Contents

Foreword by Peter Grigg   **iv**

Introduction   **iv**

About this guide   **iv**

How charities are ordered in this guide   **v**

How grant-making charities can help   **vi**

What types of help can be given?   **vi**

Advice for applicants   **vii**

Other sources of support   **viii**

How to use this guide   **xi**

How to identify sources of help – a quick reference flowchart   **xii**

How to make an application   **xiii**

Using the application form template for financial assistance   **xv**

Application form template   **xvi**

About the Directory of Social Change   **xviii**

General charities   **1**

Charities by beneficiary   **21**

Illness and disability charities   **51**

Armed forces charities   **85**

Occupational charities   **97**

Local charities   **181**

Advice organisations   **467**

Index   **485**

Foreword

It has been said that it is in the worst of times that we see the best in people. Amidst the destruction, darkness and trauma of the COVID-19 pandemic, we have also seen the most spectacular individual and collective acts of kindness. Our basic need for connection and shared purpose has been a glue to bind our social fabric, protecting and supporting us all.

It is people in communities that bring kindness to life, joining up dots and navigating towards available assets and resources. I call these brilliant people connectors. They range from those with formal roles – such as professionals providing welfare support, charities giving advice and volunteers rolling up their sleeves – to many informal roles offering sources of wisdom, advice and relationships. By making sense of the patchwork of support that exists, these invaluable connectors help bring community spirit to life.

At Home-Start, a federation of 184 charities across the UK, we work with families with young children to provide emotional and practical support. Our connectors are the 10,000 volunteers who provide compassionate, non-judgemental emotional and practical support to parents. This connection is truly inspirational and life-changing for so many families. Especially during the pandemic, when for some a phone call from our volunteer might have been the only social contact.

Never has social connection been more important than now, with the isolation, emotional strain and growing financial pressure caused by the pandemic having had such a profound impact on people's capacity to cope. At Home-Start, our staff and volunteers have dived in to play our part and have been proud to stand alongside parents in connecting communities with support. We are deeply grateful for the host of other connectors playing their part across so many aspects of society.

For all connectors, this 18th edition of *The Guide to Grants for Individuals in Need* is a vital map. It locates grant-making charities that provide much-needed resources for people in difficulty. It signposts lifeline grants for unaffordable school uniforms or to replace broken fridges and boilers. It can direct to longer-term support for people facing struggles with housing, debt, domestic violence, illness or addiction.

While I know that most connectors will race past this foreword and dive straight into the more practical parts to help people find grants, for those of you who do glance at these words I want to say thank you for all you do to keep people connected. Your contribution is seen and very much valued and appreciated by everyone. I do hope this guide makes your difficult task just a little bit easier.

Peter Grigg
Chief Executive, Home-Start UK

Introduction

Welcome to the 18th edition of *The Guide to Grants for Individuals in Need*. The main focus of the book is to list sources of non-statutory help for people in financial need. This edition details more than 1,800 charities with over £373 million available in grants for individuals. Most of this funding is given for welfare purposes but also includes, where relevant, support for educational needs, including post-16 education. The amount of support given has increased substantially since the book's first edition in 1987, in which charities gave around £66 million in welfare grants.

Since the last edition of this guide, the world has been dealing with challenges arising from the COVID-19 pandemic and the charity sector is no exception. During the course of our research, we've found that some grant programmes for individuals were cancelled or temporarily postponed; however, several charities did offer additional support directly to individuals, whether through emergency grants for basic needs or a special hamper at Christmas to raise spirits. It is promising to see that despite the impact of the COVID-19 pandemic support for individuals in need is still very much available. Assistance given by charities in this guide ranges from food vouchers to grants for domestic items (such as washing machines, fridges or cookers), educational necessities (such as school uniforms) and support towards health-related needs (such as wheelchairs and house adaptations). Although few charities will cover the whole cost of such items or needs, funders can offer a valuable contribution. This kind of help does not overcome long-term financial problems, but it can be extremely valuable in helping to meet immediate needs which the state does not currently cover.

This introduction looks at the charities included in this guide and how to locate them, before discussing what help is available and where alternative sources of help can be found. Helpful guidance that explains how to make a successful application to a relevant charity is also included; see page xiii.

A number of grant-makers that have appeared in previous editions of this guide have not been included this time as they have ceased their grant-making activities. Some may have simply ceased to exist, whereas others may now provide services instead of grants or have transferred their funds/application process to a local community foundation. The guide also features several grant-makers that have been included for the first time, some of which were only established in the two years since the last edition.

About this guide

We aim to include publicly registered charities (including those in Scotland and Northern Ireland) which give at least £500 a year to individuals in need, although most give considerably more than this.

2022/23

THE GUIDE TO
GRANTS FOR INDIVIDUALS IN NEED

18th edition

Jessica Threlfall

directory of social change

Published by the Directory of Social Change (Registered Charity
no. 800517 in England and Wales)

Office: Suite 103, 1 Old Hall Street, Liverpool L3 9HG

Tel: 020 4526 5995

Visit www.dsc.org.uk to find out more about our books,
subscription funding website and training events. You can also
sign up for e-newsletters so that you're always the first to hear
about what's new.

The publisher welcomes suggestions and comments that will help
to inform and improve future versions of this and all of our titles.
Please give us your feedback by emailing publications@dsc.org.uk.

It should be understood that this publication is intended for
guidance only and is not a substitute for professional or legal
advice. No responsibility for loss occasioned as a result of any
person acting or refraining from acting can be accepted by the
author or publisher.

First published 1987
Second edition 1990
Third edition 1992
Fourth edition 1994
Fifth edition 1996
Sixth edition 1998
Seventh edition 2000
Eighth edition 2002
Ninth edition 2004
Tenth edition 2006
Eleventh edition 2009
Twelfth edition 2011
Thirteenth edition 2013
Fourteenth edition 2014
Fifteenth edition 2016
Sixteenth edition 2018
Seventeenth edition 2020
Eighteenth edition 2022

ISBN 978 1 78482 082 4

British Library Cataloguing in Publication Data
A catalogue record for this book is available from the British
Library

Cover and text design by Kate Griffith
Typeset by Marlinzo Services, Frome
Printed and bound in the UK by Page Bros, Norwich

MIX
Paper from
responsible sources
FSC
www.fsc.org   FSC® C023114

With a few exceptions, we do not include:

- Organisations which give grants solely for higher educational purposes
- Organisations which give grants to their members only and not to dependants of such people
- Friendly societies
- Local branches of national charities, although they may raise money locally for cases of need
- Organisations only providing services (such as home visiting) rather than cash (or in-kind) grants

Over 300 of the charities support individuals towards educational needs, including post-16 education, as well as general welfare needs. In previous years, these charities have featured in the sister guide to this book, *The Guide to Educational Grants*; however, are now represented here as part of the overall support offered to individuals in need. Some charities also support organisations, such as community groups, and others have large financial commitments, such as providing housing – this will affect how much funding is available to individuals. The entries in *The Guide to Grants for Individuals in Need* concentrate solely on the charities' support to individuals in need through social welfare and, where relevant, education grants.

How charities are ordered in this guide

The charities are separated into six sections. The first five sections contain most of the grant-makers, the majority of which make grants to individuals either across the UK or at a national level in England, Northern Ireland, Scotland and Wales. Indeed, most of the money in this book is given by the charities contained in these first five sections. The final, and largest, section of the guide contains grant-makers whose assistance is restricted to those residing in defined geographical areas. The flowchart on page xii shows how the guide works.

1. General charities (page 1)

This section is mostly made up of charities which operate with very wide objectives, such as the relief of 'people in need', rather than serving a distinct beneficiary group based on, for example, age, profession/trade or disability. General charities are among the best known and tend to be heavily oversubscribed.

In this part of the guide we have also included a subsection which lists charities whose purpose is to relieve individuals with utility debt and arrears. These charities are associated with utility providers (such as the British Gas Energy Trust), and while they are generally limited to helping only the customers of a certain provider, they can operate over broad geographical areas and assist with what is a specific but common need.

This section also includes livery companies, orders and membership organisations. These charities form a distinct and unique part of the grant-making sector. They are charities affiliated with membership organisations, from historic livery companies and orders to more recently established bodies. Some of the charities in this section only support members of their associated institution (and often their dependants), while others administer a range of funds with varying eligibility criteria.

Another subsection lists charities that offer funding for personal development/extracurricular activities. These charities seek to enable individuals to partake in hobbies or experiences they wouldn't otherwise be able to, such as playing a sport, learning an instrument or volunteering for a humanitarian project abroad. Many provide funding for a range of needs including travel costs, essential kits and membership fees.

2. Charities by beneficiary (page 21)

This section features charities whose eligibility criteria is focused on individuals from defined beneficiary groups. The section contains alphabetically ordered subsections. Each subsection focuses on a specific group, including children and young people, older people, individuals belonging to a particular faith, and individuals whose needs are based on specific social circumstances, for example asylum seekers.

3. Illness and disability charities (page 51)

These charities give grants to people (and often their families/carers) who have an illness or disability and are in financial need as a result. Some have general eligibility criteria and support individuals with any kind of illness or disability; others assist only those affected by a particular condition. Many also give advisory and other support. For a detailed list of organisations providing these functions please see the 'Advice organisations' section, starting on page 467.

4. Armed forces charities (page 85)

This section contains details on exceptionally thorough charitable provision for people who have served in the forces, whether as a regular or during national service. The funders usually also provide for the widows, widowers and dependent children of the core beneficiaries. Many of these funds have local voluntary workers who provide advice and practical help and who, in turn, are backed up by professional staff and substantial resources. SSAFA, the Armed Forces Charity (Charity Commission no. 210760) is an influential member of this sector. It is often the initial contact point, as it supports all service branches and provides the application form for numerous funders, including many of the regimental funds. Since 2014 the Directory of Social Change (funded by the Forces in Mind Trust) has been undertaking research on the armed forces charity sector. See www.dsc.org.uk/armed-forces-charities for full details and ongoing findings of the project.

5. Occupational charities (page 97)

This section contains charities that benefit not only the people who worked in a particular trade but also, in many cases, their widows/widowers and dependent children. Membership or previous membership of the particular institute may be required, but many are open to non-members. Length of service can sometimes be taken into account. Some occupations are covered by a number of funds, while others do not have an established benevolent charity. Charities affiliated to trade unions can also be found in this section.

6. Local charities (page 181)

Included in this section are those charities whose support is restricted to individuals in localised geographical areas within the UK. Northern Ireland, Scotland and Wales are divided into regions and then into counties. Charities based in England are first organised by region, then subdivided into counties and then broken into districts/ boroughs. Charities which could fall under two chapters have generally been given a full record in one chapter and a cross reference in the other; charities relevant to three or more of the chapters have generally been included in the national section. Charitable help is unequally distributed across the UK, often with more money available in London and the south east of England than the rest of the UK. However, many of the largest cities contain at least one large charity that is able to give over £50,000 a year.

Charities in Northern Ireland

The number of charities giving in Northern Ireland remains limited, as there are very few grant-making charities that support individuals. However, there are now over 7,100 charities registered with the Charity Commission for Northern Ireland, and this number is continuing to grow. We hope to be able to add more Northern Irish charities in the future.

The majority of the Northern Irish charities in this guide provide support across the region and have additional criteria attached (such as type of beneficiary or occupation); therefore, they have been included under the relevant section. Only one grant-maker specified a more local beneficial area and has been placed under the local charities section, which accounts for the Northern Irish section appearing so small. It is worth noting that while the number of Northern Ireland-specific charities seems small, many general charities will fund across the UK, including Northern Ireland.

How grant-making charities can help

Some charities lament the fact that the people whom they wish to support might refuse to accept support because of a desire to maintain their independence. A charity holds public money for the benefit of a specific group of people. As such, just as people are encouraged to access any statutory funds they can, they should also be encouraged to accept all charitable money which has been set aside for them.

One of the most common charitable purposes is 'the prevention or relief of poverty', a definition of which is detailed in the section below. However, it is not just people classified as 'poor' who are eligible for support from grant-making charities. Formerly known as the 'relief

of sickness', this charitable purpose was re-defined under the provisions of the Charities Act 2006 and now comes under 'the advancement of health or the saving of lives'.

The Charity Commission's guidance for 'the advancement of health or the saving of lives' broadened the scope of the previous definition, meaning a wider range of activities became charitable. Examples of help available concentrate on the alleviation of the physical aspect of 'relief' rather than on the financial position of people who are living with an illness or disability. This is not because grants for the advancement of health are not means-tested, but simply because these charities exist to relieve a physical need rather than a financial one. There are charitable organisations that exist to carry out either or both charitable purposes; they may deal exclusively with the financial impact that an illness or disability can have on an individual's life or concentrate on the physical aspect of 'relief', or they may address both.

Although these are the areas charities *may* support, it would be wrong to believe that any given grant-making organisation will support all of these needs. Each charity in this guide has a governing document that states in which circumstances people can and cannot be supported. As noted earlier, to aid the reader in identifying those charities which are of relevance to them, we have broken the charities listed into sections, and we would strongly advise that individuals do not approach a charity for which they are not eligible.

Many trustees have complained to us that they receive applications that are outside their charity's scope; this means that the trustees might like to support them, but they do not meet the particular circumstances as stated in the charity's governing document. These applicants have no chance of being assisted by that particular charity and only serve to be a drain on the charity's valuable resources. With this in mind, please remember that it is not the number of charities you apply to which affects your chance of support but the relevance of them.

What types of help can be given?

The Charity Commission's guidance

The following guidance from the Charity Commission outlines the definition of the prevention or relief of poverty:

The prevention or relief of poverty

In the past, the courts have tended to define 'poverty' by reference to financial hardship or lack of material things but, in current social and economic circumstances, poverty includes many disadvantages and difficulties arising from, or which cause, the lack of financial or material resources.

There can be no absolute definition of what 'poverty' might mean since the problems giving rise to poverty are multidimensional and cumulative. It can affect individuals and whole communities. It might be experienced on a long or short-term basis.

Poverty can both create, and be created by, adverse social conditions, such as poor health and nutrition, and low achievement in education and other areas of human development.

The prevention or relief of poverty is not just about giving financial assistance to people who lack money; poverty is a more complex issue that is dependent upon the social and economic circumstances in which it arises. The commission recognises that many charities that are concerned with preventing or relieving poverty will do so by addressing both the causes (prevention) and the consequences (relief) of poverty.

Not everyone who is in financial hardship is necessarily poor, but it may still be charitable to relieve their financial hardship under the description of purposes relating to 'the relief of those in need by reason of youth, age, ill-health, disability, financial hardship or other disadvantage'.

In most cases, the commission will treat the relief of poverty and the relief of financial hardship the same. Generally speaking, it is likely to be charitable to relieve either the poverty or the financial hardship of anyone who does not have the resources to provide themselves, either on a short or long-term basis, with the normal things of life which most people take for granted.

Examples of ways in which charities might relieve poverty include:

- *grants of money*
- *the provision of items (either outright or on loan) such as furniture, bedding, clothing, food, fuel, heating appliances, washing machines and fridges*
- *payment for services such as essential house decorating, insulation and repairs, laundering, meals on wheels, outings and entertainment, child-minding, telephone line, rates and utilities*
- *the provision of facilities such as the supply of tools or books, payments of fees for instruction, examination or other expenses connected with vocational training, language, literacy, numerical or technical skills, travelling expenses to help the recipients to earn their living, equipment and funds for recreational pursuits or training intended to bring the quality of life of the beneficiaries to a reasonable standard*

The provision of money management and debt counselling advice are examples of the ways in which charities might help prevent poverty.

See also the commission's guidance on the prevention or relief of poverty for public benefit (www.gov.uk/government/publications/charities-supplementary-public-benefit-guidance) and social inclusion (www.gov.uk/government/publications/the-promotion-of-social-inclusion) and its decision on AITC Foundation (www.gov.uk/government/publications/aitc-foundation).

Charity Commission, 2013

One-off and recurrent grants

Some charities will only give one-off cash payments. This means that they will award a single lump sum, which is paid by cheque or postal order directly to the applicant, to the welfare agency applying on the person's behalf, or to another suitable third party or service provider. No more help will be considered until the applicant has submitted a new application, and charities are usually unwilling to give more than one such grant per person in any given year.

Other charities will only pay recurrent grants, which means they are likely to support the same individuals for sometimes long periods of time.

Some charities will give either one-off or recurrent payments according to what is more appropriate for the applicant, and some charities that give small recurrent payments may also give one-off grants for irregular expenses.

Grants in kind

Occasionally, grants are given in the form of vouchers or are paid directly to a shop or store in the form of credit to enable the applicant to obtain food, clothing or other pre-arranged items. Some charities still arrange for the delivery of coal.

More commonly, especially with disability aids or other technical equipment, the charity will either give the equipment itself (rather than the money) to the applicant or loan it free of charge or at a low rental price for as long as the applicant needs it. More common items, such as telephones and televisions, can also be given directly by the charity as equipment (the charity can get better trade terms than the individual).

Statutory funding

While there is a wide range of types of grant that can be given and a variety of reasons why they can be made, there is one area that charities cannot support. No charitable organisation is allowed to provide funds which replace statutory funding. Consider a situation where a charity gives £100 to an individual who could have received those funds from statutory sources. In such a case, it is, essentially, the state rather than the individual who is benefiting from the grant.

Advice for applicants

While there is still a large amount of money available to help applicants, the competition seems likely to remain strong. It is difficult to say how grant-makers will fare in the coming years, but it is unlikely that those who are dipping into reserves can continue to do so indefinitely, so charities will be looking to ensure that they are making the maximum possible impact with their grants.

For those individuals applying for funding the same basic principles apply – see page xiii for Ashley Wood's excellent step-by-step guide. However, in the current climate it is worth bearing a few extra things in mind:

- **Check the latest criteria**: Financial pressures and rising applications have led many charities to tighten up their eligibility criteria or limit the things for which they will give. Make sure that you have the latest guidelines and read them carefully to check that you are eligible to apply and the charity can help with your specific needs. If it has not been indicated for any given charity in this guide whether phone calls are welcome or not, it is usually appropriate to make a quick call to clear any doubts. This can definitely save time for both parties in the long run.

▶ **Be open and honest when applying:** Take care to fill in any application form as fully as possible and try to be as clear and open as you can. The same applies if you need to write a letter of application. It will help grant-makers to assess your needs quickly and advise you on any other benefits or potential sources of funding for which you may be eligible.

▶ **Don't just apply to large, well-known charities:** These charities are likely to be the most oversubscribed, leaving you with less chance of success. Take the time to look for others you may also be eligible to apply to.

▶ **Apply to all appropriate charities:** Falling average amounts of grants may mean that one grant-maker cannot offer enough to cover the full cost of the item or service you need. You may have to consider applying to several charities and asking for a small contribution from each. A quick phone call (where appropriate) can be helpful to establish how much the charity is likely to give for an individual grant.

▶ **Seek advice:** Some applications require a third-party endorsement. With advice services under increasing pressure, you may find an alternative organisation to contact in this guide; these organisations are listed on page 467. Also consider other impartial professionals who may be able to assist with an application form. Support from a school teacher can be helpful if the application is on behalf of a child, and a letter from a medical practitioner such as a GP, consultant or therapist can aid your application if it is for a medical item or is related to a medical condition. Others who may be able to help include ministers of religion, social workers, local housing associations or probation officers. It is advisable to make a quick phone call or send an email to the grant-maker to determine whether the funder can be flexible regarding who completes the application in exceptional circumstances.

Other sources of support

While there are many situations in which approaching a charity might be the best option, there is of course a limit to the support that charities can provide, individually or collectively. There are a number of alternative sources of support that should be considered in conjunction with looking at grant-makers. These are beyond the scope of this publication, but the following sections offer signposts to where to find further information.

Statutory sources

There are some funding opportunities available to individuals from the state. The exact details of these sources vary in different countries in the UK, and in some instances among different local authorities. A further complication is the impact of ongoing changes to welfare support. Consequently, comprehensive details are beyond the scope of this guide.

However, full details should be available from government departments such as benefits agencies and social services, as well as many of the welfare agencies listed in a separate section of this guide (see page 467). The government's website (www.gov.uk) and the Department for Work and Pensions (DWP) website (www.gov.uk/government/organisations/department-for-work-pensions) also have a wealth of information on what is available and how to apply.

There are a number of advice organisations that may be able to offer guidance and support to people who are unsure of their benefit entitlement or who are looking for extra support in the form of a grant. It may also prove useful to visit websites such as Turn2Us (www.turn2us.org.uk), which can offer advice on statutory and non-statutory sources of funding that are available to individuals (either directly or via charities that are working on behalf of individuals in need).

Citizens Advice provides an online advice guide (www.citizensadvice.org.uk) and offers useful information on issues relating to statutory benefits and individual entitlement. Local branches of Citizens Advice can also offer people more assistance in this area.

Food banks

Food banks exist to support people who, due to a crisis or emergency, cannot afford to feed themselves. Food banks in the UK are diverse and operate in different ways, but they are generally run by volunteers who distribute food parcels via local churches and other community organisations. In the UK, the biggest provider of emergency food relief is The Trussell Trust, which supports more than 1,200 food banks nationwide, and there are many more organisations and groups also working to support people who are facing food poverty.

The way to access assistance can vary depending on the food banks in your area; however, it is usually via referral from a care professional (such as a social worker, Citizens Advice or other welfare agency), who issues the individual who is in need of assistance with a voucher. This voucher can then be redeemed in exchange for a food parcel, which usually lasts for three to five days, depending on the food bank's policy. Some food banks can also provide support through signposting to other welfare organisations, and several charities included in this guide use food banks to reach potential applicants or liaise with existing beneficiaries. Information on food banks in your area can be found online or alternatively you can contact your local Citizens Advice.

Money advice

Many of the grant-makers in this guide specify that, before applying for a grant, individuals should seek professional financial or debt advice first. Your local Citizens Advice can provide free money advice, as can National Debtline (www.nationaldebtline.org) and Debt Advice Foundation (www.debtadvicefoundation.org), which are both accredited by the MoneyHelper (www.moneyhelper.org.uk). Alternatively, the MoneyHelper provides an easy-to-use online search for local debt advice services, which lists

Citizens Advice and other agencies that work to provide free financial advice in your area. You can also see the 'Advice organisations' section on page 467 for contact details of free-of-charge money advice providers.

Disaster appeals

In the event of a disaster or other humanitarian crisis the public's reaction is often to help the victims as quickly as possible, and one way to do so is by launching a disaster appeal. These are commonly set up as a public response to a well-publicised disaster, such as the Grenfell fire in 2017. They can also be established in response to a personal misfortune; The Mark Davies Injured Riders Fund, for instance, was established to support injured riders, by the parents of a talented rider killed during the Burghley Horse Trials. For comprehensive advice and guidance on whether to launch an appeal by an existing charity, assist an established charity in its efforts to help with the effects of the crisis or set up a non-charitable appeal fund (e.g. a fund for the benefit of a single person), please view the Charity Commission's online guidance, CC40 *Disaster Appeals*.

Companies

Many employers are concerned to see former members of staff or their dependants living in need or distress. Few have formal arrangements, but if you send a letter or make a phone call to the personnel manager, you should be able to establish whether the company will be able to assist.

Many large and some of the smaller companies give charitable grants, although most have a policy of only funding organisations. Those that will support individuals have their own charitable foundations or benevolent funds for former employees and therefore are included in this guide.

There has been a growing trend for many prominent utility companies to establish charities which give to individuals who are struggling to pay their utility bills. These charities have continued to grow and have for a number of years provided much relief to the individuals involved, lessening the financial burden on them and ensuring that no legal action will be taken against them for non-payment of bills.

Community foundations

Over recent years, community foundations have established themselves as a key community resource. According to the UK Community Foundations' website, there are 47 community foundations throughout the UK, which distribute around £100 million grants a year and hold, as of December 2021, £700 million in endowed funds.

Community foundations aim to be cause-neutral and manage funds donated to them by both individuals and organisations, which are then distributed to the local communities which they serve.

While most community foundations only support organisations, some also have funds available for individuals and are therefore included in this guide. The UK Community Foundations' website has a complete list and a map of community foundations (see www.ukcommunityfoundations.org).

Please note, as is the case with most sources of financial support, funding for individuals is subject to frequent change. Even if your local community foundation is included in this guide, it is advisable to check the availability on the relevant community foundation's website.

Ministers of religion

There may be informal arrangements within a place of worship to help people in need. Ministers of religion are often trustees of local charities that are too small to be included in this guide.

Hospitals

Most hospitals have patient welfare funds, but these funds are generally not well known, even within hospitals, and so are not used as frequently as other sources of funds. It may take some time to locate an appropriate contact. Start with the trust fund administrator or the treasurer's department of the health authority.

Local organisations

Rotary Clubs, Lions Clubs, Round Tables and so on are active in welfare provision. Usually, they support groups rather than individuals and policies vary in different towns, but some welfare agencies (such as Citizens Advice) have a working relationship with these organisations and keep up-to-date lists of contacts. All enquiries should be made by a recognised agency on behalf of the individual.

Orders

Historic organisations such as the Masonic and the Royal Antediluvian Order of Buffaloes (known as Buffs) lodges exist for the mutual benefit of their members and the wider community. Spouses and children of members (or deceased members) may also benefit, but people unconnected with these orders are unlikely to do so. Applications should be made to the lodge where the parent or spouse is (or was) a member.

Hobbies and interests

People with a particular hobby or interest should find out whether this offers any opportunities for funding. Included in this guide are a number of sporting associations which exist to relieve people who are in need, but there may be many more that are not registered with the Charity Commission, or have less than £500 a year to give, but are of great value to the people they can help. It is likely that other sports and interests have similar governing bodies that can help their members either through making a donation or organising a fundraising event.

Educational support

This guide contains information on grants for uniforms, books and equipment for schoolchildren. In a change from previous years, we have also, where applicable, included information on post-16 education support. For information on statutory funds, contact your local educational authority or enquire for information at the office of the individual's school.

Charity shops

Some charity shops will provide clothing if the applicant has a letter of referral from a recognised welfare agency.

Getting help

Unfortunately, the methods mentioned above can only offer temporary relief. Applying for grants can be a daunting experience, especially if you are unfamiliar with the process; it is probably worth starting with the help of a sympathetic advisor. Most branches of Citizens Advice have money advice workers or volunteers who are trained in money advice work. If you find that you are in financial need, try going to your nearest Citizens Advice office and talking to an advisor about your financial difficulties. They may be able to help you write an application to an appropriate charity, may know of welfare benefits you could claim or be able to re-negotiate some of your debt repayments on your behalf. They will certainly be able to help you minimise your expenditure and budget effectively.

Acknowledgements

Throughout this introduction, we have commented on the guidelines and advice from the Charity Commission for England and Wales. While we are aware that the Charity Commission for England and Wales only has rule over those countries, readers in Northern Ireland and Scotland (as well as the Isle of Man and the Channel Islands) should note that, although the exact nature of charitable law differs in these countries, the spirit and guidance remains the same throughout the UK and the Charity Commission's advice should be considered to be just as relevant.

We would like to offer a special thank you to Peter Grigg, CEO of Home-Start UK for providing a foreword for this edition of the guide.

We are extremely grateful to many people, including charity trustees, staff, volunteers and others who have helped compile this guide. To name them all individually would be impossible.

How to give us your feedback

The research for this book was done as carefully as we were able, but there will be relevant charities that we have missed, some of the information may be incomplete or will become out of date. If any reader comes across omissions or mistakes in this guide, please let us know, so we can rectify them. An email to the Research Department of the Directory of Social Change (research@dsc.org.uk) is all that is needed. We are also always looking for ways to improve our guides and would appreciate any comments, positive or negative, about this guide. We also welcome suggestions on what other information would be useful for inclusion when we research for the next edition.

References

Charity Commission for England and Wales (2013), 'Charitable purposes: The advancement of health or the saving of lives' [web page], www.gov.uk/government/publications/charitable-purposes/charitable-purposes#the-advancement-of-health-or-the-saving-of-lives, accessed January 2022.

Charity Commission for England and Wales (2013), 'Charitable purposes: The prevention or relief of poverty' [web page], www.gov.uk/government/publications/charitable-purposes/charitable-purposes#the-prevention-or-relief-of-poverty, accessed January 2022.

Charity Commission for England and Wales (2012), 'Disaster appeals: Charity Commission guidance on starting, running and supporting charitable disaster appeals (CC40)' [web page], www.gov.uk/government/publications/disaster-appeals-charity-commission-guidance-on-starting-running-and-supporting-charitable-disaster-appeals-cc40/disaster-appeals-charity-commission-guidance-on-starting-running-and-supporting-charitable-disaster-appeals, accessed January 2022.

How to use this guide

Below is a typical charity record, showing the format we have used to present the information obtained from each of the charities.

Following on from this is a flowchart. We recommend that you follow the order indicated in the flowchart to look at each section of the guide and find charities that are relevant to you. You can also use the information in the sections 'About this guide' and 'How to make an application' to help inform your applications.

The Fictitious Charity

(£) £24,000 (2019/20)

Correspondent: Ms I. M. Helpful, Charity Administrator, 7 Pleasant Road, London SN0 0ZZ (tel: 020 7123 4567; email: admin@fictitious.org.uk)

 www.fictitious.org.uk

CC number: 112234

Eligibility
People who live in London and are in need. Preference is given to older people and to single-parent families.

Types of grant
Small, one-off grants of up to £250 are given for a wide range of needs, including white goods, beds and medical equipment.

Exclusions
No grants are given for items already purchased.

Applications
Application forms are available from the charity's website. They can be submitted directly by the individual or, if necessary, by a third party such as a social worker or doctor. Applications are considered monthly.

Financial information
Year end	05/04/2020
Income	£521,000
Total expenditure	£574,000

Further financial information
The charity made grants to 251 individuals during 2019/20.

Other information
The charity also makes grants to organisations for medical research and environmental projects.

Grant total
This shows the total (or estimated) amount given in grants to individuals during the financial year in question. This will include social welfare and, where relevant, educational support.

Correspondent
This shows the name and contact details of the charity's correspondent. In many cases, this correspondent is the same contact listed on the charity's record at the Charity Commission; however, in cases where we could find a more appropriate correspondent on the charity's website, we have included their name here instead.

Registered charity number
This is the number given to a charity upon registration with the Charity Commission for England and Wales, Charity Commission for Northern Ireland or the Office of the Scottish Charity Regulator. A small number of the grant-makers detailed in this guide are not registered charities and so do not have a registered charity number.

Eligibility
This states who is eligible to apply for a grant. Among other examples, criteria can be based on place of residence, age, health or occupation.

Types of grant
This section specifies whether the charity gives one-off or recurrent grants, the size of grants given and for which items or costs grants are actually given. This section will also indicate if the charity runs various schemes.

Exclusions
This field gives information, where available, on what the charity will not fund.

Applications
This section includes information on how to apply, who should make the application (meaning the individual or a third party) and when to submit an application.

Financial information
This section includes the charity's financial year end and annual income and total charitable expenditure. The expenditure figure includes grants awarded to individuals as well as, for example, grants to organisations or the cost of service provision.

Further financial information
This field provides additional information that may be of interest, such as the number of grants made each year.

Other information
This section contains other helpful or interesting information about the charity.

How to identify sources of help – a quick reference flowchart

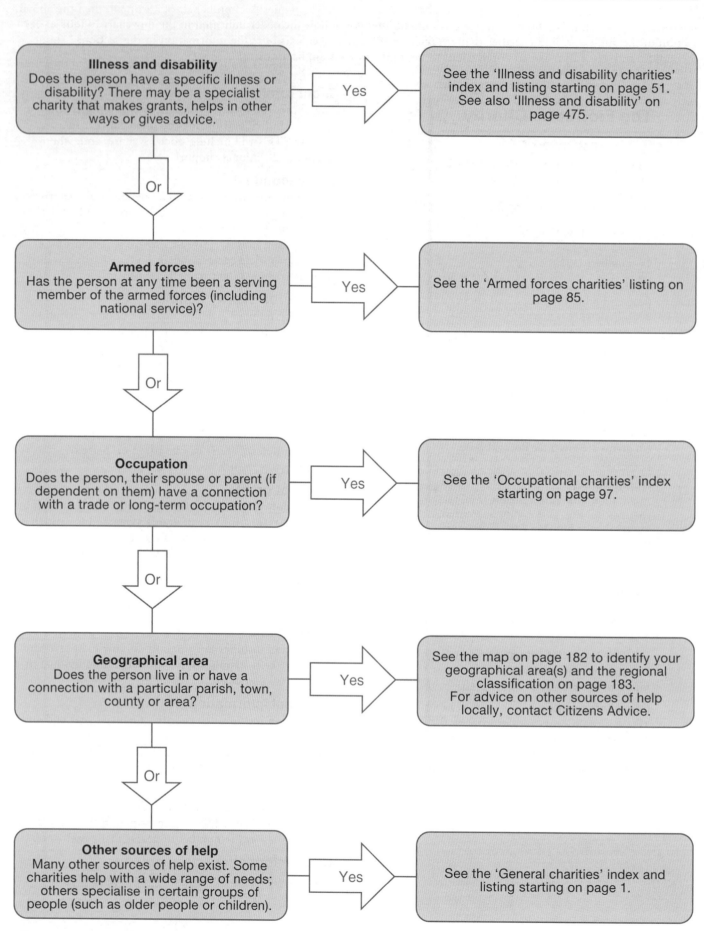

Illness and disability
Does the person have a specific illness or disability? There may be a specialist charity that makes grants, helps in other ways or gives advice.

Yes → See the 'Illness and disability charities' index and listing starting on page 51. See also 'Illness and disability' on page 475.

Or

Armed forces
Has the person at any time been a serving member of the armed forces (including national service)?

Yes → See the 'Armed forces charities' listing on page 85.

Or

Occupation
Does the person, their spouse or parent (if dependent on them) have a connection with a trade or long-term occupation?

Yes → See the 'Occupational charities' index starting on page 97.

Or

Geographical area
Does the person live in or have a connection with a particular parish, town, county or area?

Yes → See the map on page 182 to identify your geographical area(s) and the regional classification on page 183. For advice on other sources of help locally, contact Citizens Advice.

Or

Other sources of help
Many other sources of help exist. Some charities help with a wide range of needs; others specialise in certain groups of people (such as older people or children).

Yes → See the 'General charities' index and listing starting on page 1.

How to make an application

This section was kindly contributed by Ashley Wood, former Assistant Chief Executive of the Gaddum Centre, based in Manchester.

Once the appropriate charities have been identified, the next stage is the application itself. People often find making applications difficult and those who might benefit sometimes fail to do so because of the quality of the application submitted.

This article gives guidelines both to individuals applying directly and welfare agencies applying on behalf of individuals on how to make strong, clear and relevant applications.

The application form

The first stage in submitting an application is the question of application forms.

Applications on agency letter headings or personal letters directly from the applicant, no matter how well presented, are fairly pointless if the charity being approached has a specific application form which must be completed. This obvious point is often overlooked. It is frustrating when the application is returned with a blank form requesting largely the same information as has already been submitted. The resulting delay may mean missing a committee meeting where the application would have been considered and a significant wait until the next one.

Entries in this guide usually indicate when a particular application form is needed, but if there is any doubt the applicant should make a preliminary phone call to the charity.

Who submits the application?

Again, it is important that an appropriate person sends the application. The guide usually indicates whether an individual in need can apply on their own behalf, or whether a third party (professional or otherwise) must apply for them.

In recognition of 'empowerment' of service users, advisory bodies sometimes simply advise families of funds they can approach themselves. However, many charities require applications and forms (where appropriate) to be completed by a professional person who is sponsoring the application, for example. Therefore the individual in need may have to press the agency to make an application on their behalf.

The questions

When application forms are used, the questions asked can sometimes cause problems, often because they don't appear relevant. Applicants sometimes fail to realise all charities are governed by criteria laid down in their trust deeds and usually specific questions are designed to ensure these criteria are met.

For example, questions concerning date and place of birth are often answered very vaguely. 'Date of birth' is sometimes answered with 'late 50s' or, even worse, just 'elderly'. Such a reply reflects the appearance of the person in question and not their age! If the charity can only consider applications for those below a pensionable age, and the request was on behalf of a woman, then the above answers would be too imprecise.

Equally 'Place of birth' is sometimes answered with 'Great Britain' which is again not precise enough for funds whose area of benefit is regional or local. It is always better to state the place of birth as well as town and county, even if they are different from the current home address.

Where application forms are not requested, it is essential to prepare clear, concise applications that provide the following information.

A description of the person or family and the need which exists

Although applications should be concise, they must provide sufficient detail, such as:

1   The applicant's name, address, place and date of birth

2   The applicant's family circumstances (such as married/ partners, separated/divorced/single parent, widow/ widower and the number and ages of dependent children, if applicable)

3   The applicant's financial position (such as a breakdown of weekly income and expenditure, (where appropriate) DWP/housing benefit awarded/refused, savings, credit debts, rent/gas/electricity arrears, and so on)

4   Other relevant information, such as how the need arose (for example, illness, loss of job, marital separation and so on) and why other sources (especially DWP/housing departments) have not helped. If applying to a disability charity, applicants should include details of the nature and effects of the disability (although see 'Medical information' below); if applying to a local charity, how long the applicant has lived in the locality

The application which says 'this is a poor family who need their gas reconnecting' is unlikely to receive proper consideration. It is also worth mentioning that applications are dealt with in the strictest of confidence, so applicants should aim to provide as much information as is relevant. The application form template on page xvi may serve as a useful checklist to ensure that all relevant information is included for the particular application.

How much money is requested and what it will be used for

This second point tends to cause the most difficulty. Applications are often received without any indication of the amount required or without sufficient explanation as to the desired use of the money.

For example, an applicant may have multiple debts totalling over £1,000. A grant of £100 would clear one of the debts and free much-needed weekly income. So the applicant approaches a suitable charity for a grant of £100. If the applicant explains the situation clearly, trustees can see that a £100 grant in this instance would be an effective use of their charity's resources. However, if it is not made clear, trustees can only guess at the possible benefits of the grant. Because they are unwilling to take undue risks with charitable money, trustees may either turn down an incomplete application or refer it for more information, which inevitably means delays.

Charity and the state

Charities are not supposed to give grants for items that are covered by statutory sources. However, The National Lottery Community Fund and increasing reforms to the welfare state have made it much more difficult to say where statutory provision ends and charitable provision begins.

Similarly, means testing under some state provision such as Disabled Facilities Grants regulations can create shortfalls between the amount that statutory sources can and will pay, and the full costs of equipment or adaptations to properties. Sometimes, because of what can and cannot be taken into account, assessments of what families can pay appear unrealistic. Where this is the case, it should be stated.

Cuts to social care funding and changes to legislation are creating new areas of unmet need. If individuals are applying to a charity because statutory provision is clearly no longer adequate, they should make it clear in the application that they have exhausted all possible statutory sources of funding and are still left with a shortfall. A supporting reference from a knowledgeable agency may be helpful.

Where the identified need is not met, following any assessment process, applications for alternative or complementary finance should make the reasons clear.

The way that social and health care services are being provided has changed. Traditionally, the state assessed an individual's need and then provided, or arranged for those assessed services to be provided. The changes mean that money is now *given* to those assessed as eligible for services, in order to purchase the services themselves by way of an individual budget. The aim is to give more independence and a greater choice of services purchased. It is accepted that this is a radical change for many people. Applications to charities, particularly from those with social care needs, may well have to reflect the services already being purchased from an individual budget. These applications may also need a persuasive argument outlining the necessity of the thing you are applying for, and how it improves quality of life.

Realism

It helps to be realistic. Sometimes families have contributed to their own situation. An applicant who admits this and does not expect miracles, but rather seeks to hopefully plan afresh, will often be considered more positively than an applicant who philosophises about deprivation and the imperfections of the political regime of the day.

Likewise, avoid an application which tries to make the trustees feel guilty. Making them feel responsible for the impending doom which is predicted for the most vulnerable members of the family – unless money is given

– is just as unlikely to impress experienced trustees, however sympathetic.

In general, be clear and factual, not moralising and emotional. In effect, a good application attempts to identify the need and promote possible resolutions.

Applications to more than one charity

Where large amounts are being sought, it can take months to send applications one at a time and wait for the outcome of each before applying to another. However, if a number of applications are being sent out together, a paragraph explaining that other charities are being approached should be included together with a commitment to return any surplus money raised. It is also worth mentioning if any other applications have been successful in contributing to the whole – nothing succeeds like success!

The same application should not be sent off indiscriminately. For example, if somebody is applying to a trade charity on behalf of a child whose deceased father had lengthy service in that particular trade, then a detailed description of the deceased father's service would be highly relevant. If an application for the same child was being made to a local charity, it would not.

Sometimes people who are trustees of more than one charity receive three or four identical letters, none tailored to that particular charity and none indicating that other grant-making organisations have been approached. The omission of such details and the neglect of explanations will raise questions in the minds of trustees, which in the end can result in delays or even refusal.

Timing

When applying to charities, remember the time factor – particularly in cases of urgent need. Committees often sit monthly, or even quarterly. A lucky break might mean that an application is received the day before the committee's meeting. Although, if Murphy's Law is in operation, it will always arrive the day after! For the lack of a little homework, applications may not be considered in time.

From experience, few organisations object to a phone call being made to clarify criteria, dates of meetings or requests for application forms. Very often it seems that applicants leave the whole process to chance, which leads to disillusionment, frustration and wasted time for all concerned.

Savings

When awarding a grant, most trustees take the applicant's savings into account. Some applicants may think this is unnecessarily intrusive, but openness and honesty make for a better-presented application and saves time. However, sometimes savings may not need to affect trustees' calculations.

For example, if a woman has a motor accident in which she was not at fault but which leaves her with a permanent disability, she will receive compensation (often a one-off lump sum) through the guilty party's insurance company based on medical prognoses at the time. If her condition deteriorates faster and further than anticipated, requiring her to obtain an expensive item of equipment, it could well be argued that this should not be paid for out of the compensation awarded. The compensation was paid to cover factors such as loss of earnings potential, a reduced quality of life, reduced ability to easily fulfil basic household tasks and a general loss of future security, not to pay for unexpected and expensive pieces of equipment.

In such circumstances, the applicant should include a paragraph in the application to explain why their savings are not relevant to grant calculations.

In conclusion

Two final points should be borne in mind.

1. Be clear

Firstly, social and health care professionals often resort to the use of jargon when plain English would be more effective. There appear to be two extremes; one to present a report on the basis that the trustees are not very

intelligent laypeople who need to be educated, or alternatively that they are all psychotherapists who need to be impressed. Usually, this only causes confusion.

2. Medical information

Secondly, medical information should not be presented without an accurate medical diagnosis to support it. Applicants' or social workers' presumptions on medical matters are not relevant. Often what is necessary is to explain why a financial need arises from a particular condition. This may be because of the rarity of the condition or the fluctuating nature of it.

The medical information should be presented by a professional in that field. The task of the applicant or the sponsor is to explain the implications of the condition.

Ashley Wood
Former Assistant Chief Executive
Gaddum Centre

Using the application form template for financial assistance

Over the page is a general-purpose application form. It has been compiled with the help of Gaddum Centre. It can be photocopied and used whenever convenient and should enable applicants (and agencies or people applying on behalf of individuals) to state clearly the basic information required by most grant-makers.

Alternatively, applicants can use it as a checklist of points to include in the letter. Applicants using this form should note the following things in particular:

1   It is worth sending a short accompanying letter setting out the request in brief, even when using this application form.

2   Because this form is designed to be useful to a wide range of people in need, not all the information asked for in the form will be relevant to every application. For example, not all applicants are in receipt of state benefits, nor do all applicants have hire purchase commitments. In such cases, applicants should write 'N/A' (not applicable) in the box or on the line in question.

3   Similarly, if you do not have answers for all the questions at the time of applying – for example, if you have applied to other charities and are still waiting for a reply – you should write 'Pending' under the question: 'Have you written to any other charities? What was the outcome of the application?'

4   The first page is relevant to all applications; the second page is only relevant to people applying for school or college fees. If you are applying for clothing or books for a schoolchild, then it may be worth filling out only the first page of the form and then submitting a covering letter outlining the reasons for the application.

5   Filling out the weekly income and expenditure parts of the form can be worrying or even distressing. Expenditure, when itemised in this way, is usually far higher than people expect. It may be worth filling out this section with the help of a professional.

6   You should always keep a copy of the completed form in case the grant-maker has a specific query.

7   This form should not be used where the charity has its own form, which must be completed.

Application form template

Purpose for which grant is sought	Amount sought from this application £
Applicant (name)	Occupation/School
Address Telephone no.	
Date of birth Age	Place of birth
Nationality	Religion (if any)

☐ Single   ☐ Married   ☐ Divorced   ☐ Partnered   ☐ Separated   ☐ Widow/er

Family details: Name	Age	Occupation/School
Parents/ Partner	. . . . . .	. . . .
Brothers/Sisters/ Children	. . . . .	. . . .
. . . .	. . . . .	. . . .
. . . .	. . . . .	. . . .
Others (specify)	. . . . .	. . . .

Income (weekly)	£	p	**Expenditure** (weekly)	£	p
Father's/husband's wage	. . . . . .		Rent/mortgage	. . . . . .	
Mother's/wife's wage	. . . . . .		Council Tax	. . . . . .	
Partner's wage	. . . . . .		Water rate	. . . . . .	
Income Support	. . . . . .		Electricity	. . . . . .	
Jobseeker's Allowance	. . . . . .		Gas	. . . . . .	
Employment and Support Allowance	. . . . . .		Other fuel	. . . . . .	
Pension Credit	. . . . . .		Insurance	. . . . . .	
Working Tax Credit	. . . . . .		Fares/travel	. . . . . .	
Child Tax Credit	. . . . . .		Household expenses (food, laundry, etc.)	. . . . . .	
Child Benefit	. . . . . .		Clothing	. . . . . .	
Housing Benefit	. . . . . .		School dinners	. . . . . .	
Attendance Allowance	. . . . . .		Childcare fees	. . . . . .	
Disability Living Allowance	. . . . . .		Hire purchase commitments	. . . . . .	
Universal Credit	. . . . . .		Telephone	. . . . . .	
Personal Independence Payments	. . . . . .		TV rental	. . . . . .	
Maintenance payments	. . . . . .		TV licence	. . . . . .	
Pensions	. . . . . .		Other expenditure (specify)		
Other income (specify)	. . . . . .		. . . .	. . . . . .	
. . . .	. . . . . .		. . . .	. . . . . .	
. . . .	. . . . . .		. . . .	. . . . . .	
. . . .			. . . .		

Total weekly income £ [   ]   **Total weekly expenditure** £ [   ]

Savings	£

Debts/arrears
Rent, fuels, loans, hire purchase commitments, etc.

Has applicant received help from
any other source? ☐ YES ☐ NO
(If YES, please include details below)

Specify in detail	Amount owed	Sources of grant obtained	Amount
. . . .	£	. . . .	£. . . . .
. . . .	£	. . . .	£. . . . .
. . . .	£	Other sources approached	
. . . .	£	. . . .	
. . . .	£	. . . .	

Total £ _____

Total still required £ _____

Has applicant ever received previous financial help from this charity? ☐ YES ☐ NO   If so, when?

Reason for the application

Continue on a separate sheet if necessary

For applications being submitted through a welfare agency

Name of agency . . . .

Case worker . . . .

Address. . . . .

. . . .

Telephone. . . . .

How long has the applicant been known to your department/organisation?. . . . .

For all applications

Signature: **Date:**

About the Directory of Social Change

At the Directory of Social Change (DSC), we believe that the world is made better by people coming together to serve their communities and each other. For us, an independent voluntary sector is at the heart of that social change and we exist to support charities, voluntary organisations and community groups in the work they do. Our role is to:

▷ **Provide practical information** on a range of topics from fundraising to project management in both our printed publications and our e-books

▷ **Offer training** through public courses, events and in-house services

▷ **Research funders** and maintain a subscription database, *Funds Online*, with details on funding from grant-making charities, companies and government sources

▷ **Offer bespoke research** to voluntary sector organisations in order to evaluate projects, identify new opportunities and help make sense of existing data

▷ **Stimulate debate and campaign** on key issues that affect the voluntary sector, particularly to champion the concerns of smaller charities

We are a registered charity ourselves but we self-fund most of our work. We charge for services, but cross-subsidise those which charities particularly need and cannot easily afford.

Visit our website **www.dsc.org.uk** to see how we can help you to help others and have a look at **www.fundsonline. org.uk** to see how DSC could improve your fundraising. Alternatively, call our friendly team at **020 4526 5995** to chat about your needs or drop us a line at **cs@dsc.org.uk**.

General charities

This chapter includes grant-makers which could not be categorised to a specific occupation, disability, location or beneficiary group. Many have relatively broad criteria for their grant-making.

The charities listed under 'General' can give to a wide range of people, so if individuals are unable to find help from other sources in this guide then they should be able to approach one or more of these. However, note that most of these charities still have restrictions on who they can help. Applicants should not send indiscriminate applications to any charity under the 'General' heading; rather, they should first consider whether they are eligible.

The 'Utilities' section outlines charities and charitable funds, mainly set up by utility companies, with the specific purpose of providing assistance to those struggling to pay their utility bills or debts. Some of these are specific to those living in a particular geographical area, while others have a broader remit.

Many of the grant-makers included in the 'Livery companies and memberships organisations' section will only support members of their associated institutions (as well as their dependants). However, some of these charities also provide support more generally, giving funding for a wide range of causes. Some offer assistance to individuals who live in areas with which the organisation has links, while others will support people in need across the UK.

The grant-makers listed in the 'Personal development/extracurricular activities' section provide support for a range of activities and opportunities. These charities are not restricted by geographical location, with many supporting beneficiaries across the UK. Some grant-makers, however, may have additional criteria that applicants should be sure to check before applying.

The charities in both sections are listed in alphabetical order.

Index of general charities

General 1

Livery companies and membership organisations 9

Personal development/extracurricular activities 11

Utility charities 16

General

Al-Mizan Charitable Trust

 £12,500 (2019/20)

Correspondent: The Trustees, Al Mizan Charitable Trust, Can Mezzanine, 7–14 Great Dover Street, London SE1 4YR (tel: 07851 132825; email: admin@almizantrust.org.uk)

www.almizantrust.org.uk

CC number: 1135752

Eligibility
The trust's website states: 'To be eligible to apply, you must be living in the UK and have British citizenship. As well as UK nationals, this includes people who are EEA nationals; have discretionary or indefinite leave to remain; are on study or work visas; have spouse sponsorship; or are asylum seekers, refugees, have humanitarian protection, or are appealing a Home Office decision.' Preference is given to the following groups:

- Orphans (a child who has lost either both parents or one parent who was the main breadwinner in the family)
- Children and young people under the age of 19 (particularly those in care or who are carers themselves)
- Individuals who have disabilities, are incapacitated or have terminal illness (particularly those who have severe mental health issues)
- Single parents (particularly divorcees and widows/widowers with children)
- Estranged or isolated senior citizens
- Individuals with severe medical conditions or their families
- People with convictions
- People with substance-use disorders
- Victims of domestic violence and/or physical or sexual abuse
- Victims of crime, anti-social behaviour and/or terrorism.

Types of grant
One-off grants of up to £500, with the average grant being between £200 and

£250. Grants are awarded with the aims of breaking the cycle of poverty, deprivation and/or disadvantage, improving the quality of life for individuals or families who are struggling or unable to access new opportunities and helping individuals/families embark on a new start following a crisis or event. They are also given to assist with education and employability.

Exclusions
Applications for the following are not accepted:
- General appeals
- Retrospective costs (items that have already been paid for)
- Expenses relating to the practice or promotion of religion
- Debts, including rent and Council Tax arrears
- Fines or criminal penalties
- University tuition fees
- Gap year projects
- Immigration costs
- Funeral expenses
- Gifts (for birthdays or festivals)
- Holidays
- International travel
- Products/services which contravene the ethos and values of the trust

Applications from organisations or formal groups (except when assisting an individual or family) are also not accepted. The trustees stress that applicants should be claiming all benefits for which they are eligible and must not have received funding from the trust in the last 12 months.

Applications
An enquiry can be submitted through the online grants system to determine whether a full application can be considered. To reduce administrative costs, the trust does not accept enquiries by telephone.

Financial information
Year end	31/03/2020
Income	£54,800
Total expenditure	£38,600

Other information
In addition to awarding grants the trust also organises three fundraising events during the year to provide essential items for schoolchildren (Back to School Backpacks), homeless people (Winter Warmer Packs) and new parents (Mother and Baby Kits).

The Andrew Anderson Trust

(£) £277,200 (2019/20)

Correspondent: Andrew Anderson, Trustee, 1 Cote House Lane, Bristol BS9 3UW (tel: 0798 33559127; email: andrew_r_anderson@yahoo.co.uk)

CC number: 212170

Eligibility
The trust makes grants to a wide range of causes with an emphasis on religious activities, education and training, medical causes and overseas aid.

Types of grant
Grants are awarded according to need.

Applications
Apply in writing to the correspondent. Note that the trust has stated in the past that it rarely gives to people who are not known to the trustees or who have not been personally recommended by people known to the trustees.

Financial information
Year end	05/04/2020
Income	£550,000
Total expenditure	£635,900

Further financial information
We were unable to determine the split of grants between individuals and organisations. We have therefore estimated the grant total for individuals based on the trust's overall expenditure.

The Michael Barnard Charitable Trust

(£) £126,100 (2019/20)

Correspondent: The Trustees, Brown Heath Park, Gregory Lane, Durley, Southampton, Hampshire SO32 2BS (tel: 07977 403704)

CC number: 1157878

Eligibility
People living in the UK who are in need due to their social or economic circumstances, natural disasters or because of crime, injustice or violence.

Types of grant
Welfare
Grants are made for a wide range of purposes. Recent examples include a holiday, a hearing aid, accommodation costs, tickets for a theatre show and medical equipment.

Education
Grants are given for a wide range of purposes including to support the education of people in need. Previous examples of support include help towards course fees, accommodation costs and living expenses.

Applications
Apply in writing to the correspondent.

Financial information
Year end	31/03/2020
Income	£34,800
Total expenditure	£356,200

Other information
Grants are also given to organisations.

Biggart Trust

(£) £8,400 (2019/20)

Correspondent: The Trustees, c/o Shepherd and Wedderburn LLP, 1 West Regent Street, Glasgow G2 1RW

OSCR number: SC015806

Eligibility
People in need living in Scotland.

Types of grant
Grants are given according to need.

Applications
Apply in writing to the correspondent.

Financial information
Year end	05/04/2020
Income	£12,500
Total expenditure	£18,700

Further financial information
Full accounts were not available to view on the OSCR website due to the trust's low income. We have therefore estimated the grant total based on the trust's total expenditure.

The Brenley Trust

(£) £212,200 (2020/21)

Correspondent: The Trustees, 17 Prince's Drive, Oxshott, Leatherhead, Surrey KT22 0UL (tel: 01372 841801; email: patrick.riley@btinternet.com)

CC number: 1151128

Eligibility
People experiencing financial hardship.

Types of grant
Grants are awarded for general educational purposes. The 2020/21 annual report states: 'The trust does not adopt a rigid approach in ... grant making. Grants are awarded as the trustees see fit.'

Applications
Apply in writing to the correspondent.

Financial information
Year end	31/01/2021
Income	£92,900
Total expenditure	£596,300

Other information
The trust also provides grants to organisations in the UK and in South Africa.

The Alan Brentnall Charitable Trust

 £26,500 (2018/19)

Correspondent: Roger Lander, Cathkin, Nelson Road, Forres, Moray IV36 1DR (tel: 07713 878448)

CC number: 1153950

Eligibility
People experiencing financial hardship in the UK.

Types of grant
Grants are made to help individuals with their education. Grants are also occasionally awarded for welfare purposes.

Applications
Apply in writing to the correspondent.

Financial information
Year end	31/03/2019
Income	£54,000
Total expenditure	£45,900

Further financial information
Grants totalling £14,500 were given to individuals for education. In addition, a grant was awarded to one individual for medical treatment. The 2018/19 accounts were the latest available to view at the time of writing (November 2021).

Buckingham Trust

 £7,100 (2019/20)

Correspondent: The Trustees, c/o Foot Davson Ltd, 17 Church Road, Tunbridge Wells, Kent TN1 1LG (tel: 01892 774774)

CC number: 237350

Eligibility
People in need across England and Wales. Preference is given to older people, as well as people who are experiencing ill health or financial difficulty.

Types of grant
Grants are given according to need.

Applications
Apply in writing to the correspondent.

Financial information
Year end	05/04/2020
Income	£146,300
Total expenditure	£184,700

Other information
This charity also makes grants to churches and other religious charitable organisations.

The Ciao Foundation CIO

 £24,300 (2019/20)

Correspondent: The Trustees, Meridian House, 2 Russell Street, Windsor, Buckinghamshire SL4 1HQ (tel: 07745 911137; email: info@ciaofoundation.com)

🌐 https://www.ciaofoundation.com

CC number: 1165353

Eligibility
Support for individuals whose life circumstances, health or injuries have resulted in them facing challenges.

Types of grant
The majority of grants appear to go towards supporting people with disabilities to participate in sports. Occasionally, the foundation supports home adaptations.

Applications
Individuals have to be nominated. The nominator should apply on behalf of the individual using the forms provided on the foundation's website. There are also detailed guidance notes which should be read before completing the application.

Financial information
Year end	31/03/2020
Income	£14,600
Total expenditure	£53,700

Further financial information
Full accounts were not available to view on the Charity Commission's website due to the foundation's low income. We have therefore estimated the grant total based on the foundation's total expenditure.

Family Action

 £362,000 (2019/20)

Correspondent: The Grants Service, 34 Wharf Road, London N1 7GR (tel: 020 7254 6251; email: info@family-action.org.uk)

🌐 www.family-action.org.uk

CC number: 264713

Eligibility
Welfare
The charity's website states:

> In addition to living on a low income and having right of residency in the UK welfare grant applicants must fall into one or more of the following "priority areas" listed below to be eligible to apply for a grant.

Grants available nationally (including London).

- **Older People:** Support to promote independence; improve the quality of life and isolation for those aged 60 and over.
- **Disability/Sickness:** Support to pay for disability aids that will benefit the applicant in their home. Please note, we do not fund ordinary personal and household needs under this category such as cookers or clothing unless a clear case is made that they have to be specially adapted to meet the applicants needs and we may require additional information before a grants is made to support the application.
- **Mental Health:** Support for adults (over the age of 18) with a clinical diagnosis of a mental health problem.
- **Domestic Abuse:** Support for families or individuals who have recently experienced domestic abuse.

Grants available for residents of Greater London **only**.

- **Holidays for Women living in Greater London:** Support to provide recuperative holidays for women who are resident in greater London. Please note this fund is for women and their children of 16 years or less only.
- **Local Funds:** Support for any welfare needs for those living in the following locations:
- **St Pancras:** support for single parents with children under four years of age resident in the following district postcode areas: WC1 and NW1.

Education
Family Action distributes grants to individuals over the age of 14 who are looking to participate in further education.

Types of grant
Welfare
Essential personal and household needs, such as clothing or household items (e.g. furniture or white goods).

Education
Grants can be awarded for the additional costs associated with a course of study such as clothing and/or equipment required for the course, travel, examination costs, computers and laptops.

Applications
Welfare
All applications must be made online by a suitable referring agency. Suitable referring agencies include statutory agencies, charities that provide health or social care, housing associations, probation services and GPs.

Education
Applications must be made directly through a further education college affiliated with the Family Action educational grants programme. Current affiliate colleges include:

- Belfast Metropolitan College
- City and Islington College

- East Norfolk Sixth Form College
- Gower College Swansea
- South Thames College
- West London College

Financial information

Year end	31/03/2020
Income	£37,290,000
Total expenditure	£35,810,000

Other information

Family Action provides a range of advice and support services across the country – see the 'Find us' facility on the charity's website to find your local office.

The Farthing Trust

£ £15,400 (2019/20)

Correspondent: The Trustees, PO Box 276, Newmarket, Suffolk CB8 1GW (tel: 07598 565623; email: thefarthingtrust@gmail.com)

CC number: 268066

Eligibility

People in need.

Types of grant

Grants are given according to need.

Exclusions

The trust rarely supports gap year students or applications for educational courses.

Applications

Apply in writing to the correspondent.

Financial information

Year end	05/04/2020
Income	£44,600
Total expenditure	£213,700

Other information

Grants are also awarded to organisations.

The Fielding Charitable Trust

£ £2,200 (2019/20)

Correspondent: Richard Fielding, The Trustees, Ryeclose House, Bishops Down, Sherborne, Dorset DT9 5PN (tel: 01963 210234)

CC number: 1091521

Eligibility

People in need in the UK. Preference is given to older people and people who have disabilities.

Types of grant

Grants are given according to need.

Applications

Apply in writing to the correspondent.

Financial information

Year end	05/04/2020
Income	£5,000
Total expenditure	£4,800

Further financial information

Full accounts were not available to view on the Charity Commission's website due to the trust's low income. We have therefore estimated the grant total based on the trust's total expenditure.

Elizabeth Finn Care

£ £3,600,000 (2019/20)

Correspondent: Welfare Team, Hythe House, 200 Shepherds Bush Road, London W6 7NL (email: use the contact form available on the website)

 https://www.turn2us.org.uk/Get-Support/Turn2us-Funds

CC number: 207812

Eligibility

There are three grant programmes with different eligibility criteria:

- **The Elizabeth Finn Fund** – People who are British or Irish and have worked in a listed profession (available on the charity's website), and their dependants. Applicants must have a low income or be claiming benefits and have less than £4,000 in savings. Applicants must live in Britain or Ireland for at least half of every year.
- **The Edinburgh Trust** – People who live in Edinburgh and have an annual household income that is below £16,000.
- **The Turn2us Response Fund** – People who have experienced a life-changing event in the last 12 months. Grants are provided to meet specific needs to ensure the individual's/family's financial stability, well-being and independence. The website notes that 'Applications to the Response Fund can only be made through intermediaries working for our Turn2us Response Fund partner organisations – a selected group of charities and not-for-profit organisations, based across the UK.'

Types of grant

Grants are provided for specific needs which are essential to the financial stability, well-being and independence of the individual/family to help them to maintain daily living.

Applications

Information on how to apply can be found on the charity's website.

Financial information

Year end	31/03/2020
Income	£35,820,000
Total expenditure	£33,880,000

Further financial information

The charity made over 3,100 grants to individuals in 2019/20.

The Fort Foundation

£ £9,300 (2020/21)

Correspondent: The Trustees, c/o Fort Vale Engineering Ltd, Calder Vale Park, Simonstone Lane, Simonstone, Burnley BB12 7ND (tel: 01282 440000; email: info@fortvale.com)

CC number: 1028639

Eligibility

Individuals in need in England and Wales.

Types of grant

Grants are typically awarded to assist with education or amateur sport costs, or for health and welfare purposes.

Applications

Apply in writing to the correspondent.

Financial information

Year end	28/02/2021
Income	£334,000
Total expenditure	£131,500

Further financial information

The foundation made grants totalling £9,300 to individuals during 2020/21. Grants were broken down as follows: amateur sport (£9,000); education (£300). In previous years, the foundation has also made grants for welfare and health purposes.

The Hugh Fraser Foundation

£ £4,500 (2019/20)

Correspondent: The Trustees, 180 St Vincent Street, Glasgow G2 5SG (tel: 0141 441 2111; email: hughfraserfoundation@turcanconnell.com)

 https://www.turcanconnell.com/the-hugh-fraser-foundation

OSCR number: SC009303

Eligibility

People from Scotland who are in need.

Types of grant

Grants are awarded according to need.

Applications

Apply in writing to the correspondent. The trustees meet on a quarterly basis and applications should be received three months before funding is required. Note: the foundation's focus is on making grants to charitable organisations and only rarely, and in exceptional circumstances, will the trustees consider applications from individuals and their dependants.

Financial information

Year end	31/03/2020
Income	£2,880,000
Total expenditure	£2,120,000

Further financial information

Grants totalling £4,500 were made to three individuals during the year.

Other information

The foundation's 2019/20 annual report and accounts note that the trustees 'consider that better use of funds can be made by making grants to charitable bodies to assist them with their work, than by making a large number of grants to individuals'.

R. L. Glasspool Charity Trust

 £1,960,000 (2019/20)

Correspondent: Grant Officers, Saxon House (2nd Floor), 182 Hoe Street, Walthamstow, London E17 4QH (tel: 020 3141 3161; email: grants@glasspool.org.uk)

www.glasspool.org.uk

CC number: 214648

Eligibility

People in need in the UK who are on a low income.

Types of grant

The trust's Essential Living Fund provides grants for household items and essential clothing, particularly for:

- Baby equipment and clothing
- Beds and bedding (including sofa beds)
- Clothing and school uniforms
- Cookers
- Fridges, freezers or fridge-freezers
- Washing machines
- Furniture

Grants may also be given for flooring, TV licences or tumble dryers in exceptional circumstances.

Through the trust's partnership with the Smallwood Trust, grants are made to women in need. However, in February 2022, the trust's website stated that this programme was due to close at the end of March 2022. Check the trust's website for the most up-to-date information.

In 2019, the trust took over the grants administration for the Newby Trust Ltd – see the separate entry for the Newby Trust Ltd on this page.

Exclusions

Funding cannot be given for:

- Heating oil
- Vocational training
- Computers
- Household repairs
- Decorating
- Removal costs
- Debts or arrears

Applications

The trust only accepts applications from organisations on behalf of individuals. A list of criteria for organisations is available on the trust's website. Individuals should approach an approved organisation. Organisations can apply through www.grantsplus.org.uk.

Financial information

Year end	31/03/2020
Income	£2,250,000
Total expenditure	£2,330,000

Further financial information

In 2019/20, 7,969 grants were awarded.

The Houston Charitable Trust

 £2,100 (2019/20)

Correspondent: The Trustees, Little Warren, Burtons Lane, Little Chalfont, Buckinghamshire HP8 4BS (tel: 01442 873236)

CC number: 1083552

Eligibility

People in need and those seeking funding for educational purposes, or for reasons relating to the advancement of the Christian faith.

Types of grant

Grants are given according to need.

Applications

Apply in writing to the correspondent.

Financial information

Year end	05/04/2020
Income	£84,000
Total expenditure	£79,100

Other information

Grants are also made to organisations.

The National Benevolent Charity

 £205,100 (2020)

Correspondent: The Trustees, Peter Herve House, Eccles Court, Tetbury, Gloucestershire GL8 8EH (tel: 01666 505500; email: office@natben.org.uk)

https://natben.org.uk

CC number: 212450

Eligibility

The charity's website states:

To fit our criteria you (or your client) must;

- Have UK citizenship or have been granted leave to remain.
- Be over 18 years old
- Be claiming all the state benefits you are entitled to
- Be unable to fund the request yourself
- Be applying for something that would not usually be funded by the state
- Have not received an award from us in the preceding 12 months
- Have had no more than three successful applications in the preceding five years
- Have applied to other trade related benevolence funds if applicable

Types of grant

The charity's website states:

We are currently considering applications for

- White goods e.g. fridge, freezer, microwave, washing machine or cooker
- Household goods e.g. bedding and beds, bedroom furniture, kitchen equipment
- Help to buy baby equipment e.g. buggy, cot, clothes
- Help with food shopping or clothing
- Help with utility bill costs
- Help with costs of training or work tools

Applications

Applications can be made via the charity's website.

Financial information

Year end	31/12/2020
Income	£1,310,000
Total expenditure	£157,400

Newby Trust Ltd

 £49,000 (2019/20)

Correspondent: The Trustees, PO Box 87, Petworth, West Sussex GU28 8BH (email: info@newby-trust.org.uk)

www.newby-trust.org.uk

CC number: 227151

Eligibility

People in need across the UK who are experiencing 'additional misfortune' due to bereavement, divorce, abuse, homelessness, addiction, disability or ill health.

Types of grant

One-off grants of up to £250 for the following items:

- Essential furniture (beds, sofas, tables and chairs)
- Cookers and white goods (fridges/freezers or washing machines)
- Kitchen equipment
- Baby equipment

- Emergency clothing and/or school uniforms

Occasionally, grants are awarded to assist with specific costs such as:
- Rent deposits
- Household repairs or adaptations (particularly for older people or people with disabilities)
- Travel costs
- Course fees or training equipment
- Respite breaks in the UK
- Mobility equipment

Exclusions

Grants are not usually made for items such as televisions or computers, tumble dryers or dishwashers, carpets (unless there is a medical need or a baby/toddler living in the home) or curtains. Grants cannot be made for costs such as rent or Council Tax arrears, debts, bankruptcy or Debt Relief Order fees, overseas respite breaks or driving lessons.

Applications

Applications should be made through support workers (belonging to either statutory or voluntary organisations), through Glasspool at grantsplus.org.uk. All statutory sources of funding must have been exhausted before applying.

Financial information

Year end	05/04/2020
Income	£457,000
Total expenditure	£540,700

Other information

The charity makes regular grants to educational charities, to enable disadvantaged people to access or remain in education or training.

Nichol-Young Foundation

 £1,800 (2019/20)

Correspondent: The Trustees, PO Box 4757, Windsor, Berkshire SL4 9EE (tel: 07732 431385)

https://www.nicholyoung.com/copy-of-history

CC number: 259994

Eligibility

Individuals in need, with a preference for individuals living in East Anglia.

Types of grant

Grants are available to help with the cost of specific items, for example wheelchairs, travel cards or laptops. Grants are not available to cover living costs.

Applications

Apply by writing a letter to the charity, including:
- Information about yourself
- What you are applying for and how much it will cost
- A reference from a relevant third party who can confirm that the application is legitimate

Grant applications are considered on a quarterly basis.

Financial information

Year end	05/11/2020
Income	£36,700
Total expenditure	£34,300

Other information

The charity also makes grants to organisations.

The Ogilvie Charities

Correspondent: The General Manager, The Gate House, 9 Burkitt Road, Woodbridge, Suffolk IP12 4JJ (tel: 01394 388746; email: ogilviecharities@btconnect.com)

 www.ogilviecharities.org.uk

CC number: 1196197

Eligibility

The charity manages a number of funds supporting individuals in need who live in the UK. Each fund has its own eligibility criteria, please see the charity's website for specific details.

Types of grant

Support is available for the following:
- **Holidays for carers** – grants of between £200 and £300 are given towards respite holidays for carers.
- **Essential household items** – grants of between £100 and £300 are given for essential items, such as beds and bedding, cookers, refrigerators, freezers, washing machines and clothing.
- **Education and training** – grants are given towards the cost of education and training for children and young people. Preference is given to those who have lived in an orphanage and/or have been in care, those who are visually impaired and those who have been found guilty of a criminal offence in a UK court.

Exclusions

Each fund has specific exclusions, please see the charity's website for more information.

Applications

Please visit the charity's website for information on how to apply for support from a relevant fund.

Further financial information

This charity re-registered as a CIO in October 2021; therefore, we were unable to view its financial information on the Charity Commission's website at the time of writing (December 2021). We were able to determine that £5,300 was awarded in grants in 2020 towards respite holidays for carers through the Margaret Champney Rest and Holiday Fund.

The Praebendo Charitable Foundation

 £32,800 (2019/20)

Correspondent: The Trustees, 22 St Mary's Street, Stamford, Lincolnshire PE9 2DG

CC number: 1137426

Eligibility

Welfare

People living in England, Scotland or Wales who are in financial need. Preference may be given to children and young people, older individuals and people who are experiencing ill health.

Education

Educational grants are awarded to young people under the age of 30 in England, Scotland and Wales who are in higher or further education. Those preparing for entry into a professional trade upon leaving education are also eligible for support.

Types of grant

Welfare

Welfare grants are awarded according to need.

Education

Educational grants are made in the form of scholarships and maintenance allowances.

Applications

Apply in writing to the correspondent.

Financial information

Year end	30/09/2020
Income	£24,500
Total expenditure	£66,200

Further financial information

Full accounts were not available to view on the Charity Commission's website due to the foundation's low income. We have therefore estimated the foundation's grant total based on its total expenditure.

Other information

The charity recently purchased a residential home, which is being leased by another charity for the purpose of providing support for people who are currently homeless. The charity also makes grants to organisations and provides recreational facilities and facilities for learning, particularly in music and the arts.

Professionals Aid Guild

 £229,900 (2019)

Correspondent: Danielle Trevers, Company Secretary, 10 St Christopher's Place, London W1U 1HZ (tel: 020 7935 0641; email: admin@professionalsaid.org.uk)

https://www.pcac.org.uk

CC number: 207292

Eligibility

For all grants, applicants must be over 18 years of age, be resident in the UK, have already applied for assistance in the form of state benefits to which they are entitled or from their own occupational fund if appropriate, and have less than £6,000 (or £10,000 if over pension age) in savings.

Welfare

People in need who have a postgraduate degree or equivalent qualification (level 7 on the education framework).

Education

For further education grants, people in need who have an undergraduate degree or equivalent (level 6 on the education framework) and who are currently enrolled in a postgraduate (level 7) course. Applicants must have already completed one term of the relevant postgraduate course and must already have funding in place. The charity's website states that the trustees will only consider cases where the planned funding has broken down due to circumstances beyond the applicant's control.

For children's education grants, people in need who have a postgraduate degree or equivalent qualification (level 7 on the education framework) and have children who are under 18 years of age and in full-time education.

Types of grant

Welfare

Welfare grants are awarded towards living expenses, essential household furniture and white goods, essential clothing, essential home repairs (relating to safety or independent living) and home care fees.

Education

Educational grants (typically between £300 and £500) are awarded towards the cost of course fees, course-related expenses (textbooks, stationery, etc.), some travel expenses and general living expenses.

Educational grants for children under the age of 18 are made towards the cost of school uniforms, books, stationery, other school equipment, travel costs and extra tuition fees.

Exclusions

Welfare grants are not awarded for the following:

- Private medical fees (including prescription charges)
- Vet bills or pet insurance
- Debts
- Bankruptcy fees
- Electronic equipment (personal computers, laptops, stereos, etc.)
- Cars or other vehicles
- Funeral costs
- Business start-ups
- Respite breaks

Further education grants cannot be given for:

- Student sponsorships
- Study abroad
- Ordination courses
- Conversion courses
- Intercalated years or medical elective periods
- Fees for English language tests for overseas entrants to university courses

Children's education grants are not awarded for:

- School tuition fees
- School trips
- Childcare costs

Applications

Application forms and detailed guidance notes are available to download on the funder's website. Completed forms and (copies of) supporting documents must be returned via post. The charity notes that the application review process takes several weeks and applicants will be notified as soon as possible.

Financial information

Year end	31/12/2019
Income	£286,800
Total expenditure	£402,500

Further financial information

The Professionals Aid Guild (formerly Professionals Aid Council) awarded grants to 225 beneficiaries, including 39 grants to students and 15 grants towards children's education.

The School Fees Charitable Trust

 £51,800 (2019/20)

Correspondent: The Trust Secretary, 37 Swan Street, Kingsclere, Newbury, Berkshire RG20 5PR (tel: 01306 746309; email: sfct@sfs-group.co.uk)

https://www.sfs-group.co.uk/charitable-trust

CC number: 1011711

Eligibility

Children in independent schools whose parents are unable to pay their school fees because of a sudden and unforeseen change in finances. Children must be in the final year of their GCSEs, A-levels (A2) or equivalent, such as the International Baccalaureate (standard and higher level). In exceptional circumstances, children in their final year of preparatory school may be eligible for support.

Types of grant

Grants of 25% of net school fees (after the deduction of any other awards from the school or other charitable trusts) for the final year of study. In exceptional circumstances, the charity may make grants for a longer period.

Exclusions

The charity can only consider applications where the school and the parent(s) make a contribution to the fees. The charity does not normally support parents with children in state-funded boarding schools. Grants cannot be made to cover any arrears of fees incurred prior to making an application. If there are arrears, the charity will require assurance from the school that any grant made will not be used to reduce debts.

Applications

Apply in writing to the correspondent explaining your circumstances.

Financial information

Year end	31/08/2020
Income	£25,100
Total expenditure	£60,300

The Henry Smith Charity (UK)

 £1,320,000 (2020)

Correspondent: The Trustees, Sixth Floor, 65–68 Leadenhall Street, London EC3A 2AD (tel: 020 7264 4970; email: kindred@henrysmithcharity.org.uk)

www.henrysmithcharity.org.uk

CC number: 230102

Eligibility

Welfare

The descendants of the sister of Henry Smith, referred to as his 'kindred'. Support is also available to individuals who were adopted by a descendant.

Education

Kindred aged 35 and under who are studying for a first degree. Students over the age of 35 will be considered on a case-by-case basis.

Types of grant

Welfare

One-off grants are awarded for: debt relief; furniture and white goods (washing machines, fridge/freezers, etc.); boilers; laptops; moving costs; dental and optical treatment; transport (i.e. towards the cost of a car); medical bills and equipment; travel costs to hospitals/ treatment; holidays and convalescent breaks; funeral costs.

Recurrent grants for living costs are awarded to adults on low incomes (including those receiving state pensions) and adults who are moving into a nursing/residential home.

Education

University students studying for a first degree can also apply for recurrent grants for living costs. University students can request the cost of a laptop once during their course.

Grants are also made for vocational training and retraining.

Exclusions

No grants are awarded towards the cost of university fees, only towards living costs and the cost of additional courses that are relevant to the individual's studies.

Applications

Initial enquiries should be made by email or telephone. Guidance documents can be downloaded from the charity's website.

Financial information

Year end	31/12/2020
Income	£12,070,000
Total expenditure	£55,400,000

Further financial information

Grants to individuals totalled £1.32 million during the year.

Other information

The charity operates a 24/7 helpline (03332 125099) for all eligible individuals, which provides advice on mental health issues, personal troubles, finances, working conditions, etc. As of 2020, over 2,500 kindred are registered with the charity.

The Michael Sobell Welsh People's Charitable Association

£5,000 (2019/20)

Correspondent: The Trustees, Dolenog Old Hall, Llanidloes, Powys SY18 6PP (tel: 07968 958921)

CC number: 255437

Eligibility

People in need who live in Wales.

Types of grant

Grants are awarded according to need for welfare and educational purposes

Applications

Apply in writing to the correspondent.

Financial information

Year end	31/01/2020
Income	£990
Total expenditure	£11,400

Further financial information

Full accounts were not available to view on the Charity Commission's website due to the charity's low income. We have therefore estimated the charity's grant total based on its total expenditure.

Other information

Grants are also awarded to organisations.

The Talisman Charitable Trust

£191,500 (2019/20)

Correspondent: Philip Denman, Chief Executive, Lower Ground Floor Office, 354 Kennington Road, London SE11 4LD (tel: 020 7820 0254)

 www.talismancharity.org

CC number: 207173

Eligibility

People in the UK living in poverty, as defined by the Charity Commission's definition.

Types of grant

Grants are given according to need.

Applications

Applications should be made on behalf of an individual by a local authority, charitable organisation, or a social or professional worker and should be completed on letter-headed stationery. The trust's website provides a detailed list of all the information it needs to process the application. The applicant may need to provide further medical documentation, appropriate quotes for work or services and information on other assistance being received. The trust will only respond to successful applications and does not discuss applications before a decision has been made.

The trust cannot accept applications made by recorded delivery or 'signed for' services.

Financial information

Year end	05/04/2020
Income	£223,700
Total expenditure	£253,000

Further financial information

Grants were awarded to 217 individuals in 2019/20.

Grants to individuals were broken down as follows:

Housing	126	£108,100
Small means	28	£28,500
Educational	26	£26,600
Disablement and disability	15	£19,900
Child poverty	16	£7,000
Health	6	£1,400

Other information

Occasionally grants are made to organisations with similar aims.

The Vardy Foundation

£75,000 (2019/20)

Correspondent: The Trustees, 110 George Street, Edinburgh, Edinburgh EH2 4LH (tel: 0131 374 7144)

CC number: 328415

Eligibility

Grants are given to individuals in need.

Types of grant

Grants are given for a wide range of purposes. The foundation has a particular interest in early intervention, support for those who have previously offended, substance abuse, homelessness and unemployment.

Applications

Apply in writing to the correspondent.

Financial information

Year end	05/04/2020
Income	£2,230,000
Total expenditure	£2,360,000

Other information

The foundation also makes grants to organisations and is predominantly focused on funding early intervention programmes.

Livery companies and membership organisations

Auto Cycle Union Benevolent Fund

 £36,400 (2020)

Correspondent: Benevolent Fund Officers, ACU House, Wood Street, Rugby, Warwickshire CV21 2YX (tel: 01788 566400; email: dw@acu.org.uk)

https://www.acu.org.uk/General/ACU-Ben-Fund.aspx

CC number: 208567

Eligibility
Past and present members of the Auto Cycle Union (ACU), and their dependants, who are in need through an accident, illness or hardship.

Types of grant
One-off and recurrent grants. In special circumstances, the fund committee can make emergency payments or loans.

Applications
Application forms are available from your local ACU officer or centre.

Financial information
Year end	31/12/2020
Income	£206,600
Total expenditure	£69,600

Other information
A full list of ACU clubs and centres is available on the charity's website.

The Benenden Charitable Trust

 £125,400 (2020)

Correspondent: The Trustees, Holgate Park Drive, York YO26 4GG (tel: 0800 414 8450; email: charitabletrust@benenden.co.uk)

https://www.benenden.co.uk/about-benenden/charitable-trust/#

CC number: 1106287

Eligibility
Members and former members of Benenden Health, as well as friends and family named on another person's membership.

Types of grant
Grants of up to £3,000 can be made for a variety of needs including helping with the cost of medical treatments not available through the NHS or Benenden Health membership, purchasing specialist equipment and assistance with everyday living costs.

Applications
Apply via the trust's website.

Financial information
Year end	31/12/2020
Income	£80,200
Total expenditure	£211,500

British Motor Cycle Racing Club Benevolent Fund

 £3,100 (2020)

Correspondent: Mike Dommett, 3 Warren Farm Cottages, Nightingales Lane, Chalfont St Giles, Buckinghamshire HP8 4SH (tel: 01708 720305; email: mikedommett@hotmail.com)

https://www.bemsee.net/home/the-ben-fund

CC number: 213308

Eligibility
Members of the British Motor Cycle Racing Club and their dependants who are in need, with a particular focus on those who have been injured while riding.

Types of grant
One-off grants are awarded according to need, mostly towards medical care and equipment costs.

Applications
Apply in writing to the correspondent.

Financial information
Year end	31/12/2020
Income	£2,200
Total expenditure	£4,500

Further financial information
Full accounts were not available to view on the Charity Commission's website due to the fund's low income. We have therefore estimated the fund's grant total based on its total expenditure.

The Anniversaries Fund of the Worshipful Company of Founders

 £13,000 (2019/20)

Correspondent: The Trustees, The Founders Co., Founders Hall, 1 Cloth Fair, London EC1A 7JQ (tel: 020 7796 4800; email: office@foundersco.org.uk)

www.foundersco.org.uk

CC number: 1006402

Eligibility
People who are experiencing financial hardship, people with a disability and older people.

The charity's website states that 'the main focus is on young people, gifted or needy or quite often both'.

Types of grant
Small grants for welfare purposes.

Applications
Apply in writing to the correspondent.

Financial information
Year end	26/10/2020
Income	£13,800
Total expenditure	£13,800

Further financial information
Full accounts were not available to view on the Charity Commission's website due to the charity's low income. We have therefore estimated the grant total based on the charity's total expenditure.

Grand Lodge of Scotland Annuity Benevolent and Charity Funds

£87,800 (2018/19)

Correspondent: Benevolence and Care Department, c/o Freemasons' Hall, 96 George Street, Edinburgh EH2 3DH (tel: 0131 225 5577; email: use the contact form available on the website)

www.grandlodgescotland.com/charity

OSCR number: SC001996

Eligibility
Members and their dependants, and the widows and dependants of deceased members.

The charity's website states:

> The Freemason on whose membership the application has been lodged will require to have been registered in the books of Grand Lodge for at least five years and have been a Qualified Member of a Daughter Lodge during the five years

immediately preceding the date of the application for benevolence, or, if deceased at that date, he will require to have been so qualified during the five years immediately preceding the date of his death. In certain extraordinary circumstances a case may be considered where the preceding criteria is not fulfilled.

Types of grant

One-off and recurrent grants are given based on individual circumstances to assist with day-to-day living expenses.

Applications

The charity's website states:

Applications may be made for financial assistance via the Lodge with which there is, or was, a connection. If applicants are unsure about the Lodge details or require further guidance, they should contact the Benevolence and Care Department at Freemasons' Hall.

Financial information

Year end	31/05/2019
Income	£807,200
Total expenditure	£644,900

Further financial information

The 2018/19 accounts were the latest available at the time of writing (October 2021).

Masonic Charitable Foundation

 £12,950,000 (2019/20)

Correspondent: Enquiries Team, Freemasons' Hall, 60 Great Queen Street, London WC2B 5AZ (tel: 0800 035 6090; email: help@mcf.org.uk)

https://mcf.org.uk

CC number: 1164703

Eligibility

Welfare

Freemasons and their dependants who are in need. Applicants do not have to be a currently subscribing member of a lodge regulated by the United Grand Lodge of England, but must have joined before the need arose.

Education

Children or grandchildren of Freemasons, under the age of 25, who are in full-time education are eligible for funding.

Types of grant

Welfare

Grants are made to help with daily living costs as well as household arrears, support for rent and security deposit, emergency household repairs, boiler replacement, white goods and furnishings, funeral costs, childcare costs. Grants are also made for health,

care and well-being including for consultations, tests and scans, surgery, physiotherapy, manual therapy, speech therapy, occupational therapy, mobility equipment, Motability vehicle support, dental work, mental health support and short breaks for carers.

Education

Grants are made to help young people in education or training and can fund or part-fund computer equipment, educational assessments, school fees (in exceptional circumstances), higher education, apprenticeships, childcare costs and support for exceptional talent. The charity's TalentAid programme can also support children and young people who are exceptionally talented in music, sport or the performing arts. Grants can be awarded to assist with ongoing costs such as coaching, music lessons and the purchase of musical and sports equipment.

Applications

Initial enquiries should be made by contacting your Lodge Almoner or the charity directly by telephone, email or post.

Financial information

Year end	31/03/2020
Income	£88,670,000
Total expenditure	£89,110,000

Further financial information

The charity awarded grants to 6,451 beneficiaries.

Other information

Masonic care homes are operated by The Royal Masonic Benevolent Institution Care Company. The charity currently has 18 locations across England and Wales offering a range of nursing, residential and dementia care to meet the needs of older people. The charity also operates a free Counselling Careline for people experiencing mental health issues. In addition to awarding grants to individuals, the charity makes grants to local and national charities.

The Moose International Welfare Service Fund

 £18,600 (2020)

Correspondent: The Trustees, The Lighthouse Suite, Manor House, Manor Road, Burnham-on-Sea, Somerset TA8 2AS (tel: 01934 842112; email: admin@mooseintl.org.uk)

mooseintluk.org

CC number: 1153351

Eligibility

Members of the Grand Lodge of the Great Britain Loyal Order of Moose or their families who are in need.

Types of grant

Grants are given according to need.

Applications

Apply in writing to the correspondent.

Financial information

Year end	31/12/2020
Income	£84,200
Total expenditure	£99,300

Royal Antediluvian Order of Buffaloes, Grand Lodge of England War Memorial Annuities

 £11,700 (2017/18)

Correspondent: The Trustees, 17 Windsor Crescent, Dudley, West Midlands DY 8HF (tel: 07864 059365; email: webmaster@raobgle.org.uk)

www.raobgle.org.uk

CC number: 220476

Eligibility

Members of the Royal Antediluvian Order of Buffaloes who are older or who have disabilities. Members' wives or widows are also eligible.

Types of grant

Annuities.

Applications

Apply in writing to the correspondent, or through the member's lodge.

Financial information

Year end	31/03/2018
Income	£25,500
Total expenditure	£20,600

Further financial information

The 2017/18 accounts were the latest available at the time of writing (October 2021).

Other information

This charity was established by the Grand Lodge of England as a tribute to members of the order who died during the First World War.

Personal develop-ment/extra-curricular activities

Awards for Young Musicians

 £101,500 (2020)

Correspondent: Awards Team, PO Box 2754, Bristol BS4 9DA (tel: 0300 302 0023; email: awards@a-y-m.org.uk)

🌐 www.a-y-m.org.uk

CC number: 1070994

Eligibility
Musicians aged 5 to 17 who are in financial need and have exceptional musical potential in any genre. Grants are means tested; the charity's website states that applicants with household incomes of over £40,000 are likely to be ineligible.

Types of grant
Up to £2,000 can be awarded; however, the average grant is of around £500. Assistance can be given for:
- Instrumental tuition costs
- Purchasing or hiring of an instrument
- Purchasing instrumental accessories such as cases, bows or reeds
- Fees for long-term music courses such as Saturday school fees
- Travel for attending long-term music courses (where the young musician has a long journey)
- Purchasing sheet music
- Exam entry fees
- Audition fees and associated travel costs.

In exceptional circumstances assistance may be given for: holiday music courses, ensemble membership fees and computer software. See the charity's website for further details.

Exclusions
Support is not given to singers or for any of the following:
- Reimbursements for items already purchased
- Settling the balance on items paid for on credit
- Academic school fees
- Costs associated with higher education
- Foreign ensemble tours

- International travel for masterclasses or courses
- Computer hardware

Applications
Applications can be made online. Each funding round has a different application window and deadline date; sign up for the newsletter or check the website to see when the next funding round opens. Applicants must include a performance video with the application so the board can assess the level of talent or potential.

Financial information
Year end	31/12/2020
Income	£822,900
Total expenditure	£904,200

Other information
The charity also funds other music-related organisations and provides resources for music teachers on how to nurture musical potential.

The Philip Bates Trust

 £4,400 (2019)

Correspondent: The Trustees, 17 Marlborough Way, Market Harborough, Leicestershire LE16 7WL (tel: 0121 747 5705; email: info@ philipbatestrust.org.uk)

🌐 www.philipbatestrust.org.uk

CC number: 1094937

Eligibility
People under the age of 25 who wish to pursue creative and artistic achievement. According to the trust's guidelines for applicants, the trust particularly welcomes applications from individuals in the West Midlands.

Types of grant
Grants are awarded for one-off expenses that otherwise could not be afforded, for example: the purchase or repair of an instrument; the purchase of books, equipment and specialist clothing for those studying music or arts courses; the cost of attending extracurricular courses; the purchase of items necessary to complete a full- or part-time arts-based course.

The trust also supports a range of prizes and awards that are open to young composers, musicians and performers; further details can be found on the trust's website.

Exclusions
University and college course fees and related living expenses will not be funded. Grants to individuals will not be made to more than one sibling in a family unless there are exceptional circumstances. The trustees may give a second grant to a previous beneficiary but only in exceptional circumstances.

Applications
The trust accepts both postal and online applications. If sending a postal application, there is no standard application form but applicants are encouraged to include a summary of activities and requirements, details of which can be found in the guidelines for applicants, which are available to download from the trust's website. All applications for assistance will be considered at the trustees' next meeting. Where possible, the trustees prefer to receive a personal request from the applicant rather than from a parent, guardian or other adult.

Financial information
Year end	31/12/2019
Income	£9,500
Total expenditure	£9,700

Further financial information
Full accounts were not available to view on the Charity Commission's website due to the trust's low income. We have therefore estimated the grant total based on its total expenditure.

Other information
Grants are also made to charitable organisations to support projects or workshops which aim to develop creative and artistic interests and skills in young people.

The Choir Schools' Association Bursary Trust Ltd

 £222,200 (2019/20)

Correspondent: Susan Rees, Administrator, 39 Grange Close, Winchester, Hampshire SO23 9RS (tel: 01962 853508; email: admin@ choirschools.org.uk)

🌐 www.choirschools.org.uk

CC number: 1120639

Eligibility
Pupils or proposed pupils at a member school of the Choir Schools' Association.

Types of grant
Financial help is available for children who sing well, want to be a chorister and whose parents cannot afford the fees.

Applications
Applicants should contact the head of the choir or arts school concerned.

Financial information

	Year end	30/06/2020
	Income	£269,600
	Total expenditure	£256,800

Further financial information

Grants were awarded to 92 individuals.

The Alec Dickson Trust

 £10,200 (2020/21)

Correspondent: The Trustees, 18–24 Lower Clapton Road, Hackney, London E5 0PD (tel: 07737 660797; email: secretary@alecdicksontrust.org.uk)

 www.alecdicksontrust.org.uk

CC number: 1076900

Eligibility

Young people under 30 years of age who are involved in volunteering or community service in the UK.

Types of grant

Grants of up to £500 are awarded towards the costs of running projects that encourage volunteering (particularly youth volunteering) and have a positive impact on communities and individuals in need.

Exclusions

The trust does not fund overseas projects, gap year projects or grants towards college and university course fees.

Applications

Applications can be made on the trust's website and require a referee. The trustees review applications on a quarterly basis.

Financial information

	Year end	31/03/2021
	Income	£0
	Total expenditure	£11,300

Further financial information

Full accounts were not available to view on the Charity Commission's website due to the trust's low income. We have therefore estimated the trust's grant total based on its total expenditure.

The Marie Duffy Foundation

£2,600 (2019/20)

Correspondent: Mike Pask, Trustee/Secretary and Awards Manager, 2 Aspin Lodge, 38 North Park, Chalfont St Peter, Gerrard's Cross, Buckinghamshire SL9 8JP (tel: 01202 701173; email: m.pask990@btinternet.com or enquiries@marie-duffy-foundation.com)

www.marie-duffy-foundation.com

CC number: 1145892

Eligibility

Irish dancers and musicians over the age of ten who are 'passionate about excellence in dance, music, composition or choreography', as stated on the foundation's website.

Types of grant

Grants have been made for dance class fees, Step Dance Teacher (TCRG) examination fees, costs involved in attending competitions and so on. Financial support is also given in times of crisis, for example, in cases of terminal illness.

Bursaries (particularly to the University of Limerick) and scholarships to study the Irish language have also been awarded.

Applications

Application forms are available to download on the funder's website.

Financial information

	Year end	08/08/2020
	Income	£9,100
	Total expenditure	£5,800

Further financial information

Full accounts were not available to view on the Charity Commission's website due to the foundation's low income. We have therefore estimated the foundation's grant total based on its total expenditure.

Other information

Grants are mainly awarded to individuals/groups of individuals, but the charity also makes an annual donation to the World Academy of Music and Dance at the University of Limerick.

The Monica Elwes Shipway Sporting Foundation

 £800 (2019/20)

Correspondent: The Trustees, c/o McDermot Will & Emery UK LLP, 110 Bishopsgate, London EC2N 4AY (tel: 020 7570 1460; email: sgoldring@mwe.com)

CC number: 1054362

Eligibility

Children and young people in full-time education engaged in sporting activities who have limited resources.

Types of grant

One-off grants according to need.

Applications

Apply in writing to the correspondent.

Financial information

	Year end	31/03/2020
	Income	£1,000
	Total expenditure	£1,800

Further financial information

Full accounts were not available to view on the Charity Commission's website due to the foundation's low income. We have therefore estimated the foundation's grant total based on its total expenditure.

England Golf Trust

£26,000 (2019/20)

Correspondent: Di Horsley, Chair, c/o England Golf, The National Golf Centre, Woodhall Spa, Lincolnshire LN10 6PU (tel: 01526 354500; email: admin@ englandgolftrust.org)

https://www.englandgolftrust.org

CC number: 1160992

Eligibility

Individuals who are attending some form of golf coaching or are already involved with golf. Applicants must be under the age of 21, or in full-time education or pursuing a recognised continuing professional development (CPD) qualification. The applicant must have the support of two sponsors who can monitor participation and performance. The trust also has a separate grants scheme for people who meet the criteria above and who have a disability or long-term health condition.

Types of grant

General

The England Golf Trust awards grants to those in need for items such as club subscriptions, golf equipment, coaching, competition entry fees and travel/accommodation at regional and national competitions. A grant of up to £1,000 may be awarded for up to three years.

Education

There are two bursaries available for educational purposes (such as tuition fees, books and accommodation). These are:

- Angela Uzielli Bursary – between £1,250 and £2,000 per annum for up to three years awarded to girls in further or higher education who are in financial need and studying an unrelated subject to golf but who want to develop their golfing skills. For more information visit the trust's website.
- England Golf Trust Bursary – up to £1,000 per annum for up to three years awarded to anyone studying a golf-related subject or academic subject at a higher or further

education institution. For more information visit the trust's website.

Applications

Application and sponsor forms are available to download from the trust's website or by contacting the offices via telephone. Sponsors should be people who know the applicant, including one who can support their golf practice (i.e. a coach or club organiser). Check the website for the closing dates.

Financial information

Year end	30/09/2020
Income	£16,100
Total expenditure	£37,300

Further financial information

Grants totalling £26,000 were awarded to 37 young people.

The Ollie Feast Trust

 £1,900 (2019/20)

Correspondent: The Trustees, 5 Christ's Court, Victoria Street, Cambridge CB1 1JN (tel: 01223 357697; email: contact@theolliefeasttrust.com)

 www.theolliefeasttrust.com

CC number: 1177424

Eligibility

Young people who are planning to travel (particularly where the individual would otherwise be unable to travel for reasons of financial hardship or otherwise).

Types of grant

Grants of up to £500 to assist with the costs of travelling.

Applications

Application forms can be downloaded from the trust's website when funding rounds are open. Grant recipients are asked to write or give a report for the trustees following their trip.

Financial information

Year end	05/04/2020
Income	£5,300
Total expenditure	£10,200

Further financial information

Full accounts were not available to view on the Charity Commission's website due to the trust's low income. We have therefore estimated the trust's grant total based on its total expenditure.

Other information

The trust was set up to celebrate the life of Ollie Feast, who died aged just 20 and who had a passion for travel and sports. The trust also offers mentoring and coaching, and provides facilities, services and recreational activities.

The Rob George Foundation
See entry on page 64

The Reg Gilbert International Youth Friendship Trust (GIFT)

 £4,600 (2019/20)

Correspondent: The Secretary, 23 Linnet Way, Frome, Somerset BA11 2UY (tel: 01373 465225; email: Yorkie77pam@aol.co.uk)

 www.giftfriendshiptrust.org.uk

CC number: 327307

Eligibility

UK citizens aged between 16 and 24 who are undertaking a project in a financially developing country for a minimum of six weeks. Applicants must intend to live and volunteer within an indigenous community in the host country, preferably in a homestay environment. Applicants must have been vetted and accepted by an approved overseas project agency or, if travelling independently, provide a comprehensive and verifiable breakdown of their travel arrangements.

Types of grant

Bursaries of up to £500 to cover part of the cost of the trip.

Applications

Application forms and eligibility criteria can be found on the trust's website. Applicants must provide a reference from a tutor or another professional and be able to demonstrate what research and preparation they have undertaken for the trip. Applications must be received at least three months before the trip.

Financial information

Year end	05/04/2020
Income	£5,800
Total expenditure	£5,100

Further financial information

Full accounts were not available to view on the Charity Commission's website due to the trust's low income. We have therefore estimated the trust's grant total based on its total expenditure.

Other information

The trust is linked to the Rotary Club of Frome, Somerset.

Hazel's Footprints Trust

 £5,600 (2019/20)

Correspondent: Joan Scott Aiton, Company Secretary, Legerwood House, Earlston, Berwickshire TD4 6AS (tel: 01896 849677; email: info@ hazelsfootprints.org)

 www.hazelsfootprints.org

OSCR number: SC036069

Eligibility

People in the UK or Europe who wish to undertake educational voluntary work in financially developing countries. The preferred duration of a project is one year and applicants must commit to a minimum of six months in their chosen location.

Types of grant

Grants are made towards the costs of overseas volunteering.

Applications

Application forms are available to download from the trust's website and should be returned by post. Applications must be submitted by late September for January departure dates and by mid-March for summer departure dates. The trust states that the money it has available cannot meet the number of applications it receives; however, some helpful hints on how to maximise your chance of success can be found on the website. If successful, beneficiaries are required to send regular reports to the charity (with photos) during their volunteering trip, which will be posted on the trust's website and social media channels. Reports must be written in English.

Financial information

Year end	05/04/2020
Income	£27,300
Total expenditure	£53,000

Further financial information

During the financial year, the charity awarded seven grants to individuals.

Other information

Grants are also made to UK charities undertaking educational projects in financially developing countries.

The Adam Millichip Foundation
See entry on page 54

National Youth Arts Trust (NYAT)

 £12,400 (2019/20)

Correspondent: Ruth O'Brien, Director of Operations, c/o The Furniture Practice, 31 Pear Tree Street, London EC1V 3AG (tel: 07891 835589; email: admin@nationalyouthartstrust.org.uk)

https://nationalyouthartstrust.org.uk

CC number: 1152367

Eligibility

UK citizens between the ages of 12 and 25 who cannot afford access to opportunities in the arts. Applicants must be either: enrolled in full- or part-time education and eligible for Pupil Premium and/or free school meals; or (for those not in education, employment or training, and for those living in Scotland) able to provide evidence of any state benefits the applicant (or the applicant's family) receives. Applicants must be able to demonstrate talent and dedication to improving skills in their chosen art.

Types of grant

The trust offers bursaries of up to £1,000 in the fields of dance, music and drama.

- **Dance bursaries** are given to fund dance classes taught by an Imperial Society of Teachers of Dance (ISTD) teacher, or taken at a Council for Dance Education and Training (CDET) school or dance company funded by the Arts Council. Funding can also be used to cover the cost of specialist dance clothing and travel expenses
- **Music bursaries** are given to fund music lessons (instrumental and singing) taught by teachers who will enter the pupils into Associated Board of the Royal Schools of Music (ABRSM) exams. Funding can also be used to cover the costs of musical instrument hire, music ensemble membership and travel expenses. Beginner applications are only accepted from secondary school-aged individuals for singing. All other music bursary applicants must have started lessons by the age of 12

The trust provides 'access bursaries' of up to £1,000 to help with the cost of drama school audition recalls, tuition fees, books, educational materials or part-time drama classes. Drama schools must be one of the following: a former Drama UK-accredited school; a Conservatoire for Dance and Drama-accredited school; a Conservatoires UK school; or a drama school that is part of the Federation of Drama Schools.

Applications

Application forms can be completed online on the trust's website or requested from the correspondent. Applications must include the following:

- A reference that is signed, stamped and on school letterhead paper or similar
- A letter from the applicant's school confirming they receive Pupil Premium or free school meals (if applicable); otherwise, the applicant must provide evidence that they are in receipt of benefits
- A copy of a utility bill or Council Tax letter as proof of address
- A copy of the applicant's passport
- A copy of a letter of enrolment to a dance, drama or music school
- A copy of a letter of invitation to audition at an accredited drama school or conservatoire (if applicable)
- A copy of an academic transcript, CV, certificates or qualifications in the art form

A YouTube or other online video (of no more than five minutes in length) of the individual's performing arts practice can also be included but is optional.

Financial information

Year end	31/03/2020
Income	£82,800
Total expenditure	£75,000

Other information

The trust also funds a number of youth theatre projects.

Open Wing Trust

 £4,000 (2020)

Correspondent: The Trustees, Flat 2, 44 Langham Street, London W1W 7AU (email: clerk@openwing.org.uk)

www.openwing.org.uk

CC number: 1149773

Eligibility

The trust's website states that grants are available for individuals over the age of 18 in England and Wales who are 'at the beginning of their career and [who are] contemplating a radical re-orientation of their life's work or the deepening of an existing vision'. Applicants are expected to be working towards a goal that will promote social change and help other people in need.

Types of grant

One-off grants of up to £2,000 are awarded to around three individuals each year. The guidelines on the website note: 'Trustees will consider funding specific living costs such as food and rent, training programmes, or offering support during voluntary work or an internship and academic course costs specific to the intended work.'

Recent grants have been awarded for a keyboard for music therapy, living costs while developing a youth theatre and training for work with vulnerable women.

Exclusions

The trust's website states that the trustees will not fund holidays, or unspecified 'thinking time', nor will they make grants for loan and debt repayments.

Applications

Apply online via the trust's website, where full eligibility details and guidelines can also be found. Application forms can also be downloaded if necessary. The website states: 'The Trustees will expect clarity about what the applicant intends to do, what steps will be necessary to achieve it, and what they expect to be achieved during the period of the grant.' Applications made on behalf of others will not be accepted, except when there is an obvious reason.

Financial information

Year end	31/12/2020
Income	£3,500
Total expenditure	£4,600

Further financial information

Full accounts were not available to view on the Charity Commission's website due to the trust's low income. We have therefore estimated the grant total based on the trust's total expenditure.

Richard Overall Trust

 £630 (2019/20)

Correspondent: The Trustees, New Barn Cottage, Honey Lane, Selborne, Alton, Hampshire GU34 3BY (tel: 01420 511375; email: therichardoveralltrust@gmail.com)

CC number: 1088640

Eligibility

Young people with disabilities who live in the UK.

Types of grant

Grants are awarded to support participation in physical education and sports. Funding can be given towards specialist sports equipment, training, sports clothing, specialist transport and the purchase of tickets to sporting events.

Applications

Apply in writing to the correspondent. Applications can be submitted at any time.

Financial information

Year end	30/04/2020
Income	£5,800
Total expenditure	£1,400

Further financial information

Full accounts were not available to view on the Charity Commission's website due to the trust's low income. We have therefore estimated the trust's grant total based on its total expenditure.

Other information

Grants may also be given to groups or organisations.

The Ron Pickering Memorial Fund

 £61,800 (2019/20)

Correspondent: Kim Pickering, Trustee, 19 Walsingham Road, Enfield, Middlesex EN2 6EX (tel: 020 8366 2472; email: grants@rpmf.org.uk or kim.pickering1@gmail.com)

www.rpmf.org.uk

CC number: 1005166

Eligibility

Talented British track and field athletes aged between 15 and 23 years who are in financial need. This includes athletes with disabilities. Athletics coaches are also supported.

Types of grant

Grants are made for equipment, specialist coaching or travel.

The charity also administers The Jean Pickering Olympic Scholarships, originally established in the lead-up to the 2012 Olympic games. The scholarships give long-term financial support and advice to young athletes (and their coach when needed), with the aim of developing their skills to a level that gives them a good chance of being selected for the next Olympic or Paralympic Games.

Exclusions

The charity is unable to support requests for other sports. Grants to young people over the age of 23 are only made in exceptional circumstances.

Applications

Applications usually open in October and November each year, with grants being awarded the following year. When applications open, an online form becomes available on the charity's website. Check the website nearer to this time for details.

Financial information

Year end	31/07/2020
Income	£42,600
Total expenditure	£64,900

Further financial information

Grants in 2019/20 were broken down as follows: grants to 187 athletes, including 16 athletes with disabilities (£38,800); The Jean Pickering Olympic Scholarships (£22,500); grants to coaches (£500).

Other information

Grants are also made to athletics clubs and the English Schools' Athletic Association.

The RDC Foundation

 £1,400 (2019/20)

Correspondent: Nick Adlam, Trustee, Rakeshop House, Newtown Common, Newbury RG20 9DA (tel: 07734 956667; email: nick@rdc.foundation)

CC number: 1184154

Eligibility

Individuals under 21 years of age who are undertaking life-changing adventurous activities.

Types of grant

Grants of up to £1,000 are given towards the cost (including equipment) of expeditions, travels or adventurous activity.

Applications

Application forms can be downloaded from the charity's website and should be returned via email. Applications are reviewed and approved every two months.

Financial information

Year end	01/01/2020
Income	£11,800
Total expenditure	£3,100

Further financial information

Full accounts were not available to view on the Charity Commission's website due to the charity's low income. We have therefore estimated the charity's grant total based on its total expenditure.

Other information

The foundation also awards grants to organisations.

Rhona Reid Charitable Trust

 £7,700 (2019/20)

Correspondent: Kerry Clayton, c/o Rathbone Investment Management, Port of Liverpool Building, Pier Head, Liverpool, Merseyside L3 1NW (tel: 0151 236 6666; email: kerry.clayton@rathbones.com)

www.rrct.co.uk

CC number: 1047380

Eligibility

People wishing to excel in a chosen field who would be unable to do so without the trust's help. Preference is given to the study and advancement of medicine (particularly ophthalmology) and to music and the arts.

Types of grant

Grants are given according to need.

Applications

Apply in writing to the correspondent. Applications are considered in March and September.

Financial information

Year end	05/04/2020
Income	£2,100
Total expenditure	£17,000

Further financial information

Full accounts were not available to view on the Charity Commission's website due to the trust's low income. We have therefore estimated the trust's grant total based on its total expenditure.

Other information

Grants are also given to organisations.

John Taylor Foundation for Young Athletes

 £1,600 (2019/20)

Correspondent: The Trustees, 6 Sawrey Court, Broughton-in-Furness, Cumbria LA20 6JQ (tel: 01484 975487; email: enquiries@johntaylorfoundation.org.uk)

www.johntaylorfoundation.org.uk

CC number: 1101008

Eligibility

Young amateur athletes who were born and live in the UK.

Types of grant

Grants are given to allow young athletes to pursue opportunities in amateur athletics. Previous examples of support include assistance with the cost of taking part in competitions, travel, accommodation costs, equipment, sports clothing and membership fees.

Applications

Application forms can be completed on the foundation's website. Applications are considered twice a year.

Financial information

Year end	05/04/2020
Income	£100
Total expenditure	£1,800

Further financial information

Full accounts were not available to view on the Charity Commission's website due to the foundation's low income. We have therefore estimated the grant total based on the foundation's total expenditure.

Other information

The foundation also aims to promote awareness of cardiomyopathy to the public.

Sydney Dean Whitehead's Charitable Trust

£ £38,600 (2020/21)

Correspondent: The Trustees, c/o Moore Stephens, Chartered Accountants, 30 Gay Street, Bath, Somerset BA1 2PD (tel: 01225 486100; email: mark.burnett@ moorestephens.com)

CC number: 207714

Eligibility

Children under the age of 18 who have special artistic talents, especially in music, dance or ballet, and whose parents are on a low income or are unable to help them develop these talents. Preference will be given to applicants who can demonstrate their own fundraising efforts.

Types of grant

Grants are given mainly towards school fees.

Applications

Apply in writing to the correspondent.

Financial information

Year end	05/04/2021
Income	£46,900
Total expenditure	£50,400

Further financial information

Grants were awarded to 21 individuals during the year.

Other information

Grants are also awarded to organisations.

Miss E. B. Wrightson's Charitable Settlement

£ £24,200 (2019/20)

Correspondent: Trust Administrator, Swangles Farm, Cold Christmas Lane, Thundridge, Ware, Hertfordshire SG12 7SP (email: info@wrightsontrust. co.uk)

 wrightsontrust.co.uk

CC number: 1002147

Eligibility

Young musicians, usually between the ages of 11 and 18, who are in need.

Types of grant

One-off and recurrent grants ranging from £100 to £800 are given for instrumental lessons, choir/orchestra tour fees and so on. An individual may receive a maximum of three grants from the trust.

Exclusions

Assistance cannot be given towards school fees.

Applications

Application forms can be downloaded from the trust's website. Completed forms should be submitted by email using the child's name as the subject line. Applications must be submitted along with a brief music CV (for children aged 12 and above), two letters of support from teachers/tutors, details of the reasons for applying, any other supporting documents and a list of other grant-making bodies applied to. Alternatively, applications may be returned by post, sending three copies of the form, two copies of the CV and references.

Financial information

Year end	05/04/2020
Income	£20,200
Total expenditure	£86,100

Further financial information

Full accounts were not available to view on the Charity Commission's website due to the charity's low income. We have therefore estimated the grant total based on the charity's total expenditure.

Other information

The charity also supports organisations.

The Young Explorers' Trust

£ £4,100 (2020)

Correspondent: Gemma Wardle, Awards and Grants Officer, 6 Manor Road, Burnham-on-Sea, Somerset TA8 2AS (tel: 01278 784658; email: grants@theyet. org)

 https://www.theyet.org/what-we-do/grant-awards

CC number: 1006211

Eligibility

Young people under the age of 19 who wish to participate in expeditions and adventurous projects at home or abroad. Some of the trust's awards are targeted at young people who have experienced disadvantage in their lives.

Types of grant

The trust administers a number of different awards – see the website for up-to-date information. Previously, grants

have been awarded for expeditions abroad or at sea, physical adventures, community projects, conservation work, fieldwork in financially developing countries and adventure courses.

Applications

Application forms can be downloaded from the trust's website. The application deadline is currently 31 January each year; however, check the website for any changes. For further information contact the correspondent.

Financial information

Year end	31/12/2020
Income	£18,200
Total expenditure	£4,600

Further financial information

Full accounts were not available to view on the Charity Commission's website due to the trust's low income. We have therefore estimated the trust's grant total based on its total expenditure.

Utility charities

Anglian Water Assistance Fund

Correspondent: Extra Care Support Team, PO Box 4994, Lancing, West Sussex BN11 9AL (tel: 0800 975 5574)

 www.anglianwater.co.uk/awaf

Eligibility

The fund can consider helping if you are in debt with your water and/or sewerage charges to Anglian or Hartlepool Water and you are a current domestic account holder of Anglian or Hartlepool Water.

Types of grant

The fund may be able to help cover the cost of domestic water and sewerage charges, or offer alternative solutions.

Applications

An eligibility checker for support is available on Anglian Water's website on the 'Extra Care Support' page. If eligible, a contact form will be made available to you. Alternatively, you can make an enquiry by calling 0800 975 5574.

Further financial information

Financial information for the fund was not available. During the year, Anglian Water contributed £1.2 million to the fund.

Other information

The fund is no longer a registered charity. It was previously administered by Charis Grants but is now administered by Anglian Water directly.

British Gas Energy Trust

 £1,690,000 (2020/21)

Correspondent: The Trustees, Farrer & Co., 65–66 Lincoln's Inn Fields, London WC2A 3LH (tel: 020 3375 7496; email: contact@britishgasenergytrust.org.uk)

www.britishgasenergytrust.org.uk

CC number: 1179578

Eligibility
Customers of British Gas, as well as customers of other energy suppliers, can apply. Applicants must live in England, Wales or Scotland. Further information on eligibility can be found online.

Types of grant
Grants are given to clear an outstanding gas, electricity or energy debt.

Applications
Individuals can apply via the trust's online application form.

Financial information

Year end	31/03/2021
Income	£6,000,000
Total expenditure	£6,180,000

Further financial information
Grants were awarded to 1,781 individuals during the year.

E.ON Energy Fund

Correspondent: Freepost E.ON Energy Fund (tel: 0330 380 1090 (Monday to Friday 9am to 5pm); email: EONenergyfund@lets-talk.online)

 https://www.eonenergyfund.com

Eligibility
Existing or previous customers of E.ON Energy who live in England, Scotland or Wales and need help paying current or final E.ON energy bills arrears.

Types of grant
Grants are made towards current or final E.ON energy bill arrears. The fund can also help applicants replace household items such as cookers, fridges, fridge-freezers and washing machines. It may also help to replace gas boilers.

Exclusions
You must be the homeowner and an EON Energy customer to apply for a boiler replacement.

Applications
Applications can be made via the fund's website by the individual or a third party. The website states that to apply, you must demonstrate 'financial stability, a willingness to pay your ongoing energy bills and be able to evidence any benefits you are in receipt of or medical conditions. You need to have received money advice from an FCA approved agency in order to apply to the EON Energy Fund and you will need to provide evidence of this as part of your application. Priority will be given to those who have already received debt advice.' Full details of supporting documents required can be found on the website.

Further financial information
Financial information was not available for the fund.

Other information
The fund is not a registered charity. E.ON Next customers are eligible for the same support through the E.ON Next Energy Fund: https://www.eonnextenergyfund.com.

Foundations Independent Living Trust

 £381,600 (2019/20)

Correspondent: The Trustees, First Floor, 22 Norfolk Street, Glossop, Derbyshire SK13 8BS (tel: 0300 124 0316; email: info@filt.org.uk)

https://www.foundations.uk.com/filt.php

CC number: 1103784

Eligibility
To be eligible to apply for the Gas Safe Charity Hardship Fund, applicants must live in privately owned accommodation and either have a low household income and/or disability or be considered exceptionally vulnerable by the Home Improvement Agency (HIA).

Types of grant
Grants of up to £500 are awarded through the Gas Safe Charity Hardship Fund for a range of purposes including gas safety checks, gas boiler repairs/replacements, gas servicing, gas cookers and fires, gas pipework, gas meters and gas water heaters.

Exclusions
According to our previous research, the trust is unable to provide funding for the following purposes:
- Energy-efficient upgrades to existing working systems
- Routine servicing
- Payment of gas, electricity or other fuel bills/costs
- Retrospective payments

- Measures in social housing or privately rented properties
- Non-essential requirements, including cosmetic enhancements
- Replacement windows
- Fire surrounds
- Chimney sweeping
- Decorating
- Replacement of working systems
- Electrical rewiring
- Building works
- HIA fees

Applications
Application forms can be downloaded from the trust's website. Applications must be made by an HIA case worker on behalf of an individual; applications received directly from individuals will not be accepted. Further information and guidance are available on the website.

Financial information

Year end	31/03/2020
Income	£380,000
Total expenditure	£417,800

The OVO Energy Fund

Correspondent: c/o Citizens Advice Plymouth, 32 Mayflower Street, Plymouth PL1 1QX (tel: 01752 507703)

 https://www.ovoenergy.com/help/debt-and-energy-assistance

Eligibility
OVO Energy customers who have fallen into debt and are behind with their payments but want to become more financially stable in the future. The fund's website states:

You can apply to the fund if:
- You have, or have had, an account with OVO Energy
- You've run up a debt on your gas or electricity account of at least £150
- Your annual household income is £16,190 or less
- You have a valid reason affecting your ability to pay

Types of grant
Grants are made towards gas and electricity debts. Payments are made directly into the individual's OVO account or gas/electricity meter.

Applications
Applications can be made through the fund's website.

Further financial information
Financial information was not available for this funder.

Other information
The OVO Energy Fund works with Citizens Advice Plymouth to deliver grants and advice. Successful applicants will be offered a one-hour phone call

with a Citizens Advice Plymouth Energy Advisor.

Scottish Hydro Electric Community Trust

 £71,700 (2019/20)

Correspondent: Fiona Paterson, Trust Secretary, Inveralmond House, 200 Dunkeld Road, Perth, Perthshire PH1 3AQ (tel: 01738 455113)

🌐 www.shect.org

OSCR number: SC027243

Eligibility
Customers faced with high charges for an electricity connection within the Scottish Hydro-Electric Distribution area.

Types of grant
Grants towards the cost and installation of domestic electricity connections.

Applications
Applications can be made via the trust's website, where upcoming deadlines can also be found.

Financial information
Year end	31/03/2020
Income	£140,400
Total expenditure	£212,500

The Severn Trent Water Charitable Trust Fund

 £2,830,000 (2019/20)

Correspondent: The Trustees, 12–14 Mill Street, Sutton Coldfield, West Midlands B72 1TJ (tel: 0121 355 7766; email: office@sttf.org.uk)

🌐 www.sttf.org.uk

CC number: 1108278

Eligibility
People with water or sewage services provided by Severn Trent Water, or by companies or organisations which operate on behalf of Severn Trent, who are in financial difficulty and unable to pay their water charges.

Types of grant
One-off grants are given to clear or reduce water and/or sewage debt. Further assistance can be given through the purchase of essential household items or the payment of other priority bills and debts.

Exclusions
The charity's website states it will not make grants for the following:

- Court fines, catalogue debts, credit cards, personal loans or other forms of borrowing
- Social Fund loans/benefit overpayments/Tax Credit overpayments now being reclaimed

Grants cannot be made for retrospective costs.

Applications
Applications can be made through the charity's website or by using a form available to download from its website.

Financial information
Year end	31/03/2020
Income	£5,770,000
Total expenditure	£5,720,000

Other information
Grants can also be made to debt advice organisations.

South East Water's Helping Hand

Correspondent: Customer Care Team, South East Water, Rocfort Road, Snodland, Kent ME6 5AH (tel: 0333 000 2468 (Monday to Friday between 8am and 7pm); email: use the contact form available on the website)

 https://www.southeastwater.co.uk/get-help/im-struggling-to-pay-my-bill

Eligibility
South East Water customers who can demonstrate that they are taking steps to achieve financial stability but need help clearing their water and sewerage debts.

Types of grant
Grants are made towards water and sewerage debts.

Applications
Applications can be made via the South East Water website.

Further financial information
Financial information was not available.

Other information
Helping Hands is a charitable scheme funded by donations from South East Water and is not a registered charity.

South Staffordshire Water Charitable Trust

 £186,600 (2019/20)

Correspondent: The Administrator, Green Lane, Walsall, West Midlands WS2 7PD (tel: 0300 330 0033; email: SSWCharitableTrust@south-staffs-water.co.uk)

🌐 www.sswct.org/index.asp

CC number: 1043177

Eligibility
Customers who receive their water from South Staffordshire Water or Cambridge Water and who are in need of financial assistance due to reasons such as low income, unemployment, illness, redundancy, relationship breakdown or bereavement. A map of eligible areas is available on the trust's website. Priority is given to those applicants who are willing to make a contribution towards the cost of their bill (usually between £1 and £2 a week).

Types of grant
Support is given towards the costs of the individual's water bill. Funding will only cover part of the cost; however, in exceptional circumstances the entire cost of the bill may be met. Grants of up to six months' worth of payments may be made in situations of temporary hardship.

Applications
Application forms are available to download from the trust's website. Applications can be made directly by the individual or through a third party such as the Citizens Advice, local authorities, or the billing and collections team at the water company. Applications will require full information on the individual's financial situation including evidence of household income and expenditure.

Financial information
Year end	31/03/2020
Income	£215,100
Total expenditure	£215,100

Further financial information
In 2019/20, a total of 516 grants were awarded to individuals.

Other information
Those who do not qualify for a grant may be eligible to apply for the WaterSure Scheme, details of which can be found on the website.

Tackling Household Affordable Warmth Orkney (THAW Orkney)

 £13,300 (2019/20)

Correspondent: The Trustees, 5 Manse Lane, Stromness, Orkney KW16 3AP (tel: 01856 878388; email: info@thaworkney.co.uk)

🌐 www.thaworkney.co.uk

OSCR number: SC045272

Eligibility
People in need who live in Orkney.

Types of grant

The charity provides electricity vouchers and small one-off grants of up to £150 towards heating installations and repairs. It also offers 'cosy home' packs to households in need which contain a blanket, a thermal mug, clothing and more.

Applications

Application forms can be completed on the charity's website. Individuals can apply directly or organisations/agencies can apply on behalf of an individual using a separate referral form.

Financial information

Year end		31/03/2020
Income		£238,000
Total expenditure		£255,200

Further financial information

During the financial year, funding was distributed as follows: electricity vouchers (£6,400); cosy home packs (£5,900); installation grants (£1,000).

Other information

The charity also makes grants for the improvement of education in conservation and efficient use of energy and fuel.

Thames Water Trust Fund

£ £291,800 (2019/20)

Correspondent: The Trustees, Auriga Services Ltd, Emmanuel Court, 12–14 Mill Street, Sutton Coldfield, West Midlands B72 1TJ (tel: 0121 321 1324; email: office@twtf.org.uk)

 www.twtf.org.uk

CC number: 1126714

Eligibility

Thames Water customers who are in need.

Types of grant

Grants are available to people struggling to pay their water bills. Grants are also available to help towards the cost of an essential household item or other needs.

Applications

Application forms are available to download from the charity's website.

Financial information

Year end		31/03/2020
Income		£450,200
Total expenditure		£908,900

Yorkshire Water Community Trust

 £900,000 (2019/20)

Correspondent: The Trustees, PO Box 52, Bradford, West Yorkshire BD3 7YD (tel: 0345 124 2426; email: ywcommtrust@loop.co.uk)

https://www.yorkshirewater.com/billing-payments/help-paying-your-bill

CC number: 1047923

Eligibility

People who are in arrears with Yorkshire Water and have at least one other priority debt, such as gas or electricity, Council Tax, rent or mortgage repayments.

Types of grant

Payments for outstanding water bills.

Applications

Application forms are available to download from Yorkshire Water's website. Successful applicants may apply again after two years.

Financial information

Year end		31/03/2020
Income		£952,300
Total expenditure		£952,300

Further financial information

Support was given to 2,108 individuals during 2019/20.

Charities by beneficiary

This chapter includes all the charities that award grants to certain groups of beneficiary (for instance based on gender or age) or to individuals in specific circumstances (such as people experiencing homelessness or refugees and asylum seekers).

The categories in this chapter are ordered alphabetically. 'Children and young people' includes charities that specifically award grants to people aged 25 or under, while 'Older people' includes grant-makers that give to people aged 55 or older. Although this reflects the criteria of some of the grant-making charities in these chapters, the exact age restrictions specified by each individual charity do vary. The 'Miscellaneous' section includes charities with specific criteria that do not fall under any of the other categories in this guide. 'Religion' includes charities that support people of a particular religious group, while charities that specifically support those in religious occupations are listed in the 'Occupational charities' chapter in this guide (see page 97).

Please note that most of the charities within any given section still have further restrictions on who they can help. Individuals who fall into a particular category (such as 'older people') should not apply to all of the charities in the relevant section, but should first consider carefully whether they are eligible for each one.

The charities under any of the categories in this chapter are by no means the only charities in this guide that will give to that particular group of beneficiaries; they are simply the only charities that specify this group as their main criteria. For example, as well as the charities under 'Specific circumstances – Asylum seekers and refugees', there will also be charities in the 'General charities' chapter, or in local sections, that will give grants to asylum seekers and refugees as part of a wider set of criteria.

Index of charities by beneficiary

Children and young people 22

Ethnic and national minorities in the UK 30

Families 31

Gender 31

Miscellaneous 35

Older people 36

Religion 39

   General religion 39

   Christianity 39

   Islam 43

   Judaism 44

Specific circumstances 46

   Asylum seekers and refugees 47

   Homelessness 48

   People with experience of the criminal justice system 49

Children and young people

Aberlour Child Care Trust

Correspondent: Ian Black, Secretary, Kintail House, Forthside Way, Stirling, Stirlingshire FK8 1QZ (tel: 0800 085 6150; email: enquiries@aberlour.org.uk or urgentassistance@aberlour.org.uk)

 https://www.aberlour.org.uk

OSCR number: SC007991

Eligibility

Families in Scotland with children (aged 21 and under) who are experiencing severe financial hardship.

Types of grant

Grants, usually of up to £100, are available for basic needs such as food, utilities, clothing or bedding and appliance repairs/replacements. Support can also be given when emergency furniture is required, for example if the house has been flooded or if a parent has had to flee domestic abuse.

Exclusions

Grants are not made for carpets, floor coverings or electronic devices.

Applications

Applications must be completed by a sponsor, such as a social worker, teacher, clergy or third sector organisation, acting in their professional capacity. Online application forms can be found on the trust's website, along with full guidelines. As of April 2021, email applications are no longer accepted.

Financial information

Year end	31/03/2020
Income	£18,610,000
Total expenditure	£19,670,000

Further financial information

During the year, direct expenditure on activities supporting children and families totalled £16,700. We were unable to determine the figure for grants awarded.

Other information

The trust awards grants to individuals through its Urgent Assistance Fund. Grant-making is only a small part of the trust's charitable activities.

The John Maurice Aitken Trust

 £10,000 (2019/20)

Correspondent: The Trustees, c/o Nevis Capital LLP, 221 West George Street, Glasgow G2 2ND (email: info@jmatrust.com)

 www.jmatrust.com

OSCR number: SC045343

Eligibility

Young people aged 15 to 25 who are in need and live in Scotland.

Types of grant

Grants are awarded according to need. Bursaries are made to students attending university or college and who are studying mathematics or statistics.

Applications

Apply in writing to the correspondent.

Financial information

Year end	31/03/2020
Income	£111,000
Total expenditure	£96,600

Further financial information

During the financial year, the trust made grants to 23 individuals.

Other information

This trust also makes grants to organisations.

Always Look on the Bright Side of Life Charitable Trust

 £7,000 (2019/20)

Correspondent: Michael Daly, 28 Station Close, Potters Bar, Hertfordshire EN6 1TL (email: brightsidecharity@hotmail.com)

www.thebrightsideoflife.org.uk

CC number: 1150016

Eligibility

Children under the age of 18 who are disadvantaged.

Types of grant

Grants are available for items or experiences and are typically paid to a charity or organisation on the individual's behalf. The charity's website states that the trustees are 'particularly interested in applications for grants that will provide children with enjoyment, not just the basic essentials of daily life, though these may also be funded where deemed appropriate'.

Exclusions

Funding is not provided for:

- Furniture and white goods
- Fixtures and fittings
- Computers/laptops
- School/university fees
- Debts and debt management

Applications

The charity advises that a professional familiar with the applicant's situation should apply on their behalf. The application form is available on the charity's website and should be submitted by email along with the supporting documentation.

Financial information

Year end	01/10/2020
Income	£0
Total expenditure	£7,600

Further financial information

Full accounts were not available to view on the Charity Commission's website due to the trust's low income. We have therefore estimated the grant total based on the trust's total expenditure.

Bauer Radio's Cash for Kids Charities

Correspondent: Tracey Butler, Hampdon House, Unit 3, Falcon Court, Preston Farm, Stockton-on-Tees, County Durham TS18 3TS (tel: 01642 675788; email: tracey.butler@bauermedia.co.uk)

www.cashforkids.uk.com

CC number: 1122062/SC041421

Eligibility

Children under the age of 18 who are disadvantaged or have a disability and live in one of the Bauer radio areas in the UK.

Types of grant

One-off grants are available for a range of needs including bedding, appliances, sensory equipment, wheelchairs, clothing and furniture.

Applications

Applications can be made through local Bauer radio stations. A list of stations is available at www.cashforkids.uk.com. All grants are distributed through registered charities.

Financial information

Year end	31/12/2020
Income	£17,190,000
Total expenditure	£15,260,000

Further financial information

Note that the financial information refers to the combined details of both Bauer Radio's Cash for Kids Charities (England and Northern Ireland) and

Bauer Radio's Cash for Kids Charities (Scotland).

We were unable to determine the total awarded in grants to individuals. In England, Wales and Northern Ireland, grants to individuals and organisations totalled £10.7 million. In Scotland, such grants totalled £2.6 million.

In 2020, the charity's annual Mission Appeal was repurposed as an emergency appeal in response to the COVID-19 pandemic. In England, Wales and Northern Ireland, emergency grants were awarded to 23,490 children, while in Scotland, emergency grants were awarded to 16,300 children.

The Dickie Bird Foundation

 £2,300 (2019/20)

Correspondent: Grants Officer, Flat 3, The Tower, The Tower Drive, Pool-in-Wharfedale, Otley, West Yorkshire LS21 1NQ (tel: 0113 203 7196; email: warren.cowley@sky.com)

https://thedickiebirdfoundation.co.uk

CC number: 1104646

Eligibility

Disadvantaged young people aged 16 and under who are participating, or wish to participate, in sport.

Types of grant

Grants of up to £500 are available towards sports equipment and clothing. Funding will be considered for all recognised sports.

Exclusions

Grants are not available towards travel or coaching. Grants are not awarded to groups.

Applications

Applications must be submitted using the foundation's application form, which is available from its website. The form must be submitted along with two references. Completed applications should be sent by post to the Grants Officer, whose address can be found on the application form. The trustees meet every two months to consider applications.

Financial information

Year end	05/04/2020
Income	£1,900
Total expenditure	£2,500

Further financial information

Full accounts were not available to view on the Charity Commission's website due to the foundation's low income. We have therefore estimated the foundation's grant total based on its total expenditure.

The Boparan Charitable Trust

 £1,040,000 (2018/19)

Correspondent: The Trustees, Colmore Court, 9 Colmore Row, Birmingham, West Midlands B3 2BJ (tel: 0121 214 9364; email: applications@boparan.com)

www.theboparancharitabletrust.com

CC number: 1129992

Eligibility

Children and young people up to the age of 18, throughout the UK, who are disadvantaged through poverty, disability or life-limiting conditions.

Types of grant

According to the trust's website, grants are provided for the following:
- Powered and manual wheelchairs
- Specialist trikes, buggies, pushchairs and car seats
- Walkers and standing frames
- Sensory toys
- Specialist baths
- Hoists
- White goods
- Food and clothing vouchers
- P-Pod chairs
- Tough furniture beds
- Therapies (including speech and language, occupations therapy, food therapy and behavioural therapy).

The website states that if there is an item you would like funding which is not on the list, contact the trust.

Exclusions

According to the trust's website, the following are not funded (unless in exceptional circumstances):
- Donations to other charities
- Funeral services
- Service or autism dogs
- Trampolines/trampettes
- Home adaptations/renovations
- Holidays and short breaks
- Legal costs
- Warrantees
- Carpets and Flooring
- Garden Equipment/Sheds and Fencing
- Reimbursements of funds already paid out
- Repayment of loans
- Administration or salary costs
- Travelling costs
- Accommodation costs
- Safe Spaces
- Toys or computer consoles
- TVs, DVD players, PCs, laptops and tablets (including iPads)
- Hot tubs
- Sofas/settees
- Lease or purchase of cars
- Alternative therapy
- Applied Behaviour Analysis (ABA) therapy
- Room hire
- Private school fees
- Non-medical body and face enhancements

Applications

Application forms can be downloaded from the trust's website and should be returned by post. Alternatively, applications can be submitted online. Note that official written confirmation by an independent professional body will be required stating the applicant's condition or circumstances. This letter must be on company letterhead paper with contact details. An independent quote from a supplier is also required.

Financial information

Year end	29/12/2019
Income	£744,600
Total expenditure	£1,070,000

Further financial information

The 2018/19 accounts were the latest available at the time of writing (October 2021).

Grants were broken down as follows:

Disability aids	£758,000
Treatments	£53,900
Sensory items	£12,800
Holidays	£9,000
Household appliances	£5,100
Other	£4,500
Household furniture	£2,100
General household	£2,000

Buttle UK

 £2,320,000 (2019/20)

Correspondent: Grants Team, 15 Greycoat Place, London SW1P 1SB (tel: 020 7828 7311; email: info@buttleuk.org)

www.buttleuk.org

CC number: 313007/SC037997

Eligibility

Welfare

The charity's 'Chances for Children' grants are available to children and young people aged 18 and under (if living with a parent/carer) or aged 20 and under (if living independently with little or no support from their family). The young person must also be living on a low income and have experienced a crisis that has recently had a significant and enduring impact on their social and emotional well-being and their educational engagement.

A crisis may include, for example, domestic abuse, drug and alcohol misuse, estrangement, illness, distress, abuse, neglect, or behavioural or mental health issues.

In addition, the young person or their family must have recently taken action to improve the situation and be actively engaging with support so as to move on from the crisis.

Education

The charity's website states that eligibility for boarding support is as follows:

Children and young people growing up in financial hardship, aged 11-16, who are affected by at least one of the following:

- Disadvantaged by parenting capacity and at risk of family breakdown
- Who live in single parent / carer families or where there are two parents, but one or both is severely incapacitated by illness or disability
- Severe social, emotional or health problems within the family that affect the child

Types of grant

Welfare

Grants of up to £2,000 for items and activities are available through the 'Chances for Children' programme.

According to the charity's website, holistic packages of support can include, but are not limited to:

- Items and activities to support learning and development such as laptops, books, wi-fi, educational toys, tuition, etc.
- Clothing and school uniforms
- Social, sporting and leisure activities
- Family activities
- Items for children/young people's bedrooms
- Other household items that are not available from sources such as Emergency Essentials or Local Authority welfare schemes, etc.

Education

Grants are awarded to cover the full cost of boarding school fees when there is a strong case as to why a child cannot stay within the family home with their parent or carer. Note that only 10–20 boarding places are funded each year.

Exclusions

A list of exclusions for each programme can be found on the charity's website.

Applications

Welfare

Applications can be made via an online application portal on the charity's website. Applications should be completed by a frontline professional from a statutory or voluntary organisation who supports the family or the individual and is capable of assessing their needs and can also administer a grant on behalf of the charity.

Education

Applications for boarding bursaries can be made by support workers, such as

social workers and teachers, or parents and carers who have a child who will benefit from a place in a boarding school. There is a three-stage application process, details of which can be found on the charity's website. The website advises that the application process is 'lengthy and thorough'. Applications open in January each year.

Further information and regional contact details are available on the charity's website.

Financial information

Year end	31/03/2020
Income	£2,640,000
Total expenditure	£3,770,000

Further financial information

According to the 2019/20 annual report, the charity awarded grants worth £2.32 million in support of around 2,600 children and young people during the year.

Other information

As of 2018, Buttle UK no longer runs the Emergency Essentials Programme on behalf of BBC Children in Need.

The Capstone Care Leavers' Trust

£ £82,100 (2019/20)

Correspondent: Zoe Greenwood, Trust Manager, Wootton Chase, Wootton St Lawrence, Basingstoke, Hampshire RG23 8PE (tel: 0121 374 2601; email: info@capstonetrust.org)

 https://www. capstonecareleaverstrust.org

CC number: 1149717

Eligibility

Young people between the ages of 17 and 25 in England and Wales who have been in care at any time in the past and are in need. Those who have received a leaving care grant or any other financial support from a local authority department are still eligible to apply.

Types of grant

Welfare

Grants of between £300 and £2,000 are given for a range of purposes including for household furniture, kitchen appliances (such as a cooker, fridge, freezer or washing machine) and basic clothing. Grants may also be considered for driving lessons or a practical test if the applicant has already passed their driving theory test and lives in a rural area with poor transport links or needs a full licence to retain a job or complete training.

Education

Grants are awarded towards further or higher education courses and training. Funding will also be considered for items that assist with studies such as a laptop or textbooks as well as for travel to and from the place of study. Most grants will fall between £300 and £2,000; however, grants of up to £3,000 may be considered in relation to higher education fees.

Exclusions

Grants are not generally given towards the following:

- Private accommodation costs (such as deposits or rent)
- Arrears or debts
- Daily living costs
- Food or utility bills
- Credit card, overdraft or bank charges
- Overseas trips or courses
- Driving theory tests

Applications

Application forms can be completed online or downloaded from the trust's website. Applications require the names of two referees who are able to confirm the applicant's circumstances such as a support worker, social worker or tutor. The trust aims to make a decision within four weeks; however, it can take up to 12 weeks. Individuals may apply more than once but must wait 12 months before reapplying if they have already received a grant from the trust. Further guidelines are available on the trust's website.

Financial information

Year end	30/09/2020
Income	£100,300
Total expenditure	£125,700

Further financial information

In 2019/20 grants totalling £82,100 were awarded to 97 individuals.

Children of the Clergy Trust

£ £2,300 (2020)

Correspondent: The Revd I. Thomson, Trustee, 4 Keirhill Gardens, Westhill, Aberdeenshire AB32 6AZ

OSCR number: SC001845

Eligibility

Children of deceased ministers of the Church of Scotland and children of a deceased parent where the deceased parent was the principal financial provider.

Types of grant

Grants are awarded according to need.

Applications

Apply in writing to the correspondent.

Financial information

Year end	31/12/2020
Income	£2,900
Total expenditure	£2,500

Further financial information

Full accounts were not available to view on the OSCR website due to the trust's low income. We have therefore estimated the grant total based on the trust's total expenditure.

Other information

The trust is known as the Synod of Grampian Children of the Clergy Trust.

The Chizel Educational Trust

£ £12,800 (2020/21)

Correspondent: The Trustees, Burgage Manor, Burgage, Southwell, Nottingham, Nottinghamshire NG25 0EP (tel: 01636 081 685; email: thechizeleducationaltrust@gmail.com)

CC number: 1091574

Eligibility

People under the age of 24 who live in the UK and are in need of financial assistance.

Types of grant

The trust provides bursaries and maintenance allowances for students at school, university or any other educational establishment. Grants are also available towards equipment, clothing, instruments, books and travel in the UK or abroad.

Applications

Applications should be made in writing to the correspondent and must be submitted in April or October. Applications must also enclose an sae.

Financial information

Year end	05/04/2021
Income	£18,000
Total expenditure	£28,600

Further financial information

Full accounts were not available to view on the Charity Commission's website due to the trust's low income. We have therefore estimated the trust's grant total based on its total expenditure.

Other information

Financial assistance is also provided towards the maintenance of Ackworth School in Yorkshire and the Inverness Royal Academy Mollie Stephens Trust.

John Collings Educational Trust

£ £14,100 (2019/20)

Correspondent: The Trustees, 11 Church Road, Tunbridge Wells, Kent TN1 1JA (tel: 01892 526344)

CC number: 287474

Eligibility

According to its Charity Commission record, the trust supports children who 'achieve good results in both academic and other fields'.

Types of grant

Grants are made to assist beneficiaries through their education.

Applications

Apply in writing to the correspondent.

Financial information

Year end	31/08/2020
Income	£59,500
Total expenditure	£55,200

Other information

The trust also awards grants to organisations.

The Dain Fund
See entry on page 139

Eshaki Foundation

£ £1,300 (2019/20)

Correspondent: The Trustees, 85 Central Avenue, Hayes UB3 2BP (tel: 020 8581 9897; email: info@eshakifoundation.com)

 https://eshakifoundation.com

CC number: 1171109

Eligibility

Eshaki Foundation awards grants with the aim of providing opportunities for sports and academic development to young people aged 11–18 (especially those living in poverty and those who have a physical and/or mental disability).

Types of grant

Grants of up to £2,500 for sports and academic development.

Applications

Initial enquiries can be made through the form on the foundation's website. Decisions are usually made within two months of submission.

Financial information

Year end	31/08/2020
Income	£1,500
Total expenditure	£1,400

Further financial information

Full accounts were not available to view on the Charity Commission's website due to the foundation's low income. We have therefore estimated the foundation's grant total based on its total expenditure.

Other information

According to the foundation's website, the trustees hope to expand the focus on grants to individuals in the future.

The Fashion and Textile Children's Trust
See entry on page 169

The Gurney Fund

£ £713,200 (2019/20)

Correspondent: The Trustees, 9 Bath Road, Worthing, West Sussex BN11 3NU (tel: 01903 237256; email: use the contact form available on the website)

 www.gurneyfund.org

CC number: 1156903

Eligibility

Children of police officers from 22 subscribing forces in England and Wales, where a parent has died or retired on the grounds of ill health. Stepchildren may also be eligible if they were substantially supported by a deceased or medically retired officer. The list of subscribing forces can be found on the fund's website.

Types of grant

Welfare

A weekly allowance of between £20 and £100 is paid on a quarterly basis to a parent or guardian and reviewed annually. One-off additional support is available for items such as musical instruments, swimming lessons, sports and activities, bus fares and driving lessons. A Christmas gift is given to children under the age of 18.

Education

Grants are available for higher and further education students for essential costs such as course books and ancillary.

Applications

Applications for medically retired officers can be made online via the online form. Widows/widowers and guardians should contact the fund directly to discuss eligibility.

Financial information

Year end	31/03/2020
Income	£475,400
Total expenditure	£927,300

Happy Days Children's Charity

 £168,400 (2020/21)

Correspondent: Anna DaRocha, Holidays and Trusts Officer, Unit 6–7, The Glover Centre, 23–25 Bury Mead Road, Hitchin, Hertfordshire SG5 1RT (tel: 01462 530710; email: ann@happydayscharity.org or enquiries@happydayscharity.org)

www.happydayscharity.org

CC number: 1010943

Eligibility

Children and young people aged 3 to 17 years (inclusive) who have additional needs. The charity offers help to those with learning difficulties, physical or mental disabilities and with acute, chronic or life-limiting illnesses. It also helps young people who have been abused or neglected, have witnessed domestic violence, have been bereaved or act as carers for a parent or a sibling.

Types of grant

Family holidays, day trips and experiences in the UK.

Applications

Application forms are available to download from the charity's website. Applications are accepted from parents, guardians, grandparents and siblings, as well as GPs, consultants, nurses and social workers.

Financial information

Year end	31/03/2021
Income	£677,700
Total expenditure	£503,300

Other information

Grants are also made to groups of children and young people who have additional needs for day trips and holidays.

The Duchess of Leeds Foundation for Boys and Girls

 £34,000 (2020)

Correspondent: John Sinfield, Clerk to the Trustees, 19 Kenton Road, Harrow, Middlesex HA1 2BW (tel: 020 8422 1950)

CC number: 313103

Eligibility

Schoolchildren who live in England, Wales or the Channel islands and are attending a Roman Catholic school and who have lost both parents, are fatherless or whose father does not support them financially.

Types of grant

Grants are awarded per term or as a single payment towards the cost of school fees. In recent years, term-time grants have ranged between £500 and £1,700. Annual grants range from £1,500 to £3,000 for day pupils and £1,500 to £5,000 for boarders.

Applications

Apply in writing to the correspondent.

Financial information

Year end	31/12/2020
Income	£24,600
Total expenditure	£37,800

Further financial information

Full accounts were not available to view on the Charity Commission's website due to the foundation's low income. We have therefore estimated the foundation's grant total based on its total expenditure.

The Dr Thomas Lyon Bequest

 £2,500 (2020/21)

Correspondent: Gregor Murray, Secretary and Chamberlain, The Merchant Company, The Merchant Hall, 22 Hanover Street, Edinburgh EH2 2EP (tel: 0131 225 7202; email: enquiries@mcoe.org.uk or use the contact form on the website)

https://www.mcoe.org.uk

OSCR number: SC010284

Eligibility

Orphans and children of single parents in Scotland.

Types of grant

Grants are offered to children in primary and secondary education.

Applications

Contact the correspondent for more information on how to apply.

Financial information

Year end	31/07/2021
Income	£10,500
Total expenditure	£2,800

Further financial information

Full accounts were not available to view on the Charity Commission's website due to the charity's low income. We

have therefore estimated the charity's grant total based on its total expenditure.

Other information

This fund is one of nine that is administered by the Edinburgh Merchant Company.

The McAlpine Educational Endowments Ltd

 £13,700 (2019/20)

Correspondent: Gillian Bush, Secretary, Eaton Court, Maylands Avenue, Hemel Hempstead, Hertfordshire HP2 7TR (tel: 0333 566 2069; email: g.bush@srm.com)

CC number: 313156

Eligibility

Children and young people in mainstream education.

Types of grant

Grants are given for educational purposes on a yearly basis. Grants can be renewed for further years subject to a satisfactory school report.

Applications

Apply in writing to the correspondent.

Financial information

Year end	31/03/2020
Income	£9,400
Total expenditure	£15,200

Further financial information

Full accounts were not available to view on the Charity Commission's website due to the charity's low income. We have therefore estimated the charity's grant total based on its total expenditure.

Naval Children's Charity

 £795,200 (2020/21)

Correspondent: Caseworkers, 311 Twyford Avenue, Stamshaw, Hampshire PO2 8RN (tel: 023 9263 9534; email: caseworkers@navalchildrenscharity.org.uk)

www.navalchildrenscharity.org.uk

CC number: 1160182

Eligibility

Children (under the age of 25) of serving and former members of the following:
▶ The Royal Navy
▶ The Royal Marines
▶ The Queen Alexandra's Royal Naval Nursing Service

◗ The Women's Royal Naval Service
◗ The Royal Fleet Auxiliary
◗ Reserves of the above forces

Types of grant

Welfare

The charity's Emergency Essentials Grant Scheme provides grants for the purchase of day-to-day items such as groceries, children's clothing, school uniform, beds and furniture, white goods, car seats and extracurricular activities.

Grants are also available for families coping with illness or disability and range from support grants to help towards the extra costs involved in hospital visits or stays, disability equipment and, in some cases, help with house adaptations. Support when a child is bereaved is also available.

Education

Educational grants are offered to children and young people where there is a need that requires support outside that offered by the state. The charity's website states: 'Educational grants are only awarded in exceptional circumstances and there must be a supporting reason showing the child is disadvantaged academically. For example: learning disability; special needs; emotional bereavement; disability; illness.'

Applications

Contact the charity using the online form on its website.

Financial information

Year end		31/03/2021
Income		£1,090,000
Total expenditure		£1,470,000

Other information

Grants are also made for naval community projects.

The Ogilvie Charities

See entry on page 6

The Prince's Trust

£ £1,270,000 (2019/20)

Correspondent: The Trustees, 8 Glade Path, London SE1 8EG (tel: 020 7543 1234; email: info@princes-trust.org.uk)

 www.princes-trust.org.uk

CC number: 1079675/SC041198

Eligibility

Young people between the ages 11 and 30 who have struggled at school, are not in education or training, are in or leaving care, are long-term unemployed, have been in trouble with the law, are facing issues such as homelessness or mental health issues, or are otherwise disadvantaged.

Types of grant

The Prince's Trust aims to change the lives of young people, helping them to develop confidence, learn new skills and get practical and financial support. A wide range of support is offered, including:

◗ Enterprise programme – assists young people aged between 18 and 30 to start their own business through the provision of financial and mentoring support.

◗ Development awards – grants towards course fees, tools, equipment, uniforms, job licence fees or transport costs to a new job until the first payslip.

Exclusions

Restrictions and inclusions differ according to the programme being applied for. See the trust's website for further information.

Applications

Enquiries can be made via the form on the 'get in touch' page on the trust's website. Individuals who wish to speak to someone over the phone or require assistance in filling out the form can call 0800 842 842.

Financial information

Year end		31/03/2020
Income		£88,340,000
Total expenditure		£62,200,000

Further financial information

In 2019/20 a total of 5,886 grants were made to individuals totalling £1.27 million. Of this total, 793 grants totalling £398,000 were awarded through the Enterprise programme and 5,093 Development Awards were made totalling £870,000.

Other information

The Prince's Trust also has a number of programmes to help individuals into work, education or training, or to build their skills and confidence. These include work experience programmes, personal development programmes, mentoring, courses to help individuals discover new talents and courses to boost confidence and skills. For up-to-date information on the current programmes and support available, refer to the trust's website.

Rees Foundation

£ £48,500 (2019/20)

Correspondent: Janet Rees, Trustee, Rees Foundation, Craftsman House, De Salis Drive, Hampton Lovett, Droitwich, Worcestershire WR9 0QE (tel: 01527 916559; email: contactus@reesfoundation.org)

 www.reesfoundation.org

CC number: 1154019

Eligibility

Young people and adults leaving foster or residential care.

Types of grant

The foundation has a limited Crisis Fund to provide immediate financial support for emergency situations.

Applications

Applications can be made online via the foundation's website.

Financial information

Year end		31/10/2020
Income		£496,800
Total expenditure		£486,900

Other information

The foundation also offers practical advice and emotional guidance on a range of matters, as well as a mentoring service and signposting.

RMT (National Union of Rail, Maritime and Transport Workers) Orphan Fund

Correspondent: Collin Sharpe, Unity House, 39 Chalton Street, London NW1 1JD (tel: 020 7529 8291; email: info@rmt.org.uk)

 https://www.rmt.org.uk/member-benefits/orphan-benefit

Eligibility

Children of deceased members of the RMT union who are under the age of 22.

Types of grant

Grants of £12 per week are given for each child under 16 and of £12.75 per week for those between the ages of 16 and 22 who are in full-time education. Grants are payable on the member's death.

Applications

Application forms are available from the local union branch or can be downloaded from the union's website. For children over the age of 16 in full-time education, an education certificate should also be attached. All applications must be endorsed by the branch secretary.

Further financial information

There was no financial information available for this funder.

The J. C. Robinson Trust No. 3

£ £30,100 (2019/20)

Correspondent: The Trustees, Barnett Wood Bungalow, Blackboys, Uckfield, East Sussex TN22 5JL (tel: 01825 890651; email: jcrobinsontrust3@outlook.com)

CC number: 207294

Eligibility
Young and older people living in England, with a preference for East Sussex.

Types of grant
Grants are given according to need.

Applications
Apply in writing to the correspondent. Applications should be made through an organisation such as Citizens Advice or through a third party such as a social worker.

Financial information
Year end	05/04/2020
Income	£41,700
Total expenditure	£66,900

Further financial information
In 2019/20, 178 grants were awarded to organisations and individuals during the year. A breakdown of grants was not provided; therefore, we have estimated the grant total.

Royal National Children's Springboard Foundation

£ £1,860,000 (2019/20)

Correspondent: Dr Claire Hodgskiss, Director of School Relationships, 7 Grosvenor Gardens, London SW1W 0BD (tel: 01932 868622; email: admin@royalspringboard.org.uk)

 https://www.royalspringboard.org.uk

CC number: 1167491

Eligibility
Children aged 8–18 who have a low family income and:
▶ Are experiencing a lack of parental care, where suitable care is not available due to the death of a parent, a severe illness or a disability
▶ Have a sibling who has a disability that affects the well-being of the rest of the family
▶ Are experiencing a degree of social deprivation

All candidates must be British citizens or have indefinite leave to remain in the UK.

Types of grant
Bursaries for boarding schools, typically of between £4,000 and £5,000 per annum.

Exclusions
Support cannot be given on the sole basis of financial difficulties, educational preferences or special needs.

Applications
Applications can be completed on the foundation's website and submitted through the contact form. The foundation will then get in touch with all the necessary information. Partner organisations can also refer children.

Financial information
Year end	31/07/2020
Income	£2,190,000
Total expenditure	£2,860,000

Further financial information
In 2019/20, the foundation awarded grants to 422 individuals.

Sailors' Children's Society

£ £454,600 (2019/20)

Correspondent: Elizabeth Bentley, Grants Officer, Francis Reckitt House, Newland, Cottingham Road, Hull, East Yorkshire HU6 7RJ (tel: 01482 342331; email: info@sailorschildren.org.uk)

 www.sailorschildren.org.uk

CC number: 224505

Eligibility
Seafarers' children under the age of 18 who are in full-time education and whose families are in severe financial difficulties. One of the child's parents must have served in the Royal or Merchant Navy or in the fishing fleets, including on ferries, tankers, cruise ships or cargo boats. Applicants must be in receipt of Housing Benefit or Council Tax Benefit (other than single people 25% discount or disablement reduction).

Types of grant
Welfare
The charity provides financial assistance in a number of ways, including:
▶ Monthly child welfare grants – designed to boost income and enable families to provide basic essentials
▶ Clothing grants – payable per child twice a year to help children start off the new school year and to buy a new winter coat and shoes
▶ Christmas grants – to help to buy a special Christmas present
▶ Emergency heating grants – in the event of extreme winter weather
▶ Special grants – one-off grants are given in extreme cases to provide, for example, furniture for a child's bedroom
▶ Caravan holidays – the charity owns eight caravans at seaside resorts across the UK. Travel grants are given to help with the costs of public transport or fuel expenses.

Education
If the child is over the age of 18 and currently supported through the charity's child support scheme, the charity can continue to provide a welfare grant to help with their ongoing studies at university/college.

Applications
Contact the charity by phone or email to make an application.

Financial information
Year end	31/03/2020
Income	£715,000
Total expenditure	£871,000

Sailors' Orphan Society of Scotland

£ £67,800 (2019/20)

Correspondent: Claire McMillan, 18 Woodside Crescent, Glasgow G3 7UL (tel: 0141 353 2090; email: info@sailorsorphansociety.co.uk)

 www.sailorsorphansociety.co.uk

OSCR number: SC000242

Eligibility
Dependants of seafarers who are in a position of need either through disadvantage or through the death or incapacity of one or both of their parents. Support is also given to disadvantaged young people within seafaring communities in Scotland. Children must be under 16 or in full-time education if over 16.

Types of grant
The charity provides monthly grants of around £80 per child as well as two additional payments in July and December. One-off grants may also be paid at the trustees' discretion.

Applications
Application forms can be downloaded from the charity's website. Applications should include a third-party confirmation of disadvantage or death or incapacity of the parent(s). Grants are paid to the guardians of the beneficiaries.

Financial information
Year end	31/03/2020
Income	£84,400
Total expenditure	£72,800

A Smile for a Child

 £57,600 (2019/20)

Correspondent: See the charity's website for local contacts, 17 Sugarhill Crescent, Newton Aycliffe, County Durham DL5 4FH (tel: 07904 448296; email: asmileforachild@btinternet.com)

 www.asmileforachild.org

CC number: 1123357

Eligibility
Disadvantaged children or those with disabilities in the UK.

Types of grant
Grants are made for sports equipment, lessons and wheelchairs.

Applications
Application forms are available to download from the charity's website and should be returned to the correspondent.

Financial information

Year end	31/03/2020
Income	£242,100
Total expenditure	£242,800

Further financial information
The charity also gives Wembley Stadium tickets to beneficiaries. These in-kind donations totalled £28,900 in 2019/20.

Other information
The charity also helps families fundraise for their own equipment.

Grants are available to organisations to provide activities and mobility equipment.

The Spark Foundation

 £45,000 (2019/20)

Correspondent: The Trustees, Hugh House, Hugh Place, Faversham, Kent ME13 7AD (tel: 01795 534260; email: admin@sparkfoundation.org.uk)

 www.sparkfoundation.org.uk

CC number: 1097058

Eligibility
Young people under the age of 26 who either are, or have been, in care in England and Wales and are undertaking education.

Types of grant
One-off grants of up to £600 are available for a range of purposes such as household essentials, white goods, carpets, gym membership, driving lessons, activity holidays, bikes, music/drama lessons, specialist computer software and so on.

One-off grants of up to £600 are available for students and people undertaking vocational training or starting work towards tools, protective clothing, laptops and so on.

Exclusions
Grants are not given for the following:
- Things that are the responsibility of the local authority, fostering agency or care
- Renovating or decorating accommodation
- Travel expenses to get to college
- Recurring costs

Applications
Application forms can be downloaded from the foundation's website along with examples of successful applications and current deadlines.

Financial information

Year end	31/03/2020
Income	£71,400
Total expenditure	£47,900

Further financial information
During 2019/20, the foundation awarded 110 grants to individuals.

St George's Police Children Trust

 £1,100,000 (2020)

Correspondent: Trust Administrator, Northern Police Convalescent Home, St Andrews, Harlow Moor Road, Harrogate, North Yorkshire HG2 0AD (tel: 01423 504448; email: enquiries@ stgeorgespolicechildrentrust.org)

 www.stgeorgespolicechildrentrust. org

CC number: 1147445/SC043652

Eligibility
Children of serving, retired or deceased police officers who are in need due to life-changing circumstances such as the loss of a parent, or the parent who is a police officer being unable to work due to illness or injury sustained on or off duty. Each grant scheme has separate eligibility criteria; further details can be found on the trust's website. Note: to be eligible, the police officer parent typically must have donated to the trust while serving.

Types of grant
Welfare
New beneficiary grants of £1,000 are given to all eligible applicants before being given full consideration at the trustees' meeting. The trust offers a number of grant schemes:
- **St George's Police Children Trust Grants** – funding is available to eligible beneficiaries in full-time education up to statutory school leaving age, or up to the end of the school year in which they turn 19 years of age. This support is delivered in the form of weekly allowances and seasonal gifts.
- **Child Counselling Grants** – financial support of up to £1,000 is given to young people under the age of 25 who wish to access counselling to help them through a bereavement or difficult time.
- **Driving Lesson Grants** – grants of up to £1,000 are given to young people from the age of 17 up to 25 to help with the cost of learning to drive.
- **Special Needs Grants** – grants are given to children who have special needs.

Education
The trust offers three grant schemes to support education:
- **Higher Education Grants** – support is given to beneficiaries who are undertaking any form of further education such as a university degree, Higher National Certificate (HNC), Higher National Diploma (HND) or National Vocational Qualification (NVQ) level four. Grants are available from the age of 18 for a maximum of four years or up to the age of 25.
- **Ex-gratia Grant** – funding is available for trade tools, musical instruments, text books, etc.
- **School Leavers Grant** – grants of up to £500 are available for young people not attending university towards tools for apprenticeships, work uniforms and so on.

Exclusions
The trust will not support people in education beyond first-degree level. Grants are not made for gap year activities. Applicants applying for a Higher Education Grant after a gap year will only be considered if the period from education was no longer than 12 months. The trust does not pay allowances or grants to beneficiaries who are in work and earning money.

Applications
Application forms are available to download from the trust's website. Applications must be completed in full by a responsible adult or guardian, validated and countersigned either by a representative of the Police Federation office, human resources or occupational health department, or benevolent fund. Applications should be submitted along with any supporting documents such as birth, death, adoption and incapacity certificates.

Financial information

Year end	31/12/2020
Income	£1,220,000
Total expenditure	£1,320,000

Other information

The trust offers a one-week stay at its holiday home in Harrogate to all new members.

The Stanley Stein Deceased Charitable Trust

£ £34,600 (2019/20)

Correspondent: Brian Berg, Trustee, 14 Linden Lea, London N2 0RG (tel: 07968 806527; email: brianberg369@ yahoo.co.uk)

CC number: 1048873

Eligibility

People under the age of 21 or over the age of 75 who are in need and live in England or Wales. Grants are also given to people with physical disabilities (such as blindness).

Types of grant

Grants are awarded according to need.

Applications

Apply in writing to the correspondent.

Financial information

Year end	05/04/2020
Income	£6,300
Total expenditure	£38,400

Further financial information

Full accounts were not available to view on the Charity Commission's website due to the trust's low income. We have therefore estimated the grant total based on the trust's total expenditure.

Ethnic and national minorities in the UK

The Armenian Relief Society of Great Britain Trust

£ £40,000 (2019/20)

Correspondent: The Trustees, 19 Somervell Road, London HA2 8TY

CC number: 327389

Eligibility

Armenians in need as a result of illness, bereavement or financial hardship.

Types of grant

Grants are awarded according to need. Scholarships are also available.

Applications

Apply in writing to the correspondent.

Financial information

Year end	31/10/2020
Income	£75,100
Total expenditure	£80,000

Further financial information

The grant total has been estimated.

Other information

The charity collects food, medicines and clothing for distribution in disaster situations. Grants are also made to organisations, particularly relief centres and similar organisations that are involved in providing relief in times of crisis.

Koning Willem Fonds – The Netherlands Benevolent Society

£ £34,700 (2020)

Correspondent: Ms M. Koomans, Social Work Co-ordinator, 7 Austin Friars, London EC2N 2HA (tel: 07915 110590; email: info@koningwillemfonds.org.uk)

 https://www.koningwillemfonds. org.uk

CC number: 213032

Eligibility

Dutch citizens living in the UK who are in need. Support is extended to surviving widows/widowers of Dutch nationals and children with at least one parent of Dutch nationality.

Types of grant

Welfare grants are made on a one-off basis and in the form of monthly payments. Grants have been awarded for essential household items (such as furniture, bedding, white goods, etc.), clothing, utility bills and identity documents. Supermarket vouchers are also provided.

The charity has recently set up an Education Fund to deal with requests for educational support. Financial assistance has been given to students who, due to circumstances beyond their control, would otherwise be unable to finish their studies. Support has been given to those studying paramedic courses and catering diplomas.

Exclusions

The charity does not normally support university students applying for additional funding.

Applications

Initial enquiries can be made using the contact form on the charity's website. The trustees meet on a monthly basis to consider grant applications.

Financial information

Year end	31/12/2020
Income	£37,400
Total expenditure	£63,100

Further financial information

The charity awarded 94 grants to its beneficiaries. Note: the charity's Education Fund was set up over this financial year; therefore, we were unable to determine a grant total for education.

Swiss Benevolent Society

£ £16,100 (2019)

Correspondent: Petra Kehr, Welfare Officer, 79 Endell Street, London WC2H 9DY (tel: 020 7836 9119; email: info@swissbenevolent.org.uk)

 www.swissbenevolent.org.uk

CC number: 1111348

Eligibility

Swiss citizens who are experiencing hardship and are temporarily or permanently resident in the UK.

Types of grant

Monthly pensions and one-off grants towards holidays, heating costs, travel to and from day centres, therapies, household equipment, telephone and TV licences, for example.

Applications

Contact forms are available on the society's website. Additionally, the welfare officer can be contacted on 020 7836 9119 on Tuesdays and Wednesdays.

Financial information

Year end	31/12/2019
Income	£28,700
Total expenditure	£51,100

Further financial information

The 2019 annual report was the latest available at the time of writing (July 2021).

Other information

The charity has a welfare officer who supports beneficiaries by providing advice, counselling and support, offering advocacy with various agencies, co-ordinating overall care and arranging visits from volunteers to homes, hospitals and nursing homes.

Families

Child Funeral Charity

 £6,300 (2020/21)

Correspondent: The Trustees, Unit 1, The Shield Office Centre, 186A Station Road, Burton Latimer, Kettering, Northamptonshire NN15 5NT (tel: 01480 276088; email: enquiries@childfuneralcharity.org.uk)

www.childfuneralcharity.org.uk/index.html

CC number: 1156387

Eligibility
Families who are struggling to pay the costs of a funeral for a child aged 16 or under.

Types of grant
Financial support is available to help with funeral-related expenses.

Exclusions
The trustees will not consider applications for a burial plot, transport (other than hearse/hearsette), horse-drawn carriages, balloons, doves, headstones, or food and drink for a wake or gathering following the funeral.

Applications
Application forms can be downloaded from the charity's website. Applications should be made by professionals who have knowledge of the bereaved family and their circumstances. This could be funeral directors, celebrant or faith representatives, bereavement nurses or midwives, hospice managers, GPs, local authority registrars, hospital bereavement officers or registrars.

Financial information
Year end	27/02/2021
Income	£9,700
Total expenditure	£7,000

Further financial information
Full accounts were not available to view on the Charity Commission's website due to the charity's low income. We have therefore estimated the charity's grant total based on its total expenditure.

The Family Holiday Association

 £149,900 (2019/20)

Correspondent: Grants and Projects Team, Family Holiday Association, 7–14 Great Dover Street, London SE1 4YR (tel: 020 3117 0650; email: info@familyholidayassociation.org.uk)

https://www.familyholidayassociation.org.uk/apply-for-a-break/breaks

CC number: 800262

Eligibility
The Family Holiday Association was set up to help families. It considers a family to consist of dependent children and those who care for them. Carers can be parents, grandparents, guardians and others with caring responsibilities, such as an older child.

To apply, a family must:
- Be referred by someone who knows the family in a professional capacity (e.g. a social worker, health visitor, teacher or support worker), is aware of the family's circumstances and can support them until they go on the break
- Have at least one child in the family under 18 years old at the time of the holiday
- Be on a low income
- Not have had a holiday in the last four years.

Types of grant
Grants are awarded for day trips, short breaks, week-long holidays, group trips and group projects. Holidays are generally for holiday parks in the UK such as Haven or Butlins. Breaks include accommodation, linen rental (where available), entertainment passes and holiday insurance (subject to medical conditions). The charity may also make a contribution towards holiday expenses.

Exclusions
In the past, the charity has not been able to award grants to families with no recourse to public funds or those in receipt of foster care payments.

Applications
Applications can be made on behalf of families by charities, social workers, health visitors or other caring agencies. There is detailed information for both families and referrers on the association's helpful website.

Financial information
Year end	31/08/2020
Income	£1,930,000
Total expenditure	£1,200,000

Other information
If a family is caring for a child who is ill or has disabilities, they should refer to The Family Fund (www.familyfund.org.uk).

The Family Fund is an independent charity funded by the four national governments of England, Northern Ireland, Scotland and Wales that gives grants to families living in the UK who are caring for such children aged 17 years or younger. Families in these circumstances should apply to the Family Fund before making an application to the Family Holiday Association. If the family is successful in their application to the Family Fund, they will no longer be eligible for support from the Family Holiday Association.

Gender

Abortion Support Network

 £118,600 (2020)

Correspondent: The Trustees, Union House, 111 New Union Street, Coventry CV1 2NT (tel: 07897 611593 (Northern Ireland and Isle of Man); 015267370 (Ireland – calls only, no texts); email: info@asn.org.uk)

https://www.asn.org.uk

CC number: 1142120

Eligibility
Any woman from Ireland, Northern Ireland or the Isle of Man who would be unable to access an abortion without financial assistance. Women living in Malta, Gibraltar and Poland are also eligible.

Types of grant
Grants are awarded to relieve the financial burden of travelling abroad to get a safe and legal abortion. The charity's website states that funding is available on a case-by-case basis.

Applications
The charity asks applicants to call, text or email to get more information, or to discuss their circumstances. All contact information is available on the charity's website.

Financial information
Year end	31/12/2020
Income	£364,600
Total expenditure	£299,500

Other information
The charity has a network of volunteer hosts, who provide accommodation in their homes and pay for the beneficiary's food and travel. Hosts are not able to accommodate children.

Frederick Andrew Trust

 £28,000 (2019)

Correspondent: Karen Armitage, Clerk to the Trustees, PO Box 1291, Lincoln, Lincolnshire LN5 5RA (tel: 01522 810159; email: frederick.andrew@icloud.com)

www.frederickandrewtrust.org

CC number: 211029

Eligibility
Women who have been in paid employment at some point in their lives and are in need of financial assistance following an illness or injury.

Types of grant
Grants of up to £1,000 are available for respite breaks or to contribute towards the costs of domestic help to assist with cooking, cleaning and gardening. The trust also awards grants of up to £600 for therapy from therapists registered with Health Care Professions Council (HCPC). Details of such professionals can be found on the trust's or the HCPC's website. The trust's website has a useful FAQ section that provides further information on what is awarded and how.

Exclusions
The grant must be used by the applicant, it cannot cover costs for convalescing partners or children. Retrospective costs are not covered. Grants cannot be awarded within two years of a previous grant, even if that grant was not taken for any reason within the six-month period the grant remains available.

Applications
An initial assessment form can be completed online and sent to the correspondent. The trust's website provides detailed guidance on the application process.

Financial information
Year end	31/12/2019
Income	£81,100
Total expenditure	£52,200

Other information
This charity also supports organisations.

Mrs E. L. Blakeley-Marillier Charitable Fund

 £17,600 (2019/20)

Correspondent: Lynn Young, Charitable Trust Administrator, Wollens, At Harbourside, 67 The Terrace, Torquay, Devon TQ1 1DP (tel: 01803 213251; email: lynn.young@wollenmichelmore.co.uk)

CC number: 207138

Eligibility
Women over 55 who are in need and are not of the Roman Catholic faith or members of the Salvation Army.

Types of grant
Annuities of a maximum of £520 per year.

Applications
Apply in writing to the correspondent.

Financial information
Year end	05/04/2020
Income	£480
Total expenditure	£19,600

Further financial information
Full accounts were not available to view on the Charity Commission's website due to the fund's low income. We have therefore estimated the grant total based on the fund's total expenditure.

Broadlands Home Trust

 £5,400 (2019/20)

Correspondent: The Secretary, 2 Winchester Close, Newport, Isle of Wight PO30 1DR (tel: 01983 525630; email: broadlandstrust@btinternet.com)

CC number: 201433

Eligibility

Welfare

Single women and widows who are over the age of 40 and are in financial need.

Education

Educational support is also given to girls and young single women (under the age of 22) in need who are at school, starting work, or in further or higher education.

There may be some preference for women living on the Isle of Wight.

Types of grant
Grants can be made in the form of pensions or Christmas gifts to women over the age of 40. Younger women can receive grants to cover the costs of books, fees, travelling expenses or other educational equipment.

Exclusions
Grants are not made for married women or graduates.

Applications
Application forms are available from the correspondent and should be submitted either directly by the individual or by a family member. They should include the applicant's name, date of birth, address, financial details (family income and expenditure), details of the course being undertaken, a reference and confirmation of attendance, and details as to what the grant is for. Requests are considered quarterly in January, April, July and October. If you are applying by post, enclose an sae.

Financial information
Year end	31/03/2020
Income	£9,900
Total expenditure	£6,000

Further financial information
Full accounts were not available to view on the Charity Commission's website due to the trust's low income. We have therefore estimated the trust's grant total based on its total expenditure.

The Deakin and Withers Fund

 £54,400 (2019/20)

Correspondent: Karen Alsop, Fund Manager, South Yorkshire Community Foundation, Unit 9–12 Jessops Riverside, 800 Brightside Lane, Sheffield, South Yorkshire S9 2RX (tel: 0114 242 4294 or 0114 242 9003 (fund manager); email: grants@sycf.org.uk)

www.sycf.org.uk

CC number: 1140947–2

Eligibility
Single, divorced and widowed women over the age 40 who live in the UK and are in need. Applicants must be an active member of a church. The foundation will support women from a variety of denominations.

Types of grant
Grants are given towards the cost of utility bills and household items.

Exclusions
The fund will not provide grants for holidays nor will it pay for items already purchased.

Applications
Application forms can be downloaded from the South Yorkshire Community Foundation website.

Financial information
Year end	30/09/2020
Income	£58,500
Total expenditure	£79,400

Other information
This fund is administered by South Yorkshire Community Foundation.

Eaton Fund for Artists, Nurses and Gentlewomen

 £327,800 (2019/20)

Correspondent: The Trustees, PO Box 528, Fleet, Surrey GU51 9HH (tel: 020 3289 3209; email: admin@eatonfund.org.uk)

www.eatonfund.org.uk

CC number: 236060

Eligibility

The following people qualify for support:
- Artists including painters, potters, sculptors and photographers. Support may also be extended to art students.
- Male or female nurses. Examples include: state-registered or state-enrolled nurses, healthcare assistants (with relevant qualifications) or dental nurses who are in employment, retired, in hardship, or suffering with a long-term illness or disability.
- Women over the age of 18 who are experiencing hardship.

All applicants must be UK residents.

Types of grant

One-off grants of up to £300 are awarded according to need. Recent examples include: assistance towards the cost of setting up a new home after family breakdown; assistance towards the cost of wheelchairs and mobility aids; provision of white goods, furniture, carpeting or other household essentials; clothing; and grants towards artists' materials/equipment and picture framing for an exhibition.

Exclusions

Grants cannot be made for expenses such as: mortgage repayments; educational fees; rent; fuel; phone bills; special diets; care home fees; private treatments; medical care; paying off creditors. No recurrent grants are given.

Note that performing artists are not eligible to apply.

Applications

Application forms are available to download on the funder's website. Applications must include a supporting letter from a third party, such as a social worker or tutor. Applicants must also provide evidence of any benefits they are currently in receipt of. Completed forms should be sent to the correspondent by post or email.

Financial information

Year end	30/06/2020
Income	£328,700
Total expenditure	£433,900

Further financial information

During the year, grants were awarded to 1,216 individuals. According to the 2019/20 accounts, 88% of the grants supported women in need, 6% supported artists and 6% supported nurses.

Mary MacArthur Holiday Trust

 £47,100 (2019/20)

Correspondent: Cheryl Andrews, Administrator, Unite House, 1 Cathedral Road, Cardiff CF11 9SD (tel: 029 2035 9091; email: cheryl.andrews@mmht.org.uk)

www.mmht.org.uk

CC number: 209989

Eligibility

Women in need of a holiday because of age, disability, financial hardship or any other socio-economic circumstances. To qualify, applicants must:
- Be aged 18 or over
- Not have had a holiday in recent years
- Not have received a grant from the trust for at least three years

Preference is given to women who are or have normally been in employment.

Types of grant

Grants of up to £350 for holidays, coach trips, family visits and stays in caravans, hotels and self-catering accommodation in the UK and abroad.

Exclusions

The charity cannot honour any holiday booked before a decision is made. No additional funding is given to those who wish to be accompanied by someone on the holiday.

Applications

Application forms are available to download on the funder's website. Alternatively, applicants may wish to contact the administrator, who can send an application form by post. All applications must be supported by a letter from a professional third party (for example, a GP, social worker or trade union official). Friends, family or work colleagues are not permitted to sponsor an application.

Financial information

Year end	31/03/2020
Income	£62,300
Total expenditure	£82,100

The E. McLaren Fund

 £84,900 (2019)

Correspondent: The Trustees, Wright Johnston & Mackenzie LLP, 302 St Vincent Street, Glasgow G2 5RZ

OSCR number: SC004558

Eligibility

Widows and single women in need living in Scotland. Preference is given to widows and daughters of officers of certain Scottish regiments.

Types of grant

The fund provides annual pensions of £500 per individual and one-off grants given according to need.

Applications

Apply in writing to the correspondent. All applicants will be visited by a member of the fund before being added to the pension roll.

Financial information

Year end	31/12/2019
Income	£122,800
Total expenditure	£122,700

The NFL Trust

£184,000 (2019/20)

Correspondent: Mrs M. S. Chaundler, Secretary, 9 Muncaster Road, London SW11 6NY (tel: 020 7223 7133; email: nfltrust@mail.com)

www.nfltrust.org.uk

CC number: 1112422

Eligibility

Girls between the ages of 11 and 18 who are attending fee-paying schools and colleges. Priority may be given to students embarking upon public examinations in school years 10 and 11, or 12 and 13. Grants are open to girls of all faiths.

Types of grant

Recurrent bursaries are given towards school fees until the end of the course of study, usually at age 18. The trust also administers the Diana Matthews Trust Fund which is used towards educational extras, usually for girls who have already received a bursary from the trust. Recent examples include support towards a school trip and GCSE examinations. The maximum length of a bursary is seven years.

Exclusions

The trust will not usually provide support towards the cost of boarding.

Applications

Application forms and further details can be requested from the correspondent. Applications should be made in the academic year before the academic year in which the bursary is required.

Financial information

Year end	31/08/2020
Income	£102,700
Total expenditure	£212,000

Further financial information

In 2019/20 a total of £183,100 was awarded in bursaries to 46 students.

The Perry Fund

 £31,400 (2019)

Correspondent: The Trustees, c/o Underhill Langley Wright Solicitors, 7 Waterloo Road, Wolverhampton WV1 4DW (tel: 01902 423431; email: janeoliver@underhills.co.uk)

CC number: 218829

Eligibility

Women from all social and ethnic backgrounds who are in need. Older women who have difficulty managing on their very low pension are also eligible.

Types of grant

Annuities of around £3,000 for older women and one-off grants for women of all ages.

Applications

Apply in writing to the correspondent.

Financial information

Year end	31/12/2019
Income	£26,300
Total expenditure	£38,700

Further financial information

During the year, annuities were paid to six women and one-off grants were paid to 18 women. Grants were distributed as follows:

Single grant payments	£13,400
Annuities	£18,000

The Royal Society for the Support of Women of Scotland

 £1,300,000 (2019/20)

Correspondent: The Trustees, 14 Rutland Square, Edinburgh EH1 2BD (tel: 0131 229 2308; email: info@rssws. org)

www.rssws.org

OSCR number: SC016095

Eligibility

Single women in Scotland who are over the age of 50 and in need. Applicants must have been resident in Scotland for at least two years at the time of application. Further eligibility criteria is available on the charity's website.

Types of grant

The charity provides support to its beneficiaries through annual grants paid in monthly instalments. Occasionally, the trustees distribute surplus income as supplementary grants to those beneficiaries with the lowest incomes and savings.

Exclusions

One-off grants for specific items are not provided.

Applications

Application forms can be obtained from the correspondent by email.

Financial information

Year end	31/03/2020
Income	£1,830,000
Total expenditure	£1,730,000

Further financial information

Grants were made to 1,023 beneficiaries during the year.

The Sawyer Trust

 £101,100 (2019/20)

Correspondent: The Trustees, PO Box 797, Worcester, Worcestershire WR4 4BU (email: info@sawyertrust.org)

www.sawyertrust.org

CC number: 511276

Eligibility

Women over 50 who are in need through financial hardship, sickness or poor health. If there are surplus funds, men over 50 in similar circumstances may also receive assistance.

Types of grant

One-off grants of up to £500 for a range of purposes including rent, removal costs, telephone bills, medical aids and white goods. Cash is not paid directly to applicants.

Exclusions

The trust will not give funding for luxury goods or services, parties or outings, legal expenses, building repairs, credit card debt or for ongoing costs.

Applications

Application forms can be downloaded from the trust's website. Applications must be supported by a referee such as Citizens Advice, Age UK or a housing association debt officer. Applications must be accompanied by a bank statement. Visit the website for further guidance on how to apply.

Financial information

Year end	30/06/2020
Income	£67,700
Total expenditure	£115,400

Smallwood Trust

 £723,000 (2020)

Correspondent: The Trustees, Lancaster House, 25 Hornyold Road, Malvern, Worcestershire WR14 1QQ (tel: 0300 365 1886; email: info@smallwoodtrust. org.uk)

https://www.smallwoodtrust.org.uk

CC number: 205798

Eligibility

Women over the age of 18 who live alone or only with dependent children, are on a low income and in receipt of all eligible benefits to which they are entitled and can provide evidence of debt of less than £16,000 and have limited savings (less than £5,000).

Types of grant

Grants are awarded according to need. In previous years support has been given for travel costs to hospital appointments, home repairs and clothing.

Exclusions

Financial supports is not given for: the payment of white goods, tuition fees, or bankruptcy fees. The trust is also unable to offer support to those entered into an insolvency agreement such as a Debt Relief Order (DRO) or Individual Voluntary Agreement (IVA).

Applications

Applicants can either contact the trust by telephone to make an application or complete the online grant enquiry form on the trust's website. Application forms are sent out by the grants manager once the applicant has passed the initial eligibility checks.

Financial information

Year end	31/12/2020
Income	£3,730,000
Total expenditure	£5,140,000

Further financial information

During the year grants were awarded to 802 individuals.

Soroptimist International of Great Britain and Ireland Benevolent Fund

 £62,900 (2019/20)

Correspondent: The Trustees, Beckwith House, 1–3 Wellington Road North, Stockport, Cheshire SK4 1AF (tel: 0161 480 7686; email: hq@sigbi.org)

https://sigbi.org/our-charities/benevolent-fund

CC number: 211840

Eligibility
The relief of women in need who have been, for at least three consecutive years, members of a Soroptimist club within the UK (including the Channel Islands and the Isle of Man) and the Republic of Ireland.

Types of grant
One-off grants to help with a particular need, or quarterly grants to supplement income and help with day-to-day living costs.

Applications
Former soroptimists may apply to their regional representative or directly to the secretary.

Financial information
Year end	31/03/2020
Income	£44,600
Total expenditure	£71,600

Women in Prison Ltd

Correspondent: Kate Paradine, 2nd Floor, Elmfield House, 5 Stockwell Mews, London SW9 9XG (tel: 020 7359 6674; email: info@wipuk.org)

 https://www.womeninprison.org.uk

CC number: 1118727

Eligibility
Women with more than one year left to serve in prison who do not have access to monetary support. Occasionally, the charity can support women who have recently left prison.

Types of grant
One-off grants of up to £25 are available for women in prison. Women in the community who have emergency needs on leaving prison are also eligible for one-off grants for essentials like clothing, food and phone credit.

Applications
Contact the charity for more information.

Financial information
Year end	31/03/2021
Income	£2,380,000
Total expenditure	£2,300,000

Further financial information
We were unable to determine the grant total for individuals.

Miscellaneous

The Buchanan Society

 £36,800 (2019)

Correspondent: Ian Buchanan, Secretary, 16 Ribblesdale, East Kilbride, Lanarkshire G74 4QN (tel: 01355 243437; email: use the contact form available on the website)

www.buchanansociety.com

OSCR number: SC013679

Eligibility
People who through birth, adoption or marriage bear the following surnames: Buchanan, MacAuslan (all spellings), MacWattie and Risk. Those whose mother's maiden name is or was any of the above-mentioned surnames are also eligible.

Types of grant
Welfare
Pensions and one-off grants are available.

Education
Educational grants are made to students in higher and further education (including vocational training) towards costs such as purchasing equipment.

Exclusions
Grants can be paid in instalments but no grant can continue for more than three years.

Applications
Application forms are available to download on the charity's website. For educational grants, university and college students need to confirm that they have been accepted for a course. Applications for educational grants are considered in meetings in February, June and October.

Financial information
Year end	31/12/2019
Income	£64,300
Total expenditure	£58,300

East Africa Women's League (United Kingdom)

 £9,500 (2020)

Correspondent: The Trustees, Nobles Farm, Gatehouse Road, Holton-le-Moor, Market Rasen, Lincolnshire LN7 6AG (tel: 01673 828393)

https://eawl.org.uk

CC number: 294328

Eligibility
People of UK origin who have previously lived in East Africa, particularly Kenya, and their dependants.

Types of grant
Grants are given according to need.

Exclusions
Grants are not available for students.

Applications
Initial enquiries can be made using the contact form on the funder's website.

Financial information
Year end	31/12/2020
Income	£8,200
Total expenditure	£10,600

Further financial information
Full accounts were not available to view on the Charity Commission's website due to the charity's low income. We have therefore estimated the charity's grant total based on its total expenditure.

Friends of the Animals

 £117,000 (2019/20)

Correspondent: The Trustees, 17A Riverway, Newport, Isle of Wight PO3 5UX (tel: 01983 522511; email: fotaiow@hotmail.com)

https://www.friendsoftheanimals.co.uk

CC number: 1000249

Eligibility
People who are in need and live on the Isle of Wight, in Portsmouth or in the West Midlands.

Types of grant
Grants are awarded for veterinary treatments for pets, such as spaying or neutering.

Applications
Contact the correspondent in writing or by using the online form on the funder's website.

Financial information

Year end	30/09/2020
Income	£954,500
Total expenditure	£392,500

Further financial information

We have taken the figure for vet fees in the 2019/20 accounts as the grant total for the year.

Other information

The charity's activities include the rehoming of animals and the provision of free advice and information on animal welfare, as well as loans of baskets, pens and other equipment to assist with animal care.

The Agnes Macleod Memorial Fund

 £5,000 (2020/21)

Correspondent: The Trustees, Nurses Cottage, Hallin, Waternish, Isle of Skye IV55 8GJ (tel: 01470 592722; email: info@agnesmacleod.org)

 www.agnesmacleod.org

OSCR number: SC014297

Eligibility

Women in need who are over 60, living in Scotland and were born with the name Macleod or whose mothers were born Macleod.

Types of grant

One-off grants and gift vouchers when statutory funding is not available.

Applications

Apply in writing to the correspondent.

Financial information

Year end	23/03/2021
Income	£3,700
Total expenditure	£5,200

Further financial information

Full accounts were not available to view on the OSCR website due to the fund's low income. We have therefore estimated the grant total based on the fund's total expenditure.

The Vegetarian Charity

 £22,800 (2019/20)

Correspondent: The Grants Secretary, PO Box 496, Manchester M45 0FL (email: grantssecretary@ vegetariancharity.org.uk)

 www.vegetariancharity.org.uk

CC number: 294767

Eligibility

Vegetarians and vegans up to the age of 26 who are in need.

Types of grant

Welfare

One-off grants to relieve poverty and sickness, usually of up to £500. Examples include bedding, furniture and fridges.

Education

One-off grants, usually up to £500, for equipment/books, computers, art materials and so on.

Exclusions

Grants are not given to start businesses, for fundraising costs or for debt relief.

Applications

Application forms can be downloaded and completed on the charity's website. The charity prefers to receive applications via email.

Financial information

Year end	31/03/2020
Income	£47,300
Total expenditure	£45,800

Other information

Grants are also made to organisations running projects for vegetarians and vegans under the age of 26.

Older people

The Aged Christian Friend Society of Scotland

 £7,000 (2020)

Correspondent: The Trustees, Colinton Cottage Homes, 4A Redford Road, Edinburgh EH13 0AA (tel: 0131 441 2286/2502; email: office@ colintoncottages.org)

OSCR number: SC016247

Eligibility

People in need living in Scotland who are over the age of 65.

Types of grant

The charity awards annual pensions, usually of about £500 a year, paid in two half-yearly instalments.

Applications

Apply in writing to the correspondent providing full details of the applicant's need.

Financial information

Year end	31/12/2020
Income	£323,000
Total expenditure	£295,200

Other information

The charity is now a company limited by guarantee. Its principal activity is the provision of housing for older people in Scotland.

Age Sentinel Trust

 £5,900 (2019/20)

Correspondent: The Trustees, Longreach, Clay Lane, Chichester, West Sussex PO19 3PX (tel: 020 8144 4774; email: info@agesentinel.org.uk)

 agesentinel.org.uk

CC number: 1133624

Eligibility

Older people who are in need. Priority is given to people with dementia, particularly Alzheimer's disease, and those with other debilitating illnesses.

Types of grant

One-off and recurrent grants to support independent living. Grants have previously been made for items such as communication devices or home adaptations.

Applications

Apply in writing to the correspondent.

Financial information

Year end	31/03/2020
Income	£13,100
Total expenditure	£13,100

Further financial information

Full accounts were not available to view on the Charity Commission's website due to the trust's low income. We have therefore estimated the trust's grant total based on its total expenditure.

Craigcrook Mortification

 £26,500 (2019)

Correspondent: Kirsty Ashworth, Charity Accounts and Audit Services Manager, Exchange Place 3, Semple Street, Edinburgh EH3 8BL (email: SM-Charity@azets.co.uk)

 www.azets.co.uk/craigcrook-mortification

OSCR number: SC001648

Eligibility

People in need who are over 60 and were born in Scotland or have lived there for more than ten years.

Types of grant

Pensions of around £1,030 per annum are payable in half-yearly instalments.

Applications

At the time of writing (November 2021), the charity's website stated that the application process was suspended. Check the website or contact the correspondent for up-to-date information.

Financial information

Year end	31/12/2019
Income	£48,200
Total expenditure	£44,200

Further financial information
The charity supported 26 pensioners during the financial period.

Friends of the Elderly

 £179,000 (2019/20)

Correspondent: Soo Smith, Company Secretary, 40–42 Ebury Street, London SW1W 0LZ (tel: 020 7730 8263; email: enquiries@fote.org.uk)

www.fote.org.uk

CC number: 226064

Eligibility
Older people (of state retirement age) living in England or Wales who are on a low income with savings of less than £4,000.

Types of grant
One-off grants for essential items (basic furniture, flooring and household appliances), for assistance with unexpected financial bills (utility bills, household repairs and funeral costs) and towards the cost of smartphones, tablets and broadband connection. The average amount awarded for a one-off grant is £300. Recurrent grants are paid twice each year to support older people whose income does not meet their basic living standards.

Exclusions
The charity cannot fund people living in residential care or people who have served in the armed forces.

Applications
Applications must be made through a referring agent, such as someone working for a local health or social care team, Citizens Advice or another charity or community group. The referring agent can download an application form from the funder's website.

Financial information

Year end	31/03/2020
Income	£23,160,000
Total expenditure	£22,310,000

Further financial information
In 2019/20, 690 grants were awarded to individuals.

Other information
The charity offers a variety of services to support older people. These include residential care through 12 care homes, home care, four day centres, community projects and befriending services.

The Jewish Aged Needy Pension Society

 £20,300 (2019)

Correspondent: The Trustees, 34 Dalkeith Grove, Stanmore, Middlesex HA7 4SG (tel: 020 8958 5390)

CC number: 206262

Eligibility
Members of the Jewish community aged 60 or over who have lived in the UK for at least ten years or are of British nationality.

Types of grant
The charity funds pensions.

Applications
Apply in writing to the correspondent.

Financial information

Year end	31/12/2019
Income	£12,600
Total expenditure	£22,600

Further financial information
Full accounts were not available to view on the Charity Commission's website due to the charity's low income. We have therefore estimated the charity's grant total based on its total expenditure.

The William Johnston Trust Fund

£31,200 (2020)

Correspondent: The Trustees, Aspen Cottage, Apse Manor Road, Shanklin, Hampshire PO37 7PN (tel: 0151 236 6666)

CC number: 212495

Eligibility
Older people in need who live in the UK.

Types of grant
Recurrent grants are paid twice annually, usually in June and December. One-off grants and birthday gifts are also awarded.

Applications
Apply in writing to the correspondent.

Financial information

Year end	31/12/2020
Income	£36,700
Total expenditure	£57,300

Further financial information
Grants were made to 21 individuals in 2020.

Morden College

£322,000 (2019/20)

Correspondent: Maj. Gen. David Rutherford-Jones, Clerk, Clerk's House, Morden College, 19 St Germans Place, Blackheath, London SE3 0PW (tel: 020 8463 8330; email: davidrj@ mordencollege.org.uk)

www.mordencollege.org.uk

CC number: 215551

Eligibility
People in need who are aged over 50, are from a professional or managerial background, and have retired from paid employment either on medical grounds or because they have reached the statutory retirement age.

Types of grant
One-off grants and quarterly allowances to support independent living.

Exclusions
The charity does not award grants for nursing home top-up fees or any services or products which should be funded by statutory authorities. Grants are generally not awarded to individuals who have received a grant within three years.

Applications
Application forms are available from the correspondent or can be downloaded from the charity's website. Applications must include details of the applicant's income and expenditure as well as their employment history. Applicants are means tested.

Financial information

Year end	31/03/2020
Income	£15,950,000
Total expenditure	£13,350,000

Further financial information
Grants were awarded to 111 individuals during the year.

Other information
Morden College is the general title used for the administration of Sir John Morden's Charity and Dame Susan Morden's Charity. Sir John Morden's Charity provides grants and accommodation for older people. Dame Susan Morden's Charity is primarily concerned with the advancement of religion by assisting the Church of England with the upkeep of their churches and associated activities. The charity runs a care home for beneficiaries no longer capable of living independently as well as accommodation for independent and supported living.

The Roger Pilkington Young Trust

£ £53,400 (2019/20)

Correspondent: The Trustees, c/o Everys Solicitors, 104 High Street, Sidmouth, Devon EX10 8EF (tel: 01395 576113; email: info@rpyt.org.uk)

CC number: 251148

Eligibility

People aged 60 years or over who are in need.

Types of grant

Monthly allowances of £60 per month (or £720 per annum) to single people, and £80 per month (or £960 per annum) to couples/civil partners.

Applications

Apply in writing to the correspondent.

Financial information

Year end	05/04/2020
Income	£57,400
Total expenditure	£81,600

Further financial information

The trust provided financial assistance to 53 single beneficiaries and 15 couples/civil partners.

The J. C. Robinson Trust No. 3

See entry on page 28

Mr William Saunders Charity for the Relief of Indigent Gentry and Others

£ £3,100 (2019)

Correspondent: The Trustees, c/o Charles Russell LLP, 5 Fleet Street, London EC4M 7RD (tel: 020 7427 6400)

CC number: 212012

Eligibility

Older people on low incomes. According to its Charity Commission record, the charity supports 'indigent gentry tutors, governesses, merchants and others ... [and] their dependants.'

Types of grant

The charity provides pensions.

Applications

Apply in writing to the correspondent.

Financial information

Year end	31/12/2019
Income	£10,000
Total expenditure	£6,900

Further financial information

Full accounts were not available to view on the Charity Commission's website due to the charity's low income. We have therefore estimated the charity's grant total based on its total expenditure.

Other information

The charity also supports organisations.

The Shell Pensioners Benevolent Association

£ £175,000 (2020)

Correspondent: Ken Sleat, Secretary, Treasurer and Board Member, Shell Centre, London SE1 7NA (tel: 020 7934 5131; email: ken.k.sleat@shell.com)

 https://pensions.shell.co.uk/pensioners-association.html

CC number: 262049

Eligibility

UK members of the Shell Contributory Pension Fund or the Shell Overseas Contributory Pension Fund who are in need. Applicants must be members of the Shell Pensioners Association to be eligible.

Types of grant

Grants are given according to need. Examples of previous grants include: stairlifts, downstairs bathrooms, mobility aids, housing repairs and dentures. In addition, Christmas grants are awarded to around 400 pensioners each year.

Applications

Eligible candidates are generally (but not always) identified by a Shell Pensioner Programme Officer. Candidates will be required to complete an application and provide details of their financial circumstance to demonstrate the need for assistance.

Financial information

Year end	31/12/2020
Income	£231,400
Total expenditure	£223,900

Further financial information

In 2020, grants totalling £53,000 were made to 25 individuals. In addition, 305 Christmas grants were awarded, totalling £122,000.

Other information

The charity also provides interest-free loans.

St Andrew's Society for Ladies in Need

£ £68,800 (2019)

Correspondent: Maureen Pope, General Secretary, 20 Denmark Gardens, Holbrook, Ipswich, Suffolk IP9 2BG (tel: 01473 327408; email: mpope1@btinternet.com)

 https://standrewssociety.co.uk

CC number: 208541

Eligibility

Women who were born in Britain, are of retirement age or below retirement age but unable to work, live alone without dependants, have very limited savings and have achieved a 'good' standard of education or equivalent vocational qualification. Applicants are expected to be in receipt of state benefits.

Types of grant

One-off and recurrent grants. Regular grants are paid quarterly to help with day-to-day expenses. One-off grants, usually of between £250 and £750, are available to help with urgent requests for a range of goods and services, including white goods, carpets, winter clothing, household repairs (e.g. electrics and plumbing) and decoration, heating, health-related costs and funeral costs. Grants are sometimes made towards a shortfall in care home fees, or towards the cost of home-based care.

Applications

Apply in writing to the correspondent.

Financial information

Year end	31/12/2019
Income	£75,400
Total expenditure	£85,400

The Stanley Stein Deceased Charitable Trust

See entry on page 30

WaveLength

£ £148,900 (2019/20)

Correspondent: The Trustees, 159A High Street, Hornchurch, Essex RM11 3YB (tel: 017 0862 1101/ Freephone: 0800 018 2137; email: info@wavelength.org.uk)

 www.wavelength.org.uk

CC number: 207400

Eligibility

People who are lonely and have limited ability to leave their homes and are living in poverty. Preference is given to older people and people with disabilities or experiencing ill health and to cases where help will significantly relieve isolation.

Types of grant

The provision of radios, television sets and computer equipment. The charity does not provide television licences; however, in exceptional cases, licences can be funded for those with a very limited income and severe inability to leave their homes.

Applications

Application forms are available from the correspondent or can be downloaded from the charity's website. They must be submitted through a third party such as a social worker, Citizens Advice, religious organisation or other welfare agency.

Financial information

Year end	31/03/2020
Income	£402,600
Total expenditure	£377,600

Religion

General religion

Christianity

The Alexis Trust

 £15,000 (2020/21)

Correspondent: The Trustees, 14 Broadfield Way, Buckhurst Hill, Essex IG9 5AG

CC number: 262861

Eligibility

Members of the Christian faith who are in financial need. Preference may be given to older individuals or people experiencing ill health.

Types of grant

Grants are given according to need.

Applications

Apply in writing to the correspondent.

Financial information

Year end	05/04/2021
Income	£23,000
Total expenditure	£30,600

Further financial information

Full accounts were not available to view on the Charity Commission's website due to the trust's low income. We have therefore estimated the grant total based on the trust's total expenditure.

Other information

The trust usually makes grants to a list of regular recipients, but can make grants to eligible individuals not featured on the list. The trust also makes grants to organisations for Protestant Evangelical and secular education and for Christian missionary activity.

Catenian Association Benevolent and Children's Fund

 £209,300 (2020/21)

Correspondent: Phillip Roberts, Clerk to the Trustees, 2nd Floor, 1 Park House, Station Square, Coventry, Warwickshire CV1 2FL (tel: 01257 462344; email: clerk@catenianbenevolence.org)

🌐 https://catenianbenevolence.org

CC number: 214244

Eligibility

Members of The Catenian Association and their dependants who are in need.

Types of grant

Grants are given for general living expenses, debts, unexpected expenses and so on. The fund also provides loans.

Exclusions

Support is not given for the following:
▶ To finance commercial ventures
▶ To settle business debts or to provide business capital, directly or indirectly
▶ House purchases
▶ Payment of national and/or local taxes

Applications

Application forms can be downloaded from the fund's website. The trustees meet to consider applications at least four times a year, but urgent applications may be considered between the meetings.

Financial information

Year end	31/03/2021
Income	£376,300
Total expenditure	£726,500

Further financial information

Grants totalling £209,300 were awarded to 18 individuals. In addition, the fund awarded £455,000 in non-secured loans to individuals, which has not been included in the grant total.

Other information

The Catenian Association is an association of Catholic laymen.

Catenian Association Bursary Fund Ltd

 £73,200 (2019/20)

Correspondent: Bursary Fund Administrator, 1 Park House, Station Square, Coventry, West Midlands CV1 2FL (tel: 024 7622 4533; email: secretary@catenianbursary.com)

🌐 https://www.catenianbursary.com

CC number: 1081143

Eligibility

Young people (aged between 16 and 15 years) of the Catholic faith who want to work on projects for the benefit of communities in the UK or abroad. All projects must implement Christian, particularly Catholic, principles. Grants are also made to young people working as helpers or support staff in Lourdes. Support of this type is extended to young people providing the same service to assisted pilgrims on on a Jumbulance trip.

Types of grant

Bursaries are available to cover travel and other project costs.

Exclusions

Grants are not available for projects that are shorter than 17 days long (including one day of travel) or those that form a significant part of an educational course. The charity does not award retrospective grants.

Applications

Applications for individual projects can be made using an online form on the charity's website.

Financial information

Year end	31/03/2020
Income	£154,700
Total expenditure	£110,600

Further financial information

The charity awarded grants to 621 individuals.

Catholic Clothing Guild

£3,500 (2019)

Correspondent: Carmel Edwards, Trustee, 5 Dark Lane, Shrewsbury, Shropshire SY2 5LP (email: carmel.edwards17@gmail.com)

🌐 www.dioceseofshrewsbury.org/about-us/catholic-associations/catholic-clothing-guild

CC number: 277952

Eligibility

People in need of new clothing in a Catholic diocese in Brentwood, Clifton,

East Anglia, Leeds, Liverpool, Nottingham, Shrewsbury or Southwark. To qualify for support, applicants must commit to donating two new articles of clothing (or the monetary equivalent) and pay subscription fees of £1 to £2 per annum.

Types of grant

The charity supplies new clothing.

Applications

Catholic Clothing Guilds are operated by local dioceses, churches, cathedrals and other Catholic organisations. Applications should be made through a third party such as social services.

Financial information

Year end	31/12/2019
Income	£3,900
Total expenditure	£3,900

Further financial information

Full accounts were not available to view on the Charity Commission's website due to the charity's low income. We have therefore estimated the charity's grant total based on its total expenditure.

Christadelphian Benevolent Fund

£ £186,600 (2020)

Correspondent: Neville Moss, Secretary, Westhaven House, Arleston Way, Shirley, Solihull, West Midlands B90 4LH (tel: 0121 713 7100)

 christadelphianbf.com

CC number: 222416

Eligibility

Members of the Christadelphian faith who are struggling financially due to low income, unemployment, redundancy, sickness or because of an accident.

Types of grant

One-off and recurrent grants are available for fuel and water bills, and for unexpected costs caused by a job loss or illness, holidays and respite care, and nursing and residential care in Christadelphian Care Homes. Interest-free loans are also available for unexpected problems.

Applications

Applicants should contact the recording brother or secretary at their home ecclesia.

Financial information

Year end	31/12/2020
Income	£166,400
Total expenditure	£201,000

Further financial information

In 2020, grants were awarded in the following categories:

Residential care costs	£80,500
Annual holiday scheme	£26,300
Urgent help scheme	£24,700
Fuel aid	£21,000
Water aid	£12,200
Individual grants	£11,000
Iranian refugees	£7,800
Christmas bounty	£2,900
Block grants	£290

The Cross Trust

£ £36,800 (2019/20)

Correspondent: Lord Michael Farmer, Trustee and Secretary, Cansdales, Bourbon Court, Nightingales Corner, Amersham, Buckinghamshire HP7 9QS (tel: 01494 765428; email: mailto@ cansdales.co.uk)

CC number: 1127046

Eligibility

Applicants' needs must be within the objects of the charity, which fall under the broad headings of: advancing any religious or other charitable object; furtherance of religious or secular education; advancing the Christian faith in the UK or overseas; the relief of poverty and sickness; and supporting older people.

Types of grant

Grants are given according to need.

Applications

Apply in writing to the correspondent.

Financial information

Year end	04/04/2020
Income	£4,000,000
Total expenditure	£1,220,000

Further financial information

During the year, grants were made to nine individuals. Note that some recipients may have been based overseas.

Other information

The trust predominantly makes grants to organisations (£1.18 million in 2019/20).

Esdaile Trust Scheme 1968

£ £14,400 (2019/20)

Correspondent: Kirsty Ashworth, Charity Accounts, Accounts and Business Services Senior Manager, c/o Azets Accountants, Exchange Place 3, Semple Street, Edinburgh EH3 8BL (tel: 0131 473 3500; email: SM-Charity@ azets.co.uk)

 https://www.azets.co.uk/esdaile-trust

OSCR number: SC006938

Eligibility

Daughters of ministers of the Church of Scotland, daughters of missionaries appointed or nominated by the Overseas Council of the Church of Scotland, and daughters of widowed deaconesses. Applicants must be between the ages of 12 and 25. Preference is given to families with a low income.

Types of grant

Annual grants towards general educational costs.

Applications

Application forms can be obtained from the trust's website and should be submitted to the correspondent no later than 31 May each year. Grants are distributed by early September.

Financial information

Year end	31/08/2020
Income	£27,800
Total expenditure	£34,600

Further financial information

In 2019/20, the charity made grants to 20 individuals, ranging from £280 to £1,730.

William Gunn's Charity

£ £16,600 (2018/19)

Correspondent: Jane Spiers, Trustee, 3 Wesley Court, Duke Street, Broseley, Shropshire TF12 5LS (tel: 07449 983157; email: janespiers@gmail.com)

CC number: 210214

Eligibility

Members of the Society of Friends (Quakers) who are in need.

Types of grant

One-off grants are awarded according to need.

Exclusions

Grants cannot be made to cover taxes. Individuals may apply as often as necessary.

Applications

Apply in writing to the correspondent. All applications must be supported by a Friend (usually an Elder or Overseer) who knows the applicant and their circumstances. Trustees meet twice each year to consider grant applications, but are in regular contact by phone and email. Applications that clearly meet all the criteria may be responded to more quickly.

Financial information

Year end	31/03/2019
Income	£29,000
Total expenditure	£31,200

Further financial information

The 2018/19 accounts were latest available on the Charity Commission website at the time of writing (November 2021).

Hoper-Dixon Trust

£ £7,300 (2019/20)

Correspondent: The Provincial Bursar, The Dominican Council, Blackfriars Priory, St Giles, Oxford, Oxfordshire OX1 3LY (tel: 01862 88231; email: enquiries@hoperdixon.org.uk)

CC number: 231160

Eligibility

People in financial need who are connected with, or in the neighbourhood of, any house or pastoral centre of the Dominicans of the English Province of the Order of Preachers.

Types of grant

Recent grants have been made for: medical expenses not covered by public funds; help for those unable to work due to sickness or injury; help with unexpected expenses; relocation expenses; basic household equipment for those setting-up a new home; help for pilgrims going to Lourdes, both those who are sick and those caring for them; and the costs of attending a funeral for a close family member.

Exclusions

The trust is not able to help those who live elsewhere if they have no connection with Dominican friars houses or pastoral centres in England, Scotland, Grenada or Barbados.

Applications

Applications are normally made by a Dominican friar for the benefit of someone connected with the order or living in the neighbourhood of a house of the order. Although, applicants can contact their local Dominican house if they feel they may be eligible. The contact details for Dominican houses can be found on the order's website at www.english.op.org.

Financial information

Year end	30/09/2020
Income	£16,100
Total expenditure	£16,200

Further financial information

Full accounts were not available to view on the Charity Commission's website due to the trust's low income. We have therefore estimated the trust's grant total based on its total expenditure.

Other information

This charity also makes grants to organisations.

The Hounsfield Pension

£ £4,500 (2019/20)

Correspondent: The Trustees, c/o Wrigleys Solicitors, Derwent House, 15 Arundel Gate, Sheffield, South Yorkshire S1 2FN (tel: 0114 267 5596)

CC number: 221436

Eligibility

Men, unmarried women, widows and widowers who are over 50 years old, live in England or Wales and are members of the Church of England.

Types of grant

Pensions of up to £60 per year.

Applications

Apply in writing to the correspondent.

Financial information

Year end	24/06/2020
Income	£6,400
Total expenditure	£5,000

Further financial information

Full accounts were not available to view on the Charity Commission's website due to the charity's low income. We have therefore estimated the charity's grant total based on its total expenditure.

Other information

The charity tries to keep the numbers of male and female beneficiaries as equal as possible.

Sylvanus Lyson's Charity

£ £33,600 (2019/20)

Correspondent: The Trustees, c/o Tayntons Solicitors, 8–12 Clarence Street, Gloucester, Gloucestershire GL1 1DZ (tel: 01452 522047)

 https://sylvanuslysons.wordpress.com

CC number: 202939

Eligibility

Widows and dependants of the clergy of the Church of England who live in the diocese of Gloucester and are in need. Grants may occasionally be made to other members of the clergy for welfare and educational costs.

Types of grant

One-off grants according to need.

Applications

Application forms, guidelines and deadlines can be found on the charity's website.

Financial information

Year end	30/09/2020
Income	£375,700
Total expenditure	£362,600

Further financial information

Grants were awarded to 123 individuals during the year.

Other information

The charity also gives grants to organisations.

Manse Bairns Network

£ £39,900 (2019/20)

Correspondent: Kirsty Ashworth, Charity Accounts, Accounts and Business Services Senior Manager, c/o Azets Accountants, Exchange Place 3, Semple Street, Edinburgh EH3 8BL (tel: 0131 473 3500)

 mansebairnsnetwork.org

OSCR number: SC010281

Eligibility

Children of deceased ministers of the Church of Scotland who are in need. There are no geographical constraints.

Types of grant

Grants are made towards accommodation costs, tuition fees and travel costs for post-16 education (including at postgraduate level).

Applications

Application forms are available to download from the charity's website and should be submitted by 31 May each year. Grants are paid in early September.

Financial information

Year end	30/09/2020
Income	£46,600
Total expenditure	£65,700

Further financial information

The charity's website states: 'Each year an average of 16 people are supported as petitioners, each receiving between £600 and £2,430. An average of 12 educational grants are made annually ranging from £250 to £1,730.'

Other information

The registered name of the charity is: Glasgow Society of the Sons and Daughters of Ministers of the Church of Scotland.

The Morval Foundation

 £254,900 (2019/20)

Correspondent: The Trustees, Meadow Brook, Send Marsh Road, Ripley, Surrey GU23 6JR (tel: 01483 223251; email: morvalgroup@gmail.com)

CC number: 207692

Eligibility

Christian Scientists living in the UK who are in need or living with a physical disability. Preference may be given to older individuals.

Types of grant

Recurrent and one-off grants are given according to need.

Applications

Apply in writing to the correspondent.

Financial information

Year end	31/03/2020
Income	£222,900
Total expenditure	£328,400

Other information

The foundation administers four funds: The Morval Fund, The Ruston Bequest, The New Beechfield Fund and The New Chickering Fund.

The Podde Trust

 £15,300 (2020/21)

Correspondent: The Trustees, 68 Green Lane, Hucclecote, Gloucester, Gloucestershire GL3 3QX (tel: 01452 613563; email: thepodde@gmail.com)

CC number: 1016322

Eligibility

Individuals involved in Christian work in the UK and overseas.

Types of grant

The trust provides one-off and recurrent grants.

Applications

Applications may be made in writing to the correspondent. Note, the trust has previously stated that it has very limited resources and those it does have are mostly already committed. Requests from new applicants, therefore, have very little chance of success.

Financial information

Year end	05/04/2021
Income	£57,200
Total expenditure	£68,100

Other information

Grants are also awarded to organisations.

The Presbyterian Children's Society

 £657,700 (2020)

Correspondent: Jason Nicholson, Executive Secretary/Treasurer, 5th Floor, Glengall Exchange, 3 Glengall Street, Belfast BT12 5AB (tel: 028 9032 3737; email: info@presbyterianchildrenssociety. org)

🌐 https://www. presbyterianchildrenssociety.org

CCNI number: NIC101444

Eligibility

Children and young people aged 23 or under who are in full or part-time education and are in need. Beneficiaries are usually from families where a parent is deceased or absent. Families must be part of a local Presbyterian congregation and within the charity's income limits (families receiving benefits or earning below the average wage are likely to be eligible).

Types of grant

Welfare

Regular grants are paid quarterly and may also include a summer and Christmas bonus, if funds permit. One-off exceptional grants can be made for basic/essential clothing, debt repayments, funeral costs and general household expenses.

Education

Exceptional grants can also be awarded to help with educational expenses for children in full or part-time education.

Applications

Potential applicants should contact the minister of their local Presbyterian church. There is list of contact details on the charity's website. The minister will submit the application on behalf of the individual.

Financial information

Year end	31/12/2020
Income	£934,600
Total expenditure	£834,200

Other information

The charity can make small grants to recognised groups within Presbyterian congregations (youth clubs, parent and toddler groups, after-school clubs, creches, etc.) to expand or improve their facilities. The charity also makes grants to Presbyterian congregations that are seeking to improve their provision and inclusion for children and families with physical or cognitive disabilities.

The Presbyterian Old Age Fund, Women's Fund and Indigent Ladies' Fund

 £173,500 (2020)

Correspondent: The Secretary, Presbyterian Church in Ireland, Church House, Belfast BT1 6DW (tel: 028 9032 2284; email: info@presbyterianireland. org)

🌐 https://www.presbyterianireland. org/Resources/Finance-Forms/ Old-Age-Fund,-Women-s-Fund- and-Indigent-Ladies-Fu.aspx

Eligibility

Members of the Presbyterian Church in any part of Ireland who are in need. Applicants will normally: be living at home; have an income of less than £12,000/€17,500 per year; be in receipt of some type of state benefit; have less than £16,000/€20,000 in savings; have no significant support from their family members; and have medical needs requiring extra expenditure. Some, albeit not all, of the above criteria need to be satisfied. The following fund-specific criteria also apply:

▶ **Old Age Fund** – people over the age of 60.
▶ **Presbyterian Women's Fund** – applicants must be female.
▶ **Indigent Ladies' Fund** – applicants must be resident in the Republic of Ireland.

Types of grant

Grants are awarded for the following: travel allowances for hospital /home visits and funerals; laundry and household equipment; disability aids and equipment; security and safety equipment; insulation and heating; respite care. Applications may also be made for other items and services outside these categories.

Applications

Application forms and guidance can be downloaded from the fund's website. Applications should be supported by a minister.

Financial information

Year end	31/12/2020
Income	£169,000
Total expenditure	£217,500

Further financial information

During the year, a total of £173,100 was awarded to individuals, which includes £75,100 from the Old Age Fund, £54,800 from the Women's Fund and £43,200 from the Indigent Ladies' Fund.

Other information

The fund is run by the Presbyterian Church in Ireland (NIC no. 104483) and is not itself a registered charity.

Quaker Mental Health Fund

 £24,600 (2020)

Correspondent: Alison Mitchell, Mental Health Development Officer, Office 102, 51 Pinfold Street, Birmingham B2 4AY (tel: 07767 358535; email: clerk@ quakermhfund.uk)

https://www.quaker.org.uk/our-organisation/quaker-groups/quaker-mental-health-fund-uk-1

CC number: 1115135

Eligibility

Quakers, or close relatives of Quakers, who are experiencing mental health issues and are unable to afford therapeutic interventions. Applicants should also lack access to these services in the area they live in.

Types of grant

Grants, usually up to £2,000, which can be spent on mental health treatment and care. Examples of grants that have been awarded include:

- Psychological assessments
- Counselling and therapy
- Care in the home to help rehabilitation and recuperation after an illness or accident
- Support with expenses to visit relatives
- Respite care

Applications

Application forms are available to download from the fund's website and can be submitted by email or post. The trustees meet four times a year to consider applications.

Financial information

Year end	31/12/2020
Income	£76,900
Total expenditure	£121,200

Further financial information

Grants were made to 13 individuals.

Other information

The fund also awards grants to organisations to support projects which aim to promote good mental health.

The Rehoboth Trust

 £70,500 (2020)

Correspondent: The Treasurer, 9 Arlington Close, Newport NP20 6QF (email: rehobothtrust@ntlworld.com)

www.rehobothtrust.org.uk

CC number: 516295

Eligibility

People living in Wales who are Christian or have dedicated their life to Christianity through missionary work. Grants are prioritised in the following order: applicants based in Newport, South Wales; those in the combined area of Monmouthshire, Torfaen, Blaenau Gwent and Caerphilly; those in the rest of Wales.

Types of grant

Grants are given according to need.

Applications

Application forms can be downloaded from the trust's website and should be submitted with a reference.

Financial information

Year end	31/12/2020
Income	£80,000
Total expenditure	£80,000

Other information

Grants were awarded to 32 individuals.

The Westward Trust

 £8,400 (2019/20)

Correspondent: The Trustees, 12 Green Meadow Road, Birmingham, West Midlands B29 4DE (tel: 0121 475 1179; email: westwardtrust@gmail.com)

CC number: 260488

Eligibility

Quakers who live in the UK and are in need.

Types of grant

Grants are given according to need.

Applications

Apply in writing to the correspondent.

Financial information

Year end	30/09/2020
Income	£17,200
Total expenditure	£18,700

Further financial information

Full accounts were not available to view on the Charity Commission's website due to the trust's low income. We have therefore estimated the grant total based on the trust's total expenditure.

Other information

The trust makes grants to other Quaker charities and projects in which members have a substantial level of involvement.

Islam

National Zakat Foundation

 £4,688,800 (2020)

Correspondent: The Trustees, Kemp House, 152–160 City Road, London EC1 2NX (email: use the contact form available on the website)

https://www.nzf.org.uk

CC number: 1153719

Eligibility

The foundation supports UK Muslims who are in need.

Types of grant

Welfare

Grants are available from one of two funds made available by the foundation for welfare purposes: the Hardship Relief Fund for basic essentials such as food and clothing and the Housing Fund for rent and deposits, rent arrears, Council Tax arrears and furniture.

Education

Grants are available from one of two funds made available by the foundation for educational purposes: the Work Fund for vocational training courses, qualification conversion fees, certification and licence fees and tools and equipment and the Education Fund for education and training to help Muslims to better serve Islam and other Muslims in the UK.

Exclusions

Each fund has its own eligibility and exclusion criteria; see the foundation's website for the most up-to-date information.

Applications

Applications can be made via the foundation's website. Note that each fund has a separate application form.

Financial information

Year end	31/12/2020
Income	£6,350,000
Total expenditure	£5,220,000

Judaism

The Chevras Ezras Nitzrochim Trust

£ £306,200 (2019)

Correspondent: The Trustees, 53 Heathland Road, London N16 5PQ

CC number: 275352

Eligibility

People of the Jewish faith who are in need as a result of ill health or financial hardship. The trust gives mainly to those in Greater London, but support is also given elsewhere.

Types of grant

Grants are given in the form of food, medical supplies and clothing.

Applications

Apply in writing to the correspondent.

Financial information

Year end	31/12/2019
Income	£352,000
Total expenditure	£338,200

Other information

The trust also makes grants to organisations and institutions, for the purposes of education, the advancement of religion and other charitable causes.

Closehelm Ltd

£ £113,100 (2019/20)

Correspondent: The Trustees, 30 Armitage Road, London NW11 8RD (tel: 020 8201 8688)

CC number: 291296

Eligibility

People, particularly those belonging to the Jewish faith, who are in need.

Types of grant

Grants typically cover the housing costs of individuals on low incomes.

Applications

Apply in writing to the correspondent.

Financial information

Year end	30/03/2020
Income	£308,800
Total expenditure	£229,200

The Engler Family Charitable Trust

£ £7,700 (2019/20)

Correspondent: Mr J. Engler, Trustee, Sunnydale, Bowdon Road, Altrincham, Cheshire WA14 2AJ (email: jengleruk@yahoo.co.uk)

CC number: 1108518

Eligibility

Members of the Jewish faith living in England or Wales, with a particular focus on young people and older people.

Types of grant

Grants are given according to need.

Applications

Apply in writing to the correspondent.

Financial information

Year end	31/03/2020
Income	£9,400
Total expenditure	£17,000

Further financial information

Full accounts were not available to view on the Charity Commission's website due to the charity's low income. We have therefore estimated the charity's grant total based on its total expenditure.

Friends of Boyan Trust

£ £172,300 (2019)

Correspondent: Jacob Getter, Trustee, 23 Durley Road, London N16 5JW (tel: 020 8809 6051)

CC number: 1114498

Eligibility

People in need in the Orthodox Jewish community.

Types of grant

Grants are awarded according to need.

Applications

Apply in writing to the correspondent. Applications from individuals must be accompanied by a letter of recommendation by the applicant's rabbi or other known religious leader.

Financial information

Year end	31/12/2019
Income	£908,200
Total expenditure	£935,800

Other information

The trust is also involved in the running of a synagogue and awards grants to organisations.

JAT (Jewish AIDS Trust)

£ £7,200 (2019/20)

Correspondent: The Trustees, 40A Holly Park, London N3 3JD (tel: 07546 429885; email: c.spelman@jat-uk.org)

 www.jat-uk.org

CC number: 327936

Eligibility

Jewish people living with HIV/AIDS. Support is extended to their families and carers.

Types of grant

Our previous research found that grants have been awarded towards the costs of Passover food, travel expenses for respite care, washing machines, cookers and moving costs.

Applications

Prospective applicants are advised to contact the charity by telephone in the first instance.

Financial information

Year end	31/03/2020
Income	£400
Total expenditure	£8,000

Further financial information

Full accounts were not available to view on the Charity Commission's website due to the trust's low income. We have therefore estimated the trust's grant total based on its total expenditure.

Other information

The charity offers a confidential, non-judgemental counselling service for Jewish people affected by HIV/AIDS. The charity also provides sexual health and HIV awareness programmes aimed at tackling the stigma around sexually transmitted infections both in and outside the Jewish community.

Jewish Care Scotland

£ £6,900 (2020)

Correspondent: The Trustees, The Walton Community Care Centre, May Terrace, Giffnock, Glasgow G46 6LD (tel: 0141 620 1800; email: hello@jcarescot.org.uk)

 www.jcarescot.org.uk

OSCR number: SC005267

Eligibility

Jewish people who live in Scotland and are in need.

Types of grant

One-off grants are given towards clothing, food, household goods, rent, holidays, equipment and travel. The charity also runs a kosher foodbank.

Applications

Contact the charity for further information on how to make an application.

Financial information

Year end	31/12/2020
Income	£536,500
Total expenditure	£655,500

Other information

The charity mainly provides support services for the Jewish community in Scotland.

The Association of Jewish Refugees (AJR)

 £3,680,000 (2020)

Correspondent: Social Services Department, Winston House, 2 Dollis Park, Finchley, London N3 1HF (tel: 020 8385 3070; email: enquiries@ajr.org.uk)

🌐 www.ajr.org.uk

CC number: 1149882

Eligibility

Jewish refugees from Nazi oppression who settled in the UK, and their dependants and descendants. Potential applicants must be members of the Association of Jewish Refugees (AJR) or be eligible to become members and be willing to join the association.

Types of grant

The association administers emergency social, welfare and care funds on behalf of the Conference on Jewish Material Claims Against Germany, which can be used to pay for a number of services and essential items including dental treatment and specialist clothing as well as urgent house repairs, recuperative convalescence, respite breaks and homecare packages. Specifically these funds are:

- **Homecare:** grants to assist clients to live in their homes for as long as possible.
- **Emergency Fund:** grants for essential items or services such as urgent house repairs, medical consultations, dental treatment or specialist clothing.
- **Austrian Holocaust Survivors Emergency Assistance Programme:** financial assistance (up to a maximum of £10,000 in any 12-month period) for Austrian holocaust survivors on low incomes who require urgent medical attention or essential welfare services. Grants can be made for wheelchairs, disability aids, dental care, hearing aids, etc. Assistance to buy into the Austrian social security pension scheme can also be given.
- **Self-Aid:** support for AJR members on low incomes. The scheme constitutes a monthly grant with additional holiday grants paid at specific times of the year, a winter-fuel payment and awards to mark certain Jewish festivals.

Applications

Applications may be made by contacting the social work team by telephone.

Financial information

Year end		31/12/2020
Income		£4,390,000
Total expenditure		£6,500,000

Other information

The association provides claims advice for Holocaust-era compensation, runs a Meals on Wheels service and has a team of social workers to provide support for members.

The Jewish Widows and Students Aid Trust

 £67,000 (2019/20)

Correspondent: The Trustees, 5 Raeburn Close, London NW11 6UG (tel: 020 8349 7199; email: alan@gapbooks.com)

CC number: 210022

Eligibility

Jewish students (who must be from the UK, Ireland, Israel, France or the British Commonwealth and aged between 16 and 30 years old), widows and schoolchildren (not younger than ten) who reside in the UK.

Types of grant

Grants are awarded to university students to cover the cost of fees.

Applications

Apply in writing to the correspondent.

Financial information

Year end		05/04/2020
Income		£73,100
Total expenditure		£70,900

Further financial information

Grants were awarded to 39 students during the year. We were unable to determine how much was awarded to widows or schoolchildren.

Kupath Gemach Chaim Bechesed Viznitz Trust

£358,000 (2019/20)

Correspondent: The Trustees, 171 Kyverdale Road, London N16 6PS (tel: 020 8442 9604)

CC number: 1110323

Eligibility

People in need, particularly those of the Jewish faith.

Types of grant

Grants are given according to need.

Applications

Apply in writing to the correspondent. Applications by individuals must be accompanied by a letter of

recommendation by their rabbi or other known religious leader.

Financial information

Year end		31/05/2020
Income		£558,400
Total expenditure		£564,400

Other information

Grants are also made to organisations.

Machne Israel Loan Fund

£130,800 (2019)

Correspondent: The Trustees, Unit 4, Breasy Place, Burroughs Gardens, London NW4 4AT (tel: 020 3866 8888; email: info@milfcharity.com)

🌐 www.milfcharity.com

CC number: 803350

Eligibility

People of the Jewish faith who live in the UK and are in need.

Types of grant

Twice a year, grants are given to over 100 families towards making Yom Tov. Grants are also given towards Yom Tov clothes and tuition fees so a child with specific needs can attend an appropriate school abroad or in the UK. In addition, throughout the year the charity provides funding towards simchas and any other events for families in need.

Applications

Application forms can be completed on the charity's website.

Financial information

Year end		31/12/2019
Income		£183,800
Total expenditure		£149,200

Other information

The charity also provides loans to assist with a range of purposes such as buying a home, starting a business, tuition, weddings, Bar Mitzvahs, credit card debt and so on.

The Montpellier Trust

£1,300 (2019/20)

Correspondent: The Trustees, 7 Montpellier Mews, Salford, Greater Manchester M7 4ZW (tel: 0161 308 3928; email: michaelallweis@dwyers.net)

CC number: 1108119

Eligibility

People of the Orthodox Jewish faith.

Types of grant

Grants are given according to need and towards the furtherance of Orthodox Jewish education.

Applications

Apply in writing to the correspondent.

Financial information

Year end	05/04/2020
Income	£2,600
Total expenditure	£2,500

Further financial information

Full accounts were not available to view on the Charity Commission's website due to the trust's low income. We have therefore estimated the trust's grant total based on its total expenditure.

Other information

Grants may also be given to organisations.

Vyoel Moshe Charitable Trust

£ £298,000 (2020/21)

Correspondent: B. Berger, Secretary, 63A Lampard Grove, London N16 6XA (tel: 07975 952011; email: moshe@ invoicesolution.co.uk)

CC number: 327054

Eligibility

Grants are made to low-income Jewish families who are in need.

Types of grant

Grants are awarded to help with the extra expenditure incurred during Jewish religious holidays.

Applications

Individuals are referred to the trust by local rabbis.

Financial information

Year end	31/03/2021
Income	£964,500
Total expenditure	£873,900

Further financial information

Note, the grant total may include grants to organisations.

Other information

The trust also awards grants to educational and religious organisations.

The MYA Charitable Trust

£ £2,500 (2019/20)

Correspondent: The Trustees, Medcar House, 149A Stamford Hill, London N16 5LL (tel: 020 8800 3582)

CC number: 299642

Eligibility

Jewish people in need anywhere in the world.

Types of grant

Grants to people in need of financial and medical aid. Short-term interest-free loans may also be made to alleviate financial hardship.

Applications

Apply in writing to the correspondent.

Financial information

Year end	30/04/2020
Income	£177,900
Total expenditure	£141,200

Other information

The trust also makes grants to educational and religious institutions.

NJD Charitable Trust

£ £31,700 (2019/20)

Correspondent: The Trustees, c/o Berg Kaprow Lewis, 35 Ballards Lane, London N3 1XW (tel: 020 7842 7306)

CC number: 1109146

Eligibility

Members of the Jewish faith who are in need.

Types of grant

Grants are awarded according to need.

Applications

Apply in writing to the correspondent. Applications are considered throughout the year.

Financial information

Year end	31/07/2020
Income	£80
Total expenditure	£63,600

Further financial information

Full accounts were not available to view on the Charity Commission's website due to the trust's low income. We have therefore estimated the grant total based on the trust's total expenditure.

Other information

The trust also makes grants to organisations.

The ZSV Trust

£ £382,800 (2020)

Correspondent: The Trustees, 52 Darenth Road, London N16 6EJ (email: fllandzsv@gmail.com)

 www.foodlifeline.org.uk

CC number: 1063860

Eligibility

Jewish people in need.

Types of grant

One-off and recurrent grants are awarded according to need. Most of the trust's funds are spent on providing food parcels. Other recent grants have been given towards medical assistance, clothing, shoes and weddings.

Applications

Individuals need to apply through social services or be recommended by rabbis or other community leaders.

Financial information

Year end	31/12/2020
Income	£1,090,000
Total expenditure	£948,200

Further financial information

The trust also distributed food parcels worth £441,400.

The Union of Orthodox Hebrew Congregations

£ £26,000 (2019)

Correspondent: The Trustees, 140 Stamford Hall, N16 6QT (tel: 020 8800 6833)

CC number: 1158987

Eligibility

Orthodox Jewish people who live in the UK and are in need.

Types of grant

One-off grants, awarded at times of Jewish festivals, are available to assist with everyday expenses.

Applications

Apply in writing to the correspondent.

Financial information

Year end	31/12/2019
Income	£1,790,000
Total expenditure	£1,480,000

Specific circum- stances

Abortion Support Network

See entry on page 31

The Jack and Ada Beattie Foundation

 £5,900 (2019/20)

Correspondent: The Trustees, Soho Works, Unit 4.07, The Tea Building, 56 Shoreditch High Street, London E1 6JJ (email: info@beattiefoundation.com)

https://beattiefoundation.com

CC number: 1142892

Eligibility
Vulnerable or marginalised people who are facing injustice and inequality in Birmingham and London.

Types of grant
The foundation's website states that its funding priorities are 'dignity; freedom and sanctuary.' According to our previous research, grants of between £500 and £1,000 are available to individuals. In the past, support has been given for the following situations:

- A family who had escaped domestic violence and needed curtains and carpet for their new permanent accommodation
- Essential equipment and clothing to help a woman living with HIV on the arrival of her new baby
- Assistance with a rent increase for an individual living with multiple sclerosis while she waited to be rehoused

At the time of writing (November 2021) the foundation was providing grants of £100 to individuals to support basic needs in response to the COVID-19 pandemic. Check the website for the most recent information.

Applications
Contact the foundation for further information on how to apply.

Financial information
Year end	31/03/2020
Income	£18,100
Total expenditure	£13,000

Further financial information
Full accounts were not available to view on the Charity Commission's website due to the charity's low income. We have therefore estimated the charity's grant total based on its total expenditure.

The Capstone Care Leavers' Trust
See entry on page 24

The Heinz, Anna and Carol Kroch Foundation

 £203,600 (2019/20)

Correspondent: The Trustees, PO Box 327, Hampton, Middlesex TW12 9DD (tel: 020 8979 0609; email: hakf50@hotmail.com)

CC number: 207622

Eligibility
People who are in severe financial need and have ongoing medical problems. Support is also available for victims of domestic violence and people experiencing homelessness.

Types of grant
Grants tend to be of modest amounts and are given according to need. According to our previous research, grants have been given towards hospital expenses and travel costs, household bills, furniture, clothing, food, medical equipment, living costs and home adaptations and repairs.

Applications
Apply in writing to the correspondent. Most applications are submitted through other charities and local authorities. Applications are considered by the trustees at bi-monthly meetings.

Financial information
Year end	31/03/2020
Income	£317,500
Total expenditure	£316,400

Other information
The foundation also makes grants to organisations.

Asylum seekers and refugees

BMA Charities Trust Fund
See entry on page 137

Fund for Human Need

 £51,500 (2019/20)

Correspondent: Mrs G. Mason, Administrator, 6 Newlands Road, Darlington, County Durham DL3 9JL (tel: 01325 244992; email: fundhumanneed@gmail.com)

fundforhumanneed.org.uk

CC number: 208866

Eligibility
Refugees, asylum seekers, people who are experiencing homelessness and other individuals in personal distress. The fund's website states that priority is given to those 'who are destitute or have no income or benefits, who are particularly vulnerable and where amounts of up to £120 will make a major difference'.

Types of grant
Grants of up to £120 are awarded for welfare needs.

Exclusions
Grants cannot be awarded for debts, scholarships/university or college fees, or to individuals living outside the UK.

Applications
Applications can be made using an online form on the funder's website. Alternatively, applicants may wish to download a copy of the application form and send it by post to the correspondent. It is advised that applications are made through a recognised organisation, although this is not essential. The trustees meet once a month to consider grant applications.

Financial information
Year end	31/08/2020
Income	£103,800
Total expenditure	£86,400

Further financial information
Grants were awarded to 872 individuals during the year.

The Prisoners of Conscience Appeal Fund

£93,200 (2020/21)

Correspondent: Grants Officer, PO Box 61044, London SE1 1UP (tel: 020 7407 6644; email: grantsofficer@prisonersofconscience.org)

www.prisonersofconscience.org

CC number: 213766

Eligibility
People who have been persecuted for their conscientiously held beliefs. Families of such people are also eligible for assistance. Typically, the charity supports those who have had to leave their country and are seeking asylum in the UK.

Types of grant

Welfare
Relief grants are given towards food, living expenses, accommodation, furniture, travel and medical expenses. Family reunion grants are made towards

the cost of travel, emergency documentation, medical assessment, DNA testing and legal expenses to help reunite families who have been separated when seeking asylum in the UK.

Education

Educational grants are made in the form of bursaries for postgraduate or re-qualification study to improve employment prospects.

Exclusions

The charity does not help those who have used or advocated for violence, or who are members of violent organisations. Grants are not given for undergraduate university fees.

Applications

Applications for relief grants must be made through a registered and approved referral agency. To apply for a bursary or a family reunion grant, contact the correspondent via email.

Financial information

Year end	31/03/2021
Income	£275,800
Total expenditure	£289,200

Further financial information

The charity awarded 144 grants during the financial period.

Other information

The charity runs an employability panel comprising specialist organisations that can assist with finding meaningful and skills-related employment for its beneficiaries.

Homelessness

Crisis UK

 £91,000 (2019/20)

Correspondent: Welfare Team, 66 Commercial Street, London E1 6LT (tel: 0300 636 1967; email: enquiries@ crisis.org.uk)

www.crisis.org.uk

CC number: 1082947/ SC040094

Eligibility

People over 18 who are or have been homeless in the UK.

Types of grant

Grants to assist people with the costs of courses and training, equipment to get started in the world of work or towards setting up a business where a robust plan is presented.

Applications

Grant applications can be made by individuals who are supported by a coach working at a Crisis Skylight centre.

Financial information

Year end	30/06/2020
Income	£63,420,000
Total expenditure	£54,000,000

Further financial information

Grants were made to 62 members through the Crisis Changing Lives programme, with an average grant of £1,400.

Other information

Crisis is a national charity that delivers education, employment, housing and health services for people experiencing homelessness. It carries out research into the causes and consequences of homelessness and campaigns for change. Visit the charity's website for more information on its work and services.

Housing the Homeless Central Fund

 £71,900 (2020/21)

Correspondent: Frankie Salton-Cox, Clerk to the Trustees, 2A Orchard Road, Sidcup, Kent DA14 6RD (tel: 020 8309 1229; email: hhcfund@gmail.com)

CC number: 233254

Eligibility

People who are either currently experiencing or at risk of homelessness. Typical beneficiaries include: young people coming out of care; older people without family or friends and with very little savings; victims of domestic abuse; people with substance misuse disorders; people with experience of the criminal justice system; victims of theft or fire; people on very low incomes; single-parent households; parents and children involved in divorce proceedings; or people being supported by victim support schemes.

Types of grant

Grants of around £200 are given for essential household items such as beds, bedding, cots, white goods or pots and pans. Occasionally, grants are given for essential clothing and, on rare occasions, towards small rent arrears.

Applications

Applications must be made by a social care agency (such as Citizens Advice, social services, housing associations, probation services and women's welfare agencies) on behalf of an individual. Social care agencies should contact the correspondent to begin the application process.

Financial information

Year end	31/03/2021
Income	£87,200
Total expenditure	£90,600

The Heinz, Anna and Carol Kroch Foundation

See entry on page 47

The St Martin-in-the-Fields' Christmas Appeal Charity

£1,780,000 (2019/20)

Correspondent: The Trustees, 6 St Martin's Place, London WC2N 4JH (tel: 020 7766 5521; email: tim.bissett@ stmartinscharity.org.uk)

https://www.smitfc.org

CC number: 1156305

Eligibility

People living in the UK who are experiencing, or at risk of, homelessness.

Types of grant

Grants of up to £350 for:

- Accessing accommodation: rent deposits, rent in advance, admin fees, ID or temporary accommodation costs
- Preventing eviction: rent arrears, service charge arrears, Debt Relief Orders, bankruptcy fees or money to pay for a hoarding clean-up

Applications

Applications can be made through the charity's online application portal. Applications are only accepted from paid frontline workers providing support to people who are experiencing homelessness or vulnerable housing.

Financial information

Year end	31/03/2020
Income	£4,870,000
Total expenditure	£3,730,000

Further financial information

In 2019/20, 5,498 grants were awarded to 1,942 support workers who had applied on their clients' behalf. The grants were awarded to 8,760 people.

People with experience of the criminal justice system

The Hardman Trust

£ £102,200 (2019/20)

Correspondent: Administrator, PO Box 108, Newport PO30 1YN (tel: 01983 550355; email: info@hardmantrust.org.uk)

 https://www.hardmantrust.org.uk

CC number: 1042715

Eligibility

People who are serving a prison sentence of seven years or more, are within two years of release and have specific career goals upon leaving prison. Grants are currently available to people in 30 prisons across the UK. For full eligibility criteria, see the trust's website.

Types of grant

Grants of up to £900 are available for items such as laptops, printers, work clothing and tools for a trade. Grants are also available towards the cost of vocational courses, HGV and LGV training and academic study, including postgraduate courses. Grants can also be used to start up a business.

Applications

Application forms are available to download on the trust's website. The charity has staff representatives in all qualifying prisons, who prospective applicants can contact for an application form and for guidance throughout the process. All applications must include positive endorsements from two prison staff members. All applicants will be required to attend an interview with an assessor from the charity.

Financial information

Year end	31/03/2020
Income	£300,300
Total expenditure	£211,400

Further financial information

During the financial year, the trust awarded 154 grants.

Other information

The trust has an open source directory of funding sources for prisoners and people affected by the criminal justice system.

Michael and Shirley Hunt Charitable Trust

£ £3,800 (2019/20)

Correspondent: Deborah Jenkins, Trustee, Ansty House, Henfield Road, Small Dole, Henfield, West Sussex BN5 9XH (tel: 01903 817116)

CC number: 1063418

Eligibility

Grants are available for the relief of hardship of prisoners and their dependants.

Types of grant

Grants are made towards travel costs for dependent relatives of serving prisoners who wish to visit their family member in prison. Grants can also be made to prisoners to cover the cost of travel to visit family members on town visits and home leaves if the family is in hardship and cannot afford to pay the fares. Funding is also available for general welfare support.

Applications

Apply in writing to the correspondent. Applications must be supported by a probation officer, social worker, prison officer or similar third party.

Financial information

Year end	31/03/2020
Income	£242,600
Total expenditure	£72,300

Further financial information

Grants were made to 32 individuals in 2019/20.

Women in Prison Ltd
See entry on page 35

Illness and disability charities

There are many charities for people with illnesses or disabilities. The grant-makers detailed in this section are those that only give financial help. There are many others that provide non-financial support and advice and may be the starting point for getting financial help. For this reason we have a list of organisations which provide advice and support on page 467.

This section starts with an index of illness or disability. The entries are arranged alphabetically within each category, with charities supporting more than one illness or disability, or with broad criteria, listed at the start of the chapter. The 'Disability' section similarly lists charities which have a wide remit to support people with disabilities, rather than focusing on a specific condition. Individuals with any condition or disability, may therefore also look under these two general sections for support, as well as 'Other specific conditions' or any other relevant section.

The sub-section 'Children' lists charities which give exclusively to children who have an illness or disability, with age as part of their key criteria – of course, many charities in other sections will also support children.

Similarly, the charities listed under 'Mental health' are by no means the only ones that will support those with mental health problems – rather, they are the only ones that specify this as their main criteria. Many charities with a broad remit to support those with an illness or disability will include people who have mental health problems; likewise with many of the grant-makers in the 'General charities' chapter.

Index of illness and disability charities

General 51

Cancer 56

Carers 58

Children 59

Disability 70

Injuries 71

Mental health 73

Other specific conditions 73

Visual impairment 82

General

The Douglas Bader Foundation

£ £69,400 (2019/20)

Correspondent: Keith Delderfield, Bader Braves/Bader Grants Scheme Co-ordinator, Bader Grant Scheme, 45 Dundale Road, Tring, Hertfordshire HP23 5BU (tel: 01225 865172 or 07831 596015; email: douglasbaderfdn@ btinternet.com or use the contact form on the website)

 https://www.douglasbader foundation.com

CC number: 800435

Eligibility
People who were born without, or who have lost, one or more limbs, or those who have another physical disability. Adults and children with a diagnosed mental health issue can also be supported.

Types of grant
The Bader Grant Scheme provides funding to help individuals achieve personal goals in areas such as the arts, sport, education and recreation. Lady Bader Memorial grants and special awards may also be awarded at the trustees' discretion to applicants who reflect Lady Bader's own lifetime interests and achievements.

Grants can be given towards education and training (including further education) and other practical support and equipment.

Exclusions
Grants cannot be given towards living aids.

Applications

Application forms are available to download from the foundation's website.

Financial information

Year end	31/10/2020
Income	£219,100
Total expenditure	£299,100

Other information

Support is also given to organisations. The foundation administers a scheme called the Bader Braves, which offers children and young people the opportunity to fly in a light aircraft at events throughout the UK as well as the Team Bader scheme that offers children experiences that encourage teamwork to instil a sense of self-confidence. In addition, the foundation provides advice and information and a one-to-one support line named Limbline.

Barchester Health Care Foundation

 £66,000 (2019)

Correspondent: Grants Management Team, 3rd Floor, The Aspect, 12 Finsbury Square, London EC2A 1AS (tel: 0800 328 3328; email: info@bhcfoundation.org.uk)

www.bhcfoundation.org.uk

CC number: 1083272

Eligibility

Older people over the age of 65, and adults over the age of 18 with mental health problems or a physical or learning disability. Applicants must live in England, Scotland or Wales.

The direct purpose of the application should be to connect or re-connect the individual with others in their local community.

Types of grant

The foundation's website states that it helps people with:
- Mobility equipment
- Activities
- Vocational courses, if no statutory funding or student finance is available
- Equipment to help combat isolation
- UK-based holidays or a special day out

Exclusions

Grants are not normally made for:
- Disability and exercise equipment for use in the home, including specialist chairs and beds
- Repairs and maintenance of mobility equipment
- Home improvements, adaptations and property repairs, including gardens
- Household items, such as white goods, furniture and carpeting

- Medical or dental treatment, including any type of therapy or rehabilitation
- Cars, driving lessons, removal costs or holidays abroad
- Laptops and iPads
- Daily living costs (e.g. rent, utility bills, clothing, mobile phones, travel costs) or repayment of debts
- Equipment for residents in a care home operated by Barchester Healthcare or by any other care home company

Applications

Applications can be made online on the foundation's website or a form can be downloaded and submitted to the correspondent. All applications must be supported by a third-party sponsor, for example, a health or social care professional, social worker or charity representative.

Financial information

Year end	31/12/2019
Income	£317,000
Total expenditure	£210,000

Further financial information

The foundation made 87 grants during the year.

Other information

Support is also given in grants to small community groups and local charities.

The Percy Bilton Charity

 £314,500 (2019/20)

Correspondent: The Trustees, Bilton House, 7 Culmington Road, Ealing, London W13 9NB (tel: 020 8579 2829; email: information@percybiltoncharity.org)

www.percy-bilton-charity.org

CC number: 1094720

Eligibility

Individuals in financial need who have a disability or severe mental health problem, or individuals over 65 who are on a low income.

Types of grant

Examples given on the charity's website include white goods, single beds, flooring and clothing vouchers.

Exclusions

According to the charity's website, the charity cannot help with:
- General financial hardship outside the charity's specified eligibility criteria
- Payment towards items costing over £200
- Dishwashers

- Travel expenses, sponsorship, holidays or respite care
- Educational grants
- Computer equipment or software
- House alterations and maintenance
- Reimbursements for items already purchased
- Garden fencing or clearance
- Motor vehicle purchase or expenses
- Nursing and residential home fees
- Funeral expenses
- Removal expenses
- Medical treatment or therapy
- Course fees (including driving or IT lessons)

Applications

Applications can be made on the charity's website. They must be made on behalf of an individual by social workers, community psychiatric nurses or occupational therapists within a local authority or NHS trust. See the charity's website for further information and guidance on the application process.

Financial information

Year end	31/03/2020
Income	£833,000
Total expenditure	£1,010,000

Further financial information

In 2019/20, the charity made 1,701 grants to individuals totalling £314,500.

Other information

The charity also makes grants to organisations.

The Boparan Charitable Trust
See entry on page 23

Clevedon Convalescent Fund

 £52,400 (2019/20)

Correspondent: Joan Taffs, Grants Officer, 4 Kenn Road, Clevedon, Somerset BS21 6EL (tel: 01275 314777; email: joan@clevedonforbes.org)

www.clevedonforbes.org

CC number: 249313

Eligibility

People experiencing ill health or recovering from illness or medical/surgical treatment who are in need of, but cannot afford, a convalescent break. Carers of people with health problems or a disability are also eligible for funding. Preference is given to those living in the South West.

Types of grant

One-off grants towards the cost of convalescent breaks.

Exclusions

No grants are awarded for the purchase of equipment, capital goods or debt relief. Grants cannot be paid directly to the person for whom the grant is made.

Applications

Application forms are available to download on the fund's website. Applications must be made on the individual's behalf by a professional in the statutory or voluntary sector. Completed application forms should be sent to the correspondent at their postal address. If the grants officer has not met with the professional making the referral, arrangements will be made to visit them at their place of work. Subsequent referrals do not usually require a visit.

Financial information

Year end	31/03/2020
Income	£76,000
Total expenditure	£85,200

Further financial information

In the year 2019/20, the fund awarded 107 grants which assisted 311 individuals.

Other information

Unless requested otherwise, all beneficiaries receive a free Christian booklet/gospel alongside their grant. A gift of flowers is also sent to beneficiaries upon their return from convalescence.

Elifar Foundation Ltd

 £216,800 (2019/20)

Correspondent: The Trustees, Camelot, Park Road, Dormans Park, East Grinstead, Surrey RH19 2NQ (tel: 020 7318 5873; email: enquiries@ elifarfoundation.org.uk)

 www.elifarfoundation.org.uk

CC number: 1152416

Eligibility

Children and young adults (under the age of 28) with any form of physical or learning disability.

Types of grant

Grants can be made towards: manual or powered wheelchairs or other mobility aids; sensory toys and equipment; hoists; communication aids and specialised software; specialised seating, beds and sleep systems; trikes; and holidays.

Exclusions

Grants are not made for:
- Items or work for which there is statutory funding available
- Building works or garden works

- Ordinary computers/laptops/iPads
- Ordinary domestic items (e.g. furniture, flooring, white goods, clothing)
- Ordinary holidays
- Therapies
- Clothing
- Mobility scooters
- Retrospective costs

Applications

Application forms can be downloaded from the foundation's website and can be submitted by the person in need, a parent or a care professional.

Financial information

Year end	31/05/2020
Income	£274,200
Total expenditure	£256,000

Further financial information

During 2019/20, a total of 138 grants were awarded to individuals. Individual grants ranged from £100 to £6,500.

Other information

The name Elifar stands for 'Every Life is for a Reason'.

The General and Medical Foundation

 £1,400 (2020)

Correspondent: The Trustees, General & Medical Plc, 56A Napier Place, Orton Wistow, Peterborough PE2 6XN (email: enquiries@thegmfoundation.org)

https://www.generalandmedical foundation.org

CC number: 1180523

Eligibility

People with medical conditions or disabilities living in the UK.

Types of grant

Financial assistance is available to aid and improve the activities of daily living.

Applications

Applications can be made through the foundation's website.

Financial information

Year end	31/12/2020
Income	£34,000
Total expenditure	£2,800

Further financial information

We have estimated the grant total, as the foundation also awards grants to organisations.

The Hospital Saturday Fund

 £90,800 (2020)

Correspondent: Jo Moore, Charity Administrator, 24 Upper Ground, London SE1 9PD (tel: 020 7202 1334; email: charity@hsf.eu.com)

www.hospitalsaturdayfund.org

CC number: 1123381

Eligibility

People in medical need in the UK and the Republic of Ireland.

Types of grant

Partial or full grants are awarded for the following:
- Specialised mobility equipment
- Medical appliances and aids
- Specialised computer equipment
- Therapeutic equipment/treatment
- Home and car adaptations
- Respite breaks at a therapeutic centre.

A full list of examples can be found on the charity's website.

Exclusions

According to the website, the charity will not support the following:
- Treatment outside the UK and Ireland.
- Financial assistance.
- Transport costs to hospitals/clinics.
- In-home care or care home costs.
- Private hospital admission or treatment.
- Experimental drugs/medication (those not recommended by N.I.C.E).
- Purchase of a car.
- Building works to either inside or outside of the home, painting, decorating, any gardening works.
- New furniture or replacing existing furnishings.
- Installation or maintenance of any heating system.
- New or replacement carpets, electrical household goods (e.g. washing machines, bed linen, dishwashers, tumble dryers, ovens, microwaves, fridges etc).
- Holidays/trips abroad/religious pilgrimages.
- Repayment of loans or credit card debts, utility bills for household expenses (e.g. gas, water, telephone, etc), rent or mortgage arrears.
- Clothing.
- Education or tuition fees.
- Funeral expenses.
- Driving lessons.

Applications

Application forms can be completed online by a third party such as a registered health professional, social worker, hospital consultant or specialist, nurse or occupational therapist, physiotherapist or Citizens Advice. Supporting evidence must be uploaded to confirm the applicant's need. Full guidance can be found on the charity's website.

Financial information

Year end	31/12/2020
Income	£31,930,000
Total expenditure	£27,550,000

Other information

The charity also makes grants to organisations (£1.24 million in 2020).

Independence at Home

 £554,800 (2020/21)

Correspondent: The Trustees, 4th Floor, Congress House, 14 Lyon Road, Harrow, Middlesex HA1 2EN (tel: 020 8427 7929; email: iah@independenceathome.org.uk)

www.independenceathome.org.uk

CC number: 1141758

Eligibility

Individuals with long-term illness or disability who require financial assistance towards the cost of independent living.

Types of grant

Grants are available for: mobility and travel equipment; special disability equipment (including hoists, gait trainers and adjustable beds); home adaptations; communications equipment; house repairs; kitchen equipment; beds and bedding; general furnishings; and miscellaneous expenses including removal expenses.

Exclusions

According to the charity's website, grants are not considered for: medical treatment or therapies; travel to hospital appointments; debt relief or arrears; funeral expenses; telephone rental or call charges; televisions; licences or motor vehicles; equipment or work which has already been paid for.

Applications

Applications must be made on behalf of the individual by a referrer. Eligible referrers include: staff employed by a statutory health, social care or advice service; professional workers from charities that provide health, social care, welfare or advice services; Citizens Advice; and professional workers from tenancy support services, Care and Repair organisations and housing associations. Full details of the information required for applications can be found on the charity's website.

Financial information

Year end	31/03/2021
Income	£616,600
Total expenditure	£759,600

Further financial information

According to the charity's 2020/21 accounts, 1,503 grants were made to individuals during the year.

The Heinz, Anna and Carol Kroch Foundation
See entry on page 47

The Langley Foundation

 £9,100 (2019/20)

Correspondent: Grants Administrator, 408 Upper Elmers End Road, Beckenham, Greater London BR33HG (tel: 07877 997847; email: info@ langleyfoundation.org.uk)

https://langleyfoundation.org.uk

CC number: 1153706

Eligibility

Families in England and Wales where a member has been classed as having a recent onset of illness or disability. Eligible families might have their own business, be on a low income or be receiving benefits. Support is intended to help where the person's health issues bring financial hardship to the family unit.

Types of grant

Grants, usually of between £100 and £2,000, can be given for a range of purposes such as one month's rent, a family break for those families with children or one month's childcare costs.

Applications

Application forms can be downloaded from the foundation's website and posted to the address provided.

Financial information

Year end	31/03/2020
Income	£70
Total expenditure	£10,100

Further financial information

Full accounts were not available to view on the Charity Commission's website due to the foundation's low income. We have therefore estimated the foundation's grant total based on its total expenditure.

The League of the Helping Hand (LHH)

 £145,000 (2020/21)

Correspondent: The Secretary, League of the Helping Hand, PO Box 342, Burgess Hill RH15 5AQ (tel: 01444 236099; email: secretary@lhh.org.uk)

www.lhh.org.uk

CC number: 208792

Eligibility

People who have a physical disability, learning difficulty or mental health problem and are in financial need. Those who care for somebody with a disability may also be eligible.

Types of grant

One-off and recurrent payments. Grants of up to £250 are awarded towards essential household items (e.g. white goods, furniture, clothing), specialist equipment and carers' breaks. Quarterly grants are available to help with daily living costs, the beneficiaries of which also receive newsletters, birthday and Christmas cards and, where possible, an annual personal visit from the secretary.

Applications

Application forms are available to download from the charity's website. Applications must be submitted through a social worker, carers' support centre, Citizens Advice or other welfare body. If it is not possible to download the form, the correspondent should be contacted directly.

Financial information

Year end	31/03/2021
Income	£148,900
Total expenditure	£189,800

Further financial information

During the year, grants awarded were distributed as follows:

Single payments	351	£68,600
Regular beneficiaries	70	£54,000
COVID-19 grants	226	£22,400

The Adam Millichip Foundation

 £650 (2019/20)

Correspondent: The Trustees, Station House, Newnham Bridge, Tenbury Wells, Worcestershire WR15 8JE (tel: 07866 424286; email: amandamillichip@aol.com)

CC number: 1138721

Eligibility

People with disabilities (or conditions that affect their day-to-day standard of living) in the UK who wish to participate in sports.

Types of grant

Grants are given to enable participation in sports and sporting activities.

Applications

Apply in writing to the correspondent.

Financial information

Year end	05/04/2020
Income	£500
Total expenditure	£720

Further financial information

Full accounts were not available to view on the Charity Commission's website due to the foundation's low income. We have therefore estimated the foundation's grant total based on its total expenditure.

Newlife Foundation for Disabled Children

 £3,120,000 (2019/20)

Correspondent: The Care Services Team, Newlife Centre, Hemlock Way, Cannock, Staffordshire WS11 7GF (tel: 0800 902 0095; email: info@newlifecharity.co.uk)

🌐 newlifecharity.co.uk/index.php

CC number: 1170125

Eligibility

The foundation's guidelines state that the minimum eligibility requirements for a child/young person are as follows:

- A UK resident
- Has a significant disability which affects their daily like, a life threatening/life limiting condition or has been diagnosed as terminally ill
- Under 19 years of age

Types of grant

The foundation's website states:

Newlife provides funding for essential community equipment, such as beds, buggies, wheelchairs, seating systems, and much more. Our equipment grants can improve child health, reduce risk of significant injury and pain, as well as support delivery of care – while enabling childhood experiences and encouraging independence.

Applications

In the first instance, applicants should contact the Newlife Nurse Helpline (0800 902 0095) to find out if they are eligible for the equipment needed. Application forms can then be downloaded from the charity's website.

Financial information

Year end	31/03/2020
Income	£13,410,000
Total expenditure	£13,270,000

Other information

The charity also provides a helpline for families and professionals, free equipment loans and free loans of specialist toys.

The Florence Nightingale Aid-in-Sickness Trust (FNAIST)

 £383,100 (2020)

Correspondent: Ann Griffiths, Grants and Funding Manager, Community House, Room 35, South Street, Bromley, Kent BR1 1RH (tel: 020 7998 8817; email: ann.griffiths@fnaist.org.uk)

🌐 www.fnaist.org.uk

CC number: 1157980

Eligibility

People of all ages who are in poor health or have a disability and require medical items and services to improve their quality of life.

Types of grant

One-off grants for medical items and services to improve people's quality of life. According to the trust's website the following items and services can be considered:

- Medical aids such as Nebulisers and Tens machines
- Riser/recliner chairs
- Manual and Electric wheelchairs
- Standing Wheelchairs
- Specialist buggies and push chairs
- Car seats
- Car harness
- Wheelchair Power Packs
- Therapeutic Exercise Machines
- Scooters under very special circumstances
- Orthopaedic mattresses
- Washing machines
- Tumble dryers
- Mobile hoists
- Sensory equipment
- Communication aids
- Specialist software
- Computers
- Reading Aids
- Magnifiers
- Refrigerators for essential drug storage
- Secure drug cabinets
- Convalescent and Respite breaks
- Specialist mobile phones
- Telephone installation

Exclusions

According to the trust's website the following will not be considered:

- Adaptations to the home and garden
- Car purchase
- Car repairs
- Car adaptations
- Holidays
- Carer's breaks
- Nursing home fees

- Financial assistance
- Debts
- Household bills
- General clothing
- General house furnishings
- Stairlifts

Applications

Application forms are available to download from the trust's website or can be requested from the correspondent. They should be submitted by Citizens Advice, another charity, a social worker, an occupational therapist, or a doctor, health centre worker or similar professional with a medical background. Candidates should provide a brief medical history of the applicant and proof of need for assistance.

Financial information

Year end	31/12/2020
Income	£341,900
Total expenditure	£486,200

Further financial information

The charity awarded 263 grants during the year.

Miss Ada Oliver

£ £3,000 (2019/20)

Correspondent: The Trustees, c/o Marshalls Solicitors, 102 High Street, Godalming, Surrey GU7 1DS (tel: 01483 416101; email: lisa@marshalls.uk.net)

CC number: 234456

Eligibility

Individuals who have rheumatism or cancer and are in need.

Types of grant

Grants are given according to need.

Applications

Apply in writing to the correspondent.

Financial information

Year end	31/03/2020
Income	£3,600
Total expenditure	£6,700

Further financial information

Full accounts were not available to view on the Charity Commission's website due to the charity's low income. We have therefore estimated the grant total based on the charity's total expenditure.

Other information

The charity also makes grants to organisations with similar objectives.

The Royal Society for Home Relief to Incurables, Edinburgh

 £89,600 (2019)

Correspondent: Kirsty Ashworth, Charity Accounts, Accounts and Business Services Senior Manager, Azets, Exchange Place 3, Semple Street, Edinburgh EH3 8BL (tel: 0131 473 3500; email: SM-Charity@azets.co.uk)

🌐 https://www.azets.co.uk/royal-society-for-home-relief-to-incurables

OSCR number: SC004365

Eligibility

People in Scotland (normally those under retirement age) who are no longer able to work on account of having an incurable illness. The society normally considers assisting those who have ceased employment within the last ten years.

Types of grant

The society provides one-off grants and monthly allowances of around £540.

Exclusions

The society is unable to support individuals with substance misuse disorders, mental illnesses, learning difficulties, primary epilepsy, blindness or visual impairment or birth deformities where any of these is the main illness.

Applications

Application forms are available to download from the Azets website.

Financial information

Year end	31/12/2019
Income	£178,300
Total expenditure	£152,000

The Snow Sports Foundation

 £53,200 (2020)

Correspondent: The Trustees, 55 The Green, Aston Abbotts, Aylesbury HP22 4LY (tel: 07980 014134; email: ian@snowsportsfoundation.org.uk)

🌐 www.snowsportsfoundation.org.uk

CC number: 1158955

Eligibility

People who need additional support for daily living due to a sensory, intellectual, neurological or developmental disability or an acquired brain injury. Preference is given to children and young people and those experiencing financial hardship.

Types of grant

Grants are made for skiing and snowboarding lessons to help towards the development of essential skills. An assessment/taster session will be arranged, followed by ten one-to-one lessons. This may be extended if funds are available. The foundation asks for a contribution towards lessons from parents/guardians or another source. Applications are also accepted from day groups and schools. Note that the foundation pays the grant directly to the instructor.

Applications

Application forms can be completed online on the foundation's website.

Financial information

Year end	31/12/2020
Income	£106,100
Total expenditure	£106,800

Victoria Convalescent Trust

 £91,700 (2020)

Correspondent: The Trustees, 5th Floor, 14–16 Dowgate Hill, London EC4R 2SU (tel: 07768 742940; email: vic.c.trust@gmail.com)

🌐 victoriaconvalescenttrust.org.uk

CC number: 1064585

Eligibility

The charity's website states:

> Our main purpose is to make grants to fund or part-fund short breaks for those, including carers, of any age, living in England and Wales:
> ▸ Who are in need of a short break for the purpose of convalescence, recuperative care or respite care
> ▸ Who do not have adequate resources to fund themselves
> ▸ Who have been unable to obtain sufficient assistance from the statutory services.

Types of grant

Grants are available for short breaks for the purpose of convalescence, recuperative care or respite care. A small proportion of support is also given for essential equipment such as white goods, essential household items, contributions towards mobility aids and other specialist equipment. Priority for funding is given to those with a severe and enduring disability, physical or mental illness, and to carers.

Applications

Application forms are available to download from the trust's website. Applications should be by a referring agency. A list of criteria for referral

agencies can be found on the trust's website.

Financial information

Year end	31/12/2020
Income	£84,200
Total expenditure	£146,200

The Victoria Foundation

See entry on page 69

See entry on page 69

Cancer

Acheinu Cancer Support

 £5,500 (2020)

Correspondent: The Trustees, 99–101 Dunsmure Road, London N16 5HT (tel: 020 8806 7227; email: info@acscancer.org.uk)

🌐 https://acscancer.org.uk

CC number: 1181606

Eligibility

People with cancer and their families.

Types of grant

The charity can fund or partially fund the following:
▸ Treatments not funded by the NHS; these may include tests and scans, radiation, chemotherapy, monthly medications and specialist visits
▸ Basic necessities such as food and household supplies
▸ Medical equipment
▸ Travel and holidays

Applications

Contact the charity for further information.

Financial information

Year end	31/12/2020
Income	£448,400
Total expenditure	£428,200

Other information

The charity also provides a range of services to support people with cancer such as advice, patient companionship and transport services, weekend retreats and much more. Further information can be found on the charity's website.

Cancer Relief UK

 £13,100 (2019/20)

Correspondent: The Trustees, Unit B2, Holmewood Business Park, Chesterfield Road, Holmewood, Chesterfield S42 5US

https://cancerreliefuk.org

CC number: 1122929

Eligibility

People with cancer who live in the UK and are experiencing financial hardship.

Types of grant

One-off grants are awarded according to need. Grants can be made to provide direct help with utility bills, travel costs and family days out.

Applications

Contact the charity for further information.

Financial information

Year end	31/03/2020
Income	£368,200
Total expenditure	£255,000

Cost of Cancer

 £11,500 (2020)

Correspondent: The Trustees, c/o Moss Technical Services, Unit 8, Green Court, Pyle CF33 6BN (tel: 07977 584701; email: info@costofcancer.org.uk)

 https://www.costofcancer.org.uk

CC number: 1165956

Eligibility

People with cancer who are in need.

Types of grant

Grants are made towards household bills such as rent, mortgage payments, gas, electricity, etc.

Applications

Contact the charity by email or telephone, briefly explaining how much funding you are hoping to receive and what bills you need help with. If you are deemed eligible, the charity will then send you an application form.

Financial information

Year end	31/12/2020
Income	£9,200
Total expenditure	£3,300

Further financial information

Full accounts were not available to view on the Charity Commission's website due to the charity's low income. We have therefore estimated the grant total based on the charity's total expenditure.

Mark Lay Foundation

 £5,700 (2020)

Correspondent: The Trustees, 3 Rother Crescent, Gossops Green, Crawley, West Sussex RH11 8DF (tel: 07584 305006; email: grants@marklayfoundation.org.uk or use the contact form on the website)

 https://www.marklayfoundation. org.uk

CC number: 1175779

Eligibility

Families who are affected by cancer and have a household income of under £60,000. The applicant must have been diagnosed with life-limiting cancer or have been living with cancer for 18 months or more.

Types of grant

Grants are awarded to families towards a short holiday or break to enable them to spend some time together.

Applications

Applicants can register their interest on the charity's website. The applicant will require a letter from a doctor, declaring the applicant is fit for travel and confirming their diagnosis, and a payslip or P60. At the time of writing (November 2021) the grant scheme was temporarily closed due to the COVID-19 pandemic. Check the website for the most recent update.

Financial information

Year end	31/12/2020
Income	£20,900
Total expenditure	£37,400

Further financial information

The foundation's holiday grant scheme was closed during 2020/21 due to COVID-19. In 2019 grants totalling £22,200 were awarded to 25 families for holidays and short breaks.

Other information

The foundation also awards grants to charities that support people with cancer.

Leukaemia Care

 £50,900 (2020)

Correspondent: Lisa Barnett, One Birch Court, Blackpole East, Worcester WR3 8SG (tel: 0808 801 0044; email: advocacy@leukaemiacare.org.uk)

 https://www.leukaemiacare.org.uk/ support-and-information/ support-for-you

CC number: 1183890

Eligibility

The charity's website states that it can support the following:

- Patients with leukaemia, myelodysplastic syndrome (MDS) and myeloproliferative neoplasms (MPNs) that are currently undergoing treatment, chronic lymphocytic leukaemia (CLL) patients on 'watch and wait', or chronic myeloid leukaemia

(CML) patients undergoing treatment-free remission.
- Families of patients with leukaemia, myelodysplastic syndrome (MDS) and myeloproliferative neoplasms (MPNs) that are currently undergoing treatment, chronic lymphocytic leukaemia (CLL) patients on 'watch and wait', or chronic myeloid leukaemia (CML) patients undergoing treatment-free remission.

Types of grant

Grants of up to £200 for essential living costs such as:

- Travel expenses such as bus tickets, train tickets, fuel, car maintenance, parking fees and taxi fares.
- Food costs associated with a neutropenic diet, eating a high-calorie diet to avoid weight loss or simply coping with normal food costs on a reduced income.
- Utilities such as gas, electricity, or water.
- Internet access

Grants of up to £400 per applicant are available to cover the costs of a maximum of six counselling sessions, including the initial assessment. Further details can be found on the website.

Applications

Applications can be made online or by post. Full details on how to apply can be found on the charity's website.

Financial information

Year end	31/12/2020
Income	£1,190,000
Total expenditure	£1,120,000

Macmillan Cancer Support

 £9,070,000 (2020)

Correspondent: Welfare Rights Team, Camelford House, 87–90 Albert Embankment, London SE1 7UQ (tel: 0808 808 0000; email: macmillangrants@macmillan.org.uk)

 https://www.macmillan.org.uk/ cancer-information-and-support/ get-help/financial-help/ macmillan-grants

CC number: 261017

Eligibility

People of any age who have cancer, or are still seriously affected by their illness or treatment, who are in need.

Single applicants must have:
- Less than £6,000 in savings
- A weekly income of £323

Couples or families must have:
- Less than £8,000 in savings
- A weekly income of up to £442

The following are not included in the charity's definition of weekly income: Personal Independent Payment, Disability Living Allowance and Attendance Allowance.

The charity also awards grants to Macmillan professionals to support their professional development.

Types of grant

Small welfare grants (the average grant is £350) are awarded to help with the extra costs that living with cancer can bring, such as energy bills, home adaptations and the cost of travel to and from hospital. Learning and development grants are awarded to Macmillan professionals to pay for any conferences or courses that would be beneficial to their role.

Applications

Applications for welfare grants should be made through a health or social care professional. The third party can apply online through the charity's website or can request a physical copy of the application form by contacting the correspondent. Individuals can enquire directly by contacting the Welfare Rights Team on 0808 808 0000. For further information about learning and development grants contact the Service Operations Team at ServiceOpsSupport@macmillan.org.uk or 01904 651 700.

Financial information

Year end	31/12/2020
Income	£194,890,000
Total expenditure	£147,800,000

Further financial information

The charity estimates that it supported over 30,000 people with welfare grants during the year. According to Note 10 of the 2020 accounts, grants to individuals totalled £9.07 million during the year. Note, the grant total may include learning and development grants awarded to Macmillan professionals.

Other information

Grant-making is one of many charitable activities undertaken by Macmillan. The charity offers financial guidance to help people make informed decisions about pensions, savings, mortgages and other finances. The charity also operates support centres across the UK which offer face-to-face advice and information to those who need it. A free helpline is available seven days a week, 8am to 8pm, on 0808 808 0000, and a free Online Community is available for those affected by cancer to talk about their experiences.

Mummy's Star

 £72,300 (2019/20)

Correspondent: The Trustees, PO Box 428, Hadfield, Glossop SK14 9EA (tel: 07939 154217; email: info@mummysstar.org)

🌐 https://www.mummysstar.org

CC number: 1152808

Eligibility

Women who have been diagnosed with, or treated for, cancer during pregnancy or within the first year after pregnancy. Families who have lost their mother within the first year after pregnancy are also eligible for support.

Types of grant

Grants of up to £500 (£700 in cases of terminal diagnosis and £1,000 in cases of lost mothers) have been awarded towards the following:

- Travel to appointments
- Private purchase of donor breast milk (if the applicant's hospital is unwilling to fund it)
- Baby massage classes
- Counselling (if waiting lists for treatment are three months or longer)
- Holistic therapies
- Domestic help
- iPads or similar devices that allow mothers to remain in contact with their children if staying overnight in hospital
- Holidays (only in cases of terminal diagnosis)
- Prescription charges (Republic of Ireland only)

Grants have also been made to compensate partners who have had to take unpaid leave from work beyond their existing leave/paternity leave entitlements.

Exclusions

The charity is unable to award grants towards the cost of:

- Medical treatment
- Non-essential electrical equipment for the home
- Vehicles
- Rent or mortgage payments
- Interest payments
- TV licence fees

The charity cannot make grants for items and services already covered by benefits. Grants are capped at two grants in total to any one family. Once a grant has been awarded, beneficiaries cannot reapply for funding for one year (with the only exceptions being if a secondary cancer or terminal diagnosis is received, or a mother has passed away).

Applications

Application forms are available to download on the funder's website. Completed forms should be sent to the charity by email or post. All applications must include copies of photo identification, proof of address and a medical confirmation of the applicant's diagnosis.

Financial information

Year end	31/03/2020
Income	£241,300
Total expenditure	£216,500

Further financial information

In 2019/20, 132 grants were awarded to individuals.

The Shona Smile Foundation

£2,200 (2019/20)

Correspondent: The Trustees, 18 The Combers, Kesgrave, Ipswich, Suffolk IP5 2EY (tel: 01473 613489; email: theshonasmilefoundation@mail.co.uk)

CC number: 1110177

Eligibility

Children and young people under the age of 18 with cancer.

Types of grant

Financial help to grant children a wish that their families might not otherwise have been able to afford.

Applications

Apply in writing to the correspondent.

Financial information

Year end	30/06/2020
Income	£210
Total expenditure	£2,400

Further financial information

Full accounts were not available to view on the Charity Commission's website due to the foundation's low income. We have therefore estimated the foundation's grant total based on its total expenditure.

Carers

The 3H Fund

 £33,500 (2019/20)

Correspondent: The Trustees, B2 Speldhurst Business Park, Langton Road, Speldhurst, Tunbridge Wells, Kent TN3 0AQ (tel: 01892 860207; email: info@3hfund.org.uk)

🌐 https://www.3hfund.org.uk

CC number: 286306

Eligibility

Grants are given to families on a low income who have a family member with disabilities.

Types of grant

Support is provided to families to organise their own UK holiday. Grants are given for accommodation costs and are paid directly to the chosen venue. Carers can also be awarded a grant for a UK holiday away from their caring role.

Applications

Full information on the application process can be found on the charity's website.

Financial information

Year end	31/10/2020
Income	£148,200
Total expenditure	£138,100

Carers Trust

 £483,500 (2019/20)

Correspondent: Local Carers Service, Unit 101, 164–180 Union Street, London SE1 0LH (tel: 0300 772 9600; email: info@carers.org)

www.carers.org

CC number: 1145181

Eligibility

Grants are available for carers aged 16 or over.

Types of grant

Carers can apply for grants, usually of up to £300, to purchase items or activities that will benefit them in their caring role, for example: breaks or holidays, with or without the person they care for; items for the home including white goods and beds; courses and materials to develop carers' skills and for personal development; home repairs; short-term or time-limited replacement care.

Applications

Applications can be made via your local Carers Trust centre, a list of which can be found on the trust's website. Direct applications will not be considered.

Financial information

Year end	31/03/2020
Income	£6,000,000
Total expenditure	£5,760,000

Other information

The trust acts as a resource body, providing advice, information and support for carers. Carers who are in need of support can contact the online support team by emailing support@carers.org.

The Ogilvie Charities
See entry on page 6

The Respite Association

 £42,800 (2019)

Correspondent: The Trustees, Highfield Barn, Lewdown, Okehampton, Devon EX20 4DS (tel: 01566 783383; email: help@respiteassociation.org)

https://respiteassociation.org

CC number: 1086598

Eligibility

Unpaid carers. Preference is given to those with limited incomes due to the nature of their caring role.

Types of grant

Alternative appropriately qualified home carers or a temporary place in a residential care home are provided to allow the unpaid carer to take a break. A break might allow a carer to attend an evening class, or last for a weekend or for a longer period of time. Most of the grants are of a few hundred pounds. The association also owns two holiday homes which are offered to carers for a respite break away from their usual routine.

Applications

The charity's website explains that most individuals are referred from caring organisations such as Crossroads, SSAFA and Age Concern, or directly from social services. However, the charity can accept applications directly from the individual. Application forms are available on the website.

Financial information

Year end	31/12/2019
Income	£125,000
Total expenditure	£92,700

Victoria Convalescent Trust
See entry on page 56

Children

Able Kidz

 £10,000 (2019/20)

Correspondent: The Grants Officer, Able Kidz Educational Trust, Kemp House, 152–160 City Road, London EC1V 2NX (tel: 0845 123 3997; email: info@ablekidz.org)

ablekidz.org

CC number: 1114955

Eligibility

Children and young people under the age of 18 who live in the UK and have a disability.

Types of grant

Grants are given to support the education of children with disabilities. Typically funding is given towards extra tuition, computers, specialist educational equipment and educational software.

Applications

Apply in writing to the correspondent, including a summary of the child's circumstances and how Able Kidz could help them, an outline of the costs involved and a supporting letter from a teacher or educational professional.

Financial information

Year end	17/04/2020
Income	£20,200
Total expenditure	£24,700

Further financial information

Full accounts were not available to view on the Charity Commission's website due to the charity's low income. We have therefore estimated the grant total based on the charity's total expenditure.

Other information

Support is also given to schools.

The Adamson Trust

 £58,000 (2019/20)

Correspondent: The Administrator, PO Box 7227, Pitlochry, Perthshire PH16 9AL (email: info@theadamsontrust.co.uk)

www.theadamsontrust.co.uk

OSCR number: SC016517

Eligibility

Children aged between 3 and 17 who have a physical, mental or emotional disability. Preference is given to those locally resident in Scotland.

Types of grant

Grants are available for holidays or respite breaks.

Applications

Application forms can be downloaded from the trust's website. Note that applications require supporting evidence such as a letter from a GP, hospital or other health professional.

Financial information

Year end	31/03/2020
Income	£769,400
Total expenditure	£104,300

Other information

The trust also makes grants to groups and organisations.

The Amber Trust

 £143,500 (2020/21)

Correspondent: The Trustees, 64A Princes Way, London SW19 6JF (tel: 0300 323 9964; email: contact@ ambertrust.org or use the contact form on the website)

www.ambertrust.org

CC number: 1050503

Eligibility

Children and young people under the age of 18 who are blind or partially sighted and have a talent and/or passion for music.

Types of grant

Amber Music Awards are given for instrumental and singing lessons, music sessions, the purchase of musical instruments or specialist music technology, travel and accommodation to access opportunities for making music and attendance at concerts.

Exclusions

The trust is unable to make retrospective grants.

Applications

Application forms can be downloaded from the trust's website. Applications for children must be made by a parent/ guardian/carer. Young people aged 16 or over may submit an application in their own right.

Financial information

Year end	31/03/2021
Income	£399,900
Total expenditure	£266,700

Other information

The trust provides additional support through three programmes: Little Amber (ages 0–5); AmberPlus (ages 5–18) and With Music in Mind (those with neurodegenerative conditions). The programmes offer a range of resources for music-making, including sound files, video files and activity cards. The service is freely available to all families across the UK and overseas.

The Isabel Baker Foundation

 £23,200 (2019/20)

Correspondent: The Trustees, 133 Barrack Road, Christchurch, Dorset BH23 2AW (email: hello@tibf.co.uk)

https://www. theisabelbakerfoundation.co.uk

CC number: 1166529

Eligibility

The families of children with cancer.

Types of grant

Grants are available to help with essential household items, food, dry suits and gifts for children to keep them entertained during isolation.

Applications

Applications can be made via the charity's website.

Financial information

Year end	31/03/2020
Income	£38,700
Total expenditure	£57,200

Be More Bailey Charitable Foundation

 £12,300 (2019/20)

Correspondent: The Trustees, Beacon Court, Plumtree Farm Industrial Estate, Plumtree Road, Bircotes, Doncaster DN11 8EW (email: info@ bmbfoundation.co.uk)

bmbfoundation.co.uk

CC number: 1173355

Eligibility

Children and young people with disabilities.

Types of grant

Grants are available for specialist equipment to enable children with disabilities to participate in amateur sport and recreation.

Applications

Application forms are available to download from the charity's website.

Financial information

Year end	30/04/2020
Income	£22,600
Total expenditure	£19,400

Further financial information

Full accounts were not available to view on the Charity Commission's website due to the foundation's low income. We have therefore estimated the grant total based on the foundation's total expenditure.

The Campbell Burns Metabolic Trust

 £12,300 (2019/20)

Correspondent: The Trustees, 3 Merganser Way, Coalville, Leicestershire LE67 4QA (tel: 01530 482154; email: contact@campbellstrust. co.uk)

www.campbellstrust.co.uk

CC number: 1148667

Eligibility

Families of children, aged ten and under, who have been diagnosed with a metabolic disorder.

Types of grant

The trust has four grant schemes:
- **Essentials** – grants of up £100 to assist families with the financial costs of day-to-day life, such as utility bills, Council Tax or travel to hospital.
- **Experience** – grants to assist families with the cost of a day trip or social experience. Note, at the time of writing (August 2020) this programme had been temporarily suspended due to the COVID-19 pandemic.
- **Food preparation** – grants of up to £100 to help families purchase kitchen equipment to assist them in their care of a child with special dietary needs.
- **Emergency** – grants to families to help meet the financial cost of unexpected emergency situations not covered by the other grant schemes.

Applications

Application forms and guidance notes for each grant scheme can be downloaded from the trust's website. Completed forms should be submitted by post.

Financial information

Year end	30/04/2020
Income	£40,200
Total expenditure	£16,600

Further financial information

The trust awarded 124 general grants and 19 grants to support families in 2019/20.

Other information

The trust was established in the name of Campbell Burns, who was born in January 2012 and diagnosed with Leigh's disease in March 2012.

Caudwell Children

 £1,620,000 (2020)

Correspondent: The Trustees, Caudwell International Children's Centre, Innovation Way, Keele Science and Innovation Park, Newcastle-under-Lyme, Staffordshire ST5 5NT (tel: 0345 300 1348; email: applications@ caudwellchildren.com)

www.caudwellchildren.com

CC number: 1079770

Eligibility

People under 18 with a disability or serious illness who live in the UK. Support for sports equipment can be provided to people up to the age of 25.

Types of grant

The charity can provide 80% of the costs of the following equipment:

- Powered wheelchairs
- Buggies
- Car seats and harnesses
- Therapy tricycles
- Multi-sensory equipment
- Sports equipment

Applications

Applications for equipment can be made via the charity's website.

Financial information

Year end	31/12/2020
Income	£3,670,000
Total expenditure	£4,910,000

Other information

The charity provides family support services, equipment, treatment and therapies for children with disabilities and their families across the UK.

Cerebra for Brain Injured Children and Young People

 £176,000 (2020)

Correspondent: Christopher Jones, Chief Executive, Cerebra, The MacGregor Office Suite, Jolly Tar Lane, Carmarthen SA31 3LW (tel: 01267 244200; email: info@cerebra.org.uk)

www.cerebra.org.uk

CC number: 1089812

Eligibility

Children and young people aged 16 or under who have a neurodevelopmental disorder or condition. The condition may be of a physical nature, a learning disability or both. Examples of the types of conditions covered include: cerebral palsy, autistic spectrum disorders, developmental disorders, seizure disorders, ADHD, traumatic brain injuries, acquired brain injuries, Down's syndrome and other chromosomal/ genetic conditions, brain abnormalities or degenerative conditions, hydrocephalus, and conditions caused in utero. This list is by no means exhaustive and applicants who are unsure as to whether they fit the criteria should contact Cerebra directly.

Types of grant

One-off grants of up to a maximum of 80% of the total cost or of £400 (whichever is the lowest amount) are given towards equipment or resources that would improve quality of life and which are not available from statutory agencies like social services or the NHS. Examples of grants made include those towards touchscreen computers, specialist car seats, power wheelchairs, therapies, trampolines, sensory toys, and tricycles and quadricycles. For anything where there is a medical need, the charity encourages potential applicants to check to see if it can help.

Exclusions

Grants are not given for:

- Driving lessons
- Motorised vehicles such as quad bikes and motorbikes
- Anything that could be considered a home improvement such as paint for decorating, conservatories, carpet or other flooring
- Garden landscaping
- Household items such as vacuum cleaners, washing machines, wardrobes, standard beds (special beds may be considered)
- Vehicle purchase or maintenance
- Assessments
- General clothing
- Treatment centres outside the UK
- Lycra suits
- Holidays
- Educational items such as home tutors, standard teaching materials or the Son-Rise program.

Applications

Application forms and guidance notes can be downloaded from the Cerebra website.

Financial information

Year end	31/12/2020
Income	£2,920,000
Total expenditure	£2,400,000

Other information

The charity also provides other support services such as telephone counselling, parental advice and a wills and trust voucher scheme.

Childhood Eye Cancer Trust

 £8,000 (2019/20)

Correspondent: CHECT Team, The Royal London Hospital, Whitechapel Road, London E1 1FR (tel: 020 7377 5578; email: info@chect.org.uk)

https://chect.org.uk

CC number: 327493

Eligibility

Individuals and families in need due to their child's diagnosis, treatment or screening for retinoblastoma. Applicants must be UK members of the Childhood Eye Cancer Trust and/or receiving treatment under the NHS in one of the UK retinoblastoma centres at the Royal London Hospital or Birmingham Children's Hospital.

Types of grant

Grants of up to £200 per year are given towards the costs associated with retinoblastoma diagnosis, treatment or screening, such as hospital visits, or to enable access to other services provided by the charity such as regional meet-ups.

Exclusions

Grants will not be given towards travel to appointments where this cost is already being met by the NHS.

Applications

Application forms can be downloaded from the trust's website or obtained from a Childhood Eye Cancer Trust (CHECT) support worker. The trust asks that funding is first sought from other organisations as grants availability is limited. Details of other sources of funding can be found on the website.

Financial information

Year end	31/03/2020
Income	£558,600
Total expenditure	£478,700

Further financial information

In 2019/20, 40 support grants were awarded to families totalling £8,000.

Other information

The trust offers lifelong support to anyone who has been affected by retinoblastoma. The trust also provides support workers and organises events intended to bring together families and individuals. The trust also funds clinical, psycho-social and basic science research into retinoblastoma.

Children Today Charitable Trust

 £53,100 (2019/20)

Correspondent: The Trustees, 17B Telford Court, Chester Gates Business Park, Dunkirk Estate, Ellesmere Port, Cheshire CH1 6LT (tel: 01244 335622; email: info@childrentoday.org.uk)

https://www.childrentoday.org.uk

CC number: 1137436

Eligibility

Children and young people under 25 who have a disability.

Types of grant

Grants for specialist equipment such as electric wheelchairs, walking aids, adapted trikes, lifting aids and sensory equipment.

Exclusions

Grants are not available for communication equipment (including iPads and laptops), outdoor play equipment (unless it is specially adapted), adaptations (home, garden or care) or holidays or respite care.

Applications

See the charity's website for full details on how to apply. The charity strongly recommends that potential applicants call in the first instance so that it can explain the application process in detail.

Financial information

Year end	31/03/2020
Income	£308,500
Total expenditure	£338,000

Children's Hope Foundation

 £71,900 (2019/20)

Correspondent: The Trustees, 15 Palmer Place, London N7 8DH (tel: 020 7700 6855; email: info@ childrenshopefoundation.org.uk)

www.childrenshopefoundation.org.uk

CC number: 1060409

Eligibility

Children and young people up to the age of 25 who are affected by illness, disability or poverty.

Types of grant

Grants for medical equipment or treatment which may help in the management of a condition or disability. Grants are also provided for equipment such as computers for educational support.

Applications

Application forms and guidance for applicants can be found on the foundation's website.

Financial information

Year end	31/03/2020
Income	£225,800
Total expenditure	£221,300

Chips Charity

 £332,700 (2019/20)

Correspondent: The Trustees, 99 Camlet Way, Barnet EN4 0NL (email: chipscharity@aol.com)

https://www.chipscharity.org

CC number: 1173001

Eligibility

Children with disabilities who require a wheelchair to assist with mobility.

Types of grant

Grants are provided to purchase wheelchairs. The charity can consider applications that have been unsuccessful with local authorities, the NHS or wheelchair services.

Exclusions

The charity is unable to fund football or powerball wheelchairs.

Applications

Preliminary application forms can be completed on the charity's website.

Financial information

Year end	30/05/2020
Income	£374,300
Total expenditure	£375,900

CLIC Sargent (Young Lives vs Cancer)

 £1,110,000 (2019/20)

Correspondent: Grants Team, 4th Floor, Whitefriars, Lewins Mead, Bristol BS1 2NT (tel: 0300 303 5220; email: getsupport@younglivesvscancer.org.uk)

https://www.younglivesvscancer.org.uk

CC number: 1107328/SC039857

Eligibility

Children and young people in the UK who have received a confirmed cancer or bone marrow failure disorder diagnosis from an NHS cancer or haematology service before their 25th birthday. Individuals must qualify for free NHS cancer treatment in the UK.

Types of grant

Grants are given to relieve the financial pressure faced following a diagnosis.

Examples of what can be funded include hospital travel costs, extra food costs, childcare for siblings, accommodation near the hospital, household bills, private tuition to reduce the impact on education and so on.

Exclusions

The charity does not award grants for the costs of treatment, medical equipment, therapies or school fees.

Applications

Application forms can be completed online and should be supported by the patient's doctor or nurse.

Financial information

Year end	31/03/2020
Income	£31,420,000
Total expenditure	£26,790,000

Other information

The charity also provides advice and support online and in-person to families affected by cancer.

Colchester Children's Charity Appeal

 £39,500 (2019/20)

Correspondent: The Trustees, 11 Churchill Way, Colchester CO2 8ST (tel: 01206 860384)

CC number: 800485

Eligibility

Children in the Colchester area who have disabilities, illnesses or terminal illness.

Types of grant

Grants are given according to need.

Applications

Apply in writing to the correspondent.

Financial information

Year end	05/04/2020
Income	£96,100
Total expenditure	£91,400

Other information

The charity also provides (or assists in providing) facilities and accommodation in hospices for children with ill health and their families.

Henry Dancer Days

£19,300 (2019/20)

Correspondent: The Trustees, Black Horse Inn, Cornsay, Durham, County Durham DH7 9EL (tel: 07947 668993; email: henrydancerdays@aol.com)

henrydancerdays.co.uk

CC number: 1147982

Eligibility

Children and young people undergoing treatment for bone cancer.

Types of grant

Patients and families can use the grant in whichever way they feel is most appropriate and of most benefit to them. The charity's website states that grants have previously been used for:

- Transport to hospital
- Winter heating bills
- Days out as a treat for the patient and family
- Exercise bikes to aid physiotherapy
- Technology to enable patients to contact their friends when in hospital or when their immune system is compromised

Applications

Applications for grants should be made through a healthcare professional who completes the application form on the family's behalf. This may be a CLIC Sargent social worker, a Macmillan nurse, a Marie Curie nurse, or an oncology consultant.

Financial information

Year end	30/06/2020
Income	£136,200
Total expenditure	£137,100

Evie's Gift CIO

 £66,100 (2019/20)

Correspondent: The Trustees, 2 Farmhouse Court, Melksham SN12 6FG (email: Info@eviesgift.org.uk)

https://www.eviesgift.org.uk

CC number: 1177460

Eligibility

Any parent or guardian whose child has been admitted to hospital with a life-threatening or life-limiting condition.

Types of grant

Grants to cover the cost of accommodation near to the hospital where the child is being treated. Grants are also provided for associated costs such as food, travel, parking and mobile phone top-ups.

Applications

Apply online via the charity's website.

Financial information

Year end	31/03/2020
Income	£63,000
Total expenditure	£70,400

Family Fund Trust

£48,160,000 (2020/21)

Correspondent: The Trustees, Unit 4, Alpha Court, Monks Cross Drive, Huntington, York, North Yorkshire

YO32 9WN (tel: 01904 550055; email: info@familyfund.org.uk)

 www.familyfund.org.uk

CC number: 1053866/SC040810

Eligibility

Families who are caring for a child or young person aged 17 or under who has a disability or serious illness. Eligible families must show evidence of their entitlement to one of the following: Universal Credit, Child Tax Credit, Working Tax Credit, income-based Jobseeker's Allowance, income-related Employment Support Allowance, Income Support, Housing Benefit or Pension Credit. At the time of writing (November 2021) the trust was also running a grant programme for people aged 18–24 with disabilities or serious illnesses. Check the trust's website for the latest information.

Types of grant

Grants are given for a range of purposes related to the child's care needs. Examples of what can be funded include sensory toys, kitchen appliances, family breaks, bedding, furniture, outdoor play equipment, games consoles, computers and tablets, clothing, white goods and so on. Further information on the kind of things the trust will support can be found on its website.

Applications

Applications can be made via the trust's website. Alternatively, applicants can request to receive an application pack through the post.

Financial information

Year end	31/03/2021
Income	£55,410,000
Total expenditure	£52,970,000

Further financial information

During the financial year, the trust provided 124,148 grants to families across the UK. Grants were distributed as follows:

Computers	£13.1 million
Recreation/home entertainment	£9.48 million
Holidays and outings	£8.99 million
White goods	£5.1 million
Furniture	£3.1 million
Other	£2.89 million
Jet bath	£2.83 million
Clothing and bedding	£2.1 million
Hospital visiting costs	£605,000

Other information

The trust is funded entirely by the government administrations of England, Northern Ireland, Scotland and Wales. The trust also administers Take a Break Scotland on behalf of the Scottish Government – see the entry for this charity on page 68.

Fletcher's Fund

 £12,400 (2019/20)

Correspondent: The Trustees, Unit 4, Westwood Nurseries, Orton Grange, Carlisle CA5 6LB (tel: 07432 102671; email: info@fletchersfund.org.uk)

https://www.fletchersfund.org.uk

CC number: 1172985

Eligibility

Children and young people under the age of 18 who are receiving treatment for cancer in England and Wales. Applicants should be receiving treatment at the time of application or have received treatment within the past six months.

Types of grant

Cash grants to be used to allow families to spend quality time together. This could include days out, holidays, play equipment, toys, arts and crafts equipment or sensory equipment.

Exclusions

Grants cannot be used for bills, travel and other expenses.

Applications

Application forms can be downloaded from the fund's website. Applications must be supported by a Macmillan Nurse, CLIC Sargent worker or someone else involved in the child's medical care.

Financial information

Year end	30/04/2020
Income	£17,500
Total expenditure	£28,200

Further financial information

Grants were awarded to 124 individuals. In addition, the fund donated 800 arts and crafts bags.

Forbes Foundation

 £5,800 (2019/20)

Correspondent: The Trustees, Ground Floor, Oak House, 28 Sceptre Way, Walton Summit, Preston PR5 6AW (tel: 0333 207 1130; email: oliver.burton@forbessolicitors.co.uk)

https://www.forbesfoundation.org.uk

CC number: 1181535

Eligibility

Children and their families who are in need by reason of ill health, disability and/or financial hardship within England and Wales but predominantly in the north of England.

Types of grant

Grants can be given for a wide range of purposes including treatment costs.

Applications

Application forms can be requested using the contact form on the foundation's website.

Financial information

Year end	30/06/2020
Income	£17,000
Total expenditure	£6,400

Further financial information

Full accounts were not available to view on the Charity Commission's website due to the foundation's low income. We have therefore estimated the grant total based on the foundation's total expenditure.

The Rob George Foundation

 £105,500 (2019/20)

Correspondent: The Trustees, 4 Henry Villa Close, Colchester, Essex CO4 5XP (tel: 07831 504298; email: enquiries@therobgeorgefoundation.co.uk)

www.therobgeorgefoundation.co.uk

CC number: 1156026

Eligibility

The trust supports young people with life-threatening or terminal illnesses and young people who demonstrate exceptional commitment and/or ability in sport or the performing arts and who are from a low-income family.

Types of grant

Grants of up to £2,000.

Applications

Applications can be made via the foundation's website.

Financial information

Year end	31/03/2020
Income	£134,000
Total expenditure	£152,400

Further financial information

In 2019/20, 280 grants were awarded.

Get Kids Going

 £194,400 (2019/20)

Correspondent: The Trustees, Flat 4, Chandlery House, 40 Gowers Walk, London E1 8BH (tel: 020 7481 8110; email: info@getkidsgoing.com)

www.getkidsgoing.com

CC number: 1063471

Eligibility

Children and young people up to the age of 26 who have a disability and wish to participate in sport.

Types of grant

One-off grants, ranging from £500 to £15,000, are available for wheelchairs and sports equipment, repairs to sports equipment, travel to training and competitions, competition fees and sports physiotherapy.

Applications

Contact the charity for further information.

Financial information

Year end	30/06/2020
Income	£1,120,000
Total expenditure	£816,700

The Guide Dogs for the Blind Association

Correspondent: Grants Team, Hillfields, Reading Road, Burghfield Common, Reading, Berkshire RG7 3YG (tel: 0800 781 1444; email: information@guidedogs.org.uk or grants@guidedogs.org.uk)

 https://www.guidedogs.org.uk/getting-support

CC number: 209617

Eligibility

Children and young people aged up to 18 years who are (or are eligible to be) registered blind or partially sighted and live in the UK.

Types of grant

Grants are made for assistive technology such as laptops, tablets, computers, portable magnifiers, speech software, Braille devices and multi-sensory items, such as bubble tubes and dark dens.

At the time of writing (October 2021) the charity had launched a 'Tech for All' scheme, providing free Apple iPads or iPhones (depending on the child's age) for use outside school.

Applications

Application forms can be downloaded from the charity's website. Full eligibility criteria can also be found on the website.

Financial information

Year end	31/12/2020
Income	£125,900,000
Total expenditure	£111,900,000

Further financial information

According to the 2020 accounts, direct costs relating to the provision of children's services totalled £4.2 million. We were unable to determine the proportion of grants awarded to children and young people.

Other information

The charity offers a range of support, advice and services for children and young people with visual impairments and their families.

The Ben Hardwick Fund

 £9,800 (2019/20)

Correspondent: The Trustees, 12 Nassau Road, Barnes, London SW13 9QE (tel: 020 8741 8499)

CC number: 1062554

Eligibility

Children with primary liver disease, and their families, who are in need.

Types of grant

One-off and recurrent grants to help with costs which are the direct result of the child's illness, such as hospital travel costs, in-hospital expenses, telephone bills and childminding costs for other children left at home.

Applications

Applications should be submitted in writing via a hospital social worker or other welfare professional. Applications are considered at any time.

Financial information

Year end	31/05/2020
Income	£1,300
Total expenditure	£21,800

Further financial information

Full accounts were not available to view on the Charity Commission's website due to the fund's low income. We have therefore estimated the fund's grant total based on its total expenditure.

The Douglas Hay Trust

£13,300 (2019/20)

Correspondent: The Trustees, Midlothian Innovation Centre, Pentlandfield, Roslin, Midlothian EH25 9RE

www.douglashay.org.uk

OSCR number: SC014450

Eligibility

Children aged under 18 who have physical disabilities and live in Scotland.

Types of grant

One-off grants towards shoes, clothes, bedding, home improvements, holidays, computers, equipment and education.

Applications

Apply using a form available from the trust's website or by contacting the correspondent. The form should be submitted through a social worker, medical practitioner or other welfare agency. Applications are considered monthly.

Financial information

Year end	31/10/2020
Income	£34,300
Total expenditure	£30,200

Holibobs

 £2,500 (2019/20)

Correspondent: The Trustees, 46 Heol Cae-Rhys, Rhiwbina, Cardiff CF14 6AP (tel: 07496 717281; email: info@ holibobscharity.org.uk)

🌐 https://www.holibobscharity.org.uk

CC number: 1179844

Eligibility

Children and young adults (up to the age of 19) who have a cancer or leukaemia diagnosis and live in Wales.

Types of grant

Grants are provided to cover the cost of a UK holiday.

Applications

Contact the charity via email. Applicants should be made by a health professional or social worker. All applications for a holiday must be accompanied by a letter from a consultant or social worker specifying the child's medical condition.

Financial information

Year end	30/06/2020
Income	£100,500
Total expenditure	£15,600

Just Helping Children

 £1,740,000 (2019/20)

Correspondent: The Trustees, 85 Prince of Wales Road, Norwich, Norfolk NR1 1DG (tel: 0800 169 1601; email: office@just4children.org)

🌐 https://just4children.org

CC number: 1164473

Eligibility

Sick children up to the age of 25 living in the UK and Ireland. A full list of eligible conditions is available on the charity's website.

Types of grant

Grants for medical treatment, therapies, living environments, equipment and holidays.

Applications

Contact the charity for further information.

Financial information

Year end	30/09/2020
Income	£1,950,000
Total expenditure	£1,960,000

Kayleigh's Wee Stars

 £70,400 (2019/20)

Correspondent: The Trustees, Unit 4, North Meadows, Oldmeldrum, Aberdeenshire AB51 0GQ (tel: 01651 872747; email: info@kayleighsweestars. co.uk)

🌐 www.kayleighsweestars.co.uk

OSCR number: SC050136

Eligibility

Families in Scotland who have a child with a terminal illness where life expectancy is likely to be less than two years.

Types of grant

One-off grants for special holidays, travel expenses, memory keepsakes, financial pressures, specialised equipment or building modifications.

Applications

The charity's website states:

> Applications are submitted by the health professional on behalf of the family with details of the support required, and subject to approval, are typically turned round in 48 hours to ensure families receive the help at the time they need it most.

Financial information

Year end	08/05/2020
Income	£117,700
Total expenditure	£182,300

Further financial information

The charity has recently re-registered with the OSCR. The financial information relates to the previous charity (OSCR no. SC043320).

Kidney Kids Scotland Charitable Trust

 £21,500 (2019/20)

Correspondent: Grants Administrator, Merrow House, Church Street, Stenhousemuir, Stenhousemuir, Stirlingshire FK5 4BU (tel: 01324 555843; email: office@kidneykids.org.uk)

🌐 www.kidneykids.org.uk

OSCR number: SC030284

Eligibility

Children in Scotland who have renal/urological illnesses and their families who are in need.

Types of grant

Small grants to help families deal with the financial impact of having a sick child (e.g. to help with travel expenses to hospital or to support families who have taken time off from their job to be with their child).

Applications

In the first instance, contact the charity's office. Applications are usually made by a medical professional or social worker.

Financial information

Year end	30/06/2020
Income	£208,700
Total expenditure	£237,800

LATCH Welsh Children's Cancer Charity

 £317,800 (2020)

Correspondent: The Trustees, Children's Hospital for Wales, Heath Park, Cardiff CF14 4XW (tel: 029 2074 8859; email: info@latchwales.org)

🌐 www.latchwales.org

CC number: 1100949

Eligibility

Children who have cancer and leukaemia (including tumours) and have been referred to the Paediatric Oncology Unit at The Children's Hospital for Wales.

Types of grant

One-off and recurrent grants for children and their families who are in need of financial assistance towards, for example, travel costs to and from hospital, subsistence grants for daily expenses and specialist equipment.

Applications

Applications should be made through LATCH social workers, who can submit applications for consideration by the charity.

Financial information

Year end	31/12/2020
Income	£574,100
Total expenditure	£645,100

Other information

Children and their families can also be provided on-site accommodation, advocacy and information services and emotional support.

Lifeline 4 Kids (Handicapped Children's Aid Committee)

 £41,700 (2020)

Correspondent: The Trustees, 215 West End Lane, West Hampstead, London NW6 1XJ (tel: 020 7794 1661 or 020 8459 8826; email: appeals@lifeline4kids. org)

 www.lifeline4kids.org

CC number: 200050

Eligibility

Children and young people under 18 with disabilities.

Types of grant

The charity will purchase specific requested items or equipment on behalf of the individual, for example electric wheelchairs, mobility aids, specialised computers and sensory toys. The charity will also consider emergency appeals.

Exclusions

The charity does not award cash grants. According to its website, the charity will not fund:

- Therapy, treatment or assessment costs
- Building, home improvement or garden works
- Carpets
- Outside garden equipment such as trampolines
- Furniture (unless specialised)
- Ovens/Cookers
- Refrigerators (unless for medical needs)
- Washing Machines (unless for medical needs, i.e. incontinence)
- Clothing
- Shoes (unless specialist)
- Child care costs
- Vehicles
- Transport Costs
- Tuition/School Lessons or Fees
- Driving Lessons
- Recreational activities
- Holidays

Applications

Initially, potential applicants should contact the charity by email providing details on specific requirements, costs and brief factual information of the child as well as contact information.

The charity states on its website that:

Each request will be acknowledged and provided it meets our criteria, an application form will be sent by post or email. The form contains comprehensive questions relating to the child/children's medical condition and requires backup information from health professionals together with a financial statement of the applicant/organisation.

Note that initial telephone calls from applicants are not welcome as the charity does not have the staff to deal with them.

Financial information

Year end	31/12/2020
Income	£18,200
Total expenditure	£85,900

Further financial information

Full accounts were not available to view on the Charity Commission's website due to the charity's low income. We have therefore estimated the charity's grant total based on its total expenditure.

Other information

The charity also supports schools, children's hospices, respite care homes and support centres throughout the UK.

Logans Fund

 £48,100 (2019/20)

Correspondent: The Trustees, Sandyhillock, Elchies, Aberlour, Morayshire AB38 9SP (email: info@ logansfund.org)

 logansfund.org

OSCR number: SC040619

Eligibility

Children who have been affected by cancer, and their families.

Types of grant

The charity's website explains: 'Our aim is to provide a focus away from hospital and treatment with something that will bring a smile or just meet a practical need whether it be today, tomorrow or a year from now.'

Applications

Applications can be made using the form on the charity's website.

Financial information

Year end	28/02/2020
Income	£82,900
Total expenditure	£61,500

Other information

Families can also apply to spend some time together at the charity's Logan's Sunny Days caravan at Lossiemouth Bay Caravan Park. Booking requests can be made on the charity's website.

Molly Olly's Wishes

 £159,200 (2019/20)

Correspondent: Rachel Ollerenshaw, Trustee, 1 Blackwell Lane, Hatton Park, Warwick, Warwickshire CV35 7SU (tel: 01926 408480; email: rachel@ mollyolly.co.uk)

 mollyollyshop.wpengine.com

CC number: 1145312

Eligibility

Children aged between 0 and 18 who are living with a life-threatening or terminal illness, and their families.

Types of grant

The charity provides 'wishes' to individual children. These can be used for a range of purposes including for equipment to assist with day-to-day life, alternative therapy, or to attend a special occasion that a child would otherwise be isolated from due to the restrictions of their illness.

Applications

Application forms can be downloaded from the charity's website and must be completed by the child's parent or legal guardian. Applications must be supported by a healthcare professional who has been involved with the child's care.

Financial information

Year end	30/09/2020
Income	£459,300
Total expenditure	£335,600

Other information

The charity provides 'Olly the Brave' packs which include a toy lion and a book to children who require a central or a Hickman line (for nutrition, medication or bloods), either through hospitals or to individuals directly. Grants are also given to organisations.

Nicola's Fund

 £30,900 (2019/20)

Correspondent: The Trustees, The Stables, Old Meadow Court, Gresford Road, Llay, Wrexham, Clwyd LL12 0NE (tel: 01978 856120; email: info@ nicolasfund.co.uk)

 www.nicolasfund.co.uk

CC number: 1113095

Eligibility

Families of children with cancer or other long-term or terminal illnesses.

Types of grant

Grants are awarded according to need and are typically given for respite breaks in the UK.

Applications

Apply in writing to the correspondent.

Financial information

Year end	31/03/2020
Income	£65,000
Total expenditure	£51,300

Reach Charity Ltd

 £7,500 (2019/20)

Correspondent: The Trustees, c/o Tavistock Enterprise Hub, Pearl Assurance House, 2 Brook Street, Tavistock, Devon PL19 0BN (tel: 0845 130 6225 or 020 3478 0100; email: reach@reach.org.uk)

https://reach.org.uk/apply-reach-bursary

CC number: 1134544

Eligibility

Children and young people under the age of 25 who have upper limb differences and who have been a member of Reach for at least one year.

Types of grant

Grants of up to £2,000 are available. Previous grants have been given for musical instruments, car adaptations, travel, accommodation and equipment associated with sport, as well as school equipment, such as personal computers or tablets.

Applications

Application forms can be downloaded from the charity's website. The charity aims to give a decision within four weeks. Applications must include references from an appropriate third party such as an occupational therapist, GP or social services adviser.

Financial information

Year end	29/02/2020
Income	£242,600
Total expenditure	£270,200

Other information

The charity also runs events, conferences and offers support for people with upper limb differences and their families.

REACT (Rapid Effective Assistance for Children with Potentially Terminal Illnesses)

 £394,400 (2019/20)

Correspondent: The Trustees, St Luke's House, 270 Sandycombe Road, Kew, Surrey TW9 3NP (tel: 020 8940 2575; email: react@reactcharity.org)

www.reactcharity.org

CC number: 802440

Eligibility

Families caring for a child with an illness that is life-threatening or life-limiting.

Types of grant

Grants are available for a range of purposes including:

- Specialist equipment – mobility aids, medical equipment, furniture, educational or developmental equipment
- Homecare equipment – flooring, kitchen appliances, furniture, clothing and bedding
- Travel and subsistence expenses
- Respite breaks
- End-of-life support – funeral expenses and memorial headstones

Exclusions

Support cannot be given towards trips overseas, structural building works, private treatment or the purchase of a vehicle.

Applications

Application forms are available to download from the charity's website or can be requested from the correspondent.

Financial information

Year end	31/03/2020
Income	£999,300
Total expenditure	£784,300

Other information

The charity has a number of mobile homes located across the UK which families can apply to stay at for one week.

Sophie's Moonbeams Trust

 £1,000 (2019/20)

Correspondent: The Trustees, 5 Upper Heath Road, St Albans AL1 4DN (tel: 07849 358743; email: admin@sophiesmoonbeams.uk)

https://www.sophiesmoonbeams.uk

CC number: 1182086

Eligibility

Children and young people up to the age of 20 who are adopted or have special needs.

Types of grant

Grants can be used for conventional and alternative therapies. Due to the charity's size, it is unlikely the full costs of the treatment will be covered. The charity works with service providers and the grant will be paid to them, to be used by the individual within three months. Examples of therapies funded include:

- Art therapy
- Music therapy
- Cranial osteopathy
- Audio integration training
- Makaton sign language training
- TEACCH training for autism

- Adoption UK training
- Expert assessments for Education, Health and Care (EHC) plans (not including professional diagnosis of a condition)

The charity's website states: 'This list is not exhaustive and we will consider requests for other help along similar lines. However, evidence and need are at the forefront of our funding decisions.'

Exclusions

Grants for equipment and requests for donations to crowdfunding appeals will not be considered.

Applications

Application forms are available to fill in online on the charity's website. Applications are assessed twice a year, at the end of March and at the end of August. If an application is shortlisted, additional documentation will need to be provided.

Financial information

Year end	30/09/2020
Income	£1,300
Total expenditure	£1,400

Further financial information

Full accounts were not available to view on the Charity Commission's website due to the trust's low income. We have therefore estimated the grant total based on the trust's total expenditure.

Strongbones Children's Charitable Trust

 £208,600 (2020/21)

Correspondent: The Trustees, Unit B9 Romford Seedbed Centre, Davidson Way, Romford, Essex RM7 0AZ (tel: 01708 750599; email: trustees@strongbones.org.uk)

www.strongbones.org.uk

CC number: 1086173

Eligibility

Young people under the age of 21 with scoliosis, brittle bone disease, bone cancer, arthritis or any other bone condition.

Types of grant

Grants are available for disability equipment, manual wheelchairs, smart home technology, supportive seating and trikes. Up to a maximum of 70% of the cost of equipment will be provided.

Exclusions

According to the trust's website, grants are not given for the following:

- Spas/baths
- Driving lessons
- Debts/bills
- Disabled Facilities Grant top-ups

- Household appliances and furniture
- Holidays
- Clothing
- Days out (except group trips)
- Electric wheelchairs
- iPads
- Game consoles
- Garden and bedroom makeovers.

Applications

Call or email the charity to request an application form.

Financial information

Year end	28/02/2021
Income	£381,400
Total expenditure	£373,400

Sunny Days Children's Fund

 £24,000 (2019/20)

Correspondent: The Trustees (for the attention of Margaret), 4 Cressing Road, Braintree, Essex CM7 3PP (tel: 01376 528376; email: trustees@sunnydaysfund.org.uk)

www.sunnydaysfund.org.uk

CC number: 1114784

Eligibility

Children under the age of 18 who have a medical condition or disability and their families. The fund will support children with a wide range of conditions.

Types of grant

Small grants are given for a wide range of purposes including medical equipment, white goods, days out, hospital travel expenses, sensory equipment, IT equipment and clothing. Previous examples include house adaptations, a treadmill, a mobility vehicle, specialised furniture, a trampoline, lightweight laptops and so on.

Exclusions

The fund will not consider grants for iPads, mobile phones or holidays (other than those taken at its own holiday homes).

Applications

To apply for a grant, contact the charity via email at margaret@sunnydaysfund.org.uk or telephone and ask for Margaret. Applications can be made by the individual directly or through a third party such as a hospital or social worker. The trustees aim to notify applicants of the outcome within six weeks.

Financial information

Year end	30/06/2020
Income	£334,600
Total expenditure	£316,600

Other information

The charity also manages two holiday homes for families in need of crisis breaks and offers free week-long breaks to families that meet the criteria. The charity supports the Great Ormond Street Hospital Agency Care Programme which allows families of children who are undergoing home dialysis to take a break.

Take a Break Scotland

 £765,000 (2020/21)

Correspondent: Take a Break Team, Unit 4, Alpha Court, Monks Cross Drive, Huntington, York, North Yorkshire YO32 9WN (tel: 01904 571093; email: info@takeabreakscotland.org.uk)

https://takeabreakscotland.org.uk

CC number: 1053866/SC040810

Eligibility

Parents or carers of children and young people (aged between 0 and 20) who are seriously ill or have a disability. Applicants must have lived in Scotland continuously for six months or longer. Young people aged between 16 and 20 may apply in their own right.

Types of grant

Grants are given for short breaks, leisure activities, outings, sports equipment and more. Examples of what can be funded include entrance costs to theme parks and zoos, travel costs, camping equipment, horse riding lessons and gym membership fees. The average grant is of £250 to £300.

Exclusions

Grants are not given towards:
- The purchase of capital items such as vehicles
- Direct replacement of statutory funding
- Items/breaks that have already been purchased
- Items that do not meet the principles of the grant fund

Applications

Applications can be made online through the charity's website. Details of supporting evidence that needs to be submitted with the application form and the closing dates for applications can be found online. Preference is given to people applying for the first time or those who did not receive a grant in the previous year.

Financial information

Year end	31/03/2021
Income	£878,000
Total expenditure	£765,000

Further financial information

During the financial year, grants were awarded to 2,660 individuals.

Other information

The charity is administered by The Family Fund (Charity Commission No. 1053866) on behalf of the Scottish Government.

Variety, the Children's Charity

 £301,200 (2020)

Correspondent: Stanley Salter, Secretary, Variety Club House, 93 Bayham Street, London NW1 0AG (tel: 020 7428 8100; email: info@variety.org.uk)

www.variety.org.uk

CC number: 209259

Eligibility

Children (aged 18 and under) who have disabilities or are sick or disadvantaged. Applicants must be permanent residents in the UK.

Types of grant

Grants of between £100 and £6,000 can be made for medical, basic care, mobility aids or sensory play equipment. This could include monitoring equipment, feeding tubes or hoists, or specially adapted car seats.

Exclusions

The charity does not fund:
- Standard household equipment or furnishings
- Repayment of loans
- Garden adaptations
- Garden sheds or summerhouses
- The cost of a family/wheelchair adapted vehicle
- Computer hardware
- Maintenance or ongoing costs
- Travel costs
- Therapy sessions
- Reimbursement of funds already paid out
- Hire/rental costs or down payments
- Trikes/bikes or buggies
- Trips abroad or holiday costs
- Trampolines
- Medical treatment
- Education or tuition fees.

Applications

Download the relevant application form from the charity's website, where guidelines are also available.

Financial information

Year end	31/12/2020
Income	£3,670,000
Total expenditure	£3,820,000

Further financial information

Grants were awarded to 1,142 individuals during the year.

The Victoria Foundation

 £17,000 (2019/20)

Correspondent: Lorna Votier, Development Director, St David's House, 15 Worple Way, Richmond, Surrey TW10 6DG (tel: 020 8332 1788; email: enquiries@thevictoriafoundation. org.uk)

https://www.thevictoriafoundation. org.uk

CC number: 292841

Eligibility

Welfare
Children and young people who have a condition that affects mobility and are in need of financial assistance to enable them to purchase mobility aids. The foundation also supports people in need who require medical treatment that is not readily available on the NHS.

Education
UK medical students from disadvantaged backgrounds who are studying medicine at a UK university.

Types of grant

Welfare
Grants are given for a wide range of mobility aids including powered wheelchairs, buggies, specialist tricycles and lightweight wheelchairs.

Education
Support is given in the form of bursaries towards the cost of medical electives overseas. In addition, 'toolkit grants' are given towards books, equipment and medical instruments.

Applications
Application forms can be downloaded from the foundation's website and can be made directly by the individual or through a third party. Applications are reviewed each month.

Financial information

Year end	31/03/2020
Income	£18,700
Total expenditure	£21,000

Further financial information
Full accounts were not available to view on the Charity Commission's website due to the foundation's low income. We have therefore estimated the grant total based on the foundation's total expenditure.

John Watson's Trust

 £76,900 (2020)

Correspondent: Anna Bennett, Clerk and Treasurer, The Signet Library, Parliament Square, Edinburgh EH1 1RF (tel: 0131 220 3249; email: abennett@ wssociety.co.uk)

www.wssociety.co.uk/charities/jwt

OSCR number: SC014004

Eligibility
Children and young people under the age of 21 who have a physical/learning disability or are socially disadvantaged and live in Scotland. Preference is given to people living in or connected with Edinburgh or the Lothian region.

Types of grant
Grants are given towards special tuition, educational trips, laptops (especially for people with special educational needs), books, uniforms, bus passes and other expenses for further training and education. School boarding fees may be partially covered but usually in exceptional circumstances, where a personal situation makes boarding a necessary option.

Exclusions
Grants are not available for day school or university fees.

Applications
Application forms can be filled in online on the trust's website. For an application to be successful it must be supported by referees who can detail the child's situation, such as teachers, social workers or GPs. Applications must include details of the candidate's household income and specify the support required. Full details of the supporting information required can be found through the website. The grants committee meets six times each year and the application deadlines are available on the website. Applications for school trips to outdoor residential centres must be made by the school, not the individual.

Financial information

Year end	31/12/2020
Income	£145,100
Total expenditure	£187,300

Further financial information
Grants were awarded to 119 individuals in 2020 and ranged from £50 to £7,200.

Other information
The trust also awards grants to organisations and to schools for educational trips.

WellChild

 £129,200 (2020/21)

Correspondent: The Trustees, 16 Royal Crescent, Cheltenham GL50 3DA (tel: 01242 530007; email: info@ wellchild.org.uk)

https://www.wellchild.org.uk/get-support/helping-hands

CC number: 289600

Eligibility
Children under the age of 18 with a long-term serious illness or severe disability with complex care needs who would benefit from a garden or bedroom makeover.

Types of grant
Families can apply for a Helping Hands project grant, which will help them create safe, accessible and sensory gardens and bedroom spaces for children and young people with complex health needs.

Applications
At the time of writing (November 2021) Helping Hands grants were closed due to the COVID-19 pandemic. Anyone interested in the grants can complete an Expression of Interest form on the charity's website and receive notification of the scheme's reopening.

Financial information

Year end	31/03/2021
Income	£1,930,000
Total expenditure	£407,500

Other information
WellChild is a national charity that works with children and young people with exceptional health needs and helps them to be cared for at home instead of hospital, wherever possible, through a range of different projects.

Whizz-Kidz

 £1,130,000 (2020)

Correspondent: Children's Services, 2nd Floor, 30 Park Street, London SE1 9EQ (tel: 020 7233 6600; email: info@ whizz-kidz.org.uk (general enquiries) or kidzservices@whizz-kidz.org.uk)

www.whizz-kidz.org.uk

CC number: 802872

Eligibility
Parents/carers of a child with a physical disability. The charity's website states that the following should be considered before applying:
- Is your child under 18 years old? Applications must be submitted before your child's 18th birthday

▶ Does your child have a physical disability that permanently affects their mobility and participation?

▶ Have you approached your local NHS wheelchair service and found that the mobility equipment that your child needs is not available/provided?

Those that have received mobility equipment from Whizz-Kidz in the past may still apply as long as the young person still meets the above criteria and it has been two years since the last application.

Types of grant

Grants for a broad range of mobility equipment for children with a physical disability.

Applications

Applications can be made through the charity's website. Alternatively, application forms can also be downloaded and posted to the correspondent's address.

Financial information

Year end	31/12/2020
Income	£6,540,000
Total expenditure	£6,920,000

Other information

As well as providing mobility equipment, Whizz-Kidz runs a range of other services for young wheelchair users including skills training, clubs and work placements. See the charity's website for more details.

Disability

The 3H Fund
See entry on page 58

Equipment for Independent Living

 £30,200 (2020)

Correspondent: Janet Hillman, Secretary, Park Cottage, Donhead St Andrew, Shaftesbury, Dorset SP7 9DZ (tel: 01747 828789; email: equipmentforindependentliving@btinternet.com)

CC number: 228438

Eligibility

People with disabilities across the UK who are on a low income.

Types of grant

Grants are given towards mobility aids and equipment to assist with independence, for example, wheelchairs, adjustable beds and communication aids.

Exclusions

This charity does not assist children under the age of 16. Grants are not made for items the trustees believe is a legal responsibility of the NHS or other public bodies to provide.

Applications

Request an application form from the correspondent. Applications must be supported by a third party/appropriately qualified person who has assessed the condition and needs of the applicant and can confirm the suitability of the equipment requested. Applications must also include information on the individual's income and expenditure. The committee meets on a quarterly basis to consider grant applications.

Financial information

Year end	31/12/2020
Income	£22,500
Total expenditure	£30,200

Further financial information

Full accounts were not available to view on the Charity Commission's website due to the charity's low income. We have therefore estimated the grant total based on the charity's total expenditure.

Gardening with Disabilities Trust

£ £30,600 (2020)

Correspondent: The Trustees, PO Box 285, Tunbridge Wells, Kent TN2 9JD (tel: 01892 890867; email: info@gardeningwithdisabilitiestrust.org.uk)

🌐 https://www.gardeningwithdisabilitiestrust.org.uk

CC number: 255066

Eligibility

People with disabilities who wish to take up gardening as a hobby.

Types of grant

One-off grants of up to £1,000 for equipment and adaptations. Examples given on the trust's website include: raised beds, polytunnels, greenhouses, tools, small-scale garden adaptations, plants or shrubs and compost.

Exclusions

The trust's website states that it will not pay for: fencing, gates, seating, clearing, general or ongoing maintenance, turfing or tree removal. The trust has stated that it very rarely pays for decking.

Applications

Applications can be made online using a form on the trust's website. Applications require: a letter from a doctor or other healthcare professional indicating the

disability; two quotations from suppliers (for grants requesting modification to a garden); details about the project and costs, including delivery costs; and information on who will carry out the labour, which may include friends, family or voluntary organisations.

Financial information

Year end	31/12/2020
Income	£63,000
Total expenditure	£52,600

Further financial information

The trust made 92 grants during the year.

Motability

 £39,340,000 (2020/21)

Correspondent: Charitable Grants Team, Warwick House, Roydon Road, Harlow, Essex CM19 5PX (tel: 0800 500 3186)

🌐 www.motability.co.uk

CC number: 299745

Eligibility

People who receive one of the following benefits: the higher rate mobility component of Disability Living Allowance (HRMC DLA); the enhanced rate of the mobility component of Personal Independence Payment (ERMC PIP); War Pensioners' Mobility Supplement (WPMS); Armed Forces Independence Payment (AFIP).

Types of grant

The Motability Scheme helps people with disabilities by exchanging their mobility allowance to lease a car, scooter, powered wheelchair or wheelchair accessible vehicle. Additional support is provided through a range of charitable grants, details of which can be viewed on the Motability website.

Applications

Potential applicants should contact the Charitable Grants Team on 0800 500 3186.

Financial information

Year end	31/03/2021
Income	£10,190,000
Total expenditure	£61,960,000

Other information

The organisation works in conjunction with the Department for Work and Pensions.

Bruce Wake Charity

 £199,500 (2019/20)

Correspondent: Peter Hems, Trustee, Oakview House, Wakerley Road, Barrowden, Rutland, East Midlands LE15 8EP (tel: 0344 879 3349; email: info@brucewaketrust.co.uk)

 www.brucewaketrust.co.uk

CC number: 1018190

Eligibility

People with disabilities (predominantly wheelchair users) in the UK.

Types of grant

The trustees will consider grant applications related to the provision of leisure activities for people with disabilities, but particularly favour applications which meet one or all of the following criteria:

- The potential beneficiaries have a physical disability and use a wheelchair
- Improved access for wheelchair users is proposed
- A proposed sporting or leisure activity involves people with a disability who use a wheelchair

Applications

Applications should be made through the trust's website. Applications on behalf of individuals will only be accepted through a charitable organisation or equivalent recognised body. The trustees meet quarterly to consider applications.

Financial information

Year end	05/04/2020
Income	£197,000
Total expenditure	£910,000

Other information

The trust also makes grants to organisations.

WaveLength

See entry on page 38

Dennis Wise in the Community

 £51,200 (2019/20)

Correspondent: The Trustees, Stonegate Homes Ltd, Oak Green House, 250–256 High Street, Dorking, Surrey RH4 1QT (tel: 01306 884277; email: admin@dwcommunity.co.uk)

 https://dwcommunity.co.uk

CC number: 1157390

Eligibility

Children and adults with disabilities who require mobility equipment.

Types of grant

Grants are made in the form of specialist wheelchairs.

Applications

Requests for wheelchairs should be made by email.

Financial information

Year end	30/06/2020
Income	£137,300
Total expenditure	£100,100

Other information

The charity also donates minibuses to organisations, particularly schools, to help those with mobility needs and those living in areas where there are no adequate transport facilities.

Injuries

Mark Davies Injured Riders Fund

 £12,600 (2020)

Correspondent: Rosemary Lang, Administrator and Fund Co-ordinator, Lancrow Farmhouse, Penpillick Hill, Cornwall PL24 2SA (tel: 07710 788364; email: rosemary@mdirf.co.uk)

 www.mdirf.co.uk

CC number: 1022281

Eligibility

People injured in horse-related accidents and their carers.

Types of grant

One-off grants are awarded according to need. In the past grants have been given towards medical therapies, wheelchairs, specialised equipment and stable help.

Applications

Contact the correspondent via telephone or use the contact form on the fund's website.

Financial information

Year end	31/12/2020
Income	£34,600
Total expenditure	£55,400

Other information

The fund also provides medical, legal and financial advice.

The Matt Hampson Foundation

 £33,700 (2019/20)

Correspondent: The Trustees, Get Busy Living Centre, Twyford Road, Burrough-on-the-Hill, Melton Mowbray, Leicestershire LE14 2JR (tel: 01664 454155; email: info@hambo.co.uk)

 www.matthampsonfoundation.org

CC number: 1139823

Eligibility

Individuals who have been seriously injured through support.

Types of grant

One-off grants for equipment, assistive technology or everyday living expenses.

Applications

Apply in writing to the correspondent.

Financial information

Year end	31/03/2020
Income	£1,500,000
Total expenditure	£1,190,000

Further financial information

In 2019/20, grants were made to 17 individuals.

Other information

The foundation also provides advice, support, relief and treatment for anyone with a serious injury or disability primarily as the result of sport.

Headway – The Brain Injury Association

 £26,000 (2020)

Correspondent: The Trustees, Bradbury House, 190 Bagnall Road, Old Basford, Nottingham NG6 8SF (tel: 020 8640 8413; email: emergencyfund@headway.org.uk)

 https://www.headway.org.uk/supporting-you/headway-emergency-fund

CC number: 1025852/SC039992

Eligibility

Families and individuals coping with the practical implications of a sudden and catastrophic brain injury. Applicants should have less than £1,000 in savings.

Types of grant

Grants of up to £500 are provided through the Family Emergency Fund. Help can be given towards the following:

- The cost of travel to visit relatives in hospital
- Emergency accommodation

▶ Clothing needs related to the injury (e.g. sudden weight loss)
▶ Essential white goods where the individual has been made homeless and rehoused in accommodation lacking basic equipment such as a cooker or fridge
▶ A one-week self-catered carers break at a cottage in Pickering, Yorkshire

According to the charity's website, the majority of grants are for travel costs so that families can visit a loved one in a hospital following a brain injury.

Exclusions

The charity's website states that it cannot fund:

▶ Taxi journeys, flights or visa costs
▶ Costs already incurred
▶ Mortgage or rent payments
▶ Food
▶ Everyday household expenses
▶ Debts
▶ Private medical treatment
▶ Utility bills
▶ Childcare
▶ Items or services that are the responsibility of the local authority or NHS to provide
▶ Funeral costs

Applications

Application forms can be completed online or downloaded and returned to the correspondent once completed. Only one application per survivor of a brain injury can be considered.

Financial information

Year end	31/12/2020
Income	£4,550,000
Total expenditure	£4,300,000

Other information

Headway offers a range of services to people affected by a brain injury. There is a freephone helpline available (tel: 0808 800 2244; email: helpline@headway. org.uk). The Family Emergency Fund is supported by the Stewarts Law Foundation.

Regain – The Trust for Sports Tetraplegics

 £88,900 (2019)

Correspondent: Paul Lawrence, Charity Director, c/o Hewitson Moorhead, 3 Dorset Rise, London EC4Y 8EN (tel: 07572 841861; email: enquiries@ regainsportscharity.com)

https://www.regainsportscharity. com

CC number: 1030693

Eligibility

People who have sustained a sports-related spinal injury resulting in tetraplegia/quadriplegia. Support is also given to unpaid primary carers of people who have become tetraplegic as a result of a sports-related injury. Priority is given to first-time applicants.

Types of grant

Grants are made mainly for specialist equipment to help improve independence. If funds permit, other requests may be considered. Grants are also made to carers for respite breaks.

Exclusions

Grants cannot be made to provide equipment which is already available via statutory funding sources. No retrospective grants are given. Once an equipment grant has been awarded, beneficiaries cannot reapply for funding for three years. For carers respite grants, beneficiaries cannot reapply for one year.

Applications

Applications can be made online using a form on the charity's website. Applications must be accompanied by a letter of recommendation from a consultant, district occupational therapist, case manager, physiotherapist, care manager or immediate relative.

Financial information

Year end	31/12/2019
Income	£360,200
Total expenditure	£281,100

Further financial information

During the financial year, the charity awarded 36 grants. Grants were distributed as follows: £60,100 was awarded for the purchase of equipment, and a total of £28,800 was awarded to carers.

RFU Injured Players Foundation

 £242,000 (2019/20)

Correspondent: The Trustees, Rugby House, Twickenham Stadium, 200 Whitton Road, Twickenham, Greater London TW2 7BA (tel: 0800 783 1518 or 020 8831 7693; email: ipfgrants@rfu. com)

www.rfuipf.org.uk

CC number: 1122139

Eligibility

People of any age who have had a catastrophic spinal cord injury or traumatic brain injury which has resulted in permanent disability while playing rugby in England at any level. The foundation also has the Non-Catastrophic Injury (Non-CI) Grant Programme for individuals who have experienced injuries not classed as catastrophic. The injury must have taken place during a rugby match or rugby training session with a school or club approved by the Rugby Football Union (RFU). More information regarding eligibility is available from the foundation.

Types of grant

Grants are given for a range of purposes including travel for next of kin immediately following the accident, wheelchairs and equipment, physical therapy, home adaptations, mobility aids and so on.

Applications

Application forms and guidelines can be downloaded from the charity's website.

Financial information

Year end	30/06/2020
Income	£1,080,000
Total expenditure	£1,090,000

Further financial information

The foundation supported 97 individuals through its long-term grants programme totalling £270,100. It also provided a total of £17,400 to 15 individuals through the Non-CI Grants Programme.

Other information

The foundation supports injured rugby players and their families, as well as their clubs and teammates, with a range of immediate and long-term support. As part of its grants programme, the foundation also provides beneficiaries with the opportunity to experience matchday hospitality in an adapted box at Twickenham. The foundation also funds research into the causes and outcomes of serious injury, identifying the best ways to prevent and treat it and funds and informs the training of rugby coaches, players, referees and volunteers to protect players from serious injury.

Rosslyn Park Injury Trust Fund

 £1,800 (2020)

Correspondent: The Secretary, c/o Rosslyn Park FC, Priory Lane, London SW15 5JH (tel: 020 8876 1879; email: info@sportsinjurytrust.org)

sportsinjurytrust.org

CC number: 284089

Eligibility

Young people who have a disability or illness as a result of a sports injury.

Types of grant

One-off grants, preferably towards equipment.

Applications

Apply in writing to the correspondent.

Financial information

Year end	31/12/2020
Income	£20,700
Total expenditure	£2,000

Further financial information

Full accounts were not available to view on the Charity Commission's website due to the fund's low income. We have therefore estimated the fund's grant total based on its expenditure.

Mental health

The Matthew Trust

 £40,000 (2019/20)

Correspondent: Annabel Thompson, Director, PO Box 604, London SW6 3AG (tel: 020 7736 5976; email: amt@ matthewtrust.org)

www.matthewtrust.org

CC number: 294966

Eligibility

People over the age of eight who have mental health problems.

Types of grant

One-off grants are available for: clothing, furniture and equipment, respite breaks for the family, child carer holidays and second-chance education to encourage hobbies or entry into employment.

Applications

Apply in writing to the correspondent through a healthcare worker, social worker, GP, Citizens Advice or teacher including the following information:

- Name, address and age of the person requiring help
- Health and age of other close family members
- Outline background of the mental health problem
- Type of support required (including details of cost where applicable)
- Details of other organisations to whom you have applied for support

Financial information

Year end	31/03/2020
Income	£20,000
Total expenditure	£46,000

Further financial information

Full accounts were not available to view on the Charity Commission's website due to the trust's low income. We have therefore estimated the grant total based on the trust's total expenditure.

Other specific conditions

The Nihal Armstrong Trust

 £5,000 (2019/20)

Correspondent: Rahil Gupta, Trustee, 111 Chatsworth Road, London NW2 4BH (tel: 020 8459 6527; email: info@nihalarmstrongtrust.org.uk)

www.nihalarmstrongtrust.org.uk

CC number: 1107567

Eligibility

Children who are aged 18 and under, live in the UK and have cerebral palsy. Applicants must be in receipt of means-tested benefits and be able to provide supporting evidence.

Types of grant

Grants of up to £1,000 towards equipment, communication aids or a particular service that will benefit children with cerebral palsy. Items/ services must not be available from the local authority.

Exclusions

The trust does not fund holidays, refurbishment costs or household appliances. Grants are not available as part-funding for equipment or services that cost more than £1,000.

Applications

Applications can be made via the trust's website. The trust ideally needs a letter of support from a physiotherapist, occupational therapist or speech and language therapist, depending on the equipment/service needed. Where possible, parents applying for iPads should ask their child's school if they would order the iPad on their behalf and the trust will pay the school directly. Trustee meeting dates are published on the website.

Financial information

Year end	05/04/2020
Income	£6,000
Total expenditure	£5,600

Further financial information

Full accounts were not available to view on the Charity Commission's website due to the trust's low income. We have therefore estimated the trust's grant total based on its total expenditure.

Other information

The trust's website states that it receives a large number of applications for iPads.

The trust's policy is to fund the basic model of the iPad 2. Applicants will need to provide a letter of evidence from a referee which states that the child has tried one and can use it.

The Association for the Relief of Infirmity in the West of Scotland

 £164,100 (2019)

Correspondent: The Trustees, c/o Wright Johnston & Mackenzie LLP, 302 St Vincent Street, Glasgow G2 5RZ (tel: 0141 248 3434; email: enquiries@ari. scot)

https://ariws.scot

OSCR number: SC014424

Eligibility

People over 18 years of age living with an incurable contracted disease in the west of Scotland.

Types of grant

Six-monthly grants and one-off grants of up to £1,000 are available for the purchase of specific items such as appliances for the applicant's home or the cost of installing ramped access or a stairlift.

Exclusions

The charity does not assist individuals with HIV, AIDS or cancer. One-off grants are not given for the payment of debts, household bills or holidays.

Applications

Application forms can be downloaded from the charity's website. Applications should be made by a referral agency and not by the individual.

Financial information

Year end	31/12/2019
Income	£217,300
Total expenditure	£216,600

Birkdale Trust for Hearing Impaired Ltd

 £143,300 (2019/20)

Correspondent: Karen Fleetwood, Administrator, 21 Gleneagles Drive, Ainsdale, Southport, Merseyside PR8 3PP (tel: 07736 539111; email: karen_fleetwood@hotmail.com)

www.grantsforthedeaf.co.uk

CC number: 1103074

Eligibility

Children and young people up to the age of 25 with a hearing impairment.

Types of grant

Grants are given towards the purchase of specialist hearing equipment, the cost of speech/language therapy, educational support (such as extra tuition), fees for professional assessments, the cost of attending a British Sign Language course and so on.

Applications

Application forms can be downloaded from the charity's website.

Financial information

Year end	05/04/2020
Income	£200,800
Total expenditure	£265,400

Other information

Grants are also made to organisations that support young people with hearing impairments.

The British Polio Fellowship

£ £28,100 (2020)

Correspondent: The Support Services Team, CP House, Otterspool Way, Wilmington Close, Watford, Hertfordshire WD18 0FQ (tel: 01923 889758; email: dawn@britishpolio.org. uk)

 www.britishpolio.org.uk

CC number: 1108335/SC038863

Eligibility

People in need who have been affected by poliomyelitis (polio) and post-polio syndrome and who live in the UK. Carers, families and healthcare professionals may also be assisted. Only members of the fellowship may apply for assistance.

Types of grant

Welfare grants

Grants are given for disability-related equipment, such as scooters, electric or manual wheelchairs, riser/recliner chairs, specialised clothing and footwear, and specialist beds and mattresses. Household aids, equipment to enable independence, and home and car adaptations can also be supported. Assistance may occasionally be given for essential home improvement and crisis prevention.

Heating grants

Grants are made annually to members on a low income who are too young to qualify for the government's Winter Fuel Payment to help with heating costs.

Exclusions

Grants are not given to non-members, or towards hospital expenses, household bills or home carers. Statutory sources must have been exhausted before an application is made to the fellowship, as financial support will not be made to substitute statutory help.

Applications

Welfare and heating grant forms are available from the correspondent or a local branch welfare officer. Applications should be submitted by the individual or by an appropriate third party on their behalf and include a medical certificate or doctor's note stating polio-disability. Welfare applications are considered throughout the year. Heating grants are awarded once a year in the autumn. Holiday grant forms are available from the correspondent or by emailing Rosalind Evans at rosalindevans@britishpolio.org.uk. They are assessed on a bi-monthly basis.

Financial information

Year end	31/12/2020
Income	£536,500
Total expenditure	£409,100

Other information

The fellowship has over 50 local branches and there is a range of information and support services offered to people affected by polio and post-polio syndrome (some are only accessible to members).

The Brittle Bone Society

£ £38,800 (2020/21)

Correspondent: The Trustees, 30 Guthrie Street, Dundee DD1 5BS (tel: 01382 204446; email: bbs@ brittlebone.org)

 www.brittlebone.org

CC number: 272100

Eligibility

People with osteogenesis imperfecta (OI) living in the UK or the Republic of Ireland.

Types of grant

Support Grants are made towards the cost of essential equipment such as wheelchairs, trikes, buggies and other types of equipment. Assistance towards holidays and respite care can be awarded, although exceptionally. Support Grants are also awarded towards the cost of attending the charity's annual conference.

Applications

Application forms are available to download on the funder's website. A letter of support from a medical professional (an occupational therapist, physiotherapist, etc.) must accompany all applications.

Financial information

Year end	31/03/2021
Income	£191,800
Total expenditure	£203,300

Challenger Children's Fund

£ £45,400 (2019/20)

Correspondent: The Trustees, Suite 353, 44/46 Morningside Road, Edinburgh EH10 4BF (tel: 07531 580414; email: info@ccfscotland.org)

 www.ccfscotland.org

OSCR number: SC037375

Eligibility

The charity aims to help any child in Scotland under the age of 18 living with a disability through a physical impairment of the musculoskeletal, neurological or cardiorespiratory system.

Types of grant

One-off grants of up to £500. A higher amount may be granted in some circumstances. Grants can be given towards anything which is not provided by statutory sources but is required to meet the additional needs of the child. Items include clothing, apparatus, equipment, household appliances such as washing machines, furniture, travel and home or garden adaptations.

Exclusions

The charity's website states:

> The following conditions on their own however, are not accepted: mental health conditions, learning disabilities, behavioural disorders, development delay, Down's Syndrome, autism, visual or hearing impairment, cancer, diabetes, epilepsy, HIV, back pain and chronic fatigue syndrome. If they are associated with a physical disability, however, consideration will be given.

Applications

Application forms can be obtained from the correspondent or downloaded from the charity's website. Applications should be sponsored by a social worker, GP, health visitor, district nurse or therapist. Trainee workers and community care assistants may also apply.

Financial information

Year end	31/03/2020
Income	£79,200
Total expenditure	£66,700

Crohn's and Colitis UK

 £145,700 (2020)

Correspondent: Julia Devereux, Grants Assistant, 1 Bishops Square, Hatfield, Hertfordshire AL10 9NE (tel: 01727 830038; email: support.grants@crohnsandcolitis.org.uk)

www.crohnsandcolitis.org.uk

CC number: 1117148, SC038632

Eligibility

People affected by inflammatory bowel disease (IBD) who are aged 15 or older, have been resident in the UK for at least six months and are undertaking an educational or vocational training course.

Types of grant

Grants of up to £1,000 are made towards any educational or training needs, including tuition fees, books, equipment, retraining courses, additional costs of university or college and travel passes. Grants are also given for additional education needs, retraining purposes or other items and services arising as a consequence of having IBD.

Exclusions

A person can receive one grant in a five-year period. Recurring household bills or debts cannot be considered. The charity cannot reimburse for items that have already been purchased.

Applications

Application forms are available to download from the charity's website, along with guidance notes. The form has two extra sections, one of which should be completed by a doctor to confirm the individual's illness and one to be filled in by a social worker (or a health visitor, district nurse, Citizens Advice or another professional person). Full guidance, restrictions and deadlines are available online.

The grants panel meets approximately every eight weeks – refer to the website for the date of the next meeting.

Financial information

Year end	31/12/2020
Income	£4,680,000
Total expenditure	£4,030,000

Other information

Grants are also made to research institutions or to hospitals. The main role of the charity is to provide information and advice to people living with IBD. The information service can be contacted by calling 0300 222 5700 from 9am to 5pm on Monday to Friday (except English bank holidays). Outside these hours, an answerphone service is available.

The Cystic Fibrosis Holiday Fund

 £242,300 (2019)

Correspondent: The Trustees, 1 Bell Street, London NW1 5BY (tel: 020 7616 1300; email: info@cfholidayfund.org.uk)

www.cfholidayfund.org.uk

CC number: 1088630

Eligibility

Children and young people up to the age of 25 who are diagnosed with cystic fibrosis, and their families.

Types of grant

Grants of around £350 towards enabling children with cystic fibrosis to go on holidays or short trips (this may also include the child's family).

Exclusions

People who have received a grant within the previous two years cannot be assisted. The fund is usually unable to cover full costs and will not make retrospective grants (including where the trip takes place prior to the final grant approval).

Applications

Application forms can be downloaded from the charity's website or requested from the correspondent.

Financial information

Year end	31/12/2019
Income	£335,400
Total expenditure	£332,400

Further financial information

Grants of £350 were awarded to 160 individuals during the year. The charity runs the Family Revitalise programme for families that are most in need of a break. It has also provided laptops to young people in the most difficult circumstances.

Cystic Fibrosis Trust

 £385,000 (2019/20)

Correspondent: The Trustees, 1 Aldgate, Second Floor, London EC3N 1RE (tel: 020 3795 1555; email: enquiries@cysticfibrosis.org.uk)

www.cysticfibrosis.org.uk

CC number: 1079049

Eligibility

People in need who have cystic fibrosis and live in the UK.

Types of grant

The trust provides a range of grants to support people with cystic fibrosis:

- **Emergency grants** – grants of up to £150 to help in times of immediate financial need.
- **Transplant grants** – grants of up to £250 to help with the costs associated with attending a transplant assessment and having a transplant.
- **Health and well-being grants** – grants of up to £350 to fund goods or services that will improve the health and well-being of someone with cystic fibrosis (such as white goods, gym membership or exercise equipment).
- **Holiday grants** – grants of up to £300 to fund holidays, breaks, trips or days out for adults with cystic fibrosis who would not otherwise be able to afford a break.
- **Home care grants** – grants of up to £500 for times of acute illness or personal crisis. These are designed to support people with cystic fibrosis to be cared for comfortably at home.
- **Prescription pre-payment certificate grants** – one-off grants to fund the cost of a prepayment certificate for prescriptions.
- **Funeral grants** – grants of £750 to help with funeral costs.
- **Education grants** – help for adults with cystic fibrosis over the age of 18 with the costs of higher education or other professional qualifications including vocational training. The trust also accepts applications from people with cystic fibrosis aged 16 or 17 who are not moving into formal further education and who wish instead to undertake vocational training. Education grants are administered on behalf of the trust by the Joseph Levy Foundation.

Applications

Application forms can be downloaded from the trust's website.

Education grants are administered by the Joseph Levy Foundation. Further information can be found at www.jlef.org.uk.

Financial information

Year end	31/03/2020
Income	£16,530,000
Total expenditure	£16,500,000

Other information

The trust also provides confidential advice, support and information on all aspects of cystic fibrosis and a dedicated helpline which can provide advice and support on a range of issues, including help with financial issues (020 3795 1555).

Dan's Fund for Burns

 £57,600 (2019/20)

Correspondent: The Trustees, Willow House, 9 Orchard Road, Shalford, Guildford, Surrey GU4 8ER (tel: 07526 847699; email: info@dansfundforburns. org)

🌐 https://www.dansfundforburns.org

CC number: 1098720

Eligibility

Burns survivors in the UK who are in need.

Types of grant

Grants are given according to need.

Applications

Apply in writing to the correspondent, providing the following information:

▶ Name, address, phone number and email address (if possible)
▶ A brief description of the burns
▶ Details of the hospital where treatment was received
▶ A brief description of the sort of help required

Financial information

Year end	31/03/2020
Income	£91,400
Total expenditure	£187,400

Other information

This charity also makes grants to organisations for medical research and education into the treatment of burns, including first aid and nursing.

The Danny Green Fund

 £36,200 (2019/20)

Correspondent: The Trustees, 35 Hallet Road, Canvey Island, Essex SS8 8LH (tel: 07917 691593 or 07979 333283; email: info@thedannygreenfund.org.uk)

🌐 https://www.thedannygreenfund. org.uk

CC number: 1150334

Eligibility

Children with brain tumours. Priority is given to children with posterior fossa syndrome (also known as cerebellar mutism) resulting from a brain tumour.

Types of grant

One-off grants for specialist equipment such as buggies, multi-sensory equipment and iPads. Grants are also given to towards the cost of physiotherapy, hydrotherapy or horse riding sessions.

Applications

Apply in writing to the correspondent. All applications must include:

▶ Name, phone number and email address
▶ A referral form (available to download on the charity's website) signed by a health professional involved in the child's care
▶ Details of the child's needs and abilities and where you would like the child to have treatment

Financial information

Year end	07/10/2020
Income	£37,200
Total expenditure	£43,400

Other information

The charity also makes grants for research into the prevention, treatment and cure of children's brain cancer.

The Terrence Higgins Trust – Hardship Fund

 £24,000 (2019/20)

Correspondent: The Trustees, 439 Caledonian Road, London N7 9BG (tel: 0808 802 1221; email: info@tht.org. uk)

🌐 www.tht.org.uk

CC number: 288527

Eligibility

People in the UK with HIV who are in severe financial need.

Types of grant

The charity's website states:

> The Hardship Fund aims to support those clients who are experiencing the greatest level of hardship. This fund helps with:
>
> ▶ Ordinary living expenses such as food, clothing or travel
> ▶ A review/reduction/suspension of benefits due to changes in the welfare system
> ▶ A period of ill health
> ▶ Moving into a new home for the first time
> ▶ Losing a job
> ▶ Entering older age, e.g. retiring or moving into a different form of accommodation
> ▶ Starting to claim a pension
> ▶ Change in accommodation
> ▶ Contribution towards white goods such as fridges, freezers or washing machines

Exclusions

The charity's website states:

> The fund can't help with the following:
>
> ▶ Council fines, overpayment of Housing Benefit or Council Tax Benefit, court fees or immigration fees
> ▶ Travel or accommodation of any kind outside of the UK
> ▶ Respite care or holiday costs

▶ Funeral costs
▶ Credit card or loans repayments
▶ Prospective payments, e.g. rent deposit
▶ Any item for an individual without an HIV diagnosis
▶ Debt repayments/utility bills
▶ Gifts, e.g. birthday or Christmas presents
▶ Rent arrears or Council Tax arrears
▶ Professional training or education
▶ Items that are a statutory responsibility, e.g. glasses, dental work or urgent mobility equipment
▶ Other support that can be obtained through statutory support

Applications

The charity works with referral organisations across the UK. For further information contact the charity's helpline.

Financial information

Year end	31/03/2020
Income	£12,010,000
Total expenditure	£12,240,000

Other information

The charity operates service centres throughout the country for STI or HIV testing, sexual health information and advice, therapy and training. For locations, refer to the charity's website.

The Hollie Foundation

 £21,400 (2019/20)

Correspondent: Diane Waller, Secretary, 3 Stubbs Field, Shenly Brook End, Milton Keynes MK5 7GG (tel: 01908 507939; email: info@theholliefoundation. com)

🌐 https://www.theholliefoundation. com

CC number: 1156216

Eligibility

Individuals affected by the rare neurological genetic condition Niemann-Pick type C (NP-C).

Types of grant

Grants of up to £1,250 in a 12-month period are awarded where there is a recognised social or medical need. Examples of grants awarded include garden adaptations, specialist seating equipment, walking frames, sensory tools, travel expenses to a medical setting and funeral expenses.

Exclusions

Funding will not be granted where state support can cover the costs.

Applications

Initial contact can be made through the online form on the charity's website or using the contact details provided.

Financial information

Year end	31/03/2020
Income	£14,300
Total expenditure	£23,800

Further financial information

Full accounts were not available to view on the Charity Commission's website due to the foundation's low income. We have therefore estimated the foundation's grant total based on its total expenditure.

Other information

The foundation also awards grants to organisations with a common interest and raises awareness and aids research into NP-C.

June and Douglas Hume Memorial Fund

Correspondent: Jennifer McPhail, Grant Programmes Executive, Glasgow Office, Empire House, 131 West Nile Street, Glasgow G1 2RX (tel: 0141 341 4964; email: jennifer@foundationscotland.org.uk)

 https://www.foundationscotland.org.uk/apply-for-funding/funding-available/june-and-douglas-hume-memorial-fund

OSCR number: SC022910

Eligibility

Terminally ill patients who wish to spend their final days in their own home. Priority will be given to applicants from the west of Scotland and in particular the Helensburgh area.

Types of grant

One-off grants of up to £2,000 are awarded to assist patients with specialist equipment, as well as any house modifications necessary to accommodate such equipment. Grants may be used for bath and stairlifts, reclining beds and chairs, wheelchairs and zimmer frames, for example.

Applications

Applicants should contact the correspondent in the first instance and an application form will be sent out to applicants where funds are available. Individuals applying directly will need to provide a letter from a medical practitioner supporting their application.

Further financial information

No financial information was available for the fund.

Other information

The fund is administered by Foundation Scotland.

Huntington's Disease Association

 £38,600 (2019/20)

Correspondent: Specialist Huntington's Disease Advisor, Suite 24, Liverpool Science Park IC1, 131 Mount Pleasant, Liverpool, Merseyside L3 5TF (tel: 0151 331 5444; email: info@hda.org.uk)

 www.hda.org.uk

CC number: 296453

Eligibility

People with, or at risk of, Huntington's disease in England and Wales. Support is extended to the immediate families of such people.

Types of grant

The Huntington's Disease Association offers small grants for specific needs.

Applications

Initial enquiries should be made by contacting your local Specialist Huntington's Disease Advisor (SHDA). The charity's website has a search function to find your nearest SHDA.

Financial information

Year end	31/03/2020
Income	£1,680,000
Total expenditure	£1,580,000

Other information

This charity offers a variety of advice and support services, including services specifically aimed at young people affected by the juvenile form of the disease and at other young people who live in families affected by Huntington's in some form. The charity is linked to support groups across England and Wales run by teams of dedicated volunteers who provide local peer support to anyone affected by the disease. The charity's SHDAs also offer practical information, advice and emotional support at a local level.

One of the charity's main priorities is to eventually find a cure for the disease and it regularly funds research projects targeted at improving the care, treatment and prevention of Huntington's.

Kidney Care UK

 £567,500 (2020)

Correspondent: The Trustees, 3–4 The Windmills, St Mary's Close, Turk Street, Alton, Hampshire GU34 1EF (tel: 01420 541424; email: info@kidneycareuk.org)

 https://www.kidneycareuk.org

CC number: 270288

Eligibility

Dialysis patients and their families who are on a low income. Transplant patients and those receiving conservative care whose health and quality of life are being seriously affected by their renal condition are also eligible for support. Support may be extended more generally to people whose lives have been affected by kidney disease, at the trustees' discretion.

Types of grant

Grants are available for domestic costs (such as car insurance, heating costs, rent and possibly washing machines, beds and carpets), travel costs if individuals have to travel a long way to hospital, as well as grants for further education and training.

Exclusions

The charity is unable to help with travel costs for ongoing dialysis.

Applications

Application forms (and full guidelines) are available to download on the charity's website. Applications must be submitted with the input of a kidney unit social worker or a member of the kidney care team. If no member of staff can help, advocacy officers can be contacted via the charity.

Financial information

Year end	31/12/2020
Income	£1,350,000
Total expenditure	£3,300,000

Other information

The charity operates a counselling and support service for patients and their families. To access this service, contact the charity by telephone to book an appointment with a renal counsellor. It also runs a national advocacy service, with 11 advocacy officers covering different regions across the UK. The service is confidential and provides information and support to patients and their families or carers on a wide range of issues including treatment options, benefits and housing. To find your local advocacy officer, see the website.

The Kingston Trust CIO

 £26,800 (2020/21)

Correspondent: The Secretary, PO Box 6457, Basingstoke, Hampshire RG24 8LG (tel: 01256 352320; email: secretary@kingstontrust.org.uk)

 https://kingstontrust.org.uk

CC number: 1173190

Eligibility

People over the age of 16 who have an ileostomy or ileo-anal pouch and are experiencing temporary or long-term financial hardship.

Types of grant

The trust's website states that all qualifying grant applications will be considered. Examples of grants previously supported include:

- Beds and bedding
- Washing machines
- Cookers
- Bathroom modifications
- House maintenance
- Mobility aids
- Convalescent breaks (assistance for the applicant only)
- Training/education aids

Exclusions

Grants are not made to cover debts or for items already purchased (except in extreme circumstances).

Applications

Application forms can be downloaded from the trust's website along with guidance documents. Applications should be returned by post to the correspondent.

Financial information

Year end	15/02/2021
Income	£67,100
Total expenditure	£51,600

Further financial information

Full accounts were not available to view on the Charity Commission website. We have therefore estimated the trust's grant total based on previous financial information. In 2019/20, 56% of the trust's total expenditure was spent on grants to individuals.

Margaret's Fund

 £69,500 (2019/20)

Correspondent: The Trustees, PO Box 135, Buntingford, Ware SG11 2XJ (tel: 01763 274781; email: info@ margaretsfund.org)

https://margaretsfund.org

CC number: 210615

Eligibility

Women with pulmonary tuberculosis, or any other disease of the chest, who are in need. Any surplus income will be given more generally to women with other diseases.

Types of grant

Grants of up to £500 are made in support of the care, rehabilitation and aftercare of eligible people.

Applications

Apply on the funder's website. Applications must be made on the applicant's behalf by a recognised body such as a health or local authority, social services department or another charity. Grants are paid to the sponsoring agency and not directly to the applicant.

Financial information

Year end	05/04/2020
Income	£100,000
Total expenditure	£134,500

Further financial information

Grants were awarded to 99 individuals during the year.

Meningitis Now (formerly known as Meningitis Trust)

 £64,600 (2019/20)

Correspondent: The Trustees, Fern House, Daniels Industrial Estate, 104 Bath Road, Stroud, Gloucestershire GL5 3TJ (tel: 0808 801 0388; email: helpline@meningitisnow.org)

https://www.meningitisnow.org

CC number: 803016/SC037790

Eligibility

People in the UK who are in need as a result of meningitis or meningococcal septicaemia, and those who have a disability as a result of the illness. Support is extended to the immediate family (parent, step-parents, siblings, partners or grandparents) of those affected by meningitis.

Types of grant

Funding is provided through the Rebuilding Futures Fund across four separate areas:

- Health and well-being – counselling, creative therapies, travel expenses for hospital visits, swimming lessons, days out, etc.
- Opportunities – education support, books and equipment, technology to support learning, tuition and re-training costs
- Bereavement – funeral costs, headstones, bereavement counselling and so on
- Specialist equipment – mobility aids, specialist beds, sensory toys, home adaptations, specialist bikes and trikes, and prosthetics

Exclusions

According to the charity's website, funding is not given for the following:

- Holidays. Short breaks will be considered where benefit to the family unit can be demonstrated through third party supporting evidence

- Building, home and garden adaptations on a rental property, without appropriate prior written consent from the landlord
- Payment of domestic bills including arrears e.g. telephone, gas, electricity, council tax, mortgage or loan repayments
- Non-specialist clothing, bedding, furniture
- Recreational hot tubs swimming pools
- Contribution to purchase a private vehicle (it will consider funding a deposit towards a motability vehicle)
- Nursery placements
- Legal fees
- Private tuition fees
- Medical treatment
- Purchase of animals and pets
- Payments in cash

Applications

To apply for a grant, contact the charity's helpline or email address to request an application form. If the beneficiary is under the age of 18, the application must be completed on their behalf by a parent or carer. First-time applicants will have to include a written confirmation of the diagnosis. A support statement from a relevant third party (a health professional, social services, etc.) may also be required. In most cases, applications will be subject to a support assessment which involves a discussion about the individual's needs and award request with a member of the Meningitis Now Helpline or a community support officer. When appropriate, a community support officer may visit the applicant in their home to conduct the assessment.

Financial information

Year end	31/03/2020
Income	£2,810,000
Total expenditure	£3,070,000

Other information

The charity's research programmes fund projects in universities across the UK, to help improve meningitis vaccines and develop new ones. The charity also operates a free helpline on 0808 80 10 388 (Monday to Thursday 9:00 until 16:00, Fridays 9:00 until 13:00) for advice and support with meningitis-related issues. The charity has access to a telephone interpreting service in over 240 languages to ensure that the helpline is accessible to all. Those who have a hearing or speech impairment can also contact the helpline using the Next Generation Text Service, prefix 18001.

MND Scotland

 £293,000 (2019/20)

Correspondent: The Trustees, Unit 8, 76 Firhill Road, Glasgow G20 7BA (tel: 0141 332 3903; email: //info@ mndscotland.org.uk)

https://www.mndscotland.org.uk

OSCR number: SC002662

Eligibility

People affected by motor neurone disease (MND) across Scotland.

Types of grant

Grants are given in four areas:

- **Small grants scheme** – small grants of up to £1,000 for social and welfare purposes associated with the illness such as clothes, utility bills and power of attorney fees.
- **Time out grant** – grants of up to £1,000 per year to assist patients and their carers to enjoy a break from their usual routine.
- **Equipment and adaptation grant** – grants of up to £1,500 to help with the costs associated with adapting a house for someone with a disability or for essential equipment.
- **Professional development grant** – grants of up to £1,500 per year (and up to £3,000 in a lifetime) to help professionals meet the costs of attending relevant conferences and training course. They can be used to cover event fees, registration costs, travel and accommodation.

See the website for more detailed information on eligible expenditure.

Exclusions

Grants cannot be awarded retrospectively.

Applications

Application forms can be found on the charity's website. Note that each programme has a different application form.

Financial information

Year end	31/03/2020
Income	£2,810,000
Total expenditure	£2,600,000

Further financial information

In 2019/20, grants were awarded to 334 individuals and ranged from £100 to £1,500.

Other information

MND Scotland provides a range of services to those affected by MND and also supports research into MND.

Motor Neurone Disease Association

 £1,420,000 (2020)

Correspondent: Support Services, Francis Crick House, 6 Summerhouse Road, Moulton Park Industrial Estate, Northampton, Northamptonshire NN3 6BJ (tel: 01604 611802; email: support.services@mndassociation.org)

www.mndassociation.org

CC number: 294354

Eligibility

People with motor neurone disease (MND) who live in England, Wales and Northern Ireland, and their families and carers.

Types of grant

The charity offers a range of grants categorised as follows:

- **MND support (care) grant** – funding for equipment and services that people living with MND have been assessed as needing. Up to £1,500 per application predominantly for equipment or adaptations, for example stairlift purchase.
- **Quality of life grant** – improving the quality of life for anyone living with MND. Up to £500 per application to serve both the person with MND and the family, for example a short break away.
- **Carer's and young carer's grants** – for anyone aged 16 and above caring for someone with MND. Up to £500 per application to allow the person to take a break away from caring duties. Grants may be for hobbies and interests, short breaks, electronics, etc.
- **Young person's grant** – for children and young people under the age of 18 who live with someone with MND. Up to £250 per person. Examples include driving lessons, school trips and hobbies.

At the time of writing (October 2021), the charity was also offering emergency grants of up to £250 to help will additional living costs arising from the COVID-19 pandemic.

Exclusions

The charity will not support the following:

- Equipment and adaptations that are a statutory responsibility, but the charity can help with obtaining statutory funding or funding from other charitable organisations
- Retrospective funding
- Emergency healthcare needs

- Equipment for assessment for use by health and social care professionals unless with the express approval of the Director or Deputy Director of Care Improvement
- Funeral costs
- Debt repayment
- Legal costs

Applications

Each grant has a separate application form which can be downloaded from the charity's website. There is also a useful flow chart to aid the application process and policy and guidance documents.

Financial information

Year end	31/12/2020
Income	£19,910,000
Total expenditure	£15,580,000

Further financial information

According to the charity's accounts, grants were awarded to 2,479 individuals in 2020.

Other information

The charity has a network of association branches, which can offer information about the grants available and much more detailed information than is available on the website. As well as providing grants, the charity provides a wealth of services and advice for people affected by MND including an equipment loaning service.

Multiple Sclerosis Society

 £409,000 (2020)

Correspondent: The Grants Team, MS National Centre, 372 Edgware Road, Cricklewood, London NW2 6ND (tel: 020 8438 0700; email: grants@ mssociety.org.uk)

www.mssociety.org.uk

CC number: 1139257

Eligibility

People with multiple sclerosis and their families and carers living in the UK.

Types of grant

Health and well-being grants are available for items and activities that will have a significant positive impact on the individual's life, which includes everything from holidays and car adaptations to wheelchairs and exercise equipment. Carers grants can help fund activities that give unpaid carers a chance to relax or learn new skills.

Exclusions

Applicants with more than £16,000 in savings are not eligible for regular grants and those with more than £8,000 in savings are expected to contribute towards the cost of the item. Grants cannot be made:

▶ Retrospectively, for purchases already made

▶ For any ongoing or long-term financial commitments (such as living costs and bills)

▶ For debt repayments, legal fees, university fees, private purchase of cars or boilers

▶ Towards paying for treatments

▶ To people who have received a grant from the individual support grant fund within the last two years

▶ To people who have received a grant from the short breaks and activities fund within the last year.

Statutory sources should be exhausted prior to applying to the charity. Further guidance on each of the grant programmes is given on the charity's website.

Applications

Application forms are available to download from the charity's website.

Financial information

Year end	31/12/2020
Income	£20,490,000
Total expenditure	£23,460,000

Other information

The charity has a freephone helpline (tel: 0808 800 8000; email: helpline@mssociety.org.uk) and free information booklets on all aspects of living with MS for people with, or affected by, the condition. There is a network of branches, manned by volunteers, across the UK offering local support to people with MS.

Parkinson's UK

 £89,000 (2020)

Correspondent: The Trustees, 215 Vauxhall Bridge Road, London SW1V 1EJ (tel: 020 7963 3930; email: grants@parkinsons.org.uk)

https://www.parkinsons.org.uk

CC number: 258197

Eligibility

Support is available for people with Parkinson's or other forms of progressive parkinsonism and to unpaid carers. Applicants must have household savings of less than £6,000 for grants of up to £5,000 or savings of less than £16,000 for grants of over £5,000.

Types of grant

Grants are awarded for: specialist equipment or home adaptations (maximum of £1,500); electrical items such as white goods and communication technology (maximum of £500); respite care (maximum of £1,000); and recreational activities (maximum of £250).

Grants for electrical items, respite care and specialist equipment and home adaptations are limited to one application per household.

Exclusions

Grants are not awarded to pay for holidays, long-term financial commitments or daily living costs. Grants cannot be awarded for items that have already been purchased (retrospectively). Where provision of items or respite care should be the responsibility of the government or local authority, grants cannot be awarded.

Applications

Application forms are available to download on the funder's website. Annual deadlines apply – check the funder's website for up-to-date details. If you have any questions, the charity welcomes enquiries via telephone or email.

Financial information

Year end	31/12/2020
Income	£36,320,000
Total expenditure	£28,540,000

Joseph Patrick Trust

 £223,300 (2019/20)

Correspondent: The Trustees, c/o Muscular Dystropy Group of Great Britain and Northern Ireland, 61A Southwark Street, London SE1 0BU (tel: 07736 993130; email: jptgrants@muscular-dystrophy.org)

www.musculardystrophyuk.org/get-the-right-care-and-support/equipment-grants/jpt-grants

CC number: 294475

Eligibility

People with muscular dystrophy or an allied neuromuscular condition.

Types of grant

Grants are available for specialist equipment such as powered wheelchairs, adapted computers and electric beds.

Applications

Apply online via the Muscular Dystrophy UK website.

Financial information

Year end	31/03/2020
Income	£238,200
Total expenditure	£111,600

The Margaret and Alick Potter Charitable Trust

 £10,300 (2019/20)

Correspondent: Joan Miller, Trustee, Y Nyth, Capel Bangor, Aberystwyth, Dyfed SY23 3LR (tel: 07794 674339; email: joan.miller4@virgin.net)

CC number: 1088821

Eligibility

People with all types of dementia (including Alzheimer's disease), and their families and carers, who live in Ceredigion.

Types of grant

Grants are given according to need.

Applications

Apply in writing to the correspondent.

Financial information

Year end	05/04/2020
Income	£5,600
Total expenditure	£22,800

Further financial information

Full accounts were not available to view on the Charity Commission's website due to the trust's low income. We have therefore estimated the grant total based on the trust's total expenditure.

Other information

The trust also makes grants to local organisations.

Pulmonary Fibrosis Trust

£34,000 (2020)

Correspondent: The Trustees, 25 Margaret Road, Atherstone, Warwickshire CV9 1EF (tel: 01543 442191; email: info@pulmonaryfibrosistrust.org)

www.pulmonaryfibrosistrust.org

CC number: 1149901

Eligibility

People who have pulmonary fibrosis. Carers of such people are also eligible.

Types of grant

One-off grants are given for items such as stairlifts, mobility scooters, portable oxygen concentrators, etc. Funding can also be given towards transport fees to hospitals and specialist centres.

Applications

There is a short application form available to complete on the trust's website.

Financial information

Year end	31/12/2020
Income	£131,000
Total expenditure	£168,400

Other information

The trust also operates an emotional support service run by patients.

The Society for the Education of the Deaf

 £17,500 (2019/20)

Correspondent: Nancy Ward, Administrator, c/o Alexander Sloan, Chartered Accountants, 38 Cadogan Street, Glasgow G2 7HF (tel: 0141 204 8989; email: nancy.ward@alexandersloan. co.uk)

🌐 https://sed.org.uk

OSCR number: SC003804

Eligibility

Scottish individuals who are deaf and/or speech impaired.

Types of grant

Grants are awarded towards British Sign Language courses level 6 and upwards or similar activities and educational courses that will improve the applicant's ability to communicate with others.

Exclusions

Grant applications will only be considered from individuals and not course organisers or businesses.

Applications

Application forms can be completed online on the society's website or printed off and sent to the correspondent. Applications can be submitted directly by the individual or through a third party and are normally assessed within 3–8 weeks.

Financial information

Year end	31/03/2020
Income	£36,700
Total expenditure	£44,600

Further financial information

Grants totalling £22,500 were paid to 42 individuals.

Spinal Muscular Atrophy UK

 £5,200 (2020/21)

Correspondent: The Trustees, Unit 9, Shottery Brook Office Park, Timothy's Bridge Road, Stratford Enterprise Park, Stratford-upon-Avon, Warwickshire CV37 9NR (tel: 01789 267520; email: office@smauk.org.uk)

🌐 www.smasupportuk.org.uk

CC number: 1106815

Eligibility

Individuals diagnosed with any form of spinal muscular atrophy and their families.

Types of grant

Small one-off grants to assist with urgent needs, such as home adaptations and specialist equipment. The charity also provides multi-sensory toy packs to children who have been diagnosed.

Applications

Contact the charity for further information.

Financial information

Year end	31/03/2021
Income	£724,700
Total expenditure	£575,300

Further financial information

During 2020/21, support totalling £5,200 was given in welfare and equipment grants and toy packs.

Other information

The charity provides a range of support and information for individuals and families affected by spinal muscular atrophy, including support for bereavement. The charity also supports research into spinal muscular atrophy.

The Stanley Stein Deceased Charitable Trust
See entry on page 30

Tourettes Action

Correspondent: The Grants Team, Tourettes Action Grants, The Meads Business Centre, 19 Kingsmead, Farnborough, Hampshire GU14 7SR (tel: 03007778427077725819877; email: grants@tourettes-action.org.uk)

 www.tourettes-action.org.uk

CC number: 1003317

Eligibility

People with Tourette's Syndrome (TS) living in the UK. The charity is unlikely to be able to help people with a household income of over £40,000 per year or with savings of over £8,000. However, the charity tries to be as flexible as possible and will consider all applications.

Types of grant

One-off grants of up to £500 are given for equipment that supports individuals with TS in day-to-day life. Past examples include instruments for people whose tics reduce when playing music, electronic pens to help students take notes at school, and beds for people whose tics are so violent that normal beds break. The charity can be contacted to discuss the eligibility of particular items.

Exclusions

According to the charity's grant guidelines, it cannot fund:
- Home improvements, e.g. paint, conservatories, carpets or other flooring (special items which are needed because of TS but not for a medical reason may be considered)
- Household items, e.g. vacuum cleaners, washing machines, wardrobes, or standard beds or chairs (special furniture needed because of TS but not for a medical reason may be considered)
- Therapies or alternative treatments
- Educational activities, e.g. home tutors or standard teaching materials
- Activities or holidays

The charity is unlikely to fund computer equipment but will consider specialist peripherals to assist individuals with TS to make the best use of existing computer equipment. Successful applicants cannot reapply within five years of receiving a grant.

Applications

Application forms are available to download from the charity's website. Completed forms should be returned to the charity by post, along with supporting documentation.

Financial information

Year end	31/03/2020
Income	£455,400
Total expenditure	£499,200

Further financial information

During the financial year, £467,400 was awarded in grants; however, we were unable to determine the figure for individuals.

Other information

The charity also funds research into TS and offers support and information via its website.

Transplant Health Fund

 £8,000 (2018/19)

Correspondent: The Trustees, Nephrology Department, Royal Free Hospital, Pond Street, London NW3 2QG (tel: 07725 033967; email: thf. enquiry@gmail.com)

🌐 www.transplanthealthfund.org

CC number: 1154683

Eligibility

People who have had an organ transplant or those needing organ transplantation or similar care.

Types of grant

Grants are made to assist in the care and treatment of eligible people by providing, or contributing towards, equipment and services.

Exclusions

The charity does not make grants for items or services normally provided by statutory authorities.

Applications

Application forms are available to download on the funder's website from the contact page. Completed forms can be returned to the Royal Free Hospital or sent by email.

Financial information

Year end	31/03/2019
Income	£9,500
Total expenditure	£8,900

Further financial information

The 2018/19 financial information was the latest available at time of writing (November 2021). Due to the charity's low income, full accounts were not available to view. We have estimated the charity's grant total based on its expenditure.

The Tuberous Sclerosis Association

£3,300 (2020)

Correspondent: The Support Team, c/o Nightingale House, 46–48 East Street, Epsom, Surrey KT17 1HQ (tel: 0300 222 5737; email: admin@tuberous-sclerosis. org)

https://tuberous-sclerosis.org/ information-and-support/access-benefits-and-financial-aid

CC number: 1039549

Eligibility

People in need who have tuberous sclerosis complex (TSC) and their parents and carers. According to the charity's website, applicants must have photocopied evidence of their entitlement to one of the following:

- Child Tax Credit
- Working Tax Credit
- Income-based Jobseeker's Allowance
- Income Support
- Employment and Support Allowance
- Housing Benefit
- Pension Credit

If you do not receive any of the above benefits, further information may be needed to complete your application.

Types of grant

TSA Support Fund

According to the 2020 accounts, the TSA Support Fund awards small discretionary grants to offer 'a lifeline to individuals and families when the financial implications of TSC overwhelm them.' Grants can be for up to £250. Examples of what the fund can help with include:

- Home adaptations
- Household items, such as a washing machine
- A holiday or days out
- Travel costs to attend a TSA event

Exclusions

The TSA Support Fund cannot support:

- Items that are the responsibility of the local authority to provide
- Items that have already been paid for
- Ongoing or long-term costs including living costs and bills
- Costs associated with debt

Applications

Application forms are available to download from the charity's website and should be returned by post or email. Make sure to provide details of any benefits you receive as well as a quote for the item you want to purchase. Applications can be submitted all year round.

Financial information

Year end	31/12/2020
Income	£418,700
Total expenditure	£614,300

Further financial information

During the year grants were awarded in support of 14 individuals and their families.

Other information

As well as providing a range of support for people affected by TSC, the charity provides education and information about the condition. It also funds research. More information is available from the charity's informative website.

Visual impairment

BlindAid

£27,500 (2020)

Correspondent: The Trustees, Lantern House, 102 Bermondsey Street, London SE1 3UB (tel: 020 7403 6184; email: enquiries@blindaid.org.uk)

www.blindaid.org.uk

CC number: 262119

Eligibility

People aged 18 and over who are blind or visually impaired and live permanently in one of the following London boroughs: Camden, Greenwich, Hackney, Hammersmith and Fulham, Islington, the City, Kensington and Chelsea, Lewisham, Lambeth, Southwark, Tower Hamlets, Wandsworth and Westminster.

Types of grant

One-off grants, typically of up to £300, are awarded for essential items to help people maintain their independence. Recent examples include: domestic items or white goods, equipment (such as talking clocks, big button telephones, talking microwaves, etc.) and contributions towards accessible computer equipment.

Exclusions

Grants cannot be awarded towards the following:

- Payment of debts, fines, Council Tax or mortgage/rent arrears
- Smartphones/tablets
- Legal fees
- Household bills
- Carpeting, curtains or blinds
- Home adaptations
- Educational or occupational training
- Medical treatment
- Motor vehicle expenses
- Funeral costs
- Removal costs
- Pest control
- Holidays

The charity does not make retrospective grants.

Applications

Applications can be made on the funder's website using an online form. Alternatively, application forms can be downloaded from the charity's website and sent to the correspondent. Applications must be made through a third party such as social services, sensory teams, community mental health teams or other organisations. The trustees aim to process applications within 28 days. The charity can only consider one application per person/ household over a period of two years. A full list of guidelines is available to download from the charity's website.

Financial information

Year end	31/12/2020
Income	£580,800
Total expenditure	£810,500

Further financial information

During the year, 98 grants were awarded for general purposes totalling £22,100. In addition, small grants of less than £100 totalled £3,400.

Other information

The charity's Sight Support Workers make home visits to people who are blind or visually impaired, typically on a fortnightly basis, to help combat social isolation and loneliness. The charity also operates a telephone support service for those on the waiting list to see a Sight Support Worker or to those who simply choose to have a regular telephone call. The charity runs a number of community projects, which includes free classes in IT, cooking, yoga, creative writing and others, as well as local coffee events every fortnight in Tower Hamlets and Southwark.

Gardner's Trust for the Blind

 £41,400 (2019/20)

Correspondent: Angela Stewart, Suite 1, Unit 2, Stansted Courtyard, Parsonage Road, Takeley, Essex CM22 6PU (tel: 020 7253 3757)

CC number: 207233

Eligibility

Registered blind or partially sighted people who live in the UK.

Types of grant

One-off and recurrent grants of up to £600 towards the cost of household items (including some white goods), business start-ups, adapted computers and software and so on. The trust may also offer grants towards pensions.

Grants are also available for education costs such as course fees or assistive technology.

Applications

Apply in writing to the correspondent. Applications must be supported by confirmation of the applicant's disability from a third party.

Financial information

Year end	30/09/2020
Income	£96,400
Total expenditure	£103,300

Further financial information

Grants were awarded to 27 individuals during the year.

Other information

The trust may also make grants to organisations.

The Guide Dogs for the Blind Association
See entry on page 64

The Royal National Institute of Blind People (RNIB)

Correspondent: The Trustees, 105 Judd Street, London WC1H 9NE (tel: 0303 123 9999; email: helpline@rnib.org.uk)

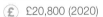 www.rnib.org.uk

CC number: 226227

Eligibility

The charity's website states that in order to receive a grant you must:
- be a resident in the UK
- be registered with your local authority as blind ("severely sight impaired") or partially sighted ("sight impaired") unless you are applying on behalf of a child who has not yet had their sight loss certified or registered
- receive a means-tested benefit and one that is not a Tax Credit. Means-tested benefits include Income Support; Pension Credit; Housing Benefit; Council Tax support; Income-related Employment and Support Allowance; Income-related Job Seeker's Allowance; and Universal Credit.
- have been refused funding from your local authority for the items you need
- have savings of less than £6,000
- have not had a grant from us in the last three years.

Types of grant

One-off grants of up to £500 for technology that can help people live more independently.

The charity's website states that it will only consider applications for the following:
- Talking phones, accessible smartphones, accessible tablets and e-readers (£350 maximum)
- Big button or talking landline telephones (£100 maximum)
- Computer accessibility software (£500 maximum)
- Electronic braille displays and notetakers (£500 maximum)
- Portable and TV video magnifiers (£500 maximum)
- DAISY players and USB players (£300 maximum)
- Smart home devices and accessories (£150 maximum)
- Wearable technology including health and fitness devices (£150 maximum)
- Voice recorders and dictaphones (£150 maximum)
- Accessible kitchen equipment including talking microwaves, talking scales and talking measuring jugs
- Talking watches and clocks (£80 maximum)
- RNIB's Penfriend 3 labelling device plus any spare labels and talking colour detectors

Exclusions

Grants cannot be made for items needed for jobs or for items which have already been purchased.

Applications

Application forms are available to download from the charity's website. Applications must be supported by a professional (social worker, occupational therapist, healthcare visitor or worker from another charity or local society) who can confirm the individual's personal circumstances.

Financial information

Year end	31/03/2020
Income	£95,930,000
Total expenditure	£92,870,000

Further financial information

We were unable to determine the grant total.

Other information

The RNIB provides a number of services for blind and partially sighted people, including in-clinic support for eye conditions in hospitals across the UK. Advice on financial issues such as benefits eligibility or other charity and statutory funding is available by email or by contacting the organisation's telephone helpline. Grants are also made to organisations.

Telephones for the Blind

 £20,800 (2020)

Correspondent: Daniel Brookbank, Honorary Treasurer, 13 Arundel Close, Pevensey Bay, Pevensey, East Sussex BN24 6SF (email: info@tftb.org.uk)

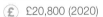 www.tftb.org.uk

CC number: 255155

Eligibility

People who are registered blind or partially sighted. Applicants must be:
- Living alone, often alone, or living with a partner who has a disability
- Living in their own room in a care home
- Unable to afford a telephone from their own resources (or their family's resources)

Types of grant

Grants are made for access to telephones. This includes providing mobile phones (Doro PhoneEasy 612), or contributing to quarterly telephone rental costs (£30 per quarter) and to cover the full cost of a new telephone line installation.

Applications

Application forms are available to
download on the charity's website.
Applications must be submitted by a
support worker, social worker or
rehabilitation worker. Completed forms
should be sent to the charity by email.

Financial information

Year end	31/12/2020
Income	£15,100
Total expenditure	£23,100

Further financial information

Full accounts were not available to view
on the Charity Commission's website
due to the charity's low income. We
have therefore estimated the charity's
grant total based on its total
expenditure.

Armed forces charities

Unlike other charities which are associated with occupations, the armed forces charities have been given their own section in this guide as there are many more relevant charities and they can support a large number of people. This branch of the sector is committed to helping anyone who has at least one day's paid service in any of the armed forces, including reserves and those who undertook National Service, and their husbands, wives, children, widows, widowers and other dependants.

These charities are exceptionally well organised. Much of this is due to the work of SSAFA, which has an extensive network of trained caseworkers around the country who act on behalf of SSAFA and other service charities. Many of the charities in this section use the same application procedures as SSAFA and assist a specified group of people within the service/ex-service community, while others (such as The Royal British Legion) have their own procedures and support the services as a whole.

Many service benevolent funds rely on trained SSAFA volunteer caseworkers to prepare applications, although some do have their own volunteers. Alternatively, some funds ask applicants to write to a central correspondent. In such cases, applicants may wish to follow the guidelines in the article 'How to make an application' on page xiii. Most entries in this section state whether the applicant should apply directly to the charity or through a caseworker. If in doubt, the applicant should ring up the charity concerned or the local SSAFA office.

Some people prefer to approach their, or their former spouse's, regimental or corps association. Many of them have their own charitable funds and volunteers, especially in their own recruiting areas. In other cases they will work through one of the volunteer networks mentioned above. Again, if in doubt or difficulty, the applicant should contact the regimental/corps association or local SSAFA office.

SSAFA is much more than just a provider of financial assistance. It also offers advice, support and training. It can assist members of the armed forces community on many issues, ranging from how to replace lost medals to advice on adoption. Its website (www.ssafa.org.uk) provides a wide range of information and useful links for members of the community.

ABF The Soldiers' Charity

£3,920,000 (2019/20)

Correspondent: The Welfare Team, Mountbarrow House, 6–20 Elizabeth Street, London SW1W 9RB (tel: 0845 241 4833; email: info@soldierscharity. org)

 www.soldierscharity.org

CC number: 1146420/SC039189

Eligibility
Members and ex-members of the British Regular Army and the Reserve Army and their dependants who are in need. Members and former members must have completed at least one year's satisfactory service. In some exceptional circumstances the charity will support individuals who were medically discharged as a direct result of an injury while training or during their first year of service.

Types of grant
Grants are awarded over several broad areas:
- Enabling independent living – through home adaptations or mobility equipment
- Care for people over the age of 65 – including stairlifts, electric beds and care home fees
- Training and education to increase employability – typically grants are for training course fees
- Increasing mental fitness – through respite breaks
- Helping army families – grants are given according to need and have included funeral costs, travel expenses and purchasing clothing and school uniforms
- Ensuring the provision of suitable housing – grants are given for essential household domestic

appliances such as fridges and washing machines

Exclusions

Grants are not awarded for medical and legal fees, non-priority debt and memorials or headstones.

Applications

The charity does not deal directly with individual cases. Applicants should first contact a relevant case-working organisation, further details of which can be found on the charity's website.

Financial information

Year end	31/03/2020
Income	£14,780,000
Total expenditure	£18,110,000

Other information

ABF also makes grants to other charities working to support current and former service people.

AJEX Charitable Foundation

 £68,700 (2020)

Correspondent: The Trustees, Shield House, Harmony Way, Hendon, London NW4 2BZ (tel: 020 8416 0164; email: headoffice@ajex.org.uk)

 www.ajex.org.uk

CC number: 1082148

Eligibility

Jewish ex-service people, and their dependants, who are in need.

Types of grant

One-off and recurrent grants are awarded according to need. Special grants are also made to cover emergencies and exceptional circumstances such as contributions towards the cost of stairlifts, electric motor scooters and so on.

Applications

Apply in writing to the correspondent.

Financial information

Year end	31/12/2020
Income	£166,200
Total expenditure	£312,300

Other information

The foundation works closely with SSAFA, Royal British Legion and other regimental associations.

ATS and WRAC Association Benevolent Fund

 £326,700 (2019/20)

Correspondent: The Trustees, Unit 11 Basepoint Business Centre, 1 Winnall

Road, Winchester, Hampshire SO23 0LD (tel: 0300 400 1992; email: penny.muxworthy@wracassociation.org.uk)

 www.wracassociation.co.uk

CC number: 206184

Eligibility

Former members of the Auxiliary Territorial Service during the Second World War and members of the Women's Royal Army Corps who served up to April 1992, who are in need and living on a basic state pension.

Types of grant

One-off grants of up to £3,000 for the payment of: house repairs and adaptations, mobility aids, funeral expenses, priority debt, clothing and food, central heating/boilers, white goods, removal and travel expenses, rent and respite breaks. The fund also offers regular payment grants. For a full list of what can be supported, visit the charity's website.

Applications

All applications for financial assistance should go through SSAFA or Royal British Legion caseworkers who will visit the applicant and submit whatever forms are necessary. Grants are distributed through these agencies.

Financial information

Year end	30/09/2020
Income	£325,700
Total expenditure	£514,600

Further financial information

Grants were awarded to 196 individuals during the year.

The Black Watch Association

 £34,200 (2020)

Correspondent: The Trustees, Balhousie Castle, Hay Street, Perth, Perthshire PH1 5HR (tel: 01738 623214; email: bwassociation@btconnect.com)

 theblackwatch.co.uk/regimental-association

OSCR number: SC016423

Eligibility

Serving and retired soldiers of the Black Watch, and their dependants, who are in need.

Types of grant

Welfare

Welfare grants have been given previously towards rent arrears, clothing, household equipment, funeral expenses and mobility aids. A holiday scheme is

also available to widows of Black Watch servicemen.

Education

Education and training grants are given to soldiers who are retired or are about to retire. In some cases, this type of grant can be awarded to spouses and dependants.

Applications

Initial enquiries should be made to SSAFA, which is responsible for making referrals to the association and administering expenditure once a grant is awarded. For details of your local SSAFA branch, see www.ssafa.org.uk.

Financial information

Year end	31/12/2020
Income	£138,000
Total expenditure	£158,900

Other information

Grants are also made to organisations, mainly to other armed forces charities.

Blind Veterans UK

 £1,830,000 (2019/20)

Correspondent: The Trustees, 12–14 Harcourt Street, London W1H 4HD (tel: 0800 389 7979; email: enquiries@blindveterans.org.uk)

 www.blindveterans.org.uk

CC number: 216227

Eligibility

All applicants must have served at any time in the regular or reserve UK armed forces (including National Service), or in the Merchant Navy during World War Two, or in the Polish or Indian forces under British command.

Blind Veterans UK uses its own criteria for the level of sight loss required to receive help and the charity's doctors will assess this. The charity's website states: 'It doesn't matter how or when your sight loss was caused, or whether you were on active service at the time.'

Types of grant

One-off grants are given to allow applicants to develop their independence through a combination of equipment, training, rehabilitation and respite care.

Exclusions

The charity typically cannot offer support where it is available from statutory services although the charity does take into consideration that applying for statutory support can be complex and have long waiting lists.

Applications

Application forms are available on the charity's website or from the correspondent. There is also a form on the website which allows potential applicants to request a call back from the charity for further information. Applications must include details of the applicant's service (including service number and dates of service) and details of their ophthalmic consultant. On receipt, the charity will contact the respective service office and ophthalmic consultant for reports. All applicants are encouraged to get in touch with the charity to discuss their needs (freephone 0800 389 7979).

Financial information

Year end	31/03/2020
Income	£28,130,000
Total expenditure	£42,210,000

Further financial information

Grants were broken down as follows:

Visual impairment and computer equipment	£838,300
Property and maintenance	£585,200
Health and well-being	£282,600
Financial assistance	£121,900

Other information

The charity's activities cover four main areas: help and training for independent living, care centre activities, welfare services and housing provision. Lifelong support and advice are offered to beneficiaries and their families. There are centres in Brighton, Sheffield and Llandudno which provide rehabilitation and training to individuals learning to cope with blindness. The Brighton and Llandudno centres also serve as nursing, residential and respite care centres.

This charity also administers the Diana Gubbay Trust, which provides support to men and women in the emergency services who have experienced sight loss while on duty. The ophthalmic criteria are the same as those for Blind Veterans UK.

British Limbless Ex-Service Men's Association (BLESMA)

 £846,700 (2020)

Correspondent: Grants Support Team, British Limbless Ex-Service Men's Association, 115 New London Road, Chelmsford, Essex CM2 0QT (tel: 020 3954 3022; email: grantsadmin@blesma. org)

www.blesma.org

CC number: 1084189

Eligibility

Serving and former members of HM or auxiliary forces who have lost a limb or eye or have a permanent loss of speech, hearing or sight, and their widows/widowers. Despite the association's

name, it helps anyone that fits the above description, regardless of gender.

Types of grant

Financial assistance is available to alleviate the additional costs and hardships of disability. Examples of items/services that grants can be used for include: mobility aids such as stairlifts, scooters, wheelchairs and walking frames; home decoration costs; garden maintenance costs.

Applications

Contact the Grants Support Team on the charity's website for further information on how to apply.

Financial information

Year end	31/12/2020
Income	£4,760,000
Total expenditure	£5,230,000

Other information

BLESMA also offers advice and support to members on a range of issues.

Churchill Lines Charitable Fund Ltd

 £32,400 (2019/20)

Correspondent: The Regimental Accountant, MOD St Athan, Barry, South Glamorgan CF62 4WA (tel: 020 7218 0906)

CC number: 1158677

Eligibility

Serving and former members of the Special Forces Support Group.

Types of grant

Grants are given according to need.

Applications

Apply in writing to the correspondent.

Financial information

Year end	30/06/2020
Income	£69,500
Total expenditure	£70,500

W. J. and Mrs C. G. Dunnachie's Charitable Trust

 £22,300 (2019/20)

Correspondent: The Trustees, c/o Low Beaton Richmond LLP, 20 Renfield Street, Glasgow G2 5AP

OSCR number: SC015981

Eligibility

People who are in poor health or who have a disability as a result of their service during the Second World War.

Types of grant

One-off and recurrent (quarterly) grants according to need.

Applications

The majority of applications are submitted via SSAFA or other appropriate sponsors.

Financial information

Year end	05/04/2020
Income	£77,800
Total expenditure	£82,000

Further financial information

Grants ranging from £90 to £750 were made to 84 individuals.

Other information

Grants are also given to organisations that support veterans and their families.

Felix Fund – The Bomb Disposal Charity

 £16,400 (2019/20)

Correspondent: Melanie Moughton, Vauxhall Barracks, Foxhall Road, Didcot, Oxfordshire OX11 7ES (tel: 07713 752901; email: enquiries@felixfund.org. uk)

 https://www.felixfund.org.uk

CC number: 1142494

Eligibility

Any serving and former military or SO15 (Metropolitan Police Counter Terrorism Unit) personnel who have conducted or assisted with Explosive Ordnance Disposal (EOD) and search duties. This includes individuals of any cap badge, including: mine clearance divers, ammunition technical officers, electronic countermeasure operators, drivers, infantry escorts, searchers, weapons intelligence specialists, dog handlers, plus any other military or police personnel who have conducted or assisted in bomb disposal duties. The families of such individuals can also be supported.

Types of grant

Grants are made for a range of purposes such as mobility aids, furniture, white goods, home adaptations, therapies (such as hydrotherapy) and sports equipment.

Applications

Application forms can be completed on the fund's website. Two forms are available, one for serving personnel and one for veterans and dependent family members.

Financial information

Year end	30/04/2020
Income	£377,500
Total expenditure	£229,400

Other information

The fund runs preventative stress training based on mindfulness. The programme is available to all serving military personnel who have assisted in bomb disposal duties to learn various tools and techniques on how to recognise the warning signs of stress and how to relax and be more positive.

Help for Heroes

 £496,000 (2019/20)

Correspondent: The Grants Team, Unit 14 Parker's Close, Downton Business Park, Downton, Salisbury, Wiltshire SP5 3RB (tel: 0300 303 9888; email: getsupport@helpforheroes.org.uk)

www.helpforheroes.org.uk

CC number: 1120920, SC044984

Eligibility

Current and former members of the armed forces who have had a life-changing injury or illness while serving, or as a result of their service, and their families.

Types of grant

Previous research suggests support is given for a range of purposes, including, but not limited to, housing adaptations, white and brown goods, sports and therapeutic equipment/activities, support with priority debts, and vocational and employment opportunities.

Applications

Applications should be made via telephone, email or the contact portal on the charity's website.

Financial information

Year end	30/09/2020
Income	£24,420,000
Total expenditure	£30,800,000

Further financial information

In 2019/20 a total of £496,000 was awarded to 416 individuals.

Other information

This charity also makes grants to organisations and provides a wide range of support, advice and other welfare services, details of which can be found on the charity's website.

Help Our Wounded Royal Marines and Supporting Arms

 £15,400 (2019/20)

Correspondent: Christian Falcke, Trustee, 20 Homewood Avenue, Sittingbourne, Kent ME10 1XL (email: chrisfalcke62@gmail.com)

 https://helpourwounded.co.uk

CC number: 1150893

Eligibility

Serving Royal Marines and their supporting arms and former troops. Dependants can also be supported.

Types of grant

One-off grants according to need.

Applications

Apply in writing to the correspondent.

Financial information

Year end	29/02/2020
Income	£24,400
Total expenditure	£25,400

Further financial information

Full accounts were not available to view on the Charity Commission's website due to the charity's low income. We have therefore estimated the grant total based on the charity's total expenditure.

Other information

The charity's website states: 'We provide long term financial help, finding physical training, emotional support and assistance in seeking suitable alternative employment given the severity of some disabilities, allowing our Royal Marines and Supporting Arms to continue with their lives.'

Honourable Artillery Company

 £17,000 (2019/20)

Correspondent: The Trustees, Honourable Artillery Co., City Road, London EC1Y 2BQ (tel: 020 7382 1537; email: hac@hac.org.uk)

www.hac.org.uk

CC number: 208443

Eligibility

Serving members of the Honorable Artillery Company (HAC) regiment and the HAC Special Constabulary, and veteran members of the HAC regiments or any other regular or reserved armed or police force, who are members of the company and their immediate dependants.

Types of grant

Grants are given according to need.

Applications

Contact the charity for more information.

Financial information

Year end	31/10/2020
Income	£3,550,000
Total expenditure	£3,790,000

Further financial information

Grants were awarded to 15 individuals through the benevolent fund.

The Household Cavalry Foundation

 £138,700 (2019/20)

Correspondent: The Trustees, Household Cavalry Foundation, Horse Guards, Whitehall, London SW1A 2AX (tel: 020 7839 4858; email: admin@hcavfoundation.org)

www.hcavfoundation.org

CC number: 1151869

Eligibility

Household Cavalrymen who have been injured on operations or veterans and their dependants.

Types of grant

Grants are given according to need.

Applications

Apply in writing to the correspondent.

Financial information

Year end	31/03/2020
Income	£499,000
Total expenditure	£378,500

Other information

Formed in January 2013, The Household Cavalry Foundation was set up to raise funds to care for the soldiers, casualties, veterans, heritage and horses of the Household Cavalry. Its aim is to bring together regimental benevolent funds such as the Operational Casualties Funds (OCF), Household Cavalry Central Charitable Fund (HCCCF) and the Regimental Associations to operate as the Household Cavalry Foundation.

The Household Division Charity

 £138,700 (2019/20)

Correspondent: Maj. William Style, Treasurer, Household Division Funds, Horse Guards, Whitehall, London SW1A 2AX (tel: 020 7414 2270; email: treasurer@householddivision.org.uk)

CC number: 1138248

Eligibility

Current and former members of the Household Division, and their dependants, who are in need.

Types of grant

One-off and recurring grants according to need.

Applications

Apply in writing to the correspondent. Applications may be submitted by the individual or by a third party such as a representative from SSAFA, Citizens Advice or other welfare organisation.

Financial information

Year end	30/09/2020
Income	£290,200
Total expenditure	£445,700

Irish Guards Charitable Fund

 £39,000 (2020)

Correspondent: The Trustees, Irish Guards Regimental Headquarters, Wellington Barracks, Birdcage Walk, London SW1A 6HQ (tel: 020 7414 3293; email: igwebmaster@btconnect.com)

CC number: 247477

Eligibility

People who are serving, or have served, in the Irish Guards. This includes officers, warrant officers, non-commissioned officers or guardsmen and their dependants.

Types of grant

Grants are given according to need.

Applications

Apply in writing to the correspondent.

Financial information

Year end	31/12/2020
Income	£118,900
Total expenditure	£177,700

Further financial information

Grants totalling £39,000 were awarded to 50 individuals during the year.

K.O.S.B. Association Funds

£13,000 (2020)

Correspondent: Maj. D. Sturrock, Trustee and Secretary, Balcladach, Easter Ulston, Jedburgh, Roxburghshire TD8 6TF

OSCR number: SC033882

Eligibility

Former members of the King's Own Scottish Borderers regiment and their families and dependants.

Types of grant

Grants are awarded according to need.

Applications

Apply in writing to the correspondent. Each application is considered on its merits.

Financial information

Year end	31/12/2020
Income	£56,200
Total expenditure	£74,200

Further financial information

Financial assistance was given in 44 cases of hardship during the year.

Other information

The trust also awards grants to organisations (£330 in 2019/20).

King Edward VII's Hospital Sister Agnes

£126,000 (2019/20)

Correspondent: Joshua Larkin, Individual Giving and Military Grants Officer, King Edward VII Hospital, Beaumont Street, London W1G 6AA (tel: 020 7486 4411; email: enquiries@ kingedwardvii.co.uk)

https://www.kingedwardvii.co.uk

CC number: 208944

Eligibility

Current and former service personnel, and their widows, widowers, spouses or ex-spouses, who are uninsured and in need.

Types of grant

Grants for medical treatment at King Edward VII's hospital only.

Exclusions

Previous research suggests grants are not made for cosmetic or bariatric surgery.

Applications

Applications should be made using the charity's online form, which must be accompanied by proof of service, full bank statements from the last three months showing the name and address of the applicant and other proof of address (e.g. utility bill).

Financial information

Year end	31/03/2020
Income	£34,710,000
Total expenditure	£33,210,000

Other information

The charity also offers subsidised treatment to eligible beneficiaries.

The Military Provost Staff Corps Benevolent Fund

£2,900 (2019/20)

Correspondent: Regimental Secretary, MPS Association, Berechurch Hall Camp, Berechurch Hall Road, Colchester, Essex CO2 9NU (tel: 01206 816795; email: regsecmpsa@mpsa.org.uk)

 www.mpsa.org.uk

CC number: 1078437

Eligibility

Former members of the former Military Provost Staff Corps and the Adjutant General's Corps (AGC) who are in need. Their widows and dependants in need are also eligible.

Types of grant

Grants are awarded according to need.

Applications

Apply in writing to the correspondent.

Financial information

Year end	31/03/2020
Income	£26,000
Total expenditure	£18,100

Further financial information

According to the charity's 2019/20 accounts, grants were broken down as follows: sports and adventure (£1,800); widows (£900); welfare (£170).

The Nash Charity

£10,000 (2019/20)

Correspondent: The Trustees, c/o Peachey & Co., 95 Aldwych, London WC2B 4JF (tel: 020 7316 5200; email: cmb@peachey.co.uk)

CC number: 229447

Eligibility

Soldiers, sailors and airmen who are in need due to disability or wounding, resulting from war.

Types of grant

Grants are given according to need.

Applications

Apply in writing to the correspondent.

Financial information

Year end	05/04/2020
Income	£17,400
Total expenditure	£22,800

Further financial information

Full accounts were not available to view on the Charity Commission's website due to the charity's low income. We have therefore estimated the charity's grant total based on its total expenditure.

Other information

This charity also makes grants to organisations.

Naval Children's Charity

See entry on page 26

Nuclear Community Charity Fund

 £48,900 (2019/20)

Correspondent: The Trustees, PO Box 8244, Castle Donington DE74 2BY (tel: 0115 888 3442; email: office@ thenccf.org)

https://thenccf.org

CC number: 1173544

Eligibility

British nuclear test survivors, particularly veterans, and their spouses and dependants.

Types of grant

Grants are given towards the costs of living adaptations, care equipment, services and therapies to enhance well-being and social inclusion.

Applications

Apply via the charity's website.

Financial information

Year end	31/03/2020
Income	£605,800
Total expenditure	£756,400

The Officers' Association

 £1,270,000 (2019/20)

Correspondent: Benevolence Team, Third Floor, 40 Caversham Road, Reading, Berkshire RG1 7EB (tel: 020 7808 4160; email: info@ officersassociation.org.uk)

www.officersassociation.org.uk

CC number: 201321

Eligibility

Former officers of the armed forces, and their widows and dependants.

Types of grant

Regular allowances to cover food and clothing costs. One-off grants can be made towards specific items such as disability aids, white or brown goods or care home top-up fees.

Applications

Apply in writing to the correspondent. The association has a network of honorary representatives throughout the UK who will normally visit the applicant to discuss their problems and offer advice.

Financial information

Year end	30/09/2020
Income	£2,647,000
Total expenditure	£3,960,000

Further financial information

Grants were awarded to 927 individuals during the year.

Other information

The association provides services and advice on money, well-being, housing, employment, health and social life.

Officers' Association Scotland

 £97,100 (2019/20)

Correspondent: Welfare Team, New Haig House, Logie Green Road, Edinburgh EH7 4HR (tel: 0131 550 1575/1581; email: GetHelp@ poppyscotland.org.uk)

www.oascotland.org.uk

OSCR number: SC010665

Eligibility

Welfare
People who have at any time held a commission in any branch of the UK armed forces who are in need. Spouses, widows/widowers, children and dependants are also eligible for support.

Education
Serving or former officers wishing to expand their learning in order to enhance their employment opportunities.

Types of grant

Welfare
The charity provides annual grants and one-off grants according to need. Previously, grants have been given towards specialist equipment, mobility aids, respite breaks, home improvements and so on.

Education
Bursaries are given towards a specific training programme, higher or further education. Support is given in the form of a single payment per year direct to the learning organisation. Consideration may also be given to study costs such as those of learning materials and childcare.

Exclusions

Grants are not made retrospectively for course fees or study materials.

Applications

To apply for a welfare grant, contact the correspondent by phone or email.

For bursary awards, application forms can be downloaded from the charity's website and should be returned to h.mcveigh@oascotland.org.uk. The bursary scheme is open all year round and applications are considered four times a year, usually in June, September, December and March.

Financial information

Year end	31/03/2020
Income	£281,100
Total expenditure	£336,800

Further financial information

During the financial period, grants were distributed as follows:

Annual grants	£62,900
Individual grants	£26,500
Vocational training grants	£3,900
Bursary awards	£3,800

Other information

The charity provides a range of other services including career advice and grants to organisations.

Poppyscotland

 £870,000 (2019/20)

Correspondent: Welfare Services Team, New Haig House, Logie Green Road, Edinburgh EH7 4HR (tel: 0131 550 1557; email: gethelp@poppyscotland.org.uk)

www.poppyscotland.org.uk

OSCR number: SC014096

Eligibility

People resident in, or born in, Scotland who have served in the UK armed forces. Support is also extended to the dependants of such people.

Employment grants are available to ex-service people who are unemployed or have a low household income. Dependants of such people are also supported.

Types of grant

The charity notes that it has deliberately broad grant-giving criteria, and examples of eligible expenditure given by the charity include home repairs or adaptations, replacement of household goods and clothing.

Exclusions

The charity cannot help with the repayment of business debts, loans, legal expenses, medical care, or casts where state assistance or statutory services are available.

Applications

In the first instance, potential applicants should call the charity's helpline (0131 550 1557) or email the Welfare Services Team to discuss their needs.

Financial information

Year end	30/09/2020
Income	£7,450,000
Total expenditure	£7,120,000

Further financial information
The charity awarded welfare grants to 1,153 individuals.

Other information
The charity operates two welfare centres, in Ayrshire and Inverness, for those needing advice on issues such as benefits or housing, debt and employment. The charity also provides financial support to various housing organisations in Scotland, to help veterans find appropriate accommodation. Poppyscotland works closely with veteran mental health organisations to ensure that veterans receive adequate support. The charity has partnered with the Scottish Association for Mental Health (SAMH) to create a specialised employment service (Employ-Able) for veterans and their partners whose mental health is having an impact on their ability to work. SAMH employment advisors can help with CV writing, finding employment and/or volunteering experience, making job applications and other employment-related issues.

Red Cypher

 £42,700 (2019/20)

Correspondent: The Trustees, Unit 5, Blue Barns Business Park, Old Ipswich Road, Ardleigh, Colchester C07 7FX (email: use the contact form available on the website)

www.redcypher.com

CC number: 1161345

Eligibility
Past and present members of 3rd Regiment Royal Horse Artillery who are in need.

Types of grant
One-off grants according to need.

Applications
Application forms are available to download from the charity's website.

Financial information

Year end	31/03/2020
Income	£68,900
Total expenditure	£66,500

The REME Charity

 £177,200 (2020)

Correspondent: The Trustees, RHQ REME, The Prince Philip Barracks, MOD Lyneham, Lyneham, Wiltshire SN15 4XX (tel: 01249 894507; email: corpssec@reme-rhq.org.uk)

remecharity.org

CC number: 1165868

Eligibility
Serving and retired members of the Corps of Royal Electrical and Mechanical Engineers who are in need. Applicants should have served for at least one year in the regular army or at least three years as a reserve.

Types of grant
Grants are given according to need.

Applications
Applications should be made through SSAFA or the Royal British Legion.

Financial information

Year end	31/12/2020
Income	£2,170,000
Total expenditure	£1,860,000

The Rifles Benevolent Trust

 £385,100 (2020)

Correspondent: The Rifles Regimental Secretary, Peninsula Barracks, Romsey Road, Winchester, Hampshire SO23 8TS (tel: 01962 828530; email: benevolence@the-rifles.co.uk)

https://theriflesnetwork.co.uk/page/benevolence

CC number: 1119071

Eligibility
Serving and former members of the Rifles, and their dependants, who are in need.

Types of grant
Welfare
Welfare grants, normally of up to £1,500, are awarded towards clothing, essential household goods, mobility equipment, home adaptations, holidays/respite breaks, rent and priority debts. Weekly pensions are also available.

Education
Educational grants, typically of up to £1,500, are made for retraining costs. Grants have been made for vocational courses for training as paramedics, plumbers, fitness instructors, etc. Grants have also been made for college courses in theology.

Applications
Initial enquiries should be made to SSAFA or the Royal British Legion.

Financial information

Year end	31/12/2020
Income	£605,200
Total expenditure	£648,800

The Rifles Officers' Fund

£1,100 (2020)

Correspondent: The Trustees, RHQ The Rifles, Peninsula Barracks, Romsey Road, Winchester, Hampshire SO23 8TP (tel: 01962 828530; email: officersfund@the-rifles.co.uk)

CC number: 1025591

Eligibility
Serving and former officers of the Rifles regiment, its territorial units and its former regiments, and their dependants, who are in need.

Types of grant
Grants are given to individuals who are in conditions of need, hardship or distress. They can cover such things as disability adaptations (e.g. stairlifts or bath hoists), mobility equipment (e.g. wheelchairs and electric-powered vehicles), rent, rates, bills, clothing or household necessities. Pensions are also available to people who are older or unable to work due to ill health.

Applications
Apply in writing to the correspondent. Applications are considered quarterly, normally in January, April, July and October. Urgent requests may be considered between meetings.

Financial information

Year end	31/12/2020
Income	£36,300
Total expenditure	£26,800

Further financial information
Benevolent grants to individual officers or their widows totalled £1,100, and grants to organisations totalled £11,600.

The Royal Air Force Benevolent Fund

£13,680,000 (2020)

Correspondent: The Trustees, 67 Portland Place, London W1B 1AR (tel: 0300 102 1919; email: mail@rafbf.org.uk)

https://www.rafbf.org

CC number: 1081009

Eligibility
Current and former members of the Royal Air Force (RAF), and their dependants, who are in need as a result of ill health, disability, financial hardship or otherwise. To qualify for support, applicants are usually required to have less than £12,000 in savings. In the case of care home top-up assistance, savings

must be less than £23,250 (£46,500 if capital savings are in joint names).

Educational grants are available to the children of deceased RAF members and those who have left the RAF unexpectedly (due to medical discharge or other unexpected life events) and are unemployed or in low-paid employment.

Types of grant

Welfare

One-off and recurrent grants are made to assist with a range of needs, including:

- Unexpected and unaffordable one-off costs, such as white goods or furniture
- Regular financial assistance (up to £30 per week) for those on a low income who are at or approaching pensionable age, or who have a long-term health condition preventing employment
- Garden maintenance allowance (up to £10 per week) for those with a disability or health condition
- Domestic assistance allowance (up to £20 per week) for those with a disability, to pay for cleaning and maintenance
- Priority bills and debts, or costs of filing for bankruptcy or a Debt Relief Order
- Temporary financial assistance, such as at times of unemployment
- Essential costs, such as a rental deposit or moving costs, for separating couples
- Funeral costs
- Immediate needs grants (up to £5,000) in case of injury or death during service

Education

Scholarships of £3,000 per annum are available to the children of service personnel who are deceased or have a disability. They can be given towards an undergraduate degree at university or a vocational course at college.

Exclusions

The charity is unable to provide support for: business and credit card debts or unsecured loans; financial advice; legal costs; private medical costs. Grants cannot be awarded retrospectively as reimbursements for funds already expended (except in exceptional circumstances).

Applications

Requests for assistance can be made using an online form on the funder's website. Alternatively, prospective applicants may wish to contact the charity's helpline on 0300 102 1919 to begin the application process.

Financial information

Year end		31/12/2020
Income		£19,140,000
Total expenditure		£31,140,000

Other information

The charity also offers a range of support and welfare services for current and former service personnel, and their dependants. See the charity's helpful website or contact the helpline for current information on the available support.

The Royal Air Forces Association

 £151,000 (2020)

Correspondent: Mr N. Bunting, Secretary General, Atlas House, 41 Wembley Road, Leicester, Leicestershire LE3 1UT (tel: 0116 464 5027; email: enquiries@rafa.org.uk)

 www.rafa.org.uk

CC number: 226686

Eligibility

Serving and former members of the Royal Air Force and their dependants. The widows and dependants of those who have died in service, or subsequently, are also eligible for assistance.

Types of grant

Grants are awarded according to need. Examples include home adaptations/improvements and respite breaks.

Applications

Initial enquiries can be made in writing or by telephone to the applicant's local branch.

Financial information

Year end		31/12/2020
Income		£13,920,000
Total expenditure		£17,240,000

Other information

The charity also provides sheltered housing, residential schemes and welfare breaks at Wings Break hotels, all at a subsidised price. The charity also offers advice about financial issues or debts and befriending services for isolated beneficiaries.

The Royal British Legion

 £10,900,000 (2019/20)

Correspondent: The Trustees, 199 Borough High Street, London SE1 1AA (tel: Helpline: 0808 802 8080 (8am to 8pm everyday); email: info@britishlegion.org.uk)

 www.britishlegion.org.uk

CC number: 219279

Eligibility

Serving and former members of the armed forces, and their dependants, who are in need. The charity is dedicated to supporting the whole armed forces community and its eligibility criteria reflects this; see the charity's website for more details.

Types of grant

Crisis grants – support for people to meet unexpected expenses. The scheme does not provide cash but can provide essentials such as vouchers to buy food and help with travel costs.

Household adaptations – support for household adaptations and facilities to help you live independently in your own home.

Employment grants – support for ex-serving personnel and their families, specifically those who are unemployed or under-employed. There are two types of grant available:

- Grants of up to £1,000 to help with the cost of travel, training, equipment and accommodation. Childcare and medical costs linked to difficulties around attending training are also considered.
- Grants of up to £250 to fund the provision of a professional licence that will assist you to find or continue work.

Applications

Initial enquiries can be made by contacting the charity by telephone or email.

Financial information

Year end		30/09/2020
Income		£143,110,000
Total expenditure		£160,970,000

Other information

The Royal British Legion's team of financial advisers can give advice and support on money management, debts and benefits. Grants are also made to organisations.

The Royal Caledonian Education Trust

 £66,600 (2019/20)

Correspondent: Karen Stock, Children and Family Support Service Co-ordinator, 15 Hill Street, Edinburgh EH2 3JP (tel: 0131 322 7350; email: familysupport@rcet.org.uk)

 www.rcet.org.uk

CC number: 310952/SC038722

Eligibility

The Scottish offspring of members of the armed forces. The parent can be non-Scottish as long as the child is Scottish (whether living with the parent or not). 'Scottish' can refer to any of the following: a born Scot; somebody living in Scotland; somebody currently being educated in Scotland

The child or children must have reached statutory pre-school age and higher/further education applicants must be under 21 at the commencement of the programme.

Exceptional circumstances may be considered at trust's discretion.

Types of grant

Individuals are supported through the following funds:

- **School Children Fund** – school uniforms/clothing, sports equipment, after-school clubs/activities, residential school trips (UK only), special equipment for educational/well-being needs and education costs in exceptional circumstances.
- **Crisis Intervention Fund/Well-being Support** – children's needs, essential clothing, essential food and groceries, essential household expenses, essential travel costs and exceptional general needs.
- **College and University Students Fund** – living expenses (undergraduate degree only), books, special equipment and essential course materials.

Exclusions

The trust will not provide funding where the need should be met by the statutory provisions.

Applications

Applications for the School Children Fund and Crisis Intervention Fund must come from a parent or guardian and be made via the local SSAFA branch.

Applications for the College and University Students Fund must come directly from the young person using the form available on the trust's website.

Documentary proof of service and place of birth will be required.

Financial information

Year end	31/03/2020
Income	£342,600
Total expenditure	£584,300

Other information

In addition to making grants to individuals, the trust also works through its education programme with schools, local authorities, armed forces charities and military communities to support armed forces children, teachers and families in the school environment, especially in relation to children's emotional well-being.

Royal Engineers Association

 £412,500 (2020)

Correspondent: The Trustees, REA, Ravelin Building, Brompton Barracks, Chatham, Kent ME4 4UG (tel: 01634 847005; email: controller@rhqre.co.uk)

www.reahq.org.uk

CC number: 258322

Eligibility

Serving or former members of the Corps of Royal Engineers, and their spouses, widows/widowers or dependants, who are in need.

Types of grant

Grants of up to £500 are awarded towards the following:

- Payment priority debts such as rent, rates or utility bills
- Bankruptcy fees and Debt Relief Orders
- Essential items such as clothing, food and household goods
- Contributions towards scooters, wheelchairs, stairlifts, bath lifts and other mobility aids not supplied by the NHS
- Contributions towards specialised medical treatments where urgent need has been identified
- Contributions towards respite breaks for beneficiaries and/or their carers
- Essential household repairs such as decorating, replacement of doors and windows, etc. Except for essential decorating, this does **not** apply to local authority or private lets.
- Bathroom or kitchen adaptations for people with medical conditions or older people (which cannot be done by the local authority or where delay is confirmed)
- Course fees and essential tools of trade required for training for employment
- Spectacles or dental treatment to people in receipt of Income Support/Pension Credit
- Repatriation costs to immediate families compassionate or medical reasons
- Weekly annuities to people over the age of 70*

In exceptional circumstances, and where an application for state benefits has been made, the charity may make a contribution towards funeral costs.

*Weekly annuities of £50 per week are awarded to older people on a low income who are living in their own homes and receive all eligible state benefits. Weekly annuities of £42.50 are awarded to older people living in local authority or private nursing/residential homes who have savings below the recognised state limits after benefits are accounted for.

Exclusions

No grants are awarded towards the cost of:

- Non-priority debts
- Car repairs or running costs
- Home adaptations when there is no medical or compassionate reason
- Mortgage arrears (unless families with young children or older people face the threat of eviction)
- Private medical treatment or medicines
- Private education
- Payment of legal fees, fines or court orders (except for bankruptcy fees or Debt Relief Orders)
- Uninsured travel or holidays
- Medical expenses resulting from an uninsured trip or holiday.

The charity does not award grants to anyone who is currently serving a prison sentence, although support may be offered to their dependants.

Applications

Contact SSAFA (tel. 0800 731 4880) or the Royal British Legion (tel. 0808 802 8080) to request a visit from a caseworker. The caseworker will then visit the applicant for an interview to assess their need. If the applicant is deemed eligible, funding will be awarded to the applicant via the caseworker.

Financial information

Year end	31/12/2020
Income	£1,180,800
Total expenditure	£1,400,400

Further financial information

During the year, the charity awarded £275,200 in welfare grants, £11,500 in Christmas grants and £125,800 in weekly allowances to older individuals.

Other information

The charity also makes grants to ABF, The Soldiers' Charity and other organisations with similar objectives and values.

The Royal Logistics Corps Association Trust Fund

 £223,900 (2019)

Correspondent: The Regimental Treasurer, Dettingen House, Princess Royal Barracks, Deepcut, Camberley GU16 6RW (tel: 01252 833334; email: regttreasurer@rhqtherlc.org.uk)

www.army.mod.uk/rlc/the_rhq/regimental_treasurer.htm

CC number: 1024036

Eligibility

People in need who have at any time served or are now serving in the Royal Logistics Corp (RLC) or its forming Corps, including the Royal Corps of Transport (RCT) and The Royal Army Services Corps (RASC). Members of the women's services and the dependants of any of the above are also eligible.

Types of grant

Grants are given according to need.

Applications

Apply in writing to the correspondent.

Financial information

Year end	31/12/2019
Income	£2,700,000
Total expenditure	£2,520,000

Royal Merchant Navy Education Foundation

 £126,600 (2019/20)

Correspondent: Cdr Charles Heron-Watson, Secretary, 1A Charnham Lane, Hungerford, Berkshire RG17 0EY (tel: 01488 567890; email: office@rmnef.orh.uk)

www.rmnef.org.uk

CC number: 1153323

Eligibility

British children of Merchant Navy seafarers, professional sea-going fishermen and RNLI lifeboat crew members, who have served or are serving at sea and who are unable to meet their children's educational needs. The foundation's website states:

> The length of sea-service is considered when determining whether a young person is eligible for support and, in all instances, the Trustees will use their discretion[...] In each case, we need to identify a genuine 'need' and this will be based upon factors such as domestic environment, locality, health, finance and education.

Types of grant

Support is available for children and young people at any stage of education from pre-school to higher education as well as for career training and apprenticeships (to professional entry qualification). Support can be given towards some or all of the following: school fees; educational extras; school uniforms; travel between home and school; educational equipment; educational visits; educational books; some university expenses.

Applications

Initial contact should be made with the correspondent via letter or email. Phone enquiries to discuss individual circumstances are also welcomed, and some applicants make contact through an associated charity (see the website for further details). Application forms will then be provided to eligible applicants. Candidates will be paid a home visit and may be required to provide an assessment by a relevant professional. A submission is then put to the trustees for a final decision.

Financial information

Year end	31/08/2020
Income	£434,500
Total expenditure	£417,700

The Royal Military Police Central Benevolent Fund

 £69,500 (2019/20)

Correspondent: Col. J. T. Green, Secretary, Regimental Headquarters, Royal Military Police, The Old Stables (Postal Point 38), Southwick Park, Fareham, Hampshire PO17 6EJ (tel: 023 9228 4206; email: cbf@rhqrmp.org)

https://www.rhqrmp.org

CC number: 248713

Eligibility

People who are serving, or have served, in the Royal Military Police and their dependants, widows or widowers.

Types of grant

Grants, generally of up to £1,500 (although larger grants may be available), are awarded for welfare needs. Christmas grants of £100 are distributed to people who have already received an individual benefit grant and are over 80 years of age. Smaller Christmas grants of £25 are awarded to RMP and WRAC in-pensioners resident at the Royal Hospital in Chelsea. In the past, £20 Amazon vouchers have also been distributed to soldiers deployed overseas over the seasonal period.

Applications

Apply in writing to the correspondent. For grant enquiries email cbf@rhqrmp.org, or to contact the secretary directly email regsec@rhqrmp.org.

Financial information

Year end	31/03/2020
Income	£275,000
Total expenditure	£278,000

Further financial information

During the year grants were awarded to 79 individuals totalling £69,500. This includes Christmas grants totalling £4,300 awarded to 40 individuals.

The Royal Naval Benevolent Trust

 £1,441,100 (2020/21)

Correspondent: Grants Administrator, Castaway House, 311 Twyford Avenue, Portsmouth, Hampshire PO2 8RN (tel: 023 9269 0112; email: rnbt@rnbt.org.uk)

www.rnbt.org.uk

CC number: 206243

Eligibility

People who are serving, or have served as ratings in the Royal Naval or as other ranks in the Royal Marines (including reservists) who are in need. Support is extended to the dependants of such people.

Types of grant

Welfare

Welfare grants are typically awarded towards the following expenses: medical and dental treatment; respite breaks; house repairs; food; clothing; furniture; household goods; energy/fuel; removals; rent; mortgage payments; Council Tax and rates; funerals; legal fees; care home top-up fees; telephone bills; domiciliary care; house adaptations (when there is a medical need); mobility aids. Weekly grants of £22 are available to those on a low income.

Education

Educational grants are made to help with costs associated with education and training for second careers.

Exclusions

The charity does not normally help with debts.

Applications

Prospective applicants should first contact their local Royal Navy/Royal Marines Welfare. Alternatively, applicants may wish to contact SSAFA or the Royal British Legion. Representatives from the above organisations will then visit the applicant to discuss their case and if eligible, will make an application on their behalf. The committee meets weekly to consider grant applications.

Financial information

Year end	31/03/2021
Income	£5,720,000
Total expenditure	£5,720,000

Other information

The trust operates a care and nursing home (Pembroke House) in Kent, as well as a subsidised housing facility at the John Cornwell VC National Memorial in Hornchurch.

The Royal Navy Officers' Charity

 £436,300 (2020)

Correspondent: The Trustees, 70 Porchester Terrace, Bayswater, London W2 3TP (tel: 020 7402 5231; email: rnoc@arno.org.uk)

https://www.arno.org.uk/rnoc

CC number: 207405

Eligibility
Serving and retired officers of the Naval Service (Royal Navy, Royal Marines and QARNNS), and their dependants, who are in need.

Types of grant
One-off and recurrent grants are awarded according to need.

Applications
Contact the charity by telephone or email. If necessary, the charity may ask serving personnel to contact the appropriate Royal Navy welfare team member, who will then apply on their behalf.

Financial information
Year end	31/12/2020
Income	£496,800
Total expenditure	£650,800

The Royal Signals Charity

 £339,600 (2020)

Correspondent: Grants Co-ordinator, RHQ Royal Signals, Griffin House, Blandford Camp, Blandford Forum, Dorset DT11 8RH (tel: 01258 482161; email: rscgrants@royalsignals.org)

https://royalsignals.org/royal-signals-charity

CC number: 284923

Eligibility
Serving and retired members and volunteer reserves of the Royal Signals. Support is extended to the dependants of such people.

Types of grant
One-off grants of up to £1,500 are given according to need. Previous examples of support include assistance towards: priority debts (rent arrears, utility bills); electric scooters; level access showers; mobility aids (riser chairs, stairlifts); replacement carpets; white goods; urgent home repairs; removals; rental bonds. The charity also makes grants towards

the cost of attending adventure training: exercises, including mountain biking trips in the USA mountaineering and trekking trips to Nepal and across Europe.

Applications
Applications should be made through SSAFA, The Royal British Legion, The Officers' Association, the British Commonwealth Ex-Services League or Veterans UK, who will complete an application form on the individual's behalf and forward it to the charity. If successful, awards will be made to the sponsoring agency and not the individual themselves.

Financial information
Year end	31/12/2020
Income	£1,250,000
Total expenditure	£1,570,000

Further financial information
The charity awarded grants to 376 beneficiaries (excluding Christmas grants) totalling £339,600. The charity notes that the number of beneficiaries was lower than usual as caseworkers were unable to make as many visits due to the COVID-19 pandemic.

Other information
The charity also operates a yacht club, where people can engage in water sports (windsurfing, kite surfing, etc.) and other sail training opportunities.

Special Boat Service Association

 £428,000 (2019/20)

Correspondent: The Trustees, RM Poole, Hamworthy, Poole, Dorset BH15 4NQ (tel: 01202 202692; email: ceo@association1664.com)

CC number: 1168876

Eligibility
Members and former members of the Special Boat Service, their families and dependants.

Types of grant
One-off grants for welfare purposes, memorials and funeral expenses.

Applications
Apply in writing to the correspondent.

Financial information
Year end	31/03/2020
Income	£2,640,000
Total expenditure	£2,670,000

SSAFA (Soldiers, Sailors, Airmen and Families Association) Forces Help

 £20,180,000 (2020)

Correspondent: The Welfare Team, Queen Elizabeth House, 4 St Dunstan's Hill, London EC3R 8AD (tel: 020 7463 9412; email: info@ssafa.org.uk)

www.ssafa.org.uk

CC number: 210760/SC038056

Eligibility
Current and former service personnel, and their immediate dependants, who are in need.

Types of grant
One-off grants are available for a variety of needs, for example, mobility aids, household goods and transition costs.

Applications
Contact the charity by using the online enquiry form on its website.

Financial information
Year end	31/12/2020
Income	£34,480,000
Total expenditure	£32,890,000

Other information
SSAFA provides a wide range of services to members of the armed forces community including mental well-being, transition support, welfare and benefit advice. The charity has branches throughout the UK and in Cyprus, France, Germany and the Republic of Ireland. Full details of the support provided can be found on the charity's website or by calling its helpline on 0800 731 4880.

UK Veterans Hearing Foundation

Correspondent: The Trustees, 6 New Buildings, Hinckley, LE10 1HW (tel: 01455 248900; email: info@ veteranshearing.org.uk)

https://www.veteranshearing.org.uk

CC number: 1188611

Eligibility
UK armed forces veterans suffering hearing loss.

Types of grant
The foundation provides hearing tests, hearing aids and accessories.

Applications
Contact the foundation via its website.

Financial information

Year end	06/04/2021
Income	£98,400
Total expenditure	£53,200

Further financial information

We were unable to determine the annual grant total.

Welsh Guards Charity

 £38,800 (2019/20)

Correspondent: Jiffy Myers, Regimental Veterans Officer, RHQ Welsh Guards, Wellington Barracks, Birdcage Walk, London SW1E 6HQ (tel: 020 7414 3288; email: welshguardsrvo@gmail.com)

https://www.welshguardscharity.co.uk

CC number: 1152766

Eligibility

Welsh Guards of all ranks, both serving soldiers and retired veterans, and their families.

Types of grant

One-off grants have been awarded in the past for medical equipment, therapy, essential items and short breaks.

Applications

The charity's website states that applicants must contact the correspondent before making an application.

Financial information

Year end	31/03/2020
Income	£424,000
Total expenditure	£537,300

WRNS Benevolent Trust

 £220,100 (2020)

Correspondent: Roger Collings, Grants Administrator, Castaway House, 311 Twyford Avenue, Portsmouth, Hampshire PO2 8RN (tel: 023 9265 5301; email: grantsadmin@wrnsbt.org.uk)

https://wrnsbt.org.uk

CC number: 206529

Eligibility

People in need who has served in the Women's Royal Naval Service (WRNS) and transferred to the Royal Navy on 1 November 1993, or anyone who has served in the WRNS since 3 September 1939, and their dependants. Preference is given to members of the Association of Wrens, but applicants need not be members.

Types of grant

Welfare

One-off and recurrent grants. Recurrent grants are given in the following categories: general amenity; care enhancement; overseas (for beneficiaries who live overseas); weekly maintenance; and weekly support supplements. One-off grants are available towards a wide range of needs, for example: household goods and repairs; priority debts and arrears; medical aids; funeral expenses; removal and travel expenses; and rent and deposits.

The trust operates a triage system such that crisis and urgent cases are dealt with as a priority. The trust's website defines urgent cases as situations where someone needs an intervention, payment or decision within 24–48 hours. If urgent cases cannot be resolved, they may be classed as a crisis case. This refers to situations where the applicant's basic needs (food, clothing and housing) are in jeopardy.

Education

Grants are also available for mature students to help with training courses, study costs, computers, books and so on.

Exclusions

The trust does not make grants for retrospective costs, nor is assistance given to settle secondary debts (e.g. credit cards or amounts owed to family or friends).

Applications

Detailed guidance on the applications process can be found on the trust's helpful website. Applicants should contact the trust via the online form, except in crisis or urgent cases in which the applicant should contact the correspondent via telephone or email (with the email subject titled 'crisis case' or 'urgent case'). Applications can be made directly by the individual or, with their consent, by a relation or friend.

Financial information

Year end	31/12/2020
Income	£321,200
Total expenditure	£329,900

Further financial information

In 2020, the trust received 170 applications.

Other information

The trust's informative website notes the following:

> Despite publicity, one of our biggest problems is raising awareness; it is surprising how many former Wrens do not even know of our existence. If you hear of a former Wren who you think may be having difficulties, do please tell her about us or, if given her permission, contact us on their behalf. Many people are too proud to ask for help, but we always stress that we are their special charity,

and one that they may well have donated to during their time in the Women's Royal Naval Service. Alternatively, you may wish to help us to help those in need by supporting our work through donations and/or legacies.

Occupational charities

This section begins with an index of categories of occupation, which are listed alphabetically.

Grant-makers include both independent charities and benevolent funds associated with particular professional bodies.

Many of the grant-making charities listed here support not only members of a particular occupation, but also their dependants (such as parents, children and partners). This may present additional options to explore when identifying a relevant occupational category.

Being a member of a particular profession or trade is not necessarily enough to be eligible for support – charities may also specify further criteria, so do read the entries in each section carefully.

We have grouped together certain occupations to make relevant charities easier to identify. For example, 'Administration and secretarial' includes charities with general criteria supporting employees in these industries, as well as charities which support a very specific type of occupation within this sector.

We have placed all 'Medicine and health' workers in the same category, as again there are charities that support workers generally and some that will only support certain specific occupations. The 'Skilled crafts and trades' section contains many different individual roles within the industry.

In some cases, paid employment is not necessary – for example, under 'Sports' there are some grant-making charities that support amateur sports people. In this edition, charities concerning clergy and missionaries have been listed under 'Religious occupations' in this chapter; for charities that give based on religious group rather than religious occupation, refer to the chapter 'Charities by beneficiary'.

Please also note that charities which specify both occupation and location are still mainly listed under the appropriate occupational heading, but those with a very specific location may be listed in the relevant geographical chapter instead.

Index of occupational charities

A

Administration and secretarial 98

Architecture and design 98

Arts and heritage 99

C

Construction 106

E

Education and training 108

Energy 111

Engineering 112

Environment and agriculture 114

F

Financial services 117

G

General 121

H

Hospitality 121

I

Information and communication 122

L

Legal 123

M

Manufacturing 125

Maritime 127

Marketing and PR 132

Media 133

Medicine and health 136

Mining and quarrying 145

O

Other specific industries 146

P

Public sector and government 148

R

Religious occupations 154

Retail 160

S

Science 166

Service industry 167

Skilled crafts and trades 167

Social care 171

Sports 172

T

Transport and travel 177

Administration and secretarial

The Chartered Secretaries' Charitable Trust

 £56,300 (2019/20)

Correspondent: The Trustees, Saffron House, 6–10 Kirby Street, London EC1N 8TS (tel: 020 7612 7048; email: CSCT@cgi.org.uk)

https://www.icsa.org.uk/about-us/charitable-trust

CC number: 1152784

Eligibility

Current and former members, employees or students of the institute, and their dependants.

Types of grant

Social welfare

Weekly allowances for everyday needs and regular support according to need, for example towards telephone line or mobile rental, broadband, white goods, house repairs, rental for emergency alarm systems and TV rental and licences. Grants are also available for one-off needs such as the replacement of household items or dental work. Christmas gifts and winter gifts are also awarded to beneficiaries.

Education

Prizes are awarded to students who obtain the highest achievements in the Chartered Governance Institute UK and Ireland's examinations. One-off grants may also be awarded for institute membership subscriptions and examination fees and towards training in secretaryship and business administration.

Applications

Application forms can be downloaded from the trust's website and should be returned by email or post. Requests can be made throughout the year. Institute members visit beneficiaries where necessary. Contact the correspondent if assistance in making the application is required.

Financial information

Year end	31/07/2020
Income	£7,800
Total expenditure	£229,500

Further financial information

The charity supported 64 individuals during the year. The following breakdown of social welfare grants was provided:

Benevolence allowances	£25,400
Rentals and licences	£7,600
Irregular grants	£4,900
Winter grants	£4,800
Christmas grants	£4,500
ICSA membership subscriptions	£2,900
Alarms	£700

In addition, education and research prizes totalled £5,400.

Architecture and design

Architects' Benevolent Society

 £1,530,000 (2019/20)

Correspondent: The Welfare Team, 6 Brewery Square, London SE1 2LF (tel: 020 7580 2823; email: help@absnet.org.uk)

www.absnet.org.uk

CC number: 265139

Eligibility

Architects, including technologists or landscape architects, and their dependants, who are in need. Employees of an architectural practice and their dependants and architecture students are also supported. Eligibility is based on work experience in the UK, rather than based on membership to any professional membership organisation.

Types of grant

One-off grants are made for adaptations for people with disabilities, or for essential living or housing costs in times of crisis. Recurrent grants are also available.

Applications

To start the application process, applicants should contact the society by telephone. Alternatively, an applicant may wish to fill out the 'Apply For Help' form on the funder's website and once completed, a representative of the society will be in touch.

Financial information

Year end	30/09/2020
Income	£790,800
Total expenditure	£2,070,000

Other information

The society offers advice services on benefits, housing, health and social care, as well as support services for people experiencing bereavement. The society works in partnership with Anxiety UK to offer a range of support to people experiencing mental health issues, such as telephone helpline support, email support, a well-being assessment (including one year's membership to Anxiety UK) and one-to-one therapy, conducted by a team of approved therapists. Therapists are trained in a range of therapeutic interventions such as cognitive behavioural therapy (CBT), clinical hypnotherapy and acupuncture, so that therapy sessions can be tailored to the individual and their needs. The society can also make referrals for specialist advice on employment, debt management, legal problems, as well as housing through its partnership with Shelter, which can provide specialist telephone casework for complex housing issues and act as an advocate for individuals facing legal trouble.

Arts and heritage

The Actors' Benevolent Fund

£ £639,500 (2020)

Correspondent: General Secretary, 6 Adam Street, London WC2N 6AD (tel: 020 7836 6378; email: office@abf. org.uk)

 www.actorsbenevolentfund.co.uk

CC number: 206524

Eligibility
Professional actors and theatrical stage managers who are unable to work because of an accident, sickness or old age.

Types of grant
Weekly and monthly grants are available for household bills, such as utilities, home insurance or car insurance, and, in some cases, the shortfall on nursing home fees. One-off grants for larger purchases or costs such as disability aids, physiotherapy, osteopathy, kitchen appliances and funeral costs are also available. The fund also awards hampers.

The fund has also launched an emergency grants programme, offering one-off grants to professional actors, actresses and stage managers experiencing financial hardship owing to the COVID-19 pandemic. See the website for details.

Exclusions
No grants are available to students.

Applications
Applications can be submitted through the fund's website. Applications are considered monthly. In cases of

emergency, where potential beneficiaries need their application to be considered before the next scheduled meeting, contact the fund's office by phone.

Financial information
Year end	31/12/2020
Income	£1,450,000
Total expenditure	£1,100,000

Further financial information
During the year the fund provided support to over 200 individuals, of whom 150 received regular financial help. Grants were paid as follows: weekly allowances (£312,200); monthly grants (£206,600); emergency COVID-19 grants (£107,700); hampers (£13,000).

Other information
The Actors' Benevolent Fund also provides support services, for example to help with the management of household expenses. If you are a member of another theatrical profession and experiencing hardship, the fund offers a list of other organisations that might be useful on its website.

The Actors' Children's Trust (ACT)

£ £634,100 (2019/20)

Correspondent: Robert Ashby, General Secretary, 58 Bloomsbury Street, London WC1B 3QT (tel: 020 7636 7868; email: robert@actorschildren.org)

 www.tactactors.org

CC number: 1177106

Eligibility
Children of professional actors. Grants are usually given to families where the household income is less than £40,000.

Types of grant
The trust's website states: 'ACT gives a range of grants and will consider most suggestions which benefit your child.' Examples of support include grants for:
- Children's activities
- School costs
- Assessments and therapy for children (up to the age of 26) with disabilities
- Childcare
- Moving home
- Help in a crisis
- New babies
- Children aged 16 to 18
- Students and apprentices over the age of 18

Exclusions
Grants are not made for legal costs or private school fees.

Applications
Contact the trust to see if you are eligible.

Financial information
Year end	31/03/2020
Income	£1,090,000
Total expenditure	£981,000

The Artistic Endeavours Trust

£ £5,200 (2019)

Correspondent: The Trustees, MHA Macintyre Hudson LLP, 30–34 New Bridge Street, London EC4V 6BJ (tel: 020 7240 4100)

CC number: 1044926

Eligibility

Welfare
Graduates who have been unable to find gainful employment within two years of finishing higher education in the arts and other creative subjects.

Education
Students undertaking higher education in the arts and other creative subjects.

Types of grant
Grants are awarded to graduate and undergraduate arts students for tuition fees, equipment, books, clothing, educational travel and anything that will assist their education in the arts. Grants are also awarded for general living costs after graduation.

Applications
Apply in writing to the correspondent.

Financial information
Year end	31/12/2019
Income	£15,000
Total expenditure	£11,300

Further financial information
Full accounts were not available to view on the Charity Commission's website due to the trust's low income. We have therefore estimated the trust's grant total based on its total expenditure.

Other information
The trust also supports organisations.

Artists' General Benevolent Institution

£ £386,400 (2019/20)

Correspondent: The Trustees, Burlington House, Piccadilly, London W1J 0BB (tel: 020 7734 1193; email: info@agbi.org.uk)

 www.agbi.org.uk

CC number: 212667

Eligibility
Professional artists (i.e. painters, sculptors, illustrators, art teachers at

A-level or above, etc.) who live in England, Wales or Northern Ireland and have earned their living (or a major part of it) from art but cannot work due to accident, illness or old age. Dependants, widows and orphaned children of artists are also eligible for assistance.

Types of grant
One-off and recurrent grants depending on need. Grants cover a wide range of items and uses, such as domestic and utility bills, repair of equipment or replacement of worn-out items, visits to family and friends, respite care and payment of assisted living.

Exclusions
The charity cannot help with career or legal difficulties, loss of earnings due to poor sales, expenses associated with exhibitions, or (except in exceptional circumstances) student fees.

Applications
Applications should initially be in writing, including a full CV listing all training, qualifications, exhibitions in professional galleries and teaching experience (if any) at GCSE, A-level or above. The secretary visits most potential beneficiaries in order to carry out an assessment and to collect original works, as well as letters from two referees and a doctor or consultant (if applicable). Enquiries from potential applicants are welcomed.

Financial information
Year end	05/04/2020
Income	£610,600
Total expenditure	£743,400

The Authors' Contingency Fund

£ £1,270,000 (2020)

Correspondent: Society of Authors, 24 Bedford Road, London WC1R 4EH (tel: 020 7373 6642; email: info@ societyofauthors.org)

 www.societyofauthors.org

CC number: 212406

Eligibility
Professional authors in the UK and their dependants. Membership of the Society of Authors is not a requirement.

Types of grant
One-off grants to relieve a temporary financial emergency.

Exclusions
The charity cannot help with the following:
- Grants to cover publication costs

- Grants to authors who are in financial difficulty through contributing towards publication costs
- Tuition fees

Applications
Application forms and guidelines are available from the charity's website. Applications should be submitted by post or email with a covering letter, which should briefly set out the circumstances that have prompted the application.

Financial information
Year end	31/12/2020
Income	£1,380,000
Total expenditure	£1,290,000

Further financial information
In 2020, 890 grants were awarded to authors.

Other information
The charity is one of three charities that provide contingency grants and are administered by the Society of Authors. The website also provides information on how to apply for several different grant programmes for works in progress.

The British Antique Dealers' Association Ltd Benevolent Fund

£ £4,400 (2018/19)

Correspondent: The Trustees, 21 John Street, London WC1N 2BF (tel: 020 7589 4128)

 www.bada.org

CC number: 238363

Eligibility
Current or former members of the British Antique Dealers' Association and their dependants. At the trustees' discretion, support may also be extended to those who have been engaged in the art trade and their dependants.

Types of grant
Grants are given according to need.

Applications
Apply in writing to the correspondent.

Financial information
Year end	30/06/2019
Income	£11,400
Total expenditure	£4,900

Further financial information
Full accounts were not available to view on the Charity Commission's website due to the fund's low income. We have therefore estimated the fund's grant total based on its total expenditure. The 2018/19 accounts were the latest available at the time of writing (November 2021).

The Concert Artistes Association Benevolent Fund

£ £30,000 (2019/20)

Correspondent: The Trustees, The Concert Artistes Association, 20 Bedford Street, London WC2E 9HP (tel: 020 7836 3172; email: office@thecaa.org)

CC number: 211012

Eligibility
Members of the association, and their dependants, who are in need. Former members who seceded from membership due to illness or misfortune may also apply.

Types of grant
Grants are available for everyday costs and medical assistance.

Applications
Apply in writing to the correspondent.

Financial information
Year end	30/09/2020
Income	£20,700
Total expenditure	£35,000

Further financial information
Full accounts were not available to view on the Charity Commission's website due to the fund's low income. We have therefore estimated the grant total based on the fund's total expenditure.

The Eaton Fund for Artists Nurses and Gentlewomen
See entry on page 33

The English National Opera Benevolent Fund

£ £14,500 (2019/20)

Correspondent: The Trustees, English National Opera, London Coliseum, St Martin's Lane, London WC2N 4ES (tel: 020 7845 9267; email: benfund@ eno.org)

 https://www.eno.org/about/eno-benevolent-fund

CC number: 211249

Eligibility
Current and former performers and backstage staff employed by the English National Opera (and its antecedent companies) who are in need due to illness, accident or some other hardship.

Dependants may also be supported in some occasions.

Types of grant

One-off and recurrent grants are given according to need. Loans are also available.

Applications

To request an application, contact the fund via email.

Financial information

Year end	31/03/2020
Income	£7,200
Total expenditure	£16,100

Further financial information

Full accounts were not available to view on the Charity Commission's website due to the fund's low income. We have therefore estimated the fund's grant total based on its total expenditure. Note that the grant total may include loans.

Equity Charitable Trust

 £250,900 (2019/20)

Correspondent: Kaethe Cherney, Company Secretary, Plouviez House, 19–20 Hatton Place, London EC1N 8RU (tel: 020 7831 1926; email: kaethe@ equitycharitabletrust.org.uk)

🌐 www.equitycharitabletrust.org.uk

CC number: 328103

Eligibility

Professional performers who are eligible for an Equity card and are in need due to unforeseen circumstances. Note, candidates do no have to be a current Equity member to be eligible.

Types of grant

Welfare

One-off welfare grants are available to assist with a range of purposes. Recent examples include household bills, medical bills, convalescence care, furniture, car repairs, mortgage arrears and so on.

Education

Grants are given to enable retraining or developing skills for a second income stream for professional performers who are able to demonstrate ten years of adult professional work.

Exclusions

The trust will not provide support for the following:

▷ Amateur performers, musicians or drama students
▷ Credit card debt
▷ Overseas courses
▷ Courses that do not lead to a recognised qualification
▷ Courses designed to improve acting and performance skills

▷ Maintenance grants
▷ Student loans
▷ Full tuition fees

Applications

Application forms for each grant can be downloaded from the trust's website. Applications should be submitted to the relevant email (details on the website). The trustees meet every two months to consider welfare grant applications. Welfare applications should include a professional CV and any supporting documentation (such as medical correspondence, copies of outstanding bills or a doctor's note). Education applications should include a personal statement of up to 500 words.

Financial information

Year end	31/03/2020
Income	£471,700
Total expenditure	£488,400

Further financial information

In 2019/20, welfare grants totalling £164,900 were awarded to 170 individuals. Education and training grants totalling £86,000 were awarded to 58 individuals.

Other information

The trust also supports theatres and theatre directors. It also administers grants for the Evelyn Norris Trust – see the charity's entry on page 104 for more information.

Francis Head Award

 £33,100 (2020)

Correspondent: The Trustees, Society of Authors, 24 Bedford Row, London WC1R 4EH (tel: 020 7373 6642; email: grants@societyofauthors.org)

🌐 www.societyofauthors.org/Grants/ Grants-for-writers-in-need

CC number: 277018

Eligibility

Published writers who were born in the UK and are over the age of 35. Priority is given to those in need due to ill health, disability or financial crisis.

Types of grant

Grants are made for a wide range of purposes including one-off expenses such as repair of a broken boiler or laptop, support for a health crisis, loss of income due to being unable to work and so on. Grants range from £500 to £2,000.

Exclusions

Grants cannot be made towards student tuition fees, specific writing projects or publication costs or to authors who are not yet working professionally and receiving income from author-related activities.

Applications

Application forms are available to download on the charity's website. Completed forms should be submitted, along with an equalities monitoring form to grants@societyofauthors.org.

Financial information

Year end	31/12/2020
Income	£19,900
Total expenditure	£49,700

Further financial information

Full accounts were not available to view on the Charity Commission's website due to the charity's low income. We have therefore estimated the grant total based on the charity's total expenditure.

Other information

The charity is one of three charities that provide contingency grants and are administered by the Society of Authors. The charity's website also provides information on how to apply for several different grant programmes for works in progress.

Help Musicians UK

 £17,490,000 (2020)

Correspondent: The Trustees, Help Musicians UK, 7–11 Britannia Street, London WC1X 9JS (tel: 020 7239 9100; email: secretariat@helpmusicians.org.uk)

🌐 www.helpmusicians.org.uk

CC number: 228089

Eligibility

Current or retired professional musicians (i.e. someone who has earned their living substantially from music, usually for more than three years). Support is also available to those who work, or have worked, in a music-related profession (i.e. work which is directly involved in the production of music or has a high level of musical training, such as a mixing desk engineer or music librarian). In some circumstances, support may be extended to the dependants and/or partners of a musician. Applicants must be current UK residents, or must have been residing in the UK for a minimum of three consecutive years during their career in music.

Types of grant

One-off grants for items services such as therapy or medical treatment, mobility aids, home adaptations and respite breaks. The charity also makes grants for household bills and other living expenses. For young artists, the charity funds a variety of learning opportunities such as masterclasses, writing retreats, short courses and so on, as well as recording costs.

Exclusions

Grants are not usually awarded to individuals with savings of more than £16,000 (£20,000 for older or retired musicians). This charity does not support amateur musicians for whom paid music work is, or was, secondary to another career.

Applications

Initial enquiries can be made by contacting the charity's helpline or email address. If deemed eligible at this stage, the applicant will be sent an application form to complete which must include evidence of finances (e.g. bank statements) and details of a musical referee who can confirm the applicant's career and status as a professional musician.

Financial information

Year end	31/12/2020
Income	£12,620,000
Total expenditure	£22,860,000

Further financial information

In 2020, £14.73 million was awarded to individuals for financial hardship relief, £1.57 million for medical and financial assistance and £1.19 million to young/emerging artists at the beginning of their careers.

Other information

The charity offers a variety of services, such as the 'Music Minds Matter' helpline operated 24/7 for musicians who need support and advice for mental health issues.

ISM Members' Fund (The Benevolent Fund of The Incorporated Society of Musicians)

 £36,000 (2019/20)

Correspondent: The Trustees, 4–5 Inverness Mews, London W2 3JQ (tel: 020 7221 3499; email: membership@ism.org)

www.ism.org

CC number: 206801

Eligibility

Members and former members of the society and their dependants who are in need.

Types of grant

One-off and recurrent grants according to need.

Applications

Contact the fund for further information.

Financial information

Year end	31/08/2020
Income	£135,400
Total expenditure	£146,900

Other information

The fund also provides counselling and physiotherapy services as well as a personal support and advice helpline.

The P.D. James Memorial Fund

 £52,500 (2020)

Correspondent: Society of Authors, 24 Bedford Row, London WC1R 4EH (tel: 020 7373 6642; email: info@societyofauthors.org)

www.societyofauthors.org/Grants/P-D-James-Memorial-Fund

CC number: 212401

Eligibility

Members of the Society of Authors (SoA) who are either aged 60 or over or are medically unable to work. Applicants must have been a member of the SoA for at least ten years and be experiencing financial hardship.

Types of grant

Annual grants of £2,200 per recipient are given in the form of regular payments.

Applications

Grants are advertised via email to members as they become available.

Financial information

Year end	31/12/2020
Income	£26,500
Total expenditure	£70,700

Further financial information

Grants were awarded to 24 individuals during the year.

Other information

The charity is one of three charities that provide contingency grants and are administered by the Society of Authors. The charity's website also provides information on how to apply for several different grant programmes for works in progress.

Line Dance Foundation

 £31,800 (2019/20)

Correspondent: The Trustees, Clare House, 166 Lord Street, Southport PR9 0QA (email: linedancefoundation@gmx.com)

www.linedancefoundation.com

CC number: 1164708

Eligibility

Support is provided to anyone involved in line dancing on a professional basis including choreographers, instructors, performers, DJs and event organisers.

Types of grant

One-off grants according to need.

Applications

Applications can be made on the funder's website. Alternatively, applicants may wish to download an application form and once completed, send it by post to the charity.

Financial information

Year end	31/03/2020
Income	£66,300
Total expenditure	£56,900

The Evelyn Norris Trust

 £40,500 (2019)

Correspondent: Kaethe Cherney, Administrator, c/o Equity Charitable Trust, Plouviez House, 19–20 Hatton Place, London EC1N 8RU (tel: 020 7831 1926; email: kaethe@equitycharitabletrust.org.uk)

www.equitycharitabletrust.org.uk/other-grants/evelyn-norris-trust

CC number: 260078

Eligibility

Members of the concert, performing or theatrical professions who are undergoing treatment or in poor health.

Types of grant

One-off holiday grants of up to £1,000.

Applications

Application forms are available to download on the trust's website. Applications are considered on a monthly basis. Grants can be requested annually, but preference is given to first-time applicants.

Financial information

Year end	31/12/2019
Income	£49,700
Total expenditure	£52,500

Further financial information

Grants were awarded to 53 individuals during the year.

Other information

The trust also makes grants to residential homes.

The Incorporated Association of Organists' Benevolent Fund

 £13,200 (2020)

Correspondent: Michael Whitehall, Secretary and Treasurer, 2 Winifred's Dale, Cavendish Road, Bath, Somerset BA1 2UD (tel: 01225 421154; email: richard.m.allen@btinternet.com)

🌐 www.iaobf.com

CC number: 216533

Eligibility
Organists and/or choirmasters who are members/former members of any association or society affiliated to the Incorporated Association of Organists, and their dependants, who are in need.

Types of grant
Recurrent grants are awarded according to need.

One-off grants are also available for young organists whose parents are unable to afford tuition fees.

Applications
An application form is available from the correspondent or can be downloaded from the fund's website. Applications can be made by the individual but should be countersigned by the secretary of the applicant's local organists' association. They should be submitted by 31 March for consideration at the trustees' annual meeting in May. In urgent cases the secretary may obtain approval at other times.

Financial information
Year end	31/12/2020
Income	£11,400
Total expenditure	£14,700

Further financial information
Full accounts were not available to view on the Charity Commission's website due to the fund's low income. We have therefore estimated the fund's grant total based on its total expenditure.

Organists' Charitable Trust

 £11,700 (2019)

Correspondent: The Grants Officer, 26 Fitzroy Square, London W1T 6BT (tel: 020 8318 1471; email: grants@organistscharitabletrust.org)

🌐 www.organistscharitabletrust.org

CC number: 225326

Eligibility
Organists who are in need as a result of disability, age, illness, infirmity or unexpected/financial difficulties, and their dependants. Support is also available to organists who are unable to afford to continue professional educational opportunities in the field.

Types of grant
Small one-off and recurrent grants are given according to need. Previously support has been given towards the cost of a carer, car repairs, home adaptations and urgent bills in times of crisis. Grants are also given for professional educational opportunities such as advanced organ lessons and attendance at a course or seminar.

Applications
Application forms are available to download from the trust's website. Completed forms should be submitted by email **and** by post to the correspondent. Applications should be submitted along with a reference form completed by two referees (e.g. a member of the clergy, doctor or solicitor). The Grants Officer will make a telephone call to at least one of the referees to confirm authenticity.

Financial information
Year end	31/12/2019
Income	£11,200
Total expenditure	£13,000

Further financial information
Full accounts were not available to view on the Charity Commission's website due to the trust's low income. We have therefore estimated the trust's grant total based on its total expenditure.

The Performing Rights Society Members' Benevolent Fund (PRS Members' Fund)

 £2,280,000 (2020)

Correspondent: The Trustees, 1st Floor, Goldings House, 2 Hay's Lane, London SE1 2HB (tel: 020 3741 4067; email: fund@prsformusic.com)

🌐 https://www.prsmembersfund.com

CC number: 1181735

Eligibility
Former and current PRS members, and their immediate families, who are experiencing financial, emotional or physical difficulties. Individuals must have held membership for at least seven years or have earned £500 in royalties.

Types of grant
Regular grants to help with daily living expenses and other essentials, as well as winter heating grants. One-off grants towards unexpected costs such as domestic appliance replacement or specialist equipment.

Exclusions
The fund will not help:
▶ With the cost of buying a home
▶ To promote any commercial venture
▶ Composers who do not have any other employment

Applications
Application forms can be downloaded from the fund's website.

Financial information
Year end	31/12/2020
Income	£2,170,000
Total expenditure	£2,700,000

Other information
The fund also provides sheltered accommodation, debt advice, career counselling services, health assessments and mental health support.

The Philharmonia Benevolent Fund

£37,400 (2019/20)

Correspondent: The Trustees, Philharmonia Ltd, 6 Chancel Street, London SE1 0UX (tel: 020 7921 3940)

CC number: 280370

Eligibility
Current and former members of the Philharmonia Orchestra, and their dependants, who are in need.

Types of grant
Grants are given according to need.

Applications
Apply in writing to the correspondent.

Financial information
Year end	31/03/2020
Income	£32,400
Total expenditure	£38,200

The Peggy Ramsay Foundation

£197,800 (2019)

Correspondent: The Trustees, 7 Savoy Court, London WC2 0EX (tel: 020 7667 5000; email: prf@harbottle.com)

🌐 www.peggyramsayfoundation.org

CC number: 1015427

Eligibility

Playwrights who are resident in the British Isles and are in need. The charity also supports musical book writers and lyricists.

Types of grant

Grants are made to theatre writers in order to afford them the time and the space to write. For example, funding could be used towards rent, bills or the cost of a laptop.

Exclusions

Support is not given to writers who write solely for media other than theatre or composers.

Applications

Apply by writing a short letter to the correspondent. Full details of what should be included can be found on the foundation's website.

Financial information

Year end	31/12/2019
Income	£267,000
Total expenditure	£317,400

Further financial information

Grants were awarded to 84 individuals in 2019.

The Royal Ballet Benevolent Fund

 £291,800 (2019/20)

Correspondent: The Trustees, Community Base, 113 Queens Road, Brighton, East Sussex BN1 3XG (tel: 01273 234011; email: info@ dancefund.org.uk)

https://www.dancefund.org.uk

CC number: 207477

Eligibility

Practicing, former or retired professional dancers, dance teachers, choreographers and choreologists with at least three years of professional experience in the UK. Dependants of such people may also be supported. Applicants must have individual savings of less than £6,000 if of working age, or £16,000 if retired, and no other significant means of support.

Types of grant

Grants, usually of between £500 and £3,000, can be awarded to help with living costs, training, medical costs, retirement and crisis funding (e.g. when facing homelessness). For further details visit the fund's website.

Exclusions

Grants are not awarded to the following individuals:

- Students training to be dancers and who are yet to commence their career

- People requiring funding for artistic work (rehearsals or production costs)
- People working in therapeutic arts (dance therapy) or movement teachers in schools

Applications

Application forms are available to download from the fund's website. Applicants must be in receipt of all the state benefits they are entitled to at the time of applying. The trustees welcome informal enquiries to discuss an application prior to the submission of a formal application.

Financial information

Year end	30/06/2020
Income	£766,200
Total expenditure	£395,600

Further financial information

During the year, grants were distributed as follows:

COVID-19 grants	£204,300
General benevolent grants	£54,000
Regular allowance for beneficiaries	£17,100
Injury grants	£10,100
Training grants	£6,400

Other information

The fund offers non-financial assistance in the form of advice services.

The Royal Literary Fund

 £1,650,000 (2019/20)

Correspondent: Eileen Gunn, Chief Executive, 3 Johnson's Court, Off Fleet Street, London EC4A 3EA (tel: 020 7353 7159; email: eileen.gunn@rlf.org.uk)

www.rlf.org.uk

CC number: 219952

Eligibility

Authors across the literary spectrum who have commercially published several pieces of work in the UK and are in need due to financial setbacks, ill health, or bereavement. Dependants of such people can also be supported.

Types of grant

One-off grants and pensions are awarded for up to five years. In the past, grants have been used for paying bills and debts, specialist equipment for people with disabilities and house adaptations for more independent living.

Exclusions

No grants for projects, work in progress or publication costs. The charity does not make loans. Self-published books and books stemming from a previous academic or practitioner career are not counted.

Applications

Application forms are available from the correspondent. When requesting a form, applicants should include a list of their publications with the names of publishers, dates and whether they are the sole author.

Financial information

Year end	31/03/2020
Income	£3,820,000
Total expenditure	£7,110,000

Further financial information

In 2019/20, 214 grants were awarded to individuals.

Other information

The charity also offers fellowships for professional writers to work in a university two days a week.

The Royal Opera House Benevolent Fund

 £105,100 (2019/20)

Correspondent: Benevolent Team, Benevolent Fund, Royal Opera House, Covent Garden, London WC2E 9DD (tel: 020 7212 9128; email: ben.fund@ roh.org.uk)

www.roh.org.uk/about/benevolent-fund

CC number: 200002

Eligibility

Past or present employees of the Royal Opera House or the Birmingham Royal Ballet, and their dependants, who are in financial need.

Types of grant

Financial support is available through monthly allowances, interest-free loans, emergency grants and one-off grants towards essential house maintenance, domestic equipment, urgent medical costs or respite breaks. The fund also provides confidential advice and emotional support.

Applications

Application forms can be downloaded from the fund's website.

Financial information

Year end	31/03/2020
Income	£145,900
Total expenditure	£519,100

Further financial information

During the year, grants awarded to individuals were distributed as follows:

Monthly allowances	£84,400
Other benevolent grants	£20,700

Other information

The fund also supports other registered charities.

The Royal Scottish Academy (RSA)

 £131,700 (2019/20)

Correspondent: The Trustees, Royal Scottish Academy, The Mound, Edinburgh EH2 2EL (tel: 0131 624 6110; email: opportunities@ royalscottishacademy.org)

www.royalscottishacademy.org

OSCR number: SC004198

Eligibility
Professional artists and art students in Scotland.

Types of grant
The charity has a number of grant schemes and eligible expenditure will vary according to the grant being offered. Awards include:
- The RSA David Michie Travel Award (£2,500) and the RSA Barns-Graham Travel Award (£2,000) for graduating and postgraduate drawing and painting students for travel and research opportunities.
- The RSA John Kinross Scholarships (£3,000) for final-year and postgraduate students to spend 6–12 weeks in Florence to research and develop their practice.
- The RSA Benevolent Awards for artists experiencing adverse financial difficulties who have had previous success such as work shown in exhibitions or who have sold their work.

Exclusions
Exclusion criteria may vary between the grant programmes; see the charity's website for further information.

Applications
Applications can be made online when the relevant grant programme is open. Further information on other grants can be also be obtained from the academy's website.

Financial information
Year end	31/03/2020
Income	£1,010,000
Total expenditure	£1,030,000

Other information
The Royal Scottish Academy is an independent membership-led organisation. It runs a programme of exhibitions, artist opportunities and educational talks and events to support artists at all stages of their careers.

The Royal Society of Musicians of Great Britain

 £576,500 (2019/20)

Correspondent: The Trustees, 26 Fitzroy Square, London W1T 6BT (tel: 020 7629 6137; email: enquiries@ royalsocietyofmusicians.org)

https://www.rsmgb.org

CC number: 208879

Eligibility
Current, former or prospective professional musicians, and their dependants, who are in need as a result of illness, accident or older age. Membership to the society is not essential, although priority may be given to members.

Types of grant
The Royal Society of Musicians of Great Britain makes grants to support household income where this is impacted by illness or accident. Grants can be given towards the cost of therapists or counsellors, unexpected bills or expenses in old age and funeral expenses.

Applications
Apply in writing to the correspondent. Applications must be supported in writing by a member or honorary member of the society, or a society-approved organisation.

Financial information
Year end	31/07/2020
Income	£929,000
Total expenditure	£1,620,000

Further financial information
During the financial year, approximately 88% of grants were made to non-members.

Other information
The society has a money adviser who is able to give practical guidance on financial problems and long-term money management and support applications for state benefits. The society also has a network of medical officers who are qualified to offer medical advice attuned to the specific needs of beneficiaries. The charity can direct unsuccessful applicants to alternative funding sources.

The Royal Theatrical Fund

 £269,400 (2019/20)

Correspondent: The Trustees, West Suite, 2nd Floor, 11 Garrick Street, London WC2E 9AR (tel: 020 7836 3322; email: admin@trtf.com)

www.trtf.com

CC number: 222080

Eligibility
People who have professionally practised or contributed to the theatrical arts (on stage, radio, film or television or any other medium) for a minimum of seven years and are in need as a result of illness, accident or old age. The dependants of such people are also eligible.

Types of grant
Monthly allowances and one-off grants towards domestic bills, shortfalls in nursing and residential fees, car tax, stairlifts, gifts, computers, insurance, TV licences and so on.

Applications
In the first instance, contact the fund via the contact section of the fund's website. The fund notes that it may later require a letter of support from a GP or hospital (or a current medical certificate) and a full CV or details of the individual's theatrical career.

Financial information
Year end	31/03/2020
Income	£630,000
Total expenditure	£492,800

Further financial information
Grants were broken down as follows:
Monthly allowances	£107,000
One-off grants (including birthday and Christmas gifts and winter fuel grants)	£104,200
Nursing/residential or home care	£58,200

Other information
The fund also provides advice on entitlement to state benefits, as well as emotional support for beneficiaries who are lonely or isolated.

Scottish Artists Benevolent Association

£17,000 (2019/20)

Correspondent: The Secretary, Regent Court, 70 West Regent Street, Glasgow G2 2QZ (email: lesley@robbferguson.co.uk)

scottishartistsbenevolentassociation.co.uk

OSCR number: SC011823

Eligibility
Scottish artists in need and their dependants. While grants are mainly given to people who are older or in poor health, the charity also receives funds from the Tod Endowment Trust (OSCR no. SC010046), which provides holidays

in Scotland for artists who have been resident in Scotland for at least two years and are experiencing difficulties.

Types of grant

Regular or one-off grants according to need.

Applications

Application forms can be requested from the correspondent. Applications are considered in March and November. Emergency applications are considered on an ongoing basis.

Financial information

Year end	31/01/2020
Income	£35,600
Total expenditure	£24,900

Scottish Showbusiness Benevolent Fund

 £16,000 (2019/20)

Correspondent: The Trustees, Centrum House, 38 Queen Street, Glasgow G1 3DX (email: use the contact form available on the website)

www.ssbf.co.uk

OSCR number: SC009910

Eligibility

Members of the Scottish Showbusiness Benevolent Fund and their dependants, including widows/widowers, who are in need.

Types of grant

One-off and recurrent grants towards, for example, clothing, fuel, living expenses, funeral costs, and TV rental and licences.

Applications

Applications should be made in writing to the correspondent.

Financial information

Year end	31/03/2020
Income	£20,600
Total expenditure	£16,900

Further financial information

Full accounts were not available to view on the OSCR website due to the fund's low income. We have therefore estimated the grant total based on the fund's total expenditure.

The Theatrical Guild

 £450,000 (2020)

Correspondent: The Trustees, The Theatrical Guild, 11 Garrick Street, London WC2E 9AR (tel: 020 7240 6062; email: admin@ttg.org.uk)

www.ttg.org.uk

CC number: 206669

Eligibility

Anyone whose career has predominantly been spent backstage or front of house in theatres in the UK. This includes stage technicians and engineers, stage managers, stagehands and flymen, anyone working in costume, hair or makeup, set or prop designers, puppet-makers, ushers and box office staff. Note that this list is not exhaustive.

Types of grant

Short-term and long-term financial help for costs including bills, medical fees, funerals, mortgage payments and childcare.

Applications

Apply online via the charity's website.

Financial information

Year end	31/12/2020
Income	£696,200
Total expenditure	£521,100

Further financial information

During the year, the charity provided grants to 1,051 individuals.

Other information

The charity also offers access to counselling, welfare support, personal and financial advice and educational sponsorship. It can also signpost individuals to other sources of support.

Construction

Builders' Benevolent Institution

 £50,400 (2020)

Correspondent: The Secretary, Sparkes Farm Cottage, Bury Road, Thorpe Morieux, Bury St Edmunds, Suffolk IP30 0NT (tel: 01284 828373; email: enquiries@bbi1847.org.uk)

https://www.bbi1847.org.uk

CC number: 212022

Eligibility

Active and retired master builders and their dependants.

Types of grant

Monthly grants are awarded according to need. One-off grants towards the cost of essential items such as stairlifts, home alterations and home repairs. The charity also distributes vouchers during Christmas.

Applications

Applications can be completed through a form available online, or they can be downloaded and posted to the correspondent.

Financial information

Year end	31/12/2020
Income	£55,100
Total expenditure	£74,200

Further financial information

During the year, grants awarded were distributed as follows: pensions (£49,700); temporary relief (£750).

Other information

The charity has a welfare advisor who visits beneficiaries regularly to offer support and to assist with applications for state benefits.

Building and Civil Engineering Charitable Trust

£142,100 (2019/20)

Correspondent: Claims Administration Team, Manor Royal, Crawley, West Sussex RH10 9QP (tel: 0300 200 0600; email: charitabletrust@bandce.co.uk)

CC number: 1004732

Eligibility

People working in, or who have worked in, the construction industry who are experiencing hardship. Applicants should have less than £3,000 in savings and must have been employed in the industry for at least 12 months.

Types of grant

Hardship grants are made for the following: essential household items, such as white goods, carpets and beds; rent/utilities arrears; rent in advance and deposits; funeral costs; bankruptcy fees; respite care; home adaptations; disability aids.

The trust also runs a grants scheme for operatives or past operatives who need to retrain due to health reasons.

Applications

Potential applicants or those acting on behalf of an individual (e.g. Citizens Advice) should contact the trust's claim administrators for further information and an application form. The trust aims to pay individuals as soon as possible; the turnaround depends on how quickly it receives supporting documentation from the applicant.

Financial information

Year end	30/09/2020
Income	£658,100
Total expenditure	£620,600

Other information

The trust has developed a free, construction worker helpline (0808 801 0372) which provides free support and guidance. The line is open from 8am to 8pm, seven days a week.

OCCUPATIONAL CHARITIES

Chartered Institute of Building Benevolent Fund

 £55,600 (2020)

Correspondent: Emma McKay, CIOB Assist Fund Manager, 1 Arlington Square, Downshire Way, Bracknell, Berkshire RG12 1WA (tel: 01344 630733; email: assist@ciob.org.uk)

https://assist.ciob.org

CC number: 1013292

Eligibility
Past and present members of the Chartered Institute of Building and their dependants who are in need.

Types of grant
According to the fund's website, it can help with:

- Financial assistance for Members and their dependent families in circumstances of crisis such as illness, unemployment and financial hardship
- Grants to help with general household costs
- Grants to help with essential travel (to work)
- Grants to help families in hardship to buy clothing, or household items
- Grants to help Members with children living at home and in hardship
- Short-term, skills-based training

Exclusions
According to its website, the fund cannot help with:

- Membership fees and medical treatment
- Legal costs
- Business-related costs
- Educational costs
- Personal or business debts
- Purchase of Motor Vehicles
- Home improvements

Applications
Application forms are available to download from the website and can be returned to the correspondent by email.

Financial information
Year end	31/12/2020
Income	£92,400
Total expenditure	£145,700

Other information
The fund provides a range of support and advice for its beneficiaries, including on work, housing, money or other welfare issues. More information on how to access support is available on the fund's informative website, or from the correspondent.

The Company of Chartered Surveyors Charitable Trust Fund (1992)

 £82,600 (2019/20)

Correspondent: The Trustees, 75 Meadway Drive, Horsell, Woking, Surrey GU21 4TF (tel: 01483 727113; email: wccsurveyors@btinternet.com)

www.surveyorslivery.org.uk

CC number: 1012227

Eligibility
Young people who wish to enter the chartered surveying profession, surveying graduates who wish to undertake a research project associated with real estate and the built environment and surveying undergraduates experiencing financial hardship.

Types of grant
Bursaries are awarded to students from four supported schools in Dagenham, Southwark, Oval and Bow. Annual awards are available for surveying graduates or surveyors to undertake a research project associated with real estate and the built environment. Grants are available for undergraduates experiencing financial hardship are awarded according to need.

Applications
Apply in writing to the correspondent.

Financial information
Year end	30/09/2020
Income	£96,800
Total expenditure	£258,300

Further financial information
Full accounts were not available to view on the Charity Commission's website at the time of writing (November 2021). We have estimated the grant total based on previous grant expenditure.

Other information
The fund mainly supports organisations and assists students by giving grants to various universities/colleges to be distributed as bursaries and prizes.

CIBSE (Chartered Institution of Building Services Engineers) Benevolent Fund Trust

 £39,700 (2020)

Correspondent: Stuart Brown, 222 Balham High Road, London SW12 9BS (tel: 020 8675 5211; email: benfund@cibse.org)

https://www.cibse.org/benfund

CC number: 1115871

Eligibility
Members and former members of CIBSE (Chartered Institution of Building Services Engineers), the Institution of Heating and Ventilating Engineers (IHVE) or the Illuminating Engineering Society of Great Britain (IES) who are in need, whether through sickness, bereavement or financial hardship. Dependants of such people are also eligible. The fund supports those who need assistance through transitional or short-term circumstances, as well as others who require ongoing support. In most cases, individuals should have been a member for at least three years.

Types of grant
Grants are awarded according to need. The fund's website states that many individuals receive a regular quarterly grant payment, while others are assisted with specific, one-off needs.

Applications
Contact the correspondent or your local almoner to request support.

Financial information
Year end	31/12/2020
Income	£58,200
Total expenditure	£43,400

Further financial information
Grants were awarded to 39 individuals during the year.

Other information
The fund's regional almoners visit applicants to assess their circumstances, as well as providing advice.

Lighthouse Construction Industry Charity (LCIC)

 £550,000 (2019)

Correspondent: The Trustees, Suffolk Enterprise Centre, Felaw Maltings, 44 Felaw Street, Ipswich IP2 8SJ (tel: 0345 609 1956; email: info@lighthouseclub.org)

www.lighthouseclub.org

CC number: 1149488

Eligibility
People who work or have recently worked in the construction industry, or in an industry associated with construction (e.g. civil engineering, demolition or design), in the UK or the Republic of Ireland. Dependants of such people are also eligible for support. The charity's website states:

You can apply for emergency financial assistance if you have worked in the construction industry for more than 5 years and one of the following applies to you:

- You have been injured at work or outside work and expected to be unable to work for more than 6 months
- You are suffering an illness that prevents you from working for a period longer than 6 months
- You are now the full time primary carer for a spouse or child
- You are suffering a long term, life changing or terminal illness

Types of grant

Grants are given according to need.

Applications

Contact the charity via the telephone or alternatively fill out the online application form. Details on how to apply are available on the website.

Financial information

Year end	31/12/2019
Income	£2,100,000
Total expenditure	£1,900,000

Other information

The charity has a helpline (0345 605 1956) that provides advice on welfare support, occupational health and mental well-being.

Lionheart (The Royal Institution of Chartered Surveyors Benevolent Fund)

£397,000 (2019/20)

Correspondent: The Trustees, Royal Institution of Chartered Surveyors Benevolent Fund, Ground Floor, 55 Colmore Row, Birmingham B3 2AA (tel: 0800 099 2960 or 0121 289 3300; email: info@lionheart.org.uk)

 www.lionheart.org.uk

CC number: 261245

Eligibility

Current and former members of the Royal Institution of Chartered Surveyors, and their dependants, who are in need. For all current eligibility criteria, see the fund's website.

Types of grant

One-off or recurrent grants (for a maximum period of two years) towards the purchase of essential items such as a fridge or cooker, or towards general living expenses. Emergency grants of up to £1,000 to members who have been affected by an unexpected environmental disaster such as a flood or earthquake.

Applications

Initial enquiries should be made by contacting the charity.

Financial information

Year end	31/03/2020
Income	£2,280,000
Total expenditure	£1,960,000

Other information

The fund offers a debt management and advice service, as well as operating workshops offering advice on how to secure a sound financial future. The fund also has a team of counsellors registered with the British Association of Counselling and Psychotherapy (BACP), who are available to speak via telephone or video call. Work-related support is also available to people who wish to build on employment skills. One-off legal support is offered to anyone experiencing legal problems.

Education and training

Church Schoolmasters and Schoolmistresses' Benevolent Institution

£104,000 (2019/20)

Correspondent: The Trustees, 3 Kings Court, Harwood Road, Horsham, West Sussex RH13 5UR (tel: 01403 250798; email: info@cssbi.org.uk)

 www.cssbi.org.uk

CC number: 207236

Eligibility

Current or former teachers and lecturers, or their immediate families, who are members of the Church of England or another recognised Christian denomination and are experiencing financial hardship. Applicants must be resident in England or Wales and be able to provide the details of two referees who can confirm their educational and church connections.

Types of grant

One-off grants are given to assist with, for example: general living expenses due to a change in circumstances such as illness, loss of employment or relationship breakdown; home repairs or adaptations; relocation costs; travel or childcare costs; purchase of essential household equipment, clothing or food; mobility equipment; short-term shortfall in care home fees; respite care; utility bill, Council Tax or rent arrears due to unavoidable circumstances. In exceptional circumstances, support over

a longer period of time may be considered.

Applications

Application forms are available to download from the website, or upon request from the correspondent.

Financial information

Year end	31/03/2020
Income	£65,300
Total expenditure	£171,000

Further financial information

Grants were awarded to 39 individuals during the year.

Education Support Partnership

£312,300 (2019/20)

Correspondent: The Grants Team, 40A Drayton Park, London N5 1EW (tel: 020 7697 2772; email: grantscaseworker@ edsupport.org.uk)

 https://www.educationsupport.org. uk

CC number: 1161436

Eligibility

People who are employed in or have been employed in primary, secondary, further or higher education in one of the following roles/areas:

- Teacher
- Teaching assistant
- Deputy head or headteacher
- Newly qualified teacher (NQT)
- Special educational needs (SEN) provision
- Lecturer
- Supply teacher
- Retired teacher
- Learning support
- Academic administration
- Academic manager

NQTs must have been employed for a minimum of one academic term.

Support can be provided if there has been a significant change in your circumstances such as:

- A sudden or unexpected loss of income
- A sudden or unexpected illness, injury or bereavement
- You are unable to meet the cost of travelling to work
- A sudden or unexpected change in living circumstances or loss of home
- A relationship breakdown
- An issue of domestic abuse

Types of grant

Grants of up to £2,000 may be able to assist with:

- Essential expenses (up to £350)
- Essential household items
- Moving costs

- Health improvement aids and adaptations
- Housing costs (rental and mortgage)
- Travel expenses to work
- Essential household repairs
- Car repairs
- Funeral costs (up to £500)
- Bankruptcy and Debt Relief Order (DRO) application fees
- Council Tax costs
- Utility bills (gas and electric)

Exclusions
The charity cannot make grants for:
- Debts – consumer credit/debt repayments, payday loans, overdraft fees
- Legal fees and costs of legal representation
- Payment of fines
- House purchase
- Private medical treatment
- Private education
- Carpets
- Benefit overpayments
- Underpayment of Income Tax
- Purchase of cars

Applications
Application forms are available to complete on the charity's website. Further information and full guidelines are also available on the website.

Financial information
Year end	31/03/2020
Income	£2,710,000
Total expenditure	£2,980,000

Other information
The charity provides resources on a range of well-being topics on its website as well as running a 24/7 phone support helpline for education staff.

Educational Institute of Scotland Benevolent Funds

£221,300 (2019/20)

Correspondent: Local Benevolent Fund Correspondent, 46 Moray Place, Edinburgh EH3 6BH (tel: 0131 225 6244; email: enquiries@eis.org.uk)

 www.eis.org.uk

OSCR number: SC007852

Eligibility
Members of the institute who are in need due to unexpected illness, long-term health problems or a sudden change in financial circumstances. Members must have held a full membership for at least one year prior to application. The widows/widowers and dependants of such people may also apply.

The charity's website gives the following examples of people who have previously received support:
- Widows and widowers facing financial difficulties
- Teachers/lecturers on long term sick leave and their families
- Former teachers/lecturers in retirement homes
- Teachers/lecturers who have faced exceptional financial difficulties
- Widows or widowers of teachers/lecturers who have no provision for a pension are also helped with grants to help with these 'extra' things which make life more pleasant
- Teachers absent through ill health who are on reduced salary may be helped depending on their circumstances.

Types of grant
Grants are given according to need. According to the website, 'emergency grants may be available to members who have had an arrestment on their salary, who face eviction, or who have their gas or electricity cut off'.

Applications
In the first instance, applicants should contact their local correspondent, details of which can be found on the charity's website.

Financial information
Year end	31/08/2020
Income	£273,700
Total expenditure	£244,900

Further financial information
Grants were awarded to 99 individuals during the year.

IAPS Charitable Trust

£94,400 (2020/21)

Correspondent: The Trustees, 11 Waterloo Place, Leamington Spa, Warwickshire CV32 5LA (tel: 01926 887833; email: jcm@iaps.uk)

 https://iaps.uk/about/fees-financial-assistance-charity.html

CC number: 1143241

Eligibility
Children in early, primary or middle school years in the UK. Support is also available to current and former members, officials or employees of the Independent Association of Prep Schools (IAPS), dependants of deceased members of IAPS, or any other person connected with education or schools who is not (for the time being) a member of the IAPS.

Types of grant
According to the trust's website, small grants may be made for teacher training or for teachers to enable them to conduct research. Grants are awarded

according to need for members or their dependants, following a needs assessment.

Exclusions
The trust does not support gap-year students.

Applications
Application forms and further guidance can be found on the trust's website.

Financial information
Year end	31/03/2021
Income	£171,100
Total expenditure	£106,900

Other information
The trust also makes grants to schools.

The Benevolent Fund of Her Majesty's Inspectors of Schools in England and Wales

£560 (2020)

Correspondent: Clive Rowe, Trustee/Honorary Treasurer, Hassocks House, 58 Main Street, Newtown Linford, Leicester, Leicestershire LE6 0AD (tel: 01530 243989; email: rowe.clive@sky.com)

CC number: 210181

Eligibility
Current or retired Her Majesty's Inspectors of Schools in England and Wales who are in need. Support is extended to the dependants of such people.

Types of grant
Grants are awarded according to need.

Applications
Apply in writing to the correspondent.

Financial information
Year end	31/12/2020
Income	£44,000
Total expenditure	£32,400

Further financial information
According to the 2020 accounts, grants totalled £560 during the year. In previous years, grants totalled over £3,000. In addition, 'charitable donations and costs incurred to support welfare' totalled £9,600. As no breakdown was provided, we have not included this figure in the grant total.

Other information
The fund also provides pastoral support and advice services to beneficiaries.

The Lloyd Foundation

 £234,400 (2019/20)

Correspondent: Rachel Boggs, Secretary, Flat 2, Pool House, Main Street, Pool-in-Wharfedale, Otley, West Yorkshire LS21 1LH (tel: 07598 444255; email: secretary@thelloydfoundation.org.uk)

https://thelloydfoundation.org.uk

CC number: 314203

Eligibility

Former employees of the English School in Cairo who worked at the school for at least five years or at the time of its closure.

Educational grants are awarded to children (aged between 5 and 25) of British citizens who are living/working overseas. Grants are also made to teaching members of staff in schools overseas which are 'conducted in accordance with British educational principles and practice'.

Types of grant

Pensions and other grants are awarded according to need.

Bursaries, scholarships and maintenance loans are awarded to help beneficiaries to obtain a 'British type education'. Grants are made to teaching staff in qualifying schools overseas for study at university.

Applications

Apply in writing to the correspondent.

Financial information

Year end	31/08/2020
Income	£165,700
Total expenditure	£234,900

Further financial information

During the financial year, the charity awarded grants to 56 beneficiaries.

The Lucy Lund Holiday Grants

£830 (2020)

Correspondent: The Trustees, 1 Lower Road, Havant, Hampshire PO9 3LH (tel: 07958 025811)

CC number: 236779

Eligibility

Teachers who are in need. Preference is given in the following order: female teachers from the West Riding of Yorkshire, female teachers in England and Wales, male teachers in England and Wales.

Types of grant

Grants are made for recuperative holidays.

Applications

Apply in writing to the correspondent.

Financial information

Year end	31/12/2020
Income	£2,000
Total expenditure	£900

Further financial information

Full accounts were not available to view on the Charity Commission's website due to the charity's low income. We have therefore estimated the charity's grant total based on its total expenditure.

NASUWT (The Teachers' Union) Benevolent Fund

 £186,800 (2020)

Correspondent: The Trustees, NASUWT Legal and Casework Team, Hillscourt Education Centre, Rose Hill, Rednal, Birmingham B45 8RS (tel: 0121 453 6150; email: legalandcasework@mail.nasuwt.org.uk)

https://www.nasuwt.org.uk

CC number: 285793

Eligibility

Members, former members and the dependants of members, former members and deceased members of NASUWT, The Teachers' Union.

Types of grant

Grants are available to relieve financial hardship that could have arisen through chronic illness, bereavement, an accident or loss of employment through redundancy or dismissal.

Applications

Further information on how to apply can be found on the union's website.

Financial information

Year end	31/12/2020
Income	£470,200
Total expenditure	£399,200

The Institute of Physics Benevolent Fund

 £39,800 (2020)

Correspondent: The Secretary of the Benevolent Fund, Institute of Physics, 37 Caledonian Road, London N1 9BU (tel: 07771 757944; email: benfund@iop.org)

www.iop.org

CC number: 209746

Eligibility

Current or former members of the institute, and their dependants, who are in need due to unemployment, ill health, financial hardship in old age, or because of an unintended career break.

Types of grant

Grants are awarded according to need. Interest-free loans are also available.

Applications

Apply in writing to the correspondent, marked 'Private and confidential'. The committee meets periodically through the year although emergency cases can be considered more urgently.

Financial information

Year end	31/12/2020
Income	£42,500
Total expenditure	£54,200

Further financial information

Grants were awarded to 17 individuals during the year.

The Association of School and College Leaders Benevolent Fund

 £73,300 (2020)

Correspondent: The Trustees, 2nd Floor, Peat House, 1 Waterloo Way, Leicester, Leicestershire LE1 6LP (tel: 0116 299 1122; email: asclbf@ascl.org.uk)

https://www.ascl.org.uk/Help-and-Advice/ASCL-Benevolent-Fund

CC number: 279628

Eligibility

The charity supports members, former members, employees and former employees of the association, and their widows, widowers, civil partners, children and dependants.

Types of grant

The charity's most recent annual report states that grants include, but are not limited to: regular payments, interest-free loans, specific grants for treatment or equipment related to illness or disability, contributions to the costs of counselling, including careers counselling in the case of unemployment and one-off grants to meet domestic emergencies.

Applications

Initial enquiries should be made by telephone or email.

Financial information

Year end	31/12/2020
Income	£81,800
Total expenditure	£85,800

Other information
The charity distributes floral tributes to families of deceased members after their funeral. Floral tributes are also gifted to members who are experiencing difficult or traumatic circumstances.

Scottish Secondary Teachers' Association Benevolent Fund

£4,100 (2020)

Correspondent: The General Secretary, West End House, 14 West End Place, Edinburgh EH11 2ED (tel: 0131 313 7300; email: info@ssta.org.uk)

 www.ssta.org.uk

OSCR number: SC011074

Eligibility
Members and retired members of the association and, in certain circumstances, their dependants and families who are in need. Spouses and dependants of deceased members are also supported.

Types of grant
One-off and recurrent grants (generally limited to a period of six months) to help members in need. The association's website notes that support is most often given 'in cases of financial hardship but can also be used to meet for requests where the member is not actually experiencing financial difficulties but for whom additional funds would be useful'; one example includes a grant for a member to visit an ill friend in hospital.

Applications
Apply in writing to the correspondent. Applications can be submitted directly by the individual or through a third party. Applicants are asked to provide details of their financial circumstances.

Financial information
Year end	31/12/2020
Income	£5,400
Total expenditure	£4,500

Further financial information
Full accounts were not available to view on the OSCR website due to the fund's low income. We have therefore estimated the grant total based on the fund's total expenditure.

The Teaching Staff Trust

£367,100 (2019/20)

Correspondent: The Grants Team, Unit 2 Bybow Farm, Orchard Way, Dartford, Kent DA2 7ER (tel: 01322 293822; email: enquiries@teachingstafftrust.org.uk)

 teachingstafftrust.org.uk

CC number: 1168445

Eligibility
People who work in or have retired from working in a school, nursery or any other educational role for under 19s. People who have benefitted from the trust in the past include nursery workers, teaching assistants and learning support staff, teachers, lunchtime supervisors and school administrators.

Types of grant
One-off grants to help people stay independent and out of financial hardship. Examples of support include: debt relief or financial support, essential household repairs, maintaining people in their homes and helping people to take or keep jobs.

Applications
Apply via the trust's website.

Financial information
Year end	31/03/2020
Income	£441,800
Total expenditure	£441,600

Energy

BP Benevolent Fund

£18,400 (2020)

Correspondent: Andrew Carter, Fund Administrator, BP Benevolent Fund Trustees Ltd, East Dalcove House, Makerstoun, Kelso TD5 7PD (tel: 020 3401 4223; email: andrew.carter@uk.bp.com)

 https://bpsociety.co.uk/about

CC number: 803778

Eligibility
Former employees of BP plc or its subsidiary or associated companies and the dependants of such people.

Types of grant
Grants are awarded for a variety of reasons. During the year payments were made towards house repairs, replacement boilers, bathroom conversions and electric mobility scooters. In previous years, car repairs and funeral costs have also been supported. Interest-free loans are also available.

Exclusions
According to the charity's website, long-term costs, such as everyday living expenses and the cost of care, are not supported.

Applications
Contact the correspondent for further information.

Financial information
Year end	31/12/2020
Income	£29,200
Total expenditure	£36,800

Further financial information
A total of 17 individuals were supported during the year. Additionally, two loans totalling £3,800 were made.

The Coal Trade Benevolent Association

£180,100 (2020)

Correspondent: The Trustees, Unit 6 Bridge Wharf, 156 Caledonian Road, London N1 9UU (tel: 020 7278 3239; email: office@coaltradebenevolent.org.uk)

 https://www.coaltradebenevolent.org.uk

CC number: 212688

Eligibility
Former non-manual workers in the coal industry in England and Wales who have worked in the production or distribution sectors and allied trades, and their dependants.

Types of grant
Weekly payments to supplement low income and help with fuel payments, telephone costs, televisions, respite holidays, birthday and Christmas cheques and shopping vouchers. Grants also available towards capital items such as stairlifts, special bathrooms, washing machines, carpets and other items.

Applications
Apply in writing to the correspondent.

Financial information
Year end	31/12/2020
Income	£161,600
Total expenditure	£309,800

The Incorporated Benevolent Fund of the Institution of Gas Engineers and Managers

£2,900 (2019)

Correspondent: The Trustees, IGEM House, 26–28 High Street, Kegworth, Derbyshire DE74 2DA (tel: 01509 678150; email: general@igem.org.uk)

 https://www.igem.org.uk/about-us/funds/benevolent-fund

CC number: 214010

Eligibility

Current members of the Institution of Gas Engineers and Managers and their immediate family (spouses, children, grandchildren and parents).

Types of grant

One-off grants, loans and regular financial support. Examples include grants to alleviate financial difficulties or illness, assistance with the costs of treating ill health and helping with property repairs.

Applications

Apply in writing to the correspondent.

Financial information

Year end	31/12/2019
Income	£13,200
Total expenditure	£3,200

Further financial information

Full accounts were not available to view on the Charity Commission's website due to the charity's low income. We have therefore estimated the charity's grant total based on its total expenditure.

The Nuclear Industry Benevolent Fund

 £53,300 (2019/20)

Correspondent: The Trustees, Unit CU1, Warrington Business Park, Long Lane, Warrington, Cheshire WA2 8TX (tel: 01925 633 005/ Confidential Helpline: 0800 587 6040; email: info@tnibf.org)

www.tnibf.org

CC number: 208729

Eligibility

Past and present employees (direct or agency supplied) of the UK nuclear industry, and their dependants.

Types of grant

Grants and allowances are awarded according to need. Previously, grants have been used for disability adaptations, essential home repairs, mobility equipment, household appliances and other tailored needs. The fund may help with short-term financial assistance while the debt issue is being addressed and appropriate debt solutions are being set up.

Exclusions

Grants are not given for private healthcare, legal, or business-related expenses, or debts to family members or friends.

Applications

To apply for funding, first contact the fund by email, telephone, or in writing.

Financial information

Year end	30/06/2020
Income	£81,600
Total expenditure	£174,500

Engineering

The British Institute of Non-Destructive Testing Benevolent Fund

 £7,600 (2019)

Correspondent: Cindy Bailey, Secretary, Midsummer House, Riverside Way, Bedford Road, Northampton NN1 5NX (tel: 01604 438320; email: cindy.bailey@bindt.org)

https://www.bindt.org/membership/for-individuals/benevolent-fund

CC number: 328481

Eligibility

Members, past or present, of the British Institute of Non-Destructive Testing and their dependants who are in need. In exceptional circumstances people who have worked in non-destructive testing but who have never been a member of the institute, and their dependants, might be considered.

Types of grant

Grants are given according to need. Previously, support has been given towards training and examination fees for those who have lost employment through illness or misfortune and towards mobility scooters, scooter hoists and stairlifts, medical expenses and so on.

Applications

In the first instance, contact the secretary of the fund for more information.

Financial information

Year end	31/12/2019
Income	£1,900
Total expenditure	£7,900

Further financial information

Full accounts were not available to view on the Charity Commission's website due to the fund's low income. We have therefore estimated the grant total based on the fund's total expenditure.

The Chemical Engineers Benevolent Fund

 £9,000 (2019)

Correspondent: Jo Downham, Secretary, c/o IChemE, Davis Building, 165–189 Railway Terrace, Rugby, Warwickshire CV21 3HQ (tel: 01788 578214; email: info@benevolentface.org)

www.benevolentface.org

CC number: 221601

Eligibility

Chemical engineers and their dependants. This includes all chemical engineers worldwide, not just members or former members of the Institution of Chemical Engineers.

Types of grant

The fund's website states:

We offer chemical engineers and their dependants a range of one-off gifts, grants and loans to help in the purchase of specialist equipment and to address financial difficulties arising through: ill health, unemployment, bereavement or other changes of circumstance. We can also support with costs arising from the pursuit of postgraduate chemical engineering studies. However, we are unable to help with postgraduate living expenses or tuition fees and any costs arising from undergraduate study.

Exclusions

The fund's website states that the following applicants are not eligible for support:

- People who cannot prove they have worked as a chemical engineer
- People who cannot prove that they have been or currently are a member of a professional institution
- Family members who have not been financially dependent upon the chemical engineer
- dependants who have been employed (although in exceptional cases this rule may be waived)
- dependants who do not or did not live with a chemical engineer
- Undergraduate students
- Postgraduate students looking for support with living expenses or tuition fees.

Applications

Applicants can register to make an initial application via the fund's website. The fund screens all initial requests prior to giving permission for a full application to be made.

Financial information

Year end	31/12/2019
Income	£64,600
Total expenditure	£22,500

The Institution of Engineering and Technology (IET)

 £626,000 (2020)

Correspondent: The Trustees, The Institution of Engineering and Technology, 2 Savoy Place, London WC2R 0BL (tel: 020 7344 5415; email: awards@theiet.org)

www.theiet.org

CC number: 211014/SC038698

Eligibility

Welfare
Grants are awarded to past and present members of the Institution of Engineering and Technology (IET) to help relieve hardship.

Education
Scholarships and awards are open to those pursuing a career in engineering whether as an apprentice, student, or researcher. There are various scholarships and awards on offer so check the IET's website to see their specific eligibility criteria. For scholarships being awarded to apprentices or students the organisation has to be linked to IET.

Types of grant

Welfare
Grants can be awarded for a variety of support needs. Past examples have included: a motorised wheelchair, counselling sessions, career support for people facing redundancy and regular monthly support to individuals and their families to help with the cost of living.

Education
The IET offers a range of scholarships, prizes and travel awards. These include undergraduate and postgraduate scholarships, travel grants to members of the IET (for study tours, work in the industry or to attend a conference), apprenticeship and technician awards, and various prizes for achievement and innovation. See the website for more information on the scholarships and how much can be awarded.

Applications
Further details and application forms are available from the IET website. The deadlines vary for different awards.

Financial information

Year end	31/12/2020
Income	£52,530,000
Total expenditure	£61,870,000

Further financial information
In 2020, scholarships, awards and prizes totalled £606,000 and were awarded to 187 individuals. Hardship grants totalled £20,000 and were awarded to 21 individuals.

The Institution of Engineering and Technology Benevolent Fund (IET Connect)

 £1,430,000 (2019/20)

Correspondent: The Trustees, Napier House, 24 High Holburn, London WC1V 6AZ (tel: 020 7344 5719; email: ietconnect@theiet.org)

www.ietconnect.org

CC number: 208925

Eligibility
Members and former members of the Institution of Engineering and Technology (IET), and their dependants, who are in need. Former members of the Institution of Electrical Engineers are also eligible.

Types of grant
Grants are given for a wide range of purposes such as:
- One-off grants to support day-to-day living costs or towards a series of counselling sessions
- Unexpected household expenses such as home repair after flood damage or boiler, fridge, washing machine or car breakdown
- Care, disability and independence support such as mobility equipment, home adaptations for accessibility, communication and assistive technology and respite breaks for carers

Grants are available to further/higher education students who need support to enable them to finish their course. Previous examples include help towards travel costs of regularly visiting home to care for a parent with mental health problems, extra counselling sessions, moving costs following a university change due to problems with visa registration and living expenses for students with additional needs. The fund also provides a range of scholarships for people studying engineering on vocational, undergraduate and postgraduate courses. Visit the fund's website for further education.

Exclusions
The fund cannot fund tuition fees, and grants cannot be used for retrospective costs.

Applications
Apply in writing to the correspondent.

Financial information

Year end	30/06/2020
Income	£1,240,000
Total expenditure	£2,590,000

Further financial information
Grants were awarded to 1,275 individuals during the year.

Other information
The charity provides free advice on a wide range of welfare-related matters. Individuals who are struggling to pay their IET membership should contact the IET membership department directly on +44 (0)1438 765 678.

The Worshipful Company of Engineers Charitable Trust Fund

 £38,400 (2020)

Correspondent: The Clerk to the Trustees, Saddlers' House, 44 Gutter lane, London EC2V 6BR (tel: 020 7726 4830; email: clerk@engineerscompany.org.uk)

www.engineerstrust.org.uk

CC number: 289819

Eligibility

Welfare
Existing Engineers' Company members, retired members, or their dependants who are in need.

Education
Qualified engineers and those training to be chartered engineers, incorporated engineers or engineering technicians. Eligibility criteria differ depending on the award. See the trust's website for more information.

Types of grant

Welfare
One-off grants are given according to need.

Education
The trust supports a number of award schemes providing monetary prizes with the aim of encouraging excellence in engineering, many of which are open to students. Visit the website for further information on the different awards.

Applications

Welfare
Apply in writing or by email to the correspondent.

Education
Each award has a different application process. See the trust's website for more details.

Financial information

Year end	31/12/2020
Income	£87,100
Total expenditure	£116,400

Other information

Support can be given to organisations concerned with engineering or organisations in the City of London. The trust also supports two Arkwright Scholarships each worth £2,000 over two years.

ICE Benevolent Fund

 £668,000 (2020)

Correspondent: The Trustees, 5 Mill Hill Close, Haywards Heath, West Sussex RH16 1NY (tel: 01444 417979; email: info@icebenfund.com)

www.icebenfund.com

CC number: 1126595

Eligibility

Welfare

Members of the Institution of Civil Engineers (ICE), and their dependants, who are in need.

Education

Support is also available to students on an ICE-accredited civil engineering degree course in the UK. Students must have reached the second year of their course.

Types of grant

Welfare

One-off grants are awarded towards: disability aids; adaptations; mobility equipment; residential/nursing home fees; home repairs or maintenance; respite breaks (for carers also). Emergency grants can be made in times of crisis. Monthly payments, typically of up to six months, are available to those who are unable to work or whose income is limited.

Education

Grants of up to £1,000 per term are awarded to students towards the cost of travel, equipment/course materials and general living expenses.

Applications

Prospective applicants should first complete the eligibility questionnaire on the funder's website. If eligible, applicants should then set up an online application account.

Financial information

Year end	31/12/2020
Income	£1,160,000
Total expenditure	£1,460,000

The Institution of Plant Engineers Benevolent Fund

 £11,300 (2019)

Correspondent: The Trustees, 87 Overdale, Ashtead, Surrey KT21 1PX (tel: 01372 277775; email: nick.jones87@btopenworld.com)

CC number: 260934

Eligibility

Current and former members of the Institution of Plant Engineers and the Bureau of Engineer Surveyors who are in need. Dependants of such people are also supported.

Types of grant

Grants are given according to need.

Applications

Apply in writing to the correspondent.

Financial information

Year end	31/12/2019
Income	£14,800
Total expenditure	£12,500

Further financial information

Full accounts were not available to view on the Charity Commission's website due to the fund's low income. We have therefore estimated the fund's grant total based on its total expenditure.

The Institution of Structural Engineers (ISTRUCTE) Benevolent Fund

£115,200 (2020)

Correspondent: The Trustees, 47–58 Bastwick Street, London EC1V 3PS (tel: 020 7235 4535; email: benfund@istructe.org)

https://www.istructe.org/about-us/funds-and-donations/benevolent-fund

CC number: 1049171

Eligibility

Members and former members of the institution and their dependants who are in financial need due to circumstances such as unemployment, illness, accidents, disability or bereavement.

Types of grant

One-off grants for an emergency or specific item, regular grants to meet continuing needs and loans.

Applications

Contact the fund to make an application.

Financial information

Year end	31/12/2020
Income	£73,900
Total expenditure	£164,900

Further financial information

Grants were awarded to 21 individuals.

Environment and agriculture

Addington Fund

 £157,200 (2019/20)

Correspondent: The Trustees, 9 Barford Exchange, Wellesbourne Road, Barford, Warwickshire CV35 8AQ (tel: 01926 620135; email: enquiries@addingtonfund.org.uk)

https://www.addingtonfund.org.uk

CC number: 1097092

Eligibility

Active and retired farmworkers in England who are in need. Families, widowers and dependants of such individuals may also apply.

Types of grant

The charity administers a number of funds:

The George Stephens Trust Fund – grants of up to £1,000 are available for essential items such as white goods, bathroom equipment or other essential furnishings. Examples include washing machines, fridges, cookers, showers, vehicle repairs, disability equipment and so on.

Trustees' Discretionary Fund for Disaster Relief – short-term financial aid for farms that have been affected by regional or national emergencies such as disease outbreak or prolonged inclement weather. The charity can provide essential commodities such as compound feeds, silage, hay, straw and straights.

Exclusions

The charity cannot provide support towards long-term business debts, routine animal vaccination costs, or problems associated with low prices for farm produce.

Applications

Individuals can apply for funding from the George Stephens Trust Fund by contacting the office for an application form. Alternatively, applications can be made by an organisation acting on the individual's behalf, such as a GP, social services, the Royal British Legion or other farming help charities. To apply to the Trustees' Discretionary Fund for Disaster Relief, contact the office via telephone or email to request an application form.

Financial information

Year end	31/03/2020
Income	£739,500
Total expenditure	£632,800

Other information

The charity also provides both affordable housing and retirement homes for farming families. The charity has recently launched the Young Entrants Scheme which matches young people wishing to start a career in agriculture with appropriate farms.

Barham Benevolent Foundation

£ £17,200 (2019/20)

Correspondent: The Trustees, 8 Stumps End, Bosham, Chichester, West Sussex PO18 8RB (tel: 07875 313365; email: mcook1158@googlemail.com)

CC number: 249922

Eligibility

Current and former employees of the dairy industry, and their dependants, who are in need.

Types of grant

Grants for hardship cases are awarded according to need. The foundation also contributes towards the costs of holidays and in some cases accommodation.

Applications

Apply in writing to the correspondent.

Financial information

Year end	31/03/2020
Income	£216,200
Total expenditure	£216,700

Other information

The foundation awards large grants to universities across the UK for research in dairy-related subjects. In 2019/20, the foundation awarded £87,300 to the University of Reading and £23,500 to the Royal Veterinary College.

The Bristol Corn Trade Guild

£ £10,400 (2020)

Correspondent: Richard Cooksley, Secretary, Portbury House, Sheepway, Portbury, Bristol BS20 7TE (tel: 01275 373539; email: richard@bcfta.com)

 https://www.bcfta.com/the-guild

CC number: 202404

Eligibility

People who have a connection with the corn, grain, feed, flour and allied trades and are in need. Dependants of such people are also eligible. Active, retired, or honorary members of the Bristol Corn and Feed Trade Association may be given preference.

Types of grant

One-off grants can be given towards medical equipment or specialist treatment, repairs and household essentials. Recurrent grants can be made for utility bills.

Applications

The charity's website states: 'To discuss potential support ring the Secretary, Richard Cooksley on 01275 373539 or mobile 07801 435772.' Enquiries can be made directly by the individual or a third party.

Financial information

Year end	31/12/2020
Income	£12,000
Total expenditure	£11,500

Further financial information

Full accounts were not available to view on the Charity Commission's website due to the charity's low income. We have therefore estimated the charity's grant total based on its total expenditure.

Other information

Members and former members of the Bristol Corn and Feed Trade Association are also invited to various activities organised by the guild, for example, sporting events or Christmas lunch.

The Worshipful Company of Farriers Charitable Trust 1994

£ £900 (2020/21)

Correspondent: The Clerk to The Worshipful Company of Farriers, 19 Queen Street, Chipperfield, Kings Langley, Hertfordshire WD4 9BT (email: theclerk@wcf.org.uk)

 https://www.wcf.org.uk/charity.php

CC number: 1044726

Eligibility

Registered farriers, their widows and dependants who are in need.

Types of grant

One-off and recurrent grants are awarded according to need. Grants are usually given to people who are unable to work through injury or sickness.

Applications

Applications should be made in writing directly to the correspondent.

Financial information

Year end	30/06/2021
Income	£60,700
Total expenditure	£40,900

Other information

The charity also makes awards for education for farriers and prospective farriers. Note that the total grant expenditure fluctuates from year to year – in 2019/20 grants totalled £8,400.

Forest Industries Education and Provident Fund

£ £3,400 (2020)

Correspondent: Edward Mills, Confederation of Forest Industries, 59 George Street, Edinburgh EH2 2JG (tel: 0131 240 1419; email: Fiona@ confor.org.uk)

 www.confor.org.uk/resources/ education-provident-fund

CC number: 1061322

Eligibility

Welfare

People who have been a member of Confor, either as a student or other individual member, continuously for one year and their dependants who are in need, for example, due to illness, personal injury, or bereavement.

Education

People who have been a member of Confor, either as a student or other individual member, continuously for one year.

Types of grant

Welfare

One-off grants are given according to need through the provident fund.

Education

Grants of up to £750 are given to students on technical and professional courses within the field of forestry. Support is also given towards educational trips, activities and professional development opportunities such as conferences.

Exclusions

Applications for retrospective funding will not be considered.

Applications

Application forms can be downloaded from the fund's website. Applicants will be required to declare any other sources of financial aid they may have received.

Financial information

Year end	31/12/2020
Income	£6,700
Total expenditure	£3,800

Further financial information

Full accounts were not available to view on the Charity Commission's website due to the fund's low income. We have therefore estimated the grant total based on the fund's total expenditure.

Other information

Successful applicants are required to write an article which may be used in the Forestry and Timber News magazine.

Gardeners' Royal Benevolent Society (Perennial)

 £273,000 (2020)

Correspondent: The Trustees, 115–117 Kingston Road, Leatherhead, Surrey KT22 7SU (tel: 0800 093 8510; email: info@perennial.org.uk)

www.perennial.org.uk

CC number: 1155156

Eligibility

People who work, or have previously worked, in the UK horticulture industry. Eligibility requirements vary between grant programmes.

Types of grant

Grants are available for:

▶ Educational school trips for the children of horticulturalists
▶ Specialised equipment for people with a long-term illness or disability
▶ Everyday essentials (food, heating and clothing) beds, household equipment and essential domestic appliances
▶ Replacement of essential tools lost due to theft, fire or flood damage
▶ Short breaks and respite support

Applications

Different schemes have different application processes; consult the charity's website for further information or contact the charity directly.

Financial information

Year end	31/12/2020
Income	£3,830,000
Total expenditure	£3,780,000

Other information

The charity provides range of resources and advice for people working in horticulture.

The Sir Percival Griffiths' Tea-Planters Trust

 £3,300 (2019)

Correspondent: The Trustees, c/o Linton Park PLC, Linton Park, Linton, Kent ME17 4AB (tel: 07375 492924)

CC number: 253904

Eligibility

Former tea-planters or people formerly engaged in the business of tea-growing, and their dependants, who are in need.

Types of grant

Grants are made according to need.

Applications

Apply in writing to the correspondent.

Financial information

Year end	31/12/2019
Income	£260
Total expenditure	£3,700

Further financial information

Full accounts were not available to view on the Charity Commission's website due to the trust's low income. We have therefore estimated the trust's grant total based on its total expenditure.

Kent Farmers Benevolent Fund

£500 (2019/20)

Correspondent: The Trustees, c/o Brachers Solicitors, Somerfield House, 57–59 London Road, Maidstone, Kent ME16 8JH (tel: 01622 690691)

CC number: 254983

Eligibility

People who have worked in agriculture and their dependants who are in need. Beneficiaries must have a connection with Kent.

Types of grant

One-off grants are awarded according to need.

Applications

Apply in writing to the correspondent.

Financial information

Year end	30/11/2020
Income	£2,700
Total expenditure	£1,000

Further financial information

Full accounts were not available to view on the Charity Commission's website due to the fund's low income. We have therefore estimated the fund's grant total based on its total expenditure.

Other information

Grants are also made to organisations that support people in the agriculture industry.

The Royal Agricultural Benevolent Institution

£2,090,000 (2020)

Correspondent: Grants Committee, Shaw House, 27 West Way, Oxford, Oxfordshire OX2 0QH (tel: 01865 724931; email: info@rabi.org.uk)

www.rabi.org.uk

CC number: 208858

Eligibility

Current and former farmers or farm workers who are in need. Support is also extended to the dependants of such people.

Types of grant

One-off grants towards the cost of essential white goods, domestic bills; rent/mortgage arrears and relief farm staff (if the applicant is unable to work due to injury or illness).

Training grants are available to established farmers on low incomes who wish to learn new skills or develop existing skills related to the trade. Recent examples include courses in tree surgery, livestock foot-trimming, forklift truck operating and website design.

Recurrent grants, paid quarterly, are available to beneficiaries aged 65 years and over towards the cost of the following: fuel; specialist equipment and mobility aids; TV licences; food vouchers; hospital travel.

Applications

Initial enquiries can be made by contacting the charity by telephone, email or post. The grants committee meets on seven occasions each year to consider applications.

Financial information

Year end	31/12/2020
Income	£5,770,000
Total expenditure	£7,900,000

Other information

The charity owns and operates two residential care homes, Beaufort House in Somerset and Manson House in Suffolk. Most residents come from farming backgrounds, but other members of the local community and people seeking respite care can be accommodated if spaces exist. The charity also has a team of caseworkers who are available to talk through any problems and concerns a farmer/farm worker may have. All caseworkers are trained in mental health first aid and suicide awareness.

RSABI (Royal Scottish Agricultural Benevolent Institution)

 £298,000 (2020/21)

Correspondent: The Welfare Team, The Rural Centre, West Mains, Newbridge, Midlothian EH28 8LT (tel: 0300 111 4166)

www.rsabi.org.uk

OSCR number: SC009828

Eligibility

People in Scotland who are involved in agriculture, crofting and growing. This includes those who are employed, self-employed, retired, unable to work or unemployed.

Types of grant

One-off and recurrent grants are given for essential items such as food, heating, counselling, disability aids, funerals, retraining and items for the home. All requests for support will be considered.

Applications

In the first instance, call the helpline on 0300 111 4166 or contact the charity using the form on its website.

Financial information

Year end	31/03/2021
Income	£4,320,000
Total expenditure	£810,800

Further financial information

Monthly payments totalling £231,000 were awarded to 251 households during the financial year. In addition, the charity awarded 203 one-off grants totalling £67,000.

Other information

The charity also provides practical support such as welfare benefits, business reviews, debt signposting, counselling and mediation services.

Financial services

The AIA Educational and Benevolent Trust

 £5,200 (2020)

Correspondent: The Trustees, The Association of International Accountants, Unit 3, Staithes, The Watermark, Metro Riverside, Tyne and Wear NE11 9SN (tel: 0191 493 0261; email: trust.fund@aiaworldwide.com)

www.aiaworldwide.com

CC number: 1118333

Eligibility

Fellows and associates of the Association of International Accountants, and their close dependants, who are in need. Registered students are also eligible to apply.

Types of grant

Grants are given according to need and towards the advancement of education in accountancy and related subjects.

Applications

Application forms can be downloaded from the trust's website.

Financial information

Year end	31/12/2020
Income	£2,000
Total expenditure	£11,800

Further financial information

Full accounts were not available to view on the Charity Commission's website due to the trust's low income. We have therefore estimated the trust's grant total based on its total expenditure.

The Bankers Benevolent Fund (The Bank Workers Charity)

 £1,000,000 (2019/20)

Correspondent: Selam Shibru, Company Secretary, Suite 686–695, Salisbury House, Finsbury Circus, London EC2M 5QQ (tel: 0800 0234 834 (9am to 5pm, Monday to Friday); email: info@ bwcharity.org.uk)

www.bwcharity.org.uk

CC number: 313080

Eligibility

Welfare

Current and former bank employees, and their families and dependants, who are in need. Applicants must work, or have worked, in the UK.

Education

Educational grants are given to the children of current or former bank workers.

Types of grant

Welfare grants are awarded towards the cost of, for example, disability aids or home adaptations, respite breaks for carers or person being cared for (or both), travel costs involved in attending hospital/medical treatment, funeral expenses and general living expenses.

Exclusions

The charity is unable to make grants for: personal debt or loans, medical fees, legal expenses, private school fees, or items or services for which statutory funding exists.

Applications

Initial enquiries can be made by contacting the charity's helpline (9am to 5pm, Monday to Friday). Alternatively, prospective applicants may wish to complete an enquiry form on the charity's website. The charity will then contact the applicant via telephone or email to discuss their application further.

Financial information

Year end	31/03/2020
Income	£1,920,000
Total expenditure	£5,190,000

Further financial information

During the year, grants were awarded to 1,221 individuals.

Other information

The charity can make referrals to therapists for those struggling with their mental health, or for those experiencing difficulties in their personal life such as relationship breakdown or bereavement. The charity also operates a range of advice services offering guidance on debt and money, disability (for information on benefit entitlements, statutory funding, etc.), housing (for information on housing benefit, repossession, eviction, etc.), as well as advice for carers.

The Chartered Accountants' Benevolent Association

 £324,000 (2020)

Correspondent: The Trustees, Merrett House, Swift Park, Old Leicester Park, Rugby, Warwickshire CV21 1DZ (tel: 01788 556366; email: enquiries@ caba.org.uk)

www.caba.org.uk

CC number: 1116973

Eligibility

Past and present Institute of Chartered Accountants in England and Wales (ICAEW) members, ICAEW staff, ACA students and their close families from across the globe.

Types of grant

One-off and recurrent grants towards fuel payments, residential care fees, adaptations and equipment, funerals and business start-up support.

Applications

Initial contact can be made by using the charity's helpline (01788 556 366), live chat, email or online enquiry form.

Financial information

Year end	31/12/2020
Income	£4,740,000
Total expenditure	£6,640,000

Further financial information

Grants were awarded to 554 individuals during the year.

Other information

The association offers a wide range of support and advice on issues such as accessing state benefits, debt and financial problems and stress management. Services are free and only the direct financial support is means tested.

The Chartered Certified Accountants' Benevolent Fund

 £75,300 (2019/20)

Correspondent: Hugh McCash, Honorary Secretary, c/o ACCA, 110 Queen Street, Glasgow G1 3BX (tel: 0141 534 4045; email: hugh. mccash@accaglobal.com)

https://www.accaglobal.com/gb/en/member/membership/benevolent-fund/about.html

CC number: 1156341

Eligibility

People who are or have been members of the Association of Chartered Certified Accountants (ACCA) or related organisations, and their dependants, who are experiencing financial difficulties.

Types of grant

One-off and recurrent (up to around £1,000 per year) grants are awarded according to need. Previous examples of support include assistance towards loss of income due to unemployment, medical costs, legal costs and carers support.

Exclusions

Previous research suggests students are not eligible for assistance.

Applications

Application forms and related guidance are available to download from the ACCA website or can be requested by telephone or by writing to the correspondent.

Financial information

Year end	31/03/2020
Income	£224,500
Total expenditure	£133,600

Other information

The charity also has a disaster fund, through which it has assisted members and their families impacted by various natural disasters such as earthquakes, floods and hurricanes. The charity also makes grants to organisations.

The Chartered Institute of Management Accountants Benevolent Fund

 £78,000 (2020)

Correspondent: Caroline Aldred, Manager, CIMA Benevolent Fund, 1 South Place, London EC2M 2RB (tel: +1 866 528 9976; email: benevolent.fund@aicpa-cima.com)

www.cimaglobal.com

CC number: 261114

Eligibility

Current or former members of the Chartered Institute of Management Accountants (CIMA) or any preceding body. Support is also extended to the dependants of such people.

Types of grant

Welfare

Grants are given towards:
- Basic living expenses
- Priority debts such as rent and Council Tax
- Mobility aids and home adaptations for people with disabilities
- Essential household goods
- Holidays and respite breaks for carers
- Medical treatments (provided that treatment is unavailable on the NHS free of charge or is delayed)
- Further professional training which is likely to alleviate financial hardship

Education

The fund awards educational grants to the dependants of members of the CIMA who are in higher education.

Exclusions

Support is not usually given for non-priority debts (such as credit card bills), school fees where education is available free-of-charge, legal costs (except for bankruptcy fees), or business or career development costs. The fund is also unable to assist student members.

Applications

Application forms and guidelines can be downloaded from the CIMA website. After receiving an application, the

manager of the benevolent fund will usually contact the applicant to ask further questions about their current circumstances.

Financial information

Year end	31/12/2020
Income	£183,000
Total expenditure	£126,000

Further financial information

During the financial year, grants were awarded to 49 beneficiaries.

Other information

The charity also funds referrals to an outplacement organisation for people who are currently out of work and need support to find employment.

The Institute of Financial Accountants and International Association of Book-Keepers Benevolent Fund

 £25,000 (2019/20)

Correspondent: Beryl Shepherd, 23 Nutbourne Road, Farlington, Portsmouth PO6 1NP (email: beryl@berylshepherd.co.uk)

www.ifaiabbenfund.org.uk

CC number: 234082

Eligibility

Current and former members of the Institute of Financial Accountants (IFA) or the International Association of Book-Keepers (IAB) and their dependants. Current students of the IFA or IAB are also eligible for support.

Types of grant

One-off grants are awarded according to need.

Exclusions

No recurrent grants or ongoing payments are made.

Applicants must be full members of the IFA. Those whose membership of the IFA is automatic by virtue of their membership of the Institute of Public Accountants (of Australia) do not qualify for assistance.

Applications

Application forms are available to download on the fund's website, or can be requested from the correspondent at their address. Completed forms can be sent by email or post.

Financial information

Year end	30/09/2020
Income	£15,800
Total expenditure	£29,400

Further financial information

Full accounts were not available to view on the Charity Commission's website due to the fund's low income. We have therefore estimated the grant total based on the fund's total expenditure.

Alfred Foster Settlement

£ £46,300 (2020/21)

Correspondent: The Trustees, c/o Zedra UK Trusts, Booths Park, Chelford Road, Knutsford, Cheshire WA16 8GS (tel: 01565 748822; email: charities@zedra.com)

CC number: 229576

Eligibility

Current and former banking employees and their dependants who are in need.

Types of grant

One-off grants of £250 to £1,000 are awarded according to need. Grants are given for welfare purposes and to assist the children of banking employees in their education.

Applications

Applications may be made in writing to the correspondent. They can be submitted directly by the individual or through the employee's bank or to their local regional office.

Previous research suggests that grants for children should be made through the school.

Financial information

Year end	01/01/2021
Income	£25,800
Total expenditure	£46,300

The Insurance Charities

£ £1,440,000 (2019/20)

Correspondent: Kirsten Hardiker, Deputy Chair and Chair of the Grants Committee, Third Floor, 2 St Andrew's Hill, London EC4V 5BY (tel: 020 7606 3763; email: info@theinsurancecharities.org.uk)

 www.theinsurancecharities.org.uk

CC number: 206860

Eligibility

The charity's website states that you can apply if you are a:
- Current or past insurance employee:
  - ideally with five years' recent work in insurance, or
  - with less than five years' insurance work but where insurance has made up the majority of your career to date, or
  - in receipt of a pension or deferred pension from an insurance employer in respect of at least five years' insurance service,

OR you are:
- A dependant of a current or former insurance employee.

In all cases:
- Service must be/have been within the UK or Irish insurance industry.
- There must be restricted financial means in terms of income and capital.
- An element of misfortune has arisen.

You do not need to be a CII member to apply for help. Employment within the industry can be in any role and is not restricted to specific insurance careers such as underwriting or broking.

Types of grant

One-off grants are awarded for essential items such as equipment to help someone with reduced mobility, an adaptation to a property which is not financed by local or central government, the replacement of an appliance or some essential property maintenance.

Ongoing payments are awarded where income is restricted or insufficient to meet higher than average costs, for example for a health condition.

Examples of grants awarded include those towards:
- Furniture and appliances
- Debt repayment
- Counselling
- Specialist assessments and therapies
- Wheelchairs, scooters and trikes
- Family holidays
- Specialist beds
- School uniforms
- Funeral expenses
- Property adaptations
- Nursing home costs
- Christmas and summer hampers

Applications

In the first instance, an initial application form is available to complete and submit online. From this, the charity may request more information or arrange a home visit or video call with a welfare advisor. The advisor will discuss your financial situation with you in detail. After this meeting, the grants committee will advise you of its decision.

Financial information

Year end	31/03/2020
Income	£1,400,000
Total expenditure	£2,210,000

Further financial information

Grants totalling £1.44 million were made to support 236 individuals.

The Lloyd's Benevolent Fund

£ £341,000 (2019/20)

Correspondent: Allan Bushnell, Secretary, Lloyd's Benevolent Fund, 1 Lime Street, London EC3M 7HA (tel: 020 7327 6453; email: lloydsbenevolentfund@lloyds.com)

CC number: 207231

Eligibility

People who work, or have worked, for Lloyd's of London Insurance who are in need. Support is extended to the dependants of such people.

Types of grant

One-off and annual grants according to need.

Exclusions

No grants are awarded to underwriting members of Lloyd's.

Applications

Apply in writing to the correspondent.

Financial information

Year end	30/09/2020
Income	£334,000
Total expenditure	£453,000

Further financial information

Grants were awarded to 28 individuals during the year.

Lloyds and TSB Staff Benevolent Fund

£ £30,200 (2020)

Correspondent: Julian Unthank, Fund Secretary, Lavender Cottage, Orchard Lane, Kingsbury Episcopi, Somerset TA12 6BA (tel: 07881 668692; email: enquiries@lloydsandtsbstaffbenevolentfund.org.uk)

 https://lloydsandtsbstaffbenevolentfund.org.uk

CC number: 276303

Eligibility

Current and former staff members of the former TSB Group plc, Lloyds TSB Group and the present Lloyds Banking Group, including their dependants and close relatives.

Types of grant

Grants are given according to need. Examples of previous support include essential home repairs, white goods, travel costs for medical appointments, mobility aids, specialist equipment, home adaptations and holidays. Hampers are distributed at Christmas.

Exclusions

The charity is unable to help with care home fees, bank or credit card debts, or funeral costs.

Applications

Initial enquiries should be made by contacting the charity. The charity aims to respond to enquiries within 48 hours.

Financial information

Year end	31/12/2020
Income	£97,700
Total expenditure	£30,300

Further financial information

As well as the £30,200 distributed to beneficiaries, the charity provided 36 Christmas hampers and an additional 43 hampers in May 2020 to raise spirits during the COVID-19 pandemic.

The NatWest Group Pensioners Benevolent Fund

 £28,000 (2020/21)

Correspondent: The Trustees, 8 Langford Road, Newcastle-under-Lyme, Staffordshire ST5 3JZ (tel: 0131 343 6467 or 07973 786097; email: contact@nwgpensbenfund.org.uk)

https://nwgpensbenfund.org.uk

CC number: 277974

Eligibility

Retired employees of the NatWest Group (including any current or former companies within the banking group) and their dependants.

Types of grant

One-off grants are given towards the cost of specific, essential items such as:
- Stairlifts
- Boiler replacements/repairs
- Large items of furniture
- Glasses
- Dentures
- White goods
- Wheelchairs
- Walk-in showers

Exclusions

Grants are not given for household bills, medical treatment or care home expenses. The fund is also unable to provide a winter fuel allowance.

Applications

Application forms can be downloaded from the fund's website.

Financial information

Year end	28/02/2021
Income	£81,500
Total expenditure	£40,300

Further financial information

The fund made 21 grants during the financial period.

Other information

This fund was formerly known as the Royal Bank of Scotland Group Pensioners' Association Benevolent Fund.

Scottish Chartered Accountants' Benevolent Association

 £84,800 (2020)

Correspondent: Kirsty Gray, Charity Manager, PO Box 28843, Edinburgh EH14 9BY (tel: 07780 435415; email: manager@scaba.org.uk)

https://www.icas.com/scaba-the-charity-for-cas-in-need

OSCR number: SC008365

Eligibility

Current and former members of the Institute of Chartered Accountants of Scotland (ICAS), and their dependants, who are in need. Prospective members of ICAS who are in higher/further education, or those who have recently entered into a training contract, are also eligible for support.

Types of grant

One-off grants have been given towards respite care, home adaptations, specialist equipment and funeral costs. Grants are normally awarded for a period of one year; however, ongoing grants and loans are also available.

Grants are also available towards the costs of retraining. Previous grants have been given for maintenance costs. Loans are also available.

Applications

Application forms are available to download on the charity's website. Completed forms should be returned to the charity by post. For any queries or help when completing the form, contact the correspondent by email or phone.

Financial information

Year end	31/12/2020
Income	£171,000
Total expenditure	£138,100

Other information

Beneficiaries will be visited by an outreach co-ordinator who will act as a listening ear and provide practical support. Beneficiaries may also be assigned a financial advisor who can help with money management.

Scottish Stockbrokers' Benevolent Fund

 £53,200 (2019/20)

Correspondent: David Crichton, Secretary, Flat 0/1, 23 Polwarth Street, Hyndland, Glasgow G12 9UD (tel: 0141 337 2949; email: secretary@ssbf.org.uk)

https://ssbf.org.uk

OSCR number: SC013429

Eligibility

Former members of the Scottish Stock Exchange and their dependants. Help has recently been extended to all employees of Scottish businesses that are members of the London Stock Exchange.

Types of grant

The fund's website states:

> The fund carries out these objectives by providing grants to individuals in need, or to prevent or relieve poverty in the form of:
> - Annuities on a discretionary basis
> - Donations to those requiring temporary help
> - Emergency grants for one-off payments
> - Help to those that are sick or with disabilities, such as for medical equipment and carers

Applications

The fund's website suggests that potential applicants should first make an informal enquiry to let the fund know about your difficulties and circumstances.

Financial information

Year end	31/03/2020
Income	£157,100
Total expenditure	£131,400

The Stock Exchange Benevolent Fund

 £755,500 (2020)

Correspondent: Robert Chambers, Secretary, 10 Paternoster Square, St Paul's, London EC4M 7DX (tel: 07494 765133 or 07957 525219; email: admin@sebf.co.uk)

www.sebf.co.uk

CC number: 245430

Eligibility

Former members of the London Stock Exchange and their dependants.

Types of grant

The following information has been taken from the charity's website:

> **One Off Payments**
> You might be awarded a one-off emergency grant or to get you through a

short term funding issue. An emergency grant can be made to cover health issues, cost of caring and more practical issues concerning motor repairs and the replacement of everyday equipment in the home.

Ongoing Grants

We offer grants on a one or two year basis if circumstances are longer term and more challenging. The payments contribute towards rent charges, the cost of living, utility costs and the reduction of excess expenditure over income.

Applications

Initial application forms are available on the website, or you can call or email to provide a brief summary of the help you need. You will then be sent an application form to complete, either by email or post. Note: applicants will be visited by the secretary of the charity as part of the application process. The trustees meet on a quarterly basis to consider grant applications.

Financial information

Year end	31/12/2020
Income	£627,800
Total expenditure	£1,060,000

Further financial information

According to the 2020 accounts, regular grants totalled £547,400, capped and emergency grants totalled £106,100 and other grants totalled £102,000.

Other information

The charity also provides debt and money management advice to eligible people.

Stock Exchange Clerks Fund

 £148,700 (2020)

Correspondent: The Trustees, 1–5 Earl Street, London EC2A 2AL (tel: 020 7797 4373; email: office@secfund.org.uk)

🌐 https://www.secfund.org.uk

CC number: 286055

Eligibility

Former members of the London Stock Exchange or member firms of the London Stock Exchange, and their dependants, who are in need.

Types of grant

Monthly payments to help with general living costs. One-off grants towards the cost of medical equipment, mobility aids, household goods and funeral expenses.

Applications

Applications can be made on the fund's website using an online form. After making an application, the fund's liaison officer will contact the applicant to talk

about the charity and offer their support through the application process.

Financial information

Year end	31/12/2020
Income	£128,300
Total expenditure	£194,400

Further financial information

The fund awarded grants to 47 beneficiaries.

The Vassar-Smith Fund

 £7,600 (2019/20)

Correspondent: The Trustees, Affinity, Bedford Heights, Brickhill Drive, Bedford MK41 7PH

CC number: 236381

Eligibility

Current or retired Lloyds Bank staff and their dependants.

Types of grant

Grants are given according to need.

Applications

Apply in writing to the correspondent.

Financial information

Year end	02/08/2020
Income	£41,400
Total expenditure	£24,100

Further financial information

Grants were awarded to nine individuals.

General

UNITE the Union Benevolent Fund

 £111,500 (2019)

Correspondent: The Trustees, Eastham Hall, 109 Eastham Village Road, Eastham, Wirral CH62 0AF (tel: 0808 196 3655; email: applications@unitebf. org)

🌐 https://unitetheunion.org/why-join/ member-offers-and-benefits/ member-offers/benevolent-fund

CC number: 228567

Eligibility

Members/former members or employees/ ex-employees of Unite the Union and their dependants.

Types of grant

One-off grants are awarded according to need.

Applications

Application forms are available to download from the fund's website.

Financial information

Year end	31/12/2019
Income	£90,900
Total expenditure	£147,200

Hospitality

The National Federation of Fish Friers Benevolent Fund

 £2,300 (2019/20)

Correspondent: The Trustees, New Federation House, 4 Greenwood Mount, Meanwood, Leeds, West Yorkshire LS6 4LQ (tel: 0113 230 7044; email: mail@nfff.co.uk)

🌐 https://www.nfff.co.uk

CC number: 229168

Eligibility

Members or former members of the federation (whether subscribers to the fund or not) and their dependants.

Types of grant

Grants are given according to need.

Applications

Apply in writing to the correspondent.

Financial information

Year end	31/05/2020
Income	£1,800
Total expenditure	£2,500

Further financial information

Full accounts were not available to view on the Charity Commission's website due to the fund's low income. We have therefore estimated the fund's grant total based on its total expenditure.

Other information

The fund also maintains respite homes.

Hospitality Action

 £1,330,000 (2020)

Correspondent: The Grants Team, 62 Britton Street, London EC1M 5UY (tel: 020 3004 5500; email: info@ hospitalityaction.org.uk)

🌐 www.hospitalityaction.org.uk

CC number: 1101083

Eligibility

People currently working in the UK hospitality industry or who have worked in the industry for a five-year period in their working life.

Types of grant

The charity offers support in the form of:

- Essential needs grants – towards the cost of an item or need considered essential for the well-being or improving the quality of life of the applicant
- Crisis grants – usually for a maximum of one year to assist with the general living costs of applicants of working age who have suffered a sudden loss of income due to bereavement, illness or injury
- Top-up grants – to assist with an individual's general living costs to ensure that an adequate standard of living is achieved
- Winter fuel grants – to pay essential fuel bills.

Exclusions

Funding is not available towards the following:

- Education-related costs, such as private school fees, fees for educational courses, student maintenance and student loan repayment
- Most private medical treatments
- Residential care fee shortfalls
- Legal costs
- Property repairs/adaptations where equity release is a viable option
- Business costs

Applications

Application forms and guidance notes can be downloaded from the charity's website.

Financial information

Year end	31/12/2020
Income	£3,240,000
Total expenditure	£2,840,000

Further financial information

The charity made 3,562 grants during the year.

Licensed Trade Charity

 £1,560,000 (2020)

Correspondent: The Trustees, Heatherley, London Road, Ascot, Berkshire SL5 8DR (tel: 01344 884440; email: james.brewster@ltcharity.org.uk)

https://www.licensedtradecharity.org.uk

CC number: 230011

Eligibility

People in need who are, or have been, employed in the licensed drinks trade for a total of five continuous years. This can be in one or more jobs. Immediate family members (i.e. those living in the same household) are also eligible for support.

Types of grant

One-off grants are available for the following:

- Utility bills
- Rent or Council Tax arrears
- Rent in advance or rent deposits
- Removal costs
- Furniture and white goods
- Decorating costs
- Funeral expenses
- Disability aids
- Wheelchairs and mobility scooters
- Convalescence breaks
- Respite breaks for carers

Education grants for the children of people in the trade are available for the following:

- School uniforms and shoes
- School trips
- Books
- Laptops

Educational grants can be awarded to adults, to support people getting back into work or furthering their career.

In exceptional circumstances, the charity can offer short-term hardship payments for around 3–12 months.

Applications

Initial enquiries should be made to the charity in writing (either by post or email) or by telephone.

Financial information

Year end	31/12/2020
Income	£21,540,000
Total expenditure	£23,180,000

Other information

The charity operates a 24/7 helpline (0808 801 0550) for those in need of advice, a counselling service and a telephone befriending service, which calls individuals in need on a weekly or fortnightly basis. Emotional support and practical advice services are available to people who have worked in the licensed trade industry for any amount of time. The charity is also able to nominate eligible single people and couples aged over 55 years for accommodation through Anchor Housing.

Information and commu-nication

BT Benevolent Fund

 £586,400 (2020)

Correspondent: Steve Melhuish, Grants Manager, Room 323, Reading Central Telephone Exchange, 41 Minister Street, Reading, Berkshire RG1 2JB (tel: 020 8726 2145; email: benevolent@bt.com)

 https://www.benevolent.bt.com

CC number: 212565

Eligibility

Present or past (whether pensionable or not) British Telecom Group employees and present or future BT Group pensioners, and their dependants, who are experiencing financial hardship. The fund's website specifies: 'Past BT employees may include workers from Telecoms side of former GPO.'

Types of grant

Assistance is provided in a wide variety of ways. According to the 2020 accounts, grants are often given towards: home adaptations and mobility aids for adults and children with disabilities; debts relating to the security of accommodation; utility bills; funeral bills; home maintenance; furniture; clothing; household appliances; fuel; hospital expenses; respite care and convalescence; and services such as shopping gardening and personal care. Weekly pensions are available to older people on a low income. Weekly grants are also awarded to assist with shortfalls in residential home fees. Recipients of weekly grants are also eligible to receive a £125 Christmas grant.

The maximum grant payment is £2,500, and up to £10,000 for home adaptations.

Exclusions

The fund is unable to help contractors or staff employed through agencies.

Applications

Current BT employees should, in the first instance, contact the Employee Assistance Programme (EAP) by calling 0800 917 6767. Former employees and BT pensioners should contact the fund directly by telephone or email. The fund's website notes that it is useful to have your BT pension number to hand when making an enquiry. BT employees based outside the UK should email the fund to enquire about their eligibility.

Financial information

Year end	31/12/2020
Income	£2,030,000
Total expenditure	£845,300

Further financial information

According to the 2020 accounts, weekly grants totalled £270,000 and single grants totalled £316,400. Overall, 388 individuals and families received grants.

Other information

The fund also operates a contact scheme to provide advice and support for BT pensioners who are over 75 years old.

Chartered Institute of Library and Information Professionals (CILIP) Benevolent Fund

 £4,500 (2020)

Correspondent: Bridget Fisher, Chair, 7 Ridgmount Street, London WC1E 7AE (tel: 01484 866697; email: benevolentfund@cilip.org.uk)

https://www.cilip.org.uk/page/benevolent

CC number: 237352

Eligibility
Members and former members of the Chartered Institute of Library and Information Professionals (CILIP) and their dependants. This includes former members of the Library Association and the Institute of Information Scientists who may not have been members of CILIP.

Types of grant
Grants are given for unexpected expenses, for example urgent house repairs, the replacement of necessary household equipment, unexpectedly large heating bills and bank overdrafts or other debts that have accumulated unavoidably as a result of illness.

Applications
An online application form can be completed on the fund's website. With the agreement of the applicant, a visit or telephone call is then arranged to discuss the application and the ways in which the fund may be able to help. The trustees meet three or four times a year to consider grant applications, but special arrangements can be made if an application is deemed urgent.

Financial information

Year end	31/12/2020
Income	£9,400
Total expenditure	£6,000

Further financial information
Full accounts were not available to view on the Charity Commission's website due to the fund's low income. We have therefore estimated the fund's grant total based on its total expenditure.

Wilshaw Benevolent Fund

 £17,900 (2019)

Correspondent: The Trustees, Eastern House, Porthcurno, Penzance TR19 6JX (tel: 01736 811910; email: chairman@telegraphmuseum.org)

CC number: 206786

Eligibility
Former employees of Cable & Wireless, and their families, who are in need.

Types of grant
One-off grants are made towards, for example, mobility aids. Monthly grants are also available.

Applications
Apply in writing to the correspondent.

Financial information

Year end	31/12/2019
Income	£86,500
Total expenditure	£30,100

Legal

Barristers Clerks Benevolent Fund

 £11,100 (2019)

Correspondent: The Trustees, 18 Woodcote Avenue, Wallington, London SM6 0QY (tel: 020 8647 0086; email: enquiries@twpllp.co.uk)

www.barristersclerksbenevolentfund

CC number: 1084609

Eligibility
Barristers' clerks, former barristers' clerks and their dependants and families.

Types of grant
Grants are given according to need.

Applications
Apply in writing to the correspondent.

Financial information

Year end	31/12/2019
Income	£9,000
Total expenditure	£12,300

Further financial information
Full accounts were not available to view on the Charity Commission's website due to the fund's low income. We have therefore estimated the fund's grant total based on its total expenditure.

The Barristers' Benevolent Association

£996,500 (2020)

Correspondent: The Trustees, 14 Gray's Inn Square, London WC1R 5JP (tel: 020 7242 4761; email: nicky@the-bba.com)

www.the-bba.com

CC number: 1106768

Eligibility
Current and former practising members of the Bar in England and Wales (including the judiciary) who are in need. Support is also extended to the dependants of such people.

Types of grant
Welfare grants are awarded towards the cost of school uniforms and other clothing, shoes, home repairs, holidays/breaks, bills (telephone bills, taxes, etc.), essential furniture (beds) and essential electronics, such as computers and laptops. Secured loans are also available.

Exclusions
The charity is unable to make grants for school fees.

Applications
Application forms are available to download on the charity's website.

Financial information

Year end	31/12/2020
Income	£1,840,000
Total expenditure	£1,290,000

Other information
The charity can offer professional advice on Individual Voluntary Agreements (IVA) or bankruptcy.

Faculty of Advocates 1985 Charitable Trust

 £138,900 (2019/20)

Correspondent: The Trustees, Advocate's Library, Parliament House, Edinburgh EH1 1RF (tel: 0131 226 5071)

www.advocates.org.uk

OSCR number: SC012486

Eligibility
Widows, widowers, children or former dependants of deceased members of the Faculty of Advocates and members who are unable to practise by reason of permanent ill health.

Types of grant
The trust awards annuities and grants according to need.

Applications
According to our previous research, the trust is regularly publicised among members and applications are often made informally by word of mouth, via a trustee. Alternatively, applications may be made in writing to the correspondent.

Financial information

Year end	31/10/2020
Income	£195,900
Total expenditure	£260,700

Further financial information

During the financial year, £107,200 was awarded to ten annuitants. In addition, five grants totalling £31,700 were paid to individual beneficiaries.

The Incorporated Benevolent Association of the Chartered Institute of Patent Attorneys

£ £46,700 (2019/20)

Correspondent: Samantha Funnell, Secretary, c/o CIPA, 2nd Floor Halton House, 20–23 Holborn, London EC1N 2JD (tel: 020 7405 9450)

CC number: 219666

Eligibility

Members and former members of the Chartered Institute of Patent Attorneys, and their dependants.

Types of grant

Grants are given according to need.

Applications

Apply in writing to the correspondent.

Financial information

Year end	05/04/2020
Income	£66,300
Total expenditure	£53,000

Further financial information

Grants were provided to four individuals in 2019/20.

The Pritt Fund

£ £17,400 (2019/20)

Correspondent: The Trustees, Second Floor, Helix, Edmund Street, Liverpool, Merseyside L3 9NY (tel: 0151 236 6998; email: charities@liverpoollawsociety.org. uk)

 https://www.liverpoollawsociety. org.uk/about/charities

CC number: 226421

Eligibility

Solicitors, university law students and/or their families in Liverpool and the metropolitan boroughs of Wirral, Knowsley and Sefton, and in Widnes and Neston in Cheshire.

Types of grant

Grants are made for the relief of financial hardship.

Applications

Apply in writing to the correspondent.

Financial information

Year end	31/05/2020
Income	£12,300
Total expenditure	£19,300

Further financial information

Full accounts were not available to view on the Charity Commission's website due to the fund's low income. We have therefore estimated the fund's grant total based on its total expenditure.

SBA The Solicitors' Charity

£ £1,270,000 (2020)

Correspondent: Casework Team, 1 Jaggard Way, London SW12 8SG (tel: 020 8675 6440; email: caseworker@ thesolicitorscharity.org)

 www.sba.org.uk

CC number: 1124512

Eligibility

Solicitors who are, or have been, admitted to the Roll for England and Wales, and their dependants, who are in need. Applicants must not have access to liquid assets of over £10,000 and must have a household income below the level indicated by the Minimum Income Standard (MIS) calculation. A link to the minimum income calculator is featured on the charity's website.

Types of grant

One-off grants are made for a range of purposes including essential household furniture, urgent home repairs or help to move house. Long-term grant funding can be given to help with day-to-day living costs. The charity may occasionally provide loans for the provision of equipment and services.

Exclusions

The charity cannot award grants for:
- Debts owed to family member or friends
- Business or partnership debts
- Business running costs
- Legal fees
- Independent school fees
- Private medical treatment
- Student loan repayments
- Professional qualification costs

Unqualified law students and trainee solicitors are not eligible for support.

Applications

Applications can be made on the charity's website. Alternatively, applicants may wish to download a copy of the application form and once completed, send it to the charity by email or post.

Financial information

Year end	31/12/2020
Income	£1,240,000
Total expenditure	£2,140,000

Further financial information

During the financial year, the charity financially supported 399 beneficiaries.

Other information

The charity makes referrals to Manchester Citizens Advice for expert advice on personal debt and welfare benefits. The charity can also make referrals to employment specialists at Renovo for a career coaching programme offering one-to-one coaching and well-being support.

Scottish Solicitors Benevolent Fund

£ £16,000 (2019/20)

Correspondent: The Secretary, 14 The Firs, Millholm Road, Cathcart G44 3YB (email: scottishlawagentssociety@gmail. com)

 https://www.scottishlawagents.org/ tod-endowment-trust

OSCR number: SC000258

Eligibility

Solicitors in Scotland who have been in practice for at least two years prior to making an application. Their spouses, partners and dependants are also eligible.

Types of grant

One-off and recurrent grants according to need.

The charity also receives funds from the Tod Endowment Trust (OSCR no. SC010046) to be used to fund short holiday respite breaks in Scotland for solicitors and their dependants. Assistance is also provided for carers or companions where reasonably required. In addition, it is possible for the charity to finance locum cover to enable solicitors to benefit from a break.

Applications

Application forms can be requested from the correspondent.

Financial information

Year end	31/10/2020
Income	£11,400
Total expenditure	£17,000

Further financial information

Full accounts were not available to view on the OSCR website due to the charity's low income. We have therefore estimated the grant total based on the charity's total expenditure.

Manufac-turing

BEN – Motor and Allied Trades Benevolent Fund

 £290,000 (2020/21)

Correspondent: Support Services Team, Lynwood Court, Lynwood Village, Rise Road, Ascot, Berkshire SL5 0FG (tel: 0808 131 1333; email: supportservices@ben.org.uk)

www.ben.org.uk

CC number: 297877

Eligibility
People who are working or have worked in the UK automotive industry and their dependants.

Types of grant
Mostly one-off grants for essential specific goods and services such as food, utility bills, household goods, essential travel costs, childcare and Council Tax.

Applications
Individuals, or somebody referring an individual, can contact the charity directly via telephone, email or post.

Financial information
Year end	31/03/2021
Income	£17,080,000
Total expenditure	£17,400,000

Other information
BEN offers free support and advice on a broad range of issues through its support services team.

The BTMA Trust

 £169,800 (2019/20)

Correspondent: Jane Pocock, Case Secretary, PO Box 3157, Caterham, Surrey CR3 4BH (tel: 01883 371280; email: secretary@bmtatrust.org.uk)

bmtatrust.org.uk

CC number: 273978

Eligibility
Welfare
People who are or have been employed in the motor industry and their children.

Education
The trust's website states that it will also support young people aged 15 to 25 who are 'are committed to pursuing a defined goal in relation to education, training or employment in the motor industry'.

Types of grant
Welfare
Grants are given for welfare purposes such as white goods, replacement carpets, respite breaks and home adaptations.

Education
Grants of up to £1,000 are awarded to young people to help them achieve their education, training or employment goals in the motor industry. Examples include course fees, tools and help with living costs.

Applications
Applicants first need to contact the case secretary by phone or email to discuss their situation. If eligible, the individual will be sent an application form to complete.

Financial information
Year end	30/06/2020
Income	£237,300
Total expenditure	£234,000

The Coats Foundation Trust

 £110,000 (2019/20)

Correspondent: Andrea McCutcheon, Coats Pensions Office, 107 West Regent Street, Glasgow G2 2BA (tel: 0141 207 6800; email: andrea.mccutcheon@coats.com)

https://www.coatspensions.co.uk/about-us/coats-foundation-trust

CC number: 268735

Eligibility
Welfare
Members of the Coats UK Pension Scheme who are in need.

Education
Students across the UK are eligible for educational assistance. Priority is given to those studying textile-related courses.

Types of grant
Grants are given according to need.

Exclusions
The trust does not normally accept applications for day-to-day items such as food or rent.

Applications
Application forms are available to download on the trust's website.

Financial information
Year end	05/04/2020
Income	£1,200
Total expenditure	£123,500

Further financial information
Full accounts were not available to view on the Charity Commission's website due to the trust's low income. We have therefore estimated the grant total based on the trust's total expenditure.

Corn Exchange Benevolent Society

 £33,600 (2019)

Correspondent: The Trustees, 38 St Mary Axe, London EC3A 8BH (tel: 020 7283 6090; email: enquiries@becf.co.uk)

https://cornexchange-charity.com

CC number: 207733

Eligibility
People who work/have worked in the UK grain trade (the corn, grain, seed, cereal, animal feeding-stuffs, pulses, malt, flour milling or granary-keeping trades) at any level (this includes the trading, processing, manufacturing, storage or transport parts of the trade), and their dependants.

Types of grant
One-off and recurrent grants are given according to need. In the past, support has been given for the payment of day-to-day expenses, holidays, decorating costs, funeral expenses, home repairs, mobility aids, house appliances and medical treatment. Heating grants and Christmas hampers are also distributed.

Exclusions
Cereal growers, farmers, bakers and pastry cooks are not eligible to apply for support.

Applications
Application forms can be downloaded from the charity's website. Alternatively, contact the correspondent by phone.

Financial information
Year end	31/12/2019
Income	£118,400
Total expenditure	£90,500

Further financial information
During the financial period, grants were made to 33 individuals.

The Cotton Industry War Memorial Trust

£5,000 (2020)

Correspondent: Phillip Roberts, Trust Secretary, 19 Shepherd Street, Nordon, Rochdale, Greater Manchester OL11 5SU (tel: 01706 631557; email: theciwmt@btinternet.com)

CC number: 242721

Eligibility

Welfare
Current and former employees of the textile industry who have been employed in the industry at some time over the last 40 years. Employees and ex-employees of the textile industry who are sick or injured (and have been certified by their doctor as being in need of respite) are also eligible for support.

Education
Educational grants are available to textile students.

Types of grant

Welfare
Welfare grants are given for recuperative breaks at commercial hotels in Blackpool. One-off grants may also be awarded for specific needs.

Education
Educational grants are awarded to help with costs associated with studying textiles. Recently, the charity awarded a bursary to a student from the Textile Conservation Foundation.

Applications
Apply in writing to the correspondent. Applications should be made by other voluntary organisations (such as the Royal British Legion, Age Concern and SSAFA) on the applicant's behalf. The trustees meet quarterly to consider grant applications.

Financial information

Year end	31/12/2020
Income	£322,000
Total expenditure	£366,400

Further financial information
During the financial year, the charity awarded 64 grants for recuperative holidays, a one-off welfare grant and a bursary. Note: we were unable to determine the grant total for recuperative holidays.

Other information
This charity also makes grants to other non-profit organisations, mainly to help with administrative and core running costs. Grants are also made in support of various textile projects.

Footwear Friends

£ £63,800 (2020/21)

Correspondent: Gabi O'Sullivan, Secretary, PO Box 77403, London SW9 1FG (tel: 07999 126572; email: info@footwearfriends.org.uk)

 www.footwearfriends.org.uk

CC number: 222117

Eligibility
People who are working or have worked in the boot trade and footwear industry, usually for a minimum of five years, and their dependants. Priority is given to people with disabilities, families with young children and older people.

Types of grant
The charity's website states:

> We may make cash grants to meet exceptional needs such as appliances, disability equipment or essential repairs. We may also offer on going support to those for whom state support is insufficient.
>
> The financial support we offer includes:
> ▷ 6-monthly grants
> ▷ Mid-Year and Christmas grants
> ▷ One off grants
> ▷ Convalescent Holiday Grants

Applications
Application forms can be completed online or downloaded and posted to the correspondent.

Financial information

Year end	31/01/2021
Income	£111,600
Total expenditure	£115,000

Further financial information
Grants were broken down as follows:

Christmas grants	£18,600
Mid-year grants	£18,000
Half-yearly grants	£15,500
Cordwainers Christmas grants	£4,000
Holiday grants	£4,000
December bonus grants	£3,700

Other information
The charity is also known as the Footwear Benevolent Society and formerly as The Boot Trade Benevolent Society.

The JIC Fund (The Charitable Fund of the Joint Industrial Council of the Match Manufacturing Industry)

£ £880 (2020)

Correspondent: The Trustees, Republic Technologies (UK) Ltd, Sword House, Totteridge Road, High Wycombe, Buckinghamshire HP13 6DG (tel: 01494 492248)

CC number: 260075

Eligibility
Current and former employees of the match manufacturing industry who are in need. Applicants must have worked in the industry for a minimum of one year. Support is also extended to the dependants of such people.

Types of grant
Grants are awarded according to need.

Applications
Apply in writing to the correspondent.

Financial information

Year end	31/12/2020
Income	£0
Total expenditure	£980

Further financial information
Full accounts were not available to view on the Charity Commission's website due to the fund's low income. We have therefore estimated the fund's grant total based on its total expenditure.

Liverpool Corn Trade Guild

£ £9,000 (2019)

Correspondent: The Trustees, 12 Birchway, Heswall, Wirral, Merseyside CH60 3SX (tel: 0151 342 4566)

CC number: 232414

Eligibility
Priority is given to members of the Liverpool Corn Trade Guild and their dependants or widows. If funds permit, the trustees may extend support to former members of the guild or the Liverpool Corn Trade Clerk's Guild, and their dependants or widows.

Types of grant
Grants and loans are awarded according to need.

Applications
Apply in writing to the correspondent.

Financial information

Year end	31/12/2019
Income	£9,900
Total expenditure	£10,000

Further financial information
Full accounts were not available to view on the Charity Commission's website due to the charity's low income. We have therefore estimated the charity's grant total based on its total expenditure.

The Society of Motor Manufacturers and Traders Charitable Trust Fund

£ £2,700 (2020)

Correspondent: The Trustees, SMMT, 71 Great Peter Street, London SW1P 2BN (tel: 020 7344 9267; email: companysecretary@smmt.co.uk)

www.smmt.co.uk

CC number: 209852

Eligibility

People in need who are associated with the motor industry, and their dependants.

Types of grant

One-off and recurrent grants according to need.

Applications

Contact the fund for further information on how to apply.

Financial information

Year end	31/12/2020
Income	£37,700
Total expenditure	£45,200

Other information

Grants are also awarded to organisations.

The National Benevolent Society of Watch and Clock Makers

 £244,100 (2019/20)

Correspondent: Anne Baker, Secretary, 5 Burleigh Park, Faygate, West Sussex KT11 2DU (tel: 07514 402607; email: sec@nbswcm.org)

🌐 www.nbswcm.org

CC number: 206750

Eligibility

Members of the UK watch and clock trade who have retired or are unable to work due to sickness or disability, and their widows/widowers and dependants who are in need. Generally, grants are given to those with an income of below £20,000, although the trustees have the discretion to act outside this guideline in certain circumstances.

Types of grant

Recurrent grants paid quarterly. Christmas, summer and heating gifts are also distributed.

Exclusions

Grants are not usually awarded for individual items such as disability aids or home adaptations; however, the charity's website states: 'If an individual has a requirement for these and cannot find the funds, their income may be such that they qualify for a recurrent grant.'

Applications

Applications should be made by requesting a form from the secretary. Completed forms should be submitted by individuals or, if they require

assistance, through a family member, social worker, welfare agency or Citizens Advice.

Financial information

Year end	31/10/2020
Income	£80,300
Total expenditure	£283,500

Further financial information

Grants were awarded to 102 individuals during the year. Grants were distributed as follows:

Heating and seasonal gifts	£120,600
Grants in aid	£107,100
Television licence fee	£16,400

The National Caravan Council (NCC) Benevolent Fund
See entry on page 147

The Spear Charitable Trust

 £24,100 (2020)

Correspondent: Hazel Spear, Trustee, Roughground House, Beggarmans Lane, Old Hall Green, Ware, Hertfordshire SG11 1HB (tel: 01920 823071)

CC number: 1041568

Eligibility

Former employees of JW Spear and Sons plc, and their families and dependants.

Types of grant

One-off and recurrent grants to relieve financial hardship.

Applications

Applications should be made in writing to the correspondent, detailing the financial need and what the grant will be used for. Proof of employment with JW Spear and Sons plc should also be included.

Financial information

Year end	31/12/2020
Income	£118,400
Total expenditure	£817,200

Further financial information

Grants were awarded to six former employees.

Other information

The majority of the charity's grant-making is to organisations (£759,000 was awarded in 2020).

W. W. Spooner Charitable Trust

£ £13,200 (2018/19)

Correspondent: The Trustees, 2 Elliot Road, Watford, Hertfordshire WD17 4DF (tel: 01923 237231)

CC number: 313653

Eligibility

Welfare
Former employees of Spooner Industries Ltd, and their dependants, who are in need.

Education
Scholarships are available to young employees of Spooner Industries Ltd.

Types of grant

Grants are given according to need.

Applications

Apply in writing to the correspondent.

Financial information

Year end	05/04/2019
Income	£92,400
Total expenditure	£122,900

Further financial information

The 2018/19 accounts were the latest available at the time of writing (November 2021).

Maritime

The Coastguard Association Charity

£ £17,300 (2019)

Correspondent: Paul Davig, Almoner, 7 Wentworth Close, Skegness, Lincolnshire PE25 1DP (tel: 01754 768094; email: almoner@ coastguardassociation.org.uk)

🌐 www.coastguardassociation.org.uk

CC number: 279359

Eligibility

Any serving or retired (by age or medically) coastguard personnel and their dependants.

Types of grant

One-off grants are awarded according to need. In the past, grants have been awarded for funeral costs, parking and fuel costs incurred as part of an extended hospital stay, special needs equipment, holidays/respite breaks and financial assistance during recovery from surgery. Gifts are distributed at Christmas to older, retired coastguards.

Applications

Apply in writing to the correspondent (ideally through a third party who can verify the claim as genuine) stating the exact hardship, a brief history of the events that led to the hardship, the applicant's age and the number of dependants.

Financial information

Year end	31/12/2019
Income	£179,600
Total expenditure	£171,400

Further financial information

During the year, hardship grants were awarded to 11 people totalling £16,000. In addition, Christmas gifts awarded to older, retired coastguards totalled £1,300.

The Corporation of Trinity House of Deptford Strond

(£) £2,771,000 (2019/20)

Correspondent: Vicki Muir, Trinity House, Tower Hill, London EC3N 4DH (tel: 020 7481 6903; email: Victoria. Muir@trinityhouse.co.uk)

 www.trinityhouse.co.uk

CC number: 211869

Eligibility

Welfare

Former seafarers, and their dependants, who are in need.

Education

Educational grants are available to young people (usually aged between 16 and 18 and a half) who are of good general health and physique, sufficient enough to pass the Maritime and Coastguard Agency medical examination. There are certain academic standards expected of applicants which differ depending on the chosen entry route. These are:

- **Foundation degree/Scottish Professional Diploma:** GCSEs at grades A to C, or Scottish Standard level 1 to 3, in English, Mathematics (grade A or B), Physics or Combined Science, and at least two other subjects. Applicants must have attained at least 120 UCAS points in any A-level subjects or equivalent. Continuation on to a full honours degree may be possible.
- **Higher National Diploma (HND):** GCSEs at grades A to C, or Scottish Standard level 1 to 3, in English, Mathematics (grade A or B), Physics or Combined Science and at least two other subjects.

United Kingdom Sailing Academy (UKSA) Superyacht Cadetships are available to young people aged 15 to 18.

Applicants are expected to have excellent oral and written skills, a good understanding of mathematics and have GCSE grades 9 to 4 (A* to C) in English, Maths and Science. If applying for a foundation degree alongside the Superyacht Cadetship, applicants must have 48 UCAS points.

Types of grant

Welfare

Grants are made in the form of annuities to residents of the Trinity Homes almshouses. One-off grants are awarded more generally to former mariners (and their dependants) who are in need.

Education

The Merchant Navy Scholarship Scheme funds cadetships for young people seeking careers in the Merchant Navy. Cadets can train as desk officers, engineer officers and electro-technical officers. The qualifications gained from a cadetship vary from an HND to a full honours degree. Grants of up to £11,000 are available for UKSA Superyacht Cadetships.

Applications

Welfare

For welfare grants, applicants are advised to contact the correspondent, who can provide an application form. The committee meets around six times a year to consider grant applications. For current application deadlines, see the funder's website.

Education

For educational grants, application forms for Merchant Navy Scholarships are available to download on the funder's website. Prospective applicants can register their interest for the UKSA Superyacht Cadetship on the website.

Financial information

Year end	31/03/2020
Income	£9,910,000
Total expenditure	£11,230,000

Further financial information

During the financial year, scholarships were awarded to 105 cadets.

Other information

The funder owns and operates 18 almshouses in Walmer (Kent), which are available to ex-mariners, typically aged 60 and above, who are in need. Residents normally have over 15 years' service at sea. Occupancy is also extended to the dependants of such people.

Fishermen's Mission

(£) £480,000 (2019/20)

Correspondent: The Trustees, The Fishermen's Mission, Mather House, 4400 Parkway, Fareham, Hampshire PO15 7FJ (tel: 01489 566910; email: enquiries@fishermensmission.org.uk)

 www.fishermensmission.org.uk

CC number: 232822

Eligibility

Current or retired commercial fishermen, and their dependants, who are in need.

Types of grant

Immediate financial assistance for costs such as food, rent, utility bills, school dinners or school uniforms. Other grants are usually one-off.

Applications

Initial enquiries should be made by contacting a local Fishermen's Mission centre, details of which can be found on the charity's website.

Financial information

Year end	31/10/2020
Income	£3,280,000
Total expenditure	£2,940,000

Other information

This charity operates a 24/7 emergency response team, to help injured, ill or shipwrecked fishermen. The charity also offers emotional support to fishermen during bereavement, family breakdown or any other adverse circumstances, as well in-person support through home and hospital visits to isolated fishermen.

Hull Trinity House Charity

(£) £343,800 (2019/20)

Correspondent: The Trustees, Hull Trinity House Charity, Trinity House, Trinity House Lane, Hull, East Yorkshire HU1 2JG (tel: 01482 324956; email: secretary@trinityhouse.karoo.co.uk)

 www.trinityhousehull.org.uk

CC number: 220331

Eligibility

Seafarers who are in ill health, retired or experiencing financial hardship and their spouses and dependants. The trustees give preference to people in need over 60 years old.

Types of grant

Annual grants paid quarterly.

Applications

Apply in writing to the correspondent.

Financial information

Year end	02/09/2020
Income	£1,430,000
Total expenditure	£1,390,000

Other information

The charity provides 'rest homes' (almshouses) which provide accommodation for recipients of grants, or non-seafarers who are in need. The charity also supports the Trinity House Academy and Welton Waters Adventure Centre.

The Guild of Benevolence of The Institute of Marine Engineering, Science and Technology

 £58,300 (2019/20)

Correspondent: The Trustees, 1 Birdcage Walk, London SW1H 9JJ (tel: 020 7382 2644; email: guild@imarest.org)

 www.imarest.org/guild

CC number: 208727

Eligibility

Past and present members or employees of The Institute of Marine Engineering, Science and Technology (IMarEST) or of The Guild of Benevolence; marine or electrical engineers, Mercantile or Naval, who possess, or have possessed, Certificates of Competency or Certificates of Service issued by the relevant governmental department or agency, or equivalent qualifications; the wives, husbands, widows, widowers, dependent children or other dependent relatives of any person qualifying under any of the previous categories.

Types of grant

Regular grants to supplement low incomes and one-off grants for home repairs, funeral expenses, respite care, debt relief, shortfalls in reasonable nursing home fees and items that are essential for the recipient's well-being. Bonuses of £100 are also distributed to regular grantees at Christmas.

Applications

Application forms can be downloaded from the charity's website. Applications can be completed by the applicant or a third party.

Financial information

Year end	30/09/2020
Income	£123,200
Total expenditure	£125,900

Further financial information

The charity awarded grants to 69 individuals. These included 33 new recipients and the remaining were existing beneficiaries who receive regular grants. During the year, the regular support grant was increased to £30 per week. Christmas bonuses awarded to regular beneficiaries totalled £2,900.

The Marine Society and Sea Cadets

 £815,000 (2019/20)

Correspondent: The Trustees, 202 Lambeth Road, London SE1 7JW (tel: 020 7654 7000; email: info@ms-sc.org)

 https://www.marine-society.org/funding

CC number: 313013/SC037808

Eligibility

Professional seafarers, active or retired, serving in the Royal Navy, the British Merchant Navy or fishing fleets, and their dependants. The charity also supports people who are serving in the navies, merchant navies or fishing fleets of other countries as the council determines. Members of the Sea Cadet Corps and those preparing to enter a maritime career are also eligible for support.

Types of grant

Welfare

Grants are given to assist with financial hardship among seafarers and their dependants.

Sea Cadet volunteers are awarded grants for the purchase and maintenance of uniforms.

Education

Bursaries, scholarships and loans are given towards education and training for those entering the maritime career. Support can be given towards fees, maintenance and other expenses. The charity administers a range of scholarships to support professional development, details of each scheme can be found on the charity's website. Grants are also available for unemployed seafarers to help them update their skills and/or revalidate specific certification requirements to increase their employability.

Applications

Application forms for each scholarship can be found on the Marine Society's website. A contact form is also available to use for any other enquiries.

Financial information

Year end	31/03/2020
Income	£17,770,000
Total expenditure	£17,320,000

Other information

According to the 2019/20 accounts, grants are also made to Sea Cadet units and support can be given to 'nautical or other schools or training establishments which are charities or to other organisations established for charitable purposes'. The charity's combined

website (Marine Society and Sea Cadets) can be found at www.ms-sc.org.

The Honourable Company of Master Mariners and Howard Leopold Davis Charity

 £62,400 (2019)

Correspondent: Honourable Company of Master Mariners, 8 Cumberland Place, Southampton, Hants SO15 2BH (tel: 023 8033 7799; email: enquiries@mnwb.org.uk)

 https://www.hcmm.org.uk/philanthropy.html

CC number: 1172234

Eligibility

Welfare

British master mariners, navigation officers of the Merchant Navy, and their wives, widows and dependants who are in need through financial hardship, sickness, disability or the effects of old age.

Education

People intending to serve in the Merchant Navy or with an interest in seamanship or sailing.

Types of grant

Welfare

One-off and recurrent grants are given according to need.

Education

The charity's website states:

> The objectives and aims of the Education Fund are to assist and encourage the education, instruction and training whether generally, technically or professionally, of persons serving or intending to serve in the Merchant Navy. Grants are available for anyone who fulfils these requirements.

Applications

Contact the charity for further information on how to apply.

Financial information

Year end	31/12/2019
Income	£103,500
Total expenditure	£140,700

The Molyneux and Warbrick Charity

 £15,400 (2019/20)

Correspondent: John Wilson, Trustee, Liverpool Seafarers Centre, 20 Crosby Road South, Liverpool, Merseyside L22 1RQ (tel: 07973 824154; email: john.wilson@liverpoolseafarerscentre.org)

CC number: 229408

Eligibility

Older seafarers or their spouses who are in need. Applicants must live in Merseyside.

Types of grant

The charity provides quarterly pensions.

Applications

Apply in writing to the correspondent.

Financial information

Year end	31/03/2020
Income	£24,100
Total expenditure	£17,100

Further financial information

Full accounts were not available to view on the Charity Commission's website due to the charity's low income. We have therefore estimated the charity's grant total based on its total expenditure.

Nautilus Welfare Fund

 £132,100 (2020)

Correspondent: Amy Johnson, Care Manager, Trinity House Hub, Webster Avenue, Mariner's Park, Wallasey, Merseyside CH44 0AE (tel: 0151 346 8840; email: welfare@nautilusint.org)

 https://www.nautiluswelfarefund.org

CC number: 218742

Eligibility

Retired seafarers and their dependants across the UK.

Types of grant

One-off grants for a range of purposes including essential household items, maintenance, independent living equipment (mobility scooters, stairlifts, etc.), outstanding bills and removal expenses.

Applications

Application forms are available from the fund's website. Alternatively, applicants can call the fund for help completing the form.

Financial information

Year end	31/12/2020
Income	£3,060,000
Total expenditure	£3,400,000

Other information

The fund also offers residential and nursing care, independent living support, specialist care at home and other services. For full information visit the fund's website.

Port of London Authority Police Charity Fund

 £4,000 (2020/21)

Correspondent: Barry Smith, Trustee, Police Headquarters, Tilbury Freeport, Tilbury Dock, Tilbury, Essex RM18 7DU (tel: 01375 846781; email: barry.smith@potll.com)

CC number: 265569

Eligibility

Former officers who have served with the Port of London Authority's police force, and their dependants, who are in need.

Types of grant

One-off grants are awarded according to need.

Applications

Apply in writing to the correspondent.

Financial information

Year end	31/03/2021
Income	£0
Total expenditure	£4,500

Further financial information

Full accounts were not available to view on the Charity Commission's website due to the fund's low income. We have therefore estimated the grant total based on the fund's total expenditure.

The Royal Liverpool Seamen's Orphan Institution (RLSOI)

 £163,600 (2020)

Correspondent: Michael Finn, Secretary, Suite 315, Cotton Exchange Building, Old Hall Street, Liverpool, Merseyside L3 9LQ (tel: 0151 227 3417 or 07831 204121 (mobile); email: enquiries@rlsoi-uk.org)

 www.rlsoi-uk.org

CC number: 526379

Eligibility

Merchant seafarers or fishermen who have had to give up their work due to the death of their partner. Widows, partners and children of deceased merchant seafarers and fishermen are also eligible for support.

Types of grant

Welfare grants are awarded according to need. Grants can be given to support the education of children in school and college, or to help with costs associated with pursuing higher or further education, including monthly maintenance allowances.

Applications

Contact the charity for more information. At the time of writing (November 2021), the charity's website stated that revised grant application forms would soon be available to download.

Financial information

Year end	31/12/2020
Income	£210,100
Total expenditure	£257,800

Sailors' Society

 £21,000 (2020)

Correspondent: The Trustees, Seafarer House, 74 St Annes Road, Southampton, Hampshire SO19 9FF (email: crisis@sailors-society.org)

 www.sailors-society.org

CC number: 237778

Eligibility

Serving merchant seafarers, retired seafarers and their dependants who find themselves in need.

Types of grant

Emergency grants to ease financial hardship.

Applications

Contact the charity for further information on how to apply.

Financial information

Year end	31/12/2020
Income	£3,660,000
Total expenditure	£7,070,000

Other information

The society maintains a network of chaplains at the various key ports around the world who carry out ship-visiting routines and minister to seafarers. It also provides centres and clubs for seafarers and associated maritime workers at strategic seaports. International disaster relief is also given and organisations are supported.

The Sailors' Children's Society
See entry on page 28

Sailors' Orphan Society of Scotland
See entry on page 28

Scottish Nautical Welfare Society

 £60,500 (2019/20)

Correspondent: Gail Haldane, Administrator, 937 Dumbarton Road, Glasgow G14 9UF (tel: 0141 337 2632; email: ghaldane@snws.org.uk)

www.snws.org.uk

OSCR number: SC032892

Eligibility
Former merchant seafarers or fishermen with ten years of sea service. Applicants with less than ten years of experience who have a specific need may be considered. Widows and widowers may also apply for financial support.

Types of grant
Regular quarterly grants and winter fuel payments.

Applications
Application forms can be downloaded from the charity's website. Some applicants may be visited by a caseworker who will provide a report and recommendations to the trustees as part of the individual's application.

Financial information
Year end	31/03/2020
Income	£112,300
Total expenditure	£119,200

Other information
The charity also provides advice and hosts social gatherings.

Seafarers Hospital Society

 £266,200 (2020)

Correspondent: Mr P. S. Coulson, Secretary, 29 King William Walk, Greenwich, London SE10 9HX (tel: 020 8858 3696; email: admin@seahospital.org.uk)

www.seahospital.org.uk

CC number: 231724

Eligibility
Current or retired merchant seafarers and fishermen and their close dependants (wives/husbands, widows/widowers or children under 18). Applicants must have at least five years sea service. Former merchant seafarers and fishermen whose service was cut short because of an accident or illness are also eligible.

Types of grant
Grants are awarded according to need. Typical examples include:

- Disability aids or equipment (stairlifts, wheelchairs, adapted bathrooms, etc.)
- Essential household items and furniture
- Assistance with priority debts (gas, electricity, Council Tax, rent, etc.)
- Essential household maintenance and repairs
- Urgent short-term living expenses
- Respite breaks or convalescence
- Clothing
- Assistance with funeral costs (maximum of £750)

Respite
The society can refer carers to two respite centres (in Cheshire and Surrey), for which it may be able to award a grant towards the cost of a stay.

Physiotherapy
The society also pays for fast-track physiotherapy, which is available for all UK-based merchant seafarers and fishers.

Applications
Application forms are available to download from the society's website or can be requested from the correspondent. Applications should be completed in conjunction with a caseworker, such as representatives from SSAFA, Shipwrecked Mariners' Society, the Fishermen's Mission or Nautilus. If you are not already in contact with a caseworker, contact the society, which will arrange for one to visit you.

Financial information
Year end	31/12/2020
Income	£290,800
Total expenditure	£761,700

Further financial information
In 2020, grants were awarded to 455 individuals as follows: general welfare assistance (£242,600); physiotherapy (£19,200); hospital travel costs (£3,500); COVID-19 grants (£960). Grants to organisations totalled £143,600.

Other information
The society operates a 24/7 advice and support service for those experiencing mental health problems. The 'Togetherall' (formerly the 'Big White Wall') service can be accessed online, and seafarers can speak with a professional via webcam, audio or instant messaging. The society also works in partnership with the Fishermen's Mission to provide free in-person physical and mental health checks to seafarers on a regular basis. Dates, times and locations of the 'SeaFit Programme' can be found on the society's website.

The Shipwrecked Fishermen and Mariners' Royal Benevolent Society

 £1,380,000 (2019/20)

Correspondent: The Grants Team, 1 North Pallant, Chichester, West Sussex PO19 1TL (tel: 01243 789329; email: grants@shipwreckedmariners.org.uk)

https://shipwreckedmariners.org.uk

CC number: 212034

Eligibility
Merchant seafarers, fishermen, and their dependants who are in need. Note that the society offers different types of financial assistance, each with different eligibility criteria.

Types of grant
According to the society's website there are five types of grant:

- **Bi-annual grants:** given twice a year to fishermen or mariners who are retired or have a permanent disability, or to their widows. A minimum of ten years of sea service is required.
- **Death benefit grants:** one-off grants for widows of life members of the society under the former beneficial membership scheme.
- **Immediate grants:** given to widows and children following the death of a serving fisherman or mariner.
- **One-off grants:** given to fishermen, mariners, and their widows and children who do not qualify for a bi-annual grant but who have a specific need. A minimum of five years of sea service is required.
- **Funeral grants:** given to next of kin if they meet the qualifying for a one-off grant subject to their having received a Department for Work and Pensions funeral grant.

Assistance is also offered to shipwrecked survivors landed on the coasts of Great Britain and Ireland.

Applications
Application forms are available from the correspondent.

Financial information
Year end	31/03/2020
Income	£1,600,000
Total expenditure	£1,970,000

Further financial information
Grants were awarded to 1,345 individuals during the year.

The Tyne Mariners' Benevolent Institution

(£) £84,400 (2020)

Correspondent: Anthony Malia, Secretary, c/o Hadaway & Hadaway, 58 Howard Street, North Shields, Tyne and Wear NE30 1AL (tel: 0191 257 0382; email: tonym@hadaway.co.uk)

CC number: 229236

Eligibility

Retired ex-seafarers living in Newcastle upon Tyne, North Tyneside, South Tyneside and Northumberland (or within a five-mile radius of the River Tyne) or their widows who are experiencing financial difficulty. Applicants must have at least five years' service at sea.

Types of grant

The charity provides monthly pensions and one-off grants according to need.

Applications

Apply in writing to the correspondent.

Financial information

Year end	31/12/2020
Income	£312,800
Total expenditure	£196,800

Other information

The charity also provides housing to ex-seafarers or their widows at the Master Mariners Homes in North Shields. Residents at the homes do not pay rent, but they do make maintenance contributions to keep them in good repair.

Marketing and PR

iprovision

 £7,100 (2019)

Correspondent: Sharon Shortland, Grants Administrator, c/o Sayer Vincent LLP, Invicta House, 108–114 Golden Lane, London EC1Y 0TL (tel: 020 8144 5536; email: support@iprovision.org.uk)

 https://www.cipr.co.uk/content/about-us/iprovision/about-iprovision

CC number: 1157465

Eligibility

Members, employees and ex-employees of the Chartered Institute of Public Relations (CIPR) and their dependants.

The charity's website states:

iprovision can offer confidential guidance and support when things get difficult for you and your family for any number of reasons, including – but not limited to:

▶ long-term or terminal illness,
▶ mental health conditions (stress, anxiety, depression),
▶ periods of unemployment or low income,
▶ relationship breakdown,
▶ caring responsibilities,
▶ bereavement,
▶ facing other set-backs.

Types of grant

The charity's website states:

If you are experiencing financial difficulties because of an unexpected need or life changing circumstance, iprovision can offer grants to help you meet the costs, including – but not limited to:

▶ short term payments towards everyday living
▶ replacement house appliances (fridge, washing machine etc.)
▶ mobility aids (wheelchair, mobility scooter etc.)
▶ home adaptations to support continued independent living
▶ clothing (such as for school uniform or job interviews)
▶ funeral costs
▶ car repair costs
▶ costs towards relocation or move home
▶ travel or hospital parking
▶ respite care, or care breaks
▶ safety and security home repairs

Applications

Initially contact the administrator in writing, by phone or by email outlining your situation and how you think the charity could help you. The trustees meet to consider applications every three months, but if the need is urgent, decisions may be made between meetings. Note: if you are contacting the administrator by post, mark your envelope 'Private and Confidential' and include your contact details in the letter.

Financial information

Year end	31/12/2019
Income	£55,400
Total expenditure	£43,000

Further financial information

A breakdown of grants was not available. The grant total has therefore been estimated.

The Market Research Benevolent Association

 £27,900 (2019/20)

Correspondent: Danielle Scott, 11 Tremayne Walk, Camberley, Surrey GU15 1AH (tel: 0345 652 0303; email: enquiries@mrba.org.uk)

🌐 www.mrba.org.uk

CC number: 274190

Eligibility

People who work, or have worked, in any aspect of market research in the UK for at least two years. Support is also available to the dependants of such people.

Types of grant

Grants are awarded according to need.

The Market Research Benevolent Association scheme aims to help young researchers, and those who are new to the industry but who may struggle to afford course fees, take the Market Research Society's Advanced Certificate in Market and Social Research qualification.

Applications

Initial enquiries should be made by email.

Financial information

Year end	31/03/2020
Income	£31,700
Total expenditure	£76,700

NABS

(£) £305,400 (2020)

Correspondent: Support Team, 10 Hills Place, London W1F 7SD (tel: 0800 707 6607 (advice line); email: support@nabs.org.uk)

🌐 https://nabs.org.uk/how-we-can-help/grants-training-awards

CC number: 1070556

Eligibility

Welfare

People who work or have worked in advertising, marketing, marketing services and related industries. Dependants of such people are also eligible.

Education

People in the industry who are out of work or their role is potentially at risk unless they upskill.

Types of grant

Welfare

One-off and ongoing assistance is given according to need.

Education

Upskilling grants of up to £1,800 are available to help with the costs of course fees.

Applications

In the first instance, contact the society's advice line (0800 707 6607) or email support@nabs.org.uk.

Financial information

Year end	31/12/2020
Income	£1,860,000
Total expenditure	£3,240,000

Further financial information
Grants were awarded to over 120 individuals during the year, including 68 crisis grants.

Other information
The society provides a wide range of advice, support, networking and career guidance for members of the advertising and media industry, including a telephone helpline, career coaching and workshops and a working parents programme.

Media

The Book Trade Charity

 £333,400 (2020)

Correspondent: The Trustees, The Foyle Centre, The Retreat, Abbots Road, Kings Langley, Hertfordshire WD4 8LT (tel: 01923 263128; email: info@btbs.org)

 https://www.btbs.org

CC number: 1128129

Eligibility
Welfare
People who have worked in the UK book trade for at least one year (normally publishing/distribution/book-selling) and are in need. Support is also extended to the dependants of such people.

Education
People (particularly those under the age of 30) who are undertaking paid internships, training or postgraduate courses in preparation for entry into the book trade are eligible for support. Unpaid internships will be considered where they adhere to government guidelines on pay (i.e. for work shadowing or mandatory internships as part of a training course). Preference is given to those at the beginning of their careers.

Types of grant
Welfare
One-off and recurrent grants are awarded according to need.

Education
Grants to improve or develop skills through training and career guidance where this will help in obtaining employment in the book trade. Support is also provided to young people (usually under 30) entering the trade through apprenticeships, internships (which must be paid) or first/second roles in the trade.

Applications
Application forms are available to download on the charity's website. If a request is urgent, applicants are advised to contact the charity by telephone.

Financial information
Year end	31/12/2020
Income	£1,270,000
Total expenditure	£780,000

Other information
The charity operates two subsidised housing facilities in Kings Langley and Whetstone, which are available to all who have worked, or are currently working in the book trade, including new entrants to the trade.

The Chartered Institute of Journalists Benevolent Fund/ Pensions Fund/Orphan Fund

 £79,600 (2020)

Correspondent: The Trustees, Institute of Journalists, PO Box 765, Waltham Abbey, Waltham Cross, Hertfordshire EN8 1NT (tel: 020 7252 1187; email: memberservices@cioj.co.uk)

 https://www.cioj.org

CC number: 208176

Eligibility
Members of The Chartered Institute of Journalists and their dependants who are in need.

Types of grant
The institute administers four charitable funds:
- The Benevolent Fund – provides grants according to need to members and their dependants
- The Orphan Fund – grants are given to the children of deceased members for educational purposes. Previously support has been given to both high school students and students in university.
- The Pension Fund – provides regular pensions to older members in need
- The Oakhill and T.P. O'Connor Fund – grants are given towards convalescent care for journalists who are in need due to illness or age

Applications
Contact the institute for information on how to apply.

Financial information
Year end	31/12/2020
Income	£119,400
Total expenditure	£111,400

Further financial information
Grants were distributed as follows: the Orphan Fund made grants totalling £32,900; the Pension Fund made grants totalling £11,200 to seven pensioners; the Oakhill and T.P. O'Connor Fund made grants totalling £11,200 to nine journalists; and the Benevolent Fund made grants totalling £24,300 to 19 members.

The Film and Television Charity

 £1,010,000 (2019/20)

Correspondent: The Trustees, 22 Golden Square, London W1F 9AD (tel: 020 7437 6567 or 0800 054 0000 (support line); email: info@filmtvcharity.org.uk)

 www.ctbf.co.uk

CC number: 1099660

Eligibility
People working in the UK film and television industry who are in need. Applicants must have at least two years of proven professional experience behind the scenes in the UK film, TV and cinema industry to be eligible.

Types of grant
One-off support grants are available for immediate and urgent needs. Grants are usually of up to £800; however, the amount could be higher in exceptional circumstances.

Exclusions
Support cannot be given to individuals that work on commercials, music videos or corporate films, or to on-screen performers. Additionally, funding is not available for:
- Business debts including accountant fees and tax debt
- Storage costs
- Repayments to family or friends
- Costs relating to county court judgements
- Driving lessons
- Vet bills
- Student living costs
- Course fees

Applications
Applications can be made through the charity's website.

Financial information
Year end	31/03/2020
Income	£1,110,000
Total expenditure	£4,210,000

Further financial information
The charity awarded 4,714 grants to individuals during 2019/20.

Other information
The charity was formerly known as The Cinema and Television Benevolent Fund. As well as making grants, the charity operates a 24/7 support line and offers information and advice to individuals.

At the time of writing (September 2021), the charity was soon to launch a new support programme alongside its support grants. Visit the website for the most up-to-date information.

Grace Wyndham Goldie (BBC) Trust Fund

 £41,500 (2019)

Correspondent: The Trustees, Pension and Benefits Centre, BBC Cymru Wales, 3 Central Square, Cardiff CF10 1FT (tel: 029 2032 2811 or 0303 0805801; email: mypension@bbc.co.uk)

https://www.bbc.com/ charityappeals/appeals/grants/ grace-wyndham-goldie

CC number: 212146

Eligibility
Individuals currently or previously engaged in broadcasting and their dependants.

Types of grant
Welfare
One-off grants are given to help relieve short-term domestic hardship not covered by assistance from other sources.

Education
One-off grants are given to help with educational costs such as travelling expenses, school outfits and books. Support can also be given to help support young people gain professional or trade qualifications.

Exclusions
The fund's application form states the following:

It is important to recognise that the fund has been established to act as a safety net and not to fund expensive lifestyle choices. If you therefore have expenses such as holidays, gym membership, digital services for tv, high mobile telephone charges or non-essential car costs then you will be expected to be able to pay for these yourself.

Applications
Application forms are available to download from the fund's page on the BBC website. Completed applications should be submitted along with supporting information by the deadline, details of which can be found on the website.

Financial information
Year end	31/12/2019
Income	£66,200
Total expenditure	£44,300

Further financial information
In 2019, the fund awarded 12 grants for education and 7 for welfare purposes.

Other information
The fund was created in memory of BBC producer Grace Wyndham Goldie, who recruited and trained many well-known broadcasters at the BBC as well as pioneering political programming such as the first televised general election.

The GPM Charitable Trust

 £3,600 (2019/20)

Correspondent: Keith Keys, Secretary, c/o 43 Spriggs Close, Clapham, Bedford MK41 6GD (tel: 07733 262991; email: gpmcharitabletrust82@gmail.com)

www.gpmtrust.org

CC number: 227177

Eligibility
Workers, former workers and their dependants in the printing, graphical, papermaking and media industries who are in need.

Types of grant
Welfare
Grants can be given to pay for goods, services, or facilities and have been made to help with the purchase of mobility aids, to finance home improvements to enable applicants to remain in their own homes and towards the cost of a respite or convalescent break.

Education
Grants are available for retraining, skills enhancement and other educational requirements especially following redundancy or other reduction in income.

Exclusions
The trust is unable to assist with regular grants or debt relief.

Applications
An application form can be downloaded from the trust's website or requested from the correspondent. It must be printed and completed in black ink before being returned to the trust. The dates of application deadlines for subsequent trustee meetings are listed on the website.

Financial information
Year end	31/03/2020
Income	£26,800
Total expenditure	£17,100

Further financial information
During the year, the trust awarded 22 grants to both individuals and organisations. As the breakdown of grants was not available, we have estimated the grant total for individuals.

Journalists' Charity

 £194,000 (2020)

Correspondent: The Trustees, 11 Ribblesdale, Roman Road, Dorking, Surrey RH4 3EX (tel: 01306 887511; email: enquiries@journalistscharity.org.uk)

www.journalistscharity.org.uk

CC number: 208215

Eligibility
People who have worked as a journalist in the UK or for a UK organisation for at least two continuous years out of the last five years or for seven years in total (if not current) with journalism being the main source of their income during that period.

Types of grant
One-off and recurrent grants are given. This charity mainly supports welfare causes such as funeral costs, bills to be paid or a wheelchair that needs replacing.

Applications
Apply via the charity's website.

Financial information
Year end	31/12/2020
Income	£518,000
Total expenditure	£1,070,000

The Guild of Motoring Writers Benevolent Fund

 £8,000 (2020)

Correspondent: Elizabeth Aves, Administrator, 23 Stockwell Park Crescent, London SW9 0DQ (tel: 020 7737 2377; email: benfundadmin@gomw.co.uk)

www.gomw.co.uk

CC number: 259583

Eligibility
Current and former members of the Guild, and their dependants, who are in need.

Types of grant
One-off grants and loans awarded according to need. Non-financial support is available in the form of professional guidance and the loan of equipment.

Applications
Apply in writing to the correspondent.

Financial information
Year end	31/12/2020
Income	£8,600
Total expenditure	£8,800

Further financial information

Full accounts were not available to view on the Charity Commission's website due to the fund's low income. We have therefore estimated the grant total based on the fund's total expenditure.

Other information

The fund's website states that it has an association with the Motor and Allied Trades Benevolent Fund (commonly known as BEN).

NUJ Extra

 £128,300 (2020)

Correspondent: The Trustees, Headland House, 72 Acton Street, London WC1X 9NB (tel: 020 7843 3738; email: extra@nuj.org.uk)

https://www.nuj.org.uk/work/nuj-extra

CC number: 1112489

Eligibility

Members and former members of the National Union of Journalists and the dependants of deceased members.

Types of grant

Support is provided to settle debts such as rent and mortgages. The charity will also consider requests for mobility equipment and minor home adaptations.

Applications

Applications can be made via the NUJ website.

Financial information

Year end	31/12/2020
Income	£164,600
Total expenditure	£122,400

The Printing Charity

 £1,131,300 (2020)

Correspondent: The Trustees, Underwood House, 235 Three Bridges Road, Crawley, West Sussex RH10 1LS (tel: 01293 542820; email: info@theprintingcharity.org.uk)

www.theprintingcharity.org.uk

CC number: 208882

Eligibility

People who work, or have worked, for at least three years (not necessarily consecutively or for the same employer) in printing, paper, publishing, packaging, graphic arts or allied trades who are in need. Emergency support may be available for people with less service. Support is extended to the dependants of such people.

Young people aged 18 to 30 years who are:

- UK residents
- Studying for a UK printing, paper, publishing, packaging or graphic arts qualification and are planning to take up their first role in the sector
- An apprentice or studying for an NVQ in a UK print-related organisation
- Already working in printing, paper, publishing, packaging or graphic arts in the UK and wish to develop their workplace skills

Types of grant

Welfare

Examples of support given by the charity include: mobility support, grants for well-being, household goods, bereavement support, housing and home repairs, and white goods.

Education

Print Futures Awards of up to £1,500 for young people working in the sector or intending to join it. Grants can be made for: post-education internships, relevant training course, professional accreditation, kit and equipment.

Applications

Contact the charity via the application form on the charity's website. Applicants will be asked to complete a financial assessment.

Financial information

Year end	31/12/2020
Income	£1,360,000
Total expenditure	£2,620,000

Further financial information

During the year, the charity made 919 grants to individuals.

Other information

Along with making Print Future Awards, the charity supports various bursaries and apprenticeships run by other organisations such as the Queen's Bindery Apprenticeship Scheme. The charity also operates two sheltered housing facilities containing 72 apartments, which are available to retired printers and their dependants.

Royal Variety Charity

 £116,900 (2020)

Correspondent: The Trustees, Brinsworth House, 72 Staines Road, Twickenham, Middlesex TW2 5AL (tel: 020 8898 8164; email: enquiries@royalvarietycharity.org)

www.royalvarietycharity.org

CC number: 206451

Eligibility

Individuals who have worked professionally in entertainment where the majority of their income came from the industry.

Types of grant

Grants are given according to need. Previous examples have included pensions and loans, funeral expenses and other expenses that ease financial hardship.

Applications

Grant application forms are available to download from the charity's website. Alternatively, applications can be made directly via the charity's website.

Financial information

Year end	31/12/2020
Income	£3,000,000
Total expenditure	£2,870,000

Other information

The charity's major fundraising event of the year is the Royal Variety Performance. The charity also has its own residential and nursing care home for older entertainment professionals and supports its residents.

The Stationers' Foundation

 £203,800 (2020)

Correspondent: Pamela Butler, Administrator, Stationers' Hall, Stationers' Hall Court, Ave Maria Lane, London EC4M 7DD (tel: 020 7246 0990; email: foundation@stationers.org)

www.stationers.org

CC number: 1120963

Eligibility

People in need, with preference given to Liverymen and Freemen of the Stationers' Company who are over 60 and their spouses, partners and dependants.

Educational support is also available for UK residents aged 25 and under who are in need of financial assistance. Preference may be given to: former pupils of the Stationers' Company School; children of Liverymen and Freemen of the Company; and those people wishing to enter the communications and content industries.

Types of grant

Welfare

The foundation offers one-off or recurrent grants through its welfare fund to people in need to relieve hardship and distress.

Education

The foundation offers support for those in education through a number of different schemes:

▶ **Postgraduate bursary scheme** – postgraduate students under the age of 25. There are 12 bursaries of £6,000 available each year for students who hold an offer on one of the specific courses listed on the foundation's website, supporting progression in or entry into the communications and content industries. Students between the ages of 25 and 30 should contact the relevant course director and the foundation's administrator

▶ **General grants** – available for students starting or continuing their education

▶ **Major awards** – awards of around £2,000 for young people under the age of 25 who wish to study a course or begin an educational project associated with printing, bookbinding, paper conservation, stationery, papermaking, publishing, bookselling or newspaper production

▶ **Francis Mathew Stationers' Company Scholarships** – travel scholarships of around £2,000 for those aged between 18 and 35 studying or working in the industries supported by the foundation

▶ **Prize and scholarship fund** – for the children of members of the Stationers' Company studying for a degree, undertaking further education, or carrying out research at a university, as well as prizes for those studying in the communication and content industries

▶ **Evening Standard Media Diversity Bursary Scheme** – two years of training, including work experience at the Evening Standard, The Independent and London Live Television for people aged 16 or over who have not been to university

Further information and guidelines for each category of grant are available on the foundation's website.

Applications

Application forms are available from the foundation's website along with detailed guidance notes and current deadlines, specific to each award. Any queries should be addressed to the foundation's administrator.

Financial information

Year end	31/12/2020
Income	£265,600
Total expenditure	£243,900

Further financial information

Grants were broken down as follows:

Postgraduate bursaries	£72,000
Educational projects	£52,000
Stationers' Crown Woods Academy	£23,500
General awards	£20,400
Queen's bindery and evening	£12,500
PhD copyright awards	£3,000

Other information

The foundation also supports a number of specific schools, organisations, charities and organises the Shine School Media Project as well as funding two Saturday supplementary schools for disadvantaged children. The foundation also administers a library.

Medicine and health

The 1930 Fund for District Nurses (No. 1)

 £41,900 (2019/20)

Correspondent: Mia Duddridge, The Trust Partnership, 6 Trull Farm Buildings, Tetbury, Gloucestershire GL8 8SQ (tel: 01285 841900; email: 1930fund@thetrustpartnership.com)

www.1930fundfornurses.org

CC number: 208312

Eligibility

Nurses who have worked or are working as community nurses, district nurses, community psychiatric nurses, community midwives, health visitors or school nurses in the community health services.

Types of grant

Recurrent grants for living expenses. One-off grants for the purchase of specialist equipment or home maintenance items.

Exclusions

Grants are not awarded to assist with care home fees, private healthcare, payment of debt, or payment of rent or Council Tax.

Applications

Application forms can be downloaded from the charity's website and can be submitted directly by the individual or through a family member, social worker, Citizens Advice or other welfare agency. Applicants must provide evidence of their employment as registered community nurses. If the application is for home adaptations, repairs or the purchase of specific items, a copy of the invoice or quote must be supplied. Successful applicants for one-off grants

can only apply once a year so it may be more appropriate to establish a short- or long-term regular payment.

Financial information

Year end	30/06/2020
Income	£53,800
Total expenditure	£76,600

The Ambulance Staff Charity

 £55,300 (2019/20)

Correspondent: The Trustees, 12 Ensign Business Centre, Westwood Way, Coventry, Warwickshire CV4 8JA (tel: 024 7798 7922; email: enquiries@theasc.org.uk)

www.theasc.org.uk

CC number: 1163538

Eligibility

The charity's website states that it helps the following:

▶ NHS ambulance staff
▶ Independent ambulance staff
▶ People who have previously worked for a UK ambulance service
▶ Family members of ambulance staff
▶ UK ambulance service volunteers
▶ Paramedic science students

Types of grant

Support is provided for help with mental health, physical rehabilitation and financial well-being.

Applications

Contact the charity using its support line on 0800 1032 999. Alternatively, complete the online enquiry form or email the charity at enquiries@theasc.org.uk.

Financial information

Year end	31/03/2020
Income	£1,080,000
Total expenditure	£990,000

Other information

The charity also provides services such as counselling, debt advice, bereavement support and rehabilitation.

Arch Support

 £21,200 (2020)

Correspondent: Helena Basarab-Horwath, Honorary Secretary, Second Floor, Quartz House, 207 Providence Square, Mill Street, London SE1 2EW (tel: 020 7234 8635; email: h.basarab-horwath@cop.org.uk)

https://rcpod.org.uk/membership/arch-support

CC number: 205684

Eligibility

Members of the Royal College of Podiatry as well as former members and dependants of deceased members.

Types of grant

Examples of support provided in the charity's application pack include: living expenses; contributions towards essential household equipment; essential clothing and assistance towards essential home repairs.

Exclusions

Grants will not be awarded for: debts arising from credit cards or loans; items of services for which there is a statutory duty from local or national government; funeral costs (except in extreme circumstances); top-up fees for care homes; legal fees and fines; private healthcare and private school fees.

Applications

Application forms are available on the charity's website.

Financial information

Year end	31/12/2020
Income	£28,800
Total expenditure	£44,100

Further financial information

During the year grants were awarded to 21 individuals.

The Barbers' Amalgamated Charity
See entry on page 167

BMA Charities Trust Fund

 £228,500 (2020)

Correspondent: BMA Advisors, BMA Charities, BMA House, Tavistock Square, London WC1H 9JP (tel: 07483 115411; email: info@bmacharities.org.uk)

https://bmacharities.org.uk

CC number: 219102

Eligibility

Welfare

The Hastings Fund – grants are made to doctors, medical students and their dependants who are experiencing financial difficulty. This fund primarily supports refugee and asylum-seeking doctors who wish to revalidate their qualifications so that they can practice in the NHS.

Individuals do not need to be a member of the British Medical Association (BMA) to apply.

Education

The Medical Education Fund – grants are made to medical students who are taking medicine as a second degree at a UK medical school and are unable to receive a statutory grant.

Types of grant

Welfare

One-off grants for essential items such as utility bills, travel and disability equipment. Grants are also given towards the General Medical Council retention fee, the Professional and Linguistic Assessments Board exams and professional indemnity insurance.

Education

Annual grants of up to £2,500 are available to support medical students to continue their studies. Grants of up to £750 are also available for medical students who are facing immediate financial hardship.

Exclusions

Welfare

The Hastings Fund does not give grants towards general living costs, legal fees, private medical treatment, conference attendance or career enhancement projects.

Education

No grants are made to students who benefit from the NHS bursary scheme or from student loans.

Applications

Welfare

Potential applicants should contact the charity by email giving a brief outline of their situation.

Education

Applications are open from November to January each academic year. Visit the charity's website for more information.

Financial information

Year end	31/12/2020
Income	£322,000
Total expenditure	£311,100

Further financial information

In 2020, grants were awarded to 143 individuals. Of them, The Hastings Fund supported 49 beneficiaries, including 36 refugee doctors, eight medical students and five other doctors, and The Medical Education Fund distributed grants to 94 beneficiaries.

Other information

The BMA also administers the Dain Fund (Charity Commission no. 313108) which provides funds for education to children of doctors. Grants are also made to medical charities.

British Dental Association (BDA) Benevolent Fund

 £218,400 (2020)

Correspondent: The Trustees, PO Box 3645, Barnet, London EN5 9TR (tel: 020 7486 4994; email: info@dentistshelp.org)

www.bdabenevolentfund.org.uk

CC number: 208146

Eligibility

Dental students, dentists and their dependants who live in the UK and are in need. Applicants must have a low income or little savings and be unable to financially support themselves due to unexpected hardship, unemployment, illness or disability, or because they are over state retirement age. Note that individuals do not need to be a member of the BDA to qualify for support but must have been registered at some time with the General Dental Council as dentists, or as a student at a UK dental school.

Types of grant

Welfare

Grants are given for a range of purposes including rent/mortgage payments, bills, food and general living expenses, electronics, white goods, home adaptations and relocation expenses. Support can also be given for retraining or development costs and towards the annual registration/retention fee.

Education

Maintenance grants are given to support individuals at university. Support is also available for travel to and from university and for laptops.

Exclusions

The fund cannot provide support towards:

- Private education
- Tuition fees/postgraduate courses
- Business costs
- Legal fees
- Tax bills or large debts

Applications

Application forms can be downloaded from the fund's website.

Financial information

Year end	31/12/2020
Income	£354,600
Total expenditure	£350,900

Other information

The fund also provides access to counselling, legal and debt advice via a 24/7 helpline, smartphone app and website.

The Association of British Dispensing Opticians (ABDO) Benevolent Fund

 £13,400 (2020)

Correspondent: Jane Burnand, 199 Gloucester Terrace, London W2 6HX (tel: 020 7298 5100; email: general@abdo.org.uk)

https://www.abdo.org.uk/dashboard/abdo-benevolent-fund

CC number: 299447

Eligibility
Members or past members of the Association of British Dispensing Opticians and their dependants.

Types of grant
The charity's website notes that grants are generally awarded for unforeseen circumstances such as redundancy, bereavement, illness and relationship breakdowns.

Exclusions
Grants are not awarded for private healthcare, private education, legal fees or for debts.

Applications
Contact the correspondent by phone or email.

Financial information
Year end	31/12/2020
Income	£11,400
Total expenditure	£14,900

Further financial information
Full accounts were not available to view on the Charity Commission's website due to the charity's low income. We have therefore estimated the charity's grant total based on its total expenditure.

The Cameron Fund

 £260,800 (2020)

Correspondent: David Harris, Company Secretary, BMA House, Tavistock Square, London WC1H 9HR (tel: 020 7388 0796; email: info@cameronfund.org.uk)

www.cameronfund.org.uk

CC number: 261993

Eligibility
Welfare
Registered and formerly registered GPs, and their dependants, who are in need. Support is also extended to doctors who are training to be GPs.

Education
The sons and daughters of existing or former beneficiaries who are in further or higher education are eligible for educational support.

Types of grant
Welfare
Welfare grants are awarded according to need. Examples include nursing home fees (when state benefits have been exhausted), school uniforms, travel to school, after-school clubs and extracurricular activities. The charity may also make contributions towards school fees, usually during an examination year or for a short period prior to joining or re-entering the state system. Grants are also made to enable beneficiaries to gain access to free financial advice from certified and insured money advisors. Interest-free loans are also available.

Education
Student allowances of £3,000 per academic year (£1,000 per term) are made towards living costs when undertaking a first-degree course or vocational training.

Applications
Application forms are available to download on the charity's website.

Financial information
Year end	31/12/2020
Income	£388,300
Total expenditure	£322,400

Further financial information
During the year the charity supported 207 individuals with 89 grants and loans.

The Care Workers Charity

 £173,600 (2019)

Correspondent: The Trustees, Suites 6–8, The Sanctuary, 23 Oakhill Grove, Surbiton KT9 6DU (email: use the contact form available on the website)

www.thecareworkerscharity.org.uk

CC number: 1132286

Eligibility
Crisis grants
The charity's website states:

> To be eligible for a Crisis Grant, you **must**:
> - Be employed in the UK social care sector, in a role that is involved in or supports the provision of adult, elderly or disability care.
> - Either have be currently employed for at least one year or have been previously employed in the care sector for at least five years

- Have experienced one of the following changes in circumstances, within the last year:
- A sudden of unexpected loss of income
- A sudden or unexpected illness or injury
- A sudden or unexpected change in living circumstances or loss of home
- A relationship breakdown
- An issue of domestic abuse
- Death of a close relative
- Not be over the 25% of the Minimum Income Standard

Types of grant
One-off payments to support someone experiencing an unforeseen or life-changing circumstance, such as bereavement, illness or injury, and who has no resources to meet associated costs.

The charity's COVID-19 Grant Fund provides emergency funding for care workers who have had a drop in income or require financial support due to COVID-19.

Applications
Applications can be made through the charity's website.

Financial information
Year end	31/12/2019
Income	£518,000
Total expenditure	£622,400

Cavell Nurses' Trust

 £797,400 (2020)

Correspondent: Welfare Team, Grosvenor House, Prospect Hill, Redditch, Worcestershire B97 4DL (tel: 01527 595999; email: admin@cavellnursestrust.org)

www.cavellnursestrust.org

CC number: 1160148

Eligibility
Working and retired nurses, midwives and healthcare assistants experiencing personal or financial hardship. Applicants should hold no more than £4,000 in savings.

Types of grant
According to its website the trust can provide assistance with:
- Short term financial emergencies
- Essential white goods
- Travelling expenses for attending medical treatment
- Mobility aids
- Home adaptations due to disability
- Rent deposits and removal costs
- Bankruptcy and Debt Relief Order fees
- Rent arrears, in some circumstances

Exclusions

The trust's website states that it is unable to provide assistance with:

- Debts
- Holidays
- Private medical treatment fees
- Private education fees
- Nursing home fees
- Educational grants, study fees or course costs
- Legal fees
- Car purchase

Applications

Application forms and guidance notes are available to download from the trust's website.

Financial information

Year end	31/12/2020
Income	£1,860,000
Total expenditure	£1,370,000

Other information

The trust also provides advice and support on issues such as domestic violence, isolation and loneliness.

Chartered Physiotherapists' Benevolent Fund

 £56,300 (2019)

Correspondent: The Trustees, CSP MBF, PO Box 17425, Sutton Coldfield, West Midlands B73 7DY (tel: 0330 678 0655; email: info@cspmbf.co.uk)

 www.csp.org.uk/about-csp/what-we-do/members-benevolent-fund

CC number: 219568

Eligibility

Past and present members in need. Members must have been a subscribing member of the Chartered Society of Physiotherapy (CSP) for two years (six months for students).

Types of grant

Monthly allowances and one-off grants according to need.

Exclusions

No grants are made towards payment of debts and loans, education, or support for family in the UK or overseas.

Applications

Application forms can be downloaded from the charity's website or requested from the correspondent.

Financial information

Year end	31/12/2019
Income	£103,700
Total expenditure	£88,300

Further financial information

During the year, grants were awarded to 37 individuals.

The Benevolent Fund of The College of Optometrists and The Association of Optometrists

 £66,300 (2019/20)

Correspondent: Lynne Brown, Administrative Secretary, 55 Colchester Road, White Colne, Colchester CO6 2PW (tel: 01787 223800; email: admin@opticalbenfund.com)

 www.opticalbenfund.com

CC number: 1003699

Eligibility

Optometrists and their families who are in need.

Types of grant

One-off grants to help with an immediate crisis or to supplement income on an ongoing basis to meet regular outgoings. As well as financial support, the fund can also assist in the purchase of equipment to meet specific health needs, such as a motorised wheelchair, IT equipment or low vision aids. It can also arrange counselling for substance misuse.

Applications

Application forms can be downloaded from the charity's website. The website states:

> Please do not be worried about contacting us. We will consider all approaches sympathetically and treat all information with absolute discretion and confidentiality. If you are not sure about what to do, make a preliminary telephone call to discuss your needs before filling in any forms. We can then give you advice about the best way to proceed.

Financial information

Year end	30/09/2020
Income	£97,500
Total expenditure	£90,700

Other information

The charity runs a peer support line for the Association of Optometrists (0800 870 8401) which provides free and confidential support to optometrists. The charity can also signpost individuals to money advice specialists.

The Dain Fund

 £40,800 (2020)

Correspondent: The Trustees, BMA Charities, BMA House, Tavistock Square, London WC1H 9JP (tel: 07483 115411; email: info@bmacharities.org.uk)

 https://bmacharities.org.uk

CC number: 313108

Eligibility

Children of doctors or deceased doctors who are in need. Most grants are awarded to children from low-income families or who have a parent that is out of work. Applications are particularly welcomed from refugee doctors.

Types of grant

Grants are given towards school uniforms, school trips, essential IT equipment, disability equipment, bedroom furniture and so on. Occasionally grants are given for short-term school fees, either until the child finishes their GCSEs or A-levels or the child is found a place in the state education system.

Exclusions

The fund is unable to provide funding for childcare costs for working doctors.

Applications

Potential applicants should contact the fund via email providing a brief outline of their situation. Applications are accepted all year round.

Financial information

Year end	31/12/2020
Income	£64,900
Total expenditure	£67,200

Further financial information

Grants were awarded to benefit 47 children and four medical students.

Other information

The British Medical Association (BMA) also administers the BMA Charities Trust Fund (Charity Commission no. 219102), which provides funding for doctors and medical students in need.

The Eaton Fund for Artists Nurses and Gentlewomen
See entry on page 33

Environmental Health Officers Welfare Fund

 £2,500 (2019)

Correspondent: The Trustees, Chartered Institute of Environmental Health, Chadwick Court, 15 Hatfields, London SE1 8DJ (tel: 020 7928 6006; email: membership@cieh.org)

 https://www.cieh.org/governance/welfare-fund

CC number: 224343

Eligibility
Members and former members of the Chartered Institute of Environmental Health (CIEH) and their families/dependants who are in need.

Types of grant
Grants are awarded according to need. Previously support has been given to fund legal advice, holidays and to supplement income when unable to work due to severe illness.

Exclusions
The fund is unable to repay debts.

Applications
Initial enquiries should be made using the contact form on the CIEH website.

Financial information
Year end	31/12/2019
Income	£200
Total expenditure	£2,800

Further financial information
Full accounts were not available to view on the Charity Commission's website due to the fund's low income. We have therefore estimated the fund's grant total based on its total expenditure.

Forth Valley Medical Benevolent Trust

 £6,900 (2020/21)

Correspondent: The Trustees, Meeks Road Surgery, 10 Meeks Road, Falkirk FK2 7ES

OSCR number: SC000014

Eligibility
Medical practitioners and their families or relatives living in the Forth Valley who are in need.

Types of grant
Grants are given according to need.

Applications
Apply in writing to the correspondent.

Financial information
Year end	11/01/2021
Income	£2,900
Total expenditure	£7,600

Further financial information
Full accounts were not available to view on the OSCR website due to the trust's low income. We have therefore estimated the grant total based on the trust's total expenditure.

Healthcare Workers' Foundation

Correspondent: The Trustees, 44 Grand Parade, Brighton, East Sussex BN2 9QA (email: contact@healthcareworkersfoundation.org)

 https://www.healthcareworkersfoundation.org

CC number: 1189737

Eligibility
NHS healthcare workers and their families living in the UK and families of frontline NHS healthcare workers who have passed away due to COVID-19.

Types of grant
Welfare
One-off grants are awarded according to need. The charity may be able to help with expenses such as transport, food and childcare.

Education
The HWF Memorial Fund provides grants of up to £5,000 to students enrolled on a higher education course to support living costs, rent, maintenance fees and educational materials.

Applications
Applications can be made via the charity's NHS Workers portal. Applicants require an NHS email address to access the portal.

Further financial information
The charity was registered with the Charity Commission in June 2020; therefore, financial information is not yet available.

Medical Research Council Staff Benevolent Fund Association

 £21,400 (2017/18)

Correspondent: James Clerkin, Secretary to the Trustees, MRC Staff Benevolent Association, Medical Research Council/UKRI, 3rd Floor, 58 Victoria Embankment, London EC4Y 0DS (tel: 020 7395 2289; email: james.clerkin@mrc.ukri.org)

 sbfa.mrc.ac.uk

CC number: 233839

Eligibility
Current and former Medical Research Council (MRC) staff and their dependants.

Types of grant
Current or former MRC employees are given quarterly grants or loans for a variety of costs. Examples include: funeral costs; car repairs; moving house costs; funds to clear Council Tax or rent arrears; funds to help when unemployed or when dependants are ill; fuel bills; study fees; solicitors bills; and unexpected childcare costs. The charity also makes grants of £150 to beneficiaries as a gift at Christmas.

Older beneficiaries receive quarterly grants to supplement their income during retirement. One-off grants have also been awarded to older people towards the cost of: replacement domestic appliances; new carpets; wheelchairs; home decorating; winter boots; spectacles; shower installations; TV repairs; roof repairs; stairlifts; and central heating systems.

The charity has also awarded grants to MRC employees with disabilities towards the cost of specialised facilities in the home, such as shower rooms and specialised beds.

Applications
Application forms are available to download on the charity's website. Physical copies can be requested from the correspondent. All applicants must provide detailed financial information, in the form of bank statements, credit card statements, loan arrangements, etc. Completed forms can be sent to the correspondent at either their email or postal address. The committee meets every three months to consider grant applications.

Financial information
Year end	30/09/2018
Income	£37,700
Total expenditure	£36,700

Further financial information
The 2017/18 annual report was the latest available at the time of writing (November 2021).

Junius S. Morgan Benevolent Fund

 £250,400 (2019)

Correspondent: Lauren George, Charity Administrator, Rathbone Trust Company Ltd, 8 Finsbury Circus, London EC2M 7AZ (tel: 020 7399 0110; email: Lauren.George@rathbones.com)

 www.juniusmorgan.org.uk

CC number: 1131892

Eligibility
Current or retired nurses, midwives and healthcare assistants who have practised

for a minimum of five years after registration.

Types of grant
One-off grants, usually of around £1,000, can be given towards rent/mortgage, Council Tax and utility bills, essential decorating, furniture and medical equipment.

Exclusions
The fund will not consider educational or funeral costs, respite care, holidays or nursing home fees. The fund cannot help carers or student nurses.

Applications
Application forms can be downloaded from the fund's website. Applications should be accompanied by a letter of support from someone in a professional capacity such as a GP, health visitor, social worker, Citizens Advice worker or housing agency worker.

Financial information
Year end	31/12/2019
Income	£417,900
Total expenditure	£325,900

Further financial information
Grants were awarded to 208 individuals.

The NHS Pensioners' Trust

 £49,500 (2020/21)

Correspondent: Frank Jackson, Director, PO Box 456, Esher, Surrey KT10 1DP (tel: 01372 805760; email: nhsptinfo@gmail.com)

 www.nhspt.org.uk

CC number: 1002061

Eligibility
Retired NHS personnel and their families, dependants, widows or widowers. This includes those who worked in any of the related health service organisations or caring professions prior to the creation of the NHS.

Types of grant
Grants of up to £350 are given according to need.

Exclusions
Grants are not given towards ongoing top-up fees in nursing or residential accommodation.

Applications
Application forms can be downloaded from the trust's website or requested from the correspondent. Third-party organisations such as the Royal British Legion, SSAFA and Care and Repair agencies, may apply on behalf of an individual.

Financial information
Year end	31/03/2021
Income	£3,400
Total expenditure	£55,000

Further financial information
Full accounts were not available to view on the Charity Commission's website due to the trust's low income. We have therefore estimated the trust's grant total based on its total expenditure.

The Nightingale Fund

 £15,900 (2019/20)

Correspondent: Katie Hyatt, Honorary Secretary, 16 Liphook Crescent, Forest Hill, London SE23 3BW (tel: 020 8291 5984; email: honorary.secretary@thenightingalefund.uk)

 www.thenightingalefund.org.uk

CC number: 205911

Eligibility
Nurses, midwives and community public health nurses who are registered with the Nursing and Midwifery Council and healthcare assistants in the UK.

Types of grant
Grants are given for course fees only. Support is given towards further education and training to allow individuals to improve and develop their nursing practice.

Applications
Candidates can apply for a grant by completing the application form and returning it to the Honorary Secretary with a current CV and two references. Application forms are available to download from the fund's website.

Financial information
Year end	30/06/2020
Income	£28,200
Total expenditure	£30,300

Further financial information
In 2019/20, 24 grants, ranging from £350 to £1,500 each, were awarded.

Other information
Each year the fund is able to support around 30 nurses, healthcare assistants, midwives and public health nurses.

The Benevolent Fund for Nurses in Scotland

 £166,800 (2020)

Correspondent: Margaret Ramsay, Liaison Officer, Mitchell Edwards, 24A Ainslie Place, Edinburgh EH3 6AJ (tel: 07584 322257; email: admin@bfns.org.uk)

 www.bfns.org.uk

OSCR number: SC006384

Eligibility
Current and former nurses, midwives or student nurses who have trained or worked in Scotland and are experiencing financial difficulties. This includes those who are unable to work due to illness.

Types of grant
Quarterly and one-off grants are given according to need, for example towards the purchase of an item of furnishing, home adaptations or equipment. The fund also gives Christmas grants.

Applications
Application forms can be obtained from the correspondent. Applications can be submitted directly by the individual or by an agency on their behalf.

Financial information
Year end	31/12/2020
Income	£238,600
Total expenditure	£244,500

Further financial information
Grants were distributed as follows:

Quarterly grants	688	£103,200
Christmas grants	174	£43,500
Single grants	43	£20,100

The Nurses' Memorial to King Edward VII Edinburgh Scottish Committee

 £132,300 (2019)

Correspondent: The Trustees, c/o Johnston Smillie Ltd, Chartered Accountants, 6 Redhueghs Rigg, Edinburgh EH12 9DQ (tel: 0131 317 7377; email: info@nursesmemorial.org.uk)

 www.nursesmemorial.org.uk

OSCR number: SC023963

Eligibility
Nurses or midwives with a strong connection to Scotland (including nurses who have worked in Scotland, or Scottish nurses working outside Scotland) who are retired, ill or otherwise in need.

Types of grant
Welfare
One-off and monthly grants towards accommodation charges, domestic bills, equipment and to supplement inadequate income.

Education
Educational bursaries are available for further education and training.

Applications

Applications can be made via the charity's website.

Financial information

Year end	31/12/2019
Income	£67,900
Total expenditure	£146,300

Pharmacist Support

 £115,300 (2020)

Correspondent: The Trustees, 5th Floor, 196 Deansgate, Manchester M3 3WF (tel: 0808 168 2233; email: info@pharmacistsupport.org)

🌐 www.pharmacistsupport.org

CC number: 1158974

Eligibility

Pharmacists registered with the General Pharmaceutical Council or the Royal Pharmaceutical Society. Dependants or widows/widowers of such people are also eligible for support, as are pre-registration trainees and pharmacy students.

Types of grant

Welfare

Financial assistance towards essential expenditure in times of difficulty. This may include fuel bills, household repairs, respite care, therapy, aids and adaptations and care home fees.

Education

One-off payments of up to £1,500 per academic year can be made to students facing unexpected hardship due to unforeseen circumstances such as ill health, bereavement or loss of income. The charity also makes awards of £3,000 or £5,000 to MPharm students entering their final year of study. To apply students must demonstrate financial hardship, outstanding and exceptional qualities to overcome an ongoing adversity, an expectation by their university of a positive contribution to pharmacy in Great Britain and a sound academic performance.

Exclusions

There are no grants available for pharmacy technicians or pharmacy assistants. Support is not available in Northern Ireland.

Applications

Apply on a form available for download from the charity's website. Applications will be considered all year round.

Financial information

Year end	31/12/2020
Income	£458,300
Total expenditure	£780,900

Other information

Pharmacist Support, formerly known as the Royal Pharmaceutical Society's Benevolent Fund, offers a range of services, information and specialist advice for pharmacists, former pharmacists and their families.

The Queen's Nursing Institute

 £105,100 (2020)

Correspondent: Joanne Moorby, Welfare and Grants Officer, 1A Henrietta Place, London W1G 0LZ (tel: 020 7594 1400; email: mail@qni.org.uk)

🌐 https://www.qni.org.uk

CC number: 213128

Eligibility

Welfare

Current or retired nurses who are in need and have worked in the community for a minimum of three years. The charity defines community work as work occurring outside hospital settings. This includes the work of district nurses, practice nurses, health visitors, etc. Beneficiaries are usually experiencing some form of personal crisis such as physical or mental illness, eviction, marriage breakdown or bereavement. For full eligibility criteria, see the charity's website.

Education

Educational grants are available to working nurses, up to and including band 6 (or equivalent), who are in need of assistance to further their education. Nurses must be studying accredited courses or modules in community nursing which demonstrate a clear clinical benefit to patients.

Types of grant

Welfare

Welfare grants are typically made towards essential household items, building repairs or adaptations, respite care, specialist equipment (walk-in baths, stairlifts, etc.) and utility bills. When appropriate, quarterly grants may be awarded.

Education

Educational grants of up £1,000 are awarded for course fees and books required for studying.

Exclusions

Welfare

Welfare grants cannot be awarded for residential or nursing home fees, debt, medical treatment or funeral expenses.

Education

Educational grants can only be paid once and are not normally given for travel costs. This charity is unable to support nurses in Scotland. Scottish nurses should instead consult The Queen's Nursing Institute Scotland.

Applications

Application forms are available to download on the funder's website. Completed forms (along with a copy of the applicant's latest bank statement and utility bill if applying for a welfare grant) should be sent to the correspondent at their postal address.

Financial information

Year end	31/12/2020
Income	£992,500
Total expenditure	£1,090,000

Further financial information

During the financial year, the charity awarded 226 welfare grants and 23 educational grants.

The RCN Foundation

 £1,907,000 (2020)

Correspondent: Ian Norris, Chair of the Grants Committee, 20 Cavendish Square, London W1G 0RN (tel: 020 7647 3599; email: rcnfoundation@rcn.org.uk)

🌐 www.rcnfoundation.org.uk

CC number: 1134606

Eligibility

Current or former nurses, midwives, healthcare assistants, nursing student and associates who are in need. Applicants do not have to be members of the Royal College of Nursing (RCN) to apply for support.

Educational grants are available to current or former nurses, midwives, nursing support workers, students and nursing associates who are looking to develop their practice. There are several grant schemes, each with their own eligibility criteria. See the foundation's website for further information.

Types of grant

Welfare

Hardship grants are awarded according to need.

Education

Student grants: one-off or recurrent grants of £2,500 for those studying nursing at undergraduate or postgraduate level.

Professional Bursary Scheme: grants of up to £5,000 for those who wish to develop their existing skills in the following fields: adult nursing; children's nursing; learning disability nursing; mental health nursing; the history of nursing (up to £1,000); occupational health nursing (up to £1,000).

Needlemakers grants: grants of up to £1,000 for nurses who use needles in their work and are studying a postgraduate or professional short course.

Kelsey Bequest: grants of up to £5,000 for nurses who work or live in the Northumberland/Tyne and Wear area who are about to begin a course that will improve patient care in adult nursing, children's nursing, learning disability nursing or mental health nursing.

Rae Bequest: grants of up to £1,000 for registered nurses currently working in Northern Ireland (in any sector), who wish to undertake a course or programme that will help their nursing practice and service delivery.

Marcia Mackie Bequest: grants of up to £300 are available to nurses currently working in Northern Ireland (in any sector) for research or personal professional development costs.

Applications

Welfare
Initial inquiries should be made by contacting the charity's Lamplight Support Service. RCN members should call Lamplight on 0345 772 6100, and non-RCN members should call on 0345 772 6200.

Education
Applicants can apply online through the funder's website. The next round of funding will be in spring 2020.

Financial information

Year end	31/12/2020
Income	£6,720,000
Total expenditure	£5,720,000

Further financial information
Grants were awarded to 3,200 individuals during the year.

Other information
Grants for research and practice development are available to organisations looking to fund a nursing-led project. Eligible organisations include registered charities, healthcare organisations, places of higher education and NHS trusts.

The Royal College of Midwives Trust

 £22,700 (2020)

Correspondent: The Trustees, 10–18 Union Street, London SE1 1SZ (tel: 0300 303 0444; email: info@rcm.org.uk)

https://www.rcm.org.uk/caring-for-you-hub-home/what-is-the-benevolent-fund

CC number: 275261

Eligibility
Current or retired midwives and nurses who are in need. Current or retired healthcare assistants/nursing auxiliary staff with experience providing care in a hospital or nursing home under the supervision of a registered nurse are also eligible. Student midwives may be supported in exceptional circumstances. According to the application guidelines, applicants to the benevolent fund should have less than £4,000 in household savings, including funds in savings and current accounts.

Types of grant
The trust works in partnership with Cavell Nurses' Trust to deliver benevolent grants. Grants are awarded towards the costs of:
- Essential white goods
- Short-term financial emergencies
- Travel expenses involved in attending medical treatment
- Mobility aids (if recommended by a medical professional)
- Home repairs (when there is a clear health and safety risk)
- Rent deposits and arrears
- Home adaptations for people with disabilities*
- Bankruptcy and Debt Relief Order fees (when this is recommended by a debt advisor)
- Removal costs

*Prospective applicants must have applied for a Disabled Facilities Grant, and have a recent occupational therapist's report recommending the adaptations in order to qualify for this type of assistance.

Exclusions
Grants cannot be awarded for the following: debts; holidays; private medical treatment; private education fees; nursing home fees; education costs, study fees or course costs; legal fees; purchasing a car.

Applications
Application forms are available to download on the trust's website. Applications must include all of the following supporting documents: evidence of employment (a letter from the Nursing and Midwifery Council, wage slip, etc.); proof of income for both you and your partner (if applicable); copy of your Universal Credit breakdown if you are not currently working; copy of bank statements for the last two full months for all accounts held by yourself and your partner (if applicable); a letter of support from a professional (GP, housing support work, manager at work, etc.); quotes/estimates if requesting a specific item.

Financial information

Year end	31/12/2020
Income	£887,100
Total expenditure	£663,500

Royal Medical Benevolent Fund (RMBF)

 £587,800 (2019/20)

Correspondent: The Casework Team, 24 King's Road, Wimbledon, London SW19 8QN (tel: 020 8540 9194 (option 1); email: help@rmbf.org)

www.rmbf.org

CC number: 207275

Eligibility

Welfare
Doctors registered with the General Medical Council, and their dependants, who are on a low income and unable to support themselves due to illness, disability, bereavement or being over state retirement age.

Education
Medical students in their final two years who are in need due to a change in circumstances caused by illness, injury, disability or bereavement. Further information on eligibility can be found on the charity's website.

Types of grant

Welfare
The fund provides monthly grants to help with essential day-to-day living costs. It also provides grants and loans for back-to-work and retraining costs, disability adaptations and specialist equipment.

Education
Grants are given to assist with essential living expenses while studying.

Exclusions
Grants are not given for the following:
- Private healthcare and medical insurance/fees
- Legal fees
- Inland revenue payments
- Debts to relatives or friends
- Private education
- Tuition fees

Support cannot be given to all family members of doctors, only their direct dependants, i.e. financially dependent children, spouses or partners.

Applications
To apply, contact the correspondent via email or by using the contact form on the website. The Grants and Awards Committee meets regularly to consider applications for assistance.

Financial information

Year end	31/03/2020
Income	£1,430,000
Total expenditure	£1,650,000

Further financial information

Note, the grant total may also include loans.

Other information

The fund provides a range of services for doctors and medical students in need including advice, well-being resources and access to a psychotherapy service.

The Royal Medical Foundation

 £196,400 (2019/20)

Correspondent: Helen Jones, Caseworker, RMF Office, Epsom College, College Road, Epsom, Surrey KT17 4JQ (tel: 01372 821010; email: rmf-caseworker@epsomcollege.org.uk or rmf@epsomcollege.org.uk)

🌐 www.royalmedicalfoundation.org

CC number: 312046

Eligibility

Doctors who are/have been registered with the General Medical Council (GMC), and their dependants, who are in need due to limited income or savings. Doctors qualified outside the UK who are currently GMC registered and have been working in the UK for three years prior to making an application, are also eligible for support.

Types of grant

One-off grants are given according to need. Examples include utility bill arrears, food and general living costs. Monthly pensions are also available. Additionally, grants can be given to assist with educational costs such as school fees when a sudden change in circumstance leads to financial difficulty.

Applications

Initial enquiries can be made on the charity's website using an online form. All applicants will be visited by the caseworker before funding is awarded. Applicants must have already applied for any state benefits to which they may be entitled before applying for funding. The board meets quarterly, usually in January, April, July and October. See the charity's website for current application deadlines.

Financial information

Year end	30/06/2020
Income	£27,500,000
Total expenditure	£26,160,000

Further financial information

Grants were awarded as follows:

Short-term payments or one-off grants where urgent assistance is required	£79,100
Financial assistance with educational expenses at Epsom College	£57,100
Financial assistance with educational expenses	£35,500
Regular payments to medical practitioners and their widows/ widowers	£24,100
Other grants	£650

Other information

This charity is one of several linked charities and funds. The charity is located at Epsom College, whose charitable activity includes providing access to day and boarding education through bursaries and scholarships.

Sandra Charitable Trust

 £150,400 (2019/20)

Correspondent: Lynne Webster, Moore Family Office Ltd, 42 Berkeley Square, London W1J 5AW (tel: 020 7318 0845; email: Lynne.Webster@ moorefamilyofficegroup.com)

CC number: 327492

Eligibility

Nurses and nursing students who are in need.

Types of grant

Welfare

According to our previous research, grants are given to nurses towards the cost of necessities and to relieve financial hardship.

Education

Our previous research states that financial assistance is available for nursing students to enable them to finish their studies. Grants can be used towards courses, equipment and so on.

Applications

Apply in writing to the correspondent. The trustees meet on a frequent basis to consider applications.

Financial information

Year end	30/06/2020
Income	£822,200
Total expenditure	£1,020,000

Further financial information

During the financial period, the trust awarded £150,300 to 148 individuals.

Other information

The trust also provides support to other charitable institutions and organisations with a wide variety of objectives including animal welfare and research, environment protection, relief of poverty and youth development. The trust's 2019/20 accounts state that it is in the process of developing a website that is due to be operational by June 2022.

Society for Assistance of Medical Families

 £98,600 (2020)

Correspondent: The Secretary, Lettsom House, 11 Chandos Street, London W1G 9EB (tel: 077 7130 0410 (Monday to Friday 10am until 4pm); email: info@ samf.org.uk)

🌐 https://www.samf.org.uk

CC number: 207473

Eligibility

Welfare

Grants are awarded to the following people (in order of priority):

- Dependants of deceased members of the society
- Members of the society
- Dependants of members
- Doctors, and their dependants, who are in need but are not currently members of the society

Education

Children of medical families who are studying for medical degrees and other medical students are eligible for educational support.

Types of grant

Welfare grants are available to cover the cost of food, household bills and home adaptations. Gifts may also be given at Christmas and Easter.

Grants are also available for course and examination fees. Grants are also made for retraining costs to help doctors remain in, or return to, work after illness or other circumstances.

Applications

Contact the charity for information on how to apply. Grant applications are considered quarterly (in February, May, August and November). If possible, the secretary or a member of the court of directors will meet applicants.

Financial information

Year end	31/12/2020
Income	£218,800
Total expenditure	£192,700

The Society of Radiographers Benevolent Fund

 £14,500 (2019/20)

Correspondent: The Trustees, 207 Providence Square, Mill Street, London SE1 2EW (tel: 0800 0778371 or 020 7740 7200; email: help@sor.org)

https://www.sor.org/About/Society-of-Radiographers/Benevolent-fund/Financial-support

CC number: 326398

Eligibility

Past and present members of the society and their dependants who are in need due to financial hardship. Individuals must have capital or savings (excluding residence) no higher than the current Department for Work and Pensions limit.

Types of grant

One-off grants are given for specific items and household bills. Examples of what can be funded include disability aids, essential building repairs, appliances, body repatriation and funeral costs.

Exclusions

Grants are not given for the following:
- Personal or business debts
- Legal costs
- Medical or dental treatment
- Private school fees
- Home purchase
- Repayment of loans
- Private healthcare

Applications

Application forms can be downloaded from the charity's website and should be returned via email.

Financial information

Year end	30/09/2020
Income	£43,400
Total expenditure	£15,900

Vetlife

 £103,100 (2020)

Correspondent: The Honorary Secretary, 7 Mansfield Street, London W1G 9NQ (tel: 020 7908 6374; email: info@vetlife.org.uk)

www.vetlife.org.uk

CC number: 224776

Eligibility

Veterinary surgeons in need who are, or have been, on the register of the Royal College of Veterinary Surgeons (including those on the supplementary veterinary register) and their dependants. Financial support is also available to the dependants of deceased or retired veterinary surgeons. All applicants must be residents in the UK.

Types of grant

Monthly grants, emergency assistance and one-off gifts awarded according to need.

Applications

Application forms can be downloaded from the Vetlife website and sent to the correspondent by post or email.

Financial information

Year end	31/12/2020
Income	£810,800
Total expenditure	£668,400

Other information

The charity also provides a helpline (0303 040 2551) and support with health issues.

Mining and quarrying

The Coal Industry Social Welfare Organisation

 £222,400 (2020)

Correspondent: The Trustees, The Old Rectory, Rectory Drive, Whiston, Rotherham, South Yorkshire S60 4JG (tel: 01709 728115; email: mail@ciswo.org.uk)

www.ciswo.org.uk

CC number: 1015581

Eligibility

Former miners and their dependants who are experiencing financial difficulties. Dependent children applying for an educational grant must be over 17 and under 25 years old at the start of the academic year for which the grant is required.

Types of grant

Welfare

Welfare grants are awarded according to need and could include medical/mobility aids, adaptations to support independent living, funeral costs, debt relief and course fees/specialist training where this will help the individual to gain employment. Specific grant assistance will be considered for individuals (or their bereaved partners) who have received an Industrial Injuries Disability Benefit award for coal workers' pneumoconiosis in the last 12 months.

Education

Educational grants are awarded for full-time higher education courses, including degrees and Higher National Diplomas.

Exclusions

The following cannot be funded by welfare grants: general household costs (utility bills/food costs), household/electrical items, IT equipment, driving lessons, holidays, repeat applications for debt relief, or goods or services that should be the responsibility of a statutory agency.

Applications

For welfare grants, applicants should contact their nearest office, details of which can be found on the charity's website. For educational grants, an application form can be requested from education@ciswo.org.uk and should be submitted between 1 March and 1 December for courses starting in September of that year.

Financial information

Year end	31/12/2020
Income	£2,990,000
Total expenditure	£3,600,000

Other information

The charity provides a range of support to former miners including a home visiting service, advocacy, emotional support, assistance applying for benefits, support on mining-related issues, support at times of hardship and reducing loneliness through a day centre and community projects.

The Members Benevolent Trust of the Institute of Materials, Minerals and Mining

 £37,900 (2019)

Correspondent: Peter Waugh, Honorary Secretary, The Member's Benevolent Trust, 297 Euston Road, London NW1 3AD (tel: 01740 645665; email: mbt@iom3.org)

www.iom3.org

CC number: 207184

Eligibility

Current and former members and employees of the Institute of Materials, Minerals and Mining, and dependants of such people, who are in need due to bereavement, illness, reduced circumstances or social distress.

Types of grant

One-off and recurrent grants are awarded according to need. For example, grants can be made for general household needs, furniture, security installations, medical aids and adaptations, clothing, respite breaks, school uniforms, school travel costs and other one-off exceptional items. The trust is also keen to help unemployed and redundant members with travel costs, subscriptions, relocation costs and short course fees (where this will widen the scope for re-employment).

Applications

The website states that applicants should contact the trust in the first instance and an application form will be provided. Once completed and returned there is a preliminary review of the returned form. This is usually followed by a visit to the applicant by an established regional visitor or a trustee to talk through the application. Following the visit, the board assesses each application thoroughly and makes its decision.

Financial information

Year end	31/12/2019
Income	£78,500
Total expenditure	£62,200

Other information

The trust also offers advice and signposting.

Mining Institute of Scotland Trust

£ £40,000 (2020)

Correspondent: The Trustees, 14/9 Burnbrae Drive, Edinburgh EH12 8AS (tel: 0131 629 7861)

 https://www.iom3.org/mining-institute-scotland/mining-institute-scotland-trust

OSCR number: SC024974

Eligibility

Former members of the Mining Institute of Scotland (MIS) and members or former members of the Institute of Materials, Minerals and Mining who live in Scotland or have worked in connection with Scottish mining for at least five consecutive years. The dependants of eligible people can also be supported.

Types of grant

Grants are awarded according to need.

Applications

Apply in writing to the correspondent.

Financial information

Year end	31/12/2020
Income	£25,100
Total expenditure	£48,300

Other information

The trust also makes grants to organisations.

The Institute of Quarrying Benevolent Fund

£ £17,100 (2019)

Correspondent: The Trustees, Quarry Managers Journal Ltd, 7 Regent Street, Nottingham, Nottinghamshire NG1 5BS (tel: 0115 945 3885; email: mail@ quarrying.org)

 https://www.quarrying.org/about-us/iqbf

CC number: 213586

Eligibility

Members or former members of the Institute of Quarrying and/or their dependants.

Types of grant

One-off grants according to need.

Exclusions

People who are involved in the quarrying industry but are not members of the institute cannot be considered.

Applications

Apply in writing to the correspondent or by completing the form on the charity's website.

Financial information

Year end	31/12/2019
Income	£47,800
Total expenditure	£20,300

Further financial information

Grants were awarded to five long-term beneficiaries for the relief of financial hardship.

South Wales Miners' Welfare Trust Fund Scheme

£ £54,500 (2019)

Correspondent: Andrew Morse, Secretary and Treasurer, c/o CISWO, Unit 5 Maritime Offices, Woodland Terrace, Maesycoed, Rhondda Cynon Taf CF37 1DZ (tel: 01443 485233; email: andrew.morse@ciswo.org.uk)

CC number: 507439

Eligibility

Miners and their dependants in South Wales.

Types of grant

Welfare

One-off grants are awarded towards the costs of home repairs, disability adaptations and other essential items.

Education

In the past, the charity awarded educational grants through the David Davies Memorial Trusts fund. This fund has now been exhausted; however, the trustees have decided to continue making educational grants through the Hafod Miners' Welfare Women's Convalescent Home and Girls' Camp fund.

Applications

Contact the correspondent for further information.

Financial information

Year end	31/12/2019
Income	£704,800
Total expenditure	£950,600

Further financial information

The majority of the charity's expenditure is spent on the upkeep of its convalescent homes and organising day trips and other social activities. Hardship grants totalling £18,200 were awarded to individuals for home adaptations and repairs. Educational grants were awarded to 37 students totalling £36,300.

Other information

The trustees are also responsible for three convalescent homes that are open to all current and former miners (and their dependants), who are eligible upon having worked a minimum of five years in the South Wales mining industry.

Other specific industries

Rowland Hill Memorial and Benevolent Fund

£ £471,300 (2019/20)

Correspondent: The Trustees, 185 Farrington Road, London EC1A 1AA (tel: 0345 600 4586; email: rowland.hill.fund@royalmail.com)

 www.rowlandhillfund.org

CC number: 207479

Eligibility

People in need who work for, have worked for or have a proven connection with:

- Royal Mail
- Post Office Ltd
- Parcelforce Worldwide
- Royal Mail Property and Facilities Solutions
- Any previously associated companies

Applicants must have completed at least six months of full or part-time service, on a permanent or fixed-term contract and have savings of less than £12,000.

Types of grant

One-off grants for specific needs such as health and ability aids, rent, mortgage and utility bill arrears.

Applications

Applications can be made via the website or by calling the charity's helpline (0345 600 4596).

Financial information

Year end	31/03/2020
Income	£565,200
Total expenditure	£682,600

Mountain and Cave Rescue Benevolent Fund

 £1,900 (2020)

Correspondent: Judy Whiteside, Secretary, 13 Maple Grove, York YO10 4EJ (tel: 07767 814051; email: secretary@rescuebenevolent.fund)

www.rescuebenevolent.fund

CC number: 1152798

Eligibility

Mountain and cave rescue team members who are experiencing hardship as a direct result of a rescue operation. This includes those who have sustained an injury while on a rescue mission. Support is extended to the families of such people.

Types of grant

Immediate support grants of up to £1,000 are awarded for unexpected expenses. Long-term financial assistance and loans are also available.

Applications

Email the secretary to request an application form. Applications must be supported by your team leader or other suitable team official. If your request relates to any physical or mental health issues, you will have to provide supporting medical evidence. Before making an application to the charity, applicants must have first visited their GP in relation to the issue they are claiming a grant for.

Financial information

Year end	31/12/2020
Income	£1,400
Total expenditure	£2,100

Further financial information

Full accounts were not available to view on the Charity Commission's website due to the charity's low income. We have therefore estimated the grant total based on the charity's total expenditure.

Other information

Through its agreements with the Fire Fighters' Charity and The Police Treatment Centres, the charity can refer injured team members for physical assessments, physiotherapy, lifestyle advice and exercise facilities. The charity also supports team members experiencing emotional trauma as a result of their work through therapy when needed.

The National Caravan Council (NCC) Benevolent Fund

 £7,900 (2017/18)

Correspondent: The Trustees, Catherine House, 74 Victoria Road, Aldershot, Hampshire GU11 1SS (tel: 01252 318251; email: info@nccbf.org.uk)

https://www.nccbenevolentfund.org.uk

CC number: 271625

Eligibility

Current and former employees of the caravan or leisure vehicle industry, and their dependants, who are in need. Qualifying trades and industries include:
- The manufacturing, sale, repair or servicing of caravans and leisure vehicles in the UK
- Suppliers of services to the caravan and leisure industry
- Caravan holiday/residential parks

Applicants must have worked in one of the above areas for a continuous period of one year. Applicants must also have less than £5,000 in savings and must be in receipt of all benefits they are entitled to. Full eligibility criteria is available to download on the charity's website.

Types of grant

Hardship grants of up to £1,500 are given towards, for example, mobility equipment and building works. Grants of up to £300 are given for general living expenses such as utility bills and travel costs. The charity can also provide holidays/respite breaks to people with a household income of less than £25,000 who have not had a holiday in the last three years.

Exclusions

Grants are not awarded for:
- Debts, court/legal fees, fines, costs or damages
- Private medical treatments that are available through the NHS or non-essential medical treatments
- Work-related expenses (excluding essential travel costs)

- Investments
- Car expenses (such as lease or hire payments)
- Non-essential household items where there is no medical need
- Regular rent or mortgage payments

The charity does not make cash grants and cannot award funding for items that have already been purchased.

Applications

Application forms are available to download from the charity's website. Completed forms can be sent to the charity by email or post. Supporting information required can be found on the website.

Financial information

Year end	31/10/2018
Income	£8,200
Total expenditure	£8,800

Further financial information

The 2017/18 financial information was the latest available on the Charity Commission at time of writing (November 2021). Due to the charity's low income, full accounts were not available to view. We have therefore estimated the charity's grant total based on its overall expenditure.

Other information

Through its partnership with PayPlan, Money Advice Service and StepChange, the charity offers support for issues relating to debt and advice on money management.

Provision Trade Charity

 £59,600 (2020)

Correspondent: Mette Barwick, Secretary, 17 Clerkenwell Green, London EC1R 0DP (tel: 020 7253 2114; email: secretary@ptbi.org.uk)

www.ptbi.org.uk

CC number: 209173

Eligibility

People in need who have worked in the provision trade or the egg industry, or their widows/widowers. The provision trade covers the following sectors: bacon, pork, canned meat/fish and dairy products.

Types of grant

The charity provides quarterly grants, summer gifts, winter gifts and one-off payments to assist with special purchases or home improvement. In past years, grants have been used for mobility aids, car repairs, travel costs from/to hospital, day-to-day expenses and household appliances.

Exclusions

The charity cannot support people employed in retail, catering or hospitality.

Applications

Application forms can be downloaded from the charity's website. Applications may be returned by email or post.

Financial information

Year end	31/12/2020
Income	£38,800
Total expenditure	£73,000

There for You (UNISON Welfare)

See entry on page 153

The Tobacco Pipe Makers and Tobacco Trade Benevolent Fund

 £164,500 (2019/20)

Correspondent: The Trustees, 2 Spa Close, Brill, Aylesbury, Buckinghamshire HP18 9RZ (tel: 020 8663 3050; email: info@tobaccocharity.org.uk)

 www.tobaccocharity.org.uk

CC number: 1135646

Eligibility

People who have worked in the tobacco trade for a substantial period time. Examples given on the charity's website include wholesalers, sales representatives and tobacconists.

Types of grant

Recurrent payments and one-off grants, mainly for household items, television licences and house repairs. Grants are also given to help with winter fuel costs and at birthdays and Christmas.

Applications

Application forms are available on the charity's website.

Financial information

Year end	31/03/2020
Income	£448,900
Total expenditure	£79,600

Other information

The charity was formed in April 2010 as a result of a merger between the Tobacco Trade Benevolent Association, the Worshipful Company of Tobacco Pipe Makers and the Tobacco Blenders Benevolent Fund.

WRVS Benevolent Trust

 £40,300 (2020)

Correspondent: John Fallon, Grants Manager, WRVS Benevolent Trust, PO Box 769, Chesterfield, Derbyshire S40 9NY (tel: 07894 060517; email: grants@wrvsbt.org.uk or enquiry@wrvsbt.org.uk)

 www.wrvsbt.org.uk

CC number: 261931

Eligibility

Welfare

People in need who have volunteered or worked for the Women's Voluntary Service (WVS), Women's Royal Voluntary Service (WRVS) or the Royal Voluntary Service.

Education

The trust also runs a bursary scheme for current or past WRVS volunteers aged 16–25 taking part in events or opportunities which will benefit their personal development and future career.

Types of grant

Welfare

One-off grants have previously been made for household items and furniture, roof repairs, dental treatment, spectacles, electric wheelchairs and stairlifts.

Education

Bursaries of up to £2,000 to help applicants take part in an unpaid event or opportunity which will assist their career development. Recent grants have been made to allow applicants to undertake medical placements, distance learning programmes for further education and residential summer courses as part of their university studies.

Applications

Applications should be made using a form available to download from the charity's website and are considered throughout the year. Applications can be made directly by the individual, or by a friend or family member on their behalf. Further information can be found on the trust's website.

Financial information

Year end	31/12/2020
Income	£28,600
Total expenditure	£49,500

Public sector and government

Avon and Somerset Constabulary Benevolent Fund

 £7,100 (2020)

Correspondent: The Administrator, PO Box 37, Valley Road, Portishead, Bristol BS20 8QJ (tel: 07802 874486; email: benevolentfund@avonandsomerset.police.uk)

 https://www.ascbenfund.org

CC number: 1085497

Eligibility

Serving and retired officers of the Avon and Somerset constabulary, their widows and dependants.

Types of grant

The charity has previously stated in its guidance notes that support can be provided for the following:

- welfare assistance in times of crisis and to help meet unexpected expenses
- specialist equipment such as mobility vehicles or equipment to enable officers to remain independent or to improve their quality of life
- adaptations to a disabled officer / former officers home to support independent living
- contributions towards the costs of children's extra-curricular activities
- help towards the incidental costs of residential care or sheltered accommodation e.g. social activities and trips

Applications

Contact the administrator by phone, email or post. The administrator will then arrange to obtain the necessary information. Third-party referrals can be made by anyone providing the person concerned knows of the referral and agrees.

Financial information

Year end	31/12/2020
Income	£39,200
Total expenditure	£34,600

PC David Rathband's Blue Lamp Foundation

 £21,400 (2019/20)

Correspondent: Peter Sweeney, 3 Front Street, Newbiggin-by-the-Sea, Northumberland NE64 6NU (tel: 0871 234 5999; email: info@ bluelampfoundation.org)

🌐 www.bluelampfoundation.org

CC number: 1138319

Eligibility
All operational personnel of the UK's police, fire and ambulance services who work on either a full-time, part-time or voluntary basis and who have sustained an injury while carrying out their duty.

Types of grant
The foundation makes four types of grants:
- **Re-enablement grants** – suited to those who have been unable to work or are medically retired, these grants help relieve financial burdens following a serious injury.
- **Specialist grant** – help with adaptations or treatment for people who are seriously injured or incapacitated, such as specialist equipment or the cost of bills.
- **Immediacy grant** – support to allow recipients to claim back the expenses that were incurred during the immediate aftermath of their injury.
- **Bereavement grant** – assistance with funeral expenses.

Applications
Applications can be made online through the foundation's website. Applications can be submitted at any time, but must be made within six months of the date of the injury, unless the trustees agree on an extension of time. Applications filled in by a nominated person will be accepted.

Financial information
Year end	30/09/2020
Income	£14,800
Total expenditure	£28,100

Further financial information
Full accounts were not available to view on the Charity Commission's website due to the foundation's low income. We have therefore estimated the grant total based on the foundation's total expenditure.

British Association of Former United Nations Civil Servants Benevolent Fund

 £21,500 (2020)

Correspondent: Geoffrey Ward, Clerk to the Trustees, Margalla, Higher Gunville, Milborne Port, Sherborne, Dorset DT9 5AW (tel: 01963 250206; email: use the contact form available on the website)

🌐 https://bafuncs.org/benevolent

CC number: 297524

Eligibility
Former employees of the United Nations or its specialised agencies and their dependants who are in need.

Types of grant
One-off grants, grants in kind and loans of between £100 and £500. Grants can be made towards a wide range of needs, including remedial medical and surgical attention, respite care to release a family carer, aids for people with disabilities, household aids for older people, assistance towards transport costs for hospital outpatient visits, assistance towards visits by family or a British Association of Former United Nations Civil Servants Benevolent (BAFUNCS) member to a hospitalised patient, convalescent visits and holidays, loans or grants to meet short-term emergencies.

Applications
Application forms are available on the website and are normally referred to a welfare officer registered with BAFUNCS for immediate follow-up. Applications are considered throughout the year.

Financial information
Year end	31/12/2020
Income	£360
Total expenditure	£23,900

Further financial information
Full accounts were not available to view on the Charity Commission's website due to the fund's low income. We have therefore estimated the grant total based on the fund's total expenditure.

British Council Benevolent Fund

 £36,000 (2019/20)

Correspondent: The Trustees, 1 Redman Place, London E20 1JQ (tel: 020 3285 3828; email: benevolent.fund@ britishcouncil.org)

CC number: 1161805

Eligibility
Past and present staff of the British Council and their families or dependants. Staff include those who work as an employee or contractor of: the British Council; any wholly owned subsidiary of the British Council; a wholly or partly owned subsidiary of BC Trading Ltd; any organisation offering services to any of the previous entities.

Types of grant
One-off, quarterly and Christmas grants.

Applications
Apply in writing to the correspondent.

Financial information
Year end	31/03/2020
Income	£21,000
Total expenditure	£39,900

Further financial information
Full accounts were not available to view on the Charity Commission's website due to the fund's low income. We have therefore estimated the grant total based on the fund's total expenditure.

The British Fire Services Association Members Welfare Fund

£8,100 (2020)

Correspondent: George Halstead, Trustee, Copthorne, 9 Home Farm Close, Wray, Lancaster, Lancashire LA2 8RG (tel: 01524 221141; email: bfsa. welfare@btinternet.com)

🌐 bfsa.org.uk/membership/members-welfare-fund

CC number: 216011

Eligibility
Current and former firefighters and who have held British Fire Services Association (BFSA) membership, and their dependants. This can be anyone from local authorities, the Ministry of Defence and private or occupational fire services.

Types of grant
Assistance may be given in the form of one-off grants to aid the purchase of mobility items, electrical appliances, furniture or repairs. Alternatively the fund may consider long-term maintenance grants to those on a limited income.

Applications
Apply in writing to the correspondent.

Financial information
Year end	31/12/2020
Income	£22,300
Total expenditure	£25,400

Further financial information

Full accounts were not available to view on the Charity Commission's website due to the fund's low income. We have therefore estimated the fund's grant total based on its total expenditure.

The Charity for Civil Servants

 £1,660,000 (2020)

Correspondent: The Trustees, 5 Anne Boleyn's Walk, Cheam, Sutton SM3 8DY (tel: 0800 056 2424; email: help@ foryoubyyou.org.uk)

www.foryoubyyou.org.uk

OSCR number: SC041956/ 1136870

Eligibility

Serving and former staff of the civil service, and their dependants, who are in need. Individuals who work for organisations directly funded by a government department may also be eligible to apply. If you are unsure of your eligibility, contact the help service.

Types of grant

One-off and occasional ongoing grants are awarded according to need. Types of financial support considered include household bills, equipment costs, funeral expenses and travel costs.

Exclusions

The charity does not help employees of the NHS, the armed forces or local authorities. According to the website, financial support will not be provided for the following:

- Car purchase
- Car repairs (except in certain exceptional circumstances)
- Hardship caused primarily by loss of earnings as a result of strike action
- Home improvements or repairs in the UK for rented properties (note that decoration or furnishing to meet a decent homes standard and which do not come under landlord responsibility may be considered for rented properties)
- Home improvements or repairs for mortgaged or outright owned properties that are not essential to meeting a decent homes standard
- Home improvements, repairs or adaptations outside the UK
- Home purchase
- Legal fees and costs of legal representation with the exception of referral to the Charity's appointed supplier for legal information
- Non-priority debts
- Payment of fines
- Private medical treatment
- Private, further and higher education
- Repatriation of person or bodies
- Treatment for infertility

Check the website for further information on eligibility.

Applications

Apply online via the charity's website.

Financial information

Year end	31/12/2020
Income	£5,330,000
Total expenditure	£8,190,000

Further financial information

Grants were broken down as follows:

Reduced or low income	£474,000
Poor well-being	£332,000
Ill health	£297,000
Disability	£186,000
Relationship breakdown	£161,000
Bereavement	£151,000
Domestic abuse	£30,000
Emergency relief	£12,000
Unstable/unsafe living arrangements	£11,000
Caring	£4,000
Community projects	£1,000

Other information

In addition to its grant-making, the charity runs services to give advice on money issues, stress and depression, carers' support, domestic abuse and mental well-being. Details regarding the full range of services provided are available on the website.

Conservative and Unionist Agents' Benevolent Association

 £249,200 (2019/20)

Correspondent: Sally Smith, Honorary Secretary, 37 Winston Close, Nether Heyford, Northampton NN7 3JX (tel: 020 7118 7475; email: sally.smith@ conservatives.com)

www.conservativeagentscharity.org. uk

CC number: 216438

Eligibility

Serving and retired Conservative Party agents and their dependants. The charity's website states:

Over the years CABA has supported those who have become seriously ill while still in employment, retired colleagues and their dependants, especially the very elderly whose salary will not have attracted a large pension, and the children and dependants of colleagues who have died in service.

Types of grant

The charity's full beneficiaries, deemed by the trustees as having a low income, receive regular monthly payments for day-to-day expenses. TV licence and telephone bill costs are covered and vouchers for newspapers are provided. The charity also awards special request

grants for mobility aids, low vision aids and call alarms. Grants are also considered for household items, white goods house repairs and other specific requests.

Exclusions

Grants cannot be made for nursing home fees.

Applications

Initial enquiries can be made by post, email or telephone to the correspondent, who will then discuss the options available to the applicant. A member of the management committee or a local serving agent will then visit the applicant to discuss their application and their need for support, which is based on an assessment of household income and other circumstances. Every beneficiary is reassessed annually, either in winter or summer.

Financial information

Year end	31/03/2020
Income	£61,200
Total expenditure	£314,500

Further financial information

Grants were broken down as follows:

Special grants	£154,300
Monthly grants	£59,300
Replace and repair grants	£15,300
Personal items grant	£6,400
Second seasonal grants	£5,900
First seasonal grants	£5,700
Newspapers grants	£1,900
TV licence grants	£260
Home items	£100

CSIS Charity Fund

 £18,800 (2020)

Correspondent: Charity Fund Secretary, 7 Colman House, King Street, Maidstone, Kent ME14 1DD (tel: 07843 342889; email: use the contact form available on the website)

www.csischarityfund.org

CC number: 1121671

Eligibility

Spouses and other dependants of deceased Civil Service Insurance Society (CSIS) policyholders.

Types of grant

One-off grants are awarded according to need.

Applications

Contact the Charity Fund Secretary to apply for a grant.

Financial information

Year end	31/12/2020
Income	£311,800
Total expenditure	£779,200

Other information
CSIS's activities are focused mainly on providing grants and assistance to charities and organisations working to support current and former civil and public servants and their dependants who are in need. The website has a helpful list of organisations with similar aims that can provide advice and financial assistance to individuals.

The Edridge Fund

 £27,900 (2019)

Correspondent: Karen Monaghan, Secretary, 65 Mortlake High Street, Boat Race House, London SW14 8HL (tel: 020 3397 7025; email: edridge.secretary@ edridgefund.org)

www.edridgefund.org

CC number: 803493

Eligibility
Members and ex-members of the probation service and family court services who are (or were) eligible to be members of Napo, and their dependants.

Types of grant
Small grants, usually of up to £350, are given for the relief of hardship as a result of unforeseen circumstances. Funding may be given towards funeral expenses, household items, disability equipment, rent arrears and so on.

Exclusions
Grants are not given for:
- School fees, funding for courses (further or higher education), student loan repayments
- House purchases
- Private medical treatment or towards travel or associated costs related to receiving treatment in another country
- Car purchases
- Legal fees, legal representation and associated costs
- Payment of fines
- Debts to family and friends
- Residential or nursing home fees
- Help to make up a loss of pay as a result of industrial action
- Applicants who have sufficient savings or monthly surplus to meet the cost of the item requested

Support will also not be given when it may lead to reputational damage to the fund.

Applications
Application forms can be completed online or downloaded from the fund's website.

Financial information
Year end	31/12/2019
Income	£57,300
Total expenditure	£46,300

Fire Fighters Charity

 £377,900 (2019/20)

Correspondent: The Trustees, Belvedere House, Basing View, Basingstoke, Hampshire RG21 4HG (tel: 01256 366566; email: administration@ firefighterscharity.org.uk)

www.firefighterscharity.org.uk

CC number: 1093387

Eligibility
Serving and retired firefighters, fire personnel and their dependants.

Types of grant
One-off grants are awarded according to need.

Applications
Contact the correspondent via the charity's website.

Financial information
Year end	31/03/2020
Income	£9,970,000
Total expenditure	£6,770,000

Other information
The charity provides personalised support to its beneficiaries, which includes online or phone support, and support in the local community or at one of its centres.

The Gurney Fund
See entry on page 25

The Benevolent Fund of Her Majesty's Inspectors of Schools in England and Wales
See entry on page 109

Metropolitan Police Benevolent Fund

£554,000 (2019)

Correspondent: Natasha Raj, Secretary, MPS Charities Section, 2nd Floor (South), Kilburn Police Station, 38 Salusbury Road, London NW6 6LT (tel: 020 7161 1481; email: natasha.p. raj@met.police.uk)

 https://www.met.police.uk

CC number: 1125409

Eligibility
Current and former officers of the Metropolitan Police, and their dependants, who are in need. Support is extended the immediate families of police officers who have lost their lives in the line of duty.

Types of grant
Grants are awarded towards furniture, mobility aids, home adaptations, dental treatment, car repairs, bills and general living expenses. Interest-free loans are also available.

Applications
Apply in writing to the correspondent.

Financial information
Year end	31/12/2019
Income	£2,530,000
Total expenditure	£2,830,000

Other information
Police officers who donate to the Give As You Earn payroll scheme are able to seek free treatment at the Police Rehabilitation Centre in Goring-on-Thames. Treatments available include physiotherapy, acupuncture, aromatherapy and hydrotherapy.

Metropolitan Police Staff Welfare Fund

£35,000 (2019/20)

Correspondent: Natasha Raj, Secretary, Metropolitan Police Services, 9th Floor, Charities Section, Empress State Building, Lillie Road, London SW6 1TR (tel: 020 7161 1481; email: natasha.p. raj@met.police.uk)

CC number: 282375

Eligibility
Current and former members of the Metropolitan Police Staff (MPS) or the Mayor's Office for Policing and Crime (MOPAC) and their dependants who are in need.

Types of grant
One-off grants, typically in the region of £100 to £2,000, are awarded according to need. Past examples include contributions towards funeral expenses, home improvements/replacements and essential furniture.

Applications
Apply in writing to the correspondent.

Financial information
Year end	31/03/2020
Income	£20,600
Total expenditure	£37,300

Further financial information

Full accounts were not available to view on the Charity Commission's website due to the fund's low income. We have therefore estimated the grant total based on the fund's total expenditure.

Northern Ireland Police Fund

 £1,110,000 (2019/20)

Correspondent: The Secretary, Maryfield Complex, 100 Belfast Road, Holywood, County Down, Northern Ireland BT18 9QY (tel: 028 9039 3556; email: admin@nipolicefund.gov.uk)

🌐 www.nipolicefund.org

Eligibility

Serving and retired police officers in Northern Ireland, and their dependants, who have been directly affected by terrorist violence whether on or off-duty. This includes those with serious physical and/or psychological injuries which would be considered sufficiently serious to warrant the award of an Injury on Duty (IOD) Band 2 medical discharge, as determined by an occupational physician. The applicant must also be able to demonstrate that the IOD was a result of the individual being the directly intended target of a terrorist attack. Our previous research found that applications are also considered from the families of officers who have died by suicide if a causal link can be established between a direct attack on the officer and their subsequent death.

Types of grant

Welfare

There are several grant programmes available to individuals. The General Support Scheme and the Disability Adaptations Scheme award grants for essential home maintenance work, household items or furniture and purchase of equipment. The Carers Respite Breaks Scheme makes grants for breaks. The Regular Payments Scheme makes two payments a year, in April and October to individuals who have an annual income of under £11,293.

Education

Educational bursaries are also available for officers with disabilities and their children who wish to study.

Applications

Applicants can find eligibility criteria and application forms on the fund's website.

Financial information

Year end	31/03/2020
Income	£36,100
Total expenditure	£1,450,000

Further financial information

The fund's accounts are available to download on its website. During the year, the fund made 188 grants to individuals for general support, disability adaptations, educational bursaries and regular payments. In addition, 497 recognition payments were made to individuals. Note, the welfare grant total includes six grants awarded to police support voluntary bodies organisations whose activities benefit individuals.

Other information

The fund was established in 2001 following the Patten Report into policing in Northern Ireland. In addition to grant-making, the fund has a team of occupational therapists who support clients.

Police Care UK

 £629,300 (2019/20)

Correspondent: The Trustees, Nova Scotia House, 70 Goldsworth Road, Woking, Surrey GU21 6LQ (tel: 0300 012 0030; email: hello@policecare.org.uk)

🌐 https://www.policecare.org.uk

CC number: 1151322

Eligibility

Welfare

Serving or veteran police officers, staff, or volunteers (including cadets and special constabulary) from any police force in the UK who are in need. Support is extended to their dependants and to the dependants of deceased police officers, staff or volunteers.

Education

Educational grants are available to the children of serving or veteran police officers, staff or volunteers who are aged 15–18 and are in full-time education. This includes stepchildren, adopted children, or grandchildren (where parental responsibility exists). Applicants must already be enrolled in, or have confirmed status of enrolment to, a higher or further education course at a recognised place of education.

Types of grant

Welfare

Welfare grants are made in the form of maintenance grants for widows of officers killed on duty, specialist equipment grants for mobility aids and home adaptations, assistance grants for furniture, household appliances, food, clothing and set-up costs associated with entering rented accommodation. Christmas grants are distributed annually for help with additional costs incurred as part of the seasonal period.

Retraining grants are available to ex-police members who are injured/medically retired, to gain access to new careers.

Education

Educational grants of up to £3,000 per year are awarded towards living costs when studying in higher or further education.

Exclusions

Grants cannot be used for repaying debts, legal costs or medical care. The charity does not make loans, nor does it award grants in cases where state assistance or statutory services are available.

Applications

Initial enquiries can be made using the 'make a referral' form featured on the charity's website. Applicants can self-refer if they wish. Alternatively, applicants may wish to contact the charity by telephone (9am to 5pm, Monday to Friday) to begin the application process. Applications for educational grants can be sent anytime up until 31 December and payments are made in January. The bursary panel meets once per year to consider grants.

Financial information

Year end	31/03/2020
Income	£1,590,000
Total expenditure	£3,790,000

Further financial information

Grants were broken down as follows:

Assistance grants	£455,100
Maintenance grants	£100,000
Educational bursaries	£65,000
Christmas grants	£9,200

Other information

The charity operates a counselling service for those struggling with mental health problems or trauma. The services encompasses a range of therapeutic interventions such as cognitive behavioural therapy (CBT), guided self-help, as well as eye movement desensitisation and reprocessing (EMDR) for people experiencing post-traumatic stress disorder.

The Royal Ulster Constabulary GC – Police Service of Northern Ireland Benevolent Fund

£93,000 (2020)

Correspondent: The Trustees, RUCGC-PSNI Benevolent Fund, 77–79 Garnerville Road, Belfast BT4 2NX (tel: 028 9076 4200; email: benevolentfund@policefedni.com)

policebenevolentfund.com

CCNI number: NIC104568

Eligibility
Members, ex-members and pensioners of the Royal Ulster Constabulary GC and/or the Police Service of Northern Ireland who are in need. Support is extended to the dependants of members or deceased members. The parents of deceased single officers are also eligible for support.

Types of grant
One-off and recurrent grants are given according to need. Interest-free loans are also available.

Applications
Initial enquiries can be made by contacting the charity. A representative from the charity may visit applicants to gain a better understanding of their personal and/or financial circumstances. The committee meets monthly to consider grant applications.

Financial information
Year end	31/12/2020
Income	£1,100,000
Total expenditure	£1,120,000

Further financial information
During the financial year, 38 grants were awarded to individuals.

Other information
The charity owns a number of holiday apartments in Northern Ireland, which are available on a weekly basis to retired ex-members and widows of ex-members. An online booking system is featured on the charity's website. The charity also supports 28 welfare groups throughout Northern Ireland, providing financial assistance towards running costs and grants for events.

Scottish Police Benevolent Fund

 £258,800 (2019/20)

Correspondent: Mairi MacGregor, Treasurer, c/o Scottish Police Federation, 28 High Street, Nairn IV12 4AU (tel: 0300 303 0028)

 www.spbf.org.uk

OSCR number: SC043489

Eligibility
Members and former members of the Scottish Police Benevolent Fund (or any former police benevolent fund within Scotland) and their dependants. People who have had some direct connection with the police service in Scotland and their dependants can also be considered.

Types of grant
Grants are awarded according to need. Emergency grants of up to £1,000 are available where there is an urgent need.

Applications
Application forms can be downloaded from the charity's website.

Financial information
Year end	31/03/2020
Income	£445,500
Total expenditure	£362,900

Other information
The charity can also provide loans to eligible individuals and awards grants to charitable organisations.

Scottish Prison Service Benevolent Fund

 £5,700 (2020/21)

Correspondent: The Trustees, HMP Shotts, Newmill/Canthill Road, Shotts ML7 4LE

OSCR number: SC021603

Eligibility
Scottish prison officers, both serving and retired, and their families who are in need.

Types of grant
Grants are given according to need.

Applications
Apply in writing to the correspondent.

Financial information
Year end	31/03/2021
Income	£21,800
Total expenditure	£12,700

Further financial information
Full accounts were not available to view on the OSCR website due to the fund's low income. We have therefore estimated the grant total based on the fund's total expenditure.

St George's Police Children Trust
See entry on page 29

See entry on page 29

The National Federation of Sub-Postmasters Benevolent Fund

 £53,500 (2019)

Correspondent: The Trustees, Post Office, Main Street, West Linton EH46 7EE (tel: 01273 458324; email: admin@nfsp.org.uk)

 www.nfsp.org.uk

CC number: 262704

Eligibility
Serving or retired sub-postmasters and current or former employees of the National Federation of SubPostmasters (NFSP) who are in need due to ill health, bereavement or domestic distress. Partners and dependants of such people may also be supported.

Types of grant
Grants are given according to need.

Applications
Apply in writing to the correspondent.

Financial information
Year end	31/12/2019
Income	£46,100
Total expenditure	£76,600

Other information
The fund also offers a trauma counselling service.

There for You (UNISON Welfare)

 £983,600 (2020)

Correspondent: Tina Willis, Casework Team, UNISON Centre, 130 Euston Road, London NW1 2AY (tel: 020 7121 5620; email: thereforyou@unison.co.uk)

 www.unison.org.uk/welfare

CC number: 1023552

Eligibility
Financial help is given to UNISON members. In certain circumstances former members of the National Association of Local Government Officers (NALGO) can also apply. Partners/dependants of deceased members can apply in their own right. Support is provided to individuals experiencing unforeseen difficulties such as redundancy, illness, bereavement or relationship breakdown.

Types of grant
The charity helps in cases of unanticipated difficulty and helps with expenses such as essential household bills and goods, disability aids, property repairs and clothing.

Applications
Individuals should first contact their branch welfare officer or secretary who will help them to fill in an application form. People who are having difficulty contacting their local branch may submit the form, which is available from the website, directly to the national office.

Financial information

Year end	31/12/2020
Income	£2,110,000
Total expenditure	£1,760,000

Further financial information

Grants were broken down as follows:

Other purposes	£470,300
Household	£176,300
Income subsidy	£122,100
Living cost	£94,000
Debt and bankruptcy	£53,200
Funeral expenses	£37,800
Employment loss	£17,700
Health	£8,900
Well-being breaks	£3,300

Other information

The charity, previously known as UNISON Welfare, provides support and advice on a variety of issues including personal debt and state benefits.

The Ulster Defence Regiment Benevolent Fund

 £199,200 (2019/20)

Correspondent: The Trustees, c/o Edwards & Co. Solicitors, 28 Hill Street, Belfast BT1 2LA (tel: 028 9040 8393; email: office@udrbenfund.com)

https://www.udrbenevolentfund. com

CCNI number: NIC107024

Eligibility

People who served in the Ulster Defence Regiment, their widows and their dependants.

Types of grant

Grants for general welfare purposes to relieve hardship, for respite activities and at Christmas.

Applications

To apply for welfare, Christmas and respite grants, contact the fund using the contact details provided. For respite breaks at Ringhaddy House, an application form is available to download from the fund's website.

Financial information

Year end	31/03/2020
Income	£223,000
Total expenditure	£480,700

Further financial information

Grants awarded in 2019/20 were broken down as follows:

Welfare grants	£103,600
Respite activities	£56,800
Christmas grants	£38,700

Other information

The fund also own 16 apartments on the north coast of Ireland which are available for eligible beneficiaries to take a respite break.

Religious occupations

Frances Ashton's Charity

 £87,100 (2020)

Correspondent: Georgina Fowle, Grants Administrator, The Old Stables, Gracious Street, Selborne, Alton GU34 3JD (tel: 01420 511310; email: francesashton@hotmail.co.uk)

www.francesashton.co.uk

CC number: 200162

Eligibility

Serving and retired Church of England clergy, and their widows/widowers, who are in need.

Types of grant

One-off grants. The charity is willing to consider any application for support. Examples of what can be funded include:

▶ The cost of new glasses
▶ A respite care break
▶ Replacement household items

The charity has a number of areas of priority including emergencies and medical or care needs for the applicant or their dependants.

Exclusions

Grants are not given towards:

▶ Educational costs
▶ Loan or debt repayments
▶ Reimbursement of costs

Applications

Apply on a form available from the correspondent, to be submitted directly by the individual.

Financial information

Year end	31/12/2020
Income	£790
Total expenditure	£96,800

Further financial information

Full accounts were not available to view on the Charity Commission's website due to the charity's low income. We have therefore estimated the charity's grant total based on its total expenditure.

Other information

The charity also makes an annual grant to the charity Royal London Society (now merged with St Giles Trust) for £95 to support people with experience of the criminal justice system and their families in need.

The Bible Preaching Trust

£6,000 (2019/20)

Correspondent: The Revd Gary Brady, Trustee, 72 Crewys Road, Childs Hill, London NW2 2AD (tel: 020 8455 2275; email: gary.bradybunch@btopenworld. com)

CC number: 262160

Eligibility

Christian preachers who are in need of support to continue preaching. Occasionally, people who wish to enter the preaching ministry are also supported.

Types of grant

Grants are given according to need.

Applications

Apply in writing to the correspondent.

Financial information

Year end	05/04/2020
Income	£4,400
Total expenditure	£7,100

Further financial information

Full accounts were not available to view on the Charity Commission's website due to the trust's low income. We have therefore estimated the grant total based on the trust's total expenditure.

Charity of Miss Ann Farrar Brideoake

£39,400 (2019/20)

Correspondent: Alan Ware, Trustee, 8 Blake Street, York, North Yorkshire YO1 8XJ (tel: 01904 625678)

CC number: 213848

Eligibility

Communicant members of the Church of England living within the dioceses of York, Liverpool and Manchester who are in need. This includes parishioners, clergy and retired clergy.

Types of grant

Grants are given according to need.

Applications

Apply in writing to the correspondent.

Financial information

Year end	05/04/2020
Income	£104,200
Total expenditure	£68,400

The Church of England Pensions Board

 £101,000 (2020)

Correspondent: The Trustees, Church of England Pensions Board, 29 Great Smith Street, London SW1P 3PS (tel: 020 7898 1000; email: housing@churchofengland.org)

https://www.cepb.org.uk

CC number: 236627

Eligibility
Retired clergy and licensed lay workers of the Church of England. Support is also available to their widows, widowers and dependants.

Types of grant
Recurrent grants in the form of pensions.

Applications
Apply in writing to the correspondent.

Financial information
Year end	31/12/2020
Income	£29,080,000
Total expenditure	£29,680,000

Other information
Another priority of the charity is to provide housing for retired clergy and their dependants under the Church's Housing Assistance for Retired Ministry (CHARM) scheme. Under CHARM, there are several housing options available to eligible people and their close families, such as access to rental property, shared ownership properties, mortgage schemes and supported housing.

The Clergy Rest Fund

 £20,500 (2020)

Correspondent: The Trustees, c/o Winckworth Sherwood LLP, Minerva House, 3–5 Montague Close, London SE1 9BB (tel: 020 7593 5000)

CC number: 233436

Eligibility
Clergy of the Church of England who are in need.

Types of grant
One-off grants ranging from £350 to £1,500.

Applications
Apply in writing to the correspondent.

Financial information
Year end	31/12/2020
Income	£47,500
Total expenditure	£68,900

Further financial information
In 2020, grants were awarded to 17 beneficiaries.

Other information
The fund also makes grants to organisations connected to the Church of England.

Clergy Support Trust

 £2,480,000 (2020)

Correspondent: The Trustees, 1 Dean Trench Street, Westminster, London SW1P 3HB (tel: 0800 389 5192; email: help@clergysupport.org.uk)

https://www.clergysupport.org.uk

CC number: 207736

Eligibility
Current and former Anglican clergy and ordinands, and their dependants, who are in need. Support is extended to the dependants of deceased Anglican clergy members and ordinands. Eligibility criteria varies between each grant scheme. The charity's website features an 'Eligibility Checker', which can be used to confirm eligibility.

Types of grant
Grants are made towards the following expenses: car deposits, car repairs, childcare, funeral costs, furniture, general living expenses, legal fees, moving costs, property maintenance and rent advances.

Emergency grants are designed to help in times of unforeseen crises or unexpected costs. These grants are smaller in value (usually of up to £500) and decisions and payments can be made more quickly than for financial support grants.

Health grants are awarded for a wide range of medical treatments, such as dental treatment, glasses, mobility aids and therapies.

Well-being grants are made towards the cost of holidays, respite breaks, retreats and leisure activities. Grants are also available for care home fees and school fees, but funding is means tested.

Applications
Applications can be made online using a form on the charity's website. Alternatively, applicants may wish to contact the charity to request that a physical copy of the application form be sent to them by post.

Financial information
Year end	31/12/2020
Income	£3,670,000
Total expenditure	£3,730,000

Further financial information
Note: the grant total includes university maintenance grants; the charity has since begun to phase out this type of support.

The Collier Charitable Trust

 £2,400 (2019)

Correspondent: The Trustees, East Haven, Church Lane, Grayshott, Hindhead GU26 6LY (tel: 01428 608740)

CC number: 251333

Eligibility
Our previous research suggests that retired Christian missionaries and teachers in the UK are eligible.

Types of grant
Grants are awarded according to need.

Applications
Apply in writing to the correspondent.

Financial information
Year end	31/12/2019
Income	£25,200
Total expenditure	£58,900

Further financial information
During the year the trust made six grants of £1,000 or below to individuals. Grants to organisations totalled £51,500.

Other information
The trust provides accommodation to individuals who are, or have been, engaged in missionary work.

The Groveland Charitable Trust

 £500 (2019/20)

Correspondent: The Trustees, 8 Fairleigh Rise, Kingron Langley, Chippenham SN15 5QF (tel: 01249 758877)

CC number: 289279

Eligibility
Gospel Standard Baptist ministers, and their dependants, who are in need.

Types of grant
Grants are given according to need.

Applications
Apply in writing to the correspondent.

Financial information
Year end	05/04/2020
Income	£45,300
Total expenditure	£14,800

Further financial information
Grants were awarded to one individual during the year.

Lady Hewley's Charity

£ £154,000 (2019/20)

Correspondent: Neil Blake, Clerk to the Trustees, Military House, 24 Castle Street, Chester CH1 2DS (tel: 01244 400315)

CC number: 230043

Eligibility

Welfare

Current or retired ministers of any United Reformed, Congregational and Baptist church. Support is extended to the dependants of such ministers, as well as members of the same churches. Dependants of former Presbyterian Church of England ministers are also eligible for support.

Education

Support is available for students who are studying for ministries in United Reformed, Congregational and Baptist churches or 'attending certain specified colleges'.

Types of grant

One-off grants according to need.

Applications

Applications are invited through contact with respective churches at local church and at regional and provincial levels. Individual applications are considered twice a year.

Financial information

Year end	05/04/2020
Income	£376,600
Total expenditure	£377,700

Other information

This charity owns and operates almshouses which are available to people belonging to the Protestant faith, aged 55 and over, who are in need.

The Leaders of Worship and Preachers Trust

£ £25,200 (2019/20)

Correspondent: Ian Buchanan, Secretary, Unit 14, Orbital 25 Business Park, Dwight Road, Watford WD18 9DA (tel: 01923 231811; email: lwptoffice@ lwpt.org.uk)

 www.lwpt.org.uk

CC number: 1107967

Eligibility

Social welfare

Preachers or leaders of worship and their families with immediate financial need.

Education

Individuals who wish to pursue their vocation in ministry. Applicants should be committed Christians and active members of a church.

Types of grant

Social welfare

The trust's hardship grants are awarded on a one-off basis according to need.

Education

The trust's vocational grants can assist with fees or materials for any recognised course or conference that enables the applicant to explore or develop their preaching skills. This can include gap year courses and those for professional development. Grants are typically in the region of £500 (maximum £1,000). The maximum for books and resource requests is £300.

Applications

Application forms are available to download from the trust's website along with guidance notes. Information about the applicant's financial circumstances will be requested by the trust in order to determine the need for support. Vocational grants are awarded in September and January following meetings in July and November. For vocational grants, applicants must have the support of a member of their church staff.

Financial information

Year end	31/08/2020
Income	£634,100
Total expenditure	£412,000

Further financial information

Grants were broken down as follows: vocational grants (£21,400) and hardship grants (£3,800).

Other information

The trust notes on its website: 'It is important to note before making an application, that your church may be able to offer you financial support.' The trust also makes grants to organisations.

The Methodist Church in Great Britain

£ £1,700,000 (2019/20)

Correspondent: The Trustees, Methodist Church House, 25 Marylebone House, London NW1 5JR (email: ministerial. grants@methodistchurch.org.uk)

 www.methodist.org.uk/for- ministers-and-office-holders/ finance/stipends-and-payroll/ ministerial-grants

CC number: 1132208

Eligibility

Methodist presbyters, deacons, lay employees and local preachers and their families.

Types of grant

The charity states in its 2019/20 accounts: 'Small grants are made to Methodist presbyters, deacons, lay employees and local preachers and their families towards the education of their children, during times of ill health and for one-off financial support.'

Applications

Application forms are available to download from the charity's website.

Financial information

Year end	31/08/2020
Income	£33,950,000
Total expenditure	£33,580,000

Ministers' Relief Society

£ £18,100 (2019)

Correspondent: The Trustees, 2 Queensberry Road, Penylan, Cardiff CV23 9JJ (tel: 029 2115 0294)

CC number: 270314

Eligibility

Protestant ministers who are in need, especially due to age or disability. Widows and children (under the age of 21) of deceased ministers are also supported. All applicants must be 'of genuine Protestant and Evangelical convictions'.

Types of grant

Grants are given according to need.

Applications

Apply in writing to the correspondent.

Financial information

Year end	31/12/2019
Income	£15,900
Total expenditure	£20,100

Further financial information

Full accounts were not available to view on the Charity Commission's website due to the charity's low income. We have therefore estimated the charity's grant total based on its total expenditure.

Other information

The charity is also known as the Society for the Relief of Necessitous Protestant Ministers, their Widows and Orphans.

Mitchell Bequest

£ £18,800 (2019/20)

Correspondent: The Trustees, Archdiocese of Glasgow, 196 Clyde Street, Glasgow G1 4JY

OSCR number: SC013478

Eligibility
Clergymen of Roman Catholic religion living in Scotland who are in need due to age or illness.

Types of grant
Annual allowances.

Applications
Apply in writing to the correspondent.

Financial information
Year end	30/11/2020
Income	£31,000
Total expenditure	£23,800

Further financial information
During the financial period, payments were made to 49 individuals.

The Ogle Christian Trust

£ £9,000 (2020)

Correspondent: The Trustees, 43 Woolstone Road, London SE23 2TR (email: oglectrust@rockuk.net)

CC number: 1061458

Eligibility
People who are in need. Preference may be given to retired missionary workers.

Types of grant
Grants are given according to need.

Applications
Apply in writing to the correspondent.

Financial information
Year end	31/12/2020
Income	£87,900
Total expenditure	£177,800

Other information
The trust's main priority is supporting new evangelism initiatives worldwide, missionary enterprises and bible student training. It also makes grants to organisations.

The Paton Trust

£ £1,400 (2018)

Correspondent: Trust Administrator, c/o Alexander Sloan Chartered Accountants, 180 St Vincent Street, Glasgow G2 5SG

OSCR number: SC012301

Eligibility
Ministers of the Established Church of Scotland who are retired or in ill health.

Types of grant
One-off grants. Grants are given to ministers who are in need of a convalescence break and to ministers who are retiring to provide them with a holiday at the time of retirement.

Applications
Application forms are available from the correspondent. Applications are considered throughout the year and should be submitted directly by the individual.

Financial information
Year end	31/12/2018
Income	£5
Total expenditure	£1,600

Further financial information
Full accounts were not available to view on the OSCR website due to the trust's low income. We have therefore estimated the grant total based on the trust's total expenditure. The 2018 financial information was the latest available at the time of writing (November 2021).

The Harry and Katie Pollard Trust

£ £11,200 (2020)

Correspondent: The Trustees, c/o The Additional Curates Society, 16 Commercial Street, Birmingham, West Midlands B1 1RS (tel: 01371 830132)

CC number: 255080

Eligibility
Widows and unmarried daughters of clergy, aged 50 or over, who are in need.

Types of grant
Grants are awarded according to need. According to the trust's application form, the trustees give priority to capital expenses rather than routine living expenses.

Applications
Application forms are available to download here: https://churchunion.co.uk/applications. The form should be submitted by post to the correspondent address.

Financial information
Year end	31/12/2020
Income	£34,000
Total expenditure	£32,600

Further financial information
During the year, grants were paid to ten individuals.

The Pyncombe Charity

£ £15,700 (2020/21)

Correspondent: Angela Robinson, Secretary, Haverbrack, Ash Priors, Taunton, Somerset TA4 3NF (tel: 01823 430861; email: angelaj.robinson@ btinternet.com)

CC number: 202255

Eligibility
Serving Anglican clergy (holding the Bishop's licence) under the age of 70, or their immediate family members who live with them, who are in need resulting from a serious illness, an injury or special circumstances.

Types of grant
The charity awards small one-off grants.

Exclusions
No grants are awarded towards educational expenses.

Applications
Applications must be made through the diocesan Bishop on a form available from the correspondent. Applications should be submitted by April. No direct applications can be considered and the charity has told us the majority of the direct applications received are ineligible. Note: it is important that the financial impact of the applicant's circumstances is clearly stated and quantified in the application.

Financial information
Year end	31/01/2021
Income	£18,000
Total expenditure	£17,400

Further financial information
Full accounts were not available to view on the Charity Commission's website due to the charity's low income. We have therefore estimated the charity's grant total based on its total expenditure.

The Retired Ministers' and Widows' Fund

£ £31,100 (2019/20)

Correspondent: Bill Allen, Secretary, Flat 7, 8 Wendover Lodge, Church Street, Welwyn Garden City, Hertfordshire AL6 9LR (tel: 01438 489171; email: billallen1960@gmail.com)

CC number: 233835

Eligibility
Retired ministers and widows/widowers of ministers of Unitarian, Free Christian, Congregational, Presbyterian, United Reformed and Baptist denominations. Single people must not have an income

exceeding £5,200 (excluding state benefits such as pensions, housing or Council Tax benefit). Married couples must not have an income exceeding £7,800 and savings of over £40,000. Priority is given to those already registered with the charity.

Types of grant

Half-yearly payments are given to eligible individuals. Christmas gifts are also awarded. One-off assistance may be provided to help in an emergency.

Exclusions

Individuals can only be awarded a maximum of two grants over a four-year period.

Applications

Contact the correspondent to request an application form.

Financial information

Year end	31/03/2020
Income	£47,100
Total expenditure	£36,300

Further financial information

In 2019/20, grants were awarded to 16 individuals, eight widows and eight ministers. Payments to widows were between £850 and £2,000, payments to ministers were £2,100 to £2,900.

Retired Missionary Aid Fund

£ £536,800 (2019/20)

Correspondent: The Trustees, 64 Callow Hill Road, Alvechurch, Birmingham B48 7LR (tel: 0121 445 2378)

 www.rmaf.co.uk

CC number: 211454

Eligibility

Retired missionaries from the Christian Brethren Assemblies who have served in a foreign mission for a significant number of years. Help may also be given to their dependants.

Types of grant

Grants are made according to need, for example for the payment of heating bills or medical costs. The fund also provides funeral grants, shopping vouchers as a birthday gift and food hampers at Christmas.

Applications

Apply in writing to the correspondent.

Financial information

Year end	30/06/2020
Income	£382,200
Total expenditure	£558,000

Further financial information

Grants were broken down as follows:

Gifts to retired missionaries	£501,900
Earmarked gifts paid to retired missionaries	£17,000
Gift vouchers and Christmas food hampers	£9,800
Funeral grants	£8,000

George Richards' Charity

£ £17,000 (2019)

Correspondent: The Trustees, Flat 96, Thomas More House, Barbican, London EC2Y 8BU (tel: 020 7588 5583)

CC number: 246965

Eligibility

Former clergy of the Church of England, who were forced to retire early as a result of ill health. Support is also available to their widows/widowers and dependants.

Types of grant

Recurrent payments in the form of pensions.

Applications

Apply in writing to the correspondent.

Financial information

Year end	31/12/2019
Income	£26,200
Total expenditure	£18,900

Further financial information

Full accounts were not available to view on the Charity Commission's website due to the charity's low income. We have therefore estimated the charity's grant total based on its total expenditure.

Samuel Robinson's Charities

£ £101,000 (2019/20)

Correspondent: Elizabeth Lawson, Grants Secretary, Bocketts, Downs Road, Epsom, Surrey KT18 5HA (tel: 01372 727777)

CC number: 222700

Eligibility

Active or retired ministers of Independent and Baptist Churches in England and Wales. Widows of such ministers are also eligible.

Types of grant

One-off grants for items, services or facilities.

Applications

Apply in writing to the correspondent.

Financial information

Year end	30/11/2020
Income	£74,500
Total expenditure	£92,800

Further financial information

Grants were awarded to 30 individuals, ranging from £1,000 to £5,000. Grants were distributed as follows:

Baptist Church	£46,500
Congregational Church	£31,200
United Reformed Church	£12,300
Assemblies of God	£5,000
Church of God	£3,000
Welsh Congregational	£3,000

Society for the Benefit of Sons and Daughters of the Clergy of the Church of Scotland

£ £25,300 (2020)

Correspondent: Kirsty Ashworth, Charity Accounts, Accounts and Business Services Senior Manager, Exchange Place, 3 Semple Street, Edinburgh EH3 8BL (email: SM-Charity@azets.co.uk)

 https://www.azets.co.uk/sons-and-daughters-of-the-clergy-of-the-church-of-scotland

OSCR number: SC008760

Eligibility

Children of ministers of the Church of Scotland aged between 12 and 25 (with preference for families on a low income), unmarried and widowed daughters of ministers and unmarried sisters over the age of 40 of ordained ministers.

Types of grant

Grants are awarded according to need.

Applications

Application forms can be downloaded from the charity's website.

Financial information

Year end	31/12/2020
Income	£44,700
Total expenditure	£49,000

Further financial information

During the year, 19 grants were awarded totalling £25,300.

Other information

The society also administers two funds to support other dependants, the John Lang Macfarlane Fund for unmarried and widowed daughters of ministers and the Robertson Chaplin Fund for unmarried sisters of ministers over the age of 40, with preference given to older individuals and those in poor health.

The Society for the Orphans and Children of Ministers and Missionaries of the Presbyterian Church in Ireland

 £40,800 (2020)

Correspondent: Jason Nicholson, Glengall Exchange, 3 Glengall Street, Belfast BT12 5AB (email: info@ presbyterianchildrenssociety.org)

presbyterianchildrenssociety.org

CCNI number: NIC101833

Eligibility

Children and young people who are orphaned and whose parents were ministers, missionaries or deaconesses of the Presbyterian Church in Ireland.

The trust also gives educational grants to the children of living ministers and missionaries.

Types of grant

One-off grants are given for general welfare purposes.

Applications

Apply in writing to the correspondent.

Financial information

Year end	31/12/2020
Income	£56,900
Total expenditure	£56,000

The Society for the Relief of Poor Clergymen

 £19,700 (2019)

Correspondent: Catherine Shearn, Secretary, SRPC, c/o CPAS, Unit 3, Sovereign Court One, Sir William Lyons Road, University of Warwick Science Park, Coventry CV4 7EZ (tel: 020 3652 0551; email: secretary@sprcaid.com)

srpc-aid.com

CC number: 232634

Eligibility

Licensed workers in the Anglican Church, which includes evangelical clergy, Evangelical Accredited Lay Workers (those who have been nationally selected, trained and licensed for Anglican ministry) and Church Army Officers who have been commissioned and hold the Bishop's licence. Support is also available to the widows/widowers or dependants of such people.

Types of grant

One-off grants are awarded to help the following categories of need, as stated on the society's website: removals, unexpected costs as a result of illness or bereavement, support to enable young people to gain ministry experience during a gap year before university, support to enable children/young people of evangelical ministers to attend Christian camps, or for any other special needs at the discretion of the trustees. While the charity does not fund school fees, it does make grants for 'special tuition fees' and for other costs associated with education.

Exclusions

Grants cannot be given for travel expenses or school fees. No recurrent grants are awarded.

Applications

Application forms are available to download from the fund's website or can be requested from the correspondent and should be returned by email or post.

The trustees meet in March, May and October to consider applications. Applications should be submitted by the second week of the preceding month.

Financial information

Year end	31/12/2019
Income	£26,200
Total expenditure	£23,400

Further financial information

Grants were broken down in the 2019 accounts as follows: special needs, including illness and encouragement (20 grants totalling £8,500); youth camps (18 grants totalling £7,200); bereavement (8 grants totalling £4,000). The average grant award was £430.

Sola Trust

 £322,800 (2019/20)

Correspondent: The Trustees, Greenend Barn, Wood End Green, Henham, Bishop's Stortford CM22 6AY (tel: 01279 850819; email: admin@solatrust.org.uk)

www.solatrust.org.uk

CC number: 1062739

Eligibility

Individuals training for full-time Christian work, either at a theological college or at a church, as well as those already involved in full-time ministry.

Types of grant

One-off grants are made according to need to support those undertaking education and training, whether at a theological college or apprentice style at a church.

Exclusions

The trust generally will not provide support beyond one year and aims to avoid being the sole source of funding for any applicant.

Applications

Apply in writing to the correspondent.

Financial information

Year end	31/03/2020
Income	£451,500
Total expenditure	£322,800

Further financial information

In 2019/20 the trust made grants as follows: theological and ministry training grants (£272,000 to 101 individuals); PhD studies (£32,500 to 6 individuals); other ministry grants (£13,000 to 4 individuals); relief of poverty (£5,300 to 2 individuals).

Other information

The charity also supports churches and the redistribution of trained gospel workers to new geographical areas.

Thornton Fund

£5,200 (2020)

Correspondent: Jane Williams, 93 Fitzjohn Avenue, Barnet, Hertfordshire EN5 2HR (tel: 020 8440 2211; email: djanewilliams@dsl.pipex. com)

CC number: 226803

Eligibility

Ministers of the Unitarian Church and students training for the Unitarian ministry.

Types of grant

Grants are given for welfare needs and towards training costs.

Applications

Apply in writing to the correspondent.

Financial information

Year end	31/12/2020
Income	£20,700
Total expenditure	£11,500

Further financial information

Full accounts were not available to view on the Charity Commission's website due to the fund's low income. We have therefore estimated the fund's grant total based on its total expenditure.

Other information

The fund occasionally for project grants to the general assembly of Unitarian and Free Christian Churches.

WODS (The Widows, Orphans and Dependants Society of the Church in Wales)

£ £92,300 (2020)

Correspondent: Louise Davies, Hon. Secretary, 2 Callaghan Square, Cardiff CF10 5BT (tel: 029 2034 8228; email: ledavies@churchinwales.org.uk)

 www.churchinwales.org.uk

CC number: 503271

Eligibility
Widows, orphans and dependants of deceased clergy of the Church in Wales who are living on a low income.

Types of grant
One-off grants according to need.

Applications
Apply in writing to the correspondent. Applications should be made through one of the six diocesan committees of the Church in Wales.

Financial information
Year end	31/12/2020
Income	£93,400
Total expenditure	£92,300

Further financial information
Grants were made to 60 individual beneficiaries in 2020.

Retail

BHS Trust Fund

£ £108,900 (2019/20)

Correspondent: The Fund Secretary, PO Box 7762, 36 Playford Close, Rothwell, Kettering NN14 6TU (tel: 07495 723550; email: contactus@bhstrustfund.com)

 https://bhstrustfund.com

CC number: 1171705

Eligibility
Former employees of BHS who were employed for a minimum of 12 months and their families.

Types of grant
Grants are given for a range of purposes including utility bill arrears, mortgage and rent arrears, white goods, household repairs, funeral costs, essential food needs, emergency travel costs, heating and so on. The fund also awards Christmas grants.

In addition to grants, the fund provides an annual holiday abroad for individuals in need of a break due to circumstances such as bereavement, recovery from surgery/illness, relationship breakdown, respite from being a carer and so on. As well as this, the fund also offers short breaks in the UK to individuals and families who are facing challenges.

Exclusions
According to its website, the fund cannot provide support for the following:
- Educational grants
- Private Health care – including dependants
- Childcare/nursery costs
- Long term financial support
- Nursing home costs
- Personal loans

Applications
Contact the fund by email, phone or social media to make an application.

Financial information
Year end	31/05/2020
Income	£90,400
Total expenditure	£211,600

Further financial information
During 2019/20, a total of 102 grants were awarded to individuals. Some individuals received more than one grant. Grants were distributed as follows: hardship grants (£85,800); annual holiday (£23,100).

Boots Benevolent Fund

£ £211,200 (2019/20)

Correspondent: Fund Administrators, D90 Boots Support Office, 1 Thane Road West, Nottingham NG90 1BS (tel: 0115 959 1285; email: bbf@boots.co.uk)

 www.boots-uk.com/corporate-social-responsibility/what-we-do/workplace/boots-benevolent-fund

CC number: 1046559

Eligibility
Current and former employees of Boots UK Ltd and their dependants.

Types of grant
Grants can be given for:
- Utility, rent and Council Tax arrears
- Funeral expenses (including travel costs)
- Essential medical aids
- Essential white goods and furniture
- Essential living expenses
- Bankruptcy and Debt Relief Order fees
- Rent and deposit if the applicant is homeless or their health and safety is at risk
- Car repairs in remote locations

Supermarket vouchers and Christmas gifts are also awarded and the fund can offer interest-free loans.

Applications
Current employees can apply through LifeWorks. Former employees can download the application form online to be submitted by email or post.

Financial information
Year end	31/08/2020
Income	£257,700
Total expenditure	£288,400

Further financial information
Grants were broken down as follows:

Financial hardship grants	195	£174,600
Supermarket vouchers	-	£36,100
Christmas grants	2	£500

The fund also offers interest-free loans. These haven't been included in the grant total but seven loans were granted in 2019/20 totalling £9,700.

BOSS Benevolent Fund

£ £74,200 (2019)

Correspondent: The Trustees, 2 Villiers Court, Meriden Business Park, Copse Drive, Coventry, Warwickshire CV5 9RN (tel: 01676 526048; email: info@bossfederation.co.uk)

 www.bossfederation.co.uk

CC number: 279029

Eligibility
Current and former employees of the office products and stationery industry who are in need. Applicants must have a minimum of two years employment within the industry. The dependants of such people are also eligible for support.

Types of grant
One-off grants towards, for example, school uniforms, mobility equipment, replacement windows and housekeeping costs. Recurrent grants are also available.

Applications
Applicants should contact the fund by telephone for an initial consultation. A representative of the charity will then make arrangements to visit the applicant in their home to get a better understanding of their current circumstances.

Financial information
Year end	31/12/2019
Income	£70,800
Total expenditure	£89,100

Further financial information
The fund awarded grants to 189 individuals.

Butchers' and Drovers' Charitable Institution (BDCI)

 £78,100 (2019)

Correspondent: The Trustees, 4 Victoria Square, St Albans, Hertfordshire AL1 3EJ (tel: 01727 896094; email: info@bdci.org.uk)

 www.bdci.org.uk

CC number: 1155703

Eligibility

People in the UK, who work or have worked in any aspect of the meat industry and their widows, widowers, partners and dependent children.

Types of grant

One-off grants are provided to help towards major expenses. Assistance is also provided for residential or nursing home fees.

Applications

Application forms can be downloaded from the charity's website.

Financial information

Year end	31/12/2019
Income	£662,100
Total expenditure	£537,600

The George Drexler Foundation

 £110,000 (2019/20)

Correspondent: The Trustees, 38–43 Lincoln's Inn Fields, London WC2A 3PE (tel: 020 7869 6086; email: info@georgedrexler.org.uk)

 www.georgedrexler.org.uk

CC number: 313278

Eligibility

Welfare

Former employees of the Ofrex group and their families. Grants are also made to individuals formerly employed in commerce and their families.

Education

Individuals engaged in full-time undergraduate or postgraduate education in any field. The foundation's website states:

It is a strict requirement of the Foundation that a personal or family link with commerce is established for an application to be considered. To qualify either the applicant, the applicant's parents or grandparents must have worked in or owned a commercial business.

Individuals studying music or medicine at one of the following universities should contact the school directly as applications for individual bursaries will not be accepted:

- University of Liverpool
- University College London
- Peninsula School of Medicine and Dentistry
- University of Nottingham, Royal Academy of Music
- Guildhall School of Music and Drama
- Royal College of Music
- Purcell School

Types of grant

Welfare

One-off grants according to need.

Education

Annual bursaries, between £500 and £2,000, to relieve financial hardship while studying.

Exclusions

Education

Support is not given for:
- Overseas students
- Volunteering
- Part-time study
- Study abroad
- Medical electives
- Gap year projects
- Non-UK citizens.

Applications

Welfare

Initial enquiries can be submitted via the contact form on the foundation's website.

Education

The application guidelines state:

Bursaries are made annually, with applications considered by the Trustees in May each year. Completed applications must be submitted online via the Foundation's website by 31 March. All applicants will be notified of the outcome by early June.

Note, at the time of writing (August 2021) the foundation was only accepting applications from those who received funding in the 2020/21 academic year. Visit the website for the most up-to-date information.

Financial information

Year end	30/06/2020
Income	£234,000
Total expenditure	£316,300

Other information

The foundation also makes grants to organisations.

The Drinks Trust

 £1,210,000 (2020)

Correspondent: Welfare Team, Unit 4, Baden Place, London SE1 1YW (tel: 020 3700 1970; email: info@drinkstrust.org.uk)

 https://www.drinkstrust.org.uk

CC number: 1023376

Eligibility

People living in the UK who have worked in the UK drinks industry. This includes any role involving production, distribution, sales, marketing and promotion of alcohol and any role working for a premise that is licensed to sell alcohol for on-or off-premise consumption. The length of time working in the industry varies based on the type of support required. See the trust's website for further information on eligibility.

Types of grant

One-off and recurrent grants are given for a range of purposes including, but not limited to, the following:
- Home adaptations
- Palliative care
- Furthering industry-specific education
- Education costs for minors
- Legal advice
- Funding unemployment, family crisis and funeral expenses
- Alleviating financial hardship relating to illness, life-changing disability
- White goods and furniture
- Rent/Council Tax/mortgage payments
- Clothing and food
- Disability aids
- Short-term help with bills

Further information can be found in the Welfare Policy guidance on the trust's website.

Exclusions

According to its website, the trust cannot support the following:
- Applicants that are retired but deferring claiming pension that they are entitled to
- Applicants that are incarcerated
- Applicants that are entitled to, but not claiming benefits may still be eligible, to be assessed by the Welfare Manager on a case by case basis

Funding is also not given for business costs, private debt (including credit cards/loans/finance agreements), vet bills, private medical costs and non-essential consumables.

Applications

Applications can be made via the trust's website.

Financial information

Year end	31/12/2020
Income	£2,400,000
Total expenditure	£2,050,000

Further financial information

During the financial period, grants were broken down as follows:

COVID-19 grants	2,598	£635,600
Beneficial grants	360	£349,200
One-off grants	142	£81,600
TV Licence grants	63	£9,700

Additionally, £129,000 was given as other support including Christmas gifts, counselling and legal advice.

Other information

This trust was formerly known as The Benevolent (The Wine and Spirits Trades' Benevolent Society). As well as grants, it also offers a range of vocational, practical and emotional support. This includes debt advice, well-being services and a 24/7 helpline (0800 915 4610).

The Fishmongers' and Poulterers' Institution

 £14,700 (2020)

Correspondent: Secretary, 49–51 East Road, London N1 6AH (tel: 020 355 7858; email: contact@fpicharity.org.uk)

https://www.fpicharity.org.uk

CC number: 209013

Eligibility

People in need who are, or have been, involved in the fish and poultry trades, and their dependants. Preference is given to those who have spent at least ten years in the trade.

Types of grant

The charity awards pensions and one-off grants. According to its website, grants have been awarded for mobility scooters, 'disability-friendly' home adaptations and respite care for long-term carers.

The charity has limited funds so will often make grants in collaboration with other charities in order to increase the amount awarded.

Exclusions

The charity does not support people who work or have worked in the fishing industry, nor those who work or have worked in fish and chip shops.

Applications

Application forms are available from the correspondent. Applications can be submitted directly by the individual; however, the charity's website states that decisions are made faster when applications have come via a third party, such as another charity, a local

authority, housing association or Citizens Advice.

Financial information

Year end	31/12/2020
Income	£19,500
Total expenditure	£26,800

Further financial information

Full accounts were not available to view on the Charity Commission's website due to the charity's low income. We have therefore estimated the charity's grant total based on information available in earlier accounts. In previous years the charity has spent between 50% and 60% of its total expenditure on grants and pensions to individuals.

Footwear Friends
See entry on page 126

See entry on page 126

The Ruby and Will George Trust

 £40,800 (2019/20)

Correspondent: The Trustees, 125 Cloverfield, West Allotment, Newcastle upon Tyne, Tyne and Wear NE27 0BE (tel: 0191 266 4527; email: admin@rwgt.co.uk)

www.rwgt.co.uk

CC number: 264042

Eligibility

People from a commerce background and their dependants.

Types of grant

One-off or recurrent grants for items which are needed but cannot be afforded.

Grants for educational purposes, predominantly to those in higher education.

Applications

Applications can be made through the trust's website. Applicants will need to provide a brief explanation of their connection to commerce and a recent payslip or a letter from an employers. Trustees meet four times a year to accept applications.

Financial information

Year end	05/04/2020
Income	£121,800
Total expenditure	£156,400

Further financial information

Grants were made to 34 individuals in 2019/20.

GroceryAid

 £2,660,000 (2019/20)

Correspondent: The Welfare Team, Unit 2, Lakeside Business Park, Swan Lane, Sandhurst, Berkshire GU47 9DN (tel: 01252 875925; email: welfare@ groceryaid.org.uk)

www.groceryaid.org.uk

CC number: 1095897

Eligibility

According to the charity's website, individuals may apply for a grant if they are currently working in the grocery industry and can provide evidence of the last six month's employment with the same company, or if they are no longer working in the grocery industry but have previously worked in the grocery industry for five years or more (the five years does not have to be continuous or with the same company).

Types of grant

Grants are available for individuals experiencing unexpected emergencies, a change in circumstances or a sudden gap in their income.

Applications

Application forms and further information on how to apply are available on the charity's website.

Financial information

Year end	31/03/2020
Income	£9,020,000
Total expenditure	£8,670,000

Further financial information

In 2019/20, a total of 802 individuals were awarded crisis grants, which totalled £603,000.

Other information

The charity runs a helpline to provide emotional support and advice to anyone who has worked in the industry regardless of length of service. The service is available 365 days a year on 08088 021 122. The charity also offers support and advice for a range of issues including relationships, critical incident support, money and legal advice.

The National Association of Co-operative Officials (NACO) Benevolent Fund

£2,700 (2020)

Correspondent: The Trustees, c/o USDAW, 188 Wilmslow Road, Manchester M14 6LJ (tel: 0161 224 2804; email: nacobenfund@usdaw.org.uk)

CC number: 262269

Eligibility

Current and former members of The National Association of Co-operative Officials, and their widows/widowers or dependants, who are in need.

Types of grant

Grants are awarded according to need. Our research shows that past grants have been awarded to help with bereavement costs and funeral expenses.

Applications

Apply in writing to the correspondent.

Financial information

Year end	31/12/2020
Income	£7,000
Total expenditure	£3,000

Further financial information

Full accounts were not available to view on the Charity Commission's website due to the fund's low income. We have therefore estimated the fund's grant total based on its total expenditure.

NewstrAid Benevolent Fund

 £753,300 (2020)

Correspondent: Welfare Team, Suites 2, Thremhall Estate, Start Hill, Bishop's Stortford, Hertfordshire CM22 7TD (tel: 0800 917 8616; email: oldben@ newstraid.org.uk)

 www.newstraid.org.uk

CC number: 1116824

Eligibility

People who are or have been employed in the selling and distribution of newspapers, magazines and periodicals in the UK. This includes:

- Newsagents
- Wholesaler employees
- Delivery drivers
- Packers
- Circulation employees
- Shop assistants
- Street vendors
- Distributor employees

The families and dependants of such people are also supported. Typically, individuals should have been employed in the industry for a minimum of five years.

Types of grant

The fund provides financial support in two ways:

- Regular grants – support towards everyday living costs. Regular assistance is awarded to individuals whose circumstances are unlikely to

change, for example, those who cannot work due to disability

- One-off grants – funding is given to address specific needs for those who are experiencing unexpected hardship. For example, essential living costs, household appliances, short-term care costs and disability equipment/ adaptations

Applications

Applications can be completed on the fund's website.

Financial information

Year end	31/12/2020
Income	£1,720,000
Total expenditure	£1,560,000

Pawnbrokers' Charitable Institution

 £91,100 (2019/20)

Correspondent: The Trustees, Grasmere, Deerleap Lane, Knockholt, Sevenoaks, Kent TN14 7NP (tel: 01959 439421; email: kay@the-pci.co.uk)

 https://www.the-pci.co.uk

CC number: 209993

Eligibility

Pawnbrokers who cannot manage on a state pension. Applicants must have worked in the industry for a minimum of five years. Support is extended to the dependants of such people.

Types of grant

One-off grants are awarded for emergency needs, such as stairlifts. Recurrent grants are awarded to supplement low incomes.

Applications

Apply in writing to the correspondent. The trustees meet on a monthly basis to consider grant applications.

Financial information

Year end	31/10/2020
Income	£113,500
Total expenditure	£150,300

Further financial information

The charity awarded grants to 23 individuals. Of these beneficiaries, 20 were over the age of 60, two were over the age of 40 and one was a 15-year-old. Of the 23 applicants, 15 were female and eight were male.

The National Federation of Retail Newsagents Convalescence Fund

 £13,300 (2020)

Correspondent: The Trustees, NFRN, Bede House, Belmont Business Park,

Durham DH1 1TW (tel: 020 7017 8880; email: connect@NFRN.org.uk)

 https://nfrnonline.com

CC number: 209280

Eligibility

Members of the National Federation of Retail Newsagents (NFRN) and their dependants.

Types of grant

One-off grants for convalescent holidays.

Applications

Apply in writing to the correspondent or by contacting the NFRN freephone helpline on 0800 121 6376 (020 7017 8880 from a mobile phone) or by email.

Financial information

Year end	31/12/2020
Income	£13,500
Total expenditure	£14,800

Further financial information

Full accounts were not available to view on the Charity Commission's website due to the fund's low income. We have therefore estimated the fund's grant total based on its total expenditure.

Retail Trust

 £435,800 (2019/20)

Correspondent: The Trustees, Marshall Hall, Marshall Estate, Hammers Lane, London NW7 4DQ (tel: 0808 801 0808; email: helpline@retailtrust.org.uk)

 www.retailtrust.org.uk

CC number: 1090136

Eligibility

People in need who have worked in retail or in manufacturing, wholesale or distribution for the supply of retail businesses, and their dependants. To be eligible for support, applicants must have worked in retail for a particular amount of time, the length of which varies depending on the applicant's employment situation (e.g. if they are currently employed in retail, unemployed, or retired). See the trust's website for more information.

Types of grant

Financial grants

Individuals can apply for a financial grant if they are at risk of becoming homeless or are unable to provide the basic essentials for their family.

Physical grants

Physical grants are available to those who need support over a longer period of time. Common requests the charity helps with include: disability items and aids, mobility items, home repairs and adaptations.

Emotional grants
Grants to help alleviate financial pressures that can affect people's emotional well-being. Common requests include: respite breaks, funeral expenses and food vouchers.

Educational grants
Education grants can cover university costs such as course fees and accommodation. The trust also offers a number of scholarships each year.

Exclusions
No grants are given for private medical treatment, legal fees, most personal debts or for items purchased prior to the application.

Applications
Applications can be made via the online grant portal. The application requirements are quite specific and potential applicants should read the information provided by the trust on its website before making an application.

Financial information

Year end	30/04/2020
Income	£8,990,000
Total expenditure	£8,760,000

Other information
Retail Trust provides free financial, legal, emotional, career and redundancy advice and support services for people who have been involved in retail through 'retailHUB'. More information on how to access these services is available on the trust's website or through its confidential helpline (0808 801 0808). The trust also operates Cottage Homes, which has five retirement estates across the UK (in London, Derby, Glasgow, Liverpool and Salford), providing sheltered and extra-care accommodation for people who have retired from the retail sector.

The Royal Pinner School Foundation

 £478,200 (2019/20)

Correspondent: David Crawford, Company Secretary, 110 Old Brompton Road, South Kensington, London SW7 3RB (tel: 020 7373 6168; email: admin@royalpinner.co.uk)

🌐 www.royalpinner.co.uk

CC number: 1128414

Eligibility
Children of commercial travellers, travelling sales and technical representatives and manufacturer's agents, where the family has experienced adversity or hardship. Preference is given

to individuals under the age of 25 and those whose parents are deceased.

Types of grant
One-off or recurrent grants are available for schoolchildren at any day or boarding school and for those preparing to start work. Grants can be used towards the costs of clothing, special educational needs, music and arts activities, tools, instruments, travel and so forth.

Grants are also available to students at university and further/higher education colleges. Support is given in the form of bursaries, maintenance allowances, grants towards accommodation and educational travel in the UK or abroad. The foundation will support a wide range of subjects.

Applications
Apply in writing to the correspondent. The foundation may arrange a home visit as part of the assessment process. The grants committee meets about five times a year to consider applications.

Financial information

Year end	31/03/2020
Income	£196,000
Total expenditure	£625,000

Further financial information
Grants were awarded to 153 individuals during the year.

Children at day and boarding schools	92	£299,100
Students at universities and colleges of further and higher education	64	£112,300
Special education needs, dance, drama, travel and clothing grants	20	£66,800

Other information
The foundation also offers pastoral support through home visits and other contact with the families it supports. Over a third of the trust's beneficiaries have lost a parent or have a parent with a long-term illness.

The Salespeople's Charity

 £701,300 (2020)

Correspondent: The Trustees, PO Box 366, Saltash PL12 9BA (tel: 020 3488 4888; email: info@salespeoplescharity.org.uk)

🌐 www.salespeoplescharity.org.uk

CC number: 1171272

Eligibility
The charity's website states:

> To be eligible for a grant from the Salespeople's Charity, an applicant must:

▸ Be resident in Great Britain and Northern Ireland.
▸ Be, or have been employed as a commercial, business-to-business salesperson, visiting client sites to sell and/or promote goods and/or services to the trade (not the public).
▸ Be, or have been employed in an appropriate sales role in Great Britain and/or Northern Ireland.
▸ Be, or have been employed in an appropriate sales role for a minimum of five years at some point during their career.
▸ Be in genuine financial need.

Applicants can be:

▸ In work and in financial need.
▸ Retired.
▸ Made redundant.
▸ Unable to work due to ill health or disability

Types of grant
One-off grants for items such as day-to-day living costs, rent and utility arrears, purchase of white goods and furniture and deposits.

Applications
Initial enquiries should be made by contacting the charity by phone, email or post. After this stage, a form is sent to the applicant. Once an application is received, the board makes a decision within 48 hours.

Financial information

Year end	31/12/2020
Income	£627,200
Total expenditure	£729,300

Scottish Grocers Federation Benevolent Fund

 £7,000 (2020)

Correspondent: The Grants Administrator, Federation House, 222–224 Queensferry Road, Edinburgh EH4 2BN (tel: 0131 343 3300; email: marion@sgfscot.co.uk)

🌐 https://www.sgfscot.co.uk/about/other-services/sgf-benevolent-fund

OSCR number: SC047273

Eligibility
Past members or employees of the independent grocery trade in Scotland who have been employed in the trade for a minimum of six months and are in need. Dependants, friends and family can also be supported.

Types of grant
One-off and recurrent grants are made according to need. Grants are also made to friends and family of grocers for funeral costs relating to death in service.

Applications
Application forms are available to download from the charity's website and should be returned to the correspondent via post.

Financial information
Year end	31/12/2020
Income	£33,700
Total expenditure	£22,500

Other information
Grants are also made to charitable organisations which provide support to those in need who work/have worked as an independent grocer in Scotland or that provide training to anyone who has worked as an independent grocer.

Sears Group Trust

 £169,600 (2019/20)

Correspondent: Gary Branston, The Trust Partnership Ltd, 6 Trull Farm Buildings, Trull, Tetbury, Gloucestershire GL8 8SQ (tel: 0800 368 8530; email: admin@searsgrouptrust.co.uk)

www.searsgrouptrust.org.uk

CC number: 1022586

Eligibility
Employees, former employees of Sears plc and their dependants of any company that is, or has been, associated with Sears Ltd, who are in financial need. Former companies include: Adams Childrenswear; British Shoe Corporation; Bentley Engineering Group; Curtess Footwear; Dolcis; Freeman Hardy Willis; Fosters Menswear (incorporating Dormie and Bradleys); Gilbert Rice Group; Hornes Bros; Hush Puppies; Lewis's; Mappin and Webb; Manfield; Miss Selfridge; Olympus Sportswear; Richards Shops; Robinson and Cleaver; Saxone; Saxone Lilley and Skinner; Selfridges; Sears; Shoe City; Shoe Express; Trueform; Wallis; Warehouse; Your Price.

Types of grant
The trust's website states that it may be able to provide financial assistance in purchasing items such as:
- Electric/mobility scooters specialist beds; rise and recline chairs
- Contributions towards the cost of installation of stair lifts
- Home furnishings items
- Electric equipment and "white goods", for instance fridges; freezers; ovens; washing machines
- Help towards the cost of home repairs/general maintenance

Exclusions
Funeral costs; long-term residential care fees; students and those employed on a casual basis.

Applications
Apply in writing to the correspondent.

Financial information
Year end	31/03/2020
Income	£371,600
Total expenditure	£404,300

The Benevolent Society of the Licensed Trade of Scotland

 £220,400 (2019/20)

Correspondent: Chris Gardner, Chief Executive, 79 West Regent Street, Glasgow G2 2AW (tel: 0141 353 3596; email: chris@bensoc.org.uk)

www.bensoc.org.uk

OSCR number: SC005604

Eligibility
People in need who live in Scotland and work or have worked in the licensed trade.

Types of grant
The charity's website lists the following examples of what it can award grants for:
- mental health issues
- support in covering utility and household bills
- the provision of home furnishings
- funding for injury rehabilitation equipment
- the supply of mobility and transport solutions

Applications
A short online form is available on the charity's website to assess applicants' eligibility. Alternatively, applicants can contact the correspondent by email or telephone (contact details are available on the website).

Financial information
Year end	29/02/2020
Income	£488,200
Total expenditure	£565,600

Further financial information
Grants were broken down as follows: pensions (£125,900); grants (£32,500); holiday gifts (£32,200); Christmas gifts (£29,900).

Other information
The charity owns the BEN Pitlochry Estate which provides accommodation for current and retired members of the industry as well respite breaks for carers. It also has a free mental health support line (0800 83 85 87).

The Timber Trades Benevolent Society

 £164,100 (2020)

Correspondent: Ivan Savage, Chief Executive Officer, 19 Church Lane, Oulton, Stone, Staffordshire ST15 8UL (tel: 0844 892 2205; email: info@ttbs.org.uk)

www.ttbs.org.uk

CC number: 207734

Eligibility
People who have worked for a minimum of ten (or five in exceptional circumstances) years for a firm engaged in the trading and distribution of wood-based products, and their dependants. Applications are also considered from employees of trussed rafter manufacturing companies, who are accredited members of the Trussed Rafter Association (TRA) subject to existing criteria and employees of accredited timber preservative processing companies.

Types of grant
Grants have been awarded towards winter fuel, phone rentals, TV sets or licences, hampers and funeral costs. Regular allowances are paid quarterly.

Exclusions
Grants are not awarded to:
- Door, window, staircase and other joinery manufacturers
- Kitchen and bedroom manufacturers
- Boat builders
- Carpenters and joiners or carpentry contractors
- Forestry operatives
- Tree Surgeons
- Furniture industry employees

Applications
Application forms are available from the correspondent. Applications can be submitted directly by the individual or through a social worker, Citizens Advice, welfare agency or other third party.

Financial information
Year end	31/12/2020
Income	£110,500
Total expenditure	£240,300

Further financial information
During the year grants were distributed as follows:
Quarterly allowances	£73,400
Winter fuel grants	£31,500
Christmas gifts	£27,000
Telephone rental	£13,300
Spring gifts	£10,200
Occasional and funeral grants	£4,500
TV rental and licences	£4,200

Science

John Murdoch's Trust

 £50,000 (2019/20)

Correspondent: Anna Bennett, The Signet Library, Parliament Square, Edinburgh, EH1 1RF (email: abennett@wssociety.co.uk)

www.wssociety.co.uk/charities/murdoch

OSCR number: SC004031

Eligibility
People in need who are over the age of 50 and have pursued science, in any of its forms, either as amateurs or professionals. Preference is given to individuals living in Scotland, or those who have a clear Scottish connection; however, people from elsewhere in the UK are also eligible.

Types of grant
Grants ranging from £500 to £2,000 are given for a range of purposes including transport, furniture, home repairs, the purchase of computers and equipment, well-being and personal expenses.

Applications
Applications can be made via the trust's website. Application forms can also be requested from the correspondent. Visit the website for current deadlines.

Financial information
Year end	05/04/2020
Income	£58,300
Total expenditure	£85,500

Further financial information
During the financial period, grants were awarded to 17 individuals.

The Royal Society of Chemistry Chemists' Community Fund

 £1,727,000 (2020)

Correspondent: Chemists' Community Fund Team, The Royal Society of Chemistry, 290–292 Science Park, Milton Road, Cambridge CB4 0WF (tel: 01223 432521; email: use the contact form available on the website)

www.rsc.org/membership-and-community/chemists-community-fund

CC number: 207890

Eligibility
Current members of the society who have been a member for a minimum of three consecutive years. Former members of the society are also eligible for support, provided they have resigned after ten years of membership rather than allowing their membership to lapse. Partners and other dependants of deceased members of the society can apply for support irrespective of membership length. There are exceptions to this criteria (particularly for students and recent graduates) so it is advised that prospective applicants contact the charity to confirm their eligibility.

Types of grant
Welfare
One-off grants have been made towards home adaptations, mobility aids, white goods and car repairs. Grants for care home top-up fees are also available. Financial grant packages are given when long-term support is needed. Packages are designed to help with general living costs for up to 12 months.

Education
Students, apprentices and those undertaking vocational training are eligible for student hardship grants. Retraining grants are available to members who wish to enhance their employment prospects. Grants can be used to help pay for course fees and other associated costs such as books and equipment. Breathing Space grants are given to recent graduates who are looking for their first jobs. One-off grants are made to help with general living costs.

Applications
Initial enquiries should be made by contacting the charity. If deemed eligible, the charity will then send you an application form. Completed forms can be sent by post or email. The committee meets quarterly to consider grant applications but if a request is deemed urgent, the committee can make decisions between meetings.

Financial information
Year end	31/12/2020
Income	£64,800,000
Total expenditure	£64,290,000

Further financial information
Grants were awarded to more than 80 individuals.

Other information
The charity provides a variety of advice and guidance services and through its partnerships with accredited counsellors, can make referrals for fast-track access to face-to-face and telephone counselling services. The charity also has a partnership with the National Autistic Society to provide its members with autism with specialist support, including guidance on how to disclose an autism diagnosis at work and tips for interacting with colleagues. The charity's Careers Team can offer confidential consultations and coaching on all aspects of job seeking, professional development and making difficult career decisions.

The Worshipful Company of Scientific Instrument Makers

 £43,900 (2019/20)

Correspondent: Clerk, Glaziers Hall, 9 Montague Close, London SE1 9DD (tel: 020 7407 4832; email: clerk@wcsim.co.uk)

https://www.wcsim.co.uk/charity/charitable-educational-trust

CC number: 221332

Eligibility
Social welfare
Members and past members of the company and their dependants.

Education
Schoolchildren, sixth formers, undergraduates and postgraduates with outstanding ability in science and mathematics and a creative and practical interest in branches of engineering connected with instrumentation and measurement.

Types of grant
Social welfare
One-off grants according to need. For example, to help with funeral costs.

Education
Postgraduate scholarships of £2,000 are awarded each year, and a further postdoctoral award (The Below Fellowship), worth £5,000, is available for continuing students. According to its website, every year the charity also funds four two-year apprenticeships for young people wishing to become apprenticed to a Liveryman. Travel grants are also available for any apprentices, scholars or freemen wishing to attend a scientific conference to present a paper.

Applications
Apply in writing to the correspondent.

Financial information
Year end	30/09/2020
Income	£90,000
Total expenditure	£101,200

Further financial information
Grants were broken down as follows: scholarships (£33,500); Beloe fellowship (£5,000); Dining scholars (£2,800); financial assistance for widows and funerals (£1,300); financial assistance to Liverymen (£1,300).

Service industry

Johnson Charitable Trust

£ £34,800 (2019/20)

Correspondent: The Trustees, Johnson Service Group plc, Unit 9, Monks Way, Preston Brook, Runcorn, Cheshire WA7 3GH (tel: 01928 704600; email: enquiries@jsg.com)

CC number: 216974

Eligibility
Current and former employees of the Johnson Group plc, and their dependants, who are in need.

Types of grant
Allowances and gifts to widows and widowers. The charity also distributes hampers at Christmas.

Applications
Apply in writing to the correspondent.

Financial information
Year end	05/04/2020
Income	£94,700
Total expenditure	£47,900

Further financial information
Grants were broken down as follows:
Christmas hampers	£34,500
Pension lunch	£270
Lifeline	£90

The Worshipful Company of Launderers Benevolent Trust Fund

£ £2,100 (2019/20)

Correspondent: Paul Higgs, Benevolent Fund Chair, Launderers Hall, 9 Montague Close, London Bridge, London SE1 9DD (email: clerk@launderers.co.uk)

 www.launderers.co.uk

CC number: 262750

Eligibility
Current or retired members of the laundry industry, and their dependants, who are in need.

Types of grant
One-off grants according to need.

Applications
Apply in writing to the correspondent.

Financial information
Year end	31/03/2020
Income	£76,800
Total expenditure	£58,700

Other information
A large portion of the fund's charitable spending is awarded to other charities local to the City of London.

Skilled crafts and trades

The Craft Bakers Benevolent and Education Fund

£ £17,400 (2020)

Correspondent: The Trustees, 21 Baldock Street, Ware, Hertfordshire SG12 9DH (tel: 01920 468061; email: info@craftbakersassociation.co.uk)

 www.craftbakersassociation.co.uk

CC number: 206691

Eligibility
Master bakers and their families who are in need. Applicants must have owned their own bakery and been a member of the National Association of Master Bakers.

Types of grant
Assistance with gas, electricity and telephone bills, decorating and equipment, or any help required which will bring relief or assistance to the beneficiary. The fund also provides quarterly grants of £200 and Christmas gifts.

Applications
Apply in writing to the correspondent.

Financial information
Year end	31/12/2020
Income	£1,000
Total expenditure	£38,600

Further financial information
Full accounts were not available to view on the Charity Commission's website due to the fund's low income. We have therefore estimated the fund's grant total based on its total expenditure.

Other information
The charity also gives grants to organisations.

The Barbers' Amalgamated Charity

£ £31,700 (2019/20)

Correspondent: The Trustees, Barber-Surgeons' Hall, 1A Monkwell Square, Wood Street, London EC2Y 5BL (tel: 020 7606 0741; email: clerk@barberscompany.org)

 www.barberscompany.org

CC number: 213085

Eligibility
Members of the medical professions or barbers' trade and their families. Preference is given to older members.

Types of grant
Pensions and one-off financial assistance.

Applications
Application forms are available on the charity website.

Financial information
Year end	31/08/2020
Income	£18,200
Total expenditure	£35,200

Further financial information
Full accounts were not available to view on the Charity Commission's website due to the charity's low income. We have therefore estimated the charity's grant total based on its total expenditure.

The Benevolent Society

£ £78,400 (2019)

Correspondent: Laura Banner, Secretary to the Trustees, Federation House, 10 Vyse Street, Hockley, Birmingham, West Midlands B18 6LT (tel: 0121 237 1138; email: laura.b.banner@gmail.com)

 www.thebenevolentsociety.co.uk

CC number: 208722

Eligibility
Welfare
People who are, or have been, engaged in the trades embraced by the British Allied Trades Federation (BATF) who are in need as a result of older age, illness, disability, or other medical conditions. Trades include the National Association of Jewellers, British Travel Goods and Accessories Association, The Giftware Association, Jewellery Distributors' Association, and the Surface Engineering Association.

Education
Education/training bursaries are available to people aged 21–35 who are planning to enter any of the trades covered by the BATF.

Types of grant

Welfare

One-off welfare grants towards the cost of, for example, white goods, carpets, televisions, clothing, shoes, spectacles and property repairs. Quarterly grants are also available.

Education

Bursaries of up £9,000 towards educational/vocational fees involved in training to work in any trade covered by the BATF.

Exclusions

Welfare

Welfare grants cannot be made for items or services where provision is deemed to be the responsibility of the Department of Social Security, the Department of Work and Pensions or local authorities.

Education

Education/training grants cannot be awarded towards the purchasing of tools and materials.

Applications

Application forms are available to download on the funder's website. The charity's qualified counsellor will usually make arrangements to visit the applicant, to fully assess their need. The charity is able to help with the completion of the application form if necessary. Trustees meet quarterly to consider grant applications.

Financial information

Year end	31/12/2019
Income	£96,300
Total expenditure	£105,500

Further financial information

During the financial year, the charity awarded 45 grants to individuals.

The Bespoke Tailors' Benevolent Association

£ £55,000 (2019/20)

Correspondent: Elizabeth Fox, Secretary, 65 Tierney Road, London SW2 4QH (tel: 07831 520801; email: elizabeth.fox@ukgateway.net)

CC number: 212954

Eligibility

Journeyman tailors and tailoresses and their dependants who are or were employed in the bespoke tailoring trade in any capacity.

Types of grant

Grants for the provision of welfare services and funding of one-off projects or treatments.

Applications

Apply in writing to the correspondent.

Financial information

Year end	03/08/2020
Income	£143,200
Total expenditure	£143,500

Further financial information

During the year grants were awarded to 28 beneficiaries.

Other information

In late 2012 the Tailors Benevolent Institute and the Master Tailors Benevolent Association merged to form the Bespoke Tailors Benevolent Association.

The Ceramic Industry Welfare Society

£ £2,700 (2020)

Correspondent: The Trustees, GMB Trade Union, Ceramics House, Garth Street, Stoke-on-Trent, Staffordshire ST1 2AB (tel: 01782 272755)

CC number: 261248

Eligibility

People employed in the ceramics industry, and their widows/widowers or dependants, who are in need.

Types of grant

Grants are given according to need.

Applications

Apply in writing to the correspondent.

Financial information

Year end	31/12/2020
Income	£3,500
Total expenditure	£2,900

Further financial information

Full accounts were not available to view on the Charity Commission's website due to the charity's low income. We have therefore estimated the charity's grant total based on its total expenditure.

Institute of Clayworkers Benevolent Fund

£ £5,200 (2019)

Correspondent: The Trustees, British Ceramic Confederation, Federation House, Station Road, Stoke-on-Trent, Staffordshire ST4 2SA (tel: 01782 572852; email: helenc@ceramfed.co.uk)

 https://www.iom3.org/international-clay-technology-association/institute-clayworkers-benevolent-fund

CC number: 212300

Eligibility

People in the clay-working industry, namely current and former employees of the British Ceramic Confederation member companies and current and former members of the institute. Dependants of such people are also eligible. Applicants will normally be unable to work due to ill health or an accident.

Types of grant

Recurrent pensions and one-off grants to relieve financial difficulty.

Applications

Application forms can be requested from the correspondent or downloaded from the fund's website.

Financial information

Year end	31/12/2019
Income	£4,000
Total expenditure	£5,800

Further financial information

Full accounts were not available to view on the Charity Commission's website due to the fund's low income. We have therefore estimated the fund's grant total based on its total expenditure.

Craft Pottery Charitable Trust

£ £5,600 (2019)

Correspondent: John Higgins, Trust Secretary and Trustee, 63 Great Russell Street, Bloomsbury, London WC1B 3BF (tel: 020 3137 0750; email: JohnHigginsceramics@gmail.com)

 https://www.craftpotters.com/craft-potters-charitable-trust

CC number: 1004767

Eligibility

People involved in the field of ceramics. Applicants must be British citizens or have permanent resident status (as defined by UK Visas and Immigration) and meet the definition of a professional artist. Further information on eligibility can be found on the trust's website.

Types of grant

The trust offers awards through the Annual Ceramic Grants programme. Awards of up to £1,000 can be given for a period of independent research, production of artworks, the development of prototypes and promotional material, participation in artists' residencies and specialised professional development activities (such as workshops or specialised training), and the production of work for public exhibitions in the UK or abroad.

Applications

Applications should include a covering email, a proposal of up to 750 words explaining why the funding is needed, a CV, an equal opportunities form (available from the trust's website) and six images of the applicant's current work. Further guidance on what should be included in the proposal can be downloaded from the trust's website.

Financial information

Year end	31/12/2019
Income	£3,500
Total expenditure	£6,200

Further financial information

The charity was not required to file accounts for the 2019 financial year; therefore, we have estimated the grant total.

The Electrical Industries Charity (also known as EEIBA)

 £732,200 (2019/20)

Correspondent: Welfare Team, Rotherwick House, 3 Thomas More Street, London E1W 1YZ (tel: 0800 652 1618; email: support@electricalcharity. org)

www.electricalcharity.org

CC number: 1012131

Eligibility

Welfare

Employees and former employees of the UK electrical and electronic industries and their families and dependants. Further eligibility guidance can be found on the charity's website. The electrical and electronic industries include: electrical and electronics retailing, lighting retailing, cable retailing, electrical and electronics distribution, lighting distribution, cable distribution, oil and gas, transmission and distribution, generation (thermal and renewables), electrical contracting and facilities management, design (electrical and mechanical engineering), lighting and cable design and installation.

Education

Apprentices who started employment after 1 July 2015, have been employed as an apprentice for at least three months and are in need. To be eligible, individuals must have obtained a GCSE grade C or above in English and Mathematics (or equivalent, for example, GCE O level or CSE grade 1) before commencing employment. If an apprentice is seeking assistance for mental health they are eligible at any time throughout their electrical apprenticeship.

Types of grant

Welfare

Grants are available for a wide range of needs, including counselling, medical costs, home repairs, disability adaptations, mobility equipment, household items, food and so on. Grants can also be given towards reskilling and training costs.

Education

Bursaries and scholarships are available to support apprentices.

Applications

Application packs and a list of guidelines are available to download from the charity's website or by calling its helpline.

Financial information

Year end	31/03/2020
Income	£2,090,000
Total expenditure	£2,580,000

Further financial information

The charity made 3,200 grants during the year. This included nine apprentice bursaries totalling £3,200.

Other information

As well as grants, the charity also provides a range of support such as legal advice, bereavement support, counselling, Employee Assistance Programmes and so on.

The Fashion and Textile Children's Trust

 £398,100 (2019/20)

Correspondent: Grants Team, The Space UK, 235 High Holborn, London WC1V 7LE (tel: 07753 605367; email: grantsadmin@ftct.org.uk)

www.ftct.org.uk

CC number: 257136

Eligibility

Children and young people under 18 whose parent(s) or full-time carer work or have worked in the UK fashion and textile retailing and manufacturing industry for at least one year (within the last nine years).

Types of grant

The trust offers the following support:

- **Grants for essential items** – such as school clothing, white goods, children's bedroom furniture, sensory toys, mobility equipment and other essential household items
- **Rehousing grants** – for families who are facing unexpected housing costs, for example if required to move by the landlord or council or where the property no longer meets the family's needs due to a health problem or disability requirements.
- **Grants for when a parent is ill** – support for parents and carers who have been diagnosed with a physical or mental condition which has affected their ability to work and the family may be struggling to provide essential items the children need.
- **Grants for kinship carers** – help for families who have taken responsibility for a child/children of a family member or friend. Grants can help to cover set-up costs for the children or support with ongoing health and well-being needs.
- **Therapy grants** – funding for a wide range of therapies to support a child's physical health, mental well-being and learning needs.
- **Specialist equipment grants** – funding for items to support children with complex health needs.

One-off grants are usually awarded but larger grants for ongoing needs can be made over a number of years. For more detailed information on all of the grant schemes visit the trust's website.

Exclusions

The trust cannot support childcare costs, house repairs/renovations, travel costs, medical and legal costs, household bills or debt repayments. See the trust's website for a more detailed list of exclusions.

Applications

In the first instance, contact the trust by telephone or by using the online enquiry form to discuss your child's needs. If the trust feels that it may be able to assist, an application form will be sent to you by post or email. Completed forms must be returned to the trust along with the required supporting documents.

Financial information

Year end	30/06/2020
Income	£371,800
Total expenditure	£849,800

Further financial information

Grants were awarded to support 824 children: 812 were new beneficiaries and 12 were ongoing. New grants were broken down as follows:

Financial hardship	£97,000
COVID-19	£80,400
Illness	£35,200
Special needs	£30,400
Redundancy	£25,400
Separation/divorce	£25,200
Disability	£16,400
Mental health	£15,700
Domestic violence	£14,500
Homelessness	£12,600
Child abuse	£4,400
Kinship carers	£4,100
Bereavement	£4,100
Substance abuse	£3,000
Harassment	£1,500

Other information

Grants may be paid directly to organisations on behalf of individuals.

The Feltmakers Charitable Foundation

 £11,800 (2019/20)

Correspondent: Clerk to the Trustees, 13 Birch Close, Farnham, Surrey GU10 4TJ (email: clerk@feltmakers.co.uk)

www.feltmakers.co.uk

CC number: 259906

Eligibility

Retired people who have been engaged in the felt or hatting trade.

Types of grant

Grants are awarded to pensioners of the trade.

Applications

Apply in writing to the correspondent.

Financial information

Year end	31/03/2020
Income	£46,200
Total expenditure	£69,400

Other information

The foundation also makes grants to organisations in the City of London.

The Furniture Makers' Company

 £124,600 (2019/20)

Correspondent: Robin Lomas, The Welfare Officer, 12 Austin Friars, London EC2N 2HE (tel: 020 7256 5558; email: clerk@furnituremakers.org.uk)

www.furnituremakers.org.uk

CC number: 1015519

Eligibility

Welfare

Current and former employees of the furnishing industry and their dependants who are in financial need. Applicants must normally have worked in the industry for a minimum of two years.

Education

People in school, college or university, or those undergoing an apprenticeship in the UK.

Types of grant

The charity's application guidelines state that grants can be awarded for:
- Essential household items
- Essential household bills
- Funeral expenses
- Disabled adaptations
- Property repairs considered essential due to age, security, or access
- Disabled/medical equipment
- Respite / convalescent breaks
- General financial hardship
- Pre-tenancy costs and removal costs
- Books to top design GCSE students
- Sponsored prizes
- Bursaries
- Seminars ran by industry-experienced individuals

The charity also provides annuities.

Bursaries are given to university students in order to complete their MA qualifications in Furniture Making and Design.

Exclusions

The charity's application guidelines state its current exclusions are:
- Assistance towards the clearance of consumer credit debt
- Bankruptcy fees and Debt Relief Orders
- Legal costs
- Private education fees
- Replacement of statutory funding
- Non-essential home improvements
- Ongoing financial assistance
- Loans of any kind
- Memorial stones
- Holidays

Applications

Application forms are available to download from the charity's website.

Financial information

Year end	30/04/2020
Income	£735,200
Total expenditure	£1,200,000

The Hair and Beauty Charity

 £264,000 (2020)

Correspondent: The Trustees, 1st Floor, 1 Abbey Court, Fraser Road, Priory Business Park, Bedford MK44 3WH (tel: 01234 831888; email: info@hairandbeautycharity.org)

https://www.hairandbeautycharity.org

CC number: 1166298

Eligibility

People who currently work in the hair and beauty industry and have done for a minimum of three years, and their families who are in need. People who have previously worked in the hair and beauty industry for at least five years may also apply, provided it was within the last 15 years.

Types of grant

Grants are given according to need.

Exclusions

Support cannot be provided for:
- Those with savings of £500, or account balances that consistently do not fall below £500
- Those with income significantly higher than their expenditure
- Business costs
- Debt (including rent arrears, bankruptcy fees, etc.)
- Major house repairs or renovations
- Training and equipment costs

Applications

Application forms are available to download from the charity's website. In order to process the application, the charity will need to know: what help is needed, why the help is needed, the applicant's length of involvement in the industry and when they last worked in the industry. The form should be completed and returned with copies of bank statements and proof of involvement in the hairdressing industry.

Financial information

Year end	31/12/2020
Income	£825,000
Total expenditure	£404,500

Leather and Hides Trades' Benevolent Institution

 £71,300 (2020)

Correspondent: Karen Harriman, Secretary, 5 Lyncroft Leys, Scraptoft, Leicester, Leicestershire LE7 9UW (tel: 07423 034807; email: lhtbisecretary@gmail.com)

www.lhtbi.org.uk

CC number: 206133

Eligibility

People who work or have worked in the leather industry for ten years or more and their dependants.

Types of grant

Quarterly recurrent grants of between £279 and £1,700 per annum. One-off grants for the payment of equipment, such as mobility scooters and stairlifts. Christmas hampers are also distributed.

Applications

Application forms can be downloaded from the charity's website and should be printed out and completed. Applications should be posted to the charity's secretary.

Financial information

Year end	31/12/2020
Income	£35,500
Total expenditure	£88,700

Scottish Association of Master Bakers Benevolent Fund

 £21,100 (2019/20)

Correspondent: The Trustees, Unit 2 Halbeath Interchange, Kingseat Road, Dunfermline, Fife KY11 8RY (tel: 01383 661555)

🌐 https://scottishbakers.org

OSCR number: SC010444

Eligibility

Members or ex-members of the Scottish Association of Master Bakers and their families who are in need. Other members of the Scottish baking industry may also be supported.

Types of grant

One-off payments for exceptional expenses such as medical equipment, mobility aids or funeral costs. The maximum grant available for one-off payments is typically £1,500.

Regular, twice-yearly payments are also available in June and December to support living expenses such as utility bills and essential travel costs or for the loss of earnings due to long-term illness or disability. The maximum grant for the twice-yearly payments is typically £500.

Exclusions

Grants are not available for:

- Expenses connected to outstanding debt, legal fees, fines, costs or damages
- Non-essential medical treatment or private medical treatment where that treatment is available through the NHS
- Work-related expenses (except for essential travel costs)
- Investments
- Car expenses
- Non-essential items where there is not a health-related need for the item
- Rent or mortgage payments
- Direct cash payments or retrospective funding

Applications

Application forms are available from the charity's website. Wherever possible, the application should be made by an employer on behalf of a former or current employee, although individuals may make applications directly if this is not possible.

Financial information

Year end	31/03/2020
Income	£23,900
Total expenditure	£23,400

Further financial information

Full accounts were not available to view on the OSCR website due to the fund's low income. We have therefore estimated the grant total based on the fund's total expenditure.

Scottish Hide and Leather Trades' Provident and Benevolent Society

 £10,000 (2020)

Correspondent: The Trustees, c/o Mitchells Roberton Solicitors, George House, 36 North Hanover Street, Glasgow G1 2AD

OSCR number: SC004504

Eligibility

Retired members of the hide and leather trades in Scotland, their widows, and children of deceased members.

Types of grant

One-off and recurrent payments in the form of grants, loans, pensions, donations and gifts.

Applications

Applications can be made in writing to the correspondent.

Financial information

Year end	31/12/2020
Income	£8,900
Total expenditure	£10,500

Further financial information

Full accounts were not available to view on the OSCR website due to the charity's low income. We have therefore estimated the grant total based on the charity's total expenditure.

The Silversmiths and Jewellers Charity

£170,000 (2020)

Correspondent: The Trustees, PO Box 61660, London SE9 9AN (tel: 020 8265 9288; email: info@thesjcharity.co.uk)

🌐 www.tsjc.org.uk

CC number: 205785

Eligibility

Any current or previous professionals in silversmithing and jewellery trades, whether in manufacturing, wholesale, retail, as an employee or self-employed.

Types of grant

The charity has two grant programmes. The Hardship Fund provides one-off grants to cover items such as wheelchairs or white goods. General Support grants are given to help with basic living costs.

Applications

Apply on a form on the charity's website or in writing to the correspondent. Applications can be submitted directly by the individual or through a social worker, Citizens Advice or other welfare agency.

Financial information

Year end	31/12/2020
Income	£95,100
Total expenditure	£201,900

Social care

Social Workers Benevolent Trust

£77,800 (2019/20)

Correspondent: Elizabeth Williams, Honorary Applications Secretary, Wellesley House, 37 Waterloo Street, Birmingham, West Midlands B2 5PP (tel: 0121 622 3911; email: swbt@basw.co.uk)

🌐 www.swbt.org

CC number: 262889

Eligibility

Social workers and their dependants who are in need. Applicants must hold a professional social work qualification. In exceptional circumstances, social workers without a professional qualification may be considered, depending on the nature and length of their employment. The charity would need to see a job description for their role, to confirm that they are in a post that would normally require a qualification.

Types of grant

Grants are made for a specific small purchases or debts.

Exclusions

Grants are not usually given for social work training and associated costs, private education fees, private health/social care or daily living expenses. Applicants are not normally considered if they have received a grant from the charity within the last year.

Applications

Application forms are available to download on the trust's website. Completed forms should be sent by email or by post to the Applications Secretary. The trustees meet approximately once every two months. For dates of upcoming meetings, see the trust's website. Applicants are advised to send their application form to the charity no later than two days before the next meeting.

Financial information

Year end	30/09/2020
Income	£83,600
Total expenditure	£82,200

Further financial information

In 2019/20, the charity received 196 applications from individuals and awarded 176 grants.

Sports

Athletics for the Young

 £12,200 (2019/20)

Correspondent: The Trustees, 12 Redcar Close, Hazel Grove, Stockport, Cheshire SK7 4SQ (tel: 0161 483 9330; email: runalan55@hotmail.com)

 www.englandathletics.org

CC number: 1004448

Eligibility

Young people aged between 13 and 25 who are in full-time education, active in athletics and eligible to compete for England.

Types of grant

Small grants of between £50 and £200 are available for costs such as equipment and travel.

Exclusions

People already receiving funding from other sources are not normally supported.

Applications

Application forms can be downloaded from the England Athletics website and should be returned via post. The deadline for applications is usually mid-February but check the website for exact dates. Note that applications should be handwritten and a reference should be attached.

Financial information

Year end	30/09/2020
Income	£5,200
Total expenditure	£13,600

Further financial information

Full accounts were not available to view on the Charity Commission's website due to the charity's low income. We have therefore estimated the charity's grant total based on its total expenditure.

BRDC Motor Sport Charity

 £20,900 (2019/20)

Correspondent: The Trustees, Eighth Floor, 6 New Street Square, London EC4A 3AQ (tel: 020 7842 2000; email: brdcmotorsportcharity@ rawlinson-hunter.com)

 www.brdc.co.uk/BRDC-Motor-Sport-Charity

CC number: 1084173

Eligibility

Members of the BRDC and other individuals involved in the motor sport industry, including their dependants.

Types of grant

According to its guidelines, the charity may help with:

- Disability equipment and adaptations
- White goods and household items
- Short-term help with living costs resulting from sickness or disability
- Nursing or residential home fees to a maximum of £100 per week (reviewed annually)
- Therapeutic support such as counselling, physiotherapy
- Debts incurred as a result of illness or disability
- Funeral costs
- Career counselling

Exclusions

According to its guidelines, the charity will not generally help with:

- Business or family debts
- Legal Fees
- Private healthcare
- Private education
- Bankruptcy fees
- University fees

Applications

Application forms can be downloaded from the charity's website.

Financial information

Year end	31/01/2020
Income	£123,400
Total expenditure	£34,400

Further financial information

In 2019/20, the charity made grants totalling £20,900 to eight individuals.

British Boxing Board of Control Charitable Trust

 £13,000 (2019)

Correspondent: Robert Smith, 14 North Road, Cardiff CF10 3DY (tel: 029 2036 7000; email: rsmith@bbbofc.com)

CC number: 1068585

Eligibility

People actively engaged, or who have been actively engaged, in the sport of professional boxing. Their dependants are also supported.

Types of grant

Grants are given according to need.

Applications

Apply in writing to the correspondent.

Financial information

Year end	31/12/2019
Income	£88,200
Total expenditure	£14,200

Further financial information

The trust's expenditure was considerably lower than in previous years.

The Joanna Brown Trust

 £3,200 (2019/20)

Correspondent: The Trustees, 13 Frederick Road, Malvern, Worcestershire WR14 1RS (tel: 01684 563235; email: info@ thejoannabrowntrust.org)

 https://www.thejoannabrowntrust. org

CC number: 1126272

Eligibility

Young athletes from across the UK who require financial support to help them excel in their chosen sport.

Types of grant

Grants of between £250 and £1,000 are available. Past examples of grants include new equipment, support with training costs and help while recovering from injuries.

Exclusions

According to the trust's website, it will not award grants for travel or accommodation costs.

Applications

Applications can be made via the trust's website.

Financial information

Year end	31/08/2020
Income	£8,000
Total expenditure	£7,000

Further financial information

Full accounts were not available to view on the Charity Commission's website due to the trust's low income. We have therefore estimated the trust's grant total based on its total expenditure.

Other information

The trust also makes grants to organisations.

The International Dance Teachers' Association Ltd Benevolent Fund

 £95,700 (2019)

Correspondent: The Trustees, International House, 76 Bennett Road, Brighton, East Sussex BN2 5JL (tel: 01273 685652; email: info@idta.co.uk)

www.idta.co.uk

CC number: 297561

Eligibility

Members and former members of the International Dance Teacher's Association, other dancers, former dancers, teachers or former teachers of dance, employees or former employees of the association, and their dependants, who are in need. Support is mainly given in cases where individuals are unable to teach or work due to sickness, injury or disability.

Types of grant

Grants of up to £1,000 are given according to need.

Applications

Apply in writing to the correspondent.

Financial information

Year end	31/12/2019
Income	£241,000
Total expenditure	£348,400

Further financial information

Grants were awarded to 45 individuals during the year.

Other information

The fund also organises various dancing events and sponsors dance-related organisations.

The Football Association Benevolent Fund

 £112,900 (2020)

Correspondent: Richard McDermott, Secretary, Wembley Stadium, PO Box 1966, London SW1P 9EQ (tel: 0800 169 1863; email: BenevolentFund@theFA.com)

www.thefa.com/about-football-association/the-fa-benevolent-fund

CC number: 299012

Eligibility

People who have been involved in Association Football in any capacity, such as players, coaches, managers and referees, and their dependants, who are in need.

Types of grant

One-off and recurrent grants are given according need.

Applications

Application forms are available from the correspondent. Applications are usually made through the County Football Associations.

Financial information

Year end	31/12/2020
Income	£135,500
Total expenditure	£164,300

Further financial information

Grants were awarded to 45 individuals in 2020.

Institute of Football Management and Administration Charity Trust

 £1,900 (2019/20)

Correspondent: The Trustees, St George's Park, Newborough Road, Needwood, Burton-on-Trent, Staffordshire DE13 9PD (tel: 01283 576350; email: ifma@lmasecure.com)

CC number: 277200

Eligibility

Current or former members of the Institute of Football Management and Administration Charity Trust, and people who work, or have worked, within professional football. Preference may be given to older people. The dependants of such people are also eligible.

Types of grant

Grants are given according to need.

Applications

Apply in writing to the correspondent.

Financial information

Year end	31/05/2020
Income	£0
Total expenditure	£4,200

Further financial information

Full accounts were not available to view on the Charity Commission's website due to the charity's low income. We have therefore estimated the charity's grant total based on its total expenditure.

Grand Prix Trust

 £41,400 (2020)

Correspondent: Sally Oliver, Client Co-ordinator, 6 New Street Square, New Fetter Lane, London EC4A 3AQ (tel: 07487 416398 or 020 7842 2000; email: sally@grandprixtrust.com or office@grandprixtrust.com)

 https://www.grandprixtrust.com

CC number: 327454

Eligibility

Current and former employees or contract staff who have been employed on Formula 1 activities for two years or more. This includes:

- F1 mechanics/operational travelling staff
- Other F1 travelling non-operational staff
- F1 factory-based personnel
- F1 contractors
- All motorsport industry employees
- Agency personnel, photographers, catering and media staff from F1-related companies
- FIA/FOM employees

Support is extended to the immediate families of such individuals.

Types of grant

Grants are given according to need. In the past, grants have been given towards respite daycare, medical costs, living costs, funeral costs and so on.

Applications

Application forms can be downloaded from the trust's website. If necessary, the trust can arrange a home visit for help with completing an application form.

Financial information

Year end	31/12/2020
Income	£163,800
Total expenditure	£143,300

Other information

The trust also offers advice and guidance to beneficiaries.

The Hornsby Professional Cricketers Fund

 £40,300 (2019/20)

Correspondent: S. P. Coverdale, Scheme Secretary, 1 Court Cottages, Overstone Park, Overstone, Northampton, Northamptonshire NN6 0AP (tel: 01604 643070; email: covers0783@gmail.com)

CC number: 235561

Eligibility

Former professional cricketers, and their dependants, who are in need.

Types of grant

One-off and recurrent grants are awarded according to need. These include monthly payments, special payments at Christmas and in summer, and grants to help with winter heating bills or to help with an urgent need. Grants are also given for medical assistance and treatment and specialist equipment (electric wheelchairs, stairlifts, etc.).

Applications

Apply in writing to the correspondent. The trustees meet twice a year.

Financial information

Year end	31/05/2020
Income	£42,200
Total expenditure	£46,800

Further financial information

During the 2019/20 financial period, the charity awarded grants to 11 individuals. Grants were broken down as follows:

Regular monthly allowances	£21,400
Summer allowances	£5,600
Winter allowances	£5,600
Heating allowances	£5,500
Allowances to former Walter Hammond Memorial Fund recipients	£1,200
Additional special grants	£1,000

The Ice Hockey Players Benevolent Fund

 £990 (2019/20)

Correspondent: Andrew Collins, Trustee, 25 Caxton Avenue, Addlestone, Surrey KT15 1LJ (tel: 01932 843660; email: info@ihpbf.com or andycollins@ihpbf.com)

www.ihpbf.com

CC number: 1053566

Eligibility

Ice hockey players, coaches and officials who are unable to earn a living as a result of illness or injury. Applicants must have been registered to play in Great Britain at some point during their career. Support is extended to the dependants of such people.

Types of grant

Grants and loans are awarded according to need. Grants have previously been made for dental and medical treatment.

Applications

Initial enquiries should be made using the form on the fund's website.

Financial information

Year end	31/05/2020
Income	£100
Total expenditure	£1,100

Further financial information

Full accounts were not available to view on the Charity Commission's website due to the fund's low income. We have therefore estimated the fund's grant total based on its total expenditure.

Other information

The charity can also provide subsidised accommodation to eligible beneficiaries.

In the Game

 £16,800 (2019/20)

Correspondent: The Trustees, National Football Centre, Newborough Road, Needwood, Burton-on-Trent DE13 9PD (tel: 01283 576350; email: lma@leaguemanagers.com)

www.leaguemanagers.com

CC number: 1016248

Eligibility

Members and former members of the League Managers Association who are in need and their wives, widows and children or dependants.

Types of grant

The charity's website suggests that grants may be used for medical and mobility expenses, education and coaching bursaries, and general welfare.

Applications

Apply in writing to the correspondent. Applications are considered throughout the year.

Financial information

Year end	30/06/2020
Income	£70,600
Total expenditure	£99,600

Other information

The charity also makes grants to organisations (£13,800 in 2019/20).

The Injured Jockeys Fund

 £664,700 (2019/20)

Correspondent: The Trustees, Peter O'Sullevan House, 7A Newmarket Road, Newmarket, Suffolk CB8 7NU (tel: 01638 662246; email: alice.wood@ijf.org.uk or use the contact form on the website)

www.injuredjockeys.co.uk

CC number: 1107395

Eligibility

Professional or amateur jockeys (including apprentice, conditional and point-to-point riders) who have been injured and their families. Applicants must hold (or have held) a licence issued by the British Horseracing Authority.

Types of grant

Immediate financial assistance for things such as temporary accommodation, travel expenses, regular bills and hospital transfers after injury. The charity also provides holidays and one-off and regular payments according to need.

Applications

Contact the fund for further information.

Financial information

Year end	31/03/2020
Income	£4,980,000
Total expenditure	£4,920,000

Further financial information

In 2019/20, grants were made to 361 injured jockeys totalling £664,700.

Other information

The Injured Jockey Fund also runs three rehabilitation and fitness centres, in Lambourn, Malton and Newmarket.

The Johnners Trust

 £13,800 (2019/20)

Correspondent: Richard Anstey, Trust Administrator, c/o The Lord's Taverners, Brian Johnston Memorial Trust, 90 Chancery Lane, London WC2A 1EU (tel: 020 7025 0000; email: bjmt@lordstaverners.org)

www.lordstaverners.org

CC number: 1045946

Eligibility

Emerging young cricketers who are in need of financial assistance to further their personal and cricketing development.

Types of grant

Scholarships are available for young cricketers at county academy and university level, towards travel, equipment and coaching.

Applications

Apply in writing to the correspondent.

Financial information

Year end	30/09/2020
Income	£54,900
Total expenditure	£42,100

Other information

The trust is administered by the Lord's Taverners. It provides the annual Brian Johnston Scholarship for promising young cricketers and also supports cricket for blind and visually impaired people.

PGA European Tour Benevolent Trust

 £112,900 (2019)

Correspondent: David Park, European Tour Building, Wentworth Drive, Virginia Water, Surrey GU25 4LX (tel: 01344 840400; email: dpark@europeantour.com)

https://www.europeantour.com/european-tour/news/articles/detail/european-tour-benevolent-trust

CC number: 327207

Eligibility
Members and former members of the PGA European Tour and other individuals whose main livelihood is, or has been, earned by providing services to professional golf. The dependants of such individuals may also apply.

Types of grant
One-off or recurrent grants are given according to need.

Applications
Contact the correspondent for more information or to make an application.

Financial information
Year end	31/12/2019
Income	£8,900
Total expenditure	£124,500

Further financial information
Full accounts were not available to view on the Charity Commission's website due to the trust's low income. We have therefore estimated the trust's grant total based on its total expenditure.

The Professional Billiards and Snooker Players Benevolent Fund

 £54,500 (2019/20)

Correspondent: Neil Tomkins, Player Relations Manager, World Snooker Ltd, 75 Whiteladies Road, Clifton, Bristol BS28 2NT (tel: 0117 317 8200; email: neil.tomkins@wpbsa.com)

https://wpbsa.com/players/support/benevolent-fund

CC number: 288352

Eligibility
Current or former professional billiards and snooker players who are or have been members of the World Professional Billiards and Snooker Association (WPBSA) and are in need as a result of ill health, disability or bereavement. Support is also extended to the dependants (aged 18 and above) of such people.

Types of grant
One-off grants are awarded according to need. According to the charity's website, the trustees currently prioritise the following:

- One-off payments to dependants following the death of a professional snooker/billiards player towards 'modest debts and immediate liabilities', including funeral expenses.
- Grants to cover the cost of private medical insurance policies for professional snooker or billiards players (past and present) who have acquired an injury related to the sport or who are of ill health.
- Loans to help with a specific temporary situation, for which repayment is possible over a specific period of time.

Exclusions
The website states the following:

'The Trustees have recently decided that they will no longer be able to provide financial assistance to tour players struggling with the cost of playing on the tour and that whilst they will consider all applications put to the board on a case by case basis, applications for such financial assistance are not likely to be approved.

Low priority is given to those who are experiencing financial hardship as a result of debt, substance misuse, gambling or any other addiction.

Applications
Application forms are available to download on the charity's website. Completed forms should be sent to the correspondent by post. For loans, applicants will have to clearly identify how the loan will be repaid over a period of time.

Financial information
Year end	30/06/2020
Income	£18,700
Total expenditure	£60,600

Further financial information
Full accounts were not available to view on the Charity Commission's website due to the fund's low income. We have therefore estimated the fund's grant total based on its total expenditure.

The Professional Footballers' Association Charity

 £1,070,000 (2019/20)

Correspondent: The Trustees, 20 Oxford Court, Bishopsgate, Manchester M2 3WQ (tel: 0161 236 0575; email: info@thepfa.co.uk)

https://www.thepfa.com/charity

CC number: 1150458

Eligibility
Former professional footballers, current and former trainee footballers and young people registered with professional football academies (or centres of excellence) associated with a football club who wish to pursue a career as a professional footballer.

Types of grant
Welfare grants are awarded according to need.

Standard grants are made for all academic courses that carry a nationally recognised qualification. Grants are given towards course fees (usually 50% up to a maximum of £1,500 per year) and can be applied for upon completion of training. University bursaries are also available.

Applications
Contact the charity for information on how to apply for a welfare grant. For educational grants, application forms are available to download on the funder's website. Full guidance notes can also be seen on the website. Completed forms should be sent to PFA Education Department, 11 Oxford Court, Bishopsgate, Manchester, M2 3WQ.

Financial information
Year end	30/06/2020
Income	£20,460,000
Total expenditure	£21,700,000

Further financial information
During the 2019/20 financial period, the charity awarded 737 welfare grants and 1,397 educational/vocational grants.

Other information
The charity operates a 24/7 counselling helpline for current and former players, and concerned family/friends to seek confidential advice and support. Contact the helpline on 07500 000 777. The charity also offers subsidised coaching courses (FA Level 2 and UEFA B qualifications) to current and former footballers. Grants are also made to organisations.

Racehorse Trainers Benevolent Fund

 £650 (2020)

Correspondent: Chief Executive, National Trainers Federation, 9 High Street, Lambourn, Hungerford, Berkshire RG17 8XL (tel: 07899 797010; email: rtbf@racehorsetrainers.org)

https://www.racehorsetrainers.org/ntf/ntf.asp

CC number: 1172296

Eligibility

Current or former racehorse trainers in the UK who are in need due to exceptional events beyond their control (such as an accident, illness, bereavement, animal disease or environmental factors). Applicants must currently be, or formerly have been, licensed by the British Horseracing Authority and have been a member of the National Trainers Federation for at least four years.

Types of grant

Grants are given according to need.

Exclusions

Grants will not be given towards the following:

▶ Anything that should be a statutory entitlement
▶ Legal fees
▶ Business finance
▶ Non-priority debts (for example, credit cards) or unsecured bank loans and loans from family and friends
▶ Applicants who could have reasonably avoided the event that has led to the grant being needed

Applications

Application forms can be downloaded from the National Trainers Federation website. Evidence of income and savings is required. All applications must include a referee.

Financial information

Year end	31/12/2020
Income	£15,100
Total expenditure	£720

Further financial information

Full accounts were not available to view on the Charity Commission's website due to the fund's low income. We have therefore estimated the grant total based on the fund's total expenditure.

Racing Welfare

 £244,000 (2020)

Correspondent: The Welfare Team, 20B Park Lane, Newmarket, Suffolk CB8 8QD (tel: 01638 560763; email: info@racingwelfare.co.uk)

 www.racingwelfare.co.uk

CC number: 1084042

Eligibility

People in need who are, or have been, employed in the horseracing and breeding industry, and their dependants.

Types of grant

Grants are made for the welfare, health and education needs. Items with which the charity may be able to help include: mobility equipment; counselling; utility bills; food; housing costs in emergency situations; physiotherapy; and white goods.

Applications

Apply in writing to the correspondent.

Financial information

Year end	31/12/2020
Income	£5,360,000
Total expenditure	£3,700,000

Other information

The charity's main activity is the provision of support and guidance through its welfare officers based all over the country, who offer information and advice, including on financial and personal issues, health and housing. There is also a 24-hour helpline (0800 6300 443) offering advice.

The Referees' Association Members Benevolent Fund

 £3,900 (2020/21)

Correspondent: The Trustees, 4 Ffinch Close, Ditton, Aylesford, Kent ME20 6ET (tel: 02476 420 360 or 07759280402; email: benevolentfund@the-ra.org)

 the-ra.org

CC number: 800845

Eligibility

Members and former members of the Referees' Association in England and their dependants who are in need.

Types of grant

Grants are given to relieve immediate financial need.

Applications

Contact the charity for further information. Members can access an application form in the members' area of the Referees' Association's website.

Financial information

Year end	31/03/2021
Income	£9,800
Total expenditure	£4,300

Further financial information

Full accounts were not available to view on the Charity Commission's website due to the fund's low income. We have therefore estimated the fund's grant total based on its total expenditure.

The RFL Benevolent Fund (Try Assist)

 £172,800 (2020)

Correspondent: The Trustees, Red Hall, Red Hall Lane, Leeds, West Yorkshire LS17 8NB (tel: 0330 111 1113; email: info@tryassist.co.uk)

 www.rflbenevolentfund.co.uk

CC number: 1109858

Eligibility

People who play or assist, or who have played or assisted, in the game of rugby league in the UK (or for a team affiliated to an association primarily based in the UK) who have sustained a serious/life-changing injury while engaging in the sport. Support is also extended to the dependants of such people.

Types of grant

Welfare

Welfare grants are available towards the costs of, for example, vehicle adaptations, housing modifications, holidays, household appliances and physiotherapy.

Education

Educational grants are available to support the education or retraining of beneficiaries.

Applications

Initial enquiries should be made by contacting the charity.

Financial information

Year end	31/12/2020
Income	£437,900
Total expenditure	£336,000

The Speedway Riders' Benevolent Fund

 £89,000 (2019)

Correspondent: S. J. Babb, Secretary, 2 Estuary View, Victory Boulevard, Lytham, Lytham St Annes FY8 5TU (tel: 07816 652107; email: ackroyd-p@hotmail.co.uk)

 https://www.srbf.co.uk

CC number: 208733

Eligibility

Speedway riders who have sustained a serious injury while speedway racing for British-based teams. Support is extended to the dependants of such people.

Types of grant

One-off grants have been given towards, for example, mobility aids and home adaptations. Long-term financial assistance is also available.

Applications

Apply in writing to the correspondent.

Financial information

Year end	31/12/2019
Income	£133,900
Total expenditure	£107,700

Further financial information

During the financial year, the charity awarded grants to 44 beneficiaries.

Tottenham Tribute Trust

 £9,800 (2019/20)

Correspondent: The Trustees, Edelman House, 1238 High Road, London N20 0LH (tel: 020 8492 5600)

 www.tottenhamtt.org

CC number: 1094092

Eligibility

Current or former players and staff in the field of professional or amateur football in the UK who are in need. Priority is given to those who work or play for (or have worked or played for) Tottenham Hotspur football club.

Types of grant

Grants are awarded according to need.

Exclusions

If a grant is awarded, beneficiaries cannot reapply for funding for two years. If unsuccessful, applicants can reapply six months after their first attempt.

Applications

Application forms are available on the trust's website. Completed application forms should be submitted to the address specified on the application form via post.

Financial information

Year end	31/03/2020
Income	£2,000
Total expenditure	£10,900

Further financial information

Full accounts were not available to view on the Charity Commission's website due to the trust's low income. We have therefore estimated the trust's grant total based on its total expenditure.

Welsh Rugby Charitable Trust

 £360,100 (2019/20)

Correspondent: Peter Owens, Trust Secretary, 48 Rhys Road, Blackwood, Caerphilly, Gwent NP12 3QR (tel: 07854 488258; email: powens@wru.wales)

 https://www.wrct.co.uk

CC number: 502079

Eligibility

Welsh Rugby Union players who have been severely injured while playing rugby, and their dependants.

Types of grant

Grants are given to help injured players regain their independence. This could include the costs of families' hospital visits, home adaptations, mobility aids, rehabilitation and retraining. The trust also provides Christmas and summer grants.

Applications

According to our previous research, applications should be made in writing to the correspondent, including the circumstances of the injury and the effect it has had on the applicant's career. Information on the applicant's financial position before and after the accident should also be included. Applications are considered every two months.

Financial information

Year end	30/11/2020
Income	£169,800
Total expenditure	£376,700

Further financial information

During 2019/20, 35 injured players were receiving ongoing support from the trust. Grants were distributed as follows:

Relief of injured rugby players	£249,400
Summer grants for injured rugby players	£58,900
Christmas grants	£30,800
Other financial support	£21,000

Welsh Rugby International Players Benevolent Association

 £18,500 (2019/20)

Correspondent: The Trustees, 75 Village Farm Road, Village Farm Industrial Estate, Pyle, Bridgend CF33 6BN (tel: 07860 739222; email: enquiries@jjwilliamsltd.com)

 wrex.co.uk

CC number: 1102484

Eligibility

Welfare

Current and former Welsh international rugby players and their families or dependants who are in need. This includes those requiring medical treatment for an injury or physical/mental health illness relating to their time playing rugby and those whose earning capacity has been adversely impacted by injuries or illnesses relating to their time in the sport.

Types of grant

One-off grants according to need.

Applications

Apply in writing to the correspondent.

Financial information

Year end	30/04/2020
Income	£16,400
Total expenditure	£20,600

Further financial information

Full accounts were not available to view on the Charity Commission's website due to the charity's low income. We have therefore estimated the charity's grant total based on its total expenditure.

Transport and travel

ABTA LifeLine (The ABTA Benevolent Trust)

 £52,100 (2020)

Correspondent: The Trustees, 30 Park Street, London SE1 9EQ (tel: 020 3117 0500; email: lifeline@abtalifeline.org.uk)

 www.abtalifeline.org.uk

CC number: 295819

Eligibility

People in need who are or have been employed by ABTA members, ABTA itself, or other organisations within the industry who are engaged in the sale of ABTA products, and their dependants.

Types of grant

Grants have been awarded for mobility equipment, disability and health needs, funeral costs, emergency home repairs, boiler breakdown costs, utility bills, and rent or mortgage arrears. Note that this list is not exhaustive.

Exclusions

The charity generally does not have any restrictions in terms of grant criteria; however, statutory help and assistance from other appropriate authorities or supportive agencies should be exhausted before applying for a grant from the charity.

Applications

There is an eligibility form that can be completed online or requested from the correspondent. Once the charity has confirmed your eligibility, an application form will be sent out.

Financial information

Year end	31/12/2020
Income	£117,800
Total expenditure	£182,100

Further financial information

57 grants were awarded to individuals during 2020.

The Air Pilots Benevolent Fund

 £9,600 (2019/20)

Correspondent: Sqn Ldr C. J. Ford, Almoner, c/o The Honourable Company of Air Pilots, Air Pilots House, 52A Borough Street, London SE1 1XN (tel: 01276 47050; email: office@airpilots. org)

https://www.airpilots.org/about-the-company/trusts/the-air-pilots-benevolent-fund

CC number: 212952

Eligibility

Members of The Honourable Company of Air Pilots and those who have been engaged professionally as air pilots or air navigators in commercial aviation, and their dependants. People who want to become pilots or wish to gain further qualifications in the aviation industry are supported by The Honourable Company of Air Pilots.

Types of grant

Social welfare

Regular and one-off grants or loans to alleviate poverty or assist in the rehabilitation of people after accidents. Examples of needs the fund may be able to help with include: home adaptations; travel for hospital visits; ongoing support to avoid fuel poverty; and funding revalidation of licences to in order to re-enter employment.

Education

Apprenticeships, scholarships and bursaries, including support for flying instructor development. Academic bursaries awarded at City University to students. Awards towards the general educational needs of the dependants of aviators.

Applications

Contact the correspondent for an application form.

Financial information

Year end	30/09/2020
Income	£37,900
Total expenditure	£20,500

Further financial information

During the year, the fund awarded £7,600 of benevolence grants and £2,000 towards flying instructor apprenticeships.

Other information

The charity was previously called The Guild of Air Pilots Benevolent Fund and provides both educational and welfare support. The fund is administered by The Honourable Company of Air Pilots, which also manages the Air Safety Trust and Air Pilots Trust.

Associated Society of Locomotive Engineers and Firemen (ASLEF) Hardship Fund

 £15,000 (2020)

Correspondent: The General Secretary, 77 St John Street, Clerkenwell, London EC1M 4NN (tel: 020 7324 2400; email: info@aslef.org.uk)

www.aslef.org.uk

Eligibility

Members of ASLEF, and their dependants, who are in need.

Types of grant

One-off grants are given according to need.

Applications

Apply in writing to the correspondent.

Further financial information

Financial information was not available for the fund. According to ASLEF's 2020 annual return, hardship payments awarded during the year totalled £15,000. We have taken this figure to be the fund's grant total.

Other information

The fund is not a registered charity.

British Airline Pilots Association Benevolent Fund (BALPA)

 £13,400 (2019/20)

Correspondent: The Trustees, 5 Heathrow Boulevard, 278 Bath Road, Sipson, West Drayton, London UB7 0DQ (tel: 020 8476 4000; email: balpa@balpa.org)

https://www.balpa.org/About/BALPA-Benevolent-Fund

CC number: 229957

Eligibility

Current or retired British commercial airline pilots, flight engineers and helicopter winchmen. Support is also available to the dependants of such people.

Types of grant

Financial assistance through grants or loans. Support may also be provided for education or retraining to realise a firm flying job offer or to pursue new opportunities beyond flying.

Applications

Application packs can be downloaded from the charity's website.

Financial information

Year end	05/04/2020
Income	£42,200
Total expenditure	£30,500

British Airways Welfare and Benevolent Fund

 £69,800 (2019)

Correspondent: The Trustees, International House, 24 Holborn Viaduct, London EC1A 2BN (email: ba.benevolentfund@ba.com)

https://www.ba-touchdown.com/bawb

CC number: 282480

Eligibility

Current and former British Airways employees (or employees of its preceding companies or corporations) who are in need. Support is extended to the spouses and dependants of such people, including the dependants of deceased employees.

Types of grant

One-off grants are given towards the purchase of necessary goods or services. Previously, grants have been given towards mobility aids or special equipment, household appliances and property maintenance/adaptations.

Exclusions

The fund cannot provide ongoing support nor can it help to clear debts or assist with the cost of private medical treatment, private education or air travel.

Applications

Contact the fund via email. All applicants will be visited by a BA-appointed caseworker, who will assist them in completing the application.

Financial information

Year end	31/12/2019
Income	£547,800
Total expenditure	£79,700

Further financial information

During 2019, grants were made to 40 individuals.

The British Guild of Tourist Guides Benevolent Fund

 £16,700 (2019)

Correspondent: Elizabeth Keatinge, c/o BGTG, Unit 5 Baden Place, London SE1 1YW (tel: 01980 623463; email: ekeatinge.lake@talk21.com)

https://www.itg.org.uk/news-and-events/tourism-industry-news/bgtg-benevolent-fund

CC number: 211562

Eligibility
Registered tourist guides who are in need and have been qualified for at least one year, and former and retired guides who have been qualified for five years or more. The dependants of guides qualified for at least five years may also be eligible for support.

Types of grant
Grants are given according to need.

Applications
Apply in writing to the correspondent. A list of trustees who may be contacted can be found online.

Financial information
Year end	31/12/2019
Income	£13,700
Total expenditure	£18,600

Further financial information
Full accounts were not available to view on the Charity Commission's website due to the fund's low income. We have therefore estimated the fund's grant total based on its total expenditure.

The London Shipowners' and Shipbrokers' Benevolent Society

£32,300 (2020)

Correspondent: Anthony Carroll, 38 St Mary Axe, London EC3A 8BH (tel: 020 7283 6090; email: anthony.carroll@becf.co.uk)

CC number: 213348

Eligibility
Shipowners and shipbrokers and their dependants who are in need.

Types of grant
Grants are given according to need.

Applications
Apply in writing to the correspondent.

Financial information
Year end	31/12/2020
Income	£12,900
Total expenditure	£35,900

Further financial information
Full accounts were not available to view on the Charity Commission's website due to the society's low income. We have therefore estimated the society's grant total based on its total expenditure.

Railway Benefit Fund

 £231,700 (2020)

Correspondent: The Trustees, 1st Floor Millennium House, 40 Nantwich Road, Crewe, Cheshire CW2 6AD (tel: 0345 241 2885; email: support@railwaybenefitfund.org.uk)

www.railwaybenefitfund.org.uk

CC number: 206312

Eligibility
Current and former railway staff with a minimum of one year's railway employment.

Types of grant
Grants are available to help people overcome life events that may impact on their financial, family, mental and physical well-being.

The charity's website states:

Unexpected life events or changes in circumstances that can affect us all include:
- Illness an health issues
- Death and bereavement
- Relationship breakdown
- Domestic violence
- Family issues
- Unexpected expenditure
- Debt and money worries
- Changes to work patterns
- Redundancy

Exclusions
The fund is unable to help with care home fees.

Applications
Application forms are available to download on the funder's website.

Financial information
Year end	31/12/2020
Income	£330,400
Total expenditure	£530,900

Removers Benevolent Association

£1,700 (2020)

Correspondent: The Trustees, Tangent House, 62 Exchange Road, Watford, Hertfordshire WD18 0TG (tel: 01923 699480; email: rba@bar.co.uk)

 https://rba-charity.org

CC number: 284012

Eligibility
Staff of British Association of Removers member companies who are in need of temporary financial assistance. A minimum of two years' continuous employment is required. Support is also available to the dependants of such people.

Types of grant
Grants are awarded according to need, (for example, to meet essential needs or to cover loss of income due to illness or injury).

Applications
Application forms are available to download from the charity's website. Applications are welcomed from the individual in need, their dependants or the member company they are/were employed by.

Financial information
Year end	31/12/2020
Income	£7,800
Total expenditure	£1,900

Further financial information
Full accounts were not available to view on the Charity Commission's website due to the charity's low income. We have therefore estimated the charity's grant total based on its total expenditure.

RMT (National Union of Rail, Maritime and Transport Workers) Orphan Fund
See entry on page 27

The Road Haulage Association Benevolent Fund

£18,800 (2019)

Correspondent: Dean Fisher, Trustee, Road Haulage Association, Roadway House, Bretton Way, Bretton, Peterborough PE3 8DD (email: d.fisher@rha.uk.net)

 www.rha.uk.net

CC number: 1082820

Eligibility

Current and former members and employees/ex-employees of the Road Haulage Association. Dependants of such people are also eligible.

Types of grant

One-off grants are awarded according to need.

Applications

Apply in writing to the correspondent.

Financial information

Year end	31/12/2019
Income	£41,400
Total expenditure	£30,800

Scottish Shipping Benevolent Association

 £30,400 (2020)

Correspondent: Support Team, c/o The Clyde Group, Seaforth House, Seaforth Road North, Hillington Park, Glasgow G52 4JQ (email: info@ scottishshippingcharity.org)

🌐 https://scottishshippingcharity.org

OSCR number: SC004018

Eligibility

Members of the Scottish Shipping Benevolent Association (SSBA), and their dependants, who are in need. If funds permit, support is then extended to non-members, and their dependants, who have a connection to the shore-side maritime industry in Scotland and are in need.

Types of grant

One-off and monthly grants are awarded according to need. Bonus payments may be given to help with extra winter heating costs.

Applications

Initial enquiries should be made by contacting the support team by email or telephone, or by using the contact form on the charity's website.

Financial information

Year end	31/12/2020
Income	£34,100
Total expenditure	£62,400

Other information

Once grants have been given to SSBA members and non-members connected to the shipping industry, the charity can then make grants to other marine and nautical charities.

The Transport Benevolent Fund CIO

 £787,000 (2019/20)

Correspondent: The Trustees, Suite 2.7, The Loom, 14 Gowers Walk, London E1 8PY (tel: 0300 333 2000; email: help@ tbf.org.uk)

🌐 www.tbf.org.uk

CC number: 1160901

Eligibility

Employees and former employees of the public transport industry who are in need (often due to sickness, disability/disabilities or convalescence), their partners and dependants. Only members of the benevolent fund are supported.

Types of grant

Grants are given to help with unexpected one-off situations, for which help is not available from other sources. Grants can be given towards bills, prescription prepayment certificates, therapies, medical costs and equipment, convalescence and recuperation, welfare and debt counselling, legal advice and costs related to bereavement.

Applications

The charity manages several different funds, forms for which can be requested on the charity's helpful website.

Financial information

Year end	31/03/2020
Income	£4,430,000
Total expenditure	£4,690,000

Local charities

This section lists local charities that award grants to individuals. The information in the following records mainly focuses on welfare support and concentrates on what the charity actually does, rather than on what its governing document allows it to do.

Regional classification

We have divided the UK into 12 geographical areas, as numbered on the map on page 182. Northern Ireland,* Scotland, Wales and England have been divided into unitary or local authorities, in some cases grouped in counties or regions. On page 183 you can find the list of unitary or local authorities within each county or area. Please note that not all of these unitary authorities have a grant-making charity included in this guide.

Please note that this section only includes grant-makers that have specified the local area in which they give. Some charities are less specific and will support beneficiaries across the country. These charities often have additional criteria and therefore have been included in the relevant chapter (such as by type of beneficiary type or occupational charities).

*Although there is a separate section for Northern Ireland, it includes just one grant-maker. This is due to the fact that only one of the Northern Irish charities in the guide operates in a specific local area. Several other charities that give across the whole region, but have additional criteria, have been included in other relevant chapters. Note that many general

charities will fund across the UK, including Northern Ireland.

Scotland
- First: Scotland is divided into electoral board areas.
- Second: Electoral board areas are further divided into council areas.

Wales
- First: Wales is subdivided into three regions. The records which apply to the whole region, or to at least two local government areas within it, appear first.
- Second: Charities are listed under the relevant local government division.

England
- First: England is divided into nine regions. The records which apply to the whole region, or to at least two counties within it, appear first.
- Second: Regions are divided into counties.
- Third: The counties are subdivided into relevant local government areas.

Greater London
- First: Charities which apply to the whole of Greater London, or to at least two boroughs, are listed.
- Second: Charities serving London are further subdivided into the relevant boroughs.

Within each geographical category, the charities are listed alphabetically.

To be sure of identifying every relevant local charity, look at the charities in each relevant category in the following order:
1 Unitary or local authority
2 County
3 Region
4 Country

For example, if you live in Liverpool, first establish which region Merseyside is in by looking at the map on page 182. Then, having established that Merseyside is in region 9, North West, look under the 'Geographical areas' list on page 183 to find the page where the records for Merseyside begin. First, look under the heading for Liverpool to see if there are any relevant charities. Then work back through the charities under Merseyside generally, and then the charities under North West generally.

Having found grant-makers covering your area, read any other eligibility requirements carefully. While some charities can and do give grants for any need for people in their area of benefit, most charities have other, more specific criteria which potential applicants must meet in order to be eligible.

Geographical areas

1. Northern Ireland 185

County Antrim 185

2. Scotland 187

Ayrshire and Arran 187

  East Ayrshire

Central Scotland 187

  Falkirk

Dumfries and Galloway 187

Dunbartonshire and Argyll and Bute 188

  Argyll and Bute; East Dumbartonshire

Fife 189

Glasgow 190

Grampian 192

  Aberdeen City; Aberdeenshire; Moray

Highlands and Western Isles 195

  Highland; Na h-Eileanan Siar (Western Isles)

Lothian 196

  City of Edinburgh

Orkney and Shetland 199

Renfrewshire 199

  East Renfrewshire; Inverclyde

Scottish Borders 200

Tayside 200

  Angus; Dundee; Perth and Kinross

3. Wales 203

Mid and West Wales 203

  Pembrokeshire – Sir Benfro; Powys

North Wales 204

  Conwy County – Conwy; Denbighshire – Sir Ddinbych; Gwynedd; Isle of Anglesey – Ynys Mon; Wrexham County – Wrecsam

South Wales 207

  Cardiff City and County – Caerdydd; Merthyr Tydfil County – Merthyr Tudful; Monmouthshire – Sir Fynwy; Newport County – Casnewydd; Swansea City and County – Abertawe; Torfaen County – Tor-faen; Vale of Glamorgan – Bro Morgannwg

4. East Midlands 211

General 211

Derbyshire 212

  Chesterfield; Derby; Derbyshire Dales; Erewash; High Peak; North East Derbyshire

Leicestershire 216

  Charnwood; Hinckley and Bosworth; Leicester; Melton; North West Leicestershire

Lincolnshire 222

  Boston; East Lindsey; Lincoln; North Kesteven; South Holland; South Kesteven; West Lindsey

Northamptonshire 228

  Daventry; Kettering; Northampton; South Northamptonshire

Nottinghamshire 234

  Ashfield; Broxtowe; Mansfield; Newark and Sherwood; Nottingham; Rushcliffe

Rutland 240

5. West Midlands Region 241

General 241

Herefordshire 243

Shropshire 245

  Telford and Wrekin

Staffordshire 248

  Cannock Chase; East Staffordshire; Lichfield; Stafford; Staffordshire and Moorlands; Stoke; Tamworth

Warwickshire 251

  North Warwickshire; Nuneaton and Bedworth; Rugby; Stratford; Warwick

West Midlands Metropolitan Area 258

  Birmingham; Coventry; Dudley; Sandwell; Solihull; Walsall; Wolverhampton

Worcestershire 267

  Malvern Hills; Worcester; Wychavon; Wyre Forest

6. East of England 271

General 271

Bedfordshire 272

  Bedford; Central Bedfordshire

Cambridgeshire 276

  Cambridge; East Cambridgeshire; Fenland; Huntingdonshire; South Cambridgeshire

Essex 279

  Braintree; Brentwood; Chelmsford; Colchester; Epping Forest; Rochford; Thurrock; Uttlesford

Hertfordshire 285

  Broxbourne; Dacorum; East Hertfordshire; North Hertfordshire; St Albans; Stevenage; Watford; Welwyn Hatfield

Norfolk 290

  Breckland; King's Lynn and West Norfolk; North Norfolk; Norwich; South Norfolk

Suffolk 299

  Babergh; East Suffolk; Ipswich; Mid Suffolk; West Suffolk

7. Greater London 305

General 305

Barnet 310

Brent 312

Bromley 312

Camden 312

City of London 313

City of Westminster 315

Ealing 317

Enfield 318

Greenwich 318

Hackney 320

Hammersmith and Fulham 320

Haringey 321

Harrow 321

Hillingdon 321

Islington 322

Kensington and Chelsea 323

Kingston upon Thames 323

Lambeth 324

Lewisham 325

Merton 325

Newham 326

Redbridge 326

Richmond upon Thames 326

Southwark 329

Sutton 330

Tower Hamlets 330

Waltham Forest 331

Wandsworth 331

8. North East 333

General 333

County Durham 336

Hartlepool; Stockton-on-Tees (north of River Tees)

North Yorkshire (formerly Cleveland) 338

Middlesbrough

Northumberland 339

Tyne and Wear 339

Gateshead; Newcastle upon Tyne; North Tyneside; Sunderland

9. North West 343

General 343

Cheshire 344

Cheshire East; Cheshire West and Chester

Cumbria 347

Allerdale; Barrow-in-Furness; Carlisle; South Lakeland

Greater Manchester 349

Bolton; Bury; Manchester; Oldham; Rochdale; Salford; Stockport; Wigan

Lancashire 356

Blackburn with Darwen; Blackpool; Chorley; Fylde; Hyndburn; Lancaster; Pendle; South Ribble; West Lancashire

Merseyside 360

Liverpool; Sefton; Wirral

10. South East 365

General 365

Berkshire 367

Reading; Slough; West Berkshire; Windsor and Maidenhead; Wokingham

Buckinghamshire 370

Aylesbury Vale; Milton Keynes; South Buckinghamshire; Wycombe

East Sussex 375

Brighton and Hove; Eastbourne; Hastings; Rother; Wealdon

Hampshire 379

Basingstoke and Deane; East Hampshire; Fareham; Gosport; New Forest; Portsmouth; Southampton; Winchester

Isle of Wight 386

Kent 386

Canterbury; Dartford; Dover; Folkestone and Hythe (formerly Shepway); Gravesham; Maidstone; Medway; Sevenoaks; Swale; Thanet

Oxfordshire 393

Cherwell; Oxford; South Oxfordshire; Vale of White Horse; West Oxfordshire

Surrey 398

Elmbridge; Epsom and Ewell; Guildford; Mole Valley; Reigate and Banstead; Runnymede; Spelthorne; Surrey Heath; Tandridge; Waverley; Woking

West Sussex 410

Crawley

11. South West 413

General 413

Bristol 414

Cornwall 417

Devon 419

East Devon; Exeter; Mid Devon; North Devon; Plymouth; South Hams; Teignbridge; Torbay; Torridge; West Devon

Dorset 428

Bournemouth, Christchurch and Poole

Gloucestershire 431

Cheltenham; Cotswold; Gloucester; South Gloucestershire; Stroud; Tewkesbury

Somerset 437

Bath and North East Somerset; Mendip; North Somerset; Somerset West and Taunton; South Somerset

Wiltshire 442

12. Yorkshire and the Humber 447

General 447

East Riding of Yorkshire 448

Kingston upon Hull

Lincolnshire (formerly part of Humberside) 450

North East Lincolnshire; North Lincolnshire

North Yorkshire 451

Craven; Hambleton; Harrogate; Scarborough; York

South Yorkshire 454

Barnsley; Doncaster; Rotherham; Sheffield

West Yorkshire 458

Bradford; Calderdale; Kirklees; Leeds; Wakefield

Northern Ireland

County Antrim

Church of Ireland Orphans and Children Society for Counties Antrim and Down

£ £54,200 (2019/20)

Correspondent: The Trustees, Church of Ireland House, Diocesan Office, 61–67 Donegall Street, Belfast BT1 2QH (tel: 028 9082 8830)

CCNI number: NIC102840

Eligibility
Children in need, mainly orphans, who live in the counties of Antrim or Down and are members of the Church of Ireland.

Types of grant
Grants are given to help orphans and other children in need, including bereavement grants on the death of a parent.

Applications
Applications can be made at any time through the rector of the parish in which the individual lives. Direct applications cannot be considered.

Financial information

Year end	30/06/2020
Income	£551,100
Total expenditure	£274,800

Other information
The society also makes grants to support parochial and diocesan projects designed to help orphans and other children.

Scotland

Ayrshire and Arran

East Ayrshire

Miss Annie Smith Mair Newmilns Trust Fund

£1,100 (2019/20)

Correspondent: Democratic Services Trusts, East Ayrshire Council, Council Headquarters, London Road, Kilmarnock, East Ayrshire KA3 7BU (tel: 01563 576093; email: admin@ east-ayrshire.gov.uk)

 https://www.east-ayrshire.gov.uk/ CouncilAndGovernment/About-the-Council/Grants-and-funding/ TrustsandBequests.aspx

OSCR number: SC021095

Eligibility
People in need who live, or were born in, Newmilns.

Types of grant
Small, one-off grants for household essentials, minor home and/or garden maintenance works and adaptations, clothing, mobility and personal aids, short breaks and help with living expenses.

Applications
Apply on a form available from the correspondent or from the East Ayrshire Council website. Applications can be made directly by the individual or through a GP, social worker, Citizens Advice or other welfare agency. Note: if an application is being made on health grounds alone, a GP's certification of need will also be required.

Financial information

Year end	31/03/2020
Income	£240
Total expenditure	£2,400

Further financial information
Full accounts were not available to view on the OSCR website due to the charity's low income. We have therefore estimated the grant total based on the charity's total expenditure.

Other information
The charity is administered by East Ayrshire Council and, in recent years, has aided more than 100 people through its grant-making activities.

Central Scotland

Falkirk

The Anderson Bequest

 £5,800 (2019/20)

Correspondent: The Trustees, c/o Johnston & Co., 13 Register Street, Bo'ness, West Lothian EH51 9AE (tel: 01506 822112)

OSCR number: SC011755

Eligibility
Pensions for people in need who live in Bo'ness.

Types of grant
Annual grants or pensions.

Applications
Apply in writing to the correspondent.

Financial information

Year end	15/05/2020
Income	£27,900
Total expenditure	£23,600

Dumfries and Galloway

The Holywood Trust

£160,200 (2019/20)

Correspondent: Claire Hanna, Grants Officer, Hestan House, Crichton Business Park, Bankend Road, Dumfries, Dumfries and Galloway DG1 4TA (tel: 01387 269176; email: funds@ holywood-trust.org.uk)

www.holywood-trust.org.uk

OSCR number: SC009942

Eligibility
Primarily, support is given to young people aged 15 to 25 living in the Dumfries and Galloway region. Occasionally, the trustees will consider applications from people under the age of 15 if there is an exceptional reason (for example, if the child has multiple disadvantages or is especially talented in a specific area such as sports or the arts).

Types of grant

Welfare
Small grants, usually up to £1,000 are given for a range of purposes such as:
- Household items, particularly for a young person leaving care
- Clothing
- Travel expenses
- Driving lessons
- Counselling
- Participation in sporting and cultural activities at regional, national or international level
- Musical instruments or sporting equipment

Education
Grants are given towards college and university expenses.

Exclusions
Grants are not given towards retrospective costs or for second or postgraduate degrees.

187

Applications

In the first instance, potential applicants should register online on the trust's website. After registering, applicants will be emailed the details needed to access the grants system.

Financial information

Year end	05/04/2020
Income	£3,190,000
Total expenditure	£2,950,000

Further financial information

Grants were awarded to 367 young people in 2019/20 for both welfare and education purposes. Grants were distributed as follows:

Personal welfare	38%
Personal development	17%
Student expenses	16%
Personal 'other'	15%
Personal challenge	14%

Other information

The majority of the trust's funds are used to award grants to organisations.

John Primrose Trust

£16,000 (2019/20)

Correspondent: The Trustees, 1 Newall Terrace, Dumfries, Dumfries and Galloway DG1 1LN (email: enquiries@ primroseandgordon.co.uk)

OSCR number: SC009173

Eligibility

People in need who live in Dumfries and Maxwelltown or who have a connection with these places by parentage.

Types of grant

One-off grants are awarded according to need.

Applications

Application forms are available from the correspondent. Applications are generally considered in June and December.

Financial information

Year end	23/03/2020
Income	£17,700
Total expenditure	£17,700

Further financial information

Full accounts were not available to view on the OSCR website due to the trust's low income. We have therefore estimated the grant total based on the trust's total expenditure.

Other information

The trust also awards grants to organisations for educational and social welfare purposes.

Wigtownshire Educational Trust

£2,000 (2020)

Correspondent: Trust Secretary, Business Support Wigtown, Dumfries and Galloway Council, Council Offices, Sun Street, Stranraer, Dumfries and Galloway DG9 7JJ (tel: 01776 888423; email: committeeadmin-communitiesdirectorate@dumgal.gov.uk)

 https://www.dumgal.gov.uk/article/ 16756/Wigtownshire- Educational-Trust

OSCR number: SC019526

Eligibility

People in need who live in the former county of Wigtownshire and have exhausted/cannot find other sources of funding. Applicants must be receiving unemployment or disability benefits; if the student is still in school, their parental circumstances will be taken into account.

Types of grant

All grants are typically of up to £300 per year.

Welfare

Grants can be made for educational excursions, with an emphasis on primary school excursions, travel expenses, special educational equipment and clothing.

Education

Grants are made to college students, undergraduates, vocational students, mature students, people with special educational needs and people seeking or starting work. Grants given include those towards, clothing/uniforms, course fees, study/travel abroad, research, equipment, sports facilities and excursions. Assistance is also given towards gaining practical experience of trades and promoting education in the visual arts, music and drama.

Applications

Application forms are available to download from the Dumfries and Galloway council website. The trust is open to applicants from the start of January each year. Application forms must be received before the end of December. The trustees meet every four months to consider applications. If the applicant is a child/young person, details of parental income are required. The application form states that the trust will accept applications from schools for school trips but only on behalf of an individual pupil.

Financial information

Year end	31/12/2020
Income	£3,900
Total expenditure	£2,300

Further financial information

Full accounts were not available to view on the OSCR website due to the trust's low income. We have therefore estimated the grant total based on the trust's total expenditure.

Dunbarton-shire and Argyll and Bute

Argyll and Bute

Glasgow Bute Benevolent Society SCIO

£10,000 (2020)

Correspondent: The Trustees, Flat 2/1, 36 Castle Street, Rothesay, Isle of Bute PA20 9HA

OSCR number: SC048945

Eligibility

People in need who live in Bute, particularly older people. The length of time a person has lived in Bute and how long they have been connected with the area is taken into consideration.

Types of grant

According to our previous research, the charity provides pensions and Christmas payments. If funds allow, grants may also be awarded for educational purposes.

Applications

Application forms are available from the correspondent. Our previous research suggests that candidates should provide a supporting recommendation from a minister of religion, doctor, solicitor or other responsible person.

Financial information

Year end	31/12/2020
Income	£9,500
Total expenditure	£11,100

Further financial information

Full accounts were not available to view on the OSCR website due to the charity's low income. We have therefore estimated the grant total based on the charity's total expenditure.

Mairi Semple Fund

£ £8,000 (2020/21)

Correspondent: Mrs M. Sinclair, 4 Barrhill, Glenbarr, Tarbert, Argyll and Bute PA29 6UT

OSCR number: SC000390

Eligibility

People who live in Kintyre and are suffering from cancer.

Types of grant

Monthly financial support.

Exclusions

No grants are given to students for research.

Applications

Apply in writing to the correspondent.

Financial information

Year end	31/03/2021
Income	£18,600
Total expenditure	£17,800

Further financial information

Full accounts were not available to view on the OSCR website due to the fund's low income. We have therefore estimated the grant total based on the fund's total expenditure.

Other information

Grants are also made to organisations.

Charles and Barbara Tyre Trust

£ £22,300 (2019/20)

Correspondent: Christine Heads, Clerk to the Governors, c/o William Duncan (Argyll) Ltd, The Old Surgery, School Road, Tarbet PA29 6UL (tel: 01880 820277; email: christine.heads@wdargyll. co.uk)

 www.charlesandbarbaratyretrust. org.uk

OSCR number: SC031378

Eligibility

Children and young people under the age of 25 who live within the former county of Argyll (which includes Kinlochleven but excludes Helensburgh and the Island of Bute), have completed their school education and are of the Protestant faith.

Types of grant

Welfare

Grants are awarded to people with physical or mental disabilities (whether temporary or permanent) for recreational holidays.

Education

Grants are given to improve individuals' qualifications or for retraining. Support can be offered towards further/higher education, Open University courses and training and development courses, such as training in leadership and initiative, which are additional to the applicant's existing degree or qualification.

Applications

Application forms can be downloaded from the trust's website and should be emailed to the correspondent by 31 May. Successful applicants will be notified by the end of August. Applications received after the closing date are not considered other than in exceptional circumstances.

Financial information

Year end	31/03/2020
Income	£36,100
Total expenditure	£35,900

Further financial information

Grants of between £500 and £2,000 were made to 13 individuals in 2019/20.

Other information

The trust notes on its website that applicants must be able to satisfy that they are of the Protestant faith and live in the former county of Argyll.

East Dumbartonshire

Lenzie Benevolent Society SCIO

£ £27,300 (2019)

Correspondent: The Trustees, c/o French Duncan LLP, 133 Finnieston Street, Glasgow G3 8HB

OSCR number: SC047694

Eligibility

People in need who live in the Lenzie area. In some circumstances, people living outside the area but who have a connection to it in some way can also be supported.

Types of grant

The charity provides monthly grants, one-off grants and holiday grants.

Applications

Apply in writing to the correspondent.

Financial information

Year end	31/12/2019
Income	£85,500
Total expenditure	£54,700

Fife

Fleming Bequest

£ £21,200 (2019/20)

Correspondent: Grants Administrator, Thorntons Law LLP, Whitehall House, 33 Yeaman Shore, Dundee DD1 4BJ

OSCR number: SC016126

Eligibility

People living in the parish of St Andrews and St Leonards in the town of St Andrews who are older, in poor health or in financial difficulty.

Types of grant

According to our previous research, grants are awarded towards clothing, carpets, fridge/freezers, special chairs and other essential household needs.

Applications

Apply in writing to the correspondent preferably through a social worker, Citizens Advice or similar welfare agency. According to our previous research, applications can be considered at any time and should include details of the applicant's postal address, date of birth and reason for requesting assistance.

Financial information

Year end	05/04/2020
Income	£21,000
Total expenditure	£23,500

Further financial information

Full accounts were not available to view on the OSCR website due to the charity's low income. We have therefore estimated the grant total based on the charity's total expenditure.

The Lethendy Charitable Trust

£ £1,000 (2020/21)

Correspondent: George Hay, Henderson Loggie LLP, The Vision Building, 20 Greenmarket, Dundee DD1 4QB (tel: 01382 200055; email: george.hay@ hlca.co.uk)

OSCR number: SC003428

Eligibility

Young people with a strong connection to the Angus, Perthshire, Dundee or Fife areas.

Types of grant

Grants of between £150 and £500 are given to young people who are travelling abroad with charitable organisations to carry out charitable activities.

Applications

Apply in writing to the correspondent. There are regular meetings throughout the year to consider applications.

Financial information

Year end	05/04/2021
Income	£85,500
Total expenditure	£105,200

Further financial information

In 2020/21, grants were made to nine individuals.

Other information

The trust also supports local charities.

George McLean Trust

£ £900 (2020/21)

Correspondent: The Trustees, Blackadders Solicitors, 30–34 Reform Street, Dundee DD1 1RJ (tel: 01382 229222; email: enquiries@blackadders.co.uk)

OSCR number: SC020963

Eligibility

People in need who are living with a mental or physical disability in Fife and Tayside. Older people may also qualify for assistance.

Types of grant

Grants typically range between £100 and £1,000 and are made towards convalescence, hospital expenses, electrical goods, clothing, travel expenses, medical equipment, furniture, disability aids and help in the home.

Applications

Apply in writing to the correspondent.

Financial information

Year end	31/03/2021
Income	£33,200
Total expenditure	£36,000

Further financial information

In previous years, the charity has distributed around £5,000 in grants to individuals.

Other information

The trust also funds local charitable organisations.

New St Andrews Japan Golf Trust

£ £7,500 (2019/20)

Correspondent: The Trustees, 7 Pilmour Links, St Andrews, Fife KY16 9JG

OSCR number: SC005668

Eligibility

Children and young people in need who live in the county of Fife and are undertaking sports and recreational activities. There is a preference for golf.

Types of grant

One-off grants are offered for the provision of sports equipment and other activities associated with the developing sports skills, such as lectures and courses.

Applications

Apply in writing to the correspondent.

Financial information

Year end	31/03/2020
Income	£19,700
Total expenditure	£6,900

Further financial information

Full accounts were not available to view on the OSCR website due to the trust's low income. We have therefore estimated the grant total based on the trust's total expenditure.

Other information

The trust supports both individuals and organisations.

Annie Ramsay McLean Trust for the Elderly

£ £4,500 (2018/19)

Correspondent: Toni McNicoll, Trust Officer, c/o Blackadders LLP, 30 and 34 Reform Street, Dundee DD1 1RJ (tel: 01382 229222; email: toni.mcnicoll@blackadders.co.uk)

OSCR number: SC014238

Eligibility

Older people who live in Fife and Tayside who are in need, particularly those with a disability or ill health.

Types of grant

Grants are awarded according to need. The trust may assist with, for example, medical treatments or equipment, clothing, holidays, or care home admission costs.

Applications

According to our previous research, application forms are available from the correspondent. Applications can be submitted directly by the individual or thorough any third party and are considered monthly.

Financial information

Year end	30/11/2019
Income	£74,400
Total expenditure	£69,600

Further financial information

The 2018/19 accounts were the latest available on the OSCR website at time of writing (November 2021). Donations of £1,000 or less made to individuals totalled £4,500 during the year.

Other information

Grants are also made to organisations.

The St Andrews Welfare Trust

£ £20,000 (2020)

Correspondent: The Trustees, Thorntons Solicitors, Whitehall House, 33 Yeaman Shore, Dundee DD1 4BJ

OSCR number: SC008660

Eligibility

People in need who live in St Andrews.

Types of grant

Annuities and one-off grants.

Applications

Apply in writing to the correspondent through a social worker, Citizens Advice or other welfare agency. Applications should include the applicant's date of birth, postal address and reason for requesting assistance. Applications are considered throughout the year.

Financial information

Year end	31/12/2020
Income	£3,800
Total expenditure	£23,900

Further financial information

Full accounts were not available to view on the OSCR website due to the trust's low income. We have therefore estimated the grant total based on the trust's total expenditure.

Glasgow

The Glasgow Care Foundation

£ £175,900 (2019/20)

Correspondent: The Trustees, Orkney Street Enterprise Centre, 18–20 Orkney Street, Glasgow G51 2BX (tel: 0141 445 2736; email: info@glasgowcarefoundation.org)

www.glasgowcarefoundation.org

OSCR number: SC000906

Eligibility

People living in Glasgow who are in need.

Types of grant

Grants are given for essential support to those in need where support is not available through local authorities or other agencies. Support is given for items such as essential white goods (e.g. cookers, fridges, freezers, washing machines), beds and bedding, basic furniture, children's clothing and holidays, mainly in the UK.

Applications

Applications can be made online, but only through a recognised agency working in the community, such as social services.

Financial information

Year end	31/05/2020
Income	£363,200
Total expenditure	£337,800

Other information

The foundation was formerly known as the City of Glasgow Society of Social Service.

James T. Howat Charitable Trust

£7,000 (2019/20)

Correspondent: The Trustees, c/o Harper Macleod LLP, The Ca'd'oro, 45 Gordon Street, Glasgow G1 3PE (tel: 0141 304 3434)

OSCR number: SC000201

Eligibility

People in need who live in Glasgow.

Types of grant

Grants are awarded according to need.

Exclusions

Support is not normally given for the following: medical electives; second or further qualifications; payment of school fees; costs incurred at tertiary educational organisations; individuals who have received a grant in the previous year.

Applications

An application form is available from the trust upon request. Regarding the application form, the trust's 2019/20 annual report states the following:

'This should be completed as fully as possible to disclose applicants' circumstances and submitted together with a summary, in their own words, extending to not more than a single A-4 sheet. If a parent is completing the form on behalf of a child, financial information is required for both parent and child. The possible costs and financial needs should be broken down, evidence of the difference which a grant would make be produced, and details given (with results) of other grants applied for.'

The trustees normally meet in March, June, September and December, and applications should be submitted by the middle of the month before a meeting. Only successful applications will usually be acknowledged.

Financial information

Year end	05/04/2020
Income	£232,800
Total expenditure	£322,400

Further financial information

In 2019/20, grants were made to 15 individuals and ranged from £250 to £1,000.

Other information

The trust also supports organisations.

The Andrew and Mary Elizabeth Little Charitable Trust

£7,800 (2019/20)

Correspondent: The Trustees, c/o Low Beaton Richmond LLP, Sterling House, 20 Renfield Street, Glasgow G2 5AP

OSCR number: SC011185

Eligibility

Residents of the city of Glasgow who are in need and whose sole source of income is income support, disability benefit or pension.

Types of grant

One-off and recurrent grants according to need.

Applications

Apply in writing to the correspondent, to be submitted through social services. Applications should include financial details and are considered monthly.

Financial information

Year end	30/06/2020
Income	£62,300
Total expenditure	£64,800

James Paterson Trust and Nursing Fund

£5,400 (2019/20)

Correspondent: The Fund Administrator, Mitchells Roberton Solicitors, George House, 36 North Hanover Street, Glasgow G1 2AD (tel: 0141 552 3422; email: info@mitchells-roberton.co.uk)

OSCR number: SC017645

Eligibility

Women who have worked in cotton factories or mills in the Glasgow area, consisting of the district of the city of Glasgow and the contiguous districts of Dumbarton, Clydebank, Bearsden and Milngavie, Bishopbriggs and Kirkintilloch, East Kilbride, Eastwood and Renfrew.

Types of grant

Grants are given for short-term convalescent accommodation and occasionally for medical expenses and private accommodation in any private hospital.

Applications

Apply in writing to the correspondent. According to our research, applications can be submitted directly by the individual or through a social worker, Citizens Advice or other welfare agency.

Financial information

Year end	24/11/2020
Income	£22,400
Total expenditure	£12,100

Further financial information

Full accounts were not available to view on the OSCR website due to the fund's low income. We have therefore estimated the grant total based on the fund's total expenditure.

The Trades House of Glasgow

£251,300 (2019/20)

Correspondent: The Trustees, Trades Hall, 85 Glassford Street, Glasgow G1 1HU (tel: 0141 553 1605; email: info@tradeshouse.org.uk)

 www.tradeshouse.org.uk

OSCR number: SC040548

Eligibility

People in need who live in Glasgow and the surrounding areas. Several funds have different eligibility criteria around age or need – consult the charity's website before making an application.

Types of grant

Welfare

Grants are given for a range of purposes – visit the website for details of each fund.

Education

The charity's education fund can provide financial help to students who lack the necessary funds to complete their studies.

Applications

Applications can be made online through the respective funding pages.

Financial information

Year end	30/09/2020
Income	£1,110,000
Total expenditure	£1,260,000

Other information

Guilds and Craft Incorporations are the Scottish equivalents of the craft guilds or livery companies that developed in the Middle Ages.

Grampian

CALICO – Cancer and Leukaemia in Children Orientated

 £4,000 (2019/20)

Correspondent: Magnus Harcus, Chair, 20 Harcourt Road, Aberdeen, Aberdeenshire AB15 5NZ (email: calicogrampian@outlook.com)

🌐 https://www.calicogrampian.org.uk

OSCR number: SC005795

Eligibility
Families living in the Grampian region who have children suffering from cancer, leukaemia or cancer-related illness.

Types of grant
Grants to alleviate, where possible, stress caused by additional expenses.

Applications
Apply in writing to the correspondent.

Financial information
Year end	31/03/2020
Income	£13,900
Total expenditure	£18,300

Further financial information
Full accounts were not available to view on the OSCR website due to the charity's low income. We have therefore estimated the grant total based on the charity's total expenditure.

North East Scotland Police Welfare Fund (NESPWF)

 £5,000 (2019/20)

Correspondent: The Secretary, 22 Union Street, Lossiemouth, Moray IV31 6BD (email: secretary@nespwf.org.uk)

🌐 www.nespwf.org.uk

OSCR number: SC044963

Eligibility
Members of the NESPWF, former officers and support staff of Grampian Police or its constituent forces, or any future police divisions covering the north-east of Scotland. Widows or widowers and/or the dependants of former officers or members are also eligible for support.

Types of grant
Grants are given according to need.

Applications
Applications can be made via the fund's website.

Financial information
Year end	31/07/2020
Income	£1,600
Total expenditure	£5,900

Further financial information
Full accounts were not available to view on the OSCR website due to the fund's low income. We have therefore estimated the grant total based on the fund's total expenditure.

Aberdeen City

Aberdeen Endowments Trust

 £837,000 (2020)

Correspondent: The Trustees, 19 Albert Street, Aberdeen, Aberdeenshire AB25 1QF (tel: 01224 646346; email: aet1909@btopenworld.com)

🌐 www.aberdeenendowmentstrust.co.uk

OSCR number: SC010507

Eligibility
Welfare
Secondary school bursaries are available to pupils from low-income families to attend secondary school.

Education
Bursaries at Robert Gordon's College are available to students before they enter the senior 1 year. To be eligible, students will be required to pass an entrance exam.

Types of grant
The majority of the trust's grants are made to cover fees at Robert Gordon's College. Bursaries for Robert Gordon's College are awarded to cover the first five years of secondary school and can be extended for a sixth year. However, grants can also be made available for:

▸ Secondary school bursaries – typically a few hundred pounds each year to help households of limited financial means that are paid up to senior year four, subject to satisfactory school reports on attendance and progress.
▸ Educational grants – these awards are means-tested and aim to improve life chances through education. Applicants must live or have a strong connection to the city of Aberdeen.
▸ School trips – the trust helps around 75 families each year with the costs of school trips.

Applications
Contact the trust for an application form.

Financial information
Year end	31/12/2020
Income	£1,180,000
Total expenditure	£1,360,000

Further financial information
In 2020, a total of £826,000 was awarded to support students through Robert Gordon's College, and £11,000 was awarded for welfare purposes to secondary school-aged pupils.

Aberdeen Female Society

 £15,200 (2019/20)

Correspondent: The Secretary, c/o Burnett & Reid LLP, Suite A, Ground Floor, 9 Queens Road, Aberdeen, Aberdeenshire AB15 4YL

OSCR number: SC016491

Eligibility
Women who have reached retirement age and are resident in Aberdeen.

Types of grant
One-off and regular grants are made according to need. Previously, funding has been given to assist with the purchase of essential household items.

Applications
According to our previous research, application forms are available on request from the secretary and must be countersigned by a third party such as a health professional, social worker or minister.

Financial information
Year end	31/10/2020
Income	£6,700
Total expenditure	£16,900

Further financial information
Full accounts were not available to view on the OSCR website due to the society's low income. We have therefore estimated the grant total based on the society's total expenditure.

Aberdeen Indigent Mental Patients Fund

 £900 (2020/21)

Correspondent: The Trustees, c/o Peterkins Solicitors, 100 Union Street, Aberdeen, Aberdeenshire AB10 1QR

OSCR number: SC003069

Eligibility
Psychiatric patients who have been discharged from hospital in Aberdeen.

Types of grant
Grants are awarded according to need.

Applications
Apply in writing to the correspondent.

Financial information

Year end	31/01/2021
Income	£670
Total expenditure	£1,000

Further financial information
Full accounts were not available to view on the OSCR website due to the fund's low income. We have therefore estimated the grant total based on the fund's total expenditure.

James Allan of Midbeltie's Fund for Widows

£ £22,000 (2019/20)

Correspondent: The Trustees, c/o Burnett & Reid LLP, Suite A, Ground Floor, 9 Queens Road, Aberdeen, Aberdeenshire AB15 4YL

OSCR number: SC003865

Eligibility
Widows who live in Aberdeen and are in need.

Types of grant
The charity provides half-yearly annuities and occasionally Christmas bonuses.

Applications
Apply in writing to the correspondent.

Financial information

Year end	31/07/2020
Income	£77,600
Total expenditure	£59,600

Dr John Calder Fund

£ £10,600 (2019/20)

Correspondent: The Trustees, St Machar's Cathedral, 18 The Chanonry, Aberdeen, Aberdeenshire AB24 1RQ

OSCR number: SC004299

Eligibility
People in need who live in the parish of Machar. Preference is given to widows with young children, where sufficient support cannot be obtained from the parish council. People in need living in Aberdeen may also be assisted.

Types of grant
Small grants are given according to need.

Applications
Apply in writing to the correspondent.

Financial information

Year end	05/04/2020
Income	£23,900
Total expenditure	£42,900

Further financial information
Full accounts were not available to view on the OSCR website due to the fund's low income. We have therefore estimated the grant total based on the fund's total expenditure.

Other information
The charity also makes grants to organisations. At the time of writing (October 2021) the trustees were intending to wind up the charity and transfer its assets and liabilities to Dr John Calder SCIO (OSCR no. SC050820), which has been established to replace it.

George, James and Alexander Chalmers Bequests

£ £34,800 (2019/20)

Correspondent: Trust Administrator, c/o Storie Cruden & Simpson Solicitors, 2 Bon-Accord Crescent, Aberdeen, Aberdeenshire AB11 6DH (email: info@storiecs.co.uk)

OSCR number: SC008818

Eligibility
Women living in Aberdeen who are in need.

Types of grant
The charity provides half-yearly annuities of around £800.

Applications
Apply on a form available from the correspondent.

Financial information

Year end	30/09/2020
Income	£149,800
Total expenditure	£202,900

Further financial information
Annuities were paid to 44 women during the 2019/20 financial period.

Other information
Grants are also made to organisations.

Mary Morrison Cox Trust

£ £11,200 (2019/20)

Correspondent: The Trustees, c/o A.C. Morrison & Richards, 18 Bon-Accord Crescent, Aberdeen, Aberdeenshire AB11 6XY

OSCR number: SC007881

Eligibility
People in need who live in the parish of Dyce, Aberdeen. Preference is given to older people and people living with disabilities.

Types of grant
One-off grants to help with general living expenses.

Applications
According to our previous research, the trust has a list of potential beneficiaries to whom it sends application forms each year, usually in November. In order to be added to this list, applicants should contact the trust.

Financial information

Year end	31/10/2020
Income	£10,000
Total expenditure	£12,400

Further financial information
Full accounts were not available to view on the OSCR website due to the trust's low income. We have therefore estimated the grant total based on the trust's total expenditure.

Miss Caroline Jane Spence's Fund

£ £5,400 (2018/19)

Correspondent: Fund Secretary, c/o Mackinnons Solicitors, 379 North Deeside Road, Cults, Aberdeen, Aberdeenshire AB15 1SX (email: cults@mackinnons.com)

OSCR number: SC006434

Eligibility
People who live in Aberdeen and the surrounding area and are in need.

Types of grant
One-off and recurrent grants according to need.

Applications
Application forms are available from the correspondent. Applications can be submitted either directly by the individual or through a social worker, Citizens Advice, welfare agency or other third party.

Financial information

Year end	20/11/2019
Income	£179,200
Total expenditure	£74,900

Further financial information
The 2018/19 accounts were the latest available at the time of writing (October 2021). Grants of £1,800 each were made to three individuals.

Aberdeenshire

Aberdeen Cheyne and Donald Trust Fund

 £88,000 (2020)

Correspondent: Trust Administrator, c/o Raeburn, Christie, Clark & Wallace, 12–16 Albyn Place, Aberdeen, Aberdeenshire AB10 1PS (tel: 01224 332400)

🌐 www.raeburns.co.uk

OSCR number: SC045666

Eligibility

People living in, or with a strong connection to, Aberdeen and Aberdeenshire who are facing financial hardship, particularly as a result of age, illness or disability.

Types of grant

One-off and recurrent (half-yearly) grants are available for the relief of poverty, depending on personal circumstances.

Applications

Applications should be made in writing to the correspondent, detailing the financial need and what the grant will be used for.

Financial information

Year end	31/12/2020
Income	£82,600
Total expenditure	£115,600

Other information

The trust gained charitable status in 2015 after the transfer of funds from the Gordon Cheyne Trust Fund, the Aberdeen Widows and Spinsters Fund, and the Donald Trust.

Aberdeenshire Educational Trust

 £100,000 (2019/20)

Correspondent: The Trustees, Aberdeenshire Council, Aberdeenshire Support and Advice Team, PO Box 18533, Aberdeen, Aberdeenshire AB51 3WA (email: asataet@ aberdeenshire.gov.uk)

🌐 https://www.aberdeenshire.gov.uk/ benefits-and-grants/educational-grants

OSCR number: SC028382

Eligibility

Students and schoolchildren of any age who, or whose immediate family, are resident in the former county of Aberdeenshire.

Types of grant

Welfare

Grants of up to £500 are awarded to schoolchildren to help with the costs of school trips. The grant is paid when the school notifies the trust that the pupil has attended the trip. Grants are means tested.

Education

Grants of up to £500 are awarded to students undertaking further or higher education courses.

Applications

Application forms are available from the correspondent via the email address provided.

Financial information

Year end	31/03/2020
Income	£180,600
Total expenditure	£153,100

Other information

Grants are also made to schools, clubs and educational groups. Annual school prizes and preference grants are also awarded to individuals.

Mrs Catherine Brook's Fund

£19,800 (2019/20)

Correspondent: The Trustees, c/o Mackinnons Solicitors, 379 North Deeside Road, Cults, Aberdeen, Aberdeenshire AB15 9SX (tel: 01224 868687; email: cults@mackinnons.com)

OSCR number: SC000675

Eligibility

People in need living in Peterhead. Preference is give to people with disabilities.

Types of grant

One-off grants of up to £600 are given according to need.

Applications

Apply in writing to the correspondent.

Financial information

Year end	05/04/2020
Income	£25,800
Total expenditure	£27,200

Further financial information

Grants were made to 33 individuals during the 2019/20 financial period.

John Harrow's Mortification

£11,900 (2019/20)

Correspondent: The Trustees, c/o Peterkins Solicitors, 100 Union Street, Aberdeen, Aberdeenshire AB10 1QR (tel: 01224 428000; email: maildesk@ peterkins.com)

OSCR number: SC003617

Eligibility

Older people in need who live in Aberdeen.

Types of grant

Grants are given according to need. The charity may also provide pensions.

Applications

Apply in writing to the correspondent.

Financial information

Year end	30/11/2020
Income	£3,900
Total expenditure	£13,200

Further financial information

Full accounts were not available to view on the OSCR website due to the charity's low income. We have therefore estimated the grant total based on the charity's total expenditure.

The Jopp Thomson Fund

£18,100 (2019/20)

Correspondent: The Trustees, c/o Ledingham Chalmers LLP, 52–54 Rose Street, Aberdeen, Aberdeenshire AB10 1HA

OSCR number: SC009106

Eligibility

People in need through age, ill health or disability. Preference is given for widowed and single women living in Aberdeenshire and those whose name or maiden name is Thomson or Middleton.

Types of grant

Annuities of £650 are given to each beneficiary, to be used at their discretion.

Applications

Apply in writing to the correspondent.

Financial information

Year end	11/11/2020
Income	£78,600
Total expenditure	£74,900

Further financial information

During the 2019/20 financial period, 22 individuals received grants of £650. An additional grant of £200 was paid to beneficiaries in response to the COVID-19 pandemic.

Other information

This fund is an amalgamation of the Henry John Jopp Fund and the Jessie Ann Thomson Fund.

Moray

Moray and Nairn Educational Trust

 £16,000 (2019/20)

Correspondent: Education and Social Care, Common Good & Trust Funds, Moray Council, Council Office, High Street, Elgin, Morayshire IV30 1BX (tel: 01343 563374; email: educationandsocialcare@moray.gov.uk)

www.moray.gov.uk/moray_standard/page_58388.html

OSCR number: SC019017

Eligibility

Students who are resident and educated in the former combined county of Moray and Nairnshire. Applicants should have resided in the area for at least five years.

Types of grant

Welfare

Travel grants for purposes of an educational nature.

Education

Bursaries are available to students (including mature and postgraduate students) in Scottish universities and people pursuing education at a Scottish central institution or training college. Financial support can also be given for study/travel overseas.

Applications

Application forms can be found on the trust's website and should be submitted before 30 September each year.

Financial information

Year end	31/03/2020
Income	£20,200
Total expenditure	£16,400

Further financial information

Full accounts were not available to view on the OSCR website due to the trust's low income. We have therefore estimated the grant total based on the trust's total expenditure.

Other information

Grants can also be made to local schools, further education centres or clubs and organisations operating in the area of benefit, for facilities, special equipment or the promotion of adult education.

Highlands and Western Isles

Highland

Dr Forbes Inverness Trust

 £2,900 (2019/20)

Correspondent: The Trustees, c/o Munro & Noble Solicitors, 26 Church Street, Inverness, Highlands IV1 1HX (tel: 01463 221727; email: legal@munronoble.com)

OSCR number: SC005573

Eligibility

People with a medical need who live within the Inverness area of the Highland Council area.

Types of grant

Generally one-off grants to help with the cost of medical treatment and equipment, convalescence or a period of residence in a nursing home, food, clothing and travel expenses to visit sick relatives.

Applications

Application forms are available from the correspondent and can be submitted by the individual or through a recognised referral agency (e.g. a social worker, Citizens Advice or a doctor) or other third party.

Financial information

Year end	05/04/2020
Income	£10,000
Total expenditure	£3,200

Further financial information

Full accounts were not available to view on the OSCR website due to the trust's low income. We have therefore estimated the grant total based on the trust's total expenditure.

Highland Children's Trust

 £22,200 (2019/20)

Correspondent: The Trustees, 105A Castle Street, Inverness, Highlands IV2 3EA (tel: 01463 243872; email: info@hctrust.co.uk)

www.hctrust.co.uk

OSCR number: SC006008

Eligibility

Children and young people in need who are under 25 and live in, or have a home address, in the area covered by the Highland Council. The charity is the successor to the Highland Orphanage Trust, so there may be preference to provide grants for orphans.

Types of grant

Welfare

Parents can apply for grants to assist with the costs of:

- A school trip (£150 for a trip within the UK and £300 for an overseas trip)
- Educational equipment for children with special educational needs
- Attendance at a local feis (up to £150 for attendance for one week per year)
- Family holidays (£350 for one UK holiday in a two-year period).

Education

Students at college or university can apply for the following:

- Hardship funding of between £1,000 and £1,500 a year if all other forms of support have been exhausted.
- Expedition grants for research purposes, or demonstrable personal development, or overseas study. The current maximum grant available is £500 per person per trip, and no more than three applications will be considered for the same trip.
- Grants to cover the expenses of travelling for a job, the cost of temporary accommodation, or the cost of training courses or apprenticeships. In exceptional circumstances, the trust can help with setting an applicant up in business or finding a home for them after their full-time education or apprenticeship is completed.

Exclusions

Grants are not given for postgraduate study, to pay off debts, or to purchase items such as clothing, footwear, food, furniture or cars.

Applications

Application forms can be downloaded from the trust's website. For applicants under 18, applications should be co-signed by a parent or guardian.

Financial information

Year end	05/04/2020
Income	£58,600
Total expenditure	£55,000

Strathnairn Community Benefit Fund

£ £212,900 (2019/20)

Correspondent: Company Secretary, Freepost RTTJ-HBSK-RRUU, SCBF, PO Box 5783, Inverness IV1 9EW (email: cosec@strathnairncbf.com)

OSCR number: SC036807

Eligibility

Residents of the Strathnairn Community Council area who are in need.

Types of grant

Grants are available for:
- Energy costs
- Energy efficiency
- The installation of renewable energy technology
- Respite and the relief of hardship

Applications

Application forms are available to download from the fund's website.

Financial information

Year end	31/08/2020
Income	£267,600
Total expenditure	£221,800

Further financial information

Note, the grant total has been estimated.

Na h-Eileanan Siar (Western Isles)

The William MacKenzie Trust

£ £17,600 (2019/20)

Correspondent: The Trustees, 26 Lewis Street, Stornoway, Isle of Lewis HS1 2JF

OSCR number: SC001598

Eligibility

Older people or those with an illness or disability living in Stornoway. Support is also given to people who are unable to work due to illness or disability.

Types of grant

Support is given towards the following:
- Enabling older people to continue living in their own homes
- Medical costs such as artificial limbs and appliances
- Assisting those who are unable to continue working in their chosen field (due to illness or disability) to enter another trade or profession

Applications

Apply in writing to the correspondent.

Financial information

Year end	05/04/2020
Income	£53,400
Total expenditure	£53,400

Lothian

Capital Charitable Trust

£ £23,800 (2019/20)

Correspondent: The Trustees, Caledonia Exchange, 19A Canning Street, Edinburgh EH3 8HE

OSCR number: SC004332

Eligibility

People in need who live in the Edinburgh and Lothians area.

Types of grant

Small, one-off grants of about £10 to £20 towards clothes, decorating, household goods and other general welfare needs.

Applications

According to our previous research, application forms can be obtained from local authority social work departments and other responsible bodies, who will forward them to the correspondent. Applications are not accepted directly from individuals.

Financial information

Year end	05/04/2020
Income	£22,600
Total expenditure	£26,400

Further financial information

Full accounts were not available to view on the OSCR website due to the trust's low income. We have therefore estimated the grant total based on the trust's total expenditure.

ECAS Ltd

£ £18,000 (2020/21)

Correspondent: The Trustees, Norton Park, 57 Albion Road, Edinburgh EH7 5QY (tel: 07500 221618; email: hello@ecas.scot or use the contact form on the website)

 https://www.ecas.scot

OSCR number: SC014929

Eligibility

People living in Edinburgh and the Lothians who have a physical disability.

Types of grant

Grants of up to £1,500 are given for items or services not available through welfare benefits and other sources. Examples include furniture, white goods, electronic goods, holidays and student fees.

Exclusions

Grants are not given for the purchase of powerchairs, scooters or battery packs. Additionally, funding cannot be given retrospectively or to pay bills or debts. According to the charity's application guidance notes, individuals with the following medical conditions are not eligible for support:

Arthritis, back pain, cardio-respiratory conditions, obesity, psychiatric disorders, learning difficulties, behavioural disorders, developmental delay, Down's syndrome, autism, visual or hearing impairment, cancer, diabetes, HIV and epilepsy.

Applications

Application forms and guidance notes can be downloaded from the charity's website.

Financial information

Year end	31/03/2021
Income	£187,200
Total expenditure	£306,600

Other information

ECAS also runs activities – ranging from arts and crafts to yoga, reading and ICT – as well as a befriending scheme, all of which aim to improve the quality of life for people living with physical disabilities.

The Edinburgh and Lothian Trust Fund

£ £183,100 (2020/21)

Correspondent: Trust Administrator, 525 Ferry Road, Edinburgh EH5 2FF (tel: 0131 555 9100; email: grants@eltf. org.uk)

 www.eltf.org.uk

OSCR number: SC031561

Eligibility

Individuals in need who live in the city of Edinburgh and the Lothians.

Types of grant

One-off grants of up to £200 where they will be of real benefit to the family or individual in need including for the following: baby equipment; furniture; bedding; household items; clothing; small electrical items; white goods; pre-paid electricity cards.

Exclusions

No grants are made for holidays (except in special circumstances, e.g. a holiday arranged by a recognised charity), student fees/equipment or the repayment of debt. Only one application per individual will be considered in a year.

Applications

Grants for individuals from the general fund can be applied for using the online form on the charity's website. Applications will only be accepted from a professional at a local authority, social services, hospital or voluntary sector agency.

Financial information

Year end	31/03/2021
Income	£254,200
Total expenditure	£300,000

Scottish Building Federation Edinburgh and District Charitable Trust

 £25,700 (2020)

Correspondent: Kirsty Ashworth, Accounts and Business Services Senior Manager, Azets, Exchange Place 3, Semple Street, Edinburgh EH3 8BL (tel: 0131 473 3500; email: SM-Charity@azets.co.uk)

https://www.azets.co.uk/scottish-building-federation

OSCR number: SC029604

Eligibility

Welfare

People in need who are, or have been, connected to the building trade in the city of Edinburgh and the Lothians. Support is extended to the dependants of such people.

Education

Students studying skills relating to the building industry in the following universities and colleges: Heriot-Watt University; Napier University; West Lothian College; and Edinburgh College).

Types of grant

Welfare

One-off grants are awarded according to need.

Education

Scholarships, bursaries and academic prizes.

Applications

Application forms are available to download from the Azets website. Applications for welfare grants should be returned to the correspondent by post. Applications for educational grants should be completed and forwarded to the appropriate department of the university or college.

Financial information

Year end	31/12/2020
Income	£44,300
Total expenditure	£83,200

John Wilson Robert Christie Bequest Fund

 £76,800 (2019/20)

Correspondent: The Trustees, c/o Geoghegans, 6 St Colme Street, Edinburgh EH3 6AD (email: mail@geoghegans.co.uk)

OSCR number: SC000465

Eligibility

People over 60 who are in need and live in Edinburgh, Midlothian, East Lothian or West Lothian. A proportion of funding is allocated to people who are suffering from acute and painful diseases.

Types of grant

Annual allowances are given according to need.

Applications

The trustees invite applications by advertising funding and contacting medical practices and other professionals in the area of benefit.

Financial information

Year end	30/09/2020
Income	£129,000
Total expenditure	£122,500

Further financial information

Grants were made to 77 beneficiaries during the year.

Other information

Grants are also made to organisations.

City of Edinburgh

The William Brown Nimmo Charitable Trust

£30,900 (2019/20)

Correspondent: The Trustees, c/o MHD Law LLP, 45 Queen Charlotte Street, Leith, Edinburgh EH6 7HT

OSCR number: SC001671

Eligibility

Women in need aged 50 or older who were born and permanently live in Leith or Edinburgh.

Types of grant

Annual grants of around £300 are given according to need.

Applications

Apply in writing to the correspondent.

Financial information

Year end	15/05/2020
Income	£47,400
Total expenditure	£36,800

Further financial information

Grants of £300 were awarded to 103 individuals in 2019/20, totalling £30,900.

Alexander Darling Silk Mercer's Fund

£2,500 (2019/20)

Correspondent: Gregor Murray, Secretary and Chamberlain, The Merchant Hall, 22 Hanover Street, Edinburgh EH2 2EP (tel: 0131 225 7202; email: gregor.murray@mcoe.org.uk)

www.mcoe.org.uk

OSCR number: SC036724

Eligibility

Women over the age of 55 who are (preferably) unmarried or widowed and who are in one of the following groups:
- Women who were born in Edinburgh
- Women who have lived in Edinburgh for the majority of their lives
- Women who were married to a man who was resident in Edinburgh
- Women who were employed in the manufacturing of ladies' and children's garments in Edinburgh

Preference is given to women with the surnames Darling, Millar, Scott and Small, as well as to women born in Lanark.

Types of grant

Grants are given according to need.

Applications

Apply in writing to the correspondent.

Financial information

Year end	31/07/2020
Income	£34,300
Total expenditure	£65,200

The Edinburgh Fire Fund

 £3,200 (2020/21)

Correspondent: The Trustees, 525 Ferry Road, Edinburgh, Edinburgh EH5 2FF (tel: 0131 555 9100; email: grants@eltf.org.uk)

https://www.eltf.org.uk/funds/the-edinburgh-fire-fund

OSCR number: SC049138

Eligibility

Individuals and families living in the Edinburgh local authority area who have been affected by fire in the last six months. Applicants must be on state benefits or earning no more than the living wage (as defined by the Living Wage Foundation).

Types of grant

Grants are made for the following: household contents, essential personal items and clothing not covered by appropriate insurance; redecoration (and any prior cleaning to remove smoke damage); and counselling or therapy needed as a result of trauma resulting from the fire.

Exclusions

Grants are not made for structural repairs or work which would usually be covered by a building insurance policy. Grants are not made to cover contents where an appropriate contents insurance policy is in place.

Applications

The fund is administered by The Edinburgh and Lothian Trust Fund. Applications can be made using the online form on the trust's website. Applications must be made by the person directly affected by the fire. An appropriate third party (e.g. a social worker, community nurse, support worker), is usually expected to verify the information provided by the applicant.

Financial information

Year end	31/03/2021
Income	£254,200
Total expenditure	£300,000

Other information

The fund, which was founded in 1824, was previously known as the Surplus Fire Fund.

Edinburgh Police Fund for Children

£ £16,600 (2019/20)

Correspondent: Trust Administrator, Edinburgh Divisional Co-ordination Unit, St Leonard's Police Station, 14 St Leonard's Street, Edinburgh EH8 9QW (tel: 0131 662 5033; email: police.fund@eltf.org.uk)

 www.eltf.org.uk/funds/edinburgh-police-fund-for-children

OSCR number: SC011164

Eligibility

School-aged children who are in need and live in the city of Edinburgh.

Types of grant

Grants of up to £50 for clothing and footwear, principally school shoes and jackets. In cases of self-referrals, a voucher will be provided.

Exclusions

The charity does not provide assistance towards school uniforms.

Applications

Grants from the fund are administered by The Edinburgh and Lothian Trust Fund. Applications are usually made through a third party (e.g. a social worker, community nurse, headteacher or police officer) using the online form, which is available on the trust's website. Families can self-refer if they do not have a suitable third party to do so on their behalf – in these cases, the Trust Administrator can be contacted directly and the family will receive an assessment visit from a police officer.

Financial information

Year end	31/03/2020
Income	£29,200
Total expenditure	£25,000

Other information

The fund, which was founded in 1892, used to be known as the Police Aided Clothing Scheme. Since January 2016, The Edinburgh and Lothian Trust Fund (OSCR no. SC031561) has administered its grant-making.

Edinburgh Royal Infirmary Samaritan Society

£ £27,000 (2019/20)

Correspondent: Mr J. Sheddan, Trustee, 7 Fountainhall Road, Edinburgh EH9 2NL

OSCR number: SC004519

Eligibility

Patients of NHS hospitals in Edinburgh who are in need. This includes Edinburgh Royal Infirmary, the City Hospital, the Royal Hospital for Sick Children and other hospitals in Edinburgh as the council may from time to time decide.

Types of grant

Grants are given for clothing, travel expenses and other purposes to assist patients while in hospital or upon discharge.

Applications

Applications can be made through the Social Service Department at the Royal Infirmary of Edinburgh or through a social worker at any of the other hospitals on the charity's list. Applications are considered fortnightly.

Financial information

Year end	30/09/2020
Income	£37,500
Total expenditure	£44,900

Further financial information

The charity made 190 grants during the 2019/20 financial period.

The Edinburgh Society for Relief of Indigent Old Men

£ £17,700 (2019/20)

Correspondent: Trust Secretary, c/o Lindsays, Caledonian Exchange, 19A Canning Street, Edinburgh EH3 8HE

OSCR number: SC005284

Eligibility

Older men living in Edinburgh who are in need.

Types of grant

The majority of spending is on monthly pensions. The charity also awards Christmas bonuses.

Applications

Applications should be made in writing to the correspondent.

Financial information

Year end	30/09/2020
Income	£58,400
Total expenditure	£43,300

Elizabeth Finn Care

See entry on page 4

The Merchant Company Endowments Trust

£ £138,100 (2019/20)

Correspondent: The Trustees, The Merchants' Hall, 22 Hanover Street, Edinburgh EH2 2EP (tel: 0131 225 7202; email: enquiries@mcoe.org.uk)

 www.mcoe.org.uk

OSCR number: SC002002

Eligibility

Men and women over the age of 55 who have worked in Edinburgh or Midlothian.

Types of grant

Assistance can be given in the form of a cash grant, biannual pension, gift or appliance, or provision and care support.

Applications

Contact the correspondent for more information. The trust employs an almoner, who assesses need and reports to the trust prior to any grant being made.

Financial information

Year end	31/07/2020
Income	£675,200
Total expenditure	£595,100

Other information

The trust also provides almshouse accommodation.

James Scott Law Charitable Fund

 £4,400 (2019/20)

Correspondent: Gregor Murray, Secretary and Chamberlain, The Merchant Company, Merchants' Hall, 22 Hanover Street, Edinburgh EH2 2EP (tel: 0131 225 7202; email: enquiries@ mcoe.org.uk or use the contact form on the website)

🌐 www.mcoe.org.uk

OSCR number: SC008878

Eligibility

Children and young people who have a link to the Edinburgh Merchant Company.

Types of grant

According to our previous research, grants are given for a wide range of purposes including school uniforms and bursaries for university.

Applications

Apply in writing to the correspondent.

Financial information

Year end	31/07/2020
Income	£10,200
Total expenditure	£4,900

Further financial information

Full accounts were not available to view on the OSCR website due to the fund's low income. We have therefore estimated the grant total based on the fund's total expenditure.

Other information

This fund is one of nine administered by the Edinburgh Merchant Company.

Orkney and Shetland

Shetland Charitable Trust

 £1,200 (2020/21)

Correspondent: Edna Flaws, Administration Manager, 22–24 North Road, Lerwick, Shetland Islands ZE1 0NQ (tel: 01595 744994; email: grants@shetlandcharitabletrust.co.uk)

🌐 www.shetlandcharitabletrust.co.uk

OSCR number: SC027025

Eligibility

Children and young people under the age of 18 who are based in Shetland and hoping to develop their art form. All forms of arts genres are supported, including the visual arts, crafts, dance, drama, dialect, film, literature, music, theatre and combined arts.

Types of grant
Shetland Arts Fund

The Shetland Arts Fund is administered by the Shetland Charitable Trust. One-off grants are awarded to support arts development. The trust will consider funding, for example:
- Training, courses, workshops and learning opportunities
- Specialist or professional fees
- Transport and accommodation fees

Exclusions

The following will not be supported: individuals seeking commercial gain will not be supported (individuals will be supported where there is deemed to be a public benefit). A full list of exclusions can be found in the guidance document.

Applications

Applications should be completed on behalf of the young person by a parent or guardian. Application forms can be downloaded from the trust's website, where full application guidelines can also be found, and should be returned by email or post.

Financial information

Year end	31/03/2021
Income	£6,570,000
Total expenditure	£12,910,000

Further financial information

During the year, grants delivered through the Arts Grants Scheme totalled £2,300. We estimate that around half of this amount was awarded to individuals.

Other information

The Shetland Arts Fund also accepts applications from organisations, projects and events. The trust also has a number of grant schemes for organisations.

Renfrewshire

East Renfrewshire

Janet Hamilton Memorial Fund

£1,100 (2020/21)

Correspondent: The Trustees, Accountancy Services, East Renfrewshire Council, Eastwood Park, Glasgow G46 6UG (tel: 0141 577 3001)

OSCR number: SC019475

Eligibility

People living in Barrhead who have an illness that requires nursing or hospital treatment. Preference may be given to older people.

Types of grant

Grants are given according to need.

Applications

Contact the correspondent to obtain an application form. Our previous research suggests that grants are distributed in December and that applications must include a signature from a doctor confirming the person's state of health, as well as a signed copy of their life certificate.

Financial information

Year end	31/03/2021
Income	£250
Total expenditure	£1,100

Further financial information

Full accounts were not available to view on the OSCR website due to the fund's low income. We have therefore estimated the grant total based on the fund's total expenditure.

Inverclyde

Gourock Coal and Benevolent Fund

£4,100 (2019/20)

Correspondent: The Trustees, 4D Cragburn Gate, Albert Road, Gourock, Renfrewshire PA19 1NZ

OSCR number: SC009881

Eligibility

Older people in need who live in the former burgh of Gourock.

Types of grant

According to our previous research, the charity provides gas and electricity vouchers as well as coal deliveries.

Applications

Our previous research indicates that applications should be made in writing to any minister or parish priest in the town. Applications can be submitted either directly by the individual or through a social worker, Citizens Advice or other welfare agency.

Financial information

Year end	25/10/2020
Income	£5,700
Total expenditure	£4,500

Further financial information

Full accounts were not available to view on the OSCR website due to the fund's low income. We have therefore estimated the grant total based on the fund's total expenditure.

Scottish Borders

Blackstock Trust

£ £20,000 (2019/20)

Correspondent: The Trustees, c/o Pike & Chapman, 36 Bank Street, Galashiels, Scottish Borders TD1 1ER

OSCR number: SC014309

Eligibility
People who are elderly or sick, or who have disabilities, and live in the counties of Roxburgh, Berwick and Selkirk. Serving and retired British police officers who have been injured or incapacitated while serving.

Types of grant
Financial assistance for accommodation, maintenance or welfare, short holiday breaks, respite care and the provision of amenities.

Applications
Apply in writing to the correspondent.

Financial information
Year end	30/09/2020
Income	£18,700
Total expenditure	£20,900

Further financial information
Full accounts were not available to view on the OSCR website due to the trust's low income. We have therefore estimated the grant total based on the trust's total expenditure.

Roxburghshire Landward Benevolent Trust

£ £1,400 (2020)

Correspondent: Mr B. Evans, Trustee, Alderwood, Main Street, St Boswells, Roxburghshire TD6 0AP

OSCR number: SC008416

Eligibility
People in need who live in the Landward area of the former Roxburgh County Council area.

Types of grant
One-off grants are awarded to assist people with health and social needs. Financial help can be given towards foods, fuel, clothing, general household requirements, medical equipment, transport and holidays. Grants may also

be given towards 'a person's maintenance or treatment in their own homes, day-care centres, nursing homes, hospices, etc.', as stated on the trust's OSCR record.

Applications
Contact the correspondent for further information.

Financial information
Year end	31/12/2020
Income	£6,100
Total expenditure	£3,000

Further financial information
Full accounts were not available to view on the OSCR website due to the trust's low income. We have therefore estimated the grant total based on the trust's total expenditure.

Other information
Grants are also made to organisations.

Tayside

George McLean Trust
See entry on page 190

Angus

Angus Council Charitable Trust

£ £7,500 (2019/20)

Correspondent: The Trustees, Angus Council, Angus House, Orchardbank Business Park, Forfar, Angus DD8 1AN (email: accesslawcommittee@angus.gov.uk)

 https://www.angus.gov.uk/council_and_democracy/councillors/strangs_mortification_and_angus_charitable_trust_applications

OSCR number: SC044695

Eligibility
People in need who live in Angus, including the wards of Kirriemuir and Dean, Brechin and Edzell, Forfar and District, Monifieth and Sidlaw, Carnoustie and District, Arbroath East and Lunan, Arbroath West and Letham, Montrose and District, as well as Angus-wide.

Types of grant
The purposes of funds available in each ward may vary; applicants should check the charity's website or contact the correspondent for further information. Residents of Forfar may also apply to

Strangs Mortification, which gives heating grants as well as one-off grants. Applicants must have lived in Forfar for at least two years and be in receipt of housing benefit.

Applications
Application forms are available to download from the charity's website or from ACCESS offices or libraries. Applications to Strangs Mortification from those who live in Forfar must be approved by a social worker, health professional or minister, from whom an application form can also be obtained.

Financial information
Year end	30/11/2020
Income	£8,300
Total expenditure	£15,500

Further financial information
Full accounts were not available to view on the OSCR website due to the trust's low income. We have therefore estimated the grant total based on the trust's total expenditure.

The Colvill Charity

£ £1,000 (2019/20)

Correspondent: Trusts Administrator, Thorntons Law LLP, Brothockbank House, Arbroath, Angus DD11 1NJ

OSCR number: SC003913

Eligibility
People who are in need and live in the town of Arbroath or the parish of St Vigeans and the surrounding area. Any surplus funds will be awarded to applicants in the district of Angus.

Types of grant
Grants are awarded according to need.

Applications
Application forms are available upon request from the correspondent.

Financial information
Year end	18/06/2020
Income	£33,000
Total expenditure	£21,800

Further financial information
Note, the grant total to individuals has been estimated.

The Lethendy Charitable Trust
See entry on page 189

The Gertrude Muriel Pattullo Advancement Award Scheme

(£) £13,000 (2019/20)

Correspondent: The Trustees, c/o Blackadders Solicitors, 30–34 Reform Street, Dundee DD1 1RJ (email: enquiries@blackadders.co.uk)

OSCR number: SC000811

Eligibility
Young people aged up to 25 who have physical disabilities and live in the city of Dundee or the county of Angus.

Types of grant
One-off and recurrent grants are given towards books, equipment, instruments, fees, living expenses and educational outings in the UK. Specialist equipment such as beds and wheelchairs can also be funded, as can clothing, travel costs to hospital and other necessities.

Applications
Application forms are available from the correspondent.

Financial information
Year end	30/09/2020
Income	£17,000
Total expenditure	£27,300

Further financial information
Full accounts were not available to view on the OSCR website due to the trust's low income. We have therefore estimated the grant total based on the trust's total expenditure.

Angus Walker Benevolent Bequest

(£) £6,100 (2019/20)

Correspondent: The Trustees, c/o T. Duncan & Co. Solicitors, 192 High Street, Montrose, Angus DD10 8NA

OSCR number: SC008129

Eligibility
People in need who live in Montrose.

Types of grant
Grants are given according to need.

Applications
According to our previous research, applications should be made via a trustee, local district councillors, the minister of Montrose Old Church or the rector of St Mary's and St Peter's Episcopal Church in Montrose.

Financial information
Year end	05/04/2020
Income	£12,100
Total expenditure	£6,800

Further financial information
Full accounts were not available to view on the OSCR website due to the charity's low income. We have therefore estimated the grant total based on the charity's total expenditure.

Dundee
The Boyack Fund

(£) £1,000 (2020)

Correspondent: The Trustees, c/o Hodge Solicitors LLP, 28 Wellmeadow, Blairgowrie, Perthshire PH10 6AX (email: info@hodgesolicitors.co.uk)

OSCR number: SC004998

Eligibility
Pensioners in need who live in Monifieth near Dundee.

Types of grant
Grants are given according to need.

Applications
Apply in writing to the correspondent.

Financial information
Year end	31/12/2020
Income	£1,000
Total expenditure	£1,200

Further financial information
Full accounts were not available to view on the OSCR website due to the fund's low income. We have therefore estimated the grant total based on the fund's total expenditure.

Broughty Ferry Benevolent Trust

(£) £15,100 (2019/20)

Correspondent: Mr G. Stirling, Trustee, 12 Tircarra Gardens, Broughty Ferry, Dundee DD5 2QF

OSCR number: SC010644

Eligibility
People in need living in the boundaries of The Ferry ward in Dundee.

Types of grant
Grants are given according to need.

Applications
Apply in writing to the correspondent.

Financial information
Year end	28/02/2020
Income	£21,100
Total expenditure	£16,800

Further financial information
Full accounts were not available to view on the OSCR website due to the trust's low income. We have therefore

estimated the grant total based on the trust's total expenditure.

The Lethendy Charitable Trust
See entry on page 189

The Mair Robertson Benevolent Fund

(£) £11,400 (2019/20)

Correspondent: The Trustees, 144 Nethergate, Dundee DD1 4EB

OSCR number: SC007435

Eligibility
Older women living in Dundee and Blairgowrie who are in need.

Types of grant
Grants are given according to need.

Applications
Apply in writing to the correspondent.

Financial information
Year end	19/01/2020
Income	£11,500
Total expenditure	£12,700

Further financial information
Full accounts were not available to view on the OSCR website due to the fund's low income. We have therefore estimated the fund's grant total based on its total expenditure.

Perth and Kinross
Mrs Agnes W. Carmichael's Trust

(£) £2,300 (2019/20)

Correspondent: The Trustees, Watson Lyall Bowie, Union Bank Buildings, Coupar Angus, Perthshire PH13 9AJ

OSCR number: SC004415

Eligibility
People in need who live in Perth and Kinross. Preference may be given to those living in Coupar Angus.

Types of grant
Grants are given according to need.

Applications
Apply in writing to the correspondent.

Financial information
Year end	05/04/2020
Income	£5,100
Total expenditure	£5,100

Further financial information

Full accounts were not available to view on the OSCR website due to the trust's low income. We have therefore estimated the grant total based on the trust's total expenditure.

Other information

The trust also makes grants to organisations.

Neil Gow Charitable Trust

£12,600 (2019/20)

Correspondent: The Trustees, c/o Miller Hendry, 10 Blackfriars Street, Perth, Perthshire PH1 5NS

OSCR number: SC012915

Eligibility

People in need who live in the district of Perth and Kinross or the immediate neighbourhood.

Types of grant

Grants are given according to need. According to our previous research, the trust also provides pensions.

Applications

Apply in writing to the correspondent.

Financial information

Year end	05/04/2020
Income	£8,500
Total expenditure	£14,000

Further financial information

Full accounts were not available to view on the OSCR website due to the trust's low income. We have therefore estimated the grant total based on the trust's total expenditure.

Guildry Incorporation of Perth

£83,700 (2020/21)

Correspondent: Secretary, 42 George Street, Perth, Perthshire PH1 5JL (email: secretary@perthguildry.org.uk)

 www.perthguildry.org.uk

OSCR number: SC008072

Eligibility

Welfare

Members of the guildry, their widows and dependants, and other people living in Perth who are in need. Assistance is only available after five years of membership if aged 40 or under and after three years of membership if aged over 40.

Education

Members of the guildry or their children who are attending a full-time course of

study at a university or college in the UK. Assistance is also given to non-members who reside in Perth or Guildtown who have a place on a full-time education course in the UK, as well as students who reside outside Perth or Guildtown but attend one of the four local secondary schools in Perth.

Types of grant

Welfare

Weekly pensions, coal allowances and Christmas gifts are awarded to members and their dependants over the state retirement age. Temporary assistance can be granted to members under state retirement age who are unable to work due to disability or who are in extreme financial difficulties.

Education

Educational bursaries are awarded to members and non-members. Travel bursaries are also available.

Applications

Contact the charity for further information.

Financial information

Year end	31/03/2021
Income	£215,500
Total expenditure	£212,800

The Lethendy Charitable Trust
See entry on page 189

Scones Lethendy Mortification

£8,100 (2020/21)

Correspondent: The Trustees, King James VI Hospital, Hospital Street, Perth, Perthshire PH2 8HP

OSCR number: SC015545

Eligibility

People over the age of 60 who are in need, and boys close to the age of 14 who can prove they are a descendant of Charles Cairnie or one of his brothers. Only residents of Perth can apply.

Types of grant

Pensions paid quarterly to older residents and bursaries (paid yearly over ten years) to young boys who can prove their relation to Charles Cairnie.

Applications

Apply on a form available from the correspondent. New applicants are added to a waiting list, although successful applicants are judged on need rather than when they applied.

Financial information

Year end	29/09/2021
Income	£181,000
Total expenditure	£143,100

Arthur and Margaret Thompson's Charitable Trust

£18,400 (2019/20)

Correspondent: The Trustees, c/o Miller Hendry, 10 Blackfriars Street, Perth, Perthshire PH1 5NS

OSCR number: SC012103

Eligibility

Residents of Kinross and the parish of Orwell who are in need.

Types of grant

The trust provides annuities and Christmas gifts.

Applications

Apply in writing to the correspondent.

Financial information

Year end	05/04/2020
Income	£174,800
Total expenditure	£96,700

Mrs A. Unwin Trust

£6,600 (2019/20)

Correspondent: The Trustees, c/o Miller Hendry, 10 Blackfriars Street, Perth, Perthshire PH1 5NS

OSCR number: SC015126

Eligibility

Residents of the city of Perth who are in need.

Types of grant

One-off and recurring grants are given according to need. Grants have previously been awarded for household goods, clothing, bedding and flooring.

Applications

The trust's 2019/20 accounts state:

> the trustees may consider written applications or specific forms from private individuals although their preference is to consider appeals made by Perth and Kinross Council Social Services Department on behalf of deserving cases.

Financial information

Year end	05/04/2020
Income	£31,700
Total expenditure	£31,800

Further financial information

Grants were awarded to 18 individuals during 2019/20.

Wales

Mid and West Wales

Pembrokeshire – Sir Benfro

Haverfordwest Freemen's Estate

£ £8,000 (2019/20)

Correspondent: The Trustees, c/o R. K. Lucas & Son, 9 Victoria Place, Haverfordwest, Pembrokeshire SA61 2JX (tel: 01437 762538)

CC number: 515111

Eligibility
Hereditary freemen of Haverfordwest aged 18 years and over.

Types of grant
Grants are given according to need.

Applications
Apply in writing to the correspondent.

Financial information

Year end	31/03/2020
Income	£56,600
Total expenditure	£18,400

Further financial information
In 2019/20, £17,700 was spent on charitable activities. A breakdown of grants was not available; therefore, we have estimated the grant total for welfare.

Other information
The charity also awards grants to organisations.

William Sanders Charity

£ £6,300 (2019/20)

Correspondent: The Trustees, St John's Community Hall, Church Street, Pembroke Dock, Pembrokeshire SA72 6AR (tel: 01646 680024)

CC number: 229182

Eligibility
Older women who are either widowed or unmarried and are experiencing financial difficulty. Applicants must live within a five-mile radius of the parish of St John's – Pembroke.

Types of grant
Grants are awarded according to need in November and December each year.

Applications
Apply in writing to the correspondent.

Financial information

Year end	30/06/2020
Income	£10,300
Total expenditure	£7,000

Further financial information
Full accounts were not available to view on the Charity Commission's website due to the charity's low income. We have therefore estimated the charity's grant total based on its total expenditure.

William Vawer

£ £3,700 (2019/20)

Correspondent: R. Lucas, c/o R. K. Lucas & Son, 9 Victoria Place, Haverfordwest, Pembrokeshire SA61 2JX (tel: 01437 762538)

CC number: 213880

Eligibility
People in need who live in the town of Haverfordwest. The charity has a preference for those who are freemen of the town of Haverfordwest.

Types of grant
Pensions and one-off grants.

Applications
Apply in writing to the correspondent.

Financial information

Year end	05/04/2020
Income	£7,400
Total expenditure	£4,100

Further financial information
Full accounts were not available to view on the Charity Commission's website due to the charity's low income. We have therefore estimated the charity's grant total based on its total expenditure.

Powys

The Brecknock Welfare Trust

£ £1,900 (2020)

Correspondent: The Trustees, Brecon Town Council, The Guildhall, High Street, Brecon LD3 7AL (tel: 01874 622884; email: office@ brecontowncouncil.org.uk)

CC number: 240671

Eligibility
Residents of the borough of Brecknock who are in need.

Types of grant
One-off grants.

Applications
Apply in writing to the correspondent.

Financial information

Year end	31/12/2020
Income	£1,300
Total expenditure	£4,200

Further financial information
Full accounts were not available to view on the Charity Commission's website due to the trust's low income. We have therefore estimated the trust's grant total based on its total expenditure.

Other information
This charity also makes grants to organisations.

Llanidloes Relief in Need Charity

£ £1,200 (2019/20)

Correspondent: Elaine Lloyd, Woodcroft, Woodlands Road, Llanidloes, Powys SY18 6HX (tel: 01686 413045; email: elainelllloyd@gmail.com)

CC number: 259955

Eligibility

People in need who live in the area of Llanidloes.

Types of grant

Grants are given according to need.

Applications

Apply in writing to the correspondent.

Financial information

Year end	29/02/2020
Income	£300
Total expenditure	£1,300

Further financial information

Full accounts were not available to view on the Charity Commission's website due to the charity's low income. We have therefore estimated the grant total based on the charity's total expenditure.

The Montgomery Welfare Fund

£ £3,100 (2020/21)

Correspondent: Edward Humphreys, 2 Rowes Terrace, Pool Road, Montgomery, Montgomeryshire SY15 6QD (tel: 01686 668790; email: montgomerycharities@gmail.com)

CC number: 214767

Eligibility

People in need who live in the borough of Montgomery.

Types of grant

Grants are given according to need.

Applications

Apply in writing to the correspondent.

Financial information

Year end	31/03/2021
Income	£4,500
Total expenditure	£3,400

Further financial information

Full accounts were not available to view on the Charity Commission's website due to the fund's low income. We have therefore estimated the fund's grant total based on its total expenditure.

The St Chad's and St Alkmund's Charity

£ £1,100 (2019/20)

Correspondent: The Trustees, 1 St Chad's Terrace, Shrewsbury, Shropshire SY1 1JL (tel: 07989 654134)

CC number: 231383

Eligibility

Welfare

People in need living in the ecclesiastical districts of St Chad's and St George's (Shrewsbury), Bicton, Oxon, Annscroft, Astley, Guilsfield, Kinnerly and Great Ness.

Education

Young people under the age of 25, living in the same parishes, are eligible for educational grants.

Types of grant

Grants are given according to need.

Applications

Apply in writing to the correspondent.

Financial information

Year end	30/09/2020
Income	£2,300
Total expenditure	£2,300

Further financial information

Full accounts were not available to view on the Charity Commission's website due to the charity's low income. We have therefore estimated the charity's grant total based on its total expenditure.

Other information

The charity also makes grants to other organisations to further the religious and charitable work of the Church of England in the local area.

Visual Impairment Breconshire (Nam Gweledol Sir Brycheiniog)

£ £3,300 (2019/20)

Correspondent: Nick Lancaster, Chair, Coed Y Wern, Pwllgloyw, Brecon LD3 9RA (tel: 01874 624949; email: vibrecon@gmail.com)

 vibreconshire.uk

CC number: 217377

Eligibility

Visually impaired people in Breconshire.

Types of grant

Grants are available to help pay for equipment, education, services training and experiences such as holidays.

Exclusions

In general, the charity will not pay for anything that should be funded by the NHS or a local authority. It will not contribute towards the rental of book reading equipment or corresponding library subscriptions, or any equipment for use in care homes or similar institutions where there exists a statutory obligation or requirement to provide for client use.

Applications

Application forms and full guidelines can be found on the charity's website. The charity notes that applicants are required to claim any relevant welfare benefits, and that a financial contribution from the applicant is expected.

Financial information

Year end	31/03/2020
Income	£2,300
Total expenditure	£3,700

Further financial information

Full accounts were not available to view on the Charity Commission's website due to the charity's low income. We have therefore estimated the charity's grant total based on its total expenditure.

Other information

This charity also runs activities and provides resources for visually impaired people in Breconshire.

North Wales

County Council of Clwyd Welsh Church Fund

£ £6,600 (2020/21)

Correspondent: Louise Elford, Flintshire County Council, Finance, County Hall, Mold, Flintshire CH7 6NA (tel: 01352 702261; email: louise.elford@flintshire.gov.uk)

CC number: 504476

Eligibility

Older people and people in need who live in Denbighshire, Flintshire and Wrexham. Preference is given to those in the county of Clwyd.

Types of grant

Grants are given according to need.

Applications

Apply in writing to the correspondent.

Financial information

Year end	31/03/2021
Income	£14,600
Total expenditure	£14,600

Further financial information

Full accounts were not available to view on the Charity Commission's website due to the fund's low income. We have therefore estimated the fund's grant total based on its total expenditure.

Other information

The charity also makes grants to organisations.

North Wales Police Benevolent Fund

£ £4,500 (2019/20)

Correspondent: Mel Jones, c/o North Wales Police Federation, 311 Abergele Road, Old Colwyn, Colwyn Bay LL29 9YF (tel: 01492 805404; email: mel. jones@nthwales.pnn.police.uk)

CC number: 505321

Eligibility

Members and former members of the North Wales Police Force and their families and immediate dependants who are in need. Former members of previous forces amalgamated to form the North Wales force are also eligible for support.

Types of grant

Grants are awarded according to need.

Applications

Contact the correspondent for further information.

Financial information

Year end	31/03/2020
Income	£6,800
Total expenditure	£5,000

Further financial information

Full accounts were not available to view on the Charity Commission's website due to the trust's low income. We have therefore estimated the grant total based on the trust's total expenditure.

The Evan and Catherine Roberts Home

£ £3,100 (2019/20)

Correspondent: The Trustees, Ael Y Garth, 81 Bryn Avenue, Old Colwyn, Colwyn Bay LL29 8AH (tel: 01492 515209; email: kenowen@uwclub.net)

CC number: 244965

Eligibility

People aged 60 years or over living within a 40-mile radius of the Bethesda Welsh Methodist Church at Old Colwyn in the county of Clwyd. Preference is given to members of the Methodist Church.

Types of grant

Grants are awarded according to need.

Applications

Apply in writing to the correspondent.

Financial information

Year end	31/03/2020
Income	£890
Total expenditure	£3,400

Further financial information

Full accounts were not available to view on the Charity Commission's website due to the charity's low income. We have therefore estimated the charity's grant total based on its total expenditure.

Conwy County – Conwy

Conwy Welsh Church Acts Fund

Correspondent: Catherine Dowber, Senior Administration Officer, Finance and Efficiencies Department, Conwy County Borough Council, Bodlondeb, Conwy LL32 8DU (tel: 01492 576201; email: welshchurchactsfund@conwy.gov. uk)

 www.conwy.gov.uk/en/Council/ Welsh-Church-Acts-Fund.aspx

Eligibility

People in need living in the county borough of Conwy.

Types of grant

One-off grants ranging from £50 to £500 are awarded for:

- The relief of poverty and sickness
- The advancement of religion
- The advancement of literature and the arts of Wales
- The advancement of education
- Medical and social research or treatment
- The relief of emergencies and disasters.

Grants are also awarded to the following people:

- People on probation
- Older people
- People who are blind or visually impaired

Exclusions

Grants are not made for tuition fees.

Applications

For further enquiries and application forms, contact the correspondent. Applications can be submitted directly by the individual or through a third party. The closing date for applications is the first week in May or October.

Further financial information

Financial information was not available for the fund.

Other information

The fund has its origins in The Welsh Church Act of 1914. There is a page about the fund on the Conwy County Borough Council website.

Denbighshire – Sir Ddinbych

Freeman Evans St David's Day Denbigh Charity

£ £23,200 (2019/20)

Correspondent: Philippa Jones, Secretary, 6 Parc Clwyd, Myddleton Park, Denbigh, Denbighshire LL16 4BA (tel: 01745 812256; email: medwynjones@btinternet.com)

CC number: 518033

Eligibility

People in need who live in Denbigh and Henllan, particularly older people and people who have an illness or disability.

Types of grant

One-off grants are given according to need.

Applications

Apply in writing to the correspondent.

Financial information

Year end	31/03/2020
Income	£188,600
Total expenditure	£50,700

Further financial information

In 2019/20, a total of £46,300 was awarded in grants. A breakdown of grants was not available.

Other information

The charity also supports organisations.

The Charity of Elizabeth Williams

£ £4,200 (2019/20)

Correspondent: Alison Alexander, 19 Roe Parc, St Asaph, Denbighshire LL17 0LD (tel: 01745 583798; email: alison.alexander@btinternet.com)

CC number: 216903

Eligibility

People in need who live in the communities of St Asaph, Bodelwyddan, Cefn and Waen in Clwyd.

Types of grant

Grants are awarded according to need.

Applications

Apply in writing to the correspondent.

Financial information

Year end	31/03/2020
Income	£8,400
Total expenditure	£4,700

Further financial information

Full accounts were not available to view on the Charity Commission's website due to the charity's low income. We have therefore estimated the charity's grant total based on its total expenditure.

Other information

One-half of the charity's income is to be awarded to Elizabeth Williams's Educational Foundation.

Gwynedd

Freeman Evans St David's Day Ffestiniog Charity

£ £51,700 (2019/20)

Correspondent: Maldwyn Evans, Treasurer, PO Box 73, Lon Merllyn, Blaenau Ffestiniog, Gwynedd LL41 9AL (tel: 07876 545786; email: swyddfa@ elusenfreemanevans.cymru)

CC number: 518034

Eligibility

People who are older, in poor health or who have disabilities and live in the districts of Blaenau Ffestiniog and Llan Ffestiniog as they were prior to the 1974 reorganisation.

Types of grant

Grants are given according to need.

Applications

Contact the correspondent for more information.

Financial information

Year end	05/04/2020
Income	£90
Total expenditure	£56,200

Further financial information

Full accounts were not available to view on the Charity Commission's website due to the charity's low income. We have therefore estimated the charity's grant total based on previous year's giving.

Isle of Anglesey – Ynys Môn

Charity of William Bold

£ £5,200 (2019/20)

Correspondent: The Trustees, Talfryn, Bodffordd, Llangefni, Anglesey LL77 7DJ (tel: 01248 750368; email: reestalfryn@ yahoo.co.uk)

CC number: 218152

Eligibility

Welfare

Residents of the parishes of Gwalchmai and Heneglwys (Bodffordd) who are in need.

Education

Educational grants are available to young people in Gwalchmai and Heneglwys (Bodffordd) for support in continuing their studies.

Types of grant

Grants are given according to need.

Applications

Apply in writing to the correspondent.

Financial information

Year end	31/03/2020
Income	£5,800
Total expenditure	£5,800

Further financial information

Full accounts were not available to view on the Charity Commission's website due to the charity's low income. We have therefore estimated the charity's grant total based on its total expenditure.

Other information

This charity also makes grants to organisations and provides other services.

Llanrhuddlad Charities (William Lloyd)

£ £1,300 (2019/20)

Correspondent: Maldwyn Roberts, Trustee, 17 Maes Cynfor, Cemaes Bay LL67 0HS (tel: 01407 710549; email: mnlroberts@gmail.com)

CC number: 238565

Eligibility

Widows and older people living in Llanrhuddlad who are in need.

Types of grant

Annual donations.

Applications

Apply in writing to the correspondent.

Financial information

Year end	31/03/2020
Income	£4,600
Total expenditure	£1,400

Further financial information

Full accounts were not available to view on the Charity Commission's website due to the charity's low income. We have therefore estimated the charity's grant total based on its total expenditure.

Other information

The charity owns two properties and pays for any maintenance and upkeep needed. The charity also provides assistance to Llanrhuddlad Church for building maintenance.

Wrexham County – Wrecsam

The Jones Trust

£ £5,000 (2020)

Correspondent: Patricia Williams, Secretary, 33 Deva Way, Wrexham, Clwyd LL13 9EU (tel: 01978 261684; email: patmwilliams@tiscali.co.uk)

CC number: 229956

Eligibility

People living in Wrexham who are in need as a result of illness, disability, convalescence, or infirmity. Support is also available to the carers of such people.

Types of grant

Grants are given for respite care.

Applications

Apply in writing to the correspondent.

Financial information

Year end	31/12/2020
Income	£32,900
Total expenditure	£23,800

Further financial information

Grants were awarded to 41 individuals during the year.

Overton United Charity

£ £1,200 (2019/20)

Correspondent: The Trustees, 6 Springfield Park, Overton, Wrexham, Clwyd LL13 0EX (tel: 01978 710567)

CC number: 1059405

Eligibility

People living in Overton who are older, ill or convalescent, or who have disabilities.

Types of grant

One-off grants are given according to need.

Applications

Apply in writing to the correspondent.

Financial information

Year end	31/05/2020
Income	£2,600
Total expenditure	£2,600

Further financial information

Full accounts were not available to view on the Charity Commission's website due to the charity's low income. We have therefore estimated the grant total based on the charity's total expenditure.

Ruabon and District Relief in Need Charity

£ £500 (2019)

Correspondent: Berwyn Thomas, 118 Pont Adam Crescent, Ruabon, Wrexham, Clwyd LL14 6AF (tel: 07399 403952; email: berwyn.thomas3@hotmail.co.uk)

CC number: 212817

Eligibility

People in need who live in the community council areas of Cefn Mawr, Pen-y-cae, Rhosllanerchrugog and Ruabon.

Types of grant

Our previous research indicates that grants have been made towards essential household items (for example, furniture, white goods and carpets), school uniforms and trips, musical instruments, clothing for adults in hospital, travel costs for hospital visits, and books and travel for university students.

Exclusions

Our previous research suggests that the charity does not make grants for private school fees or bankruptcy costs.

Applications

Our previous research suggests that applications must be made through an intermediary such as a social worker or other professional or an organisation. Applications are typically considered on the second Monday of January, April, July and October, but urgent cases may be considered at any time.

Financial information

Year end	31/12/2019
Income	£3,300
Total expenditure	£1,100

Further financial information

Full accounts were not available to view on the Charity Commission's website due to the charity's low income. We have therefore estimated the charity's grant total based on its total expenditure. The charity's expenditure was lower in 2019 than in previous years (estimated at £1,000 in 2018 and £1,300 in 2017).

Other information

This charity also makes grants to local organisations.

Wrexham and District Relief in Need Charity

£ £20,800 (2019)

Correspondent: The Trustees, Holly Chase, Pen Y Palmant Road, Minera, Wrexham, Clwyd LL11 3YW (tel: 01978 754152; email: clerk.wpef@gmail.com)

CC number: 236355

Eligibility

People living in the former borough of Wrexham who are in need. Support is also extended to residents of the following communities: Abenbury; Bersham; Bieston; Broughton; Brymbo; Esclusham Above; Esclusham Below; Gresford; Gwersyllt; Minera.

Types of grant

Grants are awarded according to need. Previous examples of items with which the charity has assisted include white goods and carpeting.

Applications

Apply in writing to the correspondent.

Financial information

Year end	31/12/2019
Income	£18,800
Total expenditure	£23,100

Further financial information

Full accounts were not available to view on the Charity Commission's website due to the charity's low income. We have therefore estimated the charity's grant total based on its total expenditure.

Other information

In previous years the charity has awarded grants to vicars in the beneficial area for distribution to individuals.

South Wales

Children's Leukaemia Society

£ £35,800 (2020/21)

Correspondent: The Trustees, Splott Library, Singleton Road, Splott, Cardiff CF24 2ET (tel: 07517 685873; email: childrensleukaemiasociety@hotmail.co.uk)

 www.childrensleukaemiasociety.co.uk

CC number: 1008634

Eligibility

Children under the age of 16 who are in need and have leukaemia. Grants are made to such children who are living in South Wales and the West Country.

Types of grant

Gifts for children who are undergoing chemotherapy, usually in the form of an Argos voucher, and holidays for children and their families following treatment.

Applications

Apply in writing to the correspondent.

Financial information

Year end	31/01/2021
Income	£44,300
Total expenditure	£59,200

Other information

The charity owns five holiday homes at Kiln Park in Tenby.

South Wales Area Miners' Benevolent Fund

£ £30,000 (2019)

Correspondent: The Trustees, NUM South Wales Area, Woodland Terrace, Maesycoed, Pontypridd, Rhondda Cynon Taf CF37 1DZ (tel: 01443 404092; email: numsouthwales@fut.net)

CC number: 500118

Eligibility

Employees and former employees of the coal mining industry in South Wales and their dependants and widows.

Types of grant

One-off grants are given according to need.

Applications

Apply in writing to the correspondent.

Financial information

Year end	31/12/2019
Income	£3,800
Total expenditure	£33,300

Further financial information

Full accounts were not available to view on the Charity Commission's website due to the fund's low income. We have therefore estimated the fund's grant total based on its total expenditure.

The South Wales Police Benevolent Fund

 £33,700 (2019/20)

Correspondent: The Trustees, South Wales Police Headquarters, Cowbridge Road, Bridgend, Wales CF31 3SU (tel: 01656 869342)

🌐 https://www.south-wales.police.uk

CC number: 501454

Eligibility

Serving and former members of the South Wales Police force and their widows/widowers, civil partners and dependants who are in need due to ill health or disability.

Types of grant

One-off grants are given according to need. The charity also provides death benefits.

Applications

Apply in writing to the correspondent.

Financial information

Year end	31/03/2020
Income	£53,600
Total expenditure	£41,600

Further financial information

In 2019/20, grants to individuals totalled £33,700. Benevolence assistance payments to 12 individuals totalled £27,100, and 22 death benefits were paid during the year totalling £6,600.

Cardiff City and County – Caerdydd

The Cardiff Blues Regional Benevolent Trust

 £30,200 (2019)

Correspondent: The Trustees, Cardiff Arms Park, Westgate Street, Cardiff CF10 1JA (tel: 07775 620266)

CC number: 1165480

Eligibility

Players or staff at a rugby club within the geographic area of the Cardiff Blues region who are in need.

Types of grant

Grants are given according to need.

Applications

Apply in writing to the correspondent.

Financial information

Year end	31/12/2019
Income	£46,300
Total expenditure	£45,600

Merthyr Tydfil County – Merthyr Tudful

Merthyr Mendicants

 £5,000 (2019)

Correspondent: The Trustees, 4 Georgetown Villas, Georgetown, Merthyr Tydfil, Mid Glamorgan CF48 1BD (tel: 01685 373308)

🌐 https://www.merthyrmendicants.org

CC number: 208105

Eligibility

People in need who live in the borough of Merthyr Tydfil.

Types of grant

Grants are awarded according to need. The charity also makes in-kind gifts.

Applications

Apply in writing to the correspondent.

Financial information

Year end	31/12/2019
Income	£14,400
Total expenditure	£11,000

Further financial information

Full accounts were not available to view on the Charity Commission's website due to the charity's low income. We have therefore estimated the charity's grant total based on its total expenditure.

Other information

The charity also makes grants to organisations.

Monmouthshire – Sir Fynwy

Monmouth Charity

 £4,200 (2019/20)

Correspondent: The Trustees, Windyridge, Ridgeway, Wyesham, Monmouth, Gwent NP25 3JX (tel: 07769 178623; email: monmouthcharity@outlook.com)

CC number: 700759

Eligibility

People living within a ten-mile radius of Monmouth town who are in need.

Types of grant

Grants are given for educational purposes and the relief of poverty and for people with disabilities.

Applications

Apply in writing to the correspondent.

Financial information

Year end	26/08/2020
Income	£9,600
Total expenditure	£9,300

Further financial information

The charity was not required to file accounts for the 2019/20 financial year; therefore, we have estimated the grant total based on previous years' giving.

Other information

This charity also makes grants to organisations.

The Monmouth Diocesan Clergy Widows and Dependants Society

 £27,200 (2020)

Correspondent: The Trustees, Llwyn-Gwyn House, Old Hereford Road, Abergavenny, Gwent NP7 7LE (tel: 01873 890265)

CC number: 1073775

Eligibility

Widows and dependants of deceased clerics of the Church in Wales who, at the time of their death, were in receipt of a stipend or pension from the Church in Wales arising from an appointment in the Diocese of Monmouth.

Types of grant

Financial support, including bereavement grants and birthday and Christmas gifts.

Applications

Apply in writing to the correspondent.

Financial information

Year end	31/12/2020
Income	£31,000
Total expenditure	£32,100

The Monmouthshire County Council Welsh Church Act Fund

 £46,900 (2019/20)

Correspondent: David Jarrett, Monmouthshire County Council, County Hall, The Rhadyr, Usk NP15 1GA (tel: 01633 644657; email: davejarrett@monmouthshire.gov.uk)

🌐 https://www.monmouthshire.gov.uk/welsh-church-fund

CC number: 507094

Eligibility

The trust covers the administrative areas of Blaenau Gwent, Caerphilly, Monmouthshire, Torfaen and the city of Newport, with Monmouthshire County Council being designated as the host authority.

Welfare

People and families in need who live in the area of benefit. Support is also given to individuals on probation and their families, people with criminal records and people with a visual impairment.

Education

People studying at school, university or any other place of education who live in the area of benefit. Grants are also made to apprentices and people starting work.

Types of grant

Welfare

Grants are given towards items and services for people in need, including essential equipment and home furnishings.

Education

Scholarships, bursaries and maintenance allowances for people undertaking education, apprenticeships or starting work. Funding can be used towards items such as tools, clothing, equipment, instruments and books. Grants are also awarded for educational travel abroad and for the study of music and the arts.

Applications

Application forms can be downloaded from the Monmouthshire County Council website and are considered seven times a year.

Financial information

Year end	31/03/2020
Income	£203,400
Total expenditure	£223,100

Other information

The charity also makes grants to organisations and assists with the provision of accommodation for older people. The charity may also offer loans to people undertaking education.

Newport County – Casnewydd

Charity of Annabelle Lady Boughey

£ £860 (2019/20)

Correspondent: Linda Palmer-Pitchford, Secretary, Bedruthan, Tibberton, Newport, Shropshire TF10 8NN (tel: 01952 550745; email: linda@ bougheyroddamha.org.uk)

🌐 https://annabelleladyboughey.org.uk

CC number: 213899

Eligibility

People living in the area covered by the TF10 postcode who are in need. This area includes: Newport; Church Aston; Chetwynd Aston; Woodcote; Moreton; Forton; Sambrook; Tibberton; Edgmond; Lilleshall.

Types of grant

Grants are awarded according to need.

Applications

Application forms are available to download on the charity's website.

Financial information

Year end	31/03/2020
Income	£2,000
Total expenditure	£1,900

Further financial information

Full accounts were not available to view on the Charity Commission's website due to the charity's low income. We have therefore estimated the charity's grant total based on its total expenditure.

Other information

This charity also makes grants to local organisations. Organisations supported recently include Church Aston Scout Group, Edgmond Scout Group, Lilleshall Memorial Hall and Newport Lions.

Swansea City and County – Abertawe

The Swansea and District Friends of the Blind

£ £12,900 (2019/20)

Correspondent: John Allan, Secretary, 3 De La Beche Street, Swansea, Wales SA1 3EY (tel: 07789 377197; email: john_allan_10@hotmail.com)

CC number: 211343

Eligibility

People who are registered blind and live in Swansea and the surrounding area. Support may be given to individuals in other parts of Wales if no other support is available locally.

Types of grant

Grants are awarded according to need.

Applications

Apply in writing to the correspondent.

Financial information

Year end	31/03/2020
Income	£230,900
Total expenditure	£84,100

Torfaen County – Tor-faen

The Cwmbran Trust

 £21,500 (2020)

Correspondent: K. Maddox, Secretary, c/o Meritor HVBS (UK) Ltd, Grange Road, Cwmbran, Gwent NP44 3XU (tel: 01633 834057 (Mondays only from 9am to 3pm); email: gifts@ cwmbrantrust.co.uk)

🌐 https://www.cwmbrantrust.co.uk

CC number: 505855

Eligibility

People in need who have lived in Cwmbran (specifically the NP44 postal district) for at least one year. Employees and ex-employees of the Girling South Wales factories are also eligible.

Types of grant

Grants are made towards, for example, furniture, white goods, carpeting and mobility equipment/aids. Interest-free loans are also available.

Applications

Application forms are available to download on the funder's website. Applications should be made on the applicant's behalf by an agency, organisation or by someone known to the applicant. The trustees meet five times per year (in February, May, July, September and December) to consider grant applications; however, they can meet/communicate between meetings if a request is deemed urgent.

Financial information

Year end	31/12/2020
Income	£85,500
Total expenditure	£53,300

Further financial information

During the year, the charity made awards to 44 individuals. Note: the grant total may include loans.

Other information

This charity also makes grants to organisations. Recently, the charity funded a sensory garden and play area at Crownbridge School.

Vale of Glamorgan – Bro Morgannwg

Cowbridge with Llanblethian United Charities

£ £12,200 (2019/20)

Correspondent: Clerk to the Trustees, 1 The Malthouse, Factory Road, Llanblethian, Cowbridge, Glamorgan CF71 7JD (tel: 01446 771816; email: cwluc.clerk@gmail.com)

CC number: 1014580

Eligibility

People in need who live in the town of Cowbridge with Llanblethian.

Types of grant

Grants are made towards clothing, fees, travel and maintenance for people in further, higher or vocational education, and towards items, services or facilities for older people.

Applications

Apply in writing to the correspondent. Applications can be submitted directly by the individual or through a third party such as a welfare agency or a school/college.

Financial information

Year end	30/09/2020
Income	£23,500
Total expenditure	£24,700

Further financial information

Full accounts were not available to view on the Charity Commission's website due to the charity's low income. We have therefore estimated the charity's grant total based on its total expenditure.

Other information

Grants are also made to local organisations.

East Midlands

General

DTD Charity

£ £40,000 (2020)

Correspondent: Zoe Lander, Fund Manager, c/o Dusk Till Dawn Ltd, G7 Ashtree Court, Mellors Way, Nottingham, Nottinghamshire NG8 6PY (tel: 07730 986000; email: zoe@dtdcharity.com)

 https://dtdcharity.com

CC number: 1104927

Eligibility
People with disabilities living in Nottinghamshire, Leicestershire, Derbyshire, the West Midlands and Warwickshire.

Types of grant
Grants of up to £5,000 are made for specific items or services which will make a positive difference to the quality of life of individuals. The majority of grants are of around £2,000.

Exclusions
The charity's website states it is unable to provide grants for the following:

> Educational grants and course fees; Debts of any kind, including utilities and rent arrears; Money direct to other charities. Reimbursement of costs for items already purchased; Motor Vehicle purchase or expenses e.g. repairs / road tax / insurance / licence; Nursing and residential home fees; Funeral expenses/ removal expenses; Driving lessons; Major home improvements including top-up grants; Therapies such as swimming with Dolphins, hyperbaric therapy etc; Deposits for housing, vehicles and loads; Alternative therapies e.g. reflexology, acupuncture, faith healing; Mobility scooters; Garden maintenance.

Applications
Applications can be made via the foundation's website. Applications can be made directly by the individual or by a professional or representative of an organisation. Where the request is from a private individual, a detailed letter of support from a professional (e.g. family doctor, hospital consultant, social worker, teacher or a worker from a community or disability organisation) is essential. If applying for specialist seating or manual or powered wheelchairs, the letter must be from an occupational therapist or physiotherapist.

Financial information

Year end	31/12/2020
Income	£66,900
Total expenditure	£62,500

Further financial information
Note: the grant total may include grants to organisations.

The Farmers' Benevolent Institution

£ £4,800 (2019/20)

Correspondent: Mark Foster, Duncan & Toplis, 3 Castlegate, Grantham, Lincolnshire NG31 6SF (tel: 01476 591200; email: mark.foster@duntop.co.uk)

CC number: 216042

Eligibility
People living within a 15-mile radius of Grantham who have been landowners and are in need.

Types of grant
Grants are given according to need.

Applications
Apply in writing to the correspondent.

Financial information

Year end	02/04/2020
Income	£4,300
Total expenditure	£5,400

Further financial information
Full accounts were not available to view on the Charity Commission's website due to the charity's low income. We have therefore estimated the charity's grant total based on its total expenditure.

The Leicester Charity Link

£ £430,200 (2019/20)

Correspondent: The Trustees, 20A Millstone Lane, Leicester, Leicestershire LE1 5JN (tel: 0116 222 2200; email: info@charity-link.org)

 www.charity-link.org

CC number: 1078271

Eligibility
People in need who live in Leicestershire, Rutland, or Northamptonshire. Beneficiaries have included those on a low income or experiencing hardship, vulnerable families, people experiencing homelessness and older people.

Types of grant
The charity makes payments from its own funds, administers funds on behalf of other charities and puts potential beneficiaries into contact with funds and charities which may be able to help. Grants are available for a wide range of needs, although the charity most commonly funds essential, everyday items such as beds, cookers and, in emergencies, food.

Applications
Applications can be made online. Full details on how to register and make an application can be found on the application form guidelines from the charity's website. Application forms are to be completed by referrers from an agency and not the applicant directly.

Financial information

Year end	31/03/2020
Income	£903,400
Total expenditure	£829,900

Further financial information
In 2019/20, the charity made 2,969 grants to individuals.

Other information
The charity also makes grants to organisations.

The Leicestershire and Rutland County Nursing Association

£ £51,200 (2019/20)

Correspondent: Edward Cufflin, Treasurer, Charles Stanley, Mercury Place, St George Street, Leicester, Leicestershire LE1 1QG (tel: 0116 366 6200; email: ed.cufflin@charles-stanley. co.uk)

CC number: 216594

Eligibility

Preference is given to current and former employees of the nursing profession in Leicestershire and Rutland who are in need as a result of age, ill health, or other medical conditions. Support is then given more generally to residents of Leicestershire and Rutland who are in need due to disability, ill health, or other medical conditions.

Types of grant

Grants are given according to need.

Applications

Apply in writing to the correspondent.

Financial information

Year end	31/03/2020
Income	£71,200
Total expenditure	£68,500

Other information

This charity also makes grants to organisations. Recently, the charity awarded a number of grants to other voluntary organisations such as the Hinckley Homeless Group and Blood Bikes.

Rycroft Children's Fund

£ £18,000 (2019/20)

Correspondent: The Trustees, Lower Dunishbooth House, Lane Head, Rochdale, Greater Manchester OL12 6BH (tel: 07778 671012; email: rycroftchildrensfund@gmx.co.uk)

 www.rycroftchildrensfund.co.uk

CC number: 231771

Eligibility

Children and young people in need living in the counties of Cheshire, Derbyshire, Greater Manchester, Lancashire, Staffordshire and South and West Yorkshire. Priority is given to residents of Manchester, Salford and Trafford.

Types of grant

Grants are given according to need.

Exclusions

Grants are not given for general living costs, housing costs such as rent or mortgage payments, building repairs, computer equipment, education, overseas travel or individual holidays.

Applications

Applications can be completed on the fund's website. Applications must be accompanied by copies of documentation from an official agency confirming the circumstances of the applicant.

Financial information

Year end	31/03/2020
Income	£37,100
Total expenditure	£51,300

Other information

The charity also makes grants to organisations.

Derbyshire

Derbyshire Community Foundation

£ £34,400 (2019/20)

Correspondent: Grants Team, Unit 2, Heritage Business Centre, Derby Road, Belper, Derbyshire DE56 1SW (tel: 01773 525860; email: hello@ foundationderbyshire.org)

 https://foundationderbyshire.org

CC number: 1039485

Eligibility

The John Weston Fund will support young people between the ages of 11 and 25 who live in certain areas of Derbyshire (a list of eligible postcodes is available on the foundation's website). The Tom Carey Fund supports individuals living in Abbey ward.

Types of grant

Welfare

The John Weston Fund offers grants of up to £500 to individuals towards experiences and projects that develop life skills and build character. Funding is given towards gap year projects, volunteering, extracurricular educational activities and the cost of pursuing excellence in sports or music.

Education

The Tom Carey Fund offers grants of up to £2,000 to individuals to help them to access education and training courses. In addition, the fund supports young people to develop their skills in sports and performing arts.

Applications

Details on how to apply can be found on the community foundation's website.

Financial information

Year end	31/03/2020
Income	£986,300
Total expenditure	£569,900

Further financial information

Grants were awarded to 103 individuals during the year.

Other information

This is one of the 47 UK community foundations, which distribute funding for a wide range of purposes. Grant schemes tend to change frequently – consult the foundation's website for details of current programmes and upcoming deadlines.

The Margaret Harrison Trust

£ £5,700 (2020)

Correspondent: Alexandra Mastin, Trustee, 273 Chesterfield Road, Matlock, Derbyshire DE4 5LE (tel: 07912 064175; email: mastinalex@aol.com)

CC number: 234296

Eligibility

'Gentlewomen of good character' in need who are aged 50 years or over and have lived within a 15-mile radius of St Giles Parish Church – Matlock for a minimum of five years, as stated on the trust's Charity Commission record.

Types of grant

The trust awards small quarterly pensions.

Applications

Apply in writing to the correspondent.

Financial information

Year end	31/12/2020
Income	£5,200
Total expenditure	£6,300

Further financial information

Full accounts were not available to view on the Charity Commission's website due to the trust's low income. We have therefore estimated the trust's grant total based on its total expenditure.

Tiny Tim Trust

 £17,600 (2019/20)

Correspondent: Jenny Anderson, Secretary, 4 Gilbert Avenue, Chesterfield S40 3EU (tel: 01246 236890; email: tinytimtrust@gmail.com)

🌐 https://tinytimtrust.org.uk

CC number: 1038669

Eligibility
Children and young adults aged 0 to 19 who have special health, educational or social needs and live in Derbyshire. Applicants over 16 years of age should be in full-time education.

Types of grant
One-off grants are available for the following: specialist therapeutic equipment; safety equipment; buggies and car seats; educational toys; sensory toys and equipment; early-learning aids; IT equipment for children over eight years of ages; and assistance with projects such as safe-play outdoor projects and fencing.

Exclusions
The trust cannot accept applications for the following: continuous or ongoing funding; clothing, except for specialist clothing; shoes; assistance with debt; or holidays.

Applications
Application forms are available to download from the trust's website. Check the website for application deadlines.

Financial information
Year end	31/03/2020
Income	£17,300
Total expenditure	£19,600

Further financial information
Full accounts were not available to view on the Charity Commission's website due to the trust's low income. We have therefore estimated the trust's grant total based on its total expenditure.

Arthur Townrow Pensions Fund

£101,900 (2020/21)

Correspondent: Samantha Dunwell, Secretary, PO Box 48, Chesterfield, Derbyshire S40 1XT (tel: 01246 231914; email: samantha.dunwell2@tiscali.co.uk)

CC number: 252256

Eligibility
Women aged 40 years or over who have never been married or are widows without children, living in Chesterfield, Bolsover and North East Derbyshire. Women of any age, living in these same areas, who are widows with children are also eligible for support. Support may be extended to women living outside the principal area of benefit, as long as they are aged 40 years or over and have never been married. All applicants must be members of the Church of England, or a Protestant Church which acknowledges the Holy Trinity as taught in the Church of England.

Types of grant
Recurrent grants of £60 a month (£720 per annum).

Applications
Apply in writing to the correspondent.

Financial information
Year end	31/03/2021
Income	£120,900
Total expenditure	£146,700

Further financial information
During the 2020/21 financial year, annuities were paid to 141 individuals.

Woodthorpe Relief-in-Need Charity

£4,800 (2020)

Correspondent: The Trustees, 8 Wigley Road, Inkersall, Chesterfield, Derbyshire S43 3ER (tel: 01246 474457)

CC number: 244192

Eligibility
Residents of the parishes of Barlborough, Staveley and Unstone who are in need.

Types of grant
Grants are given according to need.

Applications
Apply in writing to the correspondent.

Financial information
Year end	31/12/2020
Income	£6,400
Total expenditure	£5,300

Further financial information
Full accounts were not available to view on the Charity Commission's website due to the charity's low income. We have therefore estimated the charity's grant total based on its total expenditure.

Other information
Local organisations may also be supported.

Chesterfield

Chesterfield General Charitable Fund

£1,900 (2019/20)

Correspondent: The Trustees, 12 Swathwick Lane, Wingerworth, Chesterfield, Derbyshire S42 6QW (tel: 01246 234379)

CC number: 511375

Eligibility
People in need who live in the parliamentary constituency of Chesterfield.

Types of grant
Grants are awarded according to need.

Applications
Apply in writing to the correspondent.

Financial information
Year end	31/03/2020
Income	£9,300
Total expenditure	£4,300

Further financial information
Full accounts were not available to view on the Charity Commission's website due to the fund's low income. We have therefore estimated the fund's grant total based on its total expenditure.

Other information
The charity awards grants to organisations in the area of benefit.

Derby

Aston Welfare Trust

£6,400 (2019)

Correspondent: Christine Scott, 6 Lodge Estate, Aston-on-Trent, Derby, Derbyshire DE72 2AH (tel: 01332 792683; email: christine.scott1@btinternet.com)

CC number: 219985

Eligibility
People in need living in Derby.

Types of grant
One-off grants to people in need for health and social activities.

Applications
Apply in writing to the correspondent.

Financial information
Year end	31/12/2019
Income	£3,400
Total expenditure	£7,100

Further financial information
Full accounts were not available to view on the Charity Commission's website

due to the trust's low income. We have therefore estimated the trust's grant total based on its total expenditure.

The Derby City Charity

£0 (2019/20)

Correspondent: Jody Shelton, Derby City Council, Civic Services, Council House, Corporation Street, Derby, Derbyshire DE1 2FS (tel: 01332 643652; email: jody.shelton@derby.gov.uk)

CC number: 214902

Eligibility

Residents of Derby who are in need. Preference is given to residents who are under the age of 25.

Types of grant

Grants are made according to need.

Applications

Apply in writing to the correspondent.

Financial information

Year end	31/03/2020
Income	£5,700
Total expenditure	£0

Further financial information

The charity's expenditure during the 2019/20 financial year was unusually low compared to previous years (£4,100 in 2018/19 and £3,500 in 2017/18).

The Liversage Trust

£109,500 (2019/20)

Correspondent: The Trustees, 6A Liversage Almshouses, London Road, Derby, Derbyshire DE1 2QW (tel: 01332 348199; email: grants@liversagetrust.org)

 liversagetrust.org/grant-assistance

CC number: 1155282

Eligibility

Derby residents who are in need.

Types of grant

Grants can be used for winter fuel and water payments, as well as for the general relief of poverty.

Applications

Application forms can be downloaded from the trust's website. Applications should be made by an agency worker (such as a social worker, community worker or family support worker).

Financial information

Year end	31/03/2020
Income	£2,470,000
Total expenditure	£1,870,000

Other information

The trust's main concern is the management of almshouses and a care

home, Liversage Court. The charity has 160 almshouses, including historic buildings dating back to the 1800s.

Spondon Relief in Need Charity

£19,300 (2019)

Correspondent: Steve Williams, Secretary and Treasurer, 13 Chapel Street, Spondon, Derby DE21 7JP (tel: 01332 544689; email: info@spondonreliefinneedcharity.org)

 www.spondonreliefinneedcharity. org

CC number: 211317

Eligibility

People who live in the ancient parish of Spondon within the city of Derby. A boundary map can be found on the charity's website.

Types of grant

Welfare

Grants are usually paid directly to the goods or services supplier for the purchase of beds, white goods, carpets, cookers, furniture, school trips, school uniforms and childcare.

Education

Grants are made to support students in higher education who need assistance to purchase books, other equipment and travel. Help may also be given for sports. These grants are primarily for university students but can also be awarded to sixth-form college students.

Exclusions

No grants are made for the relief of rates, taxes or debts, or any expenses usually covered by statutory sources.

Repeat grants are only considered at the trustees' discretion and only if there are available funds.

Applications

Official application forms are available upon request from the correspondent. All returned applications should be accompanied by a letter of support from a social worker or other professional. Alternatively, an initial contact form is available on the charity's website. The trustees meet to consider applications in February, May, September and November.

Financial information

Year end	31/12/2019
Income	£29,200
Total expenditure	£25,300

Further financial information

In 2019, 47 grants were made for following purposes:

- White goods (17 grants)

- Others (ten grants)
- Carpets (eight grants)
- School uniforms (six grants)
- School trips (four grants)
- Furniture and bedding (two grants)

A breakdown of how much was awarded for each category was not available. At least £500 was awarded for school uniforms. During the year, no grants were awarded for higher education.

Other information

Grants are also made to organisations.

Derbyshire Dales

The Ernest Bailey Charity

£650 (2019/20)

Correspondent: Emma Mortimer, Community Development Officer, Derbyshire Dales District Council, Town Hall, Bank Road, Matlock, Derbyshire DE4 3NN (tel: 01629 761302; email: grants@derbyshiredales.gov.uk)

 https://www.derbyshiredales.gov.uk

CC number: 518884

Eligibility

People in need, sickness, old age or distress who live in Matlock and district. This area of benefit includes Bonsall, Cromford, Darley Dale, Matlock and Matlock Bath, Northwood, part of Rowsley, Starkholmes, South Darley and Tinkersley.

Types of grant

Grants are given according to need.

Applications

Application forms are available online from the Derbyshire Dales District Council website.

Financial information

Year end	31/03/2020
Income	£1,300
Total expenditure	£1,400

Further financial information

Full accounts were not available to view on the Charity Commission's website due to the charity's low income. We have therefore estimated the charity's grant total based on its total expenditure.

Other information

Grants are also awarded to organisations in Matlock.

Erewash

Charity of John and Joseph Card (also known as Draycott Charity)

£ £7,700 (2019/20)

Correspondent: The Trustees, Dairy Barn, The Street, Draycott, Cheddar BS27 3TH (tel: 01934 742811)

CC number: 203827

Eligibility

People in need who live in the hamlet of Draycott, near Cheddar, with a preference for those who receive a pension from the charity.

Types of grant

One-off and recurring grants are given according to need.

Applications

Applications for pensions can be made on a form available from the correspondent and are considered in November. Applications for hardship grants can be made in writing for consideration at any time. Applications can be submitted directly by the individual or by a family member.

Financial information

Year end	31/10/2020
Income	£8,400
Total expenditure	£8,500

Further financial information

Full accounts were not available to view on the Charity Commission's website due to the charity's low income. We have therefore estimated the charity's grant total based on its total expenditure.

Old Park Ward Old Age Pensioners Fund

£ £11,600 (2019/20)

Correspondent: The Trustees, 3 Knole Road, Nottingham, Nottinghamshire NG8 2DB (tel: 0115 913 2118)

CC number: 201037

Eligibility

People aged over 65 who are in need and live in the Old Park ward of the former borough of Ilkeston.

Types of grant

One-off cash grants are given, usually at Christmas.

Applications

Apply in writing to the correspondent.

Financial information

Year end	30/09/2020
Income	£20,200
Total expenditure	£12,900

Further financial information

Full accounts were not available to view on the Charity Commission's website due to the fund's low income. We have therefore estimated the fund's grant total based on its total expenditure.

Other information

The majority of the fund's income is spent on providing recreational facilities and events to meet social needs.

The Sawley Charities

£ £3,200 (2020)

Correspondent: The Trustees, 59 Northfield Avenue, Long Eaton, Nottingham, Nottinghamshire NG10 3FH (tel: 0115 973 3326)

CC number: 241273

Eligibility

Residents of Sawley who are in need.

Types of grant

Grants are given according to need.

Applications

Apply in writing to the correspondent.

Financial information

Year end	31/12/2020
Income	£2,400
Total expenditure	£3,600

Further financial information

Full accounts were not available to view on the Charity Commission's website due to the charity's low income. We have therefore estimated the charity's grant total based on its total expenditure.

High Peak

Mary Ellen Allen

£ £2,100 (2019/20)

Correspondent: Tony Lawton, Secretary, 8 Spinney Close, Glossop, Derbyshire SK13 7BR (tel: 07932 750693; email: tony@tlawton.co.uk)

CC number: 512661

Eligibility

People aged over 60 who are in need and live in the former borough of Glossop (as it was in 1947). There is a preference for those who have lived in the area for at least five years in total.

Types of grant

Grants are made for items and services which will reduce need and hardship.

Applications

Apply in writing to the correspondent.

Financial information

Year end	31/03/2020
Income	£6,900
Total expenditure	£4,700

Further financial information

Full accounts were not available to view on the Charity Commission's website due to the charity's low income. We have therefore estimated the charity's grant total based on its total expenditure.

Other information

The charity also awards grants to organisations.

The Bingham Trust

£ £12,800 (2019/20)

Correspondent: Ms E. Marshall, Secretary, Unit 1, Tongue Lane Industrial Estate, Dew Pond Lane, Buxton, Derbyshire SK17 7LN (tel: 07966 738546; email: binghamtrust@aol.com)

 www.binghamtrust.org.uk

CC number: 287636

Eligibility

People in need who live in and around Buxton in Derbyshire (the SK17 postcode area).

Types of grant

One-off grants ranging from £200 to £1,500 are awarded. Grants are made to individuals for a wide variety of needs, including further education. Grants to individuals are usually made by cheque to the provider of the service or goods.

Exclusions

The trustees cannot consider applications from individuals outside the SK17 postcode area. Grants are not made to repay existing debts or for higher educational purposes (university and college level). No more than one application can be accepted from the same individual in any 12-month period.

Applications

Applications can be made using the form available from the trust's website. Applications from individuals must always be supported by an agency familiar with the applicant's circumstances, such as social services or a charity or community organisation. Applications can be sent by post to the correspondent's address, or as an email attachment (with no additional attachments). All applications are acknowledged by post or email. They are usually considered in January, April, July and October/November each year; the date of the next meeting and the closing date for applications are noted on the website. In cases of more complicated applications, the trustees may find it beneficial to arrange a visit if they feel it would help.

Financial information

Year end	05/04/2020
Income	£158,000
Total expenditure	£166,400

Further financial information

The trust mainly awards grants to organisations in the area. Although a breakdown of grants was not provided in the latest accounts, previous years' expenditure suggests that around 10% of the grant total is given to individuals each year.

The Cotton Districts Convalescent Fund and the Barnes Samaritan Charity

£ £20,800 (2019)

Correspondent: Nicholas Stockton, Secretary, c/o Azets, St Crispin House, 4 St Crispin Way, Rossendale, Lancashire BB4 4PW (email: use the contact form available on the website)

 barnescottondistricts.co.uk

CC number: 224727

Eligibility

People in financial need who are suffering from a severe or incurable illness/disability and people convalescing from such illnesses who are continuing to live in their own home. Applicants should be living in one of the following areas: Lancashire, Greater Manchester, the Craven district of North Yorkshire, High Peak in Derbyshire, Macclesfield and Warrington in Cheshire and Calderdale in West Yorkshire.

Types of grant

Monthly grants of £50 are available towards the living costs of eligible people. The charity also makes grants towards subsidised holidays in Blackpool or Lytham St Annes, or can make a monetary contribution towards other UK holidays of the beneficiary's choice.

Applications

Application forms can be downloaded from the charity's website.

Financial information

Year end	31/12/2019
Income	£41,700
Total expenditure	£42,200

Further financial information

Grants were awarded to 31 individuals during the year.

Other information

This charity also makes grants to organisations.

John Mackie Memorial Ladies' Home

£ £2,600 (2020)

Correspondent: The Trustees, Rustlings, 2B Leafield Road, Disley, Stockport SK12 2JF (tel: 01663 762447; email: dhw111@hotmail.com)

CC number: 215726

Eligibility

Older single or widowed women who live in or around New Mills and are in need.

Types of grant

Grants are made according to need.

Applications

Apply in writing to the correspondent.

Financial information

Year end	31/12/2020
Income	£3,500
Total expenditure	£2,900

Further financial information

Full accounts were not available to view on the Charity Commission's website due to the charity's low income. We have therefore estimated the charity's grant total based on its total expenditure.

North East Derbyshire

The Eliza Ann Cresswell Memorial

£ £2,000 (2019)

Correspondent: The Trustees, Mill Lane, Chesterfield S45 0HS (tel: 07762 477972; email: elizacresswelltrust@gmail.com)

CC number: 230282

Eligibility

Residents of Clay Cross who are in need. Preference is given to families with young children.

Types of grant

Grants are given according to need.

Applications

Apply in writing to the correspondent.

Financial information

Year end	31/12/2019
Income	£3,100
Total expenditure	£2,200

Further financial information

Full accounts were not available to view on the Charity Commission's website due to the charity's low income. We have therefore estimated the charity's grant total based on its total expenditure.

Dronfield Relief in Need Charity

£ £1,800 (2020)

Correspondent: The Trustees, Castle Hill House, The Common, Holmesfield, Dronfield, Derbyshire S18 7WP (tel: 0114 289 1167; email: preaney@btinternet.com)

CC number: 219888

Eligibility

People in need who live in Barlow, Dronfield, Eckington, Holmesfield and Unstone.

Types of grant

Grants are given according to need.

Applications

Apply in writing to the correspondent.

Financial information

Year end	31/12/2020
Income	£5,100
Total expenditure	£4,000

Further financial information

Full accounts were not available to view on the Charity Commission's website due to the charity's low income. We have therefore estimated the grant total based on the charity's total expenditure.

Other information

Grants are also given to local organisations.

Leicestershire

Valentine Goodman (Estate Charity)

£ £14,500 (2019)

Correspondent: The Trustees, Blaston Lodge, Blaston Road, Blaston, Market Harborough, Leicestershire LE16 8DB (tel: 01858 555688)

CC number: 252108

Eligibility

Residents of the parishes of Blaston, Bringhurst, Drayton, East Magna, Hallaton and Medbourne who are in need.

Types of grant
Grants are given according to need.

Applications
Apply in writing to the correspondent.

Financial information

Year end	31/12/2019
Income	£15,600
Total expenditure	£16,100

Further financial information
Full accounts were not available to view on the Charity Commission's website due to the charity's low income. We have therefore estimated the charity's grant total based on its total expenditure.

The John Heggs Bates' Charity for Convalescents

£ £28,100 (2020)

Correspondent: Sarah Hope, Unit 5, Friars Mill, Bath Lane, Leicester, Leicestershire LE3 5BJ (tel: 0116 204 6620; email: sarah.hope@stwcharity.co.uk)

CC number: 218060

Eligibility
Residents of Leicester, Leicestershire and Rutland who are in need of a recuperative holiday because of an illness or recent medical treatment. Support is extended to the carers of such people.

Types of grant
Grants are awarded for recuperative breaks. Our previous research has found that grants are paid either to the beneficiary or directly to the provider.

Applications
Apply in writing to the correspondent.

Financial information

Year end	31/12/2020
Income	£17,800
Total expenditure	£31,200

Further financial information
Full accounts were not available to view on the Charity Commission's website due to the charity's low income. We have therefore estimated the grant total based on the charity's total expenditure.

Illston Town Land Charity

£ £5,400 (2019/20)

Correspondent: The Trustees, 5 Barnards Way, Kibworth Harcourt, Leicester, Leicestershire LE8 0RS (tel: 0116 279 2524; email: dianagaulby@aol.com)

CC number: 246616

Eligibility
Residents of Illston on the Hill who are in need.

Types of grant
Grants are given towards the cost of Council Tax.

Applications
Apply in writing to the correspondent.

Financial information

Year end	30/09/2020
Income	£6,600
Total expenditure	£6,000

Further financial information
Full accounts were not available to view on the Charity Commission's website due to the charity's low income. We have therefore estimated the charity's grant total based on its total expenditure.

Leicestershire Coal Industry Welfare Trust Fund

£ £14,600 (2020)

Correspondent: The Trustees, The Springboard Centre, Mantle Lane, Coalville, Leicester LE67 3DW (tel: 01530 832085; email: info@lciwtf.co.uk)

CC number: 1006985

Eligibility
Current and former miners and their dependants connected with the British coal mining industry in the Leicestershire area.

Types of grant
Grants are provided for welfare needs, such as holidays, disability aids and home improvements.

Applications
Apply in writing to the correspondent. Our previous research found that applications should include details of mining connections, residence in Leicestershire and dependence on the mineworker (in the case of children). The trustees meet throughout the year to consider applications.

Financial information

Year end	31/12/2020
Income	£7,000
Total expenditure	£32,400

Further financial information
Full accounts were not available to view on the Charity Commission's website due to the trust's low income. We have therefore estimated the grant total based on the trust's total expenditure.

Other information
Grants are also given to similar organisations for running costs.

Thomas Monke

£ £4,000 (2020)

Correspondent: Christopher Kitto, 29 Blacksmiths Lane, Newton Solney, Burton-on-Trent, Staffordshire DE15 0SD (tel: 01283 702129; email: thomasmonkecharity@btinternet.com)

CC number: 214783

Eligibility
People in need who live in Austrey, Measham, Shenton and Whitwick, especially people under the age of 25 who are in further or higher education.

Types of grant
Grants of up to £200 towards the cost of tools, books, fees and travelling expenses for educational purposes, including vocational training.

Exclusions
Expeditions, scholarships and university course fees are not funded.

Applications
Application forms are available from the correspondent and should be submitted directly by the individual in time for the trustees' yearly meeting, which is held in April.

Financial information

Year end	31/12/2020
Income	£3,800
Total expenditure	£4,400

Further financial information
Full accounts were not available to view on the Charity Commission's website due to the charity's low income. We have therefore estimated the charity's grant total based on its total expenditure.

Alex Neale Charity

£ £1,700 (2020)

Correspondent: Moira Bunn, Queniborough Council, Rearsby Road, Queniborough, Leicester LE7 3DH (tel: 0116 260 3313; email: clerk@queniboroughpc.org.uk)

https://www.queniboroughpc.org.uk/covid-19.html

CC number: 260247

Eligibility

Residents in the parish of Queniborough who are in need or who have a disability.

Types of grant

One-off grants are made towards the costs of items such as washing machines, tumble dryers, mobility scooters and specialist equipment (for people with disabilities). Grants are also made for travel expenses relating to hospital visits, childcare costs, gas and electricity bills, house repairs and decorating costs.

Applications

Application forms can be downloaded from the Queniborough parish council website and should be returned by post to the correspondent at: 149 The Ringway, Queniborough, Leicester, LE7 3DP.

Financial information

Year end	31/12/2020
Income	£2,300
Total expenditure	£1,900

Further financial information

Full accounts were not available to view on the Charity Commission's website due to the charity's low income. We have therefore estimated the charity's grant total based on its total expenditure.

The Nicholson Memorial Fund (The Rosehill Trust)

 £9,400 (2019/20)

Correspondent: Clerk to the Trustees, 20A Millstone Lane, Leicester, Leicestershire LE1 5JN (tel: 0116 222 2200; email: info@charity-link.org)

https://charity-link.org/trust-administration/trusts-we-administer/the-nicholson-memorial-fund

CC number: 1000860

Eligibility

According to its Charity Commission record, the trust supports young people and children 'who are delinquent, deprived, neglected or in need of care' in Leicester, Leicestershire and Rutland.

Types of grant

Grants are given according to need.

Applications

Apply using a form available from the Leicester Charity Link website.

Financial information

Year end	05/04/2020
Income	£19,200
Total expenditure	£20,900

Further financial information

Full accounts were not available to view on the Charity Commission's website due to the trust's low income. We have therefore estimated the trust's grant total based on its total expenditure.

Other information

Leicester Charity Link, the administrator of this trust, provides a wide range of support and advice to people in need. The trust also gives grants to organisations assisting children and young people.

The Thomas Rawlins Educational Foundation

 £1,900 (2020)

Correspondent: Gill Bertinat, Clerk to the Trustees, 21 Haddon Close, Syston, Leicester, Leicestershire LE7 1HZ (tel: 01162 601491 or 01509 622800; email: thomasrawlins@bertinat.me.uk)

www.woodhouseparishcouncil.org.uk

CC number: 527858

Eligibility

People under the age of 25 who live in Quorn, Woodhouse, Woodhouse Eaves or Barrow upon Soar. Preference is given to residents of Quorndon, Woodhouse and Woodhouse Eaves.

Types of grant

Welfare

Grants are made towards clothing for young people at school, college or university, or those preparing to enter work. Grants are also made towards the costs of physical or social activities, such as sports coaching, for beneficiaries who are receiving primary, secondary or further education.

Education

Scholarships, bursaries and maintenance allowances can be given to people undertaking education at a school, college or university. Grants are also available towards clothing, tools, instruments, books, extracurricular activities, educational travel and the study of music and the arts.

Applications

Application forms can be requested from the correspondent or downloaded from the Woodhouse Parish Council website. Guidance notes are available on the application form.

Financial information

Year end	31/12/2020
Income	£31,100
Total expenditure	£4,300

Further financial information

Full accounts were not available to view on the Charity Commission's website due to the foundation's low income. We have therefore estimated the foundation's grant total based on its total expenditure.

Other information

Grants are also made to organisations.

Thomas Stanley Shipman Charitable Trust

 £28,700 (2019/20)

Correspondent: The Trustees, 6 Magnolia Close, Leicester, Leicestershire LE2 8PS (tel: 07980 451336; email: info@ thomasstanleyshipmancharitabletrust. org.uk)

https://thomasstanleyshipman charitabletrust.org.uk

CC number: 200789

Eligibility

Older people in need who live in the city or county of Leicester. According to the trust's 2019/20 accounts, grants are also available for the relief of hardship and distress among other deserving individuals.

Types of grant

Grants are available for living expenses and for gifts at Christmas.

Exclusions

Grants are not awarded for educational purposes.

Applications

Apply in writing to the correspondent.

Financial information

Year end	31/05/2020
Income	£58,000
Total expenditure	£71,400

Other information

The trust also supports organisations.

Thomas Herbert Smith's Trust Fund

£6,600 (2019/20)

Correspondent: Andrew York, 6 Magnolia Close, Leicester, Leicestershire LE2 8PS (tel: 07980 451336; email: andrew_york@sky.com)

CC number: 701694

Eligibility

People in need who live in the parish of Groby in Leicestershire, including older people and people experiencing ill health or financial distress.

Types of grant

Grants are awarded for general welfare.

Applications

Applications can be made using a form available from the correspondent. They are considered throughout the year.

Financial information

Year end	05/04/2020
Income	£18,600
Total expenditure	£20,200

Further financial information

Full accounts were not available to view on the Charity Commission's website due to the trust's low income. We have therefore estimated the trust's grant total based on its total expenditure.

Other information

Grants are also made to local educational organisations and for recreational facilities.

Charnwood

The H. A. Taylor Fund

£ £9,500 (2019/20)

Correspondent: Clerk to the Trustees, c/o Charity Link, 20A Millstone Lane, Leicester, Leicestershire LE1 5JN (tel: 0116 222 2200; email: trustadmin@charity-link.org)

 charity-link.org/trust-administration/trusts-we-administer/h-a-taylor-fund

CC number: 516428

Eligibility

People in need in the town of Syston. According to the charity's website, applicants normally need to have lived in Syston for more than one year before they are eligible for a grant.

Types of grant

According to the charity's website, grants are made for a wide variety of items to people who are in need, hardship or distress.

Exclusions

Applicants should not reapply within two years of receiving a grant, except in exceptional circumstances.

Applications

Application forms are available from Syston and District Volunteer Centre, Syston Health Centre and Syston Library. They can also be downloaded from the charity's website.

Financial information

Year end	07/05/2020
Income	£44,200
Total expenditure	£29,600

Further financial information

Grants were awarded to 18 individuals in 2019/20.

Babington's Charity

£ £5,300 (2019)

Correspondent: Helen McCague, Trustee, 14 Main Street, Cossington, Leicester, Leicestershire LE7 4UU (tel: 01509 812271)

CC number: 220069

Eligibility

People in need in the parish of Cossington in Leicestershire.

Types of grant

Welfare

Welfare support includes assistance to people with disabilities and older people towards heating expenses, household equipment and travel costs to hospital; help is also offered to families suffering from hardship and other parishioners who are in distress.

Education

Educational grants are made for equipment, clothing, fees, books and other necessities, computer equipment, travel costs or maintenance expenses to people under the age of 25 to help with tertiary education costs, vocational training or entering a trade. One-off or recurrent support towards other educational needs may also be given according to need. Mature students have been supported for retraining following a redundancy.

Applications

Applications may be made in writing to the correspondent. The trustees meet at least twice a year.

Financial information

Year end	31/12/2019
Income	£36,300
Total expenditure	£16,400

Further financial information

Grants are also made to Cossington Church and Cossington School. In 2019, each received a grant of £3,000.

The Dawson and Fowler Foundation

£ £23,900 (2020)

Correspondent: Lesley Cutler, Clerk to the Trustees, PO Box 73, Loughborough, Leicestershire LE11 3XF (tel: 07765 934117; email: dawsonfowler73@gmail.com)

 www.dawsonfowler.co.uk

CC number: 527867

Eligibility

Young people between the ages of 11 and 25 who live in Loughborough or Hathern.

Types of grant

The foundation offers the following:

- Grants of up to £100 to help with the cost of school uniform for pupils in secondary school (years 7 to 11). Grants can be applied for every 12 months.
- Grants to support young people involved in scouting, guiding, sports and the Duke of Edinburgh Awards scheme.
- Scholarships to the endowed schools.

In addition, the foundation allocates a sum of money each year to local senior schools and academies to be distributed to students in need. The maximum grant per individual is £200 and can be used towards the cost of residential courses, educational visits, interview expenses, textbooks and equipment for sport, music and other activities.

Grants are also available to higher education students and apprentices towards the cost of equipment and clothing in connection with the course.

Applications

Further information and application forms can be requested from the correspondent.

Financial information

Year end	31/12/2020
Income	£48,800
Total expenditure	£41,700

Further financial information

In 2020, the foundation awarded grants totalling £23,900 to individuals. Grants were distributed as follows:

School uniform	£16,500
Scholarships	£4,100
School grants for students in need	£3,000
Other grants to individuals	£200

The Loughborough Welfare Trusts

£ £10,400 (2020)

Correspondent: The Trustees, 20 Churchgate, Loughborough, Leicestershire LE11 1UD (tel: 07765 934117; email: loughweltrsts@gmail.com)

CC number: 214654

Eligibility

People in need who live in the borough of Loughborough.

Types of grant

Grants are given according to need.

Applications

Apply in writing to the correspondent.

Financial information

Year end	31/12/2020
Income	£26,800
Total expenditure	£43,400

Further financial information

In 2020, grants totalling £7,100 were awarded for relief in need, and grants totalling £3,300 were awarded for relief in sickness.

Other information

The charity also owns two almshouses and makes grants to organisations.

Mountsorrel Relief in Need Charity

£ £98,500 (2020)

Correspondent: Rachel White, Applications Secretary, 7 Oakthorpe Avenue, Leicester LE3 0UR (tel: 0116 291 6697; email: mountsorrelunitedcharities@outlook.com)

 www.mountsorrelunitedcharities.com

CC number: 217615

Eligibility

Residents of Mountsorrel who are in need. Applicants must have lived in the parish for a minimum of six months.

Types of grant

One-off grants are given according to need. Recent examples include electrical household products, bedding, furniture, garden maintenance, decorating, carpeting, chiropody, mobility equipment (that is not supplied by social services), hospital travel expenses, home repairs and debt relief.

Applications

To apply, contact the Applications Secretary by telephone. Alternatively, prospective applicants may wish to complete the contact form on the charity's website to begin the application process. Opportunities to apply for a grant are advertised around the village and promoted to potential referrers. The trustees meet eight times per year to consider grant applications.

Financial information

Year end	31/12/2020
Income	£229,800
Total expenditure	£140,900

Further financial information

During the 2020 financial year, 14 grants were made.

Other information

This charity is administered under the Mountsorrel United Charities, as is the Mountsorrel Education Fund.

Wymeswold Parochial Charities

£ £1,800 (2019/20)

Correspondent: Jo Collington, Clerk, 94 Brook Street, Wymeswold, Loughborough, Leicestershire LE12 6TU (tel: 01509 880538; email: jocollington@sky.com)

CC number: 213241

Eligibility

Pensioners, widows/widowers and students in need who live in Wymeswold.

Types of grant

Welfare

Winter gifts are given to pensioners, widows and widowers.

Education

Educational grants are awarded through the Thompson Educational Grants scheme.

Applications

Apply in writing to the correspondent.

Financial information

Year end	31/01/2020
Income	£4,800
Total expenditure	£4,100

Further financial information

Full accounts were not available to view on the Charity Commission's website due to the charity's low income. We have therefore estimated the charity's grant total based on its total expenditure.

Other information

Grants are also made to organisations in the village.

Hinckley and Bosworth

Poor's Platt

£ £10,800 (2020)

Correspondent: The Trustees, 20A Millstone Lane, Leicester, Leicestershire LE1 5JN (tel: 0116 222 2200; email: info@charity-link.org)

 charity-link.org/trust-administration/trusts-we-administer/poors-platt

CC number: 503580

Eligibility

People in need in the ancient parish of Barwell in Leicestershire.

Types of grant

Grants are awarded according to need. The charity also awards grants to students for educational needs via the Alderman Newton's Educational Foundation (Charity Commission no. 527916).

Applications

Application forms are available to download from the Charity Link website.

Financial information

Year end	31/12/2020
Income	£26,500
Total expenditure	£25,300

Further financial information

During the year, the charity awarded eight grants directly to individuals, totalling £2,800. In addition, 13 educational grants were awarded to students via Alderman Newton's Educational Foundation.

Other information

Grants are also awarded to various organisations, projects and schools in the area of benefit.

Leicester

The Leicester Aid-in-Sickness Fund

£ £9,400 (2019/20)

Correspondent: Mark Dunkley, Charity Link, 20A Millstone Lane, Leicester, Leicestershire LE1 5JN (tel: 0116 222 2200; email: mark.dunkley@shma.co.uk)

CC number: 219785

Eligibility

People living in the city of Leicester who are experiencing ill health.

Types of grant

Grants are given according to need.

Applications

Apply in writing to the correspondent.

Financial information

Year end	05/04/2020
Income	£14,800
Total expenditure	£10,400

Further financial information
Full accounts were not available to view on the Charity Commission's website due to the fund's low income. We have therefore estimated the fund's grant total based on its total expenditure.

The Leicester Freemen's Estate

£3,800 (2020)

Correspondent: The Trustees, Estate Office, 32 Freemen's Holt, Old Church Street, Leicester, Leicestershire LE2 8NH (tel: 0116 283 4017; email: office@ leicesterfreemen.com)

 www.leicesterfreemen.com

CC number: 244732

Eligibility
Freemen of the city of Leicester, their dependants and future generations of Freemen.

Types of grant
Monthly payments and Christmas hampers.

Applications
Apply in writing to the correspondent. Beneficiaries' eligibility is reviewed annually.

Financial information

Year end	31/12/2020
Income	£267,800
Total expenditure	£234,400

Other information
The charity owns bungalows (36 as of 2020) at Freemen's Holt, which is available to retired Freemen, Freemen in need, or Freemen's widows or widowers. The cost of living in the bungalows is subsidised, and residents are asked only to contribute a small sum towards maintenance each month. The charity also hosts social events throughout the year (lunches, garden parties, etc.) with the aim of reducing isolation and loneliness.

The Leicester Indigent Old Age Society

£3,000 (2019/20)

Correspondent: The Trustees, 20A Millstone Lane, Leicester, Leicestershire LE1 5JN (tel: 0116 222 2200; email: info@charity-link.org)

 charity-link.org/trust-administration/trusts-we-administer/leicester-indigent-old-age-society

CC number: 208476

Eligibility
Older people in need living in the city of Leicester.

Types of grant
Grants are awarded according to need.

Exclusions
Assistance can only be provided once every two years unless there are exceptional circumstances.

Applications
Applications can be made via Charity Link – application forms can be found on the website. Application forms are not to be completed by the applicant unless specifically requested by Charity Link.

Financial information

Year end	31/03/2020
Income	£6,000
Total expenditure	£6,600

Further financial information
Full accounts were not available to view on the Charity Commission's website due to the charity's low income. We have therefore estimated the charity's grant total based on its total expenditure.

Other information
The charity also supports projects in Leicester that assist older people in need, hardship or distress.

Parish Piece Charity

£10,900 (2019/20)

Correspondent: Grants Administration Team, Charity Link, 20A Millstone Lane, Leicester, Leicestershire LE1 5JN (tel: 0116 222 2200; email: info@charity-link.org)

 charity-link.org/trust-administration/trusts-we-administer/st-margarets-charities

CC number: 215775

Eligibility
People in need who live in Leicester. Preference is given to those who live in the ancient parish of St Margaret.

Types of grant
Grants are given according to need.

Exclusions
Individuals living outside the city of Leicester.

Applications
Applications to the charity are administered by Charity Link. They should be made through a third party such as a healthcare professional or social worker using the form provided on the website.

Financial information

Year end	05/04/2020
Income	£10,100
Total expenditure	£12,100

Further financial information
Full accounts were not available to view on the Charity Commission's website due to the charity's low income. We have therefore estimated the charity's grant total based on its total expenditure.

The Quorn Town Lands Charity

£3,000 (2019/20)

Correspondent: The Trustees, 14 Mansfield Avenue, Quorn, Loughborough, Leicestershire LE12 8BD (tel: 01509 620701; email: quorn.townlands@gmail.com)

 quorndon.com/townlands/index.php

CC number: 216703

Eligibility
People in need who live in the village of Quorn.

Types of grant
One-off grants and recurrent grants depending on need.

Applications
Application forms are available to download from the Quorn Village website and must be posted to the correspondent.

Financial information

Year end	31/03/2020
Income	£7,500
Total expenditure	£3,300

Further financial information
Full accounts were not available to view on the Charity Commission's website due to the charity's low income. We have therefore estimated the charity's grant total based on its total expenditure.

Other information
The charity also supports organisations.

St Margaret's Charity

£ £2,000 (2019/20)

Correspondent: The Trustees, Charity Link, 20A Millstone Lane, Leicester, Leicestershire LE1 5JN (tel: 0116 222 2200; email: info@charity-link.org)

 https://charity-link.org/trust-administration/trusts-we-administer/st-margarets-charities

CC number: 234626

Eligibility
People living in the city of Leicester who are in need as a result of ill health, age or financial hardship.

Types of grant
One-off grants of up to £250 are available.

Applications
Applications must be made through Charity Link. Application forms are available to download from the Charity Link website.

Financial information
Year end	05/04/2020
Income	£3,700
Total expenditure	£4,400

Further financial information
Full accounts were not available to view on the Charity Commission's website due to the charity's low income. We have therefore estimated the grant total based on the charity's total expenditure.

Other information
This charity also makes grants to organisations.

Melton

Melton Mowbray Building Society Charitable Foundation

£ £7,600 (2019/20)

Correspondent: The Trustees, Leicester Road, Melton Mowbray, Leicestershire LE13 0DB (tel: 01664 414141; email: c.ritchie@mmbs.co.uk)

 https://www.themelton.co.uk/community-support/charitable-foundation

CC number: 1067348

Eligibility
Individuals in need within a 15-mile radius of the Melton Mowbray Building Society's branches in Melton Mowbray, Grantham and Oakham. The foundation also administers the June Roper Sporting Trust, which provides grants to

individuals from underprivileged backgrounds with a focus on sport.

Types of grant
Grants are awarded according to need.

Exclusions
The foundation is unlikely to fund running costs, expeditions or overseas travel, individuals who have applied within the previous 12 months, the restoration or upgrading of buildings (including churches), sponsorships for individuals, national charities or requests for funds that are not relevant to the foundation's local community.

Applications
Apply in writing to the correspondent.

Financial information
Year end	31/03/2020
Income	£20,000
Total expenditure	£16,900

Further financial information
Full accounts were not available to view on the Charity Commission's website due to the foundation's low income. We have therefore estimated the foundation's grant total based on its total expenditure.

The Melton Trust

£ £4,300 (2020)

Correspondent: The Trustees, c/o Melton Parish Council, 17 Riduna Park, Station Road, Melton, Woodbridge, Suffolk IP12 1QT (tel: 01394 387491; email: meltontrust.suffolk@googlemail.com)

CC number: 212286

Eligibility
People in need who live in Melton in Suffolk.

Types of grant
The trust makes grants (or pays for goods or services) according to need.

Applications
Apply in writing to the correspondent.

Financial information
Year end	31/12/2020
Income	£12,200
Total expenditure	£9,500

Further financial information
Full accounts were not available to view on the Charity Commission's website due to the trust's low income. We have therefore estimated the trust's grant total based on its total expenditure.

Other information
The trust also awards grants to organisations that help people in need in the Melton area.

North West Leicestershire

Ashby-de-la-Zouch Relief in Sickness Fund

£ £1,300 (2019/20)

Correspondent: Leanne Cooper, c/o Crane & Walton LLP, 30 South Street, Ashby-de-la-Zouch, Leicestershire LE65 1BT (tel: 01530 414111; email: leannecooper@craneandwalton.co.uk)

CC number: 508621

Eligibility
People living in the town of Ashby-de-la-Zouch who are sick or convalescent, have a disability or are caring for ill people and require financial assistance.

Types of grant
According to the charity's Charity Commission record, the trustees award small grants for the relief of its beneficiaries.

Applications
Contact the correspondent for further information.

Financial information
Year end	31/03/2020
Income	£890
Total expenditure	£1,400

Further financial information
Full accounts were not available to view on the Charity Commission's website due to the fund's low income. We have therefore estimated the grant total based on the fund's total expenditure.

Lincolnshire

Committee for Kesteven Children in Need

£ £7,100 (2019)

Correspondent: The Trustees, Nocton Rise, Lincoln, Lincolnshire LN4 2AF (tel: 01522 791217; email: enquiries@kcin.org)

 www.kcin.org

CC number: 700008

Eligibility
Children and young people up to the age of 16 who live in Kesteven (Lincolnshire) and are in need.

Types of grant
Gifts in kind or grants for essential household items, toys or clothing are

given. The charity can also help with the cost of a nursery place for children who need respite from their home lives.

Applications

The charity makes grants to people referred by social workers, health visitors, teachers and education officers and so on. Applications should include the family situation, the age of the child and their needs. Applications are considered throughout the year.

Financial information

Year end	31/12/2019
Income	£9,800
Total expenditure	£15,700

Further financial information

Full accounts were not available to view on the Charity Commission's website due to the charity's low income. We have therefore estimated the charity's grant total based on its total expenditure.

Other information

The charity also supports organisations.

Charity of Thomas Cowley Exclusive of the Cowley Education

 £5,500 (2019/20)

Correspondent: The Trustees, Holmes House, Kyme Road, Heckington Fen, Sleaford, Lincolnshire NG34 9NA (tel: 07752 183649; email: sue.hentley@hotmail.co.uk)

CC number: 249415

Eligibility

Residents of Swineshead who are in need.

Types of grant

One-off grants are given for fuel, blankets, clothing and other necessities or comforts. The charity also provides bread to residents of the parish on a weekly basis.

Applications

Apply in writing to the correspondent.

Financial information

Year end	01/04/2020
Income	£9,900
Total expenditure	£12,200

Further financial information

Full accounts were not available to view on the Charity Commission's website due to the charity's low income. We have therefore estimated the charity's grant total based on its total expenditure.

Other information

This charity also makes grants to organisations, mostly in aid of specific educational projects at Swineshead Church of England Primary School.

Freshtime Futures Trust

 £9,900 (2019/20)

Correspondent: John Stokes, Secretary, Glen Fairways, Reservoir Road, Spalding PE11 4DH (tel: 01205 312010; email: use the contact form available on the website)

🌐 https://freshtimefuturestrust.org

CC number: 1171984

Eligibility

Children and young people aged 11 to 25 years who live in Lincolnshire and are in need.

Types of grant

Welfare grants are made towards school fees, IT equipment, specialist sensory/medical equipment and for sports development.

Applications

Applications can be made on the funder's website using an online form. Alternatively, applicants may wish to download a copy of the application form and once completed, send it by post to the charity.

Financial information

Year end	31/03/2020
Income	£84,900
Total expenditure	£62,600

Gainsborough Dispensary Charity

£ £7,900 (2020)

Correspondent: The Trustees, 33 The Wharf, Morton, Gainsborough, Lincolnshire DN21 3BL (tel: 01427 615036)

CC number: 250376

Eligibility

Residents of Gainsborough and Morton who are in need.

Types of grant

Grants are given according to need.

Applications

Our previous research indicates that individuals should not apply directly; instead, a third-party professional, such as a social worker or Citizens Advice, should contact the charity on their behalf. Applications are accepted all year round.

Financial information

Year end	31/12/2020
Income	£9,400
Total expenditure	£8,700

Further financial information

Full accounts were not available to view on the Charity Commission's website due to the charity's low income. We have therefore estimated the charity grant total based on its total expenditure.

Gardiner Hill Foundation

£ £11,700 (2019/20)

Correspondent: The Trustees, NAViGO House, 3–7 Brighowgate, Grimsby, North East Lincolnshire DN32 0QE (tel: 01472 583053; email: NAV.GardinerHillFoundation@nhs.net)

🌐 https://www.navigocare.co.uk/who-we-are/the-gardiner-hill-foundation

CC number: 1146433

Eligibility

People with mental health problems who live in North East Lincolnshire. Applicants must be over the age of 16 and currently have a NAViGO care co-ordinator or a keyworker within another organisation.

Types of grant

Grants are given to enable people to access education, housing and employment opportunities.

Applications

Application forms can be downloaded from the foundation's website. Applications can be made by the individual themselves or by a carer or family member.

Financial information

Year end	31/03/2020
Income	£16,900
Total expenditure	£70,900

Further financial information

Full accounts were not available to view on the Charity Commission's website due to the foundation's low income. We have therefore estimated the foundation's grant total based on its total expenditure.

Edward Hunstone

£ £6,800 (2020)

Correspondent: The Trustees, The Old Coach House, Manor Lane, Wrangle, Boston, Lincolnshire PE22 9DE (tel: 07738 490787; email: ros@edshv.co.uk)

CC number: 214570

Eligibility

Older people and those with disabilities who are in need and live in Lincolnshire. According to the charity's Charity Commission record, there is a preference for descendants of 'Edward Hunstone, The Gedneys, Robert Smith, or the Woodliffes of 1655'. Preference is also given to retired clergymen, members of the armed forces, farmers and farm labourers.

Types of grant

Recipients receive £325 per year, paid in two instalments of £162.50 in April and October.

Applications

Apply in writing to the correspondent.

Financial information

Year end	31/12/2020
Income	£30,000
Total expenditure	£20,100

Further financial information

During the year, 21 grants were made. These were made biannually in April and October.

Other information

The charity has amended its guidelines and now accepts applications from women.

Lincolnshire Community Foundation

£ £111,200 (2019/20)

Correspondent: The Trustees, 4 Mill House, Moneys Yard, Carre Street, Sleaford, Lincolnshire NG34 7TW (tel: 01529 305825; email: info@lincolnshirecf.co.uk)

 www.lincolnshirecf.co.uk

CC number: 1092328

Eligibility

People in need who live in Lincolnshire. Visit the foundation's website for additional criteria specific to each grants programme.

Types of grant

A number of funds are available to provide individuals with support towards health, well-being and education. Visit the community foundation's website for further information on the grants available.

Applications

Details on how to apply can be found on the community foundation's website.

Financial information

Year end	31/03/2020
Income	£1,100,000
Total expenditure	£1,150,000

Other information

This is one of the 47 UK community foundations, which distribute funding for a wide range of purposes. Grant schemes tend to change frequently – consult the foundation's website for details of current programmes and upcoming deadlines.

Lincolnshire Police Charitable Fund

£ £20,200 (2019/20)

Correspondent: The Trustees, Lincolnshire Police Headquarters, Deepdale Lane, Nettleham, Lincoln, Lincolnshire LN2 2LT (tel: 01522 558238; email: charitable.fund@lincs.pnn.police.uk)

CC number: 500682

Eligibility

People in need who are present or former employees of Lincolnshire Police Authority, and their dependants. Former employees of other police authorities or committees who have retired and now live in Lincolnshire may also qualify for assistance.

Types of grant

One-off grants are awarded according to need. Interest-free loans are awarded at the discretion of the trustees.

Applications

Apply in writing to the correspondent.

Financial information

Year end	31/03/2020
Income	£30,200
Total expenditure	£29,700

Other information

The charity also makes grants to charitable organisations.

The Swineshead Poor Charities

£ £12,500 (2019/20)

Correspondent: The Trustees, Home Farm, Tumby Moorside, Boston PE22 7ST (tel: 01526 343627; email: lynne@hmtg.co.uk)

CC number: 216557

Eligibility

Residents of the parish of Swineshead who are in need.

Types of grant

Pensions and one-off grants are given.

Applications

Apply in writing to the correspondent.

Financial information

Year end	31/03/2020
Income	£43,700
Total expenditure	£24,100

Further financial information

In 2019/20, the charity awarded pensions to 11 recipients totalling £8,000 and one-off grants to individuals totalling £4,500.

Other information

This charity also makes grants to organisations, such as the Education Foundation and the Swineshead Youth Group.

Charity of Joshua Tyler for the Poor

£ £500 (2019/20)

Correspondent: Mrs M. Bradley, Clerk to the Trustees, c/o Burton & Dyson, 22 Market Place, Gainsborough, Lincolnshire DN21 2BZ (tel: 01427 010761; email: mb@burtondyson.com)

CC number: 217594

Eligibility

Residents in the parish of Morton who are in need. Applicants must be on a low income or be in receipt of benefits.

Types of grant

Grants are given according to need.

Applications

Application forms are available to download at www.burtondyson.com/about-burton-and-dyson/corporate-social-responsibility/joshua-tyler-charity. Applicants are advised to send completed application forms no later than two weeks before the trustees' next meeting. For dates of upcoming meetings, see the Burton and Dyson website.

Financial information

Year end	30/11/2020
Income	£810
Total expenditure	£550

Further financial information

Full accounts were not available to view on the Charity Commission's website due to the charity's low income. We have therefore estimated the charity's grant total based on its total expenditure.

Boston

Boston and District Sick Poor Fund

£ £600 (2020)

Correspondent: Susan Ganley, Trustee, 65 Manor Gardens, Boston PE21 6JJ (tel: 01205 368977)

CC number: 500743

Eligibility
People in need who live in Boston and the surrounding district.

Types of grant
One-off grants are given according to need.

Applications
Apply in writing to the correspondent.

Financial information
Year end	31/12/2020
Income	£2,600
Total expenditure	£1,300

Further financial information
Full accounts were not available to view on the Charity Commission's website due to the fund's low income. We have therefore estimated the grant total based on the fund's total expenditure.

Frampton Charities

£ £2,500 (2019/20)

Correspondent: The Trustees, c/o Moore Thompson, Bank House, Broad Street, Spalding, Lincolnshire PE11 1TB (tel: 01775 711333; email: louise@mooret.co.uk)

CC number: 216849

Eligibility
Residents in the parish of Frampton who are in need.

Types of grant
One-off grants are awarded according to need.

Applications
Apply in writing to the correspondent.

Financial information
Year end	31/03/2020
Income	£9,700
Total expenditure	£10,100

Further financial information
Full accounts were not available to view on the Charity Commission's website due to the charity's low income. We have therefore estimated the grant total based on the charity's total expenditure.

Other information
This charity also makes grants to organisations for specific community causes.

The Sutterton Educational Foundation (Sutterton Education Trust)

£ £720 (2020/21)

Correspondent: D. McCumiskey, 6 Hillside Gardens, Wittering, Peterborough, Cambridgeshire PE8 6DX (tel: 01780 782668; email: dpmccumiskey@gmail.com)

CC number: 527771

Eligibility
Primary and secondary schoolchildren living in the parish of Sutterton who are in need.

Types of grant
Grants are awarded towards educational costs such as books and school uniforms.

Applications
Apply in writing to the correspondent.

Financial information
Year end	31/03/2021
Income	£1,500
Total expenditure	£1,600

Further financial information
Full accounts were not available to view on the Charity Commission's website due to the foundation's low income. We have therefore estimated the foundation's grant total based on its total expenditure.

Other information
The foundation also makes grants to local schools.

Sutterton Parochial Charity Trust

£ £6,900 (2020/21)

Correspondent: Deirdre McCumiskey, 6 Hillside Gardens, Wittering, Peterborough, Cambridgeshire PE8 6DX (tel: 01780 782668; email: dpmccumiskey@gmail.com)

CC number: 234839

Eligibility
People in need who live in Sutterton and Amber Hill. Preference is given to children and older residents.

Types of grant
Grants are given according to need.

Applications
Apply in writing to the correspondent.

Financial information
Year end	31/03/2021
Income	£18,700
Total expenditure	£15,200

Further financial information
Full accounts were not available to view on the Charity Commission's website due to the charity's low income. We have therefore estimated the charity's grant total based on its total expenditure.

Other information
The trust also makes grants to organisations.

East Lindsey

Stickford Relief in Need Charity

£ £8,400 (2019)

Correspondent: The Trustees, Chattertons Solicitors, 28 Wide Bargate, Boston, Lincolnshire PE21 6RT (tel: 01205 351114)

CC number: 247423

Eligibility
People in need who live in the parish of Stickford.

Types of grant
Grants are given according to need. They can be given, for example, towards repair bills, funeral costs, costs associated with disability, transport and so on. In addition, the charity provides school uniform vouchers, birth grants and cash payments to pensioners at Christmas.

Applications
Apply in writing to the correspondent or contact any of the trustees, whose phone numbers can be found in the Stickford Parish newsletter.

Financial information
Year end	31/12/2019
Income	£19,400
Total expenditure	£18,700

Further financial information
Full accounts were not available to view on the Charity Commission's website due to the charity's low income. We have therefore estimated the charity's grant total based on its total expenditure.

Other information
The charity also runs a bus service twice a month to Boston and Horncastle for those without access to their own transport.

Lincoln

Lincoln General Dispensary Fund

£ £6,800 (2019)

Correspondent: The Trustees, Durrus, Scothern Lane, Dunholme, Lincoln, Lincolnshire LN2 3QP (tel: 01673 860660)

CC number: 220159

Eligibility

People living in the district of Lincoln who have disabilities or who are experiencing ill health.

Types of grant

Grants are given to alleviate suffering or to aid recovery.

Applications

Apply in writing to the correspondent.

Financial information

Year end	31/12/2019
Income	£11,400
Total expenditure	£15,200

Further financial information

Full accounts were not available to view on the Charity Commission's website due to the fund's low income. We have therefore estimated the fund's grant total based on its total expenditure.

Other information

The fund also supports organisations.

Lincoln Municipal Relief in Need Charity

£ £41,400 (2019/20)

Correspondent: The Trustees, PO Box 1291, Lincoln, Lincolnshire LN5 5RA (tel: 01522 810159; email: lincolnmunicipalrelief@outlook.com)

CC number: 213651

Eligibility

People in need who live in the city of Lincoln.

Types of grant

Grants of up to £500 are given according to need.

Applications

Apply in writing to the correspondent. Requests for more than £500 must be approved at a quarterly trustees' meeting.

Financial information

Year end	25/03/2020
Income	£42,100
Total expenditure	£45,000

Further financial information

In 2019/20, the charity awarded 119 grants.

Willingham and District Relief-in-Sickness Charity

£ £5,000 (2020)

Correspondent: The Trustees, 13 The Close, Sturton by Stow, Lincoln, Lincolnshire LN1 2AG (tel: 01427 788440; email: willingham.sickness. charity@mail.com)

CC number: 512180

Eligibility

People in need who are of ill health, are infirm or have a disability and live in the parishes of Corringham, Heapham, Kexby, Springthorpe, Upton and Willingham in Lincolnshire.

Types of grant

Grants of money or providing or paying for items, services or facilities which help those in need.

Applications

Apply in writing to the correspondent. The trustees meet to consider applications in February, June and October.

Financial information

Year end	31/12/2020
Income	£0
Total expenditure	£5,500

Further financial information

Full accounts were not available to view on the Charity Commission's website due to the charity's low income. We have therefore estimated the grant total based on the charity's total expenditure.

North Kesteven

The Navenby Town's Farm Trust

£ £8,100 (2020/21)

Correspondent: The Trustees, 17 North Lane, Navenby, Lincoln, Lincolnshire LN5 0EH (tel: 01522 810273)

CC number: 245223

Eligibility

People in need who live in the village of Navenby in Lincolnshire.

Students up to the age of 25 are also eligible for support. Applicants must have attended a school in the area for at least two years.

Types of grant

Grants are awarded according to need.

Exclusions

No grants can be given to individuals resident outside the village.

Applications

Application forms can be obtained from the correspondent, the village baker or butcher or the civic hall.

Financial information

Year end	31/03/2021
Income	£19,700
Total expenditure	£18,000

Further financial information

Full accounts were not available to view on the Charity Commission's website due to the trust's low income. We have therefore estimated the trust's grant total based on its total expenditure.

Other information

Grants are also made to organisations.

South Holland

Moulton Poor Trust

£ £9,800 (2020)

Correspondent: Faye Blair, Clerk to the Charity, c/o Maples & Son Solicitors LLP, 23 New Road, Spalding, Lincolnshire PE11 1DH (tel: 01775 722261)

CC number: 216630

Eligibility

People in need, generally older people, who live in Moulton village and the surrounding areas.

Types of grant

One-off grants are given according to need. The trust also provides pension credits.

Applications

Apply in writing to the correspondent.

Financial information

Year end	31/12/2020
Income	£45,900
Total expenditure	£43,300

Further financial information

During the 2020 financial year, a total of £8,100 was distributed throughout the parish of Moulton as welfare grants. A further £1,700 was given in pensions.

Other information

The trust manages almshouses, the rent from which makes up a small part of its income. Support is also given to other charities.

Phillips Charity

 £3,500 (2019)

Correspondent: The Trustees, 3 Tydd Low Road, Long Sutton, Spalding, Lincolnshire PE12 9AR (tel: 01406 363208; email: admin@proctorbros.co.uk or angelareeve10@gmail.com)

https://sutton-bridge.parish. lincolnshire.gov.uk/news/article/ 12/long-sutton-phillips- educational-charity

CC number: 213843

Eligibility

Welfare
Residents in the parishes of Long Sutton and Sutton Bridge who are in need.

Education
Students in the parishes of Long Sutton and Sutton Bridge upon transferring to secondary school and students aged 16 to 18 who are studying for A-levels or similar courses, including apprenticeships.

Types of grant

Grants are awarded according to need

Applications

Apply in writing to the correspondent. Applications for educational grants must be received by 1 October for the year of application.

Financial information

Year end	31/12/2019
Income	£3,000
Total expenditure	£3,900

Further financial information

Full accounts were not available to view on the Charity Commission's website due to the charity's low income. We have therefore estimated the charity's grant total based on its total expenditure.

Spalding Relief in Need Charity

 £21,500 (2020)

Correspondent: Rebecca Inglis, Clerk, c/o Chattertons, Dembleby House, 12 Broad Street, Spalding, Lincolnshire PE11 1ES (tel: 01775 765370; email: rebecca.inglis@chattertons.com)

https://spaldingtownhusbands.co. uk/spalding-relief-in-need-charity

CC number: 229268

Eligibility

People in need who live in the area covered by the district of South Holland. Preference is given to residents of the urban district of Spalding and the parishes of Cowbit, Deeping St Nicholas, Pinchbeck and Weston.

Types of grant

Support is given towards various items, services and facilities, including awards for furniture and domestic appliances and school uniforms. Residents of the almshouses can be helped with the cost of a TV licence.

Exclusions

Grants are not intended to be made where support can be obtained from statutory sources.

Applications

Application forms can be downloaded from the charity's website. The website states: 'Upon request applicants are asked to complete the Relief in Need application form with the assistance of the Citizens Advice.' The trustees meet fortnightly to consider applications.

Financial information

Year end	31/12/2020
Income	£40,000
Total expenditure	£32,100

Further financial information

Grants were distributed as follows:

Individuals	£18,300
Individuals – annual grants	£4,100
Individuals – TV licences for almshouse residents	£3,200

Other information

This charity is connected with the Spalding Almshouse Charity (Charity Commission no. 220077) and shares the same body of administration, the Spalding Town Husbands.

The Sutton St James United Charities

 £13,600 (2019/20)

Correspondent: Helen Minnis, Clerk, 94 Wignals Gate, Holbeach, Spalding PE12 7HR (tel: 01406 490157)

parishes.lincolnshire.gov.uk/ SuttonStJames

CC number: 527757

Eligibility

Welfare
People in need who have lived in the parish of Sutton St James and the surrounding area for at least three years.

Education
Educational grants can be made to students over the age of 16 who live within the parish of Sutton St James and the surrounding area.

Types of grant

Grants are given according to need.

Applications

Application forms can be requested from the correspondent or collected from the village post office.

Financial information

Year end	31/03/2020
Income	£23,800
Total expenditure	£15,100

Further financial information

Full accounts were not available to view on the Charity Commission's website due to the foundation's low income. We have therefore estimated the foundation's grant total based on its total expenditure.

Other information

Grants are also made to local organisations.

South Kesteven

Billingborough United Charities

£780 (2020)

Correspondent: Trevor Wells, Trustee, 9–11 Vine Street, Billingborough, Sleaford NG34 0QE (tel: 01529 241325; email: trevor_wells@btinternet.com)

CC number: 217451

Eligibility

People living in the parish of Billingborough who are in need.

Types of grant

Grants are given according to need.

Applications

Apply in writing to the correspondent.

Financial information

Year end	31/12/2020
Income	£1,900
Total expenditure	£870

Further financial information

Full accounts were not available to view on the Charity Commission's website due to the charity's low income. We have therefore estimated the charity's grant total based on its total expenditure.

Deeping St James United Charities

£ £33,900 (2020)

Correspondent: Julie Banks, Clerk, The Institute, 38 Church Street, Deeping St James, Peterborough, Cambridgeshire PE6 8HD (tel: 01778 344707; email: dsjunitedcharities@btconnect.com)

 www.dsjunitedcharities.org.uk

CC number: 248848

Eligibility

Welfare

People living in the parish of Deeping St James and Frognall who are in need due to unforeseen circumstances, ill health or an accident. Older residents who are of state pension age, have lived in the parish for at least two years and are in need can apply for a St Thomas' Day cash grant.

Education

People between the ages of 18 and 25 who are studying for their first degree or college qualification and are residents in Deeping St James can apply to the Tyghe Educational Foundation.

Types of grant

Welfare

Grants are given towards a range of purposes such as basic home essentials, replacing household equipment, visiting relatives in hospital, bills after a relationship breakdown or bereavement, driving lessons, and school uniforms and school trips. Support is also given towards medical needs such as the cost of travel to hospital appointments or therapy, special medical equipment, physiotherapy, and the cost of pre-paying prescriptions. Small cash grants are made to older residents of the parish for St Thomas' Day (21 December) each year.

Education

The Tyghe Educational Foundation provides annual grants towards the cost of studying for three years. Grants can be used towards books and equipment necessary for a degree or vocational qualification.

Applications

Welfare

Requests for assistance can be made through the charity's office, or by contacting the charity by telephone or email. Application forms for the St Thomas' Day grants can be downloaded from the charity's website; alternatively, forms are printed in the Deepings Advertiser in November. Additional forms are also made available from the charity's office (open between 10 am and 12 pm on weekdays).

Education

Application forms for the Tyghe Educational Foundation can be downloaded from the charity's website. Those who are starting higher education in the autumn are encouraged to apply as soon as their place has been awarded.

Financial information

Year end	31/12/2020
Income	£260,800
Total expenditure	£105,600

Further financial information

In 2020, a total of £33,900 was awarded to individuals. Welfare grants to individuals totalled £31,200 and were distributed as follows:

Relief in need	£25,300
Relief in sickness	£3,200
St Thomas' Day Charity	£2,700

Other information

The trust is an amalgamation of a number of small charities from the local area. The trust also gives grants to local projects which help the community.

Long Bennington Charities

£ £5,400 (2020)

Correspondent: Nicola Brown, Trustee, 61 Main Road, Long Bennington, Newark, Nottinghamshire NG23 5DJ (tel: 07901 574243; email: secretarylbcharities@gmail.com)

CC number: 214893

Eligibility

People in need who live in the parish of Long Bennington.

Types of grant

One-off grants are given according to need.

Applications

Apply in writing to the correspondent.

Financial information

Year end	31/12/2020
Income	£5,600
Total expenditure	£6,000

Further financial information

Full accounts were not available to view on the Charity Commission's website due to the charity's low income. We have therefore estimated the charity grant total based on its total expenditure.

West Lindsey

Kitchings General Charity

£ £12,900 (2020)

Correspondent: The Trustees, 42 Abbey Road, Bardney, Lincoln, Lincolnshire LN3 5XA (tel: 01526 398505; email: kitchingsgeneralcharity@outlook.com)

CC number: 219957

Eligibility

People in need who live in the parishes of Bardney, Southrey, Tupholme and Bucknall. There is a restricted fund that awards grants to widows living in the beneficial area.

Types of grant

Grants are given according to need.

Applications

Applications may be made in writing to the correspondent and should include some basic background details about the applicant and what the money is needed for.

Financial information

Year end	31/12/2020
Income	£29,300
Total expenditure	£26,100

Further financial information

Full accounts were not available to view on the Charity Commission's website due to the charity's low income. We have therefore estimated the charity's grant total based on its total expenditure.

Other information

Grants are also given to local schools and organisations.

Northamptonshire

Edmund Arnold's Charity (Poors Branch)

£ £9,600 (2020)

Correspondent: Marina Eaton, Grange Park Court, Roman Way, Grange Park, Northampton, Northamptonshire NN4 5EA (tel: 01604 876697; email: meaton@wilsonbrowne.co.uk)

CC number: 260589

Eligibility

Welfare

People in need who live in the parishes of Nether and Upper Heyford in

Northamptonshire, St Giles in Northampton and Stony Stratford in Buckinghamshire.

Education

Students under the age of 25 who have been resident in, or educated in, any of the parishes for a minimum of one year are also eligible for support.

Types of grant

One-off grants are awarded according to need for welfare and educational purposes.

Applications

Apply in writing to the correspondent.

Financial information

Year end	31/12/2020
Income	£50,100
Total expenditure	£9,800

Other information

The charity's Charity Commission record states: 'The Apprenticing and Education Branch has been amalgamated with Arnold's Educational Foundation.'

Arnold's Educational Foundation

£ £4,000 (2020)

Correspondent: Marina Eaton, Clerk to the Trustees, Grange Park Court, c/o Wilson Browne LLP, Roman Way, Grange Park, Northampton, Northamptonshire NN4 5EA (tel: 01604 876697; email: meaton@wilsonbrowne. co.uk)

CC number: 310590

Eligibility

People in need who are under 25 and live in, or were educated for at least one year in, the parishes of Stony Stratford, Nether Heyford, Upper Heyford, Stowe Nine Churches, Weedon Bec and the ancient parish of St Giles. Preference is given to members of the Church of England.

Types of grant

Welfare

Grants can be given to support the education of schoolchildren. Previously, grants have also been awarded under the category of social care to provide extra comforts to individuals in need.

Education

The foundation provides scholarships and bursaries for students in higher and further education. Grants are also given towards maintenance, clothing, tools, books and travel abroad for study.

Applications

Apply in writing to the correspondent.

Financial information

Year end	31/12/2020
Income	£24,600
Total expenditure	£9,100

Further financial information

Full accounts were not available to view on the Charity Commission's website due to the foundation's low income. We have therefore estimated the foundation's grant total based on its total expenditure.

Other information

The foundation also makes grants to Merton College at Oxford University.

The Desborough Town Welfare Committee

£ £3,500 (2020/21)

Correspondent: The Trustees, 36 Leys Avenue, Desborough, Kettering, Northamptonshire NN14 2PY (tel: 01536 764571; email: destownwelfare@gmail. com)

CC number: 235505

Eligibility

Older people in need, or people who are in need due to illness, living in Desborough.

Types of grant

Previous examples include travel costs for hospital visits or assistance towards the costs of school trips.

Applications

Apply in writing to the correspondent. Dates of upcoming committee meetings can be seen on the charity's Facebook page.

Financial information

Year end	31/03/2021
Income	£3,600
Total expenditure	£3,900

Further financial information

Full accounts were not available to view on the Charity Commission's website due to the charity's low income. We have therefore estimated the charity's grant total based on its total expenditure.

The Dorothy Johnson Charitable Trust

£ £15,600 (2019/20)

Correspondent: The Trustees, Hybank, 12 Old Road, Walgrave, Northampton, Northamptonshire NN6 9QW (tel: 01604 780662; email: zinaida@zinaidasilins. com)

CC number: 298499

Eligibility

People aged under 25 who were born and are living, have lived or were educated at some time in Northamptonshire.

Types of grant

Grants are made to schoolchildren, college students, undergraduates, vocational students, postgraduates and people with special educational needs, towards clothing/uniforms, fees, study/ travel abroad, books, equipment/ instruments, maintenance/living expenses and excursions.

Applications

Apply in writing to the correspondent.

Financial information

Year end	05/04/2020
Income	£17,200
Total expenditure	£27,300

Further financial information

Full accounts were not available to view on the Charity Commission's website due to the trust's low income. We have therefore estimated the grant total based on the trust's total expenditure.

Other information

The trust also awards grants to educational organisations.

Litchborough Parochial Charities

£ £9,000 (2019/20)

Correspondent: Maureen Pickford, Trustee, 18 Banbury Road, Litchborough, Towcester, Northamptonshire NN12 8JF (tel: 01327 830110; email: maureen@mojo1904.plus. com)

CC number: 201062

Eligibility

People in need living in the ancient parish of Litchborough.

Types of grant

One-off grants are given for heating and bills. Grants can also be made for the cost of study materials.

Applications

Apply in writing to the correspondent.

Financial information

Year end	31/05/2020
Income	£10,400
Total expenditure	£10,300

Further financial information

Full accounts were not available to view on the Charity Commission's website due to the charity's low income. We have therefore estimated the grant total based on the charity's total expenditure.

The Poors Allotment

£ £500 (2020)

Correspondent: Pam Hicks, Trustee, 1 Edwards Close, Byfield, Daventry, Northamptonshire NN11 6XP (tel: 01327 261257; email: pamhicks@uwclub.net)

CC number: 220321

Eligibility

Residents in the parish of Byfield who are in need.

Types of grant

Grants are given according to need.

Applications

Apply in writing to the correspondent.

Financial information

Year end	31/12/2020
Income	£1,000
Total expenditure	£600

Further financial information

Full accounts were not available to view on the Charity Commission's website due to the charity's low income. We have therefore estimated the charity's grant total based on its total expenditure.

The Sponne and Bickerstaffe Charity

£ £4,500 (2020)

Correspondent: The Trustees, Office, Buckingham Way, Towcester, Northamptonshire NN12 6PE (tel: 01327 351206; email: sponneandbickerstaffe@btconnect.com)

CC number: 204117

Eligibility

People in need who live in the civil parish of Towcester.

Types of grant

Grants are given according to need and food vouchers are distributed at Christmas.

Applications

Apply in writing to the correspondent.

Financial information

Year end	31/12/2020
Income	£105,900
Total expenditure	£109,800

Other information

The charity also runs almshouses for older people living in the parish.

Wappenham Poor's Land Charity

£ £4,900 (2019/20)

Correspondent: The Trustees, College Farm, College Lane, Woodend, Towcester, Northamptonshire NN12 8RY (tel: 01327 860268)

CC number: 205147

Eligibility

People in need who live in the ecclesiastical parish of Wappenham.

Types of grant

The charity gives a small standard grant to pensioners in need. Grants are also given to widows, widowers and people who are sick or who have disabilities and are in need of specific items.

Applications

Apply in writing to the correspondent.

Financial information

Year end	31/10/2020
Income	£4,100
Total expenditure	£5,400

Further financial information

Full accounts were not available to view on the Charity Commission's website due to the charity's low income. We have therefore estimated the grant total based on the charity's total expenditure.

The Wilson Foundation

£ £17,700 (2018/19)

Correspondent: Pollyanna Wilson, Trustee, The Maltings, Tithe Farm, Moulton Road, Holcot, Northamptonshire NN6 9SH (tel: 01604 782240; email: polly@tithefarm.com)

 www.thewilsonfoundation.co.uk

CC number: 1074414

Eligibility

Young people who have lived in Northamptonshire for at least a year, particularly those in financial need.

Types of grant

Grants are awarded for activities that the child may not otherwise have an opportunity to experience. Examples include school excursions, outward bound courses, sports camps, residential trips, etc. Grants can also be given for school uniforms.

Applications

Applications can be made using an online form on the funder's website. Alternatively, applicants may wish to download a form from the website and once completed, send it to the correspondent at their postal address. A reference from at least one responsible person known to the applicant is required. Applicants under the age of 18 must have the permission of their parent or guardian.

Financial information

Year end	05/04/2019
Income	£103,300
Total expenditure	£285,100

Further financial information

The 2018/19 accounts were the latest available at the time of writing (November 2021). Grants were awarded to 45 individuals during the financial year.

Yelvertoft and District Relief-in-Sickness Fund

£ £4,700 (2020)

Correspondent: The Trustees, Crick Lodge, Crick, Northampton, Northamptonshire NN6 7SN (tel: 01788 823336)

CC number: 285771

Eligibility

Residents of the parishes of Yelvertoft, West Haddon, Crick, Winwick, Clay Coton and Elkington who are in need as a result of ill health, disability or other medical conditions.

Types of grant

Grants are given towards the cost of mobility aids such as wheelchairs and walkers.

Applications

Apply in writing to the correspondent.

Financial information

Year end	31/12/2020
Income	£9,100
Total expenditure	£5,200

Further financial information

Full accounts were not available to view on the Charity Commission's website due to the fund's low income. We have therefore estimated the fund's grant total based on its total expenditure.

Daventry

The Daventry Consolidated Charity

(£) £5,500 (2020)

Correspondent: The Trustees, 15 Astbury Close, Daventry, Northamptonshire NN11 4RL (email: daventryconsolidatedcharity@gmail.com)

CC number: 200657

Eligibility
People in need who live in the borough of Daventry.

Types of grant
Grants are given according to need.

Applications
Apply in writing to the correspondent.

Financial information
Year end	31/12/2020
Income	£16,300
Total expenditure	£12,100

Further financial information
Full accounts were not available to view on the Charity Commission's website due to the charity's low income. We have therefore estimated the charity's grant total based on its total expenditure.

Other information
The charity also makes grants to organisations.

Kettering

Church and Town Allotment Charities and Others

(£) £25,000 (2020/21)

Correspondent: Anne Ireson, North Northamptonshire Council, Municipal Offices, Bowling Green Road, Kettering, Northamptonshire NN15 7QX (email: anne.ireson@northnorthants.gov.uk)

CC number: 207698

Eligibility
Welfare
Older people (i.e. those who are over the state retirement age) in Kettering and Barton Seagrave who are in need and live alone.

Education
Grants for post-secondary school education are available for students in Kettering and Barton Seagrave.

Types of grant
Welfare
Welfare grants are made towards winter fuel costs.

Education
Educational grants have previously been made towards books, equipment/ instruments and other educational needs.

Applications
Apply in writing to the correspondent.

Financial information
Year end	31/03/2021
Income	£17,000
Total expenditure	£26,900

Further financial information
Full accounts were not available to view on the Charity Commission's website due to the charity's low income. We have therefore estimated the grant total based on the charity's total expenditure.

Stockburn Memorial Trust Fund

(£) £10,300 (2020)

Correspondent: Andy Sipple, c/o Lamb and Holmes, West Street, Kettering, Northamptonshire NN16 0AZ (tel: 01536 412511; email: andy.sipple@ btinternet.com)

 https://www.kettering.gov.uk/a_to_ z/service/1228/grants_-_ stockburn_memorial_trust_fund

CC number: 205120

Eligibility
People experiencing ill health and financial hardship who live in the borough of Kettering.

Types of grant
Grants are awarded to provide temporary domestic help, the supply of special food, medicine, medical comforts, fuel, bedding and surgical appliances.

Applications
Application forms are available online.

Financial information
Year end	31/12/2020
Income	£12,600
Total expenditure	£11,400

Further financial information
Full accounts were not available to view on the Charity Commission's website due to the fund's low income. We have therefore estimated the grant total based on the fund's total expenditure.

Northampton

Gayton Relief in Need Charity

(£) £3,200 (2019/20)

Correspondent: Barry Steer, Secretary, 12 St Marys Court, Gayton, Northampton, Northamptonshire NN7 3HP (tel: 01604 858886; email: barrywendysteer@yahoo.co.uk)

 www.gayton-northants.co.uk/ organisations/charities/index. html

CC number: 201685

Eligibility
People in need who live in the parish of Gayton. In exceptional circumstances, assistance may be given to individuals who are resident in the area immediately outside the parish.

Types of grant
Small one-off grants are given to help with, for example, the purchase of food or clothing, heating costs and funeral expenses.

Applications
Application forms are available from the correspondent.

Financial information
Year end	05/04/2020
Income	£3,900
Total expenditure	£7,000

Further financial information
Full accounts were not available to view on the Charity Commission's website due to the charity's low income. We have therefore estimated the charity's grant total based on its total expenditure.

Other information
According to its Charity Commission record, the charity carries out its work under two working names: Gayton Poors, and Gayton Relief and Educational Charities. It also makes grants to organisations working to relieve poverty in the area of benefit.

The Charity of Hervey and Elizabeth Ekins

(£) £4,900 (2019/20)

Correspondent: Richard Pestell, Clerk and Trustee, 41 Thorburn Road, Northampton, Northamptonshire NN3 3DA (tel: 01604 408712; email: pestells@btinternet.com)

CC number: 309858

Eligibility

The charity supports children and young people living in the borough of Northampton or the parish of Great Doddington. Preference is given to those residing in the ecclesiastical parishes of: St Peter – Weston Favell, St Peter and St Paul – Abington and Emmanuel – Northampton.

Types of grant

Grants are awarded to children for educational visits, equipment and other aspects of education and training. Grants are also awarded to young people for university and college education.

Exclusions

Grants are not given for school fees.

Applications

Application forms can be obtained from the local parish churches or by writing to the correspondent.

Financial information

Year end	30/09/2020
Income	£38,100
Total expenditure	£23,900

Further financial information

In 2019/20, grants to young people totalled £4,900. Awards for further and higher education totalled £3,000 and grants for music and residential activities totalled £1,900.

Other information

The charity also awards grants to schools and organisations in the parishes.

The John and Mildred Law Fund

£ £1,800 (2019/20)

Correspondent: The Trustees, c/o Wilson Browne LLP, 4 Grange Park Court, Roman Way, Grange Park, Northampton, Northamptonshire NN4 5EA (tel: 01604 876697; email: meaton@wilsonbrowne.co.uk)

CC number: 1121230

Eligibility

People in need who live in the borough of Northampton.

Types of grant

Grants are given according to need.

Applications

Apply in writing to the correspondent.

Financial information

Year end	05/04/2020
Income	£22,700
Total expenditure	£8,300

Further financial information

Full accounts were not available to view on the Charity Commission's website

due to the fund's low income. We have therefore estimated the fund's grant total based on its total expenditure.

The Henry and Elizabeth Lineham Charity

£ £49,500 (2019)

Correspondent: Angela Moon, Clerk to the Trustees, c/o Hewitsons LLP, Elgin House, Billing Road, Northampton, Northamptonshire NN1 5AU (tel: 01604 233233; email: angelamoon@hewitsons.com)

CC number: 205975

Eligibility

Women in need living in the borough of Northampton, with preference given to those have lived in the area the longest.

Types of grant

Pensions, currently £512 per annum, are paid half-yearly in June and December.

Applications

Apply in writing to the correspondent.

Financial information

Year end	31/12/2019
Income	£60,800
Total expenditure	£54,700

Northampton Municipal Church Charity

£ £32,300 (2019/20)

Correspondent: Clerk to the Trustees, c/o Wilson Browne LLP, 4 Grange Park Court, Roman Way, Grange Park, Northampton, Northamptonshire NN4 5EA (tel: 01604 876697; email: NMCC@wilsonbrowne.co.uk)

CC number: 1182629

Eligibility

Residents of Northampton who are in need.

Types of grant

Any surplus income that is not required for the almshouse operated by the charity is awarded in grants, mostly to older people of retirement age, although grants are not age-restricted. The charity also distributes Christmas vouchers over the seasonal period.

Applications

Apply in writing to the correspondent.

Financial information

Year end	05/04/2020
Income	£212,200
Total expenditure	£245,900

Other information

The main priority of the charity is to operate and maintain an almshouse, known as St Thomas' House, in Northampton. The almshouse consists of 17 one-bedroom flats and is warden controlled. The charity also makes grants to other charitable organisations.

The Page Fund

£ £33,600 (2019/20)

Correspondent: The Trustees, c/o Wilson Browne LLP, 4 Grange Park Court, Roman Way, Grange Park, Northampton, Northamptonshire NN4 5EA (tel: 01604 876697; email: meaton@wilsonbrowne.co.uk)

CC number: 241274

Eligibility

Older people in need who have lived in Northampton, or within five miles of Northampton Guildhall, for a minimum of five years prior to their application.

Types of grant

Recurrent payments are distributed in the form of pensions.

Applications

Apply in writing to the correspondent. The trustees meet twice each year to consider grant applications.

Financial information

Year end	05/04/2020
Income	£37,200
Total expenditure	£32,400

Other information

The fund also makes grants to various charitable organisations.

The Betty and Charles Stilwell Fund

£ £2,300 (2019/20)

Correspondent: The Trustees, c/o Wilson Browne LLP, 4 Grange Park Court, Roman Way, Northampton, Northamptonshire NN4 5EA (tel: 01604 876697; email: meaton@wilsonbrowne.co.uk)

CC number: 1047576

Eligibility

People living in the borough of Northampton who suffer from heart diseases.

Types of grant

Grants are given to alleviate hardship associated with heart disease, for example, to purchase specialist medical equipment or aids.

Applications

Apply in writing to the correspondent.

Financial information

Year end	05/04/2020
Income	£4,100
Total expenditure	£5,000

Further financial information

Full accounts were not available to view on the Charity Commission's website due to the fund's low income. We have therefore estimated the grant total based on the fund's total expenditure.

Other information

Grants are also given to organisations and towards medical research.

Sir Thomas White's Northampton Charity

£ £236,900 (2020)

Correspondent: The Trustees, c/o Hewitsons LLP, Elgin House, Billing Road, Northampton, Northamptonshire NN1 5AU (tel: 01604 233233; email: angelamoon@hewitsons.com)

CC number: 201486

Eligibility

Welfare

People living in Northampton who are aged between 21 and 34.

Education

People aged between 16 and 25 who are living in Northampton.

Types of grant

Welfare

Interest-free loans are given for welfare purposes.

Education

One-off grants are made according to need.

Applications

Apply in writing to the correspondent.

Financial information

Year end	31/12/2020
Income	£346,600
Total expenditure	£392,000

South Northamptonshire

Blakesley Parochial Charities

£ £15,200 (2020)

Correspondent: Sally Woodman, The Bakery, Main Street, Woodend, Towcester, Northamptonshire NN12 8RX (tel: 07796 276366; email: sally.woodman@live.co.uk)

CC number: 202949

Eligibility

People in need who live in Blakesley. Funds are allocated to specifically support widows in the parish and people in higher or further education and apprentices.

Types of grant

One-off and recurrent grants are given according to need. The charity provides funds for widows and widowers in the parish and to older people who are facing financial hardship. Grants can be given in the form of cheques, vouchers for the local shop or Christmas gifts.

Grants are also given to assist people in post-16 education and those studying for a vocational qualification. Funds can be used towards the cost of books, equipment, trips and fees.

Applications

Applications may be made in writing to the correspondent at any time.

Financial information

Year end	31/12/2020
Income	£10,400
Total expenditure	£16,800

Further financial information

Full accounts were not available to view on the Charity Commission's website due to the charity's low income. We have therefore estimated the charity's grant total based on its total expenditure.

Other information

The charity also makes grants to local organisations.

Brackley United Feoffee Charity

£ £10,900 (2019/20)

Correspondent: The Trustees, 24 Broad Lane, Evenley, Brackley, Northamptonshire NN13 5SF (tel: 01280 703904; email: brackleyunitedfeoffee. charity@gmail.com)

CC number: 238067

Eligibility

People in need who live in the ecclesiastical parish of Brackley (which consists of the town of Brackley and the village of Halse only).

Types of grant

Welfare

The charity gives funding for a wide range of causes, including the distribution of Christmas donations to older residents of Brackley. In 2019/20 grants were awarded to help individuals purchase white goods, decorating

materials, adjustable beds, recliner chairs, carpets and school uniforms.

Education

The charity's education fund assists young undergraduate students with their living expenses, specifically the costs of books, laptops and other learning materials. In previous years, grants have also been given towards travel costs for schools trips.

Applications

Applications can be made in writing to the correspondent by the individual or through a social worker, Citizens Advice or other welfare agency. The trustees meet every three to four months.

Financial information

Year end	30/09/2020
Income	£36,400
Total expenditure	£43,200

Further financial information

During the year, the charity awarded £4,100 in educational grants to individuals. The charity also awarded £13,600 in social welfare grants to organisations and individuals. The specific amount awarded to individuals was not available in the 2019/20 accounts; therefore, we have estimated the amount given.

Other information

The charity also awards grants to local organisations and helps with the upkeep of St Peter's Church.

Middleton Cheney United Charities

£ £3,200 (2020)

Correspondent: The Trustees, 1 The Avenue, Middleton Cheney, Banbury, Oxfordshire OX17 2PE (tel: 01295 712650)

CC number: 202511

Eligibility

People who live in Middleton Cheney and are in need.

Types of grant

Grants are given according to need.

Applications

Apply in writing to the correspondent.

Financial information

Year end	31/12/2020
Income	£2,600
Total expenditure	£7,000

Further financial information

Full accounts were not available to view on the Charity Commission's website due to the charity's low income. We have therefore estimated the grant total based on the charity's total expenditure.

Other information

Support is also given to local organisations.

The Pattishall Parochial Charities

£ £7,600 (2020)

Correspondent: Clerk to the Trustees, Grove Close, Gayton Road, Towcester, Northamptonshire NN12 8NG (tel: 01327 830583)

 https://www.pattishallparish.org.uk/parish-council/pattishall-charities

CC number: 204106

Eligibility

People in need who live in the parish of Pattishall. Some preference is given to older people, widows and widowers.

Types of grant

Monthly pensions are awarded to 18 older widows and widowers. Others can apply separately to receive grants for fuel at Christmas. There are also funds available to support other specific, one-off requirements within the community (these grants are not age dependent).

Applications

Apply in writing to the correspondent, making sure to include details of age, marital status and the length of time the applicant has been resident in the parish. Applications are usually considered in November for fuel grants, July for pensions and throughout the year for other grants. Applications can be submitted either directly by the individual or by anybody who hears of an individual in need. Receipts (copies will do) should be included for the costs of items or travel.

Financial information

Year end	31/12/2020
Income	£11,000
Total expenditure	£8,400

Further financial information

Full accounts were not available to view on the Charity Commission's website due to the charity's low income. We have therefore estimated the charity's grant total based on its total expenditure.

Other information

The Pattishall parish website states: 'Each year the charity clerk will advertise around Pattishall and on the website for new applicants. In an effort to help identify those who would benefit from a grant, members of the parish are requested to bring forward names to the attention of the clerk.'

Roade Feoffee and Chivall Charity

£ £1,300 (2020)

Correspondent: The Trustees, Roade Library, High Street, Roade, Northampton, Northamptonshire NN7 2NW (tel: 07784 877158; email: clerk.feoffee@gmail.com)

CC number: 202132

Eligibility

People in need who live in the ancient parish of Roade.

Types of grant

Grants are given according to need.

Applications

Apply in writing to the correspondent.

Financial information

Year end	31/12/2020
Income	£20,800
Total expenditure	£171,200

Further financial information

Note: the grant total for individuals has been estimated based on information available on the charity's Charity Commission record.

Other information

The charity also makes grants to organisations.

Nottingham-shire

Dickinson Massey Underwood Charity

£ £37,600 (2019)

Correspondent: Mr C. N. Cullen, Clerk to the Trustees, Freeths LLP, Cumberland Court, 80 Mount Street, Nottingham, Nottinghamshire NG1 6HH (tel: 0115 936 9369; email: anna.chandler@freeths.co.uk)

CC number: 213884

Eligibility

Older people in need who live in the city of Nottingham or county of Nottinghamshire. Preference is given to Christians.

Types of grant

The charity provides a regular quarterly payment of £200 for pensioners. Also, an additional £200 is paid as a winter fuel grant. In addition to the regular payments, one-off grants are awarded where there is great hardship, for example when the purchase of a new bed or fridge is required.

Applications

Apply in writing to the correspondent.

Financial information

Year end	31/12/2019
Income	£70,200
Total expenditure	£69,100

Further financial information

Grants awarded in 2019 were broken down as follows:

Pensions	£28,600
Christmas/heating bonus for Pensioners	£5,800
Other grants to individuals	£3,200

The Fifty Fund

£ £16,100 (2019)

Correspondent: Craig Staten-Spencer, Nelsons Solicitors, Pennine House, 8 Stanford Street, Nottingham, Nottinghamshire NG1 7BQ (tel: 0115 989 5251; email: craig.staten-spencer@nelsonslaw.co.uk)

CC number: 214422

Eligibility

People in need who live in Nottinghamshire. Exceptionally, the trustees may choose to support people living outside the area of benefit or temporary residents in the area of benefit.

Types of grant

Recurring payments and one-off grants are given to relieve hardship.

Applications

Apply in writing to the correspondent. Applications are considered at quarterly meetings held throughout the year.

Financial information

Year end	31/12/2019
Income	£345,900
Total expenditure	£303,400

Further financial information

During 2019, the charity was able to support one individual on a regular basis and a further 44 individuals on a one-off basis.

Other information

The fund also makes grants to organisations.

The Sir Stuart and Lady Florence Goodwin Charity

 £3,900 (2019/20)

Correspondent: The Trustees, c/o Bassetlaw District Council, Queen's Buildings, Potter Street, Worksop, Nottinghamshire S80 2AH (tel: 01909 533252; email: goodwin.charity@ bassetlaw.gov.uk)

🌐 https://www.bassetlaw.gov.uk/ community-and-living/support-organisations-and-charities/sir-stuart-and-lady-florence-goodwin-charity

CC number: 216902

Eligibility
People over 60 who are on a limited income and live in the former Retford Rural District.

Types of grant
Grants are awarded towards specific needs such as disability aids, household goods and furniture, bathroom aids and mobility aids.

Exclusions
Grants cannot usually be paid retrospectively.

Applications
Application forms can be downloaded from the charity's website.

Financial information
Year end	31/03/2020
Income	£13,800
Total expenditure	£9,700

Further financial information
Full accounts were not available to view on the Charity Commission's website due to the charity's low income. We have therefore estimated the charity's grant total based on its total expenditure.

Other information
The charity may also support other organisations.

Municipal General Charities for the Poor

 £12,100 (2019)

Correspondent: Mrs E. Gamage, Clerk, c/o Payne and Gamage Solicitors, 48 Lombard Street, Newark, Nottinghamshire NG24 1XP (tel: 01636 640649)

CC number: 217437

Eligibility
People in need living in Newark, Farndon, Winthorpe, Hawton, Collingham, Coddington, Langford and Holme.

Types of grant
One-off grants are given. The charity states that grants to individuals are most commonly made for household equipment.

Applications
Apply in writing to the correspondent.

Financial information
Year end	31/12/2019
Income	£40,300
Total expenditure	£38,800

Further financial information
In 2019, £26,900 in grants was awarded to individuals and organisations. A breakdown of grants was not available; therefore, the grant total has been estimated.

Other information
The charity also makes grants to organisations.

The New Appeals Organisation

 £27,100 (2019/20)

Correspondent: Phil Everett, Grant Secretary, c/o Trent Fireplaces Ltd, Euro House, Willow Road, Nottingham, Nottinghamshire NG7 2TA (tel: 0115 979 0330; email: newappeals@gmail.com)

 newappeals.org

CC number: 502196

Eligibility
People in need who live in the city or county of Nottingham.

Types of grant
One-off grants are given towards, for example, wheelchairs, white goods, flooring, beds and bedding, rise/recliner chairs, adapted vehicles, holidays, sensory stimulation equipment, computers and other electrical goods. Christmas gifts are also given to people who are older or experiencing homelessness.

Applications
Applicants can apply using the form on the charity's website, which can be submitted online or by email.

Financial information
Year end	31/03/2020
Income	£20,300
Total expenditure	£60,200

Further financial information
Full accounts were not available to view on the Charity Commission's website due to the charity's low income. The grant total has been estimated based on the total expenditure.

Other information
The charity also awards grants to organisations and hospitals.

The Nottingham Annuity Charity

 £14,000 (2019/20)

Correspondent: Gillian Sladen, Nottingham Community Housing Association, 12–14 Pelham Road, Nottingham, Nottinghamshire NG5 1AP (tel: 0800 013 8555 or 011 5844 3401; email: gillian.sladen@ncha.org.uk)

🌐 www.ncha.org.uk

CC number: 510023

Eligibility
People in need who live in Nottinghamshire, with a preference for widows and unmarried women.

Types of grant
According to previous years' accounts, regular yearly allowances of either £260 or £520 are paid in quarterly grants and Christmas gifts are also distributed.

Applications
Apply in writing to the correspondent.

Financial information
Year end	31/03/2020
Income	£17,000
Total expenditure	£15,600

Further financial information
Full accounts were not available to view on the Charity Commission's website due to the charity's low income. We have therefore estimated the grant total based on the charity's total expenditure.

The Nottingham General Dispensary

 £18,800 (2019/20)

Correspondent: Anna Chandler, Secretary, Freeths LLP, Cumberland Court, 80 Mount Street, Nottingham, Nottinghamshire NG1 6HH (tel: 0115 901 5562; email: anna.chandler@freeths.co.uk)

CC number: 228149

Eligibility
People living in the county of Nottinghamshire who are in need as a result of illness, convalescence, disability or infirmity.

Types of grant

Grants of up to £1,000 are awarded according to need. Examples of items that can be funded include mobility scooters, respite and convalescent holidays, communication aids, adaptations to homes, stairlifts and other essential items.

Exclusions

No grants are given for items, services or facilities that are available to the individual through statutory sources.

Applications

Apply in writing to the correspondent. Applications must be supported by medical evidence and must include details of the cost of the items or facilities required.

Financial information

Year end	31/03/2020
Income	£47,100
Total expenditure	£61,400

Other information

The charity also makes grants to organisations in aid of healthcare, self-help groups, community care and disability support. In 2019/20, grants to organisations totalled £19,000.

Nottinghamshire Community Foundation

£ £4,900 (2019/20)

Correspondent: The Trustees, Pine House B, Southwell Road West, Rainworth, Mansfield, Nottinghamshire NG21 0HJ (tel: 01623 620202; email: enquiries@nottscf.org.uk)

 www.nottscf.org.uk

CC number: 1069538

Eligibility

People in need who live in Nottinghamshire. Individual funds have their own specific eligibility criteria – see the community foundation's website for details.

Types of grant

The foundation has a number of funds that are available to individuals to provide support towards food, clothing, travel, music and so on. Visit the foundation's website for further details of open grant programmes.

Applications

Details on how to apply can be found on the community foundation's website.

Financial information

Year end	31/03/2020
Income	£983,300
Total expenditure	£973,600

Other information

This is one of the 47 UK community foundations, which distribute funding for a wide range of purposes. Grant schemes tend to change frequently – consult the foundation's website for details of current programmes and upcoming deadlines.

Nottinghamshire Constabulary Benevolent Fund

£ £17,000 (2019/20)

Correspondent: Clare Gibson, West Bridgford Police Station, Rectory Road, West Bridgford, Nottingham, Nottinghamshire NG2 6BN (tel: 07595 004734; email: clare.gibson@ nottinghamshire.pnn.police.uk)

CC number: 256806

Eligibility

Members of the fund and their widows, children and dependants who are in need.

Types of grant

Cash grants are awarded according to need.

Applications

Apply in writing to the correspondent.

Financial information

Year end	31/03/2020
Income	£25,200
Total expenditure	£18,300

Further financial information

In 2019/20, the fund awarded £140 in grants to widows and children, and £5,000 in grants to subscribers of the fund.

The Nottinghamshire Miners' Welfare Trust Fund

£ £76,600 (2020)

Correspondent: The Trustees, CISWO, Welfare Offices, Berry Hill Lane, Mansfield, Nottinghamshire NG18 4JR (tel: 01623 625767; email: Pat.Charles@ ciswo.org.uk)

CC number: 1001272

Eligibility

Members of the mining community in Nottinghamshire who are in need, and their dependants.

Types of grant

One-off and recurrent grants are given to improve health and living conditions.

Applications

Apply on a form available from the correspondent, to be submitted directly by the individual or through a third party such as the Coal Industry Social Welfare Organisation (CISWO), Citizens Advice, social worker or similar welfare organisation.

Financial information

Year end	31/12/2020
Income	£154,900
Total expenditure	£166,400

Other information

Grants are also made to organisations.

The Perry Trust Gift Fund

£ £11,700 (2019/20)

Correspondent: Anna Chandler, c/o Freeths LLP, Cumberland Court, 80 Mount Street, Nottingham, Nottinghamshire NG1 6HH (tel: 0115 901 5562; email: anna.chandler@freeths. co.uk)

CC number: 247809

Eligibility

In order of preference, the following groups can be supported: friends, associates or employees of the settlor; people who have been formerly engaged in any profession or business in the city of Nottingham for a minimum of five years who, through no fault of their own, are no longer able to maintain a reasonable standard of living; residents of the city of Nottingham who have lived in the area for a minimum of five years; residents of the county of Nottingham who have lived in the area for a minimum of five years; and other deserving people.

Types of grant

Grants are given according to need.

Applications

Apply in writing to the correspondent.

Financial information

Year end	31/03/2020
Income	£13,300
Total expenditure	£13,000

Further financial information

Full accounts were not available to view on the Charity Commission's website due to the charity's low income. We have therefore estimated the charity's grant total based on its total expenditure.

St Peter's United Charities

 £7,100 (2019)

Correspondent: The Clerk, The Church Office, St Peter's Centre, St Peter's Square, Nottingham, Nottinghamshire NG1 2NW (email: stpeterscharities@ nottinghamchurches.org)

nottinghamchurches.org/church-and-community/st-peters-united-charities

CC number: 216737

Eligibility

Individuals in need living in the city of Nottingham or the surrounding districts.

Types of grant

Grants, usually up to £150, are given for essential basic items that applicants are unable to afford for themselves. Previously, grants have been given for bedding, clothing, furniture and other household items.

Applications

Application forms can be downloaded from the charity's website. Applications must be made through a third party, such as a member of the clergy or another religious leader, social workers or support organisations. Applications directly from individuals will not be accepted.

Financial information

Year end	31/12/2019
Income	£3,300
Total expenditure	£7,900

Further financial information

Full accounts were not available to view on the Charity Commission's website due to the charity's low income. We have therefore estimated the charity's grant total based on its total expenditure.

West Gate Benevolent Trust

 £37,300 (2019/20)

Correspondent: Stephen Carey, Secretary, 17 Storcroft Road, Retford, Nottinghamshire DN22 7EG (tel: 01777 707677)

CC number: 503506

Eligibility

People in need who live in Nottinghamshire.

Types of grant

One-off grants are given according to need.

Applications

Apply in writing to the correspondent. Our previous research suggests that applications should be made through a third party, such as a social worker or Citizens Advice.

Financial information

Year end	05/04/2020
Income	£40,600
Total expenditure	£40,600

Ashfield

The Hucknall Relief-in-Need Charity

 £5,200 (2019/20)

Correspondent: The Trustees, 11 Woodlands Grove, Hucknall, Nottingham, Nottinghamshire NG15 6SG (tel: 0115 953 6280)

CC number: 215974

Eligibility

People in need who live in Hucknall, with a preference for 'poor householders'.

Types of grant

One-off and recurrent grants according to need.

Applications

Apply in writing to the correspondent.

Financial information

Year end	30/04/2020
Income	£7,500
Total expenditure	£5,700

Further financial information

Full accounts were not available to view on the Charity Commission's website due to the charity's low income. We have therefore estimated the charity's grant total based on its total expenditure.

Broxtowe

Beeston Consolidated Charity

 £19,000 (2020)

Correspondent: The Trustees, PO Box 10425, Nottingham, Nottinghamshire NG9 9GN (tel: 07854 310327; email: info@beestonconsolidatedcharity.org.uk)

 www.beestonconsolidatedcharity. org.uk

CC number: 1164090

Eligibility

People in need who are residents of Beeston in Nottinghamshire.

Types of grant

One-off grants are awarded according to need.

Applications

Application forms are available to download from the charity's website.

Financial information

Year end	31/12/2020
Income	£154,100
Total expenditure	£140,500

Other information

This charity is a merger of four parochial charities for Beeston, namely the charities of Mary and Elizabeth Charlton, Henry Hanley, Elizabeth Wakefield and Henry Kirk.

Mansfield

Brunts Charity

 £11,500 (2020/21)

Correspondent: Charity Secretary, Brunts Chambers, 2 Toothill Lane, Mansfield, Nottinghamshire NG18 1NJ (tel: 01623 623055; email: paul@ bruntscharity.org.uk)

 www.bruntscharity.org.uk

CC number: 213407

Eligibility

People aged 60 or over (or aged 55 and over if they have a recognised disability) who are in need and live within the Mansfield District Council area or the surrounding area.

Types of grant

The charity provides one-off grants and pensions.

Applications

Application forms can be downloaded from the charity's website.

Financial information

Year end	31/03/2021
Income	£833,300
Total expenditure	£978,700

Further financial information

Note: the grant total for individuals was estimated based on information available in the 2020/21 accounts.

Other information

The charity's main concern is the provision of almshouses for older people who are in financial difficulty. It also makes grants to local organisations.

Warsop United Charities

£ £3,100 (2019)

Correspondent: Jean Simmons, Trustee, Newquay, Clumber Street, Warsop, Mansfield, Nottinghamshire NG20 0LX

CC number: 224821

Eligibility

People in need who live in the urban district of Warsop (Warsop, Church Warsop, Warsop Vale, Meden Vale, Spion Kop and Sookholme).

Types of grant

Grants are given according to need.

Applications

Applications may be made in writing to the correspondent.

Financial information

Year end	31/12/2019
Income	£12,500
Total expenditure	£6,900

Further financial information

Full accounts were not available to view on the Charity Commission's website due to the charity's low income. We have therefore estimated the grant total based on the charity's total expenditure.

Other information

Grants are also awarded to organisations.

Newark and Sherwood

The Balderton Parochial Charity

£ £700 (2019/20)

Correspondent: The Trustees, 16 Gardiner Avenue, Fernwood, New Balderton, Newark, Nottinghamshire NG24 3RG (tel: 07818 081490; email: louise@jimandlou.com)

CC number: 217554

Eligibility

Residents of Balderton who are in need.

Types of grant

Grants are given according to need.

Applications

Apply in writing to the correspondent.

Financial information

Year end	31/03/2020
Income	£3,000
Total expenditure	£790

Further financial information

Full accounts were not available to view on the Charity Commission's website due to the charity's low income. We have therefore estimated the charity's grant total based on its total expenditure.

Coddington United Charity

£ £4,600 (2020)

Correspondent: The Trustees, 26 Kirkgate, Newark, Nottinghamshire NG24 1AB (tel: 01636 700888)

CC number: 1046378

Eligibility

People in need who live in the village of Coddington.

Types of grant

Grants are given according to need.

Applications

Apply in writing to the correspondent.

Financial information

Year end	31/12/2020
Income	£22,900
Total expenditure	£10,200

Further financial information

Full accounts were not available to view on the Charity Commission's website due to the charity's low income. We have therefore estimated the grant total based on the charity's total expenditure.

Other information

The charity also provides and maintains almshouses in the area.

The Farnsfield Trust

£ £15,600 (2018/19)

Correspondent: Rachel Waterfield, The Administrator, PO Box 10810, Newark, Nottinghamshire NG24 9PT (tel: 07507 650337; email: office@thefarnsfieldtrust. co.uk or use the contact form on the website)

 https://thefarnsfieldtrust.co.uk

CC number: 1078367

Eligibility

People in need who live in Farnsfield in Nottinghamshire and the surrounding area.

Types of grant

Grants are given to support people in need and to assist in furthering education and personal development.

Applications

In the first instance, applicants should fill out the contact form on the trust's website. The administrator will then be in touch to discuss the application further. Alternatively, application forms can be downloaded from the trust's website and returned to the trust by post. Applications may be made on behalf of someone else provided they have given permission.

Financial information

Year end	31/03/2019
Income	£27,500
Total expenditure	£24,000

Further financial information

The 2018/19 accounts were the latest available at the time of writing (December 2021).

Other information

The trust was formerly known as The John and Nellie Brown Farnsfield Trust. It also gives grants to local organisations.

The Mary Elizabeth Siebel Charity

£ £28,800 (2019/20)

Correspondent: The Trustees, 3 Middlegate, Newark, Nottinghamshire NG24 1AQ (tel: 01636 671881)

CC number: 1001255

Eligibility

People over 60 years of age who are in poor health and live within a 12 mile radius of Newark Town Hall.

Types of grant

The trust aims to enable individual applicants to live in their own homes, for example, by helping with the cost of stairlifts, essential home repairs, aids for people with disabilities, care at home and relief for carers.

Applications

Application forms are available from the charity's office, at the address above.

Financial information

Year end	31/10/2020
Income	£85,200
Total expenditure	£96,500

Further financial information

Grants were awarded to 28 individuals during the year.

Other information

The charity also supports organisations.

Nottingham

The Charles Wright Gowthorpe Fund

£ £4,700 (2019/20)

Correspondent: The Trustees, UK Trust Centre, The Clock House, 22–26 Ock Street, Abingdon, Oxfordshire OX14 5SW (tel: 01235 232758; email: PBUKTCChairyAdmin@lloydsbanking.com)

CC number: 213852

Eligibility
Widows and other women in need who live within a 12-mile radius of the Market Square, Nottingham.

Types of grant
Grants are given according to need.

Applications
According to our previous research, application forms can be obtained from local Church of England vicars, to be returned by the end of October.

Financial information
Year end	31/01/2020
Income	£6,100
Total expenditure	£5,200

Further financial information
Full accounts were not available to view on the Charity Commission's website due to the fund's low income. We have therefore estimated the fund's grant total based on its total expenditure.

The John William Lamb Charity

£ £16,500 (2020/21)

Correspondent: Nina Dauban, c/o Nottinghamshire Community Foundation, Pine House B, Southwell Road West, Rainworth, Mansfield, Nottinghamshire NG21 0HJ (tel: 01623 620202; email: nina@nottscf.org.uk)

 www.nottscf.org.uk

CC number: 221978

Eligibility
People over the age of 55 who live within 20 miles of Nottingham City Council House.

Types of grant
Grants are awarded according to need.

Applications
Apply in writing to the correspondent.

Financial information
Year end	31/03/2021
Income	£25,000
Total expenditure	£36,600

Further financial information
Full accounts were not available to view on the Charity Commission's website due to the charity's low income. We have therefore estimated the charity's grant total based on its total expenditure.

Other information
The charity is administered by Nottinghamshire Community Foundation.

Nottingham Gordon Memorial Trust for Boys and Girls

£ £2,100 (2020)

Correspondent: Anna Chandler, Freeths LLP, Cumberland Court, 80 Mount Street, Nottingham, Nottinghamshire NG1 6HH (tel: 0115 901 5562; email: anna.chandler@freeths.co.uk)

CC number: 212536

Eligibility
Children and young people under the age of 25 who live in Nottingham and are in need.

According to its 2020 accounts, the trust helps many children of families, especially single-parent families, experiencing relationship breakdowns and financial hardship. Grants have also previously been made to asylum-seekers, who do not have recourse to public funds.

Types of grant
Welfare
Welfare grants are awarded for essential items such as cookers, washing machines, fridges and beds, as well as cots, prams and pushchairs for babies.

Education
Educational grants are made to help with costs associated with studying such as books, tools and equipment. Grants may also be made for trips in the UK and overseas.

Applications
Apply in writing to the correspondent.

Financial information
Year end	31/12/2020
Income	£31,400
Total expenditure	£32,500

Further financial information
According to the 2020 accounts, grants to individuals totalled £2,100 during the year. An exact breakdown was unavailable.

Other information
This charity also makes grants to organisations.

The Thorpe Trust

£ £23,500 (2019/20)

Correspondent: Mandy Kelly, Actons Solicitors, 20 Regent Street, Nottingham, Nottinghamshire NG1 5BQ (tel: 0115 910 0200; email: mandy.kelly@actons.co.uk)

CC number: 214611

Eligibility
Widows and unmarried women in need who live in Nottingham and the surrounding area. Applicants must be the widows or fatherless daughters of clergymen, gentlemen or professional people or of people engaged, in a skilled capacity, in trade or agriculture.

Types of grant
Recurrent grants are given according to need.

Applications
Apply in writing to the correspondent.

Financial information
Year end	05/04/2020
Income	£18,800
Total expenditure	£26,100

Further financial information
Full accounts were not available to view on the Charity Commission's website due to the trust's low income. We have therefore estimated the trust's grant total based on its total expenditure.

Rushcliffe

The Bingham Trust Scheme

£ £770 (2019/20)

Correspondent: The Trustees, 27 The Banks, Bingham, Nottingham, Nottinghamshire NG13 8BT (tel: 01949 836042; email: appletrees.hobson@gmail.com)

CC number: 513436

Eligibility
People under the age of 21 who live in Bingham.

Types of grant

Grants are given towards education, educational courses, sport, educational courses and development.

Applications

Apply in writing to the correspondent.

Financial information

Year end	31/03/2020
Income	£660
Total expenditure	£850

Further financial information

Full accounts were not available to view on the Charity Commission's website due to the trust's low income. We have therefore estimated the trust's grant total based on its total expenditure.

Bingham United Charities 2006

£ £3,100 (2019/20)

Correspondent: The Trustees, 23 Douglas Road, Bingham, Nottingham, Nottinghamshire NG13 8EL (tel: 01949 875453; email: binghamunitedcharities2006@gmail.com)

CC number: 213913

Eligibility

People in need who live in the parish of Bingham in Nottinghamshire.

Types of grant

According to our previous research, small, one-off grants can be made for items such as electrical goods, washing machines or school uniforms.

Applications

Apply in writing to the correspondent.

Financial information

Year end	31/03/2020
Income	£8,200
Total expenditure	£6,800

Further financial information

Full accounts were not available to view on the Charity Commission's website due to the charity's low income. We have therefore estimated the charity's grant total based on its total expenditure.

Other information

Grants are also made to organisations that benefit Bingham residents.

Rutland

The John Heggs Bates' Charity for Convalescents
See entry on page 217

Rutland Grants

£ £3,900 (2020)

Correspondent: The Trustees, 31 Springfield Way, Oakham, Rutland LE15 6QA (tel: 01572 756120; email: angelaandfrancis@talktalk.net)

CC number: 230188

Eligibility

Residents of Rutland who are in need. Preference is given to older residents and people (of any age) experiencing ill health or financial hardship.

Types of grant

Grants are given according to need.

Applications

Apply in writing to the correspondent.

Financial information

Year end	31/12/2020
Income	£6,000
Total expenditure	£8,500

Further financial information

Full accounts were not available to view on the Charity Commission's website due to the charity's low income. We have therefore estimated the charity's grant total based on its total expenditure.

Other information

This charity also makes grants to organisations.

The Rutland Trust

£ £9,000 (2020)

Correspondent: Richard Adams, Clerk, 35 Trent Road, Oakham, Rutland LE15 6HE (tel: 01572 756706; email: rjaadams@btinternet.com)

CC number: 517175

Eligibility

People in need living in Rutland.

Types of grant

One-off grants according to need.

Applications

Apply in writing to the correspondent.

Financial information

Year end	31/12/2020
Income	£19,100
Total expenditure	£18,800

Further financial information

Full accounts were not available to view on the Charity Commission's website due to the trust's low income. We have therefore estimated the grant total based on the trust's total expenditure.

West Midlands Region

General

Baron Davenport's Charity

 £340,500 (2020)

Correspondent: The Trustees, Portman House, 5–7 Temple Row West, Birmingham, West Midlands B2 5NY (tel: 0121 236 8004; email: enquiries@ barondavenportscharity.org)

🌐 www.barondavenportscharity.org

CC number: 217307

Eligibility

Women living in the West Midlands, no more than 60 miles from Birmingham Town Hall, who are in need.

Emergency grants are awarded to single women or single mothers living with children (children must be under 25 years old). According to the website, all applicants must be in 'reduced financial circumstances' and must be able to provide documentary evidence that all public funds have been exhausted.

Twice-yearly grants are awarded to older women, who must:
- Be single, divorced, separated or widowed
- Have lived in the area of benefit for a minimum of five years and currently live alone
- Be in receipt of State Pension and/or Pension Credit
- Have an income of less than £193 per week
- Have savings of less than £10,000
- Have a bank, building society or post office account in their sole name which can accept BACs payments*

*Post Office card accounts cannot accept BACs payments and therefore do not qualify.

Types of grant

According to the charity's guidelines, emergency grants are given mainly to help purchase an essential household item, such as:
- Gas or electric cooker
- Fridge and/or freezer
- Washing machine
- Children's beds and bedding
- Applicant single bed and bedding
- Baby equipment and, in exceptional circumstances, clothing
- Essential kitchen equipment
- Essential furniture
- Carpets and flooring

Twice-yearly grants of £260, awarded in May and November, are also available.

Exclusions

Emergency grants can only be made once every five years and, according to the charity's guidelines, cannot be made for the following items:
- General subsistence costs
- Payment of fuel, utilities, council tax or rent
- Household repairs
- House clearance costs
- Relocation costs
- Payment of loans, debts or rent deposits
- Childcare, child-minding or after school activities
- Double beds
- Children's presents
- Computers, laptops, tablets or televisions or DVD players
- Travel costs or driving lessons
- Funeral costs
- Course costs or scholarships

Applications

Applications for emergency grants must be made on the individual's behalf by a third party (tenancy support, NHS, education services, charities, etc.) supporting the woman or her family. The charity cannot accept applications from metropolitan district, unitary authority, county or district councils. Applications can be made using a system featured on the funder's website.

Applications for twice-yearly grants can be made by the individual themselves, or by an organisation on the individual's behalf. Organisations can make an application online using a system featured on the funder's website, whereas individuals should contact the charity by telephone or email to request an application form. For full details on the application processes for grants, see the guidelines on the funder's website.

Financial information

Year end	31/12/2020
Income	£877,600
Total expenditure	£1,260,000

Further financial information

During the year, 1,285 grants were awarded to individuals, totalling £340,500.

Other information

The charity also makes grants to a variety of organisations. Grants are awarded to children's charities, charities supporting older people in retirement, as well as residential homes, almshouses and hospices that support both children and older individuals. In 2020, 369 grants totalling £617,000 were awarded to organisations.

DTD Charity
See entry on page 211

The W. E. Dunn Trust

 £42,000 (2020/21)

Correspondent: Mary Touhy, Secretary to the Trustees, 30 Bentley Heath Cottages, Tilehouse Green Lane, Knowle, Solihull, West Midlands B93 9EL (tel: 01564 773407; email: wedunn@ tiscali.co.uk)

CC number: 219418

Eligibility

People in need who live in the West Midlands.

Types of grant

Welfare

One-off grants are given according to need. Grants are given for a range of purposes including clothing, furniture, convalescence holidays, household equipment and medical equipment.

Education

Grants are given towards education and training.

Exclusions

Grants will not be awarded towards debts already incurred.

Applications

Apply in writing to the correspondent. Applications for welfare grants should be made through a welfare agency. Applications for educational grants should be submitted through the individual's parent/guardian, school or welfare agency. Mature students may apply directly. Applications are considered weekly.

Financial information

Year end		05/04/2021
Income		£181,800
Total expenditure		£196,900

Further financial information

In 2020/21, a total of £52,000 was awarded to 236 individuals. Within this, grants for social welfare purposes totalled £41,600 and were distributed as follows:

Clothing and furniture	117	£19,800
Domestic equipment	104	£19,800
Social welfare	12	£1,800
Convalescence and holidays	1	£200

Education grants to two individuals totalled £400.

Jordison and Hossell Animal Welfare Charity

 £1,300 (2019/20)

Correspondent: Sally Reid, Trustee, Whitestones, Haselor, Alcester, Warwickshire B49 6LU (tel: 01789 488942; email: sallyreid@me.com)

CC number: 515352

Eligibility

People in Birmingham and Warwickshire who are on low incomes and are in need of financial assistance to meet veterinary bills for their pets.

Types of grant

One-off grants are made towards 'unpredictable' vets' bills.

Exclusions

Our previous research suggests that support is not given with vets' bills for larger animals such as horses and farm animals. Grants are not made to support the continuing care of a pet.

Applications

Apply in writing to the correspondent.

Financial information

Year end		30/06/2020
Income		£1,500
Total expenditure		£1,400

Further financial information

Full accounts were not available to view on the Charity Commission's website due to the charity's low income. We have therefore estimated the grant total based on the charity's total expenditure.

Other information

The charity may also give grants to organisations.

The Norton Foundation

 £17,000 (2019/20)

Correspondent: Richard Perkins, The Paddock, Bwlch Y Gwynt Road, Llysfaen, Colwyn Bay, Clwyd LL29 8DQ (tel: 01492 512079; email: correspondent@nortonfoundation.org)

🌐 www.nortonfoundation.org

CC number: 702638

Eligibility

Young people under the age of 25 who live in Birmingham, Coventry, Solihull or Warwickshire and are in need.

Types of grant

Grants are typically given towards clothing, household goods and education and training. Grants of up to £500 can be awarded, although they are usually within the range of £50 to £250.

Applications

Applications should be made through a third-party sponsor (such as a social worker, rotary club, scout and guide group, probation service, religious group or Citizens Advice) using the form available from the foundation's website. Applications are considered on a monthly basis. Further guidance notes can be found on the website.

Financial information

Year end		05/04/2020
Income		£201,000
Total expenditure		£261,100

Further financial information

In 2019/20, a total of £17,000 was awarded to 126 individuals.

Welfare

Welfare grants totalled £13,200 and were distributed as follows:

Household	82	£11,500
Clothing	13	£1,700

Education

A further £3,700 was awarded to 27 individuals towards education and training.

In addition, £24,100 was paid in block discretionary grants to 15 sponsors for redistribution to individuals; however, this amount is not included in the grant total.

Other information

The foundation also awards grants to organisations.

Pargeter and Wand Trust

£ £4,000 (2019/20)

Correspondent: Kay Workman, Housing and Charitable Services Manager, c/o Broadening Choices for Older People, 7–8 Imperial Court, 12 Sovereign Road, Kings Norton, Worcestershire B30 3FH (tel: 0121 459 7670; email: kay.workman@bcop.org.uk)

🌐 www.bcop.org.uk

CC number: 210725

Eligibility

Women aged 55 and over who have never been married and are in need. Preference is given to those living in the West Midlands area.

Types of grant

Grants are given according to need.

Applications

Apply in writing to the correspondent.

Financial information

Year end		31/03/2020
Income		£9,100
Total expenditure		£4,400

Further financial information

Full accounts were not available to view on the Charity Commission's website due to the trust's low income. We have therefore estimated the grant total based on the trust's total expenditure.

Pedmore Sporting Club Trust Fund

£ £9,300 (2020)

Correspondent: The Secretary, c/o Nicklin & Co. LLP, Church Court, Stourbridge Road, Halesowen, Worcestershire B63 3TT (tel: 0121 550 9916; email: psclub@pedmorehouse.co.uk)

www.pedmoresportingclub.co.uk

CC number: 263907

Eligibility
Residents in the West Midlands who are in need.

Types of grant
One-off grants according to need. Money is normally paid directly to the service/item provider, not the individual.

Applications
Apply in writing to the correspondent, providing background information about you (the applicant), details of the support required and an estimate of the cost. The trustees meet five times per year to consider grant requests. Usually, around 30 to 40 applications are considered at each meeting.

Financial information
Year end	31/12/2020
Income	£0
Total expenditure	£20,500

Further financial information
Full accounts were not available to view on the Charity Commission's website due to the trust's low income. We have therefore estimated the trust's grant total based on its total expenditure.

Other information
A large portion of the trust's grants are made to local organisations including hospices, children's homes and other charitable organisations.

Rycroft Children's Fund
See entry on page 212

The Eric W. Vincent Trust Fund

£880 (2019/20)

Correspondent: Janet Stephen, Clerk, PO Box 17146, Halesowen, West Midlands B62 2LF (email: vttrust942@gmail.com)

CC number: 204843

Eligibility
People in need living in the West Midlands.

Types of grant
The trust makes small grants to individuals, typically ranging from £100 to £150.

Exclusions
The trust does not award grants to cover debts, or to cover needs outside the local area.

Applications
Apply in writing to the correspondent.

Financial information
Year end	31/03/2020
Income	£547,900
Total expenditure	£553,200

Further financial information
During 2019/20, six grants were made to individuals.

Other information
The trust also supports organisations.

Margaret Westwood Memorial Charity

£14,600 (2019/20)

Correspondent: The Trustees, Higgs & Sons, Unit 3, Waterfront Business Park, Dudley Road, Brierley Hill, West Midlands DY5 1LX (tel: 01384 327322; email: kirsty.mcewen@higgsandsons.co.uk)

CC number: 500125

Eligibility
Children and young people who live in the former county of Worcestershire (as constituted on 18 August 1946). This includes the current county of Worcestershire and parts of the West Midlands.

Types of grant
Grants are given according to need.

Applications
Apply in writing to the correspondent.

Financial information
Year end	05/04/2020
Income	£96,400
Total expenditure	£43,000

Further financial information
The charity made 54 grants to individuals in 2019/20.

Other information
Grants are also made to organisations.

The Anthony and Gwendoline Wylde Memorial Charity

£10,200 (2019/20)

Correspondent: Kirsty McEwen, Secretary, c/o Higgs LLP, Unit 3 Waterfront Business Park, Waterfront Business Park, Dudley Road, Brierley Hill, West Midlands DY5 1LX (tel: 0345 111 5050; email: kirsty.mcewen@higgsandsons.co.uk)

 wyldecharity.weebly.com

CC number: 700239

Eligibility
People in need living in Dudley and Staffordshire. The beneficial area is defined as the DY6, DY7, DY8, DY9, DY10 and DY11 postcodes.

Types of grant
The charity offers small grants for individuals (up to £1,000) and prefers to support further education. It also awards large grants for individuals.

Applications
Application forms are available on the charity's website. Two different forms are available: an application form for small grants and an application form for large grants. According to the charity's website, applications for large grants are considered twice yearly unless there are exceptional circumstances.

Financial information
Year end	05/04/2020
Income	£84,200
Total expenditure	£42,200

Further financial information
A total of 25 grants were made to individuals in 2019/20 for both welfare and education.

Other information
The charity also gives to organisations.

Hereford-shire

All Saints Relief-in-Need Charity

£6,900 (2019/20)

Correspondent: The Trustees, 6 St Ethelbert Street, Hereford, Herefordshire HR1 2NR (tel: 01432 267821; email: carodoug@gmx.com)

CC number: 244527

Eligibility
Residents in the city of Hereford who are in need, with a preference for residents in the ancient parish of All Saints.

Types of grant
Small grants are awarded according to need.

Applications
Apply in writing to the correspondent.

Financial information
Year end	31/03/2020
Income	£7,300
Total expenditure	£7,700

Further financial information
Full accounts were not available to view on the Charity Commission's website

due to the charity's low income. We have therefore estimated the charity's grant total based on its total expenditure.

E. F. Bulmer Trust

 £47,200 (2020/21)

Correspondent: Paddy Nugent, Chief Operating Officer, The Fred Bulmer Centre, Wall Street, Hereford, Herefordshire HR4 9HP (tel: 01432 271293; email: efbulmer@gmail.com)

efbulmer.co.uk

CC number: 1188978

Eligibility

Priority is given to former employees of H P Bulmer Holdings plc (before it was acquired by Scottish and Newcastle plc) or its subsidiary companies who are in need. Grants are then made to other individuals in need in Herefordshire.

Types of grant

Small grants of up to £500 are awarded for urgent/essential items.

Applications

Application forms can be downloaded from the charity's website. Applications should be made through a recognised organisation such as social services, Citizens Advice or another reputable organisation.

Financial information

Year end	31/03/2021
Income	£245,200
Total expenditure	£219,800

Other information

Grants are also made to organisations in Herefordshire.

The Edmund Godson Charity

See entry on page 319

The Harley Charity (formerly The Honourable Miss Frances Harley Charity)

£18,500 (2019/20)

Correspondent: Edward Harley, Trustee, The Harley Estate, Brampton Bryan, Bucknell, Shropshire SY7 0DH (tel: 01547 530280)

CC number: 207072

Eligibility

Church of England clergy and their widows/widowers who are in need and live primarily, but not exclusively, in the diocese of Hereford. People with physical disabilities, primarily those who are blind, who are members of the Church of England.

Types of grant

Grants according to need.

Applications

Apply in writing to the correspondent.

Financial information

Year end	05/04/2020
Income	£37,600
Total expenditure	£37,700

Other information

The charity also seeks to support Hereford Cathedral with upkeep and repairs, as well as other local Church of England churches and registered charities.

Hereford Municipal Charities

£8,800 (2020)

Correspondent: The Clerk, 147 St Owen Street, Hereford, Herefordshire HR1 2JR (tel: 01432 354002; email: clerk@ herefordalmshouses.co.uk)

CC number: 218738

Eligibility

People in need who live in the city of Hereford.

Types of grant

Welfare

One-off grants are given according to need for a range of purposes including essential household goods and furniture.

Education

One-off grants are given towards course/ training fees and materials.

Exclusions

According to our previous research, grants are not given towards debts or nursery fees.

Applications

Application forms are available from the correspondent and should be submitted directly by the individual or through a relevant third party. Applications are considered five times a year but can be authorised within regular trustees' meetings if they are very urgent. Applicants are normally interviewed.

Financial information

Year end	31/12/2020
Income	£425,700
Total expenditure	£207,400

Other information

The charity also provides almshouse accommodation. There are two separate funds (eleemosynary and educational) administered by the grants committee.

The Hereford Society for Aiding the Industrious

£1,200 (2019/20)

Correspondent: Sally Robertson, Secretary, 18 Venns Close, Bath Street, Hereford, Herefordshire HR1 2HH (tel: 01432 274014; email: info@hsfai.co. uk)

CC number: 212220

Eligibility

People in need who live in Herefordshire who would be described as 'industrious', as stated on the Charity Commission website.

Types of grant

Grants are made to help individuals to 'get over a hurdle', as stated on the Charity Commission website. This may include grants towards education and training.

Applications

Apply in writing to the correspondent.

Financial information

Year end	05/04/2020
Income	£147,000
Total expenditure	£106,400

Further financial information

The grant total has been estimated based on the 2019/20 accounts.

Other information

The charity's main activity is providing and maintaining almshouses. It also awards grants to local organisations that are active in the community.

The Norton Canon Parochial Charities

£6,600 (2020)

Correspondent: The Trustees, Ivy Cottage, Norton Canon, Hereford, Herefordshire HR4 7BQ (tel: 01544 318984)

CC number: 218560

Eligibility

Welfare

People in need and older people who live in the parish of Norton Canon.

Education

People living in the parish of Norton Canon.

Types of grant

Welfare

One-off and recurrent grants according to need.

Education

Grants are given towards education.

Applications

Apply in writing to the correspondent.

Financial information

Year end	31/12/2020
Income	£22,500
Total expenditure	£14,700

Further financial information

Full accounts were not available to view on the Charity Commission's website due to the charity's low income. We have therefore estimated the charity's grant total based on its total expenditure.

The Rathbone Moral Aid Charity

£ £4,800 (2019)

Correspondent: The Trustees, PO Box 181, Hereford, Herefordshire HR2 9YN (tel: 01981 250899; email: carolhfdcc@btinternet.com)

CC number: 222697

Eligibility

People under the age of 25 who are in danger of lapsing into delinquency, substance misuse or who are in need of rehabilitation. Only people who live in Herefordshire are eligible for support.

Types of grant

Grants are awarded according to need.

Applications

Apply in writing to the correspondent.

Financial information

Year end	31/12/2019
Income	£17,500
Total expenditure	£10,700

Further financial information

Full accounts were not available to view on the Charity Commission's website due to the charity's low income. We have therefore estimated the charity's grant total based on its total expenditure.

Other information

Grants are also awarded to organisations.

Shropshire

Alveley Charity

£ £3,600 (2019/20)

Correspondent: Rachel Summers, Clerk to the Trustees, c/o mfg Solicitors LLP, Adam House, Birmingham Road, Kidderminster, Worcestershire DY10 2SH (tel: 01562 820181; email: rachel.summers@mfgsolicitors.com)

CC number: 1026017

Eligibility

People in need who live in the parishes of Alveley and Romsley.

Types of grant

One-off grants according to need.

Applications

Applications may be made in writing to the correspondent, either directly by the individual or through a social worker, Citizens Advice or other welfare agency.

Financial information

Year end	31/03/2020
Income	£20,000
Total expenditure	£8,100

Further financial information

Full accounts were not available to view on the Charity Commission's website due to the charity's low income. We have therefore estimated the charity's grant total based on its total expenditure.

Other information

The charity also maintains properties.

The Atherton Trust

£ £1,200 (2019/20)

Correspondent: Paul Adams, c/o Whittingham Riddell LLP, Belmont House, Shrewsbury Business Park, Shrewsbury, Shropshire SY2 6LG (tel: 01743 273273; email: pauladams797@btinternet.com)

CC number: 515220

Eligibility

People in need living in the parishes of Pontesbury and Hanwood and the villages of Annscroft and Hook-a-Gate in the county of Shropshire.

Types of grant

One-off and recurrent grants according to need.

Applications

Apply in writing to the correspondent.

Financial information

Year end	05/04/2020
Income	£44,600
Total expenditure	£58,600

Further financial information

Grants were made to two individuals in 2019/20.

Other information

The trust also awards grants to organisations.

Bridgnorth Lions Club Trust Fund

£ £4,000 (2019/20)

Correspondent: The Secretary, 11 The Ridge, Bridgnorth, Shropshire WV15 6QP (tel: 0845 833 8552; email: info@bridgnorthlions.org.uk)

 www.bridgnorthlions.org.uk

CC number: 517786

Eligibility

Residents of Bridgnorth who are in need.

Types of grant

Grants are made according to need.

Applications

Apply in writing to the correspondent.

Financial information

Year end	30/06/2020
Income	£30,100
Total expenditure	£36,200

Other information

The charity runs various community events such as the Bridgnorth Lions Walk and Marathon and an annual prostate cancer screening. Grants are also made in support of international causes, particularly major natural disasters, as well as towards local causes. Previously, the charity donated to Oak Farm in Bridgnorth, a working farm that serves as a day service for adults with learning difficulties.

The Bridgnorth Parish Charity

£ £8,500 (2019)

Correspondent: Elizabeth Smallman, Trustee, 37 Stourbridge Road, Bridgnorth, Shropshire WV15 5AZ (tel: 01746 764149)

CC number: 243890

Eligibility

People in need who live in the parish of Bridgnorth, including Oldbury, Quatford and Eardington.

Types of grant

Grants are given according to need.

Applications

Applications may be made in writing to the correspondent either directly by the individual or through a doctor, nurse, member of the local clergy, social worker, Citizens Advice or other welfare agency.

Financial information

Year end	31/12/2019
Income	£9,000
Total expenditure	£18,900

Further financial information

Full accounts were not available to view on the Charity Commission's website due to the charity's low income. We have therefore estimated the charity's grant total based on its total expenditure.

Other information

The charity also awards grants to local organisations.

The Lady Forester Trust

£ £55,400 (2020)

Correspondent: The Trustees, The Estate Office, Willey Park, Broseley, Shropshire TF12 5JN (tel: 01952 884318; email: lft@willeyestates.co.uk)

CC number: 241187

Eligibility

People who are in need as a result of illness, convalescence, disability or infirmity. Priority is given to residents of the ancient borough of Wenlock and then to residents of the wider county of Shropshire.

Types of grant

Grants are awarded according to need. Past examples include grants for medical equipment, nursing care and travel expenses to and from hospitals.

Applications

Apply in writing to the correspondent. Applications from individuals are usually made on the recommendation of GPs and social workers. The trustees meet on a quarterly basis to consider grant applications.

Financial information

Year end	31/12/2020
Income	£208,600
Total expenditure	£185,400

Gibbons Charity

£ £4,100 (2020)

Correspondent: The Trustees, 12 Shrewsbury Street, Hodnet, Market Drayton, Shropshire TF9 3NP (tel: 01630 684007)

CC number: 215171

Eligibility

Shropshire Church of England clergy and retired clergy and their widows, widowers, spouses, divorced partners and children who face hardship.

Types of grant

Grants are awarded according to need.

Applications

Apply in writing to the correspondent.

Financial information

Year end	31/12/2020
Income	£3,600
Total expenditure	£4,500

Further financial information

Full accounts were not available to view on the Charity Commission's website due to the charity's low income. We have therefore estimated the charity's grant total based on its total expenditure.

Other information

The charity's working name is Gibbons Charity. Its full name is 'William Henry Kinnaird Gibbons (including The Augmentation of the Reverend Alfred Ernest Lloyd Kenyon)'.

The Hodnet Consolidated Eleemosynary Charities

£ £1,800 (2019)

Correspondent: Mrs S. France, 26 The Meadow, Hodnet, Market Drayton, Shropshire TF9 3QF (tel: 01630 685907; email: wendy547@sky.com)

CC number: 218213

Eligibility

People in need who live in Hodnet parish.

Types of grant

Grants are given according to need.

Applications

Apply in writing to the correspondent.

Financial information

Year end	31/12/2019
Income	£3,700
Total expenditure	£4,100

Further financial information

Full accounts were not available to view on the Charity Commission's website due to the charity's low income. We have therefore estimated the charity's grant total based on its total expenditure.

The Shropshire Youth Foundation

£ £1,900 (2019/20)

Correspondent: Emily Marshall, Committee Services Officer, Democratic Services Team, Shropshire Council, The Shirehall, Abbey Foregate, Shrewsbury, Shropshire SY2 6ND (tel: 01743 257717; email: emily.marshall@shropshire.gov.uk)

CC number: 522595

Eligibility

People under the age of 25 who live in the county of Shropshire, including Telford and Wrekin.

Types of grant

Grants are given for leisure activities with the aim of developing the physical, mental and spiritual capacities of individuals so that their life conditions may be approved.

Applications

Apply in writing to the correspondent.

Financial information

Year end	31/03/2020
Income	£9,500
Total expenditure	£2,100

Further financial information

Full accounts were not available to view on the Charity Commission's website due to the foundation's low income. We have therefore estimated the foundation's grant total based on its total expenditure.

Other information

The foundation also provides assistance to organisations.

The St Chad's and St Alkmund's Charity
See entry on page 204

Thompson Pritchard Trust

 £4,200 (2019)

Correspondent: The Trustees, 8 Woodhouse Lane, Priorslee, Telford TF2 9SX (tel: 01743 241281; email: secretary@shropshirewelfaretrust.org)

https://shropshirewelfaretrust.org

CC number: 234601

Eligibility
People living in Shropshire who are in need as a result of disability or a serious health issue. Priority is given to those who have recently been discharged from a Shropshire hospital and are in need of convalescence.

Types of grant
Small one-off grants are given for a range of purposes including travel to and from hospital, convalescence, respite care, medical appliances, mobility aids and essential household appliances.

Exclusions
Grants cannot be awarded for debts, bills or expenses already incurred. The trust does not award repeat grants.

Applications
Application forms are available to download on the trust's website. Applications should be supported by a sponsor (healthcare worker, social worker, housing support officer, etc.) who can confirm the applicant's circumstances and need.

Financial information
Year end	31/12/2019
Income	£20,100
Total expenditure	£9,300

Further financial information
Full accounts were not available to view on the Charity Commission's website due to the trust's low income. We have therefore estimated the trust's grant total based on its total expenditure.

Other information
The trust also makes grants to organisations. It is part of the Shropshire Welfare Trust group of charities, which also comprises Shropshire Welfare Trust (Charity Commission no. 218206) and Dr Gardner's Trust for Nurses (Charity Commission no. 218202).

Telford and Wrekin

Basil Houghton Memorial Trust

 £6,600 (2019/20)

Correspondent: The Trustees, c/o SRCC Building, 4 The Creative Quarter, Shrewsbury Business Park, Shrewsbury, Shropshire SY2 6LG (tel: 01743 360641; email: houghton.trust@shropshire-rcc.org.uk)

www.basilhoughtontrust.org.uk

CC number: 1101947

Eligibility
People with learning disabilities who are in need and live in Shropshire or Telford and Wrekin.

Types of grant
Grants of up to £350 to enable a person with a learning disability to fulfil a dream, aspiration or improve their quality of life.

Exclusions
Grants are not given for expenditure that has already occurred.

Applications
Application forms can be downloaded from the trust's website and can be submitted at any time. The trustees meet four times a year, usually in March, June, September and December; applications should arrive at least seven days prior to the meeting. The trustees advise that applicants should apply within good time before a trip/event as it can take up to three months before the outcome is decided.

Financial information
Year end	31/03/2020
Income	£14,400
Total expenditure	£14,600

Further financial information
Full accounts were not available to view on the Charity Commission's website due to the trust's low income. We have therefore estimated the grant total based on the trust's total expenditure.

The Roddam Charity

 £2,100 (2019/20)

Correspondent: Linda Palmer-Pitchford, Secretary, Bedruthan, Tibberton, Newport, Shropshire TF10 8NN (tel: 01952 550745; email: linda@bougheyroddamha.org.uk)

https://roddamcharity.org.uk

CC number: 213892

Eligibility
People of all ages who live in the TF10 postcode area and are in need. This includes those with disabilities and illnesses and those recovering from illness.

Types of grant
Grants are made towards the cost of items, services or facilities that are not readily available from other sources which will relieve suffering or assist with recovery.

Exclusions
Grants are not made for rates, taxes or other public funds.

Applications
Application forms can be downloaded from the charity's website.

Financial information
Year end	31/03/2020
Income	£4,700
Total expenditure	£4,500

Further financial information
Full accounts were not available to view on the Charity Commission website due to the charity's low income. We have therefore estimated the charity's grant total based on its total expenditure.

Other information
The charity also awards grants to organisations.

Charity of Edith Emily Todd

£7,700 (2019/20)

Correspondent: The Grants Administrator, 4 Willmoor Lane, Lilleshall, Newport, Shropshire TF10 9EE (tel: 01952 606053)

CC number: 215058

Eligibility
People over the age of 60 who are in need and who live in the parish of Lilleshall and Donnington.

Types of grant
Monthly pensions are distributed.

Applications
Apply in writing to correspondent.

Financial information
Year end	31/03/2020
Income	£9,500
Total expenditure	£8,600

Further financial information
Full accounts were not available to view on the Charity Commission's website due to the charity's low income. We have therefore estimated the charity's grant total based on its total expenditure.

Staffordshire

The North Staffordshire Coalfield Miners Relief Fund

£ £2,500 (2019/20)

Correspondent: The Trustees, c/o Coal Industry Social Welfare Organisation, Berry Hill Lane, Penkhull, Mansfield, Nottinghamshire NG18 4JR (tel: 01623 625767)

CC number: 209616

Eligibility

Current and former mineworkers who worked in the North Staffordshire coalfield (including Cheadle), and their dependants. The mineworker must have suffered an industrial accident or illness, or died as a result of their occupation.

Types of grant

Grants according to need.

Applications

Apply in writing to the correspondent.

Financial information

Year end	30/06/2020
Income	£2,300
Total expenditure	£2,800

Further financial information

Full accounts were not available to view on the Charity Commission's website due to the fund's low income. We have therefore estimated the fund's grant total based on its total expenditure.

Other information

Grants are also made to organisations.

Persehouse Pensions Fund

£ £13,900 (2019/20)

Correspondent: The Trustees, William Lench Court, 80 Ridgacre Road, Birmingham B32 2AQ (tel: 0121 426 0455; email: jean-lucp@lenchs-trust.co.uk)

CC number: 500660

Eligibility

Older people and people in need who belong to the upper or middle classes of society and are now in need due to misfortune. Applicants must have been born in the counties of Staffordshire or Worcestershire or have lived in either county for ten years or more.

Types of grant

The fund mainly awards pensions, although one-off grants are also given occasionally.

Applications

According to our previous research, application forms are available from the correspondent and can be submitted directly by the individual.

Financial information

Year end	05/04/2020
Income	£14,000
Total expenditure	£15,500

Further financial information

Full accounts were not available to view on the Charity Commission's website due to the fund's low income. We have therefore estimated the grant total based on the fund's total expenditure.

The Community Foundation for Staffordshire

£ £11,500 (2019/20)

Correspondent: The Trustees, Communications House, University Court, Staffordshire Technology Park, Stafford, Staffordshire ST18 0ES (tel: 01785 339540; email: office@staffsfoundation.org.uk)

 https://staffsfoundation.org.uk

CC number: 1091628

Eligibility

People in need who live in Staffordshire. The community foundation operates a number of funds, each with its own eligibility criteria. See the foundation's website for more information.

Types of grant

A number of funds are available to individuals. Refer to the foundation's website for details of open grant programmes. Previously, support has been given for a range of purposes, including medical equipment, respite holidays, white goods and emergency heating repairs.

Applications

Details on how to apply can be found on the community foundation's website.

Financial information

Year end	31/03/2020
Income	£1,330,000
Total expenditure	£1,360,000

Other information

This is one of the 47 UK community foundations, which distribute funding for a wide range of purposes. Grant schemes tend to change frequently – consult the foundation's website for details of current programmes and upcoming deadlines.

Cannock Chase

Chetwynd's Charity

£ £900 (2020)

Correspondent: The Trustees, Sherwood, 17 East Butts Road, Rugeley, Staffordshire WS15 2LU (tel: 01889 800727; email: chetwyndscharity@gmail.com)

CC number: 234806

Eligibility

People in need who live in Rugeley in Staffordshire.

Types of grant

Grants are given according to need.

Applications

Apply in writing to the correspondent.

Financial information

Year end	31/12/2020
Income	£2,700
Total expenditure	£2,000

Further financial information

Full accounts were not available to view on the Charity Commission's website due to the charity's low income. We have therefore estimated the grant total based on the charity's total expenditure.

Other information

The charity also awards grants to organisations for the advancement of education, training and cultural activities.

The Rugeley Educational Endowment

£ £8,000 (2020/21)

Correspondent: The Trustees, Staffordshire County Council, Treasury and Pensions, 2 Staffordshire Place, Tipping Street, Stafford, Staffordshire ST16 2LP (tel: 01785 276330; email: melanie.stokes@staffordshire.gov.uk)

CC number: 528603

Eligibility

People under the age of 25 who live in Rugeley and have attended any secondary school in the area of benefit.

Types of grant

Grants are available to those undertaking education or leaving education to begin work.

Applications

Applications should be made through the headteacher of the school attended.

Financial information

Year end	31/03/2021
Income	£83,400
Total expenditure	£67,600

Further financial information

In 2020/21, £16,100 in grants was awarded to individuals and organisations. A breakdown of grants was not available; therefore, the grant total has been estimated.

East Staffordshire

Burton-on-Trent Nursing Endowment Fund

£ £2,000 (2020)

Correspondent: The Trustees, 141 Newton Road, Burton-on-Trent, Staffordshire DE15 0TR (tel: 01283 567900)

CC number: 239185

Eligibility

Residents of Burton-on-Trent who are in need as a result of illness.

Types of grant

Grants are awarded according to need. Past examples include chiropody treatment, bedding, removal costs, electric scooter batteries, fridge/freezers and childcare provision.

Applications

Apply in writing to the correspondent.

Financial information

Year end	31/12/2020
Income	£5,100
Total expenditure	£4,500

Further financial information

Full accounts were not available to view on the Charity Commission's website due to the fund's low income. We have therefore estimated the grant total based on the fund's total expenditure.

Other information

This fund also makes grants to organisations.

Consolidated Charity of Burton upon Trent

£ £107,700 (2019)

Correspondent: Mr J. Southwell, Clerk to the Trustees, c/o Dains LLP, 1st Floor, Gibraltar House, Crown Square, First Avenue, Burton-on-Trent, Staffordshire DE14 2WE (tel: 01283 527067; email: clerk@consolidatedcharityburton.org.uk)

 https://www.consolidatedcharity burton.org.uk

CC number: 239072

Eligibility

Welfare

People in need who live in Burton-on-Trent and the neighbouring parishes of Anslow, Barton-under-Needwood, Branston, Brizlincote, Dunstall, Hanbury, Stretton, Rolleston on Dove, Tutbury, Tatenhill, Rangemore and Outwoods.

Education

People embarking on an undergraduate course at a university who are resident with the area of benefit as defined above. The participating schools and colleges are Abbot Beyne School, Burton and South Derbyshire College, De Ferrers Specialist Technology College, John Taylor High School, Paget High School, Paulet High School, Blessed Robert Sutton Catholic Sports College and Derby Grammar School.

Types of grant

Welfare

One-off relief-in-need grants are awarded up to a maximum of £600 for essential items such as cookers, fridge freezers, washing machines, carpets, furniture, bedding, mobility aids and school uniforms.

Education

A maximum of 40 bursaries of a total value of £1,500 (£500 per year over three years) are awarded to undergraduate students each year. The charity also offers education and personal development grants of up to £300 per year towards further education, vocational training, overseas travel for personal development, sports activities and arts scholarships.

Applications

Application forms and guidance for the relief-in-need grant scheme are available online and can be downloaded and returned via post or completed online. Applications must include a signed, headed letter of support from a support worker or another suitable professional.

Applications for the bursary scheme open in January and must be submitted through – and contain a statement of support from – the applicant's school or college. Application forms and guidance for the education and personal development grant are available online and can be downloaded and returned via post or completed online. Evidence is required of acceptance onto the course or project for which the assistance is sought.

Financial information

Year end	31/12/2019
Income	£622,300
Total expenditure	£600,300

Further financial information

In 2019, the charity made welfare grants totalling £39,900 to 96 individuals and education grants totalling £50,600 to 40 individuals.

Other information

The charity also runs 29 almshouses in the local area and makes grants to organisations.

Tutbury General Charities

£ £8,200 (2019/20)

Correspondent: The Trustees, Charity House, Duke Street, Tutbury, Burton-on-Trent, Staffordshire DE13 9NE (tel: 07854 996527; email: tutburyparishcharities@gmail.com)

CC number: 215140

Eligibility

Welfare

People who are in need and live in the parish of Tutbury.

Education

Students living in Tutbury who are in college or undertaking an apprenticeship.

Types of grant

Welfare

One-off and ongoing grants are given according to need.

Education

Grants are given to assist with the expenses of further education.

Applications

Application forms can be requested from the correspondent.

Financial information

Year end	31/10/2020
Income	£23,500
Total expenditure	£9,100

Further financial information

Full accounts were not available to view on the Charity Commission's website due to the charity's low income. We have therefore estimated the charity's grant total based on its total expenditure.

Other information

The clerk has previously stated that details of the charity are well publicised within the village.

Lichfield

Michael Lowe's and Associated Charities

£ £19,700 (2019/20)

Correspondent: Simon James, Clerk to the Trustees, Ansons Solicitors, St Mary's Chambers, 5–7 Breadmarket Street, Lichfield, Staffordshire WS13 6LQ (tel: 01543 263456; email: sjames@ansonssolicitors.com)

CC number: 214785

Eligibility

People in need who live in the city of Lichfield. Fuel grant applications are accepted from those over the age of 70 who have a low income or need for heating for health reasons.

Types of grant

Fuel grants are awarded to over 70s who meet the eligibility criteria and one-off grants are awarded for domestic items; the trustees may require the recipient to make a contribution of 10% towards the cost of any item provided. Gifts in the form of second-hand furniture are also distributed through the Furniture Transfer Scheme.

Applications

Apply on a form available from the correspondent. Applications are considered on their own merits and individuals are usually interviewed before any grant is awarded. Beneficiaries of the Furniture Transfer Scheme are usually recommended to trustees through a local welfare organisation. The trustees meet on average five times a year to consider grant applications, although special meetings may be called to deal with urgent requests.

Financial information

Year end	31/03/2020
Income	£91,400
Total expenditure	£86,100

Further financial information

Grants were awarded to 142 individuals during the year.

Other information

The charity prioritises grants to individuals but also awards grants to organisations.

Stafford

Stafford Educational Endowment Charity

£ £2,000 (2020/21)

Correspondent: Melanie Stokes, Staffordshire County Council, Treasury and Pensions, 2 Staffordshire Place, Tipping Street, Stafford, Staffordshire ST16 2LP (tel: 01785 276330; email: melanie.stokes@staffordshire.gov.uk)

 www.westonroad.staffs.sch.uk/Students/Stafford-Educational-Endowment-Charity

CC number: 517345

Eligibility

Pupils and former pupils of one of the six Stafford high schools aged 25 and under. Applicants can apply up until their 26th birthday. Applicants are typically from low-income families.

Types of grant

Welfare

Grants in the past have been in the region of £150 to £250 and have been used towards a wide range of activities such as Duke of Edinburgh projects, voluntary work, sports activities and so on. Grants are also made to current students for uniforms and sportswear.

Education

Grants in the past have been in the region of £150 to £250 and have been used for a range of educational purposes such as apprentice schemes, residential courses, scientific field work, overseas travel and so on.

Exclusions

Unless there are exceptional circumstances, help is not available for the purchase of books or other materials required for courses in higher education.

Applications

Application forms can be downloaded from The Weston Road Academy website. Alternatively, the headteacher of the student's school or former school can supply an application form, as can the correspondent. Applications are usually considered in February, June and October, when the trustees meet.

Financial information

Year end	31/03/2021
Income	£18,300
Total expenditure	£18,700

Further financial information

Full accounts were not available to view on the Charity Commission's website due to the charity's low income. We have therefore estimated the charity's grant total based on the findings of our previous research.

Other information

The charity provides benefits which are not normally provided by the school or local authority.

Staffordshire and Moorlands

Carr Trust

£ £4,200 (2020)

Correspondent: The Trustees, St Luke's Church of England Church, Fountain Street, Leek, Staffordshire ST13 6JS (tel: 01538 373306; email: williamcarrtrust@gmail.com)

CC number: 216764

Eligibility

Residents of Leek, particularly older residents, who are in need.

Types of grant

Pensions are given to older residents. One-off grants are available to individuals of any age.

Applications

Apply in writing to the correspondent.

Financial information

Year end	31/12/2020
Income	£100,500
Total expenditure	£111,300

Stoke

The Lady Katherine and Sir Richard Leveson Charity

£ £680 (2020)

Correspondent: The Revd Adrian Stone, Trustee, The Vicarage, Trentham Park, Stoke-on-Trent, Staffordshire ST4 8AE (tel: 01782 691948; email: adrianstonerev@gmail.com)

CC number: 1077372

Eligibility

Welfare

People in need who live in the ancient parish of Trentham in Stoke-on-Trent and the districts of Clayton and Seabridge in Newcastle-under-Lyme.

Education

People under the age of 25 who are resident in the beneficial area and are seeking to further their education.

Types of grant

Welfare
One-off grants are awarded according to need. Grants are typically given to help buy essential household goods and services.

Education
Grants are awarded towards educational costs.

Applications
Apply in writing to the correspondent, either directly by the individual or through a third party such as an educational welfare office or school/college.

Financial information

Year end	31/12/2020
Income	£3,400
Total expenditure	£1,500

Further financial information
Full accounts were not available to view on the Charity Commission's website due to the charity's low income. We have therefore estimated the charity's grant total based on its total expenditure.

Other information
The charity also makes grants to organisations.

Edith Emily Todd (The Todd Fund)

£1,100 (2020/21)

Correspondent: The Revd Adrian Stone, Trustee, The Vicarage, Trentham Park, Stoke-on-Trent, Staffordshire ST4 8AE (tel: 01782 691948; email: adrianstonerev@gmail.com)

CC number: 209922

Eligibility
Older residents in the ecclesiastical parishes of St Mary and All Saints and Trentham and St Mathias who are in need. Also, residents of the beneficial area of any age who are in financial need.

Types of grant
The charity awards one-off grants and pensions.

Applications
Apply in writing to the correspondent.

Financial information

Year end	05/04/2021
Income	£1,800
Total expenditure	£1,200

Further financial information
Full accounts were not available to view on the Charity Commission's website due to the charity's low income. We have therefore estimated the grant total based on the charity's total expenditure.

Tamworth

Beardsley's Relief in Need Charity

£4,800 (2019/20)

Correspondent: The Trustees, Barnfield, Comberford Lane, Wigginton, Tamworth, Staffordshire B79 9DT (tel: 01543 255612; email: enquiries@tomkinsonteal.co.uk)

CC number: 214461

Eligibility
People in need who live in the borough of Tamworth, especially older people, children and people with disabilities.

Types of grant
Grants are awarded according to need.

Applications
Apply in writing to the correspondent.

Financial information

Year end	08/05/2020
Income	£14,000
Total expenditure	£10,600

Further financial information
Full accounts were not available to view on the Charity Commission's website due to the charity's low income. We have therefore estimated the charity's grant total based on its total expenditure.

Other information
The charity also makes grants to organisations.

Rawlet Trust

£23,900 (2019/20)

Correspondent: The Trustees, Lawnswood, Bowmer Lane, Fritchley, Belper, Derbyshire DE56 2FY (tel: 07850 614410; email: rawlettrust@mail.com)

CC number: 221732

Eligibility

Welfare
Residents of Tamworth who are in need, including for health reasons.

Education
Educational grants are awarded to young people in Tamworth aged under 25 years.

Types of grant
Grants are awarded according to need.

Applications
Apply in writing to the correspondent. The trustees meet quarterly, in January, April, July and October to consider grant applications.

Financial information

Year end	09/03/2020
Income	£27,000
Total expenditure	£25,500

Other information
As part of its welfare grant-making, the trust also distributes bibles to beneficiaries. The trust can also make grants to organisations.

Warwick-shire

Charities of Susanna Cole and Others

£11,000 (2020)

Correspondent: The Trustees, Central England Quakers Office, Friends Meeting House, 40 Bull Street, Birmingham B4 6AF (tel: 0121 682 7575)

CC number: 204531

Eligibility
Quakers in need who live in the West Midlands (Birmingham, Coventry, Dudley, Solihull, Sandwell, Walsall and Warwickshire) with a preference for those living in Worcester.

Types of grant
One-off grants according to need.

Applications
Applications should be made in writing to the correspondent, detailing the financial need and how the grant will be used.

Financial information

Year end	31/12/2020
Income	£12,600
Total expenditure	£12,300

Further financial information
Full accounts were not available to view on the Charity Commission's website due to the charity's low income. We have therefore estimated the grant total based on the charity's total expenditure.

William Edwards Educational Charity

£ £87,400 (2019/20)

Correspondent: Mr J. M. P. Hathaway, Clerk to the Charity, c/o Heath & Blenkinsop Solicitors, 42 Brook Street, Warwick, Warwickshire CV34 4BL (tel: 01926 492407; email: law@ heathandblenkinsop.com)

CC number: 528714

Eligibility
People in need under the age of 25 who live, or have a parent living, in the town of Kenilworth, or who attend, or have attended, a school in the town.

Types of grant
Social welfare
Grants are given for school uniforms, school trips and other similar needs for schoolchildren.

Education
Bursaries are available for postgraduate students towards tuition fees and living expenses, as well as financial assistance for undergraduates.

Applications
Apply in writing to the correspondent.

Financial information

Year end	30/06/2020
Income	£263,200
Total expenditure	£170,600

Further financial information
In 2019/20, the total sum of grants to individuals was £67,400. This amount was broken down as follows: bursaries (£37,300); awards to undergraduates (£26,300); grants to individuals for school uniform/trips (£23,800).

Other information
In 2019/20, the charity received 72 applications. A total of 67 awards were made towards the cost of school uniforms/school trips; two bursaries were made to postgraduate students, in addition to ongoing bursaries; and five awards were made to undergraduate students. The charity also supports local schools (£11,000 in 2019/20).

Leamington Relief-in-Sickness Fund

£ £1,700 (2019/20)

Correspondent: Hillary Holland, 55 West Street, Warwick, Warwickshire CV34 6AB (tel: 01926 401168; email: hilaryholland2@gmail.com)

CC number: 216781

Eligibility
People with disabilities or experiencing ill health and expectant mothers living in the former borough of Leamington Spa and its neighbourhood who are in need.

Types of grant
Grants are awarded according to need for items, services and facilities that are not readily available from other sources.

Applications
Our previous research indicates that applicants must apply in writing through a social worker, Citizens Advice, health practitioner or other welfare agency officer.

Financial information

Year end	31/03/2020
Income	£2,100
Total expenditure	£3,800

Further financial information
Full accounts were not available to view on the Charity Commission's website due to the fund's low income. We have therefore estimated the fund's grant total based on its total expenditure.

Other information
The charity also makes grants to organisations.

The Maud Beattie Murchie Charitable Trust
See entry on page 361

Newfield Charitable Trust

£ £46,100 (2020/21)

Correspondent: Eli Williams, Admin Assistant, Rotherham & Co., 8–9 The Quadrant, Coventry, Warwickshire CV1 2EG (tel: 024 7622 7331; email: m. allanson@rotherham-solicitors.co.uk)

 https://cid.coventry.gov.uk/kb5/ coventry/directory/service. page?id=O52HR2XgnIs

CC number: 221440

Eligibility
Girls and women under the age of 40 living in Coventry or Leamington Spa who are in need.

Types of grant
Welfare
Grants are given according to need towards items such as clothing, furniture, bedding, essential household items and school uniforms.

Education
Grants are given towards college fees, textbooks, educational equipment and educational trips. In addition, educational grants are given to enable young girls from disadvantaged homes to attend school residential trips.

Exclusions
Grants are not awarded for the following purposes:
- Repayment of loans from purchasing non-essential items
- Rent/community charge arrears (except in exceptional circumstances)
- Utility bills
- Private school fees
- Holidays (except in exceptional circumstances)
- Postgraduate education or second degrees.

Applications
Application forms can be downloaded from the Coventry Information Directory website and should be completed by hand and returned to Rotherham & Co. Solicitors (addressed 'FAO Mrs Mary Allanson – Clerk to Trustees' if returning by post'). Applications must be submitted along with a supporting letter from a professional which details the applicant's domestic situation and need. Applications can be submitted directly from the individual or through a third party such as social services, a teacher or health worker. See the Coventry Information Directory website for current deadlines. Grants can be awarded to an individual up to three times but cannot be applied for more than once in a year.

Financial information

Year end	31/03/2021
Income	£53,400
Total expenditure	£76,400

Further financial information
Grants were awarded to 64 individuals during the year. Grants were broken down as follows:

General	51	£34,600
Educational	2	£6,500
Clothing	11	£5,400

The Samuel Smith's and Spencer's Charities

£ £35,600 (2020)

Correspondent: Mrs E. A. Martin, Clerk, c/o Harrison Beale & Owen Ltd, Seven Stars House, 1 Wheler Road, Coventry, Warwickshire CV3 4LB (tel: 024 7630 6029; email: info@hboltd.co.uk)

CC number: 240936

Eligibility

Residents of Coventry or the parish of Bedworth who are in need.

Types of grant

Pensions are distributed to older residents and one-off grants are awarded according to need for any age group. The charity also distributes bibles to young people in the area of benefit.

Applications

Apply in writing to the correspondent.

Financial information

Year end	31/12/2020
Income	£50,600
Total expenditure	£65,400

Further financial information

Grants were broken down as follows:

Pensions	£27,600
Cash gifts in lieu of coal	£2,900
May gifts	£1,800
Relief in need	£1,800
Christmas gifts to pensioners	£720
Vision support	£500
Centenary birthday gift	£200
Bibles	£170

Tile Hill and Westwood Charities

£8,500 (2019)

Correspondent: The Trustees, 46–48 Hodgetts Lane, Burton Green, Kenilworth, Warwickshire CV8 1PJ (tel: 024 7642 1439; email: thwcharity@gmail.com)

CC number: 220898

Eligibility

People who are in need and/or in ill health who live in the parishes of Westwood and Stoneleigh or within a three-and-a-half-mile radius of 93 Cromwell Lane, Coventry.

Types of grant

Grants are given according to need.

Applications

Apply in writing to the correspondent.

Financial information

Year end	31/12/2019
Income	£23,900
Total expenditure	£9,500

Further financial information

Full accounts were not available to view on the Charity Commission's website due to the charity's low income. We have therefore estimated the charity's grant total based on its total expenditure.

Other information

The charity also supports organisations.

Warwickshire Miners' Welfare Trust Fund Scheme

£6,400 (2020)

Correspondent: Donald Brookes, CISWO, Welfare Offices, Berry Hill Lane, Mansfield, Nottinghamshire NG18 4JR (tel: 01623 625767; email: donald.brookes@ciswo.org.uk)

CC number: 519724

Eligibility

People who work or have worked within the coal mining industry in Warwickshire and their dependants. Widows, widowers and relatives of the deceased miners are eligible to apply.

Types of grant

Grants are given according to need.

Applications

Apply in writing to the correspondent.

Financial information

Year end	31/12/2020
Income	£12,300
Total expenditure	£7,100

Further financial information

Full accounts were not available to view on the Charity Commission's website due to the fund's low income. We have therefore estimated the grant total based on the fund's total expenditure.

Other information

Grants are also awarded to organisations.

The WPH Charitable Trust

£195,000 (2019/20)

Correspondent: Michael Harwood, Secretary, c/o Blythe Liggins LLP, Edmund House, Rugby Road, Leamington Spa CV32 6EL (tel: 01926 831231; email: info@warwickshirehealthcharity.org.uk)

 https://www.warwickshirehealthcharity.org.uk

CC number: 507325

Eligibility

Individuals and their close family who live with a long-term disability or chronic illness and reside in Warwickshire or Coventry.

Types of grant

Funding is awarded for medical support, healthcare needs, helping individuals to live with a disability or chronic illness as well as providing rehabilitation and respite for the individual, family or carer. The charity's website states: 'No applicant should ever think that their need is too simple or small to be considered e.g. tumble driers, carpets, mattresses, sensory items, specialist car seats.' The grants are split into three categories:

- Disability funding – support in a wide range of areas for children. Often the equipment or support required is not funded by the NHS. Examples include: specialist cycles; car seats; powered wheelchairs; home adaptations; riding courses for people with disability.
- Special needs funding – support for children and adults who are cared for at home, attend specialist schools or live independently. All types of needs and requests are considered. Examples include: special incontinence mattresses; sensory items for children; adapted computers; specialist support chairs; travel and transport costs.
- Rehabilitation funding – support to encourage rehabilitation. Short- and long-term requests are considered; help might be needed for travel, equipment or medical care, or funding may be required for a particular rehabilitation project or carer in order to pay for care and support that would otherwise be unaffordable. Examples include; special hand attachments for pots and pans; home adaptations to allow individuals to be cared for at home; specialist physiotherapy.

Applications

Application forms can be submitted via the online form or printed and sent by email or mail. The trustees meet quarterly to consider and approve applications – check the trust's website for the next meeting dates.

Financial information

Year end	30/09/2020
Income	£210,200
Total expenditure	£389,200

Further financial information

Grants were awarded to 154 individuals in 2019/20.

Other information

The charity also supports medical projects and awards grants to organisations.

North Warwickshire

The Charity of Priscilla Gent and Others

£ £2,700 (2020)

Correspondent: The Trustees, 42 King Street, Seagrave, Loughborough, Leicestershire LE12 7LY (tel: 01509 812366)

CC number: 259461

Eligibility

Residents of the parish of Atherstone who are in need.

Types of grant

Grants are given according to need.

Applications

Apply in writing to the correspondent.

Financial information

Year end	31/12/2020
Income	£7,000
Total expenditure	£5,900

Further financial information

Full accounts were not available to view on the Charity Commission's website due to the charity's low income. We have therefore estimated the charity's grant total based on its total expenditure.

Other information

The charity also makes grants to organisations with similar objectives.

Thomas Monke

See entry on page 217

Relief-in-Need Charity of Simon Lord Digby and Others

£ £5,400 (2020)

Correspondent: The Trustees, The Vicarage, High Street, Coleshill, Birmingham B46 3BP (tel: 01675 462188; email: clerk.sldigby@yahoo.com)

CC number: 237526

Eligibility

People living within the ancient parish of Coleshill, including parts of Kingshurst and Chelmsley Wood, who are in need.

Types of grant

Grants are given according to need.

Applications

Apply in writing to the correspondent. The trustees meet on a quarterly basis to consider grant applications. Special arrangements can be made for urgent applications.

Financial information

Year end	31/12/2020
Income	£13,700
Total expenditure	£6,000

Further financial information

Full accounts were not available to view on the Charity Commission's website due to the charity's low income. We have therefore estimated the charity's grant total based on its total expenditure.

Other information

This charity also makes grants to organisations.

Nuneaton and Bedworth

Exhall Educational Foundation

£ £660 (2020)

Correspondent: Carol Gough, Secretary, c/o Parish Office, St Giles Church Hall, St Giles Road, Ash Green, Coventry, Warwickshire CV7 9GZ (tel: 024 7631 8219; email: cagough@sky.com)

 www.exhalleducationalfoundation. blogspot.co.uk

CC number: 528663

Eligibility

People under the age of 25 who live, or whose parents live, in the parish of Exhall or Keresley End.

Types of grant

Grants of around £200 can be given for educational purposes, including private music tuition and dance classes, books for degree courses, field trips/ expeditions, travel to educational courses and so on.

Applications

Application forms are available from the foundation's website or can be requested from the correspondent. Applications are considered twice a year, in mid-March and mid-October. They can be submitted by post or by email in advance to the trustees' meeting.

Financial information

Year end	31/12/2020
Income	£2,700
Total expenditure	£1,400

Further financial information

Full accounts were not available to view on the Charity Commission's website due to the foundation's low income. We have therefore estimated the foundation's grant total based on its total expenditure.

Other information

The foundation also supports local schools.

The Henry Smith Charity (Bedworth)

£ £1,800 (2019/20)

Correspondent: Lesley King, Nuneaton and Bedworth Borough Council, Town Hall, Coton Road, Nuneaton, Warwickshire CV11 5AA (tel: 024 7637 6270; email: lesley.king@ nuneatonandbedworth.gov.uk)

CC number: 248109

Eligibility

Older residents of Bedworth who are in need.

Types of grant

The charity's Charity Commission record states that assistance is given in the form of annual gifts.

Applications

Apply in writing to the correspondent.

Financial information

Year end	31/03/2020
Income	£2,000
Total expenditure	£2,000

Further financial information

Full accounts were not available to view on the Charity Commission's website due to the charity's low income. We have therefore estimated the charity's grant total based on its total expenditure.

Other information

This charity is also known as the 'Consolidated Charity of Hammersley, Smith and Orton'.

Rugby

The Bilton Poor's Land and Other Charities

£ £13,800 (2019/20)

Correspondent: The Trustees, 9 Critchley Drive, Rugby, Warwickshire CV22 6PJ (tel: 01788 811030; email: biltoncharities@outlook.com)

CC number: 215833

Eligibility

Residents of Bilton who are in need as a result of ill health, old age or financial hardship.

Types of grant

Welfare grants are awarded according to need. Past examples of support include grants towards the cost of travel involved in attending hospital or medical treatments, respite breaks and domestic help.

Applications

Apply in writing to the correspondent.

Financial information

Year end	29/02/2020
Income	£35,900
Total expenditure	£29,500

Other information

Grants are made predominantly for welfare purposes, as well as to organisations whose work benefits the residents of Bilton.

The Sir Edward Boughton Long Lawford Charity

£ £11,300 (2020)

Correspondent: Debbie Groves, Clerk to the Trustees, 7 College Road, Willoughby, Rugby, Warwickshire CV23 8BN (tel: 01788 891514)

CC number: 237841

Eligibility

People who have lived in the parish of Long Lawford for a minimum of five years and are in need as a result of ill health, disability or hardship. Any surplus income may be distributed to residents of the borough of Rugby.

Types of grant

Recurrent payments in the form of pensions and Christmas bonuses. One-off grants have been awarded to cover costs such as consultants' fees, hospital expenses, mobility aids and stairlifts.

Applications

Apply in writing to the correspondent.

Financial information

Year end	31/12/2020
Income	£109,100
Total expenditure	£76,300

Further financial information

In 2020, between 64 and 66 individuals received £10,300 in pensions from the charity.

Other information

The charity makes grants to residential homes and associations that contribute towards the welfare of local residents. The charity also supports local schools by making grants to enable them to improve facilities.

Rugby Welfare Charities

£ £4,200 (2019/20)

Correspondent: Gerald Newth, Trustee, The Coach House, 27A Hillmorton Road, Rugby, Warwickshire CV22 5AB (tel: 01788 542254; email: gerald.newth@btinternet.com)

CC number: 217987

Eligibility

Residents of the ancient parish of Rugby, including St Andrew's and St Matthew's, who are in need.

Types of grant

One-off grants of up to £200 may be awarded to assist people in cases of emergency. Christmas payments may also be made to help older residents.

Exclusions

Residents of Hillmorton or Bilton, as these areas are served by alternative charities.

Applications

Application forms can be obtained from the parish office of St Andrew's church and must be completed on behalf of the applicant by professionals, such as social workers, or housing departments.

Financial information

Year end	31/05/2020
Income	£4,600
Total expenditure	£4,700

Further financial information

Full accounts were not available to view on the Charity Commission's website due to the charity's low income. We have therefore estimated the charity's grant total based on its total expenditure.

Stratford

Municipal Charities of Stratford-upon-Avon – Relief in Need Charity

£ £22,900 (2020)

Correspondent: Doug Evans, Grants Administrator, 6 Guild Cottages, Church Street, Stratford-upon-Avon, Warwickshire CV37 6HD (tel: 01789 293749; email: grants@municharities.org.uk)

 https://www.municipal-charities.org.uk

CC number: 214958

Eligibility

Residents in Stratford-upon-Avon who are in need. In exceptional circumstances, support is given to those living immediately outside the area of benefit who the trustees deem would be eligible if they were resident in the town.

Types of grant

One-off grants are awarded towards the cost of essential furniture, household equipment (beds, support chairs, white goods, etc.), mobility aids, clothing, shoes and household bills.

Exclusions

Grants are not given towards the repayment of debts, rent or Council Tax arrears. The charity is unable to provide rental deposits. Grants are not normally considered unless all available statutory benefits are being claimed.

Applications

Contact the Grants Administrator to request an application form. Applicants are required to include documentary evidence to support financial information. If applying for assistance because of a specific health condition, applicants will be asked to include, where possible, a letter of support from a relevant third party such as a GP, occupational therapist, nurse or a representative from Warwickshire County Council Adult Health and Community Services.

Financial information

Year end	31/12/2020
Income	£425,800
Total expenditure	£420,300

Other information

The Stratford-upon-Avon Municipal Charities is an amalgamation of seven different charities in the local area. A large part of the charity's activity is devoted to the provision of low-cost almshouse accommodation for older residents in the area of benefit, primarily those who are single. The charity also makes occasion donations to the trustees of the School of King Edward VI.

Stratford-upon-Avon Town Trust

£ £9,100 (2020)

Correspondent: The Trustees, 14 Rother Street, Stratford-upon-Avon, Warwickshire CV37 6LU (tel: 01789 207104; email: admin@stratfordtowntrust.co.uk)

 www.stratfordtowntrust.co.uk

CC number: 1088521

Eligibility

Stratford town residents who are in need.

Types of grant

Small one-off grants for items such as bedding, furniture, clothing, heating appliances, microwaves and fridges.

Applications

The trust requests potential applicants to first call 0300 330 1183 to discuss their eligibility.

Financial information

Year end	31/12/2020
Income	£3,140,000
Total expenditure	£3,130,000

Further financial information

The trust made 35 grants to individuals during the year.

Warwick

Barford Relief-in-Need Charity

£ £2,600 (2020)

Correspondent: The Trustees, 14 Dugard Place, Barford, Warwick, Warwickshire CV35 8DX (tel: 01926 624153)

CC number: 256836

Eligibility

People in need who live in the parish of Barford.

Types of grant

Welfare

Our previous research indicates that one-off cash grants and gifts in kind are given to help with 'any reasonable need', including hospital expenses, electric goods, convalescence, living costs, household bills, holidays, travel expenses, medical equipment, nursing fees, furniture, disability equipment and help in the home.

Education

Grants can be made to individuals who are attending school, college or university. Occasionally financial assistance is provided for specific purposes such as Raleigh International and Outward Bound-type courses.

Applications

Applications can be made in writing to the correspondent, directly by the individual or a family member. One of the trustees will then visit the applicant to obtain all necessary information. Applications are usually considered in May and October.

Financial information

Year end	31/12/2020
Income	£12,400
Total expenditure	£5,400

Further financial information

Full accounts were not available to view on the Charity Commission's website due to the charity's low income. We have therefore estimated the grant total based on the charity's total expenditure.

Other information

Grants are also made to organisations.

Austin Edwards Charity

£ £14,000 (2019/20)

Correspondent: Jackie Newton, 26 Mountford Close, Wellesbourne, Warwick, Warwickshire CV35 9QQ (tel: 01789 840135; email: jackie. newton114@gmail.com)

 www.austinedwards.org.uk

CC number: 225859

Eligibility

People living in the old borough of Warwick (generally the CV34 postcode). Our research indicates that support is normally provided to students at college or university (including mature students) or people starting work.

Types of grant

Grants, generally of no more than £300, are given for relief in need. Grants can be given for clothing, equipment, books, travel, course fees and study/travel overseas.

Exclusions

Grants cannot be provided for follow-on courses, postgraduate courses or additional degrees. The charity's website also states that 'where grants are applied for in respect of study courses, the trustees will only consider providing funding for one course per applicant'.

Applications

Application forms can be downloaded from the charity's website and should be returned to the correspondent stating the purpose of the grant and the amount required, as well as details of any other charities approached with the same request. The individual's name and address must be supplied with the application. The trustees usually hold one meeting annually in July but will consider applications throughout the year.

Financial information

Year end	05/04/2020
Income	£12,100
Total expenditure	£14,400

Further financial information

Full accounts were not available to view on the Charity Commission's website due to the charity's low income. We have therefore estimated the grant total based on the charity's total expenditure.

Hatton Consolidated Fund (Hatton Charities)

£ £4,800 (2019/20)

Correspondent: David Thompson, Clerk, 1 Gardner Way, Kenilworth, Warwickshire CV8 1QW (tel: 01926 864943; email: david@dmbfs.com)

CC number: 250572

Eligibility

Welfare

People in need who live in the parishes of Hatton, Beausale and Shrewley.

Education

Students and apprentices who live in the parishes of Hatton, Beausale and Shrewley.

Types of grant

Welfare

Grants are given for a range of social welfare purposes including the following: travel expenses for people at convalescent homes; the cost of proper care and supervision for those needing respite breaks or medical treatments; clothing, footwear, bedding, food, fuel and so on; and financial assistance in cases of sudden distress, sickness or unexpected loss.

Education

Grants are given to students, apprentices and people starting work towards fees, books, equipment, outfits, travel expenses and so on.

Applications

Contact the correspondent for more information.

Financial information

Year end	31/03/2020
Income	£13,000
Total expenditure	£10,900

Further financial information

Full accounts were not available to view on the Charity Commission's website due to the fund's low income. We have therefore estimated the fund's grant total based on its total expenditure. Note: the grant total may also include loans awarded during the year.

Other information

Grants are also given to organisations.

Kenilworth United Charities

 £16,300 (2019)

Correspondent: Mr D. J. Plant, Clerk to the Trustees, 29B Warwick Road, Kenilworth, Warwickshire CV8 1HN (tel: 01926 857741)

CC number: 215376

Eligibility

People in need who live in Kenilworth.

Types of grant

One-off grants, usually of up to £1,000, are given to relieve hardship.

Applications

Applications are usually made through referral from a care professional.

Financial information

Year end	31/12/2019
Income	£32,600
Total expenditure	£31,000

Other information

The charity also funds almshouses and the Citizens Advice in Kenilworth.

The King Henry VIII Endowed Trust, Warwick

 £5,700 (2020)

Correspondent: Jonathan Wassall, Clerk and Receiver, 12 High Street, Warwick, Warwickshire CV34 4AP (tel: 01926 495533; email: jwassall@kinghenryviii. org.uk)

www.kinghenryviii.org.uk

CC number: 232862

Eligibility

People in need who live in the former borough of Warwick. The area of benefit is roughly the CV34 postcode but exceptions apply – see the full list of eligible areas within the guidelines or contact the correspondent for clarification.

Types of grant

Grants are given according to need.

Exclusions

Grants are not given for retrospective costs.

Applications

Application forms are available to download from the trust's website. Grants are considered on a quarterly basis, usually in March, June, September and November. Check the trust's website for application deadlines.

Financial information

Year end	31/12/2020
Income	£18,090,000
Total expenditure	£10,880,000

Further financial information

Grants were awarded to three individuals during the 2020 financial period.

Other information

The majority of the trust's grants are awarded to organisations in the area.

The South Warwickshire Welfare Trust

 £7,300 (2019)

Correspondent: The Trustees, 5 Waverley Road, Kenilworth, Warwickshire CV8 1JL (tel: 01926 492226; email: valeriegrimmer34@gmail. com)

CC number: 235967

Eligibility

Residents of the district of Warwick and the former rural district of Southam who are in need as a result of illness, convalescence, disability or infirmity.

Types of grant

One-off grants are awarded according to need, including for white goods, cookers, carpets, home aids and holidays.

Exclusions

Grants cannot be awarded for items or services available to the individual through other sources (for example, statutory funds).

Applications

Application forms are available on request. Applications must be supported by an authorised agency, such as social services or a health authority.

Financial information

Year end	31/12/2019
Income	£15,900
Total expenditure	£16,100

Further financial information

Full accounts were not available to view on the Charity Commission's website due to the trust's low income. We have therefore estimated the trust's grant total based on its total expenditure.

Warwick Apprenticing Charities

 £36,300 (2019)

Correspondent: Christopher Houghton, Clerk to the Trustees, c/o Moore & Tibbits Solicitors, 34 High Street, Warwick, Warwickshire CV34 4BE (tel: 01926 491181; email: choughton@ moore-tibbits.co.uk)

www.warwickapprenticingcharities. org.uk

CC number: 528745

Eligibility

People under the age of 25 who live in Warwick.

Types of grant

Welfare

Financial assistance is available to students aged 15–19 to help with the cost of attending an Outwood Bound course or similar activity which is aimed at helping young people develop, make new friends and gain skills that will help them with their next stage of life, whether that be in further education or work.

Education

Grants are also made to students who wish to pursue further education after leaving school and can help with a range of educational pursuits including apprenticeships, college or university. Grants can assist with the costs of fees, clothing, tools, books, travel and maintenance expenses.

Applications

Applications for each type of grant can be found on the charity's website. Application forms should be printed, completed and returned by post together with a letter giving further details of the applicant, the course of study/project and the costs.

Financial information

Year end	31/12/2019
Income	£41,200
Total expenditure	£41,000

Warwick Provident Dispensary

 £10,000 (2020)

Correspondent: Christopher Houghton, Clerk to the Trustees, c/o Moore & Tibbits Solicitors, 34 High Street, Warwick, Warwickshire CV34 4BE (tel: 01926 491181; email: choughton@ moore-tibbits.co.uk)

www.warwickprovidentdispensary. org.uk

CC number: 253987

Eligibility

People living in Warwick who are in need due to illness, disability or other medical condition.

Types of grant

One-off grants are awarded according to need.

Applications

Application forms are available to download on the charity's website.

Financial information

Year end	31/12/2020
Income	£24,200
Total expenditure	£23,300

Further financial information

Full accounts were not available to view on the Charity Commission's website due to the charity's low income. We have therefore estimated the grant total based on the charity's total expenditure.

Warwick Relief in Need Charity (Warwick Combined Charity)

 £13,900 (2020)

Correspondent: Christopher Houghton, Clerk to the Trustees, c/o Moore & Tibbits Solicitors, 34 High Street, Warwick, Warwickshire CV34 4BE (tel: 01926 491181; email: choughton@ moore-tibbits.co.uk)

🌐 www.warwickreliefinneed.org.uk

CC number: 256447

Eligibility

Residents of Warwick who are in need.

Types of grant

One-off grants of up to £1,000 are awarded according to need, including for recuperative holidays, contributions towards home repairs, furniture and white goods.

Applications

Application forms are available to download on the funder's website. Applications are usually made on the individual's behalf by the social services, Citizens Advice or other recognised bodies working with the individual. Applications must include a covering letter, written by the third party, detailing the applicant's circumstances. Completed forms can be sent to the correspondent at their postal or email address.

Financial information

Year end	31/12/2020
Income	£180,200
Total expenditure	£125,700

Other information

The charity also awards grants to organisations.

West Midlands Metropolitan Area

The Birmingham and Three Counties Trust for Nurses

 £20,000 (2019/20)

Correspondent: The Trustees, 19 Hanover Gardens, Upper Holly Walk, Leamington Spa, Warwickshire CV32 4JW (tel: 07711 794049; email: bham3counties@hotmail.co.uk)

CC number: 217991

Eligibility

Nurses in Warwickshire, Worcestershire and Staffordshire who are in need. Preference is given to older nurses.

Nurses undertaking post-registration or enrolment courses who have worked in, or are currently working in, Birmingham Warwickshire, Worcestershire or Staffordshire 'for a reasonable period' are also eligible for support.

Types of grant

Grants are awarded according to need.

Applications

Apply in writing to the correspondent.

Financial information

Year end	31/03/2020
Income	£17,700
Total expenditure	£22,200

Further financial information

Full accounts were not available to view on the Charity Commission's website due to the trust's low income. We have therefore estimated the trust's grant total based on its total expenditure.

Grantham Yorke Trust

£8,400 (2019/20)

Correspondent: Christine Norgrove, Clerk to the Trustees, The Estate Office, Wharf Cottage, Broombank, Newnham Bridge, Tenbury Wells, Worcestershire WR15 8NY (tel: 07799 784019; email: chrissy@granthamyorketrust.org.uk)

CC number: 228466

Eligibility

People under the age of 25 who were born in the old West Midlands metropolitan county area (comprising Birmingham, Coventry, Dudley,

Redditch, Sandwell, Solihull, Tamworth, Walsall and Wolverhampton).

Types of grant

Welfare

One-off grants are given according to need and to assist with rehabilitation.

Education

Grants are available for people in education or apprenticeships and those starting work towards books, tools, clothing and equipment.

Applications

Application forms are available from the correspondent and can be submitted either directly by the individual or via a relevant third party such as a social worker. The trustees meet four times a year to consider applications.

Financial information

Year end	05/04/2020
Income	£298,500
Total expenditure	£359,400

Other information

The trust also provides facilities for recreational activities.

The Harborne Parish Lands Charity

£34,700 (2019/20)

Correspondent: Peter Hardisty, Grants Officer, 109 Court Oak Road, Harborne, Birmingham B17 9AA (tel: 0121 426 1600; email: peter.hardisty@hplc.org.uk or info@hplc.org.uk)

🌐 www.hplc.org.uk

CC number: 219031

Eligibility

People on a restricted income who live in the ancient parish of Harborne, which includes parts of Harborne, Smethwick, Bearwood and Quinton. There is a preference for older people, and young people at risk of becoming NEET. A map of the old parish is available to view on the charity's website and individuals are advised to check that they reside in the area of benefit before making an application.

Types of grant

One-off grants of up to £700 are awarded for essential household items such as white beds and furniture. Applications for carpets are only accepted if there is a health and safety issue.

Exclusions

Grants are not made in cash and cannot be used to pay debts such as utility bills or rent arrears.

Applications

Application forms are available from the correspondent by email or by telephone. Applications are only accepted from recognised referral agencies; those made directly by the individual will not be accepted.

Financial information

Year end	30/06/2020
Income	£1,440,000
Total expenditure	£1,300,000

Further financial information

In 2019/20, 63 grants were awarded to individuals from Birmingham and Smethwick.

Other information

The charity also provides social housing for older people, vulnerable people or people with restricted mobility.

Birmingham

Richard and Samuel Banner Trust

£ £13,000 (2019/20)

Correspondent: The Trustees, c/o Veale Wasbrough Vizards LLP, Second Floor, 3 Brindley Place, Birmingham, West Midlands B1 2JB (tel: 0121 227 3703)

CC number: 218649

Eligibility

People who are in need and live in the city of Birmingham.

Types of grant

One-off grants are awarded.

Applications

Applicants must be nominated by a trustee or doctor. Applications are considered on 1 November and grants are distributed immediately after this date.

Financial information

Year end	05/05/2020
Income	£10,400
Total expenditure	£14,600

Further financial information

Full accounts were not available to view on the Charity Commission's website due to the trust's low income. We have therefore estimated the grant total based on the trust's total expenditure.

Birmingham Bodenham Trust

£ £9,400 (2018/19)

Correspondent: Jackie Crowley, Finance, PO Box 16306, Birmingham, West Midlands B2 2XR (tel: 0121 464 3928;

email: jackie.crowley@birmingham.gov.uk)

 https://www.sportbirmingham.org/funding/588

CC number: 528902

Eligibility

Children and young people under the age of 19 living in Birmingham who have special educational needs.

Types of grant

Grants of up to £1,000 are given towards equipment or access to facilities to enhance education, care and treatment, and recreational experiences.

Applications

Application forms can be requested from the correspondent. Applications can be made at any time during the year.

Financial information

Year end	30/09/2019
Income	£24,900
Total expenditure	£21,000

Further financial information

The 2018/19 financial information was the latest available at time of writing (November 2021). The charity was not required to file accounts for the 2018/19 financial year; therefore, we have estimated the grant total.

Other information

The trust also supports organisations.

Thomas Bromwich Trust

£ £27,200 (2019/20)

Correspondent: Chrissy Norgrove, Clerk to the Trustees, The Estate Office, Wharf Cottage, Broombank, Tenbury Wells, Worcestershire WR15 8NY (tel: 07799 784019; email: chrissy@thomasbromwichtrust.org.uk)

CC number: 214966

Eligibility

People in need living in Handsworth, Great Barr and Perry Barr.

Types of grant

One-off grants of up to £1,500.

Applications

Apply in writing to the correspondent.

Financial information

Year end	28/02/2020
Income	£237,300
Total expenditure	£32,600

Further financial information

The charity made 248 grants during the year.

The Handsworth Charity

£ £1,000 (2020)

Correspondent: Dipali Chandra, Clerk to the Trustees, 109 Court Oak Road, Harborne, Birmingham, West Midlands B17 9AA (tel: 07980 555576; email: info@handsworth-charity.co.uk)

 www.handsworth-charity.co.uk

CC number: 216603

Eligibility

Residents of the ancient parish of Handsworth, which includes Handsworth, Soho, Kingstanding and parts of Ladywood, who are in need. Applicants must be permanent residents of the geographical area. Support is also given to pensioners and people who are visually impaired.

Types of grant

One-off grants of up to £500 are awarded according to need. Grants are given towards essential household items such as bedding, carpets, cookers, fridges and minor property repairs.

Exclusions

Grants are not given towards debts, legal fees, wages or retrospective funding, or for equipment/work where statutory funding is available.

Applications

Application forms can be downloaded from the charity's website and should be submitted preferably via email. Applications are only accepted from a recognised referral agency acting as a sponsoring organisation for the individual's application. Applications are accepted throughout the year and will be considered at one of the trustees' meetings, usually in March, July and November. Applications deemed to be urgent may be considered between meetings.

Financial information

Year end	31/12/2020
Income	£26,000
Total expenditure	£63,500

Further financial information

During the financial year, grants were awarded to three individuals, totalling £1,000, and pensions to an unspecified number of beneficiaries totalled £280.

Other information

Grants are also made to organisations.

The King's Norton United Charities

 £9,200 (2019)

Correspondent: The Trustees, The Rectory, 273 Pershore Road South, King's Norton, Birmingham, West Midlands B30 3EX (tel: 0121 458 3289; email: parishoffice@kingsnorton.org.uk)

www.knuc.org.uk

CC number: 202225

Eligibility

The charity is only able to assist those who live within the boundary of the ancient parish of King's Norton, formerly in Warwickshire and Worcestershire, now in Warwickshire and the West Midland. This area is much larger than the current parish of King's Norton and includes the current Church of England parishes of King's Norton, Cotteridge, Stirchley, parts of Bournville, Balsall Heath, Kings Heath, Moseley (St Anne's and St Mary's), Brandwood, Hazelwell, Highters Heath, Wythall, West Heath, Longbridge, Rubery and Rednal. There is a helpful map on the charity's website which shows the area of benefit.

Types of grant

Welfare

One-off, emergency grants of £50 to £350 are awarded to cover unforeseen expenses, such as for new essential household items or repairs.

Education

Grants of £50 to £350 are available for educational needs, such as help with fees.

For both welfare and education, the trustees may consider making a larger grant in specific cases.

Applications

The trustees prefer to receive referrals for help through a doctor or other agency; however, there is a form available on the charity's website if you wish to refer a friend or yourself. The trustees will then contact you to discuss the situation.

Financial information

Year end	31/12/2019
Income	£10,600
Total expenditure	£10,300

Further financial information

Full accounts were not available to view on the Charity Commission's website due to the charity's low income. We have therefore estimated the charity's grant total based on its total expenditure.

Charity of Harriet Louisa Loxton

 £94,000 (2018/19)

Correspondent: Trust Administrator, City Finance, PO Box 16306, Aston, Birmingham, West Midlands B2 2XR (tel: 0121 464 3003; email: Graham. Arrand@birmingham.gov.uk)

https://www.birmingham.gov.uk

CC number: 702446

Eligibility

People in need who live in Birmingham, particularly older people, young people and children and individuals with disabilities or mental health issues.

Types of grant

Grants can be awarded to buy items such as:
▶ Clothing
▶ General home furnishings and electrical goods
▶ Other equipment needed to improve the quality of life for eligible individuals and families

Exclusions

The trust cannot pay for items that should be funded by statutory bodies such as DWP, NHS or the city council.

Applications should be made to Birmingham's Welfare Provisional Fund for the following items:
▶ Single beds
▶ Double beds
▶ Fridge/fridge freezer
▶ Electric cooker
▶ Washing machine (white goods)

Applications

Application forms are available on the Birmingham City Council website, to be filled in online, along with guidance notes. Applicants should already be known to the council and therefore have a Carefirst identity number.

Financial information

Year end	31/03/2019
Income	£51,500
Total expenditure	£95,300

Further financial information

The 2018/19 accounts were the latest available at the time of writing (November 2021).

The Mitchells & Butlers Charitable Trusts

 £21,400 (2019/20)

Correspondent: The Trustees, 73–77 Euston Road, London NW1 2QS (tel: 0121 498 6514; email: charitable. trusts@mbplc.com)

www.mbtrusts.co.uk

CC number: 528922

Eligibility

The eligibility criteria for each of the charity's funds are as follows:
▶ **The Mitchell Fund** – Employees and former employees of Mitchells & Butlers, Six Continents and Bass Companies who are employed in brewing, licensed retailing or catering and are experiencing hardship.
▶ **The Welfare Fund** – People over the age of 16 who are resident in Birmingham or Smethwick and are studying at secondary school or are undertaking higher/further education in the UK. Internal applications can be made by employees, ex-employees and children of employees of Mitchells & Butlers and 'successors in business' of the company.
▶ **The Scholarship Fund** – Students studying courses relating to brewing, catering, hotel management or hospitality management

Further eligibility guidelines are available on the charity's website.

Types of grant

The charity administers a number of different funds to be distributed for educational and welfare purposes:
▶ **The Welfare Fund** – grants are available to assist students attending school, university and other places of higher education. Financial assistance can be used towards course fees, books, equipment, uniform, travel and other educational costs and necessities
▶ **The Scholarship Fund** - grants to assist with course fees, books, equipment and other necessities for courses in the following industries: brewing, catering, hotel management; and hospitality management.
▶ **The Mitchell Fund** - this fund has established links with the Licensed Trade Charity, which funds all grants given to employees and ex-employees experiencing hardship.

Exclusions

Support is not given towards master's degree courses.

Applications

Applications for the Mitchell Fund can be made through the Licensed Trade Charities website, details of which can be found on the Mitchells & Butlers Charitable Trusts' website.

Application forms for the Welfare Fund and application deadlines can be found on the trusts' website. Application forms for the Scholarship Fund can be obtained by emailing the correspondent.

Financial information

Year end	05/04/2020
Income	£125,300
Total expenditure	£181,900

Further financial information

In 2019/20, the charity awarded 79 grants to individuals totalling £21,400. Grants were distributed as follows:

The Welfare Fund	34	£16,900
The Scholarship Fund	45	£4,500

In addition, £90,300 was awarded to the Licensed Trade Charity for distribution to current and former employees experiencing hardship. As this grant was not awarded directly to individuals, we have not included it in the grant total.

Other information

The charity administers four funds (The Welfare Fund, The Scholarship Fund, The Mitchell Fund and The Common Investment Fund), which are all administered under the same Charity Commission number. The Welfare Fund and The Mitchell Fund also support organisations.

Sands Cox Relief in Sickness Charity

 £4,500 (2019/20)

Correspondent: Peter Combellack, 43 Shepherds Green Road, Erdington, Birmingham, West Midlands B24 8EU (tel: 0121 382 3295; email: pjcombellack@aol.com)

CC number: 217468

Eligibility

People who live in Birmingham and are in need due to illness, disability or other difficulties.

Types of grant

Grants are awarded according to need.

Applications

Apply in writing to the correspondent.

Financial information

Year end	30/09/2020
Income	£8,400
Total expenditure	£5,000

Further financial information

Full accounts were not available to view on the Charity Commission's website due to the charity's low income. We have therefore estimated the charity's grant total based on its total expenditure.

Other information

The charity also aims to supports other charities and organisations.

Sutton Coldfield Charitable Trust

 £59,500 (2019/20)

Correspondent: The Almshouse Manager, Lingard House, Fox Hollies Road, Sutton Coldfield, West Midlands B76 2RJ (tel: 0121 351 2262 (Tuesday to Thursday, 8.30am to 4pm); email: info@ suttoncharitabletrust.org)

🌐 www.suttoncoldfieldcharitabletrust. com

CC number: 218627

Eligibility

People in need and who have lived in the four electoral wards of Sutton Coldfield (New Hall, Four Oaks, Trinity and almost all of Vesey) for at least five years.

The parents or guardians of children at primary or secondary school can apply for school uniform vouchers if they are permanently resident in Sutton Coldfield (New Hall, Vesey, Trinity or Four Oaks wards) and are in receipt of any one of the following support payments: Income Tax Credit; Child Tax Credit; Working Tax Credit; Jobseeker's Allowance; the guarantee element of State Pension Credit; Employment and Support Allowance; Universal Credit.

Types of grant

Grants are made to help with the purchase of essential domestic equipment, to help people with disabilities, to help with education after normal schooling, to help people with long-term health problems and to meet other needs.

Vouchers for school uniforms are also available. At the time of writing (August 2020) the value of the grant was £100 per child. A maximum of four children per family can be assisted. Payment is made in the form of vouchers for use at Clive Mark Schoolwear in Boldmere.

Applications

According to the trust's annual report, potential applicants must:

- Contact the Trust, either by letter, using the registered address, by the website enquiry form, or by telephone on 0121 351 2262.
- Outline [their] needs and request a copy of the Trust's guidelines for applicants.
- If appropriate, seek a meeting with a member of staff in making [their] application.
- Ensure that all relevant documents, including estimates and accounts, reach the Trust by the requested dates.

Financial information

Year end	30/09/2020
Income	£1,910,000
Total expenditure	£1,940,000

Further financial information

In 2019/20, grants to individuals were broken down as follows: grants for school clothing (429 grants totalling £42,900), and grants for personal and educational needs (20 grants totalling £16,600).

Other information

The trust's main activity is the provision and upkeep of almshouses in Sutton Coldfield. It also awards grants to organisations (£1.15 million in 2019/20).

Yardley Educational Foundation

£ £156,700 (2019/20)

Correspondent: Derek Hackett, Clerk to the Trustees, Yardley Great Trust, 31 Brookside, Yardley Fields Road, Birmingham, West Midlands B36 8QL (tel: 0121 784 7889; email: karen.grice@ ygtrust.org.uk)

🌐 www.ygt.org.uk/yef_21674.html

CC number: 528918

Eligibility

Children and young people between the ages of 11 and 19 who have lived in the ancient parish of Yardley for at least two years and have a low household income.

Types of grant

Welfare

Grants are awarded to secondary school students for school uniforms, sports equipment, school trips and other educational needs. The foundation also awards book vouchers.

Education

The foundation provides grants to individuals aged 16–19 to undertake vocational training or apprenticeships.

Applications

Application forms can be obtained from the individual's school or college or downloaded from The Yardley Great Trust Group's website.

Financial information

Year end	31/03/2020
Income	£197,800
Total expenditure	£215,100

Further financial information

In 2019/20 a total of £156,700 was awarded in grants. We have estimated that around £65,000 was awarded towards the cost of school uniforms, school trips and sports equipment for school children, £65,000 was given towards further education and the remaining £26,700 was awarded as book tokens.

The Yardley Great Trust Group

 £29,200 (2020)

Correspondent: The Trustees, 31 Old Brookside, Yardley Fields Road, Stechford, Birmingham, West Midlands B33 8QL (tel: 0121 784 7889; email: enquiries@ygtrust.org.uk)

https://www.ygt.org.uk

CC number: 1091937

Eligibility
People living in south-east Birmingham, with preference for applicants living in the ancient parish of Yardley.

Types of grant
One-off grants are awarded towards essential items, such as washing machines, fridges, cookers, clothing, beds and bedding and household furniture.

Applications
Applications should be made through referral agencies such as Neighbourhood Offices and Citizens Advice offices. A list of authorised referral agencies is available on the trust's website.

Financial information

Year end	31/12/2020
Income	£5,700,000
Total expenditure	£5,370,000

Further financial information
In 2020, the trust received applications for grants from 114 individuals.

Other information
The trust's main activity is providing sheltered housing and residential care homes. It also awards grants to organisations.

Coventry

Coventry Children's Boot Fund

 £15,200 (2019/20)

Correspondent: Martin Harban, Trustee, Children's Boot Fund, PO Box 3124, Kenilworth, Warwickshire CV8 9ZW (tel: 024 7640 2837; email: martin@mharban.co.uk or thecoventrychildrensbootfund@gmail.com)

CC number: 214524

Eligibility
Children attending any school in Coventry who are in need. Applications for school leavers for the purpose of attending interviews are also considered.

Types of grant
Grants are given in the form of vouchers for school shoes or shoes for interviews.

Exclusions
Grants are typically limited to one child per family within a period of one year, but the charity can make exceptions in difficult circumstances or where a family has twins.

Applications
Applications should be made through the child's school. There are four application cycles per annum.

Financial information

Year end	31/05/2020
Income	£12,700
Total expenditure	£16,900

Further financial information
Full accounts were not available to view on the Charity Commission's website due to the fund's low income. We have therefore estimated the fund's grant total based on its total expenditure.

Other information
Vouchers must be used at Charles Ager shoe shop in Coventry.

The Coventry Freemen's Charity

 £585,100 (2019)

Correspondent: Robert Anderson, Azets, 3Mc Middlemarch Business Park, Siskin Drive, Coventry, Warwickshire CV3 4FJ (tel: 024 7625 8621; email: Robert.Anderson@azets.co.uk)

CC number: 229237

Eligibility
Freemen/women of the city of Coventry aged over 65 years who are fully retired and living within a seven-mile radius of St Mary's Hall. Support is also available to the widows and dependants of such people also living within a seven-mile radius of St Mary's Hall.

Types of grant
Quarterly grants are distributed in the form of pensions. One-off grants are also available.

Applications
Application forms are available from the correspondent.

Financial information

Year end	31/12/2019
Income	£909,700
Total expenditure	£900,700

Further financial information
In 2019, 2,843 pensions were awarded. Of this number, 2,186 were awarded to freemen/women, 646 to widows and 11 to special cases. In this same year, an additional £1,000 was granted for relief in need.

General Charity (Coventry)

 £251,400 (2020)

Correspondent: Susan Hanrahan, Clerk to the Trustees, General Charities Office, Old Bablake, Hill Street, Coventry, Warwickshire CV1 4AN (tel: 024 7622 2769; email: cov.genchar@outlook.com)

CC number: 216235

Eligibility
People in need living in the city of Coventry.

Types of grant

Welfare
Grants are given according to need and towards the cost of school fees. Yearly payments are made towards pensions for a maximum of 650 individuals over the age of 60.

Education
Grants are given towards the advancement of education and research. Funding is given towards books, equipment, music education and supporting individuals studying for a medical PhD.

Applications
Apply in writing to the correspondent.

Financial information

Year end	31/12/2020
Income	£4,170,000
Total expenditure	£1,600,000

Further financial information
During 2020, a total of £251,400 was awarded to individuals. Relief-in-need grants totalled £75,700 and five individuals received grants totalling £25,000 towards school fees. A further £88,700 was given in pensions to 448 individuals. Grants awarded for educational purposes totalled £62,000 and were broken down as follows:

Medical PhD students	3	£49,500
Books and equipment	102	£12,500

Other information
The charity consists of the charities formerly known as The Relief in Need Charity, Sir Thomas White's Pension Fund and Sir Thomas White's Educational Foundation. The trustees are also responsible for the administration of Lady Herbert's Homes and Eventide Homes Ltd providing accommodation for elderly people in the city of

Coventry. Grants are also given to organisations.

Doctor William MacDonald of Johannesburg Trust

£ £3,700 (2019/20)

Correspondent: Jane Barlow, Secretary, Lord Mayor's Office, Council House, Earl Street, Coventry, Warwickshire CV1 5RR (tel: 024 7683 3047; email: jane.barlow@coventry.gov.uk)

CC number: 225876

Eligibility
People in need living in the city of Coventry.

Types of grant
Grants are given according to need.

Applications
Apply in writing to the correspondent.

Financial information
Year end	30/04/2020
Income	£3,500
Total expenditure	£4,100

Further financial information
Full accounts were not available to view on the Charity Commission's website due to the trust's low income. We have therefore estimated the trust's grant total based on its total expenditure.

The Andrew Robinson Young People's Trust

£ £8,900 (2019/20)

Correspondent: The Trustees, 31 Daventry Road, Coventry, Warwickshire CV3 5DJ (tel: 024 7650 1579; email: arypt@googlemail.com)

CC number: 1094029

Eligibility
Young people who live in Coventry, particularly those who are in need.

Types of grant
Grants are given to advance the religious education of young people and to develop their faith within the Catholic Church. Support is also given to assist personal development through various leisure activities.

Applications
Apply in writing to the correspondent.

Financial information
Year end	31/05/2020
Income	£18,000
Total expenditure	£19,800

Further financial information
Full accounts were not available to view on the Charity Commission's website due to the trust's low income. We have therefore estimated the trust's grant total based on its total expenditure.

Other information
The trust also makes grants to organisations.

Soothern and Craner Educational Foundation

£ £12,200 (2019/20)

Correspondent: The Clerk, The Hollies, Priory Road, Wolston, Coventry, Warwickshire CV8 3FX (tel: 024 7655 4255; email: admin@soothernandcraner. org.uk)

 www.soothernandcraner.org.uk

CC number: 528838

Eligibility
Girls and young women who live in the city of Coventry or who are connected to Coventry Quaker Meeting. Studies may be undertaken away from Coventry but the connection with the city is crucial to eligibility.

Types of grant
Grants can be made towards the cost of school uniform, sports kits, school trips and other educational purposes for young girls who are under 16 or still attending school.

Young women over 16 can apply for grants to further their education or vocational training. This may include the cost of trips, specialist equipment and other educational needs. In some cases grants for daily travel or computer equipment will also be considered.

Exclusions
Support is rarely given to people studying beyond first-degree level.

Applications
The foundation's website provides two application forms – one for those still in school and one for school leavers. Applications can be made at any time of year and can be submitted either electronically or on paper, along with two references to support the application. Applications are usually considered in July and again in October and January providing funds are available. The foundation asks that application forms be submitted via ordinary post rather than recorded delivery, as this may result in delays.

Financial information
Year end	30/04/2020
Income	£16,200
Total expenditure	£13,400

Further financial information
Full accounts were not available to view on the Charity Commission's website due to the trust's low income. We have therefore estimated the trust's grant total based on its total expenditure.

Other information
The trust also makes grants to organisations.

Further financial information
Full accounts were not available to view on the Charity Commission's website due to the foundation's low income. We have therefore estimated the foundation's grant total based on its total expenditure.

Other information
Support may also be given to schools.

Dudley

Chris Westwood Charity

£ £83,300 (2020)

Correspondent: Chris Westwood, PO Box 7131, Stourbridge, West Midlands DY8 9FP (tel: 07968 008098; email: chriswestwood@waitrose.com)

 www.chriswestwoodcharity.co.uk

CC number: 1101230

Eligibility
Children and young people under the age of 25 who have physical disabilities and live in Stourbridge and the surrounding areas (within a 50-mile radius).

Types of grant
Grants are given for the purchase of mobility, sensory and vision equipment.

Applications
Apply in writing to the correspondent – there is no specific application form. Full information on what should be included in the application can be found on the charity's website.

Financial information
Year end	31/12/2020
Income	£76,700
Total expenditure	£83,300

Other information
The charity made 76 grants during 2020. The charity's preferred methods of contact are post and email.

The Reginald Unwin Dudley Charity

£ £4,000 (2019/20)

Correspondent: The Trustees, 53 The Broadway, Dudley, West Midlands DY1 4AP (tel: 01384 259277; email: rududley@hotmail.com)

 www.dudleyrotary.org.uk/rududley. html

CC number: 217516

Eligibility

Residents of Dudley who are in need.

Types of grant

One-off grants according to need. Examples include clothing, household appliances, respite holidays, funeral expenses, course fees, nebulisers, computers and wheelchairs.

Applications

Application forms are available to download on the charity's page on the Dudley Rotary website. Alternatively, applicants may wish to apply in writing. According to the charity's website, applications are more likely to succeed if application forms are returned with a supporting letter detailing the nature of the need for which the applicant is seeking a grant.

Financial information

Year end	06/05/2020
Income	£3,700
Total expenditure	£4,400

Further financial information

Full accounts were not available to view on the Charity Commission's website due to the charity's low income. We have therefore estimated the charity's grant total based on its total expenditure.

The Palmer and Seabright Charity

£ £11,600 (2020)

Correspondent: Susannah Griffiths, Clerk to the Trustees, c/o Wall James Chappell Solicitors, 15–23 Hagley Road, Stourbridge, West Midlands DY8 1QW (tel: 01384 371622; email: sgriffiths@wjclaw.co.uk)

CC number: 200692

Eligibility

Welfare

People in need who live in the borough of Stourbridge.

Education

Students under the age of 25 living in the borough of Stourbridge.

Types of grant

Welfare

One-off grants according to need.

Education

One-off and recurrent grants are given towards fees, books, equipment, instruments mid living expenses.

Applications

Apply in writing to the correspondent.

Financial information

Year end	31/12/2020
Income	£104,100
Total expenditure	£20,700

Further financial information

In 2020, grants totalling £11,600 were made to individuals (including £1,800 in Christmas grants).

The Dudley Charity

£ £5,000 (2019/20)

Correspondent: The Trustees, 53 The Broadway, Dudley, West Midlands DY1 4AP (tel: 01384 259277; email: dudleycharity@hotmail.co.uk)

 www.dudleyrotary.org.uk/dudleycharity.html

CC number: 254928

Eligibility

Residents of Dudley who are in need.

Types of grant

One-off grants according to need. The charity's website provides the following examples of grants that will be considered:

- Weekly allowances for a limited period
- Payments to relieve sudden distress
- Expenses for visiting people in hospitals or correctional institutions
- Assistance in meeting electricity or gas bills
- The provision of furniture, bedding, clothing, food and other household appliances
- The supply of tools, payment for training or equipment for recreational pursuits
- Respite care
- Contributions towards wheelchairs or [mobility] scooters
- Food for special diets, medical or other aids, nursing requisites or comforts

Applications

Application forms are available to download from the charity's website.

Financial information

Year end	31/03/2020
Income	£9,600
Total expenditure	£11,100

Further financial information

Full accounts were not available to view on the Charity Commission's website due to the charity's low income. We have therefore estimated the grant total based on the charity's total expenditure.

The Badley Memorial Trust

£ £27,200 (2019/20)

Correspondent: The Trustees, c/o Higgs & Sons Solicitors, Unit 3 Waterfront

Business Park, Dudley Road, Brierley Hill, Dudley, West Midlands DY5 1LX (tel: 01384 327322; email: kirsty.mcewen@higgsandsons.co.uk)

CC number: 222999

Eligibility

People in need as a result of sickness, convalescence or disability and who live within the metropolitan borough of Dudley. In exceptional cases, applications from those residing in Sandwell may also be accepted.

Types of grant

Grants are specifically provided towards white goods, flooring or carpets (when not already in the property), beds and mattresses.

Applications

Apply in writing to the correspondent.

Financial information

Year end	31/03/2020
Income	£84,600
Total expenditure	£60,800

Sandwell

The Chance Trust

£ £1,440 (2019/20)

Correspondent: The Revd Ian Shelton, Trustee, Old Church Vicarage, Church Road, Smethwick B67 6EE (tel: 0121 558 1763)

CC number: 702647

Eligibility

People in need who live in the deaneries of Warley and West Bromwich (i.e. the southern part of Sandwell).

Types of grant

Grants are awarded for both welfare and educational purposes.

Exclusions

Grants are not provided in cases where statutory funding is available.

Applications

Apply in writing to the correspondent.

Financial information

Year end	05/04/2020
Income	£2,800
Total expenditure	£1,600

Further financial information

Full accounts were not available to view on the Charity Commission's website due to the trust's low income. We have therefore estimated the trust's grant total based on its total expenditure.

The Fordath Foundation

£ £6,300 (2020)

Correspondent: The Trustees, 33 Thornyfields Lane, Stafford, Staffordshire ST17 9YS (tel: 01785 247035; email: fordath-foundation@ntlworld.com)

CC number: 501581

Eligibility

People in need who live in the metropolitan borough of Sandwell.

Types of grant

Grants are awarded according to need.

Applications

Apply in writing to the correspondent. The foundation has noted that applications will only be considered if they are received through an organisation such as Citizens Advice or via housing, social care or educational bodies.

Financial information

Year end	31/12/2020
Income	£7,100
Total expenditure	£7,000

Further financial information

Full accounts were not available to view on the Charity Commission's website due to the foundation's low income. We have therefore estimated the foundation's grant total based on its total expenditure.

The Oldbury Charity

£ £1,800 (2019/20)

Correspondent: Roland Kay, Trustee, 43 Lee Crescent, Birmingham, West Midlands B15 2BJ (tel: 0121 440 7755; email: rolandkay@tiscali.co.uk)

CC number: 527468

Eligibility

Children living in the borough of Oldbury who are in need.

Types of grant

Grants are awarded to help with welfare and educational needs. Past examples of items funded by the charity include books, clothing and equipment.

Applications

Apply in writing to the correspondent.

Financial information

Year end	30/09/2020
Income	£5,000
Total expenditure	£4,000

Further financial information

Full accounts were not available to view on the Charity Commission's website due to the charity's low income. We have therefore estimated the grant total based on the charity's total expenditure.

Other information

This charity also makes grants to organisations.

George and Thomas Henry Salter Trust

£ £5,800 (2020)

Correspondent: Mrs J. Styler, Clerk to the Trustees, 8 Yarnborough Hill, Stourbridge, West Midlands DY8 2EB (tel: 01384 316344; email: gthsaltertrust@outlook.com)

CC number: 216503

Eligibility

Welfare
People in need who live in the borough of Sandwell.

Education
Students who have lived in the borough of Sandwell for at least three years and are undertaking further or higher education. Students must have already obtained a place on a course to be eligible.

Types of grant

Welfare
Grants are given according to need.

Education
Grants of up to £350 are given to students to enable them to pursue their education, including general, professional, vocational and technical training, either in the UK or abroad.

Applications

Welfare
Apply in writing to the correspondent.

Education
Applications for student grants can be requested from the correspondent or downloaded from the Phoenix Sixth Form website. Application forms must be supported by evidence of enrolment and attendance on the course from the educational organisation that also confirms the applicant's home address. Applicants must also obtain a copy of their passport/ID photo certified as a true copy from the educational organisation.

Financial information

Year end	31/12/2020
Income	£33,700
Total expenditure	£62,800

Other information

The trust also supports local schools and organisations.

Solihull
The Lant Charity

£ £5,800 (2019/20)

Correspondent: The Trustees, 10 Orton Road, Warton, Tamworth B79 0HT (tel: 07989 741036; email: clerk.lantcharity@gmail.com)

CC number: 234841

Eligibility

People in need living in Berkswell, Balsall Common or Temple Balsall. The charity also makes grants to ministers of the Church of England holding office in the area of benefit, towards the cost of erecting or maintaining any church or church hall belonging to the Church of England.

Types of grant

Grants are given according to need.

Applications

Apply in writing to the correspondent. The trustees meet on a quarterly basis to consider grant applications.

Financial information

Year end	31/01/2020
Income	£38,200
Total expenditure	£20,700

Other information

The charity also makes grants towards the provision and maintenance of any recreation ground, open space, reading room library or village hall within the local area.

Walsall
W. J. Croft for the Relief of the Poor (W. J. Croft Charity)

£ £1,700 (2019/20)

Correspondent: Cllr Aftab Nawaz, Chair of Trustees, The Council House, Lichfield Street, Walsall, West Midlands WS1 1TW (tel: 01922 654765; email: charities@walsall.gov.uk)

🌐 https://go.walsall.gov.uk/charities#11143303-wj-croft

CC number: 702795

Eligibility

Residents of the borough of Walsall who are in hardship, need or distress due to illness, a change in personal circumstances or an exceptional culmination of events.

Types of grant

Grants are typically given for clothing (including school uniforms), footwear or household goods (such as white goods and furniture).

Exclusions

Our previous research suggests grants cannot be made for property deposits, taxes, rent arrears, mortgage payments or utility bills.

Applications

Application forms, along with guidance notes, can be found on the Walsall Council website.

Financial information

Year end	31/03/2020
Income	£2,600
Total expenditure	£1,900

Further financial information

Full accounts were not available to view on the Charity Commission's website due to the charity's low income. We have therefore estimated the charity's grant total based on its total expenditure.

The Fishley Educational and Apprenticing Foundation

 £4,800 (2019/20)

Correspondent: Clerk to the Trustees, Democratic Services, PO Box 23, Walsall, West Midlands WS1 1TW (tel: 01922 654764; email: charities@ walsall.gov.uk)

www.walsall.gov.uk/charities

CC number: 529010

Eligibility

Young people in need who are under the age of 25 and live, work or study in Walsall.

Types of grant

Welfare

Grants are made towards clothing, specialist equipment and so on for those preparing to enter work, as well as towards the cost of school trips.

Education

Grants are awarded for general educational needs including scholarships, tuition fees, maintenance allowances, travel abroad in pursuance of education, books, and the study of music and arts.

Applications

Application forms can be downloaded from the foundation's website or requested from the correspondent. Grants are considered at least twice a year. Applications must be supported by a member of teaching staff. Note that applications for grants towards educational trips should be made through the educational establishment.

Financial information

Year end	31/03/2020
Income	£22,800
Total expenditure	£5,200

Further financial information

Full accounts were not available to view on the Charity Commission's website due to the foundation's low income. We have therefore estimated the foundation's grant total based on its total expenditure.

C. C. Walker Charity

 £16,600 (2019/20)

Correspondent: Clerk to the Trustees, C. C. Walker Charity, Democratic Services, Walsall Council, Lichfield Street, Walsall, West Midlands WS1 1TW (tel: 01922 654764; email: charities@walsall.gov.uk)

https://go.walsall.gov.uk/charities

CC number: 528898

Eligibility

People who are under the age of 25 and live or study in the borough of Walsall. Preference is given to applicants whose parent/parents have died and who were either born in Walsall or whose parents or surviving parent has lived in Walsall at any time since the birth of the applicant.

Types of grant

Grants can be given for any educational purpose, including to help with the cost of school uniforms for schoolchildren.

Grants are also available in the form of scholarships and financial assistance for higher education students towards tuition fees and other course costs.

Applications

Application forms are available to download from the charity's website or can be requested from the correspondent. The trustees meet at least twice a year.

Financial information

Year end	31/03/2020
Income	£23,100
Total expenditure	£18,300

Further financial information

Full accounts were not available to view on the Charity Commission's website due to the charity's low income. We have therefore estimated the charity's grant total based on its total expenditure.

Walsall Wood (Former Allotment) Charity

 £6,000 (2019/20)

Correspondent: Paul Fantom, The Council House, Lichfield Street, Walsall, West Midlands WS1 1TW (tel: 01922 653484; email: paul.fantom@walsall.gov. uk)

https://go.walsall.gov.uk/charities

CC number: 510627

Eligibility

Residents of the borough of Walsall who are in need.

Types of grant

The remit of the charity is wide, but awards are typically made for clothing and footwear, white goods and furniture.

Applications

A form is available to download from the council website and can also be requested from the correspondent by telephone. It is helpful, but not essential, to submit supporting evidence along with an application. This could include proof of income, such as a wage slip, benefit letter or bank statement, or a supporting letter from a professional familiar with the applicant's case. The trustees meet around six times a year.

Financial information

Year end	31/03/2020
Income	£27,000
Total expenditure	£9,000

Other information

The charity is administered by the Walsall Council Democratic Services team, which also administers a number of other funds.

Wolverhampton

Albrighton Relief-in-Need Charity

£ £1,600 (2019)

Correspondent: David Beechey, Trustee, 34 Station Road, Albrighton, Wolverhampton, West Midlands WV7 3QG (tel: 01902 372779; email: davidabeechey@googlemail.com)

CC number: 240494

Eligibility

Residents in the parishes of Albrighton, Boningale and Donington who are in need.

Types of grant

Grants are awarded according to need. Previous examples of grants include contributions towards funeral costs, holidays, clothing, computer equipment and travel expenses for attending job interviews.

Applications

Apply in writing to the correspondent.

Financial information

Year end	31/12/2019
Income	£3,700
Total expenditure	£3,600

Further financial information

Full accounts were not available to view on the Charity Commission's website due to the charity's low income. We have therefore estimated the charity's grant total based on its total expenditure.

Other information

This charity also makes grants to organisations.

Bushbury (Ancient Parish) United Charities

£ £4,500 (2020)

Correspondent: The Trustees, 23 Waterloo Road, Wolverhampton, West Midlands WV1 4TJ (tel: 01902 420208)

CC number: 242290

Eligibility

People who live in the ancient parish of Bushbury who are in need. Preference may be given to older residents or people with disabilities.

Types of grant

Grants are given according to need.

Applications

Apply in writing to the correspondent.

Financial information

Year end	31/12/2020
Income	£4,600
Total expenditure	£5,000

Further financial information

Full accounts were not available to view on the Charity Commission's website due to the charity's low income. We have therefore estimated the grant total based on the charity's total expenditure.

Power Pleas Trust

£ £5,800 (2019/20)

Correspondent: Keith Berry, Trustee, 80 York Avenue, Wolverhampton, West Midlands WV3 9BU (tel: 01902 655962; email: keithoberry@hotmail.com or info@powerpleas.org)

 www.powerpleas.org

CC number: 519654

Eligibility

Mainly young people under the age of 18 with muscular dystrophy and other mobility disorders living in the Wolverhampton area.

Types of grant

Grants are given primarily towards the purchase and provision of outdoor electric powered wheelchairs, trikes and other mobility aids.

Applications

Apply in writing to the correspondent.

Financial information

Year end	31/03/2020
Income	£12,000
Total expenditure	£6,400

Further financial information

Full accounts were not available to view on the Charity Commission's website due to the trust's low income. We have therefore estimated the trust's grant total based on its total expenditure.

Worcester-shire

The Edmund Godson Charity

See entry on page 319

Malvern Hills Nils

£ £720 (2019/20)

Correspondent: Mary Walters, 52 Prospect Close, Malvern, Worcestershire WR14 2PD (tel: 07973 147423; email: malvernhillsnils@gmail.com)

 www.malvernhillsnils.co.uk

CC number: 1163579

Eligibility

Residents of the district of Malvern Hills in Worcestershire.

Types of grant

One-off grants and loans are awarded according to need.

Applications

Apply in writing to the correspondent.

Financial information

Year end	30/09/2020
Income	£880
Total expenditure	£800

Further financial information

Full accounts were not available to view on the Charity Commission's website due to the charity's low income. We have therefore estimated the charity's grant total based on its total expenditure.

Persehouse Pensions Fund

See entry on page 248

Pershore United Charity

£ £5,100 (2019/20)

Correspondent: The Trustees, 10 Hunter Rise, Pershore, Worcestershire WR10 1QZ

CC number: 200661

Eligibility

People in need, particularly older people, who live in the parishes of Pershore and Pensham.

Types of grant

Annual grants are distributed.

Applications

Apply in writing to the correspondent.

Financial information

Year end	31/01/2020
Income	£6,000
Total expenditure	£5,700

Further financial information

Full accounts were not available to view on the Charity Commission's website due to the charity's low income. We have therefore estimated the charity's grant total based on its total expenditure.

Worcester Municipal Charities (CIO)

 £116,600 (2020)

Correspondent: Office Administration, Kateryn Heywood House, Berkeley Court, The Foregate, Worcester, Worcestershire WR1 3QG (tel: 01905 317117; email: admin@wmcharities.org. uk)

www.wmcharities.org.uk

CC number: 1166931

Eligibility

Welfare

People in need living in the city of Worcester.

Education

People of any age who live in the city of Worcester or the parishes of Powick, Bransford, Rushwick and the ancient parish of Leigh who are undertaking education. Applications from people living outside these areas but who have attended a school in the city of Worcester for at least two years may also be considered. Further information on eligibility can be found on the charity's website.

Types of grant

Welfare

One-off grants are given for essential items such as cookers, fridges, fridge freezers, washing machines, clothes airers, food, clothes, fuel bills, carpeting, televisions, vacuum cleaners and other household items. In exceptional circumstances, support may be given towards holidays.

Education

Grants are given to towards equipment, supplies and other educational purposes to help an individual to complete their course.

Exclusions

Grants will not be awarded for school uniforms.

Applications in respect of fee-paying institutions, for travel abroad, and awards beyond first-degree level are normally excluded.

Applications

Welfare

Individuals should first apply to the Worcester City Council's 'Discretionary Welfare Assistance Scheme' (details can be found on Worcester Municipal Charities' website). Those who are unsuccessful in that application should then apply to this charity. Application forms can be downloaded from the charity's website and returned via email – handwritten forms will not be accepted. Applications must be made through a support worker from a statutory or voluntary organisation. Guidance, other sources of support and deadlines are also available on the website.

Education

Application forms can be downloaded from the charity's website and returned via email – handwritten forms will not be accepted. Consult the charity's website for current deadlines.

Financial information

Year end	31/12/2020
Income	£1,840,000
Total expenditure	£1,070,000

Other information

This charity is the successor of the Worcester Municipal Exhibitions Foundation and the Worcester Consolidated Municipal Charity, whose assets and liabilities were transferred to the charity on 30 June 2016. The charity owns a number of properties and affordable almshouses for retired people and young people who are experiencing homelessness. In addition, the charity provides support to organisations and helps to administer Worcester City Council's Discretionary Welfare Assistance Scheme, which gives grants to individuals in need for white goods and food.

Worcestershire Cancer Aid Committee

£10,900 (2019/20)

Correspondent: The Trustees, c/o Kennel Ground, Gilberts End, Hanley Castle, Worcestershire WR8 0AS (tel: 01684 310408)

CC number: 504647

Eligibility

People with cancer who live in Worcestershire.

Types of grant

One-off and recurrent grants are awarded for (not exclusively) special equipment, facilities, hospital visiting costs and additional domestic costs.

Applications

Applicants must be referred by a medical professional, a hospice senior staff member or a social worker, etc. Contact the correspondent for further information.

Financial information

Year end	30/09/2020
Income	£11,200
Total expenditure	£12,100

Further financial information

Full accounts were not available to view on the Charity Commission's website due to the charity's low income. We have therefore estimated the grant total based on the charity's total expenditure.

Other information

The trustees will also consider funding organisations.

Malvern Hills

The Ancient Parish of Ripple Trust

£6,900 (2020/21)

Correspondent: John Willis, Balmain, Uckinghall, Tewkesbury, Gloucestershire GL20 6EP (tel: 01684 591567; email: vwoodham09@btinternet.com)

CC number: 1055986

Eligibility

People in need, hardship or distress living in the parishes of Ripple, Holdfast, Queenhill and Bushley.

Types of grant

Grants are given according to need.

Applications

Applications may be made in writing to the correspondent. Our research suggests that the trustees meet twice a year to consider appeals and the funds are advertised locally before these meetings.

Financial information

Year end	31/01/2021
Income	£12,700
Total expenditure	£15,300

Further financial information

Full accounts were not available to view on the Charity Commission's website due to the trust's low income. We have therefore estimated the trust's grant total based on its total expenditure.

Other information

The trust's record on the Charity Commission website notes that 50% of its net income is paid to the trustees of the Ripple Ecclesiastical Charity (Charity Commission no. 1059002) for the repair of St Mary's Church, Ripple.

Worcester

The Armchair Trust CIO

Correspondent: Richard Hines, Manager, Unit 6B, Checketts Lane Trading Estate, Checketts Lane, Worcester, Worcestershire WR3 7JW (tel: 01905 456080; email: info@armchairworcester.org.uk)

 armchairworcester.org.uk

CC number: 1164966

Eligibility
People in need of furniture who have no savings and live in the city of Worcester.

Types of grant
The charity collects, recycles and provides good-quality second-hand furniture at low cost to families and individuals. Furniture provided includes beds, wardrobes, tables, chairs, desks and more.

Exclusions
The charity cannot provide electrical goods, carpets, clothing, bedding, kitchen utensils or similar items. Its website has links to other local organisations that can help source these items.

Applications
Applications should be submitted through local authorities, a social worker, Citizens Advice or other welfare agency. They are considered throughout the year. If the need is urgent, specify so in the application.

Financial information
Year end	31/03/2021
Income	£36,100
Total expenditure	£28,500

Further financial information
The charity provides gifts in kind rather than financial grants.

The Mary Hill Trust

£2,400 (2019)

Correspondent: Andrew Duncan, 16 The Tything, Worcester, Worcestershire WR1 1HD (tel: 01905 731731; email: a.duncan@wwf.co.uk)

CC number: 510978

Eligibility
People in need who live within the boundaries of the city of Worcester.

Types of grant
Grants are made according to need.

Applications
Apply in writing to the correspondent.

Financial information
Year end	31/12/2019
Income	£5,600
Total expenditure	£5,300

Further financial information
Full accounts were not available to view on the Charity Commission's website due to the trust's low income. We have therefore estimated the trust's grant total based on its total expenditure.

Other information
Grants are also made to organisations.

The United Charities of St Martin

£2,800 (2020)

Correspondent: The Trustees, 4 St Catherine's Hill, Worcester, Worcestershire WR5 2EA (tel: 01905 355585)

CC number: 200733

Eligibility
People in need who live in Worcester.

Types of grant
Grants are given according to need.

Applications
Apply in writing to the correspondent.

Financial information
Year end	31/12/2020
Income	£6,000
Total expenditure	£6,100

Further financial information
Full accounts were not available to view on the Charity Commission's website due to the charity's low income. We have therefore estimated the charity's grant total based on its total expenditure.

Other information
The charity also funds the maintenance of the parish church of St Martin with St Peter on London Road in Worcester.

Henry and James Willis Trust

£6,800 (2019/20)

Correspondent: John Wagstaff, Secretary, 4 Norton Close, Worcester, Worcestershire WR5 3EY (tel: 01905 355659; email: secretary@willistrust.org)

 www.willistrust.org

CC number: 201941

Eligibility
People living in the city of Worcester who have recently been treated in hospital or who have an ongoing medical problem.

Types of grant
One-off grants of up to £700 are awarded for the payment of short breaks away from home, either at a hotel or residential home. Help with transport costs may be provided. The trustees are willing to consider other appropriate ways of assistance.

Applications
Application forms can be downloaded from the trust's website and should be returned to the trust's secretary. Applications can be supported by a health or social care professional such as a GP, support group co-ordinator, specialist nurse or occupational therapist.

Financial information
Year end	30/06/2020
Income	£6,200
Total expenditure	£7,500

Further financial information
Full accounts were not available to view on the Charity Commission's website due to the trust's low income. We have therefore estimated the trust's grant total based on its total expenditure.

Worcester City Parish Relief in Need Charity

£6,800 (2020)

Correspondent: The Trustees, St Swithun's Institute, The Trinity, Worcester, Worcestershire WR1 2PN (tel: 01905 25952; email: worcester.cityparish@btconnect.com)

CC number: 1077788

Eligibility
People in need who reside in Worcester.

Types of grant
Grants are given according to need.

Applications
Apply in writing to the correspondent.

Financial information
Year end	31/12/2020
Income	£7,600
Total expenditure	£7,600

Further financial information
Full accounts were not available to view on the Charity Commission's website due to the charity's low income. We have therefore estimated the charity's grant total based on its total expenditure.

Wychavon

John Martin's Charity

 £255,400 (2020/21)

Correspondent: John Daniels, Clerk to the Trustees, 16 Queen's Road, Evesham, Worcester, Worcestershire WR11 4JN (tel: 01386 765440; email: enquiries@ johnmartins.org.uk)

www.johnmartins.org.uk

CC number: 527473

Eligibility

Welfare

People resident in Evesham, Worcestershire, who are in need. Grants are available for the benefit of children, families, individuals, people who have disabilities and people who are on low incomes or who are in financial difficulty due to a variety of circumstances.

Education

Individuals between the ages of 16 and state retirement age may apply for educational grants to support study in a wide variety of courses at local colleges or at universities and colleges throughout the country or the Open University. Qualifying courses include Higher National Diplomas (HND) and degree, postgraduate and part-time vocational courses. Applicants must have been a permanent resident or (if living away from home during term time) have maintained a residential address in Evesham, Worcestershire for a minimum of 12 months immediately prior to 1 September in the year of application.

Types of grant

Welfare

Grants are considered for a range of purposes including essential household items, medical and mobility equipment, utility bills, gaps in income payments and school uniforms (for children aged 4–18 who live with a parent/guardian in the town).

Emergency grants are distributed in the form of food vouchers or a small amount of cash to cover pre-payment utility meters.

Heating grants of £175 each are distributed to older people aged 63 and over. Criteria may be downloaded from the charity's website and are also advertised throughout the town and in the Evesham Journal in November.

People who are suffering from chronic ill health and live in designated parishes close to Evesham may also be able to apply for assistance with the costs of medical aids, equipment, etc. These parishes are listed on the charity's website.

Education

Grants for further and higher education are typically of up to £1,050 a year (although students living at home will receive less than this) to cover living expenses while studying.

Miscellaneous education grants of up to £175 each are awarded to students aged 4 to 18 for activities including school trips, music lessons/instrument hire and sporting activities. Applications are assessed based on the number of children and adults in the household, and housing costs are also taken into consideration. There is an easy-to-use eligibility calculator on the website

'Standards of Excellence' awards are for students aged 4 to 18 who achieve a standard of excellence in a sporting or arts/music area. Applications are not subject to a financial assessment; however, suitable evidence of the achievement must be provided.

Exclusions

The charity cannot replace statutory benefits or supply equipment that is normally available from statutory sources, nor can it pay Council Tax bills or fines.

The charity does not currently provide grants for full-time courses below HND/ degree level.

Applications

Application forms are available from the correspondent or as a download from the website, where eligibility criteria are also posted. Applications can be submitted directly by the individual or through a social worker, Citizens Advice or other welfare agency. All applications are subject to a financial assessment and evidence of income and housing costs must be provided. The charity's office can be contacted to discuss an individual's request and circumstances. The website publishes upcoming application deadlines.

Financial information

Year end	31/03/2021
Income	£684,600
Total expenditure	£655,900

Further financial information

Grants awarded in 2020/21 were broken down as follows:

Promotion of education	£166,300
Relief in need	£79,300
Religious support	£5,800
Health and other charitable purposes	£3,900

Other information

Grants are also made to organisations. The charity has an informative website.

Wyre Forest

Kidderminster Aid in Sickness Fund

 £16,600 (2019)

Correspondent: Rachel Summers, Clerk to the Trustees, c/o mfg Solicitors LLP, Adam House, Birmingham Road, Kidderminster, Worcestershire DY10 2SA (tel: 01562 820181; email: rachel.summers@mfgsolicitors.com)

kaisf.org.uk

CC number: 210586

Eligibility

People in financial need who are experiencing ill health and live in the borough of Kidderminster.

Types of grant

Grants, usually of between £100 and £2,000, are awarded towards household items, medical and other aid (for example, equipment, furniture and wheelchairs), domestic help, short holidays, respite care and, occasionally, hospice care.

Exclusions

Applications from residents of the wider Wyre Forest area cannot be considered. The fund cannot help with debt problems.

Applications

Application forms are available to download from the fund's website or hard copies can be obtained from the correspondent. Application forms must be accompanied by a covering letter and as much supporting information as possible.

Financial information

Year end	31/12/2019
Income	£20,600
Total expenditure	£36,900

Further financial information

Full accounts were not available to view on the Charity Commission's website due to the fund's low income. We have therefore estimated the fund's grant total based on its total expenditure.

Other information

The fund also supports organisations.

East of England

General

Harry Cureton Charitable Trust

 £27,200 (2019/20)

Correspondent: Grants Team, c/o Cambridgeshire Community Foundation, Hangar One, The Airport, Newmarket Road, Cambridge, Cambridgeshire CB5 8TG (tel: 01223 410535; email: info@cambscf.org.uk)

https://www.cambscf.org.uk/the-harry-cureton-charitable-trust.html

CC number: 1106206

Eligibility

People who have medical needs living in, or receiving treatment in the areas that are covered by Peterborough and Stamford hospitals.

Types of grant

Grants, generally of up to £20,000, are given towards medical equipment and minor home adaptations. Examples of previous grants include a comfort care chair for an individual with cerebral palsy, a specialist seating armchair for an individual with dementia and a Theraplay tricycle for an individual with Down's syndrome. The trustees may consider applications for larger amounts providing the applicant can demonstrate a justifiable need.

Exclusions

Grants are not made under the following circumstances: where the activity could be paid for by a surgery, the NHS or another source; where the grant will result in financial benefit of a person or group of people (e.g. improvements or alterations to a property); to cover expenditure already incurred.

Applications

Application forms can be completed on Cambridgeshire Community Foundation's website. Applications should be submitted on behalf of the individual by an occupational therapist or other medical professional who has knowledge of the individual's overall health and financial situation. Application deadlines are usually the beginning of February and August; however, check the website for current deadlines.

Financial information

Year end	31/10/2020
Income	£57,600
Total expenditure	£114,600

Further financial information

Grants in 2019/20 were awarded to seven individuals.

Other information

The trust is administered by Cambridgeshire Community Foundation and also gives funding to organisations.

Finnbar's Force

 £3,500 (2018/19)

Correspondent: The Trustees, 1 Park Green, Hethersett, Norwich NR9 3GL (email: info@finnbarsforce.co.uk)

https://www.finnbarsforce.co.uk

CC number: 1171958

Eligibility

Children (under 18 years old) living in Norfolk, Suffolk or Cambridge who have, or are under investigation for, any type of central nervous system (CNS) tumour. To be eligible, children should currently be receiving treatment, have recently received treatment (within the previous six months), be between treatments or be receiving palliative care.

Types of grant

At the time of writing (November 2021), there were two types of grant available: a £300 assistance grant for families of children who meet the eligibility criteria listed above and a £1,000 palliative assistance grant for families where the child is receiving palliative care.

Applications

Applications can be made through the charity's website.

Financial information

Year end	31/03/2019
Income	£115,900
Total expenditure	£20,900

Further financial information

The 2018/19 accounts were the latest available at the time of writing (November 2021).

Kentish's Educational Foundation

 £18,800 (2020/21)

Correspondent: Margery Roberts, Clerk to the Trustees, 7 Nunnery Stables, St Albans, Hertfordshire AL1 2AS (tel: 01727 856626)

CC number: 313098

Eligibility

Young people between the ages 11 and 25 who are in need. Applicants must be permanently resident in Hertfordshire or Bedfordshire. Preference is given to people with the family name Kentish or people related to the foundation's founder, Thomas Kentish.

Types of grant

Grants are awarded to young people attending secondary school towards educational expenses.

Grants are awarded for those undertaking a first degree, further education or an apprenticeship and for people leaving education to enter a profession or trade. Grants can be used towards associated costs including travel in pursuance of education, the study of music and the arts, books, outfits, tools and instruments. Grants for postgraduates may be considered in special circumstances.

Applications

Contact the correspondent for an application form. The trustees have noted in the 2020/21 annual report that they will ask to see school and college/

university reports and examination results in order to monitor the beneficiaries' progress and to ensure grants are being put to good use.

Financial information

Year end	31/03/2021
Income	£29,700
Total expenditure	£18,800

Further financial information

In 2020/21, the total amount awarded in grants was £18,800, which was broken down in the 2020/21 accounts as follows:

Higher/further education	£9,100
Postgraduate	£6,000
Special awards	£2,000
Apprenticeships	£1,200
Secondary education	£500

The Joe Noakes Charitable Trust

 £13,600 (2019/20)

Correspondent: Nina Noakes, Chair, Hampton House, The Street, Blo Norton, Diss, Norfolk IP22 2JB (tel: 01953 688127; email: nina@joenoakestrust.org)

www.thejoenoakestrust.org

CC number: 1153550

Eligibility

Families living in the East Anglian region (Norfolk, Suffolk, Essex and Cambridgeshire) who have a child aged under five who is on the autistic spectrum. Families applying for grants should have a combined household income of less than £45,000 per year.

Types of grant

Funding is available to cover the costs of applied behavioural analysis, a type of specialist therapy for children with autism. Grant awards will only cover the cost of therapy for one year. During this time, parents are expected to use the data collected to apply for local authority funding.

Applications

Potential applicants should email the trust, detailing their situation. If eligible, the trust will provide an application form. Completed application forms should be submitted together with the following:
- A covering letter
- A professional reference
- The child's diagnosis including all current statements, reports, etc.
- Bank statements including mortgage, overdrafts, credit card statements, etc.
- Proof of income, investments, social security benefits, maintenance payments and child support maintenance

- Details of other commitments, e.g. Council Tax, water rates, utility bills, interest on loans, food, clothing, car payments, holiday costs, etc.

Applications can be repeated annually.

Financial information

Year end	31/03/2020
Income	£2,000
Total expenditure	£15,100

Further financial information

Full accounts were not available to view on the Charity Commission's website due to the trust's low income. We have therefore estimated the trust's grant total based on its total expenditure.

Other information

The trust was founded after the parents of Joe, a child with autism who could not walk or talk, discovered applied behavioural analysis, which is currently not funded by the NHS or local education authority. Joe's parents set up the charity to help other parents provide support for their children.

Bedfordshire

Chew's Foundation at Dunstable

 £9,400 (2019/20)

Correspondent: Julie Tipler, Clerk, The Association of Dunstable Charities, Grove House, 76 High Street North, Dunstable, Bedfordshire LU6 1NF (tel: 0158 266 0008 (9am until 2pm on Tuesdays, Wednesdays and Thursdays); email: dunstablecharity@yahoo.com)

www. associationofdunstablecharities. co.uk/charities/chews-foundation

CC number: 307500

Eligibility

According to its website, the foundation supports children and young people living in Dunstable, Luton and Edlesbrough whose parent(s) is/are 'in sympathy' with the Church of England and other Christian churches, and is/are living on limited means.

Types of grant

Welfare

Welfare grants are made towards uniforms and clothing.

Education

Educational grants are made towards books and equipment. Some grants are available to young students to enable the study of music or other arts.

Exclusions

Grants are capped at a maximum of four per child.

Applications

Application forms can be downloaded from the website and should be returned by email. Proof that you are in receipt of housing benefit or Universal Credit is required. However, if you are on limited means and not on housing benefit, you should contact the clerk to arrange an interview and complete a finance form. Applications usually close at the beginning of May and payments are made in July.

Financial information

Year end	31/03/2020
Income	£19,500
Total expenditure	£10,400

Further financial information

Full accounts were not available to view on the Charity Commission's website due to the foundation's low income. We have therefore estimated the foundation's grant total based on its total expenditure.

Other information

The charity is also responsible for the upkeep and maintenance of Chew's House and the Little Theatre.

Bedford

Bedford and District Cerebral Palsy Society

 £3,700 (2019/20)

Correspondent: The Trustees, CVS Mid and North Bedfordshire, 43 Bromham Road, Bedford MK40 2AA (tel: 01234 351759; email: cp.enquiries@bdcps.org.uk)

www.bdcps.org.uk

CC number: 1156447

Eligibility

Individuals with cerebral palsy, and their families, who are in need. Individuals must be resident within the Bedford district.

Types of grant

Grants are available for customised wheelchairs, second skins, splints, short residential breaks and so on.

Applications

Contact the charity for further information.

Financial information

Year end	31/03/2020
Income	£291,000
Total expenditure	£228,800

The Harpur Trust

£ £95,000 (2019/20)

Correspondent: Lucy Bardner, Community Programmes Director, Princeton Court, The Pilgrim Centre, Brickhill Drive, Bedford, Bedfordshire MK41 7PZ (tel: 01234 369503; email: grants@harpurtrust.org.uk)

 www.harpurtrust.org.uk

CC number: 1066861

Eligibility

Adults who have been permanent residents in the borough of Bedford for at least two years who left formal education at least five years ago and are returning to work/planning a career change. Applicants must be on a low income.

Grants are also available to students aged 19 or under who are wishing to undertake an undergraduate or foundation degree course. To be eligible, students must meet all of the following criteria:

▶ Be 19 years of age or under
▶ Have lived the borough of Bedford for at least two years and attended one of the schools or colleges listed on the trust's website
▶ Have already been offered a place on a full-time course
▶ Have already applied for other forms of support
▶ Be a UK or European Union citizen, or a refugee who has been granted indefinite leave to remain in the UK

Students must also meet two of the following criteria:

▶ Be the from the first generation in their family to attend university
▶ Come from a low-income family (preference is given to families with a household income of £25,000 or less)
▶ Live independently
▶ Have additional financial difficulties arising from personal circumstances

Students who have received the trust's undergraduate bursary may be eligible to apply for a postgraduate bursary providing they graduated between 2016 and 2021 with a 2:1 or above, still have a permanent Bedford address and have been accepted onto a full-time postgraduate course (details of eligible courses can be found on the website).

Types of grant

Grants to individuals programme

Grants are given towards the cost of education for adults to support a career change or return to work. The grants aim to improve financial circumstances and quality of life.

University bursary programme

Grants of £1,200 per year for up to three years are made to students to assist with costs associated with their course.

Postgraduate bursary programme

Grants are available to support postgraduate students who have previously received the trust's undergraduate bursary. The maximum grant is £4,000.

Exclusions

Grants will not be given for PGCE courses or recreational courses, including academic courses taken for recreational purposes only. People who are part way through a course will only be supported in exceptional circumstances.

Applications

Grants to individuals

Adults returning to education or work may use the form available on the trust's website, where guidelines are also available to download. Potential applicants should contact the trust for guidance before submitting an application. Forms should be submitted by the end of May for courses beginning in September/October, and shortlisted candidates will be invited for an interview. Applicants must determine their entitlement to statutory funding before making an application.

University and postgraduate bursaries

Application forms, guidelines and current deadlines are available on the trust's website.

Financial information

Year end	30/06/2020
Income	£53,870,000
Total expenditure	£55,150,000

Further financial information

In 2019/20, grants were broken down as follows: university bursaries (£57,600); college bursaries (£20,000); school uniform grants (£17,400).

Other information

Most grants are given to registered charities, voluntary organisations and other groups. The trust also runs four independent schools (Bedford School, Bedford Modern School, Bedford Girls' School and Pilgrims Pre-Preparatory School), sponsors HEART Academies Trust and provides almshouse accommodation in Bedford.

The Kempston Charities

£ £990 (2020)

Correspondent: Christine Stewart, Clerk, 15 Loveridge Avenue, Kempston, Bedford MK42 8SF (tel: 01234 302323; email: christine.stewart17@ntlworld.com)

CC number: 200064

Eligibility

People in need who live in Kempston (including Kempston rural).

Types of grant

Grants are given according to need.

Applications

Apply in writing to the correspondent. Applications are considered three times a year.

Financial information

Year end	31/12/2020
Income	£4,800
Total expenditure	£2,200

Further financial information

Full accounts were not available to view on the Charity Commission's website due to the charity's low income. We have therefore estimated the charity's grant total based on its total expenditure.

Municipal Charities (formerly Bedford Municipal Charities)

£ £29,900 (2019/20)

Correspondent: Lynn McKenna, Bedford Borough Council, Borough Hall, Cauldwell Street, Bedford MK42 9AP (tel: 01234 228193; email: lynn.mckenna@bedford.gov.uk)

CC number: 200566

Eligibility

People in need who live in the borough of Bedford.

Types of grant

One-off grants are given for fuel, furniture, equipment and other necessities.

Applications

Apply in writing to the correspondent.

Financial information

Year end	31/03/2020
Income	£29,900
Total expenditure	£34,800

Further financial information

In 2019/20, one-off grants and fuel grants totalled £3,700, and contingency grants totalled £26,200.

The Ravensden Town and Poor Estate

£ £2,300 (2020)

Correspondent: Alison Baggott, Trustee, Westerlies, Church End, Ravensden, Bedford MK44 2RN (tel: 01234 771919; email: alisonbaggott@btinternet.com)

CC number: 200164

Eligibility
People who are in need and live in the parish of Ravensden.

Types of grant
Grants are awarded according to need.

Applications
Apply in writing to the correspondent.

Financial information
Year end	31/12/2020
Income	£3,100
Total expenditure	£2,600

Further financial information
Full accounts were not available to view on the Charity Commission's website due to the charity's low income. We have therefore estimated the charity's grant total based on its total expenditure.

Ursula Taylor Charity

£ £1,100 (2020)

Correspondent: Mavis Nicholson, 39 George Street, Clapham, Bedford MK41 6AZ (tel: 01234 405141; email: mavis.nicholson1@ntlworld.com)

CC number: 307520

Eligibility
Children and young people under the age of 25 who live in the parish of Clapham and are in full-time education or training.

Types of grant
Welfare
Grants are made to schoolchildren for books, equipment, clothing and other educational needs.

Education
Grants are made to people starting work, individuals undertaking apprenticeships and students in further/higher education. Support can be given for books, course fees, equipment/instruments, tools, clothing and so on.

Applications
Application forms can be obtained by contacting Chris Hardwick on 07971 061507.

Financial information
Year end	31/12/2020
Income	£2,500
Total expenditure	£1,200

Further financial information
Full accounts were not available to view on the Charity Commission's website due to the charity's low income. We have therefore estimated the charity's grant total based on its total expenditure.

Central Bedfordshire

Clophill United Charities

£ £2,800 (2020)

Correspondent: The Trustees, 10 The Causeway, Clophill, Bedford MK45 4BA (tel: 01525 860539)

CC number: 200034

Eligibility
People in need who live in the parish of Clophill.

Types of grant
Grants are given according to need.

Applications
Apply in writing to the correspondent.

Financial information
Year end	31/12/2020
Income	£11,700
Total expenditure	£6,200

Further financial information
Full accounts were not available to view on the Charity Commission's website due to the charity's low income. We have therefore estimated the grant total based on the charity's total expenditure.

Other information
Grants are also made to organisations in the area.

Dunstable Poor's Land Charity

£ £550 (2020)

Correspondent: Julie Tipler, Clerk, Grove House, 76 High Street North, Dunstable, Bedfordshire LU6 1NF (tel: 01582 660008; email: dunstablecharity@yahoo.com)

 www. associationofdunstablecharities. co.uk

CC number: 236805

Eligibility
Older residents on a limited income (i.e. those on Pension Credit or Housing Benefit) living in the parish of Dunstable.

Types of grant
Small grants are made annually on Maundy Thursday.

Exclusions
Only one grant can be awarded to each household.

Applications
Initial enquiries should be made by telephone.

Financial information
Year end	31/12/2020
Income	£1
Total expenditure	£610

Further financial information
Full accounts were not available to view on the Charity Commission's website due to the charity's low income. We have therefore estimated the grant total based on the charity's total expenditure.

Flitwick Combined Charities

£ £11,300 (2019/20)

Correspondent: The Revd Lucy Davis, Trustee, The Vicarage, 26 Dew Pond Road, Flitwick, Bedfordshire MK45 1RT (tel: 01525 712369; email: Lucy@ flitwickchurch.org)

 www.flitwickcombinedcharities.org. uk

CC number: 233258

Eligibility
People in need who live in the parish of Flitwick.

Grants are also awarded to students who are about to start their second year of university or are in an apprenticeship and whose home is the parish of Flitwick.

Types of grant
Grants are given according to need.

Applications
Application forms are available from the charity's website or the correspondent. The trustees' meetings are held three times a year and the dates are publicised on the website.

Financial information
Year end	31/08/2020
Income	£13,400
Total expenditure	£12,500

Further financial information
Full accounts were not available to view on the Charity Commission's website

due to the charity's low income. We have therefore estimated the charity's grant total based on its total expenditure.

Mary Lockington Charity

 £1,400 (2019/20)

Correspondent: Julie Tipler, Clerk to the Trustees, Grove House, 76 High Street North, Dunstable, Bedfordshire LU6 1NF (tel: 01582 660008; email: dunstablecharity@yahoo.com)

www. associationofdunstablecharities. co.uk/charities/mary-lockington

CC number: 204766

Eligibility
Grants are made to individuals in need who are resident in Dunstable.

Types of grant
One-off grants are given towards items, services or facilities.

Applications
Application forms can be downloaded from the charity's website. Applicants are usually referred by community health professionals and other local organisations.

Financial information
Year end	31/03/2020
Income	£12,900
Total expenditure	£3,000

Further financial information
Full accounts were not available to view on the Charity Commission's website due to the charity's low income. We have therefore estimated the charity's grant total based on its total expenditure.

Other information
This charity is part of the Association of Dunstable Charities. It also contributes to the upkeep of almshouses and makes grants to local organisations.

The Charity of Robert Lucas for the Poor and for Public Purposes

 £7,500 (2019)

Correspondent: The Trustees, 99 High Road, Shillington, Hitchin SG5 3LT (email: jacquimsmith99@gmail.com)

CC number: 204345

Eligibility
People in need who live in the ancient township of Shefford.

Types of grant
One-off or recurrent grants are given for needs which cannot be met by statutory sources. Educational grants are also awarded to university students.

Applications
Apply in writing to the correspondent. Applications should be submitted directly by the individual and are considered every two months.

Financial information
Year end	31/12/2019
Income	£132,900
Total expenditure	£74,000

Further financial information
The grant total has been estimated based on the information available in the charity's 2019 accounts.

Potton Consolidated Charity

 £26,300 (2019/20)

Correspondent: Dean Howard, Clerk, 69 Stotfold Road, Arlesey, Bedfordshire SG15 6XR (tel: 01462 735220; email: clerk@potton-consolidated-charity.co.uk)

www.potton-consolidated-charity. co.uk

CC number: 201073

Eligibility
Welfare
Residents in Potton who are in need.

Education
Educational grants are awarded to children and young people under the age of 25 who are residents of Potton. Applicants must be in further or higher education. Full guidelines can be seen on the funder's website.

Types of grant
Welfare
One-off welfare grants according to need. Grants are also distributed in November to elderly residents of Potton to help with heating costs.

Education
Educational grants are made to support those in full-time education. This includes assistance with the cost of transport.

Applications
Welfare
Apply in writing to the correspondent.

Education
Application forms are available to download on the funder's website. Alternatively, application forms can be collected from the post office.

The trustees meet between five and six times each year to consider grant applications.

Financial information
Year end	31/03/2020
Income	£152,900
Total expenditure	£172,300

Other information
This charity also makes grants to organisations, mainly to local schools and other welfare organisations assisting residents of Potton.

The Sandy Charities

 £2,500 (2020/21)

Correspondent: Valerie Haygarth, 19 The Green, Beeston, Sandy, Bedfordshire SG19 1PE (tel: 01767 680251; email: valeriehaygarth@btinternet.com)

CC number: 237145

Eligibility
People who live in Sandy and are in need.

Types of grant
Grants are given according to need. According to our previous research, previously, grants have been given towards motorised wheelchairs, decorating costs, school uniforms, school trips and so on.

Applications
Apply in writing to the correspondent.

Financial information
Year end	09/06/2021
Income	£9,721
Total expenditure	£5,600

Further financial information
Full accounts were not available to view on the Charity Commission's website due to the charity's low income. We have therefore estimated the charity's grant total based on its total expenditure.

Other information
Grants are also made to organisations.

Cambridge-shire

Cambridgeshire Community Foundation

 £115,900 (2019/20)

Correspondent: The Grants Team, Hangar One, The Airport, Newmarket Road, Cambridge CB5 8TG (tel: 01223 410535; email: info@cambscf.org.uk)

🌐 https://www.cambscf.org.uk

CC number: 1103314

Eligibility
People in need who live in Cambridgeshire.

Types of grant
A number of funds are available to individuals. Refer to the foundation's website for details of open grant programmes.

Applications
Details on how to apply can be found on the community foundation's website.

Financial information

Year end	31/03/2020
Income	£2,770,000
Total expenditure	£2,850,000

Other information
This is one of the 47 UK community foundations, which distribute funding for a wide range of purposes. Grant schemes tend to change frequently – consult the foundation's website for details of current programmes and upcoming deadlines.

The Henry Morris Memorial Trust

 £8,400 (2019)

Correspondent: Peter Hains, Chair of Trustees, 24 Barton Road, Haslingfield, Cambridge CB23 1LL (tel: 01223 870433; email: p.hains105@btinternet.com)

🌐 www.henrymorris.org

CC number: 311419

Eligibility
Young people between the ages of 13 and 19 in Cambridgeshire wanting to undertake extracurricular activities.

Types of grant
Grants are typically between £20 and £200 and are given towards project costs. Support is usually given for projects that involve travel of some kind, although home-based projects are also considered.

Past projects include a bird-spotting trip to Land's End, a trip to Gibraltar to visit the apes and a trip to the Paris Museum of Music to study the history of the piano. A list of project ideas can be found on the trust's website.

Exclusions
Grants will not normally be made for:
- The cost of a full gap year
- Foreign exchanges
- School coursework
- Holidays
- Projects managed by the applicant's school or other relevant organisation
- Projects that have already taken place before the application

The trust cannot fund 'regular activity', such as attending a drama or sports club.

Applications
Application forms are available to download on the website. Applicants under the age of 18 will have to obtain the full approval of their parent/guardian. Those applying as part of a group will have to ensure that each member of the group completes a separate application form. Applications must be returned by 31 January. Applicants who are successful after shortlisting will be invited to attend a short interview at Queens' College, Cambridge.

Financial information

Year end	31/12/2019
Income	£5,100
Total expenditure	£9,400

Further financial information
Full accounts were not available to view on the Charity Commission's website due to the trust's low income. We have therefore estimated the trust's grant total based on its total expenditure.

The Foundation of Edward Storey

 £39,400 (2020/21)

Correspondent: Clerk to the Trustees, Storey's House, Mount Pleasant, Cambridge CB3 0BZ (tel: 01223 364405; email: info@edwardstorey.org.uk)

🌐 www.edwardstorey.org.uk

CC number: 203653

Eligibility
Financially unsupported (i.e. single, separated, divorced or widowed) women who fall into one of three qualifying categories:
- Women over the age of 40 living within the county of Cambridgeshire
- Widows, ex-wives or separated spouses of clergy who have served in the Church of England, the Church in Wales or the Scottish Episcopal Church
- Clergywomen, deaconesses, missionaries, or other women with a close professional connection with the Church of England.

Types of grant
One-off grants or recurrent grants according to need. Annual grants towards living expenses are occasionally distributed (only to those over 60). Any applicant for a grant will automatically be considered for an annual grant.

Applications
Apply on a form available from the correspondent.

Financial information

Year end	31/03/2021
Income	£1,420,000
Total expenditure	£1,530,000

Other information
The charity also manages sheltered accommodation and a residential home.

The Charities of Nicholas Swallow and Others

 £1,600 (2019/20)

Correspondent: Johnny Goodman, Clerk, 56 The Lane, Barkway, Hauxton, Cambridge CB22 5HP (tel: 01223 873195; email: jg@goodmanproperty.co.uk)

CC number: 203222

Eligibility
People in need who live in the parish of Whittlesford (near Cambridge) and the adjacent area.

Types of grant
Grants are given according to need.

Applications
Apply in writing to the correspondent.

Financial information

Year end	31/03/2020
Income	£90,000
Total expenditure	£55,500

Further financial information
In 2019/20, £3,100 in grants was awarded to organisations and individuals during the year. A breakdown of grants was not available; therefore, the grant total is estimated.

Other information
The charity owns and operates 14 residential units, which are available to people in need of housing who have a strong connection to the village of Whittlesford. The charity also supports organisations.

Cambridge

Cambridge Community Nursing Trust

£ £6,400 (2020)

Correspondent: The Trustees, 38 Station Road, Whittlesford, Cambridge CB22 4NL (tel: 01223 871248; email: enquiries@cambridgecommunity nursingtrust.co.uk or use the contact form on the trust's website)

 www.cambridgecommunity nursingtrust.co.uk

CC number: 204933

Eligibility

People living in the city of Cambridge who are in need due to ill health.

Types of grant

Small grants are given according to need.

Exclusions

Grants are not made retrospectively or to assist with debts.

Applications

Applications should be made by a professional on behalf of the individual, using the referral form on the trust's website. The trustees meet regularly throughout the year and may consider applications between meetings to enable a swift response.

Financial information

Year end	31/12/2020
Income	£15,100
Total expenditure	£7,100

Further financial information

Full accounts were not available to view on the Charity Commission's website due to the trust's low income. We have therefore estimated the trust's grant total based on its total expenditure.

East Cambridgeshire

Thomas Parsons Charity

£ £1,800 (2019/20)

Correspondent: John Thorogood, The Clerk, c/o Ward Gethin Archer Ltd, Market Place, Ely, Cambridgeshire CB7 4QN (tel: 01353 662203; email: john.thorogood@wardgethinarcher.co. uk)

 www.thomasparsonscharity.org.uk

CC number: 202634

Eligibility

People in need living in the former urban district of Ely (which includes the city of Ely, Chettisham, Prickwillow, Stuntney and Queen Adelaide).

Types of grant

Grants are given to relieve financial hardship and towards medical needs.

Applications

Application forms can be downloaded from the charity's website.

Financial information

Year end	30/06/2020
Income	£330,900
Total expenditure	£187,400

Further financial information

During the year grants were awarded to three individuals.

Other information

The charity's primary activity is the management of its 27 almshouses in Ely, more details of which are available on the website.

Fenland

Chatteris Feoffee Charity

£ £2,200 (2019/20)

Correspondent: Brian Hawden, The Coach House, Beechwood Gardens, Chatteris, Cambridgeshire PE16 6PX (tel: 01354 692133; email: brian. hawden@btinternet.com)

CC number: 202150

Eligibility

People in need living in Chatteris.

Types of grant

Grants are given according to need.

Applications

Apply in writing to the correspondent.

Financial information

Year end	31/03/2020
Income	£6,200
Total expenditure	£5,000

Further financial information

Full accounts were not available to view on the Charity Commission's website due to the charity's low income. We have therefore estimated the charity's grant total based on its total expenditure.

Other information

The charity also gives grants to local organisations.

The Leverington Town Lands Charity

£ £4,500 (2019/20)

Correspondent: Mrs R. Gagen, Clerk to the Trustees, 78 High Road, Gorefield, Wisbech, Cambridgeshire PE13 4NB (tel: 01945 870454; email: levfeoffees@ aol.com)

CC number: 232526

Eligibility

People in need living in the parish of Leverington or Gorefield, or widows in need in the parish of Newton.

Types of grant

Grants are awarded according to need.

Applications

Apply in writing to the correspondent.

Financial information

Year end	30/06/2020
Income	£47,500
Total expenditure	£31,600

Further financial information

Grants to individuals totalled £4,500 during 2019/20. In previous years, the grant total has been much higher (£22,200 in 2018/19).

Other information

This charity is under the control of Leverington Feoffees Charitable Trusts. The income and expenditure figures relate to the controlling trust.

Upwell (Cambridge) Consolidated Charities

£ £1,000 (2020)

Correspondent: The Trustees, 19 Fridaybridge Road, Elm, Wisbech, Cambridgeshire PE14 0AS (tel: 01945 860902; email: yeloopelm@hotmail.co. uk)

CC number: 203558

Eligibility

Older people who are in need and live in the former isle part of the Upwell parish.

Types of grant

The charity distributes grants at Christmas.

Applications

Apply in writing to the correspondent.

Financial information

Year end	31/12/2020
Income	£6,400
Total expenditure	£1,100

Further financial information

Full accounts were not available to view on the Charity Commission's website

due to the charity's low income. We have therefore estimated the charity's grant total based on its total expenditure.

The Whittlesey Charity

£ £2,200 (2019)

Correspondent: The Trustees, 70 Mill Road, Whittlesey, Peterborough, Cambridgeshire PE7 1SN (tel: 07864 687659)

CC number: 1005069

Eligibility
People in need who live in the ancient parishes of Whittlesey Urban and Whittlesey Rural.

Types of grant
Grants are given according to need.

Applications
Apply in writing to the correspondent.

Financial information
Year end	31/12/2019
Income	£78,300
Total expenditure	£17,600

Other information
The charity makes grants to organisations and individuals for relief in need, educational purposes and general charitable purposes. It also awards grants to churches.

Elizabeth Wright's Charity

£ £7,900 (2019)

Correspondent: Iain Mason, Trustee, 13 Tavistock Road, Wisbech, Cambridgeshire PE13 2DY (tel: 01945 588646; email: i.h.mason60@gmail.com)

CC number: 203896

Eligibility
People who live in the ancient parish of Wisbech St Peter in Cambridgeshire.

Types of grant
Grants are given according to need and towards the travel costs of hospital visits. Support may also be available for schoolchildren towards school trips and so on. Grants are also given towards education including the study of music, art and religious education.

Applications
Apply in writing to the correspondent.

Financial information
Year end	31/12/2019
Income	£51,000
Total expenditure	£39,600

Other information
The charity also makes grants to organisations.

Huntingdonshire

Hilton Town Charity

£ £1,000 (2020)

Correspondent: Phil Wood, Clerk, 1 Sparrow Way, Hilton, Huntingdon, Cambridgeshire PE28 9NZ (email: phil.n.wood@btinternet.com)

CC number: 209423

Eligibility
People living in the village of Hilton in Cambridgeshire who are in need.

Types of grant
Grants are given according to need.

Applications
Apply in writing to the correspondent.

Financial information
Year end	31/12/2020
Income	£5,800
Total expenditure	£2,200

Further financial information
Full accounts were not available to view on the Charity Commission's website due to the charity's low income. We have therefore estimated the grant total based on the charity's total expenditure.

Huntingdon Freemen's Trust

£ £167,400 (2019/20)

Correspondent: Karen Clark, Grants Officer, 37 High Street, Huntingdon, Cambridgeshire PE29 3AQ (tel: 01480 414909; email: info@huntingdonfreemen.org.uk)

 www.huntingdonfreemen.org.uk

CC number: 1044573

Eligibility

Welfare

People in need who live in the area covered by Huntingdon Town Council, including Oxmoor, Hartford, Sapley, Stukeley Meadows and Hinchingbrooke Park. Applicants should have lived in the area for at least 12 months, although exceptions can be made depending on the circumstances. Applicants may be working or receiving benefits; however, their income and expenses must be assessed to verify the need for assistance.

Education

Students undertaking vocational or higher education who live in the area covered by Huntingdon Town Council, including Oxmoor, Hartford, Sapley, Stukeley Meadows and Hinchingbrooke Park. Applicants should have lived in the area for at least 12 months, although exceptions can be made depending on the circumstances.

Types of grant

Welfare

Grants are given towards a range of welfare purposes including the cost of household items, carpets, medical and mobility equipment and house adaptations.

Education

Grants of up to £1,000 per student per year. Financial assistance is available for students over the age of 16 who are undertaking vocational courses towards course fees, equipment and, in some cases, travel costs. Grants are also awarded to students who are leaving home to attend university or further education colleges to cover half of the accommodation fees.

Exclusions
The trust does not usually give grants towards rent, Council Tax, debts, fines or funerals.

Applications
Individuals applying for grants should apply in writing to the correspondent including their name, contact details and a brief description of the type of help required. Most applications will require a home visit from a grant officer, who will assess the applicants needs and financial circumstances.

Applications for student grants can be downloaded from the trust's website.

Financial information
Year end	30/04/2020
Income	£538,800
Total expenditure	£519,200

Other information
The trust also supports local organisations that cater for a wide variety or recreational activities for all ages as well as local nurseries and primary schools. The trust provides specialist equipment on long-term loan, including electric scooters.

South Cambridgeshire

Thomas Galon's Charity

 £2,600 (2020)

Correspondent: Linda Miller, Clerk, Memorial Hall, High Street, Swavesey, Cambridge, Cambridgeshire CB24 4QU (tel: 01954 202982; email: thomasgaloncharity@swavesey.org.uk)

www.swavesey.org.uk/thomas-galon-charity

CC number: 202515

Eligibility
People in need who live in the parish of Swavesey. Preference is given to older people.

Types of grant
One grant per household is given through the annual Energy Grant Scheme towards winter heating costs for elderly residents. Grants can also be made for educational or medical-related items or activities.

Applications
Apply in writing to the correspondent.

Financial information
Year end	31/12/2020
Income	£7,800
Total expenditure	£5,700

Further financial information
Full accounts were not available to view on the Charity Commission's website due to the charity's low income. We have therefore estimated the charity's grant total based on its total expenditure.

Other information
The charity also supports any social welfare organisations in Swavesey.

Girton Town Charity

 £147,000 (2019/20)

Correspondent: The Administrator, 22 High Street, Girton, Cambridge CB3 0PU (tel: 01223 276008; email: gtc@girtontowncharity.co.uk)

www.girtontowncharity.co.uk

CC number: 1130272

Eligibility
Welfare
Individuals in need living in Girton.

Education
Students living in Girton who are undertaking further or higher education.

Types of grant

Welfare
Grants are given for a range of purposes. Recent examples of grants include support towards the costs of mobility needs, the costs of adapting a home for health reasons and the costs of coping with a medical condition.

Education
Grants of up to £300 per year are given towards books, equipment, tools and other costs related to educational courses through the Educational Grant Scheme.

Applications
Contact the correspondent via email, telephone or post. Application guidelines are available on the charity's website.

Financial information
Year end	30/06/2020
Income	£1,020,000
Total expenditure	£944,000

Further financial information
Grants in 2019/20 were awarded to 22 individuals for welfare purposes and 40 individuals for educational purposes.

Other information
The charity also supports local organisations and gives funding towards village infrastructure. The charity manages a number of almshouses and runs a variety of schemes for the benefit of Girton residents, details of which can be found on its website. The charity administers the Care Plus Scheme, which aims to support independent living, provides short-term additional care and helps residents leaving hospital to return home as quickly as possible.

John Huntingdon's Charity

 £32,900 (2020)

Correspondent: Jill Hayden, Charity Manager, John Huntingdon Centre, 189 High Street, Sawston, Cambridge, Cambridgeshire CB22 3HJ (tel: 01223 492492; email: office@johnhuntingdon.org.uk)

www.johnhuntingdon.org.uk

CC number: 1118574

Eligibility
People in need who live in the parish of Sawston in Cambridgeshire.

Types of grant
Grants can be given for essential household items such as cookers, washing machines or beds. Assistance is also given towards school uniforms, school trips and, sometimes, nursery or playgroup fees.

Applications
In the first instance, call the charity's office to arrange an appointment with one of its support workers.

Financial information
Year end	31/12/2020
Income	£451,100
Total expenditure	£504,700

Further financial information
During the year, 1,284 bags of food, 160 Christmas hampers and 26 laptops were awarded to individuals.

Other information
The charity is proactive in supporting the community in Sawston and documents its activities in its informative annual report. Among its activities, the charity provides advice and housing services, sometimes in partnership with other local organisations. More details are available on the website or by contacting the charity's office.

Essex

Tom Amos Charity

 £48,000 (2020)

Correspondent: John Salmon, Secretary, Springlands, Main Road, Little Waltham, Chelmsford CM3 3PA (tel: 01245 360314; email: enquiries@tomamoscharity.org)

www.tomamoscharity.org

CC number: 1080954

Eligibility
Residents of Little Waltham, Essex, Chelmsford, Uttlesford and Braintree who are in need.

Types of grant
Grants for welfare and education purposes are awarded according to need.

Applications
Application forms, deadlines and guidance notes are available to download on the funder's website. Completed forms should be sent to the charity via email, as a PDF document.

Financial information
Year end	31/12/2020
Income	£45,000
Total expenditure	£50,100

Further financial information
During the 2020 financial year, the charity awarded grants to 13 beneficiaries.

Other information

The charity makes grants to organisations whose work coincides with its objectives (i.e. the relief of poverty and the advancement of religion and education). Grants are also made for the provision of recreational facilities in Little Waltham.

Broomfield United Charities

£ £6,000 (2019/20)

Correspondent: Brian Worboys, Trustee, 5 Butlers Close, Chelmsford CM1 7BE (tel: 01245 440540; email: brian. worboys@virgin.net)

CC number: 225563

Eligibility

People in need residing in the parish of Broomfield.

Types of grant

Grants are given according to need.

Applications

Apply in writing to the correspondent.

Financial information

Year end	31/03/2020
Income	£6,700
Total expenditure	£6,700

Further financial information

Full accounts were not available to view on the Charity Commission's website due to the charity's low income. We have therefore estimated the charity's grant total based on its total expenditure.

Other information

This charity also makes grants to local organisations with similar objectives.

The Cranfield Charitable Trust

£ £6,600 (2019/20)

Correspondent: The Trustees, 44 Lowestoft Road, Worlingham, Beccles NR34 7DY (tel: 01502 712462)

CC number: 263518

Eligibility

Welfare
People living in Norfolk, Suffolk or Essex who are in need.

Education
Educational grants are also available. Our previous research indicates that students in higher/further education (i.e. university or vocational training) are supported.

Types of grant

Grants are given according to need.

Applications

Apply in writing to the correspondent.

Financial information

Year end	15/02/2020
Income	£16,400
Total expenditure	£14,800

Further financial information

Full accounts were not available to view on the Charity Commission's website due to the trust's low income. We have therefore estimated the trust's grant total based on its total expenditure.

Other information

The trust also makes grants to organisations.

Essex Community Foundation

£ £92,000 (2019/20)

Correspondent: Grants Team, 121 New London Road, Chelmsford CM2 0QT (tel: 01245 356018; email: grants@ essexcf.org.uk)

 www.essexcommunityfoundation. org.uk

CC number: 1052061

Eligibility

Children and young adults whose financial situation is a barrier to them achieving their full potential. Applicants must live, or have lived, in Essex, Southend or Thurrock.

Types of grant

A number of funds are available to individuals to contribute towards educational opportunities and training in the arts or sports. Support is also given to individuals facing financial hardship or mental health issues. Visit the foundation's website for further information on the grants currently available.

Applications

Applications should be made to the foundation, which will match the application to the appropriate fund. Contact the grants team via telephone or email to request an application form.

Financial information

Year end	30/06/2020
Income	£6,340,000
Total expenditure	£5,740,000

Further financial information

In 2019/20, the foundation awarded grants to 97 individuals. We were unable to determine the grant total from the 2019/20 accounts; however, the foundation's Grant Supplement report,

available on its website, notes that grants to individuals totalled £92,000 and can be broken down as follows:

Education and training	25%
Financial hardship	21%
Arts and drama	20%
Sport and recreation	19%
Mental health	4%

Other information

This is one of the 47 UK community foundations, which distribute funding for a wide range of purposes. Grant schemes tend to change frequently – consult the foundation's website for details of current programmes and upcoming deadlines.

Essex Police Force Benevolent Fund

£ £62,900 (2019/20)

Correspondent: The Trustees, PO Box 2, Chelmsford CM2 6DA (tel: 01245 491491; email: loganiain@yahoo.co.uk)

CC number: 258273

Eligibility

Current or retired members of the Essex Police force and their widows/widowers, orphans and dependants.

Types of grant

Cash grants for items and adaptations such as stairlifts, reading aids and wheelchairs.

Applications

Apply in writing to the correspondent.

Financial information

Year end	31/03/2020
Income	£47,900
Total expenditure	£99,000

Essex Police Support Staff Benevolent Fund

£ £3,400 (2019/20)

Correspondent: Barry Faber, Trustee, Essex Police Headquarters, PO Box 2, Chelmsford CM2 6DA (tel: 01245 452597; email: jan.pyner@essex.pnn. police.uk)

CC number: 269890

Eligibility

People in financial need who work or have previously worked (full or part time) for the Essex Police Authority.

Types of grant

Grants are given to support welfare needs, such as the cost of essential items.

Applications

Apply in writing to the correspondent.

Financial information

Year end	31/03/2020
Income	£4,900
Total expenditure	£3,800

Further financial information

Full accounts were not available to view on the Charity Commission's website due to the charity's low income. We have therefore estimated the charity's grant total based on its total expenditure.

Other information

The charity also provides advocacy, advice and information.

The Canon Holmes Memorial Trust

 £13,100 (2019/20)

Correspondent: John Brown, Trustee, 556 Galleywood Road, Chelmsford, Essex CM2 8BX (tel: 01245 358185; email: canonjbrown@mac.com)

www.canonholmes.org.uk

CC number: 801964

Eligibility

Children between the ages of 7 and 13 who attend an independent school and whose family is in need because of a change in finances. Financial hardship may stem from, for example, illness, the death of a parent or guardian or marital breakdown. The child's parent or guardian must live within the area covered by the Roman Catholic Diocese of Brentwood or the Anglican Diocese of Chelmsford, the boundaries of which generally include the county of Essex, as well as the London boroughs of Barking and Dagenham, Havering, Newham, Redbridge and Waltham Forest. Support may be available to pupils attending any independent school across the country.

Types of grant

Grants are awarded to help cover the cost of school fees when payment is not possible at that time.

Applications

Application forms are available to download on the trust's website. Application forms must be filled out by the child's parent or guardian and, once completed, should be sent to the correspondent at their postal address. Grants are paid directly to the school.

Financial information

Year end	31/08/2020
Income	£10,200
Total expenditure	£14,600

Further financial information

Full accounts were not available to view on the Charity Commission's website due to the trust's low income. We have therefore estimated the trust's grant total based on its total expenditure.

Lenderhand

 £9,900 (2019/20)

Correspondent: The Trustees, PO Box 366, Loughton, Essex IG10 9E (tel: 020 8532 5066; email: contact@lenderhand.org)

CC number: 1161794

Eligibility

Families and individuals living in Essex who are in need.

Types of grant

One-off grants are awarded to help with essential goods and services.

Applications

Contact the charity for further information.

Financial information

Year end	31/03/2020
Income	£29,000
Total expenditure	£22,100

David Randall Foundation

£22,800 (2019/20)

Correspondent: The Trustees, 7 Browning Road, Maldon, Essex CM9 6BU (email: info@davidrandallfoundation.org)

www.davidrandallfoundation.org

CC number: 1151121

Eligibility

Welfare
Individuals with life-limiting illnesses who are living in Essex.

Education
Individuals aged between 12 and 25 who live in Essex, Suffolk or the London Borough of Havering and can demonstrate exceptional dedication to the interest they wish to pursue.

Types of grant

Welfare
The foundation offers vouchers and tickets towards a range of outings and days out such as trips to the zoo, football or theatre. The trustees try their best to provide vouchers for any outing the applicant would wish to participate in. When possible, individuals will receive a number of days out rather that just one.

Education
The David Randall Scholarship offers financial support to individuals towards pursuing their ambitions in music or sport including career development, education and training, overseas placements and assistance with kit and equipment.

Applications

Welfare
Application forms are available to download from the foundation's website.

Education
Application forms are available to download from the foundation's website. All applications should be supported by a referee who knows the applicant well and can vouch for their dedication and passion in their chosen field. Applications open at the beginning of October and must be submitted by 31 December; a decision will be made by 23 February. Applications for lesser awards can be submitted at any time.

Financial information

Year end	31/03/2020
Income	£31,000
Total expenditure	£28,200

Henry Smith's Charity (Ancient Parish of Dovercourt)

£2,700 (2018/19)

Correspondent: The Trustees, 20 Kilmaine Road, Dovercourt, Harwich, Essex CO12 4UZ (tel: 01255 503020)

CC number: 246792

Eligibility

Residents in the parishes of Dovercourt and Harwich Peninsula who are in need.

Types of grant

Grants are made in kind for domestic items, clothing, bedding, food, comforts/aids for people of ill health and towards fuel costs.

Exclusions

The charity does not normally make cash grants.

Applications

Apply in writing to the correspondent.

Financial information

Year end	23/10/2019
Income	£2,500
Total expenditure	£3,000

Further financial information

Full accounts were not available to view on the Charity Commission's website due to the charity's low income. We have therefore estimated the grant total based on the charity's total expenditure. The 2018/19 accounts were the latest available at the time of writing (December 2021).

Braintree

Braintree United Charities

 £4,100 (2019/20)

Correspondent: The Secretary, 12 Medley Road, Rayne, Braintree, Essex CM77 6TQ (tel: 01376 321651; email: info@braintreeunitedcharities.co.uk)

braintreeunitedcharities.co.uk

CC number: 212131

Eligibility
People in need who live in the parishes of St Michael's and St Paul's in Braintree. There is a map of the area covered by the charity on its website.

Types of grant
Grants are awarded according to need. For example, past grants have been given towards computers, respite day for carers and to contribute towards funeral costs. Christmas grants are also distributed.

Applications
Application forms are available from the correspondent or can be completed online. They can be submitted either directly by the individual or through a third party, such as a social worker, Citizens Advice or other welfare agency.

Financial information
Year end	31/03/2020
Income	£4,600
Total expenditure	£4,600

Further financial information
Full accounts were not available to view on the Charity Commission's website due to the charity's low income. We have therefore estimated the charity's grant total based on its total expenditure.

Other information
Grants are also made to organisations working for the benefit of local people.

Earls Colne and Halstead Educational Charity

 £6,200 (2020/21)

Correspondent: Clerk to the Trustees, 4 Mill Chase, Halstead, Essex C09 2DQ (tel: 07539 489477; email: earlscolnehalstead.edcharity@yahoo.co.uk)

www.echec.org.uk

CC number: 310859

Eligibility
Children and young people between the ages of 5 and 25 who have lived for at least one year or attended school in the charity's catchment area in North Essex. The charity's area of benefit covers most of the northern part of the Braintree district and a small part of the borough of Colchester; a helpful map is available on the charity's website.

Types of grant
The charity offers grants for books, equipment, tools, clothing and similar items to students in further education.

Project grants are available for various educational projects and educational outings for schoolchildren. For example, small grants can be given to students undertaking their Duke of Edinburgh Award.

Exclusions
Tuition fees are not normally supported and book grants cannot be awarded to students in further education (i.e. A-levels).

Applications
Application forms can be found on the website or requested from the correspondent. The trustees normally meet to consider grant applications during February, July and November. See the charity's website for details of closing dates for applications.

Financial information
Year end	28/02/2021
Income	£38,100
Total expenditure	£64,900

Other information
The charity also gives grants to local schools for educational travel or other purposes and supports voluntary bodies working for the benefit of young people in the charity's beneficial area.

Helena Sant's Residuary Trust Fund

 £5,100 (2020)

Correspondent: Malcolm Willis, Trustee, Greenway, Church Street, Gestingthorpe, Halstead, Essex CO9 3AX (tel: 01787 469920; email: willis.malcolm@gmail.com)

CC number: 269570

Eligibility
People in need who live in the parish of St Andrew with Holy Trinity, Halstead who have at any time been a member of the Church of England.

Types of grant
One-off cash grants are given according to need.

Applications
Applications can be submitted in writing to the correspondent directly by the individual, through an organisation such as Citizens Advice or through a third party such as a social worker. Applications are considered at any time.

Financial information
Year end	31/12/2020
Income	£7,300
Total expenditure	£11,400

Further financial information
Full accounts were not available to view on the Charity Commission's website due to the fund's low income. We have therefore estimated the grant total based on the fund's total expenditure.

Brentwood

White Ecclesiastical Charity of George

£14,200 (2020)

Correspondent: The Trustees, The Old Rectory, Hutton Village, Hutton, Brentwood CM13 1RX (tel: 01277 210495; email: junesykes@btinternet.com)

www.huttonchurch.org.uk

CC number: 208601

Eligibility
Elderly and young people living in the parish of All Saints, Hutton.

Types of grant
Grants are given according to need.

Applications
Apply in writing to the correspondent at any time.

Financial information
Year end	31/12/2020
Income	£15,700
Total expenditure	£15,800

Further financial information
Full accounts were not available to view on the Charity Commission's website due to the charity's low income. We have therefore estimated the charity's grant total based on its total expenditure.

Other information
The charity also provides financial support towards the repair of the church fabric in the two local parish churches.

Chelmsford

The Butler Educational Foundation

£ £4,600 (2019/20)

Correspondent: The Trustees, 88 Chichester Drive, Chelmsford, Essex CM1 7RY (tel: 07952 253991; email: butlereducational@outlook.com)

 www.borehamparishcouncil.co.uk/ breaking-news/butler-trust-applications

CC number: 310731

Eligibility

Welfare
Parents/guardians of children living in Little Baddow or Boreham who are at primary or secondary school.

Education
Students in full-time higher/further education whose parents live in the parishes of Boreham or Little Baddow.

Types of grant

Welfare
Grants are available for general educational expenses, including books, tools, educational trips, music and sports tuition and swimming lessons. Grants are usually of between £50 and £250.

Education
Grants are available for expenses related to higher and further education costs such as travel and books. Grants tend to be of £50 to £250 each, and the student will usually get a grant for each year of their course if they make a yearly application.

Exclusions

Grants are not made for school uniforms.

Applications

Application forms are available on the Boreham Parish Council website. It is the policy of the trust never to award the full amount requested. The trustees meet three times a year to review applications, usually in October, January and April.

Financial information

Year end	31/08/2020
Income	£10,800
Total expenditure	£10,200

Further financial information

Full accounts were not available to view on the Charity Commission's website due to the charity's low income. We have therefore estimated the charity's grant total based on its total expenditure.

Springfield United Charities

£ £5,400 (2019/20)

Correspondent: The Trustees, Civic Centre, Duke Street, Chelmsford, Essex CM1 2YJ (tel: 01245 606606)

CC number: 214530

Eligibility

Individuals in need living in the parish of Springfield.

Types of grant

One-off grants are given according to need.

Applications

Apply in writing to the correspondent.

Financial information

Year end	31/03/2020
Income	£8,400
Total expenditure	£6,000

Further financial information

Full accounts were not available to view on the Charity Commission's website due to the charity's low income. We have therefore estimated the charity's grant total based on its total expenditure.

Colchester

Colchester Blind Society

£ £8,200 (2019/20)

Correspondent: The Trustees, Kestrels, Harwich Road, Beaumont, Clacton-on-Sea CO16 0AU (tel: 01206 510870)

CC number: 207361

Eligibility

People who are blind, partially blind or visually impaired and live in the borough of Colchester.

Types of grant

Grants are given according to need.

Applications

Apply in writing to the correspondent.

Financial information

Year end	31/03/2020
Income	£4,000
Total expenditure	£9,100

Further financial information

Full accounts were not available to view on the Charity Commission's website due to the charity's low income. We have therefore estimated the charity's grant total based on its total expenditure.

Colchester Catalyst Charity

£ £68,900 (2020)

Correspondent: The Trustees, 14 Dedham Vale Business Centre, Manningtree Road, Dedham, Colchester CO7 6BL (tel: 01206 323420; email: info@colchestercatalyst.co.uk)

 www.colchestercatalyst.co.uk

CC number: 228352

Eligibility

People living in north-east Essex who are in need due to illness or disability. The area of benefit covers the entire CO postcode.

Types of grant

Special individual needs grants are given predominantly for mobility equipment. Grants are also awarded towards respite breaks for young carers.

Exclusions

Grants will not be made for items that have already been purchased, or for any item for which there is an obligation for provision by a statutory source. Recipients of grants are responsible for insurance, maintenance or repairs of any items funded.

Applications

Application forms for special individual needs grants can be completed on the funder's website. Applications must be supported by a third party. For enquiries about respite care, applicants should contact the charity by telephone or email.

Financial information

Year end	31/12/2020
Income	£324,300
Total expenditure	£464,300

Other information

The charity operates a counselling service through various organisations in Colchester and Tendring. This charity also makes grants to local and national organisations.

Epping Forest

The George and Alfred Lewis (of Chigwell) Memorial Fund

£ £3,600 (2020)

Correspondent: Elizabeth Smart, Trustee, 16 Forest Terrace, High Road, Chigwell, Essex IG7 5BW (tel: 020 8504 9408)

CC number: 297802

Eligibility

People who served in the armed forces during the Second World War and were living in the parishes of Chigwell and Chigwell Row at the time of their enlistment. Widows of such people are also eligible.

Types of grant

One-off grants according to need.

Applications

Apply in writing to the correspondent.

Financial information

Year end	31/12/2020
Income	£3,200
Total expenditure	£4,000

Further financial information

Full accounts were not available to view on the Charity Commission's website due to the fund's low income. We have therefore estimated the fund's grant total based on its total expenditure. Note that the grant total may include loans.

Rochford

The Canewdon Educational Foundation

£ £4,900 (2020)

Correspondent: Clerk to the Trustees, Trust House, Anchor Lane, Canewdon, Rochford, Essex SS4 3PA (tel: 07706 877437; email: clerktotrustees@gmail.com)

CC number: 310718

Eligibility

People living in the old parish of Canewdon who are under the age of 25.

Types of grant

Grants are made for extracurricular activities such as swimming, dance and drama, school and nursery costs, and Scout fees and equipment. Grants are made to assist with general expenses associated with education or if the applicant is entering a trade. Past examples of support include tuition fee

grants, travel expenses and nursing course fees.

Applications

Apply in writing to the correspondent.

Financial information

Year end	31/12/2020
Income	£35,200
Total expenditure	£27,500

Further financial information

Grants were awarded to eight individuals during the year.

Other information

The trustees use a proportion of the income to maintain Canewdon Endowed Primary School and 20% of the unrestricted fund income (after the deduction of the trustees' expenses) is paid to the Canewdon Poor's Charity (Charity Commission no. 210406). Grants are also made to organisations.

Thurrock

East Tilbury Relief in Need Charity

£ £8,200 (2020)

Correspondent: Robert Chaston, Trustee, 40 Queen Elizabeth Avenue, East Tilbury, Tilbury, Essex RM18 8SP (tel: 01375 851846)

CC number: 212335

Eligibility

People in need who live in the parish of East Tilbury.

Types of grant

One-off and recurrent grants according to need.

Applications

Apply in writing to correspondent.

Financial information

Year end	31/12/2020
Income	£9,600
Total expenditure	£9,100

Further financial information

Full accounts were not available to view on the Charity Commission's website due to the charity's low income. We have therefore estimated the charity grant total based on its total expenditure.

Uttlesford

Hatfield Broad Oak Non-Ecclesiastical Charities

£ £11,700 (2020)

Correspondent: The Trustees, Carters Barn, Cage End, Hatfield Broad Oak, Bishop's Stortford, Hertfordshire CM22 7HL (tel: 01279 718316)

CC number: 206467

Eligibility

People in need who live in Hatfield Broad Oak.

Types of grant

Grants are given according to need.

Applications

Apply in writing to the correspondent.

Financial information

Year end	31/12/2020
Income	£8,700
Total expenditure	£26,000

Further financial information

Full accounts were not available to view on the Charity Commission's website due to the charity's low income. We have therefore estimated the grant total based on the charity's total expenditure.

Other information

The charity's Charity Commission record states that it also assists with housing accommodation.

Lord Maynard's Charity

£ £2,600 (2019/20)

Correspondent: Daniel Fox, Trustee, Moulton, Vicarage Lane, Thaxted, Dunmow, Essex CM6 2QP (tel: 01371 830470; email: thaxtedfox@gmail.com)

CC number: 278579

Eligibility

Welfare

Families with more than three children under the age of 16 who live in Thaxted and who are in need. Couples who have been married in Thaxted Parish Church within the last 12 months are also eligible.

Education

Students undertaking further education (excluding sixth form colleges) or apprenticeships.

Types of grant

Grants are awarded according to need.

Applications

Apply in writing to the correspondent.

Financial information

Year end	31/08/2020
Income	£4,000
Total expenditure	£4,200

Further financial information
Full accounts were not available to view on the Charity Commission's website due to the charity's low income. We have therefore estimated the charity's grant total based on its total expenditure.

Other information
The charity also makes donations to Thaxted Parish Church for repairs and improvements.

The Saffron Walden United Charities

£ £55,400 (2019)

Correspondent: Alfred Ketteridge, Clerk to the Trustees, c/o Community Hospital, Radwinter Road, Saffron Walden, Essex CB11 3HY (tel: 01799 526122; email: alfredjames.ketteridge@ntlworld.com)

CC number: 210662

Eligibility
People in need who live in the former borough council area of Saffron Walden in Essex.

Types of grant
Grants are awarded to relieve hardship.

Applications
Apply in writing to the correspondent.

Financial information

Year end	31/12/2019
Income	£46,400
Total expenditure	£64,000

Thaxted Relief-in-Need Charities

£ £8,900 (2020)

Correspondent: Michael Hughes, Secretary, 3 Mill Row, Fishmarket Street, Thaxted, Dunmow, Essex CM6 2PD (tel: 01371 830642; email: michaelbhughes@hotmail.co.uk)

CC number: 243782

Eligibility
Residents of the parish of Thaxted who are in need.

Types of grant
Grants are given according to need.

Applications
Apply in writing to the correspondent.

Financial information

Year end	31/12/2020
Income	£45,000
Total expenditure	£428,400

Further financial information
Grants to both organisations and individuals totalled £17,800. The grant total awarded to individuals in 2020 has been estimated based on the information available in the charity's accounts.

Other information
Another priority of the charity is the provision and maintenance of almshouses for people in need. The charity also makes grants to local charitable organisations.

Hertfordshire

The Bowley Charity

£ £8,600 (2019/20)

Correspondent: The Trustees, 31 Aldenham Road, Watford, Hertfordshire WD19 4AB (tel: 07837 035591; email: bowleycharitytreasurer@gmail.com)

 www.bowleycharity.btck.co.uk

CC number: 212187

Eligibility
Disadvantaged children and young people up to 18 years old who live in the Watford and Three Rivers districts of Hertfordshire. Applications for unborn babies can be made but items cannot be purchased until after the birth of the child.

Types of grant
Small grants for children's furniture (cots, beds, etc.), baby equipment and white goods that ultimately benefit a child (cookers, freezers, etc.). Grants usually come in the form of Argos vouchers.

Exclusions
The following items are not funded: flooring, electronics (PCs, laptops, etc.), tumble dryers, school uniforms, school trips and car seats.

Applications
Application forms can be downloaded from the charity's website. Applications must be made by a practitioner such as a social worker, health visitor or support worker who knows the family and has made a home visit to confirm that assistance is needed. Check the website for upcoming application deadlines.

Financial information

Year end	30/04/2020
Income	£7,700
Total expenditure	£8,600

Further financial information
In 2019/20, a total of 36 families received grants, with the average grant being £240.

The Hertfordshire Charity for Deprived Children

£ £6,900 (2019/20)

Correspondent: David Williams, Clerk, 34 Cambridge Road, Langford, Biggleswade, Bedfordshire SG18 9PS (tel: 01992 551128; email: hertscfdc@gmail.com)

https://hertscfdc.wixsite.com/herts-charity-child

CC number: 200327

Eligibility
Disadvantaged children living in Hertfordshire who are facing difficulties that compromise their well-being and self-worth.

Types of grant
The charity provides small grants, typically towards clothing, bedding, furniture and other household goods.

Exclusions
Support is not given to children in residential care homes or foster care placement, or to families seeking assistance with loan repayments.

Applications
Apply on a form available to download from the charity's website. Applications must be made through a health visitor, social worker, housing officer or similar third party on behalf of the child.

Financial information

Year end	31/03/2020
Income	£11,100
Total expenditure	£7,700

Further financial information
Full accounts were not available to view on the Charity Commission's website due to the charity's low income. We have therefore estimated the charity's grant total based on its total expenditure.

Hertfordshire Community Foundation

 £22,900 (2019/20)

Correspondent: Grants Support Team, Foundation House, 2–4 Forum Place, Fiddlebridge Lane, Hatfield, Hertfordshire AL10 0RN (tel: 01707 251351; email: office@hertscf.org.uk)

🌐 www.hertscf.org.uk

CC number: 1156082

Eligibility
Families with young children and young people living in Hertfordshire.

Types of grant
A number of funds are available to individuals. Refer to the foundation's website for details of open grant programmes. At the time of writing (November 2021), the foundation was providing support through the following funds:
- Hertfordshire Children's Fund: grants of up to £300 for families in crisis to cover the cost of essential items such as beds, bedding and white goods.
- St Albans Care Leavers Fund: grants of up to £500 available for individuals aged 16–25 who have previously been in care in St Albans.

Exclusions
Grants are not given for clothing or school uniforms, holidays or school trips, carpeting or curtains, general furniture, gardening equipment or debt repayment.

Applications
Details on how to apply can be found on the community foundation's website.

Financial information
Year end	31/03/2020
Income	£2,060,000
Total expenditure	£1,490,000

Further financial information
In 2019/20, 101 grants were made to individuals during the year.

Other information
This is one of the 47 UK community foundations, which distribute funding for a wide range of purposes. Grant schemes tend to change frequently – consult the foundation's website for details of current programmes and upcoming deadlines.

Hertfordshire Community Nurses Charity

 £19,400 (2019/20)

Correspondent: Suzy Richardson, Trustee, 11 High Street, Barkway, Royston, Hertfordshire SG8 8EA (email: suzy@hertscommunitynursescharity.co.uk)

🌐 hertscommunitynursescharity.co.uk

CC number: 1158593

Eligibility

Welfare
According to the charity's website, in order to be eligible for a grant you must:
- Be a registered community nurse or midwife, or a retired community nurse or midwife, or a former community nurse or midwife who has worked for a minimum **of three consecutive years in the county of Hertfordshire**
- Be in financial difficulty following illness, disability or other life crisis

Education
Working registered nurses who have been working for a minimum of six months within Hertfordshire as a Community Nurse.

Types of grant

Welfare
One-off grants of up to £1,000 are awarded.

Education
Grants of up to £2,000 are awarded to help nurses undertake professional development. Nursing grants have been awarded in recent years for a wide range of studies, including part-time and full-time degree courses.

Applications
Apply via the charity's website.

Financial information
Year end	31/03/2020
Income	£88,300
Total expenditure	£48,300

Further financial information
Grants in 2019/20 totalled £19,400.

Other information
The charity occasionally makes major grants of up to £20,000 for projects which will benefit patients in Hertfordshire. The charity also provides subsidised accommodation for retired nurses who previously worked in the community in Hertfordshire.

Hertfordshire Convalescent Trust

 £17,200 (2019)

Correspondent: The Trustees, 140 North Road, Hertford, Hertfordshire SG14 2BZ (tel: 01992 505886)

CC number: 212423

Eligibility
People in need who are convalescing following an operation or period of ill health. Applicants must live in Hertfordshire.

Types of grant
One-off grants are awarded for respite breaks and holidays or recuperative stays in a nursing home.

Applications
Apply in writing to the correspondent.

Financial information
Year end	31/12/2019
Income	£25,800
Total expenditure	£28,100

Further financial information
Grants were made to approximately 100 people during the year.

The Hertfordshire Educational Foundation

£62,100 (2019)

Correspondent: Darren Tyler, c/o County Hall, Hertford, Hertfordshire SG13 8DF (tel: 01438 843319; email: darren.tyler@hertfordshire.gov.uk)

🌐 https://www.hertfordshire.gov.uk/services/schools-and-education/at-school/financial-help/hertfordshire-educational-foundation.aspx

CC number: 311025

Eligibility
Pupils and students up to 25 years of age who have a home address in Hertfordshire.

Types of grant
The foundation administers a number of different grant schemes, which are detailed on its website.

Grants for school trips (UK and abroad)
These grants are for pupils taking part in educational visits arranged by their school whose parents, due to exceptional circumstances other than financial, can't pay for all or part of the board lodging of the visit. The maximum grant is £75 per child and schools must ensure that they can match this amount.

Travel scholarships

Grants of between £100 and £500 are awarded to individuals aged 12 to 21 to undertake approved courses of study, expeditions, voluntary work and other projects in overseas countries. The usual duration is for a minimum of one month, and individuals should be able to demonstrate how their project will benefit the local community they are visiting.

The Sir George Burns Fund

Grants of between £50 and £100 are awarded to enable young people aged 16 to 21 who have a disability or are disadvantaged to purchase special equipment, take part in recreational or educational activities or participate in expeditions, educational visits, short courses or conferences, either in the UK or abroad.

Donald Mackean Trust

Grants of between £50 and £1,000 are awarded to enable young people aged 14 to 25 to participate in learning or careers in the areas of science, technology, engineering, maths or health and environment-related subjects. Grants can be used for purposes such as equipment, personal development, additional support or other costs. This fund particularly targets those who are disadvantaged – for example, looked-after children, care leavers, people who have offended, refugees, young parents, people with mental health problems or those affected by other circumstances.

Applications

Application forms are available to download from the foundation's website. Applications for the Sir George Burns Fund, travel scholarships and the Donald Mackean Trust are considered three times a year and should be sent by the head of your school or college, or by a youth leader or other sponsor. Applications for school visit grants are only considered when the headteacher gives evidence of an exceptional situation including reasons other than financial.

Applications should be submitted at least eight weeks before the activities (for which the grant is required) take place – the foundation will not consider any applications that are received less than six weeks in advance. The closing dates for applications and guidance notes for each fund are provided on the website.

Financial information

Year end	31/12/2019
Income	£29,000
Total expenditure	£62,600

Further financial information

Grants in 2019 were broken down as follows:

School trips	516	£34,100
Equipment/grants	23	£14,600
Extracurricular grants for looked-after children	-	£8,000
Travel scholarships	12	£5,400

It appears from the 2019 accounts that the grants classified as 'Equipment/grants' were made for post-16 education.

Other information

The foundation may also provide grants to organisations.

Middleton-on-the-Hill Parish Charity

 £1,500 (2020)

Correspondent: Clare Halls, Secretary, Highlands, Leysters, Leominster, Herefordshire HR6 0HP (tel: 01568 750257; email: leystershalls@aol.com)

www.middleton-leysters.com/parish-info

CC number: 527146

Eligibility

Secondary school students and people over the age of 70 living in the parish of Middleton-on-the-Hill.

Types of grant

One-off grants are given according to need.

Applications

Apply in writing to the correspondent.

Financial information

Year end	31/12/2020
Income	£3,300
Total expenditure	£3,200

Further financial information

Full accounts were not available to view on the Charity Commission's website due to the charity's low income. We have therefore estimated the charity's grant total based on its total expenditure.

Other information

The trustees also make grants to Middleton Church and St James School.

Broxbourne

Wormley Parochial Charity

 £3,200 (2020)

Correspondent: The Trustees, 43 The Oval, Broxbourne, Hertfordshire EN10 6DQ (tel: 01992 464764)

CC number: 218463

Eligibility

Welfare
People in need who live in the parish of Wormley

Types of grant

The charity provides food vouchers, bereavement grants and grants for utility bills. Grants are also made to students to support their education.

Applications

Apply in writing to the correspondent.

Financial information

Year end	31/12/2020
Income	£12,900
Total expenditure	£7,000

Further financial information

Full accounts were not available to view on the Charity Commission's website due to the charity's low income. We have therefore estimated the charity's grant total based on its total expenditure.

Other information

Grants are also made to local community organisations and to support the RVS Hospital transport scheme.

Dacorum

The Dacorum Community Trust

£21,900 (2019/20)

Correspondent: The Trustees, The Forum, Marlowes, Hemel Hempstead, Hertfordshire HP1 1DN (tel: 01442 253216; email: admin@dctrust.org.uk)

www.dctrust.org.uk

CC number: 272759

Eligibility

People in need who live in the borough of Dacorum.

Types of grant

Grants can be given towards, for example, household items, white goods, baby clothing, nursery accessories, gas or electricity vouchers and food vouchers.

Applications

Application forms are available to download on the funder's website.

Financial information

Year end	31/03/2020
Income	£63,600
Total expenditure	£79,300

Further financial information

The grant total includes £1,900 awarded as gifts in kind.

Other information

The trust also makes grants to small local groups, organisations and charities.

East Hertfordshire

The Ware Charities

 £16,800 (2019/20)

Correspondent: Susan Newman, Clerk, 2 Little Horse Lane, Ware, Hertfordshire SG12 0QB (tel: 01920 487883; email: treasurerwarecharities@gmail.com)

CC number: 225443

Eligibility

Residents in the town of Ware and the parishes of Wareside and Thundridge who are in need due to ill health or financial hardship.

Types of grant

Welfare

Welfare grants are awarded according to need. Grants have been awarded previously for school uniforms.

Education

Educational grants are given to schoolchildren, college students, people with special educational needs, people starting work and overseas students for fees, books and equipment. Grants are also made to undergraduates and vocational students for uniforms/clothing.

Applications

Apply in writing to the correspondent. All applications must be supported by a health professional, social worker, school headteacher, support worker at a children's centre or person in a similar role. If successful, grants are paid directly to the supplier or supporter and not to the individual.

Financial information

Year end	31/03/2020
Income	£46,400
Total expenditure	£65,400

Further financial information

During the 2019/20 financial year, the charity awarded grants to 19 individuals.

Other information

The charity owns and operates two almshouses, which are used by older residents in the area of benefit.

North Hertfordshire

The Letchworth Civic Trust

 £62,200 (2019/20)

Correspondent: Sally Jenkins, Secretary, 5 Gernon Walk, Letchworth Garden City, Hertfordshire SG6 3HW (email: letchworthct@gmail.com)

🌐 https://www.letchworthct.org.uk

CC number: 273336

Eligibility

People in need who live in Letchworth Garden City. Support is also given to students undertaking higher or further education who have lived in Letchworth Garden City for at least two years.

Types of grant

Welfare

School pupils whose families are in need are given grants of up to £70 towards the costs of school activities, in particular residential trips or camps. Individuals with a disability that causes mobility problems and people with particular social needs can also be given support. Bursaries are occasionally available to exceptionally talented musicians, athletes, swimmers and so on.

Education

Grants of up to £500 are awarded towards the cost of books and learning materials for university and further education students (diploma, HND, apprenticeships and so on).

Applications

Separate application forms for each type of grant are available to download from the trust's website. Applications for schoolchildren need to be supported by their headteacher. If applying for medical assistance or for a particular social need, the form must be completed by a relevant professional or social worker on behalf of the individual. University students must not apply before receiving their successful A-level results in August. Applications should be returned by the end of December, February, May, August, September and November, for consideration the following month. Applications are not usually acknowledged before the trustees' meeting.

Financial information

Year end	30/06/2020
Income	£95,300
Total expenditure	£70,900

Further financial information

Social welfare

In 2019/20, grants totalling £7,700 were awarded to 63 individuals for welfare purposes. This figure includes £3,200 for 54 schoolchildren and £4,500 to nine individuals for other welfare purposes.

Education

Educational grants totalling £54,500 were awarded to 162 university students during the year.

Other information

Around 200 individuals are supported each year, particularly young people. The trust also makes awards to around 20 local organisations per year.

James Marshall Foundation CIO

£ £165,900 (2020/21)

Correspondent: The Trustees, Unit 6, 17 Leyton Road, Harpenden, Hertfordshire AL5 2HY (tel: 01582 760735; email: grants@ jamesmarshallfoundation.co.uk)

🌐 https://www.jamesmarshall foundation.co.uk

CC number: 1181004

Eligibility

Young people under the age of 25 who live in Harpenden, Wheathampstead, Kimpton, Redbourn, Markyate or Flamstead and are in need of financial assistance. Priority is given to individuals over the age of 16.

Types of grant

Welfare

Grants are given for a range of educational purposes for schoolchildren such as school uniforms, school trips, extracurricular activities and equipment.

Education

Grants are given towards education and career development. Examples of what can be funded include:

▶ Books, equipment and materials
▶ University costs including accommodation
▶ Further education courses
▶ Travel for work and study
▶ Apprenticeships
▶ Work tools and clothing

Exclusions

According to its website, the foundation is unlikely to provide support for the following:

▶ Items that are medical rather than educational in nature
▶ Computer/Laptop repairs (unless advised by Harpenden Computer Services Ltd that this is the best approach for an older laptop)

- Items for a family, rather than for a specific child
- Activities that are primarily non-educational and not inclusive e.g. ski trips
- External/private tutoring
- Payments of rent to parents for students living at home
- Living costs
- World Challenge
- Travel grants to a station if the station is within 30 minutes walking distance from the applicant's home
- General stationery items/electronic calculators
- School bags

Applications

Application forms can be downloaded from the foundation's website. Applications can be made directly by the individual or by a parent, guardian, school or support worker.

Financial information

Year end	31/03/2021
Income	£376,900
Total expenditure	£253,600

Further financial information

During 2020/21, 326 grants were made for both welfare and educational purposes; however, we were unable to determine the split. Grants were distributed as follows:

School uniform	135
Computer	97
Degree	25
Music, drama and sport	22
Educational equipment	18
School trips	9
Travel	6
Books	5
Educational course	3
Work-related	3
Diploma	2
Other	1

St Albans

The Harpenden Trust

£ £76,600 (2019/20)

Correspondent: The Trustees, The Trust Centre, 90 Southdown Road, Harpenden, Hertfordshire AL5 1PS (tel: 01582 460457; email: admin@theharpendentrust.org.uk)

 www.theharpendentrust.org.uk

CC number: 1118870

Eligibility

People in need who live in the AL5 postal district of Harpenden.

Types of grant

One-off grants are made to assist with household bills. The trust also awards vouchers for food and clothing and for new and recycled furniture and white goods. Help can also be given to older people who have difficulty paying their winter utility bills (electricity, gas and water) and to young people and their families to help with costs of school uniforms or essential school trips. Christmas parcels are delivered to older people who are housebound during the festive period.

Applications

Contact the trust through its online form or using any of the contact details provided.

Financial information

Year end	31/03/2020
Income	£373,100
Total expenditure	£310,400

Further financial information

According to the trust's 2019/20 accounts, 834 grants were made to individuals. These grants were broken down as follows: 565 general grants totalling £41,500; 82 utilities grants totalling £22,600; 141 Christmas parcels totalling £2,600; 46 youth grants totalling £9,900.

Other information

The Harpenden Trust was founded in 1948 by Dr Charles Hill. The trust organises outings, coffee mornings, befriending and home visits for older people in the community.

Stevenage

The Stevenage Community Trust

£ £69,400 (2019/20)

Correspondent: Caroline Haskins, Manager, Stewart House, Primett Road, Stevenage, Hertfordshire SG1 3EE (tel: 01438 525390; email: enquiries@stevenagecommunitytrust.org or caroline@stevenagecommunitytrust.org)

 stevenagecommunitytrust.org

CC number: 1000762

Eligibility

People in need who live in Stevenage and the surrounding villages of Aston, Benington, Cromer, Datchworth, Graveley, Knebworth, Little Wymondley, Old Knebworth, Walkern, Watton-at-Stone, Weston and Woolmer Green.

Types of grant

Grants are given according to need.

Applications

Application forms and guidelines are available from the trust's website and can be submitted at any time. All applications must be submitted by a relevant professional (e.g. a health professional, teacher, social worker or support worker) with knowledge of the beneficiary's situation.

Financial information

Year end	31/03/2020
Income	£195,100
Total expenditure	£193,000

Other information

The trust also makes grants to local organisations.

Watford

Watford Health Trust

£ £21,400 (2019/20)

Correspondent: Ian Scleater, Treasurer, 23 Shepherds Road, Watford, Hertfordshire WD18 7HU (tel: 01923 222745; email: ian@scleater.co.uk)

CC number: 214160

Eligibility

People in need who are in poor health, convalescent or who have a disability and live in the borough of Watford or the surrounding neighbourhood.

Types of grant

One-off grants are awarded for items, services or facilities which alleviate the suffering or assist the recovery of the recipient.

Exclusions

Grants cannot be used to relieve taxes or replace statutory funding.

Applications

Applications should be made through health or social care professionals on behalf of the qualifying individual.

Financial information

Year end	30/09/2020
Income	£24,000
Total expenditure	£33,400

Further financial information

Full accounts were not available to view on the Charity Commission's website due to the trust's low income. We have therefore estimated the grant total based on the trust's total expenditure.

Welwyn Hatfield

Wellfield Trust

 £18,400 (2019/20)

Correspondent: The Trust Manager, Birchwood Leisure Centre, Longmead, Hatfield, Hertfordshire AL10 0AN (tel: 01707 251018; email: wellfieldtrust@aol.com)

 www.wellfieldtrust.co.uk

CC number: 296205

Eligibility

People in need who are on a low income and live in the parish of Hatfield. Applicants usually must have been resident in Hatfield for at least six months.

Types of grant

One-off grants are awarded towards a range of welfare needs such as appliances, beds, clothing and carpets. Grants are made for school uniforms and school trips.

Exclusions

Applications are not normally considered from individuals who have received a grant from the trust within the last two years.

Applications

There is an application form available to download from the trust's website, which must be completed by the individual or a member of the household in need and a sponsor.

Financial information

Year end	31/03/2020
Income	£73,800
Total expenditure	£68,100

Further financial information

During the year, the trust assisted 61 individuals, providing items to a value of £18,400.

Other information

The trust also gives to organisations and has a room at a local leisure centre which can be hired free of charge to charitable organisations. It also runs the Scooter Loan Scheme, through which motorised scooters are loaned to residents of Hatfield who would otherwise be 'virtually housebound' for as long as is required.

Norfolk

Benevolent Association for the Relief of Decayed Tradesmen, their Widows and Orphans

£1,800 (2020/21)

Correspondent: The Trustees, c/o Brown & Co., The Atrium, St Georges Street, Norwich, Norfolk NR3 1AB (tel: 01603 629871; email: nick.saffell@brown-co.com)

CC number: 209861

Eligibility

People who are in need and live in Norwich or the parishes of Costessey, Earlham, Hellesdon, Catton, Sprowston, Thorpe St Andrew, Trowse with Newton and Cringleford. Preference is given to those who have carried on a trade in the area of benefit and their dependants.

Types of grant

Grants are given according to need.

Applications

Apply in writing to the correspondent.

Financial information

Year end	30/04/2021
Income	£4,100
Total expenditure	£4,100

Further financial information

Full accounts were not available to view on the Charity Commission's website due to the charity's low income. We have therefore estimated the grant total based on the charity's total expenditure.

The Cranfield Charitable Trust
See entry on page 280

The Charities of Ralph Greenway

£1,200 (2019/20)

Correspondent: Robert Harris, East Barn, Hall Lane, Wiveton, Holt, Norfolk NR25 7TG (tel: 01263 740090; email: robertpharris@btinternet.com)

CC number: 207605

Eligibility

Residents in the parish of Wiveton who are in need. Preference is given to older residents of the parish.

Types of grant

Pensions and fuel grants are distributed. Grants can be given more generally for various welfare needs, at the trustees' discretion.

Applications

Apply in writing to the correspondent.

Financial information

Year end	31/05/2020
Income	£3,200
Total expenditure	£2,600

Further financial information

Full accounts were not available to view on the Charity Commission's website due to the charity's low income. We have therefore estimated the charity's grant total based on its total expenditure.

Other information

Grants are also made to organisations.

Marham Poor's Allotment

£31,800 (2018/19)

Correspondent: The Trustees, Jungfrau, The Street, Marham, King's Lynn, Norfolk PE33 9JQ (tel: 01760 337286; email: gary@tax.uk.com)

CC number: 236402

Eligibility

People living in the parish of Marham who are in financial need or distress.

Types of grant

The charity awards food and fuel vouchers. Grants are also awarded for assistance with medical treatment.

Exclusions

The charity cannot support those who are able to receive assistance from social services or other statutory sources.

Applications

Apply in writing to the correspondent.

Financial information

Year end	31/03/2019
Income	£40,000
Total expenditure	£25,600

Further financial information

The 2018/19 accounts were the latest available at time of writing (November 2021). According to the accounts, expenditure relating to medical treatment assistance totalled £23,400. Expenditure on food and fuel grants totalled £8,400.

Other information

The charity can also make grants to organisations.

Norfolk Community Foundation

£ £53,200 (2020)

Correspondent: Grants Team, Norfolk Community Foundation, St James Mill, Whitefriars, Norwich, Norfolk NR3 1TN (tel: 01603 623958; email: grants@ norfolkfoundation.com)

 www.norfolkfoundation.com

CC number: 1110817

Eligibility

People in need who live in Norfolk.

Types of grant

The foundation manages a number of funds for individuals, details of which tend to change frequently. Please see the foundation's website for details of open grant programmes.

Applications

Details on how to apply can be found on the community foundation's website.

Financial information

Year end	31/12/2020
Income	£5,800,000
Total expenditure	£4,300,000

Further financial information

Grants were awarded to 210 individuals during the year.

Other information

This is one of the 47 UK community foundations, which distribute funding for a wide range of purposes. Grant schemes tend to change frequently – consult the foundation's website for details of current programmes and upcoming deadlines.

Norfolk Constabulary Benevolent Fund

£ £10,800 (2020)

Correspondent: The Trustees, Norfolk Constabulary, Jubilee House, Falconers Chase, Wymondham, Norfolk NR18 0WW (tel: 0845 456 4567; email: benevolentfund@norfolk.pnn.police.uk)

CC number: 257462

Eligibility

Members and former members of the Norfolk Constabulary Benevolent Fund and their widows/widowers, orphans and dependants.

Types of grant

Grants are given according to need.

Applications

Apply in writing to the correspondent.

Financial information

Year end	31/12/2020
Income	£33,100
Total expenditure	£34,600

Other information

The fund owns and operates holiday homes in Kelling Heath. One of the homes is used to provide free respite care to members in need, and the other is rented to members at a subsidised cost for short holidays.

Old Buckenham Charities

£ £1,200 (2020)

Correspondent: Jenny Sallnow, Arianne, Attleborough Road, Old Buckenham, Attleborough, Norfolk NR17 1RF (tel: 01953 860166)

CC number: 206795

Eligibility

People in need who live in Old Buckenham, Norfolk. There is a preference for pensioners (over 65 years of age) but other groups are also considered.

Types of grant

Normally recurrent grants in coal, or cash in lieu for those without coal fires, are distributed, although other needs may also be addressed. Grants are usually of, or equivalent to, £50 and are distributed yearly in early December. Cases considered to be of exceptional need may be awarded more. There is a reserve of money to help those in emergencies throughout the year.

Applications

Application forms are available from the correspondent, following posted notices around the parish each autumn. Requests are usually considered in early November and can be submitted either directly by the individual or through a third party, such as any of the trustees. Any relevant evidence of need is helpful, but not essential.

Financial information

Year end	31/12/2020
Income	£2,600
Total expenditure	£1,300

Further financial information

Full accounts were not available to view on the Charity Commission's website due to the charity's low income. We have therefore estimated the charity grant total based on its total expenditure.

The Charity of Sir John Picto and Others

£ £7,400 (2019/20)

Correspondent: Stephen Pipe, Beam End, Mill Street, Buxton, Norwich, Norfolk NR10 5JE (tel: 01603 279823; email: stephenpipe@live.co.uk)

CC number: 208896

Eligibility

Residents of the parishes of Buxton Lamas, Little Hautbois, Brampton and Oxmead who are in need.

Types of grant

Welfare

Welfare grants are awarded according to need. Grants have previously been made for school uniforms.

Education

Grants for books have previously been made to college students, undergraduates, vocational students, mature students and people starting work.

Applications

Apply in writing to the correspondent.

Financial information

Year end	31/03/2020
Income	£45,100
Total expenditure	£16,700

Further financial information

Full accounts were not available to view on the Charity Commission's website due to the charity's low income. We have therefore estimated the charity's grant total based on its total expenditure.

Other information

A large portion of the charity's income is used to maintain and administer property and land owned by the charity.

The Ella Roberts Memorial Charity for Saham Toney

£ £1,300 (2019/20)

Correspondent: The Trustees, 36 Richmond Road, Saham Toney, Thetford, Norfolk IP25 7ER (tel: 01953 881844)

CC number: 1025909

Eligibility

People in need who are older or sick, or who have disabilities and live in Saham Toney.

Types of grant

One-off cash grants are awarded towards the purchase or hire of equipment, facilities and care that will provide relief to beneficiaries. Grants have previously been made to cover half the cost of dentures, glasses, physiotherapy and dental treatment, up to a maximum of £100 per application.

Applications

Application forms are available from the charity and should be submitted directly by the individual or a family member. Applications are considered on receipt.

Financial information

Year end	30/09/2020
Income	£720
Total expenditure	£1,400

Further financial information

Full accounts were not available to view on the Charity Commission's website due to the charity's low income. We have therefore estimated the charity's grant total based on its total expenditure.

South Creake Charities

£ £1,200 (2019/20)

Correspondent: Susan Hart, 26 Front Street, South Creake, Fakenham, Norfolk NR21 9PE (tel: 01328 823515; email: sccharities@hotmail.co.uk)

CC number: 210090

Eligibility

People in need who live in South Creake.

Types of grant

One-off grants according to need.

Applications

Applications may be made in writing to the correspondent.

Financial information

Year end	31/01/2020
Income	£6,200
Total expenditure	£2,600

Further financial information

Full accounts were not available to view on the Charity Commission's website due to the charity's low income. We have therefore estimated the charity's grant total based on its total expenditure.

Other information

Our research suggests that occasional awards may also be made to schools and playgroups.

The Watton Relief-in-Need Charity

£ £2,400 (2019/20)

Correspondent: The Trustees, Wayland Hall, Middle Street, Watton, Norfolk IP25 6AG (tel: 07543 651528; email: clerk.wrin@btinternet.com)

CC number: 239041

Eligibility

Residents of Watton who are in need.

Types of grant

Grants are awarded according to need, including for items, services or facilities.

Applications

Apply in writing to the correspondent.

Financial information

Year end	31/03/2020
Income	£4,300
Total expenditure	£5,300

Further financial information

Full accounts were not available to view on the Charity Commission's website due to the charity's low income. We have therefore estimated the charity's grant total based on its total expenditure.

Other information

Grants are also made to organisations.

Breckland

Edmund Atmere (Feltwell) Charity

£ £2,000 (2020)

Correspondent: P. Garland, Trustee, 16 Falcon Road, Feltwell, Thetford, Norfolk IP26 4AJ (tel: 01842 827029; email: garlandp@btinternet.com)

CC number: 270226

Eligibility

Older people, individuals with a disability, or children with a severe chronic illness who live in Feltwell.

Types of grant

Grants are given according to need.

Applications

Apply in writing to the correspondent.

Financial information

Year end	31/12/2020
Income	£3,200
Total expenditure	£2,200

Further financial information

Full accounts were not available to view on the Charity Commission's website due to the charity's low income. We

have therefore estimated the grant total based on the charity's total expenditure.

The Banham Parochial Charities

£ £9,400 (2020)

Correspondent: The Trustees, 6 Pound Close, Banham, Norwich, Norfolk NR16 2SY (tel: 01953 887008)

CC number: 213891

Eligibility

People in need who live in the parish of Banham.

Types of grant

Welfare
One-off grants according to need. Examples include assistance with heating bills or illness-related costs.

Education
One-off grants according to need.

Applications

Apply in writing to the correspondent.

Financial information

Year end	31/12/2020
Income	£11,700
Total expenditure	£10,400

Further financial information

Full accounts were not available to view on the Charity Commission's website due to the charity's low income. We have therefore estimated the charity's grant total based on its total expenditure.

Charity of Thomas Barrett

£ £2,300 (2019/20)

Correspondent: Nicholas Saffell, c/o Brown & Co., The Atrium, St Georges Street, Norwich, Norfolk NR3 1AB (tel: 01603 629871; email: nick.saffell@brown-co.com)

CC number: 207494

Eligibility

People in need who live in Swanton Morley, particularly older and younger people.

Types of grant

Grants are given according to need.

Applications

Apply in writing to the correspondent.

Financial information

Year end	30/04/2020
Income	£5,200
Total expenditure	£5,200

Further financial information

Full accounts were not available to view on the Charity Commission's website due to the charity's low income. We have therefore estimated the grant total based on the charity's total expenditure.

Other information

The trust contributes a portion of its income towards the maintenance and repair of the parish church.

East Dereham Relief-in-Need Charity

(£) £2,300 (2019/20)

Correspondent: The Trustees, 3 Breton Close, Dereham, Norfolk NR19 1JH (tel: 07810 672784)

CC number: 211142

Eligibility

People in need who live in East Dereham (and Toftwood) in Norfolk.

Types of grant

Grants are given according to need.

Applications

Apply in writing to the correspondent.

Financial information

Year end	31/03/2020
Income	£10,500
Total expenditure	£5,000

Further financial information

Full accounts were not available to view on the Charity Commission's website due to the charity's low income. We have therefore estimated the charity's grant total based on its total expenditure.

Other information

The charity also supports organisations.

Harling Combined Trust

(£) £2,000 (2019/20)

Correspondent: The Clerk, 5 The Bailiwick, East Harling, Norwich, Norfolk NR16 2NF (tel: 01953 714656; email: clerk@harlingpc.org.uk)

CC number: 211117

Eligibility

People in need living in Harling.

Types of grant

Principally one-off grants are awarded to assist with the purchase of fuel and heating costs; however, other needs may also be addressed.

Applications

Application forms are available from the correspondent. They can be submitted at

any time together with a brief financial statement.

Financial information

Year end	31/03/2020
Income	£1,700
Total expenditure	£5,000

Further financial information

Full accounts were not available to view on the Charity Commission's website due to the trust's low income. We have therefore estimated the grant total based on the trust's total expenditure.

Horstead Trust

(£) £5,000 (2020/21)

Correspondent: The Trustees, Gershom, Mill Road, Horstead, Norwich, Norfolk NR12 7AT (tel: 01603 737900; email: barbaragdn@gmail.com)

CC number: 264730

Eligibility

People in need who live in Horstead with Stanninghall.

Types of grant

One-off grants according to need.

Applications

Apply in writing to the correspondent.

Financial information

Year end	31/03/2021
Income	£6,200
Total expenditure	£10,400

Further financial information

Full accounts were not available to view on the Charity Commission's website due to the trust's low income. We have therefore estimated the grant total based on the trust's total expenditure.

Saham Toney Fuel Allotment and Perkins Charity

(£) £3,400 (2020)

Correspondent: Jill Glenn, 1 Cressingham Road, Ashill, Thetford, Norfolk IP25 7DG (tel: 01760 441738; email: jill@glenn8530.freeserve.co.uk)

CC number: 211852

Eligibility

People in need who have lived in Saham Toney for at least two years.

Types of grant

One-off grants according to need.

Applications

Apply in writing to the correspondent.

Financial information

Year end	31/12/2020
Income	£13,100
Total expenditure	£5,300

Further financial information

Full accounts were not available to view on the Charity Commission's website due to the charity's low income. We have therefore estimated the charity's grant total based on its total expenditure.

Shipdham Parochial and Fuel Allotment Charity

(£) £8,100 (2019/20)

Correspondent: The Trustees, The Rectory, Church Close, Shipdham, Thetford, Norfolk IP25 7LX (tel: 01362 822404; email: gilliewells1@btinternet.com)

 www.shipdham.org/clubs-charities

CC number: 206339

Eligibility

People in need who have lived in Shipdham for at least two years.

Types of grant

One-off grants are given towards fuel and heating, as well as medical aids, optical and dental, transport costs for medical appointments and school uniforms.

Applications

Application forms can be downloaded online or collected from the correspondent, the church or post office.

Financial information

Year end	31/10/2020
Income	£19,100
Total expenditure	£17,900

Further financial information

Full accounts were not available to view on the Charity Commission's website due to the charity's low income. We have therefore estimated the charity's grant total based on its total expenditure.

Other information

The charity also supports organisations.

Swaffham Relief in Need Charity

 £3,000 (2020/21)

Correspondent: The Trustees, The Town Hall, Swaffham, Norfolk PE37 7DQ (email: reliefinneed@ swaffhamtowncouncil.gov.uk)

🌐 www.swaffhamtowncouncil.gov.uk/ community/swaffham-town-council-12923/swaffham-relief-in-need/#

CC number: 1072912

Eligibility

People in need living in Swaffham.

Types of grant

Grants are given for welfare and educational purposes, including for kitchen appliances, furniture and household equipment, school uniforms, clothing and necessities for those returning to work and people who are re-entering education and need help with the cost of books, for example.

Applications

At the time of writing (December 2021), the charity's page on the Swaffham Town Council website stated: 'Trustees are currently undertaking a full review of the Trust as agreed at their March 2021 meeting. No new applications will be considered until this review has been completed.' Check the website for updates.

Financial information

Year end		31/03/2021
Income		£7,400
Total expenditure		£6,200

Further financial information

Full accounts were not available to view on the Charity Commission's website due to the charity's low income. We have therefore estimated the grant total based on the charity's total expenditure.

Other information

Information on the charity is available from the Swaffham Town Council website.

King's Lynn and West Norfolk

Edmund Atmere (Northwold) Charity

£ £2,500 (2019)

Correspondent: Helaine Wyett, Pangle Cottage, Church Road, Wretton, King's Lynn, Norfolk PE33 9QR (tel: 01366 500165; email: hwyett@tiscali.co.uk)

CC number: 270227

Eligibility

People in need who live in the parish of Northwold.

Types of grant

One-off grants according to need. Aids for people with disabilities are also loaned by the charity.

Applications

Apply in writing to the correspondent.

Financial information

Year end		31/12/2019
Income		£5,500
Total expenditure		£2,500

Further financial information

Full accounts were not available to view on the Charity Commission's website due to the charity's low income. We have therefore estimated the grant total based on the charity's total expenditure.

The Brancaster Educational and Almshouse Charity

£ £7,000 (2019)

Correspondent: The Trustees, Brette Cottage, Cross Lane, Brancaster, King's Lynn, Norfolk PE31 8AE (tel: 01485 210721; email: jjgould10@gmail.com)

CC number: 311128

Eligibility

Children and young people who live, or whose parents live, in the ancient parishes of Brancaster, Titchwell, Thornham and Burnham Deepdale.

Types of grant

Grants are made for educational necessities.

Applications

Apply in writing to the correspondent.

Financial information

Year end		31/12/2019
Income		£27,300
Total expenditure		£20,800

Other information

The charity also awards grants to local schools for costs not covered by the local authorities.

Downham Aid in Sickness Charity

£ £770 (2020/21)

Correspondent: The Trustees, 59 Ryston End, Downham Market, Norfolk PE38 9BA (tel: 01366 387661)

CC number: 258153

Eligibility

Residents in the Downham Market area who are in need as a result of ill health or disability.

Types of grant

Grants are awarded according to need.

Applications

Apply in writing to the correspondent.

Financial information

Year end		31/03/2021
Income		£2,000
Total expenditure		£1,700

Further financial information

Full accounts were not available to view on the Charity Commission's website due to the charity's low income. We have therefore estimated the charity's grant total based on its total expenditure.

Other information

Grants are also made to organisations.

Hall's Exhibition Foundation

£ £45,900 (2020/21)

Correspondent: Christopher Holt, Administrator, 4 Bewick Close, Snettisham, King's Lynn, Norfolk PE31 7PJ (tel: 01485 541534; email: mail@chrisholtphotographic.co.uk)

🌐 www.hallsfoundation.co.uk

CC number: 325128

Eligibility

People between the ages of 11 and 25 (as of 1 September in the year of the course) who have been resident in the village of Snettisham for at least one year and are in need for financial assistance.

Types of grant

Primary to secondary transition

Grants of up to £350 are available to students over the age of 11 who are moving on to secondary education. Grants can be used towards books, uniforms, travel costs, materials or whatever the individual feels necessary. Funding can also be given for extracurricular activities.

Education

Grants are available to further/higher education students in the following categories:

- Young people over the age of 16 who are going on to further education/undertaking A-levels can be awarded grants of up to £500 for each year of the course. This includes students undertaking apprenticeships and training courses
- Students over the age of 18 who are undertaking higher education at universities can receive grants of up to £2,000 per each year of the course (this payment will be awarded in two £1,000 grants at the start and the end of the academic year)
- Postgraduate students can be awarded a one-off grant of up to £1,000

Grants can be used towards the cost of accommodation or whatever purpose the individual requires.

Grants towards course fees and educational visits are also made at the discretion of the trustees.

Exclusions

No additional grants are made for word processors, computers, normal travelling expenses or work experience costs. Grants must be returned if any year of the course is not completed.

Applications

Application forms and further guidelines are available on the foundation's website or can be requested from the correspondent.

Financial information

Year end	31/03/2021
Income	£103,600
Total expenditure	£68,300

Further financial information

In 2020/21, a total of £45,900 was awarded to individuals. The grants were distributed in the following categories:

University/higher education	25	£33,800
Sixth form/16+ further education	34	£7,000
Pupils moving from primary to secondary school	18	£4,000
Extracurricular activities	-	£1,100

Other information

After making awards to individuals each year, the foundation may consider providing support group projects and organisations if they have an educational benefit and involve the young people of Snettisham. The foundation will support university students up to their fifth year.

Hilgay United Charities (Non-Ecclesiastical Branch)

(£) £5,300 (2020)

Correspondent: Anthony Hall, Windrush, Church Road, Ten Mile Bank, Downham Market, Norfolk PE38 0EJ (tel: 07900 518153; email: hilgay.feoffees@aol.com)

CC number: 208898

Eligibility

Welfare

Older people who live in the parish of Hilgay and are in need.

Education

People who live in the parish of Hilgay and are undertaking an apprenticeship or training.

Types of grant

Welfare

Grants are given to assist with the cost of winter fuel.

Education

Grants are given towards the cost of apprenticeships and training.

Applications

Apply in writing to the correspondent. Applications are usually considered in June each year.

Financial information

Year end	31/12/2020
Income	£53,300
Total expenditure	£29,700

Other information

The charity also supports the maintenance of two village halls and provides grants to local schools.

Hundred Acre Common Charity

(£) £8,000 (2020)

Correspondent: The Clerk, Stow Corner Farm, Wimbotsham Road, Stow Bridge, King's Lynn, Norfolk PE34 3PT (tel: 01366 386704; email: 100aclerk@gmail.com)

CC number: 208301

Eligibility

People in need, especially older people or people with disabilities, who live in the Downham Market, Downham West, Stow Bardolph and Wimbotsham areas.

Types of grant

The charity awards fuel vouchers.

Applications

Apply in writing to the correspondent.

Financial information

Year end	31/12/2020
Income	£11,000
Total expenditure	£8,900

Further financial information

Full accounts were not available to view on the Charity Commission's website due to the charity's low income. We have therefore estimated the charity's grant total based on its total expenditure.

Other information

The charity may also make grants to organisations.

The King's Lynn and West Norfolk Borough Charity

(£) £19,300 (2020)

Correspondent: Andy Stephens OBE, Secretary, 3 Heather Close, North Wooton, King's Lynn, Norfolk PE30 3RH (tel: 01553 631394; email: info@kingslynnwncharitytrust.co.uk)

 www.kingslynnwncharitytrust.co.uk

CC number: 243864

Eligibility

Residents of the borough of King's Lynn and West Norfolk who are in need as a result of financial difficulty, illness, convalescence, disability or infirmity.

Types of grant

Grants are awarded according to need. Grants have recently been given towards cookers, washing machines, carpeting, specialist clothing and assistance with the expenses of relocation within the borough.

Exclusions

Grants are not given where provision should be met by public funds.

Applications

Application forms are available from the correspondent. Applications must be endorsed with a supporting statement by a professional working with the applicant or their family. Applications must also include specific quotes for the items requested. The trustees meet on a quarterly basis to consider grant applications, but they will meet between meetings if an application is deemed urgent.

Financial information

Year end	31/12/2020
Income	£11,600
Total expenditure	£21,400

Further financial information

Full accounts were not available to view on the Charity Commission's website

due to the charity's low income. We have therefore estimated the charity grant total based on its total expenditure.

The Harold Moorhouse Charity

£ £7,000 (2019/20)

Correspondent: The Trustees, 30 Winmer Avenue, Winterton-on-Sea, Great Yarmouth, Norfolk NR29 4BA (tel: 01493 393975; email: haroldmoorhousecharity@yahoo.co.uk)

CC number: 287278

Eligibility
Individuals in need who live in Burnham Market.

Types of grant
Grants are paid biannually according to need.

Applications
Apply in writing to the correspondent.

Financial information
Year end	31/08/2020
Income	£26,500
Total expenditure	£23,800

Sir Edmund De Moundeford Charity

£ £16,100 (2020)

Correspondent: The Trustees, The Estate Office, 15 Lynn Road, Downham Market, Norfolk PE38 9NL (tel: 01366 387180; email: info@barryhawkins.co.uk)

CC number: 1075097

Eligibility
People in need who live in Feltwell.

Types of grant

Welfare
Grants are given at Christmas for heating. They can also be made to assist residents of the charity's almshouses.

Education
Grants are given towards the purchase of books for university students and to school leavers.

Applications
Apply in writing to the correspondent. Applications are considered at meetings held quarterly.

Financial information
Year end	31/12/2020
Income	£176,400
Total expenditure	£88,600

Other information
The main purpose of this charity is the provision of almshouse accommodation.

The Pentney Charity

£ £12,900 (2019/20)

Correspondent: The Trustees, Charnwood, Pentney Lane, King's Lynn, Norfolk PE32 1JE (tel: 01760 339026; email: warne100@hotmail.co.uk)

CC number: 212367

Eligibility
People who live in parish of Pentney.

Types of grant
One-off grants are awarded according to need.

Applications
Apply in writing to the correspondent.

Financial information
Year end	31/03/2020
Income	£10,900
Total expenditure	£14,300

Further financial information
Full accounts were not available to view on the Charity Commission's website due to the charity's low income. We have therefore estimated the charity's grant total based on its total expenditure.

The Southery, Feltwell and Methwold Relief in Need Charity

£ £940 (2019/20)

Correspondent: The Trustees, 22A Lynn Road, Southery, Downham Market, Norfolk PE38 0HU (tel: 01366 377571)

CC number: 268856

Eligibility
People living in the parishes of Southery, Feltwell and Methwold who are in need.

Types of grant
Grants are given according to need.

Applications
Apply in writing to the correspondent.

Financial information
Year end	31/03/2020
Income	£1,900
Total expenditure	£1,000

Further financial information
Full accounts were not available to view on the Charity Commission's website due to the charity's low income. We have therefore estimated the charity's grant total based on its total expenditure.

Town Lands Educational Foundation (Outwell Town Lands Educational Foundation)

£ £7,800 (2019)

Correspondent: The Trustees, 109 Hollycroft Road, Emneth, Wisbech, Cambridgeshire PE14 8BD (tel: 01945 580357; email: outwellpc@btinternet.com)

CC number: 311211

Eligibility

Welfare
Pensioners who live in the ancient parish of Outwell and receive benefits.

Education
Students from Outwell who are undertaking further education.

Types of grant

Welfare
Cash grants are given to local pensioners at Christmas.

Education
Grants are awarded for further education.

Applications
Contact the correspondent for an application form.

Financial information
Year end	31/12/2019
Income	£7,600
Total expenditure	£8,700

Further financial information
Full accounts were not available to view on the Charity Commission's website due to the foundation's low income. We have therefore estimated the foundation's grant total based on its total expenditure.

Walpole St Peter Poor's Estate

£ £4,400 (2020)

Correspondent: The Trustees, 1 Sutton Meadows, Leverington, Wisbech, Cambridgeshire PE13 5ED (tel: 01945 665018)

CC number: 233207

Eligibility

Welfare
Older people and people in need and who live in the parish of Walpole St Peter.

Education

Full-time college/university students from the parish of Walpole St Peter who live away from home.

Types of grant

Welfare

The charity provides annual Christmas grants.

Education

Annual grants are given for educational needs.

Applications

Apply in writing to the correspondent.

Financial information

Year end	31/12/2020
Income	£4,600
Total expenditure	£4,900

Further financial information

Full accounts were not available to view on the Charity Commission's website due to the charity's low income. We have therefore estimated the charity's grant total based on its total expenditure.

The United Walsoken and Baxter Charities

(£) £8,000 (2019)

Correspondent: Derek Mews, 7 Pickards Way, Wisbech, Cambridgeshire PE13 1SD (tel: 01945 587982; email: derek.mews@hotmail.co.uk)

CC number: 205494

Eligibility

People over the age of 65 who have lived in the ecclesiastical parish of Walsoken for at least five years. Applicants must also have been on the recipient list for at least one year prior to the upcoming round of grant distributions.

Types of grant

The charity awards small one-off grants.

Exclusions

Only one grant is permitted per household.

Applications

Applications should be made by the individual and sent directly to the correspondent.

Financial information

Year end	31/12/2019
Income	£11,500
Total expenditure	£8,900

Further financial information

Full accounts were not available to view on the Charity Commission's website due to the charity's low income. We have therefore estimated the charity's grant total based on its total expenditure.

West Norfolk and King's Lynn Girls' Schools Trust

(£) £19,800 (2019/20)

Correspondent: Miriam Aldous, Clerk, Woodstock Cottage, 2 School Lane, Little Dunham, King's Lynn, Norfolk PE32 2DQ (tel: 01760 720617)

 www.wnklgirlsschoolstrust.org.uk

CC number: 311264

Eligibility

Girls and young women over the age of 11 who are at a secondary school or in their first years after leaving school or further education. Applicants must live, or have parents living, in the borough of King's Lynn and West Norfolk. Awards to older candidates will be made in exceptional circumstances.

Types of grant

Grants are given for a range of educational needs including books, equipment, educational activities, training in music, sport or the creative arts and so on. Funding is also given towards professional and vocational training, course fees and studying abroad.

Exclusions

The trust cannot provide support for primary schoolchildren.

Applications

Apply on a form available on the trust's website. Application forms should be completed together with a supporting letter outlining the proposed venture or study course and include the details of two independent referees, one of which must be a teacher or tutor who can vouch for the suitability of the course.

Financial information

Year end	30/06/2020
Income	£33,200
Total expenditure	£25,500

Further financial information

During the 2019/20 financial period, grants totalling £19,800 were made to 20 individuals.

North Norfolk

The Blakeney Twelve

(£) £2,800 (2019/20)

Correspondent: The Trustees, 24 Kingsway, Blakeney, Holt, Norfolk NR25 7PL (tel: 01263 741020)

CC number: 276758

Eligibility

Residents in the parishes of Blakeney and Morston, and the surrounding villages, who are in need. Priority is given to older residents and people with disabilities or other medical conditions.

Types of grant

Grants are given according to need.

Applications

Apply in writing to the correspondent.

Financial information

Year end	05/04/2020
Income	£49,800
Total expenditure	£17,500

Gayton Fuel Allotment

(£) £3,000 (2019/20)

Correspondent: Tracey Haggas, Trustee, Well Hall Farm, Well Hall Lane, Gayton, King's Lynn, Norfolk PE32 1QD (tel: 07810 653788; email: traceyhaggas@icloud.com)

CC number: 243082

Eligibility

Residents of Gayton who are in need. At the trustees' discretion, grants may be awarded to temporary residents in the area of benefit or residents immediately outside the area of benefit. Applicants must be in receipt of benefits.

Types of grant

Grants are awarded according to need and are distributed before Christmas each year.

Applications

Each year a notice is placed in the parish magazine for two months (October and November) asking for applicants. Contact the correspondent for further information.

Financial information

Year end	31/03/2020
Income	£3,700
Total expenditure	£3,300

Further financial information

Full accounts were not available to view on the Charity Commission's website due to the charity's low income. We have therefore estimated the charity's grant total based on its total expenditure.

Norwich

Anguish's Educational Foundation

£ £526,700 (2019/20)

Correspondent: Grants Team, Anguish's Educational Foundation, 1 Woolgate Court, St Benedicts Street, Norwich, Norfolk NR2 4AP (tel: 01603 621023; email: information@ norwichcharitabletrusts.org.uk)

 www.norwichcharitabletrusts.org.uk

CC number: 311288

Eligibility

Individuals under the age of 25 who have been residents of the city of Norwich and the parishes of Costessey, Hellesdon, Catton, Sprowston, Thorpe and Corpusty for at least two years. Household income should not exceed £600 per week. A further allowance is made to families of up to ten children in total.

Types of grant

Welfare

Grants are made for school uniforms, educational travel and for other specialised educational needs, such as specialist equipment.

Education

Grants are made for university maintenance, further education and college fees.

Exclusions

Postgraduates are not supported.

Applications

There is no formal application form to complete. Applicants are required to write to the registered address, telephone the trust or send an email. You will then be given an interview with a Grants Officer and will be required to detail your personal or family income. You must take copies of evidence of your income (letters, wage slips, etc.).

Financial information

Year end	31/03/2020
Income	£950,200
Total expenditure	£1,620,000

Further financial information

Grants awarded in 2019/20 were distributed as follows:

School clothes	1650	£182,700
University maintenance	118	£128,500
Further education	211	£110,300
Education travel	464	£87,400
College fees	6	£9,900
Other grants	23	£7,900

Other information

In 2019/20, the foundation also made grant payments to 24 organisations across Norwich.

Anne French Memorial Trust

£ £50,500 (2019/20)

Correspondent: Coralie Nichols, Bishop's House, Norwich, Norfolk NR3 1SB (tel: 01603 629001; email: coralie.nichols@dioceseofnorwich.org)

CC number: 254567

Eligibility

Members of Church of England clergy in the diocese of Norwich.

Types of grant

Grants are awarded for holidays, general relief and courses/training.

Applications

Apply in writing to the correspondent.

Financial information

Year end	05/04/2020
Income	£264,700
Total expenditure	£226,600

Further financial information

Grants awarded in 2019/20 were broken down as follows:

Clergy support including holiday grants	£35,500
Organist training	£10,800
Other	£3,200
Training and conferences	£1,500

Other information

The trust also makes grants to local organisations.

Norwich Consolidated Charities

£ £98,900 (2020)

Correspondent: Grants Team, Norwich Consolidated Charities, 1 Woolgate Court, St Benedicts Street, Norwich, Norfolk NR2 4AP (tel: 01603 621023; email: information@ norwichcharitabletrusts.org.uk)

 www.norwichcharitabletrusts.org.uk

CC number: 1094602

Eligibility

Residents within the boundary of the Norwich City Council who are in need. Priority is given to applicants caring for a child or children.

Types of grant

One-off grants are made for welfare purposes. They can be given to help with the purchase of essential household items (cookers, fridges, beds and carpets, for example), taking out a Debt Relief Order (DRO) or applying for a personal bankruptcy order.

Applications

Applicants must contact the charity via email, telephone or post. If eligible, the charity will then arrange a meeting to discuss the application and will also visit the applicant's home to discuss specific needs. Full details are available on the charity's website.

Financial information

Year end	31/12/2020
Income	£2,270,000
Total expenditure	£2,780,000

Further financial information

During the year, 151 grants were awarded to individuals or families in need. The average grant made was of £655. Of all grants awarded, 15% were for setting up homes, 43% were for moving house, 28% were for continuing help, 11% were for Debt Relief Orders and 3% were for bankruptcy costs.

Other information

The main activity of the charity is the provision of almshouses, which include Doughty's, which acts as residence for older people, and Bakery Court, which is managed by the charity Julian Support, for people who have mental health problems.

Norwich Town Close Estate Charity

£ £150,900 (2020/21)

Correspondent: Grants Officer, 1 Woolgate Court, St Benedicts Street, Norwich, Norfolk NR2 4AP (tel: 01603 621023; email: information@ norwichcharitabletrusts.org.uk)

 https://www. norwichcharitabletrusts.org.uk

CC number: 235678

Eligibility

Freemen of the city of Norwich, and their dependants, who are in need.

Types of grant

Welfare

Grants are given for relief in need and to help with unexpected expenditure. Funding is also available towards the cost of schools clothing and school trips. The charity can provide annual pensions to those who have reached UK state pension age. It can also make grants towards the cost of obtaining a TV licence for people under the age of 75.

Education

Educational grants are awarded toward the cost of pursuing further education or vocational training (including necessary equipment), university maintenance (including support for doctorates) and personal tuition in music, the arts and sport where the beneficiary is likely to reach professional status.

Applications

In the first instance, potential applicants should contact the correspondent by email, explaining the type of grant needed. The relevant application form will then be sent to them. Completed application forms should be returned by email or post.

Financial information

Year end	31/03/2021
Income	£1,060,000
Total expenditure	£1,440,000

Further financial information

Grants were made to 142 individuals during the 2020/21 financial period. Welfare grants were broken down as follows:

Pensions	66	£68,700
Relief in need	8	£17,200
TV licences	30	£4,600
School uniforms	8	£1,500

Educational grants were broken down as follows:

College and further education	11	£39,400
Miscellaneous educational grants	11	£38,100
Talented individual grant	1	£20,800
University maintenance grants	7	£12,000

Other information

This charity is one of three amalgamated charities as part of the Norwich Charitable Trusts.

The Foundation of Joanna Scott and Others

£40,800 (2019/20)

Correspondent: Secretary to the Trustees, 21A Colegate, Norwich, Norfolk NR3 1BN (tel: 01603 224800; email: secretary@ foundationofjoannascott.org.uk)

 www.foundationofjoannascott.org. uk

CC number: 311253

Eligibility

People under the age of 25 who are being educated or live within five miles of Norwich City Hall and whose families are in financial need.

Types of grant

Welfare

Grants are given for a wide range of educational expenses including towards the costs of uniforms/other school clothing, books, equipment/instruments, childcare, educational outings in the UK, study or travel abroad and student exchanges.

Education

Grants are given for a wide range of educational expenses including towards fees, maintenance/living expenses and study or travel abroad.

Applications

Application forms are available from the foundation's website and can be posted or sent via email.

Financial information

Year end	31/03/2020
Income	£73,900
Total expenditure	£80,600

Other information

Small grants are also given to organisations and schools.

South Norfolk

Diss Parochial Charity

£7,000 (2020)

Correspondent: The Trustees, 2 The Causeway, Victoria Road, Diss, Norfolk IP22 4AW (tel: 01379 650630)

CC number: 210154

Eligibility

Residents in the parish of Diss who are in need and/or experiencing bereavement. Preference may be given to older residents. Support may be extended to temporary residents of the parish or those living outside the parish, but only in exceptional cases.

Types of grant

One-off grants are awarded towards the cost of items such as clothing, school uniforms, handrails, mobility scooters, white goods, cookers, carpets, transport costs and cleaning bills. Payments of £150 are made to individuals experiencing bereavement, which are followed up by a Christmas hamper during the seasonal period.

Applications

Apply in writing to the correspondent.

Financial information

Year end	31/12/2020
Income	£34,700
Total expenditure	£25,900

Further financial information

During the year, £4,200 was awarded in bereavement payments, £2,100 was awarded in general grants to individuals and £730 in was awarded Christmas gifts for bereaved people.

Other information

The charity owns and maintains almshouses, which are available to those in need of accommodation. The charity also makes an annual contribution to the parochial church council to maintain the tomb of William Burton and also for more general religious purposes.

The Town Estate Educational Foundation (Hempnall)

£7,400 (2019)

Correspondent: Alison Harris, Clerk to the Trustees, 1 Freemasons Cottage, Mill Road, Hempnall, Norwich, Norfolk NR15 2LP (tel: 01508 498187; email: hteefclerk@gmail.com)

CC number: 311218

Eligibility

People under the age of 25 who live in Hempnall.

Types of grant

Grants are made for educational, training, sport and recreational needs.

Applications

Grant application forms can be obtained from Hempnall Village Hall, Hempnall Mill, Hempnall Surgery, 34 Roland Drive or by emailing the clerk.

Financial information

Year end	31/12/2019
Income	£21,300
Total expenditure	£16,500

Further financial information

Full accounts were not available to view on the Charity Commission's website due to the foundation's low income. We have therefore estimated the foundation's grant total based on its total expenditure.

Suffolk

Aldeburgh United Charities

£2,100 (2020)

Correspondent: The Trustees, Moot Hall, Market Cross Place, Aldeburgh, Suffolk IP15 5DS (tel: 01728 452158; email: townclerk@aldeburghtowncouncil. co.uk)

CC number: 235840

Eligibility

Residents of Aldeburgh who are in need. The charity's Charity Commission record states that current beneficiaries include 'senior citizens, people in specific sensitive situations, young and young-minded people and people in the development stage of life's experience.'

Types of grant

Grants are given according to need.

Applications

Apply in writing to the correspondent.

Financial information

Year end	31/12/2020
Income	£6,900
Total expenditure	£4,500

Further financial information

Full accounts were not available to view on the Charity Commission's website due to the charity's low income. We have therefore estimated the charity's grant total based on its total expenditure.

Other information

This charity also makes grants to organisations.

The Cranfield Charitable Trust
See entry on page 280

See entry on page 280

The Mills Educational Foundation

 £1,500 (2020/21)

Correspondent: Chair of the Trustees, PO Box 1703, Framlingham, Woodbridge, Suffolk IP13 9WW (tel: 01728 685031; email: office@millscharity.co.uk)

www.millscharity.co.uk

CC number: 310475

Eligibility

Children who live in Framlingham and the surrounding district or who attend a school there.

Types of grant

Grants are awarded for a wide range of educational needs.

Applications

Apply in writing to the correspondent. The trustees meet every two months to consider applications.

Financial information

Year end	31/01/2021
Income	£6,700
Total expenditure	£3,400

Further financial information

Full accounts were not available to view on the Charity Commission's website due to the foundation's low income. We have therefore estimated the foundation's grant total based on its total expenditure.

Other information

The foundation also contributes directly to Thomas Mills High School.

The Seckford Foundation

 £33,000 (2019/20)

Correspondent: Graham Watson, Seckford Springboard, Marryott House, Burkitt Road, Woodbridge, Suffolk IP12 4JJ (tel: 01394 615000; email: enquiries@seckford-foundation.org.uk)

www.seckford-foundation.org.uk

CC number: 1110964

Eligibility

Individuals aged 25 and under or 65 and over who live in Suffolk.

Types of grant

Grants are given through the Seckford Springboard scheme to enable access to facilities and services that promote independent living and learning. Grants are given towards a range of purposes such as interview clothing, childcare, transport and activities that promote independence and social inclusion.

Grants of up to £500 are available for a range of purposes including travel to training/work, course costs, equipment/tools and essential equipment for an apprenticeship.

Exclusions

The foundation will not support:
- Overseas projects or gap years
- Retrospective funding
- Activities which should be funded by statutory bodies
- Building projects or refurbishments/adaptations
- Loan or debt repayments, or budget shortfalls
- Tuition fees
- Medical treatment
- Postgraduate study
- Those who have received a grant in the last 12 months
- Individuals living outside Suffolk

The foundation is unlikely to provide funding if its grant forms only a small contribution to the funding required.

Applications

Applications should be made in a letter, stating the following information: the age of the individual; where they live; what the funding is required for; and why they are unable to provide the funds themselves. Potential applicants are welcome to contact the foundation by telephone to ascertain their eligibility. Guidance notes are provided on the foundation's website and should be read before applying. In most cases, a decision can be made within three weeks of an application being received. Decisions on larger applications may take longer, in which case the foundation will notify applicants of a likely timescale.

Financial information

Year end	31/08/2020
Income	£22,780,000
Total expenditure	£23,950,000

Further financial information

In 2019/20, a total of £33,000 was awarded to ten individuals.

Other information

The foundation also provides apprenticeships and mentoring opportunities, as well as making grants to organisations. The foundation runs Woodbridge School and two free schools, as well as almshouses.

Suffolk Constabulary Benevolent Fund

 £14,500 (2019/20)

Correspondent: Trevor Barnes, Trustee, Suffolk Constabulary Headquarters, Portal Avenue, Martlesham Heath, Ipswich, Suffolk IP5 3QS (tel: 01473 613641; email: trevor.barnes@suffolk.pnn.police.uk)

CC number: 253149

Eligibility

Members of the Suffolk Constabulary Benevolent Fund who are in need.

Types of grant

Grants are given according to need.

Applications

Apply in writing to the correspondent.

Financial information

Year end	31/03/2020
Income	£36,500
Total expenditure	£28,200

Further financial information

Grants in 2019/20 were distributed as follows: Christmas grants (£6,700); grants to pensioners (£4,500); grants to serving officers (£3,300).

The Annie Tranmer Charitable Trust

(£) £21,700 (2019/20)

Correspondent: Anne-Marie Williams, Trust Administrator, 55 Dobbs Lane, Kesgrave, Ipswich, Suffolk IP5 2QA (tel: 07801 556002; email: amwilliams7903@gmail.com)

CC number: 1044231

Eligibility

Children and young people who live in the county of Suffolk.

Types of grant

To educate and support young people through their leisure-time activities to develop their mental, physical and spiritual capacities and improve their conditions of life.

Applications

Apply in writing to the correspondent.

Financial information

Year end	05/04/2020
Income	£132,100
Total expenditure	£123,800

Further financial information

Grants were awarded to 30 individuals in 2019/20.

Other information

Grants are also made to other charities and organisations.

Babergh

Sudbury Municipal Charities

(£) £5,100 (2020)

Correspondent: The Trustees, The Christopher Centre, 10 Gainsborough Street, Sudbury, Suffolk CO10 2EU (tel: 07377 330734; email: sudburymunicipalcharities@gmail.com)

CC number: 213516

Eligibility

Older people (generally those over 70) who are in need and live in the borough of Sudbury.

Types of grant

Christmas and Ascension Day gifts in the form of food and clothes vouchers.

Applications

Apply in writing to the correspondent. Grants are sometimes advertised in the local newspaper when they are available.

Financial information

Year end	31/12/2020
Income	£5,700
Total expenditure	£5,700

Further financial information

Full accounts were not available to view on the Charity Commission's website due to the charity's low income. We have therefore estimated the grant total based on the charity's total expenditure.

Other information

The charity also awards grants of up to £200 to local organisations.

East Suffolk

The Halesworth United Charities

(£) £1,600 (2019)

Correspondent: The Trustees, Hill Farm, Primes Lane, Blyford, Halesworth, Suffolk IP19 9JT (tel: 01986 872340)

CC number: 214509

Eligibility

People in need who live in the ancient parish of Halesworth. People living in the immediate vicinity of Halesworth may be supported in exceptional circumstances.

Types of grant

Grants are made according to need.

Applications

Apply in writing to the correspondent.

Financial information

Year end	31/12/2019
Income	£7,600
Total expenditure	£3,600

Further financial information

Full accounts were not available to view on the Charity Commission's website due to the charity's low income. We have therefore estimated the charity's grant total based on its total expenditure.

Other information

The charity also makes grants to organisations.

Lowestoft Church and Town Relief in Need Charity

(£) £1,500 (2019/20)

Correspondent: Matthew Breeze, 148 London Road North, Lowestoft, Suffolk NR32 1HF (tel: 01493 849200)

CC number: 1015039

Eligibility

People in need who have lived in the area of the old borough of Lowestoft for at least three years.

Types of grant

One-off grants are awarded for items and services such as childcare costs, clothing, debt relief, furniture, help for people with disabilities and help with funeral costs.

Applications

Apply in writing to the correspondent.

Financial information

Year end	05/04/2020
Income	£11,300
Total expenditure	£3,300

Further financial information

Full accounts were not available to view on the Charity Commission's website due to the charity's low income. We have therefore estimated the charity's grant total based on its total expenditure.

Other information

The charity also makes grants to organisations that assist in alleviating poverty and need in the Lowestoft area.

Lowestoft Fishermen's and Seafarers' Benevolent Society

Correspondent: Mr H. Sims, 10 Waveney Road, Lowestoft, Suffolk NR32 1BN (tel: 01502 565161; email: lowestoftfpo@hotmail.com)

 infolink.suffolk.gov.uk

Eligibility

Widows, children and dependants of fishermen and seamen lost at sea from vessels registered with the society who are in need.

Types of grant

One-off grants have previously been made for funeral costs, mobility aids and household adaptations. Monthly payments are also made.

Applications

Referrals are made via The Royal National Mission to Deep Sea Fishermen. Contact the correspondent for further information.

Further financial information

Financial information was not available for the society.

Other information

The society is not a registered charity.

The Mills Charity

£ £25,200 (2020/21)

Correspondent: Nick Corke, Chair of the Trustees, PO Box 1703, Framlingham, Woodbridge, Suffolk IP13 9WW (tel: 01728 685031; email: office@millscharity.co.uk)

 www.millscharity.co.uk

CC number: 207259

Eligibility

People in need who live in Framlingham or who are very closely associated with the town.

Types of grant

One-off grants are made to pay for items, services or facilities which will reduce need, hardship or distress.

Applications

Apply in writing to the correspondent. A supporting letter from a professional or other suitable referee to accompany the application is useful, although not essential.

Financial information

Year end	31/01/2021
Income	£257,100
Total expenditure	£259,100

Further financial information

In 2020/21, £50,300 was awarded in grants to individuals and organisations during the year. A breakdown of grants was not provided; therefore, the grant total has been estimated.

Other information

The charity also provides and maintains almshouses and makes grants to organisations.

The Reydon Trust

£ £1,400 (2019/20)

Correspondent: The Clerk, 24 Wangford, Reydon Village Hall Lowestoft Road, Reydon, Southwold, Suffolk IP18 6PY (tel: 07754 096008; email: theclerk@thereydontrust.org.uk)

CC number: 206873

Eligibility

People in need who live in the parish of Reydon.

Types of grant

One-off grants according to need. In previous years, grants have been awarded for the payment of supplies, travel costs, carpeting and clothing.

Applications

Apply in writing to the correspondent.

Financial information

Year end	31/03/2020
Income	£59,100
Total expenditure	£42,100

Mrs L. D. Rope's Third Charitable Settlement

£ £742,700 (2019/20)

Correspondent: The Trustees, Lucy House, St William Court, Kesgrave, Ipswich, Suffolk IP5 2QP (tel: 01473 333288; email: ropetrust@lucyhouse.org.uk)

CC number: 290533

Eligibility

Residents in the district of East Suffolk, particularly those in the parish of Kesgrave and the surrounding areas (including Ipswich) who are in need. Priority is given to those on a low income. Support is also available to residents of small areas of Essex and Norfolk adjacent to Suffolk.

Types of grant

One-off grants towards, for example, furniture, white goods, rent arrears and deposits.

Exclusions

No grants are awarded for private education fees, or for any cause related to the performing, literary or visual arts. The charity is not normally able to assist individuals working overseas.

Applications

Apply in writing to the correspondent. All applicants must be referred to the charity by a third party such as a housing officer, probation officer or social worker.

Financial information

Year end	05/04/2020
Income	£2,110,000
Total expenditure	£1,660,000

Further financial information

In 2019/20, the charity awarded 2,951 grants to beneficiaries. Included in the grant total is £94,200 for rent arrears and deposits.

Ipswich

John Dorkin's Charity

£ £3,800 (2020)

Correspondent: The Trustees, Holy Trinity Church, Back Hamlet, Ipswich, Suffolk IP3 8AJ (email: mail@johndorkincharityipswich.co.uk)

 www.johndorkincharityipswich.co.uk

CC number: 209635

Eligibility

People in need who live in the ancient parish of St Clement's, St Helen and Holy Trinity in Ipswich, which broadly comprises the IP3 postcode (a map of the area of benefit is provided on the charity's website). There is a preference for the widows and children of seamen.

Types of grant

Grants according to need. In previous years funding has been used for redecorating, carpeting, furnishing, furniture and white goods, toys, specialist equipment, hospital travel cost, or basic essentials.

Exclusions

Grants are not awarded for the relief of debt, taxes or other public funds.

Applications

Application forms can be downloaded from the charity's website. Applications should be made via a support worker, who must also sign the application.

Financial information

Year end	31/12/2020
Income	£10,900
Total expenditure	£8,400

Further financial information

Full accounts were not available to view on the Charity Commission's website due to the charity's low income. We have therefore estimated the charity's grant total based on its total expenditure.

Other information

The charity also makes awards to organisations.

Hope House and Gippeswyk Educational Trust

£ £8,800 (2019/20)

Correspondent: The Trustees, 4 Church Meadows, Henley, Ipswich, Suffolk IP6 0RP (tel: 07788 416722; email: clements4henley@aol.com)

CC number: 1068441

Eligibility

Young people in need who are under the age of 21 and live in Ipswich or the surrounding area.

Types of grant

Grants are made to relieve hardship and distress and can be used towards goods, food, services or facilities.

Grants are made to promote the education of young people in Ipswich and the surrounding area who are in need.

Applications

Apply in writing to the correspondent.

Financial information

Year end	30/04/2020
Income	£14,000
Total expenditure	£9,800

Further financial information

Full accounts were not available to view on the Charity Commission's website due to the trust's low income. We have therefore estimated the trust's grant total based on its total expenditure.

Other information

Financial assistance may also be given to organisations.

Mid Suffolk

Gislingham United Charity

£ £15,000 (2019)

Correspondent: Sheila Eade, Clerk, Woodberry, High Street, Gislingham, Suffolk IP23 8JD (tel: 01379 783541; email: gislinghamunitedcharity@gmail.com)

 gislingham.onesuffolk.net/organisations/gislingham-united-charity

CC number: 208340

Eligibility

People in need who live in Gislingham.

Types of grant

Welfare

One-off grants according to need.

Education

Grants are given for educational purposes through the charity's Education Branch.

Applications

Apply in writing to the correspondent.

Financial information

Year end	31/12/2019
Income	£12,300
Total expenditure	£16,800

Further financial information

Full accounts were not available to view on the Charity Commission's website due to the charity's low income. We have therefore estimated the charity's grant total based on its total expenditure.

Other information

The charity also supports the upkeep and maintenance of St Mary's Church in Gislingham.

The Stowmarket Relief Trust

£ £36,300 (2019/20)

Correspondent: The Trustees, 9 Temple Road, Stowmarket, Suffolk IP14 1AX (tel: 07414 504513; email: clerk.relieftrust@gmail.com)

CC number: 802572

Eligibility

People in need who live in the town of Stowmarket. Depending on the amount of income available, the trust can also support people living in the adjoining parishes and in the parish of Old Newton with Dagworth.

Types of grant

Grants are given for the following: the purchase and repair of white goods; the purchase and fitting of carpets and floor coverings; the purchase of beds, bedding and household furniture; the payment of living/household expenses; the purchase of clothing or footwear; the provision of specialist counselling; and the payment of court fees for individuals going into bankruptcy, including Debt Relief Orders.

Applications

Application forms are available from the correspondent. Applications should be submitted through a third party such as a social worker, probation officer, Citizens Advice or doctor. Applications are considered at trustees' meetings held three times a year, although urgent cases can be dealt with between meetings.

Financial information

Year end	30/09/2020
Income	£80,500
Total expenditure	£54,000

Town Estate Charity (Mendlesham)

£ £2,300 (2020)

Correspondent: The Trustees, 2 Old Orchard, Mendlesham, Stowmarket, Suffolk IP14 5TY (tel: 07540 288388)

CC number: 207592

Eligibility

People who are in need and live in the parish of Mendlesham in Suffolk, particularly older people and those who are suffering from an illness.

Types of grant

Grants are given according to need.

Applications

Apply in writing to the correspondent.

Financial information

Year end	31/12/2020
Income	£8,600
Total expenditure	£5,100

Further financial information

Full accounts were not available to view on the Charity Commission's website due to the charity's low income. We have therefore estimated the charity's grant total based on its total expenditure.

Other information

Grants are also made to the Church Estate Charity for the upkeep of St Mary's Church.

West Suffolk

Goward and John Evans George

£ £18,900 (2020)

Correspondent: Laura Williams, Clerk to the Trustees, 8 Woodcutters Way, Lakenheath, Brandon, Suffolk IP27 9JQ (tel: 07796 018816; email: laurawill@btinternet.com)

CC number: 253727

Eligibility

Welfare

People who are in need and live in the parish of Lakenheath in Suffolk.

Education

Students that live in the parish of Lakenheath in Suffolk.

Types of grant

Welfare

Welfare grants are available for individuals and families.

Education

Grants are given to individuals aged 16–18, further/higher education students and other young people towards educational costs.

Applications

Apply in writing to the correspondent.

Financial information

Year end	31/12/2020
Income	£33,600
Total expenditure	£33,700

Further financial information

In 2020, a total of £18,900 was awarded to individuals. Welfare grants to individuals totalled £4,400, and education-related grants totalled £14,500.

Other information

The charity also supports local schools, colleges, Sunday schools and organisations. One-eighth of the charity's income is allocated to Soham United Charities.

The Mildenhall Parish Charities

£ £4,000 (2020)

Correspondent: The Trustees, 22 Lark Road, Mildenhall, Bury St Edmunds IP28 7LA (tel: 01638 718079)

CC number: 208196

Eligibility
People, particularly older people, in need who live in the parish of Mildenhall.

Types of grant
One-off grants according to need.

Applications
Apply in writing to the correspondent.

Financial information

Year end	31/12/2020
Income	£15,000
Total expenditure	£4,500

Further financial information
Full accounts were not available to view on the Charity Commission's website due to the charity's low income. We have therefore estimated the grant total based on its total expenditure.

Pakenham Charities

£ £3,100 (2019)

Correspondent: Sally Smith, Clerk, 13 Manor Garth, Pakenham, Bury St Edmunds IP31 2LB (tel: 01359 230431; email: sally@sallysmithbooks.co.uk)

 www.pakenham-village.co.uk/main/pakenhamcharities.htm

CC number: 213314

Eligibility
People in need who live in Pakenham.

Types of grant
Small annual fuel grants are distributed to residents who are older or have an illness or disability, and one-off payments are awarded for particular needs such as hospital visits and disability aids.

Applications
Apply in writing to the correspondent. Applications are considered in early December and (for urgent requests) at midsummer too.

Financial information

Year end	31/12/2019
Income	£6,400
Total expenditure	£6,900

Further financial information
Full accounts were not available to view on the Charity Commission's website due to the charity's low income. We have therefore estimated the charity's grant total based on its total expenditure.

Other information
Local organisations can also be awarded grants.

The Risby Fuel Allotment

£ £5,500 (2019/20)

Correspondent: Penelope Wallis, Trustee, 3 Woodland Close, Risby, Bury St Edmunds IP28 6QN (tel: 01284 81064)

CC number: 212260

Eligibility
People in need who live in the parish of Risby.

Types of grant
Annual grants are distributed primarily to buy winter fuel but also for other needs.

Applications
Apply in writing to the correspondent.

Financial information

Year end	30/09/2020
Income	£7,400
Total expenditure	£6,100

Further financial information
Full accounts were not available to view on the Charity Commission's website due to the charity's low income. We have therefore estimated the charity's grant total based on its total expenditure.

The Stanton Land Fund

£ £5,400 (2019/20)

Correspondent: The Trustees, 1 Grundle Close, Stanton, Bury St Edmunds, Suffolk IP31 2DX (tel: 01359 251535)

CC number: 235649

Eligibility
People living in the parish of Stanton who are in financial need.

Types of grant
Grants are given according to need.

Applications
Apply in writing to the correspondent.

Financial information

Year end	31/01/2020
Income	£6,000
Total expenditure	£6,000

Further financial information
Full accounts were not available to view on the Charity Commission's website due to the fund's low income. We have therefore estimated the fund's grant total based on its total expenditure.

Greater London

General

Bromfield's Educational Foundation

£ £14,800 (2020)

Correspondent: Anna Paterson, Grants Officer, 5 St Andrew Street, London EC4A 3AF (tel: 020 7822 7471; email: charities@standrewholborn.org.uk)

 www.standrewholborn.org.uk

CC number: 312795

Eligibility
People under the age of 25 who, for at least the past two years, have lived in the area of the former parish of St Andrew Holborn and whose socio-economic circumstances mean that they are restricted in their ability to fully benefit from educational opportunities.

Types of grant

Welfare
One-off and termly grants are given to ensure children can participate in the opportunities that are available to them. Grants are also given towards school uniforms. Almost all the families receiving termly grants are caring for a child with a disability.

Education
Grants are given to students in further or higher education for items such as laptops, travel, books and general maintenance.

Exclusions
Grants are not given for school, college or university fees. Applications for postgraduate studies will not be considered.

Applications
Application forms can be downloaded from the foundation's website or obtained from the correspondent.

Financial information

Year end	31/12/2020
Income	£49,600
Total expenditure	£56,800

Other information
The foundation also makes grants to organisations.

The City and Diocese of London Voluntary Schools Fund

£ £5,100 (2020/21)

Correspondent: Dee Thomas, 36 Causton Street, London SW1P 4AU (tel: 020 7932 1168; email: dee.thomas@london.anglican.org)

 https://www.ldbs.co.uk

CC number: 312259

Eligibility

Welfare
Children who have attended a Church of England voluntary-aided school in the diocese of London (i.e. north of the river) for at least two years and are in need.

Education
Young people who have attended a Church of England voluntary-aided school in the diocese of London and are undertaking higher/further education or vocational training.

Types of grant

Welfare
The fund awards School Journey Grants for school trips and educational visits.

Education
Grants are available towards maintenance costs, travel, tuition and resources for individuals in higher/further education.

Applications
Application forms and guidelines are available on the fund's website.

Financial information

Year end	31/03/2021
Income	£279,900
Total expenditure	£333,700

Further financial information
During 2020/21, grants were made to 73 individuals. The accounts note that this figure would have been higher if school trips had not been cancelled due to COVID-19.

Other information
The fund also accepts group applications for school journeys.

Coopers Charity CIO

£ £46,600 (2019/20)

Correspondent: Clerk, Worshipful Company of Coopers, Coopers Hall, 13 Devonshire Square, London EC2M 4TH (tel: 020 7247 9577; email: clerk@coopers-hall.co.uk)

 https://www.coopers-hall.co.uk

CC number: 1155094

Eligibility
Members of the Worshipful Company of Coopers, and their dependants, who are in need. The charity also makes grants more generally to people in need living in Greater London or Surrey.

Types of grant
One-off grants of up to £1,000 and long-term grants of up to £5,000 per annum (for a period of up to three years) are available.

Exclusions
The charity does not normally award grants to individuals for educational purposes.

Applications
Application forms are available to download on the funder's website. Completed forms should be sent to the clerk by email or post. The committee meets quarterly in February, June, September and November to consider grant applications. The website states that gaining approval make take up to three months.

Financial information

Year end	31/03/2020
Income	£196,200
Total expenditure	£195,800

Further financial information

During the 2019/20 financial year, the charity awarded 43 grants. Of this number, 31 grants were given to people with disabilities, older people and for general welfare needs, and ten grants were given to young people.

Other information

This charity also makes grants to organisations, particularly to local organisations and causes in the City of London sponsored by the Lord Mayor. The charity does make grants to national organisations but only those financed on a local basis, such as Age Concern.

The Charles Dixon Pension Fund

 £6,200 (2020/21)

Correspondent: The Trustees, c/o The Society of Merchant Venturers, Merchants' Hall, The Promenade, Bristol BS8 3NH (tel: 0117 973 8058; email: enquiries@merchantventurers.com)

CC number: 202153

Eligibility

Merchants who are in reduced circumstances who are over 60 years of age and live in Bristol, Liverpool or London.

Types of grant

Pensions are distributed to beneficiaries.

Applications

Apply in writing to the correspondent.

Financial information

Year end	31/03/2021
Income	£9,400
Total expenditure	£6,900

Further financial information

Full accounts were not available to view on the Charity Commission's website due to the fund's low income. We have therefore estimated the fund's grant total based on its total expenditure.

Lady Gould's Charity

 £58,000 (2020)

Correspondent: The Trustees, c/o Bircham Dyson Bell, 50 Broadway, Westminster, London SW1H 0BL (tel: 020 7783 3533; email: ladygouldscharity@gmail.com)

🌐 www.ladygouldscharity.org

CC number: 1173760

Eligibility

Residents in the Highgate area of London (i.e. the N6 postal district and parts of the N2, N8, N19 and NW5

postal districts) who are in need. An index of all qualifying streets and a map of the area of benefit can be seen on the funder's website.

Types of grant

Grants of up to £600 are typically awarded for furniture, carpets, white goods, cookers, clothing and baby essentials.

Exclusions

Grants are not normally made for debt relief or educational or recreational purposes. Apart from in exceptional circumstances, grants are limited to one per individual/family per year.

Applications

Application forms are available to download from the charity's website. Applicants must submit a supporting statement from social services, another recognised state or voluntary organisation, or a professional (such as a GP) with their application. Grants are usually paid to the referring agency or supplier of goods and not directly to the applicant.

Financial information

Year end	31/12/2020
Income	£67,100
Total expenditure	£81,300

The Canon Holmes Memorial Trust
See entry on page 281

The Hornsey Parochial Charities

 £56,500 (2020)

Correspondent: Lorraine Fincham, Clerk to the Trustees, PO Box 22985, London N10 3XB (tel: 020 8352 1601; email: clerk@hornseycharities.org)

🌐 https://www.hornseycharities.org

CC number: 229410

Eligibility

People under the age of 25 who live in Hornsey, including the parish of Clerkenwell in Haringey and Hackney. Applicants must have resided in the area for at least 12 months. The charity's website has helpful maps showing the area of benefit.

Types of grant

Welfare

Grants are available for essential items such as fridges, cookers, washing machines, beds, clothing, bedding, household equipment, the cost of heating and lighting.

Education

Grants are awarded to individuals under the age of 25 to assist with educational expenses or to prepare for a career.

Applications

Applications can be made via the charity's website. Individuals applying for a welfare grant need to supply evidence of benefits, pay or an email reference from a third-party professional supporting organisation or support worker. Individuals applying for an educational grant need to supply the course enrolment letter, student loan documents (if applicable) and evidence of family income (if applicable).

Financial information

Year end	31/12/2020
Income	£70,600
Total expenditure	£51,900

Other information

Grants are also awarded to organisations.

The Hugh and Montague Leney Travelling Awards Trust

 £4,400 (2019/20)

Correspondent: Lyn Edwards, Secretary, Awards Group, Education and Libraries, Bishops Terrace, Bishops Way, Maidstone, Kent ME14 1AF (tel: 0300 041 5944; email: leneytrust@hotmail.co.uk)

🌐 www.leneytrust.org

CC number: 307950

Eligibility

Young people between the ages of 16 and 19 who are attending (or have attended within the previous 12 months) a school in Kent, Medway, Bexley or Bromley. The trust's website states that preference will be given to 'pupils who are in their final school year, who have shown qualities of leadership and whose venture is likely to help their future life and career'.

Types of grant

Grants of up to £2,500 are awarded towards charitable trips abroad, usually for a minimum of four weeks. Projects are expected to be of a humanitarian nature and to take place in financially developing regions.

Exclusions

Grants are not awarded in support of holidays, structured school visits or periods of paid employment in more developed areas.

Applications

Application forms are available to download on the trust's website. Note:

grants are not calculated to cover total costs. Therefore, the trustees take into account any contributions and other sources of fundraising/sponsorship intended to supplement funding. Completed forms should be sent to the correspondent at their postal address or email. The closing date for applications is 31 January each year.

Financial information

Year end	05/04/2020
Income	£8,500
Total expenditure	£4,800

Further financial information

Full accounts were not available to view on the Charity Commission's website due to the trust's low income. We have therefore estimated the trust's grant total based on its total expenditure.

The Mary Minet Trust

£ £18,200 (2020/21)

Correspondent: The Trustees, PO Box 53673, London SE24 4AF (tel: 07982 451082; email: admin@maryminettrust.org.uk)

CC number: 212483

Eligibility

Residents of Southwark or Lambeth who have a disability or illness and are in need.

Types of grant

One-off grants are given for specified essential items.

Applications

Applications must be made through a sponsoring organisation on behalf of an individual. Direct applications from individuals are rarely accepted. Contact the correspondent to obtain an application form. Applications are considered four times a year.

Financial information

Year end	31/03/2021
Income	£21,900
Total expenditure	£20,200

Further financial information

Full accounts were not available to view on the Charity Commission's website due to the trust's low income. We have therefore estimated the trust's grant total based on its total expenditure.

Arthur and Rosa Oppenheimer Fund

£ £3,800 (2020)

Correspondent: The Trustees, 27 Hove Park Villas, Hove, East Sussex BN3 6HH (tel: 01273 770094)

CC number: 239367

Eligibility

People of the Jewish faith who live in London and are in need as a result of ill health or disability.

Types of grant

Grants are awarded towards the cost of home visits to individuals requiring medical assistance and Kosher food.

Applications

Apply in writing to the correspondent.

Financial information

Year end	31/12/2020
Income	£2,500
Total expenditure	£8,500

Further financial information

Full accounts were not available to view on the Charity Commission's website due to the fund's low income. We have therefore estimated the fund's grant total based on its total expenditure.

Other information

The fund also makes grants to organisations, namely to the Friends of the Sick (Chevrat Bikkur Cholim) charity in London, which supports members of the Jewish Community who have fallen ill.

Dame Alice Owen's Eleemosynary Charities

£ £5,400 (2020)

Correspondent: Livery Secretary, c/o The Brewers' Company, Brewers' Hall, Aldermanbury Square, London EC2V 7HR (tel: 020 7600 1801; email: liverysecretary@brewershall.co.uk)

 https://www.brewershall.co.uk

CC number: 215543

Eligibility

Older people in need who have lived in the parishes of St Mary's Islington, St James' Clerkenwell and Christ Church Spitalfields.

Types of grant

Grants are awarded according to need.

Applications

Apply in writing to the correspondent.

Financial information

Year end	31/12/2020
Income	£12,800
Total expenditure	£6,000

Further financial information

Full accounts were not available to view on the Charity Commission's website due to the charity's low income. We have therefore estimated the charity's grant total based on its total expenditure.

Other information

The Brewers' Company acts as a trustee for this charity and manages the charity's assets.

Pusinelli Convalescent and Holiday Home

£ £930 (2019/20)

Correspondent: The Trustees, c/o Leigh Saxton Green LLP, Mutual House, 70 Conduit Street, London W1S 2GF (tel: 020 7486 5553)

CC number: 239734

Eligibility

Women and children living in London, or its vicinity, who are in need. Priority is given to those born in Germany.

Types of grant

Grants are awarded to cover the cost of staying in a holiday home.

Applications

Apply in writing to the correspondent.

Financial information

Year end	29/08/2020
Income	£8,400
Total expenditure	£1,000

Further financial information

Full accounts were not available to view on the Charity Commission's website due to the charity's low income. We have therefore estimated the grant total based on the charity's total expenditure.

Scotscare

£ £434,200 (2019/20)

Correspondent: The Trustees, 22 City Road, London EC1Y 2AJ (tel: 0800 652 2989; email: info@scotscare.com)

 www.scotscare.com

CC number: 207326

Eligibility

Scottish people, and their children and widows, who are in need, hardship or distress and live within a 35-mile radius of Charing Cross.

Types of grant

Welfare
Grants to help with, for example, essential household items, family trips and children's items, such as clothing and school uniforms.

Education
Support is available to people training for a new job or attending further education.

Applications

Apply online via the charity's website.

Financial information

Year end	31/03/2020
Income	£2,740,000
Total expenditure	£2,680,000

Other information

In addition to making grants, Scotscare also offers a range of services for beneficiaries in the areas of advocacy, employment and training, families, health, housing, money management, mental health, socialising and substance misuse.

The Sheriffs' and Recorders' Fund

 £192,400 (2019/20)

Correspondent: Secretary, Central Criminal Court, Old Bailey, London EC4M 7EH (tel: 020 7192 2734 (Tuesdays and Wednesdays 11am until 4:45pm) or 020 7248 2739; email: srfundsec@yahoo.com)

 www.srfund.org.uk

CC number: 221927

Eligibility

People who are on probation in the Greater London area. Support is also available to the families of people who are currently serving prison sentences in Greater London.

Types of grant

Welfare

Welfare grants have been given towards white goods, electrical goods, furniture, clothing (particularly for job interviews) and tools required for a trade. Grants for days out and holidays are made to the dependent families of people currently in prison. Financial help is also given to families at Christmas.

Education

Educational grants are awarded to deter people on probation from reoffending. Grants have been made towards vocational training courses (such as forklift truck driving courses) and IT courses.

Applications

Contact the secretary for information on how to apply.

Financial information

Year end	31/03/2020
Income	£309,600
Total expenditure	£307,700

Further financial information

During the 2019/20 financial year, the charity awarded 1,336 grants to individuals. Grants were distributed as follows:

Clothing	£90,700
Furnishings	£69,900
Tools	£18,300
Training	£14,900
White goods	£9,300

Other information

This charity also makes grants to organisations, particularly to other voluntary organisations that work with ex-offenders and to prisons for mentoring projects and training/job opportunities.

Skinners' Benevolent Trust

 £31,400 (2019/20)

Correspondent: Grants Administrator, Skinners Hall, 8 Dowgate Hill, London EC4R 2SP (tel: 020 7213 5629; email: svalens@skinners.org.uk)

 https://www.skinners.org.uk/grants-and-trusts/skinners-benevolent-trust

CC number: 1132640

Eligibility

Applicants must live in an area where the Skinners' Company has existing work or historical links. These areas are The City of London (the Square Mile only); the boroughs of Camden, Enfield, Hackney and Hounslow; West Kent (Tonbridge and Tunbridge Wells); and Romney Marsh (Kent). The trust's main priority is to help:
- Those living with mental health issues
- Those in recovery from substance/alcohol use
- Victims of domestic violence
- Those in receipt of a state retirement pension
- Those who have some kind of disability or chronic illness
- Families with dependent children (under 18) who are on a very low income.

Types of grant

One-off grants of up to £250 towards essential household items such as white goods, furniture or children's items.

Exclusions

The trust cannot consider:
- Applications made directly by individuals
- Applications from organisations providing one-off support or advice
- Computers
- Mobility equipment
- Debts, payment of bills, or building modifications
- Items that have already been purchased.

The trust cannot help individuals who have received a grant in the previous two years.

Applications

Application forms are available from the Grants Administrator who can be contacted by email, phone or post. Applications must be made via referral from support agencies such as social and support services, housing associations, refuge and rehabilitation organisations and local charities. The charity has a helpful website that provides further information for potential applicants. Applications are considered throughout the year.

Financial information

Year end	30/06/2020
Income	£69,700
Total expenditure	£61,100

Further financial information

Grants were awarded to 138 individuals during the year.

Society for the Relief of Distress

 £40,900 (2020)

Correspondent: Hon. Secretary, 5 Cardinal Place, London SW15 1NX (tel: 020 7371 8544; email: info@reliefofdistress.org.uk)

 https://reliefofdistress.org.uk

CC number: 207585

Eligibility

People in need living within the City of London, the City of Westminster and the following boroughs of London: Camden; Greenwich; Hackney; Hammersmith and Fulham; Islington; Kensington and Chelsea; Lambeth; Lewisham; Southwark; Tower Hamlet; and Wandsworth.

Types of grant

Grants are aimed at relieving hardship, sickness and distress. The charity typically awards one-off grants towards essential personal and household items, such as clothing, bedding, baby items, cookers, fridges, furniture and floor coverings.

Applications

Applications can be sent in writing to the correspondent and must be made through a social services department, charity, NHS trust or faith institution. There is no formal application form; instead, a letter is required that must include a summary of your personal and financial circumstances, and the particular item or expense that needs to be incurred. For more details, visit the charity's website.

Financial information

Year end	31/12/2020
Income	£36,200
Total expenditure	£40,900

Further financial information

According to the 2020 accounts, approximately 212 grants were awarded during the year. Grants were broken down as follows:

Electrical goods	£9,700
Clothes	£8,300
Furniture	£8,100
IT	£5,800
Household items	£5,600
Baby items and school uniforms	£1,500
Flooring and decorating	£1,500
Other	£590

Society of Friends of Foreigners in Distress

£21,500 (2018/19)

Correspondent: Valerie Goodhart, Trustee, 68 Burhill Road, Hersham, Walton-on-Thames, Surrey KT12 4JF (tel: 01932 244916; email: vkgoodhart@gmail.com)

CC number: 212593

Eligibility

People living in London or its surrounding area who are in need and are from countries which are not in the Commonwealth or were not once part of the British Empire.

Types of grant

The charity awards pensions, one-off grants and repatriation assistance.

Applications

Apply in writing to the correspondent.

Financial information

Year end	30/09/2019
Income	£18,400
Total expenditure	£23,900

Further financial information

The 2018/19 financial information was the latest available at time of writing (November 2021). The charity was not required to file accounts for the 2018/19 financial year; therefore, we have estimated the grant total.

St Andrew Holborn and Stafford's Charity

£226,500 (2020)

Correspondent: Anna Paterson, Grants Officer, 5 St Andrew Street, London EC4A 3AF (tel: 020 7583 7394; email: charities@standrewholborn.org.uk)

www.standrewholborn.org.uk

CC number: 1095045

Eligibility

Welfare

People in need who live in a defined area of Holborn (a map of the eligible area is available on the charity's website).

Education

People in need who have lived in a defined area of Holborn for at least two years (a map of the eligible area is available on the charity's website).

Types of grant

Welfare

Grants are given for essential household items such as kitchen appliances, beds and furniture, bedding, school uniform and clothing. Support may occasionally be given for flooring/carpets.

Education

Grants are given for computers, books, travel and general maintenance.

Exclusions

Welfare

Grants will not be given towards rent or utility arrears, credit card debt, rental deposits, holidays, school fees or for goods or services already bought.

Education

Grants will not be given towards second degrees or postgraduate courses.

Applications

Application forms can be downloaded from the charity's website. Once an application is received, a home visit will be arranged with the grants officer. Applicants must be able to provide proof of income and expenditure. Only one application per individual will be considered in any 12-month period, and only two applications will be accepted over three years.

Financial information

Year end	31/12/2020
Income	£460,400
Total expenditure	£641,300

Further financial information

In 2020, a total of £226,500 was awarded to individuals. Within this, £157,000 was given as annual awards (these were of £750 per recipient, paid half in May and half in November); at 31 December, there were 205 annual awardees. Also, £69,500 was given in individual or household grants.

Other information

Grants are also given to organisations. In 2018, the St Andrew Holborn Charity and Stafford's Charity came together to form St Andrew Holborn and Stafford's Charity.

St Giles-in-the-Fields and Bloomsbury United Charity

£14,900 (2020)

Correspondent: Clerk to the Trustees, St Giles-in-the-Fields, 60 St Giles High Street, London WC2H 8LG (tel: 07960 691436; email: clerk@stgilesandstgeorge.org.uk)

www.stgilescharities.org.uk

CC number: 1111908

Eligibility

People in need who live in the ancient parishes of St Giles-in-the-Fields, St George's Bloomsbury and St Paul's Covent Garden. A map of the area of benefit is available on the website.

Types of grant

One-off grants, usually of £500, are given towards the purchase of white goods, furniture, bedding, clothing and medical equipment. Funding is also given towards secondary school uniforms and assisted living.

Exclusions

Grants are not given towards debts or holidays.

Applications

Application forms are available to download from the charity's website.

Financial information

Year end	31/12/2020
Income	£185,800
Total expenditure	£218,800

Other information

The charity also provides almshouse accommodation, consisting of eight flats, for women over the age of 60 in the Covent Garden area. The charity also makes grants to organisations.

St Sepulchre (Finsbury) United Charities

£47,200 (2019/20)

Correspondent: Elias Poli, Clerk, Suite 1, Unit 2, Stansted Courtyard, Parsonage Road, Takeley, Essex CM22 6PU (tel: 020 7253 3757)

CC number: 213312

Eligibility

People in need who live in, or have been formerly employed in, the ecclesiastical parish of St Sepulchre or the former metropolitan borough of Finsbury.

Types of grant

Grants are given according to need. The charity also awards quarterly pensions.

Applications

Grants from the charity are administered by the Cripplegate Foundation (Charity Commission no. 207499, see entry on page 313). Most beneficiaries are referred through the Islington Resident Support Scheme. Individuals who meet the eligibility criteria can also apply to the Cripplegate Foundation directly.

Financial information

Year end	31/03/2020
Income	£99,300
Total expenditure	£99,500

Further financial information

In 2019/20, grants to individuals totalled £29,300, and quarterly pensions totalled £17,900.

Other information

The charity also awards grants to organisations within the area.

Sutton Nursing Association

£ £18,100 (2019)

Correspondent: The Trustees, 28 Southway, Carshalton SM5 4HW (tel: 020 8770 1095)

CC number: 203686

Eligibility

People who are in poor health, require financial assistance and live in the London Borough of Sutton or the surrounding area.

Types of grant

Grants are given according to need.

Applications

Apply in writing to the correspondent.

Financial information

Year end	31/12/2019
Income	£22,400
Total expenditure	£40,200

Further financial information

Full accounts were not available to view on the Charity Commission's website due to the charity's low income. We have therefore estimated the charity's grant total based on its total expenditure.

Other information

This charity also supports organisations.

Miss Vaughan's Spitalfields Charity

£ £1,600 (2019/20)

Correspondent: The Trustees, 45 Quilter Street, Bethnal Green, London E2 7BS (tel: 020 7729 2790; email: missvaughancharity@gmail.com)

CC number: 262480

Eligibility

People in need who live in the ecclesiastical parishes of Christchurch with All Saints in Spitalfields, St Matthew's in Bethnal Green and St Leonard's in Shoreditch. Preference may be given to mechanics and weavers in Spitalfields who are unable to work due to illness or an accident.

Types of grant

Small grants according to need.

Applications

Apply in writing to the correspondent.

Financial information

Year end	31/03/2020
Income	£1,400
Total expenditure	£1,700

Further financial information

Full accounts were not available to view on the Charity Commission's website due to the charity's low income. We have therefore estimated the grant total based on the charity's total expenditure.

The Charity of Sir Richard Whittington

£ £192,900 (2019/20)

Correspondent: The Trustees, c/o The Mercers' Company, 6 Frederick's Place, London EC2R 8AB (tel: 020 7726 4991; email: info@mercers.co.uk)

 https://www.mercers.co.uk/philanthropy

CC number: 1087167

Eligibility

Older people living in London who are in need.

Types of grant

Grants are awarded according to need.

Applications

All information (including guidelines and notes on exclusions) is available on The Mercers' Company website (www.mercers.co.uk/philanthropy). Note: only applications made using the application form on the website are accepted.

Financial information

Year end	31/03/2020
Income	£3,950,000
Total expenditure	£4,670,000

Further financial information

The charity made 163 grants to individuals during the year.

Other information

The Charity of Sir Richard Whittington was established by the English merchant and politician Richard Whittington. The Mercers' Company was entrusted with the care of the charity in 1424 and remains the trustee of the charity.

Barnet

The Mayor of Barnet's Benevolent Fund

£ £19,300 (2019/20)

Correspondent: Ken Argent, Grants Manager, London Borough of Barnet, 2 Bristol Avenue, London NW9 4EW (tel: 020 8359 2020; email: ken.argent@barnet.gov.uk)

 https://www.barnet.gov.uk/benefits-and-grants/grants-and-funding/apply-mayors-benevolent-fund

CC number: 1014273

Eligibility

People who have lived in the London Borough of Barnet for at least a year and are in need. Applicants must be on an income-related statutory benefit (such as Income Support).

Types of grant

Small one-off grants are given towards essential household appliances (such as cookers, refrigerators and washing machines), furnishing or equipping a new property (up to £200), school uniforms (up to £100 per child), essential items for families with a new baby, clothing for adults and support for financial hardship arising from unforeseen circumstances. Applicants can receive a maximum of two awards from the charity.

Exclusions

Children attending schools that operate their own schemes of financial assistance to parents in need will not be supported.

Applications

Apply in writing to the correspondent via email or post. Applications can be submitted directly by the individual or through a third party, such as a social worker, health visitor or an advice agency. Candidates should provide full details of their name, address, contact number, confirmation and length of residence in the borough, the number and ages of the family members, family income, proof of entitlement to a benefit, a summary of the applicant's circumstances, details of the support requested, a quotation for any items required and information on other sources of funding approached.

Financial information

Year end	31/03/2020
Income	£6,600
Total expenditure	£21,400

Further financial information

Full accounts were not available to view on the Charity Commission's website due to the charity's low income. We have therefore estimated the charity's grant total based on its total expenditure.

Jesus Hospital in Chipping Barnet

 £1,700 (2020)

Correspondent: The Trustees, Ravenscroft Lodge, 37 Union Street, Barnet, Hertfordshire EN5 4HY (tel: 020 8440 4374; email: info@ jesushospitalcharity.org.uk)

 www.jesushospitalcharity.org.uk

CC number: 1075889

Eligibility

People in need living in High Barnet, New Barnet, East Barnet and Friern Barnet.

Types of grant

Grants are given according to need.

Exclusions

Grants are not given for paying bills, arrears or salaries.

Applications

Apply on a form which can be downloaded from the charity's website. Applications are considered by the trustees, who meet every other month. Applicants may be visited by the clerk.

Financial information

Year end	31/12/2020
Income	£780,400
Total expenditure	£561,000

Other information

Grants are also made to organisations.

The Mayor's Benevolent Fund (Barnet)

Correspondent: Ken Argent, Grants Manager, Barnet Council, 2 Bristol Avenue, Colindale NW9 4EW (tel: 020 8359 2020; email: ken.argent@barnet. gov.uk)

 https://www.barnet.gov.uk/citizen-home/council-tax-and-benefits/grants-and-funding/grants-for-individuals.html

Eligibility

Residents of the London Borough of Barnet who are in financial need and have lived in the borough for at least a year and are on income-related statutory welfare benefits, such as Universal Credit.

Types of grant

Grants are awarded for the following:

- **Household goods** – help (of up to £200) is given for purchasing or replacing household appliances, such as a cooker, refrigerator or washing machine, or furnishing or equipping a new property (sourcing recycled items where possible).
- **School uniforms** – for children transferring from primary to secondary school or starting a new secondary school (up to £100 per child).
- **Clothing** – for adults with exceptional needs, such as an illness or medical condition/treatment.
- **Baby essentials** – essential items for families with new babies.
- **Relieving a financial crisis** – where financial hardship has arisen from an unforeseen circumstance.

Exclusions

Applicants can only get up to two awards from the fund. Schools uniform grants cannot be awarded when the child's school operates its own scheme for financial help.

Applications

Apply in writing to the correspondent. Details of what should be included in the application can be found on the council's website. Applications can also be accepted from a third party, such as a social worker or an advice agency.

Further financial information

Financial information was not available for the fund.

Other information

The fund is not a registered charity.

Eleanor Palmer Trust

 £43,400 (2019/20)

Correspondent: Chief Executive, 106B Wood Street, Barnet EN5 4BY (tel: 020 8441 3222; email: admin@ eleanorpalmertrust.org.uk)

 www.eleanorpalmertrust.org.uk

CC number: 220857

Eligibility

People in need who live in the former urban districts of Chipping Barnet and East Barnet. This area of benefit includes the postal codes of EN4, EN5, and part of N11 and N14. Applicants must have lived within the area for at least two years prior to submitting an application.

Types of grant

Grants are given towards the purchase of white goods and furniture.

Exclusions

No grants are available towards educational purposes, loans, settlement of debts or direct financial payments.

Applications

Application forms are available for download from the trust's website, or from the correspondent. A guide to the trust's grants is also available online.

Financial information

Year end	31/03/2020
Income	£2,330,000
Total expenditure	£1,980,000

Other information

The principal activity of the trust is providing accommodation, either within its nursing and residential care homes or in the form of sheltered housing. The trust also supports other organisations.

The Valentine Poole Charity

 £37,000 (2020)

Correspondent: The Trustees, Ewen Church Hall, Wood Street, Barnet, Hertfordshire EN5 4BW (tel: 020 8441 6893; email: clerk@valentinepoole.org. uk)

 www.valentinepoole.org.uk

CC number: 220856

Eligibility

People in need who live in Barnet, East Barnet and Chipping Barnet.

Types of grant

One-off grants are given towards essential items such as household goods, travel and school uniform costs. Pensions of £120 to £160 a month are made to older people in need. Christmas grants are also made to families at Christmas.

Applications

Applications can be made in writing to the correspondent.

Financial information

Year end		31/12/2020
Income		£60,200
Total expenditure		£61,100

Brent

Wembley Compassionate Fund

 £4,100 (2020)

Correspondent: The Trustees, St George's Catholic Church, 970 Harrow Road, Wembley, Middlesex HA0 2QE (tel: 07955 431581; email: secretary@wembleycompassionatefund. co.uk)

wembleycompassionatefund.co.uk

CC number: 211887

Eligibility

People in need living in the following Brent wards: Alperton, Barnhill, Kenton, Northwick Park, Preston, Sudbury, Tokyngton and Wembley Central.

Types of grant

Grants can be given towards essential household goods and appliances, assistance for carers, clothing and food. Funding is also given for school necessities such as uniforms, books, shoes and essential school trips.

Exclusions

Grants cannot be given towards the payment of arrears.

Applications

Application forms can be completed online on the fund's website. Applications must be submitted by a professional, such as a teacher, lawyer, doctor, therapist, legal representative, religious leader, social worker, local councillor or district nurse. Applications submitted by the individual will not be considered.

Financial information

Year end		31/12/2020
Income		£4,500
Total expenditure		£4,600

Further financial information

Full accounts were not available to view on the Charity Commission's website due to the fund's low income. We have therefore estimated the fund's grant total based on its total expenditure.

Bromley

Bromley Relief in Need Charity

 £8,100 (2019)

Correspondent: Mark Gill, Trustee, 53 Cloisters Avenue, Bromley, Kent BR2 8AN (tel: 020 8467 1260; email: mark.gill19@btinternet.com or bromleyrelief@gmail.com)

bromleyrelief.weebly.com

CC number: 262591

Eligibility

Residents of, or people who have a connection with, the ancient borough of Bromley who are in need. At the trustees' discretion, support may be extended to those living in the wider area of the modern borough of Bromley.

Types of grant

One-off grants of up to £300 are given for essential items. Recent examples of support include beds, bedding, white goods, vouchers towards decorating costs, travel expenses and stair gates.

Applications

Applications can be made on the funder's website using an online form. Applications must be made by a recognised third party (such as a social worker, healthcare professional, religious leader or representative from a voluntary organisation) on the individual's behalf. Once an application is made, the third party must send a brief email to bromleyrelief@gmail.com to confirm that they have made an application.

Financial information

Year end		31/12/2019
Income		£5,700
Total expenditure		£9,000

Further financial information

Full accounts were not available to view on the Charity Commission's website due to the charity's low income. We have therefore estimated the charity's grant total based on its total expenditure.

The Hayes (Kent) Trust

 £7,700 (2019/20)

Correspondent: The Trustees, 2 Warren Wood Close, Bromley, Kent BR2 7DU (tel: 020 8462 1915; email: hayes.kent. trust@gmail.com)

CC number: 221098

Eligibility

People in need who live in the parish of Hayes.

Types of grant

Grants are given according to need.

Applications

Apply in writing to the correspondent. The trustees meet six times a year to review applications.

Financial information

Year end		31/03/2020
Income		£54,800
Total expenditure		£55,300

Other information

The trust is an amalgamation of The Poors Land Cottage Charity, The Poors Land Eleemosynary Charity and The Hayes (Kent) Educational Foundation. It also awards grants to organisations.

Camden

Hampstead Wells and Campden Trust

£193,400 (2019/20)

Correspondent: Joanna Goga, Grants and Development Officer, 62 Rosslyn Hill, London NW3 1ND (tel: 020 7435 1570; email: grant@hwct.co.uk or joanna@hwct.co.uk)

www.hwct.org.uk

CC number: 1094611

Eligibility

Individuals and families in need who live in the former metropolitan borough of Hampstead. Individuals can check that their address is included in the trust's area of benefit using the map available on the trust's website.

Types of grant

Grants of up to a maximum of £1,000 are given for a range of purposes including for household items such as household appliances, furniture, children's items, one-off debts, clothing, travel costs and so on. In addition, seasonal Christmas vouchers are given to families in need, and the trust also offers household starter packs containing essential items for people setting up their first home.

Exclusions

The trust cannot usually cover rent arrears.

Applications

Application forms for individual grants can be downloaded from the trust's website. Applications must be made on behalf of the applicant by a local constituted group, departments/units of Camden Council or the health service, a housing association, advice agency or another voluntary agency to which the individual or family is known. Applications can be made at any time. For further information about seasonal vouchers and household starter packs, contact the correspondent.

Financial information

Year end	30/09/2020
Income	£390,600
Total expenditure	£495,200

Further financial information

During the year, 776 grants totalling £105,400 were awarded to individuals for welfare purposes, and seven grants totalling £3,100 were awarded for educational purposes. In addition, pension payments were awarded to 91 individuals totalling £84,900. The 2019/20 accounts provide the following breakdown of grants:

Pensions	91	£84,900
Furniture and starter packs	194	£54,700
Christmas vouchers	500	£15,600
COVID-19 emergency grants	9	£11,500
Other	24	£11,400
Clothing	26	£6,700
Education	7	£3,100
Help with debts	12	£2,600
Baby items	4	£1,400
Gas, electricity and fuel	2	£700
TV and phone	2	£350
Removals and transport	1	£200
Holidays	1	£150
Medical	1	£90

Other information

Historically, the trust has offered a pension award scheme, which provides support to older people in need with regular additions to their income. At the time of writing (August 2021) the trust's website stated that it would not be able to offer any new pension awards for the foreseeable future. Check the website for updates.

The trust also makes grants to organisations (16 grants totalling £130,500 in 2019/20).

St Pancras Welfare Trust

 £106,300 (2019/20)

Correspondent: The Trustees, PO Box 51764, London NW1 1EA (email: spwtrust@gmail.com)

www.spwt.org.uk

CC number: 261261

Eligibility

People who are experiencing ill health or other medical conditions, or those who are in financial need, living in the former borough of St Pancras. A map listing all qualifying streets can be seen on the trust's website.

Types of grant

One-off grants according to need.

Applications

Application forms are available to download on the funder's website and once completed, can be sent to the trust via email. All applications must be made on the individual's behalf by a sponsoring organisation such as Citizens Advice or voluntary organisation. Applications are considered monthly. The trust asks that applications are made by the 12th of each month.

Financial information

Year end	31/03/2020
Income	£123,600
Total expenditure	£130,200

Further financial information

The charity made 358 grants during the year.

City of London

Cripplegate Foundation

 £55,000 (2019)

Correspondent: The Trustees, 13 Elliott's Place, Islington, London N1 8HX (tel: 020 7288 6940; email: grants@cripplegate.org.uk)

www.cripplegate.org

CC number: 207499

Eligibility

The foundation works to bring about change that will transform the lives of disadvantaged residents in Islington and the Cripplegate ward. Applicants must be in receipt of specified benefits. Full details of eligibility criteria are available from the Cripplegate Foundation website.

Types of grant

The foundation offers grants through Islington's Residents Support Scheme (RSS) managed by Islington Council. The RSS may be able to assist with the payment of household items (fridges, beds, etc.), short-term housing costs, support with Council Tax payments, and one-off awards for food and fuel during immediate crisis.

Applications

The foundation now contributes to this scheme rather than awarding individual grants. Individuals cannot apply directly to the RSS; instead, applications are usually made through statutory services or participating community organisations. For a full list of organisations that can apply with you, email ResidentSupportTeam@islington.gov.uk.

Financial information

Year end	31/12/2019
Income	£2,350,000
Total expenditure	£2,490,000

Further financial information

No grants were awarded to individuals in 2020; therefore, the 2019 annual report was used instead.

Other information

The foundation also supports organisations through Islington Council's Community Chest.

Emanuel Hospital

 £34,800 (2019/20)

Correspondent: Gregory Moore, City of London Corporation, Aldermanbury, London EC2V 7HH (tel: 020 7332 1399; email: gregory.moore@cityoflondon.gov.uk)

www.cityoflondon.gov.uk/about-the-city/what-we-do/Pages/trusts-charities-awards.aspx

CC number: 206952

Eligibility

People who are 60 years of age or older and are in need by reason of poverty, old age, ill health, accident or infirmity. Applicants must have lived in the London boroughs of Kensington and Chelsea, Hillingdon or Westminster for at least two years.

Types of grant

Pensions together with Christmas bonuses. One-off grants are also available for essential household items.

Applications

Application forms can be requested over the phone.

Financial information

Year end	31/03/2020
Income	£415,300
Total expenditure	£37,200

Lady Elizabeth Hatton's Charity

(£) £1,200 (2020)

Correspondent: Anna Paterson, Grants Officer, 5 St Andrew Street, London EC4A 3AF (tel: 020 7583 7394; email: charities@standrewholborn.org.uk)

 www.standrewholborn.org.uk

CC number: 213720

Eligibility

Residents of the ancient parish of St Andrew Holborn who are in need. See the charity's website for a map of the beneficial area.

Types of grant

Welfare

One-off grants according to need. Most grants are given for household items such as kitchen appliances, essential furniture, bedding, carpets, school uniform and clothing. Requests for a contribution towards flooring/carpet are considered on an exceptional basis only.

Education

The charity's website states: 'Typically grants issued for educational reasons are for computers, books, travel, and general maintenance.'

Exclusions

The charity is unable to consider applications for the following:

- Debt relief including rent or utility arrears
- Credit card debt
- Rental deposits
- Holidays
- Removal costs
- School fees
- Goods or services already bought

Applications

Application forms are available to download from the charity's website and can be returned by email or post. All eligible applicants will be contacted by the Grants Officer. Only one application will be considered in any 12-month period, and only two applications can be submitted over three years.

Financial information

Year end	31/12/2020
Income	£6,500
Total expenditure	£2,700

Further financial information

Full accounts were not available to view on the Charity Commission's website due to the charity's low income. We have therefore estimated the charity's grant total based on its total expenditure.

Other information

The charity also makes grants to organisations to support the development of projects, especially through the use of church sites, for the benefit of the community.

Mitchell City of London Charity

(£) £14,600 (2019/20)

Correspondent: Lucy Jordan, Clerk to the Trustees, 24 Station Lane, Holme-on-Spalding-Moor, York YO43 4AL (tel: 01430 860089; email: mitchellcityoflondon@gmail.com)

CC number: 207342

Eligibility

Individuals of state pension age who are in need and who live or work, or have lived or worked, in the City of London for at least five years. Widows and children of such individuals are also eligible. According to the charity's Charity Commission record, there may be exceptions for people slightly below the state pension age.

Types of grant

The charity awards pensions, which are usually paid at £400 per annum, in quarterly sums of £100. Gifts are also given at Christmas (£150) and on the Queen's birthday (£150).

Exclusions

The charity's definition of the 'City of London' includes almost all of EC3 and EC4, and a small area of EC1 and EC2, but not Greater London.

Applications

Apply in writing to the correspondent.

Financial information

Year end	31/03/2020
Income	£86,900
Total expenditure	£58,400

Further financial information

In 2019/20, pensions were awarded to 19 individuals (£400 per year). A Christmas grant of £150 and a grant of £150 to celebrate the Queen's birthday were also paid to each individual.

During the year the charity also made a donation of £2,500 to the Providence Row Charity and transferred £41,300 to the Mitchell City of London Educational Foundation; these grants have not been included in the grant total.

Other information

The charity is one half of the Mitchell City of London Charity and Educational Foundation. See the entry for the Mitchell City of London Educational Foundation below.

Mitchell City of London Educational Foundation

(£) £65,400 (2019/20)

Correspondent: Lucy Jordan, Clerk to the Trustees, 24 Station Lane, Holme-on-Spalding-Moor, York, North Yorkshire YO43 4AL (tel: 01430 860089; email: mitchellcityoflondon@gmail.com)

CC number: 312499

Eligibility

People aged 11 to 19 who are either attending school in the City of London or whose parents have lived or worked there for at least five years. The City of London is defined as the area comprising almost all of EC3 and EC4, and a small area of EC1 and EC2.

Types of grant

Welfare

Grants are awarded to secondary school students who come from single-parent families and students are usually supported up to their GCSE examinations.

Education

Bursaries are awarded to students studying for their A-level or International Baccalaureate qualifications. The foundation grants Diploma Awards of £2,500 to students in need.

Applications

Apply in writing to the correspondent.

Financial information

Year end	31/03/2020
Income	£79,500
Total expenditure	£82,100

North London Welfare and Educational Foundation

(£) £1,230,000 (2019/20)

Correspondent: The Trustees, 44 Warwick Avenue, Edgware, Middlesex HA8 8UJ (tel: 020 8905 4766)

CC number: 1155103

Eligibility

People in need living primarily, but not exclusively, in North London.

Types of grant

Grants are given according to need.

Applications

Apply in writing to the correspondent.

Financial information

Year end	31/05/2020
Income	£1,870,000
Total expenditure	£1,770,000

Other information

This foundation also makes grants to education and welfare organisations.

St John Southworth Caritas Fund

 £190,000 (2019)

Correspondent: The Trustees, Diocese of Westminster, Vaughan House, 46 Francis Street, London SW1P 1QN (tel: 020 7798 9009)

https://www.caritaswestminster.org. uk/home.php

CC number: 233699

Eligibility

People in need living in the Diocese of Westminster.

Types of grant

One-off crisis grants, of between £30 and £1,500, are given for urgent items such as furniture, white good, carpets, clothing, training costs, medical needs and respite breaks. Grants of up to £1,500 are also awarded to assist with funeral costs.

Applications

Application forms can be downloaded from the website and should be completed by the applicant's parish priest. Completed application forms should be returned via post, or via email to caritasgrants@rcdow.org.uk.

Financial information

Year end	31/12/2019
Income	£50,080,000
Total expenditure	£44,360,000

Further financial information

The 2019 accounts were the latest available to view at the time of writing (November 2021). In 2019, 39 emergency grants were made to families or individuals in extreme hardship, and 41 grants were awarded to cover funeral costs when the family of the deceased was unable to do so.

Other information

The charity offers a variety of services to people in need living in the area of benefit. These include Caritas St Joseph's school for people with learning difficulties, Caritas Deaf Service, which helps those who are hard of hearing take part in church life, and Caritas Bakhita House, a refuge for women escaping human trafficking.

City of Westminster

Westminster Almshouses Foundation

 £47,100 (2020)

Correspondent: Naomi Roper, Clerk to the Trustees, Palmers House, 42 Rochester Row, London SW1P 1BU (tel: 020 7828 3131; email: clerk@ westminsteralmshouses.com)

www.westminsteralmshouses.com

CC number: 226936

Eligibility

Men and women in need living in Westminster or Greater London. In exceptional cases, support is extended to women throughout the UK.

Types of grant

One-off grants of up to £500 are given to individuals who require white goods and flooring to set up new tenancies. Grants are also made towards rent arrears.

Applications

Contact the correspondent via email to obtain an application form. Decisions are usually made within ten working days.

Financial information

Year end	31/12/2020
Income	£769,200
Total expenditure	£907,900

Other information

The priority of the charity is to provide warden-assisted sheltered housing to residents of Westminster who have lived in the city for the last ten years and are aged over 60 years. The cost of living at the almshouses is subsidised. The charity also makes larger grants of up to £30,000 to local organisations.

The Arthur Cross Charity

 £7,200 (2019/20)

Correspondent: The Trustees, The Vestry, St Michael's Church, Chester Square, London SW1W 9EF (tel: 07970 860685)

CC number: 210466

Eligibility

Residents of the ecclesiastical parish of St Michael (Chester Square) who are in need as a result of illness, disability or a medical condition.

Types of grant

Grants are given according to need.

Applications

Apply in writing to the correspondent.

Financial information

Year end	31/03/2020
Income	£6,700
Total expenditure	£8,000

Further financial information

Full accounts were not available to view on the Charity Commission's website due to the charity's low income. We have therefore estimated the charity's grant total based on its total expenditure.

Hyde Park Place Estate Charity

 £16,800 (2019/20)

Correspondent: Shirley Vaughan, Clerk to the Trustees, St George's Hanover Square, The Vestry, 2A Mill Street, London W1S 1FX (tel: 020 7629 0874; email: hppec@stgeorgeshanoversquare. org)

www.stgeorgeshanoversquare.org

CC number: 212439

Eligibility

People in need who live in the City of Westminster.

Types of grant

Small grants in the region of £50 to £200 are given to individuals in need.

Applications

Apply in writing to the correspondent. Applications should be made by a recognised welfare organisation on behalf of the individual or family.

Financial information

Year end	25/03/2020
Income	£628,600
Total expenditure	£586,300

Other information

The charity also supports organisations and churches in the area. In addition, discretionary grants are given to clergy working in local churches.

St Marylebone Educational Foundation

 £31,400 (2019/20)

Correspondent: Caroline Grant, Clerk to the Trustees, 12 Melcombe Place, Marylebone Station, Marylebone, London NW1 6JJ (tel: 020 7139 5017; email: applications@ stmaryboneeducationalfoundation.org)

https://stmaryleboneeducational
foundation.org

CC number: 312378

Eligibility

Young people under the age of 25 who have received primary or secondary education in the City of Westminster and young people who live, or whose parents have lived, in the area for at least two years. Preference is given to those in the old London Borough of St Marylebone and to individuals who are experiencing unforeseen circumstances which are affecting their financial situation or for whom boarding school is a preferred option due to a parental illness or specific educational need. Assistance is also given to students who have studied at the Royal Academy of Music or the Royal College of Music.

Types of grant

School fees (see the website for specific eligibility criteria) and financial assistance for uniforms, clothing, tools, instruments, books and laptops are given to assist with education, including the study of music and other arts. Grants can also be awarded for extracurricular activities, such as music lessons. Financial assistance can also be given to those at the specified music institutions.

Exclusions

Grants are not given for further/higher education.

Applications

To apply, first complete an expression of interest form through the website. If you are eligible, the clerk will send an application form. Postgraduate students should apply through one of the specified schools.

Financial information

Year end	31/08/2020
Income	£264,900
Total expenditure	£241,600

Further financial information

Grants were paid to ten individuals in 2019/20.

Other information

The foundation also awards capital grants to Westminster-based schools and organisations (£180,900 in 2019/20).

The United Charities of St Paul's Covent Garden

£ £5,200 (2019/20)

Correspondent: Maggie Rae, Flat 9, 19 Henrietta Street, London WC2E 8QH (tel: 020 3871 2906; email: mrae@ clintons.co.uk)

CC number: 209568

Eligibility

People in need who live in the City of Westminster.

Types of grant

One-off grants are awarded.

Applications

Apply in writing to the correspondent.

Financial information

Year end	22/01/2020
Income	£5,900
Total expenditure	£5,800

Further financial information

Full accounts were not available to view on the Charity Commission's website due to the charity's low income. We have therefore estimated the charity's grant total based on its total expenditure.

Strand Parishes Trust

 £23,400 (2020)

Correspondent: Roy Sully, Clerk to the Trustees, 169 Strand, London WC2R 2LS (tel: 020 7848 4275; email: sptwestminster@aol.com)

 www.strandparishestrust.org.uk

CC number: 1121754

Eligibility

Welfare

People who are disadvantaged through physical or mental disability or financial hardship and who live and/or work in the City of Westminster.

Education

People under the age of 25 who have lived or worked in Westminster and are seeking advancement in life through education or training.

Types of grant

Welfare

Grants of between £50 and £500 are given according to need. The average grant is of £250.

Education

Small grants of up to £500 are available for educational needs such as books, tools, instruments and essential equipment and clothing.

Exclusions

Welfare

Grants are not given for holidays abroad or towards the clearance of debt. Multiple applications within a 12-month period are not usually considered apart from in exceptional circumstances.

Education

Grants are not given towards medical or dental electives, private school fees or postgraduate study.

Applications

Application forms are available to download from the trust's website or can be requested from the correspondent. For welfare grants, applications must be supported by a sponsor, such as social services or Citizens Advice.

Financial information

Year end	31/12/2020
Income	£244,100
Total expenditure	£242,900

Further financial information

During 2020, grants totalling £10,000 were made to 31 individuals. Additionally, the trust provided pensions totalling £13,400.

Other information

The Isaac Duckett's Charity, St Mary le Strand Charity and St Clement Danes Parochial Charities were amalgamated with other charities to form the Strand Parishes Trust.

Westminster Amalgamated Charity

£ £35,600 (2019)

Correspondent: Julia Moorcroft, School House, Drury Lane, London WC2B 5SU (tel: 020 7395 9460; email: wac@3chars. org.uk)

 www.w-a-c.org.uk

CC number: 207964

Eligibility

People who live, work or study in the borough of Westminster, and people who have lived, worked or studied in Westminster for at least five years. Grants are awarded to those on low incomes or in receipt of benefits, those with disabilities on a low income, and those without a permanent residence who are currently residing in a hostel.

Types of grant

One-off grants of between £100 and £400 are awarded for clothing, household items (such as white goods and furniture), decor (including carpets and flooring) and UK holidays (for over 60s only). If the grant is for household repairs or items, the money will be paid directly to the supplier.

Exclusions

Grants will not be given for: TVs; CD/DVD players; mobile phones; computers/software; educational needs; holidays abroad; debt repayment or fees.

No retrospective or emergency grants will be awarded.

Applications

Application forms are available to download from the charity's website and must be sponsored by a recognised agency, such as social services or Citizens Advice. Applicants are expected to have sought out all the statutory support to which they may be entitled before applying.

Financial information

Year end	31/12/2019
Income	£354,800
Total expenditure	£425,100

Further financial information

During 2019, 125 grants were awarded; they were distributed as follows:

Discretionary	63	£15,800
Household	42	£14,400
Holidays	9	£3,900
Clothing	10	£1,300
Other	1	200

Other information

The charity also makes grants to local organisations in the area.

Ealing

Acton (Middlesex) Charities – Relief in Need Fund

 £7,900 (2019)

Correspondent: Julian Gallant, Clerk to the Trustees, c/o St Mary's Parish Office, 1 The Mount, Acton High Street, London W3 8HA (email: actoncharities@gmail.com)

www.actoncharities.co.uk

CC number: 211446

Eligibility

People in need who have lived in the former ancient parish of Acton for at least three years can apply to the Relief in Need Fund. The John Perryn Relief in Need Fund considers applicants who have lived in the parish for less than three years.

Types of grant

The John Perryn Relief in Need Fund awards grants according to need. The Relief in Need Fund awards grants for furniture, white goods and other household items.

Exclusions

The charity cannot support anyone outside the area of benefit (a map is available to view on the charity's website).

Applications

Application forms are available from the charity's website or the correspondent; however, referrals must be made by a professional third party, such as a doctor, district health visitor or social services.

Financial information

Year end	31/12/2019
Income	£8,700
Total expenditure	£7,900

Further financial information

Full accounts were not available to view on the Charity Commission's website due to the fund's low income. We have therefore estimated the grant total based on the fund's total expenditure.

Other information

This charity, together with Acton (Middlesex) Educational Charity (Charity Commission no. 312312), is one of the Acton (Middlesex) Charities. The charities are administered by the same body of trustees and provide welfare, educational and arts grants.

The Ealing Aid-in-Sickness Trust

 £3,700 (2019/20)

Correspondent: The Trustees, The William Hobbayne Community Centre, St Dunstan's Road, London W7 2HB (tel: 020 8810 0277; email: hobbaynecharity@btinternet.com)

www.williamhobbaynecharity.co.uk/causes/grants

CC number: 212826

Eligibility

People in need who live in the London Borough of Ealing (this includes Hanwell, Ealing, Greenford, Perivale and Northolt) and are incurring extra expenses due to a long- or short-term medical condition.

Types of grant

Grants are awarded according to need, to assist with the extra costs incurred through illness.

Exclusions

Grants are not awarded to individuals living in Acton or Southall.

Applications

Application forms are available from the correspondent. Applications must be made through a sponsor. Sponsors may include social service officers, school administrators, medical practitioners or members of the clergy.

Financial information

Year end	30/09/2020
Income	£5,100
Total expenditure	£4,100

Further financial information

Full accounts were not available to view on the Charity Commission's website due to the trust's low income. We have therefore estimated the trust's grant total based on its total expenditure.

Other information

The trust is one of three schemes, alongside The Eleemosynary Charity of William Hobbayne, and The Educational Foundation of William Hobbayne.

The Eleemosynary Charity of William Hobbayne

 £30,300 (2019/20)

Correspondent: The Trustees, The William Hobbayne Centre, St Dunstan's Road, London W7 2HB (tel: 020 8810 0277; email: anita@williamhobbaynecharity.co.uk)

www.williamhobbaynecharity.co.uk

CC number: 211547

Eligibility

Primarily people in need who live in the civil parish of Hanwell (the W7 postcode).

Types of grant

One-off grants are given for clothing, furniture and domestic appliances. Grants are paid directly to the sponsors or suppliers.

Applications

Apply on a form available from the correspondent, to be submitted through third-party sponsors such as social services officers, members of the clergy, school teachers/administrators or medical practitioners.

Financial information

Year end	30/09/2020
Income	£229,200
Total expenditure	£196,500

Other information

The charity is one of three schemes, alongside The Ealing Aid in Sickness Trust and The Educational Foundation of William Hobbayne. The charity owns the William Hobbayne Centre, which runs activities and events for local people. It also has an outreach worker who, aside from encouraging grant applications, organises Christmas toy collections in more affluent parts of Hanwell for redistribution to families with difficult financial circumstances and works with foodbanks. The charity also supports people who are experiencing homelessness and helps young people in gaining work experience.

Enfield

Edmonton Aid-in-Sickness and Nursing Fund

 £9,000 (2020)

Correspondent: The Secretary, 21 Cheyne Walk, London N21 1DP (tel: 07956 370615; email: secretary@eais. org.uk)

https://eais.org.uk

CC number: 210623

Eligibility

People in need who are in poor health (physically or mentally) and live in the old borough of Edmonton (mainly the N9 and N18 postcodes). The fund also covers a very small part of Bush Hill Park and the eastern edge of Winchmore Hill.

Types of grant

Grants are given according to need. Examples of support include special food, medicine, medical equipment, furniture, fuel, white goods, special clothing and rehabilitation or respite.

Applications

Applications can be made by email to the correspondent, either directly by the individual or through a third party. Details of what to include can be found on the website.

Financial information

Year end	31/12/2020
Income	£7,900
Total expenditure	£10,000

Further financial information

Full accounts were not available to view on the Charity Commission's website due to the fund's low income. We have therefore estimated the fund's grant total based on its total expenditure.

The Old Enfield Charitable Trust

 £245,900 (2019/20)

Correspondent: The Trust Team, 22 The Town, Enfield, Middlesex EN2 6LT (tel: 020 8367 8941; email: enquiries@ thetrustenfield.org.uk)

https://www.thetrustenfield.org.uk

CC number: 207840

Eligibility

People who live in the ancient parish of Enfield and are in need. Beneficiaries can include individuals who are undertaking further education or training. An eligibility checker is available to use on the trust's website. In exceptional circumstances, the trustees may award a grant to an applicant living outside the ancient parish of Enfield.

Types of grant

Welfare

One-off grants are given to help with unexpected expenses, household goods, furniture, bedding and items to support individuals with disabilities and chronic illnesses.

Education

Grants are given to assist with living costs, equipment, childcare, travel and other educational expenses to help the individual complete their course.

Exclusions

The trust will not provide support where local authority or central government should be assisting.

Applications

Application forms and further guidance can be found on the trust's website.

Financial information

Year end	31/03/2020
Income	£648,700
Total expenditure	£724,700

Other information

The trust makes community grants to local organisations and manages Enfield Market Place. The trust also administers Ann Crowe's and Wright's Almshouse Charity, and administers two sets of almshouses.

Greenwich

Sir William Boreman's Foundation

 £45,500 (2019/20)

Correspondent: Clerk to the Trustees, The Drapers' Company, Drapers' Hall, Throgmorton Avenue, London EC2N 2DQ (tel: 020 7588 5001; email: charities@thedrapers.co.uk)

https://thedrapers.co.uk/sir-william-boremans-foundation

CC number: 312796

Eligibility

Young people who are permanent residents in Greenwich and Lewisham, are full or part-time students, aged below 25 and from a low-income/disadvantaged background. The young

person's annual gross household income must be of £30,000 or less. The young person must be a UK national or have settled status under the terms of the Immigration Act 1971. Preference is given to practising members of the Church of England and to sons and daughters of seamen, watermen and fishermen, particularly those who have served in the armed forces.

Types of grant

Social welfare

Small hardship grants are awarded to under 16s and can be used for:

- School uniform and sports kits
- Travel costs to and from school
- School trips that are part of the curriculum
- Other necessary educational expenses

These grants are awarded to primary and secondary schoolchildren through block grants administered on behalf of the foundation by the relevant Attendance and Inclusion Department at Greenwich and Lewisham councils.

Education

Grants of up to £3,000 per year are awarded to over 16s in further, higher or postgraduate education and can be used to help cover expenses while continuing study, including:

- Daily living costs such as rent and food
- Travel costs to and from college or university
- Educational materials, books and equipment
- Childcare costs

Grants are made towards expenses in the current academic year only.

Exclusions

Grants are not made for:

- A-level studies (except for post-19-year-old students)
- Qualifications below Level 4
- Students aged over 25 or pre-schoolchildren
- Non-UK citizens or individuals without settled status under the terms of the Immigration Act 1971
- Postgraduate students who have attained a 2.2 or lower in their undergraduate degree
- Overseas study/travel or exchange visits
- Retrospective appeals
- Tuition fees
- Loans or debts that are not related to education
- Setting up business ventures
- Independent school fees

Applications

To apply for a grant for a primary or secondary school student, contact the local (Greenwich/Lewisham) Attendance and Welfare Services. Details can be found on the foundation's website.

Application forms for young people aged between 16 and 25 can be found on the website along with the guidelines for applicants. Applications can be submitted at any time. The trustees meet three times a year, in November, February and May. Check the website to see the next meeting dates – applications should be submitted at least three weeks before these meeting dates.

Financial information

Year end	31/07/2020
Income	£147,700
Total expenditure	£132,000

Further financial information

Social welfare

Block grants of £6,000 and £4,000 were made to the Attendance and Welfare Services of Lewisham and Greenwich boroughs, respectively, for administration to primary and secondary schoolchildren.

Education

Grants of £35,500 were awarded to 28 individuals studying at further or higher education institutions.

Other information

The foundation also supports organisations with similar objectives. Grants to organisations are usually one-off awards of up to £5,000.

The Edmund Godson Charity

£4,500 (2019/20)

Correspondent: The Trustees, 30 Hemingford Road, Cambridge CB1 3BZ (tel: 07866 267692; email: info@edmundgodson.org)

CC number: 227463

Eligibility

People in need residing in the following parishes: Pencowe with Marston; Stannett, Pudleston-cum-Whyle; Leominster; St Mary the Virgin; Middleton-on-the-Hill; St Michael and All Angels; Tenbury and Tenbury Wells; St Mary and Shinfield; All Saints Eltham; All Saints Shooters Hill; The Church of Ascension Plumstead; The Good Shepherd with St Peter Lee; Holy Trinity Eltham; St Barnabas Eltham; St James Kidbrooke; St John with St James and St Paul Plumstead; St Luke Eltham Park; St Luke with Holy Trinity Charlton; St Mark and St Margaret Plumstead; St Mary Magdalene with St Michael and All Angels Woolwich; St Michael and All Angels Abbey Wood; St Nicholas Plumstead; St Saviour Eltham; and St Thomas Woolwich.

Types of grant

Grants are made for the relief of need and to help people start new careers in other countries.

Applications

Apply in writing to the correspondent.

Financial information

Year end	05/04/2020
Income	£17,800
Total expenditure	£9,400

Further financial information

Full accounts were not available to view on the Charity Commission's website due to the charity's low income. We have therefore estimated the grant total based on the charity's total expenditure.

Other information

This charity also makes grants to organisations.

The Greenwich Charities

£12,500 (2019/20)

Correspondent: The Trustees, c/o St Alfege Church, Greenwich Church Street, London SE10 9BJ (email: thegreenwichcharities@gmail.com)

 thegreenwichcharities.com

CC number: 252262, 216731, 1074816

Eligibility

Residents living within the SE10, SE3, SE7, SE13 and SE8 postcode areas whose Council Tax is paid to The Royal Borough of Greenwich.

Types of grant

One-off small grants are awarded, for example to the cover the cost of an unexpected telephone bill, a new washing machine or clothing.

Applications

Applicants can download the application form on the charity's website.

Financial information

Year end	31/03/2020
Income	£18,500
Total expenditure	£26,200

Further financial information

Full accounts were not available to view on the Charity Commission's website due to the charity's low income. We have therefore estimated the grant total based on the charity's total expenditure.

Other information

The Greenwich Charities is a group of three charities that share common objects and have a single application process. They consist of the Charity of Charles Soames (Charity Commission no. 252262), Randall's Charity (Charity Commission no. 216731) and The Greenwich Charity (Charity Commission no. 1074816).

Greenwich Charities of William Hatcliffe and The Misses Smith

£15,100 (2019/20)

Correspondent: Linda Clayton, Clerk to the Trustees, Greenwich Hatcliffe Charities, PO Box 70569, London SE9 9DT (email: clerk@greenwich-hatcliffe.org.uk)

CC number: 227721

Eligibility

People in need who are over 60 years of age and live in East Greenwich or the south side of the River Thames, up to a radius of five miles from the charity's almshouses.

Types of grant

'Help at home' grants of up to £600 are given to enable beneficiaries to live independently in their own homes. Residents of the charity's almshouses are awarded a small grant annually at Christmas.

Applications

Apply in writing to the correspondent. Applications for individual grants are usually referred through agencies such as Age UK.

Financial information

Year end	30/09/2020
Income	£527,000
Total expenditure	£164,300

Further financial information

Grants in 2019/20 were broken down as follows: £14,000 awarded in individual grants to residents of East Greenwich and £1,100 awarded in the form of one-off gifts to residents of the almshouses at Christmas.

Other information

The charity's priority is to provide almshouses for older residents of East Greenwich, or those living within a five-mile radius of the almshouses. The age restriction for beneficiaries at the almshouses has been reduced to 55 years. In 2019/20, expenditure on letting costs and general maintenance of the almshouses totalled £72,000. The charity also makes grants to organisations (£15,000 in 2019/20).

The Woolwich and Plumstead Relief-in-Sickness Fund

£ £5,900 (2019/20)

Correspondent: Dave Lucas, Royal Borough of Greenwich, The Woolwich Centre, 35 Wellington Street, Woolwich, London SE18 6HQ (tel: 020 8921 5261; email: dave.lucas@royalgreenwich.gov.uk)

CC number: 212482

Eligibility

People in need who have a physical illness or disability and live in the parishes of Woolwich and Plumstead. When funds allow, applications may be accepted from people living in the borough of Greenwich.

Types of grant

One-off grants are given according to need.

Applications

Apply in writing to the correspondent.

Financial information

Year end	31/03/2020
Income	£19,400
Total expenditure	£13,000

Further financial information

Full accounts were not available to view on the Charity Commission's website due to the fund's low income. We have therefore estimated the fund's grant total based on its total expenditure.

Other information

The fund also makes grants to organisations.

Hackney

Hackney Benevolent Pension Society

£ £3,300 (2019/20)

Correspondent: Frances Broadway, Trustee, 39 Sydner Road, London N16 7UF (tel: 020 7254 6145; email: fm.broadway@gmail.com)

CC number: 212731

Eligibility

People who live in Hackney, are older and in need.

Types of grant

Three annual payments are awarded to pensioners, at Christmas, on their birthday and at the society's annual general meeting in November. Payments are delivered in person through home visits.

Applications

Apply in writing to the correspondent.

Financial information

Year end	30/06/2020
Income	£2,600
Total expenditure	£3,700

Further financial information

Full accounts were not available to view on the Charity Commission's website due to the society's low income. We have therefore estimated the grant total based on the society's total expenditure.

Hackney Parochial Charities

£ £65,300 (2019/20)

Correspondent: Clerk to the Trustees, Hackney Parochial Charities, Unit 11, 8–20 Well Street, London E9 7PX (tel: 01285 841900; email: office@thetrustpartnership.com)

 www.hackneyparochialcharities.org.uk

CC number: 219876

Eligibility

People in need who live in the former metropolitan borough of Hackney (as it was before 1970).

Types of grant

One-off grants, typically up to £500, are awarded for the purchase of clothing and essential household equipment, although grants can be given for many other welfare purposes, such as travel expenses for hospital visits. On the website there is a helpful list which shows the guideline amounts for certain household items (for example £120 for a single bed).

Applications

Applications can be made via a form available on the website. Applications must be made through a supporting agency such as a church or social worker, whose details need to be included on the online form.

Financial information

Year end	31/03/2020
Income	£477,500
Total expenditure	£302,700

Further financial information

Grants were awarded to 113 individuals in 2019/20.

Other information

The annual report states: 'During 2009 and 2010 all assets and liabilities of the Hackney District Nursing Association were transferred to the Hackney Parochial Charities and are administered as a restricted fund. The objectives of the Hackney District Nursing Association are the training, education and support of nurses and midwives, the provision of equipment and services to support them, and also to relieve the poverty of persons resident within the London Borough of Hackney.'

Hammersmith and Fulham

Dr Edwards and Bishop King's Fulham Charity

£ £176,500 (2019/20)

Correspondent: Jonathan Martin, Clerk to the Trustees, Percy Barton House, 33–35 Dawes Road, Fulham, London SW6 7DT (tel: 020 7386 9387; email: clerk@debk.org.uk)

 www.debk.org.uk

CC number: 1113490

Eligibility

People in need who live in the old metropolitan borough of Fulham. A full list of eligible addresses is available to view on the charity's website.

Types of grant

Grants are given according to need towards essential items such as kitchen appliances, flooring, beds, furniture and clothing.

Grants are given towards education and training. Recent examples of funded items have included furnishings, white goods and flooring.

Exclusions

According to its website, the charity does not normally help homeowners, nor will it provide support for the following:

- Applications from those not in the area of benefit
- Cash grants (unless they are to be administered by an agency)
- Retrospective grants or arrears on utility bills
- Funding for funerals
- Wheelchairs or electric scooters
- Computer equipment of any sort, unless for an applicant that is housebound
- Dishwashers (unless there is a medical need)
- Equipment where the government, or local government, or any other agency is required to provide that equipment by law

Items where the individual purchase value is of less than £15

Applications

Application forms are available to download from the charity's website and can be submitted directly by the individual or through a supporting agency such as social services.

Financial information

Year end	31/03/2020
Income	£514,200
Total expenditure	£537,700

Further financial information

According to the charity's 2019/20 accounts, 249 grants were awarded during the year.

Other information

The charity also gives grants to organisations and runs summer schemes whereby funding is given to projects that allow children to enjoy a break during the summer holidays that they would otherwise not have access to.

Haringey

Tottenham District Charity

 £100,000 (2020/21)

Correspondent: Carolyn Banks, Secretary, PO Box 365, Loughton, Essex LG10 9EU (email: charities@ tottenhamdistrictcharity.org.uk)

www.tottenhamdistrictcharity.org. uk

CC number: 207490

Eligibility

People in need, particularly older people, who live in Tottenham. Eligible individuals aged 65 and over can apply for a pension.

Types of grant

One-off grants of up to £400 are available towards basic household items or furniture, white goods (such as fridges and washing machines), clothing, hospital visits expenses, educational expenses (such as books, fees for further education and transport costs for college), recuperative holidays, and home improvements and repairs. Pensions are also available to people over the state pension age who have lived in Tottenham for over seven years.

Exclusions

No grants are made to help with bills or debts.

Applications

Applications can be made through the charity's website.

Financial information

Year end	31/03/2021
Income	£142,900
Total expenditure	£133,500

Wood Green (Urban District) Charity

 £11,300 (2019/20)

Correspondent: The Trustees, 43 Kenilworth Crescent, Enfield, Middlesex EN1 3RE (tel: 07740 456581)

CC number: 206736

Eligibility

People in need, especially widows and older people, who have lived in the former urban district of Wood Green for at least seven years.

Types of grant

Grants are made according to need. Pensions are given to eligible older people.

Applications

Apply in writing to the correspondent.

Financial information

Year end	30/06/2020
Income	£8,700
Total expenditure	£12,500

Further financial information

Full accounts were not available to view on the Charity Commission's website due to the charity's low income. We have therefore estimated the charity's grant total based on its total expenditure.

Harrow

Mayor of Harrow's Charity Fund

£3,400 (2019/20)

Correspondent: The Trustees, London Borough of Harrow, Civic Centre, Harrow, Middlesex HA1 2UH (tel: 020 8424 1232; email:mayor@harrow.gov.uk)

CC number: 219034

Eligibility

People in need who live in the borough of Harrow.

Types of grant

One-off grants are given for basic items such as food, clothing, heating, beds, cookers, childcare equipment and health treatments. Grants are also given

towards holidays/school trips for children.

Applications

Apply in writing to the correspondent.

Financial information

Year end	19/05/2020
Income	£3,300
Total expenditure	£3,800

Further financial information

Full accounts were not available to view on the Charity Commission's website due to the fund's low income. We have therefore estimated the fund's grant total based on its total expenditure.

Hillingdon

The Harefield Parochial Charities

£5,600 (2020)

Correspondent: The Trustees, 11 Burberry Close, Harefield, Uxbridge, Middlesex UB9 6QP (tel: 07546 979971; email: hpc@harefieldcharities.co.uk)

www.harefieldcharities.co.uk

CC number: 210145

Eligibility

Residents in the ancient parish of Harefield who are in need.

Types of grant

One-off grants are awarded towards the cost of:
- Bedding
- Clothing
- Food
- Fuel
- Furniture
- Recuperative holidays
- Domestic help
- Travelling to and from hospital
- Tools, equipment and course fees involved in training for any trade or profession

Coal allowances are distributed at Christmas to older residents. The charity may also distribute weekly allowances.

Applications

Apply in writing to the correspondent. The trustees meet 12 times each year and communicate by email and telephone between meetings if a matter arises.

Financial information

Year end	31/12/2020
Income	£138,900
Total expenditure	£102,800

Other information

The charity also provides almshouse accommodation to older women and families in Harefield.

Uxbridge United Welfare Trust

 £92,400 (2020)

Correspondent: Grants Officer, Charter Building, Charter Place, Uxbridge, Middlesex UB8 1JG (tel: 01895 232976; email: universal@uuwt.org)

https://www.uuwt.org

CC number: 1181683

Eligibility

People who are in need and live in the postcodes of UB8, UB9 and UB10 and, in exceptional cases, the surrounding area.

Types of grant

Welfare

One-off grants are awarded to relieve hardship. Examples include grants towards furniture, white goods, clothing, baby equipment and help with fuel bills.

Education

One-off educational grants are awarded to support people to attend educational courses and apprenticeships.

Exclusions

Previous research suggests that grants are not normally given for school fees. Funding is not intended to be provided where statutory support is available.

Applications

Application forms can be requested in writing from the correspondent or through the trust's website. Applications are typically made in person or over the phone. The trust's website notes that it aims to have a quick turnaround.

Financial information

Year end	31/12/2020
Income	£715,700
Total expenditure	£447,800

Further financial information

In 2020, the trust made 48 welfare grants, and a further three educational grants were awarded through the Lord Ossulton Fund.

Other information

The trust also runs almshouses and makes grants to local organisations.

Islington

Cloudesley

 £176,800 (2019/20)

Correspondent: The Trustees, Office 1.1, Resource for London, 356 Holloway Road, London N7 6PA (tel: 020 7697 4094; email: info@cloudesley.org.uk)

www.cloudesley.org.uk

CC number: 205959

Eligibility

Cloudesley provides small grants to Islington residents with health problems (physical or mental) and/or a disability who are facing financial hardship. Cloudesley Partner grants can be used for a variety of purposes but must help to relieve ill health or disability.

Types of grant

One-off grants are awarded for a wide range of purposes.

Exclusions

Grants cannot be made for any item or service that is readily available from central or local government, landlords or the health service. Grants are one-off interventions and cannot be used for recurring needs, although several small grants may be considered necessary in a crisis situation.

Applications

Grants are distributed through a number of locally based voluntary organisations and charities known as Cloudesley Partners. A list of the current Cloudesley Partners is available on the charity's website. Cloudesley does not make individual grants directly but can give further information and refer individuals to the appropriate partner agency.

Financial information

Year end	30/06/2020
Income	£1,760,000
Total expenditure	£1,740,000

Further financial information

in 2019/20, 1,407 grants were made to individuals.

The Pilion Trust Ltd

 £900 (2019/20)

Correspondent: Dolores Steadman, The Ringcross Community Centre, 60 Lough Road, Islington, London N7 8RH (tel: 020 7700 2498; email: dolores.mc@ piliontrust.org.uk)

piliontrust.info

CC number: 1122628

Eligibility

Vulnerable people who live in Islington and are struggling to maintain a home and a basic lifestyle or to get to the next level of their life and seek to be independent.

Types of grant

One-off grants are awarded.

Applications

Apply in writing to the correspondent.

Financial information

Year end	31/01/2020
Income	£112,900
Total expenditure	£95,100

Worrall and Fuller Exhibition Fund

 £5,800 (2019/20)

Correspondent: The Clerk, St Luke's Community Centre, 90 Central Street, London EC1V 8AJ (tel: 020 7549 8181; email: worrall&fuller@slpt.org.uk)

 www.worrallandfuller.org

CC number: 312507

Eligibility

Children and young people between the ages of 5 and 25 who are resident in the old borough of Finsbury (now part of Islington). Preference is given to those who live in the parish of St Luke, Old Street and those whose parents have had their business or employment there in previous years.

Types of grant

Welfare

Grants are awarded for school uniform and study equipment costs, organised educational trips, and extracurricular, non-mainstream and out-of-school activities. The website states that the later 'should be related to arts, sports, music lessons, dance, scouting, Duke of Edinburgh's Award, etc., for primary and secondary school-age children. We can support fees, equipment, clothing, and trips, etc. The activity should be structured and taught in groups or individually, and progress reports/ certificates awarded that show attendance and progress.' Grants are typically between £250 and £750.

Education

Students in further and higher education can be supported with grants towards study materials including laptops and IT equipment, but not course fees. Grants are typically between £250 and £750.

Applications

Application forms can be found on the website. The charity meets four times a year to consider applications but can also take urgent requests.

Financial information

Year end	31/03/2020
Income	£20,300
Total expenditure	£12,900

Further financial information

Full accounts were not available to view on the Charity Commission's website due to the fund's low income. We have therefore estimated the grant total based on the fund's total expenditure.

Other information

The charity is administered by St Luke's Community Centre and Trust. They carry out all aspects of the grants and financial administration.

Kensington and Chelsea

The Campden Charities

 £1,830,000 (2019/20)

Correspondent: Outreach Officer, Studios 3 and 4, 27A Pembridge Villas, London W11 3EP (tel: 020 7243 0551; email: chris-stannard@campdencharities. org.uk)

🌐 www.campdencharities.org.uk

CC number: 1104616

Eligibility

Residents of Kensington, London who are:

▶ A British or European Union citizen (or have indefinite leave to remain)
▶ Not a homeowner
▶ In low-paid work or receiving benefits

Support is also available for young people from disadvantaged backgrounds who are undertaking education.

Types of grant

Welfare

Grants are given to supplement income for people in low-paid employment to improve their future employment prospects. Examples of what may be funded include childcare costs, travel to work, training costs and so on. Funding is also given to help individuals who are unable to work to improve their home environment. As well as grants, pensions are distributed to older residents of Kensington.

Education

Grants are given to promote education and training (vocational, social, recreational and physical). Campden Scholarships are awarded to young people studying at university, towards the costs of accommodation, books and materials. Vocational training grants are also available to individuals who wish to gain qualifications via the Employment Routes programme. Support is also given to young people who are leaving school and undertaking training, and to those beginning apprenticeships.

Exclusions

Grants will not be made to replace statutory services.

Applications

Applications can be completed online or by contacting the correspondent by telephone. Alternatively, referrals can be made on behalf of an individual by a professional. Referral forms can be downloaded from the charity's website.

Financial information

Year end	31/03/2020
Income	£4,040,000
Total expenditure	£3,760,000

Kensington and Chelsea District Nursing Trust

 £75,500 (2019/20)

Correspondent: Margaret Rhodes, Clerk to the Trustees, Richford House, Grove Mews, London W6 7HS (tel: 07801 105374; email: kcdntrust@gmail.com)

CC number: 210931

Eligibility

People living in Kensington and Chelsea who have a disability or who are experiencing ill health. In exceptional circumstances, support may be given to people outside the beneficial area.

Types of grant

Grants are given for items and services that may alleviate suffering or assist with recovery.

Applications

Apply in writing to the correspondent.

Financial information

Year end	31/03/2020
Income	£97,600
Total expenditure	£109,600

Further financial information

We were unable to view the trust's full 2019/20 accounts; therefore, the grant total has been estimated based on its expenditure.

Westway Trust

 £130,300 (2019/20)

Correspondent: Grants Team, 1 Thorpe Close, London W10 5XL (tel: 020 8962 5720; email: grants@westway.org)

🌐 www.westway.org

CC number: 1123127

Eligibility

People in need who live in the borough of Kensington and Chelsea and can demonstrate a commitment to sports and fitness/health. The recipient (or the recipient's family if the applicant is under the age of 18) must be in receipt of one of the following benefits:

Universal Credit, Housing Benefit, Personal Independence Payment (PIP) or Carer's Allowance. Applicants who have disabilities or a long-term health condition are encouraged to apply.

Types of grant

The trust offers sports bursaries of up to £500 for adults or children who want to take part in sports and fitness activities at Westway Sports and Fitness facilities but find it difficult to pay the fees. There are three separate bursary schemes for training, coaching and NGB training courses (Levels 1 and 2).

Exclusions

The trust does not fund retrospective costs and cannot award grants for any accrued debts for activities.

Applications

Application forms and further details can be found on the website. There is an option to sign up to grants alerts to receive a notification when applications open.

Financial information

Year end	31/03/2020
Income	£6,060,000
Total expenditure	£6,130,000

Other information

The trust runs education and training programmes, sports facilities and health and fitness services. It also provides facilities for arts, culture and other events. Grants are also made to local community groups and charities.

Kingston upon Thames

Chessington Charities

 £1,600 (2020)

Correspondent: The Trustees, The Vicarage, Garrison Lane, Chessington KT9 2LB (tel: 020 8397 3016; email: stmaryschessington@hotmail.co.uk)

CC number: 209241

Eligibility

People in need who live in the parish of St Mary the Virgin, Chessington.

Types of grant

Welfare

One-off grants are made according to need. Our previous research suggests that past grants have included Christmas grants for older people in need.

Education

Children and young people under the age of 21 who are students or apprentices are eligible for one-off educational or training grants.

Exclusions

Grants are not given to pay debts and cannot be given regularly.

Applications

Apply in writing to the correspondent.

Financial information

Year end	31/12/2020
Income	£4,500
Total expenditure	£3,500

Further financial information

Full accounts were not available to view on the Charity Commission's website due to the charity's low income. We have therefore estimated the charity's grant total based on its total expenditure.

Other information

Grants are also made to local charitable organisations.

Lambeth

The Clapham Relief Fund

 £12,100 (2019)

Correspondent: Clerk to the Trustees, PO Box 37978, London SW4 8WX (email: enquiries@claphamrelieffund. org)

claphamrelieffund.org

CC number: 1074562

Eligibility

People in need who live in Clapham (the local authority wards of Larkhall, Clapham Town, Ferndale, Clapham Common, Brixton Hill and Thornton). A map of the area of benefit is available on the fund's website.

Types of grant

Grants typically range from £100 to £300 and can be awarded for the following items and services, especially where the grant will help relieve pain, suffering or distress:

▸ Household appliances and furnishings, bedding, floor coverings, etc.
▸ Home improvements and repair costs, such as decorating and insulation
▸ Home adaptations for people who are infirm or have a disability
▸ Training fees and equipment, such as books, tools, exam costs and tuition fees
▸ Clothing and footwear

▸ Travel and accommodation costs for visiting relatives in hospital, care homes, children's homes, prison, etc.
▸ Recuperative or respite holiday.
▸ Food for special diets, medical or other aids, nursing requisites or comforts.

The website notes that 'assistance will normally only be granted where insufficient funds are available from public sources (e.g. local authority or DWP).'

Exclusions

The fund does not meet the costs of any debts already incurred.

Applications

Application forms and guidance notes can be downloaded from the fund's website. The trustees meet quarterly to consider applications, usually in early March, June, September and December. Completed application forms should be submitted two weeks before meetings. In exceptional circumstances, applications may be considered at other times by the chair and treasurer.

Financial information

Year end	31/12/2019
Income	£28,900
Total expenditure	£23,600

Further financial information

According to the 2019 accounts, 48 grants totalling £11,900 were awarded to individuals during the year. None of these grants exceeded £400. In addition, two Christmas vouchers of £100 each were awarded to individuals. Grants to organisations totalled £9,500.

Other information

The fund also makes grants to organisations.

South London Relief-in-Sickness Fund

 £7,900 (2019)

Correspondent: Fiona Rae, Clerk to the Trustees, Room 154, Wandsworth Town Hall, Wandsworth High Street, London SW18 2PU (tel: 020 8871 7857; email: fiona.rae@richmondandwandsworth.gov. uk)

www.slrsf.org.uk

CC number: 210939

Eligibility

People in need who live in Lambeth and Wandsworth and have disabilities or are experiencing ill health.

Types of grant

One-off grants of up to £300 (average £130) are given towards, for example,

furnishings, kitchen appliances, clothing and holidays.

Applications

Applications can be made using a form, which is available to download online and should be submitted through a social worker, Citizens Advice or other welfare agency.

Financial information

Year end	31/12/2019
Income	£15,100
Total expenditure	£17,600

Further financial information

Full accounts were not available to view on the Charity Commission's website due to the fund's low income. We have therefore estimated the grant total based on the fund's total expenditure.

Waterloo Parish Charity

 £770 (2019/20)

Correspondent: The Trustees, c/o The Vicarage, 1 Secker Street, London SE1 8UF (tel: 020 7633 9819; email: admin@stjohnswaterloo.org)

www.stjohnswaterloo.org

CC number: 251594

Eligibility

Residents in the ecclesiastical parish of St John with St Andrew in Waterloo who are in need. Preference is given to those resident in the former ecclesiastical parish of St John the Evangelist in Lambeth.

Types of grant

Grants are awarded according to need.

Applications

Apply in writing to the correspondent.

Financial information

Year end	11/09/2020
Income	£980
Total expenditure	£1,700

Further financial information

Full accounts were not available to view on the Charity Commission's website due to the charity's low income. We have therefore estimated the charity's grant total based on its total expenditure.

Other information

This charity also makes grants to organisations.

Lewisham

Sir William Boreman's Foundation
See entry on page 318

The Deptford Pension Society

£ £6,400 (2019)

Correspondent: The Trustees, 144 Farnaby Road, Bromley BR1 4BW (tel: 020 8402 0775; email: mjpbaker@hotmail.co.uk)

CC number: 219232

Eligibility
People over the age of 60 who live in Deptford.

Types of grant
Monthly pensions are distributed.

Applications
Apply in writing to the correspondent.

Financial information
Year end	31/12/2019
Income	£5,400
Total expenditure	£7,200

Further financial information
Full accounts were not available to view on the Charity Commission's website due to the charity's low income. We have therefore estimated the charity's grant total based on its total expenditure.

Sir John Evelyn's Charity

£ £8,400 (2019)

Correspondent: Colette Saunders, Clerk, Armada Court Hall, 21 McMillan Street, Deptford, London SE8 3EZ (tel: 020 8694 8953)

CC number: 225707

Eligibility
People in need residing in the ancient parish of St Nicholas and St Luke in Deptford in south-east London.

Types of grant
Grants are awarded according to need. Pensions are paid recurrently to older beneficiaries.

Applications
Apply in writing to the correspondent.

Financial information
Year end	31/12/2019
Income	£85,300
Total expenditure	£65,300

Further financial information
The grant total for 2019 is made up of pensions paid to older people and the cost of outings/meals for older people only.

Other information
The charity provides a range of activities and services for older people, which include the following: a weekly lunch club; a summer excursion to a coastal resort; a Christmas party including lunch and a gift; and one-to-one support and advice on welfare issues and applying for benefits for individuals in financial need. The charity also supports the Armada Community Project, which gives individuals in need access to services, including childcare creches, family arts and crafts, women's support groups and advice on welfare.

The Lee Charity of William Hatcliffe

£ £3,900 (2019)

Correspondent: The Trustees, PO Box 7041, Bridgnorth, Shropshire WV16 9EL (tel: 07517 527849; email: annewilsontc@hotmail.co.uk)

CC number: 208053

Eligibility
People in Lewisham who are in need, hardship or distress, with preference given to those living in the ancient parish of Lee.

Types of grant
Grants are awarding according to need.

Applications
Apply in writing to the correspondent.

Financial information
Year end	31/12/2019
Income	£76,200
Total expenditure	£21,400

Further financial information
During the year, grants were awarded to eight individuals.

Other information
The charity also supports other registered charities in Lewisham.

Lewisham Relief in Need Charity

£ £8,000 (2019/20)

Correspondent: The Finance and Administration Manager, Clerk's Office, Lloyd Court, Slagrove Place, London SE13 7LP (tel: 020 8690 8145; email: admin@lpcharities.co.uk)

 www.lpcharities.co.uk

CC number: 1025779

Eligibility
People in need, including those who are older, disadvantaged or have disabilities, who live in the ancient parish of Lewisham, which does not include Deptford or Lee.

Types of grant
Small one-off grants of up to £500 for essential items such as kitchen equipment, beds or carpets.

Applications
Apply in writing to the Finance and Administration Manager clearly stating your requirements and enclosing quotes and examples of goods required, including as much information as you think will aid the trustees in making their decision. Check the charity's website for application deadlines.

Financial information
Year end	31/03/2020
Income	£159,400
Total expenditure	£110,700

Other information
The charity is primarily engaged in providing sheltered accommodation for older people at its almshouse, Lloyd Court. Funding is available for larger organisations working in the ancient parish of Lewisham that require funding for projects. Grants of up to £1,000 are awarded.

Merton

Alf and Hilda Leivers Charity Trust

£ £9,800 (2019/20)

Correspondent: The Trustees, Rosewood End, Windsor Road, Chobham, Surrey GU24 8NA (tel: 01276 58575)

CC number: 299267

Eligibility
Young people under the age of 18 who either live or attend schools in the London Borough of Merton. At least one of the applicant's parents/guardians must have been resident in Merton for the last five years.

Types of grant

Welfare
Grants are made in support of mental, physical and emotional health and well-being.

Education

Grants are made for educational purposes, particularly for support in the fields of the arts and athletics.

Applications

Apply in writing to the correspondent.

Financial information

Year end	31/03/2020
Income	£21,200
Total expenditure	£21,700

Further financial information

Full accounts were not available to view on the Charity Commission's website due to the trust's low income. We have therefore estimated the trust's grant total based on its total expenditure.

Other information

The trust also makes grants to organisations, in particular to support the provision of recreational facilities.

Wimbledon Guild of Social Welfare (Incorporated)

£311,700 (2019/20)

Correspondent: The Trustees, Guild House, 30–32 Worple Road, Wimbledon, London SW19 4EF (tel: 020 8946 0735; email: info@wimbledonguild.co.uk)

 www.wimbledonguild.co.uk

CC number: 200424

Eligibility

Individuals in need who live in the borough of Merton. The guild's activities focus on fighting poverty, reducing social isolation and loneliness, and encouraging older people to be active and healthy.

Types of grant

Small grants are awarded to pay for items such as kitchen equipment, children's clothing and school uniforms, furniture and school trips (up to £300 for white goods and £75 for school uniforms). The guild also provides support for unexpected costs arising from major changes to personal circumstances such as disability, redundancy or bereavement. Specific funds are available for individuals with armed forces connections.

Exclusions

Grants are not awarded for:
- Continued funding
- Payment of debts or arrears
- Improvements to council or privately rented property

Applications

Application forms are available to download from the website and may be completed by individuals or their social/health worker with the individual's consent. Where possible, applications must be supported by the professional or social worker by a letter detailing their involvement. Applications can be returned via post or sent via email to welfare@wimbledonguild.co.uk. Alternatively, applications can also be made in person through an appointment with the Welfare Team. Applications are considered as they are received and a decision is usually made within two weeks. Applicants cannot apply more than once a year.

Financial information

Year end	31/03/2020
Income	£1,840,000
Total expenditure	£2,610,000

Other information

The guild also donates to other charities and organisations with similar objectives, and runs counselling and outreach services.

Newham

Mary Curtis' Maternity Charity

£1,400 (2019/20)

Correspondent: The Trustees, Durning Hall, Earlham Grove, London E7 9AB (tel: 020 3740 8114; email: eileen.da-silva@aston-mansfield.org.uk)

CC number: 235036

Eligibility

Pregnant women or mothers with children under the age of one living in Newham. Preference is given to women living within a one-mile radius of St John's Church, Stratford.

Types of grant

Grants are made according to need.

Applications

Apply in writing to the correspondent.

Financial information

Year end	31/03/2020
Income	£2,400
Total expenditure	£1,500

Further financial information

Full accounts were not available to view on the Charity Commission's website due to the charity's low income. We have therefore estimated the charity's grant total based on its total expenditure.

Redbridge

Ethel Baker Bequest

£1,800 (2020/21)

Correspondent: The Trustees, 35 Stanley Road, London E18 2NR (tel: 020 3245 1046)

CC number: 270274

Eligibility

Individuals who are resident in the London Borough of Redbridge or are connected with Woodford Baptist Church and are in need.

Types of grant

Grants are made according to need.

Applications

Apply in writing to the correspondent.

Financial information

Year end	31/03/2021
Income	£400
Total expenditure	£3,900

Further financial information

Full accounts were not available to view on the Charity Commission's website due to the charity's low income. We have therefore estimated the charity's grant total based on its total expenditure.

Other information

The charity also makes grants to organisations.

Richmond upon Thames

The Barnes Workhouse Fund

£43,100 (2020)

Correspondent: Katy Makepeace-Gray, Director, PO Box 347, Hampton, Middlesex TW12 9ED (tel: 07484 146802; email: kmakepeacegray@barnesworkhousefund.org.uk)

 www.barnesworkhousefund.org.uk

CC number: 200103

Eligibility

Welfare

Residents in the parish of Barnes (roughly the SW13 postal district) who are in need as a result of ill health, age or financial hardship.

Education

Students living in the parish of Barnes (roughly the SW13 postal district).

Types of grant

Welfare

Grants have previously been made towards the cost of utility bills, household items, furniture, school trips and uniform, and food vouchers.

Education

Educational grants are awarded towards the cost of fees, maintenance, equipment, travel and childcare.

Applications

Welfare

Applications must be made on the individual's behalf by referral agencies such as Citizens Advice, social services, housing associations and so on. The charity is unable to accept applications from individuals directly.

Education

Applications can be made via the charity's website.

Financial information

Year end	31/12/2020
Income	£720,000
Total expenditure	£806,300

Further financial information

In 2020, the charity awarded 89 grants for welfare and 17 for education.

Other information

The charity operates and maintains a sheltered housing facility, Walsingham Lodge, which provides accommodation for approximately 40 residents. The charity also makes grants to local voluntary organisations.

Hampton Fuel Allotment Charity

 £828,400 (2019/20)

Correspondent: The Trustees, 15 High Street, Hampton, Middlesex TW12 2SA (tel: 020 8941 7866; email: david@hfac. co.uk)

www.hamptonfund.co.uk

CC number: 211756

Eligibility

People in need living in Hampton, Hampton Hill, Hampton Wick, Teddington, Twickenham and Whitton. Applicants must either work part time or be on a low wage, in receipt of state benefits, in receipt of help with rent or Council Tax or living on a pension.

Types of grant

Grants are awarded to help with the cost electricity and gas, the purchase of white goods and furniture, and school journey costs.

Applications

Application forms are available to download from the website, the charity's office or from Greenwood Centre, Twickenham Citizens Advice or the White House. Applications should be submitted by post either directly by the individual or by a third party.

Financial information

Year end	30/06/2020
Income	£1,950,000
Total expenditure	£2,420,000

Further financial information

In 2019/20, 1,653 grants were awarded to individuals and were distributed as follows:

Fuel grants	1,591	£770,700
Essential items and furniture	-	£53,300
Careline	41	£2,200
School journey grants	9	£1,300
Children's disability fund	2	£1,200
School uniform grants	10	£1,000

Other information

The charity also supports organisations.

The Hampton Wick United Charity

 £29,200 (2019/20)

Correspondent: Paul Barnfield, The Clerk, 258 Hanworth Road, Hounslow, London TW3 3TY (tel: 020 8737 0371; email: info@hwuc.org)

https://hwuc.org

CC number: 1010147

Eligibility

Welfare

People in need living in the parishes of St John the Baptist in Hampton Wick, St Mark in Teddington, and St Mary with St Alban in Teddington. Beneficiaries are usually in receipt of a state benefit and proof of this may be required.

Education

Residents and their dependants under the age of 25 who have lived in the parishes of St John the Baptist in Hampton Wick, St Mark in Teddington, and St Mary with St Alban in Teddington for at least 12 months.

Types of grant

Welfare

Relief-in-need grants are given for a range of purposes, such as towards the purchase of a wheelchair, furniture, medical equipment and travel expenses to visit relatives in hospital. Grants are also given for school uniforms and school trips.

Education

Grants can be awarded for educational costs such as academic books and travel expenses.

Applications

Contact the clerk for an informal discussion regarding making an application. The trustees consider applications three times a year. In the case of an emergency, special arrangements can be made to consider the request without delay.

Financial information

Year end	31/03/2020
Income	£55,100
Total expenditure	£41,800

Further financial information

We estimate that during 2019/20 around £15,900 was given to individuals for welfare purposes (including grants for schoolchildren) and around £13,300 was given to individuals for educational purposes.

The Petersham United Charities

£ £20,000 (2020)

Correspondent: The Trustees, The Vicarage, Bute Avenue, Richmond, Surrey TW10 7AX (tel: 020 8940 8435; email: st.peters.petersham@googlemail. com)

CC number: 200433

Eligibility

Residents in the ecclesiastical parish of Petersham who are in need.

Types of grant

Grants are made for welfare and educational purposes.

Applications

Apply in writing to the correspondent.

Financial information

Year end	31/12/2020
Income	£10,400
Total expenditure	£10,100

Further financial information

Full accounts were not available to view on the Charity Commission's website due to the charity's low income. We have therefore estimated the grant total based on the charity's total expenditure.

Other information

This charity also makes grants to organisations.

The Richmond Aid-in-Sickness Fund

 £5,200 (2020)

Correspondent: The Trustees, 95 Sheen Road, Richmond, Surrey TW9 1YJ (tel: 020 8948 4188; email: info@ richmondcharities.org.uk)

www.richmondcharities.org.uk

CC number: 200434

Eligibility

People in need who live in the borough of Richmond.

Types of grant

One-off grants ranging up to £250 are awarded towards utility bills, bankruptcy fees, mobility aids and white goods. For a full list of eligible items, visit the fund's website.

Exclusions

Funding will not be awarded for:
- Flooring/carpets
- Educational courses or materials
- Anything with a religious or political purpose
- TVs
- Home improvement for owner occupiers
- Treatments (for example, massages)
- Complementary therapies

Applications

The fund has selected 11 charities through which individuals can apply for a grant – visit its website for the full list of selected organisations.

Financial information

Year end	31/12/2020
Income	£5,800
Total expenditure	£5,800

Further financial information

Full accounts were not available to view on the Charity Commission's website due to the fund's low income. We have therefore estimated the fund's grant total based on its total expenditure.

Other information

The fund receives a grant from the Henry Smith Charity to distribute to people in need.

Richmond Parish Lands Charity

 £208,200 (2019/20)

Correspondent: Eleanor Rees, Grants Manager, The Vestry House, 21 Paradise Road, Richmond, Surrey TW9 1SA (tel: 020 8948 5701; email: grants@rplc. org.uk)

www.rplc.org.uk

CC number: 200069

Eligibility

Welfare

People living in the areas covered by the TW9, TW10, SW13 and SW14 postcodes who are in times of critical need.

Education

People over the age of 18 who are living in the areas covered by the TW9, TW10, SW13 and SW14 postcodes, who are studying at a state-run school, college, university or training provider. Our previous research suggests that support may be extended to students aged between 16 and 18, and that non-residents who have worked for a charitable organisation/social enterprise within the borough, or non-residents who have at one time been educated in the borough may also be eligible for funding.

Types of grant

Welfare

Welfare grants are awarded towards, for example, white goods, furniture or household items, utility bills and child-related expenses. Adult-only households are eligible for £300 per year. Households with one dependant are eligible for up to £500 per year. Households with two or more dependants are eligible for up to £600 per year.

Education

Educational grants, usually of up to £1,500, are made to help with the cost of any additional qualifications or training needed for employment. The charity has previously funded courses in literacy, gas fitting, plumbing, beauty therapy, hairdressing, first aid, IT, HGV driving, nursing, teaching and accounting. Other fees associated with studying for a course (such as transport, childcare, books/equipment or general living costs) are also covered. Support is also available for undergraduate programmes.

Grants of up to £400 are also available to full-time carers and retired residents for a recreational course to improve their socialisation and quality of life, and to residents recovering from a mental or physical condition for a therapeutic course.

Exclusions

Welfare

Welfare grants can only be made in cases where there are either no statutory funds or all statutory sources have been exhausted.

Education

Educational grants can only be awarded for study at private institutions when courses or training programmes are not available within the state sector. The

charity does not usually support master's degrees.

Applications

Welfare

An online application form can be completed on the website. Applications must be made on the individual's behalf by a local agency such as Richmond Borough Council support teams, Citizens Advice, social services, Age UK Richmond or the Community Mental Health Teams. Schools in the catchment area can also act as referees. Completed forms should be sent to the charity by email.

Education

For educational grants, applications can be made using an online form on the charity's website. Note: there are two different forms for applicants: one for requesting grants of up to £1,500, and another for requesting grants greater than £1,500.

Financial information

Year end	30/06/2020
Income	£2,740,000
Total expenditure	£3,310,000

Further financial information

During the 2019/20 financial year, the charity awarded 426 grants to individuals for both welfare and educational needs.

Other information

The charity also provides regular funding to local charities for support with administration costs/core operation activities. The charity also makes grants to schools and various non-statutory educational initiatives that promote learning opportunities for children and adults in the area of benefit.

Richmond Philanthropic Society

 £14,000 (2020)

Correspondent: The Trustees, 95 Sheen Road, Richmond, Surrey TW9 1YJ (tel: 020 8948 4188; email: info@ richmondcharities.org.uk)

www.richmondcharities.org.uk

CC number: 212941

Eligibility

People in need who live in the former borough of Richmond (with a preference for TW9 or TW10) and, ideally, have lived there for at least two years.

Types of grant

One-off grants of up to £250 are awarded to help with the costs of furniture, white goods, general household items, basic living expenses, bedding, utility bills, Council Tax and mobility aids. For a full list of approved items, visit the charity's website.

Exclusions

No grants are given for flooring/carpets, educational courses or materials, anything with religious or political purposes, TVs, home improvements or complementary therapies.

Applications

Applications must be made through one of the 11 organisations the charity has selected to distribute its funds (a list is available on the website): individuals cannot apply directly.

Financial information

Year end	31/12/2020
Income	£15,700
Total expenditure	£15,500

Further financial information

Full accounts were not available to view on the Charity Commission's website due to the charity's low income. We have therefore estimated the charity's grant total based on its total expenditure.

Other information

Richmond Charities runs nine almshouses and two other welfare charities – Richmond Aid in Sickness Fund, and the Misses Thomson and Whipple Charity.

Henry Smith's Charity (Richmond)

 £4,400 (2020)

Correspondent: The Trustees, 95 Sheen Road, Richmond, Surrey TW9 1YJ (tel: 020 8948 4188; email: info@ richmondcharities.org.uk)

www.richmondcharities.org.uk

CC number: 200431–4

Eligibility

People experiencing hardship or distress who live in the former borough of Richmond (Richmond, Kew, Petersham and Ham – the TW9 and TW10 postcodes).

Types of grant

One-off grants ranging up to £250 are awarded towards, for example, white goods, furniture, household items, assistance with utility costs, basic living expenses and special equipment.

Applications

Apply in writing to the correspondent.

Financial information

Year end	31/12/2020
Income	£4,450,000
Total expenditure	£3,800,000

Other information

The charity is administered by the Richmond Charities, along with the Richmond Aid-in-Sickness Fund, the Richmond Philanthropic Society (see separate entries) and the Misses Thompson and Whipple Charity. Its funds, however, are entirely separate and do not form part of the Richmond Charities' investments.

Southwark

Camberwell Consolidated Charities

 £50,000 (2019/20)

Correspondent: The Trustees, c/o HFM Tax Accounts, 180 Piccadilly, London W1J 9HF (tel: 07931 464882; email: norahjanet@aol.com)

CC number: 208441

Eligibility

Older people living in the former parish of Camberwell (which includes Dulwich and Peckham) whose income is at or a little above the minimum State Pension level.

Types of grant

Annual pensions, paid at a rate of £350 per individual or £525 per couple, are awarded. The charity also provides £80 grants at Christmas to eight people.

Applications

Application forms can be requested from the correspondent.

Financial information

Year end	31/03/2020
Income	£57,700
Total expenditure	£57,500

Further financial information

Grants were made to 141 individuals during the year.

Rotherhithe Consolidated Charities

 £36,200 (2020)

Correspondent: The Trustees, c/o HB Accountants, Plumpton House, Plumpton Road, Hoddesdon, Hertfordshire EN11 0LB (tel: 01992 444466; email: keith@hbaccountants.co. uk)

CC number: 211980

Eligibility

Widows who are in need and have lived in the ancient parish of Rotherhithe for at least ten years. Help is also given for the general benefit of those in need who live in the parish.

Types of grant

One-off grants are awarded for relief in need. Annual pensions are also provided to widows in need.

Applications

Apply in writing to the correspondent.

Financial information

Year end	31/12/2020
Income	£139,900
Total expenditure	£163,000

Other information

The charity also supports organisations.

Southwark Charities

 £3,900 (2019/20)

Correspondent: Chris Wilson, Clerk to the Trustees, c/o 39 Edward Edwards' House, Nicholson Street, London SE1 0XL (tel: 020 7593 2000; email: clerk@southwarkcharities.org.uk)

www.southwarkcharities.co.uk

CC number: 1137760

Eligibility

Older people in need who are over 60 and have lived in the former metropolitan borough of Southwark for at least five years.

Types of grant

Grants of up to £200 are awarded for holidays.

Applications

Application forms for holiday grants can be downloaded from the website.

Financial information

Year end	30/12/2020
Income	£771,500
Total expenditure	£807,400

Other information

The charity's main objective is the maintenance of almshouses for the benefit of older people who are facing financial difficulties. Grants are also made to four named Church of England schools within the ancient parish of St Mary Newington and to local organisations working with older people.

The Mayor of Southwark's Common Good Trust (The Mayor's Charity)

£ £4,500 (2019/20)

Correspondent: The Trustees, 1 Therapia Road, London SE22 0SF (email: karoncook@infinityaccountants. co.uk)

CC number: 280011

Eligibility

People in need who live in, or have a connection with, the London Borough of Southwark. Those living in the immediate neighbourhood are also eligible.

Types of grant

Grants are given according to need.

Applications

Apply in writing to the correspondent.

Financial information

Year end	31/03/2020
Income	£8,100
Total expenditure	£18,800

Further financial information

Full accounts were not available to view on the Charity Commission's website due to the trust's low income. We have therefore estimated the grant total based on the trust's total expenditure.

Other information

The trust also makes grants to organisations.

The United Charities of St George the Martyr

£ £75,200 (2020)

Correspondent: Andrew Murphy, Marshall House, 66 Newcomen Street, London SE1 IYT (tel: 020 7407 2994; email: visitor@stgeorge1584.org.uk)

 https://www.stgeorgethemartyr charity.com

CC number: 208732

Eligibility

People in need who are aged 55 or older and live within or very near the boundaries of the former (pre-1965) metropolitan borough of Southwark. There is an area of benefit map on the charity's website.

Types of grant

Grants are awarded for items such as furniture, white goods, bedding or winter clothing. The charity also

provides Christmas hampers and trips/ outings for its beneficiaries.

Exclusions

Grants will not be awarded for items or services that are the responsibility of a landlord or statutory body.

Applications

Contact the charity to make an application.

Financial information

Year end	31/12/2020
Income	£252,300
Total expenditure	£412,000

Further financial information

Grants in 2020 were distributed as follows:

Grants to individuals	£43,900
Hampers and Christmas parties	£24,500
Pensioners' trips and outings	£6,600
Pensioners' holiday costs	£100

St Olave, St Thomas and St John United Charity

£ £262,000 (2019/20)

Correspondent: The Trustees, 6–8 Druid Street, London SE1 2EU (tel: 020 7407 2530; email: st.olavescharity@btconnect. com)

CC number: 211763

Eligibility

Welfare
People living in the former metropolitan borough of Bermondsey in the London Borough of Southwark who are in need.

Education
Young people under the age of 25 living in the former metropolitan borough of Bermondsey in the London Borough of Southwark.

Types of grant

Welfare
Grants are given according to need. The charity also provides annual birthday gifts to people over 65 as well as Christmas gifts and holidays for older people and families in need.

Education
Grants are given for educational purposes.

Applications

Apply in writing to the correspondent.

Financial information

Year end	31/03/2020
Income	£587,700
Total expenditure	£605,200

Other information

Grants are also awarded to organisations.

Sutton

Cheam Consolidated Charities

£ £2,400 (2020)

Correspondent: The Trustees, St Dunstan's Church, Church Road, Cheam, Surrey SM3 8QH (tel: 020 8641 1284)

CC number: 238392

Eligibility

Residents of Cheam who are in need.

Types of grant

Grants are given according to need.

Applications

Apply in writing to the correspondent.

Financial information

Year end	31/12/2020
Income	£5,000
Total expenditure	£5,400

Further financial information

Full accounts were not available to view on the Charity Commission's website due to the charity's low income. We have therefore estimated the grant total based on the charity's total expenditure.

Other information

This charity also makes grants to organisations in the local area.

Tower Hamlets

Stepney Relief-in-Need Charity

£ £10,300 (2019/20)

Correspondent: Jean Partleton, Clerk to the Trustees, Rectory Cottage, 5 White Horse Lane, Stepney, London E1 3NE (tel: 020 7790 3598; email: jeanpartleton194@btinternet.com)

CC number: 250130

Eligibility

People in need who live within the old metropolitan borough of Stepney.

Types of grant

One-off grants, usually of £100 to £1,000, are considered for a wide range of needs, including household items, clothing, holidays (when an individual would benefit from a short break), hospital travel expenses and funeral costs. Grants are also given in the form of Sainsbury's vouchers.

Applications

An application form is available from the correspondent and may be submitted either directly by the individual or through a relative, social worker or other welfare agency. The trustees usually meet four times a year, but some applications can be considered between meetings at the chair's discretion.

Financial information

Year end	30/06/2020
Income	£26,700
Total expenditure	£21,500

Waltham Forest

Walthamstow and Chingford Almshouse Charity

 £50,700 (2019/20)

Correspondent: The Trustees, Monoux Hall, Church End, Walthamstow, London E17 9RL (tel: 020 8520 0295; email: office@wcac.org.uk)

wcac.org.uk

CC number: 1116355

Eligibility

Individuals and families in crisis who have a limited income and live in Walthamstow or Chingford.

Types of grant

Grants are awarded according to need.

Applications

The majority of grants are made as a result of referrals from social or health services. Application forms are available online if an individual wishes to refer themselves. Most applicants will be visited at their home before a decision is made.

Financial information

Year end	31/03/2020
Income	£993,800
Total expenditure	£745,100

Further financial information

According to the charity's 2019/20 accounts, 68 grants were made to individuals during the year.

Other information

The charity is an almshouse charity, providing accommodation for older people in Walthamstow and Chingford. Among its activities, the charity also makes grants to organisations working to prevent or relieve financial need in Walthamstow and Chingford, as well as occasionally to students and apprentices who live in the area and have limited family income for books, equipment or tools.

Wandsworth

Battersea United Charities

 £14,800 (2019/20)

Correspondent: Stephen Willmett, Clerk to the Trustees, Battersea Library, 265 Lavender Hill, Battersea, London SW11 1JB (tel: 07813 668897; email: batterseacharities@gmail.com)

https://batterseaunitedcharities.org. uk

CC number: 312153

Eligibility

People in need who live or attend an educational establishment in the former metropolitan borough of Battersea.

Types of grant

Welfare

Grants are available for the relief of poverty, in particular, but not exclusively, through the payment of pensions or the provision of other financial support. Examples of grants include furniture, clothing and other items for children.

Education

Grants are available for the advancement of education. For example, the charity has previously funded an International Citizen's Service (ICS) placement for a young Battersea resident to enhance their development and career prospects.

Applications

Contact the charity via the form available on the website with an initial enquiry, and you will be sent the relevant application form.

Financial information

Year end	31/03/2020
Income	£22,900
Total expenditure	£23,700

Further financial information

Full accounts were not available to view on the Charity Commission's website due to the charity's low income. According to the charity's website, in the preceding three years, its charitable giving has ranged from £13,800 to £15,900. We have used this information to estimate the charity's grant total.

Other information

Grants are also given to organisations.

Fuelbanks and Families

 £2,000 (2019/20)

Correspondent: The Trustees, 108 Battersea High Street, London SW11 3HP (tel: 020 3696 5335; email: admin@fuelbanksandfamilies.com)

www.fuelbanksandfamilies.com

CC number: 1161459

Eligibility

Families with children in need who live in Wandsworth.

Types of grant

The charity provides the following types of support for families in need:

- Debt repayment on prepay meters
- Credit on prepayment meters
- Power provisions for families, to enable them to cook food and heat their homes

Applications

Contact the charity for further information.

Financial information

Year end	31/03/2020
Income	£90
Total expenditure	£2,000

Further financial information

Full accounts were not available to view on the Charity Commission's website due to the charity's low income. We have therefore estimated the grant total based on the charity's total expenditure.

Other information

The charity has partnered with Centre 70 (www.centre70.org.uk) to offer specialist debt, benefits and housing support advice.

South London Relief-in-Sickness Fund

See entry on page 324

Wandsworth Combined Charity

 £5,000 (2019/20)

Correspondent: The Trustees, 179 Upper Richmond Road West, London SW14 8DU (tel: 020 8876 4478)

CC number: 210269

Eligibility

Older people who have lived in Wandsworth for at least three years.

Types of grant

The charity provides regular pensions.

Applications

Applications should be made in writing
to the correspondent.

Financial information

Year end	31/03/2020
Income	£9,500
Total expenditure	£5,500

Further financial information

Full accounts were not available to view
on the Charity Commission's website
due to the charity's low income. We
have therefore estimated the charity's
grant total based on its total
expenditure.

North East

General

The Christina Aitchison Trust

£ £700 (2020/21)

Correspondent: The Trustees, The Old Post Office, The Street, West Raynham, Fakenham, Norfolk NR21 7AD (tel: 07725 575210)

CC number: 1041578

Eligibility

Welfare

People living in the north-east or south-west of England who are in need as a result of blindness or any other ophthalmic disease. Support is also extended to people suffering from terminal illness.

Education

Educational grants are made to young people under the age of 25, who live in the north-east or south-west of England, to promote, improve, develop and maintain the education and appreciation of music.

Types of grant

Grants are given according to need.

Applications

Apply in writing to the correspondent.

Financial information

Year end	05/04/2021
Income	£2,200
Total expenditure	£1,600

Further financial information

Full accounts were not available to view on the Charity Commission's website due to the trust's low income. We have therefore estimated the trust's grant total based on its total expenditure.

Other information

The trust also makes grants to organisations, to promote research into ophthalmic diseases and to advance the education and appreciation of the arts, science and music.

Chloe and Liam Together Forever Trust

£ £67,800 (2020)

Correspondent: The Trustees, c/o KP Simpson, 172–174 Albert Road, Jarrow NE32 5JA (email: candltft@gmail.com)

 togetherforevertrust.co.uk

CC number: 1178806

Eligibility

Young people who are engaged in the fields of sport and the performing arts.

Types of grant

Grants are awarded to assist with costs for auditions, exams, coaching, qualifications, equipment and travel expenses at the beginning of young people's careers.

Applications

Applications can be made through the online form on the trust's website.

Financial information

Year end	31/12/2020
Income	£57,300
Total expenditure	£68,700

Other information

The trust was set up to honour Chloe and Liam, who lost their lives in the Manchester bombing in 2017. They loved to inspire others to follow their dreams and reach their goals. The trust also makes grants to organisations.

Lord Crewe's Charity

£ £189,500 (2020)

Correspondent: Mr C. Smithers, Clerk to the Trustees, The Miners' Hall, Durham, County Durham DH1 4BD (tel: 0191 384 7736; email: enquiries@ lordcrewescharity.co.uk)

 www.lordcrewescharity.org.uk

CC number: 1155101

Eligibility

Members of the Church of England clergy, and their dependants, who live in the dioceses of Durham and Newcastle and are in need.

The children of clergy members are eligible for educational grants.

Types of grant

Welfare grants are made to clergy to assist with specific cases of hardship, and to assist clergy when moving out of church housing upon retirement.

Educational grants are awarded to support the children of clergy members through their studies, up to postgraduate level.

Exclusions

The charity is unable to make grants to individuals who are not clergy members, or dependants of clergy in the two dioceses. The charity is also unable to support applications for church buildings or church projects, except in a very small number of parishes in which the charity holds property or has rights of presentation.

Applications

Apply in writing to the correspondent.

Financial information

Year end	31/12/2020
Income	£1,450,000
Total expenditure	£1,430,000

Further financial information

In 2020, the charity awarded 117 educational grants totalling £144,000 to members of the clergy in support of the education of their children. In addition, 21 grants totalling £24,500 were awarded to members of the clergy to assist with specific instances of hardship, and 12 grants totalling £21,000 were given to assist clergy moving out of church housing on retirement.

Other information

This charity is linked to the Lord Crewe's Library and Archives Trust (Charity Commission no. 1155101–3). The charity makes a small annual grant to the Lord Crewe's Durham Apprenticeship Fund, to assist young people in learning a trade or occupation.

The charity also makes grants to the dioceses of Newcastle and Durham for projects designed to support clergy members such as pastoral care and counselling, mentoring and continuing ministerial development.

The Olive and Norman Field Charity

£ £23,400 (2019)

Correspondent: The Trustees, Carrick House, Thurston Road, Northallerton, North Yorkshire DL6 2NA (tel: 01609 766322; email: office@oliveandnorman. co.uk)

 www.oliveandnormanfieldcharity. co.uk

CC number: 208760

Eligibility

People in need living in the following local government areas: North Yorkshire County Council, York City Council, Durham County Council, Darlington Borough Council, Hartlepool Borough Council, Middlesbrough Council, Redcar and Cleveland Borough Council and Stockton-on-Tees Borough Council.

Types of grant

One-off grants (reapplication can be made after 12 months) to cover costs where the outcome will improve the individual's quality of life. Awards have previously been made for respite and short breaks, household goods and electronics, specialist equipment (e.g. sensory toys, specialised seating and car seats), home adaptations (after a Disabled Facilities Grant has already been awarded) and mobility aids (e.g. wheelchairs).

Exclusions

Grants cannot be given for the following: building work (unless a Disabled Facilities Grant has been secured); equipment or work for which statutory funding is available (although contributions towards shortfalls in funding may be considered); retrospective funding; or the settlement of debts.

Applications

Applications can be completed online, or the application form can be downloaded from the website, completed and returned to the charity's address. Applications should be supported by a professional support worker such as a GP or professional/social worker, or Citizens Advice. Also note that if the application is for specialist equipment, the trustees require confirmation from an appropriate specialist therapist.

Financial information

Year end	31/12/2019
Income	£24,500
Total expenditure	£26,000

Further financial information

Full accounts were not available to view on the Charity Commission's website due to the charity's low income. We have therefore estimated the charity's grant total based on its total expenditure.

The Greggs Foundation

£ £794,600 (2020)

Correspondent: The Trustees, Q9, Quorum Business Park, Newcastle upon Tyne, Tyne and Wear NE12 8BU (tel: 0191 212 7626; email: greggsfoundation@greggs.co.uk)

 www.greggsfoundation.org.uk

CC number: 296590

Eligibility

People in need who live in the North East (Northumberland, Tyne and Wear, Durham and Teesside). Priority is given to families over individuals, the most financially excluded people and items that will make the most difference.

Types of grant

BACs payments of up to £150 can be made towards items including beds and bedding, baby equipment, clothing and flooring. Supermarket vouchers of up to £100 are available for food. White goods are supplied directly to families in need in partnership with East Durham Partnership.

Exclusions

Grants cannot be awarded for:
- Unspecified costs
- Loan repayments
- Bankruptcy fees
- Holidays
- Funeral expenses
- Medical equipment
- Computer equipment

Once a grant is awarded, beneficiaries cannot reapply for one year. If unsuccessful, applicants can reapply after 12 weeks.

Applications

Applications can be made online using a form featured on the foundation's website. Applications must be made by a third party (such as registered charities, housing associations or social services) on the individual's behalf. Applications are considered weekly – applicants can expect a response within two weeks of applying. Submit applications by 4pm on Friday to be considered in the following week's assessment.

Financial information

Year end	31/12/2020
Income	£3,890,000
Total expenditure	£3,630,000

Further financial information

During the year, the foundation made 2,747 hardship grants.

Other information

The foundation has separate grant programmes for organisations. The Local Community Projects Fund makes grants of up to £2,000 to organisations to deliver activities that would not be possible without funding. North East Core Funding grants of up to £45,000 are made to charitable organisations in the North East for support in providing quality services. The charity also operates breakfast clubs in local schools, to ensure that pupils are provided with a nutritious breakfast each morning.

Hylton House and Specialist Support Fund

£ £7,000 (2020/21)

Correspondent: Grants Team, County Durham Community Foundation, Victoria House, 2 Whitfield Court, St John's Road, Meadowfield Industrial Estate, Durham, County Durham DH7 8XL (tel: 0191 378 6340; email: info@cdcf.org.uk)

 www.cdcf.org.uk

CC number: 1047625–2

Eligibility

People in the North East (County Durham, Darlington, Gateshead, South Shields, Sunderland and Cleveland) with cerebral palsy and related neurological conditions. Support is also extended to the families and carers of such people.

Types of grant

Grants of up to £1,000 are available for a range of purposes including the purchase of essential household items (e.g. a cooker, fridge freezer or a washing machine), specialist equipment (e.g. mobility aids, specialist car seat, sensory equipment) and therapy.

Exclusions

The fund cannot reimburse applicants for any items already purchased. Additionally, it cannot provide support for purchasing a vehicle or driving lessons.

Applications

Complete the registration process on County Durham Community Foundation's website to receive an application form. Applications must be made by a recognised supporting organisation such as a professionally qualified health/social care worker, statutory organisation or registered charity. Grants are typically awarded up to eight weeks from application submission.

Financial information

Year end	31/03/2021
Income	£4,900
Total expenditure	£7,000

Further financial information

Full accounts were not available to view on the Charity Commission's website due to the fund's low income. We have therefore estimated the grant total based on the fund's total expenditure.

Other information

The fund is administrated by County Durham Community Foundation (Charity Commission no. 1047625).

North East Area Miners' Social Welfare Trust Fund

 £730 (2019/20)

Correspondent: Rick O'Toole, The Old Rectory, Rectory Drive, Whiston, Rotherham S60 4JG (tel: 01709 728115; email: rick.otoole@ciswo.org.uk)

www.ciswo.org.uk

CC number: 504178

Eligibility

People in need living in Durham, Tyne and Wear and Northumberland who are, or have been, employed in the coal industry. Support is extended to the dependants of such people.

Types of grant

One-off grants are awarded for holidays/respite breaks. Grants are also made for general welfare needs.

Applications

Apply in writing to the correspondent.

Financial information

Year end	30/09/2020
Income	£74,600
Total expenditure	£178,000

Further financial information

In previous years, the charity has awarded around £80,000 in grants for holidays and convalescence.

Northern Ladies Annuity Society

 £175,300 (2019/20)

Correspondent: Jean Ferry, MEA House, Ellison Place, Newcastle upon Tyne, Tyne and Wear NE1 8XS (tel: 0191 232 1518; email: jean.ferry@nlas.org.uk)

CC number: 1097222

Eligibility

Single, unmarried and widowed women over state retirement age who are in need. To be eligible, applicants must live or have lived in the north of England for many years, have an income of no more than £69,500 per annum and have savings of no more than £10,000.

Types of grant

Annuities are paid quarterly. One-off grants are also available for those in receipt of an annuity for expenses such as furniture, white goods, glasses, travel costs and other unexpected costs. Christmas hampers are also distributed to most annuitants.

Exclusions

The society does not give one-off grants to non-annuitants.

Applications

Applications to become an annuitant should be made on a form available from the correspondent. Completed forms can be submitted directly by the individual or through a third party such as Citizens Advice or a social worker.

Financial information

Year end	31/03/2020
Income	£261,800
Total expenditure	£372,200

Further financial information

During 2019/20, the society supported 120 annuitants.

Other information

The society also provides subsidised accommodation.

The Gus Robinson Foundation

 £12,400 (2019/20)

Correspondent: Jeanette Henderson, 69 Gala Close, Hartlepool, Cleveland TS25 1GB (tel: 07306 160229; email: jeanette_henderson@sky.com)

www.gusrobinson.com/foundation

CC number: 1156290

Eligibility

Individuals in need who are under the age of 25 and live in the Tees Valley.

Types of grant

Grants are available to support individuals with education, training, sports, music, art and entrepreneurship.

Applications

Apply in writing to the correspondent.

Financial information

Year end	30/11/2020
Income	£700
Total expenditure	£13,800

Further financial information

Full accounts were not available to view on the Charity Commission's website due to the foundation's low income. We have therefore estimated the foundation's grant total based on its total expenditure.

Other information

In May 2018, Hartlepool Youth became linked to the foundation and its funds were transferred across.

The Ropner Centenary Trust

£24,000 (2019/20)

Correspondent: Alan Theakston, Trustee, 15 The Green, High Coniscliffe, Darlington, County Durham DL2 2LJ (tel: 07954 192754; email: alantheakston@btinternet.com)

CC number: 269109

Eligibility

Ex-seafarers who are in need, and their dependants. Preference is generally given to people living in the North East, particularly those who have worked for Ropner Shipping Company Ltd.

Types of grant

Grants are given according to need.

Applications

Apply in writing to the correspondent.

Financial information

Year end	31/03/2020
Income	£45,100
Total expenditure	£25,700

Tees Valley Community Foundation

£60,200

Correspondent: Peter Rowley, Secretary, Tees Valley Community Foundation, Wallace House, Falcon Court, Preston Farm Industrial Estate, Stockton-on-Tees, County Durham TS18 3TX (tel: 01642 260860; email: info@teesvalleyfoundation.org)

www.teesvalleyfoundation.org

CC number: 1111222

Eligibility

People in need who live in the Tees Valley. Specific criteria apply depending on the fund.

Types of grant

The community foundation manages a number of different funds, each of which has its own specific criteria for what it can fund.

Applications

Visit the community foundation's website to see details of funds that are currently open to individuals, including specific eligibility criteria and how to make an application.

Financial information

Year end	31/03/2020
Income	£614,500
Total expenditure	£734,200

Further financial information

Grants were awarded to 248 individuals during the year.

Other information

This is one of the 47 UK community foundations, which distribute funding for a wide range of purposes. Grant schemes tend to change frequently – consult the foundation's website for up-to-date information.

The Teesside Family Foundation

£ £2,500 (2020)

Correspondent: The Trustees, 64–66 Borough Road, Middlesbrough TS1 2JH (email: enquiries@ theteessidefamily.com)

 https://www.theteessidefamily.com

CC number: 1179360

Eligibility

People in need living on Teesside.

Types of grant

One-off welfare grants are made according to need. Support may also be available for holidays and specialist equipment for people with disabilities.

Applications

Apply via the charity's website.

Financial information

Year end	31/12/2020
Income	£82,200
Total expenditure	£84,700

Further financial information

The grant total has been estimated based on information available in the foundation's latest accounts.

Community Foundation serving Tyne and Wear and Northumberland

 £90,200 (2020/21)

Correspondent: The Grants Team, Philanthropy House, Woodbine Road, Gosforth, Newcastle upon Tyne NE3 1DD (tel: 0191 222 0945; email: general@communityfoundation.org.uk)

🌐 www.communityfoundation.org.uk

CC number: 700510

Eligibility

People in need living in Tyne and Wear or Northumberland. Support may also be available to individuals living in other parts of the North East.

Types of grant

A number of funds are available to individuals. Refer to the foundation's website for details of open grant programmes.

Exclusions

According to its website, the foundation does not support:

- contributions to general appeals or circulars;
- religious activity which is not for wider public benefit;
- where the primary benefit is to enable a public body to carry out its statutory obligations;
- activities where the primary benefit is the advancement of animal welfare;
- activities which have already taken place;
- grant making, or equivalent gifts in kind, by other organisations;
- privately owned and profit-distributing companies or limited partnerships

Applications

Details on how to apply can be found on the community foundation's website.

Financial information

Year end	31/03/2021
Income	£12,690,000
Total expenditure	£8,120,000

Further financial information

Grants were awarded to 123 individuals during the year.

Other information

This is one of the 47 UK community foundations, which distribute funding for a wide range of purposes. Grant schemes tend to change frequently – consult the foundation's website for details of current programmes and upcoming deadlines.

County Durham

Bull Piece Charity

£ £500 (2019/20)

Correspondent: The Trustees, The Garden House, Hamsterley, Bishop Auckland DL13 3PT (tel: 07787 507816)

CC number: 237477

Eligibility

Residents in the parishes of Copley, Hamsterley, South Bedburn, Lynesack and Softley who are in need.

Types of grant

Grants are given according to need.

Applications

Apply in writing to the correspondent.

Financial information

Year end	30/06/2020
Income	£3,000
Total expenditure	£1,000

Further financial information

Full accounts were not available to view on the Charity Commission's website due to the charity's low income. We have therefore estimated the charity's grant total based on its total expenditure.

Other information

The charity's income is received from the rent of Bull Piece Farm in County Durham. Grants are also made to organisations.

County Durham Community Foundation

 £101,000 (2020/21)

Correspondent: Grants Team, Victoria House, Whitfield Court, St John's Road, Meadowfield Industrial Estate, Durham, County Durham DH7 8XL (tel: 0191 378 6340; email: info@cdcf.org.uk)

🌐 www.cdcf.org.uk

CC number: 1047625

Eligibility

People in need who live in County Durham and Darlington.

Types of grant

A number of funds are available to individuals. Refer to the foundation's website for details of current and open grant programmes.

Applications

Details on how to apply can be found on the community foundation's website.

Financial information

Year end	31/03/2021
Income	£6,040,000
Total expenditure	£5,460,000

Further financial information

During 2020/21, a total of £101,000 was awarded to 380 individuals, with the average grant being £265.

Other information

This is one of the 47 UK community foundations, which distribute funding for a wide range of purposes. Grant schemes tend to change frequently – consult the foundation's website for details of current programmes and upcoming deadlines.

The Hartwell Educational Foundation

 £1,700 (2019/20)

Correspondent: Jayne Dobson, Hillfield, Cotherstone, Barnard Castle DL12 9PG (tel: 07738 873152; email: jayned11@hotmail.com)

https://democracy.durham.gov.uk/mgOutsideBodyDetails.aspx?ID=487

CC number: 527368

Eligibility

People aged between 11 and 21 who live in the civil parish of Stanhope. Eligibility is dependent on parental income.

Types of grant

One-off grants can be given to secondary school students from low-income families towards the cost of uniforms, clothing, books and other educational expenses.

Recurrent grants are available for students who are attending university or college towards the cost of fees, living expenses and books.

Applications

Application forms can be requested from the correspondent.

Financial information

Year end	31/03/2020
Income	£1,500
Total expenditure	£1,900

Further financial information

Full accounts were not available to view on the Charity Commission's website due to the foundation's low income. We have therefore estimated the foundation's grant total based on its total expenditure.

Johnston Educational Foundation

 £1,000 (2020/21)

Correspondent: Grants Team, County Durham Community Foundation, Victoria House, 2 Whitfield Court, St John's Road, Meadowfield Industrial Estate, Durham, County Durham DH7 8XL (tel: 0191 378 6340; email: info@cdcf.org.uk)

https://www.cdcf.org.uk

CC number: 1047625

Eligibility

People under the age of 24 who have attended one of the following schools for at least two years: Belmont Community School; Durham Community Business College; Durham Johnston Comprehensive School; Durham Sixth Form Centre; Durham Trinity School and Sports College; Framwellgate School; St Leonard's RC Comprehensive School. Priority is given to applicants who currently live in Durham and have done for at least two years. Those who live elsewhere for university but have parents residing in Durham may still apply.

Types of grant

Welfare

Grants of between £100 and £250 are given to support those seeking employment towards interview clothes, work clothes, uniforms, tools equipment and books. Assistance is also available for schoolchildren towards equipment, uniforms and so on.

Education

Grants of between £100 and £250 are available to college and university students towards equipment, educational trips, research trips, books, instruments and so on.

Exclusions

The foundation will not fund the following:

- Items that have already been purchased or activities that have already taken place
- Term fees for specialist educational organisations
- Items that are the responsibility of an employer or third party to provide
- Any item/activity whose provision is a statutory obligation
- Gap year activities unless there is a well demonstrated educational element
- Any individual need for which the need for funding is not well demonstrated

- IT equipment (except adaptive computer equipment for users with a disability)

Applications

Application forms and guidelines are available on the County Durham Community Foundation website and can be submitted at any time. Applications must be supported by an independent referee such as a school tutor, a college mentor, a social worker or other professional.

Financial information

Year end	31/03/2021
Income	£4,500

Further financial information

During the 2020/21 financial year, the foundation made grants totalling £1,000. We estimate that £500 was awarded for welfare purposes and £500 was awarded for education.

Other information

This charity is administered by County Durham Community Foundation (1047625).

The Sedgefield District Relief in Need Charity (The Sedgefield Charities)

£15,000 (2020)

Correspondent: The Trustees, 46 While House Drive, Sedgefield, Stockton-on-Tees, County Durham TS1 3BU (tel: 01740 620811; email: sedgefieldcharities@gmail.com)

CC number: 230395

Eligibility

Residents in the parishes of Bishop Middleham, Bradbury, Cornforth, Fishburn, Mordon, Sedgefield and Trimdon who are in need.

Types of grant

Welfare grants are made mainly towards basic furniture. Christmas gifts of £20 are distributed to older residents in the area of benefit.

Applications

Apply in writing to the correspondent. Applications are usually made by social services, Citizen Advice or professionals on the applicant's behalf.

Financial information

Year end	31/12/2020
Income	£12,000
Total expenditure	£19,400

Further financial information

Full accounts were not available to view on the Charity Commission's website due to the charity's low income. We have therefore estimated the grant total based on the charity's total expenditure.

Other information
Grants are also made to local organisations.

Hartlepool

The Furness Seamen's Pension Fund

£ £10,400 (2019/20)

Correspondent: Heather O'Driscoll, Secretary, c/o Waltons Clark Whitehill, Maritime House, Harbour Walk, Hartlepool TS24 0UX (tel: 01429 234414; email: heather.odriscoll@waltonscw.co.uk)

CC number: 226655

Eligibility
Older or retired seamen who live in the borough of Hartlepool, including West Hartlepool, and are in need.

Types of grant
Grants are paid quarterly.

Applications
Apply in writing to the correspondent.

Financial information

Year end	30/06/2020
Income	£9,800
Total expenditure	£11,600

Further financial information
Full accounts were not available to view on the Charity Commission's website due to the fund's low income. We have therefore estimated the fund's grant total based on its total expenditure. Note that the grant total may include loans.

Stockton-on-Tees (North of River Tees)

John T. Shuttleworth Ropner Memorial Fund

£ £1,600 (2020/21)

Correspondent: Grants and Donor Services, Victoria House, Whitfield Court, St John's Road, Meadowfield Industrial Estate, Durham, County Durham DH7 8XL (tel: 0191 378 6340; email: info@cdcf.org.uk)

 www.cdcf.org.uk

CC number: 1047625–1

Eligibility
People who live in the Tees Valley area and are sick or older, or who have a disability, and their carers. Support is given to those who are in need of respite care or temporary support following hospitalisation or bereavement, or due to dependency treatment. Applicants must live in Darlington, Hartlepool, Middlesbrough, Redcar and Cleveland or Stockton-on-Tees.

Types of grant
Grants of up to £1,000 are awarded for recuperative or respite care, home help, bereavement-related costs, travel and accommodation for individuals (and for their families) who are undergoing dependency treatment at a clinic or centre away from their place of residence.

Applications
At the time of writing (October 2021), applications for the fund were not being accepted; unsolicited requests submitted while the fund is closed to applications will not receive a response. Refer to the County Durham Community Foundation website for updates.

Financial information

Year end	31/03/2021
Income	£23,600
Total expenditure	£1,600

Further financial information
Full accounts were not available to view on the Charity Commission's website due to the fund's low income. We have therefore estimated the grant total based on the fund's total expenditure.

North Yorkshire (formerly Cleveland)

Fisher Charity Elizabeth

£ £3,200 (2019)

Correspondent: Enid Roberts, 28 Broadacres, Carlton, Goole, East Yorkshire DN14 9NF (tel: 01405 947328)

CC number: 1071754

Eligibility
Residents of the parishes of Carlton and Drax who are in need.

Types of grant
One-off grants according to need.

Applications
Apply in writing to the correspondent.

Financial information

Year end	31/12/2019
Income	£7,200
Total expenditure	£7,000

Further financial information
Full accounts were not available to view on the Charity Commission's website due to the charity's low income. We have therefore estimated the charity's grant total based on its total expenditure.

The Rowlandson and Eggleston Relief-in-Need Charity

£ £4,900 (2019/20)

Correspondent: Peter Vaux, Clowbeck Farm, Barton, Richmond, North Yorkshire DL10 6HP (tel: 01325 377236; email: petervaux@brettanbymanor.co.uk)

CC number: 515647

Eligibility
People in the parishes of Barton and Newton Morrell who are in need.

Types of grant
One-off grants are awarded, usually in the range of £100 to £500. Recent grants have been given towards funeral expenses, medical equipment, disability aids and lifeline telephone systems for older people.

Applications
Apply in writing to the correspondent including details of circumstances and the specific need(s). Applications may be submitted directly by the individual or through a social worker, Citizens Advice or other third party.

Financial information

Year end	29/02/2020
Income	£4,900
Total expenditure	£5,400

Further financial information
Full accounts were not available to view on the Charity Commission's website due to the charity's low income. We have therefore estimated the charity's grant total based on its total expenditure.

Other information
The charity also provides other facilities and can make grants to individuals for educational purposes.

Middlesbrough

The Lady Crosthwaite Bequest

£ £1,100 (2019/20)

Correspondent: The Trustees, Strategic Resources, PO Box 506, Middlesbrough, North Yorkshire TS1 9GA (tel: 01642 729556)

CC number: 234932

Eligibility
Older people in need living in the county borough of Middlesbrough.

Types of grant
Grants are given according to need.

Applications
Apply in writing to the correspondent.

Financial information
Year end	31/03/2020
Income	£2,700
Total expenditure	£1,200

Further financial information
Full accounts were not available to view on the Charity Commission's website due to the charity's low income. We have therefore estimated the charity's grant total based on its total expenditure.

Northumber-land

The Eleemosynary Charity of Giles Heron

£ £12,400 (2020/21)

Correspondent: The Trustees, Walwick Farm, Humshaugh, Hexham, Northumberland NE46 4BJ (tel: 01434 681203; email: office@chestersestate.co.uk)

CC number: 224157

Eligibility
People in need who live in the parish of Wark and Simonburn.

Types of grant
Grants are awarded according to need.

Applications
Apply in writing to the correspondent.

Financial information
Year end	31/03/2021
Income	£21,000
Total expenditure	£13,800

Further financial information
Full accounts were not available to view on the Charity Commission's website due to the charity's low income. We have therefore estimated the charity's grant total based on its total expenditure.

Morpeth Dispensary

£ £2,300 (2020)

Correspondent: The Trustees, 2 Shadfen Farm Mews, Shadfen, Morpeth, Northumberland NE61 6NP (tel: 01670 512484; email: johnslogger@aol.com)

CC number: 222352

Eligibility
Residents of Morpeth who are experiencing ill health and/or financial hardship.

Types of grant
One-off grants are awarded according to need. Recent examples include grants for white goods, furnishing, decorating and clothing.

Applications
Apply in writing to the correspondent.

Financial information
Year end	31/12/2020
Income	£3,300
Total expenditure	£2,500

Further financial information
Full accounts were not available to view on the Charity Commission's website due to the charity's low income. We have therefore estimated the charity's grant total based on its total expenditure.

The John Routledge Hunter Memorial Fund

£ £4,400 (2019/20)

Correspondent: The Trustees, c/o Womble Bond Dickinson LLP, One Trinity Gardens, Broad Chare, Newcastle upon Tyne, Tyne and Wear NE1 2HF (tel: 0191 279 9000)

CC number: 225619

Eligibility
People living Northumberland and Tyne and Wear who are in need as a result of illness, convalescence, infirmity or disability. Priority is given to residents of the former county of Northumberland prior to the 1974 reorganisation. In exceptional cases, temporary residents of the area of benefit, or residents outside the area of benefit, may also be eligible for assistance.

Types of grant
Grants for essential items, services or facilities are awarded to relieve suffering or assist recovery. The fund may award cash grants or pay for goods on behalf of the individual.

Applications
Apply in writing to the correspondent.

Financial information
Year end	31/10/2020
Income	£16,200
Total expenditure	£4,900

Further financial information
Full accounts were not available to view on the Charity Commission's website due to the fund's low income. We have therefore estimated the fund's grant total based on its total expenditure.

Other information
Grants are also awarded to organisations.

Tyne and Wear

Gateshead

Gateshead Relief-in-Sickness Fund

£ £720 (2020)

Correspondent: Rachel Ray, c/o Thomas Magnay & Co., 8 St Mary's Green, Whickham, Newcastle upon Tyne, Tyne and Wear NE16 4DN (tel: 0191 488 7459; email: rachelray@thomasmagnay.co.uk)

CC number: 234970

Eligibility
People living in Gateshead who are in need as a result of ill health, disability or other medical conditions.

Types of grant
The charity makes grants for items, services or facilities which assist the recovery or relief of its beneficiaries. Grants are made towards items that are not readily available from other sources.

Applications
Apply in writing to the correspondent.

Financial information
Year end	31/12/2020
Income	£2,200
Total expenditure	£1,600

Further financial information
Full accounts were not available to view on the Charity Commission's website due to the fund's low income. We have therefore estimated the grant total based on the fund's total expenditure.

Other information
This charity also makes grants to organisations.

Newcastle upon Tyne

The Non-Ecclesiastical Charity of William Moulton

£ £33,500 (2019)

Correspondent: Roger Gray, Clerk to the Trustees, 42 Richardson Gardens, Shiremoor, Newcastle upon Tyne NE27 0FH (tel: 0191 253 7693; email: williammoulton.charity@gmail.com)

CC number: 216255

Eligibility
People in need who have lived within the boundaries of the city of Newcastle upon Tyne for at least the past 12 months.

Types of grant
One-off grants are awarded according to need.

Exclusions
Only one grant will be given to an applicant in any 12-month period. Our previous research indicates that the charity does not assist with: education or training; repaying debts or arrears, such as Council Tax arrears; or day-to-day living expenses, such as food.

Applications
Application forms can be requested from the charity.

Financial information
Year end	31/12/2019
Income	£42,800
Total expenditure	£63,900

The Town Moor Money Charity

£ £22,700 (2019/20)

Correspondent: The Trustees, Moor Bank Lodge, Claremont Road, Newcastle upon Tyne, Tyne and Wear NE2 4NL (tel: 0191 261 5970; email: admin@ freemenofnewcastle.org)

 www.freemenofnewcastle.org

CC number: 227620–1

Eligibility
Freemen of Newcastle upon Tyne, and their spouses, who are in need. The widows of deceased freemen are also eligible for support. Educational grants are available to the children of freemen,

aged 18 to 20, who are in full-time further education.

Types of grant
Welfare
Grants are awarded towards the cost of mobility aids.

Education
Grants are awarded towards the costs of further education.

Applications
The website states that application forms are available in April and October from 'the Senior Steward of the Company through which the applicant's family hail'. Grants are awarded twice a year, in June and December.

Financial information
Year end	29/09/2020

Further financial information
During the 2019/20 financial year, the charity awarded £11,500 in December to 115 individuals and £11,200 in June to 112 individuals.

The charity does not disclose its income or total expenditure in The Town Moor Charity's accounts.

Other information
This charity is linked to The Town Moor Charity.

North Tyneside

Victor Mann Trust (also known as The Wallsend Charitable Trust)

£ £6,700 (2019)

Correspondent: The Trustees, North Tyneside Council, 16 The Silverlink North, Newcastle upon Tyne, Tyne and Wear NE27 0BY (tel: 0191 643 7006)

CC number: 215476

Eligibility
Older people who are in need and live in the former borough of Wallsend.

Types of grant
Grants are given according to need.

Applications
Apply in writing to the correspondent.

Financial information
Year end	31/12/2019
Income	£122,500
Total expenditure	£28,600

Other information
The trust also provides housing for older people and awards grants to organisations with similar objectives.

Sunderland

George Hudson's Charity

£ £22,200 (2019/20)

Correspondent: George Johnston, Secretary, 47 John Street, Sunderland, Tyne and Wear SR1 1QU (tel: 0191 567 4857; email: georgejohnston@ mckenzie-bell.co.uk)

CC number: 527204

Eligibility
People under the age of 18 whose father has died or is unable to work and who are living in Sunderland. First preference is given to children of seafarers or pilots belonging to the Port of Sunderland, and second preference is given to those born and resident in the ancient township of Monkwearmouth.

Types of grant
The charity gives regular grants and clothing vouchers.

Applications
Contact the correspondent for more information.

Financial information
Year end	05/04/2020
Income	£35,100
Total expenditure	£42,500

Further financial information
Grants awarded in 2019/20 were broken down as follows: monthly cash payments (£10,500); clothing and footwear (£10,500); Christmas bonuses (£1,200).

Sunderland Guild of Help

£ £14,300 (2019/20)

Correspondent: The Trustees, Bede Tower, Burdon Road, Sunderland SR2 7EA (tel: 0191 6310 992 (Wednesdays from 9.30am only); email: info@guildofhelp.co.uk)

 www.guildofhelp.co.uk

CC number: 229656

Eligibility
People living in Sunderland who are in need as a result of illness or financial difficulty. The charity has a particular interest in supporting people who have been affected by domestic abuse and families of children with a disability.

Types of grant
Support is given for the provision of essential items such as beds, washing machines and fridges.

Exclusions

The charity does not provide cash grants or loans, nor does it give grants for new goods or goods made to order.

Applications

Application forms can be downloaded from the charity's website and must be submitted by a social worker or other professional.

Financial information

Year end	31/03/2020
Income	£9,500
Total expenditure	£15,900

Further financial information

Full accounts were not available to view on the Charity Commission's website due to the charity's low income. We have therefore estimated the charity's grant total based on its total expenditure.

The Sunderland Orphanage and Educational Foundation

£ £18,000 (2019/20)

Correspondent: The Trustees, 47 John Street, Sunderland, Tyne and Wear SR1 1QU (tel: 0191 565 6561; email: georgejohnston@mckenzie-bell.co.uk)

CC number: 527202

Eligibility

Young people under the age of 25 who live in or around Sunderland and attend a school, college or university approved by the trustees. The applicant's parents should be separated or divorced, have a disability, or one or both parents should be deceased.

Types of grant

Grants are awarded for the following purposes:

- Provision of tools, equipment, books and other physical necessities for education
- Purchasing school uniforms or job-related clothing
- Scholarships, bursaries and maintenance allowances tenable at any place of learning approved by the trustees
- Financial assistance for people leaving school and about to enter employment or trade
- Provision and tutoring of musical instruments
- Travelling abroad for study
- Coaching and training in sports and athletics
- Financial assistance to study music and the arts.

The foundation also provides grants in the form of boarding and pocket money to young people in financial need.

Applications

Apply in writing to the correspondent.

Financial information

Year end	05/04/2020
Income	£21,800
Total expenditure	£20,000

Further financial information

Full accounts were not available to view on the Charity Commission's website due to the foundation's low income. We have therefore estimated the foundation's grant total based on its total expenditure.

North West

General

The Cotton Districts Convalescent Fund and the Barnes Samaritan Charity
See entry on page 216

Community Foundations for Lancashire and Merseyside

£ £91,000 (2019/20)

Correspondent: The Trustees, 43 Hanover Street, Liverpool, Merseyside L1 3DN (tel: 0151 232 2420; email: applications@cflm.email)

 www.cfmerseyside.org.uk

CC number: 1068887

Eligibility
People in need who live in Merseyside.

Types of grant
A number of funds are available to individuals. Refer to the foundation's website for details of current and open grant programmes.

Applications
Details on how to apply can be found on the community foundation's website.

Financial information

Year end	31/03/2020
Income	£3,880,000
Total expenditure	£3,230,000

Further financial information
Based on the information gathered from the foundation's website, we have estimated that a total of £91,000 was awarded to individuals in 2019/20, with around £52,200 being awarded for social welfare purposes and £37,700 for education purposes.

Other information
This is one of the 47 UK community foundations, which distribute funding for a wide range of purposes. Grant schemes tend to change frequently – consult the foundation's website for details of current programmes and upcoming deadlines.

The Lancashire Infirm Secular Clergy Fund

£ £110,600 (2019/20)

Correspondent: The Revd Simon Hawksworth, Treasurer, Christ the Good Shepherd, Banklands, Workington CA14 3EP (email: simon.hawksworth@hotmail.co.uk)

CC number: 222796

Eligibility
Catholic secular clergy of the dioceses of Liverpool, Salford and Lancaster who are sick or retired and are in need of support.

Types of grant
One-off or recurrent grants are awarded according to need.

Applications
Apply in writing to the correspondent.

Financial information

Year end	05/04/2020
Income	£153,300
Total expenditure	£115,400

The North West Police Benevolent Fund

£ £42,600 (2019)

Correspondent: J. Smithies, Secretary, St Michael's Lodge, Northcote Road, Langho, Lancashire BB6 8BG (tel: 01254 244980; email: enquiries@nwpbf.org)

 https://www.thebenfund.co.uk

CC number: 503045

Eligibility
Serving and retired officers of Cheshire Constabulary, Greater Manchester Police, Lancashire Constabulary, Cumbria Constabulary, Merseyside Police, the National Crime Agency (NCA) and previous police forces amalgamated within the constituent forces, and their dependants, who are in need. Officers must be members of the fund and contribute a monthly membership fee.

Types of grant
One-off and recurrent grants and interest-free loans are given to pay for items or services that will alleviate suffering. In the event of the death of a serving police officer, a grant of £5,000 is paid to their dependants.

Exclusions
Grants are not given for private healthcare, nursing home fees, private education or legal fees.

Applications
Contact the fund for more information.

Financial information

Year end	31/12/2019
Income	£1,600,000
Total expenditure	£1,610,000

Further financial information
During 2019, grants to serving officers totalled £8,500 and those to retired officers £5,100. Additionally, loans paid out totalled £11,900, which has not been included in the grant total.

Other information
As well as grants, the fund offers a range of services such as physiotherapy and mental health support. It also owns a lodge, which is used for convalescence and well-being breaks.

Northern Ladies Annuity Society
See entry on page 335

Lancashire County Nursing Trust

 £17,000 (2020)

Correspondent: Hadyn Gigg, Trustee, Plumpton House, Plumpton Lane, Great Plumpton, Preston, Lancashire PR4 3NE (tel: 01772 673618; email: hadyngigg@yahoo.co.uk)

www.lcnt.org.uk

CC number: 224667

Eligibility
People in need due to illness or financial difficulty who live in Lancashire, Greater Manchester, South Cumbria, Liverpool or Sefton. Support is also available to retired district nursing staff who have worked within the same areas.

Types of grant
According to the trust's website, previous grants have been used towards replacement washing machines, food for people with special dietary requirements, assistance with home adaptations, radios or TVs for individuals who are housebound, and Amazon Kindles and downloadable books.

Applications
Apply in writing to the correspondent.

Financial information
Year end	31/12/2020
Income	£15,500
Total expenditure	£18,900

Further financial information
Full accounts were not available to view on the Charity Commission's website due to the trust's low income. We have therefore estimated the grant total based on the trust's total expenditure.

Roundhouse Foundation

 £5,900 (2019/20)

Correspondent: The Trustees, 3 Roundhouse Court, South Rings Office Village, Bamber Bridge, Preston, Lancashire PR5 6DA (tel: 01772 312579; email: rhf@roundhouseproperties.co.uk)

CC number: 1104085

Eligibility
Residents in the counties of Cumbria, Lancashire and Greater Manchester who are in need. Children attending any educational organisation in these same counties are also eligible for support.

Types of grant
Grants are given according to need.

Applications
Apply in writing to the correspondent.

Financial information
Year end	31/03/2020
Income	£5,600
Total expenditure	£13,200

Further financial information
Full accounts were not available to view on the Charity Commission's website due to the foundation's low income. We have therefore estimated the grant total based on the foundation's total expenditure.

Other information
The foundation also makes grants to organisations.

Rycroft Children's Fund
See entry on page 212

United Utilities Trust Fund

 £2,880,000 (2019/20)

Correspondent: The Trustees, Emmanuel Court, 12–14 Mill Street, Sutton Coldfield, West Midlands B72 1TJ (tel: 0300 790 6172; email: contact@uutf.org.uk)

www.uutf.org.uk

CC number: 1108296

Eligibility
People in need who live in the area supplied by United Utilities Water (predominantly the north-west of England).

Types of grant
Payments are given to meet water and/or sewerage charges related to United Utilities Water, white goods and other household needs, bankruptcy orders, Debt Relief Orders and funeral costs.

Exclusions
The trust cannot help with the following: household bills such as gas and electricity or rent arrears; court fines; catalogue debts; credit cards; personal loans or other forms of borrowing; Social Fund loans; benefit over payments; tax credit overpayment; bills that have already been paid; items that have already been bought.

Applications
Application forms and full guidelines are available from the trust's website.

Financial information
Year end	31/03/2020
Income	£3,500,000
Total expenditure	£3,460,000

Cheshire

The Grant, Bagshaw, Rogers and Tidswell Fund

 £21,000 (2019/20)

Correspondent: Lawrence Downey, Ripley House, 56 Freshfield Road, Formby, Liverpool, Merseyside L37 3HW (tel: 07785 768270; email: lawrencedowney@btconnect.com)

CC number: 216948

Eligibility
Older people in need who live, or were born in, Liverpool, the Wirral, Ellesmere Port or Chester.

Types of grant
Small pensions and grants are given.

Applications
Apply in writing to the correspondent.

Financial information
Year end	30/09/2020
Income	£16,000
Total expenditure	£23,300

Further financial information
Full accounts were not available to view on the Charity Commission's website due to the fund's low income. We have therefore estimated the grant total based on the fund's total expenditure.

John Holford's Charity

 £36,100 (2019)

Correspondent: Kerris Owen, Clerk to the Trustees, Parish Office, St Peter's Church, The Cross, Chester CH1 2LA (tel: 07794 654212; email: jholfordcharity@gmail.com)

www.johnholfordcharity.org

CC number: 223046

Eligibility
People in need who live in one of the following parishes: Alsager, Astbury, Brereton, Church Lawton, Clutton, Congleton, Eaton, Goostrey, Holmes Chapel, Hulme Walfield, Middlewich, Mow Cop, North Rode, Odd Rode, Rode Heath, Sandbach, Sandbach Heath, Smallwood, Swettenham and Wheelock.

Types of grant

Grants are given for a range of purposes. In the past, support has been given towards white goods and furniture, school uniforms, mobility and communication aids, and retraining expenses.

Exclusions

Grants cannot be given to eradicate debt.

Applications

Application forms can be downloaded from the charity's website.

Financial information

Year end	31/12/2019
Income	£89,200
Total expenditure	£80,200

Further financial information

Based on the financial information available on the charity's Charity Commission record, we estimate that around £36,100 was awarded to individuals in 2019.

Other information

This charity also makes grants to organisations.

Cheshire East

Alsager Educational Foundation

£ £8,900 (2019/20)

Correspondent: Catherine Lovatt, Secretary, 6 Pikemere Road, Alsager, Stoke-on-Trent, Staffordshire ST7 2SB (tel: 01270 873680; email: colovatt@ hotmail.com)

CC number: 525834

Eligibility

Children and young people who live in the parish of Alsager, Cheshire East.

Types of grant

The foundation awards scholarships, bursaries and maintenance allowances for a range of educational purposes and recreational activities. Support may be given towards the costs of, for example, books, travel (including abroad in pursuance of education), religious education and the study of music.

Applications

Apply in writing to the correspondent.

Financial information

Year end	30/06/2020
Income	£25,700
Total expenditure	£23,400

Further financial information

In 2019/20, grants to individuals totalled £8,900.

Other information

The foundation also supports organisations (£13,600 in 2019/20). Special benefits are provided to the Alsager Church of England Junior School.

The Congleton Town Trust

£ £1,800 (2020)

Correspondent: Jo Money, Clerk to the Trustees, Congleton Town Hall, High Street, Congleton, Cheshire CW12 1BN (tel: 01260 270908; email: info@ congletontowntrust.co.uk)

 www.congletontowntrust.co.uk

CC number: 1051122

Eligibility

Residents within the area administered by Congleton Town Council who are in need.

Types of grant

Welfare grants are awarded according to need.

Applications

The website states, 'If you are applying as an individual, contact the Clerk directly.' The trustees meet quarterly to consider grant applications.

Financial information

Year end	31/12/2020
Income	£15,600
Total expenditure	£14,600

Further financial information

Full accounts were not available to view on the Charity Commission's website due to the trust's low income. We have therefore estimated the trust's grant total based on its total expenditure.

Other information

The trust also makes grants to organisations.

Lindow Workhouse Charity

£ £6,800 (2019/20)

Correspondent: The Trustees, 1 Thornfield Hey, Wilmslow, Cheshire SK9 2NF (tel: 01625 533950)

CC number: 226023

Eligibility

Residents of Wilmslow who are in need.

Types of grant

Grants are given according to need.

Applications

Apply in writing to the correspondent.

Financial information

Year end	31/10/2020
Income	£11,900
Total expenditure	£7,500

Further financial information

Full accounts were not available to view on the Charity Commission's website due to the charity's low income. We have therefore estimated the grant total based on the charity's total expenditure.

Macclesfield and District Relief-in-Sickness Charity

£ £4,500 (2019/20)

Correspondent: The Trustees, 35 Ivy Road, Macclesfield, Cheshire SK11 8QN (tel: 01625 420530)

CC number: 501631

Eligibility

People who have a disability or are sick, convalescent or infirm and live in the Macclesfield borough area.

Types of grant

One-off grants according to need.

Applications

Apply in writing to the correspondent.

Financial information

Year end	31/03/2020
Income	£3,000
Total expenditure	£5,000

Further financial information

Full accounts were not available to view on the Charity Commission's website due to the charity's low income. We have therefore estimated the charity's grant total based on its total expenditure.

Wilmslow Aid Trust (Incorporating Amos Johnson Fund)

£ £1,100 (2019/20)

Correspondent: David Pincombe, Trustee, 7 Brereton Road, Handforth, Cheshire SK9 3AN (tel: 01625 526352; email: dhpincombe@btinternet.com)

CC number: 253340

Eligibility

Residents of Wilmslow and the surrounding neighbourhood who are in need. Priority is given to those in need due to ill health or disability.

Types of grant

Grants are given according to need.

Applications

Apply in writing to the correspondent.

Financial information

Year end	31/08/2020
Income	£3,400
Total expenditure	£2,300

Further financial information

Full accounts were not available to view on the Charity Commission's website due to the trust's low income. We have therefore estimated the trust's grant total based on its total expenditure.

Other information

This trust also makes grants to organisations.

The Consolidated Charity of the Parish of Wrenbury

£4,600 (2019)

Correspondent: Rachel Cope, Trustee, 2 Belmont Villa, Frith Lane, Wrenbury, Nantwich, Cheshire CW5 8HQ (tel: 01270 780262; email: rachelcope27@ yahoo.co.uk)

CC number: 241778

Eligibility

People in need who live in the parishes of Chorley, Sound, Broomhall, Newhall, Wrenbury-cum-Frith and Dodcott-cum-Wilkesley. There is a preference for older people and students.

Types of grant

Grants are awarded according to need for the welfare of older people and the welfare and education of students.

Applications

Apply in writing to the correspondent.

Financial information

Year end	31/12/2019
Income	£10,800
Total expenditure	£10,300

Further financial information

Full accounts were not available to view on the Charity Commission's website due to the charity's low income. We have therefore estimated the charity's grant total based on its total expenditure.

Other information

Grants are also given to churches, the village hall and to local schools.

The Wybunbury United Charities

£3,000 (2020)

Correspondent: The Trustees, c/o Barnabas Pettman & Co. Ltd, 12 Lyndhurst Grove, Stone, Staffordshire ST15 8TP (tel: 01785 819677; email: barnabaspettman@hotmail.co.uk)

CC number: 227387

Eligibility

People in need living within the parishes of the Cheshire East Council area (formerly known as the borough of Crewe and Nantwich), with some preference for residents of Wybunbury and its vicinity.

Types of grant

Grants are awarded according to need with the aim of alleviating poverty.

Applications

Apply in writing to the correspondent.

Financial information

Year end	31/12/2020
Income	£5,000
Total expenditure	£6,600

Further financial information

Full accounts were not available to view on the Charity Commission's website due to the charity's low income. We have therefore estimated the charity's grant total based on its total expenditure.

Other information

The charity also makes grants to organisations.

Cheshire West and Chester

Chester Parochial Charity

£49,100 (2019/20)

Correspondent: The Trustees, Parish Office, St Peter's Church, Watergate Street, Chester CH1 2LA (tel: 07794 654212; email: cprncharity@gmail.com)

CC number: 1001314

Eligibility

People in need who live in the city of Chester.

Types of grant

One-off grants are given for a range of purposes including furniture, white goods, school uniforms and so on. According to our previous research, the charity also runs a supermarket vouchers

scheme to help low-income families, mainly over the Christmas period.

Applications

Apply in writing to the correspondent. Applicants are usually visited by a trustee, who will then report back to the sub-committee for a final decision.

Financial information

Year end	08/11/2020
Income	£29,300
Total expenditure	£61,800

The Ursula Keyes Trust

£8,000 (2019)

Correspondent: The Trustees, c/o RSM, One City Place, Queens Street, Chester CH1 3BQ (tel: 01244 505100)

 www.ursula-keyes-trust.org.uk

CC number: 517200

Eligibility

People in need, especially those with a medical condition, who live in the area administered by Chester District Council, in particular those within the boundaries of the former city of Chester and the adjoining parishes of Great Boughton and Upton.

Types of grant

One-off grants according to need.

Applications

Apply in writing to the correspondent. A summary form is available to download from the website and should be submitted along with your application. Applications must be supported by a social worker, a doctor (if relevant) or another professional or welfare agency. Applications are considered by the trustees at their quarterly meetings, which take place on Fridays at the end of January, April, July and October. Applications should be received at least two weeks before these dates to be certain of consideration at any particular meeting. Dates of forthcoming meetings are posted on the trust's website.

Financial information

Year end	31/12/2019
Income	£351,400
Total expenditure	£378,700

Further financial information

Grants were awarded to two individuals in 2019.

Other information

The trust also gives grants to organisations.

Cumbria

Agnes Backhouse Annuity Fund

(£) £14,900 (2020)

Correspondent: The Trustees, c/o Temple Heelis Solicitors, 1 Kent View, Kendal, Cumbria LA9 4DZ (tel: 01539 723757)

CC number: 224960

Eligibility
Unmarried or widowed women in need who are over 50 years of age and live in the parish of Ambleside, Cumbria.

Types of grant
Annuities or yearly donations are awarded according to need.

Applications
Apply in writing to the correspondent.

Financial information
Year end	31/12/2020
Income	£18,000
Total expenditure	£33,100

Further financial information
Full accounts were not available to view on the Charity Commission's website due to the fund's low income. We have therefore estimated the fund's grant total based on its total expenditure.

Other information
This fund also makes grants directly to, or through, other charitable organisations.

Barrow Thornborrow Charity

(£) £3,900 (2019)

Correspondent: The Trustees, 6 Murley Moss, Kendal, Cumbria LA9 7RW (tel: 01539 722956; email: walkerg8@sky.com)

CC number: 222168

Eligibility
People with disabilities or those with ill health who reside in the following areas: the former county of Westmorland; the former county borough of Barrow; the former rural districts of Sedbergh and North Lonsdale; or the former urban districts of Dalton-in-Furness, Grange and Ulverston.

Types of grant
Grants are given according to need.

Applications
Apply in writing to the correspondent.

Financial information
Year end	31/12/2019
Income	£3,100
Total expenditure	£4,300

Further financial information
Full accounts were not available to view on the Charity Commission's website due to the charity's low income. We have therefore estimated the charity's grant total based on its total expenditure.

Cumbria Community Foundation

(£) £153,200 (2019/20)

Correspondent: The Trustees, Cumbria Community Foundation, Dovenby Hall, Dovenby, Cockermouth CA13 0PN (tel: 01900 825760; email: enquiries@cumbriafoundation.org)

 www.cumbriafoundation.org

CC number: 1075120

Eligibility
People in need who live in Cumbria.

Types of grant
A number of funds are available to individuals. Refer to the foundation's website for details of current and open grants.

Applications
Details on how to apply can be found on the community foundation's website.

Financial information
Year end	31/03/2020
Income	£8,470,000
Total expenditure	£2,530,000

Further financial information
In 2019/20, a total of £153,200 was awarded to 180 individuals.

Other information
This is one of the 47 UK community foundations, which distribute funding for a wide range of purposes. Grant schemes tend to change frequently – consult the foundation's website for details of current programmes and upcoming deadlines.

The Jane Fisher Trust

(£) £1,200 (2019/20)

Correspondent: Deborah Yearnshire, c/o Brown Barron, 65 Duke Street, Barrow-in-Furness, Cumbria LA12 7AU (tel: 01229 828814; email: deborah.yearnshire@brown-barron.co.uk)

CC number: 225401

Eligibility
People in need who are aged 55 years and over and have lived in Ulverston, Osmotherly or Pennington for 20 years.

Types of grant
Grants are given according to need.

Applications
Apply in writing to the correspondent.

Financial information
Year end	05/04/2020
Income	£4,700
Total expenditure	£1,500

Further financial information
Full accounts were not available to view on the Charity Commission's website due to the trust's low income. We have therefore estimated the grant total based on the trust's total expenditure.

Kirkby Lonsdale Relief in Need Charity

(£) £1,500 (2019/20)

Correspondent: The Trustees, 19 Fairgarth Drive, Kirkby Lonsdale, Carnforth, Lancashire LA6 2DT (tel: 01524 271985; email: dquinn1716@btinternet.com)

CC number: 224872

Eligibility
People who live in the parish of Kirkby Lonsdale and are in need.

Types of grant
Grants are awarded according to need.

Applications
Apply in writing to the correspondent. Awards are usually distributed in December.

Financial information
Year end	30/11/2020
Income	£1,300
Total expenditure	£1,700

Further financial information
Full accounts were not available to view on the Charity Commission's website due to the charity's low income. We have therefore estimated the grant total based on the charity's total expenditure.

The Mary Grave Trust

(£) £32,800 (2019/20)

Correspondent: Gary Higgs, Cumbria Community Foundation, Dovenby Hall, Dovenby, Cockermouth, Cumbria CA13 0PN (tel: 01900 825760; email: gary@cumbriafoundation.org)

 https://www.cumbriafoundation.org/fund/mary-grave-trust-fund

CC number: 1075120

Eligibility
Young people aged between 11 and 21 who live in the old county of Cumberland (excluding Carlisle, unless the applicant's mother was resident outside Carlisle at the time of birth). Applicants must have attended full time education within the last two years prior to application. Priority will be given to people living in the areas of Workington, Maryport and Whitehaven. Grants are means tested; to be eligible, the applicant's household income must be less than £590 per week.

Types of grant
Grants are available for individuals to travel abroad for educational purposes. The trust's website gives the following examples: school or youth organisation trips, gap year activities and work-experience.

Exclusions
The trust will not fund group or family holidays.

Applications
Application forms and guidelines are available from the Cumbria Community Foundation's website. Applications are considered three times a year, usually in January, June and November, and applications deadlines fall a month before each meeting. Applicants are required to submit a full copy of their birth certificate along with the application form.

Financial information
Year end	31/03/2020
Income	£67,200
Total expenditure	£34,200

Further financial information
In 2019/20, the trust made grants totalling £32,800 to 41 individuals.

Other information
The trust is administered by the Cumbria Community Foundation.

Allerdale

Cockermouth Relief-in-Need Charity

£ £3,000 (2020)

Correspondent: The Trustees, The Rectory, Lorton Road, Cockermouth CA13 9DU (tel: 01900 821288)

CC number: 221297

Eligibility
People in need who live in Cockermouth.

Types of grant
One-off grants are awarded according to need.

Applications
Apply in writing to the correspondent.

Financial information
Year end	31/12/2020
Income	£3,000
Total expenditure	£3,400

Further financial information
Full accounts were not available to view on the Charity Commission's website due to the charity's low income. We have therefore estimated the grant total based on the charity's total expenditure.

Fawcett Johnston Charity

£ £2,000 (2019)

Correspondent: The Trustees, The Town Hall, Senhouse Street, Maryport, Cumbria CA15 6BH (tel: 01900 813205; email: maryport.council@talk21.com)

CC number: 208326

Eligibility
Sailors and ship carpenters living in Maryport who are in need. The widows and children of such individuals are also supported.

Types of grant
Grants are given according to need.

Applications
Apply in writing to the correspondent.

Financial information
Year end	31/12/2019
Income	£2,500
Total expenditure	£2,200

Further financial information
Full accounts were not available to view on the Charity Commission's website due to the charity's low income. We have therefore estimated the charity's grant total based on its total expenditure.

Barrow-in-Furness

Billincoat Charities

£ £8,600 (2019/20)

Correspondent: Clerk to the Trustees, Dalton Town Council Offices, Station Road, Dalton-in-Furness, Cumbria LA15 8DT (tel: 07708 425503; email: townclerk@daltoncouncil.org.uk)

 https://daltoncouncil.org.uk/billincoat-charity

CC number: 233409

Eligibility

Welfare
Older people and people with disabilities who live in Barrow-in-Furness.

Education
Young people who live in Barrow-in-Furness.

Types of grant
One-off grants are given according to need.

Applications
Application forms can be obtained from the correspondent.

Financial information
Year end	30/06/2020
Income	£3,400
Total expenditure	£9,600

Further financial information
Full accounts were not available to view on the Charity Commission's website due to the charity's low income. We have therefore estimated the charity's grant total based on its total expenditure.

Carlisle

Carlisle Sick Poor Fund

£ £5,200 (2019)

Correspondent: The Trustees, 15 Fisher Street, Carlisle, Cumbria CA3 8RW

CC number: 223124

Eligibility
People living in Carlisle and its vicinity who are in financial hardship due to ill health.

Types of grant
One-off grants are awarded towards items such as bedding, food, fuel, medical aids and equipment. Grants are also given towards the payment of recuperative holidays, home help and convalescent care homes.

Applications
Apply in writing to the correspondent.

Financial information
Year end	31/12/2019
Income	£9,700
Total expenditure	£11,600

Further financial information
Full accounts were not available to view on the Charity Commission's website due to the fund's low income. We have therefore estimated the fund's grant total based on its total expenditure.

Other information

This fund also supports local organisations that provide care and relief to people who are sick or in financial need.

South Lakeland

Ambleside Welfare Charity

£8,800 (2020)

Correspondent: The Trustees, 36 Hill Top View, Bowburn, Durham, County Durham DH6 5BU (tel: 0191 377 2756; email: mjohn59655uk@yahoo.com)

CC number: 214759

Eligibility

People in need who live in the parish of Ambleside.

Types of grant

Grants are given according to need.

Applications

Apply in writing to the correspondent.

Financial information

Year end	31/12/2020
Income	£15,300
Total expenditure	£27,100

Further financial information

Full accounts were not available to view on the Charity Commission's website due to the charity's low income. We have therefore estimated the charity's grant total based on its total expenditure.

Lakeland Disability Support CIO

£43,000 (2020)

Correspondent: The LDS Correspondent, 46 Victoria Road North, Windermere, Cumbria LA23 2DS (tel: 01539 442800)

 www.amblesideonline.co.uk/useful-information/clubs/lakeland-disability-support

CC number: 1184060

Eligibility

People with physical disabilities who live in South Lakeland, Cumbria.

Types of grant

One-off grants ranging from £200 to £5,000 are awarded towards, for example, the cost of respite care, garden access, special education or equipment (such as electric scooters, special chairs or computers).

Exclusions

No grants are given towards term care provision.

Applications

Application forms can be downloaded from the Ambleside Online website or requested from the correspondent. Applications may be made by the individual or a third party and should be accompanied by a reference from a carer, doctor or social worker. Applications are considered quarterly, usually in March, June, September and December each year.

Financial information

Year end	31/12/2020
Income	£47,300
Total expenditure	£92,800

Other information

This charity was formerly known as Lakeland Disability Support (Charity Commission no. 1102609) but re-registered as Lakeland Disability Support CIO in June 2019.

Greater Manchester

The Believe and Achieve Trust

£20,600 (2019/20)

Correspondent: Alison Williams, Executive Founder, 1 Sugden Street, Ashton-Under-Lyne, Lancashire OL6 6PT (tel: 0161 330 2501; email: hello@believeandachieve.org.uk)

 believeandachieve.org.uk

CC number: 1157173

Eligibility

Young people who live in Greater Manchester and are disadvantaged. The trust's website states that, for its purposes, "disadvanatged" means someone with physical or learning disabilities, or is socially or financially deprived'.

Types of grant

Grants are given to improve the beneficiary's life (for example, their emotional welfare, social inclusion or level of independence). A past example is a grant for a light weight wheelchair that allowed the young person to gain a lot more independence.

Applications

There is an initial contact form on the website. Alternatively, you can contact the trust via email, telephone or social media.

Financial information

Year end	30/06/2020
Income	£22,100
Total expenditure	£22,900

Further financial information

Full accounts were not available to view on the Charity Commission's website due to the trust's low income. We have therefore estimated the trust's grant total based on its total expenditure.

Other information

The charity was established in 2014 in honour of Alex Williams, who was a dedicate meningitis campaigner. Alongside awarding grants to both individuals and organisations, the trust also raises awareness of meningitis.

J. T. Blair's Charity

£25,300 (2019/20)

Correspondent: Emma Willder, Secretary, Room G104, Bolton Arena, Arena Approach, Bolton BL6 4GH (tel: 01204 414317; email: jtblairs@gmail.com)

https://jtblairscharity.btck.co.uk

CC number: 221248

Eligibility

People in need over the age of 65 who live in Manchester and Salford.

Types of grant

Pensions of up to £10 per week are available towards the cost of utility bills.

Applications

Application forms are available to download on the charity's website or can be requested from the correspondent.

Financial information

Year end	30/06/2020
Income	£14,400
Total expenditure	£28,100

Further financial information

Full accounts were not available to view on the Charity Commission's website due to the charity's low income. We have therefore estimated the charity's grant total based on its total expenditure.

Other information

The charity also provides a befriending service for socially isolated people, as well as supporting other charitable organisations.

George House Trust

 £43,000 (2019/20)

Correspondent: The Trustees, 75–77 Ardwick Green North, Manchester M12 6FX (tel: 0161 274 4499; email: ght@ght.org.uk)

🌐 www.ght.org.uk

CC number: 1143138

Eligibility

People with HIV who live in the north-west of England and have accessed services at George House Trust.

Types of grant

Grants are available for beds and mattresses, white goods, clothing and bedding.

Exclusions

Individuals who have not contacted George House Trust before must book an appointment with an adviser before applying for a grant.

Applications

Applications can be made via the trust's website.

Financial information

Year end	31/03/2020
Income	£638,100
Total expenditure	£684,200

Further financial information

According to the trust's 2019/20 accounts, 242 grants were made to individuals during the year.

Other information

The trust's activities range from raising awareness through its information and community services, to providing advice, counselling and support for people affected by HIV and AIDS.

Manchester District Nursing Institution Fund

 £9,000 (2020)

Correspondent: The Trustees, Beyond Profit Ltd, G104 Bolton Arena, Arena Approach, Horwich, Bolton, Greater Manchester BL6 6LB (tel: 01204 414317; email: admin@reliefinneed.co.uk)

🌐 https://www.reliefinneed.co.uk/ district-nursing-fund

CC number: 235916

Eligibility

People living in Manchester, Salford or Trafford who are on a low income and whose need is further exacerbated by illness, convalescence or disability.

Types of grant

Grants of up to £500 are available for specific purposes that alleviate the individual's distress and assist in recovery. In some cases, grants of over £500 may be considered.

Exclusions

Grants are not given to relieve rates, taxes or other public funds.

Applications

Application forms can be downloaded from the charity's website. Forms must be submitted on behalf of an individual by a health or social care worker or a registered charity/voluntary organisation. The trustees meet once a month to consider applications. Applications should be submitted by the 15th of each month, excluding December where the deadline is the 12th, to be considered at the next meeting.

Financial information

Year end	31/12/2020
Income	£27,500
Total expenditure	£22,000

Further financial information

In 2020, 37 grants were awarded to individuals.

Other information

The charity is administered by Beyond Profit, along with Manchester Children's Relief in Need Charity (Charity Commission no. 249657) and Manchester Relief in Need Charity (Charity Commission no. 224271). The charity also encompasses The Levenshulme Trust for the Relief of Sickness, which supports residents of Levenshulme and the M19 postcode who are in need due to illness or disability.

Manchester Relief-in-Need Fund and Manchester Children's Relief-in-Need Fund

 £32,700 (2019/20)

Correspondent: The Trustees, Beyond Profit Ltd, Bolton Arena, Arena Approach, Horwich, Bolton, Greater Manchester BL6 6LB (tel: 01204 414317; email: admin@reliefinneed.co.uk)

🌐 https://www.reliefinneed.co.uk

CC number: 224271 and 249657

Eligibility

People in need who live in the city of Manchester.

Types of grant

One-off grants are available for domestic appliances, furniture, clothing, and other general necessities.

Exclusions

According to the application guidelines, support will not be given for: rates, Council Tax, taxes or other public costs; mortgages; funeral costs or memorials; items for residences other than where the claimant lives. The trustees have also noted in the application guidelines that they do not generally provide the same item to an applicant more than once.

Applications

Application forms and guidelines can be found on the website. According to the application guidelines, applications must be completed by the support worker who is working most closely with the client. Examples given include social workers, health visitors and any other professional from a statutory or voluntary organisation.

Financial information

Year end	31/03/2020
Income	£86,400
Total expenditure	£89,100

Further financial information

The financial information has been combined for both charities and the grant total has been estimated due to the Manchester Children's Relief in Need Charity's low income.

Other information

Grants are also made to organisations.

The Middleton Relief-in-Need Charity

£500 (2019/20)

Correspondent: The Trustees, c/o 4 Chaffinch Close, Thornton-Cleveleys, Wyre, Lancashire FY5 2UR (email: mrint@outlook.com)

CC number: 200079

Eligibility

People in need who live in the former borough of Middleton.

Types of grant

Grants are awarded according to need.

Applications

Apply in writing to the correspondent.

Financial information

Year end	31/03/2020
Income	£590
Total expenditure	£850

Further financial information

Full accounts were not available to view on the Charity Commission's website due to the charity's low income. We have therefore estimated the charity's grant total based on its total expenditure.

The Pratt Charity

Correspondent: Lynne Stafford, Chief Executive, c/o St Wilfrid's Enterprise Centre, Royce Road, Hulme, Manchester M15 5BJ (tel: 0161 834 6069; email: trustfunds@gaddum.org.uk)

 https://www.gaddumcentre.co.uk

CC number: 507162–1

Eligibility
Women over the age of 60 who live in the city of Manchester and are in need.

Types of grant
Small grants are awarded according to need.

Applications
Contact the Gaddum Centre by telephone or email to request an application form. All applications must be submitted on the individual's behalf by a social worker, health visitor, teacher or other professional. Applications can only be sent to statutory or voluntary organisations.

Further financial information
Financial information for the Pratt Charity was unavailable at the time of writing (November 2021). This charity (along with several other small charities) is administered by The Gaddum Centre.

Bolton

The Bolton Guild of Help Incorporated

£58,600 (2019)

Correspondent: The Trustees, Scott House, 27 Silverwell Street, Bolton BL1 1PP (tel: 01204 524858; email: guildofhelp@btconnect.com)

CC number: 224760

Eligibility
The charity has several funds to assist people living in Bolton who are in need: The Louisa Alice Kay Fund supports individuals and families; the Bolton Veterans Fund assists veterans and their families; and the Bolton Mother and Child Welfare Association supports expectant and nursing mothers and young children.

Types of grant
One-off grants are awarded according to need. This may include, for example, furniture and white goods, bedding, prams, school uniforms, the costs of funerals, debt management, cleaning and painting, removals, counselling and specialist holidays for clients with medical needs. The Louisa Alice Kay Fund makes grants for the purchase of urgently required items and services.

Applications
Contact the charity for further information.

Financial information
Year end	31/12/2019
Income	£133,600
Total expenditure	£172,400

Further financial information
The 2019 accounts were the latest available at the time of writing (November 2021). During the year, grants to individuals were awarded through the following funds:
- Louisa Alice Kay Fund – a total of £57,700 was awarded to 196 families. The average grant was for £273.
- Bolton Mother and Child Welfare Association – £600 was awarded to expecting and new mothers.
- Bolton Veterans Fund – £270 was awarded to Bolton veterans and their families.

Other information
The charity also makes grants to organisations, including Citizens Advice Bolton and Bury and animal charities.

Bury

Bury Relief in Sickness Fund

£10,200 (2019)

Correspondent: The Trustees, 2 Park Crescent, Haslingden, Rossendale, Lancashire BB4 6PS (tel: 01706 223578)

CC number: 256397

Eligibility
Residents of Bury who are in need as a result of illness, disability or other medical conditions.

Types of grant
The fund provides or pays for items, services or facilities that will alleviate suffering or assist with recovery.

Exclusions
Grants cannot be made for items or services available to the individual through other sources.

Applications
Apply in writing to the correspondent.

Financial information
Year end	31/12/2019
Income	£70
Total expenditure	£22,600

Further financial information
Full accounts were not available to view on the Charity Commission's website due to the fund's low income. We have therefore estimated the fund's grant total based on its total expenditure.

Other information
The fund also makes grants to organisations working in the same area.

The Mellor Fund

£3,100 (2019)

Correspondent: Gillian Critchley, Chair of Trustees, 17 Marle Croft, Whitefield, Manchester M45 7NB (tel: 0161 766 8086)

CC number: 230013

Eligibility
People living in Whitefield, Unsworth or Radcliffe who are in financial need as result of ill health or disability. Support is extended to those who care for such people.

Types of grant
Grants are made for items and services, including holidays.

Exclusions
People with a position of professional responsibility to eligible individuals do not qualify for support.

Applications
Apply in writing to the correspondent.

Financial information
Year end	31/12/2019
Income	£8,400
Total expenditure	£3,400

Further financial information
Full accounts were not available to view on the Charity Commission's website due to the charity's low income. We have therefore estimated the charity's grant total based on its total expenditure.

Manchester

The Dean of Manchester Crosland Fund

£5,800 (2019/20)

Correspondent: The Trustees, Manchester Cathedral, Victoria Street, Manchester M3 1SX (tel: 0161 833 2220)

 www.manchestercathedral.org/ crosland

CC number: 242838

Eligibility
Residents of Manchester who are in need.

Types of grant

Grants are awarded according to need.

Exclusions

The fund does not make recurrent grants. Grants cannot be made for the relief of rates, taxes or other public funds.

Applications

Apply online on the fund's website (paper applications are no longer accepted). Applications must be submitted by a recognised organisation on the individual's behalf. Grants are distributed on a quarterly basis in March, June, September and December, and applications should be submitted by the end of the previous month. Closing dates for applications can be seen on the fund's website.

Financial information

Year end	31/03/2020
Income	£7,900
Total expenditure	£6,400

Further financial information

Full accounts were not available to view on the Charity Commission's website due to the fund's low income. We have therefore estimated the fund's grant total based on its total expenditure.

We Love Manchester Charity

 £52,400 (2019/20)

Correspondent: The Trustees, c/o Lord Mayor's Office, Room 412, Level 4, Town Hall, Manchester M60 2LA (tel: 0161 234 3229; email: welovemcrcharity@manchester.gov.uk)

www.welovemcrcharity.org

CC number: 1066972

Eligibility

The Sir Howard Bernstein Endowment Fund was established for young people from Manchester to help them gain the knowledge, skills and confidence they need to succeed in education, employment and enterprise. Families from Manchester are also eligible for short breaks at the Ghyll Head Outdoor Learning Centre in the Lake District.

Types of grant

Grants are awarded according to need.

Applications

Application forms and guidance on how to apply can be found on the charity's website.

Financial information

Year end	31/03/2020
Income	£160,400
Total expenditure	£355,200

Oldham

The Sarah Lees Relief Trust

£3,600 (2019/20)

Correspondent: Margaret Struthers, Trustee, Rose Cottage, Beckett Street, Lees, Oldham OL4 3JY (tel: 01606 205343; email: m.struthers@mmu.ac.uk)

CC number: 514240

Eligibility

People who live in Oldham and are sick or convalescent, or have a disability.

Types of grant

Grants are awarded according to need.

Applications

Contact the correspondent for further information.

Financial information

Year end	31/03/2020
Income	£4,000
Total expenditure	£8,100

Further financial information

Full accounts were not available to view on the Charity Commission's website due to the trust's low income. We have therefore estimated the trust's grant total based on its total expenditure.

Other information

The trust also awards grants to organisations.

Oldham United Charity

£1,300 (2019/20)

Correspondent: Phil Higgins, 130 Denbydale Way, Royton, Oldham, Greater Manchester OL2 5TE (tel: 0161 624 2034; email: phil.higgins11@gmail.com)

CC number: 221095

Eligibility

People in need who live in the metropolitan borough of Oldham.

Types of grant

Grants are given according to need. According to our previous research, in the past grants have been given for medical needs such as wheelchairs and washing machines for people who are incontinent.

Applications

Apply in writing to the correspondent.

Financial information

Year end	31/08/2020
Income	£4,800
Total expenditure	£2,800

Further financial information

Full accounts were not available to view on the Charity Commission's website due to the charity's low income. We have therefore estimated the charity's grant total based on its total expenditure.

Rochdale

The Norman Barnes Fund

£5,200 (2019/20)

Correspondent: The Trustees, Rochdale Borough Council, Tax and Treasury Team, Floor 2, Number One Riverside, Smith Street, Rochdale, Lancashire OL16 1XU (tel: 01706 924872; email: committee.services@rochdale.gov.uk)

 www.rochdale.gov.uk/council-and-democracy/grants//Pages/charitable-trusts.aspx

CC number: 511646

Eligibility

People over the age of 60 who are retired and live in Rochdale, Castleton, Norden or Bamford.

Types of grant

Grants of up to £250 are awarded according to need. Examples include:
- Household appliances and furniture
- Essential house decorating and repairs
- Recuperative holidays
- Travel costs
- Tools, equipment and books

Exclusions

No payments are made for tax, Council Tax or other statutory payments, except where relief or assistance is already provided out of public funds.

Applications

Application forms are available to download from the Rochdale Council website or by contacting the correspondent. It is recommended that applicants include a supporting comment from a doctor, social worker, Age UK representative or some other relevant professional. If applying for items such as carpets and beds, the trustees require written quotations to be submitted with the application. Only one application can be made within any 12-month period.

Financial information

Year end	31/03/2020
Income	£9,400
Total expenditure	£5,800

Further financial information

Full accounts were not available to view on the Charity Commission's website

due to the fund's low income. We have therefore estimated the fund's grant total based on its total expenditure.

Other information
The fund can also make grants to organisations.

Heywood Relief-in-Need Trust Fund

 £4,100 (2019/20)

Correspondent: The Trustees, c/o 4 Chaffinch Close, Thorton-Cleveleys, FY5 2UR (tel: 07833 249318; email: phoenixtrust@outlook.com)

www.rochdale.gov.uk/council-and-democracy/grants/Pages/charitable-trusts.aspx# HeywoodPhoenix

CC number: 517114

Eligibility
People in need who live in the former municipal borough of Heywood. In exceptional cases, applications may be considered from those who are only temporarily located within the borough.

Types of grant
The charity offers grants for items, services or facilities.

Applications
Apply in writing to the correspondent.

Financial information
Year end	31/03/2020
Income	£4,100
Total expenditure	£4,600

Further financial information
Full accounts were not available to view on the Charity Commission's website due to the charity's low income. We have therefore estimated the grant total based on the charity's total expenditure.

Littleborough Nursing Association Fund

 £1,000 (2020)

Correspondent: Marilyn Aldred, Trustee, 26 Hodder Avenue, Littleborough, Greater Manchester OL15 8EU (tel: 01706 370738; email: marilyn41@talktalk.net)

CC number: 222482

Eligibility
People living in the former urban district of Littleborough who are in need as a result of ill health or disability.

Types of grant
Grants are given according to need.

Applications
Apply in writing to the correspondent.

Financial information
Year end	31/12/2020
Income	£2,500
Total expenditure	£2,200

Further financial information
Full accounts were not available to view on the Charity Commission's website due to the fund's low income. We have therefore estimated the fund's grant total based on its total expenditure.

Other information
This fund also makes grants to organisations.

The Rochdale Fund for Relief-in-Sickness

 £10,300 (2019/20)

Correspondent: Susan Stoney, Clerk to the Trustees, The Old Parsonage, 2 St Mary's Gate, Rochdale, Lancashire OL16 1AP (tel: 01706 644187)

https://www.rochdaleonline.co.uk/sites/the-rochdale-fund-for-relief-in-sickness

CC number: 222652

Eligibility
People living in the borough of Rochdale (including Wardle, Littleborough, Middleton, Heywood, Norden, Birtle, Milnrow and Newhey) who are in need as a result of sickness, injury or a disability. This also extends to any physical or mental illnesses resulting from financial instability or other adverse circumstances.

Types of grant
One-off grants are made according to need. Grants have been awarded for wheelchairs, hoists, IT equipment, adaptations to homes, special leisure equipment, medical aids, washing machines, cookers, clothing, beds, bedding, respite in the form of holidays and outings, nursing aid or comfort and help for close relatives to visit or care for patients.

Exclusions
Grants are not given for the payment of debts, including utility bills, Council Tax and Inland Revenue payments or to help with hardship not directly related to, or caused as a result of, sickness.

Applications
Applicants can download an application form on the funder's website. Completed forms should be sent to the correspondent at their address.

Financial information
Year end	05/04/2020
Income	£75,900
Total expenditure	£53,300

Other information
This fund also makes grants to organisations.

Rochdale United Charity

 £6,300 (2019/20)

Correspondent: The Trustees, Saddleworth Parish Council, Civic Hall, Lee Street, Uppermill, Oldham, Lancashire OL3 6AE (tel: 01457 876665; email: enquiries@ saddleworthparishcouncil.org.uk)

www.rochdale.gov.uk/council-and-democracy/grants/Pages/charitable-trusts.aspx# RochdaleUnited

CC number: 224461

Eligibility
People in need who live in the ancient parish of Rochdale (the former county borough of Rochdale, Castleton, Wardle, Whitworth, Littleborough, Todmorden and Saddleworth).

Types of grant
One-off grants are available for household items. Examples include white goods (washing machines, cookers fridges, etc.), furniture and carpets.

Exclusions
The charity cannot award cash grants.

Applications
Application forms are available to download from the charity's website. Applications should include supporting information from a third party (a social worker, health visitor or other professional). Grants are valid for a period of three months from the date of notification. Grants not claimed within this period will be withdrawn.

Financial information
Year end	31/03/2020
Income	£6,500
Total expenditure	£7,000

Further financial information
Full accounts were not available to view on the Charity Commission's website due to the charity's low income. We have therefore estimated the charity's grant total based on its total expenditure.

Other information
This charity also makes grants to organisations.

Salford

The Booth Charities

£ £1,100 (2020/21)

Correspondent: Jonathan Aldersley, Clerk to the Trustees, c/o Butcher & Barlow LLP, 3 Royal Mews, Gadbrook Road, Rudheath, Northwich, Cheshire CW9 7UD (tel: 01606 334309; email: jaldersley@butcher-barlow.co.uk)

CC number: 221800

Eligibility

People in need residing in the City of Salford, with priority given to people on low incomes, people who are sick, people with disabilities and older people over the age of 60.

Types of grant

Grants are given mainly for TV licences. In 2020/21, the maximum grant for TV licences was £157.50. Pensions are available to residents over the age of 60.

Applications

Apply in writing to the correspondent.

Financial information

Year end	31/03/2021
Income	£1,520,000
Total expenditure	£1,010,000

Further financial information

During the financial year, the charity awarded 22 grants to individuals totalling £1,100, of which £980 was awarded for TV licences.

Other information

The charity offers drop-in services for people who are currently homeless. The charity also operates and maintains almshouses which are available to Salford residents who are in need, with preference given to those over the age of 60 years. Grants are also made to organisations.

The Salford Foundation Trust

£ £16,200 (2019/20)

Correspondent: Peter Collins, Company Secretary, Heywood Hall, Bolton Road, Pendlebury, Swinton, Greater Manchester M27 8UX (tel: 0161 727 4335; email: mail@salfordfoundationtrust.org.uk)

 www.salfordfoundationtrust.org.uk

CC number: 1105303

Eligibility

Young people in need between the ages of 5 and 25 who have lived in Salford for at least three years. Priority is given to applicants under 21.

Types of grant

Welfare

Grants of up to £500 are given for opportunities that allow personal development and promote good mental health, that may otherwise be inaccessible due to financial circumstances. Previous examples include music tuition, sports, participation in competitions, sports clothing, equipment and so on.

Education

Our previous research notes that grants of up to £500 are given towards training, vocational courses, performing arts qualifications and so on. The trust also provides apprenticeship toolkits and college resources for young people living on their own or for people who are solely responsible for dependants.

Exclusions

Funding will not be considered for the following:

▶ Driving lessons and associated items
▶ Childcare costs
▶ Course fees or living expenses
▶ Membership fees
▶ Remedial intervention (speech/language/occupational therapies)
▶ Retrospective funding
▶ Standard school/college and sports trips or residential excursions
▶ Activities with political or religious focus
▶ Needs that should be financed by statutory services.
▶ Activities that are for the benefit of a group of people

Applications

Application forms and further guidance notes can be downloaded from the trust's website. Applications can be made directly by the individual or their parent/legal guardian, or through a third party such as a teacher, youth worker, mentor or welfare agency. Applicants who may have difficulty completing application forms may apply with an acoustic or visual recording in which the answers to the questions on the application form are spoken rather than written. Applications must be supported by two referees and returned by post. There are four application rounds a year; see the trust's website for full details.

Financial information

Year end	31/03/2020
Income	£41,800
Total expenditure	£37,500

Further financial information

In 2019/20, 59 grants were awarded to individuals.

Mary Strand Charitable Trust

£ £23,900 (2020)

Correspondent: Mark Wiggin, Trustee, Cathedral Centre, 3 Ford Street, Salford M3 6DP (tel: 0161 817 2222; email: m. wiggin@caritassalford.org.uk)

CC number: 800301

Eligibility

People who live in Salford and are in need due to poverty, sickness or old age.

Types of grant

Grants of around £200 to £250 are made towards items like household goods, pilgrimages, travel costs and clothing.

Applications

Apply in writing to the correspondent. Applications should be submitted through a local priest, charity or welfare agency.

Financial information

Year end	31/12/2020
Income	£11,000
Total expenditure	£26,500

Further financial information

Full accounts were not available to view on the Charity Commission's website due to the trust's low income. We have therefore estimated the trust's grant total based on its total expenditure.

Other information

The trustees occasionally publish a column in each edition of The Catholic Universe, a weekly Catholic newspaper. The column contains details of deserving causes, with names changed to preserve anonymity, and appeals are made for specific requirements. Donations from readers are received in answer to these appeals and then distributed. The trustees also award grants to organisations.

Stockport

The Ephraim Hallam Charity

£ £11,400 (2020)

Correspondent: The Trustees, 3 Highfield Road, Poynton, Stockport, Cheshire SK12 1DU (tel: 01625 874445; email: hallam@stogrants.onmicrosoft.com)

CC number: 525975

Eligibility

Welfare
People who are resident in the Metropolitan Borough of Stockport and are in need.

Education
People under the age of 25 in higher or further education.

Types of grant

Welfare
Grants are offered to help to relieve financial hardship and poor health of individuals living in Stockport.

Education
The charity also awards scholarships, maintenance allowances or grants tenable at any university, college or institution of higher/further education. In addition, grants are given towards the cost of travel associated with furthering education as well as to assist with entry into any occupation, profession or trade for those leaving an educational establishment.

Applications

Apply in writing to the correspondent.

Financial information

Year end	31/12/2020
Income	£13,600
Total expenditure	£12,600

Further financial information

Full accounts were not available to view on the Charity Commission's website due to the charity's low income. We have therefore estimated the charity's grant total based on its total expenditure.

Other information

Grants are also made to local charities whose aims include advancing the education of young people.

Sir Ralph Pendlebury's Charity for Orphans

£ £10,800 (2020)

Correspondent: The Trustees, c/o Stockport Lads Club, Hempshaw Lane, Stockport, Cheshire SK1 4NT (tel: 07773 421209; email: pendlebury@ stockportgrants.onmicrosioft.com)

CC number: 213927

Eligibility

Orphans who have lived, or whose parents have lived, in the borough of Stockport for at least two years and who are in need.

Types of grant

Grants are given according to need.

Applications

Apply in writing to the correspondent.

Financial information

Year end	31/12/2020
Income	£11,400
Total expenditure	£24,000

Further financial information

Full accounts were not available to view on the Charity Commission's website due to the charity's low income. We have therefore estimated the charity's grant total based on its total expenditure.

Sir Ralph Pendlebury's Charity for the Aged

£ £11,000 (2020)

Correspondent: The Trustees, c/o Stockport Lads Club, Hempshaw Lane, Stockport SK1 4NT (tel: 07773 421209; email: pendlebury@stockportgrants. onmicrosoft.com)

CC number: 213928

Eligibility

People in need above pensionable age who live in the borough of Stockport.

Types of grant

Grants are given according to need.

Applications

Apply in writing to the correspondent.

Financial information

Year end	31/12/2020
Income	£9,000
Total expenditure	£12,200

Further financial information

Full accounts were not available to view on the Charity Commission's website due to the charity's low income. We have therefore estimated the charity's grant total based on its total expenditure.

Other information

The charity also awards grants to organisations that support older people.

Wigan

The Golborne Charities – Charity of William Leadbetter

£ £6,400 (2019/20)

Correspondent: Paul Gleave, 56 Nook Lane, Golborne, Warrington, Cheshire WA3 3JQ (tel: 01942 727627)

CC number: 221088

Eligibility

People in need who live in the parish of Golborne as it was in 1892.

Types of grant

The charity awards one-off grants, usually of between £70 and £100, although larger sums may be given. Grants are usually cash payments for items, services and facilities, although in-kind support is also given occasionally.

Applications

Apply in writing to the correspondent.

Financial information

Year end	30/04/2020
Income	£7,300
Total expenditure	£7,100

Further financial information

Full accounts were not available to view on the Charity Commission's website due to the charity's low income. We have therefore estimated the charity's grant total based on its total expenditure.

The Lowton United Charity

£ £4,700 (2019/20)

Correspondent: The Trustees, 51 Kenilworth Road, Lowton, Warrington, Cheshire WA3 2AZ (tel: 01942 741583)

CC number: 226469

Eligibility

People in need who live in the parishes of St Luke's and St Mary's in Lowton.

Types of grant

Grants can be given for urgent need towards the cost of goods and materials.

Applications

Apply in writing to the correspondent.

Financial information

Year end	31/03/2020
Income	£8,000
Total expenditure	£5,200

Further financial information

Full accounts were not available to view on the Charity Commission's website due to the charity's low income. We have therefore estimated the charity's grant total based on its total expenditure.

Other information

Some assistance may also be given to organisations.

Lancashire

The Cottam Charities

£ £48,200 (2019/20)

Correspondent: The Trustees, c/o Blackhurst Swainson Goodier LLP, 3–4 Aalborg Place, Lancaster, Lancashire LA1 1BJ (tel: 01524 386500; email: eje@bsglaw.co.uk)

CC number: 223936/223925

Eligibility

People in need who are aged over 50 and have lived in Caton-with-Littledale in Lancashire for at least five years.

Types of grant

Grants are awarded according to need.

Applications

Apply in writing to the correspondent.

Financial information

Year end	11/11/2020
Income	£19,100
Total expenditure	£53,600

Further financial information

The financial information for the Alice Cottam Charity and the Edward Cottam Charity has been combined. The charities were not required to file accounts for the 2019/20 financial year; therefore, the grant total has been estimated based on the combined expenditure of both charities.

Other information

'The Cottam Charities' refers to Edward Cottam Charity (Charity Commission no. 223936) and Alice Cottam Charity (Charity Commission no. 223925).

The Goosnargh and Whittingham United Charity

£ £3,200 (2020)

Correspondent: Cllr J. Singleton, Parish Council Representative, Lower Stanalee Farm, Stanalee Lane, Goosnargh, Preston, Lancashire PR3 2EQ (tel: 01995 640224)

CC number: 233744

Eligibility

People in need living in the parishes of Goosnargh, Whittingham and Barton. Some preference may be given to older residents.

Types of grant

Grants are awarded according to need.

Applications

Apply in writing to the correspondent.

Financial information

Year end	31/12/2020
Income	£4,800
Total expenditure	£3,600

Further financial information

Full accounts were not available to view on the Charity Commission's website due to the charity's low income. We have therefore estimated the charity's grant total based on its total expenditure.

The Harris Charity

£ £2,000 (2019/20)

Correspondent: David Ingram, Secretary, c/o Moore and Smalley, Richard House, 9 Winckley Square, Preston, Lancashire PR1 3HP (tel: 01772 821021; email: harrischarity@mooreandsmalley.co.uk)

 theharrischarity.co.uk

CC number: 526206

Eligibility

People in need under the age of 25 who live in the 'old' Lancashire boundaries as defined in 1972, with a preference for the Preston district. Applicants must be permanent residents of the UK.

Types of grant

Welfare

One-off grants to alleviate hardship.

Education

One-off grants for training and education, including apprenticeships. Grants are also awarded for associated costs, such as books, tools, equipment, clothing and musical instruments.

Exclusions

The charity will not fund course fees, living expenses or groups travelling overseas.

Applications

Application forms are available to download from the charity's website. The half-yearly dates by which the applications must be submitted are 31 March and 30 September. Successful applicants are notified in July and January, respectively. Individual applicants may be required to supply supporting references from responsible referees, such as a faith leader, employer or local authority.

Financial information

Year end	05/04/2020
Income	£127,400
Total expenditure	£80,500

Further financial information

In 2019/20, £650 was awarded to individuals in the Preston area and £1,300 in the Lancashire area for both welfare and education purposes.

Other information

The original charity, known as the Harris Orphanage Charity, dates back to 1883. A new charitable scheme was established in 1985 following the sale of the Harris Orphanage premises in Garstang Road, Preston. The charity also supports other charitable organisations.

John Parkinson (Goosnargh and Whittingham United Charity)

£ £1,400 (2020)

Correspondent: The Trustees, Lower Stanalee Farm, Stanalee Lane, Goosnargh, Preston, Lancashire PR3 2EQ (tel: 01995 640224)

CC number: 526060

Eligibility

People under the age of 25 who live in the parishes of Goosnargh, Whittingham and the part of Barton that lies west of the Lancaster to Preston railway.

Types of grant

Grants are made towards fees, books, tools, outfits, travel and maintenance expenses for people entering a profession, trade or service.

Applications

Apply in writing to the correspondent.

Financial information

Year end	31/12/2020
Income	£3,100
Total expenditure	£1,500

Further financial information

Full accounts were not available to view on the Charity Commission's website due to the charity's low income. We have therefore estimated the charity's grant total based on its total expenditure.

Swallowdale Children's Trust

£ £61,200 (2019/20)

Correspondent: The Trustees, 13 Newlands Avenue, Blackpool FY3 9PG (tel: 07984 539657; email: secswallowdale@hotmail.co.uk)

CC number: 526205

Eligibility

People who live in the boroughs of Blackpool, Wyre and Fylde who are under the age of 25.

Types of grant

The trust provides grants for general welfare purposes and relief in need, for example living expenses, essential items and recreational equipment. It can also make grants for educational purposes, such as fees for training and educational courses.

Exclusions

Grants are not awarded where support is available from family or community sources.

Applications

Apply in writing to the correspondent.

Financial information

Year end	31/03/2020
Income	£33,600
Total expenditure	£92,200

Other information

The trust also assists charities working with young people in its operating area.

Blackburn with Darwen

It's Your Wish – The John Bury Trust

£ £6,800 (2019/20)

Correspondent: The Trustees, 2 Eckersley Close, Blackburn, Lancashire BB2 4FA (tel: 07834 738356; email: treasurer@thejohnburytrust.co.uk)

 www.johnburytrust.co.uk

CC number: 1108181

Eligibility

Young people aged 10–25 who live in the borough of Blackburn with Darwen.

Types of grant

Grants are given towards a wide range of activities aimed to support the personal development of young people. Examples include purchasing equipment, extracurricular activities, travelling overseas, short-term projects, other travel costs, gaining new skills, sporting activities and so on. All grants are expected to be spent within a 12-month period of receiving the award.

Applications

Application forms and full terms and conditions are available to download from the trust's website. Applicants who are successful after the first consideration will be invited to an interview.

Financial information

Year end	30/04/2020
Income	£9,900
Total expenditure	£7,500

Further financial information

Full accounts were not available to view on the Charity Commission's website due to the trust's low income. We have therefore estimated the grant total based on the trust's total expenditure.

The W. M. and B. W. Lloyd Trust

£ £43,800 (2019/20)

Correspondent: John Jacklin, Trustee/Secretary, Gorse Barn, Rock Lane, Tockholes, Darwen, Lancashire BB3 0LX (tel: 01254 771367; email: johnjacklin@homecall.co.uk)

CC number: 503384

Eligibility

People who live in, or have been educated in, the borough of Darwen who are in need.

Types of grant

Welfare grants are awarded according to need. The trust also makes grants for the advancement of education.

Applications

Apply in writing to the correspondent either by post or email. Applications should be sponsored by a third party such as a social worker, doctor, minister or someone known to the applicant who can support their application.

Financial information

Year end	05/04/2020
Income	£127,300
Total expenditure	£117,300

Other information

The trust also makes grants to organisations and towards the improvement of public amenities.

Blackpool

Baines's Charity

£ £7,700 (2020)

Correspondent: The Trustees, 45 Durham Avenue, Thornton-Cleveleys, Lancashire FY5 2DP (tel: 07583 029539; email: A_KAY4@sky.com)

CC number: 224135

Eligibility

People in need who live in the area of Blackpool, Fylde and Wyre, specifically Carleton, Hardhorn-with-Newton, Marlton, Poulton-Le-Fylde and Thornton. If there are surplus funds available, people who are temporarily resident in the beneficial area can be supported. Educational grants are given

to those about to start vocational or further education.

Types of grant

The trustees award small grants according to need. Occasionally, they purchase equipment, books or other goods on behalf of the applicant.

Applications

Apply in writing to the correspondent.

Financial information

Year end	31/12/2020
Income	£12,400
Total expenditure	£8,600

Further financial information

Full accounts were not available to view on the Charity Commission's website due to the charity's low income. We have therefore estimated the charity's grant total based on its total expenditure. This total may also include grants for education.

Other information

Grants can be made to individuals and organisations for both welfare and educational purposes, including support to schools. The charity works in conjunction with John Sykes Dewhurst Bequest (Charity Commission no. 224133).

The Blackpool Ladies' Sick Poor Association

£ £18,600 (2019/20)

Correspondent: The Trustees, 22 James Avenue, Blackpool FY4 4LB (tel: 07592 703579; email: blackpoollspa@gmail.com)

CC number: 220639

Eligibility

People in need who live in Blackpool.

Types of grant

Grants are awarded towards essential household items, living costs and fuel payments. Food vouchers are also distributed.

Applications

Apply in writing to the correspondent.

Financial information

Year end	31/03/2020
Income	£21,000
Total expenditure	£20,700

Further financial information

Full accounts were not available to view on the Charity Commission's website due to the charity's low income. We have therefore estimated the charity's grant total based on its total expenditure.

Other information

The charity occasionally makes grants to organisations with similar objectives.

The Foxton Dispensary

 £13,000 (2020)

Correspondent: Robert Dunn, Clerk, PO Box 227, Lytham St Annes, Lancashire FY8 9BJ (email: clerk@foxtoncharity.co.uk)

www.foxtoncharity.co.uk

CC number: 224312

Eligibility

People in need as a result of ill health, disability, convalescence or infirmity living in the borough of Blackpool and Poulton-le-Fylde. Applicants of ill health must be on prescribed medication.

Types of grant

One-off grants are awarded according to need. Examples include white goods, carpets and beds.

Exclusions

Grants are not awarded for items and services that should be covered through statutory support.

Applications

There is an online application form on the charity's website. Applications should be made through a third party (GPs, healthcare professionals, mental health workers, social workers, etc.).

Financial information

Year end	31/12/2020
Income	£19,800
Total expenditure	£18,600

Further financial information

Full accounts were not available to view on the Charity Commission's website due to the charity's low income. We have therefore estimated the charity's grant total based on its total expenditure. In previous years, around 65–70% of the charity's total expenditure was spent on grants.

Gerry Richardson Trust

 £670 (2020/21)

Correspondent: The Trustees, Northdene, Stoney Lane, Hambleton, Poulton-le-Fylde FY6 9AF (tel: 01253 700879 or 07799 763108; email: david@davidwilliamsonaccountants.co.uk)

https://gerryrichardsontrust.org

CC number: 504413

Eligibility

Young people under the age of 25 who live or work within 15 miles of

Blackpool Town Hall. Some preference is given to young people with disabilities or special needs.

Types of grant

Grants are given to encourage young people to attend courses and activities of an educational, cultural, sporting, adventuresome or character-building nature.

Applications

Applications can be made on the trust's website or in writing to the correspondent. Unsuccessful applicants are not notified.

Financial information

Year end	31/03/2021
Income	£8,700
Total expenditure	£740

Further financial information

Full accounts were not available to view on the Charity Commission's website due to the trust's low income. We have therefore estimated the trust's grant total based on its total expenditure.

Other information

The trust also provides grants to organisations.

Chorley

The Shaw Charities

£1,100 (2020/21)

Correspondent: The Trustees, 99 Rawlinson Lane, Heath Charnock, Chorley, Lancashire PR7 4DE (tel: 01257 480515; email: woodrows@tinyworld.co.uk)

CC number: 214318

Eligibility

People in need who are over 60 and live in Rivington, Anglezarke, Heath Charnock or Anderton. People under the age of 21 who would like to advance their education and have lived in one of the four parishes for at least two years are also supported.

Types of grant

Grants are awarded according to need.

Applications

Apply in writing to the correspondent.

Financial information

Year end	30/06/2021
Income	£2,600
Total expenditure	£1,200

Further financial information

Full accounts were not available to view on the Charity Commission's website due to the charity's low income. We have therefore estimated the charity's

grant total based on its total expenditure.

Fylde

The Lytham St Anne's Relief-in-Sickness Charity

£1,600 (2020/21)

Correspondent: Jill Walker, Fylde YMCA, St Alban's Road, St Annes on Sea, Lancashire FY8 1XD (tel: 01253 895115; email: jill.walker@fyldecoastymca.org)

CC number: 500498

Eligibility

People with physical or mental health needs who live in Fylde. This need must be verified by a medical report.

Types of grant

One-off grants of between £50 and £600 are made towards equipment/training or household appliances.

Applications

Apply in writing to the correspondent.

Financial information

Year end	14/01/2021
Income	£2,500
Total expenditure	£1,800

Further financial information

Full accounts were not available to view on the Charity Commission's website due to the charity's low income. We have therefore estimated the charity's grant total based on its total expenditure.

Hyndburn

The Accrington and District Helping Hands Fund

£4,300 (2020)

Correspondent: The Trustees, 4 Grindleton Road, West Bradford, Clitheroe BB7 4TE (tel: 01200 422062; email: maryann.renton2@btinternet.com)

CC number: 222241

Eligibility

People living in Accrington, Clayton-Le-Moors and Altham, who are in poor health and/or on a low income.

Types of grant

One-off grants are made towards the cost of the following: special foods and medicines; medical equipment and comforts; domestic help; mobile physiotherapy services and staff required for the operation of such treatment.

Applications

Apply in writing to the correspondent.

Financial information

Year end	31/12/2020
Income	£14,500
Total expenditure	£9,500

Further financial information

Full accounts were not available to view on the Charity Commission's website due to the fund's low income. We have therefore estimated the fund's grant total based on its total expenditure.

Other information

The fund also makes grants to organisations.

Lancaster

James Bond/Henry Welch Trust

£7,900 (2019/20)

Correspondent: The Trustees, Democratic Services, Lancaster Town Hall, Dalton Square, Lancaster, Lancashire LA1 1PJ (tel: 01524 582135; email: democracy@lancaster.gov.uk)

 https://www.lancaster.gov.uk

CC number: 222791

Eligibility

People in need within the administrative district covered by Lancaster City Council who are affected by any of the chest and lung diseases. Children with disabilities and other special needs in the area are also eligible.

Types of grant

Grants are awarded according to need.

Applications

Apply in writing to the correspondent.

Financial information

Year end	31/03/2020
Income	£11,200
Total expenditure	£8,800

Further financial information

Full accounts were not available to view on the Charity Commission's website due to the trust's low income. We have therefore estimated the trust's grant total based on its total expenditure.

Brockbank's Annuities Trust

£9,800 (2019)

Correspondent: The Trustees, c/o Blackhurst Swainson Goodier LLP, 3 and 4 Aalborg Square, Lancaster, Lancashire LA1 1GG (tel: 01524 32471; email: eje@bsglaw.co.uk)

CC number: 223595

Eligibility

Single people aged over 50 who have lived in Lancaster for a minimum of three years and have an income of less than £12,000 per annum.

Types of grant

The trust awards quarterly grants.

Applications

Apply in writing to the correspondent.

Financial information

Year end	31/12/2019
Income	£8,000
Total expenditure	£10,900

Further financial information

Full accounts were not available to view on the Charity Commission's website due to the trust's low income. We have therefore estimated the trust's grant total based on its total expenditure.

Pendle

Nelson District Nursing Association Fund

£8,000 (2020/21)

Correspondent: Joanne Eccles, Democratic and Legal Services, Pendle Borough Council, Nelson Town Hall, Market Street, Nelson, Lancashire BB9 7LJ (tel: 01282 661654; email: joanne.eccles@pendle.gov.uk)

CC number: 222530

Eligibility

People who are sick or in financial need and live in the borough of Nelson, Lancashire.

Types of grant

Grants are awarded according to need.

Applications

Apply in writing to the correspondent.

Financial information

Year end	05/04/2021
Income	£4,400
Total expenditure	£8,900

Further financial information

Full accounts were not available to view on the Charity Commission's website due to the fund's low income. We have therefore estimated the grant total based on the fund's total expenditure.

South Ribble

Balshaw's Educational Foundation

£1,120 (2020)

Correspondent: The Trustees, 8 Beechfield Road, Leyland, Lancashire PR25 3BG (tel: 01772 421009)

CC number: 526595

Eligibility

Young people who live, or whose parents live, in the parish of Leyland. Our research suggests preference is given to current and former pupils of Balshaw's Church of England High School.

Types of grant

Grants are awarded for clothing, extracurricular activities and other costs related to educational needs of people under the age of 16.

People in secondary, further and higher education can receive grants for books, instruments, equipment, educational trips abroad and other education-related costs.

Assistance is also given to people preparing to enter a profession or trade (for tools, equipment, clothing or similar items) and to enable young people to study music or other arts.

Applications

Apply in writing to the correspondent.

Financial information

Year end	31/12/2020
Income	£2,700
Total expenditure	£2,500

Further financial information

Full accounts were not available to view on the Charity Commission's website due to the foundation's low income. We have estimated the foundation's grant total based on its total expenditure.

Other information

Grants are also made to organisations.

West Lancashire

Peter Lathom (including the Lathom Educational Foundation)

£ £9,000 (2020)

Correspondent: Karen Thompson, c/o Advance Accountancy Ltd, 71–73 Hoghton Street, Southport, Merseyside PR9 0PR (tel: 07845 798400; email: karen.thompson1624@gmail.com)

CC number: 228828

Eligibility

Welfare

Residents in Chorley and West Lancashire who are in need.

Education

Educational grants are available to children and young people under the age of 25 living in Chorley and West Lancashire.

Types of grant

Grants are awarded according to need for both welfare and educational purposes.

Applications

Apply in writing to the correspondent.

Financial information

Year end	31/12/2020
Income	£53,600
Total expenditure	£57,300

Further financial information

According to the 2020 accounts, educational grants totalling £2,000 were awarded to four individuals via The Lathom Educational Foundation. In addition, welfare grants totalling £7,000 were awarded from the Estate or Mixed Account.

Other information

The Lathom Educational Foundation forms part of the charity and makes grants to individuals and schools for educational purposes. Welfare grants are awarded from the charity's Estate or Mixed Account. These welfare grants are distributed by 12 local bodies of trustees in their respective districts.

Merseyside

Channel – Supporting Family Social Work in Liverpool

£ £14,000 (2019/20)

Correspondent: Rebecca Black, Trustee, St Bede's Centre, Fern Grove, Liverpool L8 0RZ (tel: 0151 734 5404; email: beccavblack@hotmail.com)

CC number: 257916

Eligibility

Families with young children living in Merseyside who are in need.

Types of grant

One-off grants of up to £100. The charity also provides beneficiaries with second-hand household goods and clothing.

Applications

Apply in writing to the correspondent.

Financial information

Year end	31/03/2020
Income	£18,900
Total expenditure	£15,500

Further financial information

Full accounts were not available to view on the Charity Commission's website due to the charity's low income. We have therefore estimated the grant total based on the charity's total expenditure.

Other information

This charity also supports statutory caring services and other charitable organisations, operating within the area of benefit.

Girls Welfare Fund

£ £9,800 (2020)

Correspondent: The Trustees, PO BOX 2031752, Heswall, Wirral CH60 0AJ (email: gwf_charity@hotmail.co.uk)

 https://www.seftondirectory.com/kb5/sefton/directory/service.page?id=jUMs5kLBGKQ

CC number: 220347

Eligibility

Girls and young women, usually those aged between 15 and 25, who were born, educated and are living in Merseyside.

Types of grant

The following information has been taken from Sefton Council's website: 'One-off and recurrent grants for leisure and creative activities, sports, welfare and the relief of poverty. Grants may be given to schoolchildren and mature students for uniforms / clothing, college students and undergraduates for uniforms / clothing, study / travel overseas and books, vocational students for uniforms / clothing and equipment / instruments. The fund is particularly interested in helping individual girls and young women of poor or deferred education to establish themselves. Grants range from £50 to £750.'

Applications

Apply in writing to the correspondent via post or email. Applications can be submitted directly by the individual or through a social worker, Citizens Advice, other welfare agency or college/educational establishment. Applications are considered quarterly in March, June, September and December, and should include full information about the college, course and particular circumstances.

Financial information

Year end	31/12/2020
Income	£10,900
Total expenditure	£10,900

Further financial information

Full accounts were not available to view on the Charity Commission's website due to the fund's low income. We have therefore estimated the grant total based on the fund's total expenditure.

The Grant, Bagshaw, Rogers and Tidswell Fund

See entry on page 344

The James Greenop Foundation

£ £10,000 (2019)

Correspondent: Russell Greenop, Trustee, 4 Eaton Place, Prescot, Merseyside L34 6ND (tel: 07799 620644; email: russgreenop@msn.com)

 www.thejamesgreenopfoundation.org

CC number: 1164640

Eligibility

Disadvantaged children and young adults, and their families or carers, who live in Merseyside.

Types of grant

The foundation's website states:

The purpose of our small grants scheme is to fund activities that promote inclusion, enhance wellbeing, improve prospects and raise aspirations. This may be through purchasing assistive technology and adaptations, equipment, training, educational resources, and activities that encourage personal and social development.

Up to £500 can be awarded to individuals, their families or carers. Individual small grants may cover all or part of a purchase but must NOT be less than half the total cost.

Exclusions

Applications for funding towards any activities, services or products exceeding £1,000 are not supported.

Applications

Online application forms can be completed on the foundation's website.

Financial information

Year end	31/12/2019
Income	£12,000
Total expenditure	£22,500

Further financial information

Full accounts were not available to view on the Charity Commission's website due to the foundation's low income. We have therefore estimated the foundation's grant total based on its total expenditure.

Other information

The foundation also funds small community projects.

Liverpool Marine Engineers' and Naval Architects' Guild

£ £26,300 (2020)

Correspondent: The Trustees, c/o James Troop & Co. Ltd, 4 Davy Road, Astmoor Industrial Estate, Runcorn, Cheshire WA7 1PZ (tel: 07477 535255)

 liverpoolmarineengineersguild.org.uk

CC number: 224856

Eligibility

People who are, or have been, members of the guild, employees of the guild, marine engineer officers* and consulting engineers or naval architects in the Liverpool and Merseyside area. Support is also available to the families, spouses and widows/widowers of such people.

*marine engineer officers who have worked in any vessel owned or managed by member of the Port of Manchester, or any firm or company owned by members or directors of the Port of Manchester are also eligible.

Types of grant

Recurrent or one-off grants are awarded according to need. Examples include regular financial assistance to older or retired beneficiaries, assistance with nursing home fees and the provision of mobility equipment.

Applications

Apply in writing to the correspondent.

Financial information

Year end	31/12/2020
Income	£26,800
Total expenditure	£27,900

Other information

The charity states that once the needs of individuals are met, any surplus funding goes towards the charitable promotion of education (particularly marine-related education), the needs of the local young people and local charities involved in the marine industry.

Merseyside Jewish Community Care

£ £24,600 (2019/20)

Correspondent: The Trustees, Shifrin House, 433 Smithdown Road, Liverpool, Merseyside L15 3JL (tel: 0151 733 2292; email: info@mjccshifrin.co.uk)

CC number: 1122902

Eligibility

People of the Jewish faith who live in Merseyside and are in need.

Types of grant

Grants are made towards basic essentials, such as food and clothing, and also to fund Jewish burials.

Applications

Apply in writing to the correspondent.

Financial information

Year end	31/03/2020
Income	£356,800
Total expenditure	£396,800

Other information

Merseyside Jewish Community Care provides a care and welfare service for Jewish people in Merseyside.

The Maud Beattie Murchie Charitable Trust

£ £6,800 (2019/20)

Correspondent: The Trustees, c/o DSG, Castle Chambers, 43 Castle Street, Liverpool, Merseyside L2 9TL (tel: 0151 243 1209)

CC number: 265281

Eligibility

Retired members of James Beattie plc stores, who live in Cheshire, Warwickshire or the Wirral and are in need. The trust also makes grants more generally to residents in the Wirral who are in need.

Types of grant

Grants are given according to need.

Applications

Apply in writing to the correspondent.

Financial information

Year end	05/04/2020
Income	£40,100
Total expenditure	£35,000

Other information

The trust also makes small grants to charitable organisations.

Liverpool

The Charles Dixon Pension Fund
See entry on page 306

Gregson Memorial Annuities

£ £2,300 (2019/20)

Correspondent: Jane Fagan, Trustee, c/o Brabners LLP, Horton House, Exchange Flags, Liverpool, Merseyside L2 3YL (tel: 0151 600 3448; email: jane.fagan@brabners.com)

CC number: 218096

Eligibility

Women over the age of 50 who live in Liverpool, Southport, Malpas and the surrounding district. The following people are eligible for support:
- Domestic servants who have been in service for a minimum of ten years and can no longer work for health reasons
- Governesses
- Gentlewomen, widows or unmarried daughters or sisters of professional men and merchants
- Members of the Church of England who are in need

Types of grant

Grants are made in the form of annuities.

Applications

Apply in writing to the correspondent.

Financial information

Year end	05/04/2020
Income	£3,900
Total expenditure	£2,500

Further financial information

Full accounts were not available to view on the Charity Commission's website due to the charity's low income. We have therefore estimated the charity's grant total based on its total expenditure.

The Johnston Family Trust

£ £15,000 (2019)

Correspondent: The Trustees, Aspen Cottage, Apse Manor Road, Shanklin, Hampshire PO37 7PN (tel: 0151 236 6666)

CC number: 207512

Eligibility

Members of the upper and middle classes (and widows and daughters of such people) who, through no fault of their own, have fallen into impoverished circumstances. Assistance is limited to men over 50 and women over 40.

Types of grant

Grants are given according to need.

Applications

Apply in writing to the correspondent.

Financial information

Year end	31/12/2019
Income	£22,000
Total expenditure	£307,000

Further financial information

Full accounts were not available to view on the Charity Commission's website due to the trust's low income. We have therefore estimated the grant total based on the trust's total expenditure.

The Liverpool Caledonian Association

£ £16,900 (2019)

Correspondent: The Trustees, 47 Primrose Lane, Helsby, Frodsham, Cheshire WA6 0HH (tel: 01928 722182)

CC number: 250791

Eligibility

People of Scottish descent who live in Liverpool or within a 15-mile radius of Liverpool Town Hall and are in need.

Types of grant

Grants are given according to need.

Applications

Apply in writing to the correspondent.

Financial information

Year end	31/12/2019
Income	£12,800
Total expenditure	£18,800

Further financial information

Full accounts were not available to view on the Charity Commission's website due to the charity's low income. We have therefore estimated the charity's grant total based on its total expenditure.

The Liverpool Ladies' Institution

£ £4,200 (2020)

Correspondent: David Anderton, Trustee, 15 Childwall Park Avenue, Childwall, Liverpool, Merseyside L16 0JE (tel: 0151 722 9823; email: d.anderton68@btinternet.com)

CC number: 209490

Eligibility

Single women in need who were either born in the city of Liverpool or live in Merseyside. Preference is given to women who are members of the Church of England.

Types of grant

The charity makes recurrent grants.

Applications

Apply in writing to the correspondent. Applications should be submitted, at any time, through a social worker, Citizens Advice or other welfare agency.

Financial information

Year end	31/12/2020
Income	£4,600
Total expenditure	£4,700

Further financial information

Full accounts were not available to view on the Charity Commission's website due to the charity's low income. We have therefore estimated the charity's grant total based on its total expenditure.

The Liverpool Merchants' Guild

£ £1,210,000 (2019/20)

Correspondent: The Trustees, Moore Stephens LLP, 110–114 Duke Street, Liverpool, Merseyside L1 5AG (tel: 0151 703 1080; email: info@liverpoolmerchantsguild.org.uk)

 www.liverpoolmerchantsguild.org.uk

CC number: 206454

Eligibility

People over 50 who currently live or have lived in Merseyside for a continuous period of at least 15 years, and work or have worked in a professional, self-employed, supervisory, clerical, or non-manual capacity, and with savings of less than £23,250.

Types of grant

One-off grants of up to £6,000 are available for the purchase of personal mobility/technology aids or necessary adaptations, such as bathroom conversions, purchase of stairlifts and white goods or insulation/energy-saving work.

Regular payments of up to £6,000 per year (paid in two half-yearly instalments) are also available to bring up income to a level set by the trustees.

Exclusions

Grants are not awarded for:
▹ Rent arrears or debt
▹ Legal fees
▹ Private medical treatment

Applications

Applicants can apply online through the website or download the application form from the website and email/post it back to the correspondent.

Financial information

Year end	30/10/2020
Income	£1,210,000
Total expenditure	£1,490,000

The Liverpool Provision Trade Guild

£ £5,900 (2019/20)

Correspondent: The Trustees, c/o KBH Accountants Ltd, 255 Poulton Road, Wallasey, Merseyside CH44 4BT (tel: 0151 638 8550)

CC number: 224918

Eligibility

Members of the guild, and their dependants, who are in need. If funds permit, the charity may extend support to other members of the Liverpool provision trade and their dependants.

Types of grant

Grants are awarded according to need.

Applications

Apply in writing to the correspondent.

Financial information

Year end	30/11/2020
Income	£800
Total expenditure	£6,600

Further financial information

Full accounts were not available to view on the Charity Commission's website due to the charity's low income. We have therefore estimated the charity's grant total based on its total expenditure.

Liverpool Shipbrokers' Benevolent Society Incorporated

 £283,800 (2019)

Correspondent: The Trustees, 4th Floor, Melbourne Buildings, 21 North John Street, Liverpool, Merseyside L2 5QU (tel: 0151 236 0101)

CC number: 226072

Eligibility

Members and former members of the Liverpool Shipbrokers' Benevolent Society, including their partners, widows, children or dependants. People who are or have been in the business of shipbroking or shipowning and similar in Liverpool, including members of the Liverpool Shipping Staffs' Association, and their partners, widows, children or dependants.

Types of grant

One-off grants are awarded according to need. Additional support is available for holiday grants, assistance with winter fuel bills and Christmas expenses.

Applications

Apply in writing to the correspondent.

Financial information

Year end	31/12/2019
Income	£222,400
Total expenditure	£401,900

Further financial information

During 2019, grants were distributed to 48 individuals.

Merseyside Medical Benevolent Fund

 £12,200 (2020)

Correspondent: Dr Anne Monk, Secretary/Trustee, Liverpool Medical Institution, 24 Reservoir Road North, Birkenhead, Merseyside CH42 8LU (tel: 0151 608 2228; email: gillazurdia24@gmail.com)

https://www.mmbf.org.uk

CC number: 247161

Eligibility

Doctors in need who are practising, or have practiced, in the Merseyside area. Support is extended to the immediate families of such people. A map of the catchment area can be seen on the charity's website.

Types of grant

Grants are typically made to cover fuel/heating costs and priority debts. Gifts are also given twice-annually in the summer and at Christmas. Occasionally, the charity may award grants for younger members of eligible families to buy books and equipment.

Exclusions

The charity does not make grants to supplement income when going through a divorce.

Applications

Applications can be made on the charity's website. Applications should be made on the individual's behalf by a referee, such as a medical practitioner, healthcare professional, medical staffing officer or any other person who has a genuine concern for the applicant.

Financial information

Year end	31/12/2020
Income	£19,500
Total expenditure	£13,500

Further financial information

Full accounts were not available to view on the Charity Commission's website due to the charity's low income. We have therefore estimated the charity's grant total based on its total expenditure.

Other information

For many years, the charity belonged to the Royal Medical Benevolent Fund (Charity Commission no. 207275) as its Liverpool branch. Today, while the charity is now a separate fund, it still works closely with the Royal Medical Benevolent Fund and will take on cases of theirs that are local to the Merseyside area.

John James Rowe's Foundation for Girls

£3,600 (2019/20)

Correspondent: The Trustees, 18–28 Seel Street, Liverpool, Merseyside L1 4BE (tel: 0151 702 5555)

CC number: 526166

Eligibility

Girls between the ages of 11 and 25 who live in Merseyside and who have lost either or both of their parents, whose parents are separated/divorced or whose home conditions are especially difficult.

Types of grant

Grants can contribute to the costs of clothing, boarding out and the cost of holidays.

Grants are also available to promote the education of young women in secondary and further education, apprenticeships

and to assist those preparing to enter a profession trade or calling.

Applications

Apply in writing to the correspondent.

Financial information

Year end	31/03/2020
Income	£17,300
Total expenditure	£8,100

Further financial information

Full accounts were not available to view on the Charity Commission's website due to the foundation's low income. We have therefore estimated the grant total based on the foundation's total expenditure.

West Derby Waste Lands Charity

£6,000 (2020)

Correspondent: Lawrence Downey, Secretary, Ripley House, 56 Freshfield Road, Formby, Liverpool, Merseyside L37 3HW (tel: 01704 879330; email: lawrence@westderbywastelands.co.uk)

www.westderbywastelands.co.uk

CC number: 223623

Eligibility

People who are in financial need and live within the boundaries of West Derby Waste Lands area (this includes parts, but not all, of the L7, L11, L12, L13 and L14 postcodes; the secretary holds a map of the defined area). Priority is given to older people and children/younger people.

Types of grant

One-off grants are given according to need.

Applications

Application forms are available to download from the website or can be requested from the correspondent. Applicants are required to attend an interview before the grant can be awarded.

Financial information

Year end	31/12/2020
Income	£52,400
Total expenditure	£62,900

Other information

This charity also makes grants to organisations. The charity's website states that it helps an average of 50 individuals and organisations each year.

Sefton

The Southport and Birkdale Provident Society

£ £19,100 (2020)

Correspondent: The Trustees, 84 Lexton Drive, Southport, Merseyside PR9 8QW (tel: 01704 214023; email: sandbprov@mail.com)

CC number: 224460

Eligibility

People in need who live in the metropolitan borough of Sefton.

Types of grant

Grants are awarded according to need.

Applications

Apply in writing to the correspondent.

Financial information

Year end	31/12/2020
Income	£27,100
Total expenditure	£19,200

Further financial information

Full accounts were not available to view on the Charity Commission's website due to the charity's low income. We have therefore estimated the charity's grant total using accounts from previous years. Note, the grant total may include grants to organisations.

Other information

In previous years the charity has also awarded grants to organisations.

Wirral

The Conroy Trust

£ £1,500 (2020)

Correspondent: The Trustees, 16 Teesdale Road, Wirral, Merseyside CH63 3AS (tel: 07875 091831; email: bryantehiggins@gmail.com)

CC number: 210797

Eligibility

People in need who live in the parish of Bebington, including young people, older people and people with disabilities.

Types of grant

Grants are awarded according to need.

Applications

Apply in writing to the correspondent.

Financial information

Year end	31/12/2020
Income	£6,300
Total expenditure	£3,300

Further financial information

Full accounts were not available to view on the Charity Commission's website due to the trust's low income. We have therefore estimated the trust's grant total based on its total expenditure.

Other information

The trust also awards grants to organisations.

Thomas Robinson Charity

£ £1,300 (2020)

Correspondent: The Trustees, 1 Blakeley Brow, Wirral, Merseyside CH63 0PS

CC number: 233412

Eligibility

People in need who live in Higher Bebington.

Types of grant

One-off grants are made according to need.

Applications

Apply in writing to the correspondent.

Financial information

Year end	31/12/2020
Income	£4,700
Total expenditure	£1,500

Further financial information

Full accounts were not available to view on the Charity Commission's website due to the charity's low income. We have therefore estimated the charity's grant total based on its total expenditure.

West Kirby Charity

£ £3,100 (2019)

Correspondent: The Trustees, 2 The Roscote, Wallrake, Heswall, Wirral CH60 8QW (tel: 07773 449123; email: westkirbycharity@hotmail.com)

CC number: 218546

Eligibility

People in need who have lived in the old urban district of Hoylake (i.e. Hoylake, Meols, Greasby, Frankby, Caldy, Grange, Newton and West Kirby) for at least three years.

Types of grant

The charity awards small pensions and Christmas gifts to older people. It also awards one-off grants and pays for items, services or facilities for people in need.

Applications

Apply in writing to the correspondent.

Financial information

Year end	31/12/2019
Income	£25,100
Total expenditure	£26,800

Further financial information

Grants to individuals were broken down as follows:

Heswall Disabled Children's Holiday Fund – support for two residents	£2,000
Access ramp for a resident	£590
Pensions	£270
Christmas gifts to pensioners	£130
Christmas hampers	£100

Other information

The charity also makes grants to local schools and churches for distribution to individuals and families in need. Each year, half of the charity's net income is awarded to The Bennett Trust for use by the pupils of Calday Grange Grammar School. In 2019, the trust received £8,000.

South East

General

Berkshire Nurses and Relief-in-Sickness Trust

£ £19,100 (2019/20)

Correspondent: The Trustees, Box 7482, Hook, Hampshire RG27 7NW (tel: 07860 166858; email: thebnrst@gmail.com)

CC number: 205274

Eligibility
People who live in the geographical area of Berkshire and South Oxfordshire, whether or not they are nurses. Applicants must be under the care of the medical profession due to illness or disability.

Types of grant
One-off grants are given according to need. In the past, grants have been used for the payment of basic household items, furniture, clothing, white goods, electric wheelchairs and home adaptations.

Applications
Apply on a form available from the correspondent. Applications must be made through a third party such as a social worker, support and housing worker or community nurse.

Financial information
Year end	31/03/2020
Income	£75,700
Total expenditure	£35,000

Further financial information
During the financial period, grants were awarded to 67 individuals. The average grant was of £290.

Other information
The charity also supports organisations that are directly involved with illness or disability.

East Sussex Farmers' Benevolent Fund

£ £8,600 (2019/20)

Correspondent: Desmond Lambert, Honorary Secretary, Filsham Lodge, Horsted Lane, Isfield, Uckfield, East Sussex TN22 5TX (tel: 01825 751207; email: des.lambert@btinternet.com)

 https://www.eastsussexfarmers benevolentfund.co.uk

CC number: 271188

Eligibility
Farmers, farmworkers or those involved in the wider land-based industry who are in need. Preference is given to those in East or West Sussex, and then to those in the adjoining counties of Kent and Surrey. Support is also available to the dependants of such people.

Types of grant
One-off or long-term grants are available. The trust also distributes hampers.

Applications
Contact the correspondent by telephone.

Financial information
Year end	05/04/2020
Income	£73,000
Total expenditure	£44,000

Further financial information
The fund awarded £8,600 in grants to individuals and a further £5,200 in hampers.

Other information
The fund's website states that it offers business support.

Ewelme Exhibition Endowment

£ £216,800 (2020)

Correspondent: James Oliver, Clerk and Trust Manager, c/o HMG-Law, 126 High Street, Oxford, Oxfordshire OX1 4DG (tel: 01865 244661; email: ewelme.exhibition@gmail.com)

 www.ewelme-education-awards.info

CC number: 309240

Eligibility
Young people (both in state and independent education) aged between 11 and 24 who live in Oxfordshire, Berkshire, Buckinghamshire, Ramridge in Hampshire and Conock in Wiltshire and demonstrate exceptional talent or need. The combined family income must be less than £75,000 a year.

Types of grant
Bursaries are awarded to young people with exceptional talent, specific educational needs or unexpected financial crises or bereavement. They are usually made on first entry into secondary education although later applications are considered. Some awards are aimed towards gifted young people unable to consider an independent school education without substantial financial support and a number of these are made every year in partnership with schools already willing to make a contribution to the fees. Bursaries are between £2,400 to £5,000 per year.

Grants can also be given to secondary school pupils for books, travel, uniforms, sports training, extra tuition, equipment and so on.

Awards, usually of between £250 and £1,500, are provided towards the costs of vocational training, apprenticeships and the development of skills and costs associated with a university or any other tertiary education course, such as travel expenses. Grants can also be awarded for extra tuition and masterclasses while engaged in tertiary education.

Applications
Application forms and further information on how to apply can be found on the charity's website.

Financial information
Year end	31/12/2020
Income	£270,000
Total expenditure	£235,300

365

German Society of Benevolence

£ £7,100 (2019/20)

Correspondent: The Trustees, c/o Leigh Saxton Green LLP, Mutual House, 70 Conduit Street, London W1S 2GF (tel: 020 7486 5553)

CC number: 247379

Eligibility

People who are, or were, citizens of the German Federal Republic, the German Democratic Republic, the Republic of Austria or who were citizens of the former German Empire. Support is also extended to the dependants of such people. Applicants must live in Greater London, Essex, Hertfordshire, Kent or Surrey.

Types of grant

Grants are given to supplement income.

Applications

Apply in writing to the correspondent.

Financial information

Year end	30/11/2020
Income	£14,200
Total expenditure	£7,900

Further financial information

Full accounts were not available to view on the Charity Commission's website due to the charity's low income. We have therefore estimated the charity's grant total based on its total expenditure.

Margaret Jeannie Hindley Charitable Trust

£ £14,000 (2019/20)

Correspondent: The Trustees, c/o Marshalls Solicitors, 102 High Street, Godalming, Surrey GU7 1DS (tel: 01483 416101; email: lisa@marshalls.uk.net)

CC number: 272140

Eligibility

People 'in reduced or destitute circumstances'.

Types of grant

Grants are given according to need.

Applications

Apply in writing to the correspondent.

Financial information

Year end	31/03/2020
Income	£18,100
Total expenditure	£28,200

Further financial information

Full accounts were not available to view on the Charity Commission's website due to the trust's low income. We have therefore estimated the grant total based on the trust's total expenditure.

Hyde Charitable Trust

£ £82,000 (2019/20)

Correspondent: Zoe Ollerearnshaw, Hyde Housing Association, 30 Park Street, London SE1 9EQ (tel: 020 3207 2762; email: zoe.ollerearnshaw@ hyde-housing.co.uk)

 https://www.hyde-housing.co.uk/ corporate/our-social-purpose/ the-hyde-charitable-trust

CC number: 289888

Eligibility

Residents of Hyde Group housing association who are in need.

Types of grant

The trust runs grant programmes that help Hyde Group residents maintain their tenancies and support them to find work.

Applications

Further information can be found on the trust's website.

Financial information

Year end	31/03/2020
Income	£392,000
Total expenditure	£297,000

Other information

As part of an ongoing review the trust's grant programmes may change. Applicants are advised to check the website for current details before making an application.

MidasPlus

£ £6,700 (2019/20)

Correspondent: The Trustees, 20 Island Close, Staines, Middlesex TW18 4YZ (tel: 07803 706440; email: info@ midasplus.org.uk)

 www.midasplus.org.uk

CC number: 1110699

Eligibility

Individuals with physical or learning disabilities who are experiencing difficult circumstances. Applicants must have lived within the South Middlesex and North Surrey borders and the surrounding areas (East Berkshire) for at least six months. The charity's main area of focus is Spelthorne and Runnymede.

Types of grant

One-off grants, usually of up to £500, are given for specific items or services. Previous examples include medical and disability aids (e.g. wheelchairs or scooters), holidays, equipment, carpeting, communication aids and garden or home adaptations. In certain circumstances, the trustees may consider awarding grants of over £500.

Exclusions

Grants cannot be made to:
- People planning to move out of the area of benefit
- Those who have received three grants in the past
- Pay for general living costs
- Pay off debts
- Buy floor coverings of any type (unless there are very exceptional circumstances)
- Buy non-essential items

Applications

Application forms can be downloaded from the charity's website. Applicants must be able to supply a letter of support from their GP confirming hardship or distress.

Financial information

Year end	30/06/2020
Income	£11,900
Total expenditure	£14,900

Further financial information

Full accounts were not available to view on the Charity Commission's website due to the charity's low income. We have therefore estimated the grant total based on the charity's total expenditure.

Other information

Organisations and community groups are also assisted.

The Florence Reiss Trust for Old People

£ £4,500 (2019/20)

Correspondent: The Trustees, 94 Tinwell Road, Stamford, Lincolnshire PE9 2SD (tel: 01780 762710)

CC number: 236634

Eligibility

Women aged over 55 and men aged over 60 who are in need. Priority is given to those living in the parishes of Streatley in Berkshire and Goring-on-Thames in Oxfordshire.

Types of grant

Grants are given according to need.

Applications

Apply in writing to the correspondent.

Financial information

Year end	31/03/2020
Income	£12,000
Total expenditure	£10,000

Further financial information

Full accounts were not available to view on the Charity Commission's website due to the trust's low income. We have therefore estimated the trust's grant total based on its total expenditure.

Other information

The trust also makes grants to charitable organisations that support older people across Great Britain.

The Thames Valley Police Benevolent Fund

£27,300 (2019/20)

Correspondent: Jackie Johnson, Finance Accounting, PO Box 238, Kidlington, Oxfordshire OX5 1XS (email: j.johnson@tv.polfed.org)

 https://www.tvpfed.org/benevolent-fund

CC number: 256865

Eligibility

Serving or retired police officers who are members of the benevolent fund. Members must have been subscribed to the fund for a minimum of one year before grants can be awarded. Support is also available to the widows/widowers and dependants of such people.

Types of grant

One-off grants are given according to need. Examples of grants include medical scans and treatment, travel costs and deposits for accommodation.

Applications

Application forms are available to download on the funder's website. Completed forms should be sent to the correspondent.

Financial information

Year end	31/03/2020
Income	£116,600
Total expenditure	£114,300

The Vokins Charitable Trust

£2,300 (2020)

Correspondent: David Vokins, Trustee, The Old Barn, School Road, Amberley, Arundel BN18 9NA (tel: 01798 839086)

CC number: 801487

Eligibility

People who live in Brighton and Hove and East and West Sussex, particularly

people with disabilities or those suffering from ill health.

Types of grant

Grants are given according to need. The trust also provides mobility scooters to individuals with disabilities.

Applications

Apply in writing to the correspondent.

Financial information

Year end	31/12/2020
Income	£4,500
Total expenditure	£5,000

Further financial information

Full accounts were not available to view on the Charity Commission's website due to the trust's low income. We have therefore estimated the grant total based on the trust's total expenditure.

Other information

The trust also awards grants to organisations.

Whitton's Wishes (The Kathryn Turner Trust)

£21,000 (2019)

Correspondent: Kathryn Turner, Trustee, Unit 3, Suffolk Way, Abingdon, Oxfordshire OX14 5JX (tel: 01235 527310; email: kathrynturnertrust@hotmail.co.uk)

CC number: 1111250

Eligibility

Children, young people, older people and people with disabilities/special needs in the historic county of Middlesex. Grants can also be made in relieving the need, suffering and distress of members and former members of the services, their wives, husbands, widows, widowers and dependants.

Types of grant

One-off grants are awarded according to need.

Applications

Apply in writing to the correspondent.

Financial information

Year end	31/12/2019
Income	£155,300
Total expenditure	£163,500

Other information

The trust also makes grants to organisations.

Berkshire

The Edmund Godson Charity
See entry on page 319

The Polehampton Charity

 £6,400 (2020)

Correspondent: Caroline White, Clerk to the Trustees, 65 The Hawthorns, Charvil, Reading, Berkshire RG10 9TS (tel: 0118 934 0852; email: polehampton.applications@gmail.com)

www.thepolehamptoncharity.co.uk

CC number: 1072631

Eligibility

Residents of Twyford, Ruscombe and Charvil who are in need.

Types of grant

Welfare grants are awarded according to need.

Applications

Applications should be made in writing, providing full details and costings, to the assistant clerk: Miss E. Treadwell, by email (polehampton.applications@gmail.com) or by post to 114 Victoria Road, Wargrave, Berkshire, RG10 8AE.

Financial information

Year end	31/12/2020
Income	£97,400
Total expenditure	£88,700

Twyford and District Nursing Association

£2,000 (2020)

Correspondent: Giselle Letchworth, Trustee, Sunnyside, High Street, Twyford, Winchester, Hampshire SO21 1RG (tel: 01962 712158; email: giselleletchworth@btinternet.com)

CC number: 800876

Eligibility

People who are in need and live in the parishes of Twyford, Compton and Shawford, Colden Common and Owslebury, in the county of Hampshire. Preference is given for applicants who are experiencing or recovering from ill health or who have a disability.

Types of grant

Short-term grants are awarded for relief in need, including for medical care.

Exclusions

The charity will not offer long-term care.

Applications

Apply in writing to the correspondent.

Financial information

Year end	31/12/2020
Income	£7,800
Total expenditure	£2,200

Further financial information

Full accounts were not available to view on the Charity Commission's website due to the charity's low income. We have therefore estimated the charity's grant total based on its total expenditure.

Reading

The Earley Charity

 £9,200 (2020)

Correspondent: Jane Wittig, Clerk to the Trustees, St Nicolas Centre, Sutcliffe Avenue, Earley, Reading, Berkshire RG6 7JN (tel: 0118 926 1068; email: ec@ earleycharity.org.uk)

www.earleycharity.org.uk

CC number: 244823

Eligibility

People in need who have lived in Earley and the surrounding neighbourhood for at least six months. A map of the beneficial area is available to view on the charity's website. Applicants must be living in permanent accommodation and have UK citizenship or have been granted indefinite leave to remain in the UK. If in doubt, get in touch with the correspondent to confirm.

Types of grant

Welfare

One-off grants are given for the purchase of a specific item, equipment or service. Grants have been given for household goods, such as washing machines, cookers, fridges/freezers, beds and bedding, other furniture, kitchen appliances and also mobility aids (wheelchairs, scooters, etc.) and sensory equipment. Grants do not normally exceed £400.

Education

Grants are given to support young people who are learning a trade.

Exclusions

According to the charity's website, grants are not given for the following:

- Postgraduate education
- General running/living costs
- Core costs
- Open-ended salaries
- General appeals
- Religious activities
- National organisations operating in the area of benefit without a local office
- General public sector appeals (apart from in a few very exceptional cases)
- Applications from outside the area of benefit

Applications

Application forms can be requested from the correspondent or by using the enquiry form on the website. They can be submitted either directly by the individual or through a social worker, Citizens Advice or other welfare agency. Applications for grants under £500 and applications for grants over £500 are considered at separate meetings around five times each year. The dates of these meetings, along with application submission deadlines, are published on the website.

Financial information

Year end	31/12/2020
Income	£262,300
Total expenditure	£755,200

Further financial information

Grants were made to 31 individuals out of 37 applications.

Other information

Grants are also made to organisations and local voluntary and community groups.

Reading Dispensary Trust

 £15,400 (2019)

Correspondent: The Clerk, 16 Wokingham Road, Reading, Berkshire RG6 1JQ (tel: 0118 926 5698; email: theclerk@readingdispensarytrust.org.uk)

www.readingdispensarytrust.org.uk

CC number: 203943

Eligibility

People in need who are in poor health, convalescent or who have a physical or mental disability or illness and live in Reading and the surrounding area (within a seven-mile radius of the centre of Reading).

Types of grant

One-off grants for equipment and services not available through statutory sources, such as household items, fridges, washing machines, carpeting, house clearance, therapy and furniture. In 2019, grants ranged from £69 to £1,300.

Exclusions

The charity cannot fund services or goods which are available from statutory sources.

Applications

Application forms can be downloaded from the trust's website, along with guidelines. Applications must be made through doctors, nurses, NHS departments, local councils, social workers or voluntary organisations. Grant applications are considered monthly; however, applications requesting over £500 are taken to the quarterly trustees' meeting for approval.

Financial information

Year end	31/12/2019
Income	£57,300
Total expenditure	£43,300

Further financial information

The 2019 annual report was the latest available at the time of writing (October 2021). A breakdown of grants was not available. The grant total has therefore been estimated.

Other information

The trust also supports organisations.

Tilehurst Poor's Land Charity

 £7,300 (2019)

Correspondent: Clerk to the Trustees, PO Box 2802, Reading, Berkshire RG30 4GE (tel: 07899 798335; email: clerk@tilehurstplc.org.uk)

www.tilehurstplc.org.uk

CC number: 204048

Eligibility

People in need in the ancient parish of Tilehurst, which covers mainly, but not exclusively, postcodes RG30 and RG31.

Types of grant

Small grants for the purchase of appliances, furniture, house adaptations, and clothing.

Applications

Application forms can be downloaded from the charity's website and should be printed out, completed and then posted to the contact address. Wherever possible, applications should include a supporting letter from a third-party organisation, describing the applicant's personal circumstances.

Financial information

Year end	31/12/2019
Income	£18,800
Total expenditure	£16,100

Further financial information

Full accounts were not available to view on the Charity Commission's website due to the charity's low income. We have therefore estimated the charity's grant total based on its total expenditure.

Other information

The charity also owns allotments that are rented, which contributes to the annual sum available for charitable activities.

Slough

The Slough and District Community Fund

£ £810 (2020)

Correspondent: David Nicks, Trustee, 7 Sussex Place, Slough, Berkshire SL1 1NH (tel: 01753 577475; email: dave.nicks@btinternet.com)

CC number: 201598

Eligibility

People who are in need and live in and around the Borough of Slough.

Types of grant

One-off grants are awarded according to need.

Applications

Application forms are available from the correspondent.

Financial information

Year end	31/12/2020
Income	£3,900
Total expenditure	£900

Further financial information

Full accounts were not available to view on the Charity Commission's website due to the fund's low income. We have therefore estimated the fund's grant total based on its total expenditure.

West Berkshire

The Newbury and Thatcham Welfare Trust

£ £2,300 (2020)

Correspondent: Jacqui Letsome, Clerk, 1 Bolton Place, Northbrook Street, Newbury, Berkshire RG14 1AJ (tel: 07340 731631; email: ntwt@hotmail.com)

 www.newburyandthatcham welfaretrust.org

CC number: 235077

Eligibility

People who live in any parish belonging to the district of West Berkshire and are in both financial *and* medical need as a result of illness, convalescence, disability or infirmity.

Types of grant

One-off grants of up to £250. Recent examples include a wheelchair, specialist medical equipment and bedding/mattresses.

Exclusions

Grants are not given towards debts, Council Tax, rent or mortgage payments.

Applications

Application forms are available to download on the trust's website. Applications must be completed by a third party, such as a health professional, recognised support agency or another charitable organisation on the individual's behalf. The trustees meet three times per year to consider grant applications.

Financial information

Year end	31/12/2020
Income	£3,400
Total expenditure	£2,500

Further financial information

Full accounts were not available to view on the Charity Commission's website due to the trust's low income. We have therefore estimated the trust's grant total based on its total expenditure.

Windsor and Maidenhead

Datchet United Charities

£ £10,000 (2018/19)

Correspondent: The Trustees, 24 Holmlea Walk, Datchet, Slough, Berkshire SL3 9HZ (tel: 07762 607358; email: triciamaryjames@btinternet.com)

CC number: 235891

Eligibility

People in need who live in the ancient parish of Datchet.

Types of grant

Monetary assistance to individuals and families in need. Vouchers are also awarded annually at Christmas.

Exclusions

The area of application is confined to the parish of Datchet only. Applications outside this area will not be accepted.

Applications

Apply in writing to the correspondent.

Financial information

Year end	30/09/2019
Income	£32,200
Total expenditure	£58,500

Further financial information

The charity's 2019/20 accounts were not accessible at the time of writing (August 2021). In 2018/19, the charity awarded monetary assistance totalling £7,600 and Christmas vouchers in the amount of £2,400.

Other information

The charity also operates a day centre.

The Spoore, Merry and Rixman Foundation

£ £246,200 (2019)

Correspondent: Clerk to the Trustees, PO Box 4787, Maidenhead, Berkshire SL60 1JA (tel: 020 3286 8300; email: clerk@smrfmaidenhead.org)

 www.smrfmaidenhead.org.uk

CC number: 309040

Eligibility

People under the age of 25 who are in need and live in Maidenhead and the surrounding areas (postcodes SL6 1–9). There is a handy map on the foundation's website which shows the area of benefit.

Types of grant

Grants can be given for a range of needs to help individuals in education and their families. Funding may help with, for example: school uniforms; musical or arts tuition; books; musical instruments and sporting equipment; school trips; residential courses; recreational activities such as swimming lessons; special educational needs and aids, such as laptops for children with dyslexia. Assistance is also available people in further or higher education and may include support towards the cost of a university course for students from low-income families.

Individuals who have been accepted on an apprenticeship can apply for up to £1,500 (for those living independently) and up to £1,000 (for those living with parents/guardians).

Applications

Application forms can be downloaded from the foundation's website.

Financial information

Year end	31/12/2019
Income	£409,000
Total expenditure	£753,000

Other information

Grants are also given to schools for educational facilities not funded by school budgets (e.g. development of school grounds or specialist equipment), as well as to youth clubs and other organisations for wider educational facilities. Every child leaving a local authority maintained primary school in the foundation's area of benefit receives a dictionary from the foundation.

Sunninghill Fuel Allotment Trust

 £17,200 (2019/20)

Correspondent: The Clerk, The Sunninghill Trust, PO Box 4712, Ascot, Berkshire SL5 9AA (tel: 01344 206320; email: help@thesunninghilltrust.org)

🌐 thesunninghilltrust.org

CC number: 240061

Eligibility

Residents of Sunninghill, Ascot or South Ascot who are in need. Preference may be given to older residents or those who are suffering with ill health.

Types of grant

One-off grants are awarded according to need. Recent examples include grants to cover the cost of medical care, day care and home adaptations.

Exclusions

No retrospective funding is awarded (i.e. for needs that have already been addressed). Grants cannot be made for items or services where provision is the responsibility of central or local government, health trust or health authority.

Applications

Applications should be made in writing to the correspondent and should detail:
▶ Why the grant is needed/what difference it will make
▶ What the applicant has done so far to find assistance
▶ Why funding is unavailable elsewhere
▶ When the funding is needed by and the level of urgency for funding
▶ Full contact details

The trustees meet on a quarterly basis to consider applications. Emergency applications are considered as they are received.

Financial information

Year end	31/03/2020
Income	£141,700
Total expenditure	£74,600

Further financial information

In the year 2019/20, 11 grants were awarded to individuals. Nine cash grants were made and two grants were awarded to cover day care and physiotherapy costs. Grants to organisations totalled £44,500.

Other information

A large portion of the trust's grants are made to organisations. The trust makes donations to day centres, hospices, sports and recreation facilities and schools situated within the area of benefit.

Wokingham

The Finchampstead and Barkham Relief-in-Sickness Fund

 £2,700 (2020)

Correspondent: Gaynor Popplestone, Chair, 175 Nine Mile Ride, Finchampstead, Wokingham, Berkshire RG40 4JD (tel: 0118 973 3553; email: gaynorpoppelstone@doctors.org.uk)

CC number: 259206

Eligibility

People with disabilities who live in the parishes of Finchampstead and Barkham and are in need. Support may be extended to those experiencing ill health or other medical conditions.

Types of grant

One-off grants are awarded towards, for example, clothing, electrical goods, holidays, travel expenses, medical equipment, nursing fees, household bills and general living costs.

Exclusions

Grants cannot be used for the relief of rates or taxes. Once a grant is awarded, it cannot be repeated or renewed.

Applications

Apply in writing to the correspondent.

Financial information

Year end	31/12/2020
Income	£4,000
Total expenditure	£3,000

Further financial information

Full accounts were not available to view on the Charity Commission's website due to the fund's low income. We have therefore estimated the fund's grant total based on its total expenditure. Note that the grant total may include loans.

Wokingham United Charities

 £14,600 (2019/20)

Correspondent: Tracey Hedgecox, Operations Manager, Westende, London Road, Wokingham, Berkshire RG40 1YA (tel: 07598 583513; email: chiefadmin@ wokinghamunitedcharities.org.uk)

🌐 wokinghamunitedcharities.org.uk

CC number: 1107171

Eligibility

People in need who live in the civil parishes of Wokingham, Wokingham Without, St Nicholas Hurst, Ruscombe or Finchampstead.

Types of grant

One-off grants, typically of under £500, are available towards household items, school trips and clothing.

Exclusions

According to our previous research, the charity is unable to fund general living costs, debts, floor coverings, non-essential items or item that have already been purchased.

Applications

In the first instance, contact should be made through Citizens Advice Wokingham by calling 0300 330 1189.

Financial information

Year end	31/03/2020
Income	£520,500
Total expenditure	£567,500

Further financial information

In 2019/20, grants were awarded to 39 individuals. The average grant was £350.

Other information

The main activity of the charity is the provision of almshouses in the area. Grants are also awarded to local charitable organisations.

Buckingham-shire

The Archdeaconry of Buckingham Clergy Charity

 £27,000 (2019)

Correspondent: The Trustees, Archdeacons House, Stone, Aylesbury, Buckinghamshire HP17 8RZ (tel: 01865 208266; email: archdeacon.buckingham@ oxford.anglican.org)

CC number: 1052475

Eligibility

Members of the clergy who are serving or who have served in Buckinghamshire Archdeaconry of the Oxfordshire Diocese and their dependants.

Types of grant

One-off grants are awarded according to need.

Applications

Apply in writing to the correspondent.

Financial information

Year end	31/12/2019
Income	£21,200
Total expenditure	£30,800

Further financial information

Full accounts were not available to view on the Charity Commission's website due to the charity's low income. We have therefore estimated the grant total based on the charity's total expenditure.

The Hitcham Poor Lands Charity

£1,800 (2019/20)

Correspondent: Joyce Brown, Trustee, 20 Wethered Drive, Burnham, Slough, Berkshire SL1 7NG (tel: 01628 664662; email: joybrown02@aol.com)

CC number: 203447

Eligibility

People in need who live in the parishes of Hitcham and Burnham.

Types of grant

Grants are given for furniture, white goods, school uniforms, school trips, carer's holidays and so on. The charity also distributes around 300 Christmas parcels of £20 each every year.

Applications

Apply in writing to the correspondent.

Financial information

Year end	31/03/2020
Income	£7,100
Total expenditure	£4,000

Further financial information

Full accounts were not available to view on the Charity Commission's website due to the charity's low income. We have therefore estimated the charity's grant total based on its total expenditure.

Other information

The charity also supports The Burnham Lighthouse Project and Thames Hospice Care, which operate in the local area.

Iver Heath Care Fund

£1,400 (2020)

Correspondent: The Trustees, 15 Warren Field, Iver, Buckinghamshire SL0 0RU (tel: 07816 514489)

CC number: 231111

Eligibility

People living in the Iver Heath ward in the parish of Iver and part of the parish of Wexham who are in need as a result of ill health, disability and other medical conditions.

Types of grant

Grants are given according to need.

Applications

Apply in writing to the correspondent.

Financial information

Year end	31/12/2020
Income	£4,600
Total expenditure	£3,200

Further financial information

Full accounts were not available to view on the Charity Commission's website due to the charity's low income. We have therefore estimated the grant total based on the charity's total expenditure.

Other information

This charity also makes grants to organisations.

The Saye and Sele Foundation

£4,800 (2020)

Correspondent: Tim Friedlander, Clerk to the Trustees, 18 Lower Street, Quainton, Aylesbury, Buckinghamshire HP22 4BJ (tel: 01296 318500; email: friedlandertim24@gmail.com)

CC number: 310554

Eligibility

People under the age of 25 who live in the parishes of Grendon Underwood and Quainton.

Types of grant

Welfare

One-off grants are given to help schoolchildren with educational needs. Grants have been made towards computers for people from low-income families and equipment for people with disabilities. Support can also be given for activities that increase life skills and experience.

Education

One-off grants are given to help college and university students with books, equipment and training costs.

Applications

Apply in writing to the correspondent.

Financial information

Year end	31/12/2020
Income	£23,100
Total expenditure	£10,700

Further financial information

Full accounts were not available to view on the Charity Commission's website due to the foundation's low income. We have therefore estimated the foundation's grant total based on its total expenditure.

Other information

The foundation also provides building space in the community and can support local schools.

The Stoke Mandeville and Other Parishes Charity

£35,600 (2020)

Correspondent: Caroline Dobson, Administrator, 17 Elham Way, Aylesbury, Aylesbury, Buckinghamshire HP21 9XN (tel: 07966 442036; email: smandopc@gmail.com)

 smandopc.org

CC number: 296174

Eligibility

People in need who live in the parishes of Stoke Mandeville, Great Missenden and Great and Little Hampden, Buckinghamshire. Applicants should have been resident in the area of benefit for at least two years.

Types of grant

Grants are available for the following:
- Lifeline alarms for older residents
- Senior citizens railcards to residents of Stoke Mandeville who are over 60 years old
- An annual grant to residents of Stoke Mandeville who are over 70 years old at Christmas time
- Family day trips for families of Stoke Mandeville with children under the age of 12

An annual educational grant is available to assist with the costs of books and equipment for further or higher education courses. University students can receive £500 and college students can receive £300.

Exclusions

Students undertaking GCSEs, AS or A-levels cannot apply for an educational grant. Grants for tuition fees are not available.

Applications

Application forms are available to download from the charity's website.

Financial information

Year end	31/12/2020
Income	£87,000
Total expenditure	£89,600

Aylesbury Vale

John Bedford's Charity

 £1,900 (2019)

Correspondent: The Trustees, 14 Bourbon Street, Aylesbury, Buckinghamshire HP20 2RS (tel: 01296 318500)

CC number: 202972

Eligibility

Older people in need living in Aylesbury.

Types of grant

Grants are given according to need.

Applications

Apply in writing to the correspondent.

Financial information

Year end	31/12/2019
Income	£3,000
Total expenditure	£2,100

Further financial information

Full accounts were not available to view on the Charity Commission's website due to the charity's low income. We have therefore estimated the charity's grant total based on its total expenditure.

Other information

The charity also provides support for the repair of highways in Aylesbury.

Cheddington Town Lands Charity

 £9,330 (2019/20)

Correspondent: Mr M. Watson, Treasurer, The Chase, Chaseside Close, Cheddington, Leighton Buzzard, Bedfordshire LU7 0SA (tel: 01296 662400; email: mcwatson@hotmail.co.uk)

CC number: 235076

Eligibility

People in need who live in the parish of Cheddington.

Types of grant

Welfare

Grants are given towards hospital transport and travel.

Education

Grants are given towards educational needs. According to our previous research, support is given to students in further and higher education to help with the cost of educational materials and equipment.

Applications

Apply in writing to the correspondent.

Financial information

Year end	31/03/2020
Income	£29,900
Total expenditure	£32,800

Other information

One-third of the charity's income goes to the maintenance of the parish church. The remainder is divided between village organisations, volunteer hospital drivers, students and people in need.

Charity of Elizabeth Eman

 £67,900 (2019)

Correspondent: Mr N. Freeman, Clerk to the Trustees, Horwood & James Solicitors, 7 Temple Square, Aylesbury, Buckinghamshire HP20 2QB (tel: 01296 487361; email: enquiries@horwoodjames.co.uk)

🌐 www.emans.co.uk

CC number: 215511

Eligibility

Women and men who are resident in Aylesbury Vale and are widowed, single or divorced and eligible to receive their pension.

Types of grant

Allowances of £111 per quarter are paid at the end of March, June, September and December. Grants are for life.

Applications

Application forms can be completed online through the charity's website.

Financial information

Year end	31/12/2019
Income	£61,000
Total expenditure	£68,700

Other information

The charity was originally set up for women who were widowed and born in Aylesbury; therefore, priority is given to such individuals, even though the criteria for receiving a pension has now been extended.

William Harding's Charity

 £248,600 (2019)

Correspondent: The Trustees, c/o Parrott & Coales Solicitors LLP, 14 Bourbon Street, Aylesbury, Buckinghamshire HP20 2RS (tel: 01296 318501; email: doudjag@pandcllp.co.uk)

🌐 https://www.leapwithus.org.uk/funding/william-hardings-charity

CC number: 310619

Eligibility

People under the age of 25 who live in the town of Aylesbury.

Types of grant

One-off grants are made to schoolchildren towards uniforms, clothing, fees, travel, books, educational outings, equipment, maintenance/living expenses or for special educational needs.

Young people in further/higher education and vocational training can apply for one-off awards towards, for example, living expenses.

Facilities for recreation and social or physical training may be provided to people in further education and children in primary or secondary school.

Applications

Application forms are available on request from the charity. Applications may be submitted at any time.

Financial information

Year end	31/12/2019
Income	£1,180,000
Total expenditure	£915,400

Further financial information

Grants to individuals were broken down as follows in the accounts: individual pupil support (£246,400); equipment and tools for young people (£2,200). Grants to organisations totalled £302,500.

Other information

The charity also owns almshouses and supports local educational institutions, youth groups and organisations.

Thomas Hickman's Charity

£66,800 (2019)

Correspondent: Clerk to the Trustees, c/o Parrott & Coales LLP, 14–16 Bourbon Street, Aylesbury, Buckinghamshire HP20 2RS (tel: 01296 318500; email: doudjag@pandcllp.co.uk)

🌐 thomashickmancharity.co.uk

CC number: 202973

Eligibility

People in need who live in Aylesbury town.

Types of grant

Grants are typically given for essential household items such as carpets, washing machines, cookers and fridges. Grants can also be made for school uniforms.

Applications

Application forms can be downloaded from the charity's website.

Financial information

Year end	31/12/2019
Income	£875,900
Total expenditure	£720,700

Further financial information

Grants were awarded to 104 individuals.

Other information

The charity's main activity is the upkeep of almshouses in the area.

Milton Keynes

The Ancell Trust

£ £7,000 (2019/20)

Correspondent: Karen Phillips, 78 London Road, Stony Stratford, Milton Keynes, Buckinghamshire MK11 1JH (tel: 01908 563350; email: karen.phillips440@gmail.com)

CC number: 233824

Eligibility

People in need in the town of Stony Stratford.

Types of grant

Welfare

One-off grants are awarded according to need. Historically grants have been given for healthcare and travelling expenses.

Education

One-off grants are awarded according to need for education, training and apprenticeships.

Applications

Apply in writing to the correspondent.

Financial information

Year end	05/04/2020
Income	£14,300
Total expenditure	£14,800

Further financial information

Full accounts were not available to view on the Charity Commission's website due to the trust's low income. We have therefore estimated the grant total based on the trust's total expenditure.

Other information

The trust owns the sports ground in Stony Stratford, which provides cricket, football, bowls, croquet and tennis facilities. Support is also given to organisations.

Edmund Arnold's Charity (Poors Branch)
See entry on page 228

Calverton Apprenticing Charity

£ £7,600 (2020/21)

Correspondent: Karen Phillips, 78 London Road, Stony Stratford, Milton Keynes, Buckinghamshire MK11 1JH (tel: 01908 563350; email: karen.phillips440@gmail.com)

CC number: 239246

Eligibility

People in need who have lived in the parish of All Saints, Calverton. Preference is given to people over the age of 65 and young people under the age of 21, particularly apprentices.

Types of grant

Welfare

Grants can be awarded for essential items such as clothing, medical equipment, nursing fees, furniture, heating and so on.

Education

Educational grants can be given for uniforms or clothing, fees, books, equipment and instruments.

Applications

Application forms can be requested from the correspondent. They can be submitted directly by the individual or a family member.

Financial information

Year end	31/03/2021
Income	£34,100
Total expenditure	£135,700

Other information

The charity also makes grants to organisations.

Catherine Featherstone

£ £6,500 (2020)

Correspondent: Karen Phillips, Secretary, 78 London Road, Stony Stratford, Milton Keynes, Buckinghamshire MK11 1JH (tel: 01908 563350; email: karen.phillips440@gmail.com)

CC number: 242620

Eligibility

Residents of Wolverton who are in need. Priority is given to people who attend church regularly.

Types of grant

Grants are given according to need. According to our previous research, past grants have been given towards household bills, food, medical and disability equipment, electrical goods, living costs and domestic help.

Applications

Apply in writing to the correspondent.

Financial information

Year end	31/12/2020
Income	£9,600
Total expenditure	£14,500

Further financial information

Full accounts were not available to view on the Charity Commission's website due to the charity's low income. We have therefore estimated the charity's grant total based on its total expenditure.

Other information

Grants are also given to local organisations.

Fuel Allotment

£ £1,600 (2019/20)

Correspondent: The Trustees, 9 Katrine Place, Bletchley, Milton Keynes, Buckinghamshire MK2 3DW (tel: 01908 642713)

CC number: 251127

Eligibility

Widows who live in Water Eaton and are in need. Any surplus income of the charity is distributed more generally to residents of Water Eaton who are in need.

Types of grant

Grants are given mainly towards fuel payments.

Applications

Apply in writing to the correspondent.

Financial information

Year end	30/11/2020
Income	£2,800
Total expenditure	£1,800

Further financial information

Full accounts were not available to view on the Charity Commission's website due to the charity's low income. We have therefore estimated the grant total based on the charity's total expenditure.

Great Linford Relief in Need Charity

£ £2,400 (2020)

Correspondent: The Trustees, 2 Lodge Gate, Great Linford, Milton Keynes, Buckinghamshire MK14 5EW (tel: 01908 605664)

CC number: 237373

Eligibility

People in need who live in the parish of Great Linford.

Types of grant
Grants are awarded according to need.

Applications
Apply in writing to the correspondent.

Financial information
Year end	31/12/2020
Income	£1,100
Total expenditure	£2,700

Further financial information
Full accounts were not available to view on the Charity Commission's website due to the charity's low income. We have therefore estimated the charity's grant total based on its total expenditure.

The Poor's Allotments Charity

 £810 (2019/20)

Correspondent: The Trustees, 6 Pigott Drive, Shenley Church End, Milton Keynes, Buckinghamshire MK5 6BY (tel: 01908 507474)

CC number: 240164

Eligibility
Widows in Bletchley who are in need.

Types of grant
The charity makes payments for fuel.

Applications
Apply in writing to the correspondent.

Financial information
Year end	30/11/2020
Income	£4,300
Total expenditure	£900

Further financial information
Full accounts were not available to view on the Charity Commission's website due to the charity's low income. We have therefore estimated the charity's grant total based on its total expenditure.

Tyringham Pension Fund for the Blind

 £1,000 (2019/20)

Correspondent: The Trustees, 6 St Faiths Close, Newton Longville, Milton Keynes, Buckinghamshire MK17 0BA (tel: 01908 643816; email: davan6@icloud.com)

CC number: 210332

Eligibility
People in need who are blind or partially sighted and live in Newport Pagnell and Wolverton.

Types of grant
The charity provides pensions.

Applications
Apply in writing to the correspondent.

Financial information
Year end	31/03/2020
Income	£1,900
Total expenditure	£1,100

Further financial information
Full accounts were not available to view on the Charity Commission's website due to the charity's low income. We have therefore estimated the grant total based on the charity's total expenditure.

South Buckinghamshire

Stoke Poges Hastings Community Fund

 £1,900 (2019)

Correspondent: The Trustees, Village Hall, 129 Rogers Lane, Stoke Poges, Slough, Berkshire SL2 4LP (tel: 01753 646323; email: SPHCF11@outlook.com)

stokepogescharities.uk/stoke-poges-hastings-community-fund

CC number: 206915

Eligibility
People in need resident in the parish of Stoke Poges.

Types of grant
Grants are given for a range of purposes such as kitchen appliances, furniture, debts, wheelchairs and other independence aids, school uniforms, non-university courses and breaks for carers.

Applications
Application forms can be either downloaded from the charity's website and returned by post or completed online.

Financial information
Year end	31/12/2019
Income	£22,400
Total expenditure	£4,300

Further financial information
Full accounts were not available to view on the Charity Commission's website due to the charity's low income. We have therefore estimated the charity's grant total based on its total expenditure.

Other information
Grants are also made to local organisations.

Stoke Poges United Charity

 £7,100 (2019)

Correspondent: The Trustees, Kidd Rapinet Llp, 392 Edinburgh Avenue, Wooburn Green, Slough, Berkshire SL1 4UF (tel: 01753 532541; email: pastles@kiddrapinet.co.uk)

www.stokepogescharities.com

CC number: 205289

Eligibility
People who are in need and live in the parish of Stoke Poges and the surrounding area. A map of the charity's area of benefit is available on its website.

Types of grant
Grants can be given for items such as furniture, clothing, fuel, hospital travel expenses and home adaptations. For a full list of eligible expenditure visit the charity's website.

Applications
Application forms can be either downloaded from the charity's website and returned by post or completed online.

Financial information
Year end	31/12/2019
Income	£10,600
Total expenditure	£15,700

Further financial information
Full accounts were not available to view on the Charity Commission's website due to the charity's low income. We have therefore estimated the grant total based on the charity's total expenditure.

Other information
The charity also supports organisations.

Wycombe

High Wycombe Central Aid Society

 £24,000 (2019/20)

Correspondent: The Trustees, High Wycombe Central Aid Society, West Richardson Street, High Wycombe, Buckinghamshire HP11 2SB (tel: 01494 535890; email: office@central-aid.org.uk)

www.central-aid.org.uk

CC number: 201445

Eligibility
People in need, including those in receipt of benefits, who live in the old borough of High Wycombe. The society will also help ex-service personnel and their dependants.

Types of grant

Grants can be made for furniture, white goods and carpet tiles. Work experience opportunities are available for those with learning and social communication difficulties.

Applications

Apply in writing to the correspondent, including details of income, savings, family situation and a quote for the goods needed along with any relevant supporting documents. Applications can be submitted through a social worker, local council, SSAFA, Citizens Advice or other welfare agency.

Financial information

Year end	31/03/2020
Income	£290,900
Total expenditure	£183,400

Further financial information

During the year, furniture grants were awarded to 121 families.

Other information

The society has a second-hand furniture warehouse and clothes and soft furnishings store (tel: 01494 4434 59, email: furniture@central-aid.org.uk).

Wooburn, Bourne End and District Relief-in-Sickness Charity

(£) £17,600 (2020)

Correspondent: The Trustees, 11 Telston Close, Bourne End SL8 5TY (tel: 01628 523498)

CC number: 210596

Eligibility

People who are experiencing ill health or who have disabilities and who live in the parishes of Wooburn and Hedsor and the part of Bourne End which is in the parish of Little Marlow.

Types of grant

Grants are awarded for items, services or facilities that will alleviate suffering or assist in recovery, and which are not readily available from other sources.

Applications

Apply in writing to the correspondent.

Financial information

Year end	31/12/2020
Income	£22,900
Total expenditure	£19,500

Further financial information

Full accounts were not available to view on the Charity Commission's website due to the charity's low income. We have therefore estimated the charity's grant total based on its total expenditure.

East Sussex

Carlton Colville Fuel or Poor's Allotment

(£) £8,500 (2019)

Correspondent: The Trustees, 23 Wannock Close, Carlton Colville, Lowestoft, Suffolk NR33 8DW (tel: 01502 518197)

CC number: 242083

Eligibility

People in need who live in the ancient parish of Carlton Colville. Priority is given to older residents of the parish.

Types of grant

Recurrent grants are awarded for fuel and heating costs. Any surplus income is distributed in the form of one-off grants.

Applications

Apply in writing to the correspondent.

Financial information

Year end	31/12/2019
Income	£19,600
Total expenditure	£18,800

Further financial information

Full accounts were not available to view on the Charity Commission's website due to the charity's low income. We have therefore estimated the charity's grant total based on its total expenditure.

Other information

This charity also makes grants to local organisations.

The Chownes Foundation

(£) £19,100 (2019/20)

Correspondent: Sylvia Spencer, Secretary, Stable Cottage, Whiteway Lane, Rodmell, Steyning, Lewes BN7 3EX (tel: 07736 354139; email: ianhazeel@btopenworld.com)

CC number: 327451

Eligibility

Former employees of Sound Diffusion plc who lost their pensions when the company went into receivership. Our research indicates that grants are also made to assist older people who live in mid-Sussex and are in need.

Types of grant

One-off and recurrent grants are given according to need.

Applications

Apply in writing to the correspondent.

Financial information

Year end	31/03/2020
Income	£4,300
Total expenditure	£42,300

Further financial information

Full accounts were not available to view on the Charity Commission's website due to the foundation's low income. We have therefore estimated the foundation's grant total based on its total expenditure.

Other information

The majority of the foundation's funds are committed to long-term support for poor and vulnerable beneficiaries, so very few applications are successful.

Corton Poor's Land Trust

(£) £4,000 (2019/20)

Correspondent: The Trustees, 49 Darby Road, Beccles, Suffolk NR34 9XX (email: boyneclaire@gmail.com)

CC number: 206067

Eligibility

People in need who live in the ancient parish of Corton in Suffolk.

Types of grant

Grants are given to according to need and as Christmas gifts for people in need.

Applications

Apply in writing to the correspondent.

Financial information

Year end	31/10/2020
Income	£25,300
Total expenditure	£9,800

Other information

The trust also maintains almshouses and makes grants to organisations.

Miss Ethel Mary Fletcher's Charitable Bequest

(£) £5,500 (2019/20)

Correspondent: The Trustees, c/o Thomson, Snell & Passmore, 3 Lonsdale Gardens, Tunbridge Wells, Kent TN1 1NU (tel: 01892 510000)

CC number: 219850

Eligibility

Older people in need due to ill health, age or otherwise.

Types of grant

Gifts in kind, pensions, and grants for clothing, fuel, medical attention and treatments, food and other essential items.

Applications

Apply in writing to the correspondent.

Financial information

Year end	18/06/2020
Income	£7,600
Total expenditure	£12,200

Further financial information

Full accounts were not available to view on the Charity Commission's website due to the charity's low income. We have therefore estimated the charity's grant total based on its total expenditure.

Other information

The charity also makes grants towards improving access to education for children and to other charitable organisations.

Hastings Area Community Trust

 £46,100 (2018/19)

Correspondent: John Enefer, Bolton Tomson House, 49 Cambridge Gardens, Hastings, East Sussex TN34 1EN (tel: 01424 718880; email: clerk.relief@ gmail.com)

reliefhastings.weebly.com

CC number: 1002470

Eligibility

People in need who live in Hastings and Rother.

Types of grant

Grants are given according to need.

Applications

Apply on a form available from the correspondent. Grant applications must be made via a referring agency.

Financial information

Year end	31/03/2019
Income	£82,000
Total expenditure	£93,200

Other information

The trust also provides accommodation and administration services to other local charities and organisations.

Kirkley Poor's Land Estate

 £27,100 (2019/20)

Correspondent: Lucy Walker, Clerk to the Trustees, 4 Station Road, Lowestoft, Suffolk NR32 4QF (tel: 01502 514964; email: kirkleypoors@gmail.com)

www.kirkleypoorslandestate.co.uk

CC number: 210177

Eligibility

Welfare

Older people in need who live in the parish of Kirkley.

Education

Students who are undertaking their first degree and live in the parish of Kirkley.

Types of grant

Welfare

Vouchers of £25 are available to pensioners each winter to help with the cost of groceries.

Education

Grants are awarded to help towards university degree expenses throughout the course of the degree.

Applications

Apply in writing to the correspondent.

Financial information

Year end	30/04/2020
Income	£99,900
Total expenditure	£78,800

Further financial information

In 2019/20, the charity distributed food vouchers to 673 pensioners.

Other information

The boundaries of the parish are fully defined on the charity's website. The charity also awards grants to local organisations.

The Mrs A. Lacy Tate Trust

 £25,300 (2019/20)

Correspondent: The Trustees, Heringtons LLP, 37–39 Gildredge Road, Eastbourne, East Sussex BN21 4RX (tel: 01323 411020)

CC number: 803596

Eligibility

People in need and schoolchildren undertaking education who live in East Sussex.

Types of grant

Grants are awarded according to need, including to further the education of children.

Applications

Apply in writing to the correspondent.

Financial information

Year end	05/04/2020
Income	£68,500
Total expenditure	£60,500

Further financial information

In 2019/20, 95 grants were awarded to individuals totalling £25,300. In

addition, grants to organisations totalled £31,500.

Other information

Grants are also made to organisations and towards animal welfare.

MacAndrew Sussex Trust

£26,400 (2019/20)

Correspondent: The Trustees, 4th Floor, Park Gate, 161–163 Preston Road, Brighton, East Sussex BN1 6AF (tel: 01273 562563; email: roger@ friend-james.co.uk)

CC number: 206900

Eligibility

Young and older people who live in East and West Sussex. The trust's objects are as follows:

▶ Supporting boys through sea training, with a focus on character building
▶ Helping young people, as part of their education, to extend their knowledge of other nations
▶ Supporting disadvantaged young people to get a good start in life
▶ Supporting older people in difficult financial circumstances

Types of grant

Grants are awarded in support of the trust's objects.

Applications

Apply in writing to the correspondent.

Financial information

Year end	31/03/2020
Income	£1,000
Total expenditure	£58,600

Further financial information

Full accounts were not available to view on the Charity Commission's website due to the trust's low income. We have therefore estimated the trust's grant total based on its total expenditure.

Other information

The trust also gives grants to organisations.

Smith and Fermor Charities

£1,900 (2020)

Correspondent: Clerk, 82 Fermor Way, Crowborough, East Sussex TN6 3BJ (tel: 01892 664245; email: clerk@ rotherfieldparishcouncil.co.uk)

www.rotherfieldparishcouncil.co.uk

CC number: 235516

Eligibility
Residents of Rotherfield and Crowborough civil parishes who are in need.

Types of grant
The annual report and accounts were unavailable for 2020; however, previous examples of support include grants towards mobility aids, travel costs for regular hospital visits and court fees.

Applications
Apply in writing to the correspondent.

Financial information
Year end	31/12/2020
Income	£2,600
Total expenditure	£4,200

Further financial information
Full accounts were not available to view on the Charity Commission's website due to the charity's low income. We have therefore estimated the grant total based on the charity's total expenditure.

Other information
This charity also makes grants to other voluntary organisations whose work supports people in the area of benefit, particularly those involved in supporting older people, those supporting the care and rehabilitation of people with physical or mental illnesses and those whose work helps to provide recreational or educational activities.

Sussex County Football Association Benevolent Fund

£1,500 (2019/20)

Correspondent: Nigel Williams, Honorary Secretary, Sussex County Football Association, Culver Road, Lancing, West Sussex BN15 9AX (tel: 01903 753547)

CC number: 217496

Eligibility
Members of clubs affiliated with Sussex County Football Association, or people who have 'rendered services to the game', who are in need because of a football-related injury. Support is extended to the dependants of such people.

Types of grant
One-off grants or a series of periodical payments.

Exclusions
Claims for one week's incapacity are rarely approved and should only be submitted in exceptional circumstances.

Applications
To request an application form, contact the correspondent. Requests for forms must be made within 28 days of injury and applications must be returned within a further 28 days upon receiving a form. All applications must include a medical certificate or equivalent.

Financial information
Year end	30/04/2020
Income	£10,600
Total expenditure	£1,700

Further financial information
Full accounts were not available to view on the Charity Commission's website due to the fund's low income. We have therefore estimated the fund's grant total based on its total expenditure.

Sussex Police Charitable Trust

£53,800 (2020)

Correspondent: The Trustees, Malling House, Church Lane, Lewes, East Sussex BN7 2DZ (tel: 01273 470101 (ext. 540703); email: spct@sussex.pnn.police.uk)

 www.sussex.police.uk/SPCT

CC number: 257564

Eligibility
Current or retired members of the trust, and their dependants, who are in need, hardship or distress.

Types of grant
One-off grants for various welfare needs. The most common grants awarded in 2020 included: therapies for mental and physical health and well-being; food vouchers and other living costs; hospital or health travel and accommodation; recuperative breaks.

Applications
Apply in writing to the correspondent.

Financial information
Year end	31/12/2020
Income	£188,200
Total expenditure	£209,500

Further financial information
In 2020, the average grant made by the trust was £350. The largest grant was £2,000 and the lowest grant was £30.

Other information
The trust owns a bungalow in Dorset, which is available to members in need of a recuperative break for up to six days at a time. Interest-free loans are available to members of the trust who are still employed by Sussex Police if they do not already qualify for a 'high street' loan and have the ability to pay back the loan over a term agreed with the trust (but no longer than five years). These loans are repayable through deductions to payroll.

Brighton and Hove
The Brighton Fund

£62,900 (2020/21)

Correspondent: Nicci Grundy, Brighton and Hove City Council, Financial Accounting, 3rd Floor Bartholomew House, Bartholomew Square, Brighton, East Sussex BN1 1JE (tel: 01273 291259; email: accountancy@brighton-hove.gov.uk)

https://www.brighton-hove.gov.uk/content/life-events-and-communities/community-and-voluntary-sector-support/brighton-fund

CC number: 1011724

Eligibility
Individuals in need who live within the administrative boundary of Brighton and Hove.

Types of grant
One-off grants of up to £500 are given for essential items such as white goods, flooring, clothing, furniture and so on.

Exclusions
The charity does not provide the following:
- Crisis loans
- Support for people who are currently homeless
- Grants for consumer electrics (such as laptops or phones)
- Direct payment of debts (although Debt Relief Orders are funded)
- Grants for ongoing costs

Applications
Application forms can be completed online on the charity's website or downloaded and completed by hand. All applications to the charity must be made by support workers on behalf of the applicant. It can take up to a month for applications to be considered.

Financial information
Year end	31/03/2021
Income	£53,300
Total expenditure	£63,100

Further financial information
Grants were distributed as follows: grants to individuals in need over 60 years old (£8,100); grants to individuals in need under 60 years old (£54,800).

The Newick Distress Trust

£ £8,500 (2020)

Correspondent: Ian Reekie, Trustee, 3 High Hurst Close, Newick, Lewes, East Sussex BN8 4NJ (tel: 01825 722512; email: ianreekie24@gmail.com)

CC number: 291954

Eligibility

Residents of the village of Newick. The trust states that people whose income has been 'drastically reduced' as a result of ill health, bereavement, unemployment or marriage breakdown constitute the most common causes for help.

Types of grant

Grants are awarded according to need. Examples include assistance to cover the cost of heating bills in periods of cold weather and school uniforms on a change of school.

Exclusions

Applications outside the Newick village will not be accepted.

Applications

Apply in writing to the correspondent. The trustees meet twice each year (or when necessary) to consider grant applications.

Financial information

Year end	31/12/2020
Income	£21,000
Total expenditure	£19,000

Further financial information

Full accounts were not available to view on the Charity Commission's website due to the trust's low income. We have therefore estimated the trust's grant total based on its total expenditure.

Eastbourne

The Mayor's Poor Fund, Eastbourne

£ £1,300 (2019/20)

Correspondent: The Trustees, Town Hall, Grove Road, Eastbourne, East Sussex BN21 4UG (tel: 01323 415002; email: mayorsoffice@lewes-eastbourne.gov.uk)

CC number: 210664

Eligibility

People who live in the borough of Eastbourne and are in need of temporary financial assistance due to illness, unemployment or similar circumstances.

Types of grant

One-off grants are awarded according to need.

Applications

Apply in writing to the correspondent.

Financial information

Year end	30/06/2020
Income	£1,100
Total expenditure	£1,500

Further financial information

Full accounts were not available to view on the Charity Commission's website due to the charity's low income. We have therefore estimated the grant total based on the charity's total expenditure.

Hastings

The Isabel Blackman Foundation

£ £45,100 (2019/20)

Correspondent: John Francis Lamplugh, Secretary, Stonehenge, 13 Laton Road, Hastings, East Sussex TN34 2ES (tel: 01424 431756; email: ibfoundation@uwclub.net)

CC number: 313577

Eligibility

Welfare
People who live in Hastings and St Leonards-on-Sea and require financial assistance. Preference may be given to older people.

Education
Students who live in Hastings and St Leonards-on-Sea that require financial assistance.

Types of grant

Welfare
Grants are given to support the social well-being and health of residents.

Education
Grants are available to support education.

Applications

Apply in writing to the correspondent. The foundation's 2019/20 accounts state: 'Applications for grants are more likely to succeed where it can be shown that the applicants are helping themselves as well as seeking assistance.'

Financial information

Year end	05/04/2020
Income	£296,500
Total expenditure	£328,200

Further financial information

Welfare grants were broken down as follows:

Health	6	£6,700
Culture and recreation	1	£1,000
Youth clubs	1	£1,000

Education grants were awarded to 26 individuals.

Other information

The foundation also makes grants to organisations active in the community.

William Shadwell Charity

£ £7,500 (2020)

Correspondent: The Trustees, 205 St Helens Road, Hastings, East Sussex TN34 3EA (tel: 07814 102210; email: williamshadwellcharity@btinternet.com)

CC number: 207366

Eligibility

People with disabilities or experiencing ill health who live in the borough of Hastings.

Types of grant

Grants are given according to need.

Applications

Apply in writing to the correspondent.

Financial information

Year end	31/12/2020
Income	£11,600
Total expenditure	£16,500

Further financial information

Full accounts were not available to view on the Charity Commission's website due to the charity's low income. We have therefore estimated the grant total based on the charity's total expenditure.

Rother

The Battle Charities

£ £750 (2020)

Correspondent: The Trustees, The Hurst, Netherfield Hill, Battle, East Sussex TN33 0LA (tel: 01424 774435; email: thebattlecharities@gmail.com)

CC number: 206591

Eligibility

People in need who live in Battle and Netherfield, East Sussex.

Types of grant

Grants are given according to need.

Applications

Apply in writing to the correspondent.

Financial information

Year end	31/12/2020
Income	£3,300
Total expenditure	£830

Further financial information

Full accounts were not available to view on the Charity Commission's website due to the charity's low income. We have therefore estimated the charity's grant total based on its total expenditure.

Wealdon

The Mayfield Trust

 £2,300 (2020)

Correspondent: Brenda Hopkin, Appletrees, Alexandra Road, Mayfield, East Sussex TN20 6UD (tel: 01435 873279; email: brendahopkin@tiscali.co.uk)

https://mayfieldfiveashes.org.uk/about-us/the-mayfield-trust

CC number: 212996

Eligibility

People in need who live in the parish of Mayfield, which includes Mayfield, Five Ashes and part of Hadlow Down.

Types of grant

Welfare
One-off grants are given towards health and social needs. Examples of support include medical or mobility equipment and help with family emergencies.

Education
Grants are awarded according to need for education.

Exclusions

Grants are not made for religious or political causes.

Applications

Apply in writing to the correspondent.

Financial information

Year end	31/12/2020
Income	£5,000
Total expenditure	£5,500

Further financial information

Full accounts were not available to view on the Charity Commission's website due to the trust's low income. We have therefore estimated the trust's grant total based on its total expenditure.

Other information

The trust also makes grants to organisations.

Warbleton Charity

 £3,400 (2020)

Correspondent: The Trustees, 3 Benhall Mill Place, Benhall Mill Road, Tunbridge Wells, Kent TN2 5EE (tel: 01892 513899; email: leeves@freenetname.co.uk)

https://www.warbletonchurch.org.uk/info

CC number: 208130

Eligibility

People who live in the parish of Warbleton, particularly those on low income.

Types of grant

Welfare
One-off grants are awarded according to need. The charity also provides a number of local people with Christmas hampers.

Education
The charity awards small vocational training and apprenticeship grants.

Applications

Apply in writing to the correspondent.

Financial information

Year end	31/12/2020
Income	£3,700
Total expenditure	£3,700

Further financial information

Full accounts were not available to view on the Charity Commission's website due to the charity's low income. We have therefore estimated the charity's grant total based on its total expenditure.

Hampshire

Aldworth's Educational Trust (Aldworth Trust Foundation)

£5,900 (2019/20)

Correspondent: Debbie Reavell, 25 Cromwell Road, Basingstoke, Hampshire RG21 5NR (tel: 01256 473390; email: reavell@btinternet.com)

CC number: 307259

Eligibility

Children and young people who are either resident in or were educated/are currently attending school in Basingstoke and Deane.

Types of grant

Grants are awarded towards the cost of travel, books, equipment and clothing.

Applications

Apply in writing to the correspondent.

Financial information

Year end	31/03/2020
Income	£6,600
Total expenditure	£6,600

Further financial information

Full accounts were not available to view on the Charity Commission's website due to the trust's low income. We have therefore estimated the trust's grant total based on its total expenditure.

The Fareham Welfare Trust

£9,200 (2019/20)

Correspondent: The Trustees, 44 Old Turnpike, Fareham, Hampshire PO16 7HA (tel: 01329 235186)

CC number: 236738

Eligibility

People in need who live in the ecclesiastical area of Fareham. This includes the parishes of St Peter and Paul, St John and Holy Trinity. Priority is given to widows.

Types of grant

Grants are given according to need.

Applications

Apply in writing to the correspondent.

Financial information

Year end	31/10/2020
Income	£11,600
Total expenditure	£10,200

Further financial information

Full accounts were not available to view on the Charity Commission's website due to the trust's low income. We have therefore estimated the trust's grant total based on its total expenditure.

The Farnborough (Hampshire) Welfare Trust

£1,200 (2019)

Correspondent: The Trustees, 45 Church Avenue, Farnborough, Hampshire GU14 7AP (tel: 01252 542726; email: evans.bowmarsh@ntlworld.com)

CC number: 236889

Eligibility

Residents of Farnborough and Cove who are in financial need.

Types of grant

Grants are given according to need.

Applications

Apply in writing to the correspondent.

Financial information

Year end	31/12/2019
Income	£4,900
Total expenditure	£2,600

Further financial information

Full accounts were not available to view on the Charity Commission's website due to the trust's low income. We have therefore estimated the trust's grant total based on its total expenditure.

The Hampshire and Isle of Wight Military Aid Fund

£ £18,700 (2019)

Correspondent: Lt Col. Colin Bulleid, Secretary, Serle's House, Southgate Street, Winchester, Hampshire SO23 9EG (tel: 01263 852933; email: secretary@hantsMAF.org)

 www.hantsmaf.org/index.htm

CC number: 202363

Eligibility

Members, or former members, of the British Army (whether regular, territorial, militia, yeomanry or volunteer), and their dependants, who are in need. Eligible applicants should be:

▷ Members or former members of any Regiment or Corps raised in Hampshire.
▷ Members or former members of The Princess of Wales's Royal Regiment (Queen's and Royal Hampshires) who were resident in Hampshire or the Isle of White at the time of their enlistment.

Territorial Army (TA) soldiers must have had at least four years service with a TA unit in Hampshire or operational service.

Types of grant

One-off grants are awarded for services or items such as rent arrears, debts/bankruptcy, household and boiler repairs, white goods and furnishings, nursing home fees, funeral costs, respite care and holidays, removals, house deposits, travel costs and home adaptations (for example, stairlifts, riser chairs/beds, EPVs, wheelchairs and showers).

Applications

The fund should not normally be approached directly. The following information is taken from the fund's website:

Like all other military charities access to assistance is via a report from either SSAFA Forces Help or The Royal British Legion.

A caseworker from your chosen organisation will visit you and complete a Form A with details about your connection to the Army, financial situation, your need, and a recommendation for appropriate assistance.

Consult the website for detailed information about the application process and how the money will be paid.

Financial information

Year end	31/12/2019
Income	£25,000
Total expenditure	£24,900

Further financial information

Full accounts were not available to view on the Charity Commission's website due to the fund's low income. We have therefore estimated the fund's grant total based on previous years' accounts. In previous years the fund has spent around 75% of its total expenditure on grants.

Hampshire Constabulary Welfare Fund

£ £17,500 (2019/20)

Correspondent: Mr G. Smith, Secretary, Federation House, 1490 Parkway, Solent Business Park, Whiteley, Hampshire PO15 7AF (tel: 023 8047 8920; email: hampshire@polfed.org)

CC number: 291061

Eligibility

Serving officers and staff of Hampshire Constabulary, as well as retired members of any UK Police Force connected with Hampshire Constabulary, and the dependants of such people, who are in need. Support is also extended to Special Constables injured while on Hampshire Constabulary duties.

Types of grant

One-off welfare grants to cover the cost of, for example, mobility aids, home adaptations, priority debts and rent deposits. Recurrent gifts of £25 are distributed at Christmas to widows and children. Loans are also available.

Applications

Apply in writing to the correspondent.

Financial information

Year end	31/03/2020
Income	£16,000
Total expenditure	£266,300

Further financial information

Full accounts were not available to view on the Charity Commission's website due to the fund's low income. We have therefore estimated the grant total based on the fund's total expenditure.

Other information

The fund also donates to other charitable organisations which support police officers.

Hampshire Football Association Benevolent Fund

£ £4,100 (2019/20)

Correspondent: The Trustees, Winklebury Football Complex, Winklebury Way, Basingstoke, Hampshire RG23 8BF (tel: 01256 853000)

CC number: 232359

Eligibility

People who are in need as a result of accident or injury while participating in association football, under the administration of Hampshire Football Association.

Types of grant

Grants are given according to need.

Applications

Apply in writing to the correspondent.

Financial information

Year end	30/06/2020
Income	£2,100
Total expenditure	£4,600

Further financial information

Full accounts were not available to view on the Charity Commission's website due to the fund's low income. We have therefore estimated the grant total based on the fund's total expenditure.

Hawley Almshouses

£ £900 (2020/21)

Correspondent: The Manager, Trustees' Office, Ratcliffe House, Blackwater, Camberley GU17 9DD (tel: 01276 33515; email: hawleyalmshouses@btconnect.com)

 https://www.hawleyalmshouses.org.uk/reliefinneed.html

CC number: 204684

Eligibility

People in need who live in the area covered by Hart District Council and Rushmoor Borough Council.

Types of grant

One-off grants are awarded according to need. Examples of grants made include funding towards school trips for families on a low income, the purchase of special equipment for people with disabilities and contributions to specialist medical assessments.

Applications

Apply in writing to the correspondent. Applications must be made through a third-party professional body, such as a health professional, school, another charity or voluntary organisation and so on.

Financial information

Year end	31/03/2021
Income	£159,400
Total expenditure	£147,900

Further financial information

The annual grant total has been larger in previous years.

Other information

The charity also runs almshouses.

Hollis Charity

£ £5,000 (2019/20)

Correspondent: The Trustees, 2 Winchester Close, Newport, Isle of Wight PO30 1DR (tel: 01983 525630; email: cvhollistrust@btinternet.com)

CC number: 257875

Eligibility

Widows or unmarried women, aged 40 years or over, living in Hampshire or the Isle of Wight who are in need. Support is also available to younger women who are preparing to enter, or are currently engaged in, any profession or trade.

Types of grant

Recurrent grants in the form of pensions are awarded to women aged 40 years or over. One-off grants for tools, books, fee payments, travelling expenses and so on are made to younger current or aspiring professionals or tradeswomen.

Applications

Apply in writing to the correspondent.

Financial information

Year end	31/03/2020
Income	£5,500
Total expenditure	£5,300

Further financial information

Full accounts were not available to view on the Charity Commission's website due to the charity's low income. We have therefore estimated the grant total based on the charity's total expenditure.

The Richard Kirkman Trust

£ £15,900 (2019/20)

Correspondent: The Trustees, Ashton House, 12 The Central Precinct, Winchester Road, Chandler's Ford, Eastleigh, Hampshire SO53 2GB (tel: 023 8027 4555; email: ashton.house@btconnect.com)

CC number: 327972

Eligibility

People in need who live in Hampshire.

Types of grant

One-off grants are awarded according to need.

Applications

Apply in writing to the correspondent.

Financial information

Year end	05/04/2020
Income	£82,200
Total expenditure	£99,800

Further financial information

Note: the grant total has been estimated and may include grants to organisations.

Portsmouth Victoria Nursing Association

£ £26,900 (2019)

Correspondent: The Trustees, 14 Clegg Road, Southsea, Portsmouth, Hampshire PO4 9DQ (tel: 07434 617947; email: pvnacharity@gmail.com)

CC number: 203311

Eligibility

People in both medical and financial need who live in the areas covered by the Portsmouth City Primary Care Trust, the Fareham and Gosport Primary Care Trust and the East Hampshire Primary Care Trust.

Types of grant

Grants are given towards the purchase of medical equipment, furniture, electrical goods and special clothing as well as for respite care (requests for respite care in the form of nursery places for children will be funded if there is a special need).

Exclusions

Grants cannot be given for items that should be provided by the NHS.

Applications

All applications must be made through nurse representatives from district nurses, health visitors and other community nurses. Referrals are also accepted from social services, school nurses, occupational therapists and Citizens Advice personnel. Referrals are considered by the committee at monthly meetings.

Financial information

Year end	31/12/2019
Income	£53,300
Total expenditure	£48,800

South Central Ambulance Service (Incorporating Hampshire Ambulance Service) Benevolent Fund

£ £3,600 (2019/20)

Correspondent: Philip Pimlott, Trustee, 170 Knapp Lane, Ampfield, Romsey, Hampshire SO51 9BT (tel: 01794 368424; email: scasbftreasurer@gmail.com)

CC number: 1041811

Eligibility

Serving and retired members of Hampshire Ambulance Service/South Central Ambulance Service NHS Trust and their dependants.

Types of grant

One-off grants can be awarded according to need.

Applications

Apply in writing to the correspondent.

Financial information

Year end	31/03/2020
Income	£2,500
Total expenditure	£4,000

Further financial information

Full accounts were not available to view on the Charity Commission's website due to the fund's low income. We have therefore estimated the grant total based on the fund's total expenditure.

Basingstoke and Deane

Ashford Hill Educational Trust

£ £780 (2020)

Correspondent: The Trustees, Minnesota, Ashford Hill Road, Headley, Thatcham, Berkshire RG19 8AB (tel: 01635 269596)

CC number: 1040559

Eligibility

People who live in the parish of Ashford Hill with Headley or the surrounding area. There is no age limit.

Types of grant

Grants can be given towards recreational activities for all ages and also for educational purposes.

Applications

Apply in writing to the correspondent.

Financial information

Year end	31/12/2020
Income	£5,800
Total expenditure	£1,700

Further financial information

Full accounts were not available to view on the Charity Commission's website due to the trust's low income. We have therefore estimated the trust's grant total based on its total expenditure.

Other information

The trust also makes grants to organisations.

Kingsclere Welfare Charities

£ £10,400 (2020)

Correspondent: The Trustees, Russell House, Ashford Hill Road, Headley, Thatcham RG19 8AB (tel: 01635 269184; email: kingsclerecharities@iname.com)

CC number: 237218

Eligibility

Residents in the parishes of Kingsclere and Ashford Hill with Headley who are in need as a result of ill health, disability or other medical conditions.

Types of grant

Grants are awarded according to need. Assistance is given in cases where help has not been available elsewhere.

Applications

Apply in writing to the correspondent.

Financial information

Year end	31/12/2020
Income	£2,000
Total expenditure	£11,600

Further financial information

Full accounts were not available to view on the Charity Commission's website due to the charity's low income. We have therefore estimated the charity's grant total based on its total expenditure.

East Hampshire

The Tantum Trust

£ £16,800 (2019/20)

Correspondent: The Trustees, The Tantum Trust, Room 60, Building 51, Bordon Enterprise Park, GU35 0FJ (tel: 01420 477787; email: info@blhcharity.co.uk)

 www.blhcharity.co.uk

CC number: 1153712

Eligibility

People in need who live in the north-east of Hampshire and south-west of Surrey.

Types of grant

One-off grants and supermarket vouchers are available. Grants are made for items such as furniture, electrical goods and carpets.

Applications

Apply on a form available from the correspondent or to download from the website. Applications can be made either directly by the individual or through a social worker, Citizens Advice, other welfare agency, parent support advisor, health visitor or district nurse.

Financial information

Year end	31/03/2020
Income	£228,100
Total expenditure	£232,500

Further financial information

Grants to individuals have been estimated based on the charity's overall grant giving.

Other information

The charity raises money through its four charity shops in Bordon, Haslemere, Grayshott and Liphook and provides support to both individuals and organisations. It registered as a CIO in 2013.

Fareham

The William Price Charitable Trust

£ £31,400 (2019/20)

Correspondent: Christopher Thomas, Clerk, 24 Cuckoo Lane, Fareham, Hampshire PO14 3PF (tel: 01329 663685; email: mazchris@tiscali.co.uk)

 www.pricestrust.org.uk

CC number: 307319

Eligibility

Children and young people under the age of 25 who live in the parishes of St Peter and St Paul, Holy Trinity with St Columba and St John the Evangelist (the same area as the original Fareham town parish but not the whole area of the Fareham borough).

Types of grant

Education

Grants are awarded to students for university, college and apprenticeship costs.

Welfare

Grants are awarded for pupils whose families are in financial need to take part

in educational visits, purchase of school uniforms, tools and equipment.

Applications

Where possible, applications should be made through a school/college; however, individual applications will also be considered, particularly from people in further/higher education. Application forms can be downloaded from the trust's website or requested from the correspondent. Bursaries and college/university grants are considered twice a year, normally in March and September, and applications should be received by the first day of these months. Applications for smaller hardship grants can be made at any time and will be paid through a school/college.

Financial information

Year end	31/03/2020
Income	£197,300
Total expenditure	£255,600

Further financial information

In 2019/20, 44 grants were awarded to individuals for welfare purposes, and 16 grants were awarded for education.

Other information

Grants are also made to churches and schools/colleges, and there is an annual grant to the Fareham Welfare Trust.

The Earl of Southampton Trust

£ £29,300 (2019/20)

Correspondent: Tracey Kenney, Clerk to the Trustees, 24 The Square, Titchfield, Hampshire PO14 4RU (tel: 01329 513294; email: info@eost.org.uk)

 eost.org.uk

CC number: 238549

Eligibility

Residents of the ancient parish of Titchfield, which is comprised mainly of Sarisbury and Whiteley, Titchfield, Locks Heath, Warsash, Stubbington and Lee on the Solent. A map of the area of benefit can be found on the trust's website.

Types of grant

Grants are awarded according to need. Previously support has been given towards furniture, food vouchers, household bills, household appliances, rent arrears, transport, holidays, respite care, childcare, medical equipment and computer equipment.

Applications

Application forms are available to download from the trust's website. All applications must be made on the individual's behalf by a recognised agency such as social services, schools, health visitors and so on.

Financial information

Year end		31/03/2020
Income		£112,900
Total expenditure		£102,600

Further financial information

Grants were broken down as follows:

Carpet/flooring	£10,900
Debt repayment	£6,100
Home improvements	£4,200
Medical equipment	£3,400
Household appliances	£2,600
Childcare	£850
Transport	£660
Food/vouchers	£370
Cleaning	£250

Other information

The trust owns a number of almshouses for people in need and runs a day centre for older people.

Gosport

The Alverstoke Trust

 £1,000 (2020)

Correspondent: Clerk, 5 Constable Close, Gosport, Hampshire PO12 2UF (tel: 023 9258 9822; email: use the contact form available on the website)

 stmarysalverstoke.org.uk/the-alverstoke-trust

CC number: 239303

Eligibility

Residents in the ecclesiastical parish of Alverstoke who are in need. A list of all qualifying streets can be seen on the trust's website. The trust may also make grants to residents immediately outside the parish in the wider area of Gosport, although exceptionally.

Types of grant

The trust awards small grants, typically in the range of £100 to £200. According to the trust's website, around eight grants are awarded each year.

Exclusions

Once awarded, grants cannot be repeated or renewed. Grants cannot be used for the relief of rates, taxes or other public funds.

Applications

Initial enquiries can be made using a form on the trust's website. The trustees meet throughout the year but hold formal meetings in April and November.

Financial information

Year end		31/12/2020
Income		£1,600
Total expenditure		£6,300

Further financial information

Full accounts were not available to view on the Charity Commission's website due to the trust's low income. We have therefore estimated the trust's grant total based off information available on its website.

Thorngate Trust

 £9,800 (2020/21)

Correspondent: The Clerk, 52 Brooklands Road, Bedhampton, Havant, Hampshire PO9 3NT (tel: 07954 411852; email: info@thorngatecharity.co.uk)

 www.thorngatecharity.co.uk

CC number: 210946

Eligibility

People in need who live in Gosport.

Types of grant

Welfare

Grants are given for furniture, bedding, white goods, heating, school uniforms, travel to hospital appointments and so on.

Education

Grants are given towards further education and vocational courses. Previously, support has been given towards fees for veterinary school, ballet or drama courses and theological college fees.

Exclusions

Grants are not given for rates, taxes or other public funds.

Applications

Welfare

Relief-in-need application forms can be downloaded from the trust's website. It is strongly recommended that all applications for relief-in-need grants are submitted by an agency.

Education

Educational grant application forms can be downloaded from the trust's website and should be sent directly to the clerk by email or post.

Financial information

Year end		31/03/2021
Income		£7,300
Total expenditure		£16,300

Further financial information

Full accounts were not available to view on the Charity Commission's website due to the trust's low income. We have therefore estimated the grant total based on the trust's total expenditure.

Other information

Grants are also awarded to local organisations.

New Forest

Dibden Allotments Fund

 £171,600 (2019/20)

Correspondent: The Trustees, 7 Drummond Court, Prospect Place, Hythe, Southampton, Hampshire SO45 6HD (tel: 023 8084 1305; email: dibdenallotments@btconnect.com)

 daf-hythe.org.uk

CC number: 255778

Eligibility

People in need who have lived in the parishes of Hythe, Dibden, Marshwood or Fawley in Hampshire for at least 12 months. Priority is given to Hythe and Dibden. Support may also be given to ex-service personnel and their dependants.

Types of grant

Welfare

One-off grants are given for a range of purposes including food vouchers, clothing, household items or white goods and furniture.

The Shoe Voucher Scheme provides vouchers, generally to children and older people, for the purchase of shoes at one of a number of participating local shoe retailers.

The Garden Support Scheme runs in conjunction with a number of local gardeners to help older people to manage their garden work, such as grass cutting and hedge trimming. The scheme runs from March to November. Participants of the scheme are expected to make a small contribution towards its costs.

Education

One-off grants are given towards educational costs, for example educational travel.

Exclusions

The fund will not usually award a grant to someone who has previously received a grant from the fund within the last 12 months.

Applications

Application forms for general support can be downloaded from the fund's website. Completed forms should be submitted along with a supporting statement from a professional such as a health or social worker, midwife or teacher.

Shoe vouchers are mainly distributed through schools and participating organisations; however, those who don't have access to either may make an application using the application form available on the website.

Applications for the Garden Support Scheme can be made at any time by writing a letter or making a phone call; however, the fund encourages applications to be made during January and February. Once the application has been received, the fund will arrange a visit to discuss requirements.

Financial information

Year end	31/03/2020
Income	£428,600
Total expenditure	£399,300

Further financial information

Grants were distributed as follows:

General	136	£89,500
Gardening	165	£64,300
Shoe project	592	£17,200
Education	2	£580

Other information

Grants are also made to organisations.

Groome Trust

(£) £2,500 (2020)

Correspondent: The Trustees, 70 Carrington Lane, Milford on Sea, Lymington, Hampshire SO41 0RB (tel: 01590 622303; email: patd2@btinternet.com)

CC number: 204829

Eligibility

People in need who live in the parish of Brockenhurst.

Types of grant

One-off grants are available towards lifelines for people living alone, and as gifts and food vouchers for older people at Christmas.

Applications

Apply in writing to the correspondent.

Financial information

Year end	31/12/2020
Income	£6,600
Total expenditure	£5,500

Further financial information

Full accounts were not available to view on the Charity Commission's website due to the trust's low income. We have therefore estimated the grant total based on the trust's total expenditure.

Other information

The trust also provides support to local organisations.

The Hordle District Nursing Association

(£) £900 (2019/20)

Correspondent: The Trustees, 7 Firmount Close, Everton, Lymington, Hampshire SO41 0JN (tel: 01590 642272)

CC number: 201328

Eligibility

People in need who live in the parish of Hordle.

Types of grant

Grants are given to help with medical costs.

Applications

Apply in writing to the correspondent.

Financial information

Year end	31/10/2020
Income	£1,300
Total expenditure	£1,000

Further financial information

Full accounts were not available to view on the Charity Commission's website due to the charity's low income. We have therefore estimated the grant total based on the charity's total expenditure.

The Lyndhurst Welfare Charity

(£) £900 (2019/20)

Correspondent: The Trustees, 59 The Meadows, Lyndhurst, Hampshire SO43 7EJ (tel: 023 8028 3895; email: lyndhurstwelfare@outlook.com)

CC number: 206647

Eligibility

People in need who live in the parish of Lyndhurst.

Types of grant

Grants are normally one-off and are made towards items, services or facilities, such as household items, respite care and counselling.

Applications

Apply in writing to the correspondent.

Financial information

Year end	31/03/2020
Income	£6,100
Total expenditure	£970

Further financial information

Full accounts were not available to view on the Charity Commission's website due to the charity's low income. We have therefore estimated the grant total based on the charity's total expenditure.

Other information

Grants can also be made to organisations.

The New Forest Keepers Widows Fund

(£) £10,700 (2019/20)

Correspondent: Secretary, Forestry England, The Queens House, High Street, Lyndhurst, Hampshire SO43 7NH (tel: 0300 067 4616; email: secretary.nfkwf@forestryengland.uk)

CC number: 1016362

Eligibility

Retired and serving keepers of the New Forest, and their dependants, who are in need. Dependants of deceased keepers are also eligible.

Types of grant

Grants are given according to need.

Applications

Apply in writing to the correspondent.

Financial information

Year end	06/04/2020
Income	£13,500
Total expenditure	£11,900

Further financial information

Full accounts were not available to view on the Charity Commission's website due to the fund's low income. We have therefore estimated the fund's grant total based on its total expenditure.

The Sway Welfare Aid Group (SWAG)

(£) £17,900 (2019/20)

Correspondent: Jeremy Stevens, Trustee and Treasurer, Driftway, Mead End Road, Sway, Lymington, Hampshire SO41 6EH (tel: 01590 681 500 (Select option 2 for financial grants); email: info@swaghants.org.uk)

 www.swaghants.org.uk

CC number: 261220

Eligibility

Residents of the parish of Sway, and its immediate vicinity, who are in need. A map of the area of benefit can be found on the charity's website.

Types of grant

One-off emergency grants are awarded for a variety of welfare purposes. Recent examples include: rent or Council Tax arrears; school trips; nursery fees; replacement carpets and boilers; car repairs; food. The charity also awards recurrent grants, in the form of twice-yearly payments of £250 (£500 per annum) towards heating costs.

Applications
Applicants should contact the charity by telephone to make an initial enquiry.

Financial information
Year end	30/09/2020
Income	£88,900
Total expenditure	£48,000

Further financial information
Grants to individuals were broken down as follows in the accounts: COVID-19 grants (£9,700); heating grants (£6,400); hardship grants (£1,800).

Other information
The charity operates a transport service for people who have difficulty attending medical appointments, as well as a twice-monthly Lunch Club for residents of Sway who are aged over 65 and live alone. Transport to the Lunch Club is also provided.

Portsmouth

Isaac and Annie Fogelman Relief Trust

(£) £6,800 (2019/20)

Correspondent: Stephen Forman, Trustee, 51 Barham Avenue, Elstree, Borehamwood, Hertfordshire WD6 3PW (tel: 020 8953 8678; email: stephenjforman1@gmail.com)

CC number: 202285

Eligibility
People of the Jewish faith who primarily attend the Portsmouth and Southsea Hebrew Congregation.

Types of grant
Grants are given according to need.

Applications
Apply in writing to the correspondent.

Financial information
Year end	05/04/2020
Income	£20,900
Total expenditure	£7,600

Further financial information
Full accounts were not available to view on the Charity Commission's website due to the charity's low income. We have therefore estimated the charity's grant total based on its total expenditure.

The John Henry King Fund

(£) £49,300 (2020)

Correspondent: The Trustees, Presbytery, The Close, Ringwood, Hampshire BH24 1LA (tel: 01481 720755; email: anne@adh-consulting.co.uk)

 https://www.portsmouthdiocese.org.uk

CC number: 224437

Eligibility
Sick or retired members of the Catholic clergy of the Portsmouth Diocese.

Types of grant
Grants are awarded according to need.

Applications
Apply in writing to the correspondent.

Financial information
Year end	31/12/2020
Income	£54,500
Total expenditure	£61,500

Further financial information
During the year, grants were paid to 34 individuals totalling £49,300.

Southampton

The Southampton (City Centre) Relief-in-Need Charity

(£) £3,600 (2019)

Correspondent: The Trustees, 12 Westgate Street, Southampton, Hampshire SO14 2AY (tel: 023 8033 2030)

CC number: 255617

Eligibility
Residents of Southampton City Centre who are in need.

Types of grant
Grants are made according to need. The charity supplies a leaflet detailing the types of grant it can give.

Applications
Applications should be made to the charity by a statutory or voluntary organisation on the individual's behalf.

Financial information
Year end	31/12/2019
Income	£11,200
Total expenditure	£4,000

Further financial information
Full accounts were not available to view on the Charity Commission's website

due to the charity's low income. We have therefore estimated the charity's grant total based on its total expenditure.

Southampton and District Sick Poor Fund and Humane Society (Southampton Charitable Trust)

(£) £7,800 (2019)

Correspondent: Dave Richards, The Quay, 30 Channel Way, Ocean Village, Southampton SO14 3TG (tel: 023 8082 1522; email: dave.richards@moorestephens.com)

CC number: 201603

Eligibility
People who are poor and experiencing ill health, and who live in Southampton and the immediate surrounding area. Grants and certificates are also awarded to people for saving or attempting to save someone from drowning or other dangers.

Types of grant
Grants are given according to need.

Applications
Apply in writing to the correspondent.

Financial information
Year end	31/12/2019
Income	£20,200
Total expenditure	£17,500

Further financial information
Full accounts were not available to view on the Charity Commission's website due to the charity's low income. We have therefore estimated the charity's grant total based on its total expenditure.

Winchester

The Winchester Rural District Welfare Trust

(£) £2,400 (2019/20)

Correspondent: Penny Russell, Trustee, Nutley, Manor Road, Twyford, Winchester, Hampshire SO21 1RJ (tel: 07765 068556; email: winchestervillagestrust@gmail.com)

CC number: 246512

Eligibility
Residents in the Winchester rural district. This includes the parishes of: Bighton, Bramdean, Compton, Headbourne Worthy and Abbot's Barton, Hursley, Itchen Valley, King's

Worthy, Micheldever, Old Alresford, Owslebury, Sparsholt, Twyford, Wonston, Beauworth, Bishop's Sutton, Cheriton, Chilcomb, Crawley, Itchen Stoke and Ovington, Kilmeston, Littleton, New Alresford, Northington, and Oliver's Battery and Tichborne.

Types of grant

Welfare

Welfare grants are made towards, for example: travel expenses to and from hospital or residential homes (for those receiving treatment and for visiting relatives); extracurricular activities (for children and young people whose parents cannot afford such costs); essential needs, such as furniture, bedding, clothing, food, fuel or household appliances; and payments towards utility bills and rent. Food vouchers are also awarded at Christmas time.

Education

Educational grants are awarded to students in the area of benefit for costs associated with study, such as books, tools, exam or tuition fees and travel expenses. Help is also given to those seeking employment.

Exclusions

Grants are not made for items or services available through public funds.

Applications

Apply in writing to the correspondent.

Financial information

Year end	31/03/2020
Income	£4,900
Total expenditure	£5,500

Further financial information

Full accounts were not available to view on the Charity Commission's website due to the trust's low income. We have therefore estimated the trust's grant total based on its total expenditure.

Other information

This trust also makes grants to organisations.

Isle of Wight

Community Action Isle of Wight

£ £11,100 (2019/20)

Correspondent: Helping Hands Administrator, Riverside Centre, The Quay, Newport, Isle of Wight PO30 2QR (tel: 01983 524058; email: mbulpitt@actioniw.org.uk)

 www.communityactioniw.org.uk

CC number: 1063737

Eligibility

People who live on the Isle of Wight and are in need.

Types of grant

Small, one-off grants are made to assist people in crisis or immediate need.

Applications

Applications must be made through a referring agent, such as a housing association or local charity.

Financial information

Year end	31/03/2020
Income	£1,690,000
Total expenditure	£1,900,000

Charity of Edgar Ralph Dore

£ £12,000 (2019/20)

Correspondent: The Trustees, 62–66 Lugley Street, Newport, Isle of Wight PO30 5EU (tel: 01983 524431; email: ab@roachpittis.co.uk)

CC number: 255520

Eligibility

People in need on the Isle of Wight.

Types of grant

Grants are awarded according to need.

Applications

Apply in writing to the correspondent.

Financial information

Year end	05/04/2020
Income	£16,700
Total expenditure	£25,200

Further financial information

Full accounts were not available to view on the Charity Commission's website due to the charity's low income. We have therefore estimated the grant total based on the charity's total expenditure.

Other information

The charity also makes grants for the purpose of protecting, and preventing cruelty to, animals on the Isle of Wight.

Greater Ryde Benevolent Trust

£ £6,900 (2019)

Correspondent: Tricia Cotton, 40 Buckland Gardens, Ryde, Isle of Wight PO33 3AG (tel: 01983 612913; email: cottontricia1956@gmail.com)

CC number: 249832

Eligibility

Residents of the borough of Ryde in the Isle of Wight who have health needs and are experiencing financial difficulty.

Types of grant

Small grants are awarded according to need.

Applications

Apply in writing to the correspondent.

Financial information

Year end	31/12/2019
Income	£8,300
Total expenditure	£7,700

Further financial information

Full accounts were not available to view on the Charity Commission's website due to the trust's low income. We have therefore estimated the trust's grant total based on its total expenditure.

Tom Woolgar

£ £800 (2020)

Correspondent: The Trustees, The Riverside Centre, The Quay, Newport, Isle of Wight PO30 2QR (tel: 01983 559119; email: clerk@newportwight.org.uk)

CC number: 204080

Eligibility

People in need aged 65 and over who live in the former borough of Newport.

Types of grant

Winter fuel allowances.

Applications

Apply in writing to the correspondent.

Financial information

Year end	31/12/2020
Income	£1,700
Total expenditure	£850

Further financial information

Full accounts were not available to view on the Charity Commission's website due to the charity's low income. We have therefore estimated the grant total based on the charity's total expenditure.

Kent

Headley-Pitt Charitable Trust

£ £67,000 (2019/20)

Correspondent: The Administrator, Old Mill Cottage, Ulley Road, Kennington, Ashford, Kent TN24 9HX (tel: 01233 626189; email: thelma.pitt7@gmail.com)

 https://headleypitt.site123.me

CC number: 252023

Eligibility

People in need who live in East Kent, which comprises the district council areas of Ashford, Canterbury, Dover, Folkestone and Hythe, Maidstone, Medway Unitary Authority, Swale and Thanet.

Types of grant

Small grants are given to people in need.

Applications

Apply in writing to the correspondent, either by email or by post. Applications should include the name, address and contact details of the applicant (and of the beneficiary if different) as well as brief details of the amount needed, how the money would be used and any other steps to find funding that have been taken. The name and address in which the cheque should be made out to must also be included.

Financial information

Year end	31/01/2020
Income	£81,500
Total expenditure	£131,200

Other information

The trust administers ten bungalows to be used for the benefit of older people. In addition, the trust may support any charitable objects in connection with the town of Ashford in Kent as well as the Religious Society of Friends.

Kent Community Foundation

 £37,100 (2019/20)

Correspondent: Grants Team, Evegate Park Barn, Evegate Business Park, Ashford, Kent TN25 6SX (tel: 01303 814500; email: admin@kentcf.org.uk)

 www.kentcf.org.uk

CC number: 1084361

Eligibility

Individuals and families living in Kent or Medway who are in need. Each funding stream has its own specific eligibility criteria – see the foundation's website for more information.

Types of grant

A number of funds are available to individuals. Refer to the foundation's website for details of open grants. In the past, support has been given for respite and short breaks for children with illnesses or disabilities and holidays for adult carers.

Applications

Application forms can be downloaded from the foundation's website. Note that individuals must be nominated by a professional third party (such as a

charity employee, social worker or GP) and individuals cannot apply directly.

Financial information

Year end	31/03/2020
Income	£8,670,000
Total expenditure	£4,520,000

Other information

This is one of the 47 UK community foundations, which distribute funding for a wide range of purposes. Grant schemes tend to change frequently – consult the foundation's website for details of current programmes and upcoming deadlines.

The Kent County Football Association Benevolent Fund

 £3,000 (2019)

Correspondent: Darryl Haden, Trustee, Invicta House, London Road, Ditton, Aylesford, Kent ME20 6DQ (tel: 01622 791850; email: darryl.haden@kentfa.com)

 www.kentfa.com

CC number: 273118

Eligibility

Footballers, other members or officials of affiliated bodies under the jurisdiction of Kent FA and people who, in the opinion of Kent FA, have rendered service to football in the county who have experienced injury or illness attributable to participation in football. Support is extended to the dependants of the above people.

Types of grant

Grants are made according to need.

Exclusions

Grants are not typically made to members of clubs or competitions who have not previously contributed to the fund.

Applications

Application forms are available to download on the fund's website and must be accompanied by a medical certificate.

Financial information

Year end	31/12/2019
Income	£6,200
Total expenditure	£3,300

Further financial information

Full accounts were not available to view on the Charity Commission's website due to the fund's low income. We have therefore estimated the fund's grant total based on its total expenditure.

Kent Nursing Institution

 £5,000 (2019)

Correspondent: The Trustees, Michaelmas Cottage, Stan Lane, West Peckham, Maidstone, Kent ME18 5JT (tel: 01622 817693)

CC number: 211227

Eligibility

People in need who have disabilities or are experiencing ill health and live in Kent.

Types of grant

Grants are available for the purchase of equipment.

Applications

Apply in writing to the correspondent.

Financial information

Year end	31/12/2019
Income	£5,400
Total expenditure	£5,600

Further financial information

Full accounts were not available to view on the Charity Commission's website due to the charity's low income. We have therefore estimated the charity's grant total based on its total expenditure.

Other information

The charity also supports organisations.

The Hugh and Montague Leney Travelling Awards
See entry on page 306

See entry on page 306

The Elaine and Angus Lloyd Charitable Trust

 £4,400 (2019/20)

Correspondent: The Trustees, Ground Floor, 45 Pall Mall, London SW1Y 5JG (tel: 020 7930 7797; email: ross.badger@hhllp.co.uk)

CC number: 237250

Eligibility

People in need who live in Kent or Surrey. Preference may be given to people with disabilities or health problems.

Types of grant

Grants are given according to need.

Applications

Apply in writing to the correspondent.

Financial information

Year end	05/04/2020
Income	£139,000
Total expenditure	£145,900

Other information

This charity predominantly makes grants to schools, churches and other charitable organisations.

Red Eagle Foundation

 £14,300 (2019)

Correspondent: Wayne Hodgson, Chair, Shakespeare House, 147 Sandgate Road, Folkestone, Kent CT20 2DA (tel: 07967 664960; email: wayne@ redeaglefoundation.org)

🌐 https://www.redeaglefoundation.org

CC number: 1179117

Eligibility

Children from Kent with mobility, mental health and learning difficulties, and those from a disadvantaged financial background.

Types of grant

Grants are usually between £100 and £5,000 and focus on improving the applicant's mental or physical health. The charity particularly focuses its support on grants for equipment not provided by the NHS. Past examples include: a wheelchair for a a person with cerebral palsy; funding for qualifications for a child with severe dyslexia; a tricycle for a boy affected by Down's Syndrome.

Applications

Application forms should be completed online on the charity's website.

Financial information

Year end	31/12/2019
Income	£27,800
Total expenditure	£29,700

Skinners' Benevolent Trust

See entry on page 308

Sir Thomas Smythe's Poor Fund (Skinners' Company)

 £6,200 (2019/20)

Correspondent: Grants Administrator, Skinners' Hall, 8 Dowgate Hill, London EC4R 2SP (tel: 020 7236 5629; email: charitiesadmin@skinners.org.uk)

🌐 https://www.skinners.org.uk

CC number: 210775

Eligibility

People in need who live in one the 26 designated parishes in Kent. Applicants must be living on a low income and/or living in their own home either as a tenant or owner-occupier. There is a historic preference to support older people. A full list of eligible parishes can be found on the charity's website.

Types of grant

One-off grants, usually of up to £250, are typically made for unexpected household repairs, domestic appliance replacement, hospital travel costs and one-off expenses such as deep cleaning.

Applications

Contact the correspondent for an application form. Applications must be made through agencies such as social and support services, housing associations, refuge and rehabilitation organisations and local charities.

Financial information

Year end	30/06/2020
Income	£36,600
Total expenditure	£25,700

Other information

The charity also supports organisations.

Whitstable Non-Ecclesiastical Charities

£ £32,100 (2019)

Correspondent: G. S. Wootton, Clerk to the Trustees, c/o Furley Page LLP, 52–54 High Street, Whitstable, Kent CT5 1BG (tel: 01227 863179; email: gsw@furleypage.co.uk)

CC number: 248134

Eligibility

Residents of Whitstable who are in need.

Types of grant

One-off and recurrent grants are awarded according to need.

Applications

Apply in writing to the correspondent.

Financial information

Year end	31/12/2019
Income	£173,800
Total expenditure	£151,600

Other information

This charity also makes grants to organisations, mostly to local schools, educational foundations and almshouse charities.

Canterbury

The Appleton Trust (Canterbury)

£ £3,800 (2018)

Correspondent: The Trustees, Diocesan Board of Finance, Diocesan House, Lady Wootton's Green, Canterbury CT1 1NQ (tel: 01227 459401)

CC number: 250271

Eligibility

People associated with the Church of England in the diocese of Canterbury who are in need.

Types of grant

One-off grants are awarded according to need. The trust also makes loans to members of the clergy, parishes and lay workers of the Diocese of Canterbury to assist mainly with the purchasing of cars and computer equipment.

Applications

Apply in writing to the correspondent.

Financial information

Year end	31/12/2018
Income	£32,500
Total expenditure	£27,200

Further financial information

The 2018 accounts were the latest available at the time of writing (November 2021).

Other information

The trust also makes grants to organisations with similar objectives.

The Canterbury United Municipal Charities

£ £7,400 (2019)

Correspondent: The Trustees, c/o Furley Page Solicitors, 39–40 St Margaret's Street, Canterbury, Kent CT1 2TX (tel: 01227 863140; email: aas@ furleypage.co.uk)

CC number: 210992

Eligibility

People who live in the city of Canterbury and are in need.

Types of grant

Welfare

Welfare grants are awarded according to need. Small pensions are given to older residents, and food and clothing vouchers are distributed at Christmas.

Education

According to our previous research, educational grants can be made to students in higher and further education towards books and equipment.

Applications
Apply in writing to the correspondent.

Financial information
Year end	31/12/2019
Income	£9,600
Total expenditure	£8,100

Further financial information
Full accounts were not available to view on the Charity Commission's website due to the charity's low income. We have therefore estimated the charity's grant total based on its total expenditure.

The Lord Mayor of Canterbury's Christmas Gift Fund

 £13,800 (2019/20)

Correspondent: The Trustees, Lord Mayor of Canterbury Christmas Gift Fund, Robert Brett House, Ashford Road, Chartham, Canterbury, Kent CT4 7PP (tel: 01227 471509; email: christmasgiftfund@gmail.com)

 www.christmasgiftfund.co.uk

CC number: 278803

Eligibility
People in need who live in Canterbury and the surrounding area that forms the former district of Bridge Blean. Preference is given to older people and to families with young children.

Types of grant
The fund distributes food parcels and toy vouchers at Christmas.

Applications
Applicants should be referred to the fund by a local third party (for example, a health centre, school, member of clergy or social services agency). Gifts are delivered personally by volunteers.

Financial information
Year end	05/04/2020
Income	£15,000
Total expenditure	£15,300

Further financial information
Full accounts were not available to view on the Charity Commission's website due to the fund's low income. We have therefore estimated the fund's grant total based on its total expenditure.

The Herne Bay Parochial Charity

£720 (2020)

Correspondent: Susan Record, Clerk, c/o Hadfield Bull & Bull, Unit 1, 2B The Links, Herne Bay, Kent CT6 7GQ (tel: 01227 742660; email: srecord@hbbsolicitors.co.uk)

CC number: 1069542

Eligibility
People in need who live in Herne Bay. In exceptional cases, those living immediately outside the area may be eligible. Our previous research suggests that applicants preferably should be on income support or in receipt of similar financial assistance.

Types of grant
Our previous research suggests that both one-off and regular grants are awarded, usually in the form of food and fuel vouchers, during the year and at Christmas.

Applications
Apply in writing to the correspondent. Applications can be made through a social worker, Citizens Advice or other welfare agency or directly by the individual.

Financial information
Year end	31/12/2020
Income	£2,000
Total expenditure	£1,600

Further financial information
Full accounts were not available to view on the Charity Commission's website due to the charity's low income. We have therefore estimated the charity's grant total based on its total expenditure.

Other information
Grants are also made to organisations.

Streynsham's Charity

£25,600 (2019)

Correspondent: Clerk to the Trustees, PO Box 970, Canterbury, Kent CT1 9DJ (tel: 0845 094 4769)

CC number: 214436

Eligibility
People who live in the ancient parish of St Dunstan's in Canterbury.

Types of grant
One-off grants are awarded for essential good and purchases. Grants are also available for schoolchildren to help them participate in educational activities and to assist students with further or higher education fees.

Applications
Apply in writing to the correspondent.

Financial information
Year end	31/12/2019
Income	£75,700
Total expenditure	£70,500

Dartford

Wilmington Parochial Charity

£5,400 (2019/20)

Correspondent: The Trustees, 101 Birchwood Road, Dartford, Kent DA2 7HQ (tel: 01322 662342)

CC number: 1011708

Eligibility
People in need who live in the parish of Wilmington, Kent.

Types of grant
Grants are given according to need.

Applications
Apply in writing to the correspondent. Our previous research suggests that applications should be submitted by the individual or through a social worker, Citizens Advice or other welfare agency. The trustees meet twice a year to consider applications.

Financial information
Year end	31/10/2020
Income	£12,300
Total expenditure	£12,100

Further financial information
Full accounts were not available to view on the Charity Commission's website due to the charity's low income. We have therefore estimated the charity's grant total based on its total expenditure.

Other information
Grants are also awarded to local organisations and schools.

Dover

The R. V. Coleman Trust

£32,900 (2020)

Correspondent: Mrs G. Farthing, Clerk to the Trustees, 3 Church Farm Mews, The Street, East Langdon, Dover, Kent CT15 5FE (tel: 01304 851878; email: colemantrustclerk@btinternet.com)

CC number: 237708

Eligibility

Residents of Dover, and its immediate neighbourhood, who are in need as a result of illness, convalescence or disability.

Types of grant

Grants are awarded according to need. An example of previous support includes funding to undertake specialist medical treatment abroad.

Applications

Apply in writing to the correspondent. According to the 2020 annual report, the trustees actively seek potential beneficiaries, largely by regular contact with local GPs.

Financial information

Year end	31/12/2020
Income	£73,700
Total expenditure	£48,800

Further financial information

During 2020, grants were awarded to 43 individuals.

Folkestone and Hythe (formerly Shepway)

Folkestone Municipal Charity

 £101,200 (2020/21)

Correspondent: The Trustees, Romney House, Cliff Road, Hythe, Kent CT21 5XA (tel: 01303 260144; email: gillyjc@btinternet.com)

CC number: 211528

Eligibility

People in need who live in the borough of Folkestone.

Types of grant

The charity provides both monthly grants and one-off grants according to need.

Applications

Apply in writing to the correspondent.

Financial information

Year end	31/03/2021
Income	£129,600
Total expenditure	£107,500

Further financial information

Note: the grant total may include some grants to organisations.

Other information

The charity also supports organisations.

Anne Peirson Charitable Trust

 £8,800 (2019)

Correspondent: The Trustees, 11 Summer Close, Hythe, Kent CT21 4DR (tel: 01303 264976; email: theannepeirsontrust@gmail.com)

🌐 www.annepeirsontrust.co.uk

CC number: 800093

Eligibility

People who live in the parish of Hythe and are in need due to, for example, hardship, disability or sickness. Our research suggests that support is primarily given for children's educational needs but other people will be supported if financial hardship is demonstrated.

Types of grant

Grants have been made towards, for example, equipment for children who have disabilities, school trips and household goods.

Applications

Applications should be made in writing to the correspondent. Grants are considered at quarterly meetings of the trustees, but emergency applications can be considered in the interim.

Financial information

Year end	31/12/2019
Income	£17,800
Total expenditure	£19,600

Further financial information

Full accounts were not available to view on the Charity Commission's website due to the trust's low income. We have therefore estimated the trust's grant total based on its total expenditure.

Gravesham

William Frank Pinn Charitable Trust

 £165,400 (2019/20)

Correspondent: HSBC Trust Company (UK) Ltd, Forum 1, Second Floor, Parkway, Whiteley, Fareham, Hampshire PO15 7PA (tel: 023 8072 2225)

CC number: 287772

Eligibility

People of state pensionable age who live in the borough of Gravesham. Priority is given to those on lower incomes.

Types of grant

One-off grants are awarded, typically, to purchase clothing and to cover general household expenses.

Applications

Apply in writing to the correspondent.

Financial information

Year end	05/04/2020
Income	£315,600
Total expenditure	£397,400

Further financial information

The trust awarded 1,285 grants in 2019/20.

Maidstone

The Mike Collingwood Memorial Fund

 £3,100 (2019/20)

Correspondent: Ken Townsend, Trustee, Delmede, North Street, Sutton Valence, Maidstone, Kent ME17 3HU (tel: 07883 097811; email: mcmf@wealdofkentrotary. org.uk)

🌐 www.wealdofkentrotary.org.uk/ MCMF.html

CC number: 288806

Eligibility

Young people who live within a 20-mile radius of the Who'd A Thought It pub in Grafty Green, Kent, where the Rotary Club of the Weald of Kent holds its weekly meetings.

Types of grant

Grants are given towards educational and personal challenges both at home and overseas. This could include participating in an overseas trip or attaining excellence in a particular sport or chosen vocation. Due to the limited amount available, support is only supplementary and the applicants are expected to raise the balance by other means.

Exclusions

The fund is not able to help with recurring costs such as university fees.

Applications

Application forms can be found on the Rotary Club of The Weald of Kent website or requested from the correspondent. Applications are invited each year, generally in March and October, and are considered in November and April.

Financial information

Year end	30/06/2020
Income	£10,500
Total expenditure	£3,400

Further financial information

Full accounts were not available to view on the Charity Commission's website due to the fund's low income. We have therefore estimated the fund's grant total based on its total expenditure.

Edmett and Fisher Charity

£ £8,100 (2019/20)

Correspondent: The Trustees, Whitehead Monckton, Eclipse Park, Sittingbourne Road, Maidstone, Kent ME14 3EN (tel: 01622 698000)

CC number: 241823

Eligibility
People in need who are aged over 60 and live in the former borough of Maidstone (as it was before April 1974).

Types of grant
Grants are given according to need.

Applications
Apply in writing to the correspondent.

Financial information
Year end	30/04/2020
Income	£10,800
Total expenditure	£9,000

Further financial information
Full accounts were not available to view on the Charity Commission's website due to the charity's low income. We have therefore estimated the charity's grant total based on its total expenditure.

Maidstone Relief-in-Need Charities

£ £1,900 (2019/20)

Correspondent: Debbie Snook, Maidstone Borough Council, Maidstone House, King Street, Maidstone, Kent ME15 6JQ (tel: 01622 602030; email: debbiesnook@maidstone.gov.uk)

CC number: 210539

Eligibility
People who live in Maidstone, Kent and are in need.

Types of grant
Grants are given according to need.

Applications
Apply in writing to the correspondent.

Financial information
Year end	31/03/2020
Income	£5,900
Total expenditure	£4,300

Further financial information
Full accounts were not available to view on the Charity Commission's website due to the charity's low income. We have therefore estimated the charity's

grant total based on its total expenditure.

Other information
This charity also makes grants to organisations.

Medway

Cliffe and Cliffe Woods Community Trust

£ £2,600 (2019/20)

Correspondent: Paul Kingman, 52 Reed Street, Cliffe, Rochester, Kent ME3 7UL (tel: 01634 220422; email: mrpaulkingman@gmail.com)

CC number: 220855

Eligibility
People in need who live in the ancient parish of Cliffe-at-Hoo.

Types of grant
Grants are given according to need.

Applications
Apply in writing to the correspondent. Applications can be submitted directly by the individual or a family member, or through a third party such as a social worker or teacher.

Financial information
Year end	31/03/2020
Income	£14,900
Total expenditure	£2,900

Further financial information
Full accounts were not available to view on the Charity Commission's website due to the trust's low income. We have therefore estimated the trust's grant total based on its total expenditure.

Other information
Grants are also made to organisations in the area.

The Dobson Trust

£ £800 (2019/20)

Correspondent: Ellen Wright, Medway Council, Gun Wharf, Dock Road, Chatham ME4 4TR (tel: 01634 332319; email: ellen.wright@medway.gov.uk)

CC number: 283158

Eligibility
Residents of Gillingham who are aged over 60 and in financial need.

Types of grant
Grants are awarded for 'enjoyment and welfare'.

Applications
Apply in writing to the correspondent.

Financial information
Year end	31/03/2020
Income	£1,600
Total expenditure	£1,800

Further financial information
Full accounts were not available to view on the Charity Commission's website due to the trust's low income. We have therefore estimated the trust's grant total based on its total expenditure.

Other information
This charity also makes grants to organisations that support the welfare of older people in the local area.

Arthur Ingram Trust

£ £55,500 (2019/20)

Correspondent: Robin Baker, Medway Council, Gun Wharf, Dock Road, Chatham ME4 4TR (tel: 01634 332319; email: robin.baker@medway.gov.uk)

CC number: 212868

Eligibility
Young people in need between the ages of 14 and 20 who are in full time education or training, live in the Medway council area and are on a low income/from a low-income family.

Types of grant
The 2019/20 annual report states that grants are provided for the following purposes:
- To families with young persons in further education, (or to independent students where they have no family).
- For the purchase of school uniforms.
- For specialist equipment needed for training in a profession.
- To school voluntary funds to meet special hardship cases.
- Towards school trips which are identified as being linked to exam related studies.

Applications
Application forms can be requested from the correspondent.

Financial information
Year end	31/03/2020
Income	£75,400
Total expenditure	£88,000

Further financial information
According to the 2019/20 annual report, grants to individuals were distributed as follows:

Bursary grants	37	£53,900
Continuing education	4	£1,600

No grants were made for school uniforms during the year.

Other information
Grants are also awarded to schools for field trips and equipment/books.

Richard Watts and The City of Rochester Almshouse Charities

(£) £9,000 (2020)

Correspondent: Jane Rose, Clerk to the Trustees and Chief Officer, Administrative Offices, Watts Almshouses, Maidstone Road, Rochester, Kent ME1 1SE (tel: 01634 842194; email: admin@richardwatts.org.uk)

 www.richardwatts.org.uk

CC number: 212828

Eligibility

Welfare

Residents of Rochester (within the ME1 and ME2 postcode areas) who are in need.

Education

Educational grants are available to support residents within the postcode areas of ME1 and ME2. Trade apprentices under the age of 25 are also eligible for support.

Types of grant

Welfare

Welfare grants are awarded towards the cost of essential items such as clothing (including school uniforms) and white goods. Pension payments of £15 per week are also available to older people.

Education

Educational grants are awarded for costs associated with education and training. Apprenticeship grants are made to cover the cost of tools, protective clothing, equipment, travel costs and any additional study costs.

Applications

Application forms are available to download on the charity's website. For full guidelines for each grant scheme, see the website.

Financial information

Year end	31/12/2020
Income	£1,260,000
Total expenditure	£1,160,000

Other information

The charity operates and maintains almshouses, which are available to people aged 65 and over who are 'in reasonable health'. The charity also operates a subsidised home help service for older residents in the area of benefit. The service can provide help with general housework, taking out rubbish, shopping, personal paperwork, making telephone calls and so on. A lawn cutting service is also provided by the charity, designed for older individuals or people with disabilities who are unable to cut their lawn themselves.

Sevenoaks

Kate Drummond Trust

(£) £1,000 (2020/21)

Correspondent: The Trustees, 25 Bankside, Dunton Green, Sevenoaks, Kent TN13 2UA (tel: 01732 740920; email: kdtrustees@gmail.com)

CC number: 246830

Eligibility

People in need who live in Sevenoaks urban district and neighbourhood, with preference given to older people and young girls.

Types of grant

The majority of grants are one-off, given according to need. Educational grants are given towards education, recreation or training, including vocational training for people entering a trade.

Applications

Applications can be made in writing to the correspondent. Include an sae if a reply is required.

Financial information

Year end	05/04/2021
Income	£12,900
Total expenditure	£33,000

Further financial information

Full accounts were not available to view on the Charity Commission's website due to the trust's low income. We have therefore estimated the grant total based on the trust's total expenditure.

Other information

The trust owns and operates a residential house offering either rent-free or subsidised accommodation. Grant-making is available when there is surplus money. It can also give grants to organisations.

Leigh United Charities

(£) £31,300 (2019/20)

Correspondent: Sally Bresnahan, Clerk, 3 Oak Cottages, High Street, Leigh, Tonbridge, Kent TN11 8RW (tel: 07835 984060; email: sally@bresnahan.co.uk)

CC number: 233988

Eligibility

People in need who live in the parish of Leigh in Kent. If funds permit, support may be extended to residents of the old parish of Leigh and the Hollanden portion of Leigh in Hildenborough.

Types of grant

Grants are awarded according to need.

Applications

Apply in writing to the correspondent.

Financial information

Year end	31/01/2020
Income	£54,500
Total expenditure	£34,200

The Dorothy Parrott Memorial Trust Fund

(£) £4,100 (2019)

Correspondent: The Trustees, 10 The Landway, Kemsing, Sevenoaks, Kent TN15 6TG (tel: 01732 760263)

CC number: 278904

Eligibility

Residents in the area administered by Sevenoaks Town Council (TN13, TN14 and TN15 postcodes). Preference may be given to young children and older people.

Types of grant

Grants are given according to need.

Applications

Apply in writing to the correspondent.

Financial information

Year end	31/12/2019
Income	£14,200
Total expenditure	£9,000

Further financial information

Full accounts were not available to view on the Charity Commission's website due to the charity's low income. We have therefore estimated the charity's grant total based on its total expenditure.

Other information

This charity also makes grants to local organisations.

Swale

Boughton Almsland Charities

(£) £4,600 (2020/21)

Correspondent: Patricia Saunders, Trustee, 45C The Street, Boughton-Under-Blean, Faversham, Kent ME13 9BA (tel: 01227 750747; email: pat.saunders23@ntlworld.com)

CC number: 213399

Eligibility

People in need who live in the parish of Boughton-Under-Blean.

Types of grant

Grants are given according to need.

Applications

Apply in writing to the correspondent.

Financial information

Year end	31/03/2021
Income	£7,300
Total expenditure	£5,100

Further financial information

Full accounts were not available to view on the Charity Commission's website due to the charity's low income. We have therefore estimated the charity's grant total based on its total expenditure.

The William Barrow's Charity

 £78,200 (2020)

Correspondent: Stuart Mair, Clerk to the Trustees, c/o George Webb Finn, 43 Park Road, Sittingbourne, Kent ME10 1DY (tel: 01795 470556; email: stuart@georgewebbfinn.com)

www.thewilliambarrowscharity.org. uk

CC number: 1172933

Eligibility

Welfare

People in need who live in the parish of Borden, Kent. Priority is given to people over the age of 60.

Education

Students under the age of 25 who live in the parish of Borden, Kent and are in full time education. Priority is given to students entering tertiary education.

Types of grant

Welfare

One-off and recurrent grants are given according to need. Previous grants have been given towards goods, services, clothing, school fees, medical equipment and support for people with disabilities.

Education

Scholarships and bursaries are given to assist students undertaking further education and can be used towards books, travel, living expenses and so on.

Applications

Applications can be made through the charity's website. Those who have previously received a grant from the charity may apply to renew their educational grant. Applicants must provide their exam results and confirmation of acceptance at a college/ university. Applications should be submitted before the end of August prior to the academic year. Consult the website for current deadlines.

Financial information

Year end	31/12/2020
Income	£302,800
Total expenditure	£207,800

Further financial information

Grants were awarded to 30 students attending college or university. Grants were also awarded to eight older people, eight people with disabilities and four other individuals in need.

Other information

The charity also provides grants to local schools and organisations.

Thanet

Margate and Dr Peete's Charity

 £4,000 (2019/20)

Correspondent: Dorothy Collins, 31 Avenue Gardens, Cliftonville, Margate, Kent CT9 3AZ (tel: 01843 226173; email: dorothy_collins@talktalk. net)

CC number: 212503

Eligibility

People in need who live in the former borough of Margate (as constituted before 1974).

Types of grant

Small one-off and recurrent grants.

Applications

Apply on a form available from the correspondent. Applications should be submitted either directly by the individual or, where applicable, through a social worker, Citizens Advice or other welfare agency.

Financial information

Year end	31/10/2020
Income	£7,900
Total expenditure	£4,400

Further financial information

Full accounts were not available to view on the Charity Commission's website due to the charity's low income. We have therefore estimated the charity's grant total based on its total expenditure.

Other information

The charity was established in 1907 following the death of Dr Thomas Peete, who left his entire estate – a total of £50,000 – to the Margate Philanthropic Institution. Since then, the charity has supported many of Margate's neediest residents.

Oxfordshire

The Appleton Trust (Abingdon)

 £5,000 (2020)

Correspondent: David Dymock, 73 Eaton Road, Appleton, Abingdon, Oxfordshire OX13 5JJ (tel: 01865 863709; email: appleton.trust@yahoo.co. uk)

CC number: 201552

Eligibility

People who live in Appleton with Eaton and are in need or suffer from sickness, disability or other hardship.

Types of grant

One-off and recurrent grants.

Applications

Apply in writing to the correspondent. Applications can be made either directly by the individual or through an appropriate third party.

Financial information

Year end	31/12/2020
Income	£6,800
Total expenditure	£5,500

Further financial information

Full accounts were not available to view on the Charity Commission's website due to the trust's low income. We have therefore estimated the trust's grant total based on its total expenditure.

Other information

Grants are also given to local organisations and for educational purposes to former pupils of Appleton Primary School.

Arnold's Educational Foundation

See entry on page 229

The Bartlett Taylor Charitable Trust

 £8,500 (2019/20)

Correspondent: The Trustees, c/o John Welch and Stammers, 24 Church Green, Witney, Oxfordshire OX28 4AT (tel: 01993 703941; email: galty@ johnwelchandstammers.co.uk)

www.btctrust.org.uk

CC number: 285249

Eligibility

People in need who live in West Oxfordshire.

Types of grant

Grants are given according to need.

Applications

Apply using an online form on the trust's website. A letter from a recognised professional (for example, a doctor) should be attached to all applications. The trustees meet around six times each year to consider grant applications but can deal with emergency requests between meetings.

Financial information

Year end	05/04/2020
Income	£97,200
Total expenditure	£142,000

Other information

The trust makes regular grants to medical, social and welfare organisations, both national and local. The trust has also donated to international emergencies.

The J. I. Colvile Charitable Trust

£ £2,200 (2020)

Correspondent: The Trustees, 1 Weald Manor Cottages, Weald, Bampton, Oxfordshire OX18 2HH (tel: 01993 850736; email: jicolvilecharitabletrust@ gmail.com)

CC number: 1067274

Eligibility

People in need who live in Gloucestershire or Oxfordshire.

Types of grant

According to our previous research, the trust makes small, one-off grants, usually ranging from £250 to £500.

Applications

Apply in writing to the correspondent. Applications can be submitted directly by the individual or family member, or by an organisation such as Citizens Advice.

Financial information

Year end	31/12/2020
Income	£2,600
Total expenditure	£2,500

Further financial information

Full accounts were not available to view on the Charity Commission's website due to the trust's low income. We have therefore estimated the trust's grant total based on its total expenditure.

Henley Educational Trust

 £19,600 (2019/20)

Correspondent: Mrs C. Brown, Clerk, 1A Coldharbour Close, Henley-on-Thames RG9 1QF (tel: 01491 524994; email: clerk@henleyeducationaltrust. com)

🌐 www.henleyeducationaltrust.com

CC number: 309237

Eligibility

Young people under the age of 25 who live in, or currently attend a school in, the parishes of Henley, Bix and Assendon, Remenham and Rotherfield Greys. Those who have previously attended a school within the area of benefit for a minimum of two years are also eligible.

Types of grant

Grants are made towards the cost of the following:

- School trips (under £20)
- Music tuition
- Playgroup fees
- Homework clubs
- Sports club fees (up to 90% of total)
- Sports equipment
- School uniforms (up to £75 for primary school and £120 for secondary school)
- Shoe vouchers (£45 in total)
- Gap year educational electives
- Apprentice tools
- Assistance for promising sportspeople to attend specialised training

Applications

Application forms are available to download on the charity's website. All applications must be sponsored by an educational or healthcare professional. Note, there are different application forms for individuals with incomes of over £16,190 and individuals who are in receipt of free school meals. Applicants who are entitled to free school meals (FSM) should include a written letter of FSM entitlement if possible. If not, the sponsor will have to confirm that the applicant is listed as an FSM recipient on the Department of Education online checking service. Full guidance on the application process can be seen on the application form. The trustees meet six times a year to consider grant applications.

Financial information

Year end	31/03/2020
Income	£157,800
Total expenditure	£156,500

Further financial information

Grants were awarded to 80 individuals during the year.

Other information

This charity also makes grants to organisations, particularly to local schools for teaching aids (not normally provided by a local education authority), and more generally to colleges, local air cadets, music schools and other organisations and projects for wider educational support.

The John Hodges Charitable Trust

£ £18,000 (2019/20)

Correspondent: Julie Griffin, 3 Berkshire Road, Henley-on-Thames, Oxfordshire RG9 1ND (tel: 01491 572621; email: juliegriffin2004@googlemail.com)

CC number: 304313

Eligibility

Residents in the ecclesiastical parish of St Mary the Virgin in Henley-on-Thames, and the surrounding area, who are in need.

Types of grant

Grants have previously been given for white goods, carpets and flooring, clothing, mobility aids, bankruptcy fees and heating bills.

Applications

Apply in writing to the correspondent.

Financial information

Year end	31/03/2020
Income	£16,000
Total expenditure	£20,000

Further financial information

Full accounts were not available to view on the Charity Commission's website due to the trust's low income. We have therefore estimated the trust's grant total based on its total expenditure.

Other information

This trust also makes grants to organisations.

Tetsworth Cozens Bequest

£ £1,500 (2019/20)

Correspondent: The Trustees, 12 The Mount, Tetsworth, Thame, Oxfordshire OX9 7AF (tel: 07985 197513; email: steve.lingard@vorticity-systems.com)

CC number: 204368

Eligibility

People need who live in the parishes of Tetsworth, Thame, Great Haseley, Stoke Talmage, Wheatfield, Adwell, South Weston, Lewknor and Aston Rowant.

Types of grant

Grants are given according to need.

Applications

Apply in writing to the correspondent.

Financial information

Year end	31/10/2020
Income	£4,700
Total expenditure	£1,700

Further financial information

Full accounts were not available to view on the Charity Commission's website due to the charity's low income. We have therefore estimated the charity's grant total based on its total expenditure.

Cherwell

Banbury Charities

 £55,800 (2020)

Correspondent: Ms M. J. Tarrant, Clerk to the Trustees, 36 West Bar, Banbury, Oxfordshire OX16 9RU (tel: 01295 251234)

 https://banburycharities.co.uk

CC number: 201418

Eligibility

Welfare

People who live within a five-mile radius of Banbury Cross (or a ten-mile radius in the case of Banbury Poor Trust) and are in need.

Education

Educational grants are available to students under the age of 25 who live within a five-mile radius of Banbury Cross.

Types of grant

Welfare

Welfare grants are given according to need. Examples include special foods and medicines, extra bedding, medical comforts, medical/surgical appliances, fuel and domestic help.

Education

Educational grants are made for a range of needs such as books and equipment. Specific grant schemes are available for apprentices and those studying STEM subjects or subjects involving literature and the arts. For full details, see the charity's website.

Applications

Apply in writing to the correspondent.

Financial information

Year end	31/12/2020
Income	£270,700
Total expenditure	£251,800

Further financial information

The charity awarded grants to 197 individuals.

Other information

Banbury Charities is a group of eight registered charities, comprised of the following: Bridge Estate Charity; Countess of Arran's Charity; Banbury Arts and Educational Charity; Banbury Almshouses Charity; Banbury Sick Poor Fund; Banbury Welfare Trust; Banbury Poor Trust; and Banbury Recreation Charity. One of the objectives of the Banbury Charities is to provide and maintain almshouses accommodation for people in financial need.

The Souldern United Charities

 £3,600 (2019/20)

Correspondent: Susan Jones, Trustee, Yew Cottage, Bates Lane, Souldern, Bicester, Oxfordshire OX27 7JU (tel: 01869 345707; email: susan.jones@ headlinersgroup.com)

CC number: 1002942

Eligibility

People in need who live in the parish of Souldern in Oxfordshire.

Types of grant

One-off and recurrent grants are made according to need.

Applications

Apply in writing to the correspondent.

Financial information

Year end	31/03/2020
Income	£13,200
Total expenditure	£8,000

Further financial information

Full accounts were not available to view on the Charity Commission's website due to the charity's low income. We have therefore estimated the charity's grant total based on its total expenditure.

Other information

The charity also provides housing.

Oxford

The City of Oxford Charity

£66,000 (2020)

Correspondent: Grants Administrator, The Office, Stones Court, St Clements, Oxford, Oxfordshire OX14 1AP (tel: 01865 247161; email: enquiries@ oxfordcitycharity.org.uk)

https://www.oxfordcitycharity.org. uk

CC number: 1172230

Eligibility

Welfare

Residents in the city of Oxford who are in need as a result of ill health, disability or financial hardship. Applicants must have lived in the city for a minimum of three years.

Education

Educational grants are available to young residents in the city of Oxford who are aged under 25 years. Applicants must have lived in the city for a minimum of three years.

Types of grant

Welfare

Welfare grants are awarded according to need. Grants have been made towards the cost of school uniforms and bankruptcy/Debt Relief Order court fees.

Education

Educational grants are made to students in any level of education, up to the age of 25. Grants have been awarded towards the cost of books, material and equipment for college and undergraduate students. Students can also apply for grants to help cover the cost of a bus pass for travel to and from their place of education.

Exclusions

The trustees do not normally make grants to those studying beyond a first degree.

Applications

Application forms are available to download on the charity's website. For welfare grants, all applications must include a letter of support from a third party such as a social worker, health visitor or advice agency/organisation active within the community.

Financial information

Year end	31/12/2020
Income	£416,900
Total expenditure	£393,700

Further financial information

Welfare grants were made to 176 people and education grants were made to 14 people. The grant total may include grants to organisations.

Other information

The charity is an amalgamation of several ancient charities working for the benefit of the people of Oxford city. The charity owns and operates almshouses at Stone's Court in St Clements, which are available to residents in the city who are in need. Preference is given to older residents.

South Oxfordshire

Thame Charities (The Thame Welfare Trust)

£ £6,300 (2019/20)

Correspondent: John Gadd, 2 Cromwell Avenue, Thame, Oxfordshire OX9 3TD (tel: 01844 212564; email: johngadd4@gmail.com)

CC number: 241914

Eligibility

People in need who live in Thame and the immediately adjoining villages.

Types of grant

Grants are given according to need. According to our previous research, examples of previous support include a grant for a single parent's mortgage repayments and a wheelchair for a person who has disabilities. Grants can also be given for educational purposes.

Applications

Apply in writing to the correspondent.

Financial information

Year end	09/02/2020
Income	£16,800
Total expenditure	£14,000

Further financial information

Full accounts were not available to view on the Charity Commission's website due to the charity's low income. We have therefore estimated the charity's grant total based on its total expenditure.

Other information

Grants are also given to organisations.

Wallingford Relief in Need Charity

£ £3,800 (2019/20)

Correspondent: Pat Hayton, Chair of Trustees, Raggalds, Nuneham Courtenay, Oxford, Oxfordshire OX44 9PP (tel: 01491 835373; email: raggalds@btinternet.com)

CC number: 292000

Eligibility

People in need who live in Wallingford and the surrounding neighbourhood.

Types of grant

Grants are made according to need.

Applications

Apply in writing to the correspondent.

Financial information

Year end	31/03/2020
Income	£9,400
Total expenditure	£4,200

Further financial information

Full accounts were not available to view on the Charity Commission's website due to the charity's low income. We have therefore estimated the charity's grant total based on its total expenditure.

The Wheatley Charities

£ £1,100 (2020)

Correspondent: The Trustees, 24 Old London Road, Wheatley, Oxford, Oxfordshire OX33 1YW (tel: 01865 874676)

CC number: 203535

Eligibility

Welfare
People in need who live in the parish of Wheatley, South Oxfordshire.

Education
Educational grants are made to parishioners under the age of 25.

Types of grant

Welfare
Grants are awarded according to need.

Education
The charity awards educational grants and assistance for young people preparing to enter work.

Applications

Apply in writing to the correspondent.

Financial information

Year end	31/12/2020
Income	£3,500
Total expenditure	£2,400

Further financial information

Full accounts were not available to view on the Charity Commission's website due to the charity's low income. We have therefore estimated the charity's grant total based on its total expenditure.

Other information

Grants are also made to local organisations.

Vale of White Horse

The Ray Collins Charitable Trust

£ £10,700 (2019)

Correspondent: The Trustees, 88 Springfield Road, Wantage OX12 8EZ (email: info@raycollinstrust.org)

 https://www.raycollinstrust.org

CC number: 1173358

Eligibility

People in need who live in Wantage and its surrounding villages (within a five-mile radius).

Types of grant

One-off grants are awarded according to need. The charity has previously provided garden makeovers, household appliances and furnishings. It also provides hampers and Easter eggs.

Applications

Application forms can be downloaded from the charity's website or requested by emailing the correspondent.

Financial information

Year end	31/12/2019
Income	£27,700
Total expenditure	£31,800

Further financial information

Grants were broken down as follows:

Hampers	£5,200
Cash donations	£3,900
Easter eggs	£1,000
Electrical goods	£600

Faringdon United Charities

£ £16,800 (2019/20)

Correspondent: Vivienne Checkley, c/o Bunting & Co., Brunel House, Volunteer Way, Faringdon, Oxfordshire SN7 7YR (tel: 01367 243789; email: vivienne.checkley@buntingaccountants.co.uk or use the contact form available on the website)

 faringdonunitedcharities.co.uk

CC number: 237040

Eligibility

People who are in need and live in the parishes of Great Faringdon, Littleworth or Little Coxwell, in Oxfordshire. Preference is given to older people, children and people with illnesses.

Types of grant

Grants are given for a range of purposes including carpets, sports activities, white goods, computers, sports trips and so on. Support may also be given for other medical, educational or additional needs.

Applications

Applications can be downloaded from the charity's website and can be submitted directly by the individual or by a healthcare professional or other third party on behalf of an individual. The charity aims to make contact within 48 hours.

Financial information

Year end	31/03/2020
Income	£48,700
Total expenditure	£39,800

Further financial information

Grants were distributed as follows:

Families	£9,000
People with illnesses	£3,100
Young people	£2,700
Older people	£2,000

Other information

The charity also supports organisations and groups.

The Tony Loy Trust

 £1,600 (2020)

Correspondent: The Trustees, 24 Grahame Close, Blewbury, Oxfordshire OX11 9QE (tel: 01235 850537; email: sloy24@gmail.com)

https://www.thetonyloytrust.org

CC number: 1163810

Eligibility

Children and young people under the age of 25 who live in and around Blewbury, South Oxfordshire.

Types of grant

The trust aims to promote art, sport and education among young people. This is done by providing grants for projects, training and travel to events.

Applications

Apply in writing to the correspondent with a brief outline of how the financial support would be used.

Financial information

Year end	31/12/2020
Income	£690
Total expenditure	£3,700

Further financial information

Full accounts were not available to view on the Charity Commission's website due to the trust's low income. We have therefore estimated the trust's grant total based on its total expenditure.

Other information

The trust also makes grants to organisations and projects that promote arts and sports.

The Steventon Allotments and Relief-in-Need Charity

£8,740 (2021)

Correspondent: The Trustees, 19 Lime Grove, Southmoor, Abingdon, Oxfordshire OX13 5DN (tel: 01865 821055; email: info@sarinc.org.uk)

CC number: 203331

Eligibility

People who are in need and live in Steventon.

Types of grant

One-off grants for welfare and education are awarded according to need. Birthday grants of £50 are also given.

Applications

Apply in writing to the correspondent. The charity advertises regularly in the local parish magazine. Applications should include full details of the applicant's income and expenditure.

Financial information

Year end	31/12/2021
Income	£116,900
Total expenditure	£105,100

Other information

Grants are also made to organisations.

The Wantage District Coronation Memorial and Nursing Amenities Fund

£5,600 (2019/20)

Correspondent: The Trustees, 21 Church Green, Stanford in the Vale, Faringdon, Oxfordshire SN7 8HU (tel: 01367 718395; email: wantagecoronationfund@gmail.com)

CC number: 234384

Eligibility

People who live in the area covered by Wantage and Grove medical practices, and are in need as a result of illness, disability or financial difficulty.

Types of grant

According to our previous research, the charity awards one-off and recurrent grants, typically ranging from around £20 to £100.

Applications

Apply in writing to the correspondent.

Financial information

Year end	30/11/2020
Income	£5,500
Total expenditure	£6,200

Further financial information

Full accounts were not available to view on the Charity Commission's website due to the charity's low income. We have therefore estimated the charity's grant total based on its total expenditure.

Other information

This charity may also make grants to organisations.

West Oxfordshire

The Bampton Welfare Trust

£5,600 (2020)

Correspondent: Peter Alcock, Clerk to the Trustees, Well Place, Cheapside, Bampton, Oxfordshire OX18 2JL (tel: 01993 852196; email: peter@peteralcock.co.uk)

CC number: 202735

Eligibility

People in need, especially those experiencing ill health, who live in the parishes of Bampton, Aston and Lew.

Types of grant

Grants can be made for travelling to hospital expenses, to help with fuel and food costs or to relieve other immediate need.

Applications

Apply in writing to the correspondent.

Financial information

Year end	31/12/2020
Income	£16,200
Total expenditure	£12,500

Further financial information

Full accounts were not available to view on the Charity Commission's website due to the trust's low income. We have therefore estimated the trust's grant total based on its total expenditure.

Other information

The trust also makes grants to local primary schools, playgroups and clubs for older people in the area.

The Burford Relief-in-Need Charity

£4,600 (2020)

Correspondent: The Trustees, Whitehill Farm, Burford, Oxfordshire OX18 4DT (tel: 01993 822894)

CC number: 1036378

Eligibility

People who live within a seven-mile radius of The Tolsey in Burford and are in need.

Types of grant

Grants are given according to need. Funding is also given towards education to enable the recipient to earn a living.

Applications

Apply in writing to the correspondent.

Financial information

Year end	31/12/2020
Income	£29,100
Total expenditure	£5,200

Further financial information

Full accounts were not available to view on the Charity Commission's website due to the charity's low income. We have therefore estimated the charity's grant total based on its total expenditure.

Ducklington and Hardwick-with-Yelford Charity

 £1,600 (2019)

Correspondent: The Clerk, 10 Lovell Close, Ducklington, Witney, Oxfordshire OX29 7YQ (tel: 01993 702261)

CC number: 237343

Eligibility

People in need or hardship who live in the villages of Ducklington and Hardwick-with-Yelford.

Types of grant

Welfare

One-off grants of up to £200 can be given towards heating, transport costs, assistance with playgroup fees, furniture, funeral expenses, conversion of rooms for people who are older or have disabilities, provision of telephones, spectacles, school holiday assistance, help with rent arrears and other needs.

Education

Book grants are awarded for those starting university courses. Grants are also given to people starting apprenticeships who cannot afford equipment or clothing.

Applications

Applications may be made in writing to the correspondent. The trustees normally meet in March and November, but applications can be submitted at any time.

Financial information

Year end	31/12/2019
Income	£5,600
Total expenditure	£3,200

Further financial information

Full accounts were not available to view on the Charity Commission's website due to the charity's low income. We have therefore estimated the charity's grant total based on its total expenditure.

Other information

Grants are also made to organisations, clubs and schools.

Eynsham Consolidated Charity

 £1,700 (2019)

Correspondent: Robin Mitchell, Clerk to the Trustees, 20 High Street, Eynsham, Oxfordshire OX29 4HB (tel: 01865 880665)

 https://eynsham-pc.gov.uk/org.aspx?n=Eynsham-Consolidated-Charity

CC number: 200977

Eligibility

People in need who live in the ancient parish of Eynsham (which covers Eynsham and part of Freeland) in Oxfordshire (see the charity's website for further detail, including a map). In exceptional circumstances, grants can be made to people who live immediately outside the parish; therefore, people living anywhere in Freeland are encouraged to apply.

Types of grant

One-off grants of up to £4,000 can be given to support directly in times of financial crisis and also towards goods (e.g. spectacles, furniture or special equipment for people with disabilities) or services (e.g. an insurance premium or utilities).

Exclusions

Grants are not made to help with payment of rates, taxes or other public charges. Support is not given on a recurrent basis or in the form of personal loans.

Applications

Apply in writing to the correspondent by post or email. The trustees typically meet four times per year (February, May, August or September and November) to review applications.

Financial information

Year end	31/12/2019
Income	£6,700
Total expenditure	£3,800

Further financial information

Full accounts were not available to view on the Charity Commission's website due to the charity's low income. We have therefore estimated the charity's grant total based on its total expenditure.

Other information

The charity will consider sharing costs with other grant-making organisations when costs are high. This charity also supports local organisations.

Surrey

Banstead United Charities

 £1,800 (2019)

Correspondent: The Trustees, 6 Garratts Lane, Banstead, Surrey SM7 2DZ (tel: 01737 355827)

CC number: 233339

Eligibility

People in need who live in the wards of Banstead village, Burgh Heath, Kingswood, Nork, Preston, Tadworth and Tattenhams.

Types of grant

Grants are given according to need.

Applications

Apply in writing to the correspondent.

Financial information

Year end	31/12/2019
Income	£7,000
Total expenditure	£4,000

Further financial information

Full accounts were not available to view on the Charity Commission's website due to the charity's low income. We have therefore estimated the charity's grant total based on its total expenditure.

John Beane's Charity CIO

 £75,300 (2019/20)

Correspondent: Nicola Willshire, PO Box 607, Guildford, Surrey GU2 8WR (tel: 05603 870633; email: use the contact form available on the website)

 https://www.johnbeane.org.uk

CC number: 1161716

Eligibility

Families in need who live in the administrative county of Surrey.

Types of grant

Grants are provided for items such as white goods, carpeting for children's bedrooms, school uniform and so on.

Applications

Application forms are available to download from the charity's website.

Financial information

Year end	31/03/2020
Income	£337,000
Total expenditure	£350,100

Other information

Grants are also provided to United Reformed Church churches for capital projects.

Bletchingley United Charities

 £6,800 (2019/20)

Correspondent: Christine Bolshaw, Clerk, Cleves, Castle Street, Bletchingley, Surrey RH1 4QA (tel: 01883 743000; email: chrisbolshaw@hotmail.co.uk)

 www.bletchingley.org.uk

CC number: 236747

Eligibility

Residents in the parish of Bletchingley who are in need.

Types of grant

Grants are awarded according to need. Vouchers are distributed twice each year, at Christmas and in summer. Previous examples of support include a holiday for a child with a disability, a grant for glasses, food vouchers and quarterly alarm rentals for older people.

Exclusions

Grants cannot be made for the relief of rates, taxes or other public funds.

Applications

Apply in writing to the correspondent. According to the charity's website, requests for assistance can be made to David Martin at 94 High Street, Bletchingley, Surrey, RH1 4PA (tel: 01883 743 144), or to the correspondent.

Financial information

Year end	30/09/2020
Income	£17,500
Total expenditure	£15,000

Further financial information

Full accounts were not available to view on the Charity Commission's website due to the charity's low income. We have therefore estimated the charity's grant total based on its total expenditure.

Other information

The charity also makes grants to organisations. The charity consists of the following: The Charity of William Evans; The Charity of William Hampton; Site of the Old Almshouses; and the share of the Charity of Henry Smith (Worth Estate) applicable in Bletchingley.

The Godstone United Charities

 £5,900 (2019/20)

Correspondent: The Trustees, Bassett Villa, Oxted Road, Godstone, Surrey RH9 8AD (tel: 01883 742625; email: clerk@godstonepc.org.uk)

 www.godstonepc.org.uk

CC number: 200055

Eligibility

People in need who live in the old parish of Godstone (Blindley Heath, South Godstone and Godstone Village).

Types of grant

Food vouchers are usually given in December and March. The charity may also assist with educational, personal and domestic needs and through one-off grants.

Applications

Apply in writing to the correspondent.

Financial information

Year end	31/03/2020
Income	£6,600
Total expenditure	£6,600

Further financial information

Full accounts were not available to view on the Charity Commission's website due to the charity's low income. We have therefore estimated the charity's grant total based on its total expenditure.

Other information

The charity also supports organisations.

The Elaine and Angus Lloyd Charitable Trust
See entry on page 387

The Henry Smith Charity (Ash and Normandy)

 £2,200 (2020/21)

Correspondent: Alan Coomer, 84 Queenhythe Road, Jacob's Well, Guildford, Surrey GU4 7NX (tel: 01483 300103; email: alancoomer2@gmail.com)

CC number: 240485

Eligibility

Residents in the parishes of Ash and Normandy who are in need.

Types of grant

Grants are awarded according to need.

Applications

Apply in writing to the correspondent.

Financial information

Year end	31/03/2021
Income	£4,600
Total expenditure	£4,900

Further financial information

Full accounts were not available to view on the Charity Commission's website due to the charity's low income. We have therefore estimated the charity's grant total based on its total expenditure.

Other information

Grants are also made to organisations.

The Henry Smith Charity (Bramley)

 £2,300 (2019/20)

Correspondent: The Trustees, Bramley Village Hall, Hall Road, Bramley, Guildford, Surrey GU5 0AX (tel: 01483 894138; email: bramleyparish@gmail.com)

CC number: 200128

Eligibility

Residents of the parish of Bramley who are in need. If funds permit, support is extended to residents outside the area of benefit.

Types of grant

Grants are given according to need.

Applications

Apply in writing to the correspondent.

Financial information

Year end	30/09/2020
Income	£3,600
Total expenditure	£2,500

Further financial information

Full accounts were not available to view on the Charity Commission's website due to the charity's low income. We have therefore estimated the charity's grant total based on its total expenditure.

Other information

This charity is also known as Smith's Charity.

The Surrey Association for Visual Impairment

 £128,600 (2019/20)

Correspondent: Bob Hughes, Chief Executive, Sight for Surrey, Rentwood, School Lane, Fetcham, Leatherhead, Surrey KT22 9JX (tel: 01372 377701; email: info@sightforsurrey.org.uk)

https://sightforsurrey.org.uk

CC number: 1121949

Eligibility

People who are blind or partially sighted and who live in the administrative county of Surrey.

Types of grant

Small, one-off grants are given when absolutely necessary. Grants are usually to help pay for equipment required to overcome a sight problem or a sudden domestic need. Applications for small, interest-free loans are also occasionally considered.

Applications

Apply on a form available from the correspondent. Applications can be submitted at any time by the individual or through a social worker, welfare agency, club or any recognised organisation for blind or partially sighted people.

Financial information

Year end	31/03/2020
Income	£2,450,000
Total expenditure	£2,470,000

Other information

The association's main focus is the provision of services, advice, IT training and information for visually impaired people. It runs a resource centre equipped with a wide range of aids and equipment as well as a home visiting scheme and outreach groups. The association has a successful children's services division and also provides support for those struggling to navigate the benefits system.

Elmbridge

Jemima Octavia Cooper for the Poor (Stoke D'Abernon Charities)

 £2,700 (2019/20)

Correspondent: The Trustees, Old Timbers, Manor Way, Oxshott, Leatherhead, Surrey KT22 0HU (tel: 07785 272590; email: ronandjackie@ tecres.net)

CC number: 200187

Eligibility

People in need who live in the ancient parish of Stoke D'Abernon and Oxshott.

Types of grant

Grants are given according to need.

Applications

Apply in writing to the correspondent.

Financial information

Year end	31/03/2020
Income	£2,800
Total expenditure	£3,000

Further financial information

Full accounts were not available to view on the Charity Commission's website due to the charity's low income. We have therefore estimated the charity's grant total based on its total expenditure.

Walton-on-Thames Charity

 £70,900 (2018/19)

Correspondent: The Trustees, Walton-on-Thames Charity, Charities House, 1 and 2 The Quintet, Churchfield Road, Walton on Thames, Surrey KT12 2TZ (tel: 01932 220242; email: admin@ waltoncharity.org.uk)

www.waltoncharity.org.uk

CC number: 1185959

Eligibility

People in need living in the borough of Elmbridge, with a preference for residents of Walton-on-Thames.

Types of grant

One-off grants can be given for:
- Essential furniture and household items (see below for exclusions)
- Transport (such as bicycles or public transport)
- Training or support for getting back into work (such as course fees, equipment, work-related clothing or short-term childcare)
- Extracurricular activities and holiday clubs for children and young people

Exclusions

Grants cannot be awarded for:
- Non-essential furniture or household goods (such as dishwashers, tumble dryers or wardrobes)
- Rent deposits, rent in advance or rent arrears
- Degree course tuition fees or postgraduate qualifications
- Medical equipment, aids and adaptations normally provided by the NHS or other statutory agencies

- Catalogue debts, credit cards bills, personal loans or debt to central or local government departments
- Funeral costs
- Holidays

Applications

Applicants must be referred to the charity by a local organisation before making an application. Full details of the application process can be found on the charity's website.

Financial information

Year end	31/03/2019
Income	£2,220,000
Total expenditure	£1,900,000

Further financial information

The charity has recently re-registered with the Charity Commission and therefore full accounts were not available to view. The financial information relates to the previous charity (Charity Commission no. 230652), as its financial details were the latest available to view at the time of writing (November 2021).

Other information

Grants are also awarded to local charities.

Weybridge Poor's Land (Weybridge Land Charity)

 £5,100 (2019)

Correspondent: Howard Turner, Treasurer, Weybridge Charity, Allotments Gate, Curzon Road, Weybridge, Surrey KT13 8UN (tel: 07768 351999; email: treasurer@ weybridgelandcharity.org.uk)

weybridgecharity.org.uk

CC number: 200270

Eligibility

People in need who live in Weybridge.

Types of grant

Emergency grants can be made to help with the cost of food, essential furniture, flooring, white goods, and children's expenses such as prams. Note that necessary items are purchased directly by the charity.

Exclusions

Grants are not awarded for credit card or other debt relief.

Applications

Applicants for an emergency grant must be referred to the charity through an agent such as the local Citizens Advice, Home-Start Elmbridge, Walton Family Centre, local church, or the applicant's social worker.

Financial information

Year end	31/12/2019
Income	£61,000
Total expenditure	£38,100

Other information

The charity also owns and operates the Churchfields Allotments.

Epsom and Ewell

Epsom Parochial Charities (Epsom Almshouse Charity)

£ £10,300 (2019)

Correspondent: The Trustees, Farm View Suite, 42 Canons lane, Burgh Heath, Tadworth, Surrey KT20 6DP (tel: 01737 361243; email: vanstonewalker@ntlworld.com)

CC number: 200571

Eligibility

People in need who live in the ancient parish of Epsom.

Types of grant

One-off grants according to need are given through the Epsom Relief in Need Charity.

Applications

Apply in writing to the correspondent.

Financial information

Year end	31/12/2019
Income	£91,400
Total expenditure	£133,800

Other information

The charity also manages a number of almshouses.

Ewell Parochial Trusts

£ £20,800 (2020)

Correspondent: Miriam Massey, Clerk, 19 Cheam Road, Epsom, Surrey KT17 1ST (tel: 020 8394 0453; email: mirimas@globalnet.co.uk)

CC number: 201623

Eligibility

People in need who live, work or are being educated in the ancient ecclesiastical parish of Ewell and the domain of Kingswood, Surrey.

Types of grant

Grants are given according to need.

Applications

Apply in writing to the correspondent. Individuals can be referred by a third party, such as a health visitor, social care team or Citizens Advice.

Financial information

Year end	31/12/2020
Income	£53,700
Total expenditure	£53,700

Further financial information

We estimate that around £20,800 was awarded to individuals.

Other information

The trust also supports organisations.

The Henry Smith Charity (Headley)

£ £4,100 (2019/20)

Correspondent: The Trustees, Broom Cottage, Crabtree Lane, Headley, Epsom, Surrey KT18 6PS (tel: 01372 374728; email: tony.vinelott@btinternet.com)

CC number: 237927

Eligibility

Residents of Headley and Epsom who are in need.

Types of grant

Grants are given according to need.

Applications

Apply in writing to the correspondent.

Financial information

Year end	30/09/2020
Income	£5,100
Total expenditure	£4,600

Further financial information

Full accounts were not available to view on the Charity Commission's website due to the charity's low income. We have therefore estimated the charity's grant total based on its total expenditure.

Guildford

Guildford Poyle Charities

£ £19,800 (2020)

Correspondent: The Trustees, 208 High Street, Guildford, Surrey GU1 3JB (tel: 01483 303678; email: admin@guildfordpoylecharities.org)

 www.guildfordpoylecharities.org

CC number: 1145202

Eligibility

People in need who live in the borough of Guildford, as constituted prior to 1 April 1974, and part of the ancient parish of Merrow. A map showing the beneficial area can be viewed on the website.

Types of grant

The charity mainly awards one-off grants for kitchen items and appliances, furniture, baby equipment, travel and training costs. Grants are in the form of cheques or vouchers for suppliers with which the charity has arrangements or as a cheque made out to the referral agency.

Exclusions

Grants are usually not made to pay for basic items such as food, rent and utility bills. No help is given towards debts or arrears.

Applications

Application forms are available from the correspondent or to download from the website. Applications can be submitted at any time through a social worker, Citizens Advice or other welfare agency. Individuals may apply directly, although the charity states that an application has more chance of being successful if it is supported by a letter from a health or welfare professional who is familiar with the individual's circumstances.

Financial information

Year end	31/12/2020
Income	£149,100
Total expenditure	£164,700

The Mayor of Guildford's Local Support Fund

£ £7,900 (2019/20)

Correspondent: Annette Stone, Guildford Borough Council, Millmead House, Millmead, Guildford, Surrey GU2 4BB (email: civilsecretary@guildford.gov.uk)

 https://www.guildford.gov.uk/article/24412/Apply-for-the-Mayor-of-Guildford-s-Local-Support-Fund

CC number: 258388

Eligibility

Residents of Guildford who are in need. Preference is given to older residents or people with disabilities. While support is available to former residents of Guildford, priority is given to those living in the area at the time of application.

Types of grant

One-off grants of up to £250 are available towards, for example, kitchen items and appliances, furniture, carpeting, clothing and Debt Relief Orders.

Exclusions

Grants cannot be awarded to cover ongoing expenses such as rent, utility bills or debts. One application per applicant can be considered in a year.

Applications

Applications should be made on the individual's behalf by a third party (such as an officer of Guildford Borough Council, Citizens Advice or social services) The third party must email civicsecretary@guildford.gov.uk requesting a username and password to begin the application process.

Financial information

Year end	31/03/2020
Income	£4,300
Total expenditure	£7,900

Further financial information

The charity awarded 38 grants during the year.

The Pirbright Relief-in-Need Charity

£ £2,300 (2019/20)

Correspondent: Hugh Dennis, Hayloft, Mill Lane, Pirbright, Woking, Surrey GU24 0BN (tel: 01483 473108; email: hugh.dennis@ukgateway.net)

CC number: 238494

Eligibility

Residents in the parish of Pirbright who are in need.

Types of grant

Grants are awarded according to need.

Applications

Apply in writing to the correspondent.

Financial information

Year end	30/09/2020
Income	£4,900
Total expenditure	£5,000

Further financial information

Full accounts were not available to view on the Charity Commission's website due to the charity's low income. We have therefore estimated the charity's grant total based on its total expenditure.

Other information

The charity also makes grants to organisations.

The Henry Smith Charity (Send and Ripley)

£ £4,300 (2019/20)

Correspondent: The Trustees, 2 Rose Lane, Ripley, Surrey GU23 6NE (tel: 01483 225322; email: shop@ richardsonsflorist.co.uk)

CC number: 200496

Eligibility

People in need who live in Send and Ripley.

Types of grant

One-off grants are awarded to older people at Christmas.

Applications

Apply in writing to the correspondent.

Financial information

Year end	31/03/2020
Income	£4,900
Total expenditure	£4,800

Further financial information

Full accounts were not available to view on the Charity Commission's website due to the charity's low income. We have therefore estimated the charity's grant total based on its total expenditure.

Smiths Charity (Shalford)

£ £3,200 (2019/20)

Correspondent: Shalford Parish Council, Shalford Village Hall Kings Road, Shalford, Guildford, Surrey GU4 8HA (tel: 01483 459108; email: clerk@ shalfordpc.org.uk)

 https://shalford-pc.gov.uk

CC number: 240135

Eligibility

Residents of Shalford in Guilford who are in need.

Types of grant

Grants are awarded according to need.

Applications

Apply in writing to the correspondent.

Financial information

Year end	31/10/2020
Income	£3,600
Total expenditure	£3,500

Further financial information

Full accounts were not available to view on the Charity Commission's website due to the charity's low income. We have therefore estimated the charity's

grant total based on its total expenditure.

West Clandon Parochial Charities

£ £2,500 (2020)

Correspondent: The Trustees, 11 Bennett Way, West Clandon, Guildford, Surrey GU4 7TN (tel: 01486 212640)

CC number: 200165

Eligibility

People in need, mainly older people, who have lived in the parish of West Clandon for at least five years.

Types of grant

Grants are given according to need.

Applications

Apply in writing to the correspondent.

Financial information

Year end	31/12/2020
Income	£3,000
Total expenditure	£2,700

Further financial information

Full accounts were not available to view on the Charity Commission's website due to the charity's low income. We have therefore estimated the charity's grant total based on its total expenditure.

The Wonersh Charities

£ £1,400 (2019/20)

Correspondent: The Trustees, The Vicarage, Church Hill, Shamley Green, Guildford, Surrey GU5 0UG (tel: 01483 892030; email: wonershunitedcharities@ gmail.com)

CC number: 200086

Eligibility

People with disabilities or in need, especially children and older people, who live in the parishes of Wonersh, Shamley Green and Blackheath.

Types of grant

Grants are given according to need.

Applications

Apply in writing to the correspondent.

Financial information

Year end	30/06/2020
Income	£5,300
Total expenditure	£3,200

Further financial information

Full accounts were not available to view on the Charity Commission's website due to the charity's low income. We have therefore estimated the charity's grant total based on its total expenditure.

Other information
The charity also supports organisations.

Worplesdon United Charities

(£) £2,700 (2018/19)

Correspondent: The Trustees, 171 Glaziers Lane, Normandy, Guildford, Surrey GU3 2EH (tel: 01483 811847)

CC number: 200382

Eligibility
People, mainly older people, who are in need and live in the parish of Worplesdon.

Types of grant
Grants of about £80 are available according to need.

Applications
Apply in writing to the correspondent.

Financial information

Year end	31/10/2019
Income	£3,100
Total expenditure	£3,000

Further financial information
Full accounts were not available to view on the Charity Commission's website due to the charity's low income. We have therefore estimated the charity's grant total based on its total expenditure.

Mole Valley

The Abinger Consolidated Charities

(£) £3,800 (2019/20)

Correspondent: The Trustees, The Rectory, Abinger Lane, Abinger Common, Dorking, Surrey RH5 6HZ (tel: 01306 737160)

CC number: 200124

Eligibility
People in need who live in the ancient parish of Abinger.

Types of grant
Grants are given according to need, for example towards the purchase of logs or heaters.

Applications
Apply in writing to the correspondent.

Financial information

Year end	30/09/2020
Income	£9,900
Total expenditure	£8,500

Further financial information
Full accounts were not available to view on the Charity Commission's website due to the charity's low income. We have therefore estimated the charity's grant total based on its total expenditure.

Other information
The charity also supports organisations.

Betchworth United Charities

(£) £11,900 (2020)

Correspondent: Andrea Brown, Clerk to the Trustees, 15 Nutwood Avenue, Brockham, Betchworth, Surrey RH3 7LT (tel: 01737 843806 or 07788 194972; email: clerkofbuc@btinternet.com)

 https://www.betchworth-pc.gov.uk/betchworth-united-charities-2

CC number: 200299

Eligibility
People in need who live in the ancient parish of Betchworth (including Brockham and surrounding areas).

Types of grant
Grants are given according to need. Support is also available for educational purposes for children and young people.

Applications
In the first instance, contact the correspondent.

Financial information

Year end	31/12/2020
Income	£12,100
Total expenditure	£13,300

Further financial information
Full accounts were not available to view on the Charity Commission's website due to the charity's low income. We have therefore estimated the grant total based on the charity's total expenditure.

The Bookhams, Fetcham and Effingham Nursing Association Trust

(£) £3,600 (2019/20)

Correspondent: Jenny Peers, Trustee, 1 Manor Cottages, Manor House Lane, Bookham, Leatherhead, Surrey KT23 4EW (tel: 01372 456752; email: j.peers@tiscali.co.uk)

CC number: 265962

Eligibility
People who are in need as a result of ill health, disability or any other medical condition and live in Great Bookham, Little Bookham, Fetcham and Effingham.

Types of grant
Grants are given for medical items, services or facilities.

Applications
Apply in writing to the correspondent.

Financial information

Year end	31/03/2020
Income	£9,300
Total expenditure	£8,000

Further financial information
Full accounts were not available to view on the Charity Commission's website due to the charity's low income. We have therefore estimated the charity's grant total based on its total expenditure.

Other information
The charity also makes grants to organisations.

Henry Smith and Michael Earle Charities

(£) £5,300 (2019/20)

Correspondent: The Trustees, The Birches, Ifield Road, Charlwood, Horley, Surrey RH6 0DR (tel: 01293 862129; email: gillespie2@btinternet.com)

CC number: 200043

Eligibility
People in need who live in the old parish of Charlwood.

Types of grant
Grants are given according to need.

Applications
Apply using a form available from the correspondent.

Financial information

Year end	30/09/2020
Income	£6,000
Total expenditure	£5,900

Further financial information
Full accounts were not available to view on the Charity Commission's website due to the charity's low income. We have therefore estimated the charity's grant total based on its total expenditure.

Leatherhead United Charities

 £22,600 (2020)

Correspondent: The Trustees, Homefield, Forty Foot Road, Leatherhead, Surrey KT22 8RP (tel: 01372 370073; email: enquiries@lucharity.co.uk)

🌐 https://www.lucharity.co.uk

CC number: 200183

Eligibility

People in need who live in the former urban district of Leatherhead (Ashtead, Bookhams, Fetcham and Leatherhead). Preference is given to those who live in the area of the Parish of Leatherhead as constituted on 27 September 1912. Pensions are also available to people over 55 on a low income who have lived in the area for at least two years.

Types of grant

The charity provides one-off grants according to need as well as pensions.

Applications

Apply in writing to the correspondent. Applications must be supported by a professional agency such as The Citizens Advice.

Financial information

Year end	31/12/2020
Income	£347,100
Total expenditure	£228,100

Further financial information

We estimate that around £22,600 was awarded to individuals in grants and pensions during the financial year.

Other information

The charity's main purpose is to provide accommodation to older people living in the area. It also makes grants to local community organisations.

John Bristow and Thomas Mason Trust

 £16,300 (2019/20)

Correspondent: Sam Songhurst, Trust Secretary, Beech Hay, Ifield Road, Charlwood, Surrey RH6 0DR (tel: 01293 862734; email: trust.secretary@jbtmt.org.uk)

🌐 www.jbtmt.org.uk

CC number: 1075971

Eligibility

People in need who live in the ancient parish of Charlwood as constituted in 1926. This includes Hookwood and Lowfield Heath. A map of the area of

benefit can be found on the trust's website.

Types of grant

Welfare
Welfare grants are awarded according to need.

Education
Educational grants are awarded to young people to help with costs associated with further education.

Applications

Application forms can be downloaded from the trust's website and should be returned to the secretary by post. The trustees meet every alternate month to consider grant applications. Applications for educational grants need to be received by the trust secretary at least two weeks before the meeting. For dates of upcoming meetings, see the website.

Financial information

Year end	30/09/2020
Income	£92,400
Total expenditure	£62,900

Further financial information

During the financial year, welfare grants were awarded to seven individuals and educational grants were awarded to five individuals.

Other information

The trust also supports schools, churches and the overall improvement of the area of benefit.

Ockley United Charities

£6,500 (2019/20)

Correspondent: Tim Pryke, Trustee, Danesfield, Stane Street, Ockley, Dorking, Surrey RH5 5SY (tel: 01306 711511)

CC number: 200556

Eligibility

People in need who live in Ockley (primarily older people living in sheltered accommodation provided by Ockley Housing Association or rented housing).

Types of grant

The charity gives recurrent annual cash gifts of £110. Assistance is also given to local families for nursery fees.

Applications

Apply in writing to the correspondent. Applications should include details of the individual's income, housing situation and need for which funds are requested. Applications are considered on a regular basis.

Financial information

Year end	30/09/2020
Income	£10,000
Total expenditure	£7,200

Further financial information

Full accounts were not available to view on the Charity Commission's website due to the charity's low income. We have therefore estimated the charity's grant total based on its total expenditure.

Henry Smith (Worth Estate)

£4,800 (2018/19)

Correspondent: The Trustee, Limeway Cottage, Hogspudding Lane, Newdigate, Dorking, Surrey RH5 5DS (tel: 01306 631536)

CC number: 200062

Eligibility

People in need who live in the parish of Newdigate.

Types of grant

Grants are given according to need.

Applications

Apply in writing to the correspondent.

Financial information

Year end	30/09/2019
Income	£5,000
Total expenditure	£5,400

Further financial information

The 2018/19 accounts were the latest available at the time of writing (November 2021). The charity's accounts were not available to view on the Charity Commission's website due to its low income. We have estimated the charity's grant total based on its expenditure.

The Henry Smith Charity (Capel)

£2,000 (2019/20)

Correspondent: Jenny Richards, Trustee, Old School House, Coldharbour, Dorking, Surrey RH5 6HF (tel: 01306 711885; email: jennyrichards1885@gmail.com)

CC number: 201507

Eligibility

People who live in Capel, Surrey.

Types of grant

Grants are given according to need.

Applications

Apply in writing to the correspondent.

Financial information

Year end	31/03/2020
Income	£2,400
Total expenditure	£2,200

Further financial information

Full accounts were not available to view on the Charity Commission's website due to the charity's low income. We have therefore estimated the charity's grant total based on its total expenditure.

Other information

The charity is administered by the Warbleton Estate of the Henry Smith Charity.

The Henry Smith Charity (Effingham)

£ £4,100 (2019/20)

Correspondent: Effingham Parish Council, The Parish Room, 3 Home Barn Court, The Street, Effingham, Surrey KT24 5LG (tel: 01372 454911; email: clerk2010@ effinghamparishcouncil.gov.uk)

CC number: 237703

Eligibility

Older people and people in financial hardship who live in the parish of Effingham.

Types of grant

Grants are given according to need.

Applications

Apply in writing to the correspondent.

Financial information

Year end	30/09/2020
Income	£3,500
Total expenditure	£5,600

Further financial information

Full accounts were not available to view on the Charity Commission's website due to the charity's low income. We have therefore estimated the grant total based on the charity's total expenditure.

Other information

This charity also makes grants to organisations.

Henry Smith Fund (Shere)

£ £5,300 (2019/20)

Correspondent: The Clerk, The Cottage, Lower Street, Shere, Guildford, Surrey GU5 9HX (tel: 07929 396533; email: clerk.hsfs@gmail.com)

CC number: 239115

Eligibility

Residents of the parish of Shere who are in need.

Types of grant

Grants are given according to need.

Applications

Apply in writing to the correspondent.

Financial information

Year end	31/10/2020
Income	£17,500
Total expenditure	£11,700

Further financial information

Full accounts were not available to view on the Charity Commission's website due to the charity's low income. We have therefore estimated the grant total based on the charity's total expenditure.

Other information

This charity makes grants to local voluntary organisations that provide social activities for older residents in Shere.

Henry Smith's Charity (East Horsley)

£ £770 (2020)

Correspondent: The Trustees, Parish Court, Kingston Avenue, East Horsley, Leatherhead, Surrey KT24 6QT (tel: 01483 281148; email: parishcouncil@easthorsleypc.org)

CC number: 200796

Eligibility

Residents of East Horsley who have lived in the parish for a minimum of five years. Preference is given to older residents and those in need due to ill health or financial hardship.

Types of grant

Grants are awarded according to need.

Applications

Apply in writing to the correspondent.

Financial information

Year end	31/12/2020
Income	£2,000
Total expenditure	£1,700

Further financial information

Full accounts were not available to view on the Charity Commission's website due to the charity's low income. We have therefore estimated the grant total based on the charity's total expenditure.

Other information

This charity also makes grants to organisations with similar objectives.

Reigate and Banstead

Walton Parochial Charities

£ £1,800 (2019/20)

Correspondent: The Trustees, St Peter's Church, Breech Lane, Walton-on-the-Hill, Surrey KT20 7SD (tel: 01737 668254)

CC number: 200568

Eligibility

People in need who live within the parish of Walton-on-the-Hill.

Types of grant

One-off or recurrent grants are given according to need.

Applications

Apply in writing to the correspondent.

Financial information

Year end	31/03/2020
Income	£3,200
Total expenditure	£4,000

Further financial information

Full accounts were not available to view on the Charity Commission's website due to the charity's low income. We have therefore estimated the charity's grant total based on its total expenditure.

Runnymede

Chertsey Combined Charity

£ £13,600 (2020/21)

Correspondent: Secretary and Treasurer, PO Box 89, Weybridge, Surrey KT13 8HY (tel: 01932 700906; email: secretary@chertsey-combined-charity. org)

🌐 chertsey-combined-charity.org

CC number: 200186

Eligibility

People in need who live in the former urban district of Chertsey (this includes Addlestone, Chertsey, Lyne, Ottershaw, Rowtown and parts of Woodham).

Types of grant

One-off grants are awarded according to need. This can include support towards the cost of books, clothing and other essentials for those in education.

Applications

Application forms are available to download from the website or from the correspondent.

Financial information

Year end	31/03/2021
Income	£55,200
Total expenditure	£35,100

Other information

Grants are also made to organisations.

The Egham United Charity

£ £17,000 (2020)

Correspondent: The Trustees, c/o Gladstone House, 77–79 High Street, Egham, Surrey TW20 9HY (tel: 01784 472742; email: eghamunitedcharity@ outlook.com)

 www.eghamunitedcharity.org

CC number: 205885

Eligibility

Welfare

People in need who have lived in Egham, Englefield Green (West and East), Hythe or Virginia Water for at least five years. Support is typically given to families, older people, people who have physical and mental disabilities and their carers, people who are recuperating from mental illness, and parents in need. For further detail see the charity's website.

Education

Students up to the age of 25 who have lived in the area of benefit for at least five years.

Types of grant

Welfare

One-off grants are awarded according to need. Grants can be made towards, for example, fuel bills, household essentials, mobility aids and for school uniforms, trips and travel fares. In most cases, payments are made directly to the supplier/provider (in the case of settling bills) or to the referring agency for distribution.

Education

Financial assistance for educational purposes can be given as follows:

▶ To meet the costs of secondary, further and/or vocational educational courses. If appropriate, the grant may be repeated annually throughout the student's full course of study.
▶ To help with the initial expenses when a student first leaves home to take up a course.
▶ For students studying courses that involve exceptionally costly items, such as musical instruments and specialist project work.

▶ Towards the costs relating to extracurricular activities offered by youth groups, such as Guides, Scouts and the Duke of Edinburgh Award. This may include equipment costs.
▶ To help with exceptional travel costs relating to education.

Exclusions

The website states that the charity cannot: fund necessities which are provided by local or central government (although it may top up partial provision); make up for income deficiencies or make recurring grants; pay for necessities which 'applicants, albeit with appropriate advice and befriending, could provide for themselves'; offer loans; or commit to any support outside a trustees' meeting.

Applications

Application forms are available to download from the website. The trustees prefer to receive welfare applications through a referral agency, such as Citizens Advice or a social worker. Applications are only ever considered at trustees' meetings held every six weeks. On occasion, the trustees may arrange to visit an applicant.

Financial information

Year end	31/12/2020
Income	£22,400
Total expenditure	£18,900

Further financial information

Full accounts were not available to view on the Charity Commission's website due to the charity's low income. We have therefore estimated the charity's grant total based on its total expenditure.

Other information

The charity also administers two groups of almshouses in Egham.

The Henry Smith Charity (Chertsey)

£ £8,600 (2019/20)

Correspondent: The Trustees, c/o Runnymede Borough Council, Runnymede Civic Centre, Station Road, Addlestone, Surrey KT15 2AH (tel: 01932 425620)

CC number: 233531

Eligibility

Older people and people with disabilities who live in Chertsey and are in need.

Types of grant

The charity awards fuel vouchers.

Applications

Apply in writing to the correspondent.

Financial information

Year end	30/09/2020
Income	£21,000
Total expenditure	£19,000

Further financial information

Full accounts were not available to view on the Charity Commission's website due to the charity's low income. We have therefore estimated the grant total based on the charity's total expenditure.

Other information

Grants are also awarded to organisations that support older people and people with disabilities.

The Thorpe Parochial Charities

£ £3,200 (2019/20)

Correspondent: The Trustees, 21 The Gower, Egham, Surrey TW20 8UB (tel: 01932 560459; email: TWRA@ Patenall.org.uk)

CC number: 205888

Eligibility

People in need who live in the ancient parish of Thorpe, especially those over 60 years of age.

Types of grant

Financial assistance with fuel bills.

Applications

Apply in writing to the correspondent.

Financial information

Year end	29/02/2020
Income	£5,300
Total expenditure	£3,500

Further financial information

Full accounts were not available to view on the Charity Commission's website due to the charity's low income. We have therefore estimated the charity's grant total based on its total expenditure.

Spelthorne

Ashford Relief in Need Charities

£ £18,300 (2019/20)

Correspondent: The Trustees, c/o St Matthews Church Hall, Muncaster Close, Ashford, Middlesex TW15 2EE (tel: 01784 259093; email: arin@smam. org.uk)

CC number: 231441

Eligibility

People in need who live in the parish of Ashford or within the area covered by the TW15 postcode.

Types of grant

Grants are made according to need.

Applications

Apply in writing to the correspondent.

Financial information

Year end	31/03/2020
Income	£7,200
Total expenditure	£20,300

Further financial information

Full accounts were not available to view on the Charity Commission's website due to the charity's low income. We have therefore estimated the charity's grant total based on its total expenditure.

Staines Parochial Charity

£ £7,000 (2019/20)

Correspondent: The Trustees, 11 Budebury Road, Staines-upon-Thames, Middlesex TW18 2AZ (tel: 01784 462539)

CC number: 211653

Eligibility

Older people and people with disabilities who live in the urban district of Staines.

Types of grant

Grants are given according to need.

Applications

Apply in writing to the correspondent.

Financial information

Year end	31/03/2020
Income	£4,600
Total expenditure	£7,800

Further financial information

Full accounts were not available to view on the Charity Commission's website due to the charity's low income. We have therefore estimated the charity's grant total based on its total expenditure.

Surrey Heath

Chobham Poor Allotment Charity

£ £9,500 (2019/20)

Correspondent: The Trustees, 46 Chertsey Road, Windlesham, Surrey GU20 6EP (tel: 01276 475392)

CC number: 200154

Eligibility

People in need who live in the ancient parish of Chobham, which includes the civil parishes of Chobham and West End.

Types of grant

Grants are given according to need.

Applications

Apply in writing to the correspondent.

Financial information

Year end	30/04/2020
Income	£56,500
Total expenditure	£52,600

Further financial information

The charity awarded a total of £1,200 in grants to individuals. In addition, it provided vouchers totalling £8,300 to eligible parishioners as part of its 'annual distribution'.

Other information

The main activities of the charity are the provision and maintenance of allotments, almshouses, and recreational and educational facilities. Grants are also made to organisations.

Frimley Fuel Allotments CIO

£ £56,600 (2020)

Correspondent: The Trustees, High Cross Church, Camberley GU15 3SY (tel: 01276 28719; email: ffa.office1@gmail.com)

 www.frimleyfuelallotments.org.uk

CC number: 1161717

Eligibility

People in need who live in the parish of Frimley. Priority is given to people who are older or who have a disability, and to those who care for them.

Types of grant

One-off grants are made according to need.

Applications

Apply on a form available from the secretary or a local Citizens Advice, church or social services centre.

Financial information

Year end	31/12/2020
Income	£241,800
Total expenditure	£131,400

Henry Smith (Chobham)

£ £9,300 (2019/20)

Correspondent: The Trustees, 46 Chertsey Road, Windlesham, Surrey GU20 6EP (tel: 01276 475936; email: cpa1831@aol.com)

CC number: 200155

Eligibility

People in need who live in the ancient parish of Chobham (roughly the current civil parishes of Chobham and West End) in Surrey. The charity's Charity Commission record suggests it has some preference for supporting older people and people with disabilities.

Types of grant

Our previous research has shown that small, one-off grants are awarded according to need.

Applications

Apply in writing to the correspondent.

Financial information

Year end	29/02/2020
Income	£24,000
Total expenditure	£10,300

Further financial information

Full accounts were not available to view on the Charity Commission's website due to the charity's low income. We have therefore estimated the charity's grant total based on its total expenditure.

Other information

This charity is a local branch of the wider Henry Smith Charity network.

The Henry Smith Charity (Bisley)

£ £2,300 (2020)

Correspondent: Alexandra Gunn, Trustee, 213 Guildford Road, Bisley, Woking, Surrey GU24 9DL (tel: 01483 838329; email: sandygunn213@gmail.com)

CC number: 200157

Eligibility

Residents of Bisley who are in need. Preference is given to older residents and people experiencing financial hardship.

Types of grant

Grants are given according to need.

Applications

Apply in writing to the correspondent.

Financial information

Year end	31/12/2020
Income	£2,500
Total expenditure	£2,500

Further financial information

Full accounts were not available to view on the Charity Commission's website due to the charity's low income. We have therefore estimated the grant total based on the charity's total expenditure.

The Henry Smith Charity (Frimley)

(£) £1,600 (2019/20)

Correspondent: The Trustees, Surrey Heath Borough Council, Surrey Heath House, Knoll Road, Camberley, Surrey GU15 3HD (tel: 01276 707335; email: democratic.services@surreyheath.gov.uk)

CC number: 236367

Eligibility
Residents in the parish of Frimley who are in need.

Types of grant
Grants are made in kind for clothing, linen, bedding, fuel, tools and medical aids.

Applications
Apply in writing to the correspondent.

Financial information
Year end	31/03/2020
Income	£4,000
Total expenditure	£1,800

Further financial information
Full accounts were not available to view on the Charity Commission's website due to the charity's low income. We have therefore estimated the charity's grant total based on its total expenditure.

Windlesham United Charities

(£) £2,500 (2020)

Correspondent: Carol Robson, 4 James Butler Almshouses, Guildford Road, Bagshot, Surrey GU19 5NH (tel: 01276 476158; email: jamesbutleroffice@ btinternet.com)

CC number: 200224

Eligibility
Mainly elderly individuals and people with disabilities who are in need and have lived in the parishes of Bagshot, Lightwater and Windlesham (Surrey) for at least two years.

Types of grant
The charity awards one-off grants, mainly in the form of small heating grants.

Applications
Apply in writing to the correspondent at any time.

Financial information
Year end	31/12/2020
Income	£55,200
Total expenditure	£42,200

Other information
Windlesham United Charities consists of four separate funds: R. E. Cooper Educational Fund, The Duchess of Gloucester Educational Fund, Windlesham Poors Allotments and Windlesham United Charities. The charity also maintain allotments.

Tandridge

The Oxted United Charities

(£) £4,100 (2020/21)

Correspondent: The Trustees, 9 Paddock Way, Oxted, Surrey RH8 0LF (tel: 01883 818549; email: cjboxted@aol.co.uk)

CC number: 200056

Eligibility
People in need or with disabilities who live in the parish of Oxted.

Applications
Apply in writing to the correspondent.

Financial information
Year end	28/02/2021
Income	£5,500
Total expenditure	£4,600

Further financial information
Full accounts were not available to view on the Charity Commission's website due to the charity's low income. We have therefore estimated the charity's grant total based on its total expenditure.

Smith's Charity (Nutfield)

(£) £2,700 (2019/20)

Correspondent: The Trustees, 7 Morris Road, South Nutfield, Redhill, Surrey RH1 5SB (tel: 01737 823348; email: smithsnutfield@aol.com)

CC number: 255839

Eligibility
Residents of Nutfield who are in need as a result of low income or temporary financial hardship.

Types of grant
Grants are awarded according to need.

Applications
Apply in writing to the correspondent.

Financial information
Year end	30/09/2020
Income	£5,400
Total expenditure	£5,900

Further financial information
Full accounts were not available to view on the Charity Commission's website due to the charity's low income. We have therefore estimated the charity's grant total based on its total expenditure.

Other information
This charity also makes grants to organisations whose work involves providing services to children and older people in need.

Waverley

The Churt Welfare Trust

(£) £1,500 (2020/21)

Correspondent: John Brain, Chair/Trustee, Hearn Lodge, Spats Lane, Headley Down, Bordon GU35 8SU (email: john@regalarch.f9.co.uk)

 https://www.churt.org/churt-welfare-trust

CC number: 210076

Eligibility
Residents of Churt, and its neighbourhood, who are in need.

Types of grant
One-off grants are awarded according to need. The trust's website states:

> Examples of ways in which the Trust has helped and can consider applications for contributory or full assistance in appropriate cases are:-
> - General assistance towards the welfare of individuals or families in the local community.
> - Assistance towards heating costs in winter for the elderly or frail.
> - Equipment, furnishings or improvement of general comfort for the physically or mentally ill.
> - Specialist or household equipment or nursing, educational or home help facilities to assist or comfort the temporarily or terminally ill or injured.
> - Travel or holiday arrangements.
> - Medical expenses.
> - Occasional taxi or transport for the elderly or long distance medical appointments.
> - Facilities for educational or community welfare for all age groups.
> - Local charities.
> - Household repairs and maintenance.
> - Help at a time of financial difficulty.

Applications
Apply in writing to the correspondent.

Financial information
Year end	31/01/2021
Income	£9,300
Total expenditure	£7,600

Further financial information

Full accounts were not available to view on the Charity Commission's website due to the trust's low income. We have therefore estimated the grant total based on the trust's total expenditure.

Other information

Any surplus income is awarded to local organisations.

The Cranleigh and District Nursing Association

£2,100 (2020)

Correspondent: The Trustees, 14 Dukes Close, Cranleigh, Surrey GU6 7JU (tel: 01483 274162)

CC number: 200649

Eligibility

People in need and who are experiencing ill health and live in the Cranleigh district.

Types of grant

One-off grants.

Applications

Apply in writing to the correspondent through a social worker, Citizens Advice or other welfare agency.

Financial information

Year end	31/12/2020
Income	£2,000
Total expenditure	£2,300

Further financial information

Full accounts were not available to view on the Charity Commission's website due to the charity's low income. We have therefore estimated the charity's grant total based on its total expenditure.

Dempster Trust

 £11,200 (2020/21)

Correspondent: Jon Curtis, Trustee, 21 Broomleaf Road, Farnham, Surrey GU9 8DG (tel: 01252 710673; email: joncurtis@thedempstertrust.org.uk)

https://thedempstertrust.org.uk

CC number: 200107

Eligibility

Welfare

People in need, hardship or distress who live in Farnham and the general neighbourhood.

Education

University students who reside in Farnham or its surrounding area who

are finding it difficult to find funds for study-related costs.

Types of grant

Welfare

The trust rarely offers cash grants as it prefers to purchase goods on behalf of individuals. In the past, the trust has assisted with school uniforms and school trips, care alarms for older people, travel costs to hospitals, and furnishings.

Education

Following the death of a long-standing trustee, the trust established The Jack Mayhew Education Grant to support students who may be in need of books, computers or other significant costs to start their studies at university. Cash grants are not given but the trust will purchase the equipment on the student's behalf.

Exclusions

Grants are not awarded for the payment of debts.

Applications

Welfare

An application form and guidance notes can be downloaded from the trust's website and should be returned by email or post. Applications are generally not considered unless they are supported by a referee, such as a doctor, social worker, headteacher, hospital, Citizens Advice or another welfare agency. Applications can be considered at any time.

Education

Schools and colleges in Farnham should apply on behalf of the individual. An application form can be downloaded from the website.

Financial information

Year end	31/03/2021
Income	£7,900
Total expenditure	£12,500

Further financial information

Full accounts were not available to view on the Charity Commission's website due to the trust's low income. We have therefore estimated the trust's grant total based on its total expenditure.

Shottermill United Charities

£1,300 (2020/21)

Correspondent: Hilary Bicknell, 7 Underwood Road, Haslemere, Surrey GU27 1JQ (tel: 01428 651276; email: hilary.bicknell@gmail.com)

CC number: 200394

Eligibility

People on a low income, individuals with disabilities or older people who live in the parish of Shottermill, Surrey.

Types of grant

The charity distributes grocery vouchers during Christmas.

Applications

Apply in writing to the correspondent.

Financial information

Year end	15/03/2021
Income	£3,100
Total expenditure	£2,900

Further financial information

Full accounts were not available to view on the Charity Commission's website due to the charity's low income. We have therefore estimated the charity's grant total based on its total expenditure.

Other information

The charity also gives grants to organisations.

The Witley Charitable Trust

£3,200 (2019)

Correspondent: Julie Grist, Chair of Trustees, Holmbury, Wheeler Lane, Witley, Godalming, Surrey GU8 5QU (tel: 01428 683448; email: witleycharitabletrust@gmail.com)

 witley-pc.gov.uk/parish-council/witley-charitable-trust

CC number: 200338

Eligibility

People in need who live in the parishes of Witley and Milford.

Types of grant

Grants are made according to need. Our previous research indicates that support has been given towards telephone, electricity and gas debts, for medical appliances not available through the NHS, and to help a pupil attend a local pre-school. The trust has also previously distributed Christmas gifts, benefitting between 40 and 50 individuals.

Applications

Applications on behalf of individuals, for example from health visitors, district nurses and churches, should be made in writing.

Financial information

Year end	31/12/2019
Income	£4,400
Total expenditure	£3,500

Further financial information

Full accounts were not available to view on the Charity Commission's website due to the trust's low income. We have therefore estimated the trust's grant total based on its total expenditure.

Woking

The Byfleet United Charity

 £204,500 (2020)

Correspondent: Grants Manager, Stoop Court, Leisure Lane, West Byfleet, Surrey KT14 6HF (tel: 01932 340532; email: buc@byfleetunitedcharity.org.uk)

🌐 byfleetunitedcharity.org.uk

CC number: 1167753

Eligibility

People in need who have lived in the ancient parish of Byfleet or West Byfleet area for at least a year immediately prior to their application.

Types of grant

Welfare

The charity has different grant programmes providing welfare grants. Essential Grants provide everyday items and services for families and individuals. Family Support Grants provide help for families in financial need. Regular monthly payments can help towards the cost of raising a family, household bills, debts and arrears. Short Term Support Grants provide help for families and individuals who find themselves in temporary financial difficulty.

Education

The charity's Bursary Award can purchase educational equipment for students or help towards course fees.

Applications

Applications are available to download from the charity's website. Applications can be made directly by the individual or through a third party, such as a social worker, Citizens Advice, local GP or church. Candidates are usually visited and assessed.

Financial information

Year end	31/12/2020
Income	£531,700
Total expenditure	£570,700

Further financial information

Grants totalling £40,700 were made to 99 individuals. Allowances totalling £163,800 were given to 84 people.

Other information

The charity also gives money to local organisations. This charity is an amalgamation of smaller trusts, including the Byfleet Pensions Fund.

Henry Smith (Share Warbleton Estate)

£ £2,700 (2019/20)

Correspondent: The Trustees, Flat 40, Park Heights, Constitution Hill, Woking, Surrey GU22 7RT (tel: 07800 844877)

CC number: 232281

Eligibility

Residents of Woking who are in need.

Types of grant

Cash grants are awarded according to need.

Applications

Apply in writing to the correspondent. Grants are distributed by vicars of the seven parishes within the area of benefit.

Financial information

Year end	31/05/2020
Income	£6,000
Total expenditure	£6,000

Further financial information

Full accounts were not available to view on the Charity Commission's website due to the charity's low income. We have therefore estimated the charity's grant total based on its total expenditure.

West Sussex

The Ashington, Wiston, Warminghurst Sick Poor Fund

£ £5,000 (2020)

Correspondent: Rod Shepherd, Trustee, c/o Sheen Stickland LLP, 7 East Pallant, Chichester, West Sussex PO19 1TR (tel: 01243 781255; email: rod.shepherd@btinternet.com)

CC number: 234625

Eligibility

People who live in the county of West Sussex and are in need as a result of illness or financial difficulty. Preference is given to residents of Ashington, Wiston and Warminghurst.

Types of grant

Small grants (£300 on average) are given according to need. Most grants are made for equipment deemed to improve the daily life of beneficiaries.

Applications

Apply in writing to the correspondent.

Financial information

Year end	31/12/2020
Income	£450
Total expenditure	£5,500

Further financial information

Full accounts were not available to view on the Charity Commission's website due to the fund's low income. We have therefore estimated the fund's grant total based on its total expenditure.

The Chownes Foundation
See entry on page 375

MacAndrew Sussex Trust
See entry on page 376

The Pest House Charity

£ £5,800 (2020)

Correspondent: Tim Rudwick, Clerk, Lavender Cottage, The Street, Midhurst, West Sussex GU29 0NJ (tel: 07969 365370; email: pesthousecharity@gmail.com)

CC number: 227479

Eligibility

People who live in the parish of Midhurst and are in need due to illness or financial difficulty.

Types of grant

Grants are given according to need.

Exclusions

The area of application is restricted to the parish of Midhurst. Applications from its vicinity will not be accepted.

Applications

Apply in writing to the correspondent.

Financial information

Year end	31/12/2020
Income	£12,100
Total expenditure	£12,800

Further financial information

Full accounts were not available to view on the Charity Commission's website due to the charity's low income. We have therefore estimated the charity's grant total based on its total expenditure.

Other information

This charity also makes grants to organisations.

Sussex County Football Association Benevolent Fund
See entry on page 377

Sussex Police Charitable Trust
See entry on page 377

The West Sussex County Nursing Benevolent Fund

£ £1,900 (2020)

Correspondent: Rod Shepherd, Trustee, c/o Sheen Stickland LLP, 7 East Pallant, Chichester PO19 1TR (tel: 01243 781255; email: rod.shepherd@btinternet.com)

CC number: 234210

Eligibility
Retired community nurses who practised in West Sussex and who are in need as a result of ill health, convalescence, disability, infirmity or financial difficulty. Retired general or specialist nurses who practised in West Sussex may also be considered.

Types of grant
Grants are awarded according to need.

Applications
Apply in writing to the correspondent.

Financial information
Year end	31/12/2020
Income	£2,200
Total expenditure	£2,100

Further financial information
Full accounts were not available to view on the Charity Commission's website due to the fund's low income. We have therefore estimated the fund's grant total based on its total expenditure.

Crawley

Lichfield Municipal Charities

£ £9,000 (2020)

Correspondent: Jane Bethell, Administrator, c/o Ansons Solicitors Ltd, St Marys Chambers, 5–7 Breadmarket Street, Lichfield, Staffordshire WS13 6LQ (tel: 01543 267982; email: jbethell@ansonssolicitors.com)

 https://lichfieldmunicipal.org.uk

CC number: 254299

Eligibility
Residents of Lichfield who are in need.

Types of grant
One-off grants are awarded according to need. The charity's website states that it can help by making grants of money or paying for items, services or facilities to reduce the need, hardship or distress.

Exclusions
Individuals outside the area of benefit, as detailed on the charity's website, are not eligible.

Applications
Applications can be made online using the form on the charity's website. Alternatively, application forms are available to download on the charity's website and, once completed, can be sent to the correspondent at their postal or email address. As part of the application process, a representative of the charity will make arrangements to visit the individual at their home to further discuss their application. If arrangements are made and the applicant fails to meet with the representative, the application will no longer be considered.

Financial information
Year end	31/12/2020
Income	£87,100
Total expenditure	£105,000

Further financial information
During 2020, the trust made 22 grants to individuals.

Other information
Lichfield Municipal Charities comprises of thirteen almshouses known as William Lunn's Homes, which are available for occupation by local people who are in need. Four of the homes are suitable for single people, while the remaining nine homes are designed for married couples. The charity also makes grants to local organisations, namely the St Mary's public library situated in the area of benefit.

South West

General

The Christina Aitchison Trust

See entry on page 333

Children's Leukaemia Society

See entry on page 207

The Heathcoat Trust

£ £135,800 (2019/20)

Correspondent: Helen Isaac, Secretary, The Factory, West Exe, Tiverton, Devon EX16 5LL (tel: 01884 244296; email: heathcoattrust@heathcoat.co.uk)

CC number: 203367

Eligibility

People who are older, in poor health or in financial need and live in Cornwall and Devon, or in the operating areas of the firms John Heathcoat and Co. Ltd and Lowman Manufacturing Co. Ltd and their subsidiaries. Some preference is given to employees and dependants of these firms.

Types of grant

One-off and recurrent grants can be awarded according to need. Examples include: hospital visits; dentist, optician and chiropody charges; hardship grants; employee sickness grants; and bereavement support.

Applications

Applications should be made in writing to the correspondent. The trustees meet regularly to consider applications.

Financial information

Year end	05/04/2020
Income	£858,300
Total expenditure	£886,100

Further financial information

Grants were broken down as follows:

Bereavement grants	£40,000
Hospital visits	£32,500
Opticians charges	£23,200
Chiropody charges	£20,700
Dentists charges	£13,600
Hardship grants	£5,300
Communication grants	£540

Other information

The trust also awards grants for educational advancement and provides grants to organisations.

Sam Pilcher Trust

 £18,000 (2020)

Correspondent: The Trustees, Springhill Barn, Upper Slaughter, Cheltenham GL54 2JH (tel: 01451 810845; email: info@sampilchertrust.org.uk)

🌐 www.sampilchertrust.org.uk

CC number: 1151779

Eligibility

Families of children with cancer. The trust's focus is helping patients during and after treatment at the Bristol Royal and Gloucester Royal Children's Hospital.

Types of grant

One-off grants are available to assist with the costs associated with having a child with cancer. In the past, grants have been given towards travel expenses, computer equipment (e.g. iPads), clothes, washing machines, holiday insurance and passports.

Applications

Apply in writing to the correspondent.

Financial information

Year end	31/12/2020
Income	£27,300
Total expenditure	£20,000

Further financial information

Note: the grant total for individuals has been estimated, based on the information gathered in the trust's accounts.

Other information

The trust was established after the death of 11-year-old Sam Pilcher, who died from leukaemia. Before his death, Sam began fundraising to help other children suffering from cancer. The trust mainly supports hospitals and other cancer care units. For example, it helped to establish a dedicated Teenage Cancer Care Unit and helped to refurbish the activity rooms in Bristol Royal Children's Hospital and Gloucester Royal Children's Hospital. The trust also provides cuddly toys for new patients at Gloucester Royal Children's Hospital and gives goody bags to inpatients at Bristol Royal Children's Hospital.

The Plymouth and Cornwall Cancer Fund

 £19,400 (2019/20)

Correspondent: The Trustees, 80A Hyde Park Road, Plymouth PL3 4RQ (tel: 01752 220587; email: admin@pccf.org.uk)

🌐 https://www.plymouthandcornwall cancerfund.org.uk

CC number: 262587

Eligibility

Welfare
People with cancer who are under the care of Derriford Hospital or any other health organisation within the catchment area, a map of which can be seen on the fund's website.

Education
The fund also makes grants to healthcare professionals and staff involved in cancer treatment to support them in further education.

Types of grant

Welfare
Welfare grants of up to £500 can be made towards the cost of travel for patients and carers, and more general living expenses.

Education

Educational grants are awarded to healthcare professionals or staff involved in caring for cancer patients to attend courses, conferences and to access postgraduate training opportunities.

Applications

Apply in writing to the correspondent. Applications must be made by a recognised healthcare professional on the individual's behalf. Applications for support should include:

▶ Details of why the support is needed
▶ Explanation of what the funding is for
▶ Confirmation that a financial assessment has been undertaken, that the patient has received all relevant entitlements and that the costs and expenses are reasonable

Financial information

Year end	31/10/2020
Income	£58,200
Total expenditure	£63,200

Other information

The fund operates a charity shop in Hyde Park Village, which is run by a team of over 20 volunteers. The shop generates a large portion of the fund's income. The fund also makes grants in support of local research projects related to improving the treatment of cancer and to Derriford Hospital to help improve its facilities.

The Royal Bath and West of England Society

 £4,000 (2020)

Correspondent: The Trustees, The Bath and West Showground, Shepton Mallett, Somerset BA4 6QN (tel: 01749 822201; email: Rupert.Cox@bathandwest.co.uk)

🌐 www.bathandwestsociety.com

CC number: 1039397

Eligibility

Individuals from Somerset, Dorset, Devon, Wiltshire, Gloucestershire and Bristol studying relevant courses related to agriculture and the rural economy.

Types of grant

Scholarships and grants are given towards courses and projects that promote agriculture and rural economy. Previously support has been given to individuals attending agricultural colleges, veterinary schools, livestock photography courses or forestry courses, undertaking an NVQ and so on. Applications for PhDs and second degrees will be considered.

Applications

Contact the correspondent for further information and to request an application form. The deadline for scholarship and grant applications falls on 1 June each year. Further information can be found on the society's website.

Financial information

Year end	31/12/2020
Income	£700,000
Total expenditure	£3,290,000

Further financial information

The grant total has been estimated, based on the information gathered in the charity's annual report and accounts.

Other information

The society aims to promote agriculture and rural economy through seminars, conferences and open days. In addition, it administers a range of events and awards for both organisations and individuals. The society sponsors the West Country Dairy Awards, which offer support to individuals undertaking further education courses related to the dairy industry.

South West Peninsula Football League Benevolent Fund

 £1,400 (2019/20)

Correspondent: The Trustees, 45A Serge Court, Commercial Road, Exeter EX2 4EB (tel: 01392 493995; email: phil@swpleague.co.uk)

🌐 www.swpleague.co.uk

CC number: 1079397

Eligibility

People in need who live in the counties of Devon and Cornwall and who are or were involved with, or connected to, the South West Peninsula Football League. Support is extended to referees in the league.

Types of grant

Grants are awarded according to need.

Applications

Apply in writing to the correspondent.

Financial information

Year end	31/03/2020
Income	£2,200
Total expenditure	£1,600

Further financial information

Full accounts were not available to view on the Charity Commission's website due to the fund's low income. We have therefore estimated the fund's grant total based on its total expenditure.

Bristol

The Anchor Society

 £41,600 (2020)

Correspondent: Catherine Watts, Administrator, 29 Alma Vale Road, Clifton, Bristol BS8 2HL (tel: 0117 973 4161; email: admin@anchorsociety.co.uk)

🌐 www.anchorsociety.co.uk

CC number: 1167933

Eligibility

Isolated, older people who are over the age of 55 and live in the Greater Bristol area.

Types of grant

One-off grants are made to help older people stay independent and in their own homes. Typical awards include home repairs and adaptations, mobility aids, boiler/heating systems, essential appliances, carpets and flooring and essential household furniture.

Exclusions

The charity does not give grants for general living expenses, moving costs or travel expenses, holidays, respite breaks, insurance costs, funeral costs, clothing, crockery and kitchen utensils or cleaning services, or to pay off outstanding bills and debts.

Applications

Applications should be made through the grants request form available on the charity's website. The form should be completed by a third party responsible for referring the individual for a grant.

Financial information

Year end	31/12/2020
Income	£168,800
Total expenditure	£240,300

Further financial information

Note that the grant total may include loans.

Other information

The charity operates a befriending service that is provided by volunteers. It has also invested in the development of sheltered housing and day care provisions for older people.

Elizabeth Blanchard's Charity

 £1,900 (2019)

Correspondent: Ruth Mico, Trustee, 3 Springfield Grove, Bristol BS6 7XG (tel: 07576 710918; email: ruthmico@gmail.com)

CC number: 243122

Eligibility

Women in need, with preference given to women belonging to the Old King Street Chapel in Bristol.

Types of grant

Grants are given according to need.

Applications

Apply in writing to the correspondent.

Financial information

Year end	31/12/2019
Income	£2,300
Total expenditure	£2,200

Further financial information

Full accounts were not available to view on the Charity Commission's website due to the charity's low income. We have therefore estimated the charity's grant total based on its total expenditure.

The Bristol Benevolent Institution

 £555,100 (2020)

Correspondent: Maureen Nicholls, Secretary, 45 High Street, Nailsea, Bristol BS48 1AW (tel: 01275 810365; email: secretary@bristolbenevolent.org)

 bristolbenevolent.org

CC number: 204592

Eligibility

People over the age of 60 with small fixed incomes and little or no capital, living in or around the city of Bristol. People over the age of 55 who have chronic illness or severe disabilities are also eligible.

Types of grant

Recurrent annual grants are paid quarterly and usually total between £320 and £1,300 per annum. One-off grants for specific needs, such as removal fees, furniture, household appliances or general help with repairs, are also available. Those who own their own homes, free of mortgage, can apply for small interest-free loans to help supplement a low income or to help make essential repairs.

Applications

Potential applicants should contact the correspondent in writing or by phone or email.

Financial information

Year end	31/12/2020
Income	£463,700
Total expenditure	£613,500

Bristol Charities

 £307,600 (2019/20)

Correspondent: Grants Committee, 17 St Augustines Parade, Bristol BS1 4UL (tel: 0117 930 0301; email: info@bristolcharities.org.uk)

 www.bristolcharities.org.uk

CC number: 1109141

Eligibility

People who live in Bristol and are in need or suffering from ill health. The charity also supports carers and young people under 25 who may need help funding after school activities, school trips or certain educational materials.

Types of grant

Grants are available for white goods, small electrical equipment (such as hoovers and microwaves), flooring, basic furniture (including beds, sofas, tables and chairs) and cutlery and crockery.

Exclusions

Grants are not made for clothing, tumble dryers or dishwashers, gas cookers, TVs, PCs, audio equipment, rent arrears, Debt Relief Orders or any other kind of debt.

Applications

Applicants should nominate a sponsor from a professional background to apply on their behalf. Sponsors can register with the charity via its website and, once approved, will receive an application form to complete on behalf of the applicant.

Financial information

Year end	31/03/2020
Income	£1,010,000
Total expenditure	£1,470,000

The Lord Mayor of Bristol's Children Appeal

 £57,500 (2019/20)

Correspondent: The Trustees, 3 Park Crescent, Frenchay, Bristol BS16 1PD (tel: 07768 077864; email: info@lordmayorofbristolappeal.com)

 https://www.lordmayorofbristolappeal.com

CC number: 288262

Eligibility

Children under the age of 16 (or aged under 18 if a child has a disability) who live in Bristol and are in need.

Types of grant

Grants in the form of food, clothing and toy vouchers are distributed at

Christmas. Each child receives a £20 voucher for gifts or clothing, and another £20 for food.

Applications

Social workers liaise with the charity and make referrals for funding.

Financial information

Year end	30/06/2020
Income	£55,500
Total expenditure	£60,300

Further financial information

During the year, £57,500 was spent on food, clothing and toy vouchers for children. The charity aims to award grants to around 1,650 children each year.

Christ Church Exhibition Fund

 £2,200 (2020)

Correspondent: The Trustees, 1 All Saints Court, Bristol BS1 1JN (tel: 0117 929 2709; email: ascl.charity@btconnect.com)

CC number: 325124

Eligibility

Boys and girls who live in the city and county borough of Bristol. Students in higher/further education who have attended school in the city and county borough of Bristol are also eligible, with a preference for those who have lived in the ecclesiastical parish of Christ Church with St Ewen for at least two years.

Types of grant

Grants are awarded to promote the education of schoolchildren and to aid students at university or further education institutions.

Applications

Apply in writing to the correspondent.

Financial information

Year end	31/12/2020
Income	£12,700
Total expenditure	£2,500

Further financial information

Full accounts were not available to view on the Charity Commission's website due to the charity's low income. We have therefore estimated the charity's grant total based on its total expenditure.

Other information

The charity provides funding towards the running of a Sunday school in St Ewen. The charity also supports the education of choristers of the parish church of Christ Church with St Ewen.

The Charles Dixon Pension Fund

See entry on page 306

Dolphin Society

 £37,500 (2019/20)

Correspondent: Sean Hollinswaite, Administrator, Kitale, Wills Lane, Bristol BS9 1FH (tel: 0117 929 9649; email: enquiries@dolphinsociety.org.uk)

https://www.dolphin-society.org.uk

CC number: 203142

Eligibility

Older people or people with disabilities who live in Bristol and its adjoining local authority areas. Applicants should be on a low income and need help to maintain their independence and safety in their own homes.

Types of grant

Free pendant alarms are given to individuals who do not qualify for local authority assistance. The charity also channels funding through the charity WE Care and Repair to facilitate home adaptations and emergency repairs (e.g. for central heating).

Applications

For more information on pendant alarms, and how to apply for one, contact the correspondent. Further information on assistance with home adaptations and heating repairs is available from WE Care and Repair (tel: 0117 954 2222; email: info@ bristolcareandrepair.org.uk).

Financial information

Year end	30/09/2020
Income	£177,400
Total expenditure	£184,400

Edmonds and Coles Scholarships (Edmonds and Coles Charity)

 £6,100 (2019/20)

Correspondent: The Trustees, The Society of Merchant Venturers, Merchants' Hall, The Promenade, Clifton Down, Bristol BS8 3NH (tel: 0117 973 8058; email: treasurer@ merchantventurers.com)

merchantventurers.com/charitable-activities/edmonds-and-coles-scholarships

CC number: 311751

Eligibility

People in need who are under the age of 25 and live in the area of benefit, which includes: Aust, Avonmouth, Bishopston, Brentry, Charlton Mead, Coombe Dingle, Cotham, Durdham Down, Hallen, Henbury, Henleaze, Horfield, Kingsweston, Kingsdown, Lawrence Weston, New Passage, Northwick, Pilning, Redland, Redwick, Sea Mills, Severn Beach, Shirehampton, Southmead, Stoke Bishop, Tyndalls Park, Westbury-on-Trym, Westbury Park and Woolcott Park.

Types of grant

The charity can help with the costs associated with a schoolchild's education. Awards are made towards general educational expenses, including the cost of books, equipment/ instruments or travel. Support can also be given to people at school or college/ university and those undertaking vocational training.

Exclusions

At primary and secondary school level, grants are not normally given to enable children to enter private education when parents cannot afford the cost. Help may, however, be given in respect of children already in private education when there has been a change in financial circumstances (through, for example, death of a parent, divorce or unemployment) and there are good reasons for avoiding disruption of a child's education.

Applications

Application forms are available from the charity's website or the correspondent. They can be submitted by the individual or, if the applicant is under 16, a third party. Grants are usually considered in February, July and September.

Financial information

Year end	31/08/2020
Income	£12,300
Total expenditure	£6,800

Further financial information

Full accounts were not available to view on the Charity Commission's website due to the charity's low income. We have therefore estimated the charity's grant total based on its total expenditure.

Other information

Our research shows that this charity consults and co-operates with Bristol Municipal Charities in some cases.

Anthony Edmonds Charity

 £11,600 (2019/20)

Correspondent: Fran Greenfield, Clerk, 43 Meadowland Road, Bristol BS10 7PW (tel: 0117 909 8308; email: fran. greenfield@blueyonder.co.uk)

www.aedmondscharity.org

CC number: 286709

Eligibility

Children and young people up to the age of 25 who live in any of the ancient parishes of Henbury, Westbury and Horfield.

Types of grant

Grants are awarded to help with activities of a broadly educational nature. This can include apprenticeships, courses and less formal projects, whether or not they lead to qualifications, which may be academic, artistic, technical, social or sporting.

Applications

An application form can be downloaded from the charity's website and should be returned by email or post. You can contact the clerk for a hard copy.

Financial information

Year end	30/09/2020
Income	£1,100
Total expenditure	£12,900

Further financial information

Full accounts were not available to view on the Charity Commission's website due to the charity's low income. We have therefore estimated the grant total based on the charity's total expenditure.

The Portishead Nautical Trust

 £8,200 (2019/20)

Correspondent: Mrs E. Knight, Secretary, 108 High Street, Portishead, Bristol BS20 6AJ (tel: 01275 847463)

https://www. portisheadnauticaltrust.org

CC number: 228876

Eligibility

Young people under the age of 25 who are in need as a result of difficult circumstances such as ill health, financial difficulty or parental neglect. Preference is given to those based in North Somerset, Bristol or surrounding areas.

Types of grant

One-off grants are given for urgent needs. Small grants and bursaries are also given for educational/specialised courses or trips.

Applications

Application forms can be downloaded from the charity's website. Completed forms can be returned either by email or post. Applications must be supported by a third party (such as a GP or social worker) who can confirm the applicant's circumstances. The trustees meet on a quarterly basis to consider grant applications.

Financial information

Year end	31/03/2020
Income	£92,700
Total expenditure	£108,500

Other information

This charity makes grants to organisations that support children in the same area of benefit.

The Redcliffe Parish Charity

(£) £3,800 (2019/20)

Correspondent: The Trustees, 18 Kingston Road, Nailsea, Bristol, North Somerset BS48 4RD (tel: 01275 854057; email: redcliffeparishclerk@mail. com)

CC number: 203916

Eligibility

Residents of Bristol who are in need, with preference given to those living in the ecclesiastical parish of St Mary Redcliffe with Temple and St John the Baptist in Bedminster.

Types of grant

One-off grants are awarded according to need.

Exclusions

The charity does not award grants for school/college fees or recurring expenses. Loans are unavailable.

Applications

Applications should be made through third-party organisations (social services, housing associations, etc.) Prospective applicants should consult a third party to apply on their behalf.

Financial information

Year end	30/06/2020
Income	£8,000
Total expenditure	£8,500

Further financial information

Full accounts were not available to view on the Charity Commission's website due to the charity's low income. We have therefore estimated the charity's grant total based on its total expenditure.

St Monica Trust

(£) £232,300 (2020)

Correspondent: Community Fund Team, Cote Lane, Westbury-on-Trym, Bristol BS9 3UN (tel: 0117 949 4006; email: info@stmonicatrust.org.uk)

 www.stmonicatrust.org.uk

CC number: 202151

Eligibility

People who have a physical disability or long-term physical health problem and live in Bristol, South Gloucestershire, North Somerset or Bath and North East Somerset. Applicants must have a low income, limited savings and be over 40 years old.

Types of grant

Gifts

One-off grants to help towards disability-related items or adaptations, domestic appliances, and furniture and flooring. This list is not exhaustive and gifts will be considered for anything that will make a positive difference to the applicant's everyday life.

Short-term grants

Monthly payments, mostly of £110 for an average of three to six months, designed to help during a time of crisis. Grants may help with, for example, debt relief, adjusting to a sudden loss of income, unexpected medical costs or while claiming for disability benefits.

Exclusions

Grants are not awarded for: holidays, gardening, bankruptcy fees, funeral expenses, decorating labour costs, respite care, care home fees and daily living costs.

Applications

Apply on a form available online or by contacting the trust. Applicants can apply directly or through a third party.

Financial information

Year end	31/12/2020
Income	£44,110,000
Total expenditure	£47,540,000

Further financial information

During the year, 329 gifts and 192 short-term grants were awarded.

Other information

Grants are also made to organisations whose aim is to support a similar group of beneficiaries. The trust also provides sheltered housing and retirement accommodation, support services, and nursing and residential care.

Cornwall

The Beckly Trust

(£) £5,900 (2019/20)

Correspondent: Stephen Trahair, Trustee, 10 South Hill, Stoke, Plymouth, Devon PL1 5RR (tel: 01752 675071; email: stephentrahair@blueyonder.co.uk)

CC number: 235763

Eligibility

Children who live in either the city of Plymouth or the district of Caradon (Cornwall) and are in need as result of illness or disability.

Types of grant

Grants are given according to need.

Applications

Apply in writing to the correspondent.

Financial information

Year end	11/06/2020
Income	£9,200
Total expenditure	£13,000

Further financial information

Full accounts were not available to view on the Charity Commission's website due to the trust's low income. We have therefore estimated the trust's grant total based on its total expenditure.

Other information

This trust also makes grants to other charitable organisations that provide for children who are disadvantaged or have disabilities.

Cornwall Community Foundation

(£) £153,700 (2020)

Correspondent: The Grants Team, Suite 1, Sheers Barton, Lawhitton, Launceston, Cornwall PL15 9NJ (tel: 01566 779333; email: office@cornwallfoundation.com)

https://www. cornwallcommunityfoundation. com

CC number: 1099977

Eligibility

People in need who live in Cornwall and the Isles of Scilly.

Types of grant

A number of funds are available to individuals. Refer to the foundation's website for details of current and open grants. Grants for individuals tend to be between £200 and £1,000 and focus on young carers, young people who are disadvantaged, mental health and well-being, warmth and health in winter and people who are in crisis.

Exclusions

See the relevant fund on the website for details of exclusions.

Applications

Details on how to apply can be found on the community foundation's website.

Financial information

Year end	31/12/2020
Income	£3,140,000
Total expenditure	£1,960,000

Further financial information

In 2020, the foundation awarded £1.64 million to 741 community projects and individuals. A breakdown of the proportion given to individuals was not provided. The grant total has been estimated by totalling grants awarded from the following funds, which, according to the website, make grants to individuals: Crisis Fund, The Duke of Cornwall's Benevolent Fund, Emily Bolitho Trust Fund and The Worval Foundation.

Other information

This is one of the 47 UK community foundations, which distribute funding for a wide range of purposes. Grant schemes tend to change frequently – consult the foundation's website for details of current programmes and upcoming deadlines.

The Cornwall Retired Clergy, Widows of the Clergy and their Dependants Fund

£ £11,700 (2019)

Correspondent: The Trustees, Truro Diocesan Board of Finance Ltd, Church House, Woodland Court, Truro Business Park, Threemilestone, Cornwall TR4 9NH (tel: 01872 274351; email: finance@truro.anglican.org)

CC number: 289675

Eligibility

Widows/widowers, former/separated spouses or children of deceased members of the clergy who live in, or have worked in, the diocese of Truro. Retired Anglican and Church of England clergy who are resident in, or have connections with, the diocese of Truro are also eligible for support.

Types of grant

Grants are given according to need.

Applications

Apply in writing to the correspondent.

Financial information

Year end	31/12/2019
Income	£12,400
Total expenditure	£13,000

Further financial information

Full accounts were not available to view on the Charity Commission's website due to the fund's low income. We have therefore estimated the fund's grant total based on its total expenditure.

Charity of John Davey

£ £7,700 (2019/20)

Correspondent: The Trustees, Tregenna Lodge, Crane, Camborne, Cornwall TR14 7QX (tel: 01209 718853; email: pbfhayle@hotmail.co.uk)

CC number: 232127

Eligibility

Ex-miners, or their widows, who live in the parish of Gwenapp, are aged 70 and over and have worked in a mine for a minimum of five consecutive years. Support is also available to miners, of whatever age, who have worked in a mine for any period of time and are unable to work either temporarily or permanently due to illness, accident, disability or other medical conditions.

Types of grant

Grants are awarded according to need.

Applications

Apply in writing to the correspondent.

Financial information

Year end	30/06/2020
Income	£13,800
Total expenditure	£8,600

Further financial information

Full accounts were not available to view on the Charity Commission's website due to the charity's low income. We have therefore estimated the charity's grant total based on its total expenditure.

The Helston Welfare Trust

£ £500 (2019/20)

Correspondent: The Trustees, The Guildhall, Helston, Cornwall TR13 8ST (tel: 01326 572063; email: townclerk@helstontc.com)

CC number: 1014972

Eligibility

People in need who live in the area administered by Helston Town Council (parish of Helston as constituted on 1 April, 1985).

Types of grant

Grants are given according to need.

Applications

Apply in writing to the correspondent. Applications can be submitted directly by the individual or through a third party, such as a social worker or Citizens Advice.

Financial information

Year end	31/03/2020
Income	£2,700
Total expenditure	£1,440

Further financial information

Full accounts were not available to view on the Charity Commission's website due to the trust's low income. We have therefore estimated the trust's grant total based on its total expenditure.

Charity of Thomas Henwood

£ £6,600 (2020)

Correspondent: Jennifer Moyle, Trustee, Homeleigh, Gunwalloe, Helston, Cornwall TR12 7QG (tel: 01326 564806)

CC number: 206765

Eligibility

People who live in the parish of Gunwalloe and are unemployed, sick or retired and in need.

Types of grant

One-off or recurrent grants are made according to need. The charity also awards grants for the provision of nurses and to assist people recovering from illness. Its income is also used to care for graves in the churchyard if no relatives are still alive.

Applications

Apply in writing to the trustees. Applications are considered in March and December.

Financial information

Year end	31/12/2020
Income	£6,800
Total expenditure	£7,300

Further financial information

Full accounts were not available to view on the Charity Commission's website due to the charity's low income. We have therefore estimated the charity's grant total based on its total expenditure.

United Charities of Liskeard

£ £850 (2020)

Correspondent: The Trustees, 12 Trecarne View, St Cleer, Liskeard, Cornwall PL14 5BS (tel: 07989 320193; email: haywards.334@gmail.com)

CC number: 215173

Eligibility

Residents of Liskeard who are in need.

Types of grant

Grants are awarded according to need.

Applications

Apply in writing to the correspondent.

Financial information

Year end	31/12/2020
Income	£2,000
Total expenditure	£1,900

Further financial information

Full accounts were not available to view on the Charity Commission's website due to the charity's low income. We have therefore estimated the charity's grant total based on its total expenditure.

Other information

The charity also awards grants to organisations.

Devon

Brixton Feoffee Trust

£ £4,900 (2020/21)

Correspondent: The Trustees, 15 Cherry Tree Drive, Brixton, Plymouth, Devon PL8 2DD (tel: 01752 880262; email: brixtonfeoffeetrust@googlemail.com)

CC number: 203604

Eligibility

People in need who live in the parish of Brixton, near Plymouth.

Types of grant

One-off and recurrent grants are available according to need. Grants have been given for disability aids, essential household items, school travel costs, independent living alarms and assistance with rent payments.

Applications

Application forms are available from the correspondent or to download from the charity's website. They can be submitted directly by the individual or through a social worker, Citizens Advice or other welfare agency or third party. They are considered throughout the year.

Financial information

Year end	31/03/2021
Income	£38,500
Total expenditure	£35,500

Crediton United Charities

£ £810 (2019/20)

Correspondent: Karen Limon, Clerk to the Trustees, The Armstrong Room, 5 Parr House, Lennard Road, Crediton, Devon EX17 2AP (tel: 01363 776529)

CC number: 247038

Eligibility

Residents in the town of Crediton and the parish of Crediton Hamlets who are in need.

Types of grant

Grants are awarded according to need for goods and services.

Exclusions

The charity does not award cash grants. Grants cannot be used for the relief of public funds such as rates or taxes, nor for items or services that are available to the applicant through statutory benefits.

Applications

Applicants should contact the clerk in writing, by email or by telephone to request an application form.

Financial information

Year end	31/08/2020
Income	£16,300
Total expenditure	£9,400

Further financial information

During the year, three grants totalling £810 were awarded to individuals.

Other information

The charity owns and operates eight almshouses facilities. Residents' water bills are paid for by the charity and gifts are distributed to residents at Christmas. Grants are also made to organisations.

Devon Community Foundation

£ £24,100 (2019/20)

Correspondent: The Grants Team, The Factory, Leat Street, Tiverton EX16 5LL (tel: 01884 235887; email: grants@devoncf.com)

 devoncf.com/apply/apply-for-a-grant/individual-grants

CC number: 1057923

Eligibility

People in need who live in Devon.

Types of grant

A number of funds are available to individuals. Refer to the foundation's website for details of current and open grants.

Applications

Details on how to apply can be found on the community foundation's website.

Financial information

Year end	31/03/2020
Income	£2,270,000
Total expenditure	£1,720,000

Further financial information

Grants totalling £24,100 were awarded to 16 individuals during 2019/20.

Other information

This is one of the 47 UK community foundations, which distribute funding for a wide range of purposes. Grant schemes tend to change frequently – consult the foundation's website for details of current programmes and upcoming deadlines.

The Devon Educational Trust

£ £7,600 (2020)

Correspondent: The Trustees, PO Box 86, Teignmouth, Devon TQ14 8ZT (tel: 01626 776653; email: devonedtrust@talktalk.net)

 devoneducationaltrust.co.uk

CC number: 1157674

Eligibility

Children and young people under the age of 25 who live in Devon. Applicants must live in Devon on a permanent basis for at least twelve months. Temporary residence while at university does not qualify.

Types of grant

Welfare

Grants are available for clothing, equipment, tools and travel for people getting into work and to help with medical, emotional and learning support for children with special needs. Grants can also be provided for tuition and school trips for school-aged children.

Education

Grants for books, laptops, expeditions and travel costs are available for students in higher education. Grants for equipment, lessons and travel are also provided for people involved in sports and the arts.

Exclusions

Support for higher degree courses and boarding/school fees is only provided in exceptional circumstances.

Applications

Application forms can be downloaded from the trust's website. Application deadlines fall on 1 February, 1 June and 1 October each year.

Financial information

Year end	31/12/2020
Income	£43,900
Total expenditure	£21,700

Further financial information

Grants were awarded to 37 individuals.

Other information

The trust also provides assistance to organisations for the promotion of education or improvement in conditions of life.

Exminster Feoffees

£ £1,500 (2020)

Correspondent: The Trustees, 2 Dryfield, Exminster, Exeter, Devon EX6 8AL (email: exminster.feoffees@ gmail.com)

CC number: 212497

Eligibility

People in need who live in the parish of Exminster, Devon.

Types of grant

One-off grants are made according to need.

Applications

Apply in writing to the correspondent.

Financial information

Year end	31/12/2020
Income	£2,400
Total expenditure	£1,700

Further financial information

Full accounts were not available to view on the Charity Commission's website due to the charity's low income. We have therefore estimated the grant total based on the charity's total expenditure.

The Maudlyn Lands Charity

£ £5,800 (2019/20)

Correspondent: The Trustees, Blue Haze, Down Road, Tavistock, Devon PL19 9AG (tel: 01822 612983; email: avda10@dsl.pipex.com)

CC number: 202577

Eligibility

People who live in the Plympton and Sparkwell areas of Devon who are in need.

Types of grant

Grants are awarded according to need.

Applications

Apply in writing to the correspondent.

Financial information

Year end	31/10/2020
Income	£7,300
Total expenditure	£6,400

Further financial information

Full accounts were not available to view on the Charity Commission's website due to the charity's low income. We have therefore estimated the charity's grant total based on its total expenditure.

Northcott Devon Foundation

 £174,700 (2019/20)

Correspondent: The Trustees, 1B Victoria Road, Exmouth, Devon EX8 1DL (tel: 01395 269204; email: emmap893@btconnect.com)

🌐 https://northcottdevonfoundation. com

CC number: 201277

Eligibility

People who live in Devon and are in need as the result of illness, injury, bereavement or exceptional disadvantage.

Types of grant

Grants are typically one-off payments that rarely exceed £200. According to the foundation's website, applicants requesting household goods are encouraged to buy good quality second-hand items from recycling centres or charity shops.

Exclusions

According to the foundation's website, grants are not available for debts such as Council Tax or energy bills, but other debts may be considered if the applicant has negotiated a substantial reduction in the amount owed.

Applications

Application forms are available on the foundation's website and require a sponsor. Examples of sponsors given on the foundation's website include doctors, social workers, Citizens Advice, health visitors, headteachers, and priests or other faith leaders.

Financial information

Year end	31/05/2020
Income	£190,600
Total expenditure	£250,700

Other information

The foundation also supports organisations.

Saint Petrox Trust Lands

£ £20,500 (2019/20)

Correspondent: Hilary Bastone, Clerk/ Treasurer, Apartment 12, Vavasour House, North Embankment, Dartmouth, Devon TQ6 9PW (tel: 01803 835455; email: hilarybastone@hotmail.co.uk)

CC number: 230593

Eligibility

People in need who live in the parish of Dartmouth, with a preference for residents of the parish of St Petrox and St Saviour with St Clement.

Types of grant

Grants are given according to need.

Applications

Apply in writing to the correspondent.

Financial information

Year end	31/03/2020
Income	£70,100
Total expenditure	£50,300

Other information

The charity also funds the repair and restoration of historical buildings in the area of benefit.

Sidmouth Consolidated Charities

£ £27,300 (2020)

Correspondent: The Administrator, PO Box 99, Sidmouth, Devon EX10 1DH (tel: 01395 516956; email: info@ sidmouthconsolidatedcharities.co.uk)

 https://www. sidmouthconsolidatedcharities. co.uk

CC number: 207081

Eligibility

Residents in the area covered by the Sidmouth Town Council who are in need. This includes Sidford, Sidbury and Salcombe Regis.

Types of grant

Grants have been made towards furnishings, appliances (washing machines, fridge/freezers, etc.), medical equipment, mobility aids, rent deposits and funeral costs.

Applications

Applications can be made online using a form on the funder's website.

Financial information

Year end	31/12/2020
Income	£44,600
Total expenditure	£69,600

Further financial information
The grant total has been estimated.

The Sidmouth Educational Foundation

 £2,600 (2020)

Correspondent: The Administrator, PO Box 99, Sidmouth, Devon EX10 1DH (tel: 01395 513079; email: info@ sidmouthconsolidatedcharities.co.uk)

https://sidmouthconsolidated charities.co.uk

CC number: 306892

Eligibility
Children and adults who live in the area covered by the Sidmouth Town Council. This includes Sidmouth, Sidford, Sidbury and Salcombe Regis.

Types of grant
Grants are awarded towards school uniforms, school trips, extra tuition costs, books, computers, travel expenses and course fees.

Applications
Applications can be made online using a form on the foundation's website.

Financial information
Year end	31/12/2020
Income	£9,300
Total expenditure	£2,900

Further financial information
Full accounts were not available to view on the Charity Commission's website due to the foundation's low income. We have therefore estimated the foundation's grant total based on its total expenditure.

Other information
This foundation also makes grants to organisations.

Nicholas Watts' Gift (Brownsdon and Tremayne Estate)

 £8,600 (2019/20)

Correspondent: The Trustees, 17 Chapel Street, Tavistock, Devon PL19 8DX (tel: 01822 612822)

CC number: 203271

Eligibility
People who live in Tavistock and are in need.

Types of grant
Grants are given according to need.

Applications
Apply in writing to the correspondent.

Financial information
Year end	30/06/2020
Income	£24,000
Total expenditure	£9,600

Further financial information
Full accounts were not available to view on the Charity Commission's website due to the charity's low income. We have therefore estimated the charity's grant total based on its total expenditure.

East Devon

Adventure Trust for Girls

 £1,200 (2019/20)

Correspondent: The Trustees, 28 Richmond Road, Exmouth, Devon EX8 2NB (tel: 01395 265391; email: info@adventuretrustforgirls.org.uk)

www.adventuretrustforgirls.org.uk

CC number: 800999

Eligibility
Girls and young women aged 10–23 on the first day of the venture who live or attend school within eight miles of Exmouth Town Hall. This excludes areas west of the River Exe estuary and north of the M5. Consult the trust's website for a map of eligible areas.

Types of grant
Grants are given to help with the costs of an adventure. This could include travelling, volunteering, teaching English abroad, music camps and any other activity that develops the individual's self-confidence, personal skills, physical development, character, leadership, team spirit and sense of social responsibility.

Applications
Application forms can be downloaded from the trust's website and must be submitted directly by the individual.

Financial information
Year end	30/09/2020
Income	£9,400
Total expenditure	£1,300

Further financial information
Full accounts were not available to view on the Charity Commission's website due to the trust's low income. We have therefore estimated the trust's grant total based on its total expenditure.

Exmouth Welfare Trust

 £21,000 (2020)

Correspondent: The Trustees, PO Box 16, Exmouth, Devon EX8 3YT (tel: 01395 274473)

CC number: 269382

Eligibility
People who live in the former urban district of Exmouth, comprising the parishes of Withycombe Raleigh and Littleham-cum-Exmouth, and are in need.

Types of grant
Grants of up to £250 are given according to need.

Applications
Apply in writing to the correspondent.

Financial information
Year end	31/12/2020
Income	£21,300
Total expenditure	£23,300

Further financial information
Full accounts were not available to view on the Charity Commission's website due to the trust's low income. We have therefore estimated the trust's grant total based on its total expenditure.

The David Gibbons Foundation

 £10,500 (2020/21)

Correspondent: The Trustees, 24 Philip Avenue, Barnstaple, Devon EX31 3AQ (tel: 07483 335759; email: enquiries@ gibbonstrusts.org)

gibbonstrusts.org.uk

CC number: 1134727

Eligibility
Older people, people with physical or mental illnesses or disabilities and people in financial hardship in Devon, with a preference for those from East Devon.

Types of grant
Grants are awarded according to need.

Exclusions
Grants are not made for: fees or payments of an ongoing nature (such as payments for education); trips overseas for any reason; private schools; restrospective expenditure.

Applications
Application forms and further information on how to apply can be found on the foundation's website.

Financial information
Year end	31/03/2021
Income	£119,000
Total expenditure	£121,100

Other information
Grants are also made to organisations.

Honiton United Charities

(£) £1,600 (2020)

Correspondent: The Trustees, Ford Simey, 118 High Street, Honiton, Devon EX14 1JP (tel: 01404 540024; email: psl@fordsimey.co.uk)

CC number: 200900

Eligibility

People in need who live in the borough of Honiton.

Types of grant

Our previous research suggests that the charity awards one-off and recurrent grants, and that pensions are paid quarterly.

Applications

Apply in writing to the correspondent.

Financial information

Year end	31/12/2020
Income	£9,100
Total expenditure	£3,600

Further financial information

Full accounts were not available to view on the Charity Commission's website due to the charity's low income. We have therefore estimated the charity's grant total based on its total expenditure.

Other information

The charity also makes grants to organisations.

The Ottery Feoffee Charity

(£) £1,500 (2020)

Correspondent: The Trustees, c/o Gilbert Stephens, 7 Broad Street, Ottery St Mary, Devon EX11 1BS (email: osmlaw@gilbertstephens.co.uk)

CC number: 202095

Eligibility

People in need who live in the ancient parish of Ottery St Mary. Priority is usually given to older people and people with disabilities.

Types of grant

One-off grants are made according to need.

Applications

Apply in writing to the correspondent.

Financial information

Year end	31/12/2020
Income	£79,400
Total expenditure	£78,300

Other information

The charity also runs a small day centre.

Thomas Axe's Non-Ecclesiastical

(£) £1,400 (2019)

Correspondent: David Coral, 50 Claremont Field, Ottery St Mary, Devon EX11 1NP (tel: 01404 813961; email: david.coral683844@btinternet.com)

CC number: 202725

Eligibility

People in need who live in Ottery St Mary, Devon, with a preference for older people.

Types of grant

Grants are made according to need.

Applications

Apply in writing to the correspondent.

Financial information

Year end	31/12/2019
Income	£1,800
Total expenditure	£1,600

Further financial information

Full accounts were not available to view on the Charity Commission's website due to the charity's low income. We have therefore estimated the charity's grant total based on its total expenditure.

Exeter

Central Exeter Relief-in-Need Charity

(£) £7,100 (2019)

Correspondent: The Trustees, 1 Fairview Terrace, Exeter, Devon EX1 3SQ (tel: 07968 338371)

CC number: 1022288

Eligibility

People in need who live in the parish of Central Exeter.

Types of grant

According to our previous research, the charity provides one-off grants, usually of £50 to £150, for basic needs such as furniture, assistance with heating bills, children's clothing and mobility aids.

Applications

Applications are accepted through established care agencies such as social services or other welfare organisations.

Financial information

Year end	31/12/2019
Income	£5,400
Total expenditure	£7,900

Further financial information

Full accounts were not available to view on the Charity Commission's website due to the charity's low income. We have therefore estimated the charity's grant total based on its total expenditure.

Exeter Dispensary Charity

(£) £36,700 (2020)

Correspondent: David Bostock, Applications Secretary, Ridge Farm, Broadhembury, Honiton, Devon EX14 3LU (tel: 01404 841401; email: applications@exeterdispensary.org.uk)

 https://www.exeterdispensary.org.uk

CC number: 1189534

Eligibility

People who live in Exeter and are in need due to illness, disability or financial hardship.

Types of grant

Around 90% of the charity's disposable income is given as supportive grants to individuals. These grants can be given for a range of purposes such as medical aids, clothing, footwear, beds and bedding, kitchen appliances, utility and telephone bills, carpets and so on.

Exclusions

The charity does not normally provide grants for purely educational purposes, computers or home adaptations unless essential.

Applications

Application forms can be downloaded from the charity's website and must be made on behalf of the individual by a support worker or advocate.

Financial information

Year end	31/12/2020
Income	£42,100
Total expenditure	£39,000

Further financial information

The charity provided 200 supportive grants to individuals during the financial period.

Other information

This charity was formerly known as Exeter Dispensary and Aid-In-Sickness Fund. In May 2020 it re-registered as a CIO and changed its name to Exeter Dispensary Charity. Grants are also given to other organisations with similar objectives.

Exeter Homes Trust

 £10,100 (2020)

Correspondent: The Trustees, 6 Southernhay West, Exeter EX1 1JG (tel: 01392 421162; email: info@exeterhomestrust.com)

https://www.exeterhomestrust.com

CC number: 201530

Eligibility

Welfare
People who live within a ten-mile radius of Exeter centre and are in need.

Education
Educational grants are made to students under the age of 25 who live within a 15-mile radius of Exeter centre.

Types of grant

Welfare
Welfare grants are awarded according to need.

Education
Educational grants are made to help with higher education costs.

Applications
Contact the charity to request an application form. Application forms are sent by email or post. As part of the application process, all applicants will be interviewed by one of the charity's directors.

Financial information

Year end	31/12/2020
Income	£693,300
Total expenditure	£1,020,000

Other information
Welfare grants are made by the amalgamated Exeter Relief in Need (Charity Commission no. 1002152) and educational grants by Exeter Advancement in Life (Charity Commission no. 1002151). The priority of Essex Homes Trust is to provide accommodation to people aged 55 and over who have lived in Exeter, or within a ten-mile radius of Exeter, and are in financial need. The trust currently owns and operates 143 housing facilities in eight different locations, all within a reasonable distance to the city of Exeter.

The Exeter Nursing Association Trust

£16,600 (2019/20)

Correspondent: John Redwood, Trustee, Lower Hawkerland, Sidmouth Road, Aylesbeare, Exeter, Devon EX5 2JJ (tel: 01395 232122; email: johncredwood@btinternet.com)

CC number: 202314

Eligibility
People in need who are receiving, or in need of, medical/nursing care, and employees or ex-employees of the association and the nursing profession who live in the city and county of Exeter.

Types of grant
The trust provides and supplements nursing services of any kind. One-off grants are also made.

Applications
Apply in writing to the correspondent. Patients should write via their attending health visitor or district nurse; nurses should write via a senior nurse at Community Nursing Services Exeter Localities.

Financial information

Year end	31/03/2020
Income	£9,900
Total expenditure	£36,800

Further financial information
Full accounts were not available to view on the Charity Commission's website due to the trust's low income. We have therefore estimated the trust's grant total based on its total expenditure.

Other information
The trust also supports organisations concerned with nursing.

The Exeter Relief-in-Need Charity

£9,800 (2020)

Correspondent: Steven Sitch, 6 Southernhay West, Exeter, Devon EX1 1JG (tel: 01392 421162; email: info@exetermunicipalcharity.org.uk)

CC number: 1002152

Eligibility
People in need who live within a ten-mile radius of Exeter centre.

Types of grant
One-off grants, usually of between £50 and £150, can be made towards the purchase of clothing, children's shoes, school uniforms, bedding, soft furnishings and floor coverings. Assistance can also be given with the settlement of fuel, heating and lighting bills.

Exclusions
Grants cannot be made for debt repayment, interest on loans, rent, mortgage or Council Tax arrears.

Applications
Application forms are available from the correspondent and are dispatched by post or email. Grants are means tested and all applicants are interviewed by one of the directors.

Financial information

Year end	31/12/2020
Income	£11,800
Total expenditure	£10,900

Further financial information
Full accounts were not available to view on the Charity Commission's website due to the charity's low income. We have therefore estimated the charity's grant total based on its total expenditure.

Other information
This charity is part of Exeter Municipal Charities.

The Charity of John Shere and Others

£3,600 (2020)

Correspondent: David Tucker, 5 Elm Grove Gardens, Topsham, Exeter, Devon EX3 0EL (tel: 01392 873168; email: tucker-david@talktalk.net)

CC number: 220736

Eligibility
Older people in need who have lived in the parish of Topsham for at least three years.

Types of grant
Grants are given according to need.

Applications
Apply in writing to the correspondent.

Financial information

Year end	31/12/2020
Income	£3,900
Total expenditure	£4,000

Further financial information
Full accounts were not available to view on the Charity Commission's website due to the charity's low income. We have therefore estimated the charity's grant total based on its total expenditure.

Mid Devon

Charity of Edward Blagdon

£11,000 (2019/20)

Correspondent: The Trustees, 29 Lime Tree Mead, Tiverton, Devon EX16 4PX (tel: 01884 258595)

CC number: 244676

Eligibility

Residents of Tiverton and Washfield who are in need.

Types of grant

Grants are awarded according to need.

Applications

Apply in writing to the correspondent.

Financial information

Year end	05/04/2020
Income	£16,600
Total expenditure	£12,300

Further financial information

Full accounts were not available to view on the Charity Commission's website due to the charity's low income. We have therefore estimated the grant total based on the charity's total expenditure.

Silverton Parochial Trust

£ £7,600 (2020)

Correspondent: Maggie Smith, Secretary to the Trustees, 52 Wyndham Road, Silverton, Exeter, Devon EX5 4JZ (tel: 01392 860235; email: silvertonparochialtrust@gmail.com or use the contact form on the website)

 www.silvertonparochialtrust.co.uk

CC number: 201255

Eligibility

People in need who live in the parish of Silverton.

Types of grant

Awards are given towards anything that will help relieve hardship or need, such as stairlifts, personal alarm systems, respite holidays and carpets.

Exclusions

Funding is not given for the relief of rates or towards taxes.

Applications

Application forms are available to download from the trust's website. Paper forms can also be obtained from a number of locations around Silverton, details of which can be found on the website. The trustees meet ten times a year to consider applications.

Financial information

Year end	31/12/2020
Income	£36,600
Total expenditure	£25,500

Further financial information

The 2020 annual report states that grants totalling £15,300 were awarded to individuals and community projects during the year. We have estimated that around £7,600 was awarded to individuals.

Other information

Grants are also made to organisations providing assistance for people in need who live in the parish.

North Devon

Barnstaple Almshouses

 £930 (2020/21)

Correspondent: Mrs J. Northridge, Charity Manager, Chudleigh House, Grange Road, Bideford EX39 4AR

https://www.barnstaplealmshouses.co.uk

CC number: 1186225

Eligibility

Welfare

People in need who live in Barnstaple.

Education

Students who live in Barnstaple and the surrounding five-mile area who either attend a local school or college or require support for university.

Types of grant

Welfare

The charity's website states:

Applications for the Relief in Need Grant are not exclusive to, but may include:
- Immediate aid in the event of an emergency.
- Travel and other expenses for visiting people in hospital or other institutions which are out of the area.
- Provision of essential goods to maintain an acceptable standard of living such as bedding, clothing, heating appliances, white goods, furniture and carpets.
- Provisions for home repairs such as repainting, insulation, carpentry and skilled engineering works.
- Payments towards the cost of adaptation to the homes of the disabled
- Payments for food for special diets, medical or other aids, nursing requisites or comforts
- Provision of invalid chairs for the disabled, handicapped or infirm.
- Provisions to support the elderly or lonely
- Special payments to relieve sudden distress

Education

The charity's website states:

Applications for the Apprentice / Educational Grant are not exclusive to but may include:
- Supply of tools or books
- Payment of fees for instruction or examination
- Travelling expenses

Applications

Welfare

Application forms can be downloaded from the charity's website. The charity favours applications requested through a recognised agency, for example social services or another public authority or charity.

Education

Application forms can be downloaded from the charity's website. Applications require a professional reference from a tutor, teacher or faculty head, which must be submitted with the application stating that the grant is to assist the applicant's progression into further education or apprenticeship.

Financial information

Year end	30/06/2021
Income	£175,500
Total expenditure	£183,500

The Barnstaple and North Devon Dispensary Fund

£ £2,900 (2020)

Correspondent: The Trustees, 17 Sloc Lane, Landkey, Barnstaple, Devon EX32 0UF (tel: 01271 831551; email: bandnddf@gmail.com)

CC number: 215805

Eligibility

People in need who live in Barnstaple and surrounding parishes in North Devon.

Types of grant

One-off grants are given according to need. This includes safety and medical equipment/appliances, hospital travel expenses and specialised communication equipment.

Exclusions

Grants are not available for the following:
- To alleviate financial hardship
- For non-medical equipment or services
- For education and/or training
- For applicants living outside the charity's catchment area

Applications

Apply in writing to the correspondent via a healthcare/social care professional.

Financial information

Year end	31/12/2020
Income	£10,200
Total expenditure	£3,200

Further financial information

Full accounts were not available to view on the Charity Commission's website due to the fund's low income. We have therefore estimated the fund's grant total based on its total expenditure.

Bridge Trust

 £2,400 (2020)

Correspondent: Chamberlain, The Bridge Trust, 7 Bridge Chambers, The Strand, Barnstaple, Devon EX31 1HB (tel: 01271 343995; email: chamberlain@ barumbridgetrust.org)

 www.barumbridgetrust.org

CC number: 1184834

Eligibility
People in need who live within a five-mile radius of the Guild Hall in Barnstaple.

Types of grant
Samaritan Grants of up to £200 (£400 with the approval of the Chair of the Grants Committee) are available to individuals towards the cost of furniture or domestic appliances.

Applications
Apply in writing to the correspondent, including as much information as possible. Applications can be made at any time. Payments are normally made to organisations or the supplier of items/ services, not the applicant.

Financial information
Year end	31/12/2020
Income	£4,760,000
Total expenditure	£242,400

Other information
The trust's main priority is the maintenance of properties in Barnstaple and making grants to local organisations.

The Elizabeth Smith Trust for Widows

 £2,000 (2019/20)

Correspondent: The Revd John Roles, Trustee, 6 Adelaide Terrace, Ilfracombe, Devon EX34 9JR (tel: 01271 863350; email: frjohnroles@gmail.co.uk)

CC number: 206557

Eligibility
Widows in Devon who are in need.

Types of grant
Pensions are paid half yearly.

Applications
Apply in writing to the correspondent.

Financial information
Year end	05/04/2020
Income	£4,800
Total expenditure	£2,200

Further financial information
Full accounts were not available to view on the Charity Commission's website due to the charity's low income. We have therefore estimated the charity's grant total based on its total expenditure.

Plymouth

The Beckly Trust
See entry on page 417

Joseph Jory's Charity

 £8,800 (2019)

Correspondent: The Trustees, c/o Wolferstans Solicitors, 60–66 North Hill, Plymouth, Devon PL4 8EP (tel: 01752 292382)

CC number: 235138

Eligibility
Widows on a low income who are aged 50 years or over and have resided in Plymouth, or its neighbouring area, for a minimum of seven years.

Types of grant
Recurrent payments in the form of pensions.

Applications
Apply in writing to the correspondent.

Financial information
Year end	31/12/2019
Income	£15,200
Total expenditure	£9,800

Further financial information
Full accounts were not available to view on the Charity Commission's website due to the charity's low income. We have therefore estimated the grant total based on the charity's total expenditure.

The Ladies Aid Society and the Eyre Charity

 £8,700 (2020)

Correspondent: The Trustees, 14 Court Park, Thurlestone, Kingsbridge, Devon TQ7 3LX (tel: 01548 560891)

CC number: 202137

Eligibility
Unmarried women, widows and divorcees who are in need and live, or have lived, in Plymouth.

Types of grant
Grants are made according to need.

Applications
Apply in writing to the correspondent.

Financial information
Year end	31/12/2020
Income	£12,500
Total expenditure	£19,300

Further financial information
Full accounts were not available to view on the Charity Commission's website due to the charity's low income. We have therefore estimated the charity's grant total based on its total expenditure.

Orphan's Aid Educational Foundation (Plymouth)

 £1,400 (2020)

Correspondent: Vanessa Steer, 184 Mannamead Road, Plymouth, Devon PL3 5RE (tel: 01752 703280; email: v_steer@yahoo.co.uk)

CC number: 306770

Eligibility
Children and young people who live in Plymouth and are in need. Preference is given to children with one parent or families experiencing severe hardship.

Types of grant
Grants are awarded in the form of higher education scholarships. Grants for clothing, tools, books and more general financial assistance required for entry into a trade or profession are also available.

Applications
Apply in writing to the correspondent.

Financial information
Year end	31/12/2020
Income	£3,000
Total expenditure	£1,500

Further financial information
Full accounts were not available to view on the Charity Commission's website due to the foundation's low income. We have therefore estimated the foundation's grant total based on its total expenditure.

Plymouth Public Dispensary

 £15,600 (2020)

Correspondent: Clerk to the Trustees, 81D Higher Compton Road, Plymouth, Devon PL3 5JD (tel: 01752 782758; email: admin@ppdtrust.co.uk)

www.ppdtrust.co.uk

CC number: 267658

Eligibility
Permanent residents of Plymouth who are experiencing financial hardship, whose need is further exacerbated by ill health, disability or any other medical condition.

Types of grant
Grants are awarded according to need.

Applications
Applications must be made on the individual's behalf by professionally qualified staff from the NHS, social workers, or from representatives of care agencies or charities. The nominated third party can request an application form from the clerk by email or telephone. Completed forms can be sent to the clerk at their postal or email address.

Financial information
Year end	31/12/2020
Income	£56,100
Total expenditure	£50,700

Further financial information
The smallest grant awarded to individuals during the year was £95 and the largest grant awarded was £2,000.

Other information
The charity also makes grants to organisations and charities whose work benefits people living in Plymouth.

South Hams

The Dodbrooke Parish Charity (Dodbrooke Feoffees)

 £8,100 (2021)

Correspondent: The Trustees, Springfield House, Ashleigh Road, Kingsbridge, Devon TQ7 1HB (tel: 01548 854321)

CC number: 800214

Eligibility
People in need who live in the parish of Kingsbridge in South Devon.

Types of grant
Grants are given according to need.

Applications
Apply in writing to the correspondent.

Financial information
Year end	31/12/2021
Income	£24,100
Total expenditure	£18,000

Further financial information
Full accounts were not available to view on the Charity Commission's website due to the charity's low income. We have therefore estimated the grant total based on the charity's total expenditure.

Other information
The charity also supports the parish church and rents property out to local residents.

Parish Lands (South Brent Feoffees)

£29,000 (2020)

Correspondent: John Blackler, Clerk to the Trustees, c/o Luscombe Maye Ltd, 6 Fore Street, South Brent, Devon TQ10 9BQ (tel: 01364 646180)

https://www.southbrent.org.uk/organisations/feoffes

CC number: 255283

Eligibility
Welfare
Residents of South Brent who are in need.

Education
Educational grants are available to current or former residents of the parish who are in post-18 education or training.

Types of grant
Welfare
Grants are awarded according to need.

Education
Educational grants are made to young people in post-18 education for support with costs associated with vocational training and university studies. The South Brent Community website states: 'Grants are not income related but reflect whether the student is studying away from home or living locally and in what year of study the application is made.'

Applications
Welfare
Applications for welfare grants should be made in writing to the correspondent.

Education
Application forms for educational grants are usually available to download on the charity's website. At the time of writing (November 2021) the charity's website was down; therefore, we advise applicants to contact the correspondent for an application form. All applications must include written evidence from the applicant's head of department or tutor confirming their attendance. Written evidence confirming an offer to a place of higher education will not suffice. Applicants should have already started their course before applying for funding. Each individual can apply once a year for three years. Application deadlines are available to view on the South Brent Community website.

Financial information
Year end	31/12/2020
Income	£63,300
Total expenditure	£56,200

Further financial information
Grants totalled £43,400 during the year. According to the charity's accounts, a third of the charity's annual income is awarded in welfare grants, a third is awarded in educational grants and a third is applied to the upkeep of the local parish church. We have used this framework to estimate the grant total.

Teignbridge

Cranbrook Charity

£3,500 (2019/20)

Correspondent: Stephen Purser, Trustee, Venn Farm, Bridford, Exeter, Devon EX6 7LF (tel: 01647 252328; email: purseratvenn@hotmail.com)

CC number: 249074

Eligibility
People in need who live in the parishes of Dunsford, Doddiscombsleigh and some parts of Holcombe Burnel.

Types of grant
Grants are given according to need. Grants may also be available for educational purposes for those under the age of 25.

Applications
Apply in writing to the correspondent.

Financial information
Year end	29/02/2020
Income	£13,100
Total expenditure	£7,700

Further financial information
Full accounts were not available to view on the Charity Commission's website due to the charity's low income. We have therefore estimated the grant total based on the charity's total expenditure.

Other information

Grants are also made to local organisations.

Torbay

Paignton Parish Charity

£ £2,500 (2019/20)

Correspondent: The Trustees, The Parish Office, The Vicarage, Palace Place, Paignton, Devon TQ3 3AQ (tel: 01803 551866; email: paigntonparishoffice@ gmail.com)

CC number: 240509

Eligibility

People in need who live in Paignton, particularly the wards of Preston, Blatchcombe, Coverdale and St Michaels with Goodrington.

Types of grant

Grants are awarded according to need. Previously, grants have been made for mobility scooters and safety improvements to homes.

Applications

Apply in writing to the correspondent.

Financial information

Year end	31/03/2020
Income	£52,000
Total expenditure	£38,100

Further financial information

According to the charity's accounts for 2019/20, the charity made grants totalling £5,100 to organisations and individuals. We have estimated that approximately half of the grant total was awarded to individuals.

Other information

Grants are also made to organisations. The charity also operates the Paignton Community Larder (food bank).

Torridge

The Bridge Trust (Bideford Bridge Trust)

£ £273,700 (2019/20)

Correspondent: The Steward, 23A The Quay, Bideford, Devon EX39 2PS (tel: 01237 473122; email: info@ bidefordbridgetrust.org.uk)

 https://www.bidefordbridgetrust. org.uk

CC number: 204536

Eligibility

Welfare

Residents of Bideford, and its immediate neighbourhood, who are in need.

Education

Students who are either resident in, or studying in, Bideford and its immediate neighbourhood are eligible for support. For full eligibility criteria, see the funder's website.

Types of grant

Welfare

The following grants are available:
- Support for people experiencing hardship
- Taxi vouchers for people over the age of 85 or people suffering from an illness or disability
- Business start-up grants for people who are currently unemployed or anticipating becoming unemployed and seeking to become self-employed or start a new business.

Education

The following educational grants are available from the trust. See the trust's website for eligibility criteria.
- Book and equipment grants of up to £300
- Hardship grants of £250
- Educational bursaries of up to £600 for students on their first, second or third year of a degree course
- Apprenticeship grants and vocational grants

Exclusions

The charity does not support postgraduate courses/students.

Applications

Application forms are available to download on the charity's website. Completed forms should be sent to the charity by post.

Financial information

Year end	21/12/2020
Income	£854,100
Total expenditure	£750,200

Other information

The charity also makes grants to organisations and to local schools to help with the cost of funding swimming lessons for pupils.

Peter Speccott

£ £1,500 (2020)

Correspondent: Claire Woolsey, Peter Peter and Wright, 6–8 Fore Street, Holsworthy, Devon EX22 6ED (tel: 01409 253262; email: clairewoolsey@ peterslaw.co.uk)

CC number: 203987

Eligibility

People in need who live in Holsworthy, Holsworthy Hamlets or the parish of Black Torrington, Devon.

Types of grant

Grants are given according to need.

Applications

Apply in writing to the correspondent.

Financial information

Year end	31/12/2020
Income	£3,800
Total expenditure	£1,600

Further financial information

Full accounts were not available to view on the Charity Commission's website due to the charity's low income. We have therefore estimated the charity's grant total based on its total expenditure.

West Devon

Okehampton United Charity

£ £3,600 (2020)

Correspondent: The Trustees, 15 Upper Crooked Meadow, Okehampton, Devon EX20 1WW (tel: 01837 55179; email: use the contact form available on the website)

 https://www.okehamptoncharities. org.uk

CC number: 202686

Eligibility

People who have lived in Okehampton for over 12 months and are in need.

Types of grant

One-off grants are made according to need. Welfare grants are paid from the Chairs Crisis Fund.

Applications

Application forms for the Chairs Crisis Fund are available online alongside the supporting policy documents. Professional written support has to be included with the request.

Financial information

Year end	31/12/2020
Income	£403,400
Total expenditure	£359,700

Further financial information

Grants to individuals were broken down as follows: adult education (£2,100); sporting achievement (£900); crisis/ hardship (£600).

Other information

The website refers to both this charity and the Okehampton Educational Foundation (Charity Commission no.

306677) collectively know as Okehampton United Charities. The charity awards both individuals and organisations for educational and welfare needs and the application forms for different awards are available on the website.

Dorset

Beaminster Relief in Need Charity

£ £6,600 (2019)

Correspondent: The Trustees, 24 Church Street, Beaminster, Dorset DT8 3BA (tel: 01308 862192; email: cnj@hand-n-head.uk)

CC number: 200685

Eligibility

People in need who live in the parish of Beaminster. Preference is given to children.

Types of grant

One-off grants are given for a wide range of purposes.

Applications

Apply in writing to the correspondent.

Financial information

Year end	31/12/2019
Income	£13,900
Total expenditure	£14,600

Further financial information

Full accounts were not available to view on the Charity Commission's website due to the charity's low income. We have therefore estimated the charity's grant total based on its total expenditure.

Other information

The charity also makes grants to organisations.

Blandford Forum Charities

£ £11,100 (2019/20)

Correspondent: Rene Prior, Clerk to the Trustees, Barnes Homes, Salisbury Road, Blandford Forum, Dorset DT11 7HU (tel: 01258 451810; email: clerkbfc@googlemail.com)

CC number: 230853

Eligibility

Welfare
Residents of Blandford Forum who are in need. The T.E.D. George Fund provides support to children under the age of 12 who are residents in the area.

Education
Young people under the age of 25 who live in, or have been educated in, Blandford Forum for at least two years.

Types of grant

Welfare
Grants are given according to need.

Education
Grants are given for educational purposes through the Apprenticing and Educational Foundation Charity.

Applications

Apply in writing to the correspondent.

Financial information

Year end	31/03/2020
Income	£238,200
Total expenditure	£182,700

Further financial information

Grants were distributed as follows: relief in need (£7,100); grants for children under 12 through the T.E.D. George Fund (£2,000); apprenticing and education (£2,000).

Other information

The Blandford Forum Charities comprises the following: Blandford Forum Almshouses Charity, the Relief in Need Fund, Blandford Forum Apprenticing and Educational Foundation Charity, The Charity of Christopher JK Robert Pitt and the T.E.D. George Fund.

Boveridge Charity

£ £2,400 (2020/21)

Correspondent: The Trustees, Brinscombe House, Lower Blandford Road, Cann, Shaftesbury, Dorset SP7 0BG (tel: 01747 852511; email: ceh75@hotmail.co.uk)

CC number: 231340

Eligibility

People in need who are in the ancient parish of Cranborne and Edmondsham for a minimum of two years. At the trustees' discretion, support may be extended to those living outside the area of benefit.

Types of grant

One-off grants and pensions.

Applications

Apply in writing to the correspondent.

Financial information

Year end	08/01/2021
Income	£7,100
Total expenditure	£5,300

Further financial information

Full accounts were not available to view on the Charity Commission's website due to the charity's low income. We have therefore estimated the charity's grant total based on its total expenditure.

The Bridge Educational Trust (1996)

£ £79,600 (2020/21)

Correspondent: The Trustees, c/o Piddle Valley First School, Piddletrenthide, Dorchester, Dorset DT2 7QL (tel: 07501 225054; email: bridgeeducationaltrust@outlook.com)

 www.bridgeeducationaltrust.org.uk

CC number: 1068720

Eligibility

People who live, or who were born, in the county of Dorset, primarily in the parishes of Piddletrenthide (with Plush), Piddlehinton and Alton St Pancras. This excludes residents of the South East Dorset conurbation including Bournemouth, Poole and Christchurch. The trust provides grants for people in the following circumstances:

- Students undertaking a first degree or other qualification in order to further their career who are experiencing financial difficulty
- Mature students who are retraining
- Students, whether studying or on a gap year, who wish to undertake an educational expedition or course
- Individuals working with support agencies looking to improve their life chances
- Students of school age with special educational needs that cannot be met by the local authority
- Single parents, or those with a partner who has a disability, undertaking training to support their children or family members
- Individuals recommended by probation services for training to help rehabilitation

Types of grant

One-off and recurrent grants are offered to people in education at school, college or other educational establishment. Grants are not normally paid to individuals directly unless a prior arrangement has been made. Grants are awarded towards fees, accommodation, educational travel, books, equipment, exhibitions, visits and other expenses.

Exclusions

The trust will not provide grants for fees which can be covered by student loans or for retrospective purchases. People who have a temporary address in Dorset for student accommodation do not meet the Dorset resident criterion.

Applications

Application forms are available on the trust's website, with full details and guidance on how to complete them.

Financial information

Year end	31/03/2021
Income	£82,300
Total expenditure	£87,000

Further financial information

In 2020/21, grants totalling £79,600 were given to 61 people. This was broken down as follows: £55,100 for 36 younger students at university or college who have shown evidence of exceptional financial difficulty; £9,200 for ten mature students; £5,400 for five single parents on courses or training to support dependants; £4,800 for four students for educational visits; £2,600 for three individuals of school age with special needs not met within the state sector or as contributions to fees at independent schools; £2,500 for three individuals for miscellaneous grants to resolve a short-term problem.

Brown Habgood Hall and Higden Charity

£ £16,000 (2020)

Correspondent: The Trustees, White Oaks, Colehill Lane, Wimborne, Dorset BH21 7AN (tel: 01202 886303; email: bhhh.charity@btinternet.com)

CC number: 204101

Eligibility

People in need living in the ancient parish of Wimborne Minster in Dorset.

Types of grant

Grants and gifts in kind.

Applications

Apply in writing to the correspondent.

Financial information

Year end	31/12/2020
Income	£17,800
Total expenditure	£16,900

Further financial information

Full accounts were not available to view on the Charity Commission's website due to the charity's low income. We have therefore estimated the grant total based on the charity's total expenditure.

Charmouth United Charities

£ £1,000 (2020)

Correspondent: The Trustees, Swansmead, Riverway, Charmouth, Bridport DT6 6LS (tel: 01297 560465; email: gilly@swansmead.co.uk)

CC number: 201885

Eligibility

People in need who, or whose immediate family, live in the parish of Charmouth.

Types of grant

One-off and recurrent grants. Grants have been given for hospital expenses, nursing fees, funeral expenses, special needs, health needs and general living expenses.

Applications

Apply in writing to the correspondent. Applications can be submitted directly by the individual or through a third party such as a rector, doctor or trustee. They are usually considered at quarterly periods; emergencies can be considered at other times.

Financial information

Year end	31/12/2020
Income	£3,700
Total expenditure	£2,500

Further financial information

Full accounts were not available to view on the Charity Commission's website due to the charity's low income. We have therefore estimated the grant total based on the charity's total expenditure.

Corfe Castle Charity

£ £28,800 (2019/20)

Correspondent: Clerk to the Trustees, 2 Battlemead, Corfe Castle, Wareham, Dorset BH20 5ER (tel: 01929 480873; email: CCcharity1602@outlook.com)

 https://www.corfecastlepc.org.uk/the-corfe-castle-charity

CC number: 1055846

Eligibility

People in need who live in the parish of Corfe Castle (including Kingston) or who have a strong local connection.

Types of grant

Welfare

Welfare grants are given according to need. Grants are also available towards pre-school fees, after-school clubs and holiday clubs at the Corfe Castle Community Pre-School.

Education

Grants are given towards the cost of education and training, including higher education courses.

Applications

Apply in writing to the correspondent.

Financial information

Year end	31/03/2020
Income	£291,000
Total expenditure	£245,200

Further financial information

During 2019/20, grants totalling £28,800 were awarded to 47 individuals. This included 34 general grants (£21,100) and 13 educational grants (£7,700).

Other information

The charity also makes grants to local organisations and administers both almshouse accommodation and affordable housing. The charity also provides interest-free loans to individuals in need.

Dorchester Relief in Need Charity

£ £3,600 (2019/20)

Correspondent: The Trustees, 5 Copper Crescent, Dorchester, Dorset DT1 1GL (tel: 01305 262041; email: robjoy1@talktalk.net)

CC number: 286570

Eligibility

People in need who live in the ecclesiastical parish of Dorchester.

Types of grant

Grants are given according to need.

Applications

Application forms are available from the correspondent and can be submitted by the individual or through a social worker, health visitor and so on.

Financial information

Year end	22/04/2020
Income	£4,900
Total expenditure	£4,000

Further financial information

Full accounts were not available to view on the Charity Commission's website due to the charity's low income. We have therefore estimated the grant total based on the charity's total expenditure.

Dorset Cancer Care Foundation

£ £62,200 (2020)

Correspondent: Nikki Davis-Thomas, Secretary, The Factory, 14 Alder Hills, Poole BH12 4AS (tel: 07593 890879; email: info@dccf.co.uk)

 https://www.dccf.co.uk

CC number: 1151603

Eligibility

People with cancer, and their families, who live in Dorset.

Types of grant

Grants can be awarded towards the following:

- Food
- Childcare
- Counselling
- Transport/parking costs incurred while receiving treatment
- Overnight accommodation during treatment
- Accommodation payments while out of work
- Wigs and prosthetics
- Home adaptations
- Special equipment
- Domestic help
- Respite breaks
- Family days out

Applications

Applications can be made on the charity's website. Alternatively, applicants can download a copy of the application form and, once completed, send it by post to the charity.

Financial information

Year end	31/12/2020
Income	£109,200
Total expenditure	£112,800

Further financial information

During the financial year, the charity awarded 116 grants to individuals. The largest award given was £2,100 and the smallest £70.

Grants were broken down as follows:

Bills	44	£23,400
Transport costs	31	£16,600
Household goods	16	£8,600
Specialised items	14	£7,400

Note that grants were also provided in three smaller categories; however, details of these were not provided.

Other information

This charity also makes grants to organisations and hospitals involved in the treatment and care of cancer patients. Grants are typically made in support of research in cancer cure and for medical equipment for the treatment of cancer patients.

John Foyle's Charity

£ £3,000 (2020)

Correspondent: The Trustees, c/o 41 Homefield, Shaftesbury, Dorset SP7 8DT (email: trustees@johnfoyles.org.uk)

 https://www.johnfoyles.org.uk

CC number: 202959

Eligibility

People in need who live in the town of Shaftesbury and the parishes of Melbury and Cann.

Types of grant

One-off grants are made according to need. Examples of grants include awards for:

- Computer equipment
- Employment training costs
- Hospital travel expenses
- Installation of telephone helplines
- Play equipment
- Books and tools
- Home broadband connections
- Funding towards wheelchairs
- Equipment for people with disabilities
- Essential household goods
- Essential furnishings

Applications

Apply via the charity's website.

Financial information

Year end	31/12/2020
Income	£6,400
Total expenditure	£4,000

Further financial information

Full accounts were not available to view on the Charity Commission's website due to the charity's low income. We have therefore estimated the grant total based on the charity's total expenditure.

The Litton Cheney Trust

£ £3,200 (2019)

Correspondent: The Trustees, Skep House, The Paddocks, Litton Cheney, Dorchester, Dorset DT2 9AF (tel: 01308 482602; email: skephouse@btinternet.com)

CC number: 231388

Eligibility

Welfare

People in need who live in the parish of Litton Cheney.

Education

Students who live in the parish of Litton Cheney.

Types of grant

Welfare

Grants are given to people who are in need due to sudden illness or bereavement. Support is also given to older people in need towards the cost of heating.

Education

Grants are given to those who are leaving school and are about to start a career, undertake an apprenticeship or embark on a university course.

Applications

Apply in writing to the correspondent.

Financial information

Year end	31/12/2019
Income	£7,500
Total expenditure	£7,100

Further financial information

Full accounts were not available to view on the Charity Commission's website due to the trust's low income. We have therefore estimated the trust's grant total based on its total expenditure.

Other information

Grants are also awarded to local organisations including schools, churches and community associations.

The MacDougall Trust

£ £27,100 (2019/20)

Correspondent: The Trustees, 9 Egdon Drive, Wimborne, Dorset BH21 1TY (email: use the contact form available on the website)

 www.macdougalltrust.org

CC number: 209743

Eligibility

People in need who live in Dorset.

Types of grant

One-off grants of up to £300 are given according to need.

Exclusions

The charity cannot consider making grants for the following:

- Sponsorship
- Childcare
- Debt
- People living outside Dorset
- Organisations

Applications

An application form can be completed online or downloaded from the website. Applications need to be supported by a recognised agency or primary healthcare worker. This may inlcude support workers, social services, Citizens Advice, The You Trust or other similar organisations.

Financial information

Year end	31/03/2020
Income	£29,400
Total expenditure	£27,100

St Martin's Trust

£ £3,400 (2017/18)

Correspondent: The Revd David Ayton, Trustee, 201 Kinson Road, Bournemouth BH10 5HB (tel: 01202 547054; email: davidj.ayton@ntlworld.com)

 www.stmartinsbooks.co.uk

CC number: 1065584

Eligibility

People in need who live in Dorset.

Types of grant

Grants are given according to need.

Applications

Apply in writing to the correspondent.

Financial information

Year end	31/10/2018
Income	£5,900
Total expenditure	£7,500

Further financial information

Full accounts were not available to view on the Charity Commission's website due to the trust's low income. We have therefore estimated the trust's grant total based on its total expenditure. Financial information from 2017/18 was the latest available at the time of writing (October 2021).

Other information

The trust runs a bookshop. Funds raised by the sale of books are used to support good causes. The trust awards grants to organisations too.

The Charity of William Williams

 £220,200 (2019)

Correspondent: The Clerk to the Trustees, Burraton House, 5 Burraton Square, Poundbury, Dorchester, Dorset DT1 3GR (tel: 01305 571274; email: enquiries@williamwilliams.org.uk)

www.williamwilliams.org.uk

CC number: 202188

Eligibility

People in need who live in the ancient parishes of Blandford Forum, Shaftesbury or Sturminster Newton. Individuals must reside in one of the specific postcodes listed on the charity's website.

Types of grant

Welfare

Grants are awarded according to need.

Education

Educational grants are made to students, mature students or apprentices embarking on higher education or recognised training schemes.

Exclusions

Typically, applications from young people for educational grants are not considered in cases where parents' annual income exceeds £40,000.

Applications

Details of how to apply, application forms and guidance can be found on the charity's website. For educational grants, both parts of the application (to be completed by the applicant and the applicant's parent or guardian, respectively) must be received before the deadline (which is usually in September).

Financial information

Year end	31/12/2019
Income	£490,300
Total expenditure	£385,000

Other information

Grants are also made to local organisations.

Bournemouth, Christchurch and Poole

Clingan's Trust

 £19,500 (2020)

Correspondent: David Richardson, Clerk, 4 Bournewood Drive, Bournemouth, Dorset BH4 9JP (tel: 01202 766838; email: jdavidhrichardson4@gmail.com)

https://www.clinganstrust.co.uk

CC number: 307085

Eligibility

Young people aged under 25 who are in need and live (or whose parent/guardian lives) in Christchurch (see the trust's website for the catchment area map) and who have also attended some stage of education in the area. Parental income is taken into account.

Types of grant

Grants are made towards costs and activities related to education or training. Previous grants have included assistance towards travel requirements, general maintenance, uniforms, clothing, tools, musical instruments, computer equipment and books.

Applications

Application forms and guidance notes can be downloaded from trust's website and should be returned by post or email. The trustees meet five times per year, typically in January, April, July, September and November. Application forms must be received at least a month in advance to be considered at that particular meeting.

Financial information

Year end	31/12/2020
Income	£63,600
Total expenditure	£64,600

Other information

This charity also makes grants to organisations.

Legate's Charity

£4,900 (2019)

Correspondent: Sarah Culwick, Christchurch Borough Council, Civic Offices, Bridge Street, Christchurch, Dorset BH23 1AZ (tel: 01202 795273; email: sculwick@ christchurchandeastdorset.gov.uk)

CC number: 215712

Eligibility

People in need who live in the borough of Christchurch and the immediate surrounding area.

Types of grant

The charity provides one-off grants towards specific items and small monthly allowances.

Applications

Apply in writing to the correspondent.

Financial information

Year end	31/12/2019
Income	£10,800
Total expenditure	£5,400

Further financial information

Full accounts were not available to view on the Charity Commission's website due to the charity's low income. We have therefore estimated the charity's grant total based on its total expenditure.

Gloucester-shire

Barnwood Trust

 £1,680,000 (2020)

Correspondent: Funding Team, Overton House, Overton Road, Cheltenham, Gloucestershire GL50 3BN (tel: 01242 539935; email: grants@barnwoodtrust.org)

www.barnwoodtrust.org

CC number: 1162855

Eligibility

People in need who live in Gloucestershire and have a disability or a diagnosed mental health challenge.

Types of grant

Grants are made under three categories: home (white goods, beds and flooring), well-being (televisions, laptops and tablets, online courses, home exercise equipment and material for hobbies) and mobility (riser recliners, mobility scooters and disability aids).

Exclusions

The trust will not fund:
▶ Activities against government safety guidelines during the COVID-19 pandemic
▶ Holidays and days out
▶ Ongoing expenses such as household bills
▶ Anything that has already been purchased or ordered
▶ Anything that the trust has already awarded the applicant funding for
▶ Anything available from the council or NHS

Applications

Applications can be made on the trust's website. Individuals who cannot complete the application online can call the Funding Team when the grants programme is open.

Financial information

Year end	31/12/2020
Income	£3,020,000
Total expenditure	£5,380,000

Further financial information

Grants made during the year were broken down into the following categories: well-being grants (£1.48 million); community spaces grants (£175,000); opportunity awards (£27,000); small sparks (£3,000).

The Gloucester Charities Trust

 £44,100 (2019/20)

Correspondent: The Trustees, Century House, 100 London Road, Gloucester, Gloucestershire GL1 3PL (tel: 01452 500429; email: info@gloschar.org.uk)

 www.gloucestercharitiestrust.co.uk

CC number: 205177

Eligibility

Older people and nurses in need who live in the county of Gloucestershire, and retired nurses who were formerly employed by the Gloucester District Nursing Society.

Types of grant

Grants of between £100 and £300 are made according to need, including: essential domestic equipment and appliances, children's equipment, furniture, school uniforms and essential clothing, decorating materials and specialist equipment for medical conditions.

Exclusions

The trust will not generally fund:
▶ Items that have already been purchased

▶ Payment of bills (such as heating or Council Tax)
▶ Payment of debts or arrears

Applications

Application forms are available to download on the trust's website. Applications must be made through a social worker or other professional in related fields.

Financial information

Year end	30/09/2020
Income	£4,570,000
Total expenditure	£4,310,000

Other information

The charity additionally provides sheltered flats for older people living within Gloucestershire, as well as residential and nursing homes to people from any location.

Gloucester Relief in Sickness Fund

 £8,100 (2019/20)

Correspondent: T. Bennett, Clerk to the Trustees, 85 Sapperton Road, Gloucester, Gloucestershire GL4 6UN (tel: 07765 864460; email: traceyatgrisf@hotmail.co.uk)

 gloucesterreliefinsickness.org.uk

CC number: 243548

Eligibility

Residents of the city of Gloucester (under the 1969 boundary) who are in need as a result of illness *and* financial difficulty.

Types of grant

Grants are awarded according to need. Recent examples include funding to cover the cost of furniture, bedding, white goods, food, clothing, electricity bill arrears, travel expenses to and from hospitals and bankruptcy fees.

Exclusions

Grants cannot be made for the relief of rates or taxes, or as reimbursement for items that have already been purchased. Recurrent grants are not made.

Applications

Application forms are available to download from the website, although most of the organisations the charity works with will already have application forms. Applications must be supported by evidence of poor health and financial hardship, so it may be beneficial to ask a representative from a recognised support agency (a social worker, health visitor, etc.) to assist in preparing an application. Applications must also evidence either that an applicant is not entitled to state benefits or that benefits

do not fully meet their needs. The trustees meet on a monthly basis, usually on the second Monday of each month, to consider grant applications.

Financial information

Year end	31/08/2020
Income	£10,300
Total expenditure	£9,100

Further financial information

Full accounts were not available to view on the Charity Commission's website due to the fund's low income. We have therefore estimated the grant total based on the fund's total expenditure.

The Gloucestershire Association for Disability

 £51,000 (2019/20)

Correspondent: The Trustees, c/o Centre for Deaf People, Colin Road, Barnwood, Gloucester, Gloucestershire GL4 3JL (tel: 01452 614890 (Tuesday or Thursday 10am–1pm); email: info@glosdisabilityfund.org.uk)

 www.glosdisabilityfund.org.uk

CC number: 1048489

Eligibility

Welfare

Gloucestershire residents of any age with a physical, sensory or learning disability who are in receipt of a disability benefit.

Education

Gloucestershire residents aged 18 with a disability who are pursuing education or training.

Types of grant

Welfare

Well-being grants of up to £1,000 are given to help with one-off exceptional needs. Examples include wheelchair adaptations, household goods, play equipment to aid development, holidays, disability equipment, participation and training in sporting activities and so on.

Education

The charity's Your Future grants provide support to individuals over the age of 18 for education, training for work or excellence in the fields of arts and sport. Grants can be given towards course and travel fees, computer equipment and so on.

Exclusions

According to the charity's grant application guidance notes, support is not given for the following:
▶ Goods/services already ordered or purchased **prior** to making an application **or** before a grant decision is made

- To help pay off outstanding debts
- For the "client contribution" element of Disabled Facilities Grants (DFG)
- The cost of day to day social or health care, medical procedures, rehabilitation or therapy courses,
- Personal income, routine household expenses or for services that are normally available from statutory agencies.

The charity is not able to support applicants whose disability arises from a mental illness.

Applications
Application forms can be downloaded from the charity's website. Applications should be supported by a health, social care or education professional, support worker or another independent person able to comment on the individuals needs and circumstances.

Financial information
Year end	31/03/2020
Income	£201,900
Total expenditure	£163,100

Further financial information
Well-being grants totalled £41,400, and Your Future grants totalled £9,600.

Other information
Grants are also made to organisations. In 2019/20, the charity received 96 well-being applications and approved 74. A total of six Your Future grant applications were received during the period and all six were approved.

Gloucestershire Football Association – Benevolent Fund

£6,900 (2019/20)

Correspondent: Operations Manager, Gloucestershire FA Ltd, Oaklands Park, Gloucester Road, Almondsbury, Gloucestershire BS32 4AG (tel: 01454 615888)

 https://www.gloucestershirefa.com/players/benevolent-fund

CC number: 249744

Eligibility
Players or referees of clubs affiliated with the Gloucestershire Football Association, and players or referees of Representative League and County Teams, who have been injured while playing football in a recognised match. Applicants must be unable to follow their usual employment for a minimum of two weeks.

Types of grant
One-off or recurrent grants are awarded according to need.

Applications
Application forms are available to download on the fund's website. Applications must be made within 28 days of injury. Applications made after this period may be accepted, although exceptionally. A doctor's certificate stating the nature and duration of the injury must accompany all applications. Completed forms should be sent to the Operations Manager by post.

Financial information
Year end	30/06/2020
Income	£5,500
Total expenditure	£7,700

Further financial information
Full accounts were not available to view on the Charity Commission's website due to the fund's low income. We have therefore estimated the grant total based on the fund's total expenditure.

The Gloucestershire Society

£87,600 (2020)

Correspondent: See the website for relevant contact, Saffery Champness, St Catherines Court, Berkeley Place, Bristol BS8 1BQ

 https://www.gloucestershiresociety.org.uk

CC number: 203159

Eligibility
Individuals in need who live in the ceremonial county of Gloucestershire.

Types of grant
One-off grants are available according to need.

Exclusions
Grants cannot be awarded to fund therapeutic services or to assist with debt.

Applications
Applications can be made via the society's website. Applications can only be made by professional staff, working at agencies or organisations recognised by The Gloucestershire Society.

Financial information
Year end	31/12/2020
Income	£150,800
Total expenditure	£95,900

Severn Wye Energy Agency

£1,290,000 (2019/20)

Correspondent: The Trustees, Unit 15, Highnam Business Centre, Highnam, Gloucester, Gloucestershire GL2 8DN

(tel: 01452 835060; email: info@severnwye.org.uk)

 https://www.severnwye.org.uk

CC number: 1083812

Eligibility
People in need who live in Gloucestershire. Individual funds have different criteria, please contact the charity for further information.

Types of grant
One-off grants according to need are available to improve the energy efficiency of properties.

Applications
Apply in writing to the correspondent.

Financial information
Year end	31/03/2020
Income	£3,190,000
Total expenditure	£3,160,000

Further financial information
The grant total reported may also include grants made for educational purposes.

Other information
Through its helpline, the charity also provides advice on how to reduce fuel bills and detailed bespoke advice on energy efficiency measures and renewable technologies.

Edith Strain Nursing Charity

£1,300 (2019/20)

Correspondent: Joan Deveney, 85 Shepherds Leaze, Wotton-under-Edge, Gloucestershire GL12 7LJ (tel: 01458 44370)

CC number: 204598

Eligibility
People who live in the town of Wotton-under-Edge and are in need due to medical problems.

Types of grant
One-off and recurrent grants.

Applications
Apply in writing to the correspondent, either directly by the individual, or via a social worker, Citizens Advice or other welfare agency. An sae is required. Applications are usually considered in May and November.

Financial information
Year end	30/09/2020
Income	£3,300
Total expenditure	£2,800

Further financial information
Full accounts were not available to view on the Charity Commission's website

due to the charity's low income. We have therefore estimated the charity's grant total based on its total expenditure.

Other information
Grants are also made to local organisations which care for people who are sick.

Weston-sub-Edge Educational Charity

 £5,200 (2019/20)

Correspondent: Rachel Hurley, Clerk, Longclose Cottage, Weston-sub-Edge, Chipping Campden, Gloucestershire GL55 6QX (tel: 01386 841808; email: hurleyrac@gmail.com)

www.westonsubedge.com/?page_id=143

CC number: 297226

Eligibility
Children and young people under the age of 25 who, or whose parents, live in Weston-sub-Edge, or who have at any time attended (or whose parents have attended) Weston-sub-Edge Church of England Primary School.

Types of grant
Grants of between £10 and £500 can be given for costs associated with pre-school, reception (to year six) and year seven to eleven.

Grants of between £10 and £500 can be given for costs associated with further and higher education.

Exclusions
Retrospective applications are unlikely to be considered.

Applications
Application forms can be obtained from the correspondent and should be submitted directly by the individual in question, unless they are under 16, in which case a parent or guardian can apply. The trustees meet on the fourth Monday in January, March, May, July, September and November, and applications must be received at least ten days in advance of a meeting. Only one application per student per term will be considered.

Financial information
Year end	31/08/2020
Income	£5,400
Total expenditure	£5,700

Further financial information
Full accounts were not available to view on the Charity Commission's website due to the charity's low income. We have therefore estimated the charity's

grant total based on its total expenditure.

Cheltenham

Charlton Kings Relief in Need Charity

 £2,100 (2019/20)

Correspondent: Martin Fry, Clerk to the Trustees, 7 Branch Hill Rise, Charlton Kings, Cheltenham GL53 9HN (tel: 01242 239903; email: applications@CKreliefinneed.org or use the contact form available on the website)

ckreliefinneed.org

CC number: 204597

Eligibility
People in need who live in the former urban district of Charlton Kings.

Types of grant
Grants are given according to need.

Applications
Application forms can be downloaded from the charity's website and must include two letters of reference as well as an sae. Completed applications should be sent to the clerk by post, at least two weeks before a trustee meeting. Dates of upcoming meetings can be found on the charity's website.

Financial information
Year end	31/03/2020
Income	£4,100
Total expenditure	£4,500

Further financial information
Full accounts were not available to view on the Charity Commission's website due to the charity's low income. We have therefore estimated the charity's grant total based on its total expenditure.

Other information
Grants are also awarded to organisations.

Higgs and Cooper's Educational Charity

 £11,000 (2019/20)

Correspondent: Martin Fry, Clerk to the Trustees, 7 Branch Hill Rise, Charlton Kings, Cheltenham GL53 9HN (tel: 07813 955008; email: applications@higgsandcooper.org)

www.higgsandcooper.org

CC number: 311570

Eligibility
People under the age of 25 who were born or live in the former Charlton

Kings civil parish. Preference is given to people from single-parent families.

Types of grant
Grants are awarded for costs associated with secondary education. Support is mainly given towards educational outings and study/travel overseas.

Awards are also made for further/higher education students and people starting work/entering a trade. Support is given for general educational expenditure, including books, equipment/instruments, fees and so on. Grants can also be given for postgraduate degrees and training.

Applications
Application forms can be found on the website and must be submitted to the clerk by post or hand two weeks before the meeting at which they are to be considered. Two reference letters must be submitted along with the application: one professional reference (school/institution for which the applicant needs support) and one personal reference from someone who has known the applicant for a number of years (other than a family member). An sae should accompany the application. The trustees meet four times a year, normally in March, June, September and December.

Financial information
Year end	31/03/2020
Income	£20,200
Total expenditure	£24,200

Further financial information
Full accounts were not available to view on the Charity Commission's website due to the charity's low income. We have therefore estimated the charity's grant total based on its total expenditure.

Other information
The charity also supports local schools and youth organisations.

The Prestbury Charity (Prestbury United Charities)

 £8,700 (2019)

Correspondent: J. Montgomery, Clerk, The Prestbury United Charities, The Coach House Mews, The Burgage, Prestbury, Cheltenham, Gloucestershire GL52 3DN (tel: 07710 141355; email: clerk@puc.org.uk)

puc.org.uk

CC number: 202655

Eligibility
People in need who live in the ecclesiastical parish of Prestbury and the adjoining parishes of Southam and

Swindon village or immediately adjoining areas (most of North Cheltenham).

Types of grant

Grants are awarded according to need. Previously support has been given towards: the purchase of white goods, furniture, school clothing, repairs and decorating costs, counselling and assistance for single-parent families.

Applications

Application forms are available to download from the charity's website and should be printed and returned directly to the clerk. Applications need to be supported by an independent professional person such as social worker, family support worker, housing advisor and so on.

Financial information

Year end	31/12/2019
Income	£26,400
Total expenditure	£19,200

Further financial information

Grants were awarded to 30 individuals during the year.

Other information

Local organisations, groups and societies are also supported. The charity has an almshouse branch responsible for providing accommodation to those in need.

Cotswold

Smith's Cirencester Poor Charity

 £3,000 (2019/20)

Correspondent: The Trustees, 7 Dollar Street, Cirencester, Gloucestershire GL7 2AS (tel: 01285 650000)

CC number: 232383

Eligibility

Residents of Cirencester who are in need. Applicants must have lived in the town for a minimum of three consecutive years before applying for funding.

Types of grant

Grants are given according to need.

Applications

Applicants should be referred through local agencies such as a medical practice or hospital, social services, Citizens Advice or another voluntary organisation. The trustees meet quarterly to consider grant applications.

Financial information

Year end	31/05/2020
Income	£5,200
Total expenditure	£6,700

Further financial information

Full accounts were not available to view on the Charity Commission's website due to the charity's low income. We have therefore estimated the grant total based on the charity's total expenditure.

Gloucester

The Fluck Convalescent Fund

 £48,900 (2019/20)

Correspondent: The Trustees, Tracy House, Houndscroft, Stroud, Gloucestershire GL5 5DG (tel: 01453 872300; email: flucktrust@gmail.com)

🌐 https://www.fluckfund.org.uk

CC number: 205315

Eligibility

Women of all ages and children under 16 who live in the city of Gloucester and its surrounding area and are in poor health or convalescing after illness or operative treatment.

Types of grant

Grants are awarded for: clothing, bedding, furniture, food, refrigerators and freezers, vacuum cleaners, fuel, medical or other aids, other comforts, recuperative holidays, domestic help for respite care and assistance with nursery fees in conjunction with respite care.

Exclusions

Grants are not awarded for the relief of taxes or other public funds, or repayment of debts. The charity will not award recurring grants.

Applications

Apply in writing to the correspondent through a professional third party, such as a social worker, medical professional or officer from the Health Trust or Citizens Advice.

Financial information

Year end	31/03/2020
Income	£49,800
Total expenditure	£50,700

Further financial information

A total of 159 grants were awarded during the year.

United Charity of Palling Burgess and Others

💷 £2,100 (2019/20)

Correspondent: The Trustees, Glasfryn, Cwmcarvan, Monmouth, Gwent NP25 4JP (tel: 01600 740433; email: jessica@malcolmbruno.com)

CC number: 236440

Eligibility

People in need who live within the boundaries of the Gloucester city council administrative area. Preference is given to residents living in the ecclesiastical parishes of St John the Baptist, St Mary de Crypt and St Michael.

Types of grant

Grants are given according to need.

Applications

Apply in writing to the correspondent.

Financial information

Year end	31/03/2020
Income	£2,200
Total expenditure	£2,300

Further financial information

Full accounts were not available to view on the Charity Commission's website due to the charity's low income. We have therefore estimated the charity's grant total based on its total expenditure.

South Gloucestershire

Almondsbury Charity

💷 £8,800 (2019/20)

Correspondent: Peter Orford, Secretary, Wayside, Shepperdine Road, Oldbury Naite, Oldbury-on-Severn, Bristol BS35 1RJ (tel: 01454 415346; email: peter.orford@gmail.com)

🌐 www.almondsburycharity.org.uk

CC number: 202263

Eligibility

Individuals who are in need and have lived in the parish of Almondsbury, as it existed in 1881 (that is, in Almondsbury, Patchway, Easter Compton and parts of Pilning and Bradley Stoke North), for at least one year. Young people who are in education are also supported.

Types of grant

One-off grants can be given according to need. Previous grants have included those for white goods, furniture, computer equipment and other household necessities such as carpets. Grants to young people in education have previously included grants towards books or equipment. Previous research suggests that, occasionally, grants are made for educational trips.

Exclusions

Previous research suggests grants are not given towards fuel bills, or school or course fees. The charity does not make cash grants.

Applications
Application forms can be downloaded from the charity's website. Completed applications should be sent via post to the correspondent.

Financial information
Year end	30/09/2020
Income	£65,600
Total expenditure	£64,000

Further financial information
In 2019/20, grants were made to 15 individuals.

Other information
The charity also makes grants to local organisations.

Chipping Sodbury Town Lands Charity

 £19,100 (2020)

Correspondent: Nicola Gideon, Clerk to the Trustees, Town Hall, 57–59 Broad Street, Chipping Sodbury, Bristol BS37 6AD (tel: 01454 852223; email: nicola.gideon@chippingsodburytownhall.co.uk)

 www.chippingsodburytownhall.co.uk

CC number: 236364

Eligibility
Residents in the parish of Sodbury who are in need.

Types of grant
Welfare
Grants are given according to need, for example towards the cost of white goods or heating bills and other winter expenses.

Education
Educational grants are made for the promotion of education, including further education courses.

Applications
Apply in writing to the correspondent.

Financial information
Year end	31/12/2020
Income	£321,100
Total expenditure	£224,200

Further financial information
Welfare grants were awarded to 152 households.

Other information
The charity also makes grants to local schools and organisations.

St Monica Trust
See entry on page 417

Thornbury Town Trust

 £21,800 (2020)

Correspondent: Sally Bertram, Clerk to the Trust, 23 Cumbria Close, Thornbury, Bristol BS35 2YE (tel: 07835 110766; email: sallytowntrust@gmail.com or use the contact form on the website)

 www.thornburytowntrust.uk

CC number: 238273

Eligibility
Residents of Thornbury who are in need.

Types of grant
Grants are given for nursing home fees and for other miscellaneous welfare purposes. Grants are also awarded as gifts at Christmas.

Applications
Apply in writing to the correspondent.

Financial information
Year end	31/12/2020
Income	£54,900
Total expenditure	£48,300

Other information
The trust owns 126 allotments and four almshouses in the town. Grants are also awarded to organisations.

Stroud
The Charity of the Ancient Parish of Bisley

 £8,100 (2019/20)

Correspondent: Mrs J. Bentley, Secretary, The Old Post Office, High Street, Bisley, Stroud, Gloucestershire GL6 7AA (tel: 01452 770756; email: bisleycharity.capb@gmail.com)

 www.bisleycharity-capb.org

CC number: 237229

Eligibility
Residents of the ancient parish of Bisley who are in need as a result of illness, convalescence, disability, financial difficulty or other forms of hardship. Preference is given to older people and children and young people.

Types of grant
One-off or in-kind grants are awarded according to need. Recent examples include items such as white goods and

assistance towards the cost of home repairs and funerals.

Exclusions
Recurrent awards are not made. Grants cannot be awarded towards the relief of rates or taxes.

Applications
Application forms can be completed online on the charity's website.

Financial information
Year end	31/08/2020
Income	£10,700
Total expenditure	£9,000

Further financial information
Full accounts were not available to view on the Charity Commission's website due to the charity's low income. We have therefore estimated the charity's grant total based on its total expenditure.

Lady Downe's Charity

 £7,000 (2019/20)

Correspondent: The Clerk, The Coach House at Well Close, Painswick Road, Brockworth, Gloucestershire GL3 4RZ (email: clerk@ladydowne.org)

 https://ladydowne.org

CC number: 286577

Eligibility
Welfare
People in need who live in Upton St Leonards, Gloucestershire.

Education
People under 25 who live in Upton St Leonards and are going on to further education or training.

Types of grant
Welfare
One-off grants are awarded according to need. Grants can be made for items such as disability aids, respite care, personal alarm systems and household equipment.

Education
Grants are available for books or equipment.

Applications
Application forms can be downloaded from the charity's website.

Financial information
Year end	31/03/2020
Income	£28,700
Total expenditure	£33,400

The Stroud and Rodborough Educational Charity

£ £14,000 (2019/20)

Correspondent: Shani Baker, Clerk to the Trustees, 14 Green Close, Uley, Dursley, Gloucestershire GL11 5TH (tel: 01453 860379; email: info@ stroudrodboroughed.org)

 www.stroudrodboroughec.org

CC number: 309614

Eligibility

Children and young people in need who are under the age of 25 and resident in the parishes comprising the old Stroud rural district (Bisley-with-Lypiatt, Chalford, Cranham, Horsley, Kings Stanley, Leonard Stanley, Minchinhampton, Miserden, Oakridge, Painswick, Pitchcombe, Randwick, Rodborough, Stonehouse, Thrupp, Whiteshill, Woodchester and Nailsworth urban district).

Types of grant

Grants can be given towards general educational needs including for primary schoolchildren to undertake educational and residential school trips, towards music and drama lessons, to help with the costs of study/travel overseas, equipment, clothing, books and course-related necessities and so on.

Exclusions

Support is not given in the cases where funding should be provided by the local authority.

Applications

Application forms are available on the charity's website or from the correspondent. The trustees meet four times a year – see the website for the next application deadline. Applications should include a reference from a teacher and be submitted in advance to the meetings.

Financial information

Year end	31/03/2020
Income	£83,200
Total expenditure	£105,100

Further financial information

A breakdown of grants was not available.

Other information

The priority of the charity is to assist Marling School, Stroud High School and Archway School, where support is not already provided by the local authority. The charity also gives grants to local charitable organisations working for the benefit of young people and administers a number of prize funds tenable at the local schools.

Tewkesbury

The Gyles Geest Charity

£ £7,500 (2019/20)

Correspondent: The Trustees, 10 Troughton Place, Tewkesbury, Gloucestershire GL20 8EA (tel: 01684 850697; email: simmondskandm@ btinternet.com)

CC number: 239372

Eligibility

Residents of the borough of Tewkesbury who are in need. Preference may be given to older residents.

Types of grant

Grants are given according to need.

Applications

Apply in writing to the correspondent.

Financial information

Year end	31/10/2020
Income	£8,500
Total expenditure	£8,300

Further financial information

Full accounts were not available to view on the Charity Commission's website due to the charity's low income. We have therefore estimated the charity's grant total based on its total expenditure.

Other information

The charity has been in existence since 1551.

Somerset

Archdeaconry of Bath Clerical Families Fund

£ £7,800 (2019/20)

Correspondent: The Trustees, The Bath and Wells Diocesan Board of Finance, 2 Cathedral Avenue, Wells, Somerset BA5 1FD (tel: 01749 670777)

CC number: 230676

Eligibility

Families of clergy in the Deaneries of Bath, Chew Magna, Locking, Midsomer Norton or Portishead who are in need. Widows and children of deceased clergymen who have been beneficed or licensed within the same deaneries are also eligible.

Types of grant

Grants are given according to need.

Applications

Apply in writing to the correspondent.

Financial information

Year end	31/10/2020
Income	£4,300
Total expenditure	£7,800

Further financial information

Full accounts were not available to view on the Charity Commission's website due to the fund's low income. We have therefore estimated the grant total based on the fund's total expenditure.

Cannington Combined Charity

£ £1,300 (2020/21)

Correspondent: The Trustees, 4A Gurney Street, Cannington, Bridgwater, Somerset TA5 2HW (tel: 01278 653256)

CC number: 290789

Eligibility

People who live in the parish of Cannington and are in need.

Types of grant

According to our previous research, grants have been given for school trips, clothing, heating bills and for the replacement of essential electrical equipment.

Applications

Apply in writing to the correspondent.

Financial information

Year end	30/06/2021
Income	£4,100
Total expenditure	£2,900

Further financial information

Full accounts were not available to view on the Charity Commission's website due to the charity's low income. We have therefore estimated the grant total based on the charity's total expenditure.

Other information

This charity also makes grants to organisations.

The Ilminster Educational Foundation

£ £25,300 (2019/20)

Correspondent: Edward Wells, Clerk, Larkhill, Chardstock, Axminster, Devon EX13 7BR (tel: 01460 53029; email: e. wells125@btinternet.com)

CC number: 310265

Eligibility

People under the age of 25 who live in the parish of Ilminster, Somerset or have attended an educational institution in the parish for at least two years.

Types of grant

Social welfare

Grants can be made to schoolchildren for educational trips.

Education

Grants are available to students for costs associated with university and college, including scholarships, bursaries and maintenance allowances.

Applications

Apply in writing to the correspondent.

Financial information

Year end	31/07/2020
Income	£203,400
Total expenditure	£193,100

Further financial information

Grants to schoolchildren totalled £8,700, and a further £16,600 was paid to students in higher education.

Other information

The foundation also awards grants to five local schools in the parish (£8,200 in 2019/20).

J. A. F. Luttrell Memorial Charity

£ £7,400 (2019/20)

Correspondent: Clerk to the Trustees, The Old Hospital, Redlands Lane, Edington, Bridgwater, Somerset TA7 9JW (tel: 01278 723192; email: JAFLMCclerk@hotmail.com)

CC number: 201495

Eligibility

People in need who live in Edington, Catcott, Chilton Polden, Burtle and Cossington.

Types of grant

Grants can be made for transport, respite care, gardening, heating, house maintenance and equipment, and musical instruments.

Applications

Application forms are available by contacting the correspondent. Applications are considered twice a year, in spring and autumn.

Financial information

Year end	31/07/2020
Income	£11,700
Total expenditure	£8,200

Further financial information

Full accounts were not available to view on the Charity Commission's website due to the charity's low income. We have therefore estimated the charity's grant total based on its total expenditure.

Other information

Grants are also awarded to local organisations.

The Nuttall Trust

£ £14,400 (2019/20)

Correspondent: Nicholas Redding, Trustee, c/o Barrington & Sons, 60 High Street, Burnham-on-Sea, Somerset TA8 1AG (tel: 01278 782371; email: nredding@barrington-sons.co.uk)

CC number: 1085196

Eligibility

People in need who live in the parishes of Brent Knoll, East Brent, Mark and Lympsham in Somerset.

Types of grant

Grants are given according to need.

Applications

Apply in writing to the correspondent.

Financial information

Year end	31/01/2020
Income	£33,900
Total expenditure	£37,100

Further financial information

A breakdown of grants was not available. Grant total has therefore been estimated.

Somerset Local Medical Benevolent Fund

£ £23,000 (2019/20)

Correspondent: The Trustees, Somerset LMC, The Crown Medical Centre, Crown Industrial Estate, Venture Way, Taunton, Somerset TA2 8QY (tel: 01823 331428; email: lmcoffice@somersetlmc.nhs.uk)

 www.somersetlmc.co.uk

CC number: 201777

Eligibility

General medical practitioners who are practising or have practised in Somerset and their dependants who are in need.

Types of grant

Grants are awarded according to need.

Applications

Apply in writing to the correspondent.

Financial information

Year end	31/03/2020
Income	£23,100
Total expenditure	£34,100

Further financial information

Full accounts were not available to view on the Charity Commission's website due to the fund's low income. We have

therefore estimated the grant total based on the fund's total expenditure.

The Tamlin Charity

£ £2,500 (2020)

Correspondent: The Trustees, 5 Channel Court, Burnham-on-Sea, Somerset TA8 1NE (tel: 01278 789859)

CC number: 228586

Eligibility

Older people in need living in Bridgwater, Somerset.

Types of grant

Small grants are awarded in the form of pensions.

Applications

Apply in writing to the correspondent.

Financial information

Year end	31/12/2020
Income	£2,000
Total expenditure	£2,800

Further financial information

Full accounts were not available to view on the Charity Commission's website due to the charity's low income. We have therefore estimated the charity's grant total based on its total expenditure.

Bath and North East Somerset

Bath Disability Trust

£ £7,100 (2019/20)

Correspondent: The Trustees, 5 Napier Road, Bath BA1 4LN (tel: 01225 315647; email: contact@bathdisabilitytrust.org)

 https://www.bathdisabilitytrust.org

CC number: 231502

Eligibility

People with disabilities who live in the City of Bath and adjoining parishes.

Types of grant

One-off grants are available according to need. Grants can be awarded for items such as wheelchairs, entrance ramps, hoists, postural chairs and beds and accessible showers.

Applications

Application forms can be downloaded from the trust's website.

Financial information

Year end	31/03/2020
Income	£43,400
Total expenditure	£64,200

Mayor of Bath's Relief Fund

£ £5,000 (2020)

Correspondent: Mandy Majendie, Funding and Impact Officer, c/o St John's Hospital, 4–5 Chapel Court, Bath, Somerset BA1 1SQ (tel: 01225 486400)

 https://www.stjohnsbath.org.uk

CC number: 204649

Eligibility

People in need who live in Bath. Note: grants are only made as a last resort for those who have already exhausted all other funding channels such as social services and other local charities.

Types of grant

One-off grants ranging from £50 to £350 are given for carpets, second-hand furniture and appliances, bills, and school uniforms and other clothing.

Exclusions

No grants are given for tuition fees or rent arrears.

Applications

Applications must be made through agencies such as social services or Citizens Advice and not directly via the individual in need.

Financial information

Year end	31/12/2020
Income	£5,400
Total expenditure	£5,500

Further financial information

Full accounts were not available to view on the Charity Commission's website due to the fund's low income. We have therefore estimated the fund's grant total based on its total expenditure.

Other information

The fund is administered by the St John's Foundation.

Combe Down Holiday Trust

£ £10,700 (2020)

Correspondent: The Trustees, c/o Combe Down Surgery, The Avenue, Combe Down, Bath, Somerset BA2 5EG (tel: 01225 837181; email: gr@cdht.org.uk)

 www.cdht.org.uk

CC number: 1022275

Eligibility

People who have disabilities, including as a result of an illness (such as cancer), who live in the Bath and North East Somerset area. Families and carers of such people are also eligible.

Types of grant

One-off grants are available towards the cost of a holiday, short break or respite care.

Applications

Apply on a form available from the correspondent, to be submitted directly by the individual or through a social worker, Citizens Advice or other welfare agency.

Financial information

Year end	31/12/2020
Income	£86,300
Total expenditure	£37,000

The Henry Smith Charity (Longney)

£ £1,600 (2020/21)

Correspondent: John Irons, Trustee, 48 Northend, Batheaston, Bath, Somerset BA1 7ES (tel: 01225 852440; email: johnirons35@gmail.com)

CC number: 204620

Eligibility

Widows who live in Batheaston and are in need. Support is also given more generally to residents of Batheaston who are experiencing financial hardship.

Types of grant

One-off grants are given for fuel costs.

Applications

Apply in writing to the correspondent.

Financial information

Year end	28/02/2021
Income	£1,800
Total expenditure	£1,800

Further financial information

Full accounts were not available to view on the Charity Commission's website due to the charity's low income. We have therefore estimated the charity's grant total based on its total expenditure.

St John's Hospital (Bath)

£ £241,500 (2020)

Correspondent: The Trustees, 4–5 Chapel Court, Bath, Somerset BA1 1SQ (tel: 01225 486400; email: grants@stjohnsbath.org.uk)

 www.stjohnsbath.org.uk

CC number: 201476

Eligibility

People who live Bath and the surrounding area and are in need due to age, ill health, disability, financial hardship or other circumstances.

Types of grant

Grants of up to £1,500 can be made towards a wide range of essential items and services such as furniture, white goods, carpets, counselling, clothing vouchers, funeral costs, and basic employment skills and training. Payment of debts may be considered if it will enable the individual to get back on their feet and move forward.

Exclusions

Grants are not awarded for loans, fines (including Magistrate Court fines), deposits or rent in advance, retrospective funding, gap year projects, gifts, holidays, legal aid, or to applicants who have already received three awards in the last three years, repeat applicants for the same item and residents of St John's Almshouses.

Applications

Applications can only be made through professional referrers, such as Citizens Advice, housing advice centres, health professionals or the Genesis Trust. There is an online system where applications can be made on behalf of the individual. Direct applications from those in need are not accepted.

Financial information

Year end	31/12/2020
Income	£5,200,000
Total expenditure	£5,740,000

Further financial information

During the year, grants were awarded to 600 individuals.

Other information

The foundation also provides accommodation for people over 65 and in financial need. It also supports other organisations.

St Monica Trust

See entry on page 417

Mendip

Charity of George Cox

£ £2,300 (2020)

Correspondent: The Trustees, The Mission Church, Vestry Road, Street, Somerset BA16 0HZ (tel: 01458 442671)

CC number: 240491

Eligibility

Residents in the parish of Street who are in need.

Types of grant

Grants are given according to need. The charity will also pay for items, services or facilities that will reduce hardship.

Applications

Apply in writing to the correspondent. Applications are usually submitted through a third party on the individual's behalf.

Financial information

Year end	31/12/2020
Income	£3,300
Total expenditure	£5,000

Further financial information

Full accounts were not available to view on the Charity Commission's website due to the charity's low income. We have therefore estimated the grant total based on the charity's total expenditure.

Other information

Grants are also made to organisations.

The Wells Clerical Charity

£ £1,260 (2020)

Correspondent: The Trustees, 6 The Liberty, Wells, Somerset BA5 2SU (tel: 01749 670777; email: general@bathwells.anglican.org)

CC number: 248436

Eligibility

Clergy of the Church of England who have served in the historic archdeaconry of Wells, and their families who are in need.

People under the age of 25 who are the children of clergy members of the Church of England, including retired or deceased members who have served in the historic archdeaconry of Wells.

Types of grant

One-off grants are made according to need, including towards education and to people preparing to enter a trade or profession (for example, for travel costs, maintenance or clothing).

Applications

Apply in writing to the correspondent.

Financial information

Year end	31/12/2020
Income	£9,800
Total expenditure	£1,400

Further financial information

Full accounts were not available to view on the Charity Commission's website due to the charity's low income. We have therefore estimated the charity's grant total based on its total expenditure.

North Somerset

The Backwell Foundation

£ £1,400 (2019)

Correspondent: The Trustees, Sedalia, Brockley Hall, Brockley Lane, Brockley, Bristol BS48 3AZ (tel: 01275 463261)

CC number: 1086036

Eligibility

People in need who live in the civil parishes of Backwell and Brockley.

Types of grant

Grants are awarded according to need.

Applications

Apply in writing to the correspondent.

Financial information

Year end	31/12/2019
Income	£1,500
Total expenditure	£1,500

Further financial information

Full accounts were not available to view on the Charity Commission's website due to the charity's low income. We have therefore estimated the charity's grant total based on its total expenditure.

Marchioness of Northampton (Wraxall Parochial Charities)

£ £4,200 (2020)

Correspondent: The Trustees, The Cross Tree Centre, Bristol Road, Wraxall BS48 1LB (tel: 07543 613278; email: info.wraxallcharities@gmail.com)

 https://www.wraxallcharities.com

CC number: 230410

Eligibility

Residents of the parish of Wraxall and Failand who are in need.

Types of grant

Welfare

Grants are awarded according to need. Examples include: essential household items (e.g. washing machines); clothing and/or shoes; school uniforms; travel expenses for medical care or hospital visits; respite breaks; convalescent assistance; special food; medical aids or equipment.

Education

The charity can help with the fees for a course or travelling expenses to assist people on a course.

Applications

Application forms can be requested from the charity. Completed forms can be returned either by email or post.

Financial information

Year end	31/12/2020
Income	£26,600
Total expenditure	£16,600

Other information

This charity also makes grants to organisations.

Nailsea Community Trust Ltd

£ £3,400 (2020/21)

Correspondent: The Secretary, 1st Nailsea Scouts Training and Activity Centre, Clevedon Road, Nailsea, North Somerset BS48 1EH (email: info@nailseacommunitytrust.org.uk)

 https://www.nailseacommunitytrust.org.uk

CC number: 900031

Eligibility

Individuals who have lived in Nailsea, Backwell, Chelvey, Tickenham and Wraxall for at least 12 months.

Types of grant

Welfare

Grants are given according to need. Support has previously been given for essential repairs, household goods, counselling services, attendance at after school clubs and so on.

Education

Grants are given to assist with education, particularly in the areas of science, the arts, religion, commerce and healthcare.

Applications

Application forms can be downloaded from the trust's website. Applications are considered on a weekly basis. To discuss an urgent request or to check eligibility, contact the trust directly via email.

Financial information

Year end	31/03/2021
Income	£4,700
Total expenditure	£7,700

Further financial information

Full accounts were not available to view on the Charity Commission's website due to the trust's low income. We have therefore estimated the grant total based on the trust's total expenditure.

Other information

Grants are also awarded to organisations.

The Portishead Nautical Trust

See entry on page 416

St Monica Trust

See entry on page 417

Charles Graham Stone's Relief-in-Need Charity

 £1,200 (2019)

Correspondent: The Trustees, The Boardroom, Sidney Hill Cottage Homes, Front Street, Churchill, Winscombe, Somerset BS25 5NE (email: clerkhillarmshouses@gmx.co.uk)

CC number: 260044

Eligibility

People in need who live in North Somerset, although in practice many of the grants are awarded to people who live in Langford.

Types of grant

Grants are given according to need.

Exclusions

Previous research suggests that grants are not made for payment of national or local taxes or rates.

Applications

Applications may be made in writing to the correspondent providing a full explanation of the applicant's personal circumstances. Previous research suggests that requests should be submitted by the end of February or August for consideration in the following month.

Financial information

Year end	31/12/2019
Income	£3,700
Total expenditure	£2,600

Further financial information

Full accounts were not available to view on the Charity Commission's website due to the charity's low income. We have therefore estimated the grant total based on the charity's total expenditure.

Somerset West and Taunton

The Rogers and Holes Charities

 £1,200 (2020)

Correspondent: The Trustees, Steepholme, Bossington Lane, Porlock, Minehead TA24 8HD (tel: 01643 863124; email: ruthehyett@gmail.com)

CC number: 290787

Eligibility

Older people who live in Porlock.

Types of grant

One-off grants and small monthly payments.

Applications

Apply in writing to the correspondent.

Financial information

Year end	31/12/2020
Income	£2,700
Total expenditure	£2,600

Further financial information

Full accounts were not available to view on the Charity Commission's website due to the charity's low income. We have therefore estimated the charity's grant total based on its total expenditure.

The Taunton Aid in Sickness Fund

£20,400 (2019/20)

Correspondent: The Clerk, Lower Orchard, Spearcey Lane, Trull, Taunton, Somerset TA3 7HW (email: info@ tauntonaidinsicknessfund.co.uk)

www.tauntonaidinsicknessfund.co. uk

CC number: 260716

Eligibility

People who live within a five-mile radius of St Mary's Church in Taunton and are ill or have a disability.

Types of grant

One-off grants are made according to need. Examples include washing machines, cookers, flooring, mobility equipment and garden adaptations.

Applications

Application forms are available to download on the funder's website. Applications should be made on the individual's behalf by a third party, such as the Citizens Advice, and should include quotes of the items requested.

Financial information

Year end	31/03/2020
Income	£27,000
Total expenditure	£45,600

Further financial information

In the financial year, the charity made 41 grants to individuals.

Other information

The charity also makes small donations to organisations.

Taunton Heritage Trust

£56,200 (2019/20)

Correspondent: The Trustees, Huish Homes, Magdalene Street, Taunton, Somerset TA1 1SG (tel: 01823 335348; email: info@tauntonheritagetrust.org.uk)

www.tauntonheritagetrust.org.uk

CC number: 1177162

Eligibility

People who live in the borough of Taunton Deane and are in need.

Types of grant

One-off grants are given for a wide range of purposes including:

- Furniture
- Clothing
- Freestanding white goods (fridges, freezers, cookers, washing machines, etc.)
- Flooring
- Disability aids, home adaptations and mobility scooters
- School uniform (basic clothing essentials only)
- Home computers
- Respite holidays
- Nursery fees

Exclusions

Grants are not given for the following:

- To replace statutory support (supplementary grants may be available, however)
- School trips, school bags, stationery or other non-essential school items
- Retrospective applications
- Further/higher education course fees or books/materials
- Deposits for accommodation
- Funeral expenses
- Bankruptcy costs

Applications

Application forms can be downloaded from the trust's website and must be completed by a recognised referral agency such as social services or Citizens Advice. Further guidelines are available to download on the trust's website.

Financial information

Year end	30/08/2020
Income	£733,200
Total expenditure	£617,300

Other information

The primary role of the trust is to provide sheltered accommodation for people over the age of 60. Grants are also given to organisations.

South Somerset

The Ilchester Relief in Need and Educational Charity (IRINEC)

£16,600 (2020)

Correspondent: Kaye Elston, Clerk to the Trustees, 15 Chilton Grove, Yeovil, Somerset BA21 4AN (tel: 07782 251464)

 www.ilchesterparishcouncil.gov.uk

CC number: 235578

Eligibility

People in need who live in the parish of Ilchester.

Types of grant

Welfare

One-off grants are given for goods and services to relieve need, hardship and distress. The charity can also provide financial assistance towards leisure activities where they will help the applicant's well-being.

Education

One-off grants are given to help with expenses at schools, universities, colleges or other educational organisations. They can help to provide books, tools or other equipment, or help with travel expenses.

Exclusions

Grants are not available where support should be received from statutory sources.

Applications

Application forms are available to request from the correspondent. The clerk welcomes initial telephone contact to discuss need and eligibility. Check the website for dates applications should be received by.

Financial information

Year end	31/12/2020
Income	£43,100
Total expenditure	£25,900

Other information

Grants are also awarded to organisations for educational purposes.

John Nowes Exhibition Foundation

£6,000 (2019/20)

Correspondent: Amanda Goddard, Clerk to the Trustees, Battens Solicitors, Mansion House, 54–58 Princes Street, Yeovil, Somerset BA20 1EP (tel: 01935 846000; email: amanda.goddard@battens. co.uk)

 https://www.battens.co.uk/news-events/news/john-nowes-exhibition-foundation-applications-2

CC number: 309984

Eligibility

Children and young people between the ages of 16 and 25 who live in the borough of Yeovil and surrounding parishes (including Alvington, Barwick, Brympton, Chilthorne Domer, East Coker, Limington, Mudford, Preston Plucknett, Yeovil Without or West Coker). Applicants must have a household income of less than £33,000 per annum.

Types of grant

Financial assistance can be given towards facilities not normally provided by the Local Education Authority for recreation, social and physical training, including coaching for sports, athletics and games.

Scholarships, bursaries, and maintenance allowances are provided to those in school, university or college. Small grants are awarded towards clothing, equipment, or books for those preparing to enter work. There are also grants available for travel abroad for educational purposes.

Applications

An application form can be downloaded from the foundation's website or requested from the correspondent. It should be submitted along with a parental declaration, evidence of household income and a reference from the head of the student's current educational establishment. Check the website for the closing date, which is usually in June so the grants can be awarded in September.

Financial information

Year end	31/03/2020
Income	£5,400
Total expenditure	£6,700

Further financial information

Full accounts were not available to view on the Charity Commission's website due to the foundation's low income. We have therefore estimated the foundation's grant total based on its total expenditure.

Wiltshire

Aldbourne Poors' Gorse

£4,200 (2019/20)

Correspondent: Terry Gilligan, 9 Cook Road, Aldbourne, Marlborough, Wiltshire SN8 2EG (tel: 01672 540205; email: terrygilliganaldbourne@gmail. com)

CC number: 202958

Eligibility

People in need who live in the parish of Aldbourne, with a preference for those over 65.

Types of grant

One-off grants towards fuel costs.

Applications

Apply in writing to the correspondent, directly by the individual, usually on the charity's invitation.

Financial information

Year end	12/12/2020
Income	£4,500
Total expenditure	£4,700

Further financial information

Full accounts were not available to view on the Charity Commission's website due to the charity's low income. We have therefore estimated the grant total based on the charity's total expenditure.

The Ashton Keynes Charity

£3,000 (2020)

Correspondent: The Trustees, Coulston, High Road, Ashton Keynes, Swindon SN6 6NX (tel: 01285 861461; email: recsmith4@gmail.com)

CC number: 205302

Eligibility

People in need who live in Ashton Keynes, and young people under the age of 25 who are undertaking an apprenticeship.

Types of grant

Grants are given according to need.

Applications

Apply in writing to the correspondent.

Financial information

Year end	31/12/2020
Income	£7,300
Total expenditure	£6,100

Further financial information

Full accounts were not available to view on the Charity Commission's website

due to the charity's low income. We have therefore estimated the grant total based on the charity's total expenditure.

C. N. W. Blair Charity

 £5,000 (2019/20)

Correspondent: The Trustees, Castle House, Castle Place, Trowbridge, Wiltshire BA14 8AX (tel: 01225 755621)

CC number: 202446

Eligibility
People in need who live in Trowbridge, particularly those with a low income. Christmas vouchers are available for residents who are able to provide proof of being in receipt of benefits.

Types of grant
Grants are awarded for food, fuel and clothing. Each year, Christmas vouchers are distributed at the Guide Hall in the People's Park.

Applications
The trust has previously advertised the date of distribution each year in the local press, with details of how to apply. Contact the correspondent for more information.

Financial information
Year end	31/03/2020
Income	£8,500
Total expenditure	£11,200

Further financial information
Full accounts were not available to view on the Charity Commission's website due to the charity's low income. We have therefore estimated the charity's grant total based on its total expenditure.

Other information
The charity also supports organisations.

Charity of William Botley

 £11,100 (2020)

Correspondent: Clerk to the Trustees, Trinity Hospital, Trinity Street, Salisbury, Wiltshire SP1 2BD (tel: 01722 325640; email: clerk@ salisburyalmshouses.co.uk)

www.salisburyalmshouses.co.uk

CC number: 268418

Eligibility
Women who live in Salisbury and are in need.

Types of grant
One-off grants are awarded according to need. Examples include: clothing and school uniforms; furniture; beds and

bedding; carpets; kitchen appliances; specialist disability/mobility aids and equipment; hospital visits; removal costs; funeral expenses. Interest-free loans are also awarded, although exceptionally.

Exclusions
Grants cannot be awarded to top up income, repay debts or as reimbursement for items already purchased. Repeat grants are not usually given.

Applications
Application forms are available from the Salisbury City Almshouse and Welfare Charities website. The trustees meet once every month to consider grant applications. Applications should be made on the individual's behalf by a recognised third party, such as a social worker or Citizens Advice.

Financial information
Year end	31/12/2020
Income	£7,500
Total expenditure	£12,300

Further financial information
Full accounts were not available to view on the Charity Commission's website due to the charity's low income. We have therefore estimated the charity's grant total based on its total expenditure.

Other information
The charity is administered under the umbrella of the Salisbury City Almshouse and Welfare Charities (Charity Commission no. 202110).

Chippenham Borough Lands Charity

 £39,600 (2019/20)

Correspondent: Grants Officer, Jubilee Building, 32 Market Place, Chippenham, Wiltshire SN15 3HP (tel: 01249 658180; email: admin@cblc.org.uk)

www.cblc.org.uk

CC number: 270062

Eligibility
People in need who are living within the parish of Chippenham at the date of application, and have been for a minimum of two years immediately prior to applying.

Types of grant
Welfare
One-off grants and loans are made according to need. Recent grants have included white goods, furniture, food vouchers, debt relief, funeral costs and mobility aids.

Education
Grants are available to individuals studying up to and including level 3. Support may include help with equipment such as laptops, course fees and transport costs.

Applications
Potential applicants should contact the charity via telephone or email to discuss their need and eligibility. Application forms will then be provided by the correspondent.

Financial information
Year end	31/03/2020
Income	£626,100
Total expenditure	£555,600

Other information
Other welfare organisations in the area work closely with the charity to support people in need. There are also funds provided to local organisations with similar objectives to the charity. Note that after the changes to the parish boundary both the Cepen Park North and Cepen Park South estates are included.

The Community Foundation for Wiltshire and Swindon

 £385,100 (2019/20)

Correspondent: Grants Team, Ground Floor, Sandcliff House, 21 Northgate Street, Devizes, Wiltshire SN10 1JT (tel: 01380 729284; email: info@ wiltshirecf.org.uk)

https://www.wiltshirecf.org.uk

CC number: 1123126

Eligibility
People in need who live in Wiltshire. Visit the foundation's website for additional criteria specific to each grant.

Types of grant
Welfare
The foundation administers the Surviving Winter Campaign which provides grants of £300 towards winter fuel costs for people in need. Support is mostly given to older people. Visit the website for further information and specific criteria.

Education
The foundation provides up to £1,000 to children and young people who need educational support due to a disability or illness through the educational support scheme. Funding can be given towards extracurricular activities, therapeutic equipment such as music, educational resources, travel costs and so on.

The foundation currently provides a number of educational grant schemes:

- **University bursary – one degree more:** Supports individuals between 17 and 24 who are about to begin, or who are already studying for, an undergraduate degree at a UK university. Bursaries of £1,500 are awarded each year of the course towards living expenses, travel expenses (not including study abroad), books and course costs. In some cases, an additional £500 can be granted for certain courses or situations

- **Vocational grants:** Grants are given to young people in need between 14 and 24 to support those at school/college (including sixth form) and people undertaking vocational courses and apprenticeships. Grants of up to £1,000 can be used towards travel costs, IT equipment course-related field trips, educational resources and so on.

Visit the website for further information and specific criteria for each grant scheme.

Applications

Application packs for the educational support grant can be requested from the foundation's website. Application forms for the Surviving Winter Campaign can be requested from the correspondent. Applications should be made through a third-party organisation, such as Age UK, Aster Living, Credit Union or Citizens Advice.

Financial information

Year end	31/03/2020
Income	£2,190,000
Total expenditure	£1,860,000

Further financial information

Grants were awarded to 391 individuals during the year. 125 grants were awarded for education and 266 grants for welfare.

Other information

This is one of the 47 UK community foundations, which distribute funding for a wide range of purposes. Grant schemes tend to change frequently – consult the foundation's website for details of current programmes and upcoming deadlines.

The Ernest and Marjorie Fudge Trust

 £31,800 (2019/20)

Correspondent: Fran Pearson, Trustee/Chair, 12 Rock Lane, Warminster, Wiltshire BA12 9JZ (tel: 01985 213440; email: info@fudgetrust.co.uk)

 www.fudgetrust.co.uk

CC number: 1168096

Eligibility

Residents of Warminster and the surrounding area who are in need. Preference is given to people with learning difficulties.

Types of grant

Welfare
Grants are awarded according to need. Grants have previously been given towards wheelchairs, stairlifts, scooters, furniture, appliances, winter fuel bills and respite breaks for full-time carers.

Education
According to the trust's website, grants may be awarded for personal and professional development courses.

Applications

Application forms can be completed on the trust's website. A copy should be saved and printed before submission. Note: all payments are made by cheque directly to suppliers. Applicants should be sure that their chosen suppliers can accept this form of payment.

Financial information

Year end	05/04/2020
Income	£72,400
Total expenditure	£65,300

Further financial information

During the financial year, the charity awarded grants to 20 individuals. It also awarded grants to 14 organisations totalling £17,200.

Other information

Grants are also made to local organisations. The charity continues to support applications from local schools for specialist computer equipment and software to help children with special educational needs.

Malmesbury Area Community Trust

 £18,000 (2019/20)

Correspondent: Phil Rice, Trustee, 49 Bonners Close, Malmesbury, Wiltshire SN16 9UF (tel: 07973 646869; email: tony.moore49@outlook.com)

 www.mact.org.uk

CC number: 1018458

Eligibility

People in need who live in Malmesbury and the surrounding area, with priority given to older residents.

Types of grant

The trust is able to make emergency grants of up to £500. Grants are also available for disability scooters and aids, essential household equipment, equipment for young children with special needs, school uniforms, school trips, musical instruments for young people, books, travel costs and work equipment for those on apprenticeship schemes.

Applications

Application forms are available on the trust's website.

Financial information

Year end	31/03/2020
Income	£8,000
Total expenditure	£20,000

Further financial information

Full accounts were not available to view on the Charity Commission's website due to the trust's low income. We have therefore estimated the grant total based on the trust's total expenditure.

Salisbury City Almshouse and Welfare Charities

 £25,100 (2020)

Correspondent: Clerk to the Trustees, Trinity Hospital, Trinity Street, Salisbury, Wiltshire SP1 2BD (tel: 01722 325640; email: clerk@salisburyalmshouses.co.uk)

 www.salisburyalmshouses.co.uk

CC number: 202110

Eligibility

People in need who live in Salisbury.

Types of grant

One-off grants are given according to need. Funding can be given towards household items, white goods, furniture, clothing, school uniform, beds, bedding and carpets, as well as specialist disability/mobility aids and equipment, hospital visits, removal costs and funeral expenses.

Exclusions

Grants are not made to cover debts, top up income or reimburse individuals for purchases already made. It is unusual for the charity to make more than one grant to an applicant in any one year.

Applications

Application forms and full guidelines are available on the charity's website. All applications must be sponsored by a recognised professional.

Financial information

Year end	31/12/2020
Income	£1,830,000
Total expenditure	£1,650,000

Other information

The charity's main concern is the maintenance of almshouses in and around Salisbury. This mainly includes housing for older people; however, accommodation is also offered to young families, especially single parents. Educational support is given through Salisbury City Educational and Apprenticing Charity (Charity Commission no. 309523).

Salisbury City Educational and Apprenticing Charity

£ £2,800 (2020)

Correspondent: Clerk to the Trustees, Trinity Hospital, Trinity Street, Salisbury, Wiltshire SP1 2BD (tel: 01722 325640; email: clerk@almshouses.demon.co.uk)

 www.salisburyalmshouses.co.uk

CC number: 309523

Eligibility

Young people under the age of 25 who live in the district of Salisbury.

Types of grant

Education

Educational and apprenticing grants are available to young people. Awards are given for education in the broadest sense, for example for courses, trips, books, equipment and tools, vocational training and professional qualifications.

Welfare

Welfare grants are awarded for trips, play schemes, adventure activities, expeditions and voluntary work abroad.

Exclusions

Grants are not given for postgraduate study or for daily subsistence expenses (e.g. while at university). Regular payments towards fees or expenses are rarely made.

Applications

Application forms and full guidelines, stating what should be included, are available on the charity's website. Requests are considered on a monthly basis.

Financial information

Year end	31/12/2020
Income	£2,800
Total expenditure	£3,200

Further financial information

Full accounts were not available to view on the Charity Commission's website due to the charity's low income. We have therefore estimated the charity's grant total based on its total expenditure.

Other information

The charity shares the trustees with Salisbury City Almshouse and Welfare Charities (Charity Commission no. 202110), which maintains almshouses and may also provide emergency welfare support.

The Henry Smith Charity (Westbury)

£ £1,800 (2019)

Correspondent: The Trustees, c/o Pinniger Finch & Co. Solicitors, 35 Church Street, Westbury, Wiltshire BA13 3BZ (tel: 01373 823791; email: info@pinnigerfinch.co.uk)

CC number: 243888

Eligibility

Older people and people with disabilities living in Westbury.

Types of grant

Grants are given according to need.

Applications

Apply in writing to the correspondent.

Financial information

Year end	31/12/2019
Income	£2,000
Total expenditure	£2,000

Further financial information

Full accounts were not available to view on the Charity Commission's website due to the charity's low income. We have therefore estimated the charity's grant total based on its total expenditure.

Wiltshire Ambulance Service Benevolent Fund

£ £15,000 (2019/20)

Correspondent: The Trustees, 82 Dunch Lane, Melksham, Wiltshire SN12 8DX (tel: 07966 534713; email: charliecopter@msn.com)

CC number: 280364

Eligibility

Current and former members of the benevolent fund, and their dependants, who are in need.

Types of grant

Grants are given according to need.

Applications

Apply in writing to the correspondent.

Financial information

Year end	31/03/2020
Income	£22,800
Total expenditure	£15,800

Further financial information

Full accounts were not available to view on the Charity Commission's website due to the fund's low income. We have therefore estimated the grant total based on the fund's total expenditure.

Other information

The fund also provides holiday accommodation, which is available for eligible people to use.

Wiltshire Police Benevolent Trust

£ £21,400 (2019/20)

Correspondent: The Trustees, Wiltshire Constabulary Headquarters, London Road, Devizes SN10 2DN (tel: 01380 861043; email: federation@wiltshire.pnn.police.uk)

CC number: 1117765

Eligibility

Serving and retired Wiltshire Police staff, special constables and their dependants.

Types of grant

Grants are awarded according to need.

Applications

Apply in writing to the correspondent.

Financial information

Year end	31/03/2020
Income	£12,100
Total expenditure	£23,800

Further financial information

Full accounts were not available to view on the Charity Commission's website due to the trust's low income. We have therefore estimated the trust's grant total based on its total expenditure.

Yorkshire and the Humber

General

The Cotton Districts Convalescent Fund and the Barnes Samaritan Charity
See entry on page 216

The Hesslewood Children's Trust (Hull Seamen's and General Orphanage)

£ £32,200 (2019/20)

Correspondent: Lynne Bullock, 62 The Meadows, Cherry Burton, East Yorkshire HU17 7RQ (tel: 01964 550882; email: misslynneb@aol.com)

CC number: 529804

Eligibility
People under the age of 25 who live, or have a parent that lives, in the former county of Humberside or in the districts of Gainsborough or Caistor in Lincolnshire. Former residents of the Hull Seamen's and General Orphanage are also eligible, with preference given to children of seamen.

Types of grant
Grants are given according to need.

Exclusions
Applicants based outside the beneficial areas.

Applications
Apply in writing to the correspondent.

Financial information

Year end	31/03/2020
Income	£116,900
Total expenditure	£102,300

Other information
The trust also awards grants to organisations active in the local communities.

Humberside Police Welfare and Benevolent Fund

£ £12,000 (2020)

Correspondent: The Trustees, c/o Humberside Police, Police Station, Priory Road, Hull HU5 5SF (tel: 0845 606 0222; email: webmail@humberside. pnn.police.uk)

CC number: 503762

Eligibility
Grants are awarded for: serving and retired officers of the Humberside Police and retired officers from other forces who live in Humberside, and their partners and dependants; and civilian employees of Humberside Police Authority, retired civilian employees, and their partners and dependants.

Types of grant
One-off and recurrent grants can be awarded to help individuals through a particularly difficult time. Loans are also provided.

Applications
Apply in writing to the correspondent.

Financial information

Year end	31/12/2020
Income	£15,100
Total expenditure	£13,700

Further financial information
Full accounts were not available to view on the Charity Commission's website due to the fund's low income. We have therefore estimated the grant total based on the fund's total expenditure.

Rycroft Children's Fund
See entry on page 212

York Dispensary Sick Poor Fund

£ £22,000 (2020)

Correspondent: The Trustees, c/o Grays Solicitors, Duncombe Place, York, North Yorkshire YO1 7DY (tel: 01904 634771; email: iainmilne@grayssolicitors.co.uk)

CC number: 221277

Eligibility
People who live in York and the surrounding districts and are suffering from both poverty and ill health.

Types of grant
Grants are given according to need.

Applications
Apply in writing to the correspondent.

Financial information

Year end	31/12/2020
Income	£21,000
Total expenditure	£24,200

Further financial information
Full accounts were not available to view on the Charity Commission's website due to the fund's low income. We have therefore estimated the fund's grant total based on its total expenditure.

Other information
The fund also supports organisations.

Yorkshire Children's Trust

 £15,700 (2020/21)

Correspondent: Rachael Administration Assistant, YCT House, 70 Commercial Street, Halifax, West Yorkshire HX1 2JE (tel: 01422 728008; email: rachael@yctrust.uk or charity@yctrust.uk)

🌐 https://www.yctrust.uk

CC number: 1146884

Eligibility

Families who live in Yorkshire with children who are sick or have a disability up to the age of 18.

Types of grant

At the time of writing (October 2021) the trust offered the following grants.

Hospital Stay Grant

One-off grants of £150 to help cover the costs associated with having a child in hospital for an extended duration (eight days or more), such as travel costs, parking charges and food.

50:50 Grant

The grant covers 50% of the cost of equipment and therapies that will improve the health or well-being of a child with physical or mental illness or disability. Items must cost up to £1,000 (the charity's maximum contribution is £500).

Previous examples include: specialist car seats; wheelchair ramps; hydrotherapy sessions; sensory equipment; specialist cutlery; specialist buggies; a washer dryer for a child with incontinence; Apple iPad.

Applications

Online applications forms are available on the trust's website.

Hospital Stay Grant

Applications are only accepted from parents, medical professionals, social workers or key workers. Applications will take between one and four weeks to process.

50:50 Grant

Applications are welcomed from parents, carers, teachers, social/support workers and medical professionals. Applications take about 30 days to process.

Financial information

Year end	28/02/2021
Income	£137,100
Total expenditure	£91,500

Other information

The trust also offers free respite breaks for families at its holiday home at Butlins, as well as a counselling service.

East Riding of Yorkshire

Aldbrough Poor Fields

 £630 (2020/21)

Correspondent: Nicola Salvidge, Clerk, 17 Spring Field Close, Sigglesthorne, Hull HU11 5QP (tel: 01964 533148; email: clerk@aldbroughparishcouncil.co.uk)

🌐 https://www.aldbroughparish council.co.uk

CC number: 222569

Eligibility

Men aged over 65 and children with disabilities who are in need and live in Aldbrough village and the surrounding area of West Newton.

Types of grant

Grants are given in the form of vouchers and are distributed at Christmas.

Applications

Apply in writing to the correspondent.

Financial information

Year end	31/03/2021
Income	£880
Total expenditure	£700

Further financial information

Full accounts were not available to view on the Charity Commission's website due to the charity's low income. We have therefore estimated the charity's grant total based on its total expenditure.

The Bridlington Charities (Henry Cowton)

 £30,400 (2020)

Correspondent: The Trustees, 118 St James Road, Bridlington, East Yorkshire YO15 3NJ (tel: 01262 403333; email: bridlingtoncharities@yahoo.co.uk)

CC number: 224609

Eligibility

People in need who live in the parish of Bridlington.

Types of grant

Grants are given according to need.

Applications

Apply in writing to the correspondent.

Financial information

Year end	31/12/2020
Income	£94,300
Total expenditure	£81,900

Further financial information

In 2020, the charity awarded grants totalling £60,700. We estimate that around £30,400 was awarded to individuals.

Other information

This charity also makes grants to organisations.

The Hedon Haven Trust

 £1,700 (2019)

Correspondent: The Trustees, 1 Pasture Terrace, Beverley, East Yorkshire HU17 8DR (tel: 01482 864331; email: sngreen@epea.karoo.co.uk)

CC number: 500259

Eligibility

Residents of Hedon who are in need.

Types of grant

Grants are allocated according to need.

Applications

Apply in writing to the correspondent.

Financial information

Year end	31/12/2019
Income	£5,200
Total expenditure	£3,800

Further financial information

Full accounts were not available to view on the Charity Commission's website due to the trust's low income. We have therefore estimated the trust's grant total based on its total expenditure.

Other information

This charity also makes grants to local organisations.

Heron Educational Foundation (Heron Trust)

 £1,100 (2020/21)

Correspondent: The Trustees, Hill Farm House, Sproatley Road, Flinton, Hull HU11 4NE (tel: 01964 529668; email: herontrustcio@gmail.com)

🌐 www.humbleton.org.uk/new-page-3.aspx

CC number: 1187969

Eligibility

People under the age of 25 who live in the parish of Humbleton and the nearby villages of Flinton and Fitling.

Types of grant

Grants are available to students starting school and further/higher education. People entering a trade/profession may also be assisted.

Applications

Apply in writing to the correspondent.

Financial information

Year end	31/03/2021
Income	£50,300
Total expenditure	£43,800

Other information

This charity also awards grants to organisations.

The Nafferton Feoffees Charities Trust

 £12,400 (2020)

Correspondent: Secretary, c/o South Cattleholmes, White Dike, Wansford, Driffield, East Yorkshire YO25 8NW (tel: 01377 254293; email: secretary@ feoffeetrust.co.uk)

 www.feoffeetrust.co.uk

CC number: 232796

Eligibility

Welfare

People in need who live in the parish of All Saints Nafferton with St Mary's Wansford.

Education

Individuals who live in the parish of All Saints Nafferton with St Mary's Wansford and are intending to undertake a first degree at a UK university or college.

Types of grant

Grants are given according to need. Previous grants have been given towards the cost of music and sports lessons, laptops, a wheelchair, travel costs and educational materials.

Bursaries are available to local students who are undertaking a first degree. Up to £2,100 per year for each year of the course can be awarded towards books, course materials, study visits and other educational expenses. The trust will provide support for mature students.

Applications

Application forms and guidance can be downloaded from the trust's website.

Financial information

Year end	31/12/2020
Income	£34,300
Total expenditure	£36,000

Further financial information

In 2020, a total of £600 was awarded for welfare purposes. Scholarships totalled £11,800.

Other information

Grants are also made to local organisations.

The Sir James Reckitt Charity

 £95,400 (2020)

Correspondent: The Trustees, 7 Derrymore Road, Willerby, Hull, East Yorkshire HU10 6ES (tel: 01482 655861; email: jim@derrymore.karoo.co.uk)

www.thesirjamesreckittcharity.org. uk

CC number: 225356

Eligibility

People in need, with a high priority given to those residing in Hull and the East Riding of Yorkshire.

Types of grant

One-off grants ranging from £500 to £5,000. Grants are usually given in the form of vouchers to be exchanged at local suppliers for an item of furniture or household equipment.

Exclusions

No repeat grants are made over a two-year period.

Applications

Applications for individual grants must be made to the Consortium of Grant Giving Trusts (Hull and East Yorkshire). Application forms can be downloaded on the funder's website and should be completed by a sponsoring agency, such as a social worker or health visitor, working with the applicant.

Financial information

Year end	31/12/2020
Income	£1,580,000
Total expenditure	£1,480,000

Other information

The charity also makes grants to young people to help them attend overseas events run by local Scouting and Guiding Associations, as well as those organised by Children's International Summer Villages.

Robert Towrie's Charity

£4,600 (2019/20)

Correspondent: The Trustees, Stud Farm, Hull Road, Aldbrough, Hull, East Yorkshire HU11 4RE (tel: 01964 527580; email: roberttowerytrust@googlemail. com)

CC number: 222568

Eligibility

Residents in the parishes of Aldbrough and Burton Constable who are in need, particularly older individuals and people with disabilities.

Types of grant

Welfare

Examples of grants from the charity's 2019/20 accounts included awards to help with the cost of painting ceilings, chimney sweeping, plastering walls and bathroom sink repair.

Education

According to the charity's 2019/20 accounts, all education grants were given as university payments.

Applications

Apply in writing to the correspondent.

Financial information

Year end	01/04/2020
Income	£158,200
Total expenditure	£7,400

Other information

The charity makes grants to individuals and organisations for both educational and welfare needs.

Kingston upon Hull

The Charity of Miss Eliza Clubley Middleton

£20,000 (2019/20)

Correspondent: Harriet Wheeldon, c/o Rollitts LLP, Citadel House, 58 High Street, Hull HU1 1QE (tel: 01482 323239; email: Harriet.Wheeldon@rollits. com)

CC number: 229134

Eligibility

Women of the Roman Catholic faith who are experiencing financial difficulty and live in Kingston upon Hull (or within ten miles of its boundaries).

Types of grant

One-off or recurrent grants are made in the form of pensions.

Applications

Apply in writing to the correspondent.

Financial information

Year end	05/04/2020
Income	£5,600
Total expenditure	£21,000

Further financial information

Full accounts were not available to view on the Charity Commission's website due to the charity's low income. We have therefore estimated the grant total based on the charity's total expenditure.

The Hull Aid in Sickness Trust

 £6,100 (2019/20)

Correspondent: Clerk to the Trustees, Hull CVS Ltd, The Strand, 75 Beverley Road, Hull, East Yorkshire HU3 1XL (tel: 07415 105494 or 01482 595564; email: info@hullaidinsickness.co.uk)

🌐 www.hullaidinsickness.co.uk

CC number: 224193

Eligibility

People who live in the city and county of Kingston upon Hull and are in need as a result of low household income, ill health or disability.

Types of grant

One-off grants are given towards items or services that will provide a clear benefit to the applicant's health and quality of life. Examples include household furnishings, carpets or appliances; mobility aids; appliances or equipment that must be modified for specialist needs (for example, talking microwaves for those who are partially sighted); other medical/nursing aids. Grants tend to be between £150 and £600; however, larger grants will be considered.

Exclusions

Grants are not given for items that are available through other sources (i.e. alternative funding, family assistance or social services) or items that are affordable by way of monthly payments. Grants cannot be used towards debts or as reimbursement for items that have already been purchased.

Applications

Application forms are available to download from the trust's website. Those with disabilities or suffering ill health must provide recent medical evidence alongside their application. Further guidance on what to include can be found on the website.

Financial information

Year end	30/08/2020
Income	£36,700
Total expenditure	£27,000

Further financial information

The funder's website states that the maximum grant considered is usually in the region of £150 to £600 per application.

Other information

This trust also makes grants to organisations.

The Mother Humber' Memorial Fund

 £13,500 (2019/20)

Correspondent: Malcolm Welford, Secretary to the Trustees, Suite 1, The Riverside Building, Livingstone Road, Hessle, Hull, East Yorkshire HU13 0DZ (tel: 0845 463 4727; email: info@ motherhumber.org.uk)

🌐 www.motherhumber.org.uk

CC number: 225082

Eligibility

People in need who live within the city of Kingston upon Hull.

Types of grant

Grants are typically under £500 and can cover, for example, items such as electrical equipment/white goods, essential furniture, clothing and bedding.

Exclusions

Our previous research suggests that the charity does not awards grants for tumble dryers, nor does it make grants for debt repayments.

Applications

Application forms are available to download on the funder's website and should be returned via email. A supporting letter from a third party (such as Citizens Advice or a social worker or health visitor) may help an individual's application, but is not considered mandatory. The trustees usually meet once per month.

Financial information

Year end	31/05/2020
Income	£40,600
Total expenditure	£40,100

Further financial information

Full accounts were not available to view on the Charity Commission's website due to the charity's low income. We have therefore estimated the charity's grant total based on its total expenditure.

Other information

This charity also makes grants to organisations.

The Joseph Rank Benevolent Fund

 £84,000 (2020)

Correspondent: Debby Burman, Clerk to the Trustees, Artlink Centre, 87 Princes Avenue, Hull, East Yorkshire HU5 3QP (tel: 01482 225542; email: debbyburman@icloud.com)

🌐 www.josephrankfund.org.uk

CC number: 225318

Eligibility

Retired people who are in need and have resided in Hull for at least ten years within the past 15 years with less than £10,000 in savings. People aged over 55 with a long-term health condition will also be considered.

Types of grant

Recurrent grants are paid quarterly.

Applications

Application forms can be requested from the correspondent by telephone or using the contact form on the fund's website. Completed forms should be posted to the correspondent.

Financial information

Year end	31/12/2020
Income	£119,300
Total expenditure	£184,200

Further financial information

In 2020, the fund made quarterly payments of £45 to 396 single beneficiaries and payments of £90 to 46 married couples.

Other information

This fund also makes small grants to charities whose work is largely based in Hull. This occurs annually in December.

Lincolnshire (formerly part of Humberside)

North East Lincolnshire

Sir Alec Black's Charity

£ £22,100 (2019/20)

Correspondent: The Trustees, 27 Osborne Street, Grimsby, North East Lincolnshire DN31 1NU (tel: 01472 348315; email: sabc@wilsonsharpe.co.uk)

CC number: 220295

Eligibility

Fishermen and dockworkers in Grimsby, and their dependants, who are in need as a result of illness or financial hardship. Pensions are available to employees of Sir Alec Black during his lifetime. The charity will also support residents of Grimsby who are experiencing ill health or financial hardship.

Types of grant

Grants and pensions are awarded according to need.

Applications

Apply in writing to the correspondent.

Financial information

Year end	12/04/2020
Income	£331,900
Total expenditure	£78,100

Further financial information

During the year, the charity awarded grants to 42 individuals.

Other information

This charity also provides bed linen and pillows to voluntary organisations caring for people experiencing ill health.

Grimsby Sailors and Fishing Charity

£ £19,400 (2019)

Correspondent: Judi Coultas, Manager, Office Suite 1, Alexandra Dock Business Centre, Fishermans Wharf, Grimsby, Lincolnshire DN31 1UL (tel: 01472 347914; email: judicoultas12@gmail.com)

CC number: 500816

Eligibility

Children of deceased fishermen who are in full-time education and are in need.

Types of grant

Weekly and quarterly grants.

Applications

Apply in writing to the correspondent.

Financial information

Year end	31/12/2019
Income	£750,500
Total expenditure	£508,400

Other information

Retired sailors and fish trade workers (and their dependants) are eligible for accommodation at the charity's almshouses in Grimsby, Waltham, New Waltham and Scartho.

North Lincolnshire

Beeton, Barrick and Beck Relief-in-Need Charity

£ £4,300 (2019/20)

Correspondent: The Trustees, Barrow Wold Farm, Deepdale, Barton-upon-Humber, North Lincolnshire DN18 6ED (tel: 01469 531928; email: audrey.lawe@hotmail.co.uk)

CC number: 234571

Eligibility

Older residents in the parish of Barrow-upon-Humber.

Types of grant

Annual grants are awarded at Christmas.

Applications

Apply in writing to the correspondent.

Financial information

Year end	22/09/2020
Income	£19,400
Total expenditure	£17,300

Further financial information

Full accounts were not available to view on the Charity Commission's website due to the charity's low income. We have therefore estimated the grant total based on the charity's total expenditure.

Blue Coat Charity

£ £18,000 (2019/20)

Correspondent: The Trustees, c/o B. G. Solicitors LLP, Market Place, Barton-upon-Humber, North Lincolnshire DN18 5DD (tel: 01652 632215)

CC number: 237891

Eligibility

Residents of Barton-upon-Humber who are in need.

Types of grant

Grants are awarded in the form of vouchers, mostly for food, bedding, school uniforms and other essential items.

Applications

Apply in writing to the correspondent.

Financial information

Year end	31/03/2020
Income	£18,500
Total expenditure	£22,700

Further financial information

Full accounts were not available to view on the Charity Commission's website due to the charity's low income. We have therefore estimated the charity's grant total based on its total expenditure.

Epworth Charities

£ £1,000 (2019/20)

Correspondent: The Trustees, 6 Rectory Street, Epworth, Doncaster, South Yorkshire DN9 1HB (tel: 01427 872466; email: jrlambert@doctors.org.uk)

CC number: 219744

Eligibility

People in need who live in Epworth.

Types of grant

One-off and recurrent grants are made according to need.

Applications

Apply in writing to the correspondent. Applications can be made directly by the individual and are considered on an ongoing basis.

Financial information

Year end	30/04/2020
Income	£4,100
Total expenditure	£1,300

Further financial information

Full accounts were not available to view on the Charity Commission's website due to the charity's low income. We have therefore estimated the grant total based on the charity's total expenditure.

North Yorkshire

Bedale Welfare Charity (The Rector and Four and Twenty of Bedale)

£ £1,400 (2019/20)

Correspondent: Judi Asquith, 11A Meadowfield, Aiskew, Bedale, North Yorkshire DL8 1EA (tel: 07454 822008; email: judiasquith@yahoo.com)

CC number: 224035

Eligibility

Residents in the parishes of Aiskew, Bedale, Burrill with Cowling, Crakehall, Firby, Langthorne and Rand Grange who are in need.

Types of grant

Grants are awarded according to need for items, services and facilities.

Applications

Apply in writing to the correspondent.

Financial information

Year end	31/03/2020
Income	£19,900
Total expenditure	£3,200

Further financial information

Full accounts were not available to view on the Charity Commission's website due to the charity's low income. We have therefore estimated the charity's grant total based on its total expenditure.

Other information

This charity also makes grants to organisations.

Craven

The Gertrude Beasley Charitable Trust

£ £1,400 (2019/20)

Correspondent: J. Mewies, Trustee, c/o J. P. Mewies and Co. Solicitors, Clifford House, Keighley Road, Skipton, North Yorkshire BD23 2NB (tel: 01756 799000; email: j.mewies@mewiessolicitors.co.uk)

CC number: 1074589

Eligibility

Individuals under the age of 18 who have a disability and are resident in Craven, North Yorkshire.

Types of grant

Grants are made according to need.

Applications

Apply in writing to the correspondent.

Financial information

Year end	31/03/2020
Income	£5,600
Total expenditure	£3,100

Further financial information

Full accounts were not available to view on the Charity Commission's website due to the trust's low income. We have therefore estimated the trust's grant total based on its total expenditure.

Other information

This trust also makes grants to organisations.

The Craven Trust

£ £6,000 (2019/20)

Correspondent: Rowena Garton, PO Box 126, Skipton, BD23 9FT (tel: 07954 803327; email: enquiries@craventrust. org.uk)

 www.craventrust.org.uk

CC number: 1045419

Eligibility

People resident within the Craven area who are in need, hardship or distress. The area of benefit includes Settle, Skipton and Bornoldswick and is bordered by Sedbergh to the north, Keighley to the east, Denholme and Hurst Green to the south, and Ingleton to the west. See the map on the website for the exact area.

Types of grant

One-off grants are available to applicants for 'items, services or facilities which help to reduce their difficulties'.

Exclusions

Grant are not given to students, for foreign travel or to help with rates, taxes or other public funds. The trust cannot commit itself to repeat or renew a grant.

Applications

Application forms are available from the website. Preferably, they should be submitted through a referral agency or referee, such as Citizens Advice, social services or a vicar or doctor.

Financial information

Year end	31/03/2020
Income	£30,600
Total expenditure	£45,000

Further financial information

£24,800 in grants was awarded to organisations during the year.

The Gargrave Poor's Land Charity

£ £17,900 (2019/20)

Correspondent: The Trustees, Higherland House, West Street, Gargrave, Skipton BD23 3RJ (tel: 01756 749913)

CC number: 225067

Eligibility

People who are in need and are permanently resident in Gargrave, Banknewton, Coniston Cold, Flasby, Eshton or Winterburn.

Types of grant

Welfare

One-off and recurrent grants are awarded to relieve financial hardship. Christmas gifts, principally for fuel bills, are also made each year to permanent residents who are poor, older, disadvantaged or have a disability.

Education

Grants are awarded to students towards the costs of maintenance, books and tuition fees. Support is also provided to students taking vocational further education courses and other vocational training.

Applications

Applications can be made on a form, which is available from the correspondent, and can be submitted at any time.

Financial information

Year end	05/04/2020
Income	£26,500
Total expenditure	£36,200

Hambleton

The Grace Gardner Trust

£ £2,100 (2019/20)

Correspondent: Cllr David Richardson, c/o Town Council Office, Town Hall, High Street, Northallerton, North Yorkshire DL7 8QR (tel: 01609 776718; email: cllr.david.richardson@ northallertontowncouncil.gov.uk)

CC number: 511030

Eligibility

Older people in need who live within the boundary of Northallerton parish.

Types of grant

Grants are made for day trips, annual Christmas parties and to relieve hardship.

Applications

Apply in writing to the correspondent.

Financial information

Year end	31/03/2020
Income	£5,400
Total expenditure	£4,600

Further financial information

Full accounts were not available to view on the Charity Commission's website due to the trust's low income. We have therefore estimated the trust's grant total based on its total expenditure.

Other information

The trust also makes grants to local organisations.

Harrogate

Knaresborough Relief in Need Charity

£ £15,700 (2019)

Correspondent: The Trustees, 9 Netheredge Drive, Knaresborough, North Yorkshire HG5 9DA (tel: 01423 863378; email: thedixongang2@gmail. com)

CC number: 226743

Eligibility

People in need who live in the parish of Knaresborough.

Types of grant

Grants are given according to need.

Applications

Apply in writing to the correspondent.

Financial information

Year end	31/12/2019
Income	£38,200
Total expenditure	£31,400

Scarborough

The Scarborough Municipal Charity

£ £8,000 (2020)

Correspondent: The Trustees, Flat 2, 126 Falsgrave Road, Scarborough, North Yorkshire YO12 5BE (email: scar. municipalcharity@yahoo.co.uk)

CC number: 217793

Eligibility

People who have lived in the borough of Scarborough for at least five years and are in need, hardship or distress.

Types of grant

Modest grants and the provision of goods, services and facilities to assist those who are in financial need or hardship.

Applications

Application forms can be requested from the correspondent.

Financial information

Year end	31/12/2020
Income	£222,600
Total expenditure	£239,000

Scarborough United Scholarships Foundation

£ £7,400 (2019/20)

Correspondent: Anne Marr, Secretary, 11A Lightfoots Close, Scarborough, North Yorkshire YO12 5NR (tel: 01723 375908; email: a.j.marr3@outlook.com)

CC number: 529678

Eligibility

People under the age of 25 who live in the borough of Scarborough. Previous research suggests applicants should have attended education in the area for at least three years.

The foundation administers the John Kendall Trust, which supports young people under the age of 18 who live in Scarborough and are in need but cannot be helped by a parent or guardian. Previous research suggests that consideration can also be given to children or young people from abroad who may not be receiving state benefits but otherwise are eligible.

Types of grant

Education

Grants are given to assist with the cost of education. In the past the foundation has awarded grants towards specific items with an educational benefit, such as computers, travel expenses, projects or equipment, as well as supporting study of music and the arts, vocational studies, educational visits, work experience opportunities and children with special needs.

The John Kendall Trust also makes grants towards education.

Welfare

The John Kendall Trust provides support towards maintenance and clothing for young people.

Applications

Apply in writing to the correspondent.

Financial information

Year end	31/03/2020
Income	£9,000
Total expenditure	£8,300

Further financial information

Full accounts were not available to view on the Charity Commission's website due to the foundation's low income. We have therefore estimated the foundation's grant total based on its total expenditure.

Other information

The John Kendall Trust may also support organisations with similar aims.

York

Norman Collinson Charitable Trust

£ £14,100 (2020)

Correspondent: Dianne Hepworth, Clerk to the Trustees, Fairfield, The Mile, Pocklington, York, North Yorkshire YO42 1TW (tel: 01759 322102; email: info@ncct.org.uk)

 www.ncct.org.uk

CC number: 277325

Eligibility

Residents of York and surrounding areas who are in need.

Types of grant

Grants, typically in the region of £200 to £2,000, are awarded for welfare needs.

Exclusions

Grants are not usually made towards rent arrears or holidays, and do not normally exceed the value of £5,000.

Applications

Application forms are available to download on the trust's website. Applications must be made on the individual's behalf by a recognised third party (health workers, mental health workers, child support services, etc.) working for agencies such as the City of York Council, Leeds and York PFT, North Yorkshire County Council or Changing Lives. Completed forms can be submitted by either post or email.

Financial information

Year end	31/12/2020
Income	£28,300
Total expenditure	£67,900

Further financial information

In 2020, the trust awarded grants to 52 individuals.

Other information

The trust also makes grants to organisations based in, or working within, the area of York (20-mile radius). National charities carrying out work in the area of benefit may also be supported.

The Isabel Ward (York) Charitable Trust

£ £12,500 (2020)

Correspondent: Mark Kingaby-Daly, 2 Cromarty Cottages, Birdsall, Malton, North Yorkshire YO24 1DL (tel: 01904 593608; email: info@isabelwardtrust.org. uk)

 https://isabelwardtrust.org.uk

CC number: 1094334

Eligibility

Residents of the city of York who are in need.

Types of grant

One-off awards according to need.

Applications

Apply in writing to the correspondent.

Financial information

Year end	31/12/2020
Income	£11,000
Total expenditure	£24,900

Further financial information

Full accounts were not available to view on the Charity Commission's website due to the trust's low income. We have therefore estimated the trust's grant total based on its total expenditure.

The Purey Cust Trust CIO

 £11,500 (2019/20)

Correspondent: Kathryn Hodges, Trust Secretary, c/o Garbutt & Elliott, Triune Court, Monks Cross, York YO32 9GZ (tel: 01937 834730; email: pureycusttrust@btinternet.com)

https://pureycusttrust.org

CC number: 1159079

Eligibility
People in need who live in the City of York and the surrounding area.

Types of grant
The trust's website states: 'Grants should aim to prevent, treat or alleviate illness, injury, disability or related conditions and disorders whether physical or related to mental health and well-being.' Grants are normally one-off.

Applications
Applications can be made via the trust's website or by downloading an application form from the site. Applications for individuals must be made by a third-party referee or organisations, such as a social worker, health professional or Citizens Advice. Applications are considered throughout the year.

Financial information
Year end	05/04/2020
Income	£85,500
Total expenditure	£115,900

Further financial information
Grants were awarded to 33 individuals during the year.

Other information
Grants are also made to organisations (£71,800 in 2019/20).

Feoffee Estate of St Michael-le-Belfrey York

 £4,000 (2020)

Correspondent: The Trustees, c/o Grays Solicitors, Duncombe Place, York, North Yorkshire YO1 7DY (tel: 01904 634771)

CC number: 222051

Eligibility
People in need who live near the parish of St Michael-le-Belfrey.

Types of grant
Grants are given according to need.

Applications
Apply in writing to the correspondent.

Financial information
Year end	31/12/2020
Income	£6,900
Total expenditure	£8,900

Further financial information
Full accounts were not available to view on the Charity Commission's website due to the charity's low income. We have therefore estimated the charity's grant total based on its total expenditure.

Other information
This charity also makes grants to organisations.

Robert Winterscale's Charity

 £1,100 (2019)

Correspondent: The Trustees, c/o Crombie Wilkinson Solicitors, 17–19 Clifford Street, York, North Yorkshire YO1 9RJ (tel: 01904 624185)

CC number: 224230

Eligibility
People in need who are aged over 65 and have lived in the parishes of St Margaret's or St Denys's for a minimum of five years.

Types of grant
Grants are made in the form of small pensions.

Applications
Apply in writing to the correspondent.

Financial information
Year end	31/12/2019
Income	£2,100
Total expenditure	£1,200

Further financial information
Full accounts were not available to view on the Charity Commission's website due to the charity's low income. We have therefore estimated the charity's grant total based on its total expenditure.

York Children's Trust

 £39,000 (2019)

Correspondent: The Trustees, 29 Whinney Lane, Harrogate, North Yorkshire HG2 9LS (tel: 01423 504765; email: yorkchildrenstrust@hotmail.co.uk)

CC number: 222279

Eligibility
Children and young people under 25 who live within 20 miles of the centre of York.

Types of grant
Grants are awarded under three categories: educational; social and medical; travel and fostering talents.

Applications
According to our previous research, application forms are available from the correspondent and can be submitted directly by the individual, by the individual's school, college or educational welfare agency, or by a third party such as a health visitor or social worker. Applications are considered quarterly, although urgent grants of up to £500 can be approved outside the quarterly trustee meetings.

Financial information
Year end	31/12/2019
Income	£114,300
Total expenditure	£131,500

Further financial information
In 2019, grants were awarded to 101 individuals. Of this, £32,600 was awarded under the 'social and medical' category, £5,900 under the 'travel and fostering talents' category and the remaining £470 under the 'educational' category.

Other information
The trust was established through the amalgamation of five existing charities: St Stephen's Orphanage, Blue Coat Boys' and Grey Coat Girls' Schools, The William Richard Beckwith Fund, The Charity of Reverend A.A.R. Gill and The Matthew Rymer Girls Education Fund. Grants are also awarded to children's organisations.

South Yorkshire

The Sheffield West Riding Charitable Society Trust

 £11,100 (2020)

Correspondent: The Trustees, Diocesan Church House, 95–99 Effingham Street, Rotherham, South Yorkshire S65 1BL (tel: 01709 309100; email: westriding@sheffield.anglican.org)

www.sheffield.anglican.org

CC number: 1002026

Eligibility
Clergy, deaconesses and licensed lay people in Sheffield, and their dependants. Also housekeepers who have worked for any member of the clergy

who have been resident or served in the Diocese of Sheffield.

Types of grant
One-off, small grants to provide relief for those in need.

Applications
Applications can be made by email to the correspondent.

Financial information
Year end	31/12/2020
Income	£15,100
Total expenditure	£12,300

Further financial information
Full accounts were not available to view on the Charity Commission's website due to the trust's low income. We have therefore estimated the trust's grant total based on its total expenditure.

South Yorkshire Community Foundation

Correspondent: Grants Team, Unit 9–12 Jessops Riverside, 800 Brightside Lane, Sheffield, South Yorkshire S9 2RX (tel: 0114 242 4857; email: grants@sycf.org.uk)

 www.sycf.org.uk

CC number: 1140947

Eligibility
People in need who live in South Yorkshire.

Types of grant
A number of funds are available to individuals. Refer to the foundation's website for details of current and open grants.

Applications
Details on how to apply can be found on the community foundation's website.

Financial information
Year end	30/09/2020
Income	£4,480,000
Total expenditure	£3,710,000

Further financial information
Overall, grants totalling £3.1 million were distributed during the financial year; however, we were unable to determine the split between organisations and individuals.

Other information
This is one of the 47 UK community foundations, which distribute funding for a wide range of purposes. Grant schemes tend to change frequently – consult the foundation's website for details of current programmes and upcoming deadlines.

Barnsley

Rebecca Guest Robinson (The Robinson Bequest)

£720 (2019/20)

Correspondent: The Trustees, 10 St Mary's Gardens, Worsbrough, Barnsley, South Yorkshire S70 5LU (tel: 01226 290179)

CC number: 247266

Eligibility
Residents in the villages of Birdwell and Worsbrough who are in need.

Types of grant
Grants are awarded according to need to relieve hardship which cannot be relieved from public funds.

Applications
Apply in writing to the correspondent.

Financial information
Year end	30/09/2020
Income	£2,200
Total expenditure	£1,600

Further financial information
Full accounts were not available to view on the Charity Commission's website due to the charity's low income. We have therefore estimated the charity's grant total based on its total expenditure.

Other information
This charity also makes grants to organisations that provide assistance to residents in the area of benefit.

Doncaster

Armthorpe Poors Estate Charity

£1,700 (2019/20)

Correspondent: The Trustees, 6 The Lings, Armthorpe, Doncaster, South Yorkshire DN3 3RH (tel: 07725 636432; email: apecharity@gmail.com)

CC number: 226123

Eligibility
People resident in Armthorpe who are in need, hardship or distress.

Types of grant
Grants are awarded according to need.

Applications
Previous research suggests individuals should not apply directly but through an intermediary, such as a social worker. The full postal address of the applicant should be included within the application.

Financial information
Year end	31/03/2020
Income	£37,000
Total expenditure	£3,700

Further financial information
Full accounts were not available to view on the Charity Commission's website due to the charity's low income. We have therefore estimated the charity's grant total based on its total expenditure.

Other information
Grants are also made to local organisations supporting people in need.

Cantley Poor's Land Trust

£18,200 (2019/20)

Correspondent: Elizabeth Forbes, Clerk, 27 Acacia Road, Doncaster, South Yorkshire DN4 6NR (tel: 01302 536106; email: artfelt@hotmail.co.uk)

 www.cantleywithbrantonparish.co.uk/parish/cantley-poors-land-trust

CC number: 224787

Eligibility
People in financial need who live in Doncaster or South Yorkshire, with priority given to residents of Cantley with Branton.

Types of grant
Grants are given according to need.

Exclusions
Grants cannot be used for the relief of rates, taxes or other public funds. Repeated grants are not made.

Applications
Apply in writing to the correspondent.

Financial information
Year end	31/03/2020
Income	£164,000
Total expenditure	£157,600

Further financial information
During the financial year, the charity awarded 45 grants to individuals.

J. W. Chapman Earlesmere Charitable Trust

 £47,600 (2019/20)

Correspondent: The Trustees, c/o Jordans, 4 Priory Place, Doncaster, South Yorkshire DN1 1BP (tel: 01302 365374; email: info@chapmantrust.org)

🌐 https://chapman-trust.org

CC number: 223002

Eligibility
Residents of Doncaster Metropolitan Borough who are in need.

Types of grant
Grants are awarded according to need.

Exclusions
Grants for non-essential items will not be considered.

Applications
Application forms and guidelines can be found on the trust's website. Note that applications require a letter of support, and eligible individuals who may provide the letter of support include health visitors, GPs, probation officers or social services.

Financial information
Year end	31/03/2020
Income	£188,800
Total expenditure	£197,000

Other information
The trust also makes grants to organisations.

Rotherham

Aston Charities

£ £11,100 (2019)

Correspondent: James Nuttall, Trustee, 3 Rosegarth Avenue, Aston, Sheffield, South Yorkshire S26 2DB (tel: 0114 287 6047; email: jimnuttall@talktalk.net)

CC number: 225071

Eligibility
Older people living in Aston-cum-Aughton who are in need. Support is also available to residents of any age experiencing other forms of disadvantage.

Types of grant
Grants are given according to need.

Applications
Apply in writing to the correspondent.

Financial information
Year end	31/12/2019
Income	£21,600
Total expenditure	£24,700

Further financial information
Full accounts were not available to view on the Charity Commission's website due to the charity's low income. We have therefore estimated the charity's grant total based on its total expenditure.

Other information
This charity also makes grants to organisations.

Aston-with-Aughton Educational Foundation

£ £900 (2020)

Correspondent: James Nuttall, Trustee, 3 Rosegarth Avenue, Aston, Sheffield, South Yorkshire S26 2DB (tel: 0114 287 6047; email: jimnuttall@talktalk.net)

CC number: 529424

Eligibility
Support is available to disadvantaged young people in education. Applicants should have attended a public elementary school for at least three years, and their parents should be resident in Aston-with-Aughton.

Types of grant
Grants are awarded according to need.

Applications
Apply in writing to the correspondent.

Financial information
Year end	31/12/2020
Income	£10,900
Total expenditure	£2,000

Further financial information
Full accounts were not available to view on the Charity Commission's website due to the charity's low income. We have therefore estimated the charity's grant total based on its total expenditure.

Other information
Grants may also be made to organisations.

Brampton Bierlow Welfare Trust

£ £2,600 (2020)

Correspondent: Jill Leece, c/o Newman & Bond Solicitors, 35 Church Street, Barnsley, South Yorkshire S70 2AP (tel: 01226 213434; email: jill.leece@ newmanandbond.co.uk)

CC number: 249838

Eligibility
Residents of the parish of Brampton Bierlow, the wards of Melton and Winterwell in Wath-upon-Deane and the ward of Elsecar in Hoyland who are in need.

Types of grant
Grants are given according to need.

Applications
Apply in writing to the correspondent.

Financial information
Year end	31/12/2020
Income	£11,400
Total expenditure	£5,700

Further financial information
Full accounts were not available to view on the Charity Commission's website due to the trust's low income. We have therefore estimated the trust's grant total based on its total expenditure.

Other information
The trust also makes grants to organisations.

The Common Lands of Rotherham Charity

£ £5,600 (2019)

Correspondent: The Trustees, 66 Moorgate Road, Rotherham, South Yorkshire S60 2AU (tel: 01709 365032; email: info@rotherhamfeoffees.org.uk)

 https://rotherhamfeoffees.org.uk/ index.html

CC number: 223050

Eligibility

Welfare
People in need who live in Rotherham. Priority is usually given to older people and individuals in financial difficulty.

Education
Students living in Rotherham.

Types of grant

Welfare
Grants are given according to need.

Education
Small scholarship awards and bursaries are given to local students to assist them in continuing their studies.

Applications
Apply in writing to the correspondent.

Financial information
Year end	31/12/2019
Income	£22,200
Total expenditure	£12,300

Further financial information

Full accounts were not available to view on the Charity Commission's website due to the charity's low income. We have therefore estimated the charity's grant total based on its total expenditure.

Other information

This charity also makes grants to organisations.

Stoddart Samaritan Fund

£7,200 (2019/20)

Correspondent: The Trustees, 7 Melrose Grove, Rotherham, South Yorkshire S60 3NA (tel: 01709 376448; email: charlie0358-stoddartcfund@yahoo.co.uk)

CC number: 242853

Eligibility

Residents of Rotherham, and areas in its vicinity, who are in need of financial assistance because of medical problems.

Types of grant

Financial assistance towards people's recovery from medical problems.

Applications

Apply in writing to the correspondent.

Financial information

Year end	30/09/2020
Income	£14,200
Total expenditure	£8,000

Further financial information

Full accounts were not available to view on the Charity Commission's website due to the fund's low income. We have therefore estimated the grant total based on the fund's total expenditure.

Sheffield

Beighton Relief-in-Need Charity

£5,400 (2019)

Correspondent: The Trustees, The Lifestyle Centre, High Street, Beighton, Sheffield, South Yorkshire S20 1ED (email: beightonrelief@hotmail.co.uk)

CC number: 225416

Eligibility

People in need who live in the former parish of Beighton.

Types of grant

Grants are given according to need.

Applications

Apply in writing to the correspondent.

Financial information

Year end	31/12/2019
Income	£11,800
Total expenditure	£11,900

Further financial information

Full accounts were not available to view on the Charity Commission's website due to the charity's low income. We have therefore estimated the charity's grant total based on its total expenditure.

Other information

The charity also awards grants to organisations.

Church Burgesses Educational Foundation

£20,300 (2020)

Correspondent: Ian Potter, Law Clerk, Wrigleys Solicitors LLP, Derwent House, 150 Arundel Gate, Sheffield, South Yorkshire S1 2FN (tel: 0114 267 5596)

 www.sheffieldchurchburgesses.org. uk

CC number: 529357

Eligibility

Children and young people under the age of 25 who (or whose parents) have lived in Sheffield for at least three years.

Types of grant

Grants are given to support the education of schoolchildren and towards gap years, expeditions, travel overseas, art and sport activities, and special educational needs. Grants towards attendance at independent schools will only be considered where a special need is demonstrated, for example the death of a parent or sudden financial hardship.

Exclusions

The foundation does not normally provide support for higher education courses, A-level courses or postgraduate studies except in exceptional cases.

Applications

Application forms can be downloaded from the foundation's website. The trustees usually meet four times a year, in January, May, August and November.

Financial information

Year end	31/12/2020
Income	£153,500
Total expenditure	£110,000

Other information

Grants are also made for church-based youth work, to organisations and for supporting music in the local area. In very exceptional cases the foundation may support higher/further education.

Sir George Franklin's Pension Charity

£6,200 (2019/20)

Correspondent: The Trustees, Allen, West and Foster Ltd, Omega Court, 364–366 Cemetery Road, Sheffield, South Yorkshire S11 8FT (tel: 0114 268 9950)

CC number: 224883

Eligibility

People in financial need who are over 50 years of age and live in Sheffield.

Types of grant

Grants are given according to need.

Applications

Apply in writing to the correspondent.

Financial information

Year end	25/07/2020
Income	£9,400
Total expenditure	£6,900

Further financial information

Full accounts were not available to view on the Charity Commission's website due to the charity's low income. We have therefore estimated the grant total based on the charity's total expenditure.

Hollowford Trust

£4,200 (2020)

Correspondent: Lucy Nunn, Sheffield Diocesan Church House, 95–99 Effingham Street, Rotherham, South Yorkshire S65 1BL (tel: 01709 309135; email: lucy.nunn@sheffield. anglican.org)

 www.sheffield.anglican.org/ hollowford-trust

CC number: 523918

Eligibility

Young people between the ages of 10 and 25 who are resident in, or near, the diocese of Sheffield.

Types of grant

Grants of up to £300 for individuals to help 'develop their physical, mental and spiritual capabilities', in contributing towards the cost of taking up voluntary experience both in the UK and overseas. Grants of up to £75 are awarded for short trips in the UK of less than three months. Grants of up to £400 are available to groups of individuals for start-ups and for concerts, outreach events and more general events. Groups of individuals can apply for a grant of up to £50 per person for trips in the UK.

Exclusions

The trust is unable to fund the following:

- ▶ Musical instruments
- ▶ Formal qualifications/education
- ▶ Activities where evangelism is primary purpose
- ▶ Employment of youth/child workers

The trust does not make grants to other charitable organisations, nor can it support repeat applications from a previous beneficiary/beneficiaries.

Applications

Application forms are available to download on the trust's website. For current closing dates for applications, see the guidelines which are also available to download on the website.

Financial information

Year end	31/12/2020
Income	£12,900
Total expenditure	£4,700

Further financial information

Full accounts were not available to view on the Charity Commission's website due to the trust's low income. We have therefore estimated the trust's grant total based on its total expenditure.

The Sheffield Bluecoat and Mount Pleasant Educational Foundation

£ £17,400 (2019/20)

Correspondent: Ms S. M. Greaves, Secretary, Wrigleys Solicitors, 3rd Floor, Fountain Precinct, Balm Green, Sheffield, South Yorkshire S1 2JA (tel: 01426 75588; email: sue.greaves@ wrigleys.co.uk)

CC number: 529351

Eligibility

Young people under the age of 25 who live within a 20-mile radius of Sheffield city centre and are in need.

Types of grant

Welfare

Grants are available for a range of purposes such as gap years, travel and extracurricular activities as well as towards clothing, books, tools and instruments to support people preparing to start work.

Education

Grants can assist with a wide range of educational purposes including course fees, maintenance allowances, educational travel and the study of music and the arts.

Applications

Applications can be requested from the correspondent and are available in both hard and digital copy. Application forms should be submitted along with supporting documents and evidence of financial need. The trustees usually meet twice a year to consider applications.

Financial information

Year end	31/03/2020
Income	£68,600
Total expenditure	£83,000

Further financial information

25 grants were awarded to individuals during the year.

Other information

The foundation also supports local organisations.

Sheffield Grammar School Exhibition Foundation

£ £39,800 (2019/20)

Correspondent: Gillian Mills, Charity Administrator, c/o Wrigleys Solicitors LLP, 3rd Floor, Fountain Precinct, Balm Green, Sheffield, South Yorkshire S1 2JA (tel: 0114 267 5596; email: sheffieldgrammarschool@wrigleys.co.uk)

 www.sgsef.org.uk/index.htm

CC number: 529372

Eligibility

People who have lived in the City of Sheffield for at least three years, with a preference for those who are attending/ have attended King Edward VII School for at least two years. A map of eligible areas can be found on the foundation's website.

Types of grant

Welfare

Grants are awarded for a wide range of purposes including gap years, character-building opportunities, extracurricular activities, retraining, childcare and support for schoolchildren with special educational needs. Financial assistance is also given towards the cost of books, clothing and tools for people preparing to enter work.

Education

Grants can be used for a number of educational purposes such as costs associated with courses (e.g. degree, master's and PhD), studying overseas and travel to pursue education.

Exclusions

The foundation does not award grants to individuals outside Sheffield.

Applications

Application forms can be downloaded from the foundation's website or can be requested from the correspondent.

Completed applications must be returned as a hard copy by post. The trustees meet four times a year to consider applications, usually in March, June, September and December. Check the website for current deadlines.

Financial information

Year end	31/03/2020
Income	£193,200
Total expenditure	£227,600

Further financial information

Grants were awarded to 62 individuals during the year.

West Yorkshire

Brook Charitable Trust

£ £8,400 (2019/20)

Correspondent: Richard Mills, Trustee, 9 Camborne Drive, Fixby, Huddersfield, West Yorkshire HD2 2NF (tel: 01484 544749; email: richard.mills136@ outlook.com)

CC number: 1068335

Eligibility

People in need who live in Bradford, Calderdale, Wakefield, Kirkless or Leeds city. Preference may be given to children and young people, older people and people with disabilities.

Types of grant

Grants are given according to need.

Applications

Apply in writing to the correspondent.

Financial information

Year end	05/04/2020
Income	£12,500
Total expenditure	£18,700

Further financial information

Full accounts were not available to view on the Charity Commission's website due to the trust's low income. We have therefore estimated the grant total based on the trust's total expenditure.

Community Foundation for Leeds

£ £961,000 (2019/20)

Correspondent: Grants Committee, 1st Floor, 51A St Paul's Street, Leeds, West Yorkshire LS1 2TE (tel: 0113 242 2426; email: grants@leedcf.org.uk)

 www.leedscf.org.uk

CC number: 1096892

Eligibility

People in need who live in Leeds and Bradford.

Types of grant

A number of funds are available to individuals. Refer to the foundation's website for details of open grants.

Applications

Details on how to apply can be found on the community foundation's website.

Financial information

Year end	31/03/2020
Income	£5,850,000
Total expenditure	£4,570,000

Other information

This is one of the 47 UK community foundations, which distribute funding for a wide range of purposes. Grant schemes tend to change frequently – consult the foundation's website for details of current programmes and upcoming deadlines.

The Lady Elizabeth Hastings Estate Charity

(£) £343,600 (2019/20)

Correspondent: Andrew Fallows, Clerk, c/o Carter Jonas, 82 Micklegate, York, North Yorkshire YO1 6LF (tel: 01904 558250; email: leh.clerk@carterjonas.co.uk)

 www.ladyelizabethhastingscharities.co.uk

CC number: 224098

Eligibility

Welfare

Residents of the ecclesiastical parishes of Collingham with Harewood, Ledsham with Fairburn and Thorp Arch.

Education

People living in the ecclesiastical parishes of Bardsey with East Keswick, Collingham with Harewood, Ledsham with Fairburn, Shadwell, Thorp Arch and the civil parish of Burton Salmon. Grants can also be made to those who have at any time attended one of the Lady Elizabeth Hastings schools in Collingham, Thorp Arch or Ledston, irrespective of whether they are still resident in the area of benefit.

Types of grant

One-off grants are awarded according to need.

Applications

Application forms can be downloaded from the charity's website.

Financial information

Year end	24/06/2020
Income	£629,400
Total expenditure	£618,800

Other information

The Lady Elizabeth Hastings Estate Charity (Charity Commission no. 224098) administers The Lady Elizabeth Hastings Educational Foundation (Charity Commission no. 224098-1) and The Lady Elizabeth Hastings Non-Educational Foundation (Charity Commission no. 224098-2). Half of the charity's income is distributed to the Non-Educational Charity and the other half to the Education Foundation.

The William and Sarah Midgley Charity

(£) £3,500 (2020/21)

Correspondent: The Trustees, 9 Norbreck Drive, Cross Roads, Keighley, West Yorkshire BD22 9DT (tel: 01535 957927)

CC number: 500095

Eligibility

People who are in need, hardship or distress and live 'in the localities of Barcroft Lees and Cross Roads' in the former borough of Keighley, West Yorkshire.

Types of grant

One-off grants according to need.

Applications

Apply in writing to the correspondent.

Financial information

Year end	05/04/2021
Income	£5,300
Total expenditure	£3,900

Further financial information

Full accounts were not available to view on the Charity Commission's website due to the charity's low income. We have therefore estimated the grant total based on the charity's total expenditure.

West Yorkshire Police (Employees) Benevolent Fund

(£) £4,000 (2020/21)

Correspondent: The Trustees, Finance Department, PO Box 9, Wakefield, West Yorkshire WF1 3QP (tel: 01924 296989; email: diane.nelson@westyorkshire.pnn.police.uk)

CC number: 701817

Eligibility

Employees and ex-employees of the West Yorkshire Police Force or the West Yorkshire Metropolitan County Council under the direct control of the chief constable who are in need, and their widows, orphans and other dependants.

Types of grant

One-off and ongoing grants are given according to need.

Applications

Contact the correspondent for further information.

Financial information

Year end	31/03/2021
Income	£4,100
Total expenditure	£8,900

Further financial information

Full accounts were not available to view on the Charity Commission's website due to the fund's low income. We have therefore estimated the fund's grant total based on its total expenditure.

The West Yorkshire Police Benevolent and Loans Fund

(£) £63,400 (2019/20)

Correspondent: Andrea North, The Trustees, Finance Department, Laburnum Road, Wakefield, West Yorkshire WF1 3QP (tel: 01924 295493)

CC number: 505514

Eligibility

Serving or former members of the force and their dependants. In addition, interest-free loans are also awarded to members of the West Yorkshire Metropolitan Police who face temporary financial difficulties.

Types of grant

One-off grants according to need.

Applications

Contact the correspondent for further information.

Financial information

Year end	31/03/2020
Income	£45,000
Total expenditure	£70,300

Bradford

John Ashton (including the Gift of Hannah Shaw)

£ £2,300 (2020)

Correspondent: Ruth Richardson, 16 Mostyn Grove, Bradford, West Yorkshire BD6 3RB (tel: 01274 608741; email: ruthrichardson26@gmail.com)

CC number: 233661

Eligibility

People in need who live in the Great Horton area of Bradford and other parts of the city that were originally part of the parish of Horton.

Types of grant

Small grants are given according to need.

Applications

Apply in writing to the correspondent. Grants are distributed in June and December each year.

Financial information

Year end	31/12/2020
Income	£2,300
Total expenditure	£2,500

Further financial information

Full accounts were not available to view on the Charity Commission's website due to the charity's low income. We have therefore estimated the charity's grant total based on its total expenditure.

Bowcocks Trust Fund for Keighley

£ £4,300 (2019/20)

Correspondent: Wendy Docherty, 17 Farndale Road, Wilsden, Bradford BD15 0LW (tel: 01535 272657; email: wendy.docherty4@btinternet.com)

CC number: 223290

Eligibility

People in need who live in the municipal borough of Keighley as constituted on 31 March 1974.

Types of grant

One-off grants of no more than £350 are given according to need.

Applications

Apply in writing to the correspondent.

Financial information

Year end	31/03/2020
Income	£7,900
Total expenditure	£9,500

Further financial information

Full accounts were not available to view on the Charity Commission's website due to the fund's low income. We have therefore estimated the grant total based on the fund's total expenditure.

Other information

Grants are also awarded to local charitable organisations.

The Bradford and District Wool Association Benevolent Fund

£ £1,800 (2018/19)

Correspondent: The Trustees, 1 Roseville, Moor Lane, Menston, Ilkley, West Yorkshire LS29 6AP (tel: 01943 874624; email: sirjameshill@btconnect.com)

CC number: 518439

Eligibility

Former employees of the wool trade in Bradford or their spouses who are in need. Preference is given to older people and those with disabilities.

Types of grant

One-off grants are given according to need.

Applications

Apply in writing to the correspondent.

Financial information

Year end	31/08/2019
Income	£2,000
Total expenditure	£2,000

Further financial information

The 2018/19 accounts were the latest available at the time of writing (November 2021). Full accounts were not available to view due to the fund's low income. We have therefore estimated the fund's grant total based on its expenditure.

The Butterfield Trust

£ £1,400 (2020)

Correspondent: The Revd Sandra Benham, Trustee, The Vicarage, Church Hill, Baildon, Shipley, West Yorkshire BD17 6NE (tel: 01274 589005)

CC number: 216821

Eligibility

People in need who live in the parish of Baildon.

Types of grant

One-off grants for emergencies.

Applications

Apply in writing to the correspondent. Decisions can be made immediately.

Financial information

Year end	31/12/2020
Income	£3,500
Total expenditure	£1,600

Further financial information

Full accounts were not available to view on the Charity Commission's website due to the trust's low income. We have therefore estimated the trust's grant total based on its total expenditure.

The Moser Benevolent Trust Fund

£ £5,900 (2019/20)

Correspondent: The Trustees, 33 Mossy Bank Close, Queensbury, Bradford, West Yorkshire BD13 1PX (tel: 01274 817414; email: moser@donaldstokes.co.uk)

CC number: 222868

Eligibility

People in financial need who are over 60 years of age and have resided or worked in Bradford for a minimum of three years.

Types of grant

Recurrent grants in the form of a pension, to be spent on items, services and facilities calculated to reduce the need of beneficiaries.

Applications

Apply in writing to the correspondent.

Financial information

Year end	31/03/2020
Income	£7,600
Total expenditure	£6,500

Further financial information

Full accounts were not available to view on the Charity Commission's website due to the trust's low income. We have therefore estimated the trust's grant total based on its total expenditure.

Joseph Nutter's Foundation

£ £26,900 (2019/20)

Correspondent: John Lambert, 7 Southway, Eldwick, Bingley BD16 3EW (tel: 01274 561838; email: johnlambert2009@hotmail.co.uk)

CC number: 507491

Eligibility

Children and young people who live in the metropolitan district of Bradford and have suffered the loss of a parent.

Types of grant

Our previous research indicates that the foundation awards one-off grants which are given towards clothing, bedding, beds and other household items that will specifically benefit the child. Other needs may occasionally be considered on an individual basis.

Applications

Apply in writing to the correspondent.

Financial information

Year end	31/03/2020
Income	£17,200
Total expenditure	£29,900

Further financial information

Full accounts were not available to view on the Charity Commission's website due to the foundation's low income. We have therefore estimated the grant total based on the foundation's total expenditure.

Sir Titus Salt's Charity

£ £3,900 (2019/20)

Correspondent: The Trustees, 6 Carlton Road, Shipley, West Yorkshire BD18 4NE (tel: 01274 599540)

CC number: 216357

Eligibility

Older people who are experiencing ill health and live in Saltaire or the surrounding area.

Types of grant

Grants towards food, medicine, medical comforts, bedding and the provision of domestic help. Loans may also be available.

Applications

Apply in writing to the correspondent.

Financial information

Year end	31/03/2020
Income	£6,500
Total expenditure	£4,300

Further financial information

Full accounts were not available to view on the Charity Commission's website due to the charity's low income. We have therefore estimated the charity's grant total based on its total expenditure.

Paul and Nancy Speak's Charity

£ £4,000 (2020)

Correspondent: The Trustees, 506 Thornton Road, Thornton, Bradford BD13 3JD (tel: 01274 770878; email: sblakeley@blakeleysolicitors.co.uk)

CC number: 231339

Eligibility

Women in need who are aged over 50 and live in Bradford.

Types of grant

Regular payments in the form of allowances.

Applications

Apply in writing to the correspondent.

Financial information

Year end	31/12/2020
Income	£11,900
Total expenditure	£9,900

Further financial information

Full accounts were not available to view on the Charity Commission's website due to the charity's low income. We have therefore estimated the grant total based on the charity's total expenditure.

Samuel Sunderland Relief-in-Need Charity

£ £6,700 (2020)

Correspondent: The Trustees, 4 College Road, Bingley BD16 4UG (tel: 01274 568074; email: dennis.child@me.com)

CC number: 225745

Eligibility

People in need residing in the former parish of Bingley, with a preference for children and older people.

Types of grant

Grants are given according to need.

Applications

Apply in writing to the correspondent.

Financial information

Year end	31/12/2020
Income	£8,200
Total expenditure	£7,400

Further financial information

Full accounts were not available to view on the Charity Commission's website due to the charity's low income. We have therefore estimated the charity's grant total based on its total expenditure.

Other information

The charity also makes grants to local organisations.

Calderdale

Bearder Charity

£ £213,500 (2019/20)

Correspondent: Secretary, 5 King Street, Brighouse, West Yorkshire HD6 1NX

(tel: 01484 710571; email: beardercharity@gmail.com)

 www.bearder-charity.org

CC number: 1010529

Eligibility

People in need who live in Calderdale, West Yorkshire.

Types of grant

Grants to individuals are awarded under the categories of welfare, education and the arts.

Applications

All applicants are asked to apply in writing to the secretary. Applications may be made directly or through a local third-party organisation. The trustees meet six times a year to assess grant applications.

Financial information

Year end	05/04/2020
Income	£126,800
Total expenditure	£331,400

Further financial information

In 2019/20, grants to individuals were awarded under the following categories: general welfare grants (£144,600); education grants (£66,800); grants for the arts and artists (£2,100). Grants to organisations totalled £93,600.

Other information

The charity also makes grants to organisations.

Community Foundation for Calderdale

£ £116,300 (2019/20)

Correspondent: Grants Team, The 1855 Building (first floor), Discovery Road, Halifax, West Yorkshire HX1 2NG (tel: 01422 349700; email: grants@cffc.co.uk)

 www.cffc.co.uk

CC number: 1002722

Eligibility

People in need who live in Calderdale.

Types of grant

Welfare

Grants from the Individual Fund are awarded to help alleviate personal needs. These grants are made to individuals through referring agencies.

Education

The foundation also awards bursaries to students through the Calderdale College Education Fund. Bursaries can be used for travel assistance and educational materials or can be awarded as scholarships.

Applications

Details on how to apply can be found on the community foundation's website.

Financial information

Year end	30/06/2020
Income	£2,470,000
Total expenditure	£1,860,000

Further financial information

In 2019/20, grants awarded through the Individual Fund totalled £109,600. In addition, we estimate that student bursaries awarded through the Calderdale College Education Fund totalled £6,700.

Other information

This is one of the 47 UK community foundations, which distribute funding for a wide range of purposes. Grant schemes tend to change frequently – consult the foundation's website for details of current programmes and upcoming deadlines.

Mary Farrar's Benevolent Trust Fund

(£) £5,000 (2019/20)

Correspondent: Peter Haley, c/o P. Haley & Co., Poverty Hall, Lower Ellistones, Saddleworth Road, Halifax, West Yorkshire HX4 8NG (tel: 01422 376690)

CC number: 223806

Eligibility

Women in financial need who are aged 55 or older and who were born in the parish of Halifax or have lived there for a minimum of five years.

Types of grant

Recurrent grants in the form of pensions.

Applications

Apply in writing to the correspondent.

Financial information

Year end	31/05/2020
Income	£5,300
Total expenditure	£5,500

Further financial information

Full accounts were not available to view on the Charity Commission's website due to the fund's low income. We have therefore estimated the fund's grant total based on its total expenditure.

The Goodall Trust

(£) £3,300 (2020)

Correspondent: Andrew Buck, 122 Skircoat Road, Halifax, West Yorkshire HX1 2RE (tel: 07758 609341; email: atbuck@tiscali.co.uk)

CC number: 221651

Eligibility

Widows, women living alone with their children and unmarried women on low income who reside in the present ward of Skircoat, Calderdale or the parts of the parishes of St Jude and All Saints (Halifax), which are within the ancient township of Skircoat.

Types of grant

Grants are made according to need, including household and living expenses.

Applications

Apply in writing to the correspondent.

Financial information

Year end	31/12/2020
Income	£3,700
Total expenditure	£3,700

Further financial information

Full accounts were not available to view on the Charity Commission's website due to the trust's low income. We have therefore estimated the trust's grant total based on its total expenditure.

Halifax Society for the Blind

(£) £940 (2019/20)

Correspondent: The Trustees, 36 Clare Road, Halifax, West Yorkshire HX1 2HX (tel: 01422 352383; email: info@ halifaxblindsociety.org.uk)

 www.halifaxblindsociety.org.uk

CC number: 224258

Eligibility

People living in Calderdale who are registered blind or partially sighted.

Types of grant

Grants are mainly made towards specialist equipment.

Applications

Apply in writing to the correspondent.

Financial information

Year end	31/03/2020
Income	£174,000
Total expenditure	£141,000

Other information

The charity offers a range of services including home visiting services and social groups. This charity also makes grants to organisations.

Charity of Ann Holt

(£) £13,500 (2019/20)

Correspondent: The Trustees, 26 Westacre, Lyndhurst Road, Brighouse,

West Yorkshire HD6 3SH (tel: 01484 717172; email: oakey9uk@outlook.com)

CC number: 502391

Eligibility

Single women over the age of 55 who have lived in Halifax for (at least) the previous five years and are in need.

Types of grant

Quarterly pensions.

Applications

Apply in writing to the correspondent.

Financial information

Year end	31/03/2020
Income	£16,200
Total expenditure	£15,000

Further financial information

Full accounts were not available to view on the Charity Commission's website due to the charity's low income. We have therefore estimated the grant total based on the charity's total expenditure.

Todmorden War Memorial Fund (1914/1918)

(£) £2,100 (2019)

Correspondent: The Trustees, 8 Walton Fold, Todmorden, West Yorkshire OL14 5TE (tel: 01706 812146)

CC number: 219673

Eligibility

Veterans of the Second World War in need who live or have lived in the former borough of Todmorden. Dependants of First World War and Second World War veterans are also supported. Other Todmorden residents in need can also be assisted.

Types of grant

Grants are given according to need.

Applications

Apply in writing to the correspondent.

Financial information

Year end	31/12/2019
Income	£3,600
Total expenditure	£4,600

Further financial information

Full accounts were not available to view on the Charity Commission's website due to the fund's low income. We have therefore estimated the fund's grant total based on its total expenditure.

Other information

The charity also makes grants to organisations.

Kirklees

The Beaumont and Jessop Relief-in-Need Charity

£ £1,300 (2019/20)

Correspondent: The Trustees, Moorview, Briar Court, Holmfirth, West Yorkshire HD9 2JJ (tel: 01484 767827; email: lesbuk@gmail.com)

CC number: 504141

Eligibility

People in need who are over 65 and live in Honley. In exceptional circumstances grants might be awarded to people under 65.

Types of grant

Grants are given according to need.

Applications

Apply in writing to the correspondent.

Financial information

Year end	30/09/2020
Income	£3,800
Total expenditure	£2,900

Further financial information

Full accounts were not available to view on the Charity Commission's website due to the charity's low income. We have therefore estimated the charity's grant total based on its total expenditure.

Charles Brook Convalescent Fund

£ £14,500 (2019/20)

Correspondent: The Trustees, Mistal Barn, Almondbury, Huddersfield, West Yorkshire HD4 6TA (tel: 01484 532183)

CC number: 229445

Eligibility

People who are recuperating after treatment at Huddersfield hospitals.

Types of grant

One-off grants are awarded according to need. Examples include: special food or medicines; medical comforts; medical/surgical appliances; fuel; transport expenses; extra bedding; clothing; white goods (washing machines, fridges, etc.); floor coverings; cleaning services; domestic help; convalescent holidays.

Applications

Apply in writing to the correspondent.

Financial information

Year end	30/04/2020
Income	£13,900
Total expenditure	£16,100

Further financial information

Full accounts were not available to view on the Charity Commission's website due to the fund's low income. We have therefore estimated the grant total based on the fund's total expenditure.

Dewsbury and District Sick Poor Fund

£ £13,100 (2020)

Correspondent: The Trustees, 130 Boothroyd Lane, Dewsbury, West Yorkshire WF13 2LW (tel: 01924 463308; email: alanwwayside@talktalk.net)

CC number: 234401

Eligibility

People who live in the county borough of Dewsbury and the ecclesiastical parish of Hanging Heaton and are in need as a result of illness and/or financial difficulty.

Types of grant

One-off grants for household goods, convalescent holidays and the purchase of medical aids. This charity also provides vouchers for food and clothing.

Applications

Apply in writing to the correspondent.

Financial information

Year end	31/12/2020
Income	£4,700
Total expenditure	£14,500

Further financial information

Full accounts were not available to view on the Charity Commission's website due to the fund's low income. We have therefore estimated the grant total based on the fund's total expenditure.

The H. P. Dugdale Foundation

£ £53,000 (2019/20)

Correspondent: Trevor Balderson, Charity Administrator, c/o Simpson Wood, Bank Chambers, Market Street, Huddersfield, West Yorkshire HD1 2EW (tel: 07907 294129; email: trevor.balderson@simpson-wood.co.uk)

CC number: 200538

Eligibility

People in need who live in the county borough of Huddersfield (comprising the urban districts of Colne Valley, Kirkburton, Meltham and Holmfirth).

Types of grant

One-off and recurrent grants according to need.

Applications

Application forms are given to local organisations such as social services and churches and may be submitted by or on behalf of the individual.

Financial information

Year end	05/07/2020
Income	£70,700
Total expenditure	£77,800

Further financial information

During the financial period, grants were awarded to 61 individuals.

Huddersfield and District Army Veterans' Association Benevolent Fund

£ £12,100 (2019)

Correspondent: The Trustees, 10 Belton Grove, Huddersfield, HD3 3RF (tel: 01484 310193)

 https://hdava.co.uk

CC number: 222286

Eligibility

Veterans of the Army, Royal Navy or the Royal Air Force who are in need. Applicants must be over the age of 55, live in Huddersfield or within its vicinity and have been discharged from the forces with good character.

Types of grant

One-off grants for clothing, trips and special aid.

Applications

Contact the charity for further information.

Financial information

Year end	31/12/2019
Income	£39,000
Total expenditure	£29,000

Further financial information

Grants were broken down as follows: special aid (£11,500); clothing and uniforms (£580).

Other information

The fund also provides services such as community support, outings, events, home/hospital visits, advice for funerals and general assistance in times of need.

Leeds

Chapel Allerton and Potter Newton Relief-in-Need Charity

£ £2,500 (2020)

Correspondent: The Trustees, 6 Grosvenor Park, Leeds, West Yorkshire LS7 3QD (tel: 0113 268 0600; email: cacharities@btinternet.com)

CC number: 245504

Eligibility

Residents in the parishes of Chapel Allerton and Potter Newton who are in need.

Types of grant

Grants are given mainly for white goods and debt relief.

Applications

Applicants must be referred to the charity by a professional caring agency, which will then make an application on their behalf.

Financial information

Year end	31/12/2020
Income	£2,500
Total expenditure	£2,800

Further financial information

Full accounts were not available to view on the Charity Commission's website due to the charity's low income. We have therefore estimated the charity's grant total based on its total expenditure.

Kirke's Charity

£ £2,400 (2019/20)

Correspondent: The Trustees, 8 St Helens Croft, Leeds, West Yorkshire LS16 8JY (tel: 0113 267 9780)

CC number: 246102

Eligibility

People in need who live in the ancient parish of Adel.

Types of grant

Grants are given according to need, including for education and training purposes.

Applications

Applications can be submitted directly by the individual or through a social worker, Citizens Advice or other welfare agency.

Financial information

Year end	31/10/2020
Income	£9,400
Total expenditure	£5,500

Further financial information

Full accounts were not available to view on the Charity Commission's website due to the charity's low income. We have therefore estimated the grant total based on the charity's total expenditure.

Other information

Grants are also awarded to local organisations.

Leeds Benevolent Society for Single Ladies

£ £30,000 (2020)

Correspondent: Anona Everett, Trustee, West Cottage, 12 Eastgate, Bramhope LS16 9AB (tel: 0113 284 3815; email: anonaeverett@gmail.com)

CC number: 1155794

Eligibility

Single women who live in the Leeds district.

Types of grant

One-off grants are awarded according to need.

Applications

Apply in writing to the correspondent.

Financial information

Year end	31/12/2020
Income	£144,000
Total expenditure	£214,500

The Leeds Community Trust

£ £27,600 (2019)

Correspondent: The Trustees, The Community Shop Trust, Suite 23, McCarthy's Business Centre, Education Road, Leeds, West Yorkshire LS7 2AL (tel: 0113 237 9685; email: info@leedscommunitytrust.org)

 www.leedscommunitytrust.org

CC number: 701375

Eligibility

Families who are in need and live in the Leeds area with an LS postcode.

Types of grant

The trust provides assistance in a number of forms:

▸ **Emergency grants** – One-off grants are given for needs such as beds, bedding, carpets, washing machines and removal costs. The website states: 'Families with children are usually given priority, but we try to help all families in need who have problems such as physical or mental disabilities,

child protection issues, homelessness or similar situations.'

▸ **Holiday grants** – One-off grants are given to enable children and their families to go away on holiday; this could be to a caravan, a bed and breakfast or a guesthouse

▸ **Christmas grants** – One-off grants are given to disadvantaged families with children to cover the cost of food and gifts. Where funds permit, a grocery voucher is issued before Christmas

Applications

Applications can only be submitted by a third-party care agency such as social services, health visitors or housing officers. Applications must be on office-headed paper and include the following information: full names and ages of everyone in the applicant's household; the applicant's address; the background circumstances of the applicant; what help is requested. The referrer should follow up the written application with a phone call after 10–14 days.

Financial information

Year end	31/12/2019
Income	£26,700
Total expenditure	£27,600

Further financial information

Grants were broken down as follows:

Emergency grants	80	£15,600
Christmas grants	109	£7,600
Holidays	10	£4,400

Other information

The trust runs two charity shops and distributes the profits to individuals in need, particularly people who are in vulnerable situations.

Leeds Convalescent Society

£ £6,500 (2019)

Correspondent: Alison Gallant, 25 Clarence Mews, Horsforth, Leeds, West Yorkshire LS18 4EP (tel: 0113 259 1014; email: alison.gallant1962@gmail.com)

CC number: 223831

Eligibility

People who live in Leeds and are in need as a result of sickness, disability, convalescence or financial difficulty.

Types of grant

Cash grants are given according to need. Examples include special equipment such as wheelchairs or baths.

Applications

Apply in writing to the correspondent.

Financial information

Year end	31/12/2019
Income	£15,300
Total expenditure	£14,500

Further financial information

Full accounts were not available to view on the Charity Commission's website due to the charity's low income. We have therefore estimated the charity's grant total based on its total expenditure.

Other information

This charity also makes grants to organisations.

Metcalfe Smith Trust CIO

 £30,200 (2019/20)

Correspondent: The Trustees, c/o Voluntary Action Leeds, Stringer House, 34 Lupton Street, Hunslett, Leeds, West Yorkshire LS10 2QW (email: metcalfesmithbs@gmail.com)

www.metcalfesmithtrust.org.uk

CC number: 1164280

Eligibility

Adults or children who live in the Leeds Metropolitan District and have a physical disability, long-term illness or difficulties with their mental health.

Types of grant

One-off grants, usually ranging from £250 to £2,500. The trust's website states: 'Grants can be made for convalescent or respite care; for purchasing necessary equipment and household items and for meeting other costs which living with disabilities inevitably incur.' The trust also makes small emergency grants of up to £150.

Exclusions

According to its website, the trust does not fund:
- General appeals
- Research costs
- General fundraising initiatives
- Administrative costs or fees
- Tuition fees
- General living costs such as rent or utility bills

Applications

Application forms can be downloaded from the website. Alternatively, potential applicants can first complete an eligibility assessment form on the website. Eligible applicants will then receive an email with the application form to complete. Applications from individuals must be accompanied by a letter from a charity, voluntary organisation, school or professional such as their GP or social worker. Completed

applications should be submitted by post. The trustees meet twice a year to consider applications; however, emergency grants can be made in between meetings.

Financial information

Year end	30/06/2020
Income	£46,600
Total expenditure	£61,400

Further financial information

The trust supported 168 individuals during the financial period. Within this, grants totalling £10,000 were made for the benefit of 26 individuals and emergency grants totalling £20,200 were awarded to 142 individuals.

Other information

Grants are also made to organisations.

Wakefield

Lady Bolles Foundation

 £8,000 (2020)

Correspondent: The Trustees, Wakefield Cathedral, The Westmoreland Centre, 8–10 Westmorland Street, Wakefield, West Yorkshire WF1 1PJ (tel: 01924 250473; email: bev.howes@ wakefield-cathedral.org.uk)

CC number: 529344

Eligibility

People under the age of 24 who live in the county borough of Wakefield who are preparing to enter work. At the trustees' discretion support may be continued up to the age of 26.

Types of grant

Welfare

Financial assistance towards clothing, travel, maintenance expenses or any other purpose that enables applicants to earn a living.

Education

Financial assistance towards fees associated with preparing to enter work, including grants for apprenticeships.

Applications

Apply in writing to the correspondent.

Financial information

Year end	31/12/2020
Income	£9,400
Total expenditure	£8,700

Further financial information

Full accounts were not available to view on the Charity Commission's website due to the foundation's low income. We have therefore estimated the foundation's grant total based on its total expenditure.

The Brotherton Charity Trust

£2,900 (2020)

Correspondent: The Trustees, PO Box 374, Harrogate, North Yorkshire HG1 4YW

CC number: 221006

Eligibility

People in need who are over 60 years old and live in Wakefield on a low income.

Types of grant

Small annual pensions are paid to long-standing Wakefield residents on low incomes.

Applications

Apply in writing to the correspondent.

Financial information

Year end	31/12/2020
Income	£5,400
Total expenditure	£3,200

Further financial information

Full accounts were not available to view on the Charity Commission's website due to the trust's low income. We have therefore estimated the trust's grant total based on its total expenditure.

Horbury Common Lands Trust

£5,500 (2019)

Correspondent: The Clerk, Meadow View, Haigh Moor Road, Tingley, Wakefield, West Yorkshire WF3 1EJ (tel: 07550 085465; email: milner. martin@gmail.com)

www.horburycommonlandstrust. org.uk

CC number: 214613

Eligibility

Residents aged over 70 who have lived the urban district of Horbury for ten years or more are invited to apply for a Christmas grant from the trust. Other grants are available for individuals in need.

Types of grant

One-off grants according to need.

Applications

Application forms can be downloaded from the trust's website. Applications can be submitted at any time of the year. Decisions are made in March, June, September and December. Applications need to be with the correspondent at the latest by the first day of the month of a meeting.

Financial information

Year end	31/12/2019
Income	£71,300
Total expenditure	£41,400

Further financial information

In 2019, £5,000 was awarded to older people in need, and £500 was distributed in grants to other individuals.

St Leonards Hospital – Horbury

(£) £2,300 (2019)

Correspondent: The Trustees, 15 Tyndale Avenue, Horbury, Wakefield, West Yorkshire WF4 5QT (tel: 01924 379256)

CC number: 243977

Eligibility

Residents of Horbury who are in need.

Types of grant

Grants are given according to need.

Applications

Apply in writing to the correspondent.

Financial information

Year end	31/12/2019
Income	£4,000
Total expenditure	£5,000

Further financial information

Full accounts were not available to view on the Charity Commission's website due to the charity's low income. We have therefore estimated the charity's grant total based on its total expenditure.

Other information

This charity also makes grants to organisations.

Advice organisations

The following section lists the names and contact details of voluntary organisations that offer advice and support to individuals in need. The list is split into two sections – 'Welfare' and 'Illness and disability'. Each section begins with an index before listing the organisations by category.

The listings are a useful reference guide to organisations that individuals can contact to discuss their situation and receive advice and support. These organisations will have experience in tackling the sorts of problem that other individuals have faced and will know the most effective and efficient ways of dealing with them. They may also be able to arrange for people to meet others in a similar situation. As well as providing advice and support, many of the organisations will be happy to help individuals submit applications to the funders included in this guide. They may also know of other sources of funding available.

Some organisations included in this list have their own financial resources available to individuals. We have marked these with an asterisk (*). This list should not be used as a quick way of identifying potential funding – the organisations will have criteria and policies that may mean they are unable to support all the needs under that category and the guide will include many more potential sources of funding than the organisations listed below.

Some organisations have local branches, which are better placed to have a personal contact with the individual and have a greater local knowledge of the need. We have only included the headquarters of such organisations, which will be happy to provide details for the relevant branches.

If you are requesting information by post from any of the organisations listed, it is helpful to include an sae.

This list is by no means comprehensive and should only be used as a starting point. It only contains organisations that have a national remit and does not include organisations that provide general advice and support solely to members of a particular religion, country or ethnic group. For further details of groups, look for charitable and voluntary organisations in online directories, or contact your local council for voluntary service (CVS) (sometimes called Voluntary Action) or community foundation, details of which can be found online.

The following general welfare section includes 'Benefit and grants information' and 'Debt and financial advice', which may be of particular relevance during these difficult times.

Welfare

General 468

Benefit and grants information 468

Bereavement 468

    Children 469

    Parents 469

Carers 469

Children and young people 469

    Bullying 469

Debt and financial advice 469

Families 470

Housing 470

Legal 470

Missing people 470

People with experience of the criminal justice system 470

Families of people with experience of the criminal justice system 470

Women with experience of the criminal justice system 471

Older people 471

Parenting 471

    Abduction 471

    Adoption and fostering 471

    Childcare 471

    Divorce 471

    Grandparents 471

    Mothers 472

    Pregnancy 472

    Single parents 472

Poverty 472

Refugees and asylum seekers 472

Relationships 472

ADVICE ORGANISATIONS

Social isolation 472

Squatters 472

Victims of accidents and crimes 472

    Abuse 472

    Crime 473

    Disasters 473

    Domestic violence 473

    Medical accidents 473

    Rape 473

    Road accidents 473

Work issues 473

Women 473

General

Advice NI, Forestview, Purdy's Lane, Newtownbreda, Belfast BT8 7AR (tel: 0800 915 4604; email: advice@adviceni.net; website: www.adviceni.net). For information on sources of advice and support in Northern Ireland.

Citizens Advice, 3rd Floor North, 200 Aldersgate Street, London EC1A 4HD (Adviceline: 0800 144 8848 [England], 0800 702 2020 [Wales], 0800 144 8884 [Text Relay]; website: www.citizensadvice.org.uk). For details of your local Citizens Advice office see the website.

The Salvation Army, Territorial Headquarters, 101 Newington Causeway, London SE1 6BN (tel: 020 7367 4500; email: info@salvationarmy.org.uk; website: www.salvationarmy.org.uk)

Samaritans, The Upper Mill, Kingston Road, Ewell, Surrey KT17 2AF (tel: 020 8394 8300; 24-hour helpline: 116 123; see the website for local numbers; email: admin@samaritans.org [general] or jo@samaritans.org [helpline]; website: www.samaritans.org)

Benefit and grants information

Child Benefit, PO Box 1, Newcastle upon Tyne NE88 1AA (helpline: 0300 200 3100 [Mon–Fri, 8am–8pm; Sat, 8am–4pm]; NGT Text relay: dial 18001 then 0300 200 3100; website: www.gov.uk/child-benefit) Contact can also be made through an online live chat feature or by using the online form.

Child Maintenance Options, (tel: 0800 953 0191 [Mon–Fri, 8am–8pm]; website: www.gov.uk/making-child-maintenance-arrangement). Contact can also be made through an online live chat feature or by using the online form.

Disability Service Centre, (Disability Living Allowance helpline: 0800 121 4600 [Mon–Fri, 9am–5pm]; Attendance Allowance helpline: 0800 731 0122; Personal Independence Payment (PIP) helpline: 0800 121 4433; website: www.gov.uk/pip)

Gov.uk, general information on money, tax and benefits (website: www.gov.uk)

Jobseeker's Allowance (JSA) (Universal Credit helpline: 0800 169 0310 [Mon–Fri, 8am–5pm]; textphone: 0800 169 0314; website: www.gov.uk/jobseekers-allowance). You may also make a claim online.

Pension Credit Claim Line; (tel: 0800 731 0469 [Mon–Fri, 9.30am–3.30pm]; textphone: 0800 169 0133; website: www.gov.uk/pension-credit) See the website for information on local offices.

Tax Credits helpline, Tax Credit Office, Preston PR1 4AT; (tel: 0345 300 3900 [Mon–Fri, 8am–6pm]; textphone 0345 300 3900; website: www.gov.uk/government/organisations/hm-revenue-customs/contact/tax-credits-enquiries)

Veterans UK, Ministry of Defence, Norcross, Thornton Cleveleys, Lancashire FY5 3WP; (helpline: 0808 191 4218 [Mon–Fri, 8am–5pm]; email: veterans-uk@mod.uk; website: www.gov.uk/government organisations/veterans-uk)

Winter Fuel Payments, Winter Fuel Payment Centre, Mail Handling Site A, Wolverhampton WV98 1LR; (helpline: 0800 731 0160 [Mon–Fri, 8am–6pm]; textphone: 0800 731 0176; website: www.gov.uk/winter-fuel-payment)

Bereavement

Cruse Bereavement Care, PO Box 800, Richmond, Surrey TW9 1RG; (tel: 020 8939 9530; helpline: 0808 808 1677 [Mon and Fri, 9.30am–5pm; Tues, Wed and Thurs, 9.30am–8pm; Sat and Sun, 10am–2pm]; website: www.cruse.org.uk) See the website for information on local offices.

Natural Death Centre, In The Hill House, Watley Lane, Twyford, Winchester SO21 1QX; (tel: 01962 712690; email: rosie@naturaldeath.org.uk; website: www.naturaldeath.org.uk)

Stillbirth and Neonatal Death Society (SANDS), CAN Mezzanine, 49–51 East Road, London N1 6AH (tel: 020 7436 7940; helpline: 0808 164 3332 [Mon–Fri, 10am–3pm; Tues and Thurs evenings, 6pm–9pm]; email: helpline@sands.org.uk or use the online form; website: www.sands.org.uk)

Survivors of Bereavement by Suicide (SOBS), The Flamsteed Centre, Albert Street, Ilkeston, Derbyshire DE7 5GU; (tel: 0115 944 1117; helpline: 0300 111 5065 [Mon–Sun, 9am–9pm]; email: admin@uksobs.org; helpline: email.support@uksobs.org; website: www.uksobs.org)

Children

Child Bereavement UK; (helpline: 0800 028 8840; email: enquiries@ childbereavementuk.org; website: www.childbereavement.org.uk); See the website for information on local offices.

Grief Encounter, Crystal House, Daws Lane, London NW7 4ST; (tel: 020 8371 8455; helpline: 0808 802 0111 [Mon–Fri, 9am–9pm]; email: grieftalk@griefencounter.org.uk; website: www.griefencounter.org.uk)

Winston's Wish, 17 Royal Crescent, Cheltenham GL50 3DA; (tel: 01242 515157; helpline: 0808 802 0021 [Mon–Fri, 9am–5pm]; email: info@ winstonswish.org.uk or ask@winstonswish.org; website: www. winstonswish.org.uk)

Parents

Child Death Helpline, Barclay House, 37 Queen Square, London WC1N 3BH; (tel: 020 7813 8416 [admin]; helpline: 0800 282986 [Mon, Thurs and Fri, 10am–1pm; Tues and Wed, 10am–4pm; and every evening, 7pm–10pm]; website: www. childdeathhelpline.org.uk)

The Compassionate Friends, Kilburn Grange, Priory Park Road, London NW6 7UJ; (tel: 0345 120 3785; helpline: 0345 123 2304 [10am–4pm and 7pm–10pm daily]; email: info@ tcf.org.uk or helpline@tcf.org.uk; website: www.tcf.org.uk)

The Lullaby Trust, CAN Mezzanine 7–14 Dover Street, London SE1 4YR (tel: 020 7802 3200; helpline: 0808 802 6868 [Mon–Fri, 10am–5pm; weekends and public holidays, 6pm–10pm]; email: office@ lullabytrust.org.uk or support@lullabytrust.org.uk; website: www.lullabytrust.org.uk)

Carers

Carers UK, 20 Great Dover Street, London SE1 4LX; (tel: 020 7378 4999; Carers UK Adviceline: 0808 808 7777 [Mon–Fri, 9am–6pm]; email: advice@ carersuk.org; website: www.carersuk. org)

Leonard Cheshire Disability, 66 South Lambeth Road, London SW8 1RL; (tel: 020 3242 0200; email: use the online form; website: www. leonardcheshire.org)

Children and young people

Action for Children, 3 The Boulevard, Ascot Road, Watford WD18 8AG (tel: 01923 361500 [Mon–Fri, 9am–5pm]; email: ask.us@actionforchildren.org. uk; website: www.actionforchildren. org.uk)

Catch 22, 27 Pear Tree Street, London EC1V 3AG (tel: 020 7336 4800; email: use the online form; website: www. catch-22.org.uk)

ChildLine, 42 Curtain Road, London EC2A 3NH (tel: 020 7825 2500; 24-hour advice helpline: 08001111; website: www.childline.org.uk). A personal inbox can be set up on the site which will allow you to send emails to ChildLine and save replies in a similar way to a normal email service. Alternatively, send a message without signing in through the 'send Sam a message' function. You can also chat online with a ChildLine counsellor by going to www.childline. org.uk/get-support/1-2-1-counsellor-chat.

The Children's Society, Whitecross Studio, Banner Street, London EC1Y 8ST (tel: 0300 303 7000; email: supportercare@childrenssociety.org. uk; website: www.childrenssociety. org.uk)

Child Law Advice, (tel: 0300 330 5480 [Mon–Fri, 8am–6pm]; email: online form; website www.childlawadvice. org.uk)

National Youth Advocacy Service, Tower House, 1 Tower Road, Birkenhead CH41 1FF (tel: 0151 649 8700; helpline: 0808 808 1001 [Mon–Fri, 9am–6pm]; email: main@ nyas.net or help@nyas.net; website: www.nyas.net)

NSPCC, Weston House, 42 Curtain Road, London EC2A 3NH (tel: 020 7825 2505; helpline for adults concerned about a child: 0808 800 5000 [Mon–Fri, 8am–10pm; Sat–Sun, 9am–6pm]; for children and young people, call ChildLine: 08001111; email: help@nspcc.org.uk or use the

online form; website: www.nspcc.org. uk)

Become, 15–18 White Lion Street, London N1 9PG (tel: 020 7251 3117; care advice line: 0800 023 2033 [Mon–Fri, 10.30am–5pm]; email: advice@becomecharity.org.uk; website: www.becomecharity.org.uk)

Youth Access, 1–2 Taylors Yard, 67 Alderbrook Road, London SW12 8AD (tel: 020 8772 9900 email: admin@youthaccess.org.uk; website: www.youthaccess.org.uk [for an online directory of information, advice and support services for young people])

Bullying

The Anti-Bullying Alliance, National Children's Bureau, 23 Mentmore Terrace, London E8 3PN (email: aba@ncb.org.uk; website: www.anti-bullyingalliance.org.uk)

Kidscape, 8–10 South Street, Epsom Surrey KT18 7PF (tel: 020 7730 330; parent advice line: 020 7823 5430 [Mon–Tues, 9.30am–2.30pm]; email: parentsupport@kidscape.org.uk [parent advice line], info@kidscape.org.uk; website: www. kidscape.org.uk)

Young People Leaving Care, Catch22, National Care Advisory Service (NCAS), 27 Pear Tree Street, London EC1V 3AG; (tel: 020 7336 4824; email: nlcbf@catch-22.org.uk; website: www.leavingcare.org)

Debt and financial advice

Age UK Money Matters, provides a range of advice on topics such as pensions, tax, financial management, legal matters and benefits (website: www.ageuk.org.uk/money-matters; Age UK Advice line: 0800 678 1602 [8am–7pm daily). See the website for information on local offices.

Business Debtline, 21 Garlick Hill, London EC4V 2AU (tel: 0800 197 6026 [Mon–Fri, 9am–8pm]; a webchat and email feature is also available; website: www. businessdebtline.org)

Gamblers Anonymous, The Wellness Centre, 45 Montrose Avenue, Intake, Doncaster DN2 6PL (tel: 0330 094 0322 [national hotline]; email: info@ gamblersanonymous.org.uk; website: www.gamblersanonymous.org.uk)

GamCare, 1st Floor, 91–94 Saffron Hill, London EC1N 8QP (tel: 020 7801 7000; helpline: 0808 802 0133 [24 hours a day, seven days a week]; email: info@gamcare.org.uk; website: www.gamcare.org.uk; an online chat feature and group chat is also available)

MoneyHelper, Holborn Centre, 120 Holborn, London EC1N 2TD (tel: 0800 138 7777; typetalk: 18001 0800 915 4622 [Mon–Fri, 8am–6pm]; website: www.moneyhelper.org.uk; an online chat and WhatsApp chat facility are also available)

National Debtline, Tricorn House, 51–53 Hagley Road, Edgbaston, Birmingham B16 8TP (helpline: 0808 808 4000 [Mon–Fri, 9am–8pm; Sat, 9.30am–1pm]; website: www. nationaldebtline.org; an online chat facility is also available [Mon–Fri, 9am–8pm; Sat, 9.30am–1pm])

StepChange Debt Charity, 123 Albion Street, Leeds LS2 8ER (helpline: 0800 138 1111 [Mon–Fri, 8am–8pm; Sat, 8am–4pm]; website: www.stepchange. org; an online chat feature is also available on the website)

TaxAid, Unit 2, 33 Stannary Street, London SE11 4AA (tel: helpline: 0345 120 3779 [Mon–Fri, 9am–5pm]; email: use the online form; website: www.taxaid.org.uk)

MoneyHelper (pensions and retirement), 120 Holborn, London EC1N 2TD (tel: 0800 011 3797 [Mon–Fri, 9am–5pm]; helpline for self-employed: 0345 602 7021 [Mon–Fri, 9am–5pm]; email: use the online form; website:www. moneyhelper.org.uk/en/pensions-and-retirement; an online chat facility is also available [Mon–Fri, 9am–6pm])

Families

Care for the Family, Tovey House, Cleppa Park, Newport NP10 8BA (tel: 029 2081 0800 [Mon, 10am–5pm; Tues–Thurs, 9am–5pm; Fri 9am–4.30pm]; email: mail@cff.org.uk; website: www.careforthefamily.org. uk)

Home-Start UK, The Crescent, King Street, Leicester LE1 6RX (tel: 0116 464 5490; email: info@home-start.org. uk or use the online form; website: www.home-start.org.uk)

Housing

Homes England (tel: 0300 1234 500; email: enquiries@homesengland.gov. uk [Mon–Fri, 9am–5pm]; website: www.gov.uk/government/ organisations/homes-england). See the website for information on local offices.

Shelter, 88 Old Street, London EC1V 9HU (tel: 0300 330 1234 [Mon–Fri, 9am–6pm]; helpline: 0808 800 4444 [Mon–Fri, 8am–8pm; Sat, 9am–5pm]; email: info@shelter.org. uk; website: www.shelter.org.uk)

Legal

Advocate (Bar Pro Bono), 50–52 Chancery Lane, London WC2A 1HL (tel: 020 7092 3960; email: enquiries@weareadvocate.org. uk or use the online form; website: www.weareadvocate.org.uk)

Civil Legal Advice, (helpline: 0345 345 4 345 [Mon–Fri, 9am–8pm; Sat, 9am–12.30pm]; text 'legalaid' and your name to 80010 for a call back; website: www.gov.uk/civil-legal-advice)

Law Centres Network, 1 Lady Hale Gate, Gray's Inn, London WC1X 8BS (tel: 020 3637 1330 [note this is not an advice line but LCN's office line]; email: use the online form; website: www.lawcentres.org.uk). See the website for information on your local law centre.

LawWorks, National Pro Bono Centre, 50–52 Chancery Lane, London WC2A 1HL (email: use the online form; website: www.lawworks. org.uk). See the website for information on your local legal advice clinic.

LGBTQ+

Beaumont Society, 27 Old Gloucester Street, London WC1N 3XX (24-hour helpline: 01582 412220; email: use the online form; website: www. beaumontsociety.org.uk)

LGBT Foundation, St George's House, 215–219 Chester Road, Manchester M15 4JE (helpline: 0345 330 30 30 [Mon–Fri, 9am–9pm]; email: info@lgbt.foundation, helpline: helpline@lgbt.foundation; website: www.lgbt.foundation)

Stonewall, 192 St John Street, Clerkenwell, London EC1V 4JY

(office [admin] tel: 020 7593 1850; information line: 0800 050 2020 [Mon–Fri, 9.30am–4.30pm]; email: info@stonewall.org.uk; website: www. stonewall.org.uk)

Missing people

Missing People, 284 Upper Richmond Road West, London SW14 7JE; (helpline: 116 000; text: 116 000 [9am–11pm daily]; email: 116000@ missingpeople.org.uk or use the online form [to report someone missing]; website: www. missingpeople.org.uk)

People with experience of the criminal justice system

APEX Trust, 13–15 North Road, St Helens, Merseyside WA10 2TW (tel: 01744 612898; email: sthelens@ apextrust.com or use the online contact form; website: www.apextrust. com)

Hardman Trust, PO Box 108, Newport, IW PO30 1YN (tel: 01983 550355; email: info@hardmantrust. org.uk; website: www.hardmantrust. org.uk)

National Association for the Care and Rehabilitation of Offenders (NACRO), 16–17 Devonshire Square, London EC2M 4SQ (tel: 0300 123 1999 [Resettlement Advice Service; Mon–Thurs, 9am–3pm; Fri, 1pm–5pm]; email: helpline@nacro. org.uk; website: www.nacro.org.uk)

Prisoners Abroad, 89–93 Fonthill Road, Finsbury Park, London N4 3JH (tel: 020 7561 6820; helpline: 0808 172 0098 [Mon–Fri, 9.30am–4.30pm; email: info@prisonersabroad.org.uk or use the online enquiry form; website: www.prisonersabroad.org.uk)

Unlock, Maidstone Community Support Centre, 39–48 Marsham Street, Maidstone, Kent ME14 1HH (tel: 01622 230705 [admin]; helpline: 01634 247350 [Mon–Fri, 10am–4pm]; text: 07824 113848; email: use the online form; website: www.unlock. org.uk)

Families of people with experience of the criminal justice system

Prisoners' families helpline, Pact, 29 Peckham Road, London SE5 8UA (helpline: 0808 808 2003 [Mon–Fri, 9am–8pm; Sat–Sun, 10am–3pm];

email: info@prisonersfamilies.org or use the online form; website: www. prisonersfamilies.org)

Partners of Prisoners and Families Support Group, POPS 1079 Rochdale Road, Blackley, Manchester M9 8AJ (tel: 0161 702 1000; helpline: 0808 808 2003 [Mon–Fri, 9am–8pm; Sat–Sun, 10am–3pm]; email: mail@ partnersofprisoners.co.uk or use the online form; website: www. partnersofprisoners.co.uk)

The Prison Advice and Care Trust (Pact), 29 Peckham Road, London SE5 8UA (tel: 020 7735 9535; helpline: 0808 808 2003; email: info@ prisonadvice.org.uk; website: www. prisonadvice.org.uk)

Women with experience of the criminal justice system

Working Chance, Claremont Building, 24–27 White Lion Street, London N1 9PD (tel: 020 7278 1532; email: info@workingchance.org or use the online form; website: www. workingchance.org)

Older people

Age UK, 6th Floor, Tavis House, 1–6 Tavistock Square, London WC1H 9NA (tel: 0800 169 8080 helpline: 0800 678 1602 [8am–7pm daily]; email: contact@ageuk.org.uk or by using the online form; website: www.ageuk.org.uk)

The Age and Employment Network, Headland House, 207–221 Pentonville, Road, London N1 9UZ, (tel: 020 7843 1590; email: taen@helptheaged.org.uk; website: www.taen.org.uk)

Care & Repair, Unit 9, The Renewal Trust Business Centre, 3 Hawksworth Street, Nottingham NG3 2EG (tel: 0115 950 6500; email: info@ careandrepair-england.org.uk; website: careandrepair-england.org.uk)

*Friends of the Elderly, 40–42 Ebury Street, London SW1W 0LZ (tel: 020 7730 8263; email: enquiries@fote.org. uk or use the online form; website: www.fote.org.uk)

Independent Age, 18 Avonmore Road, London W14 8RR, (tel: 020 7605 4200; helpline: 0800 319 6789 [Mon–Fri, 8.30am–6.30pm]; email: charity@independentage.org; website: www.independentage.org)

Parenting

Family Lives, 15–17 The Broadway, Hatfield, Hertfordshire AL9 5HZ (tel: 020 7553 3080; helpline: 0808 800 2222 [Mon–Fri, 9am–9pm; Sat–Sun, 10am–3pm]; email: askus@ familylives.org.uk; website: www. familylives.org.uk)

Twins Trust Manor House, Church Hill, Aldershot, Hampshire GU12 4JU (tel: 01252 332344; helpline: 0800 138 0509 [Mon–Fri, 10am–1pm and 7pm–10pm]; email: enquiries@ twinstrust.org; website: www. twinstrust.org)

Abduction

Reunite (National Council for Abducted Children), PO Box 7124, Leicester LE1 7XX (tel: 0116 255 5345; advice line: 0116 255 6234; email: reunite@dircon.co.uk or use the online form; website: www. reunite.org)

Adoption and fostering

Adoption UK, Units 11 and 12, Vantage Business Park, Bloxham Road, Banbury OX16 9UX (tel: 01295 752240; helpline: 0300 666 0006 [England, Mon–Fri, 10am–2.30pm; Northern Ireland, Mon–Fri, 9am–5pm; Scotland, Mon–Fri, 10am–2.30pm; Wales, Mon–Fri, 10am–2.30pm]; email: helpline@ adoptionuk.org.uk; website: www. adoptionuk.org.uk)

CoramBAAF Adoption & Fostering Academy, Coram Campus, 41 Brunswick Square, London WC1N 1AZ (tel: 020 7520 0300; members advice line: 0300 222 5775 [Mon–Fri, 9am–1pm]; email: use the online messaging feature [members only]; website: www.corambaaf.org. uk)

The Fostering Network, 87 Blackfriars Road, London SE1 8HA (tel: 020 7620 6400; Fosterline: 020 7401 9582 [England], 0800 316 7664 [Wales], 0141 204 1400 [Scotland], 028 9070 5056 [Northern Ireland], 01384 885734 [24-hour legal helpline], 01384 885734 [stress counselling helpline]; email: info@fostering.net; website: www.thefosteringnetwork. org.uk)

National Association of Child Contact Centres, 5 Russell Place, Nottingham NG1 5HJ (tel:0115 948 4557 [Mon–Fri, 9am–1pm]; email:

contact@naccc.org.uk or use the online form; website: www.naccc.org. uk)

Post-Adoption Centre (PAC-UK), Family Action Head Office, 34 Wharf Road, London N1 7GR (tel: 020 7284 0555; London advice line: 020 7284 5879 [Mon, Tues and Fri, 10am–4pm; Wed and Thurs 2pm–7.30pm]; Leeds advice line 0113 230 2100 [Mon, Thurs and Fri, 10am–1pm, Tues and Wed, 4pm–7pm]; education advice line: 020 7284 5879 [Thurs, 12am–2pm]; email: advice@pac-uk. org or use the online form; website: www.pac-uk.org)

Childcare

Family and Childcare Trust, Coram Campus, 41 Brunswick Square, London WC1N 1AZ (tel: 020 7239 7535; email: info@ familyandchildcaretrust.org.uk; website: www. familyandchildcaretrust.org)

Family Rights Group, Second Floor, The Print House, 18 Ashwin Street, London E8 3DL (tel: 020 7923 2628; advice line: 0808 801 0366 [Mon–Fri, 9.30am–3pm]; textphone: dial 18001 and then 0808 801 0366; email: office@frg.org.uk [admin]; website: www.frg.org.uk)

Divorce

Cafcass (Children and Family Court Advisory and Support Service), 3rd Floor, 21 Bloomsbury Street, London WC1B 3HF [national office] and Cafcass PO Box 5076, Slough SL1 0RX [national postal address] (tel: 0300 456 4000; email: use the online contact form; website: www. cafcass.gov.uk)

Families Need Fathers, Unit 501, The Pill Box Building, 115 Coventry Road, London E2 6GG (tel: 0300 0300 110 [admin], helpline: 0300 0300 363 [Mon–Fri, 9am–10pm, Sat–Sun, 10am–3pm]; email: fnf@fnf.org.uk; website: www.fnf.org.uk)

National Family Mediation, Civic Centre, Paris Street, Exeter (tel: 0300 4000 636; email: general@nfm.org.uk or use the online form; website: www. nfm.org.uk)

Grandparents

Kinship (Grandparents Plus), The Foundry, 17 Oval Way, London SE11 5RR (tel: 03300 167 235; advice

line: 0300 123 7015; email: info@
kinship.org.uk, advice@kinship.org.uk
[advice line] or use the online form;
website: www.kinship.org.uk)

Mothers

Mothers Apart from their Children
(MATCH), BM Box No. 6334,
London WC1N 3XX (helpline: 0800
689 4104 [9am–1pm and
7pm–9.30pm]; email: enquiries@
matchmothers.org; website: www.
matchmothers.org)

Mumsnet, (email: contactus@
mumsnet.com; website: www.
mumsnet.com)

Pregnancy

ARC (Antenatal Results and Choices),
12–15 Crawford Mews, York Street,
London W1H 1LX (tel: 020 7713
7356 [admin], helpline: 020 7713
7486 [Mon–Fri, 10am–5.30pm];
email: info@arc-uk.org or use the
online form; website: www.arc-uk.
org)

British Pregnancy Advisory Service
(BPAS), 20 Timothy's Bridge Road,
Stratford Enterprise Park, Stratford-
upon-Avon, Warwickshire CV37 9BF
(tel: 0345 365 5050 [head office];
advice line: 03457 30 40 30 [Mon–Fri,
7am–7pm; Sat, 8am–4pm; Sun,
9.30am–2.30pm]; email: info@bpas.
org; website: www.bpas.org)

Brook (sexual health and wellbeing
for under 25s) (email: admin@brook.
org.uk; website: www.brook.org.uk).
Resources and advice are available on
the website. See the website for
information on local clinics.

Disability Pregnancy and Parenthood
International (DPPI), 106 Muswell
Hill Road, London N10 3JR (email:
info@disabledparent.org.uk or use the
online contact form; website: www.
disabledparent.org.uk)

Maternity Action, Second Floor,
3–4 Wells Terrace, London N4 3JU
(tel: 020 7253 2288; email: info@
maternity.org.uk; website: www.
maternityaction.org.uk)

National Childbirth Trust, Brunel
House, 11 The Promenade, Clifton
Down, Bristol BS8 3NG (helpline:
0300 330 0700; email: enquiries@nct.
org.uk or use the online form;
website: www.nct.org.uk)

Single parents

Gingerbread, 54–74 Holmes Road,
London NW5 3AQ (tel: 020 7428
5400 [admin]; helpline: 0808 802
0925 [Mon, 10am–6pm; Tues, Thurs
and Fri, 10am–4pm; Wed, 10am–1pm
and 5pm–7pm]; email: use the online
form; website: www.gingerbread.org.
uk)

Single Parents (website: www.
singleparents.org.uk)

Poverty

Care International, Supporter Care
Team, CARE International, c/o
Ashurst LLP, London Fruit and Wool
Exchange, 1 Duval Square, London
E1 6PW (tel: 020 7091 6000; email:
info@careinternational.org; website:
www.careinternational.org.uk)

*Family Action, 34 Wharf Road,
London N1 7GR (tel: 020 7254 6251
[general] or 0808 802 6666 [helpline];
text: 07537 404282 [helpline]; email:
info@family-action.org.uk or
familyline@family-action.org.uk
[helpline]; website: www.family-
action.org.uk)

The Trussell Trust, Unit 9, Ashfield
Trading Estate, Ashfield Road,
Salisbury SP2 7HL (tel: 01722 580180;
email: enquiries@trusselltrust.org or
use the online contact form; website:
www.trusselltrust.org). You can also
use the website's search facility to
find your nearest food bank.

Refugees and asylum seekers

Consonant, Berol House, 25 Ashley
Road, London N17 9LJ (tel: 020 7354
9631; email: hello@consonant.org.uk;
website: www.consonant.org.uk)

Migrant Help, Charlton House, Dour
Street, Dover, Kent CT16 1AT (tel:
01304 203977, helpline: 0808 801
0503 [24-hour]; email: info@
migranthelpuk.org or use the online
contact form; website: www.
migranthelpuk.org)

Refugee Action, 179 Royce Road,
Manchester M15 5TJ (website: www.
refugee-action.org.uk)

Refugee Council, PO Box 68614,
London E15 1NS (tel: 020 7346 6700
[head office]; website: www.
refugeecouncil.org.uk). Visit the
website for signposting to a specific
service.

Relationships

Albany Trust Counselling, 239A
Balham High Road, London
SW17 7BE (tel: 020 8767 1827; email:
info@albanytrust.org; website: www.
albanytrust.org)

Marriage Care, Huntingdon House,
278–290 Huntingdon St, Nottingham
NG1 3LY (tel: 0800 389
3801[Mon–Thurs, 9am–6pm];
helpline: 0845 660 6000 [Mon–Fri,
9am–9pm; Sat–Sun, 10am–3pm];
email: appointments@marriagecare.
org.uk or use the online contact
form; website: www.marriagecare.org.
uk)

Relate Premier House, Carolina
Court, Lakeside, Doncaster DN4 5RA
(email: use the online form; website:
www.relate.org.uk; a live chat service,
webcam counselling and telephone
counselling are also available on the
website). See the website for
information on local offices.

Social isolation

The Farming Community Network,
Manor Farm, West Haddon,
Northampton NN6 7AQ (tel: 01788
510866; helpline: 0300 0111999;
email: help@fcn.org.uk; website:
www.fcn.org.uk)

Squatters

Advisory Service for Squatters (ASS),
Angel Alley, 84B Whitechapel High
Street, London E1 7QX (tel:
07545508628; email:
advice4squatters@gmail.com; website:
www.squatter.org.uk)

Victims of accidents and crimes

Abuse

Hourglass (formerly Action on Elder
Abuse), Office 8, Unit 5, Stour Valley
Business Centre, Brundon Lane,
Sudbury, Suffolk CO10 7GB
(helpline: 0808 808 814; free text:
07860 052906; email: enquiries@
wearehourglass.org,
helpline@wearehourglass.org
[helpline] or use the online form;
website: www.wearehourglass.org)

NSPCC, Weston House, 42 Curtain
Road, London EC2A 3NH (tel: 020
7825 2505 [Mon–Fri, 9am–5pm];
helpline for adults concerned about a
child: 0808 800 5000 [Mon–Fri,
8am–10pm; Sat–Sun, 9am–6pm]; for

children and young people, call ChildLine: 08001111 [24/7]; email: help@nspcc.org.uk or use the online form; website: www.nspcc.org.uk). A one-to-one counsellor chat feature is also available on the website.

Crime

Victim Support, 1 Bridge Street, Derby DE1 3HZ (Supportline: 0808 168 9111 [24-hour]; text relay: 18001 08 08 16 89 111; victims' information service: 0808 168 9293 [24-hour]; email: use the online contact form to contact the support line via email; website: www.victimsupport.org.uk). For details on the regional offices see the website. A live chat feature is also available on the website.

Disasters

Disaster Action, No. 4, 71–73 Upper Berkeley Street, London W1H 7DB (email: admin@disasteraction.org.uk; website: www.disasteraction.org.uk)

Domestic violence

ManKind Initiative, Flook House, Belvedere Road, Taunton, Somerset TA1 1BT (helpline: 01823 334244 [weekdays, 10am–4pm]; email: admin@mankind.org.uk [admin]; website: www.mankind.org.uk)

Men's Aid Charity (helpline: 0333 567 0556; email: help@mensaid.co.uk; website: www.mensaid.co.uk)

National Centre for Domestic Violence, Edgeborough House, Upper Edgeborough Road, Guildford, Surrey GU1 2BJ (24-hour helpline: 0800 970 2070; text: 'NCDV' to 60777 for call back; email: office@ncdv.org.uk; website: www.ncdv.org.uk)

Respect (tel: 0808 802 4040 [Mon–Fri, 9am–8pm]; email: info@respectphoneline.org.uk [Mon–Fri, 9am–8pm; Sat–Sun, 10am–12pm and 4pm–6pm]; website: www.respectphoneline.org.uk) A webchat feature is also available on the website.

Refuge, Fourth Floor, International House, 1 St Katharine's Way, London E1W 1UN (tel: 020 7395 7700 [general]; 24-hour helpline: 0808 200 0247; email: use the online form to contact the helpline via email; website: www.refuge.org.uk)

Women's Aid Federation, PO Box 3245, Bristol BS2 2EH (tel: 24-hour helpline: 0808 200 0247; email: info@

womensaid.org.uk or helpline@womensaid.org.uk; website: www.womensaid.org.uk). A live chat feature is also available on the website. See the website for details on the regional offices.

Medical accidents

Action against Medical Accidents (AVMA), 117 High Street, Croydon, London CR0 1QG (tel: 020 8688 9555 [admin]; helpline: 0845 123 2352 [Mon–Fri, 10am–3.30pm]; email: admin@avma.org.uk [admin only]; website: www.avma.org.uk)

Rape

Rape Crisis Centre, Suite E4, Joseph's Well, Hanover Walk, Leeds LS3 1AB (helpline: 0808 802 9999 [12pm–2.30pm and 7pm–9.30pm daily]; email: rcewinfo@rapecrisis.org.uk; website: www.rapecrisis.org.uk). A live chat feature is also available on the website. See website for information on local rape crisis centres.

Safeline, 6A New Street, Warwick, Warwickshire CV34 4RX (tel: 01926 402498; national male survivor helpline: 0808 800 5005; email: use the online form; website: www.safeline.org.uk). A live chat feature is also available on the website.

The Survivors Trust, Unit 2, Eastlands Court Business Centre, St Peter's Road, Rugby, Warwickshire CV21 3QP (tel: 01788 550554; helpline: 0808 801 0818 [Mon–Thurs, 10am–12.30pm, 1.30pm–5.30pm and 6pm–8pm, Fri, 10am-12.30pm and 1.30pm-5.30pm; Sat, 10am–1pm; Sun, 5pm–8pm]; email: info@thesurvivorstrust.org; website: www.thesurvivorstrust.org) See the website for information on support in your local area. A live chat feature is also available on the website.

Women Against Rape (WAR) and Black Women's Rape Action Project, Crossroads Women's Centre, 25 Wolsey Mews NW5 2DX (tel: 020 7482 2496; email: war@womenagainstrape.net or asylumfromrape@womenagainstrape.net; website:www.womenagainstrape.net)

Road accidents

Brake, PO Box 548, Huddersfield HD1 2XZ (tel: 01484 559909; helpline: 0808 800 0401; email: help@

brake.org.uk; website: www.brake.org.uk)

RoadPeace, 3Space International House, 6 Canterbury Crescent, London SW9 7QD (tel: 020 7733 1603; helpline: 0845 450 0355 [Mon–Fri, 10am–1pm]; email: info@roadpeace.org or use the online form; website: www.roadpeace.org)

Work issues

Acas, 8th Floor Windsor House, 50 Victoria Street, London SW1H 0TL; (helpline: 0300 123 1100 [Mon–Fri, 8am–6pm]; text relay: 18001 0300 123 1100; website: www.acas.org.uk)

Employment Tribunals Enquiry Line, (public enquiry line: 0300 123 1024 and textphone: 18001 0300 123 1024 [England and Wales]; public enquiry line: 0300 790 6234 and textphone: 18001 0300 790 6234 [Scotland]; website: www.gov.uk/courts-tribunals/employment-tribunal). See website for the contact details of local employment tribunals.

Protect (formerly Public Concern at Work), The Green House, 244–254 Cambridge Heath Road, London E2 9DA, (whistleblowing advice line: 020 3117 2520 [Mon, Tues and Thurs, 9.30am–1pm and 2pm–5.30pm; Wed and Fri, 9.30am–1pm]; email: whistle@protect-advice.org.uk or use the contact form on the website; website: www.protect-advice.org.uk)

Trades Union Congress, Congress House, Great Russell Street, London WC1B 3LS (tel: 020 7636 4030; email: info@tuc.org.uk; website: www.tuc.org.uk)

Women

Women and Girls Network, PO Box 13095, London W13 3BJ (tel: 020 7610 4678 [general]; advice line: 0808 801 0660 [Mon–Fri, 10am–4pm; Wed, 6pm–9pm]; Sexual Violence Helpline: 0808 801 0770 [see website for opening times]; email: info@wgn.org.uk or use the online form; website: www.wgn.org.uk; an online chat feature is also available)

Women's Health Concern, Spracklen House, Dukes Place, Marlow, Buckinghamshire SL7 2QH (tel: 01628 890199 [telephone and email advice is available for a small fee,

check the website for more details];
website: www.womens-health-
concern.org)

Illness and disability

Disability (general) 476

Addiction 476

Ageing 476

AIDS/HIV 476

Alcohol 476

Allergy 477

Alopecia areata and alopecia androgenetica 477

Alzheimer's disease/dementia 477

Arthritis/rheumatic diseases 477

Arthrogryposis 477

Asthma 477

Ataxia 477

Autism 477

Back pain 477

Blind/partially sighted 477

Bone marrow 477

Brain injury 477

Brain tumours 477

Brittle bones 477

Burns 478

Cancer and leukaemia 478

Cerebral palsy 478

Chest/lungs 478

Cleft lip/palate disorder 478

Coeliac disease 478

Colostomy 478

Counselling 478

Crohn's disease and colitis 478

Cystic fibrosis 478

Deafblind 478

Deafness/hearing difficulties 479

Depression 479

Diabetes 479

Disfigurement 479

Down's syndrome 479

Drugs 479

Dyslexia 479

Dyspraxia 479

Dystonia 479

Eating disorders 479

Eczema 480

Endometriosis 480

Epilepsy 480

Growth conditions 480

Haemophilia 480

Heart attacks/heart disease 480

Hemiplegia 480

Hodgkin's disease 480

Huntington's disease 480

Hyperactivity and ADHD 480

Incontinence 480

Industrial diseases 480

Infertility 480

Irritable bowel syndrome 480

Kidney disease 480

Learning disabilities 481

Limb conditions 481

Literacy/learning difficulties 481

Liver disease 481

Lupus 481

Mastectomy 481

Meningitis 481

Menopause 481

Mental health 481

Metabolic disorders 481

Migraine 481

Miscarriage 481

Motor neurone disease 482

Multiple sclerosis 482

Muscular dystrophy 482

Myalgic Encephalopathy/Chronic Fatigue Syndrome(ME/CFS) 482

Myotonic dystrophy 482

Narcolepsy 482

Neurofibromatosis 482

Osteoporosis 482

Paget's disease 482

Parkinson's disease 482

Pituitary disorders 482

Poliomyelitis 482

Postnatal depression 482

Prader-Willi syndrome 482

Pre-eclampsia 482

Psoriasis 482

Rett syndrome 482

Reye's syndrome 482

Sarcoidosis 483

Schizophrenia 483

Scoliosis 483

Sexually transmitted infections 483

Sickle cell disease 483

Smoking 483

Solvent abuse 483

Speech and language difficulties 483

Spina bifida 483

Spinal injuries 483

Stroke 483

Sudden infant death syndrome (SIDS) 483

Suicide 483

Tinnitus 483

Tourette's syndrome 483

Tracheo-oesophageal fistula 483

Tuberous sclerosis 484

Urostomy 484

Williams syndrome 484

ADVICE ORGANISATIONS

Disability (general)

Action Medical Research, Vincent House, Horsham, West Sussex RH12 2DP (tel: 01403 210406; email: info@action.org.uk or use the online form; website: www.action.org.uk)

Contact a Family, 209–211 City Road, London EC1V 1JN (tel: 020 7608 8700; helpline: 0808 808 3555; email: info@contact.org.uk or use the online form; website: www.cafamily.org.uk)

Disabled Living Foundation (DLF), Black Country House, Rounds Green Road, Oldbury B69 2DG (tel: 030 123 3084; helpline: 0300 999 0004 [Mon–Fri, 9am–5pm]; email: info@dlf.org.uk; website: www.livingmadeeasy.org.uk). An online self-help feature called AskSARA is available to use on the website.

Disabilities Trust, 32 Market Place, Burgess Hill, West Sussex RH15 9NP (tel: 01444 239123; email: info@thedtgroup.org or use the online contact form; website: www.thedtgroup.org)

Disability Law Service (DLS), The Foundry, 17 Oval Way, London SE11 5RR (tel: 020 7791 9800; email: advice@dls.org.uk or use the online contact form; website: www.dls.org.uk)

Disability Pregnancy and Parenthood International (DPPI), 106 Muswell Hill Road, London N10 3JR (email: info@disabledparent.org.uk or use the online contact form; website: www.disabledparent.org.uk)

Disability Rights UK, Plexal, 14 East Bay Lane, Here East, Queen Elizabeth Olympic Park, Stratford, London E20 3BS (tel: 0330 995 0400; email: enquiries@disabilityrightsuk.org or use the online contact form; website: www.disabilityrightsuk.org)

I CAN, 2 Angel Gate, Hall Street, London EC1V 2PT (tel: 020 7843 2510; helpline for parent support: 020 7843 2544; email: info@ican.org.uk; website: www.ican.org.uk)

Jewish Care, Amélie House, Maurice and Vivienne Wohl Campus, 221 Golders Green Road, London NW11 9DQ (tel: 020 8922 2000; helpline: 020 8922 2222; email: info@jcare.org or helpline@jcare.org or use the online contact form; website: www.jewishcare.org)

Kids, 7–9 Elliott's Place, London N1 8HX (tel: 020 7359 3635; email: use the online form; website: www.kids.org.uk)

PHAB England, Summit House, 50 Wandle Road, Croydon CR0 1DF (tel: 020 8667 9443; email: info@phab.org.uk; website: www.phab.org.uk)

Queen Elizabeth's Foundation (QEF), Leatherhead Court, Woodlands Road, Leatherhead, Surrey KT22 0BN (tel: 01372 841100; email: info@qef.org.uk or use the online form; website: www.qef.org.uk)

Respond, 3rd Floor, Windover House, St Ann Street, Salisbury SP1 2DR (tel: 020 7383 0700; email: admin@respond.org.uk or use the online contact form; website: www.respond.org.uk)

Scope, 2nd Floor, Here East Press Centre, 14 East Bay Lane, London E15 2GW (helpline: 0808 800 3333; textphone: 18001 0808 800 3333 [Mon–Fri, 9am–6pm; Sat–Sun, 10am–6pm]; email: helpline@scope.org.uk; website: www.scope.org.uk)

Addiction

Action on Addiction, Unit 106–107, Edinburgh House, 170 Kennington Lane, London SE11 5DP (tel: 020 3981 5525; email: enquiries@actiononaddiction.org.uk; website: www.actiononaddiction.org.uk). An online advice chat service is also available to use on the website.

DrugFAM (for families who have been affected by addiction), Oakley Hall, 8 Castle Street, High Wycombe HP13 6RF (helpline: 0300 888 3853 [9am–9pm daily]; email: office@drugfam.co.uk or use the online contact form; website: www.drugfam.co.uk)

We Are With You (formerly Addaction), 1–3 St John's Square, London EC1M 4DH (tel: 020 7251 5860; email: use the online form or the webchat feature; website: www.addaction.org.uk). See the website for information on local services.

Ageing

Age UK, Tavis House (6th Floor), 1–6 Tavistock Square, London WC1H 9NA (advice line: 0800 678 1602 [8am–7pm daily]; email: use the online form; website: www.ageuk.org.uk)

Independent Age, 18 Avonmore Road, London W14 8RR, (tel: 020 7605 4200; helpline: 0800 319 6789 [Mon–Fri, 8:30am–6:30pm]; email: charity@independentage.org; website: www.independentage.org)

AIDS/HIV

National Aids Trust, Aztec House, 397–405 Archway Road, London N6 4EY (tel: 020 7814 6767; email: info@nat.org.uk; website: www.nat.org.uk)

*Positive East, 159 Mile End Road, London E1 4AQ (tel: 020 7791 2855; email: talktome@positiveeast.org.uk or use the online form; website: www.positiveeast.org.uk)

*Terrence Higgins Trust, 437 and 439 Caledonian Road, London NV 9BG (tel: 020 7812 1600; advice and support line: 0808 802 1221 [Mon–Fri, 10am–6pm]; email: info@tht.org.uk or use the online form; website: www.tht.org.uk)

Alcohol

Al-Anon Family Groups UK and Eire (AFG), 57B Great Suffolk Street, London SE1 0BB (helpline: 0800 008 6811 [10am–10pm daily]; email: use the online form; website: www.al-anonuk.org.uk)

Alcohol Change UK (formerly Alcohol Research UK and Alcohol Concern), 27 Swinton Street, London WC1X 9NW (tel: 020 3907 8480; email: contact@alcoholchange.org.uk; website: www.alcoholchange.org.uk)

Alcoholics Anonymous (AA), General Service Office, PO Box 1, 10 Toft Green, York YO1 7NJ (tel: 01904 644026; helpline: 0800 917 7650; email: help@aamail.org; website: www.alcoholics-anonymous.org.uk)

Drinkaware, Upper Ground Floor (Room 264), Salisbury House), London EC2M 5QQ (tel: 020 7766 9900; email: contact@drinkaware.co.uk; website: www.drinkaware.co.uk)

Drinkline (helpline: 0300 123 1110 [Mon–Fri, 9am–8pm; Sat–Sun, 11am–4pm])

Phoenix Futures, 68 Newington Causeway, London SE1 6DF (tel: 020 7234 9740; website: www.phoenix-futures.org.uk)

Turning Point, Standon House, 21 Mansell Street, London E1 8AA (tel: 020 7481 7600; email: info@ turning-point.co.uk or use the online form; website: www.turning-point.co.uk)

Allergy

Action Against Allergy, PO Box 278, Twickenham TW1 4QQ (tel: 020 8892 4949; helpline: 020 8892 2711; email: aaa@actionagainstallergy.freeserve.co.uk; website: www.actionagainstallergy.co.uk)

Allergy UK, Planwell House, LEFA Business Park, Edgington Way Sidcup, Kent DA14 5BH (helpline: 01322 619898 [Mon–Fri, 9am–5pm]; email: info@allergyuk.org; website: www.allergyuk.org). A live chat facility is also available on the website.

Alopecia areata and alopecia androgenetica

Alopecia UK, PO Box 341, Baildon, Shipley BD18 9EH (tel: 0800 101 7025 [Mon–Fri, 10am–4pm]; email: info@alopecia.org.uk or use the online form; website: www.alopecia.org.uk)

Alzheimer's disease/dementia

Alzheimer's Society, Scott Lodge, Scott Road, Plymouth PL2 3DU (tel: 0330 333 0804; helpline: 0333 150 3456 [8am–10pm daily]; email: use the online form; website: www.alzheimers.org.uk)

Dementia UK, Head Office, 7th Floor, One Aldgate, London EC3N 1RE (tel: 020 8036 5400; helpline: 0800 888 6678 [Mon–Fri, 9am–9pm; Sat–Sun, 9am–5pm] email: info@dementiauk.org; website: www.dementiauk.org)

Arthritis/rheumatic diseases

Versus Arthritis (formerly Arthritis Care and Arthritis Research UK), Copeman House, St Mary's Court, St Mary's Gate, Chesterfield S41 7TD (tel: 0300 790 0400; helpline: 0800 520 0520; email: enquiries@ versusarthritis.org; website: www.versusarthritis.org)

Arthrogryposis

The Arthrogryposis Group (TAG), 37 Brynteg Avenue, Pontllanfraith, Blackwood, Gwent NP12 2BY (helpline: 07508 679351; email: help@ arthrogryposis.co.uk or use the online form; website: www.arthrogryposis.co.uk)

Asthma

Asthma UK, 18 Mansell Street, London E1 8AA (tel: 0300 222 5800; advice line: 0300 222 5800 (option 1) [Mon–Fri, 9am–5pm]; email: info@ asthma.org.uk; website: www.asthma.org.uk)

Ataxia

Ataxia UK, 12 Broadbent Close, London N6 5JW (tel: 020 7582 1444; helpline: 0800 995 6037 [Mon–Thurs, 10.30am–2.30pm]; email: office@ ataxia.org.uk or helpline@ataxia.org.uk; website: www.ataxia.org.uk)

Autism

National Autistic Society (NAS), 393 City Road, London EC1V 1NG (tel: 020 7833 2299; details of numerous helplines are available on the website; email: nas@nas.org.uk; website: www.autism.org.uk)

Back pain

BackCare, 29 Bridge Street, Hitchen SG5 2DF (tel: 020 8977 5474; email: info@backcare.org.uk; website: www.backcare.org.uk)

Blind/partially sighted

Calibre Audio (Cassette Library of Recorded Books), New Road, Aston Clinton, Aylesbury, Buckinghamshire HP22 5XQ (tel: 01296 432339; email: enquiries@calibre.org.uk; website: www.calibreaudio.org.uk)

Glaucoma UK, Woodcote House, 15 Highpoint Business Village, Henwood, Ashford, Kent TN24 8DH (tel: 01233 648164; helpline: 01233 648170 [Mon–Fri, 9:30am–5pm]; email: help@glaucoma.uk; website: www.glaucoma.uk)

Listening Books, 12 Lant Street, London SE1 1QH (tel: 020 7407 9417; email: info@listening-books.org.uk; website: www.listening-books.org.uk)

National Federation of the Blind of the UK (NFBUK), Sir John Wilson House, 215 Kirkgate, Wakefield WF1 1JG (tel: 01924 291313; email: admin@nfbuk.org or use the online form; website: www.nfbuk.org)

Partially Sighted Society, 1 Bennetthorpe, Doncaster DN2 6AA (tel: 01302 965195; email: reception@ partsight.org.uk; website: www.partsight.org.uk)

Royal National Institute for the Blind (RNIB), 105 Judd Street, London WC1H 9NE (helpline: 0303 123 9999 [Mon–Fri, 8am–8pm; Sat, 9am–1pm]; email: helpline@rnib.org.uk or use the online form; website: www.rnib.org.uk)

Retina UK, Wharf House, Stratford Road, Buckingham MK18 1TD (tel: 01280 821334; helpline: 0300 111 4000; email: helpline@retinauk.org.uk; website: www.retinauk.org.uk)

Voluntary Transcribers' Group, Apartment 005, Bournville Gardens, 49 Bristol Road South, Birmingham B31 2FR (tel: 0121 227 9005; email: braillist@btinternet.com)

Bone marrow

Anthony Nolan Trust, 2 Heathgate Place, 75–87 Agincourt Road, London NW3 2NU (tel: 0303 303 0303; email: use the online form; website: www.anthonynolan.org)

Brain injury

British Institute for Brain-Injured Children (BIBIC), Old Kelways, Somerton Road, Langport, Somerset TA10 9SJ (tel: 01458 253344; email: info@bibic.org.uk or use the online form; website: www.bibic.org.uk)

*Headway, Bradbury House, 190 Bagnall Road, Old Basford, Nottingham NG6 8SF (tel: 0115 924 0800; helpline: 0808 800 2244; email: enquiries@headway.org.uk; website: www.headway.org.uk)

Brain tumours

The Brain Tumour Charity, Fleet 27, Rye Close, Fleet, Hampshire GU51 2UH (tel: 01252 749990; information and support line: 0808 800 0004 [Mon–Fri, 9am–5pm]; email: support@ thebraintumourcharity.org or use the online form; website: www.thebraintumourcharity.org)

Brittle bones

Brittle Bone Society, Grant-Paterson House, 30 Guthrie Street, Dundee DD1 5BS (tel: 01382 204446; email:

bbs@brittlebone.org; website: www.
brittlebone.org)

Burns

British Burn Association, Royal
College of Surgeons of England,
35–43 Lincoln's Inn Fields, London
WC2A 3PE (tel: 020 7869 6923;
email: info@britishburnassociation.
org; website: www.
britishburnassociation.org)

Children's Burns Trust, 13 The Vale,
Stock, Ingatestone, Essex CM4 9PW
(tel: 07802 635590; email: info@
cbtrust.org.uk or use the online form;
website: www.cbtrust.org.uk)

Cancer and leukaemia

Action Cancer, 20 Windsor Avenue,
Belfast BT9 6EE (tel: 028 9080 3344;
email: info@actioncancer.org or use
the online form; website: www.
actioncancer.org)

Cancer Support Scotland, The
Calman Centre, 75 Shelley Road,
Glasgow G12 0ZE (tel: 0800 652 4531;
email:
info@cancersupportscotland.org or
use the online form; website: www.
cancersupportscotland.org)

*CLIC Sargent Cancer Care for
Children (operating as Young Lives vs
Cancer), No. 1 Farriers Yard,
Assembly London, 77–85 Fulham
Palace Road, London W6 8JA (tel:
0300 330 0803 [Mon–Fri, 9am–5pm];
email: use the online form; website:
www.younglivesvscancer.org.uk)

*Leukaemia Care Society, One Birch
Court, Blackpole East, Worcester
WR3 8SG (tel: 01905 755977;
helpline: 0808 801 0444 [Mon–Fri,
9am–5pm; Thurs–Fri, 7pm–10pm];
email: support@leukaemiacare.org.uk;
website: www.leukaemiacare.org.uk)

*Macmillan Cancer Support,
89 Albert Embankment, London
SE1 7UQ (tel: 020 7840 7840;
helpline: 0808 808 0000 [8am–8pm
daily]; email: use the online form;
website: www.macmillan.org.uk)

Marie Curie Foundation, 89 Albert
Embankment, London SE1 7TP (tel:
0800 716146; helpline: 0800 090 2309;
email: supporter.relations@
mariecurie.org.uk; website: www.
mariecurie.org.uk)

Tenovus Cancer Care, Brunel House
(15th Floor), 2 Fitzalan Road, Cardiff

CF24 0EB (tel: 029 2076 8850;
helpline: 0808 808 1010; email: info@
tenovuscancercare.org.uk; website:
www.tenovuscancercare.org.uk) There
is also an 'Ask the Nurse' enquiry
form on the website.

Cerebral palsy

SCOPE, Here East Press Centre,
14 East Bay Lane, London E15 2GW
(helpline: 0808 800 3333 [Mon–Fri,
9am–6pm; Sat–Sun, 10am–6pm];
email: helpline@scope.org.uk; website:
www.scope.org.uk) See the website
for information on local offices.

Chest/lungs

British Lung Foundation, 18 Mansell
Street, London E1 8AA (helpline:
0300 003 0555 [Mon–Fri, 9pm–5pm];
email: use the online form; website:
www.blf.org.uk)

Roy Castle Lung Cancer Foundation,
Cotton Exchange Building, Old Hall
Street, Liverpool L3 9LQ (tel: 0333
323 7200; email: foundation@
roycastle.org or use the online form;
website: www.roycastle.org)

Cleft lip/palate disorder

Cleft Lip and Palate Association
(CLAPA), The Green House,
244–254 Cambridge Heath Road,
London E2 9DA (tel: 020 7833 4883
[Mon–Fri, 9am–5pm]; email: info@
clapa.com or use the online form;
website: www.clapa.com)

Coeliac disease

Coeliac UK, 3rd Floor, Apollo Centre,
Desborough Road, High Wycombe
HP11 2QW (helpline: 0333 332 2033
[Mon–Fri, 9am–5pm]; email: use the
online form; website: www.coeliac.
org.uk)

Colostomy

Colostomy UK, Enterprise House,
95 London Street, Reading, Berkshire
RG1 4QA (tel: 0118 939 1537
[Mon–Fri, 9am–5pm]; 24-hour
helpline: 0800 328 4257; email: info@
colostomyuk.org or use the online
form; website: www.colostomyuk.org)

Counselling

British Association for Counselling
and Psychotherapy, 15 St John's
Business Park, Lutterworth
LE17 4HB, (tel: 01455 883300; email:

bacp@bacp.co.uk; website: www.bacp.
co.uk)

Samaritans, The Upper Mill, Kingston
Road, Ewell, Surrey KT17 2AF (tel:
020 8394 8300; 24-hour helpline: 116
123; see the website for local
numbers; email: admin@samaritans.
org [general] or jo@samaritans.org
[helpline]; website: www.samaritans.
org)

SupportLine, PO Box 2860, Romford,
Essex RM7 1JA (tel: 01708 765222;
helpline: 01708 765200; email: info@
supportline.org.uk; website: www.
supportline.org.uk)

Crohn's disease and colitis

Children with Crohn's and Colitis
(CICRA), Pat Shaw House,
13–19 Ventnor Road, Sutton, Surrey
SM2 6AQ (tel: 020 8949 6209; email:
support@cicra.org or use the online
form; website: www.cicra.org)

Crohn's and Colitis UK, 1 Bishops
Square (Helios Court), Hatfield
Business Park, Hatfield, Hertfordshire
AL10 9NE (tel: 01727 830038;
helpline: 0300 222 5700 [Mon–Fri,
9am–5pm]; email: helpline@
crohnsandcolitis.org.uk; website:
www.crohnsandcolitis.org.uk)

Cystic fibrosis

Butterfly Trust, 109/3 Swanston Road,
Edinburgh EH10 7DS (tel: 0131 445
5590; email: info@butterflytrust.org.
uk; website: www.butterflytrust.org.
uk)

*Cystic Fibrosis Trust, One Aldgate,
Second Floor, London EC3N 1RE
(tel: 020 3795 1555; helpline: 0300
373 1000 [see website for current
opening hours]; email: enquiries@
cysticfibrosis.org.uk or
helpline@cysticfibrosis.org.uk;
website: www.cysticfibrosis.org.uk)

Deafblind

Deafblind UK, National Centre for
Deafblindness, 19 Rainbow Court,
Paston Ridings, Peterborough,
Cambridgeshire PE4 7UP (tel: 0800
132320; textphone: 07903 572885;
email: info@deafblind.org.uk or use
the online form; website: www.
deafblind.org.uk)

Sense, 101 Pentonville Road, London
N1 9LG (tel: 0300 330 9256;
textphone: 18001 0300 330 9256;
email: info@sense.org.uk or use the

online form; website: www.sense.org.uk)

Deafness/hearing difficulties

Royal National Institute for Deaf People – RNID (formerly Action on Hearing Loss), Information Line, RNID, 9 Bakewell Road, Orton Southgate, Peterborough PE2 6XU (tel: 0808 808 0123; text: 07800 000360; textphone: 0808 808 9000; relay: 18001 then 0808 808 0123; email: information@rnid.org.uk; website: www.rnid.org.uk)

British Deaf Association (BDA), St John's Deaf Community Centre, 258 Green Lanes, London N4 2HE (text: 07795 410724; email: bda@bda.org.uk or use the online form; website: www.bda.org.uk)

The Guide Dogs for the Blind Association, Burghfield Common, Reading RG7 3YG (tel: 0118 983 5555; advice line: 0800 781 1444 [Mon–Fri, 9am–5pm]; email: information@guidedogs.org.uk; website: www.guidedogs.org.uk)

Hearing Dogs for Deaf People, The Grange, Wycombe Road, Saunderton, Buckinghamshire HP27 9NS (tel: 01844 348100; text relay: 18001 01844 348100; email: info@hearingdogs.org.uk; website: www.hearingdogs.org.uk)

National Deaf Children's Society, Ground Floor South, Castle House, 37–45 Paul Street, London EC2A 4LS (tel: 020 7490 8656; helpline: 0808 800 8880 [Mon–Fri, 9am–5pm]; text: 07860 022888 [Mon–Fri, 9am–5pm] email: ndcs@ndcs.org.uk or use the contact form; website: www.ndcs.org.uk). Live chat and sign video features are also available.

Royal Association for Deaf People (RAD), Block F, Parkside Office Village, Knowledge Gateway, Nesfield Road, Colchester CO4 3ZL (tel: 0300 688 2525; textphone: 0300 688 2527; text: 07851 423866; email: info@royaldeaf.org.uk; website: www.royaldeaf.org.uk)

Depression

Mind, 2 Redman Place, London E20 1JQ; infoline address: Mind Infoline, PO Box 75225, London E15 9FS (tel: 020 8519 2122; infoline: 0300 123 3393 [Mon–Fri, 9am–6pm, except for bank holidays]; email: info@mind.org.uk; website: www.mind.org.uk)

Depression UK, Lytchett House, 13 Freeland Park, Wareham Road, Poole, Dorset BH16 6FA (email: info@depressionuk.org; website: www.depressionuk.org)

Samaritans, The Upper Mill, Kingston Road, Ewell, Surrey KT17 2AF (tel: 020 8394 8300; 24-hour helpline: 116 123; see website for local numbers; email: admin@samaritans.org [general] or jo@samaritans.org [helpline]; website: www.samaritans.org)

Diabetes

Diabetes UK, Wells Lawrence House, 126 Back Church Lane, London E1 1FH (tel: 0345 123 2399; [Mon–Fri, 9am–6pm]; 0141 212 8710 [Scotland; Mon–Fri, 9am–6pm] email: helpline@diabetes.org.uk; helpline.scotland@diabetes.org.uk [Scotland]; website: www.diabetes.org.uk)

Disfigurement

Disfigurement Guidance Centre, PO Box 7, Cupar, Fife KY15 4PF (tel: 01334 839084)

Changing Faces, PO Box 76751, London WC1A 9QR (tel: 0345 450 0275; email: info@changingfaces.org.uk; website: www.changingfaces.org.uk)

Down's syndrome

Down's Syndrome Association, Langdon Down Centre, 2A Langdon Park, Teddington, Middlesex TW11 9PS (helpline: 0333 1212 300 [Mon–Fri, 10am–4pm]; email: info@downs-syndrome.org.uk; website: www.downs-syndrome.org.uk)

Drugs

ADFAM National, 27 Swinton Street, London WC1X 9NW (tel: 07442 137421 or 07552 986887; email: admin@adfam.org.uk; website: www.adfam.org.uk)

Cocaine Anonymous UK, PO Box 1337, Enfield EN1 9AS (helpline: 0800 612 0225 [10am–10pm daily]; email: helpline@cauk.org.uk; website: www.cocaineanonymous.org.uk)

Early Break, Annara House, 7–9 Bury Road, Radcliffe M26 2UG (tel: see website for local numbers; email:

info@earlybreak.co.uk or use the online form; website: www.earlybreak.co.uk)

Families Anonymous, Doddington and Rollo Community Association, Charlotte Despard Avenue, Battersea, London SW11 5HD (tel: 020 7498 4680; helpline: 020 7498 4680; email: office@famanon.org.uk; website: www.famanon.org.uk)

FRANK (National Drugs Helpline), (24-hour helpline: 0300 123 6600; text: 82111; email: frank@talktofrank.com or use the online form; website: www.talktofrank.com). Contact can also be made via an online chat facility 2pm–6pm daily.

Narcotics Anonymous (NA), 202 City Road, London EC1V 2PH (helpline: 0300 999 1212 [10am–12am]; email: pi@ukna.org; website: www.ukna.org)

Turning Point, Standon House, 21 Mansell Street, London E1 8AA (tel: 020 7481 7600; email: info@turning-point.co.uk or use the online form; website: www.turning-point.co.uk)

Dyslexia

British Dyslexia Association, Unit 6A, Bracknell Beeches, Old Bracknell Lane, Bracknell RG12 7BW (tel: 0333 405 4555; helpline: 0333 405 4567 [Tues–Wed, 10am–3pm; Thurs, 1pm–3pm]; email: helpline@bdadyslexia.org or use the online form; website: www.bdadyslexia.org.uk)

Dyspraxia

Dyspraxia Foundation, 8 West Alley, Hitchin, Hertfordshire SG5 1EG (tel: 01462 455016; helpline: 01462 454986 [at the time of writing (December 2021) the helpline was temporarily closed]; email: info@dyspraxiafoundation.org.uk; website: www.dyspraxiafoundation.org.uk)

Dystonia

*Dystonia Society, Second Floor, 89 Albert Embankment, London SE1 7TP (tel: 020 7793 3651; email: info@dystonia.org.uk; website: www.dystonia.org.uk)

Eating disorders

Eating Disorders Association (Beat), Unit 1 Chalk Hill House, 19 Rosary Road, Norwich, Norfolk NR1 1SZ (tel: 0300 123 335; helpline [Mon–Fri, 9am–12am; Sat–Sun, 4pm–12am]: 0808 801 0677 [England], 0808 801 0432 [Scotland], 0808 801 0433 [Wales], 0808 801 0434 [Northern Ireland]; youth helpline: 0808 801 0711; email: help@ beateatingdisorders.org.uk or see the website for the relevant email address; website: www.beateatingdisorders.org.uk)

Eczema

National Eczema Society, 11 Murray Street, London NW1 9RE (tel: 020 7281 3553; helpline: 0800 448 0818 [Mon–Fri, 10am–4pm]; email: helpline@eczema.org; website: www.eczema.org)

Endometriosis

Endometriosis UK, 10–18 Union Street, London SE1 1SZ (tel: 020 7222 2781; helpline: 0808 808 2227; email: admin@endometriosis-uk.org or use the online form; website: www.endometriosis-uk.org)

Epilepsy

Epilepsy Action, New Anstey House, Gate Way Drive, Yeadon, Leeds LS19 7XY (tel: 0113 210 8800; helpline: 0808 800 5050 [Mon–Tues, 8.30am–7pm; Wed–Fri, 8.30am–4.30pm; Sat, 10am–4pm]; email: epilepsy@epilepsy.org.uk or helpline@epilepsy.org.uk; website: www.epilepsy.org.uk)

Epilepsy Society, Chesham Lane, Chalfont St Peter, Buckinghamshire SL9 0RJ (tel: 01494 601300; helpline: 01494 601400 [Mon–Tues, 9am–4pm; Wed, 9am–7:30pm]; email: enquiries@epilepsysociety.org.uk or helpline@epilepsysociety.org.uk; website: www.epilepsysociety.org.uk)

Growth conditions

Child Growth Foundation (helpline: 020 8995 0257 [Mon–Fri, 9:30am–4pm]; email: info@ childgrowthfoundation.org or use the online form; website: www.childgrowthfoundation.org)

Restricted Growth Association (RGA), PO Box 88, Presteigne LD1 9BL (helpline: 0300 111 1970; email: office@restrictedgrowth.co.uk [general] or medical@restrictedgrowth.co.uk [for

medical advice]; website: www.rgauk.org)

Haemophilia

*The Haemophilia Society, 52B Borough High Street, London SE1 1L (tel: 020 7939 0780; email: info@ haemophilia.org.uk; website: www.haemophilia.org.uk)

Heart attacks/heart disease

British Heart Foundation, Compton House, 2300 The Crescent, Birmingham Business Park, Birmingham B37 7YE (tel: 0300 330 3322 [Mon–Fri, 9am–5pm]; textphone: 1800 1030 0330 3322; helpline: 0300 330 3311 [Mon–Fri, 9am–5pm]; email: heretohelp@bhf.org.uk or use the online form; website: www.bhf.org.uk). An online chat feature is also available on the website.

Heartline Families, 14 Nobles Close, Coates, Whittlesey, Peterborough PE7 2BT (email: intouch@heartline.org.uk; website: www.heartline.org.uk)

Hemiplegia

HemiChat, 17 Lower School Drive, Ruabon, Wrexham, North Wales LL14 7RP (tel: 0844 802 3203; email: info@hemichat.org or use the online form; website: www.hemichat.org)

Hodgkin's disease

Lymphoma Action, 3 Cromwell Court, New Street, Aylesbury HP20 2PB (tel: 01296 619400; helpline: 0808 808 5555 (option 1)[Mon–Fri, 10am–3pm]; email: enquiries@lymphoma-action.org.uk or information@lymphoma-action.org.uk; website: www.lymphoma-action.org.uk). A live chat feature is also available on the website.

Huntington's disease

*Huntington's Disease Association, Suite 24, Liverpool Science Park IC1, 131 Mount Pleasant Liverpool L3 5TF (tel: 0151 331 5444; email: info@hda.org.uk; website: www.hda.org.uk)

Hyperactivity and ADHD

ADHD Foundation, 3rd Floor, 54 St James Street, Liverpool L1 0AB (tel: 0151 541 9020; email: info@

adhdfoundation.org.uk; website: www.adhdfoundation.org.uk)

The Hyperactive Children's Support Group, 71 Whyke Lane, Chichester, West Sussex PO19 7PD (tel: 01243 539966 [Mon–Fri, 2.30pm–4.30pm]; email: hacsg@hacsg.org.uk; website: www.hacsg.org.uk)

Incontinence

Incontinence UK (email: use the online form; website: www.incontinence.co.uk)

Association for Continence Advice (ACA), Fitwise Management Ltd, Blackburn House, Redhouse Road, Seafield, Bathgate, West Lothian EH47 7AQ (tel: 01506 811077; email: aca@fitwise.co.uk; website: www.aca.uk.com)

Industrial diseases

Mesothelioma UK, 235 Loughborough Road, Mountsorrel, Loughborough, Leicestershire LE12 7AS (tel: 0800 169 2409 [Mon–Fri, 8:30am–4:30pm]; email: support@mesothelioma.uk.com or use the online form; website: www.mesothelioma.uk.com)

Action on Asbestos (formerly Clydeside Action on Asbestos), 245 High Street, Glasgow G4 0QR (freephone: 0800 089 1717 [Mon–Fri, 9am–5pm]; email: admin@ clydesideaction.co.uk; website: www.clydesideactiononasbestos.org.uk)

Infertility

Fertility Network UK, Forum at Greenwich, Trafalgar Road, Greenwich SE10 9EQ (tel: 01424 732361 [info line] or 0121 323 5025 [support line]; email info@fertilitynetworkuk.org or support@fertilitynetworkuk.org; website: www.fertilitynetworkuk.org)

Irritable bowel syndrome

The IBS Network, Unit 1.16 SOAR Works, 14 Knutton Road, Sheffield S5 9NU (tel: 0114 272 3253 [Mon–Fri, 9am–4:30pm]; email: info@theibsnetwork.org; website: www.theibsnetwork.org)

Kidney disease

*Kidney Care UK, 3 The Windmills, St Mary's Close, Turk Street, Alton GU34 1EF (tel: 01420 541424

[Mon–Fri, 9am–5pm]; email: info@kidneycareuk.org; website: www.kidneycareuk.org)

National Kidney Federation, The Point, Coach Road, Shireoaks, Worksop, Nottinghamshire S81 8BW (tel: 01909 544999; helpline: 0800 169 0936; email: use the online form; website: www.kidney.org.uk)

Learning disabilities

Mencap, Mencap National Centre, 123 Golden Lane, London EC1Y 0RT (tel: 020 7454 0454; helpline: 0808 808 1111 [Mon–Fri, 9am–3pm]; email: help@mencap.org.uk; website: www.mencap.org.uk)

Limb conditions

*Blesma, 115 New London Road, Chelmsford CM2 0QT (tel: 020 8590 1124 [Mon–Fri, 9am–5pm]; email: info@blesma.org; website: www.blesma.org)

Limbless Association, Unit 10, 2 Cromar Way, Chelmsford CM1 2QE (helpdesk: 0800 644 0185 [Mon–Fri, 9am–5pm; email: use the online form; website: www.limbless-association.org)

Reach, Pearl Assurance House, Brook Street, Tavistock, Devon PL19 0BN (helpline: 0845 130 6225 or 020 3478 0100; email: reach@reach.org.uk or use the online form; website: www.reach.org.uk)

STEPS (a charity for people affected by childhood lower limb conditions), The White House, Wilderspool Business Park, Greenall's Avenue, Warrington WA4 6HL (helpline: 01925 750271; email: info@steps-charity.org.uk; website: www.steps-charity.org.uk)

Literacy/learning difficulties

Learning and Work Institute, 4th Floor, Arnhem House, 31 Waterloo Way, Leicester LE1 6LP (tel: 0116 204 4200; email: enquiries@learningandwork.org.uk; website: www.learningandwork.org.uk)

Liver disease

British Liver Trust, 1st Floor Offices, Venta Court, 20 Jewry Street, Winchester SO23 8FE (tel: 01425 481320 [Mon–Fri, 9am–5pm]; helpline: 0800 652 7330 [Mon–Fri, 10am–3pm]; email: info@britishlivertrust.org.uk or use the online form; website: www.britishlivertrust.org.uk)

Liver4Life, Holme Cottage, Croft Road, Neacroft, Christchurch BH23 8JS (helpline: 0800 074 3494; email: info@liver4life.org.uk; website: www.liver4life.org.uk)

Lupus

Lupus UK, St James House, Eastern Road, Romford RM1 3NH (tel: 01708 731251; email: headoffice@lupusuk.org.uk; website: www.lupusuk.org.uk)

Scleroderma & Raynaud's UK, 18–20 Bride Lane, London EC4Y 8EE (tel: 020 3893 5998; email: info@sruk.co.uk; website: www.sruk.co.uk)

Mastectomy

Breast Cancer Now, Fifth Floor, Ibex House, 42–47 Minories, London EC3N 1DY (tel: 0333 20 70 300; helpline: 0808 800 6000 [Mon–Fri, 9am–4pm; Sat, 9am–1pm]; email: hello@breastcancernow.org; website: www.breastcancernow.org.uk)

Meningitis

*Meningitis Now, Fern House, Bath Road, Stroud, Gloucestershire GL5 3TJ (tel: 01453 768000; nurse-led helpline: 0808 801 0388 [Mon–Thurs, 9am–4pm; Fri, 9am–1pm]; email: info@meningitisnow.org or helpline@meningitisnow.org; website: www.meningitisnow.org)

Menopause

The Daisy Network Premature Menopause Support Group, PO Box 71432, London SW6 9HJ (tel: 07870 904457; email: info@daisynetwork.org; website: www.daisynetwork.org)

Mental health

Anxiety UK, Nunes House, 447 Chester Road, Manchester M16 9HA (helpline: 03444 775 774 [Mon–Fri, 9:30am–5:30pm]; text service: 07537 416905; email: support@anxietyuk.org.uk; website: www.anxietyuk.org.uk)

Bipolar UK, 32 Cubitt Street, London WC1X 0LR (tel: use the online chat feature to arrange a call; email: info@bipolaruk.org.uk; website: www.bipolaruk.org.uk)

Mental Health Foundation, Studio 2, 197 Long Lane, London SE1 4PD (tel: 020 7803 1100; website: www.mentalhealth.org.uk). Note: the foundation does not offer a help or advice line and should not be contacted unless specific information on its work is required or you wish to collaborate with the foundation in a professional capacity. Its website advises that other organisations, such as Samaritans, can offer emotional support. Samaritans can be contacted by calling 116 123 or by emailing jo@samaritans.org.

Mind, 2 Redman Place, London E20 1JQ; infoline address: Mind Infoline, PO Box 75225, London E15 9FS (tel: 020 8519 2122; infoline: 0300 123 3393 [Mon–Fri, 9am–6pm, except for bank holidays]; email: info@mind.org.uk or supporterrelations@mind.org.uk; website: www.mind.org.uk)

SANE (The Mental Health Charity), St Mark's Studios, 14 Chillingworth Road, Islington, London N7 8QJ (tel: 020 3805 1790; helpline: 0300 304 7000 [this number was temporarily unavailable at the time of writing (January 2021), please check the website for updates]; email: support@sane.org.uk; website: www.sane.org.uk). A Textcare service is also available to access via the website.

Metabolic disorders

Metabolic Support, Unit 11–12 Gwenfro, Technology Park, Croesnewydd Road, Wrexham, Wales LL13 7YP (tel: 0845 241 2173; helpline: 0800 652 3181 [Mon–Fri, 10am–4pm]; email: contact@metabolicsupportuk.org or use the online form; website: www.metabolicsupportuk.org)

Migraine

Migraine Trust, 4th Floor, Mitre House, 44–46 Fleet Street, London EC4Y 1BN (tel: 020 3951 0150; helpline: 0808 802 0066 [Mon–Fri, 10am–2pm]; email: info@migrainetrust.org or use the online form; website: www.migrainetrust.org)

Miscarriage

The Miscarriage Association, 17 Wentworth Terrace, Wakefield, West Yorkshire WF1 3QW (tel: 01924 200795; helpline: 01924 200799 [Mon–Fri, 9am–4pm]; email: info@

miscarriageassociation.org.uk; website: www.miscarriageassociation. org.uk)

Tommy's, Nicholas House, 3 Laurence Pountney Hill, London EC4R 0BB (tel: 020 7398 3400; PregnancyLine: 0800 014 7800 [Mon–Fri, 9am–5pm]; email: midwife@tommys.org or mailbox@tommys.org; website: www. tommys.org)

Motor neurone disease

*Motor Neurone Disease Association (MND), Francis Crick House, 6 Summerhouse Road, Moulton Park, Northampton NN3 6BJ (tel: 01604 250505; helpline: 0808 802 6262 [Mon–Fri, 9am–5pm and 7pm–10:30pm]; email:mndconnect@mndassociation.-org; website: www.mndassociation. org)

Multiple sclerosis

*Multiple Sclerosis Society, 10 Queen Street Place, London EC4R 1AG (helpline: 0808 800 8000 [Mon–Fri, 9am–7pm]; email: helpline@ mssociety.org.uk or use the online form; website: www.mssociety.org.uk)

Muscular dystrophy

Muscular Dystrophy UK, 61A Great Suffolk Street, London SE1 0BU (tel: 020 7803 4800; helpline: 0800 652 6352 [Mon–Thurs, 10am–2pm]; email: info@musculardystrophyuk. org; website: www. musculardystrophyuk.org)

Myalgic Encephalopathy/ Chronic Fatigue Syndrome(ME/CFS)

Action for ME, 42 Temple Street, Keynsham BS31 1EH (tel: 0117 927 9551; email: questions@actionforme. org.uk; website: www.actionforme. org.uk)

ME Association, 7 Apollo Office Court, Radclive Road, Gawcott, Buckinghamshire MK18 4DF (tel: 01280 81896; helpline: 0344 576 5326 [10am–12pm, 2pm–4pm and 7pm–9pm daily]; email: meconnect@ meassociation.org.uk; website: www. meassociation.org.uk)

Myotonic dystrophy

Myotonic Dystrophy Support Group, 19–21 Main Road, Gedling, Nottingham NG4 3HQ (tel: 0115 987 5869; helpline: 0808 169 1960 [Tues–Thurs, 9am–1pm]; email: contact@mdsguk.org; website: www. myotonicdystrophysupportgroup.org)

Narcolepsy

Narcolepsy UK, PO Box 701, Huntingdon PE29 9LR (helpline: 0345 450 0394; email: info@ narcolepsy.org.uk; website: www. narcolepsy.org.uk)

Neurofibromatosis

Nerve Tumours UK, 1st Floor, 44 Combe Lane, London SW20 0LA (tel: 020 8439 1234; helpline: 07939 046030 [Mon and Wed, 9am–5pm]; email: info@nervetumours.org.uk; website: www.nervetumours.org.uk)

Osteoporosis

Royal Osteoporosis Society, Manor Farm, Skinners Hill, Camerton, Bath BA2 0PJ (tel: 01761 471771; helpline: 0808 800 0035 [Mon–Fri, 9am–1pm and 2pm–5pm]; email: nurses@ theros.org.uk; website: www.theros. org.uk)

Paget's disease

The Paget's Association, Suite 5, Moorfield Road, Swinton, Manchester M27 0EW (helpline: 0161 799 4646; email: helpline@paget.org.uk or the use the online form; website: www. paget.org.uk)

Parkinson's disease

*Parkinson's UK, 215 Vauxhall Bridge Road, London SW1V 1EJ (tel: 020 7931 8080; helpline: 0808 800 0303 [Mon–Fri, 9am–6pm; Sat, 10am–2pm]; text relay: 18001 0808 800 0303; email: hello@parkinsons. org.uk; website: www.parkinsons.org. uk)

Pituitary disorders

Pituitary Foundation, 86 Colston Street, Bristol BS1 5BB (helpline: 0117 370 1320 [Mon–Fri, 10am–4pm]; endocrine nurse helpline: 0117 370 1317 [Mon, 10am–2pm; Tues, 8.30am–3pm; Weds, 10am–2pm; Thurs, 10am–2pm]; website: www.pituitary. org.uk)

Poliomyelitis

*British Polio Fellowship, CP House, Otterspool Way, Watford WD25 8HR (tel: 0800 043 1935; email: info@ britishpolio.org.uk; website: www. britishpolio.org.uk)

Postnatal depression

Association for Post-Natal Illness, 145 Dawes Road, Fulham, London SW6 7EB (tel: 020 7386 0868 [Mon–Fri, 10am–2pm]; email: info@ apni.org; website: www.apni.org)

Prader-Willi syndrome

Prader-Willi Syndrome Association, PWSA UK, PO Box 8478, Derby DE1 9HT (tel: 01332 365676 [Mon–Thurs, 9am–5pm; Fri, 9am–1pm]; email: admin@pwsa.co. uk; website: www.pwsa.co.uk)

Pre-eclampsia

Action on Pre-Eclampsia, The Stables, 80B High Street, Evesham, Worcestershire WR11 4EU (tel: 01386 761848; email: info@apec.org.uk; website: www.action-on-pre-eclampsia.org.uk)

Psoriasis

Psoriasis Association, Dick Coles House, 2 Queensbridge, Northampton NN4 7BF (tel: 01604 251620; WhatsApp: 07387716439; email: mail@psoriasis-association.org. uk; website: www.psoriasis-association.org.uk)

Scleroderma & Raynaud's UK, 18–20 Bride Lane, London EC4Y 8EE (tel: 020 3893 5998; email: info@sruk. co.uk; website: www.sruk.co.uk)

Rett syndrome

Rett Syndrome Association UK, Victory House, Chobham Street, Luton LU1 3BS (helpline: 01582 798911; email: info@rettuk.org or support@rettuk.org; website: www. rettuk.org)

Reye's syndrome

National Reye's Syndrome Foundation of the UK (NRSF), 5–11 Theobald's Road, London WC1X 8SH (email: use the online form; website: www.reyessyndrome. co.uk)

Sarcoidosis

SarcoidosisUK, 214 China Works, 100 Black Prince Road, London SE1 7SJ (tel: 020 3389 7221 or 0800 014 8821 [Mon–Fri, 10am–6pm]; email: info@sarcoidosisuk.org; website: www.sarcoidosisuk.org)

Schizophrenia

Hearing Voices Network, 86–90 Paul Street, London EC2A 4NE (email: info@hearing-voices.org; website: www.hearing-voices.org)

Scoliosis

Scoliosis Association (UK) (SAUK), 4 Ivebury Court, 325 Latimer Road, London W10 6RA (tel: 020 8964 5343; helpline: 020 8964 1166; email: info@sauk.org.uk; website: www.sauk.org.uk)

Sexually transmitted infections

BASHH (British Association for Sexual Health and HIV), c/o Executive Business Support Ltd, Unit E1, Davidson Road, Lichfield, Staffordshire WS14 9DZ (tel: 01543 442190; email: admin@bashh.org; website: www.bashh.org)

Brook, Penhaligon House, Green Street, Truro TR1 2LH (tel: 020 3949 6720; email: admin@brook.org.uk; website: www.brook.org.uk)

Sickle cell disease

Sickle Cell Society (SCS), 54 Station Road, London NW10 4UA (tel: 020 8961 7795; email: info@sicklecellsociety.org or use the online form; website: www.sicklecellsociety.org)

Smoking

Action on Smoking and Health (ASH), Unit 2.9, The Foundry, 17 Oval Way, London SE11 5RR (email: enquiries@ash.org.uk or use the online form; website: www.ash.org.uk)

Solvent abuse

Re-Solv, 30A High Street, Stone, Staffordshire ST15 8AW (tel: 01785 817885; helpline: 01785 810762; text: 07496 959930; email: info@re-solv.org or use the online form; website: www.re-solv.org). An online chat feature is available on the website.

Speech and language difficulties

Association for All Speech-Impaired Children (AFASIC), 15 Old Ford Road, London E2 9PJ (tel: 020 7490 9410; helpline: 0300 666 9410; email: use the online form; website: www.afasic.org.uk)

Stamma, 15 Old Ford Road, London E2 9PJ (tel: 020 8983 1003; helpline: 0808 802 0002 [Mon–Fri, 10am–12pm and 6pm–8pm]; email: mail@stamma.org or help@stamma.org [helpline]; website: www.stamma.org). An online chat feature is also available on the website.

Royal Association for Deaf People (RAD), Block F, Parkside Office Village, Knowledge Gateway, Nesfield Road, Colchester CO4 3ZL (tel: 0300 688 2525; textphone: 0300 688 2527; text: 07467 914175; email: info@royaldeaf.org.uk; website: www.royaldeaf.org.uk). A live chat feature is also available on the website.

Spina bifida

SHINE, 42 Park Road, Peterborough PE1 2UQ (tel: 01733 555988; email: info@shinecharity.org.uk or firstcontact@shinecharity.org.uk; website: www.shinecharity.org.uk)

Spinal injuries

Spinal Injuries Association, SIA House, 2 Trueman Place, Oldbrook, Milton Keynes MK6 2HH (tel: 01908 604191; advice line: 0800 980 0501 [Mon–Fri, 10am–4:30pm]; email: sia@spinal.co.uk or support@spinal.co.uk; website: www.spinal.co.uk)

Stroke

Stroke Association, 240 City Road, London EC1V 2PR (helpline: 0303 303 3100 [Mon, Thurs and Fri, 9am–5pm; Tues and Wed, 8am–6pm; Sat, 10am–1pm]; email: info@stroke.org.uk or helpline@stroke.org.uk; website: www.stroke.org.uk)

Sudden infant death syndrome (SIDS)

Compassionate Friends, Kilburn Grange, Priory Park Road, London NW6 7UJ (helpline: 0345 123 2304 [10am–4pm and 7pm–10pm daily]; email: info@tcf.org.uk or helpline@tcf.org.uk; website: www.tcf.org.uk)

The Lullaby Trust (formerly Foundation for the Study of Infant Deaths), CAN Mezzanine, 7–14 Great Dover Street, London SE1 4YR (tel: 020 7802 3200; bereavement support: 0808 802 6868; information and advice: 0808 802 6869 [Mon–Fri, 10am–5pm; Sat–Sun, 6pm–10pm]; email:office@lullabytrust.org.uk, support@lullabytrust.org.uk or info@lullabytrust.org.uk; website: www.lullabytrust.org.uk)

Suicide

Maytree, 72 Moray Road, Finsbury Park, London N4 3LG (helpline: 020 7263 7070; email: maytree@maytree.org.uk or use the online form; website: www.maytree.org.uk)

Papyrus, Bankside 2, Crosfield Street, Warrington, Cheshire WA1 1UP (tel: 01925 572444; helpline: 0800 068 4141 [9am–12am daily]; text: 07860 039967; email: admin@papyrus-uk.org or pat@papyrus-uk.org [helpline]; website: www.papyrus-uk.org)

Tinnitus

British Tinnitus Association (BTA), Unit 5, Acorn Business Park, Woodseats Close, Sheffield S8 0TB (tel: 0114 250 9933; helpline: 0800 018 0527 [Mon–Fri, 9am–5pm]; text: 07537 416841; email: info@tinnitus.org.uk or helpline@tinnitus.org.uk; website: www.tinnitus.org.uk). A webchat feature is also available on the website.

Tourette's syndrome

*Tourettes Action, Kings Court, The Meads Business Centre, 19 Kingsmead, Farnborough, Hampshire GU14 7SR (tel: email help@tourettes-action.org.uk to request a call back; email: use the online form; website: www.tourettes-action.org.uk). A live chat feature is available on the website (Mon–Fri, 10am–3pm).

Tracheo-oesophageal fistula

Tracheo-Oesophageal Fistula Support Group (TOFS), St George's Centre, 91 Victoria Road, Netherfield, Nottingham NG4 2NN (tel: 0115 961 3092; email: info@tofs.org.uk; website: www.tofs.org.uk)

Tuberous sclerosis

The Tuberous Sclerosis Association, c/o Nightingale House, 46–48 East Street, Epsom, Surrey KT17 1HQ (tel: 0300 222 5737; helpline: 0808 801 0700; email: admin@tuberous-sclerosis.org or support@tuberous-sclerosis.org; website: www.tuberous-sclerosis.org). A webchat feature is also available on the website.

Urostomy

Urostomy Association, 2 Tyne Place, Mickleton, Chipping Campden GL55 6UG (tel: 01386 430140; email: info@urostomyassociation.org.uk; website: www.urostomyassociation.org.uk)

Williams syndrome

Williams Syndrome Foundation, Box 103, Charter House, Lord Montgomery Way, Portsmouth PO1 2SN (tel: 020 8567 1374; email: enquiries@williams-syndrome.org.uk; website: www.williams-syndrome.org.uk)

Index

1930: The 1930 Fund for District Nurses (No. 1) 136

3H: The 3H Fund 58

Aberdeen: Aberdeen Cheyne and Donald Trust Fund 194
Aberdeen Endowments Trust 192
Aberdeen Female Society 192
Aberdeen Indigent Mental Patients Fund 192

Aberdeenshire: Aberdeenshire Educational Trust 194

Aberlour: Aberlour Child Care Trust 22

ABF: ABF The Soldiers' Charity 85

Abinger: The Abinger Consolidated Charities 403

Able: Able Kidz 59

Abortion: Abortion Support Network 31

ABTA: ABTA LifeLine (The ABTA Benevolent Trust) 177

Accrington: The Accrington and District Helping Hands Fund 358

Acheinu: Acheinu Cancer Support 56

Acton: Acton (Middlesex) Charities – Relief in Need Fund 317

Actors': The Actors' Benevolent Fund 99
The Actors' Children's Trust (ACT) 99

Adamson: The Adamson Trust 59

Addington: Addington Fund 114

Adventure: Adventure Trust for Girls 421

Age: Age Sentinel Trust 36

Aged: The Aged Christian Friend Society of Scotland 36

AIA: The AIA Educational and Benevolent Trust 117

Air: The Air Pilots Benevolent Fund 178

Aitchison: The Christina Aitchison Trust 333

Aitken: The John Maurice Aitken Trust 22

AJEX: AJEX Charitable Foundation 86

Albrighton: Albrighton Relief-in-Need Charity 267

Aldbourne: Aldbourne Poors' Gorse 442

Aldbrough: Aldbrough Poor Fields 448

Aldeburgh: Aldeburgh United Charities 299

Aldworth's: Aldworth's Educational Trust (Aldworth Trust Foundation) 379

Alexis: The Alexis Trust 39

All: All Saints Relief-in-Need Charity 243

Allan: James Allan of Midbeltie's Fund for Widows 193

Allen: Mary Ellen Allen 215

Al-Mizan: Al-Mizan Charitable Trust 1

Almondsbury: Almondsbury Charity 435

Almshouses: Westminster Almshouses Foundation 315

Alsager: Alsager Educational Foundation 345

Alveley: Alveley Charity 245

Alverstoke: The Alverstoke Trust 383

Always: Always Look on the Bright Side of Life Charitable Trust 22

Amber: The Amber Trust 60

Ambleside: Ambleside Welfare Charity 349

Ambulance: The Ambulance Staff Charity 136

Amos: Tom Amos Charity 279

Ancell: The Ancell Trust 373

Anchor: The Anchor Society 414

Anderson: The Anderson Bequest 187
The Andrew Anderson Trust 2

Andrew: Frederick Andrew Trust 32

Anglian: Anglian Water Assistance Fund 16

Anguish's: Anguish's Educational Foundation 298

Angus: Angus Council Charitable Trust 200

Appleton: The Appleton Trust (Abingdon) 393

The Appleton Trust (Canterbury) 388

Arch: Arch Support 136

Architects': Architects' Benevolent Society 98

Armchair: The Armchair Trust CIO 269

Armenian: The Armenian Relief Society of Great Britain Trust 30

Armstrong: The Nihal Armstrong Trust 73

Armthorpe: Armthorpe Poors Estate Charity 455

Arnold's: Edmund Arnold's Charity (Poors Branch) 228

Arnold's: Arnold's Educational Foundation 229

Artistic: The Artistic Endeavours Trust 99

Artists': Artists' General Benevolent Institution 99

Ashby-de-la-Zouch: Ashby-de-la-Zouch Relief in Sickness Fund 222

Ashford: Ashford Hill Educational Trust 381

Ashington: The Ashington, Wiston, Warminghurst Sick Poor Fund 410

Ashton: John Ashton (including the Gift of Hannah Shaw) 460
The Ashton Keynes Charity 442

Ashton's: Frances Ashton's Charity 154

Associated: Associated Society of Locomotive Engineers and Firemen (ASLEF) Hardship Fund 178

Association: The Association for the Relief of Infirmity in the West of Scotland 73

Aston: Aston Charities 456
Aston Welfare Trust 213

Aston-with-Aughton: Aston-with-Aughton Educational Foundation 456

Atherton: The Atherton Trust 245

Athletics: Athletics for the Young 172

Atmere: Edmund Atmere (Feltwell) Charity 292

Edmund Atmere (Northwold) Charity 294

ATS: ATS and WRAC Association Benevolent Fund 86

Authors': The Authors' Contingency Fund 100

Auto: Auto Cycle Union Benevolent Fund 9

Avon: Avon and Somerset Constabulary Benevolent Fund 148

Awards: Awards for Young Musicians 11

Babington's: Babington's Charity 219

Backhouse: Agnes Backhouse Annuity Fund 347

Backwell: The Backwell Foundation 440

Bader: The Douglas Bader Foundation 51

Badley: The Badley Memorial Trust 264

Bailey: The Ernest Bailey Charity 214

Baines's: Baines's Charity 357

Baker: Ethel Baker Bequest 326

The Isabel Baker Foundation 60

Balderton: The Balderton Parochial Charity 238

Balshaw's: Balshaw's Educational Foundation 359

Bampton: The Bampton Welfare Trust 397

Banbury: Banbury Charities 395

Banham: The Banham Parochial Charities 292

Bankers: The Bankers Benevolent Fund (The Bank Workers Charity) 117

Banner: Richard and Samuel Banner Trust 259

Banstead: Banstead United Charities 398

Barbers': The Barbers' Amalgamated Charity 167

Barchester: Barchester Health Care Foundation 52

Barford: Barford Relief-in-Need Charity 256

Barham: Barham Benevolent Foundation 115

Barnard: The Michael Barnard Charitable Trust 2

Barnes: The Norman Barnes Fund 352

The Barnes Workhouse Fund 326

Barnet's: The Mayor of Barnet's Benevolent Fund 310

Barnstaple: Barnstaple Almshouses 424

The Barnstaple and North Devon Dispensary Fund 424

Barnwood: Barnwood Trust 431

Barrett: Charity of Thomas Barrett 292

Barristers: Barristers Clerks Benevolent Fund 123

Barristers': The Barristers' Benevolent Association 123

Barrow: Barrow Thornborrow Charity 347

Bartlett: The Bartlett Taylor Charitable Trust 393

Bates: The Philip Bates Trust 11

Bath: Archdeaconry of Bath Clerical Families Fund 437

Bath Disability Trust 438

Bath's: Mayor of Bath's Relief Fund 439

Battersea: Battersea United Charities 331

Battle: The Battle Charities 378

Bauer: Bauer Radio's Cash for Kids Charities 22

Be: Be More Bailey Charitable Foundation 60

Beaminster: Beaminster Relief in Need Charity 428

Beane's: John Beane's Charity CIO 398

Bearder: Bearder Charity 461

Beardsley's: Beardsley's Relief in Need Charity 251

Beasley: The Gertrude Beasley Charitable Trust 452

Beattie: The Jack and Ada Beattie Foundation 47

Beaumont: The Beaumont and Jessop Relief-in-Need Charity 463

Beckly: The Beckly Trust 417

Bedale: Bedale Welfare Charity (The Rector and Four and Twenty of Bedale) 451

Bedford: Bedford and District Cerebral Palsy Society 272

Bedford's: John Bedford's Charity 372

Beeston: Beeston Consolidated Charity 237

Beeton: Beeton, Barrick and Beck Relief-in-Need Charity 451

Beighton: Beighton Relief-in-Need Charity 457

Believe: The Believe and Achieve Trust 349

BEN: BEN – Motor and Allied Trades Benevolent Fund 125

Benenden: The Benenden Charitable Trust 9

Benevolent: The Craft Bakers Benevolent and Education Fund 167

Benevolent Association for the Relief of Decayed Tradesmen, their Widows and Orphans 290

The Benevolent Society 167

Berkshire: Berkshire Nurses and Relief-in-Sickness Trust 365

Bespoke: The Bespoke Tailors' Benevolent Association 168

Betchworth: Betchworth United Charities 403

BHS: BHS Trust Fund 160

Bible: The Bible Preaching Trust 154

Biggart: Biggart Trust 2

Billincoat: Billincoat Charities 348

Billingborough: Billingborough United Charities 227

Bilton: The Percy Bilton Charity 52

The Bilton Poor's Land and Other Charities 254

Bingham: The Bingham Trust 215

The Bingham Trust Scheme 239

Bingham United Charities 2006 240

Bird: The Dickie Bird Foundation 23

Birkdale: Birkdale Trust for Hearing Impaired Ltd 73

Birmingham: The Birmingham and Three Counties Trust for Nurses 258

Birmingham Bodenham Trust 259

Bisley: The Charity of the Ancient Parish of Bisley 436

Black: The Black Watch Association 86

Blackman: The Isabel Blackman Foundation 378

Blackpool: The Blackpool Ladies' Sick Poor Association 357

Black's: Sir Alec Black's Charity 450

Blackstock: Blackstock Trust 200

Blagdon: Charity of Edward Blagdon 423

Blair: C. N. W. Blair Charity 443

Blair's: J. T. Blair's Charity 349

Blakeley-Marillier: Mrs E. L. Blakeley-Marillier Charitable Fund 32

Blakeney: The Blakeney Twelve 297

Blakesley: Blakesley Parochial Charities 233

Blanchard's: Elizabeth Blanchard's Charity 414

Blandford: Blandford Forum Charities 428

Bletchingley: Bletchingley United Charities 399

Blind: Blind Veterans UK 86

BlindAid: BlindAid 82

Blue: Blue Coat Charity 451

PC David Rathband's Blue Lamp Foundation 149

BMA: BMA Charities Trust Fund 137

Bold: Charity of William Bold 206

Bolles: Lady Bolles Foundation 465

Bolton: The Bolton Guild of Help Incorporated 351

Bond/Henry: James Bond/Henry Welch Trust 359
Book: The Book Trade Charity 133
Bookhams: The Bookhams, Fetcham and Effingham Nursing Association Trust 403
Booth: The Booth Charities 354
Boots: Boots Benevolent Fund 160
Boparan: The Boparan Charitable Trust 23
Boreman's: Sir William Boreman's Foundation 318
BOSS: BOSS Benevolent Fund 160
Boston: Boston and District Sick Poor Fund 225
Botley: Charity of William Botley 443
Boughey: Charity of Annabelle Lady Boughey 209
Boughton: Boughton Almsland Charities 392
The Sir Edward Boughton Long Lawford Charity 255
Boveridge: Boveridge Charity 428
Bowcocks: Bowcocks Trust Fund for Keighley 460
Bowley: The Bowley Charity 285
Boyack: The Boyack Fund 201
BP: BP Benevolent Fund 111
Brackley: Brackley United Feoffee Charity 233
Bradford: The Bradford and District Wool Association Benevolent Fund 460
Braintree: Braintree United Charities 282
Brampton: Brampton Bierlow Welfare Trust 456
Brancaster: The Brancaster Educational and Almshouse Charity 294
BRDC: BRDC Motor Sport Charity 172
Brecknock: The Brecknock Welfare Trust 203
Brenley: The Brenley Trust 2
Brentnall: The Alan Brentnall Charitable Trust 3
Brideoake: Charity of Miss Ann Farrar Brideoake 154
Bridge: The Bridge Educational Trust (1996) 428
Bridge Trust 425
The Bridge Trust (Bideford Bridge Trust) 427
Bridgnorth: Bridgnorth Lions Club Trust Fund 245
The Bridgnorth Parish Charity 245
Bridlington: The Bridlington Charities (Henry Cowton) 448
Brighton: The Brighton Fund 377
Bristol: The Bristol Benevolent Institution 415

Bristol Charities 415
The Bristol Corn Trade Guild 115
Bristol's: The Lord Mayor of Bristol's Children Appeal 415
British: British Airline Pilots Association Benevolent Fund (BALPA) 178
British Airways Welfare and Benevolent Fund 178
The British Antique Dealers' Association Ltd Benevolent Fund 100
British Association of Former United Nations Civil Servants Benevolent Fund 149
British Boxing Board of Control Charitable Trust 172
British Council Benevolent Fund 149
British Dental Association (BDA) Benevolent Fund 137
The Association of British Dispensing Opticians (ABDO) Benevolent Fund 138
The British Fire Services Association Members Welfare Fund 149
British Gas Energy Trust 17
The British Guild of Tourist Guides Benevolent Fund 179
The British Institute of Non-Destructive Testing Benevolent Fund 112
British Limbless Ex-Service Men's Association (BLESMA) 87
British Motor Cycle Racing Club Benevolent Fund 9
The British Polio Fellowship 74
Brittle: The Brittle Bone Society 74
Brixton: Brixton Feoffee Trust 419
Broadlands: Broadlands Home Trust 32
Brockbank's: Brockbank's Annuities Trust 359
Bromfield's: Bromfield's Educational Foundation 305
Bromley: Bromley Relief in Need Charity 312
Bromwich: Thomas Bromwich Trust 259
Brook: Brook Charitable Trust 458
Charles Brook Convalescent Fund 463
Brook's: Mrs Catherine Brook's Fund 194
Broomfield: Broomfield United Charities 280
Brotherton: The Brotherton Charity Trust 465
Broughty: Broughty Ferry Benevolent Trust 201
Brown: Brown Habgood Hall and Higden Charity 429

The William Brown Nimmo Charitable Trust 197
The Joanna Brown Trust 172
Brunts: Brunts Charity 237
BT: BT Benevolent Fund 122
BTMA: The BTMA Trust 125
Buchanan: The Buchanan Society 35
Buckingham: The Archdeaconry of Buckingham Clergy Charity 370
Buckingham Trust 3
Builders': Builders' Benevolent Institution 106
Building: Building and Civil Engineering Charitable Trust 106
Chartered Institute of Building Benevolent Fund 107
Bull: Bull Piece Charity 336
Bulmer: E. F. Bulmer Trust 244
Burford: The Burford Relief-in-Need Charity 397
Burns: The Campbell Burns Metabolic Trust 60
Burton: Burton on Trent Nursing Endowment Fund 249
Consolidated Charity of Burton upon Trent 249
Bury: Bury Relief in Sickness Fund 351
Bushbury: Bushbury (Ancient Parish) United Charities 267
Butchers': Butchers' and Drovers' Charitable Institution (BDCI) 161
Butler: The Butler Educational Foundation 283
Butterfield: The Butterfield Trust 460
Buttle: Buttle UK 23
Byfleet: The Byfleet United Charity 410
Calder: Dr John Calder Fund 193
CALICO: CALICO – Cancer and Leukaemia in Children Orientated 192
Calverton: Calverton Apprenticing Charity 373
Camberwell: Camberwell Consolidated Charities 329
Cambridge: Cambridge Community Nursing Trust 277
Cambridgeshire: Cambridgeshire Community Foundation 276
Cameron: The Cameron Fund 138
Campden: The Campden Charities 323
Cancer: Cancer Relief UK 56
Canewdon: The Canewdon Educational Foundation 284
Cannington: Cannington Combined Charity 437
Canterbury: The Canterbury United Municipal Charities 388

Canterbury's: The Lord Mayor of Canterbury's Christmas Gift Fund 389

Cantley: Cantley Poor's Land Trust 455

Capital: Capital Charitable Trust 196

Capstone: The Capstone Care Leavers' Trust 24

Card: Charity of John and Joseph Card (also known as Draycott Charity) 215

Cardiff: The Cardiff Blues Regional Benevolent Trust 208

Care: The Care Workers Charity 138

Carers: Carers Trust 59

Carlisle: Carlisle Sick Poor Fund 348

Carlton: Carlton Colville Fuel or Poor's Allotment 375

Carmichael's: Mrs Agnes W. Carmichael's Trust 201

Carr: Carr Trust 250

Catenian: Catenian Association Benevolent and Children's Fund 39

Catenian Association Bursary Fund Ltd 39

Catholic: Catholic Clothing Guild 39

Caudwell: Caudwell Children 61

Cavell: Cavell Nurses' Trust 138

Central: Central Exeter Relief-in-Need Charity 422

Ceramic: The Ceramic Industry Welfare Society 168

Cerebra: Cerebra for Brain Injured Children and Young People 61

Challenger: Challenger Children's Fund 74

Chalmers: George, James and Alexander Chalmers Bequests 193

Chance: The Chance Trust 264

Channel: Channel – Supporting Family Social Work in Liverpool 360

Chapel: Chapel Allerton and Potter Newton Relief-in-Need Charity 464

Chapman: J. W. Chapman Earlesmere Charitable Trust 456

Charlton: Charlton Kings Relief in Need Charity 434

Charmouth: Charmouth United Charities 429

Chartered: The Chartered Accountants' Benevolent Association 117

The Chartered Certified Accountants' Benevolent Fund 118

The Chartered Institute of Journalists Benevolent Fund/ Pensions Fund/Orphan Fund 133

The Chartered Institute of Management Accountants Benevolent Fund 118

Chartered Physiotherapists' Benevolent Fund 139

The Chartered Secretaries' Charitable Trust 98

The Company of Chartered Surveyors Charitable Trust Fund (1992) 107

Chatteris: Chatteris Feoffee Charity 277

Cheam: Cheam Consolidated Charities 330

Cheddington: Cheddington Town Lands Charity 372

Chemical: The Chemical Engineers Benevolent Fund 112

Chertsey: Chertsey Combined Charity 405

Chessington: Chessington Charities 323

Chester: Chester Parochial Charity 346

Chesterfield: Chesterfield General Charitable Fund 213

Chetwynd's: Chetwynd's Charity 248

Chew's: Chew's Foundation at Dunstable 272

Child: Child Funeral Charity 31

Childhood: Childhood Eye Cancer Trust 61

Children: Children of the Clergy Trust 24

Children Today Charitable Trust 62

Children's: Children's Leukaemia Society 207

Children's: Children's Hope Foundation 62

Chippenham: Chippenham Borough Lands Charity 443

Chipping: Chipping Sodbury Town Lands Charity 436

Chips: Chips Charity 62

Chizel: The Chizel Educational Trust 25

Chloe: Chloe and Liam Together Forever Trust 333

Chobham: Chobham Poor Allotment Charity 407

Choir: The Choir Schools' Association Bursary Trust Ltd 11

Chownes: The Chownes Foundation 375

Christ: Christ Church Exhibition Fund 415

Christadelphian: Christadelphian Benevolent Fund 40

Church: Church and Town Allotment Charities and Others 231

Church Burgesses Educational Foundation 457

The Church of England Pensions Board 155

Church of Ireland Orphans and Children Society for Counties Antrim and Down 185

Church Schoolmasters and Schoolmistresses' Benevolent Institution 108

Churchill: Churchill Lines Charitable Fund Ltd 87

Churt: The Churt Welfare Trust 408

Ciao: The Ciao Foundation CIO 3

CIBSE: CIBSE (Chartered Institution of Building Services Engineers) Benevolent Fund Trust 107

City: The City and Diocese of London Voluntary Schools Fund 305

Civil: The Charity for Civil Servants 150

Clapham: The Clapham Relief Fund 324

Clayworkers: Institute of Clayworkers Benevolent Fund 168

Clergy: The Clergy Rest Fund 155

Clergy Support Trust 155

Clevedon: Clevedon Convalescent Fund 52

CLIC: CLIC Sargent (Young Lives vs Cancer) 62

Cliffe: Cliffe and Cliffe Woods Community Trust 391

Clingan's: Clingan's Trust 431

Clophill: Clophill United Charities 274

Closehelm: Closehelm Ltd 44

Cloudesley: Cloudesley 322

Clubley: The Charity of Miss Eliza Clubley Middleton 449

Clwyd: County Council of Clwyd Welsh Church Fund 204

Coal: The Coal Industry Social Welfare Organisation 145

The Coal Trade Benevolent Association 111

Coastguard: The Coastguard Association Charity 127

Coats: The Coats Foundation Trust 125

Cockermouth: Cockermouth Relief-in-Need Charity 348

Coddington: Coddington United Charity 238

Colchester: Colchester Blind Society 283

Colchester Catalyst Charity 283

Colchester Children's Charity Appeal 62

Cole: Charities of Susanna Cole and Others 251

Coleman: The R. V. Coleman Trust 389

College: The Benevolent Fund of The College of Optometrists and The Association of Optometrists 139

Collier: The Collier Charitable Trust 155

Collings: John Collings Educational Trust 25

Collingwood: The Mike Collingwood Memorial Fund 390

Collins: The Ray Collins Charitable Trust 396

Collinson: Norman Collinson Charitable Trust 453

Colvile: The J. I. Colvile Charitable Trust 394

Colvill: The Colvill Charity 200

Combe: Combe Down Holiday Trust 439

Committee: Committee for Kesteven Children in Need 222

Common: The Common Lands of Rotherham Charity 456

Community: Community Action Isle of Wight 386

Community Foundation for Calderdale 461

Community Foundation for Leeds 458

The Community Foundation for Wiltshire and Swindon 443

Concert: The Concert Artistes Association Benevolent Fund 100

Congleton: The Congleton Town Trust 345

Conroy: The Conroy Trust 364

Conservative: Conservative and Unionist Agents' Benevolent Association 150

Conwy: Conwy Welsh Church Acts Fund 205

Cooper: Jemima Octavia Cooper for the Poor (Stoke D'Abernon Charities) 400

Coopers: Coopers Charity CIO 305

Corfe: Corfe Castle Charity 429

Corn: Corn Exchange Benevolent Society 125

Cornwall: Cornwall Community Foundation 417

The Cornwall Retired Clergy, Widows of the Clergy and their Dependants Fund 418

Corporation: The Corporation of Trinity House of Deptford Strond 128

Corton: Corton Poor's Land Trust 375

Cost: Cost of Cancer 57

Cottam: The Cottam Charities 356

Cotton: The Cotton Districts Convalescent Fund and the Barnes Samaritan Charity 216

The Cotton Industry War Memorial Trust 125

County: County Durham Community Foundation 336

Coventry: Coventry Children's Boot Fund 262

The Coventry Freemen's Charity 262

Cowbridge: Cowbridge with Llanblethian United Charities 210

Cowley: Charity of Thomas Cowley Exclusive of the Cowley Education 223

Cox: Charity of George Cox 440

Craft: Craft Pottery Charitable Trust 168

Craigcrook: Craigcrook Mortification 36

Cranbrook: Cranbrook Charity 426

Cranfield: The Cranfield Charitable Trust 280

Cranleigh: The Cranleigh and District Nursing Association 409

Craven: The Craven Trust 452

Crediton: Crediton United Charities 419

Cresswell: The Eliza Ann Cresswell Memorial 216

Crewe's: Lord Crewe's Charity 333

Cripplegate: Cripplegate Foundation 313

Crisis: Crisis UK 48

Croft: W. J. Croft for the Relief of the Poor (W. J. Croft Charity) 265

Crohn's: Crohn's and Colitis UK 75

Cross: The Arthur Cross Charity 315
The Cross Trust 40

Crosthwaite: The Lady Crosthwaite Bequest 339

CSIS: CSIS Charity Fund 150

Cumbria: Cumbria Community Foundation 347

Cureton: Harry Cureton Charitable Trust 271

Curtis': Mary Curtis' Maternity Charity 326

Cwmbran: The Cwmbran Trust 209

Cystic: The Cystic Fibrosis Holiday Fund 75

Cystic Fibrosis Trust 75

Dacorum: The Dacorum Community Trust 287

Dain: The Dain Fund 139

Dance: The International Dance Teachers' Association Ltd Benevolent Fund 173

Dancer: Henry Dancer Days 62

Dan's: Dan's Fund for Burns 76

Darling: Alexander Darling Silk Mercer's Fund 197

Datchet: Datchet United Charities 369

Davenport's: Baron Davenport's Charity 241

Daventry: The Daventry Consolidated Charity 231

Davey: Charity of John Davey 418

Davies: Mark Davies Injured Riders Fund 71

Deakin: The Deakin and Withers Fund 32

Deeping: Deeping St James United Charities 228

Dempster: Dempster Trust 409

Deptford: The Deptford Pension Society 325

Derby: The Derby City Charity 214

Derbyshire: Derbyshire Community Foundation 212

Desborough: The Desborough Town Welfare Committee 229

Devon: Devon Community Foundation 419

The Devon Educational Trust 419

Dewsbury: Dewsbury and District Sick Poor Fund 463

Dibden: Dibden Allotments Fund 383

Dickinson: Dickinson Massey Underwood Charity 234

Dickson: The Alec Dickson Trust 12

Diss: Diss Parochial Charity 299

District: Nelson District Nursing Association Fund 359

Dixon: The Charles Dixon Pension Fund 306

Dobson: The Dobson Trust 391

Dodbrooke: The Dodbrooke Parish Charity (Dodbrooke Feoffees) 426

Dolphin: Dolphin Society 416

Dorchester: Dorchester Relief in Need Charity 429

Dore: Charity of Edgar Ralph Dore 386

Dorkin's: John Dorkin's Charity 302

Dorset: Dorset Cancer Care Foundation 429

Downe's: Lady Downe's Charity 436

Downham: Downham Aid in Sickness Charity 294

Drexler: The George Drexler Foundation 161

Drinks: The Drinks Trust 161

Dronfield: Dronfield Relief in Need Charity 216

Drummond: Kate Drummond Trust 392

DTD: DTD Charity 211

Ducklington: Ducklington and Hardwick-with-Yelford Charity 398

Dudley: The Dudley Charity 264

Duffy: The Marie Duffy Foundation 12

Dugdale: The H. P. Dugdale Foundation 463
Dunn: The W. E. Dunn Trust 241
Dunnachie's: W. J. and Mrs C. G. Dunnachie's Charitable Trust 87
Dunstable: Dunstable Poor's Land Charity 274
E.ON: E.ON Energy Fund 17
Ealing: The Ealing Aid-in-Sickness Trust 317
Earle: Henry Smith and Michael Earle Charities 403
Earley: The Earley Charity 368
Earls: Earls Colne and Halstead Educational Charity 282
East: East Africa Women's League (United Kingdom) 35
East Dereham Relief-in-Need Charity 293
East Sussex Farmers' Benevolent Fund 365
East Tilbury Relief in Need Charity 284
Eaton: Eaton Fund for Artists, Nurses and Gentlewomen 33
ECAS: ECAS Ltd 196
Ecclesiastical: White Ecclesiastical Charity of George 282
Edinburgh: The Edinburgh and Lothian Trust Fund 196
The Edinburgh Fire Fund 197
Edinburgh Police Fund for Children 198
Edinburgh Royal Infirmary Samaritan Society 198
The Edinburgh Society for Relief of Indigent Old Men 198
Edmett: Edmett and Fisher Charity 391
Edmonds: Edmonds and Coles Scholarships (Edmonds and Coles Charity) 416
Anthony Edmonds Charity 416
Edmonton: Edmonton Aid-in-Sickness and Nursing Fund 318
Edridge: The Edridge Fund 151
Education: Education Support Partnership 108
Educational: Educational Institute of Scotland Benevolent Funds 109
Edwards: Dr Edwards and Bishop King's Fulham Charity 320
Austin Edwards Charity 256
William Edwards Educational Charity 252
Egham: The Egham United Charity 406
Electrical: The Electrical Industries Charity (also known as EEIBA) 169
Elifar: Elifar Foundation Ltd 53
Elizabeth: Fisher Charity Elizabeth 338

Elwes: The Monica Elwes Shipway Sporting Foundation 12
Eman: Charity of Elizabeth Eman 372
Emanuel: Emanuel Hospital 313
Engineering: The Institution of Engineering and Technology (IET) 113
The Institution of Engineering and Technology Benevolent Fund (IET Connect) 113
Engineers: The Worshipful Company of Engineers Charitable Trust Fund 113
England: England Golf Trust 12
Engler: The Engler Family Charitable Trust 44
English: The English National Opera Benevolent Fund 100
Environmental: Environmental Health Officers Welfare Fund 139
Epsom: Epsom Parochial Charities (Epsom Almshouse Charity) 401
Epworth: Epworth Charities 451
Equipment: Equipment for Independent Living 70
Equity: Equity Charitable Trust 101
Esdaile: Esdaile Trust Scheme 1968 40
Eshaki: Eshaki Foundation 25
Essex: Essex Community Foundation 280
Essex Police Force Benevolent Fund 280
Essex Police Support Staff Benevolent Fund 280
Evans: Freeman Evans St David's Day Ffestiniog Charity 206
Evelyn's: Sir John Evelyn's Charity 325
Evie's: Evie's Gift CIO 63
Ewell: Ewell Parochial Trusts 401
Ewelme: Ewelme Exhibition Endowment 365
Exeter: Exeter Dispensary Charity 422
Exeter Homes Trust 423
The Exeter Nursing Association Trust 423
The Exeter Relief-in-Need Charity 423
Exhall: Exhall Educational Foundation 254
Exminster: Exminster Feoffees 420
Exmouth: Exmouth Welfare Trust 421
Eynsham: Eynsham Consolidated Charity 398
Faculty: Faculty of Advocates 1985 Charitable Trust 123
Family: Family Action 3
Family Fund Trust 63
The Family Holiday Association 31
Fareham: The Fareham Welfare Trust 379
Faringdon: Faringdon United Charities 396

Farmers': The Farmers' Benevolent Institution 211
Farnborough: The Farnborough (Hampshire) Welfare Trust 379
Farnsfield: The Farnsfield Trust 238
Farrar's: Mary Farrar's Benevolent Trust Fund 462
Farriers: The Worshipful Company of Farriers Charitable Trust 1994 115
Farthing: The Farthing Trust 4
Fashion: The Fashion and Textile Children's Trust 169
Fawcett: Fawcett Johnston Charity 348
Feast: The Ollie Feast Trust 13
Featherstone: Catherine Featherstone 373
Felix: Felix Fund – The Bomb Disposal Charity 87
Feltmakers: The Feltmakers Charitable Foundation 170
Field: The Olive and Norman Field Charity 334
Fielding: The Fielding Charitable Trust 4
Fifty: The Fifty Fund 234
Film: The Film and Television Charity 133
Financial: The Institute of Financial Accountants and International Association of Book-Keepers Benevolent Fund 118
Finchampstead: The Finchampstead and Barkham Relief-in-Sickness Fund 370
Finn: Elizabeth Finn Care 4
Finnbar's: Finnbar's Force 271
Fire: Fire Fighters Charity 151
Fish: The National Federation of Fish Friers Benevolent Fund 121
Fisher: The Jane Fisher Trust 347
Fishermen's: Fishermen's Mission 128
Fishley: The Fishley Educational and Apprenticing Foundation 266
Fishmongers': The Fishmongers' and Poulterers' Institution 162
Fleming: Fleming Bequest 189
Fletcher's: Miss Ethel Mary Fletcher's Charitable Bequest 375
Fletcher's: Fletcher's Fund 63
Flitwick: Flitwick Combined Charities 274
Fluck: The Fluck Convalescent Fund 435
Fogelman: Isaac and Annie Fogelman Relief Trust 385
Folkestone: Folkestone Municipal Charity 390
Football: The Football Association Benevolent Fund 173

Institute of Football Management and Administration Charity Trust 173
Footwear: Footwear Friends 126
Forbes: Forbes Foundation 63
Dr Forbes Inverness Trust 195
Fordath: The Fordath Foundation 265
Forest: Forest Industries Education and Provident Fund 115
Forester: The Lady Forester Trust 246
Fort: The Fort Foundation 4
Forth: Forth Valley Medical Benevolent Trust 140
Foster: Alfred Foster Settlement 119
Foundations: Foundations Independent Living Trust 17
Founders: The Anniversaries Fund of the Worshipful Company of Founders 9
Fowler: The Dawson and Fowler Foundation 219
Foxton: The Foxton Dispensary 358
Foyle's: John Foyle's Charity 430
Frampton: Frampton Charities 225
Franklin's: Sir George Franklin's Pension Charity 457
Fraser: The Hugh Fraser Foundation 4
French: Anne French Memorial Trust 298
Freshtime: Freshtime Futures Trust 223
Friends: Friends of Boyan Trust 44
Friends of the Animals 35
Friends of the Elderly 37
Frimley: Frimley Fuel Allotments CIO 407
Fudge: The Ernest and Marjorie Fudge Trust 444
Fuel: Fuel Allotment 373
Fuelbanks: Fuelbanks and Families 331
Fund: Fund for Human Need 47
Furness: The Furness Seamen's Pension Fund 338
Furniture: The Furniture Makers' Company 170
Gainsborough: Gainsborough Dispensary Charity 223
Galon's: Thomas Galon's Charity 279
Gardeners': Gardeners' Royal Benevolent Society (Perennial) 116
Gardening: Gardening with Disabilities Trust 70
Gardiner: Gardiner Hill Foundation 223
Gardner: The Grace Gardner Trust 452
Gardner's: Gardner's Trust for the Blind 83
Gargrave: The Gargrave Poor's Land Charity 452

Gas: The Incorporated Benevolent Fund of the Institution of Gas Engineers and Managers 111
Gateshead: Gateshead Relief-in-Sickness Fund 339
Gayton: Gayton Fuel Allotment 297
Gayton Relief in Need Charity 231
Geest: The Gyles Geest Charity 437
General: The General and Medical Foundation 53
General Charity (Coventry) 262
Gent: The Charity of Priscilla Gent and Others 254
George: Goward and John Evans George 303
The Rob George Foundation 64
The Ruby and Will George Trust 162
German: German Society of Benevolence 366
Get: Get Kids Going 64
Gibbons: Gibbons Charity 246
The David Gibbons Foundation 421
Gilbert: The Reg Gilbert International Youth Friendship Trust (GIFT) 13
Gippeswyk: Hope House and Gippeswyk Educational Trust 302
Girls: Girls Welfare Fund 360
Girton: Girton Town Charity 279
Gislingham: Gislingham United Charity 303
Glasgow: Glasgow Bute Benevolent Society SCIO 188
The Glasgow Care Foundation 190
Glasspool: R. L. Glasspool Charity Trust 5
Gloucester: The Gloucester Charities Trust 432
Gloucester Relief in Sickness Fund 432
Gloucestershire: The Gloucestershire Association for Disability 432
Gloucestershire Football Association – Benevolent Fund 433
The Gloucestershire Society 433
Godson: The Edmund Godson Charity 319
Godstone: The Godstone United Charities 399
Golborne: The Golborne Charities – Charity of William Leadbetter 355
Goldie: Grace Wyndham Goldie (BBC) Trust Fund 134
Goodall: The Goodall Trust 462
Goodman: Valentine Goodman (Estate Charity) 216
Goodwin: The Sir Stuart and Lady Florence Goodwin Charity 235

Goosnargh: The Goosnargh and Whittingham United Charity 356
Gould's: Lady Gould's Charity 306
Gourock: Gourock Coal and Benevolent Fund 199
Gow: Neil Gow Charitable Trust 202
Gowthorpe: The Charles Wright Gowthorpe Fund 239
GPM: The GPM Charitable Trust 134
Grand: Grand Lodge of Scotland Annuity Benevolent and Charity Funds 9
Grand Prix Trust 173
Grant: The Grant, Bagshaw, Rogers and Tidswell Fund 344
Grantham: Grantham Yorke Trust 258
Great: Great Linford Relief in Need Charity 373
Greater: Greater Ryde Benevolent Trust 386
Green: The Danny Green Fund 76
Greenop: The James Greenop Foundation 360
Greenway: The Charities of Ralph Greenway 290
Greenwich: The Greenwich Charities 319
Greggs: The Greggs Foundation 334
Gregson: Gregson Memorial Annuities 361
Griffiths': The Sir Percival Griffiths' Tea-Planters Trust 116
Grimsby: Grimsby Sailors and Fishing Charity 451
GroceryAid: GroceryAid 162
Groome: Groome Trust 384
Groveland: The Groveland Charitable Trust 155
Guest: Rebecca Guest Robinson (The Robinson Bequest) 455
Guide: The Guide Dogs for the Blind Association 64
Guildford: Guildford Poyle Charities 401
Guildford's: The Mayor of Guildford's Local Support Fund 401
Guildry: Guildry Incorporation of Perth 202
Gunn's: William Gunn's Charity 40
Gurney: The Gurney Fund 25
Hackney: Hackney Benevolent Pension Society 320
Hackney Parochial Charities 320
Hair: The Hair and Beauty Charity 170
Halesworth: The Halesworth United Charities 301
Halifax: Halifax Society for the Blind 462
Hallam: The Ephraim Hallam Charity 354

Hall's: Hall's Exhibition Foundation 294

Hamilton: Janet Hamilton Memorial Fund 199

Hampshire: The Hampshire and Isle of Wight Military Aid Fund 380

Hampshire Constabulary Welfare Fund 380

Hampshire Football Association Benevolent Fund 380

Hampson: The Matt Hampson Foundation 71

Hampstead: Hampstead Wells and Campden Trust 312

Hampton: Hampton Fuel Allotment Charity 327

The Hampton Wick United Charity 327

Handsworth: The Handsworth Charity 259

Happy: Happy Days Children's Charity 26

Harborne: The Harborne Parish Lands Charity 258

Harding's: William Harding's Charity 372

Hardman: The Hardman Trust 49

Hardwick: The Ben Hardwick Fund 64

Harefield: The Harefield Parochial Charities 321

Harley: The Harley Charity (formerly The Honourable Miss Frances Harley Charity) 244

Harling: Harling Combined Trust 293

Harpenden: The Harpenden Trust 289

Harpur: The Harpur Trust 273

Harris: The Harris Charity 356

Harrison: The Margaret Harrison Trust 212

Harrow's: Mayor of Harrow's Charity Fund 321

John Harrow's Mortification 194

Hartwell: The Hartwell Educational Foundation 337

Hastings: Hastings Area Community Trust 376

Hatcliffe: Greenwich Charities of William Hatcliffe and The Misses Smith 319

Hatfield: Hatfield Broad Oak Non-Ecclesiastical Charities 284

Hatton: Hatton Consolidated Fund (Hatton Charities) 256

Hatton's: Lady Elizabeth Hatton's Charity 314

Haverfordwest: Haverfordwest Freemen's Estate 203

Hawley: Hawley Almshouses 380

Hay: The Douglas Hay Trust 64

Hayes: The Hayes (Kent) Trust 312

Hazel's: Hazel's Footprints Trust 13

Head: Francis Head Award 101

Headley-Pitt: Headley-Pitt Charitable Trust 386

Headway: Headway – The Brain Injury Association 71

Healthcare: Healthcare Workers' Foundation 140

Heathcoat: The Heathcoat Trust 413

Hedon: The Hedon Haven Trust 448

Heggs: The John Heggs Bates' Charity for Convalescents 217

Help: Help for Heroes 88

Help Musicians UK 101

Help Our Wounded Royal Marines and Supporting Arms 88

Helston: The Helston Welfare Trust 418

Henley: Henley Educational Trust 394

Hereford: Hereford Municipal Charities 244

The Hereford Society for Aiding the Industrious 244

Herne: The Herne Bay Parochial Charity 389

Heron: The Eleemosynary Charity of Giles Heron 339

Heron Educational Foundation (Heron Trust) 448

Hertfordshire: The Hertfordshire Charity for Deprived Children 285

Hertfordshire Community Foundation 286

Hertfordshire Community Nurses Charity 286

Hertfordshire Convalescent Trust 286

The Hertfordshire Educational Foundation 286

Hervey: The Charity of Hervey and Elizabeth Ekins 231

Hesslewood: The Hesslewood Children's Trust (Hull Seamen's and General Orphanage) 447

Hewley's: Lady Hewley's Charity 156

Heywood: Heywood Relief-in-Need Trust Fund 353

Hickman's: Thomas Hickman's Charity 372

Higgins: The Terrence Higgins Trust – Hardship Fund 76

Higgs: Higgs and Cooper's Educational Charity 434

High: High Wycombe Central Aid Society 374

Highland: Highland Children's Trust 195

Hilgay: Hilgay United Charities (Non-Ecclesiastical Branch) 295

Hill: Rowland Hill Memorial and Benevolent Fund 146

The Mary Hill Trust 269

Hilton: Hilton Town Charity 278

Hindley: Margaret Jeannie Hindley Charitable Trust 366

Hitcham: The Hitcham Poor Lands Charity 371

Hobbayne: The Eleemosynary Charity of William Hobbayne 317

Hodges: The John Hodges Charitable Trust 394

Hodnet: The Hodnet Consolidated Eleemosynary Charities 246

Holford's: John Holford's Charity 344

Holibobs: Holibobs 65

Hollie: The Hollie Foundation 76

Hollis: Hollis Charity 381

Hollowford: Hollowford Trust 457

Holmes: The Canon Holmes Memorial Trust 281

Holt: Charity of Ann Holt 462

Holywood: The Holywood Trust 187

Honiton: Honiton United Charities 422

Honourable: Honourable Artillery Company 88

Hoper-Dixon: Hoper-Dixon Trust 41

Horbury: Horbury Common Lands Trust 465

Hordle: The Hordle District Nursing Association 384

Hornsby: The Hornsby Professional Cricketers Fund 173

Hornsey: The Hornsey Parochial Charities 306

Horstead: Horstead Trust 293

Hospital: The Hospital Saturday Fund 53

Hospitality: Hospitality Action 121

Houghton: Basil Houghton Memorial Trust 247

Hounsfield: The Hounsfield Pension 41

House: George House Trust 350

Household: The Household Cavalry Foundation 88

The Household Division Charity 88

Housing: Housing the Homeless Central Fund 48

Houston: The Houston Charitable Trust 5

Howat: James T. Howat Charitable Trust 191

Hucknall: The Hucknall Relief-in-Need Charity 237

Huddersfield: Huddersfield and District Army Veterans' Association Benevolent Fund 463

Hudson's: George Hudson's Charity 340

Hull: The Hull Aid in Sickness Trust 450

Hull Trinity House Charity 128

Humberside: Humberside Police Welfare and Benevolent Fund 447

Hume: June and Douglas Hume Memorial Fund 77

Hundred: Hundred Acre Common Charity 295

Hunstone: Edward Hunstone 224

Hunt: Michael and Shirley Hunt Charitable Trust 49

Huntingdon: Huntingdon Freemen's Trust 278

Huntingdon's: John Huntingdon's Charity 279

Huntington's: Huntington's Disease Association 77

Hyde: Hyde Charitable Trust 366
Hyde Park Place Estate Charity 315

Hylton: Hylton House and Specialist Support Fund 334

IAPS: IAPS Charitable Trust 109

ICE: ICE Benevolent Fund 114
The Ice Hockey Players Benevolent Fund 174

Ilchester: The Ilchester Relief in Need and Educational Charity (IRINEC) 442

Illston: Illston Town Land Charity 217

Ilminster: The Ilminster Educational Foundation 437

In: In the Game 174

Independence: Independence at Home 54

Ingram: Arthur Ingram Trust 391

Injured: The Injured Jockeys Fund 174

Inspectors: The Benevolent Fund of Her Majesty's Inspectors of Schools in England and Wales 109

Insurance: The Insurance Charities 119

iprovision: iprovision 132

Irish: Irish Guards Charitable Fund 89

Isabel: The Isabel Ward (York) Charitable Trust 453

ISM: ISM Members' Fund (The Benevolent Fund of The Incorporated Society of Musicians) 102

It's: It's Your Wish – The John Bury Trust 357

Iver: Iver Heath Care Fund 371

James: The P.D. James Memorial Fund 102

JAT: JAT (Jewish AIDS Trust) 44

Jesus: Jesus Hospital in Chipping Barnet 311

Jewish: The Jewish Aged Needy Pension Society 37
Jewish Care Scotland 44
The Association of Jewish Refugees (AJR) 45

The Jewish Widows and Students Aid Trust 45

JIC: The JIC Fund (The Charitable Fund of the Joint Industrial Council of the Match Manufacturing Industry) 126

Johnners: The Johnners Trust 174

Johnson: Johnson Charitable Trust 167
The Dorothy Johnson Charitable Trust 229

Johnston: Johnston Educational Foundation 337
The Johnston Family Trust 362
The William Johnston Trust Fund 37

Jones: The Jones Trust 206

Jopp: The Jopp Thomson Fund 194

Jordison: Jordison and Hossell Animal Welfare Charity 242

Jory's: Joseph Jory's Charity 425

Journalists': Journalists' Charity 134

Just: Just Helping Children 65

K.O.S.B.: K.O.S.B. Association Funds 89

Kayleigh's: Kayleigh's Wee Stars 65

Kempston: The Kempston Charities 273

Kenilworth: Kenilworth United Charities 257

Kensington: Kensington and Chelsea District Nursing Trust 323

Kent: Kent Community Foundation 387
The Kent County Football Association Benevolent Fund 387
Kent Farmers Benevolent Fund 116
Kent Nursing Institution 387

Kentish's: Kentish's Educational Foundation 271

Keyes: The Ursula Keyes Trust 346

Kidderminster: Kidderminster Aid in Sickness Fund 270

Kidney: Kidney Care UK 77
Kidney Kids Scotland Charitable Trust 65

King: King Edward VII's Hospital Sister Agnes 89
The John Henry King Fund 385
The King Henry VIII Endowed Trust, Warwick 257

King's: The King's Lynn and West Norfolk Borough Charity 295

King's: The King's Norton United Charities 260

Kingsclere: Kingsclere Welfare Charities 382

Kingston: The Kingston Trust CIO 77

Kirkby: Kirkby Lonsdale Relief in Need Charity 347

Kirke's: Kirke's Charity 464

Kirkley: Kirkley Poor's Land Estate 376

Kirkman: The Richard Kirkman Trust 381

Kitchings: Kitchings General Charity 228

Koning: Koning Willem Fonds – The Netherlands Benevolent Society 30

Kroch: The Heinz, Anna and Carol Kroch Foundation 47

Kupath: Kupath Gemach Chaim Bechesed Viznitz Trust 45

Lacy: The Mrs A. Lacy Tate Trust 376

Ladies: The Ladies Aid Society and the Eyre Charity 425

Lady: The Lady Elizabeth Hastings Estate Charity 459

Lakeland: Lakeland Disability Support CIO 349

Lamb: The John William Lamb Charity 239

Lancashire: Community Foundations for Lancashire and Merseyside 343
The Lancashire Infirm Secular Clergy Fund 343

Langley: The Langley Foundation 54

Lant: The Lant Charity 265

LATCH: LATCH Welsh Children's Cancer Charity 65

Lathom: Peter Lathom (including the Lathom Educational Foundation) 360

Launderers: The Worshipful Company of Launderers Benevolent Trust Fund 167

Law: The John and Mildred Law Fund 232

Lay: Mark Lay Foundation 57

Leaders: The Leaders of Worship and Preachers Trust 156

League: The League of the Helping Hand (LHH) 54

Leamington: Leamington Relief-in-Sickness Fund 252

Leather: Leather and Hides Trades' Benevolent Institution 170

Leatherhead: Leatherhead United Charities 404

Lee: The Lee Charity of William Hatcliffe 325

Leeds: Leeds Benevolent Society for Single Ladies 464
The Leeds Community Trust 464
Leeds Convalescent Society 464
The Duchess of Leeds Foundation for Boys and Girls 26

Lees: The Sarah Lees Relief Trust 352

Legate's: Legate's Charity 431

Leicester: The Leicester Aid-in-Sickness Fund 220
The Leicester Charity Link 211

The Leicester Freemen's Estate 221

The Leicester Indigent Old Age Society 221

Leicestershire: The Leicestershire and Rutland County Nursing Association 212

Leicestershire Coal Industry Welfare Trust Fund 217

Leigh: Leigh United Charities 392

Leivers: Alf and Hilda Leivers Charity Trust 325

Lenderhand: Lenderhand 281

Leney: The Hugh and Montague Leney Travelling Awards Trust 306

Lenzie: Lenzie Benevolent Society SCIO 189

Letchworth: The Letchworth Civic Trust 288

Lethendy: The Lethendy Charitable Trust 189

Leukaemia: Leukaemia Care 57

Leverington: The Leverington Town Lands Charity 277

Leveson: The Lady Katherine and Sir Richard Leveson Charity 250

Lewis: The George and Alfred Lewis (of Chigwell) Memorial Fund 284

Lewisham: Lewisham Relief in Need Charity 325

Library: Chartered Institute of Library and Information Professionals (CILIP) Benevolent Fund 123

Licensed: Licensed Trade Charity 122

Lichfield: Lichfield Municipal Charities 411

Lifeline: Lifeline 4 Kids (Handicapped Children's Aid Committee) 66

Lighthouse: Lighthouse Construction Industry Charity (LCIC) 107

Lincoln: Lincoln General Dispensary Fund 226

Lincoln Municipal Relief in Need Charity 226

Lincolnshire: Lincolnshire Community Foundation 224

Lincolnshire Police Charitable Fund 224

Lindow: Lindow Workhouse Charity 345

Line: Line Dance Foundation 102

Lineham: The Henry and Elizabeth Lineham Charity 232

Lionheart: Lionheart (The Royal Institution of Chartered Surveyors Benevolent Fund) 108

Litchborough: Litchborough Parochial Charities 229

Little: The Andrew and Mary Elizabeth Little Charitable Trust 191

Littleborough: Littleborough Nursing Association Fund 353

Litton: The Litton Cheney Trust 430

Liverpool: The Liverpool Caledonian Association 362

Liverpool Corn Trade Guild 126

The Liverpool Ladies' Institution 362

Liverpool Marine Engineers' and Naval Architects' Guild 361

The Liverpool Merchants' Guild 362

The Liverpool Provision Trade Guild 362

Liverpool Shipbrokers' Benevolent Society Incorporated 363

Liversage: The Liversage Trust 214

Llanidloes: Llanidloes Relief in Need Charity 204

Llanrhuddlad: Llanrhuddlad Charities (William Lloyd) 206

Lloyd: The Elaine and Angus Lloyd Charitable Trust 387

The Lloyd Foundation 110

The W. M. and B. W. Lloyd Trust 357

Lloyd's: The Lloyd's Benevolent Fund 119

Lloyds: Lloyds and TSB Staff Benevolent Fund 119

Lockington: Mary Lockington Charity 275

Logans: Logans Fund 66

London: The London Shipowners' and Shipbrokers' Benevolent Society 179

Long: Long Bennington Charities 228

Loughborough: The Loughborough Welfare Trusts 219

Lowe's: Michael Lowe's and Associated Charities 250

Lowestoft: Lowestoft Church and Town Relief in Need Charity 301

Lowestoft Fishermen's and Seafarers' Benevolent Society 301

Lowton: The Lowton United Charity 355

Loxton: Charity of Harriet Louisa Loxton 260

Loy: The Tony Loy Trust 397

Lucas: The Charity of Robert Lucas for the Poor and for Public Purposes 275

Lund: The Lucy Lund Holiday Grants 110

Luttrell: J. A. F. Luttrell Memorial Charity 438

Lyndhurst: The Lyndhurst Welfare Charity 384

Lyon: The Dr Thomas Lyon Bequest 26

Lyson's: Sylvanus Lyson's Charity 41

Lytham: The Lytham St Anne's Relief-in-Sickness Charity 358

MacAndrew: MacAndrew Sussex Trust 376

MacArthur: Mary MacArthur Holiday Trust 33

Macclesfield: Macclesfield and District Relief-in-Sickness Charity 345

MacDonald: Doctor William MacDonald of Johannesburg Trust 263

MacDougall: The MacDougall Trust 430

Machne: Machne Israel Loan Fund 45

MacKenzie: The William MacKenzie Trust 196

Mackie: John Mackie Memorial Ladies' Home 216

Macleod: The Agnes Macleod Memorial Fund 36

Macmillan: Macmillan Cancer Support 57

Maidstone: Maidstone Relief-in-Need Charities 391

Malmesbury: Malmesbury Area Community Trust 444

Malvern: Malvern Hills Nils 267

Manchester: The Dean of Manchester Crosland Fund 351

Manchester District Nursing Institution Fund 350

Manchester Relief-in-Need Fund and Manchester Children's Relief-in-Need Fund 350

Mann: Victor Mann Trust (also known as The Wallsend Charitable Trust) 340

Manse: Manse Bairns Network 41

Marchioness: Marchioness of Northampton (Wraxall Parochial Charities) 440

Margaret's: Margaret's Fund 78

Margate: Margate and Dr Peete's Charity 393

Marham: Marham Poor's Allotment 290

Marine: The Guild of Benevolence of The Institute of Marine Engineering, Science and Technology 129

The Marine Society and Sea Cadets 129

Market: The Market Research Benevolent Association 132

Marshall: James Marshall Foundation CIO 288

Martin's: John Martin's Charity 270

Mary: The Mary Grave Trust 347

Marylebone: St Marylebone Educational Foundation 315

Mason: John Bristow and Thomas Mason Trust 404

Masonic: Masonic Charitable Foundation 10

Master: The Honourable Company of Master Mariners and Howard Leopold Davis Charity 129

Matthew: The Matthew Trust 73

Maudlyn: The Maudlyn Lands Charity 420

Mayfield: The Mayfield Trust 379

Maynard's: Lord Maynard's Charity 284

Mayor's: The Mayor's Poor Fund, Eastbourne 378

Mayor's: The Mayor's Benevolent Fund (Barnet) 311

McAlpine: The McAlpine Educational Endowments Ltd 26

McLaren: The E. McLaren Fund 33

McLean: George McLean Trust 190

Medical: Medical Research Council Staff Benevolent Fund Association 140

Mellor: The Mellor Fund 351

Melton: Melton Mowbray Building Society Charitable Foundation 222

The Melton Trust 222

Members: The Members Benevolent Trust of the Institute of Materials, Minerals and Mining 145

Meningitis: Meningitis Now (formerly known as Meningitis Trust) 78

Merchant: The Merchant Company Endowments Trust 198

Merseyside: Merseyside Jewish Community Care 361

Merseyside Medical Benevolent Fund 363

Merthyr: Merthyr Mendicants 208

Metcalfe: Metcalfe Smith Trust CIO 465

Methodist: The Methodist Church in Great Britain 156

Metropolitan: Metropolitan Police Benevolent Fund 151

Metropolitan Police Staff Welfare Fund 151

MidasPlus: MidasPlus 366

Middleton: Middleton Cheney United Charities 233

The Middleton Relief-in-Need Charity 350

Middleton-on-the-Hill: Middleton-on-the-Hill Parish Charity 287

Midgley: The William and Sarah Midgley Charity 459

Mildenhall: The Mildenhall Parish Charities 304

Military: The Military Provost Staff Corps Benevolent Fund 89

Millichip: The Adam Millichip Foundation 54

Mills: The Mills Charity 302

The Mills Educational Foundation 300

Minet: The Mary Minet Trust 307

Mining: Mining Institute of Scotland Trust 146

Ministers': Ministers' Relief Society 156

Mitchell: Mitchell Bequest 157

Mitchell City of London Charity 314

Mitchell City of London Educational Foundation 314

Mitchells: The Mitchells and Butlers Charitable Trusts 260

MND: MND Scotland 79

Molly: Molly Olly's Wishes 66

Molyneux: The Molyneux and Warbrick Charity 129

Monke: Thomas Monke 217

Monmouth: Monmouth Charity 208

The Monmouth Diocesan Clergy Widows and Dependants Society 208

Monmouthshire: The Monmouthshire County Council Welsh Church Act Fund 208

Montgomery: The Montgomery Welfare Fund 204

Montpellier: The Montpellier Trust 45

Moorhouse: The Harold Moorhouse Charity 296

Moose: The Moose International Welfare Service Fund 10

Moray: Moray and Nairn Educational Trust 195

Morden: Morden College 37

Morgan: Junius S. Morgan Benevolent Fund 140

Morpeth: Morpeth Dispensary 339

Morris: The Henry Morris Memorial Trust 276

Morrison: Mary Morrison Cox Trust 193

Morval: The Morval Foundation 42

Moser: The Moser Benevolent Trust Fund 460

Moshe: Vyoel Moshe Charitable Trust 46

Motability: Motability 70

Mother: The Mother Humber' Memorial Fund 450

Motor: Motor Neurone Disease Association 79

Motoring: The Guild of Motoring Writers Benevolent Fund 134

Moulton: The Non-Ecclesiastical Charity of William Moulton 340

Moulton Poor Trust 226

Moundeford: Sir Edmund De Moundeford Charity 296

Mountain: Mountain and Cave Rescue Benevolent Fund 147

Mountsorrel: Mountsorrel Relief in Need Charity 220

Multiple: Multiple Sclerosis Society 79

Mummy's: Mummy's Star 58

Municipal: Municipal Charities (formerly Bedford Municipal Charities) 273

Municipal Charities of Stratford-upon-Avon – Relief in Need Charity 255

Municipal General Charities for the Poor 235

Murchie: The Maud Beattie Murchie Charitable Trust 361

Murdoch's: John Murdoch's Trust 166

MYA: The MYA Charitable Trust 46

NABS: NABS 132

Nafferton: The Nafferton Feoffees Charities Trust 449

Nailsea: Nailsea Community Trust Ltd 440

Nash: The Nash Charity 89

NASUWT: NASUWT (The Teachers' Union) Benevolent Fund 110

National: The National Association of Co-operative Officials (NACO) Benevolent Fund 162

The National Benevolent Charity 5

The National Caravan Council (NCC) Benevolent Fund 147

National Youth Arts Trust (NYAT) 14

National Zakat Foundation 43

NatWest: The NatWest Group Pensioners Benevolent Fund 120

Nautilus: Nautilus Welfare Fund 130

Naval: Naval Children's Charity 26

Navenby: The Navenby Town's Farm Trust 226

Neale: Alex Neale Charity 217

New: The New Appeals Organisation 235

The New Forest Keepers Widows Fund 384

New St Andrews Japan Golf Trust 190

Newbury: The Newbury and Thatcham Welfare Trust 369

Newby: Newby Trust Ltd 5

Newfield: Newfield Charitable Trust 252

Newick: The Newick Distress Trust 378

Newlife: Newlife Foundation for Disabled Children 55

NewstrAid: NewstrAid Benevolent Fund 163

NFL: The NFL Trust 33

NHS: The NHS Pensioners' Trust 141

Nicholson: The Nicholson Memorial Fund (The Rosehill Trust) 218

Nichol-Young: Nichol-Young Foundation 6

Nicola's: Nicola's Fund 66

Nightingale: The Florence Nightingale Aid-in-Sickness Trust (FNAIST) 55

The Nightingale Fund 141

Nitzrochim: The Chevras Ezras Nitzrochim Trust 44

NJD: NJD Charitable Trust 46

Noakes: The Joe Noakes Charitable Trust 272

Norfolk: Norfolk Community Foundation 291

Norfolk Constabulary Benevolent Fund 291

Norris: The Evelyn Norris Trust 102

North: North East Area Miners' Social Welfare Trust Fund 335

North East Scotland Police Welfare Fund (NESPWF) 192

North London Welfare and Educational Foundation 314

The North Staffordshire Coalfield Miners Relief Fund 248

North Wales Police Benevolent Fund 205

The North West Police Benevolent Fund 343

Northampton: Northampton Municipal Church Charity 232

Northcott: Northcott Devon Foundation 420

Northern: Northern Ireland Police Fund 152

Northern Ladies Annuity Society 335

Norton: The Norton Canon Parochial Charities 244

The Norton Foundation 242

Norwich: Norwich Consolidated Charities 298

Norwich Town Close Estate Charity 298

Nottingham: The Nottingham Annuity Charity 235

The Nottingham General Dispensary 235

Nottingham Gordon Memorial Trust for Boys and Girls 239

Nottinghamshire: Nottinghamshire Community Foundation 236

Nottinghamshire Constabulary Benevolent Fund 236

The Nottinghamshire Miners' Welfare Trust Fund 236

Nowes: John Nowes Exhibition Foundation 442

Nuclear: Nuclear Community Charity Fund 90

The Nuclear Industry Benevolent Fund 112

NUJ: NUJ Extra 135

Nurses: The Benevolent Fund for Nurses in Scotland 141

Nurses': The Nurses' Memorial to King Edward VII Edinburgh Scottish Committee 141

Nursing: Lancashire County Nursing Trust 344

Nuttall: The Nuttall Trust 438

Nutter's: Joseph Nutter's Foundation 460

Ockley: Ockley United Charities 404

Officers': The Officers' Association 90

Officers' Association Scotland 90

Ogilvie: The Ogilvie Charities 6

Ogle: The Ogle Christian Trust 157

Okehampton: Okehampton United Charity 427

Old: Old Buckenham Charities 291

The Old Enfield Charitable Trust 318

Old Park Ward Old Age Pensioners Fund 215

Oldbury: The Oldbury Charity 265

Oldham: Oldham United Charity 352

Oliver: Miss Ada Oliver 55

Open: Open Wing Trust 14

Oppenheimer: Arthur and Rosa Oppenheimer Fund 307

Organists': The Incorporated Association of Organists' Benevolent Fund 103

Organists' Charitable Trust 103

Orphan's: Orphan's Aid Educational Foundation (Plymouth) 425

Ottery: The Ottery Feoffee Charity 422

Overall: Richard Overall Trust 14

Overton: Overton United Charity 206

OVO: The OVO Energy Fund 17

Owen's: Dame Alice Owen's Eleemosynary Charities 307

Oxford: The City of Oxford Charity 395

Oxted: The Oxted United Charities 408

Page: The Page Fund 232

Paignton: Paignton Parish Charity 427

Pakenham: Pakenham Charities 304

Palling: United Charity of Palling Burgess and Others 435

Palmer: The Palmer and Seabright Charity 264

Eleanor Palmer Trust 311

Pargeter: Pargeter and Wand Trust 242

Parish: Parish Lands (South Brent Feoffees) 426

Parish Piece Charity 221

Parkinson: John Parkinson (Goosnargh and Whittingham United Charity) 356

Parkinson's: Parkinson's UK 80

Parrott: The Dorothy Parrott Memorial Trust Fund 392

Parsons: Thomas Parsons Charity 277

Patent: The Incorporated Benevolent Association of the Chartered Institute of Patent Attorneys 124

Paterson: James Paterson Trust and Nursing Fund 191

Paton: The Paton Trust 157

Patrick: Joseph Patrick Trust 80

Pattishall: The Pattishall Parochial Charities 234

Pattullo: The Gertrude Muriel Pattullo Advancement Award Scheme 201

Pawnbrokers': Pawnbrokers' Charitable Institution 163

Pedmore: Pedmore Sporting Club Trust Fund 242

Peirson: Anne Peirson Charitable Trust 390

Pendlebury's: Sir Ralph Pendlebury's Charity for Orphans 355

Sir Ralph Pendlebury's Charity for the Aged 355

Pentney: The Pentney Charity 296

Performing: The Performing Rights Society Members' Benevolent Fund (PRS Members' Fund) 103

Perry: The Perry Fund 34

The Perry Trust Gift Fund 236

Persehouse: Persehouse Pensions Fund 248

Pershore: Pershore United Charity 267

Pest: The Pest House Charity 410

Petersham: The Petersham United Charities 327

PGA: PGA European Tour Benevolent Trust 175

Pharmacist: Pharmacist Support 142

Philharmonia: The Philharmonia Benevolent Fund 103

Phillips: Phillips Charity 227

Physics: The Institute of Physics Benevolent Fund 110

Pickering: The Ron Pickering Memorial Fund 15

Picto: The Charity of Sir John Picto and Others 291

Pilcher: Sam Pilcher Trust 413

Pilion: The Pilion Trust Ltd 322

Pilkington: The Roger Pilkington Young Trust 38

Pinn: William Frank Pinn Charitable Trust 390

Pirbright: The Pirbright Relief-in-Need Charity 402

Plant: The Institution of Plant Engineers Benevolent Fund 114

Plymouth: The Plymouth and Cornwall Cancer Fund 413

Plymouth Public Dispensary 426

Podde: The Podde Trust 42

Polehampton: The Polehampton Charity 367

Police: Police Care UK 152

Pollard: The Harry and Katie Pollard Trust 157

Poole: The Valentine Poole Charity 311

Poors: The Poors Allotment 230

Poor's: The Poor's Allotments Charity 374

Poor's Platt 220

Poppyscotland: Poppyscotland 90

Port: Port of London Authority Police Charity Fund 130

Portishead: The Portishead Nautical Trust 416

Portsmouth: Portsmouth Victoria Nursing Association 381

Potter: The Margaret and Alick Potter Charitable Trust 80

Potton: Potton Consolidated Charity 275

Power: Power Pleas Trust 267

Praebendo: The Praebendo Charitable Foundation 6

Pratt: The Pratt Charity 351

Presbyterian: The Presbyterian Children's Society 42

The Presbyterian Old Age Fund, Women's Fund and Indigent Ladies' Fund 42

Prestbury: The Prestbury Charity (Prestbury United Charities) 434

Price: The William Price Charitable Trust 382

Primrose: John Primrose Trust 188

Prince's: The Prince's Trust 27

Printing: The Printing Charity 135

Prisoners: The Prisoners of Conscience Appeal Fund 47

Pritt: The Pritt Fund 124

Professional: The Professional Billiards and Snooker Players Benevolent Fund 175

The Professional Footballers' Association Charity 175

Professionals: Professionals Aid Guild 7

Provision: Provision Trade Charity 147

Pulmonary: Pulmonary Fibrosis Trust 80

Purey: The Purey Cust Trust CIO 454

Pusinelli: Pusinelli Convalescent and Holiday Home 307

Pyncombe: The Pyncombe Charity 157

Quaker: Quaker Mental Health Fund 43

Quarrying: The Institute of Quarrying Benevolent Fund 146

Queen's: The Queen's Nursing Institute 142

Quorn: The Quorn Town Lands Charity 221

Racehorse: Racehorse Trainers Benevolent Fund 175

Racing: Racing Welfare 176

Railway: Railway Benefit Fund 179

Ramsay: The Peggy Ramsay Foundation 103

Annie Ramsay McLean Trust for the Elderly 190

Randall: David Randall Foundation 281

Rank: The Joseph Rank Benevolent Fund 450

Rathbone: The Rathbone Moral Aid Charity 245

Ravensden: The Ravensden Town and Poor Estate 274

Rawlet: Rawlet Trust 251

Rawlins: The Thomas Rawlins Educational Foundation 218

RCN: The RCN Foundation 142

RDC: The RDC Foundation 15

Reach: Reach Charity Ltd 67

REACT: REACT (Rapid Effective Assistance for Children with Potentially Terminal Illnesses) 67

Reading: Reading Dispensary Trust 368

Reckitt: The Sir James Reckitt Charity 449

Red: Red Cypher 91

Red Eagle Foundation 388

Redcliffe: The Redcliffe Parish Charity 417

Rees: Rees Foundation 27

Referees': The Referees' Association Members Benevolent Fund 176

Regain: Regain – The Trust for Sports Tetraplegics 72

Rehoboth: The Rehoboth Trust 43

Reid: Rhona Reid Charitable Trust 15

Reiss: The Florence Reiss Trust for Old People 366

Relief: Ashford Relief in Need Charities 406

Knaresborough Relief in Need Charity 452

Relief-in-Need: Relief-in-Need Charity of Simon Lord Digby and Others 254

REME: The REME Charity 91

Removers: Removers Benevolent Association 179

Respite: The Respite Association 59

Retail: The National Federation of Retail Newsagents Convalescence Fund 163

Retail Trust 163

Retired: The Retired Ministers' and Widows' Fund 157

Retired Missionary Aid Fund 158

Reydon: The Reydon Trust 302

RFL: The RFL Benevolent Fund (Try Assist) 176

RFU: RFU Injured Players Foundation 72

Richards': George Richards' Charity 158

Richardson: Gerry Richardson Trust 358

Richmond: The Richmond Aid-in-Sickness Fund 328

Richmond Parish Lands Charity 328

Richmond Philanthropic Society 328

Rifles: The Rifles Benevolent Trust 91

The Rifles Officers' Fund 91

Ripple: The Ancient Parish of Ripple Trust 268

Risby: The Risby Fuel Allotment 304

RMT: RMT (National Union of Rail, Maritime and Transport Workers) Orphan Fund 27

Road: The Road Haulage Association Benevolent Fund 179

Roade: Roade Feoffee and Chivall Charity 234

Roberts: The Evan and Catherine Roberts Home 205

The Ella Roberts Memorial Charity for Saham Toney 291

Robertson: The Mair Robertson Benevolent Fund 201

Robinson: Thomas Robinson Charity 364

The Gus Robinson Foundation 335

The J. C. Robinson Trust No. 3 28

The Andrew Robinson Young People's Trust 263

Robinson's: Samuel Robinson's Charities 158

Rochdale: The Rochdale Fund for Relief-in-Sickness 353

Rochdale United Charity 353

Roddam: The Roddam Charity 247

Rogers: The Rogers and Holes Charities 441

Rope's: Mrs L. D. Rope's Third Charitable Settlement 302

Ropner: The Ropner Centenary Trust 335

Rosslyn: Rosslyn Park Injury Trust Fund 72

Rotherhithe: Rotherhithe Consolidated Charities 329

Roundhouse: Roundhouse Foundation 344

Routledge: The John Routledge Hunter Memorial Fund 339

Rowe's: John James Rowe's Foundation for Girls 363

Rowlandson: The Rowlandson and Eggleston Relief-in-Need Charity 338

Roxburghshire: Roxburghshire Landward Benevolent Trust 200

Royal: The Royal Agricultural Benevolent Institution 116

The Royal Air Force Benevolent Fund 91

The Royal Air Forces Association 92

Royal Antediluvian Order of Buffaloes, Grand Lodge of England War Memorial Annuities 10

The Royal Ballet Benevolent Fund 104

The Royal Bath and West of England Society 414

The Royal British Legion 92

The Royal Caledonian Education Trust 92

The Royal College of Midwives Trust 143

Royal Engineers Association 93

The Royal Literary Fund 104

The Royal Liverpool Seamen's Orphan Institution (RLSOI) 130

The Royal Logistics Corps Association Trust Fund 93

Royal Medical Benevolent Fund (RMBF) 143

The Royal Medical Foundation 144

Royal Merchant Navy Education Foundation 94

The Royal Military Police Central Benevolent Fund 94

Royal National Children's Springboard Foundation 28

The Royal National Institute of Blind People (RNIB) 83

The Royal Naval Benevolent Trust 94

The Royal Navy Officers' Charity 95

The Royal Opera House Benevolent Fund 104

The Royal Pinner School Foundation 164

The Royal Scottish Academy (RSA) 105

The Royal Signals Charity 95

The Royal Society for Home Relief to Incurables, Edinburgh 56

The Royal Society for the Support of Women of Scotland 34

The Royal Society of Chemistry Chemists' Community Fund 166

The Royal Society of Musicians of Great Britain 105

The Royal Theatrical Fund 105

The Royal Ulster Constabulary GC – Police Service of Northern Ireland Benevolent Fund 152

Royal Variety Charity 135

RSABI: RSABI (Royal Scottish Agricultural Benevolent Institution) 117

Ruabon: Ruabon and District Relief in Need Charity 207

Rugby: Rugby Welfare Charities 255

Rugeley: The Rugeley Educational Endowment 248

Rutland: Rutland Grants 240

The Rutland Trust 240

Rycroft: Rycroft Children's Fund 212

Saffron: The Saffron Walden United Charities 285

Saham: Saham Toney Fuel Allotment and Perkins Charity 293

Sailors': Sailors' Society 130

Sailors': Sailors' Children's Society 28

Sailors' Orphan Society of Scotland 28

Saint: Saint Petrox Trust Lands 420

Salespeople's: The Salespeople's Charity 164

Salford: The Salford Foundation Trust 354

Salisbury: Salisbury City Almshouse and Welfare Charities 444

Salisbury City Educational and Apprenticing Charity 445

Salt's: Sir Titus Salt's Charity 461

Salter: George and Thomas Henry Salter Trust 265

Sanders: William Sanders Charity 203

Sandra: Sandra Charitable Trust 144

Sands: Sands Cox Relief in Sickness Charity 261

Sandy: The Sandy Charities 275

Sant's: Helena Sant's Residuary Trust Fund 282

Saunders: Mr William Saunders Charity for the Relief of Indigent Gentry and Others 38

Sawley: The Sawley Charities 215

Sawyer: The Sawyer Trust 34

Saye: The Saye and Sele Foundation 371

SBA: SBA The Solicitors' Charity 124

Scarborough: The Scarborough Municipal Charity 453

School: The Association of School and College Leaders Benevolent Fund 110

The School Fees Charitable Trust 7

Scientific: The Worshipful Company of Scientific Instrument Makers 166

Scones: Scones Lethendy Mortification 202

Scotscare: Scotscare 307

Scott: The Foundation of Joanna Scott and Others 299

James Scott Law Charitable Fund 199

Scottish: Scottish Artists Benevolent Association 105

Scottish Association of Master Bakers Benevolent Fund 171

Scottish Building Federation Edinburgh and District Charitable Trust 197

Scottish Chartered Accountants' Benevolent Association 120

Scottish Grocers Federation Benevolent Fund 164

Scottish Hide and Leather Trades' Provident and Benevolent Society 171

Scottish Hydro Electric Community Trust 18

Scottish Nautical Welfare Society 131

Scottish Police Benevolent Fund 153

Scottish Prison Service Benevolent Fund 153

Scottish Secondary Teachers' Association Benevolent Fund 111

Scottish Shipping Benevolent Association 180

Scottish Showbusiness Benevolent Fund 106

Scottish Solicitors Benevolent Fund 124

Scottish Stockbrokers' Benevolent Fund 120

Seafarers: Seafarers Hospital Society 131

Sears: Sears Group Trust 165

Seckford: The Seckford Foundation 300

Sedgefield: The Sedgefield District Relief in Need Charity (The Sedgefield Charities) 337

Semple: Mairi Semple Fund 189

Severn: The Severn Trent Water Charitable Trust Fund 18

Severn Wye Energy Agency 433

Shadwell: William Shadwell Charity 378

Shaw: The Shaw Charities 358

Sheffield: The Sheffield Bluecoat and Mount Pleasant Educational Foundation 458

Sheffield Grammar School Exhibition Foundation 458

The Sheffield West Riding Charitable Society Trust 454

Shell: The Shell Pensioners Benevolent Association 38

Shere: The Charity of John Shere and Others 423

Sheriffs': The Sheriffs' and Recorders' Fund 308

Shetland: Shetland Charitable Trust 199

Shipdham: Shipdham Parochial and Fuel Allotment Charity 293

Shipman: Thomas Stanley Shipman Charitable Trust 218

Shipwrecked: The Shipwrecked Fishermen and Mariners' Royal Benevolent Society 131

Shona: The Shona Smile Foundation 58

Shottermill: Shottermill United Charities 409

Shropshire: The Shropshire Youth Foundation 246

Shuttleworth: John T. Shuttleworth Ropner Memorial Fund 338

Sidmouth: Sidmouth Consolidated Charities 420

The Sidmouth Educational Foundation 421

Siebel: The Mary Elizabeth Siebel Charity 238

Silversmiths: The Silversmiths and Jewellers Charity 171

Silverton: Silverton Parochial Trust 424

Skinners': Skinners' Benevolent Trust 308

Slough: The Slough and District Community Fund 369

Smallwood: Smallwood Trust 34

Smile: A Smile for a Child 29

Smith: Henry Smith (Chobham) 407

Henry Smith (Share Warbleton Estate) 410

Henry Smith (Worth Estate) 404

Smith and Fermor Charities 376

The Henry Smith Charity (Ash and Normandy) 399

The Henry Smith Charity (Bedworth) 254

The Henry Smith Charity (Bisley) 407

The Henry Smith Charity (Bramley) 399

The Henry Smith Charity (Capel) 404

The Henry Smith Charity (Chertsey) 406

The Henry Smith Charity (Effingham) 405

The Henry Smith Charity (Frimley) 408

The Henry Smith Charity (Headley) 401

The Henry Smith Charity (Longney) 439

The Henry Smith Charity (Send and Ripley) 402

The Henry Smith Charity (UK) 7

The Henry Smith Charity (Westbury) 445

Henry Smith Fund (Shere) 405

Miss Annie Smith Mair Newmilns Trust Fund 187

The Elizabeth Smith Trust for Widows 425

Smith's: Henry Smith's Charity (East Horsley) 405

Smith's Charity (Nutfield) 408

Smith's Cirencester Poor Charity 435

Smith's: The Samuel Smith's and Spencer's Charities 252

Henry Smith's Charity (Ancient Parish of Dovercourt) 281

Henry Smith's Charity (Richmond) 329

Smiths: Smiths Charity (Shalford) 402

Smith's: Thomas Herbert Smith's Trust Fund 218

Smythe's: Sir Thomas Smythe's Poor Fund (Skinners' Company) 388

Snow: The Snow Sports Foundation 56

Sobell: The Michael Sobell Welsh People's Charitable Association 8

Social: Social Workers Benevolent Trust 171

Society: Society for Assistance of Medical Families 144

Society for the Benefit of Sons and Daughters of the Clergy of the Church of Scotland 158

The Society for the Education of the Deaf 81

The Society for the Orphans and Children of Ministers and Missionaries of the Presbyterian Church in Ireland 159

Society for the Relief of Distress 308

The Society for the Relief of Poor Clergymen 159

Society of Friends of Foreigners in Distress 309

The Society of Motor Manufacturers and Traders Charitable Trust Fund 126

The Society of Radiographers Benevolent Fund 145

The Benevolent Society of the Licensed Trade of Scotland 165

The National Benevolent Society of Watch and Clock Makers 127

Sola: Sola Trust 159

Somerset: Somerset Local Medical Benevolent Fund 438

Soothern: Soothern and Craner Educational Foundation 263

Sophie's: Sophie's Moonbeams Trust 67

Soroptimist: Soroptimist International of Great Britain and Ireland Benevolent Fund 35

Souldern: The Souldern United Charities 395

South: South Central Ambulance Service (Incorporating Hampshire Ambulance Service) Benevolent Fund 381

South Creake Charities 292

South East Water's Helping Hand 18

South London Relief-in-Sickness Fund 324

South Staffordshire Water Charitable Trust 18

South Wales Area Miners' Benevolent Fund 207

South Wales Miners' Welfare Trust Fund Scheme 146

The South Wales Police Benevolent Fund 208

The South Warwickshire Welfare Trust 257

South West Peninsula Football League Benevolent Fund 414

South Yorkshire Community Foundation 455

Southampton: The Southampton (City Centre) Relief-in-Need Charity 385

Southampton and District Sick Poor Fund and Humane Society (Southampton Charitable Trust) 385

The Earl of Southampton Trust 382

Southery: The Southery, Feltwell and Methwold Relief in Need Charity 296

Southport: The Southport and Birkdale Provident Society 364

Southwark: Southwark Charities 329

Southwark's: The Mayor of Southwark's Common Good Trust (The Mayor's Charity) 330

Southworth: St John Southworth Caritas Fund 315

Spalding: Spalding Relief in Need Charity 227

Spark: The Spark Foundation 29

Speak's: Paul and Nancy Speak's Charity 461

Spear: The Spear Charitable Trust 127

Speccott: Peter Speccott 427

Special: Special Boat Service Association 95

Speedway: The Speedway Riders' Benevolent Fund 176

Spence's: Miss Caroline Jane Spence's Fund 193

Spinal: Spinal Muscular Atrophy UK 81

Spondon: Spondon Relief in Need Charity 214

Sponne: The Sponne and Bickerstaffe Charity 230

Spooner: W. W. Spooner Charitable Trust 127

Spoore: The Spoore, Merry and Rixman Foundation 369

Springfield: Springfield United Charities 283

SSAFA: SSAFA (Soldiers, Sailors, Airmen and Families Association) Forces Help 95

Saint: St Andrew Holborn and Stafford's Charity 309

St Andrew's Society for Ladies in Need 38

The St Andrews Welfare Trust 190

The St Chad's and St Alkmund's Charity 204

Freeman Evans St David's Day Denbigh Charity 205

The United Charities of St George the Martyr 330

St George's Police Children Trust 29

St Giles-in-the-Fields and Bloomsbury United Charity 309

St John's Hospital (Bath) 439

St Leonards Hospital – Horbury 466

St Margaret's Charity 222

The United Charities of St Martin 269

The St Martin-in-the-Fields' Christmas Appeal Charity 48

St Martin's Trust 430

Feoffee Estate of St Michael-le-Belfrey York 454

St Monica Trust 417

St Olave, St Thomas and St John United Charity 330

St Pancras Welfare Trust 313

The United Charities of St Paul's Covent Garden 316

St Peter's United Charities 237

St Sepulchre (Finsbury) United Charities 309

Stafford: Stafford Educational Endowment Charity 250

Staffordshire: The Community Foundation for Staffordshire 248

Staines: Staines Parochial Charity 407

Stanton: The Stanton Land Fund 304

Stationers': The Stationers' Foundation 135

Stein: The Stanley Stein Deceased Charitable Trust 30

Stepney: Stepney Relief-in-Need Charity 330

Stevenage: The Stevenage Community Trust 289

Steventon: The Steventon Allotments and Relief-in-Need Charity 397

Stickford: Stickford Relief in Need Charity 225

Stilwell: The Betty and Charles Stilwell Fund 232

Stock: The Stock Exchange Benevolent Fund 120

Stock Exchange Clerks Fund 121

Stockburn: Stockburn Memorial Trust Fund 231

Stoddart: Stoddart Samaritan Fund 457

Stoke: The Stoke Mandeville and Other Parishes Charity 371

Stoke Poges Hastings Community Fund 374

Stoke Poges United Charity 374

Stone's: Charles Graham Stone's Relief-in-Need Charity 441

Storey: The Foundation of Edward Storey 276

Stowmarket: The Stowmarket Relief Trust 303

Strain: Edith Strain Nursing Charity 433

Strand: Mary Strand Charitable Trust 354

Strand Parishes Trust 316

Stratford-Upon-Avon: Stratford-Upon-Avon Town Trust 255

Strathnairn: Strathnairn Community Benefit Fund 196

Streynsham's: Streynsham's Charity 389

Strongbones: Strongbones Children's Charitable Trust 67

Stroud: The Stroud and Rodborough Educational Charity 437

Structural: The Institution of Structural Engineers (ISTRUCTE) Benevolent Fund 114

Sub-Postmasters: The National Federation of Sub-Postmasters Benevolent Fund 153

Sudbury: Sudbury Municipal Charities 301

Suffolk: Suffolk Constabulary Benevolent Fund 300

Sunderland: Sunderland Guild of Help 340

The Sunderland Orphanage and Educational Foundation 341

Samuel Sunderland Relief-in-Need Charity 461

Sunninghill: Sunninghill Fuel Allotment Trust 370

Sunny: Sunny Days Children's Fund 68

Surrey: The Surrey Association for Visual Impairment 400

Sussex: Sussex County Football Association Benevolent Fund 377

Sussex Police Charitable Trust 377

Sutterton: The Sutterton Educational Foundation (Sutterton Education Trust) 225

Sutterton Parochial Charity Trust 225

Sutton: Sutton Coldfield Charitable Trust 261

Sutton Nursing Association 310

The Sutton St James United Charities 227

Swaffham: Swaffham Relief in Need Charity 294

Swallow: The Charities of Nicholas Swallow and Others 276

Swallowdale: Swallowdale Children's Trust 356

Swansea: The Swansea and District Friends of the Blind 209

Sway: The Sway Welfare Aid Group (SWAG) 384

Swineshead: The Swineshead Poor Charities 224

Swiss: Swiss Benevolent Society 30

Tackling: Tackling Household Affordable Warmth Orkney (THAW Orkney) 18

Take: Take a Break Scotland 68

Talisman: The Talisman Charitable Trust 8

Tamlin: The Tamlin Charity 438

Tantum: The Tantum Trust 382

Taunton: The Taunton Aid in Sickness Fund 441

Taunton Heritage Trust 441

Taylor: Ursula Taylor Charity 274

John Taylor Foundation for Young Athletes 15

The H. A. Taylor Fund 219

Teaching: The Teaching Staff Trust 111

Tees: Tees Valley Community Foundation 335

Teesside: The Teesside Family Foundation 336

Telephones: Telephones for the Blind 83

Tetsworth: Tetsworth Cozens Bequest 394

Thame: Thame Charities (The Thame Welfare Trust) 396

Thames: The Thames Valley Police Benevolent Fund 367

Thames Water Trust Fund 19

Thaxted: Thaxted Relief-in-Need Charities 285

Theatrical: The Theatrical Guild 106

There: There for You (UNISON Welfare) 153

Thomas: Thomas Axe's Non-Ecclesiastical 422

Charity of Thomas Henwood 418

Thompson: Thompson Pritchard Trust 247

Thompson's: Arthur and Margaret Thompson's Charitable Trust 202

Thornbury: Thornbury Town Trust 436

Thorngate: Thorngate Trust 383

Thornton: Thornton Fund 159

Thorpe: The Thorpe Parochial Charities 406

The Thorpe Trust 239

Tile: Tile Hill and Westwood Charities 253

Tilehurst: Tilehurst Poor's Land Charity 368

Timber: The Timber Trades Benevolent Society 165

Tiny: Tiny Tim Trust 213

Tobacco: The Tobacco Pipe Makers and Tobacco Trade Benevolent Fund 148

Todd: Charity of Edith Emily Todd 247

Edith Emily Todd (The Todd Fund) 251

Todmorden: Todmorden War Memorial Fund (1914/1918) 462

Tottenham: Tottenham District Charity 321

Tottenham Tribute Trust 177

Tourettes: Tourettes Action 81

Town: Town Estate Charity (Mendlesham) 303

The Town Estate Educational Foundation (Hempnall) 299

Town Lands Educational Foundation (Outwell Town Lands Educational Foundation) 296

The Town Moor Money Charity 340

Townrow: Arthur Townrow Pensions Fund 213

Towrie's: Robert Towrie's Charity 449

Trades: The Trades House of Glasgow 191

Tranmer: The Annie Tranmer Charitable Trust 301

Transplant: Transplant Health Fund 81

Transport: The Transport Benevolent Fund CIO 180

Tuberous: The Tuberous Sclerosis Association 82

Tutbury: Tutbury General Charities 249

Twyford: Twyford and District Nursing Association 367

Tyler: Charity of Joshua Tyler for the Poor 224

Tyne: Community Foundation serving Tyne and Wear and Northumberland 336

The Tyne Mariners' Benevolent Institution 132

Tyre: Charles and Barbara Tyre Trust 189

Tyringham: Tyringham Pension Fund for the Blind 374

UK: UK Veterans Hearing Foundation 95

Ulster: The Ulster Defence Regiment Benevolent Fund 154

Union: The Union of Orthodox Hebrew Congregations 46

UNITE: UNITE the Union Benevolent Fund 121

United: United Charities of Liskeard 419

Scarborough United Scholarships Foundation 453

United Utilities Trust Fund 344

Unwin: The Reginald Unwin Dudley Charity 263

Mrs A. Unwin Trust 202

Upwell: Upwell (Cambridge) Consolidated Charities 277

Uxbridge: Uxbridge United Welfare Trust 322

Vardy: The Vardy Foundation 8

Variety: Variety, the Children's Charity 68

Vassar-Smith: The Vassar-Smith Fund 121

Vaughan's: Miss Vaughan's Spitalfields Charity 310

Vawer: William Vawer 203

Vegetarian: The Vegetarian Charity 36

Vetlife: Vetlife 145

Victoria: Victoria Convalescent Trust 56

The Victoria Foundation 69

Vincent: The Eric W. Vincent Trust Fund 243

Visual: Visual Impairment Breconshire (Nam Gweledol Sir Brycheiniog) 204

Vokins: The Vokins Charitable Trust 367

Wake: Bruce Wake Charity 71

Walker: Angus Walker Benevolent Bequest 201

C. C. Walker Charity 266

Wallingford: Wallingford Relief in Need Charity 396

Walpole: Walpole St Peter Poor's Estate 296

Walsall: Walsall Wood (Former Allotment) Charity 266

Walsoken: The United Walsoken and Baxter Charities 297

Walthamstow: Walthamstow and Chingford Almshouse Charity 331

Walton: Walton on Thames Charity 400

Walton Parochial Charities 405

Wandsworth: Wandsworth Combined Charity 331

Wantage: The Wantage District Coronation Memorial and Nursing Amenities Fund 397

Wappenham: Wappenham Poor's Land Charity 230

Warbleton: Warbleton Charity 379

Ware: The Ware Charities 288

Warsop: Warsop United Charities 238

Warwick: Warwick Apprenticing Charities 257

Warwick Provident Dispensary 257

Warwick Relief in Need Charity (Warwick Combined Charity) 258

Warwickshire: Warwickshire Miners' Welfare Trust Fund Scheme 253

Waterloo: Waterloo Parish Charity 324

Watford: Watford Health Trust 289

Watson's: John Watson's Trust 69

Watton: The Watton Relief-in-Need Charity 292

Watts: Richard Watts and The City of Rochester Almshouse Charities 392

Watts': Nicholas Watts' Gift (Brownsdon and Tremayne Estate) 421

WaveLength: WaveLength 38

We: We Love Manchester Charity 352

WellChild: WellChild 69

Wellfield: Wellfield Trust 290

Wells: The Wells Clerical Charity 440

Welsh: Welsh Guards Charity 96

Welsh Rugby Charitable Trust 177

Welsh Rugby International Players Benevolent Association 177

Wembley: Wembley Compassionate Fund 312

West: West Clandon Parochial Charities 402

West Derby Waste Lands Charity 363

West Gate Benevolent Trust 237

West Kirby Charity 364

West Norfolk and King's Lynn Girls' Schools Trust 297

The West Sussex County Nursing Benevolent Fund 411

West Yorkshire Police (Employees) Benevolent Fund 459

The West Yorkshire Police Benevolent and Loans Fund 459

Westminster: Westminster Amalgamated Charity 316

Weston-sub-Edge: Weston-sub-Edge Educational Charity 434

Westward: The Westward Trust 43

Westway: Westway Trust 323

Westwood: Chris Westwood Charity 263

Margaret Westwood Memorial Charity 243

Weybridge: Weybridge Poor's Land (Weybridge Land Charity) 400

Wheatley: The Wheatley Charities 396

White's: Sir Thomas White's Northampton Charity 233

Whitehead's: Sydney Dean Whitehead's Charitable Trust 16

Whitstable: Whitstable Non-Ecclesiastical Charities 388

Whittington: The Charity of Sir Richard Whittington 310

Whittlesey: The Whittlesey Charity 278

Whitton's: Whitton's Wishes (The Kathryn Turner Trust) 367

Whizz-Kidz: Whizz-Kidz 69

Wigtownshire: Wigtownshire Educational Trust 188

William: The William Barrow's Charity 393

The Charity of William Williams 431

Williams: The Charity of Elizabeth Williams 205

Willingham: Willingham and District Relief-in-Sickness Charity 226

Willis: Henry and James Willis Trust 269

Wilmington: Wilmington Parochial Charity 389

Wilmslow: Wilmslow Aid Trust (Incorporating Amos Johnson Fund) 345

Wilshaw: Wilshaw Benevolent Fund 123

Wilson: The Wilson Foundation 230

John Wilson Robert Christie Bequest Fund 197

Wiltshire: Wiltshire Ambulance Service Benevolent Fund 445

Wiltshire Police Benevolent Trust 445

Wimbledon: Wimbledon Guild of Social Welfare (Incorporated) 326

Winchester: The Winchester Rural District Welfare Trust 385

Windlesham: Windlesham United Charities 408

Winterscale's: Robert Winterscale's Charity 454

Wise: Dennis Wise in the Community 71

Witley: The Witley Charitable Trust 409

WODS: WODS (The Widows, Orphans and Dependants Society of the Church in Wales) 160

Wokingham: Wokingham United Charities 370

Women: Women in Prison Ltd 35

Wonersh: The Wonersh Charities 402

Wooburn: Wooburn, Bourne End and District Relief-in-Sickness Charity 375

Wood: Wood Green (Urban District) Charity 321

Woodthorpe: Woodthorpe Relief-in-Need Charity 213

Woolgar: Tom Woolgar 386

Woolwich: The Woolwich and Plumstead Relief-in-Sickness Fund 320

Worcester: Worcester City Parish Relief in Need Charity 269

Worcester Municipal Charities (CIO) 268

Worcestershire: Worcestershire Cancer Aid Committee 268

Wormley: Wormley Parochial Charity 287

Worplesdon: Worplesdon United Charities 403

Worrall: Worrall and Fuller Exhibition Fund 322

WPH: The WPH Charitable Trust 253

Wrenbury: The Consolidated Charity of the Parish of Wrenbury 346

Wrexham: Wrexham and District Relief in Need Charity 207

Wright's: Elizabeth Wright's Charity 278

Wrightson's: Miss E. B. Wrightson's Charitable Settlement 16

WRNS: WRNS Benevolent Trust 96

WRVS: WRVS Benevolent Trust 148

Wybunbury: The Wybunbury United Charities 346

Wylde: The Anthony and Gwendoline Wylde Memorial Charity 243

Wymeswold: Wymeswold Parochial Charities 220

Yardley: Yardley Educational Foundation 261

The Yardley Great Trust Group 262

Yelvertoft: Yelvertoft and District Relief-in-Sickness Fund 230

York: York Children's Trust 454

York Dispensary Sick Poor Fund 447

Yorkshire: Yorkshire Children's Trust 448

Yorkshire Water Community Trust 19

Young: The Young Explorers' Trust 16

ZSV: The ZSV Trust 46